MICHIGAN

RULES OF COURT

STATE

2003

INCLUDING AMENDMENTS RECEIVED
THROUGH JANUARY 1, 2003

THOMSON

WEST

MAT #40059218

COPYRIGHT © 2003
by
WEST GROUP
All rights reserved.

ISBN 0–314–10345-7

PRINTED ON 10% POST CONSUMER RECYCLED PAPER

PREFACE

This two–volume set of *Michigan Rules of Court, State and Federal, 2003* supersedes the 2002 set, including the 2002 supplements affixed to the inside back covers. It provides in convenient form the current text of court rules governing state and federal practice in Michigan, with amendments received through January 1, 2003.

State Rule Changes

New and amended rules in the State volume include:

Michigan Court Rules of 1985

Administrative Orders of the Michigan Supreme Court

New or amended local rules for the following jurisdictions:

Thirty–Sixth Judicial Circuit [City of Detroit]

Rules Concerning the State Bar

Staff Comments

As noted in several of the Staff Comments that follow some rules, the staff comment is published only for the benefit of the bench and bar and is not an authoritative construction by the Court.

In addition, when the Supreme Court amends a rule, the order often contains a Staff Comment pertaining to the amendment. The text of the new Staff Comment is usually added following the text of any existing Staff Comments. Therefore, in using the Staff Comments to track changes, the reader should consult the text of *all* Staff Comments to a particular rule. As a research aid, we have inserted bold headings indicating dates that correspond to the dates of adoption or amendment of the rule.

Updating Court Rules

Judicial amendments to the rules in this edition are published, as received, in the preliminary pages of advance sheets as follows:

State rules	*North Western Reporter 2d*
	Michigan Reporter
Federal Rules of Civil Procedure	*Federal Reporter 3d*
Federal Rules of Evidence	*Federal Supplement*
Federal Rules of Appellate Procedure	*Supreme Court Reporter*
	Federal Rules Decisions
	Bankruptcy Reporter
U.S. Court of Appeals rules (Sixth Circuit)	*Federal Reporter 3d*
	Michigan Reporter
	Ohio Cases
	Tennessee Decisions
Rules of Procedure of the Judicial Panel on	*Federal Reporter 3d*

Multidistrict Litigation	*Federal Supplement*
	Federal Rules Decisions
Federal Courts	*Federal Reporter 3d*
Miscellaneous	*Federal Supplement*
Fee Schedules	*Supreme Court Reporter*

Amendments to the state rules are also published in Michigan Legislative Service.

Westlaw® may also be used to update court rules. The MI–RULES database contains state rules and local rules of the U.S. District and Bankruptcy Courts in Michigan; US–RULES contains federal rules. An "UPDATE" command from a rule in the MI–RULES database will retrieve, from the MI–ORDERS database (which serves as an electronic "pocket part" to the MI–RULES database), judicial amendments to that rule. Similarly, an "UPDATE" command from a rule in the US–RULES database will retrieve judicial and legislative amendments from US–ORDERS or US–PL. See the Scope Screens for these Westlaw databases for further information.

Research Tips

The RULES and ORDERS databases described above may be searched on Westlaw to find specific court rules and terms.

Case law databases may also be used to find cases citing specific court rules.

See the Research Note preceding each set of rules for further information.

THE PUBLISHER

COORDINATED RESEARCH IN MICHIGAN FROM WEST

MICHIGAN COMPILED LAWS ANNOTATED

WEST's MICHIGAN COMPILED LAWS–COMPACT EDITION

WEST'S MICHIGAN DIGEST, 2D

MICHIGAN REPORTER

MICHIGAN COURT RULES PRACTICE

Text and Forms

James A. Martin, Robert Dean, Robert B. Webster, Elizabeth Norma Mckenna, Alan Saltzman, Sheila Robertson Deming & Ronald S. Longhofer

Courtroom Handbook on Michigan Civil Procedure

Ronald S. Longhofer

Evidence

James K. Robinson, Ronald S. Longhofer & Norman C. Ankers

Courtroom Handbook on Michigan Evidence

James K. Robinson & Ronald S. Longhofer

TREATISES

Callaghan's Michigan Civil Jurisprudence

Callaghan's Michigan Pleading & Practice, 2d

Callaghan's Michigan Civil Practice Forms

Gillespie Michigan Criminal Law & Procedure with Forms, 2d

Michigan Administrative Law

Don LeDuc

Michigan Probate: A Practice Systems Library Manual

Leonard Edelman & updates by John Payne

Michigan Nonstandard Jury Instructions: Civil and Criminal

Timothy Baughman, David C. Chardavoyne, Kenneth Mogill & Judge Cynthia Stephens

COORDINATED RESEARCH

MICHIGAN PRACTICE GUIDES
Alternative Dispute Resolution
U.S. District Court Chief Judge Richard A. Enslen, Pamela Chapman–Enslen & Mary A. Bedikian
Civil Trials and Evidence
Judge Gerald E. Rosen, Judge Kurtis T. Wilder, Rodger D. Young & Thomas W. Cranmer
Civil Appeals
Michigan Supreme Court Justice Stephen J. Markman
Enforcing Judgments and Debts
U.S. Bankruptcy Court Judge James D. Gregg, Linda C. Scheuerman & Stephen S. LaPlante
Torts
Michigan Supreme Court Justice Clifford W. Taylor, George A. Googasian & Allen S. Falk

---

FORMS
Michigan SCAO Approved Forms
MCLA: Uniform Commercial Code Forms with Practice Comments
Bradford Stone

HANDBOOKS & PAMPHLETS
Official Michigan Tax Guide
Michigan Criminal Law & Rules
Michigan Probate Law
Michigan Family Law
Michigan Rules of Court—State & Federal
Michigan Sentencing Guidelines
Michigan Child Support Formula Manual
Michigan Law Finder

ONLINE RESEARCH
Westlaw®
KeyCite[2F]
WEST*Check*®

CONTACT US

For more information about any of these Michigan research tools,
please call your West Representative or **1–800–328–9352.**

COORDINATED RESEARCH

NEED RESEARCH HELP?

You can get quality research results with free help—call the West Reference Attorneys when you have questions concerning Westlaw or West Publications at 1–800–733–2889.

INTERNET ACCESS

Contact the West Editorial Department directly with your questions and suggestions by e-mail at editor@westgroup.com. Visit West's home page on the World Wide Web at http://www.westgroup.com.

*

TABLE OF CONTENTS

TABLE OF CONTENTS

MICHIGAN COURT RULES OF 1985

Effective March 1, 1985

Research Note

Consult Michigan Court Rules Practice—Text, *for commentary and caselaw annotations to Michigan Court Rules of 1985.*

Use Westlaw ® *to find cases citing or applying specific rules. Westlaw may also be used to search for specific terms in court rules or to update court rules. See the MI–RULES and MI–ORDERS Scope Screens for detailed descriptive information and search tips, and Michigan Legislative Service.*

Amendments to these rules are published, as received, in the N.W.2d and Michigan Reporter *advance sheets, and Michigan Legislative Service.*

Table of Rules

3

CHAPTER 1. GENERAL PROVISIONS

Effective March 1, 1985

[For Table of Rules, see page 1 et seq.]

SUBCHAPTER 1.100 APPLICABILITY; CONSTRUCTION

RULE 1.101 TITLE; CITATION

These rules are the "Michigan Court Rules of 1985". An individual rule may be referred to as "Michigan Court Rule _____", and cited by the symbol "MCR _____". For example, this rule may be cited as MCR 1.101.

[Effective March 1, 1985.]

1985 Staff Comment

MCR 1.101 corresponds to the second paragraph of GCR 1963, 11.1.

The Michigan Court Rules of 1985 are based on the proposal of the Committee To Revise and Consolidate the Court Rules, which was originally published in 1978. See 402A Mich. Revisions were made in response to comments received, and additional proposals were developed that had not been included in the earlier publication. On July 29, 1983, the Supreme Court ordered that the revised draft be published for comment. See 417A Mich. A committee of judges and lawyers was appointed to review the comments and to advise the Court as to whether further modifications should be made. After the submission of the committee report, the Supreme Court again considered the rules and adopted them in the present form.

These rules replace the General Court Rules of 1963, the Rules of the Court of Claims, the District Court Rules, the Probate Court Rules of 1972, and the Juvenile Court Rules of 1969. They take into account all amendments of the former rules through July 31, 1984. The Michigan Court Rules do not replace the Michigan Rules of Evidence, the Code of Professional Responsibility and Canons, the Code of Judicial Conduct, the Rules Concerning the State Bar, and the Rules for the Board of Law Examiners.

The notes [staff comments] that follow each rule were prepared by the Supreme Court staff to assist the reader in identifying the substantive changes that the rules make from prior Michigan practice. They have not been approved by the Supreme Court, and should not be considered an authoritative construction of the rules.

RULE 1.102 EFFECTIVE DATE

These rules take effect on March 1, 1985. They govern all proceedings in actions brought on or after that date, and all further proceedings in actions then pending. A court may permit a pending action to proceed under the former rules if it finds that the application of these rules to that action would not be feasible or would work injustice.

[Effective March 1, 1985.]

1985 Staff Comment

MCR 1.102 is comparable to GCR 1963, 14.

RULE 1.103 APPLICABILITY

The Michigan Court Rules govern practice and procedure in all courts established by the constitution and laws of the State of Michigan. Rules stated to be applicable only in a specific court or only to a specific type of proceeding apply only to that court or to that type of proceeding and control over general rules.

[Effective March 1, 1985.]

1985 Staff Comment

MCR 1.103 revises GCR 1963, 11, covering the applicability of the rules to the various courts. The Michigan Court Rules differ from the General Court Rules of 1963 in that a single set of rules is made applicable to all courts. However, various rules are by their terms applicable only in certain courts or to certain types of proceedings. Several chapters include provisions as to the applicability of the rules within each. See MCR 3.001, 4.001, 5.001, 6.001.

RULE 1.104 STATUTORY PRACTICE PROVISIONS

Rules of practice set forth in any statute, if not in conflict with any of these rules, are effective until superseded by rules adopted by the Supreme Court.

[Effective March 1, 1985.]

1985 Staff Comment

MCR 1.104 is substantially the same as GCR 1963, 16.

RULE 1.105 CONSTRUCTION

These rules are to be construed to secure the just, speedy, and economical determination of every action and to avoid the consequences of error that does not affect the substantial rights of the parties.

[Effective March 1, 1985.]

1985 Staff Comment

MCR 1.105 is substantially the same as GCR 1963, 13.

RULE 1.106 CATCH LINES

The catch lines of a rule are not part of the rule and may not be used to construe the rule more broadly or more narrowly than the text indicates.

[Effective March 1, 1985.]

1985 Staff Comment

MCR 1.106 is substantially the same as GCR 1963, 15.

RULE 1.107 NUMBER

Words used in the singular also apply to the plural, where appropriate.

[Effective March 1, 1985.]

1985 Staff Comment

MCR 1.107 is new.

RULE 1.108 COMPUTATION OF TIME

In computing a period of time prescribed or allowed by these rules, by court order, or by statute, the following rules apply:

(1) The day of the act, event, or default after which the designated period of time begins to run is not included. The last day of the period is included, unless it is a Saturday, Sunday, legal holiday, or holiday on which the court is closed pursuant to court order; in that event the period runs until the end of the next day that is not a Saturday, Sunday, legal holiday, or holiday on which the court is closed pursuant to court order.

(2) If a period is measured by a number of weeks, the last day of the period is the same day of the week as the day on which the period began.

(3) If a period is measured by months or years, the last day of the period is the same day of the month as the day on which the period began. If what would otherwise be the final month does not include that day, the last day of the period is the last day of that month. For example, "2 months" after January 31 is March 31, and "3 months" after January 31 is April 30.

[Effective March 1, 1985.]

1985 Staff Comment

MCR 1.108 includes the provisions of GCR 108.6 regarding computation of time.

In addition, new language is added covering computation of time periods measured in weeks, months, and years, based in part on PCR 108.4.

RULE 1.109 LETTER–SIZE PAPER STANDARD

All pleadings and other papers prepared for filing in the courts of this state must be on good quality paper not exceeding 8½ inches wide by 11 inches long. This requirement does not apply to attachments and exhibits, but parties are encouraged to reduce or enlarge such papers to 8½ by 11 inches, if practical. Court clerks may not accept nonconforming papers except on written direction of a judge.

[Adopted effective January 1, 1991.]

1991 Staff Comment

A proposal to require the use of letter-size paper for pleadings and other papers filed in Michigan courts has been under consideration for several years. See Administrative Order 1987–8.

New MCR 1.109, effective January 1, 1991, adopts such a requirement, consistent with the trend in many other jurisdictions, including the federal courts.

The requirement does not apply to attachments, though parties are encouraged to reproduce them on 8½-by-11-inch paper as well.

RULE 1.110 COLLECTION OF FINES AND COSTS

Fines, costs, and other financial obligations imposed by the court must be paid at the time of assessment, except when the court allows otherwise, for good cause shown.

[Adopted effective January 1, 2002.]

2001 Staff Comment

The October 23, 2001 addition of MCR 1.110, effective January 1, 2002, stated the expectation that fines, fees, costs, and other financial obligations imposed by courts are due at the time of assessment, absent good cause shown. This is consistent with pilot programs that have been conducted in some courts, and with the assessment standards set forth in *Michigan Trial Court Collections: A Design and Implementation Guide for Collections Programs.*

The staff comment is published only for the benefit of the bench and bar and is not an authoritative construction by the Court.

SUBCHAPTER 1.200 AMENDMENT OF MICHIGAN COURT RULES

RULE 1.201 AMENDMENT PROCEDURE

(A) Notice of Proposed Amendment. Before amending the Michigan Court Rules or other sets of rules within its jurisdiction, the Supreme Court will notify the secretary of the State Bar of Michigan and the state court administrator of the proposed amendment, and the manner and date for submitting comments. The notice also will be posted on the Court's website, www.supremecourt.state.mi.us.

(B) Notice to Bar. The state bar secretary shall notify the appropriate state bar committees or sections of the proposed amendment, and the manner and date for submitting comments. Unless otherwise directed by the Court, the proposed amendment shall be published in the Michigan Bar Journal.

(C) Notice to Judges. The state court administrator shall notify the presidents of the Michigan Judges Association, the Michigan District Judges Association, and the Michigan Probate and Juvenile Court Judges Association of the proposed amendment, and the manner and date for submitting comments.

(D) Exceptions. The Court may modify or dispense with the notice requirements of this rule if it determines that there is a need for immediate action or if the proposed amendment would not significantly affect the delivery of justice.

(E) Administrative Public Hearings. The Court will conduct a public hearing pursuant to Supreme Court Administrative Order 1997–11 before acting on a proposed amendment that requires notice, unless there is a need for immediate action, in which event the amendment will be considered at a public hearing following adoption. Public hearing agendas will be posted on the Court's website.

[Effective March 1, 1985; amended effective September 1, 2001.]

1985 Staff Comment

MCR 1.201 retains the basic procedure for amendment of the rules found in GCR 1963, 933.

Subrule (B) adds a reference to publication in the Michigan Bar Journal because of the practice of publishing proposed amendments.

In subrule (C) the reference to the committees of the "judicial conference" is replaced by references to notification of the presidents of the various judges associations.

Staff Comment to 2001 Amendment

The July 30, 2001, amendment of subrule (A), effective September 1, 2001, added notice that rule proposals are posted on the Supreme Court's website. The amendment also recognized that the notice process applies to other sets of rules within the Court's jurisdiction, *e.g.*, the Michigan Rules of Evidence, the Michigan Rules of Professional Conduct, the Rules Governing the State Bar of Michigan, the Rules for the Board of Law Examiners, and the Michigan Code of Judicial Conduct. The amendment of subrule (D) provided that the Court may dispense with the notice requirements for changes that do not significantly affect the delivery of justice. The addition of subrule (E) incorporated the public hearing provisions of Supreme Court Administrative Order 1997–11.

CHAPTER 2. CIVIL PROCEDURE

Effective March 1, 1985

[For Table of Rules, see page 1 et seq.]

SUBCHAPTER 2.000 GENERAL PROVISIONS

RULE 2.001 APPLICABILITY

The rules in this chapter govern procedure in all civil proceedings in all courts established by the constitution and laws of the State of Michigan, except where the limited jurisdiction of a court makes a rule inherently inapplicable or where a rule applicable to a specific court or a specific type of proceeding provides a different procedure. •

[Effective March 1, 1985.]

1985 Staff Comment

MCR 2.001 is new, and states the applicability of the rules of civil procedure in chapter 2. They apply to all cases in all courts unless there is a specific rule applicable to the matter or the civil procedure rules are inherently inapplicable because of the limited jurisdiction of a court.

RULE 2.002 WAIVER OR SUSPENSION OF FEES AND COSTS FOR INDIGENT PERSONS

(A) Applicability.

(1) Only a natural person is eligible for the waiver or suspension of fees and costs under this rule.

(2) Except as provided in subrule (F), for the purpose of this rule "fees and costs" applies only to filing fees required by law.

(B) Execution of Affidavits. An affidavit required by this rule may be signed either

(1) by the party in whose behalf the affidavit is made; or

(2) by a person having personal knowledge of the facts required to be shown, if the person in whose behalf the affidavit is made is unable to sign it because of minority or other disability. The affidavit must recite the minority or other disability.

(C) Persons Receiving Public Assistance. If a party shows by ex parte affidavit or otherwise that he or she is receiving any form of public assistance, the payment of fees and costs as to that party shall be suspended.

(D) Other Indigent Persons. If a party shows by ex parte affidavit or otherwise that he or she is unable

because of indigency to pay fees and costs, the court shall order those fees and costs either waived or suspended until the conclusion of the litigation.

(E) Domestic Relations Cases; Payment of Fees and Costs by Spouse.

(1) In an action for divorce, separate maintenance, or annulment or affirmation of marriage, the court shall order suspension of payment of fees and costs required to be paid by a party and order that they be paid by the spouse, if that party

(a) is qualified for a waiver or suspension of fees and costs under subrule (C) or (D), and

(b) is entitled to an order requiring the spouse to pay attorney fees.

(2) If the spouse is entitled to have the fees and costs waived or suspended under subrule (C) or (D), the fees and costs are waived or suspended for the spouse.

(F) Payment of Service Fees and Costs of Publication for Indigent Persons. If payment of fees and costs has been waived or suspended for a party and service of process must be made by an official process server or by publication, the court shall order the service fees or costs of publication paid by the county or funding unit in which the action is pending, if the party submits an ex parte affidavit stating facts showing the necessity for that type of service of process.

(G) Reinstatement of Requirement for Payment of Fees and Costs. If the payment of fees or costs has been waived or suspended under this rule, the court may on its own initiative order the person for whom the fees or costs were waived or suspended to pay those fees or costs when the reason for the waiver or suspension no longer exists.

[Effective March 1, 1985; amended effective July 1, 1995.]

1985 Staff Comment

MCR 2.002 is substantially the same as GCR 1963, 120.

Staff Comment to 1995 Amendment

The amendments of MCR 2.002, effective July 1, 1995, add a new subrule (A)(2) defining "fees and costs," as meaning only filing fees required by law, excluding such costs and expenses as transcript preparation. There are corresponding adjustments in subrules (C) and (D).

RULE 2.003 DISQUALIFICATION OF JUDGE

(A) Who May Raise. A party may raise the issue of a judge's disqualification by motion, or the judge may raise it.

(B) Grounds. A judge is disqualified when the judge cannot impartially hear a case, including but not limited to instances in which:

(1) The judge is personally biased or prejudiced for or against a party or attorney.

(2) The judge has personal knowledge of disputed evidentiary facts concerning the proceeding.

(3) The judge has been consulted or employed as an attorney in the matter in controversy.

(4) The judge was a partner of a party, attorney for a party, or a member of a law firm representing a party within the preceding two years.

(5) The judge knows that he or she, individually or as a fiduciary, or the judge's spouse, parent or child wherever residing, or any other member of the judge's family residing in the judge's household, has an economic interest in the subject matter in controversy or in a party to the proceeding or has any other more than de minimis interest that could be substantially affected by the proceeding;

(6) The judge or the judge's spouse, or a person within the third degree of relationship to either of them, or the spouse of such a person:

(a) is a party to the proceeding, or an officer, director or trustee of a party;

(b) is acting as a lawyer in the proceeding;

(c) is known by the judge to have a more than de minimis interest that could be substantially affected by the proceeding;

(d) is to the judge's knowledge likely to be a material witness in the proceeding.

A judge is not disqualified merely because the judge's former law clerk is an attorney of record for a party in an action that is before the judge or is associated with a law firm representing a party in an action that is before the judge.

(C) Procedure.

(1) *Time for Filing.* To avoid delaying trial and inconveniencing the witnesses, a motion to disqualify must be filed within 14 days after the moving party discovers the ground for disqualification. If the discovery is made within 14 days of the trial date, the motion must be made forthwith. If a motion is not timely filed, untimeliness, including delay in waiving jury trial, is a factor in deciding whether the motion should be granted.

(2) *All Grounds to Be Included; Affidavit.* In any motion under this rule, the moving party must include all grounds for disqualification that are known at the time the motion is filed. An affidavit must accompany the motion.

(3) *Ruling.* The challenged judge shall decide the motion. If the challenged judge denies the motion,

(a) in a court having two or more judges, on the request of a party, the challenged judge shall refer the motion to the chief judge, who shall decide the motion de novo;

(b) in a single-judge court, or if the challenged judge is the chief judge, on the request of a party, the challenged judge shall refer the motion to the state court administrator for assignment to another judge, who shall decide the motion de novo.

(4) *Motion Granted.* When a judge is disqualified, the action must be assigned to another judge of the same court, or, if one is not available, the state court administrator shall assign another judge.

(D) Remittal of Disqualification. If it appears that there may be grounds for disqualification, the judge may ask the parties and their lawyers to consider, out of the presence of the judge, whether to waive disqualification. If, following disclosure of any basis for disqualification other than personal bias or prejudice concerning a party, the parties without participation by the judge, all agree that the judge should not be disqualified, and the judge is then willing to participate, the judge may participate in the proceedings. The agreement shall be in writing or placed on the record.

[Effective March 1, 1985; amended effective September 1, 1995.]

1985 Staff Comment

MCR 2.003 is based on GCR 1963, 912.

Under subrule (B)(3) a judge is disqualified not only as to a proceeding in which the judge was consulted or employed as counsel (see GCR 1963, 912.2[a][3]), but also when the judge was consulted or employed as counsel in the matter in controversy, even before it reached the litigation stage.

Subrule (C)(1) changes the time when the motion must be filed. A party must file a motion within 14 days after learning of the ground for disqualification, rather than 10 days after the case is assigned to a judge or 10 days before trial. However, if the discovery is made within 14 days of trial, the motion must be made forthwith. This would cover situations in which the assignment of the judge is not made until shortly before the trial date.

Subrule (C)(2) removes the language limiting a party to one motion to disqualify per judge. Additional grounds for disqualification might be discovered later. However, the party must include all grounds that are known at the time the motion is filed.

Staff Comment to 1995 Amendment

The July 10, 1995 amendments of MCR 2.003, and Rules 3A, 3D, 6C, and 7B of the Michigan Code of Judicial Conduct, and new MCR 9.227 and Rule 7D of the Michigan Code of Judicial Conduct, are based on the proposed revision of the Michigan Code of Judicial Conduct submitted by the State Bar Representative Assembly. See 442 Mich 1216 (1993). They are effective September 1, 1995.

RULE 2.004 INCARCERATED PARTIES

(A) This rule applies to

(1) domestic relations actions involving minor children, and

(2) other actions involving the custody, guardianship, neglect, or foster-care placement of minor children, or the termination of parental rights,

in which a party is incarcerated under the jurisdiction of the Department of Corrections.

(B) The party seeking an order regarding a minor child shall

(1) contact the department to confirm the incarceration and the incarcerated party's prison number and location;

(2) serve the incarcerated person with the petition or motion seeking an order regarding the minor child, and file proof with the court that the papers were served; and

(3) file with the court the petition or motion seeking an order regarding the minor child, stating that a party is incarcerated and providing the party's prison number and location; the caption of the petition or motion shall state that a telephonic hearing is required by this rule.

(C) When all the requirements of subrule (B) have been accomplished to the court's satisfaction, the court shall issue an order requesting the department, or the facility where the party is located if it is not a department facility, to allow that party to participate with the court or its designee by way of a noncollect and unmonitored telephone call in a hearing or conference, including a friend of the court adjudicative hearing or meeting. The order shall include the date and time for the hearing, and the prisoner's name and prison identification number, and shall be served by the court upon the parties and the warden or supervisor of the facility where the incarcerated party resides.

(D) All court documents or correspondence mailed to the incarcerated party concerning any matter covered by this rule shall include the name and the prison number of the incarcerated party on the envelope.

(E) The purpose of the telephone call described in this rule is to determine

(1) whether the incarcerated party has received adequate notice of the proceedings and has had an opportunity to respond and to participate,

(2) whether counsel is necessary in matters allowing for the appointment of counsel to assure that the incarcerated party's access to the court is protected,

(3) whether the incarcerated party is capable of self-representation, if that is the party's choice,

(4) how the incarcerated party can communicate with the court or the friend of the court during the pendency of the action, and whether the party needs special assistance for such communication, including participation in additional telephone calls, and

(5) the scheduling and nature of future proceedings, to the extent practicable, and the manner in which the incarcerated party may participate.

(F) A court may not grant the relief requested by the moving party concerning the minor child if the incarcerated party has not been offered the opportunity to participate in the proceedings, as described in this rule. This provision shall not apply if the incarcerated party actually does participate in a telephone call, or if the court determines that immediate action is necessary on a temporary basis to protect the minor child.

(G) The court may impose sanctions if it finds that an attempt was made to keep information about the case from an incarcerated party in order to deny that party access to the courts.

[Formerly rule 3.220, adopted effective January 1, 2003. Renumbered rule 2.004 and amended effective January 1, 2003.]

Staff Comment to 2003 Adoption

The November 1, 2002, enactment of MCR 3.220, effective January 1, 2003, is based on a proposal made in conjunction with the settlement agreement in the Court of Claims of that portion of *Cain v Dep't of Corrections*, 88–61119–AZ, 93–15000–CM, and 96–16341–CM, that pertains to women prisoners.

The staff comment is published only for the benefit of the bench and bar and is not an authoritative construction by the Court.

Staff Comment to 2002 Renumber and Amendment

MCR 2.004, effective January 1, 2003, is based on a proposal made in conjunction with the settlement agreement in the Court of Claims of that portion of *Cain v Dep't of Corrections*, 88–61119–AZ, 93–15000–CM, and 96–16341–CM, that pertains to women prisoners. The rule initially was adopted in November 2002 as MCR 3.220, but was amended and renumbered as Rule 2.004 in December 2002 to clarify the scope of the rule and to eliminate other potential confusion.

The staff comment is published only for the benefit of the bench and bar and is not an authoritative construction by the Court.

SUBCHAPTER 2.100   COMMENCEMENT OF ACTION; SERVICE OF PROCESS; PLEADINGS; MOTIONS

RULE 2.101   FORM AND COMMENCEMENT OF ACTION

(A) Form of Action. There is one form of action known as a "civil action".

(B) Commencement of Action. A civil action is commenced by filing a complaint with a court.

[Effective March 1, 1985.]

1985 Staff Comment

MCR 2.101 includes the provisions of GCR 1963, 12 (subrule [A]) and 101 (subrule [B]).

RULE 2.102   SUMMONS; EXPIRATION OF SUMMONS; DISMISSAL OF ACTION FOR FAILURE TO SERVE

(A) Issuance. On the filing of a complaint, the court clerk shall issue a summons to be served as provided in MCR 2.103 and 2.105. A separate summons may issue against a particular defendant or group of defendants. A duplicate summons may be issued from time to time and is as valid as the original summons.

(B) Form. A summons must be issued "In the name of the people of the State of Michigan", under the seal of the court that issued it. It must be directed to the defendant, and include

(1) the name and address of the court,

(2) the names of the parties,

(3) the file number,

(4) the name and address of the plaintiff's attorney or the address of a plaintiff appearing without an attorney,

(5) the defendant's address, if known,

(6) the name of the court clerk,

(7) the date on which the summons was issued,

(8) the last date on which the summons is valid,

(9) a statement that the summons is invalid unless served on or before the last date on which it is valid,

(10) the time within which the defendant is required to answer or take other action, and

(11) a notice that if the defendant fails to answer or take other action within the time allowed, judgment may be entered against the defendant for the relief demanded in the complaint.

(C) Amendment. At any time on terms that are just, a court may allow process or proof of service of process to be amended, unless it clearly appears that to do so would materially prejudice the substantive rights of the party against whom the process issued. An amendment relates back to the date of the original issuance or service of process unless the court determines that relation back would unfairly prejudice the party against whom the process issued.

(D) Expiration. A summons expires 91 days after the date the complaint is filed. However, within that 91 days, on a showing of good cause, the judge to whom the action is assigned may order a second summons to issue for a definite period not exceeding 1 year from the date the complaint is filed. If such an extension is granted, the new summons expires at the end of the extended period. The judge may impose just conditions on the issuance of the second summons. Duplicate summonses issued under subrule (A) do not extend the life of the original summons. The running of the 91-day period is tolled while a motion challenging the sufficiency of the summons or of the service of the summons is pending.

(E) Dismissal as to Defendant Not Served.

(1) On the expiration of the summons as provided in subrule (D), the action is deemed dismissed without prejudice as to a defendant who has not been served with process as provided in these rules, unless the defendant has submitted to the court's jurisdiction. As to a defendant added as a party after the filing of the first complaint in the action, the time provided in this rule runs from the filing of the first pleading that names that defendant as a party.

(2) After the time stated in subrule (E)(1), the clerk shall examine the court records and enter an order dismissing the action as to a defendant who has not been served with process or submitted to the court's jurisdiction. The clerk's failure to enter a dismissal order does not continue an action deemed dismissed.

(3) The clerk shall give notice of the entry of a dismissal order under MCR 2.107 and record the date of the notice in the case file. The failure to give notice does not affect the dismissal.

(F) Setting Aside Dismissal. A court may set aside the dismissal of the action as to a defendant under subrule (E) only on stipulation of the parties or when all of the following conditions are met:

(1) within the time provided in subrule (D), service of process was in fact made on the dismissed defendant, or the defendant submitted to the court's jurisdiction;

(2) proof of service of process was filed or the failure to file is excused for good cause shown;

(3) the motion to set aside the dismissal was filed within 28 days after notice of the order of dismissal was given, or, if notice of dismissal was not given, the

motion was promptly filed after the plaintiff learned of the dismissal.

(G) Exception; Summary Proceedings to Recover Possession of Realty. Subrules (D), (E), and (F) do not apply to summary proceedings governed by MCL 600.5701–600.5759; MSA 27A.5701–27A.5759 and by subchapter 4.200 of these rules.

[Effective March 1, 1985; amended effective October 1, 1991.]

1985 Staff Comment

MCR 2.102 is comparable to GCR 1963, 102 and DCR 102.7.

Subrule (A) corresponds to GCR 1963, 102.1. The rule is revised to make clear that, while the clerk issues the summons, the clerk is not responsible for having it served.

Subrule (B) is similar to GCR 1963, 102.2, covering the requirements for the information to be included in the summons. The new provision adds several items, including the date of issuance, the file number, the defendant's address, the last date on which the summons is valid, and a statement that the summons is invalid unless served before that date. There is also a change in the language of subrule (B)(11). GCR 1963, 102.2 states that a judgment "will be" rendered against a defendant who fails to answer. Subrule (B)(11) says that judgment "may be" entered.

Subrule (C) includes additional language regarding the effective date of an amendment: The amendment relates back to the date of the original issuance or service of process unless the court determines that relation back would unfairly prejudice the opposing party.

Subrule (D) is comparable to GCR 1963, 102.4. A provision is added that the 182-day life of a summons is tolled while a motion challenging the summons or its service is pending.

Subrule (E) is comparable to GCR 102.5. Language is added in subrule (E)(1) to clarify the application of the rule to a defendant who is added after the first complaint is filed. The 182-day period runs from the filing of the first pleading that names that defendant as a party.

Subrule (F) is based on GCR 1963, 102.6. Language is added allowing a dismissal to be set aside on stipulation.

In subrule (F)(1) the condition of a motion to set aside a dismissal is changed from a requirement that service was made within 180 days to a requirement that service was made within the time permitted by subrule (D). This takes account of the possibility that the court may have extended the time for service or that the time may have been tolled while a motion challenging service was pending.

In subrule (F)(3) language is added to cover the time for filing a motion to set aside a dismissal in circumstances in which the clerk failed to give notice of the dismissal. In such a case the motion must be filed promptly after the plaintiff learns of the dismissal.

MCR 2.102(G) excepts summary proceedings to recover possession of real estate from the dismissal rule, as had DCR 102.7. The rules governing those procedures include their own provisions regarding service. See subchapter 4.200.

Staff Comment to 1991 Amendment

The [October 1, 1991] amendment of MCR 2.102(D) shortens the time for expiration of a summons from 182 days to 91 days.

RULE 2.103 PROCESS; WHO MAY SERVE

(A) Service Generally. Process in civil actions may be served by any legally competent adult who is not a party or an officer of a corporate party.

(B) Service Requiring Seizure of Property. A writ of restitution or process requiring the seizure or attachment of property may only be served by

(1) a sheriff or deputy sheriff, or a bailiff or court officer appointed by the court for that purpose,

(2) an officer of the Department of State Police in an action in which the state is a party, or

(3) a police officer of an incorporated city or village in an action in which the city or village is a party.

A writ of garnishment may be served by any person authorized by subrule (A).

(C) Service in a Governmental Institution. If personal service of process is to be made on a person in a governmental institution, hospital, or home, service must be made by the person in charge of the institution or by someone designated by that person.

(D) Process Requiring Arrest. Process in civil proceedings requiring the arrest of a person may be served only by a sheriff, deputy sheriff, or police officer, or by a court officer appointed by the court for that purpose.

[Effective March 1, 1985.]

1985 Staff Comment

MCR 2.103 includes provisions from both GCR 1963, 103 and DCR 103.

Subrule (A) is similar to GCR 1963, 103(1), and allows any competent adult other than a party or an officer of a corporate party to serve a summons and complaint. The effect is to expand the class of persons who can serve process in the district court. Compare DCR 103.1, under which persons other than the officers listed in MCL 600.8321; MSA 27A.8321 could serve process only with leave of court. As under GCR 1963, 103(1), the attorney for a party may serve process.

In addition, the term "any person of suitable age and discretion" in GCR 1963, 103(1) is changed to "any legally competent adult".

Subrule (B) contains the substance of DCR 103.3, regarding service requiring seizure of property.

Subrule (C) is similar to GCR 1963, 103(2) and DCR 103.2. However, the rule is modified to allow the person in charge of the institution to designate anyone to serve process, not only a member of the institution staff. See PCR 103.2.

Subrule (D) is based on GCR 1963, 103(3) and DCR 103.3. Process requiring the arrest of a person may only be served by a law enforcement officer or a court officer appointed for that purpose.

RULE 2.104 PROCESS; PROOF OF SERVICE

(A) Requirements. Proof of service may be made by

(1) written acknowledgment of the receipt of a summons and a copy of the complaint, dated and signed by the person to whom the service is directed or by a person authorized under these rules to receive the service of process;

(2) a certificate stating the facts of service, including the manner, time, date, and place of service, if service is made within the State of Michigan by

(a) a sheriff,

(b) a deputy sheriff or bailiff, if that officer holds office in the county in which the court issuing the process is held,

(c) an appointed court officer,

(d) an attorney for a party; or

(3) an affidavit stating the facts of service, including the manner, time, date, and place of service, and indicating the process server's official capacity, if any.

The place of service must be described by giving the address where the service was made or, if the service was not made at a particular address, by another description of the location.

(B) Failure to File. Failure to file proof of service does not affect the validity of the service.

(C) Publication, Posting, and Mailing. If the manner of service used requires sending a copy of the summons and complaint by mail, the party requesting issuance of the summons is responsible for arranging the mailing and filing proof of service. Proof of publication, posting, and mailing under MCR 2.106 is governed by MCR 2.106(G).

[Effective March 1, 1985.]

1985 Staff Comment

MCR 2.104 is comparable to GCR 1963, 104.

In subrule (A)(2)(b) references to "coroners" and "constables" are deleted.

Subrule (A)(2)(d) adds the attorney for a party to the list of persons who may prove service by filing a certificate of service.

Language is added at the end of subrule (A) to require greater specificity regarding the place of service than is found in GCR 1963, 104(1).

New subrule (C) makes clear that MCR 2.106(G) governs proof of publication, posting, and mailing under that rule.

The [March 1, 1985] amendment of MCR 2.104(C) adds an explicit statement that when a copy of the summons and complaint are required to be sent by mail, the party who secured the issuance of the summons is responsible for the mailing and proof of service.

RULE 2.105 PROCESS; MANNER OF SERVICE

(A) Individuals. Process may be served on a resident or nonresident individual by,

(1) delivering a summons and a copy of the complaint to the defendant personally; or

(2) sending a summons and a copy of the complaint by registered or certified mail, return receipt requested, and delivery restricted to the addressee. Service is made when the defendant acknowledges receipt of the mail. A copy of the return receipt signed by the defendant must be attached to proof showing service under subrule (A)(2).

(B) Individuals; Substituted Service. Service of process may be made

(1) on a nonresident individual, by

(a) serving a summons and a copy of the complaint in Michigan on an agent, employee, representative, sales representative, or servant of the defendant, and

(b) sending a summons and a copy of the complaint by registered mail addressed to the defendant at his or her last known address;

(2) on a minor, by serving a summons and a copy of the complaint on a person having care and control of the minor and with whom he or she resides;

(3) on a defendant for whom a guardian or conservator has been appointed and is acting, by serving a summons and a copy of the complaint on the guardian or conservator;

(4) on an individual doing business under an assumed name, by

(a) serving a summons and copy of the complaint on the person in charge of an office or business establishment of the individual, and

(b) sending a summons and a copy of the complaint by registered mail addressed to the individual at his or her usual residence or last known address.

(C) Partnerships; Limited Partnerships. Service of process on a partnership or limited partnership may be made by

(1) serving a summons and a copy of the complaint on any general partner; or

(2) serving a summons and a copy of the complaint on the person in charge of a partnership office or business establishment and sending a summons and a copy of the complaint by registered mail, addressed to a general partner at his or her usual residence or last known address.

(D) Private Corporations, Domestic and Foreign. Service of process on a domestic or foreign corporation may be made by

(1) serving a summons and a copy of the complaint on an officer or the resident agent;

(2) serving a summons and a copy of the complaint on a director, trustee, or person in charge of an office or business establishment of the corporation and sending a summons and a copy of the complaint by registered mail, addressed to the principal office of the corporation;

(3) serving a summons and a copy of the complaint on the last presiding officer, president, cashier, secretary, or treasurer of a corporation that has ceased to do business by failing to keep up its organization by the appointment of officers or otherwise, or whose term of existence has expired;

(4) sending a summons and a copy of the complaint by registered mail to the corporation or an appropriate corporation officer and to the Michigan Corporation and Securities Bureau if

(a) the corporation has failed to appoint and maintain a resident agent or to file a certificate of that appointment as required by law;

(b) the corporation has failed to keep up its organization by the appointment of officers or otherwise; or

(c) the corporation's term of existence has expired.

(E) Partnership Associations; Unincorporated Voluntary Associations. Service of process on a partnership association or an unincorporated voluntary association may be made by

(1) serving a summons and a copy of the complaint on an officer, director, trustee, agent, or person in charge of an office or business establishment of the association, and

(2) sending a summons and a copy of the complaint by registered mail, addressed to an office of the association. If an office cannot be located, a summons and a copy of the complaint may be sent by registered mail to a member of the association other than the person on whom the summons and complaint was served.

(F) Service on Insurer. If service on an insurer is made by serving the Commissioner of Insurance, as permitted by statute, 2 summonses and a copy of the complaint must be delivered or mailed by registered mail to the office of the Commissioner of Insurance.

(G) Public Corporations. Service of process on a public, municipal, quasi-municipal, or governmental corporation, unincorporated board, or public body may be made by serving a summons and a copy of the complaint on:

(1) the chairperson of the board of commissioners or the county clerk of a county;

(2) the mayor, the city clerk, or the city attorney of a city;

(3) the president, the clerk, or a trustee of a village;

(4) the supervisor or the township clerk of a township;

(5) the president, the secretary, or the treasurer of a school district;

(6) the president or the secretary of the Michigan State Board of Education;

(7) the president, the secretary, or other member of the governing body of a corporate body or an unincorporated board having control of a state institution;

(8) the president, the chairperson, the secretary, the manager, or the clerk of any other public body organized or existing under the constitution or laws of Michigan, when no other method of service is specially provided by statute.

The service of process may be made on an officer having substantially the same duties as those named or described above, irrespective of title. In any case, service may be made by serving a summons and a copy of the complaint on a person in charge of the office of an officer on whom service may be made and sending a summons and a copy of the complaint by registered mail addressed to the officer at his or her office.

(H) Agent Authorized by Appointment or by Law.

(1) Service of process on a defendant may be made by serving a summons and a copy of the complaint on an agent authorized by written appointment or by law to receive service of process.

(2) Whenever, pursuant to statute or court rule, service of process is to be made on a nongovernmental defendant by service on a public officer, service on the public officer may be made by registered mail addressed to his or her office.

(I) Discretion of the Court.

(1) On a showing that service of process cannot reasonably be made as provided by this rule, the court may by order permit service of process to be made in any other manner reasonably calculated to give the defendant actual notice of the proceedings and an opportunity to be heard.

(2) A request for an order under the rule must be made in a verified motion dated not more than 14 days before it is filed. The motion must set forth sufficient facts to show that process cannot be served under this rule and must state the defendant's address or last known address, or that no address of the defendant is known. If the name or present address of the defendant is unknown, the moving party must set forth facts showing diligent inquiry to ascertain it. A hearing on the motion is not required unless the court so directs.

(3) Service of process may not be made under this subrule before entry of the court's order permitting it.

(J) Jurisdiction; Range of Service; Effect of Improper Service.

(1) Provisions for service of process contained in these rules are intended to satisfy the due process requirement that a defendant be informed of an action by the best means available under the circumstances. These rules are not intended to limit or expand the jurisdiction given the Michigan courts over a defendant. The jurisdiction of a court over a defendant is governed by the United States Constitution and the constitution and laws of the State of Michigan. See MCL 600.701 et seq.; MSA 27A.701 et seq.

(2) There is no territorial limitation on the range of process issued by a Michigan court.

(3) An action shall not be dismissed for improper service of process unless the service failed to inform the defendant of the action within the time provided in these rules for service.

(K) Registered and Certified Mail.

(1) If a rule uses the term "registered mail", that term includes the term "certified mail", and the term "registered mail, return receipt requested" includes the term "certified mail, return receipt requested". However, if certified mail is used, the receipt of mailing must be postmarked by the post office.

(2) If a rule uses the term "certified mail", a postmarked receipt of mailing is not required. Registered mail may be used when a rule requires certified mail.

[Effective March 1, 1985.]

1985 Staff Comment

MCR 2.105 is based on GCR 1963, 105, and includes some provisions from GCR 1963, 106.1.

Subrule (A)(2) provides that service on an individual may be made by registered or certified mail with delivery restricted to the addressee. A copy of the return receipt signed by the defendant must be attached to the proof of service.

There are corresponding changes in subrules (C)–(E) that would permit service by mail on persons who are served as representatives of organizations. The prior rule spoke of "leaving" the summons and a copy of the complaint with these persons. GCR 1963, 105.3–105.6.

In subrule (B), regarding substituted service on individuals, a person's conservator is added as a representative on whom service may be made.

The provisions of GCR 1963, 105.4 regarding service on insurers are moved from the section dealing with private corporations to a new subrule (F) in recognition that insurance companies need not be corporations. MCL 500.106; MSA 24.1106. The reference to service on a "resident agent" is deleted. The statute from which that term was drawn (CL 1970, 500.1404) has been repealed.

Additional detail has been added in subrule (I) regarding court orders for service where service under the rule cannot reasonably be made. Some of the procedural provisions are taken from GCR 1963, 106.1. The authority to order such other methods of service on the ground that the defendant resides outside of Michigan is deleted.

In subrule (J)(1), regarding the limits on jurisdiction of the courts, a reference to the United States Constitution is added.

Subrule (J)(3) is a new provision regarding the remedy when service is found to have been improper. Dismissal is required only if the attempt to serve did not give the defendant notice of the action within the time provided for service by the rules.

Subrule (K) clarifies the use of the terms "registered mail" and "certified mail".

The forms contained in GCR 1963, 105.10–105.15 are deleted. The function of approving forms had been delegated to the state court administrator.

RULE 2.106   NOTICE BY POSTING OR PUBLICATION

(A) Availability. This rule governs service of process by publication or posting pursuant to an order under MCR 2.105(I).

(B) Procedure. A request for an order permitting service under this rule shall be made by motion in the manner provided in MCR 2.105(I). In ruling on the motion, the court shall determine whether mailing is required under subrules (D)(2) or (E)(2).

(C) Notice of Action; Contents.

(1) The order directing that notice be given to a defendant under this rule must include

    (a) the name of the court,

    (b) the names of the parties,

    (c) a statement describing the nature of the proceedings,

    (d) directions as to where and when to answer or take other action permitted by law or court rule, and

    (e) a statement as to the effect of failure to answer or take other action.

(2) If the names of some or all defendants are unknown, the order must describe the relationship of the unknown defendants to the matter to be litigated in the best way possible, as, for example, unknown claimants, unknown owners, or unknown heirs, devisees, or assignees of a named person.

(D) Publication of Order; Mailing. If the court orders notice by publication, the defendant shall be notified of the action by

(1) publishing a copy of the order once each week for 3 consecutive weeks, or for such further time as the court may require, in a newspaper in the county where the defendant resides, if known, and if not, in the county where the action is pending; and

(2) sending a copy of the order to the defendant at his or her last known address by registered mail, return receipt requested, before the date of the last publication. If the plaintiff does not know the present or last known address of the defendant, and cannot

ascertain it after diligent inquiry, mailing a copy of the order is not required. The moving party is responsible for arranging for the mailing and proof of mailing.

(E) Posting; Mailing. If the court orders notice by posting, the defendant shall be notified of the action by

(1) posting a copy of the order in the courthouse and 2 or more other public places as the court may direct for 3 continuous weeks or for such further time as the court may require; and

(2) sending a copy of the order to the defendant at his or her last known address by registered mail, return receipt requested, before the last week of posting. If the plaintiff does not know the present or last known address of the defendant, and cannot ascertain it after diligent inquiry, mailing a copy of the order is not required. The moving party is responsible for arranging for the mailing and proof of mailing.

The order must designate who is to post the notice and file proof of posting. Only a person listed in MCR 2.103(B)(1), (2), or (3) may be designated.

(F) Newspaper Defined.

(1) The term "newspaper" as used in this rule is limited to a newspaper published in the English language for the dissemination of general news and information or for the dissemination of legal news. The newspaper must have a bona fide list of paying subscribers or have been published at least once a week in the same community without interruption for at least 2 years, and have been established, published, and circulated at least once a week without interruption for at least 1 year in the county where publication is to occur.

(2) If no newspaper qualifies in the county where publication is to be made under subrule (D)(1) the term "newspaper" includes a newspaper that by this rule is qualified to publish notice of actions commenced in an adjoining county.

(G) Proof of Service. Service of process made pursuant to this rule may be proven as follows:

(1) Publication must be proven by an affidavit of the publisher or the publisher's agent

(a) stating facts establishing the qualification of the newspaper in which the order was published,

(b) setting out a copy of the published order, and

(c) stating the dates on which it was published.

(2) Posting must be proven by an affidavit of the person designated in the order under subrule (E) attesting that a copy of the order was posted for the required time in the courthouse in a conspicuous place open to the public and in the other places as ordered by the court.

(3) Mailing must be proven by affidavit. The affiant must attach a copy of the order as mailed, and a return receipt.

[Effective March 1, 1985.]

1985 Staff Comment

MCR 2.106 is similar to GCR 1963, 106. The principal change is the deletion of the limitation of GCR 106 to actions in which personal jurisdiction is not required. Rather, MCR 2.106 is written to prescribe the procedure for giving of notice by publication or posting where such notice is authorized by order under MCR 2.105(I). The procedures for requesting an order are placed in MCR 2.105(I).

The [March 1, 1985] amendment of MCR 2.106(C)(1) modifies the language to make clear that when an order is entered permitting notice by publication or posting, the order itself must include the specific information required by the rule.

Subrule (D)(1) requires that a publication be made in the county in which the defendant resides, if known. Under GCR 1963, 106.4, the publication must be made in the county in which the action is pending. Subrule (D)(1) also reduces the required number of weeks of publication from 4 (see GCR 1963, 106.3[1]) to 3.

Subrule (E) adds provisions specifying the manner of notice by posting applicable when posting is ordered by the court.

Subrules (D)(2) and (E)(2) provide that it is the plaintiff who is responsible for the mailing that accompanies notice under this rule. In addition, those provisions specify that the mailing in conjunction with a publication or posting of notice must be by registered mail.

The forms found in GCR 1963, 106.8–106.12 are deleted.

RULE 2.107   SERVICE AND FILING OF PLEADINGS AND OTHER PAPERS

(A) Service; When Required.

(1) Unless otherwise stated in this rule, every party who has filed a pleading, an appearance, or a motion must be served with a copy of every paper later filed in the action. A nonparty who has filed a motion or appeared in response to a motion need only be served with papers that relate to that motion.

(2) Except as provided in MCR 2.603, after a default is entered against a party, further service of papers need not be made on that party unless he or she has filed an appearance or a written demand for service of papers. However, a pleading that states a new claim for relief against a party in default must be served in the manner provided by MCR 2.105.

(3) If an attorney appears on behalf of a person who has not received a copy of the complaint, a copy of the complaint must be delivered to the attorney on request.

(4) All papers filed on behalf of a defendant must be served on all other defendants not in default.

(B) Service on Attorney or Party.

(1) Service required or permitted to be made on a party for whom an attorney has appeared in the action must be made on the attorney except as follows:

(a) The original service of the summons and complaint must be made on the party as provided by MCR 2.105;

(b) When a contempt proceeding for disobeying a court order is initiated, the notice or order must be personally delivered to the party, unless the court orders otherwise;

(c) After a final judgment has been entered and the time for an appeal of right has passed, papers must be served on the party unless the rule governing the particular postjudgment procedure specifically allows service on the attorney;

(d) The court may order service on the party.

(2) If two or more attorneys represent the same party, service of papers on one of the attorneys is sufficient. An attorney who represents more than one party is entitled to service of only one copy of a paper.

(3) If a party prosecutes or defends the action on his or her own behalf, service of papers must be made on the party in the manner provided by subrule (C).

(C) Manner of Service. Service of a copy of a paper on an attorney must be made by delivery or by mailing to the attorney at his or her last known business address or, if the attorney does not have a business address, then to his or her last known residence address. Service on a party must be made by delivery or by mailing to the party at the address stated in the party's pleadings.

(1) *Delivery to Attorney.* Delivery of a copy to an attorney within this rule means

(a) handing it to the attorney personally;

(b) leaving it at the attorney's office with the person in charge or, if no one is in charge or present, by leaving it in a conspicuous place; or

(c) if the office is closed or the attorney has no office, by leaving it at the attorney's usual residence with some person of suitable age and discretion residing there.

(2) *Delivery to Party.* Delivery of a copy to a party within this rule means

(a) handing it to the party personally; or

(b) leaving it at the party's usual residence with some person of suitable age and discretion residing there.

(3) *Mailing.* Mailing a copy under this rule means enclosing it in a sealed envelope with first class postage fully prepaid, addressed to the person to be served, and depositing the envelope and its contents in the United States mail. Service by mail is complete at the time of mailing.

(D) Proof of Service. Except as otherwise provided by MCR 2.104, 2.105, or 2.106, proof of service of papers required or permitted to be served may be by written acknowledgment of service, affidavit of the person making the service, a statement regarding the service verified under MCR 2.114(A), or other proof satisfactory to the court. The proof of service may be included at the end of the paper as filed. Proof of service must be filed promptly and at least at or before a hearing to which the paper relates.

(E) Service Prescribed by Court. When service of papers after the original complaint cannot reasonably be made because there is no attorney of record, because the party cannot be found, or for any other reason, the court, for good cause on ex parte application, may direct in what manner and on whom service may be made.

(F) Numerous Parties. In an action in which there is an unusually large number of parties on the same side, the court on motion or on its own initiative may order that

(1) they need not serve their papers on each other;

(2) responses to their pleadings need only be served on the party to whose pleading the response is made;

(3) a cross-claim, counterclaim, or allegation in an answer demanding a reply is deemed denied by the parties not served; and

(4) the filing of a pleading and service on an adverse party constitutes notice of it to all parties.

A copy of the order must be served on all parties in the manner the court directs.

(G) Filing With Court Defined. The filing of pleadings and other papers with the court as required by these rules must be with the court clerk, except that the judge may permit papers to be filed with him or her in which event the judge shall note the filing date on the papers and forthwith transmit them to the office of the court clerk.

[Effective March 1, 1985.]

1985 Staff Comment

MCR 2.107 is based on GCR 1963, 107.

In subrule (A)(1) a provision is added requiring that a nonparty who has filed a motion or appeared in response to a motion be served with papers that relate to the motion. This would be expected to arise most commonly with motions to intervene or motions with regard to discovery requests directed to a nonparty.

Subrule (A)(2), covering service of papers on a party in default, includes a cross-reference to MCR 2.603, which adds several requirements of notice to a defaulted party.

Subrule (B)(1)(c) specifies for how long parties may continue to serve an attorney who has appeared in the action. This addition is related to MCR 2.117(C), covering the duration of an attorney's appearance.

Subrule (D) permits a proof of service of papers to be included in the body of the document itself. Subrule (D) also adds language regarding the time for filing a proof of service to cover the circumstance in which there is no hearing involved. In such cases proof of service must be filed "promptly".

RULE 2.108   TIME

(A) Time for Service and Filing of Pleadings.

(1) A defendant must serve and file an answer or take other action permitted by law or these rules within 21 days after being served with the summons and a copy of the complaint in Michigan in the manner provided in MCR 2.105(A)(1).

(2) If service of the summons and a copy of the complaint is made outside Michigan, or if the manner of service used requires the summons and a copy of the complaint to be sent by registered mail addressed to the defendant, the defendant must serve and file an answer or take other action permitted by law or these rules within 28 days after service.

(3) When service is made in accordance with MCR 2.106, the court shall allow a reasonable time for the defendant to answer or take other action permitted by law or these rules, but may not prescribe a time less than 28 days after publication or posting is completed.

(4) A party served with a pleading stating a cross-claim or counterclaim against that party must serve and file an answer or take other action permitted by law or these rules within 21 days after service.

(5) A party served with a pleading to which a reply is required or permitted may serve and file a reply within 21 days after service of the pleading to which it is directed.

(6) In an action alleging medical malpractice filed on or after October 1, 1986, unless the defendant has responded as provided in subrule (A)(1) or (2), the defendant must serve and file an answer within 21 days after being served with the notice of filing the security for costs or the affidavit in lieu of such security required by MCL 600.2912d; MSA 27A.2912d.

(B) Time for Filing Motion in Response to Pleading.
A motion raising a defense or an objection to a pleading must be served and filed within the time for filing the responsive pleading or, if no responsive pleading is required, within 21 days after service of the pleading to which the motion is directed.

(C) Effect of Particular Motions and Amendments.
When a motion or an amended pleading is filed, the time for pleading set in subrule (A) is altered as follows, unless a different time is set by the court:

(1) If a motion under MCR 2.116 made before filing a responsive pleading is denied, the moving party must serve and file a responsive pleading within 21 days after notice of the denial. However, if the moving party, within 21 days, files an application for leave to appeal from the order, the time is extended until 21 days after the denial of the application unless the appellate court orders otherwise.

(2) An order granting a motion under MCR 2.116 must set the time for service and filing of the amended pleading, if one is allowed.

(3) The response to a supplemental pleading or to a pleading amended either as of right or by leave of court must be served and filed within the time remaining for response to the original pleading or within 21 days after service of the supplemental or amended pleading, whichever period is longer.

(4) If the court has granted a motion for more definite statement, the responsive pleading must be served and filed within 21 days after the more definite statement is served.

(D) Time for Service of Order to Show Cause.
An order to show cause must set the time for service of the order and for the hearing, and may set the time for answer to the complaint or response to the motion on which the order is based.

(E) Extension of Time.
A court may, with notice to the other parties who have appeared, extend the time for serving and filing a pleading or motion or the doing of another act, if the request is made before the expiration of the period originally prescribed. After the expiration of the original period, the court may, on motion, permit a party to act if the failure to act was the result of excusable neglect. However, if a rule governing a particular act limits the authority to extend the time, those limitations must be observed. MCR 2.603(D) applies if a default has been entered.

(F) Unaffected by Expiration of Term.
The time provided for the doing of an act or the holding of a proceeding is not affected or limited by the continuation or expiration of a term of court. The continuation or expiration of a term of court does not affect the power of a court to do an act or conduct a proceeding in a civil action pending before it.

[Effective March 1, 1985; amended effective December 12, 1986.]

1985 Staff Comment

MCR 2.108 is based on GCR 1963, 108. Throughout the Michigan Court Rules, time limits for periods of up to 6 months are expressed in multiples of 7 days, except for very short periods, certain statutorily prescribed times, and certain administrative provisions that do not affect the conduct of litigation.

The provisions of GCR 1963, 108.6, regarding computation of time, are moved to MCR 1.108.

The [March 1, 1985] amendment of MCR 2.108(A)(1) and (2) changes the time within which a defendant served by registered or certified mail under MCR 2.105(A)(2) must respond from 21 days to 28 days.

The [March 1, 1985] amendment of MCR 2.108(A)(4) corrects a typographical error, substituting "permitted" for "permitting".

Subrule (C)(4) is slightly different from GCR 1963, 108.3(4). The provision regarding the time for filing a more definite statement is omitted; that subject is covered by MCR 2.115. Subrule (C)(4) only states when the responsive pleading is required.

GCR 1963, 108 was not consistent in its use of the terms "file" and "serve". In several provisions, only one of those terms was used, while the intention seemed to be that both filing and service were required. See, e.g., GCR 1963, 108.2, 108.4. Both terms are used in MCR 2.108.

The time for service of motions and affidavits, covered by GCR 1963, 108.4, is moved to the motion practice rule, MCR 2.119.

GCR 1963, 108.7(1), which provided an extra 2 days to act when a paper was mailed out of the county, is omitted.

Language is added in MCR 2.108(E) regarding the trial judge's authority to extend the time for various acts. If a specific rule places limitations on the judge's authority to do so, the specific provision controls, rather than this general one.

RULE 2.109 SECURITY FOR COSTS

(A) Motion. On motion of a party against whom a claim has been asserted in a civil action, if it appears reasonable and proper, the court may order the opposing party to file with the court clerk a bond with surety as required by the court in an amount sufficient to cover all costs and other recoverable expenses that may be awarded by the trial court, or, if the claiming party appeals, by the trial and appellate courts. The court shall determine the amount in its discretion. MCR 3.604(E) and (F) govern objections to the surety.

(B) Exceptions. Subrule (A) does not apply in the following circumstances:

(1) The court may allow a party to proceed without furnishing security for costs if the party's pleading states a legitimate claim and the party shows by affidavit that he or she is financially unable to furnish a security bond.

(2) Security shall not be required of

(a) the United States or an agency or instrumentality of the United States;

(b) the State of Michigan or a governmental unit of the state, including but not limited to a public, municipal, quasi-municipal or governmental corporation, unincorporated board, public body, or political subdivision; or

(c) an officer of a governmental unit or agency exempt from security who brings an action in his or her official capacity.

(C) Modification of Order. The court may order new or additional security at any time on just terms,

(1) if the party or the surety moves out of Michigan, or

(2) if the original amount of the bond proves insufficient.

A person who becomes a new or additional surety is liable for all costs from the commencement of the action, as if he or she had been the original surety.

[Effective March 1, 1985; amended effective December 12, 1986; April 1, 1998.]

1985 Staff Comment

MCR 2.109 corresponds to GCR 1963, 109. The principal change is that the court will have the authority to require the posting of security not only by a plaintiff, but also by any other party asserting a claim in the action. Some counterclaims or cross-claims might greatly expand the scope of the litigation, making it appropriate to require a defendant to post security.

In subrule (A) a cross-reference is added to the provisions of the general bond rule regarding objections to sureties.

In subrule (B)(1) the language of GCR 1963, 109(1), regarding the showing required to avoid the need to post security, is modified slightly in light of *Gaffier v. St Johns Hospital*, 68 Mich App 474 (1976).

Staff Comment to 1998 Amendment

The March 24, 1998, amendments [effective April 1, 1998] of 2.109, 2.111, 2.112, 2.119, 8.103, 8.106, 8.110, 8.111, 9.114, and 9.203, make technical changes necessary in light of statutory amendments and correct cross-references.

The amendments of MCR 2.109 and 2.112 relate to amendments of MCR 600.2912d, 600.2912e; MSA 27A.2912(d), 27A.2912(e), by 1993 PA 78.

The amendments of MCR 2.111 and 2.119 are based on statutes amended by 1996 PA 388. The change in MCR 2.111(B)(2) applies to actions filed on or after January 1, 1998, the effective date of the statute increasing the jurisdictional limit of the district court.

The amendment of MCR 8.106 corrects a statutory reference in light of 1993 PA 189.

The remaining amendments make changes in cross-references necessitated by earlier amendments. Some published versions of the rules already include several of these corrections.

RULE 2.110 PLEADINGS

(A) Definition of "Pleading". The term "pleading" includes only:

(1) a complaint,

(2) a cross-claim,

(3) a counterclaim,

(4) a third-party complaint,

(5) an answer to a complaint, cross-claim, counterclaim, or third-party complaint, and

(6) a reply to an answer.

No other form of pleading is allowed.

(B) When Responsive Pleading Required. A party must file and serve a responsive pleading to

(1) a complaint,

(2) a counterclaim,

(3) a cross-claim,

(4) a third-party complaint, or

(5) an answer demanding a reply.

(C) Designation of Cross-Claim or Counter-claim. A cross-claim or a counterclaim may be combined with an answer. The counterclaim or cross-claim must be clearly designated as such.

(1) A responsive pleading is not required to a cross-claim or counterclaim that is not clearly designated as such in the answer.

(2) If a party has raised a cross-claim or counter-claim in the answer, but has not designated it as such, the court may treat the pleading as if it had been properly designated and require the party to amend the pleading, direct the opposing party to file a responsive pleading, or enter another appropriate order.

(3) The court may treat a cross-claim or counter-claim designated as a defense, or a defense designated as a cross-claim or counterclaim, as if the designation had been proper and issue an appropriate order.

[Effective March 1, 1985.]

1985 Staff Comment

MCR 2.110 is based on GCR 1963, 110.1 and 111.7.

Subrule (A) defines the term "pleading," and subrule (B) specifies when a responsive pleading is required. In addition to the required responsive pleadings, the party always has the option of filing a reply to an answer.

Subrule (C) provides more detail regarding the treatment of misdesignated cross-claims and counterclaims than was found in GCR 1963, 111.7.

Several provisions of GCR 1963, 110 are not included in MCR 2.110. The provisions on motions (GCR 1963, 110.2) are moved to the motion practice rule, MCR 2.119. The rule of construction found in GCR 1963, 110.3 is deleted as unnecessary in light of MCR 1.105.

RULE 2.111   GENERAL RULES
OF PLEADING

(A) Pleading to Be Concise and Direct; Inconsistent Claims.

(1) Each allegation of a pleading must be clear, concise, and direct.

(2) Inconsistent claims or defenses are not objectionable. A party may

   (a) allege two or more statements of fact in the alternative when in doubt about which of the statements is true;

   (b) state as many separate claims or defenses as the party has, regardless of consistency and whether they are based on legal or equitable grounds or on both.

All statements made in a pleading are subject to the requirements of MCR 2.114.

(B) Statement of Claim. A complaint, counter-claim, cross-claim, or third-party complaint must contain the following:

(1) A statement of the facts, without repetition, on which the pleader relies in stating the cause of action, with the specific allegations necessary reasonably to inform the adverse party of the nature of the claims the adverse party is called on to defend; and

(2) A demand for judgment for the relief that the pleader seeks. If the pleader seeks an award of money, a specific amount must be stated if the claim is for a sum certain or a sum that can by computation be made certain, or if the amount sought is $25,000 or less. Otherwise, a specific amount may not be stated, and the pleading must include allegations that show that the claim is within the jurisdiction of the court. Declaratory relief may be claimed in cases of actual controversy. See MCR 2.605. Relief in the alternative or relief of several different types may be demanded.

(C) Form of Responsive Pleading. As to each allegation on which the adverse party relies, a responsive pleading must

(1) state an explicit admission or denial;

(2) plead no contest; or

(3) state that the pleader lacks knowledge or information sufficient to form a belief as to the truth of an allegation, which has the effect of a denial.

(D) Form of Denials. Each denial must state the substance of the matters on which the pleader will rely to support the denial.

(E) Effect of Failure to Deny.

(1) Allegations in a pleading that requires a responsive pleading, other than allegations of the amount of damage or the nature of the relief demanded, are admitted if not denied in the responsive pleading.

(2) Allegations in a pleading that does not require a responsive pleading are taken as denied.

(3) A pleading of no contest, provided for in subrule (C)(2), permits the action to proceed without proof of the claim or part of the claim to which the pleading is directed. Pleading no contest has the effect of an admission only for purposes of the pending action.

(F) Defenses; Requirement That Defense Be Pleaded.

(1) *Pleading Multiple Defenses.* A pleader may assert as many defenses, legal or equitable or both, as the pleader has against an opposing party. A defense is not waived by being joined with other defenses.

(2) *Defenses Must Be Pleaded; Exceptions.* A party against whom a cause of action has been asserted by complaint, cross-claim, counterclaim, or third-party claim must assert in a responsive pleading the defenses the party has against the claim. A defense not asserted in the responsive pleading or by motion as

provided by these rules is waived, except for the defenses of lack of jurisdiction over the subject matter of the action, and failure to state a claim on which relief can be granted. However,

　(a) a party who has asserted a defense by motion filed pursuant to MCR 2.116 before filing a responsive pleading need not again assert that defense in a responsive pleading later filed;

　(b) if a pleading states a claim for relief to which a responsive pleading is not required, a defense to that claim may be asserted at the trial unless a pretrial conference summary pursuant to MCR 2.401(C) has limited the issues to be tried.

(3) *Affirmative Defenses.* Affirmative defenses must be stated in a party's responsive pleading, either as originally filed or as amended in accordance with MCR 2.118. Under a separate and distinct heading, a party must state the facts constituting

　(a) an affirmative defense, such as contributory negligence; the existence of an agreement to arbitrate; assumption of risk; payment; release; satisfaction; discharge; license; fraud; duress; estoppel; statute of frauds; statute of limitations; immunity granted by law; want or failure of consideration; or that an instrument or transaction is void, voidable, or cannot be recovered on by reason of statute or nondelivery;

　(b) a defense that by reason of other affirmative matter seeks to avoid the legal effect of or defeat the claim of the opposing party, in whole or in part;

　(c) a ground of defense that, if not raised in the pleading, would be likely to take the adverse party by surprise.

[Effective March 1, 1985; amended effective December 1, 1989; April 1, 1992; April 1, 1998, to apply to actions filed on or after January 1, 1998.]

1985 Staff Comment

MCR 2.111 is based on GCR 1963, 111. The provisions are reorganized, and several are moved to other rules. GCR 1963, 111.8, concerning counterclaims, is relocated to MCR 2.203, which contains the general counterclaim provisions. GCR 1963, 111.10, which provided for submission of a case to the court on stipulated facts, is relocated to the summary disposition rule, MCR 2.116.

In addition, there are several other changes. Subrule (B)(2) includes a requirement that a pleader include a statement of a specific ad damnum if the claim is for a sum certain or an amount that can be computed. In addition, a specific amount must always be stated in actions in which no more than $10,000 is sought.

Subrule (F)(2) includes a slight modification of GCR 1963, 111.3. In general, a defense that a party is not required to plead can be raised at trial. However, a pretrial order under MCR 2.401(C) may limit the issues to be tried.

The [March 1, 1985] amendment of MCR 2.111(F)(3)(a) adds "immunity granted by law" to the list of affirmative defenses that must be pleaded.

GCR 1963, 111.6, regarding unwarranted claims and denials, is omitted. A much more detailed rule covering that subject is included as MCR 2.114.

Staff Comment to 1992 Amendment

The [April 1,] 1992 amendments to MCR 2.111 and 2.116 were designed to confirm the right of a party to amend a pleading to add or modify affirmative defenses. This right of amendment is governed by MCR 2.118. To the extent that *Campbell v St John Hospital*, 434 Mich 608, 615–617; 455 NW2d 695 (1990) had been understood to preclude amendment of affirmative defenses, including defenses related to the Malpractice Arbitration Act (MCL 600.5040 et seq; MSA 27A.5040 et seq), the rule of *Campbell* was modified by these amendments.

Staff Comment to 1998 Amendment

The March 24, 1998 [effective April 1, 1998], amendments of 2.109, 2.111, 2.112, 2.119, 8.103, 8.106, 8.110, 8.111, 9.114, and 9.203, make technical changes necessary in light of statutory amendments and correct cross-references.

The amendments of MCR 2.109 and 2.112 relate to amendments of MCR 600.2912d, 600.2912e; MSA 27A.2912(d), 27A.2912(e), by 1993 PA 78.

The amendments of MCR 2.111 and 2.119 are based on statutes amended by 1996 PA 388. The change in MCR 2.111(B)(2) applies to actions filed on or after January 1, 1998, the effective date of the statute increasing the jurisdictional limit of the district court.

The amendment of MCR 8.106 corrects a statutory reference in light of 1993 PA 189.

The remaining amendments make changes in cross-references necessitated by earlier amendments. Some published versions of the rules already include several of these corrections.

RULE 2.112　PLEADING SPECIAL MATTERS

(A) Capacity; Legal Existence.

(1) Except to the extent required to show jurisdiction of a court, it is not necessary to allege

　(a) the capacity of a party to sue,

　(b) the authority of a party to sue or be sued in a representative capacity, or

　(c) the legal existence of an organized association of persons that is made a party.

(2) A party wishing to raise an issue about

　(a) the legal existence of a party,

　(b) the capacity of a party to sue or be sued, or

　(c) the authority of a party to sue or be sued in a representative capacity,

must do so by specific allegation, including supporting facts peculiarly within the pleader's knowledge.

(B) Fraud, Mistake, or Condition of Mind.

(1) In allegations of fraud or mistake, the circumstances constituting fraud or mistake must be stated with particularity.

(2) Malice, intent, knowledge, and other conditions of mind may be alleged generally.

(C) Conditions Precedent.

(1) In pleading performance or occurrence of conditions precedent, it is sufficient to allege generally that all conditions precedent have been performed or have occurred.

(2) A denial of performance or occurrence must be made specifically and with particularity.

(D) Action on Policy of Insurance.

(1) In an action on a policy of insurance, it is sufficient to allege

  (a) the execution, date, and amount of the policy,

  (b) the premium paid or to be paid,

  (c) the property or risk insured,

  (d) the interest of the insured, and

  (e) the loss.

(2) A defense of

  (a) breach of condition, agreement, representation, or warranty of a policy of insurance or of an application for a policy; or

  (b) failure to furnish proof of loss as required by the policy

must be stated specifically and with particularity.

(E) Action on Written Instrument.

(1) In an action on a written instrument, the execution of the instrument and the handwriting of the defendant are admitted unless the defendant specifically denies the execution or the handwriting and supports the denial with an affidavit filed with the answer. The court may, for good cause, extend the time for filing the affidavits.

(2) This subrule also applies to an action against an indorser and to a party against whom a counterclaim or a cross-claim on a written instrument is filed.

(F) Official Document or Act. In pleading an official document or official act, it is sufficient to allege that the document was issued or the act done in compliance with law.

(G) Judgment. A judgment or decision of a domestic or foreign court, a tribal court of a federally recognized Indian tribe, a judicial or quasi-judicial tribunal, or a board or officer, must be alleged with sufficient particularity to identify it; it is not necessary to state facts showing jurisdiction to render it.

(H) Statutes, Ordinances, or Charters. In pleading a statute, ordinance, or municipal charter, it is sufficient to identify it, without stating its substance.

(I) Special Damages. When items of special damage are claimed, they must be specifically stated.

(J) Law of Other Jurisdictions; Notice in Pleadings. A party who intends to rely on or raise an issue concerning the law of

(1) a state other than Michigan,

(2) a United States territory,

(3) a foreign nation or unit thereof, or

(4) a federally recognized Indian tribe

must give notice of that intention either in his or her pleadings or in a written notice served by the close of discovery.

(K) Fault of Nonparties; Notice.

(1) *Applicability.* This rule applies to actions for personal injury, property damage, and wrongful death to which MCL 600.2957; MSA 27A.2957 and MCL 600.6304; MSA 27A.6304, as amended by 1995 PA 249, apply.

(2) *Notice Requirement.* Notwithstanding MCL 600.6304; MSA 27A.6304, the trier of fact shall not assess the fault of a nonparty unless notice has been given as provided in this subrule.

(3) *Notice.*

  (a) A party against whom a claim is asserted may give notice of a claim that a nonparty is wholly or partially at fault. A notice filed by one party identifying a particular nonparty serves as notice by all parties as to that nonparty.

  (b) The notice shall designate the nonparty and set forth the nonparty's name and last known address, or the best identification of the nonparty that is possible, together with a brief statement of the basis for believing the nonparty is at fault.

  (c) The notice must be filed within 91 days after the party files its first responsive pleading. On motion, the court shall allow a later filing of the notice on a showing that the facts on which the notice is based were not and could not with reasonable diligence have been known to the moving party earlier, provided that the late filing of the notice does not result in unfair prejudice to the opposing party.

(4) *Amendment Adding Party.* A party served with a notice under this subrule may file an amended pleading stating a claim or claims against the nonparty within 91 days of service of the first notice identifying that nonparty. The court may permit later amendment as provided in MCR 2.118.

(L) Medical Malpractice Actions. In an action alleging medical malpractice filed on or after October 1, 1993, each party must file an affidavit as provided in MCL 600.2912d, 600.2912e; MSA 27A.2912(4), 27A.2912(5). Notice of filing the affidavit must be promptly served on the opposing party. If the opposing party has appeared in the action, the notice may be served in the manner provided by MCR 2.107. If the opposing party has not appeared, the notice must be served in the manner provided by MCR 2.105. Proof of service of the notice must be promptly filed with the court.

[Effective March 1, 1985; amended effective July 1, 1996; February 1, 1997; April 1, 1998.]

1985 Staff Comment

MCR 2.112 is comparable to GCR 1963, 112. The only change is the addition of a requirement that a party intending to rely on foreign law must give notice of that intention by the close of discovery. See subrule (J).

The provisions of GCR 1963, 602, regarding actions on written instruments, are moved to this rule as subrule (E).

Staff Comment to 1996 Amendment

The 1996 amendment of MCR 2.112(G) and (J) and the 1996 promulgation of MCR 2.615 were prompted by proposals from the Indian Tribal Court/State Trial Court Forum and from the State Bar of Michigan. The adopted rules reflect a synthesis of those sources, of a corresponding rule of the North Dakota Supreme Court, and of the model rules generated by the Michigan Indian Judicial Association.

Staff Comment to 1997 Amendment

The November 6 amendments of MCR 2.112, 2.222, 2.223, and 2.403, and the repeal of MCR 2.224, effective February 1, 1997, relate to statutory changes made by 1995 PA 161 and 1995 PA 249.

New MCR 2.112(K) governs the procedure for identifying nonparties whose conduct is claimed to be a cause of the injury, and for adding them as parties. See MCL 600.2957; MSA 27A.2957 and MCL 600.6304; MSA 27A.6304.

Staff Comment to 1998 Amendment

The March 24, 1998 [effective April 1, 1998], amendments of 2.109, 2.111, 2.112, 2.119, 8.103, 8.106, 8.110, 8.111, 9.114, and 9.203, make technical changes necessary in light of statutory amendments and correct cross-references.

The amendments of MCR 2.109 and 2.112 relate to amendments of MCR 600.2912d, 600.2912e; MSA 27A.2912(d), 27A.2912(e), by 1993 PA 78.

The amendments of MCR 2.111 and 2.119 are based on statutes amended by 1996 PA 388. The change in MCR 2.111(B)(2) applies to actions filed on or after January 1, 1998, the effective date of the statute increasing the jurisdictional limit of the district court.

The amendment of MCR 8.106 corrects a statutory reference in light of 1993 PA 189.

The remaining amendments make changes in cross-references necessitated by earlier amendments. Some published versions of the rules already include several of these corrections.

RULE 2.113   FORM OF PLEADINGS AND OTHER PAPERS

(A) Applicability. The rules on the form, captioning, signing, and verifying of pleadings apply to all motions, affidavits, and other papers provided for by these rules. However, an affidavit must be verified by oath or affirmation.

(B) Preparation. Every pleading must be legibly typewritten or printed in ink in the English language.

(C) Captions.

(1) the first part of every pleading must contain a caption stating

    (a) the name of the court;

    (b) the names of the parties or the title of the action, subject to subrule (D);

    (c) the case number, including a prefix of the year filed and a two-letter suffix for the case-type code from a list provided by the State Court Administrator pursuant to MCR 8.117 according to the principal subject matter of the proceeding;

    (d) the identification of the pleading (see MCR 2.110[A]);

    (e) the name, business address, telephone number, and state bar number of the pleading attorney;

    (f) the name, address, and telephone number of a pleading party appearing without an attorney; and

    (g) the name and state bar number of each other attorney who has appeared in the action.

(2) The caption of a complaint must also contain either (a) or (b) as a statement of the attorney for the plaintiff, or of a plaintiff appearing without an attorney:

    (a) There is no other pending or resolved civil action arising out of the transaction or occurrence alleged in the complaint.

    (b) A civil action between these parties or other parties arising out of the transaction or occurrence alleged in the complaint has been previously filed in [this court]/[_____ Court], where it was given docket number _____ and was assigned to Judge _____. The action [remains]/[is no longer] pending.

(3) If an action has been assigned to a particular judge in a multi-judge court, the name of that judge must be included in the caption of a pleading later filed with the court.

(D) Names of Parties.

(1) In a complaint, the title of the action must include the names of all the parties, with the plaintiff's name placed first.

(2) In other pleadings, it is sufficient to state the name of the first party on each side with an appropriate indication of other parties, such as "et al."

(E) Paragraphs; Separate Statements.

(1) All allegations must be made in numbered paragraphs, and the paragraphs of a responsive pleading must be numbered to correspond to the numbers of the paragraphs being answered.

(2) The content of each paragraph must be limited as far as practicable to a single set of circumstances.

(3) Each statement of a claim for relief founded on a single transaction or occurrence or on separate

transactions or occurrences, and each defense other than a denial, must be stated in a separately numbered count or defense.

(F) Exhibits; Written Instruments.

(1) If a claim or defense is based on a written instrument, a copy of the instrument or its pertinent parts must be attached to the pleading as an exhibit unless the instrument is

(a) a matter of public record in the county in which the action is commenced and its location in the record is stated in the pleading;

(b) in the possession of the adverse party and the pleading so states;

(c) inaccessible to the pleader and the pleading so states, giving the reason; or

(d) of a nature that attaching the instrument would be unnecessary or impractical and the pleading so states, giving the reason.

(2) An exhibit attached or referred to under subrule (F)(1)(a) or (b) is a part of the pleading for all purposes.

(G) Adoption by Reference. Statements in a pleading may be adopted by reference only in another part of the same pleading.

[Effective March 1, 1985; amended effective July 1, 1989; November 1, 1991; November 30, 1999; May 23, 2000.]

1985 Staff Comment

MCR 2.113 includes provisions from GCR 1963, 110.2(2) and 113. The rules regarding the form of pleadings and papers are included in this rule. Signing of papers is covered in rule 2.114.

Under subrule (A), the rules on the form, captioning, and signing of pleadings apply to all papers. However, affidavits must be verified by oath or affirmation.

Subrule (C)(1), which covers the contents of the caption, adds several new requirements. The case-type code (see MCR 8.117) must be included. In addition, the telephone number of the attorney, or of a pleading party appearing without an attorney, must be included. And subrule (C)(1)(h) requires the name and state bar number of each attorney who has appeared. The requirement was adopted in Supreme Court Administrative Order No. 1983–5.

Subrule (C)(2) specifies the language in which the plaintiff must make the required certification (see MCR 8.112 and GCR 1963, 926.4) regarding prior or pending actions involving the same parties and subject matter. In addition, the rule covers the possibility that an earlier action may have been transferred, rather than dismissed.

In subrule (E)(1) language is added requiring that the paragraphs of the responsive pleading be numbered to correspond to the numbering of the pleading being answered.

Subrule (F) eliminates the exception for insurance policies from the general rule that written instruments on which a claim or defense is based must be attached. Compare GCR 1963, 113.4.

Under subrule (G) adoption by reference is permitted only with regard to other parts of the same document. Compare GCR 1963, 113.5.

Staff Comment to 1989 Amendment

The [April 13, 1989] amendment to MCR 2.113(C)(2) requires the filing attorney's statement to include a reference to other known cases arising out of the same transaction or occurrence as the action being filed, even where such other cases do not involve the same parties.

Staff Comment to 1991 Amendment

The [November 1,] 1991 amendment of MCR 2.113(C)(2) was designed to clarify a plaintiff's initial obligation to disclose the existence of related civil litigation.

Staff Comment to 1999 Amendment

The amendments of MCR 2.113, 5.113, 5.901, 7.210, 8.105, 8.110, 8.116, 8.203, 8.205, and 8.302 [effective November 30, 1999] and the addition of MCR 2.518 and 8.119 [effective November 30, 1999] are to accommodate statewide records standards applicable to all courts and all clerks of the courts as developed and recommended by the Michigan Trial Court Case File Management Standards Committee.

Staff Comment to 2000 Amendment

These amendments [effective May 23, 2000] are made to allow for flexibility in making changes to case classification codes. Case classification codes are used principally for administrative purposes by trial courts and the State Court Administrator for collecting management information regarding case and for identifying the administrative processing of cases.

The notice requirements of MCR 1.201 were dispensed with in order that several changes in case classification codes required with the implementation of the Estates and Protected Individuals Code, MCL 700.1101 et seq.; MSA 27.11101 et seq. could be implemented immediately by the State Court Administrator. The Estates and Protected Individuals Code became effective April 1, 2000. This matter will be included on the Court's future public hearing agenda for the purpose of receiving comments.

The State Court Administrator will incorporate case classification codes in the Case File Management Standards maintained by that office. The State Court Administrator will publish a revised case classification code schedule immediately, and will periodically publish case classification codes for the benefit of the public and the bar.

RULE 2.114 SIGNATURES OF ATTORNEYS AND PARTIES; VERIFICATION; EFFECT; SANCTIONS

(A) Applicability. This rule applies to all pleadings, motions, affidavits, and other papers provided for by these rules. See MCR 2.113(A). In this rule, the term "document" refers to all such papers.

(B) Verification.

(1) Except when otherwise specifically provided by rule or statute, a document need not be verified or accompanied by an affidavit.

(2) If a document is required or permitted to be verified, it may be verified by

(a) oath or affirmation of the party or of someone having knowledge of the facts stated; or

(b) except as to an affidavit, including the following signed and dated declaration: "I declare that the statements above are true to the best of my information, knowledge, and belief."

In addition to the sanctions provided by subrule (E), a person who knowingly makes a false declaration under subrule (B)(2)(b) may be found in contempt of court.

(C) Signature.

(1) *Requirement.* Every document of a party represented by an attorney shall be signed by at least one attorney of record. A party who is not represented by an attorney must sign the document.

(2) *Failure to Sign.* If a document is not signed, it shall be stricken unless it is signed promptly after the omission is called to the attention of the party.

(D) Effect of Signature. The signature of an attorney or party, whether or not the party is represented by an attorney, constitutes a certification by the signer that

(1) he or she has read the document;

(2) to the best of his or her knowledge, information, and belief formed after reasonable inquiry, the document is well grounded in fact and is warranted by existing law or a good-faith argument for the extension, modification, or reversal of existing law; and

(3) the document is not interposed for any improper purpose, such as to harass or to cause unnecessary delay or needless increase in the cost of litigation.

(E) Sanctions for Violation. If a document is signed in violation of this rule, the court, on the motion of a party or on its own initiative, shall impose upon the person who signed it, a represented party, or both, an appropriate sanction, which may include an order to pay to the other party or parties the amount of the reasonable expenses incurred because of the filing of the document, including reasonable attorney fees. The court may not assess punitive damages.

(F) Sanctions for Frivolous Claims and Defenses. In addition to sanctions under this rule, a party pleading a frivolous claim or defense is subject to costs as provided in MCR 2.625(A)(2). The court may not assess punitive damages.

[Effective March 1, 1985; amended effective December 12, 1986; April 1, 1991; January 1, 1995.]

1985 Staff Comment

MCR 2.114 covers the subjects of the signing of papers and the sanctions for unwarranted allegations or denials. These provisions, which are based on the recent amendment of FR Civ P 11, differ considerably from the corresponding provisions in the prior Michigan rules, GCR 1963, 114 and 111.6.

Although the rule uses the term "pleading," it also applies to other papers. See MCR 2.113(A).

Subrule (A) provides that pleadings need not be verified or accompanied by an affidavit in the absence of a specific rule

or statute so requiring. However, pleadings must be signed (see subrule [B]), and subrule (D) provides that the signature operates as a certification of the signer's knowledge of the contents of the pleading, of the signer's good faith belief that the pleading is warranted by the law and facts, and that the pleading is not interposed for improper purposes.

When verification is required by statute or rule, subrule (A) permits the verification to be either by oath or affirmation or by signing a declaration like that found in GCR 1963, 114.3. FR Civ P 11 does not include such a provision, but a federal statute allows the use of a similar declaration. See 28 USC 1746.

The [March 1, 1985] amendment of MCR 2.114(A)(2)(a) corrects a typographical error, substituting "oath or affirmation" for "oath of affirmation".

Subrule (E) authorizes the court to impose sanctions for a signature in violation of the rule.

Staff Comment to 1991 Amendment

The [April 1,] 1991 amendment to MCR 2.114(E) and (F) resolves a split in the Court of Appeals by making clear that punitive damages are not a permissible sanction under these subrules.

Staff Comment to 1995 Amendment

The November 16, 1994, amendment of MCR 2.114 (effective January 1, 1995) clarifies that the rule applies not only to "pleadings," as defined in MCR 2.110(A), but also to other papers provided for by the rules. See MCR 2.113(A), and *Bechtold* v *Morris*, 443 Mich 105 (1993).

RULE 2.115 MOTION TO CORRECT OR TO STRIKE PLEADINGS

(A) Motion for More Definite Statement. If a pleading is so vague or ambiguous that it fails to comply with the requirements of these rules, an opposing party may move for a more definite statement before filing a responsive pleading. The motion must point out the defects complained of and the details desired. If the motion is granted and is not obeyed within 14 days after notice of the order, or within such other time as the court may set, the court may strike the pleading to which the motion was directed or enter an order it deems just.

(B) Motion to Strike. On motion by a party or on the court's own initiative, the court may strike from a pleading redundant, immaterial, impertinent, scandalous, or indecent matter, or may strike all or part of a pleading not drawn in conformity with these rules.

[Effective March 1, 1985.]

1985 Staff Comment

MCR 2.115 is substantially the same as GCR 1963, 115.

RULE 2.116 SUMMARY DISPOSITION

(A) Judgment on Stipulated Facts.

(1) The parties to a civil action may submit an agreed-upon stipulation of facts to the court.

(2) If the parties have stipulated to facts sufficient to enable the court to render judgment in the action, the court shall do so.

(B) Motion.

(1) A party may move for dismissal of or judgment on all or part of a claim in accordance with this rule. A party against whom a defense is asserted may move under this rule for summary disposition of the defense. A request for dismissal without prejudice under MCL 600.2912c; MSA 27A.2912(3) must be made by motion under MCR 2.116 and MCR 2.119.

(2) A motion under this rule may be filed at any time consistent with subrule (D) and subrule (G)(1), but the hearing on a motion brought by a party asserting a claim shall not take place until at least 28 days after the opposing party was served with the pleading stating the claim.

(C) Grounds. The motion may be based on one or more of these grounds, and must specify the grounds on which it is based:

(1) The court lacks jurisdiction over the person or property.

(2) The process issued in the action was insufficient.

(3) The service of process was insufficient.

(4) The court lacks jurisdiction of the subject matter.

(5) The party asserting the claim lacks the legal capacity to sue.

(6) Another action has been initiated between the same parties involving the same claim.

(7) The claim is barred because of release, payment, prior judgment, immunity granted by law, statute of limitations, statute of frauds, an agreement to arbitrate, infancy or other disability of the moving party, or assignment or other disposition of the claim before commencement of the action.

(8) The opposing party has failed to state a claim on which relief can be granted.

(9) The opposing party has failed to state a valid defense to the claim asserted against him or her.

(10) Except as to the amount of damages, there is no genuine issue as to any material fact, and the moving party is entitled to judgment or partial judgment as a matter of law.

(D) Time to Raise Defenses and Objections. The grounds listed in subrule (C) must be raised as follows:

(1) The grounds listed in subrule (C)(1), (2), and (3) must be raised in a party's first motion under this rule or in the party's responsive pleading, whichever is filed first, or they are waived.

(2) The grounds listed in subrule (C)(5), (6), and (7) must be raised in a party's responsive pleading, unless

the grounds are stated in a motion filed under this rule prior to the party's first responsive pleading. Amendment of a responsive pleading is governed by MCR 2.118.

(3) The grounds listed in subrule (C)(4), (8), (9), and (10) may be raised at any time.

(E) Consolidation; Successive Motions.

(1) A party may combine in a single motion as many defenses or objections as the party has based on any of the grounds enumerated in this rule.

(2) No defense or objection is waived by being joined with one or more other defenses or objections.

(3) A party may file more than one motion under this rule, subject to the provisions of subrule (F).

(F) Motion or Affidavit Filed in Bad Faith. A party or an attorney found by the court to have filed a motion or an affidavit in violation of the provisions of MCR 2.114 may, in addition to the imposition of other penalties prescribed by that rule, be found guilty of contempt.

(G) Affidavits; Hearing.

(1) Except as otherwise provided in this subrule, MCR 2.119 applies to motions brought under this rule.

(a) Unless a different period is set by the court,

(i) a written motion under this rule with supporting brief and any affidavits must be filed and served at least 21 days before the time set for the hearing, and

(ii) any response to the motion (including brief and any affidavits) must be filed and served at least 7 days before the hearing.

(b) If the court sets a different time for filing and serving a motion or a response, its authorization must be endorsed in writing on the face of the notice of hearing or made by separate order.

(c) A copy of a motion or response (including brief and any affidavits) filed under this rule must be provided by counsel to the office of the judge hearing the motion. The judge's copy must be clearly marked JUDGE'S COPY on the cover sheet; that notation may be handwritten.

(2) Except as to a motion based on subrule (C)(8) or (9), affidavits, depositions, admissions, or other documentary evidence may be submitted by a party to support or oppose the grounds asserted in the motion.

(3) Affidavits, depositions, admissions, or other documentary evidence in support of the grounds asserted in the motion are required

(a) when the grounds asserted do not appear on the face of the pleadings, or

(b) when judgment is sought based on subrule (C)(10).

(4) A motion under subrule (C)(10) must specifically identify the issues as to which the moving party

believes there is no genuine issue as to any material fact. When a motion under subrule (C)(10) is made and supported as provided in this rule, an adverse party may not rest upon the mere allegations or denials of his or her pleading, but must, by affidavits or as otherwise provided in this rule, set forth specific facts showing that there is a genuine issue for trial. If the adverse party does not so respond, judgment, if appropriate, shall be entered against him or her.

(5) The affidavits, together with the pleadings, depositions, admissions, and documentary evidence then filed in the action or submitted by the parties, must be considered by the court when the motion is based on subrule (C)(1)–(7) or (10). Only the pleadings may be considered when the motion is based on subrule (C)(8) or (9).

(6) Affidavits, depositions, admissions, and documentary evidence offered in support of or in opposition to a motion based on subrule (C)(1)—(7) or (10) shall only be considered to the extent that the content or substance would be admissible as evidence to establish or deny the grounds stated in the motion.

(H) Affidavits Unavailable.

(1) A party may show by affidavit that the facts necessary to support the party's position cannot be presented because the facts are known only to persons whose affidavits the party cannot procure. The affidavit must

(a) name these persons and state why their testimony cannot be procured, and

(b) state the nature of the probable testimony of these persons and the reason for the party's belief that these persons would testify to those facts.

(2) When this kind of affidavit is filed, the court may enter an appropriate order, including an order

(a) denying the motion, or

(b) allowing additional time to permit the affidavit to be supported by further affidavits, or by depositions, answers to interrogatories, or other discovery.

(I) Disposition by Court; Immediate Trial.

(1) If the pleadings show that a party is entitled to judgment as a matter of law, or if the affidavits or other proofs show that there is no genuine issue of material fact, the court shall render judgment without delay.

(2) If it appears to the court that the opposing party, rather than the moving party, is entitled to judgment, the court may render judgment in favor of the opposing party.

(3) A court may, under proper circumstances, order immediate trial to resolve any disputed issue of fact, and judgment may be entered forthwith if the proofs show that a party is entitled to judgment on the facts as determined by the court. An immediate trial may

be ordered if the grounds asserted are based on subrules (C)(1) through (C)(6), or if the motion is based on subrule (C)(7) and a jury trial as of right has not been demanded on or before the date set for hearing. If the motion is based on subrule (C)(7) and a jury trial has been demanded, the court may order immediate trial, but must afford the parties a jury trial as to issues raised by the motion as to which there is a right to trial by jury.

(4) The court may postpone until trial the hearing and decision on a matter involving disputed issues of fact brought before it under this rule.

(5) If the grounds asserted are based on subrule (C)(8), (9), or (10), the court shall give the parties an opportunity to amend their pleadings as provided by MCR 2.118, unless the evidence then before the court shows that amendment would not be justified.

(J) Motion Denied; Case Not Fully Adjudicated on Motion.

(1) If a motion under this rule is denied, or if the decision does not dispose of the entire action or grant all the relief demanded, the action must proceed to final judgment. The court may:

(a) set the time for further pleadings or amendments required;

(b) examine the evidence before it and, by questioning the attorneys, ascertain what material facts are without substantial controversy, including the extent to which damages are not disputed; and

(c) set the date on which all discovery must be completed.

(2) A party aggrieved by a decision of the court entered under this rule may:

(a) seek interlocutory leave to appeal as provided for by these rules;

(b) claim an immediate appeal as of right if the judgment entered by the court constitutes a final judgment under MCR 2.604(B); or

(c) proceed to final judgment and raise errors of the court committed under this rule in an appeal taken from final judgment.

[Effective March 1, 1985; amended effective December 12, 1986; January 1, 1991; April 1, 1992; September 19, 1995; January 1, 2001.]

1985 Staff Comment

MCR 2.116 consolidates and reorganizes the provisions regarding summary disposition of claims or defenses found in GCR 1963, 111.10, 116, and 117. Much of the substance of the rules remains the same, although procedural provisions formerly applicable only to rule 116 or rule 117 are made applicable to all portions of the new rule.

Subrule (A) is the procedure for judgment on stipulated facts found in GCR 1963, 111.10.

Subrule (B) is derived from GCR 1963, 117.1. The language is modified to indicate that not all such motions seek "judgment" on a claim. Sometimes the relief sought is dismissal (for example, when the motion challenges service of process or jurisdiction).

Under GCR 1963, 117.1 a party seeking to recover on a claim could not file a motion until the adverse party had responded. Under subrule (B)(2), the motion may be *filed* at any time, but the claimant may not notice it for hearing until the time for answer has passed.

The [March 1, 1985] amendment of MCR 2.116(B)(2) corrects the cross-reference to subrule (D), which covers the time for raising defenses.

Subrule (C) collects the various grounds for accelerated and summary judgment found in GCR 1963, 116.1 and 117.2.

Subrule (D) collects the various provisions regarding the time when these grounds must be raised. See GCR 1963, 116.1, 116.2. The provision should be read in conjunction with MCR 2.111(F), which covers the subject of when defenses must be raised, and MCR 2.118(D), under which an amended pleading relates back to the date the original pleading was filed.

Subrule (E) is based on GCR 1963, 116.2.

Subrule (F) replaces the provisions of GCR 1963, 116.5, regarding affidavits made in bad faith, with a reference to MCR 2.114, which covers the subject of bad faith signing of papers.

Subrule (G), regarding affidavits, is based on GCR 116.3 and 117.3. The rule makes clear that affidavits as well as other evidentiary materials submitted in connection with a motion must be considered by the court when the motion is based on subrules (C)(1)–(7) or (10). However, when the motion is based on subrule (C)(8) (failure to state a claim) or subrule (C)(9) (failure to state a defense), only the pleadings may be considered.

Subrule (G)(4) is new. It requires a party moving for summary judgment under subrule (C)(10) (lack of genuine issue of material fact) to specify the issues as to which it is claimed that there is no factual dispute. Further, language taken from FR Civ P 56(e) is added, requiring the party opposing the motion to respond with affidavits or other evidentiary materials to show the existence of a factual dispute, rather than relying on the allegations or denials in pleadings.

Subrule (H) covers procedure when a party shows that affidavits are unavailable. It is derived from GCR 1963, 116.6.

Subrule (I) includes the provisions regarding disposition of the motion found in GCR 1963, 116.3 and 117.3. In addition, under subrule (I)(2), an immediate trial of disputed factual issues raised by a motion under subrule (C)(7) may be held despite the fact that a jury has been demanded. The immediate trial would, however, be by jury.

The [March 1, 1985] amendment of MCR 2.116(I)(1) adds the word "material" in the reference to genuine issues of fact, making the language consistent with MCR 2.116(C)(10).

Subrule (J) includes the provisions regarding further proceedings when the motion is denied or the case is not fully decided on motion. See GCR 1963, 117.4. In addition, subrule (J)(2) contains new provisions clarifying the appellate options of a party aggrieved by the court's decision.

In addition, the provisions of GCR 1963, 116.4 regarding the form of affidavits are moved to the motion practice rule, MCR 2.119. The motion practice rule is expressly made applicable to MCR 2.116. See MCR 2.116(G)(1).

Staff Comment to 1990 Amendment

The 1990 amendments to MCR 2.116(G)(1) [effective January 1, 1991] were designed to give the parties and the court additional time to prepare for a hearing on a motion for summary disposition. The 1990 amendments to MCR 2.116(B)(2) [effective January 1, 1991] added a cross-reference to MCR 2.116(G)(1) and clarified a previously ambiguous provision concerning the scheduling of a hearing on a motion brought by a party asserting a claim.

Staff Comment to 1992 Amendment

The [April 1,] 1992 amendments to MCR 2.111 and 2.116 were designed to confirm the right of a party to amend a pleading to add or modify affirmative defenses. This right of amendment is governed by MCR 2.118. To the extent that *Campbell* v *St John Hospital*, 434 Mich 608, 615–617; 455 NW2d 695 (1990) had been understood to preclude amendment of affirmative defenses, including defenses related to the Malpractice Arbitration Act (MCL 600.5040 et seq; MSA 27A.5040 et seq), the rule of *Campbell* was modified by these amendments.

Staff Comment to 1995 Amendment

The amendments of MCR 2.116(J)(1), 2.119(F)(1), 2.204(A)(4), and 2.614(G) correct cross-references to MCR 2.604 that were no longer correct after MCR 2.604 was amended on May 16, 1995, and further amended on September 19, 1995.

Staff Comment to 2000 Amendment

The October 3, 2000, amendment of MCR 2.116(G), effective January 1, 2001, specifies that materials submitted in support of or opposition to a motion under MCR 2.116 (C)(1)—(7) or (10) may only be considered to the extent that their content or substance would be admissible. See *Maiden* v *Rozwood*, 461 Mich 109 (1999).

RULE 2.117   APPEARANCES

(A) Appearance by Party.

(1) A party may appear in an action by filing a notice to that effect or by physically appearing before the court for that purpose. In the latter event, the party must promptly file a written appearance and serve it on all persons entitled to service. The party's address and telephone number must be included in the appearance.

(2) Filing an appearance without taking any other action toward prosecution or defense of the action neither confers nor enlarges the jurisdiction of the court over the party. An appearance entitles a party to receive copies of all pleadings and papers as provided by MCR 2.107(A). In all other respects, the party is treated as if the appearance had not been filed.

(B) Appearance by Attorney.

(1) *In General.* An attorney may appear by an act indicating that the attorney represents a party in the action. An appearance by an attorney for a party is deemed an appearance by the party. Unless a particular rule indicates otherwise, any act required to be performed by a party may be performed by the attorney representing the party.

(2) *Notice of Appearance.*

(a) If an appearance is made in a manner not involving the filing of a paper with the court, the attorney must promptly file a written appearance and serve it on the parties entitled to service. The attorney's address and telephone number must be included in the appearance.

(b) If an attorney files an appearance, but takes no other action toward prosecution or defense of the action, the appearance entitles the attorney to service of pleadings and papers as provided by MCR 2.107(A).

(3) *Appearance by Law Firm.*

(a) A pleading, appearance, motion, or other paper filed by a law firm on behalf of a client is deemed the appearance of the individual attorney first filing a paper in the action. All notices required by these rules may be served on that individual. That attorney's appearance continues until an order of substitution or withdrawal is entered. This subrule is not intended to prohibit other attorneys in the law firm from appearing in the action on behalf of the party.

(b) The appearance of an attorney is deemed to be the appearance of every member of the law firm. Any attorney in the firm may be required by the court to conduct a court ordered conference or trial.

(C) Duration of Appearance by Attorney.

(1) Unless otherwise stated or ordered by the court, an attorney's appearance applies only in the court in which it is made, or to which the action is transferred, until a final judgment is entered disposing of all claims by or against the party whom the attorney represents and the time for appeal of right has passed. The appearance applies in an appeal taken before entry of final judgment by the trial court.

(2) An attorney who has entered an appearance may withdraw from the action or be substituted for only on order of the court.

[Effective March 1, 1985.]

1985 Staff Comment

MCR 2.117 is largely new and governs appearances by parties and attorneys.

Under subrule (A) a party may appear by filing a written notice of appearance, which may follow a physical appearance before the court. The only effect of such an appearance is to entitle the party to receive copies of papers as provided by MCR 2.107(A).

Subrule (B) governs appearances by attorneys. In general, an attorney who has appeared for a party may act for the party in the action. See subrule (B)(1). As in the case of a party, an attorney's appearance may be in the form of filing a notice of appearance, with no further action being taken. The effect is the same: the attorney is entitled to receive copies of papers filed. See subrule (B)(2)(b).

Subrule (B)(3) governs appearances by a law firm. Notices may be served on the individual attorney who first signs

a paper filed in the case. However, the rule is not meant to prevent other attorneys in the firm from appearing. The appearance is also deemed to be the appearance of every other member of the law firm, and the court may order another attorney in the firm to appear at a conference or for trial.

Subrule (C) governs the duration of an attorney's appearance. An appearance applies only until the time for an appeal of right from the final judgment has passed. Thereafter, the attorney is deemed not to represent the party, and service of further notices must be on the party. The attorney's appearance does apply in an appeal taken before entry of final judgment. See subrule (C)(1). Otherwise, an appearance in the trial court does not apply on appeal. The rules governing appeals to circuit court (MCR 7.101[D][1]) and the Court of Appeals (MCR 7.204[G]) require the filing of a new appearance for an appellee.

Under subrule (C)(2) a court order is required for withdrawal or substitution of an attorney.

RULE 2.118   AMENDED AND SUPPLEMENTAL PLEADINGS

(A) Amendments.

(1) A party may amend a pleading once as a matter of course within 14 days after being served with a responsive pleading by an adverse party, or within 14 days after serving the pleading if it does not require a responsive pleading.

(2) Except as provided in subrule (A)(1), a party may amend a pleading only by leave of the court or by written consent of the adverse party. Leave shall be freely given when justice so requires.

(3) On a finding that inexcusable delay in requesting an amendment has caused or will cause the adverse party additional expense that would have been unnecessary had the request for amendment been filed earlier, the court may condition the order allowing amendment on the offending party's reimbursing the adverse party for the additional expense, including reasonable attorney fees.

(4) Amendments must be filed in writing, dated, and numbered consecutively, and must comply with MCR 2.113. Unless otherwise indicated, an amended pleading supersedes the former pleading.

(B) Response to Amendments. Within the time prescribed by MCR 2.108, a party served with an amendment to a pleading requiring a response under MCR 2.110(B) must

(1) serve and file a pleading in response to the amended pleading, or

(2) serve and file a notice that the party's pleading filed in response to the opposing party's earlier pleading will stand as the response to the amended pleading.

(C) Amendments to Conform to the Evidence.

(1) When issues not raised by the pleadings are tried by express or implied consent of the parties, they are treated as if they had been raised by the pleadings. In that case, amendment of the pleadings to conform to the evidence and to raise those issues may be made on motion of a party at any time, even after judgment.

(2) If evidence is objected to at trial on the ground that it is not within the issues raised by the pleadings, amendment to conform to that proof shall not be allowed unless the party seeking to amend satisfies the court that the amendment and the admission of the evidence would not prejudice the objecting party in maintaining his or her action or defense on the merits. The court may grant an adjournment to enable the objecting party to meet the evidence.

(D) Relation Back of Amendments. An amendment that adds a claim or a defense relates back to the date of the original pleading if the claim or defense asserted in the amended pleading arose out of the conduct, transaction, or occurrence set forth, or attempted to be set forth, in the original pleading.

(E) Supplemental Pleadings. On motion of a party the court may, on reasonable notice and on just terms, permit the party to serve a supplemental pleading to state transactions or events that have happened since the date of the pleading sought to be supplemented, whether or not the original pleading is defective in its statement of a claim for relief or a defense. The court may order the adverse party to plead, specifying the time allowed for pleading.

[Effective March 1, 1985; amended effective January 1, 2001.]

1985 Staff Comment

MCR 2.118 is based on GCR 1963, 118.

Under subrule (A)(3), the court may order the amending party to compensate the opposing party for the additional expense caused by a late amendment.

Subrule (B) modifies the language of GCR 1963, 118.2 regarding responses to amended pleadings. Within the time allowed, the party must either serve and file a responsive pleading or serve and file a notice that the pleading on file in response to the earlier pleading will stand as the response to the amended one.

Staff Comment to 2000 Amendment

The October 24, 2000, amendment of MCR 2.118, effective January 1, 2001, clarifies that the relation-back doctrine pertains to the addition of claims and defenses.

RULE 2.119 MOTION PRACTICE

(A) Form of Motions.

(1) An application to the court for an order in a pending action must be by motion. Unless made during a hearing or trial, a motion must

(a) be in writing,

(b) state with particularity the grounds and authority on which it is based,

(c) state the relief or order sought, and

(d) be signed by the party or attorney as provided in MCR 2.114.

(2) A motion or response to a motion that presents an issue of law must be accompanied by a brief citing the authority on which it is based. Except as permitted by the court, the combined length of any motion and brief, or of a response and brief, may not exceed 20 pages double spaced, exclusive of attachments and exhibits. Quotations and footnotes may be single-spaced. At least one-inch margins must be used, and printing shall not be smaller than 12–point type. A copy of a motion or response (including brief) filed under this rule must be provided by counsel to the office of the judge hearing the motion. The judge's copy must be clearly marked JUDGE'S COPY on the cover sheet; that notation may be handwritten.

(3) A motion and notice of the hearing on it may be combined in the same document.

(4) If a contested motion is filed after rejection of a proposed order under subrule (D), a copy of the rejected order and an affidavit establishing the rejection must be filed with the motion.

(B) Form of Affidavits.

(1) If an affidavit is filed in support of or in opposition to a motion, it must:

(a) be made on personal knowledge;

(b) state with particularity facts admissible as evidence establishing or denying the grounds stated in the motion; and

(c) show affirmatively that the affiant, if sworn as a witness, can testify competently to the facts stated in the affidavit.

(2) Sworn or certified copies of all papers or parts of papers referred to in an affidavit must be attached to the affidavit unless the papers or copies:

(a) have already been filed in the action;

(b) are matters of public record in the county in which the action is pending;

(c) are in the possession of the adverse party, and this fact is stated in the affidavit or the motion; or

(d) are of such nature that attaching them would be unreasonable or impracticable, and this fact and the reasons are stated in the affidavit or the motion.

(C) Time for Service and Filing of Motions and Responses.

(1) Unless a different period is set by these rules or by the court for good cause, a written motion (other than one that may be heard ex parte), notice of the hearing on the motion, and any supporting brief or affidavits must be served as follows:

(a) at least 9 days before the time set for the hearing, if served by mail, or

(b) at least 7 days before the time set for the hearing, if served by delivery under MCR 2.107(C)(1) or (2).

(2) Unless a different period is set by these rules or by the court for good cause, any response to a motion (including a brief or affidavits) required or permitted by these rules must be served as follows:

(a) at least 5 days before the hearing, if served by mail, or

(b) at least 3 days before the hearing, if served by delivery under MCR 2.107(C)(1) or (2).

(3) If the court sets a different time for serving a motion or response its authorization must be endorsed in writing on the face of the notice of hearing or made by separate order.

(4) Unless the court sets a different time, a motion must be filed at least 7 days before the hearing, and any response to a motion required or permitted by these rules must be filed at least 3 days before the hearing.

(D) Uncontested Orders.

(1) Before filing a motion, a party may serve on the opposite party a copy of a proposed order and a request to stipulate to the court's entry of the proposed order.

(2) On receipt of a request to stipulate, a party may

(a) stipulate to the entry of the order by signing the following statement at the end of the proposed order: "I stipulate to the entry of the above order"; or

(b) waive notice and hearing on the entry of an order by signing the following statement at the end of the proposed order: "Notice and hearing on entry of the above order is waived."

A proposed order is deemed rejected unless it is stipulated to or notice and hearing are waived within 7 days after it is served.

(3) If the parties have stipulated to the entry of a proposed order or waived notice and hearing, the court may enter the order. If the court declines to enter the order, it shall notify the moving party that a hearing on the motion is required. The matter then proceeds as a contested motion under subrule (E).

(4) The moving party must serve a copy of an order entered by the court pursuant to subrule (D)(3) on the parties entitled to notice under MCR 2.107, or notify them that the court requires the matter to be heard as a contested motion.

(5) Notwithstanding the provisions of subrule (D)(3), stipulations and orders for adjournment are governed by MCR 2.503.

(E) Contested Motions.

(1) Contested motions should be noticed for hearing at the time designated by the court for the hearing of motions. A motion will be heard on the day for which it is noticed, unless the court otherwise directs. If a motion cannot be heard on the day it is noticed, the court may schedule a new hearing date or the moving party may renotice the hearing.

(2) When a motion is based on facts not appearing of record, the court may hear the motion on affidavits presented by the parties, or may direct that the motion be heard wholly or partly on oral testimony or deposition.

(3) A court may, in its discretion, dispense with or limit oral arguments on motions, and may require the parties to file briefs in support of and in opposition to a motion.

(4) Appearance at the hearing is governed by the following:

(a) A party who, pursuant to subrule (D)(2), has previously rejected the proposed order before the court must either

(i) appear at the hearing held on the motion, or

(ii) before the hearing, file a response containing a concise statement of reasons in opposition to the motion and supporting authorities.

A party who fails to comply with this subrule is subject to assessment of costs under subrule (E)(4)(c).

(b) Unless excused by the court, the moving party must appear at a hearing on the motion. A moving party who fails to appear is subject to assessment of costs under subrule (E)(4)(c); in addition, the court may assess a penalty not to exceed $100, payable to the clerk of the court.

(c) If a party violates the provisions of subrule (E)(4)(a) or (b), the court shall assess costs against the offending party, that party's attorney, or both, equal to the expenses reasonably incurred by the opposing party in appearing at the hearing, including reasonable attorney fees, unless the circumstances make an award of expenses unjust.

(F) Motions for Rehearing or Reconsideration.

(1) Unless another rule provides a different procedure for reconsideration of a decision (see, e.g., MCR 2.604[A], 2.612), a motion for rehearing or reconsideration of the decision on a motion must be served and filed not later than 14 days after entry of an order disposing of the motion.

(2) No response to the motion may be filed, and there is no oral argument, unless the court otherwise directs.

(3) Generally, and without restricting the discretion of the court, a motion for rehearing or reconsideration which merely presents the same issues ruled on by

the court, either expressly or by reasonable implication, will not be granted. The moving party must demonstrate a palpable error by which the court and the parties have been misled and show that a different disposition of the motion must result from correction of the error.

(G) Motion Fees. The following provisions apply to actions in which a motion fee is required by MCL 600.2529(1)(e); MSA 2529(1)(e) or MCL 600.8371(10); MSA 27A.8371(10):

(1) A motion fee must be paid on the filing of any request for an order in a pending action, whether the request is entitled "motion," "petition," "application," or otherwise.

(2) The clerk shall charge a single motion fee, in the amount specified by MCL 600.2529(1)(e); MSA 27A.2529(1)(e) or MCL 600.8371(10); MSA 27A.8371(10), for all motions filed at the same time in an action regardless of the number of separately captioned documents filed or the number of distinct or alternative requests for relief included in the motions.

(3) A motion fee may not be charged:

(a) in criminal cases;

(b) for a notice of settlement of a proposed judgment or order under MCR 2.602(B);

(c) for a request for an order waiving fees under MCR 2.002 or MCL 600.2529(4); MSA 27A.2529(4) or MCL 600.8371(6); MSA 27A.8371(6); T21☐(d) if the motion is filed at the same time as another document in the same action as to which a fee is required by another provision of MCL 600.2529; MSA 27A.2529 or MCL 600.8371; MSA 27A.8371; or

(e) for entry of an uncontested order under subrule (D).

[Effective March 1, 1985; amended effective October 1, 1989; October 1, 1991; September 1, 1995; September 19, 1995; February 4, 1997; April 1, 1998.]

1985 Staff Comment

MCR 2.119 provides considerably more detail than did the prior motion practice rule, GCR 1963, 119. It brings together a number of provisions from various sections of the General Court Rules and adds several new provisions.

Subrule (A)(1), governing the basic form of motions, is taken from GCR 1963, 110.2. The signing requirements of MCR 2.114 apply. The remainder of subrule (A) consists of new provisions allowing a notice of hearing to be combined with the motion in a single document, and requiring that a rejected order be attached to a contested motion filed thereafter.

Subrule (B), governing the form of affidavits, is taken from GCR 1963, 116.4.

Subrule (C) replaces GCR 1963, 108.4, which provided for 4 days' notice of motions. The notice time is lengthened to 9 days if the motion is served by mail and 7 days if it is delivered to the opposing party. Similarly, subrule (C)(2) changes the time for response by the opposing party to 5 days (service by mail) or 3 days (delivery). Finally, the rule expressly provides the times by which the motions and responses must be filed. See subrule (C)(4). The court is authorized to set different time limits, but must do so in writing on the notice of hearing or in a separate order. See subrule (C)(3).

The [March 1, 1985] amendment of MCR 2.119(C)(4) explicitly authorizes the court to modify the time for filing motions and responses to motions.

Subrule (D) is a new provision creating an optional procedure for seeking uncontested orders. A party may serve a proposed order on the other parties, requesting stipulation to the entry of the order. The other parties may stipulate to the entry of the order or waive notice of hearing on its entry with language specified in subrule (D)(2). If they do, the court shall either enter the order or notify the moving party that a hearing is required. The moving party is responsible for notice of the court's actions. Subrule (D)(5) provides that MCR 2.503 governs stipulations for adjournment. A party may choose to file the motion without having used the uncontested order procedure, or may use a less formal method of seeking agreement; however, the opposing party would not be subject to the cost sanctions of subrule (E)(4).

Subrule (E) governs the procedure regarding contested motions, which may be used: (1) without resort to the uncontested order procedure, (2) following rejection of a proposed order under the uncontested order procedure, or (3) because the court has declined to enter an order to which the parties have stipulated. Subrules (E)(1) and (3) are based on the current motion practice provisions of GCR 1963, 119. Subrule (E)(4) creates the requirement that the moving party, and any other party who has previously rejected the proposed order, appear at the hearing or face the possible imposition of costs.

Subrule (E)(2) is a new provision based on FR Civ P 43(e). It gives the judge the option of making certain factual decisions relevant to motions on the affidavits filed, or of directing that depositions or in-court testimony be taken. The rule would not apply to at least some motions under MCR 2.116, which has its own provisions regarding the manner in which the judge is to consider a motion.

Subrule (F) adds a new provision covering motions for rehearing or reconsideration. It is similar to local rule 17(k) of the United States District Court for the Eastern District of Michigan. Such a motion must be filed and served within 7 days after the entry of the order disposing of the motion, and there is to be no response or oral argument unless directed by the court.

Subrule (G) contains the motion fee provisions found in Administrative Order 1978–6. Under the present statute, MCL 600.2529; MSA 27A.2529, motion fees are required only in circuit court in counties with populations of more than 100,000. Another exception is added: no fee is required for entry of an uncontested order under subrule (D).

Staff Comment to 1989 Amendment

There are two changes [in the October 1, 1989 amendment] in MCR 2.119(F)(1). First, the rule is expressly made inapplicable where other rules provide different procedures for seeking reconsideration of decisions. Second, the time limit on motions for reconsideration is increased from 7 to 14 days.

Staff Comment to 1991 Amendment

The [October 1,] 1991 amendment of Rule 2.119(A) was the product of a proposal by the Michigan Judges Association and of earlier proposals that had been developed in conjunction with the work of the Caseflow Management Coordinating Committee and the Caseflow Management Rules Committee. The 20–page limit on briefs accords with rules that have been promulgated by the United States District Court for the Eastern District of Michigan and for the Western District of Michigan.

Staff Comment to September 1, 1995 Amendment

The 1995 amendment of MCR 2.119(A)(2) changed some of the technical requirements for motions, responses, and accompanying briefs.

Staff Comment to September 19, 1995 Amendment

The amendments of MCR 2.116(J)(1), 2.119(F)(1), 2.204(A)(4), and 2.614(G) correct cross-references to MCR 2.604 that were no longer correct after MCR 2.604 was amended on May 16, 1995, and further amended on September 19, 1995.

Staff Comment to 1997 Amendment

The February 4, 1997, amendment to MCR 2.119(G) adjusts the reference to the statute that establishes the fees for filing motions.

Staff Comment to 1998 Amendment

The March 24, 1998 [effective April 1, 1998], amendments of 2.109, 2.111, 2.112, 2.119, 8.103, 8.106, 8.110, 8.111, 9.114, and 9.203, make technical changes necessary in light of statutory amendments and correct cross-references.

The amendments of MCR 2.109 and 2.112 relate to amendments of MCR 600.2912d, 600.2912e; MSA 27A.2912(d), 27A.2912(e), by 1993 PA 78.

The amendments of MCR 2.111 and 2.119 are based on statutes amended by 1996 PA 388. The change in MCR 2.111(B)(2) applies to actions filed on or after January 1, 1998, the effective date of the statute increasing the jurisdictional limit of the district court.

The amendment of MCR 8.106 corrects a statutory reference in light of 1993 PA 189.

The remaining amendments make changes in cross-references necessitated by earlier amendments. Some published versions of the rules already include several of these corrections.

SUBCHAPTER 2.200   PARTIES; JOINDER OF CLAIMS AND PARTIES; VENUE; TRANSFER OF ACTIONS

RULE 2.201   PARTIES PLAINTIFF AND DEFENDANT; CAPACITY

(A) Designation of Parties. The party who commences a civil action is designated as plaintiff and the adverse party as defendant. In an appeal the relative position of the parties and their designations as plaintiff and defendant are the same, but they are also designated as appellant and appellee.

(B) Real Party in Interest. An action must be prosecuted in the name of the real party in interest, subject to the following provisions:

(1) A personal representative, guardian, conservator, trustee of an express trust, a party with whom or in whose name a contract has been made for the benefit of another, or a person authorized by statute may sue in his or her own name without joining the party for whose benefit the action is brought.

(2) An action on the bond of a public officer required to give bond to the people of the state may be brought in the name of the person to whom the right on the bond accrues.

(3) An action on a bond, contract, or undertaking made with an officer of the state or of a governmental unit, including but not limited to a public, municipal, quasi-municipal, or governmental corporation, an unincorporated board, a public body, or a political subdivision, may be brought in the name of the state or the governmental unit for whose benefit the contract was made.

(4) An action to prevent illegal expenditure of state funds or to test the constitutionality of a statute relating to such an expenditure may be brought:

(a) in the name of a domestic nonprofit corporation organized for civic, protective, or improvement purposes; or

(b) in the names of at least 5 residents of Michigan who own property assessed for direct taxation by the county where they reside.

(C) Capacity to Sue or Be Sued.

(1) A natural person may sue or be sued in his or her own name.

(2) A person conducting a business under a name subject to certification under the assumed name statute may be sued in that name in an action arising out of the conduct of that business.

(3) A partnership, partnership association, or unincorporated voluntary association having a distinguishing name may sue or be sued in its partnership or association name, in the names of any of its members designated as such, or both.

(4) A domestic or a foreign corporation may sue or be sued in its corporate name, unless a statute provides otherwise.

(5) Actions to which the state or a governmental unit (including but not limited to a public, municipal, quasi-municipal, or governmental corporation, an unincorporated board, a public body, or a political subdivision) is a party may be brought by or against the state

or governmental unit in its own name, or in the name of an officer authorized to sue or be sued on its behalf. An officer of the state or governmental unit must be sued in the officer's official capacity to enforce the performance of an official duty. An officer who sues or is sued in his or her official capacity may be described as a party by official title and not by name, but the court may require the name to be added.

(D) Unknown Parties; Procedure.

(1) Persons who are or may be interested in the subject matter of an action, but whose names cannot be ascertained on diligent inquiry, may be made parties by being described as:

(a) unknown claimants;

(b) unknown owners; or

(c) unknown heirs, devisees, or assignees of a deceased person who may have been interested in the subject matter of the action.

If it cannot be ascertained on diligent inquiry whether a person who is or may be interested in the subject matter of the action is alive or dead, what disposition the person may have made of his or her interest, or where the person resides if alive, the person and everyone claiming under him or her may be made parties by naming the person and adding "or [his or her] unknown heirs, devisees, or assignees".

(2) The names and descriptions of the persons sought to be made parties, with a statement of the efforts made to identify and locate them, must be stated in the complaint and verified by oath or affirmation by the plaintiff or someone having knowledge of the facts in the plaintiff's behalf. The court may require a more specific description to be made by amendment.

(3) A publication giving notice to persons who cannot be personally served must include the description of unknown persons as set forth in the complaint or amended complaint.

(4) The publication and all later proceedings in the action are conducted as if the unknown parties were designated by their proper names. The judgment rendered determines the nature, validity, and extent of the rights of all parties.

(5) A person desiring to appear and show his or her interest in the subject matter of the action must proceed under MCR 2.209. Subject to that rule, the person may be made a party in his or her proper name.

(E) Minors and Incompetent Persons. This subrule does not apply to proceedings under chapter 5.

(1) *Representation.*

(a) If a minor or incompetent person has a conservator, actions may be brought and must be defended by the conservator on behalf of the minor or incompetent person.

(b) If a minor or incompetent person does not have a conservator to represent the person as plaintiff, the court shall appoint a competent and responsible person to appear as next friend on his or her behalf, and the next friend is responsible for the costs of the action.

(c) If the minor or incompetent person does not have a conservator to represent the person as defendant, the action may not proceed until the court appoints a guardian ad litem, who is not responsible for the costs of the action unless, by reason of personal misconduct, he or she is specifically charged costs by the court. It is unnecessary to appoint a representative for a minor accused of a civil infraction.

(2) *Appointment of Representative.*

(a) Appointment of a next friend or guardian ad litem shall be made by the court as follows:

(i) if the party is a minor 14 years of age or older, on the minor's nomination, accompanied by a written consent of the person to be appointed;

(ii) if the party is a minor under 14 years of age or an incompetent person, on the nomination of the party's next of kin or of another relative or friend the court deems suitable, accompanied by a written consent of the person to be appointed; or

(iii) if a nomination is not made or approved within 21 days after service of process, on motion of the court or of a party.

(b) The court may refuse to appoint a representative it deems unsuitable.

(c) The order appointing a person next friend or guardian ad litem must be promptly filed with the clerk of the court.

(3) *Security.*

(a) Except for costs and expenses awarded to the next friend or guardian ad litem or the represented party, a person appointed under this subrule may not receive money or property belonging to the minor or incompetent party or awarded to that party in the action, unless he or she gives security as the court directs.

(b) The court may require that the conservator representing a minor or incompetent party give security as the court directs before receiving the party's money or property.

(4) *Incompetency While Action Pending.* A party who becomes incompetent while an action is pending may be represented by his or her conservator, or the court may appoint a next friend or guardian ad litem as if the action had been commenced after the appointment.

[Effective March 1, 1985; amended effective April 1, 1992.]

1985 Staff Comment

MCR 2.201 is substantially the same as GCR 1963, 201.

The term "conservator" is added in subrule (B)(1) to conform to the Revised Probate Code.

Language is added to subrule (E)(1)(c) to make clear that it is not necessary to appoint a representative for a minor accused of a civil infraction. See MCL 257.741(5); MSA 9.2441(5).

Staff Comment to 1992 Amendment

Subrule (E) is amended [effective April 1, 1992] to make clear that its terms do not apply to proceedings under chapter 5.

RULE 2.202   SUBSTITUTION OF PARTIES

(A) Death.

(1) If a party dies and the claim is not thereby extinguished, the court may order substitution of the proper parties.

(a) A motion for substitution may be made by a party, or by the successor or representative of the deceased party.

(b) Unless a motion for substitution is made within 91 days after filing and service of a statement of the fact of the death, the action must be dismissed as to the deceased party, unless the party seeking substitution shows that there would be no prejudice to any other party from allowing later substitution.

(c) Service of the statement or motion must be made on the parties as provided in MCR 2.107, and on persons not parties as provided in MCR 2.105.

(2) If one or more of the plaintiffs or one or more of the defendants in an action dies, and the right sought to be enforced survives only to the surviving plaintiffs or only against the surviving defendants, the action does not abate. A party or attorney who learns that a party has died must promptly file a notice of the death.

(B) Transfer or Change of Interest. If there is a change or transfer of interest, the action may be continued by or against the original party in his or her original capacity, unless the court, on motion supported by affidavit, directs that the person to whom the interest is transferred be substituted for or joined with the original party, or directs that the original party be made a party in another capacity. Notice must be given as provided in subrule (A)(1)(c).

(C) Public Officers; Death or Separation From Office. When an officer of the class described in MCR 2.201(C)(5) is a party to an action and during its pendency dies, resigns, or otherwise ceases to hold office, the action may be continued and maintained by or against the officer's successor without a formal order of substitution.

(D) Substitution at Any Stage. Substitution of parties under this rule may be ordered by the court either before or after judgment or by the Court of Appeals or Supreme Court pending appeal. If substi-

tution is ordered, the court may require additional security to be given.

[Effective March 1, 1985.]

1985 Staff Comment

MCR 2.202 is based on GCR 1963, 202.

Subrule (A)(1)(b) sets a 91-day time limit for moving to substitute following the death of a party. This makes the rule consistent with FR Civ P 25. However, later substitution is allowed if the party seeking it shows that no other party will be prejudiced because of the late motion.

Language is added in subrule (A)(2) to make clear that any attorney or party who learns of the death is to file a notice.

RULE 2.203   JOINDER OF CLAIMS, COUNTERCLAIMS, AND CROSS–CLAIMS

(A) Compulsory Joinder. In a pleading that states a claim against an opposing party, the pleader must join every claim that the pleader has against that opposing party at the time of serving the pleading, if it arises out of the transaction or occurrence that is the subject matter of the action and does not require for its adjudication the presence of third parties over whom the court cannot acquire jurisdiction.

(B) Permissive Joinder. A pleader may join as either independent or alternate claims as many claims, legal or equitable, as the pleader has against an opposing party. If a claim is one previously cognizable only after another claim has been prosecuted to a conclusion, the two claims may be joined in a single action; but the court may grant relief only in accordance with the substantive rights of the parties.

(C) Counterclaim Exceeding Opposing Claim. A counterclaim may, but need not, diminish or defeat the recovery sought by the opposing party. It may claim relief exceeding in amount or different in kind from that sought in the pleading of the opposing party.

(D) Cross-Claim Against Co-party. A pleading may state as a cross-claim a claim by one party against a co-party arising out of the transaction or occurrence that is the subject matter of the original action or of a counterclaim, or that relates to property that is the subject matter of the original action. The cross-claim may include a claim that the party against whom it is asserted is or may be liable to the cross-claimant for all or part of a claim asserted in the action against the cross-claimant.

(E) Time for Filing Counterclaim or Cross-Claim. A counterclaim or cross-claim must be filed with the answer or filed as an amendment in the manner provided by MCR 2.118. If a motion to amend to state a counterclaim or cross-claim is denied, the litigation of that claim in another action is not precluded unless the court specifies otherwise.

(F) Separate Trials; Separate Judgment. If the court orders separate trials as provided in MCR

2.505(B), judgment on a claim, counterclaim, or cross-claim may be rendered in accordance with the terms of MCR 2.604 when the court has jurisdiction to do so. The judgment may be rendered even if the claims of the opposing party have been dismissed or otherwise disposed of.

[Effective March 1, 1985; amended effective June 1, 1999.]

1985 Staff Comment

MCR 2.203 is based on GCR 1963, 203. It includes a new subrule (C), which is taken from GCR 1963, 111.8.

Subrule (A) includes modifications of the provision regarding waiver of objections to failure to join claims. First, a party may object to failure to join claims in a pleading, as well as by motion or at the pretrial conference. Second, language is added to the effect that the rule does not affect collateral estoppel or the prohibition on relitigation of a claim under a different theory.

Subrule (E) is a new provision setting the time for filing a counterclaim or cross-claim. Under MCR 2.110, these are classified as pleadings, unlike the practice under GCR 1963, 110.1. Counterclaims or cross-claims must be filed either with the answer or within the time for answering. The usual principles regarding amendment apply. See MCR 2.118. In addition, unless the court specifies otherwise, the rules regarding compulsory joinder do not apply if the court denies a motion to amend to add such a claim.

Staff Comment to 1998 Amendment

The February 2, 1999 amendment of subrule (A), effective June 1, 1999, omitted the provision that made failure to object to improper joinder a waiver of the joinder rules. The amendment was recommended by the State Bar of Michigan to facilitate operation of the common law doctrine of res judicata, and to make Michigan practice more consistent with practice in other jurisdictions.

RULE 2.204 THIRD–PARTY PRACTICE

(A) When Defendant May Bring in Third Party.

(1) Subject to the provisions of MCL 500.3030; MSA 24.13030, any time after commencement of an action, a defending party, as a third-party plaintiff, may serve a summons and complaint on a person not a party to the action who is or may be liable to the third-party plaintiff for all or part of the plaintiff's claim. The third-party plaintiff need not obtain leave to make the service if the third-party complaint is filed within 21 days after the third-party plaintiff's original answer was filed. Otherwise, leave on motion with notice to all parties is required. Unless the court orders otherwise, the summons issued on the filing of a third-party complaint is valid for 21 days after it is issued, and must include the expiration date. See MCR 2.102(B)(8).

(2) Within the time provided by MCR 2.108(A)(1)–(3), the person served with the summons and third-party complaint (the "third-party defendant") must respond to the third-party plaintiff's claim as provided in MCR 2.111, and may file counterclaims against the third-party plaintiff and cross-claims against other parties as provided in MCR 2.203. The

third-party defendant may assert against the plaintiff any defenses which the third-party plaintiff has to the plaintiff's claim. The third-party defendant may also assert a claim against the plaintiff arising out of the transaction or occurrence that is the subject matter of the plaintiff's claim against the third-party plaintiff.

(3) The plaintiff may assert a claim against the third-party defendant arising out of the transaction or occurrence that is the subject matter of the plaintiff's claim against the third-party plaintiff, and the third-party defendant must respond as provided in MCR 2.111 and may file counterclaims and cross-claims as provided in MCR 2.203.

(4) A party may move for severance, separate trial, or dismissal of the third-party claim. The court may direct entry of a final judgment on either the original claim or the third-party claim, in accordance with MCR 2.604(B).

(5) A third-party defendant may proceed under this rule against a person not a party to the action who is or may be liable to the third-party defendant for all or part of a claim made in the action against the third-party defendant.

(B) When Plaintiff May Bring in Third Party. A plaintiff against whom a claim or counterclaim is asserted may bring in a third party under this rule to the same extent as a defendant.

(C) Exception; Small Claims. The provisions of this rule do not apply to actions in the small claims division of the district court.

[Effective March 1, 1985; amended effective September 19, 1995.]

1985 Staff Comment

The [March 1, 1985] amendment of MCR 2.204(A)(1) modifies the provisions regarding the filing and serving of a third-party complaint. Leave of court is not required if the third-party complaint is filed within 21 days after the defendant's original answer, and served within 21 days thereafter. Language is also added requiring that the summons specify its expiration date.

The [March 1, 1985] amendment of MCR 2.204(A)(2) makes explicit the requirement that a party served with a third-party complaint must answer or otherwise respond within the same time limits as applicable to other complaints. See MCR 2.108(A)(1)–(3).

Staff Comment to 1995 Amendment

The amendments of MCR 2.116(J)(1), 2.119(F)(1), 2.204(A)(4), and 2.614(G) correct cross-references to MCR 2.604 that were no longer correct after MCR 2.604 was amended on May 16, 1995, and further amended on September 19, 1995.

RULE 2.205 NECESSARY JOINDER OF PARTIES

(A) Necessary Joinder. Subject to the provisions of subrule (B) and MCR 3.501, persons having such interests in the subject matter of an action that their presence in the action is essential to permit the court to render complete relief must be made parties and aligned as plaintiffs or defendants in accordance with their respective interests.

(B) Effect of Failure to Join. When persons described in subrule (A) have not been made parties and are subject to the jurisdiction of the court, the court shall order them summoned to appear in the action, and may prescribe the time and order of pleading. If jurisdiction over those persons can be acquired only by their consent or voluntary appearance, the court may proceed with the action and grant appropriate relief to persons who are parties to prevent a failure of justice. In determining whether to proceed, the court shall consider

(1) whether a valid judgment may be rendered in favor of the plaintiff in the absence of the person not joined;

(2) whether the plaintiff would have another effective remedy if the action is dismissed because of the nonjoinder;

(3) the prejudice to the defendant or to the person not joined that may result from the nonjoinder; and

(4) whether the prejudice, if any, may be avoided or lessened by a protective order or a provision included in the final judgment.

Notwithstanding the failure to join a person who should have been joined, the court may render a judgment against the plaintiff whenever it is determined that the plaintiff is not entitled to relief as a matter of substantive law.

(C) Names of Omitted Persons and Reasons for Nonjoinder to Be Pleaded. In a pleading in which relief is asked, the pleader must state the names, if known, of persons who are not joined, but who ought to be parties if complete relief is to be accorded to those already parties, and must state why they are not joined.

[Effective March 1, 1985.]

1985 Staff Comment

MCR 2.205 is substantially the same as GCR 1963, 205.

RULE 2.206   PERMISSIVE JOINDER OF PARTIES

(A) Permissive Joinder.

(1) All persons may join in one action as plaintiffs

(a) if they assert a right to relief jointly, severally, or in the alternative, in respect of or arising out of the same transaction, occurrence, or series of transactions or occurrences and if a question of law or fact common to all of the plaintiffs will arise in the action; or

(b) if their presence in the action will promote the convenient administration of justice.

(2) All persons may be joined in one action as defendants

(a) if there is asserted against them jointly, severally, or in the alternative, a right to relief in respect of or arising out of the same transaction, occurrence, or series of transactions or occurrences and if a question of law or fact common to all of the defendants will arise in the action; or

(b) if their presence in the action will promote the convenient administration of justice.

(3) A plaintiff or defendant need not be interested in obtaining or defending against all the relief demanded. Judgment may be rendered for one or more of the parties against one or more of the parties as the rights and liabilities of the parties are determined.

(B) Separate Trials. The court may enter orders to prevent a party from being embarrassed, delayed, or put to expense by the joinder of a person against whom the party asserts no claim and who asserts no claim against the party, and may order separate trials or enter other orders to prevent delay or prejudice.

[Effective March 1, 1985.]

1985 Staff Comment

MCR 2.206 is substantially the same as GCR 1963, 206.

RULE 2.207   MISJOINDER AND NONJOINDER OF PARTIES

Misjoinder of parties is not a ground for dismissal of an action. Parties may be added or dropped by order of the court on motion of a party or on the court's own initiative at any stage of the action and on terms that are just. When the presence of persons other than the original parties to the action is required to grant complete relief in the determination of a counterclaim or cross-claim, the court shall order those persons to be brought in as defendants if jurisdiction over them can be obtained. A claim against a party may be severed and proceeded with separately.

[Effective March 1, 1985.]

1985 Staff Comment

MCR 2.207 is substantially the same as GCR 1963, 207.

RULE 2.209   INTERVENTION

(A) Intervention of Right. On timely application a person has a right to intervene in an action:

(1) when a Michigan statute or court rule confers an unconditional right to intervene;

(2) by stipulation of all the parties; or

(3) when the applicant claims an interest relating to the property or transaction which is the subject of the action and is so situated that the disposition of the action may as a practical matter impair or impede the applicant's ability to protect that interest, unless the

applicant's interest is adequately represented by existing parties.

(B) Permissive Intervention. On timely application a person may intervene in an action

(1) when a Michigan statute or court rule confers a conditional right to intervene; or

(2) when an applicant's claim or defense and the main action have a question of law or fact in common.

In exercising its discretion, the court shall consider whether the intervention will unduly delay or prejudice the adjudication of the rights of the original parties.

(C) Procedure. A person seeking to intervene must apply to the court by motion and give notice in writing to all parties under MCR 2.107. The motion must

(1) state the grounds for intervention, and

(2) be accompanied by a pleading stating the claim or defense for which intervention is sought.

(D) Notice to Attorney General. When the validity of a Michigan statute or a rule or regulation included in the Michigan Administrative Code is in question in an action to which the state or an officer or agency of the state is not a party, the court may require that notice be given to the Attorney General, specifying the pertinent statute, rule, or regulation.

[Effective March 1, 1985.]

1985 Staff Comment

MCR 2.209 is based on GCR 1963, 209. A requirement of a timely application to exercise intervention of right is added in subrule (A). See FR Civ P 24(a).

There is a corresponding change in subrule (C), to recognize that a motion to intervene is always required.

RULE 2.221 MOTION FOR CHANGE OF VENUE

(A) Time to File. A motion for change of venue must be filed before or at the time the defendant files an answer.

(B) Late Motion. Untimeliness is not a ground for denial of a motion filed after the answer if the court is satisfied that the facts on which the motion is based were not and could not with reasonable diligence have been known to the moving party more than 14 days before the motion was filed.

(C) Waiver. An objection to venue is waived if it is not raised within the time limits imposed by this rule.

[Effective March 1, 1985.]

1985 Staff Comment

MCR 2.221 includes the provisions found in GCR 1963, 401, 402, and 409.

The only substantive changes are in subrule (B). Unlike the practice under GCR 1963, 402, a plaintiff is permitted to file a late motion for a change of venue.

In addition, the language of GCR 1963, 402 is modified to remove the possible implication that the judge must grant the motion if the moving party demonstrates that the grounds are newly discovered. The fact that the grounds are newly discovered only removes untimeliness as a basis for denying the motion.

RULE 2.222 CHANGE OF VENUE; VENUE PROPER

(A) Grounds. The court may order a change of venue of a civil action, or of an appeal from an order or decision of a state board, commission, or agency authorized to promulgate rules or regulations, for the convenience of parties and witnesses or when an impartial trial cannot be had where the action is pending. In the case of appellate review of administrative proceedings, venue may also be changed for the convenience of the attorneys.

(B) Motion Required. If the venue of the action is proper, the court may not change the venue on its own initiative, but may do so only on motion of a party.

(C) Multiple Claims. If multiple claims are joined in an action, and the venue of one or more of them would have been improper if the claims had been brought in separate actions, the defendant may move to separate the claims and to transfer those as to which venue would have been improper. The court has discretion to

(1) order the transfer of all claims,

(2) order the separation and transfer moved for, or

(3) retain the entire action for trial.

(D) Filing and Jury Fees After Change of Venue.

(1) An order changing venue under this rule shall require the party who moved for a change of venue to pay the statutory filing fee applicable to the court to which the action is transferred.

(2) If the jury fee has been paid, the clerk of the transferring court shall forward it to the clerk of the court to which the action is transferred.

(E) In tort actions filed between October 1, 1986, and March 28, 1996, if venue is changed because of hardship or inconvenience, the action may be transferred only to the county in which the moving party resides.

[Effective March 1, 1985; amended effective February 1, 1997.]

1985 Staff Comment

MCR 2.222 includes provisions from GCR 1963, 403 and 406.

A new subrule (B) is added to emphasize that if the venue of a civil action is proper, the court may not change venue on its own initiative.

Subrule (C) includes the provisions formerly found in GCR 1963, 406(2), covering the possible remedies when multiple claims are joined and there would not be an independent basis for venue as to some of them. The provisions of GCR 1963, 406(1) regarding improperly joined claims are deleted.

New subrule (D) provides that if a change of venue is granted, the moving party is required to pay the filing fee applicable in the court to which the case is transferred.

The [March 1, 1985] amendments of MCR 2.222(D), 2.223(B), and 2.225 add provisions regarding the transfer of jury fees when venue is changed. If the fee had been paid in the court in which the action was filed, the clerk is to forward it to the clerk of the court to which the action is to be transferred.

The references in the former rules to the "county" in which the action is pending are changed because of the application of the rules to the district court.

Staff Comment to 1997 Amendment

The November 6 amendments of MCR 2.112, 2.222, 2.223, and 2.403, and the repeal of MCR 2.224, effective February 1, 1997, relate to statutory changes made by 1995 PA 161 and 1995 PA 249.

The repeal of MCR 2.224 and the inclusion of several of its former provisions in MCR 2.222 and 2.223 conform the venue rules to MCL 600.1629(2); MSA 27A.1629(2), as amended by 1995 PA 161 and 1995 PA 249.

RULE 2.223   CHANGE OF VENUE; VENUE IMPROPER

(A) Motion; Court's Own Initiative. If the venue of a civil action is improper, the court

(1) shall order a change of venue on timely motion of a defendant, or

(2) may order a change of venue on its own initiative with notice to the parties and opportunity for them to be heard on the venue question.

If venue is changed because the action was brought where venue was not proper, the action may be transferred only to a county in which venue would have been proper.

(B) Costs; Fees.

(1) The court shall order the change at the plaintiff's cost, which shall include the statutory filing fee applicable to the court to which the action is transferred, and which may include reasonable compensation for the defendant's expense, including reasonable attorney fees, in attending in the wrong court.

(2) After transfer, no further proceedings may be had in the action until the costs and expenses allowed under this rule have been paid. If they are not paid within 56 days from the date of the order changing venue, the action must be dismissed by the court to which it was transferred.

(3) If the jury fee has been paid, the clerk of the transferring court shall forward it to the clerk of the court to which the action is transferred.

(4) MCL 600.1653; MSA 27A.1653 applies to tort actions filed on or after October 1, 1986.

[Effective March 1, 1985; amended effective February 1, 1997.]

1985 Staff Comment

MCR 2.223 is comparable to GCR 1963, 404.

Subrule (A)(2) adds a requirement that before the court may change venue on its own initiative it must give the parties notice and opportunity to be heard on the venue question.

Subrule (B)(1) provides that one of the costs that the plaintiff must pay is a new filing fee in the court to which the action is transferred. Unlike the comparable provision in MCR 2.222(D), this cost will always be imposed on the plaintiff, rather than on whichever party moved for a change of venue, because it is the plaintiff who selected the wrong forum.

The [March 1, 1985] amendments of MCR 2.222(D), 2.223(B), and 2.225 add provisions regarding the transfer of jury fees when venue is changed. If the fee had been paid in the court in which the action was filed, the clerk is to forward it to the clerk of the court to which the action is to be transferred.

Staff Comment to 1997 Amendment

The November 6 amendments of MCR 2.112, 2.222, 2.223, and 2.403, and the repeal of MCR 2.224, effective February 1, 1997, relate to statutory changes made by 1995 PA 161 and 1995 PA 249.

The repeal of MCR 2.224 and the inclusion of several of its former provisions in MCR 2.222 and 2.223 conform the venue rules to MCL 600.1629(2); MSA 27A.1629(2), as amended by 1995 PA 161 and 1995 PA 249.

RULE 2.224   CHANGE OF VENUE IN TORT ACTIONS [REPEALED]

[Repealed effective February 1, 1997.]

RULE 2.225   JOINDER OF PARTY TO CONTROL VENUE

(A) Joinder Not in Good Faith. On a defendant's motion, venue must be changed on a showing that the venue of the action is proper only because of the joinder of a codefendant who was not joined in good faith but only to control venue.

(B) Transfer Costs. A transfer under this rule must be made at the plaintiff's cost, which shall include the statutory filing fee applicable to the court to which the action is transferred, and which may include reasonable compensation for the defendant's expense, including reasonable attorney fees, necessary to accomplish the transfer.

(C) Jury Fee. If the jury fee has been paid, the clerk of the transferring court shall forward it to the clerk of the court to which the action is transferred.

[Effective March 1, 1985.]

1985 Staff Comment

MCR 2.225 is comparable to GCR 1963, 407.

In subrule (A) the word "may" is changed to "must" to require a change of venue on the showing of bad faith joinder of parties.

As in MCR 2.222 and 2.223, the rule requires the payment of an additional filing fee in the court to which the action is transferred. This cost will always be imposed on the plaintiff because the transfer results from the bad faith of the plaintiff in joining parties.

References to the "county" in which the action is pending are changed because of the application of the rule to the district court. In addition, the reference to a defendant being "established" in the county is changed in view of the amendment of the venue statute to delete that concept. See 1976 PA 375, amending MCL 600.1621; MSA 27A.1621.

The [March 1, 1985] amendments of MCR 2.222(D), 2.223(B), and 2.225 add provisions regarding the transfer of jury fees when venue is changed. If the fee had been paid in the court in which the action was filed, the clerk is to forward it to the clerk of the court to which the action is to be transferred.

RULE 2.226   CHANGE OF VENUE; ORDERS

The court ordering a change of venue shall enter all necessary orders pertaining to the certification and transfer of the action to the court to which the action is transferred.

[Effective March 1, 1985.]

1985 Staff Comment

MCR 2.226 is substantially the same as GCR 1963, 408.

The reference to the transferring court making "rules" is deleted, as is the reference to the "county" to which the action is being transferred.

RULE 2.227   TRANSFER OF ACTIONS ON FINDING OF LACK OF JURISDICTION

(A) Transfer to Court Which Has Jurisdiction.

(1) When the court in which a civil action is pending determines that it lacks jurisdiction of the subject matter of the action, but that some other Michigan court would have jurisdiction of the action, the court may order the action transferred to the other court in a place where venue would be proper. If the question of jurisdiction is raised by the court on its own initiative, the action may not be transferred until the parties are given notice and an opportunity to be heard on the jurisdictional issue.

(2) As a condition of transfer, the court shall require the plaintiff to pay the statutory filing fee applicable to the court to which the action is to be transferred, and to pay reasonable compensation for the defendant's expense, including reasonable attorney fees, in attending in the wrong court.

(3) If the plaintiff does not pay the filing fee to the clerk of the court transferring the action and submit proof to the clerk of the payment of any other costs imposed within 28 days after entry of the order of transfer, the clerk shall notify the judge who entered the order, and the judge shall dismiss the action for lack of jurisdiction. The clerk shall notify the parties of the entry of the dismissal.

(4) After the plaintiff pays the fee and costs, the clerk of the court transferring the action shall promptly forward to the clerk of the court to which the action is transferred the original papers filed in the action and the filing fee and shall send written notice of this action to the parties. If part of the action remains pending in the transferring court, certified copies of the papers filed may be forwarded, with the cost to be paid by the plaintiff.

(B) Procedure After Transfer.

(1) The action proceeds in the court to which it is transferred as if it had been originally filed there. If further pleadings are required or allowed, the time for filing them runs from the date the clerk sends notice that the file has been forwarded under subrule (A)(4). The court to which the action is transferred may order the filing of new or amended pleadings.

(2) If a defendant had not been served with process at the time the action was transferred, the plaintiff must obtain the issuance of a new summons by the court to which the action is transferred.

(3) A waiver of jury trial in the court in which the action was originally filed is ineffective after transfer. A party who had waived trial by jury may demand a jury trial after transfer by filing a demand and paying the applicable jury fee within 28 days after the clerk sends the notice that the file has been forwarded under subrule (A)(4). A demand for a jury trial in the court in which the action was originally filed is preserved after transfer. If the jury fee had been paid, the clerk shall forward it with the file to the clerk of the court to which the action is transferred.

(C) Relation to Other Transfer Provisions. This rule does not affect transfers (pursuant to other rules or statutes) of actions over which the transferring court had jurisdiction.

[Effective March 1, 1985.]

1985 Staff Comment

MCR 2.227 creates a new procedure permitting a court which determines that it lacks jurisdiction of an action to transfer it to an appropriate court, rather than dismiss it. Under subrule (A)(1) the procedure is discretionary, and the court may not make such an order on its own initiative without giving the parties an opportunity to be heard.

Under subrule (A)(2), as a condition of transfer the court is to require the plaintiff to pay appropriate costs. In effect, this gives the plaintiff control over whether the case will be transferred. If the plaintiff does not pay the costs within the appropriate period, the court is to dismiss the action. In many cases, the plaintiff might prefer to simply start a new action in the appropriate court.

Subrule (B) includes provisions covering procedure after transfer, including such matters as the time for further pleadings after the records are sent by the transferring court, issuance of a new summons if the defendant had not been served at the time of transfer, and the continuing effect of a demand for or waiver of jury trial after transfer.

Subrule (C) makes clear that these provisions do not affect the transfer of cases pursuant to other rules or statutes when the transferring court had jurisdiction. See, e.g., MCR 4.002, 4.003; MCL 700.022(3); MSA 27.5022(3).

SUBCHAPTER 2.300 DISCOVERY

RULE 2.301 COMPLETION OF DISCOVERY

(A) In circuit and probate court, the time for completion of discovery shall be set by an order entered under MCR 2.401(B)(2)(a).

(B) In an action in which discovery is available only on leave of the court or by stipulation, the order or stipulation shall set a time for completion of discovery. A time set by stipulation may not delay the scheduling of the action for trial.

(C) After the time for completion of discovery, a deposition of a witness taken solely for the purpose of preservation of testimony may be taken at any time before commencement of trial without leave of court. [Effective March 1, 1985; amended effective October 1, 1991.]

1985 Staff Comment

MCR 2.301 covers the time for completion of discovery. The corresponding provision of the General Court Rules is GCR 1963, 301.7, which sets the discovery cutoff at the pretrial conference or the waiver of a pretrial conference. Under MCR 2.301 discovery must be completed 1 year after an answer is filed unless the court sets another date.

Subrule (B) is related to MCR 2.302(A)(2), which provides that in district court discovery is available only by stipulation or a court order. In such a case, the order or stipulation providing for discovery is to set the time for completion of discovery, but is not to delay trial of the action.

Subrule (C) creates an exception for the taking of a deposition to preserve testimony. Such a deposition may be taken without court order at any time before commencement of trial.

Staff Comment to 1991 Amendment

MCR 2.301(A) is amended [effective October 1, 1991] by deleting the provision setting one year as the time for completion of discovery in the absence of an order providing otherwise. Setting the time for completion of discovery, and other events in the case, is to be done by scheduling orders under MCR 2.401(B)(2).

RULE 2.302 GENERAL RULES GOVERNING DISCOVERY

(A) Availability of Discovery.

(1) After commencement of an action, parties may obtain discovery by any means provided in subchapter 2.300 of these rules.

(2) In actions in the district court, no discovery is permitted before entry of judgment except by leave of the court or on the stipulation of all parties. A motion for discovery may not be filed unless the discovery sought has previously been requested and refused.

(3) Notwithstanding the provisions of this or any other rule, discovery is not permitted in actions in the small claims division of the district court or in civil infraction actions.

(B) Scope of Discovery.

(1) *In General.* Parties may obtain discovery regarding any matter, not privileged, which is relevant to the subject matter involved in the pending action, whether it relates to the claim or defense of the party seeking discovery or to the claim or defense of another party, including the existence, description, nature, custody, condition, and location of books, documents, or other tangible things and the identity and location of persons having knowledge of a discoverable matter. It is not ground for objection that the information sought will be inadmissible at trial if the information sought appears reasonably calculated to lead to the discovery of admissible evidence.

(2) *Insurance Agreements.* A party may obtain discovery of the existence and contents of an insurance agreement under which a person carrying on an insurance business may be liable to satisfy part or all of a judgment which may be entered in the action or to indemnify or reimburse for payments made to satisfy the judgment. Information concerning the insurance agreement is not by reason of disclosure admissible at trial. For purposes of this subrule, an application for insurance is not part of an insurance agreement.

(3) *Trial Preparation; Materials.*

(a) Subject to the provisions of subrule (B)(4), a party may obtain discovery of documents and tangible things otherwise discoverable under subrule (B)(1) and prepared in anticipation of litigation or for trial by or for another party or another party's representative (including an attorney, consultant, surety, indemnitor, insurer, or agent) only on a showing that the party seeking discovery has substantial need of the materials in the preparation of the case and is unable without undue hardship to obtain the substantial equivalent of the materials by other means. In ordering discovery of such materials when the required showing has been made, the court shall protect against disclosure of the mental impressions, conclusions, opinions, or legal theories of an attorney or other representative of a party concerning the litigation.

(b) Without the showing required by subrule (B)(3)(a), a party or a nonparty may obtain a statement concerning the action or its subject matter previously made by the person making the request. A nonparty whose request is refused may move for a court order. The provisions of MCR 2.313(A)(5) apply to the award of expenses incurred in relation to the motion.

(c) For purposes of subrule (B)(3)(b), a statement previously made is

(i) a written statement signed or otherwise adopted or approved by the person making it; or

(ii) a stenographic, mechanical, electrical, or other recording, or a transcription of it, which is a substantially verbatim recital of an oral statement by the person making it and contemporaneously recorded.

(4) *Trial Preparation; Experts.* Discovery of facts known and opinions held by experts, otherwise discoverable under the provisions of subrule (B)(1) and acquired or developed in anticipation of litigation or for trial, may be obtained only as follows:

(a)(i) A party may through interrogatories require another party to identify each person whom the other party expects to call as an expert witness at trial, to state the subject matter about which the expert is expected to testify, and to state the substance of the facts and opinions to which the expert is expected to testify and a summary of the grounds for each opinion.

(ii) A party may take the deposition of a person whom the other party expects to call as an expert witness at trial.

(iii) On motion, the court may order further discovery by other means, subject to such restrictions as to scope and such provisions (pursuant to subrule [B][4][c]) concerning fees and expenses as the court deems appropriate.

(b) A party may not discover the identity of and facts known or opinions held by an expert who has been retained or specially employed by another party in anticipation of litigation or preparation for trial and who is not expected to be called as a witness at trial, except

(i) as provided in MCR 2.311, or

(ii) where an order has been entered on a showing of exceptional circumstances under which it is impracticable for the party seeking discovery to obtain facts or opinions on the same subject by other means.

(c) Unless manifest injustice would result

(i) the court shall require that the party seeking discovery under subrules (B)(4)(a)(ii) or (iii) or (B)(4)(b) pay the expert a reasonable fee for time spent in a deposition, but not including preparation time; and

(ii) with respect to discovery obtained under subrule (B)(4)(a)(ii) or (iii), the court may require, and with respect to discovery obtained under subrule (B)(4)(b) the court shall require, the party seeking discovery to pay the other party a fair portion of the fees and expenses reasonably incurred by the latter party in obtaining facts and opinions from the expert.

(d) A party may depose a witness that he or she expects to call as an expert at trial. The deposition may be taken at any time before trial on reasonable notice to the opposite party, and may be offered as evidence at trial as provided in MCR 2.308(A). The court need not adjourn the trial because of the unavailability of expert witnesses or their depositions.

(C) Protective Orders. On motion by a party or by the person from whom discovery is sought, and on reasonable notice and for good cause shown, the court in which the action is pending may issue any order that justice requires to protect a party or person from annoyance, embarrassment, oppression, or undue burden or expense, including one or more of the following orders:

(1) that the discovery not be had;

(2) that the discovery may be had only on specified terms and conditions, including a designation of the time or place;

(3) that the discovery may be had only by a method of discovery other than that selected by the party seeking discovery;

(4) that certain matters not be inquired into, or that the scope of the discovery be limited to certain matters;

(5) that discovery be conducted with no one present except persons designated by the court;

(6) that a deposition, after being sealed, be opened only by order of the court;

(7) that a deposition shall be taken only for the purpose of discovery and shall not be admissible in evidence except for the purpose of impeachment;

(8) that a trade secret or other confidential research, development, or commercial information not be disclosed or be disclosed only in a designated way;

(9) that the parties simultaneously file specified documents or information enclosed in sealed envelopes to be opened as directed by the court.

If the motion for a protective order is denied in whole or in part, the court may, on terms and conditions as are just, order that a party or person provide or permit discovery. The provisions of MCR 2.313(A)(5) apply to the award of expenses incurred in relation to the motion.

(D) Sequence and Timing of Discovery. Unless the court orders otherwise, on motion, for the convenience of parties and witnesses and in the interests of justice, methods of discovery may be used in any sequence, and the fact that a party is conducting discovery, whether by deposition or otherwise, does not operate to delay another party's discovery.

(E) Supplementation of Responses.

(1) *Duty to Supplement.* A party who has responded to a request for discovery with a response that was complete when made is under no duty to supplement the response to include information acquired later, except as follows:

(a) A party is under a duty seasonably to supplement the response with respect to a question directly addressed to

(i) the identity and location of persons having knowledge of discoverable matters; and

(ii) the identity of each person expected to be called as an expert witness at trial, the subject matter on which the expert is expected to testify, and the substance of the expert's testimony.

(b) A party is under a duty seasonably to amend a prior response if the party obtains information on the basis of which the party knows that

(i) the response was incorrect when made; or

(ii) the response, though correct when made, is no longer true and the circumstances are such that a failure to amend the response is in substance a knowing concealment.

(c) A duty to supplement responses may be imposed by order of the court, agreement of the parties, or at any time before trial through new requests for supplementation of prior responses.

(2) *Failure to Supplement.* If the court finds, by way of motion or otherwise, that a party has not seasonably supplemented responses as required by this subrule the court may enter an order as is just, including an order providing the sanctions stated in MCR 2.313(B), and, in particular, MCR 2.313(B)(2)(b).

(F) Stipulations Regarding Discovery Procedure. Unless the court orders otherwise, the parties may by written stipulation:

(1) provide that depositions may be taken before any person, at any time or place, on any notice, and in any manner, and when so taken may be used like other depositions; and

(2) modify the procedures of these rules for other methods of discovery, except that stipulations extending the time within which discovery may be sought or for responses to discovery may be made only with the approval of the court.

(G) Signing of Discovery Requests, Responses, and Objections; Sanctions.

(1) In addition to any other signature required by these rules, every request for discovery and every response or objection to such a request made by a party represented by an attorney shall be signed by at least one attorney of record. A party who is not represented by an attorney must sign the request, response, or objection.

(2) If a request, response, or objection is not signed, it shall be stricken unless it is signed promptly after the omission is called to the attention of the party making the request, response, or objection, and another party need not take any action with respect to it until it is signed.

(3) The signature of the attorney or party constitutes a certification that he or she has read the request, response, or objection, and that to the best of the signer's knowledge, information, and belief formed after a reasonable inquiry it is:

(a) consistent with these rules and warranted by existing law or a good faith argument for the extension, modification, or reversal of existing law;

(b) not interposed for any improper purpose, such as to harass or to cause unnecessary delay or needless increase in the cost of litigation; and

(c) not unreasonable or unduly burdensome or expensive, given the needs of the case, the discovery already had in the case, the amount in controversy, and the importance of the issues at stake in the litigation.

(4) If a certification is made in violation of this rule, the court, on the motion of a party or on its own initiative, shall impose upon the person who made the certification, the party on whose behalf the request, response, or objection is made, or both, an appropriate sanction, which may include an order to pay the amount of the reasonable expenses incurred because of the violation, including reasonable attorney fees.

(H) Filing and Service of Discovery Materials.

(1) Unless a particular rule requires filing of discovery materials, requests, responses, depositions, and other discovery materials may not be filed with the court except as follows:

(a) If discovery materials are to be used in connection with a motion, they must either be filed separately or be attached to the motion or an accompanying affidavit;

(b) If discovery materials are to be used at trial they must be either filed or made an exhibit;

(c) The court may order discovery materials to be filed.

(2) Copies of discovery materials served under these rules must be served on all parties to the action, unless the court has entered an order under MCR 2.107(F).

(3) On appeal, only discovery materials that were filed or made exhibits are part of the record on appeal.

(4) Removal and destruction of discovery materials are governed by MCR. 2.316.

[Effective March 1, 1985; amended effective June 1, 1989; March 1, 1991; June 1, 1993; September 1, 1994.]

1985 Staff Comment

MCR 2.302 collects the general provisions governing discovery. There was no counterpart to the rule in the General Court Rules, although certain aspects of it were covered by rules spread throughout the discovery subchapter. The rule is organized in the manner of FR Civ P 26. Although the discovery rules continue to include some provisions not found in the federal rules, in general, the Michigan Court Rules make Michigan discovery practice far more like federal procedure than was the case under the General Court Rules.

Subrule (A) includes the general statement as to the availability of discovery. Subrule (A)(1) is based on FR Civ P 26(a). The General Court Rules had comparable provisions at the beginning of the rule covering each method of discovery. See, e.g., GCR 1963, 302.1 (depositions), 309.1 (interrogatories), 310.1 (motion to produce or permit inspection).

In addition, the rule retains two major limitations on discovery applicable to the district court. As under DCR 302.2, no discovery is allowed except on court order or stipulation. See subrule (A)(2). Additional language is included to make clear that discovery is allowed after judgment, for example, under MCR 2.621 or 3.101(J). Second, subrule (A)(3) carries forward the provision of DCR 302.6 that discovery is not allowed in the small claims division of the district court, and adds a prohibition on discovery in civil infraction actions.

Subrule (B) governs the general subject of the scope of discovery. It is modeled on FR Civ P 26(b). Most of the material was not included in the General Court Rules.

Subrule (B)(1) changes the scope of discovery to the federal formulation by eliminating the admissibility requirement found in GCR 1963, 302.2(1) (and incorporated in GCR 1963, 309.4 and 310.1). The second paragraph of FR Civ P 26(b)(1), covering court orders limiting discovery, is omitted; however, such orders would be allowed under subrules (A)(1) and (C).

Subrule (B)(1)(b) retains the substance of GCR 1963, 302.2(1), forbidding a party who has invoked a privilege at a deposition from introducing at trial the testimony of the witness pertaining to the evidence objected to at the deposition. Note that there is a related provision regarding privileges with respect to medical information in MCR 2.314(B).

Subrules (B)(2), covering discovery of insurance agreements, and (B)(3), limiting the discoverability of documents and things prepared by the other party in anticipation of litigation or trial, are basically the same as FR Civ P 26(b)(2) and (3). There were no corresponding provisions in the former Michigan rules.

In subrule (B)(4), in addition to the methods of discovery regarding expert witnesses that are provided by FR Civ P 26(b)(4), a party is permitted to take the deposition of an expert witness that the opposing party intends to call at trial. This is consistent with prior Michigan practice. The cost provisions in subrule (B)(4)(c) are modified from the corresponding provisions of the federal rule because of the availability of depositions of experts.

Subrule (B)(4)(d) is a provision not found in FR Civ P 26. It permits a party to take the deposition of a witness whom that party expects to call as an expert at trial. Use of such a deposition at trial is governed by MCR 2.308(A)(1)(c)(i). The General Court Rules included such a provision only with regard to the Wayne and Genesee circuit courts. GCR 1963, 302.7, 302.8.

Subrule (C) is based on FR Civ P 26(c). The prior Michigan rules had several provisions regarding protective orders. For example, GCR 1963, 306.2, 307.4, and 309.5 included many of the same principles as subrule (C). However, several new protective order provisions are added. Subrule (C)(5), like FR Civ P 26(c)(5), permits the court to order that a deposition is to be taken with no one present except those permitted by the order. By contrast, GCR 1963, 306.2 did not allow exclusion of a party. Second, subrule (C)(7) adds to the list of possible protective orders found in FR Civ P 26(c) and GCR 1963, 306.2, that a deposition may be taken only for the purpose of discovery and will not be admissible at trial.

The [March 1, 1985] amendment of MCR 2.302(C)(7) specifies that a protective order that a deposition is to be taken only for the purpose of discovery and will not be admissible in evidence does not preclude the use of the deposition for purpose of impeachment.

Subrule (D), covering the sequence and timing of discovery, is taken from FR Civ P 26(d). There was no comparable provision in the General Court Rules.

Subrule (E), supplementation of responses, is based on FR Civ P 26(e). There was no comparable Michigan provision, although GCR 1963, 309.2 (applicable only in Wayne circuit court) treated interrogatories asking for the identification of witnesses as "continuing" questions. In addition to the provisions of the federal rule, subrule (E)(2) provides sanctions for failure to supplement.

Subrule (F), governing stipulations regarding discovery, is taken from FR Civ P 29. The only similar provision in the General Court Rules was GCR 1963, 302.2(2), which applied only to depositions.

Subrule (G) is based on the August 1, 1983, amendment of FR Civ P 26, which added the provisions regarding the signing of discovery requests and responses, and sanctions for violation of the rule. The rule is similar to MCR 2.114, governing signing of other papers. In addition to any other signature required (see, e.g., MCR 2.309[B][3]), discovery requests and responses must be signed by an attorney if the party is represented by an attorney. The effect of a signature on a discovery request or response is a certification similar to that required by MCR 2.114 as to other papers. See subrule (G)(3). Similar sanctions are imposed for a certification made in violation of the rule. See subrule (G)(4).

Subrule (H) is a new provision governing the filing of discovery materials, which differs from both prior Michigan practice and the federal rules. Unless a particular rule requires a filing (see, e.g., MCR 2.312[F]), filing is required only when the materials are to be used in connection with a motion or at trial. Only those discovery materials that were filed or made an exhibit are considered part of the record on appeal. In a number of places throughout the other discovery rules, references to filing of various papers are deleted to be consistent with subrule (H).

The [March 1, 1985] amendment of MCR 2.302(H) adds a requirement that discovery materials be served on all parties. The general rule requiring service, MCR 2.107(A)(1), applies to papers "filed". Under MCR 2.302(H), most discovery materials will not be filed.

Staff Comment to 1989 Amendment

MCR 2.302(H)(4) was amended [June 1, 1989] to add reference to a new rule, MCR 2.316, authorizing removal and destruction of certain discovery material.

Staff Comment to 1991 Amendment

The [March 1,] 1991 amendment changed a cross-reference in subrule (B)(4)(d) in order to acknowledge a previous amendment to MCR 2.308(A).

Staff Comment to 1993 Amendment

The March 5, 1993, amendment of MCR 2.302(B)(4)(b), effective June 1, 1993, deals with the subject of discovery of the identity of experts who have been retained or specially employed in anticipation of or during litigation but who are not expected to be called as witnesses. Case law has produced varying answers regarding whether the limitations on discovery of facts known or opinions held by such experts also extends to their identities. Decisions such as *Sucoe* v. *Oakwood Hosp Corp*, 185 MichApp 484 (1990), *vacated in part* 439 Mich 914 (1992), have held that a party seeking the identity of such experts need not show exceptional circumstances. Others, such as *Ager* v. *Jane C Stormont Hosp*, 622 F2d 496 (CA 10, 1980), have held that the extraordinary circumstances requirement does apply to identity. The amendment adopts the latter view.

The remaining changes in the language and structure of the rule are meant to clarify, rather than change, the current provision.

Staff Comment to 1994 Amendment

[Under the amendment effective September 1, 1994,] the language of former MCR 2.302(B)(1)(b) is moved to the deposition rule as new MCR 2.306(D)(4), and a cross-reference to MCR 2.314 is added.

RULE 2.303 DEPOSITIONS BEFORE ACTION OR PENDING APPEAL

(A) Before Action.

(1) *Petition.* A person who desires to perpetuate his or her own testimony or that of another person, for use as evidence and not for the purpose of discovery, regarding a matter that may be cognizable in a Michigan court may file a verified petition in the circuit court of the county of the residence of an expected adverse party. The petition must be entitled in the name of the petitioner and must show:

(a) that the petitioner expects to be a party to an action cognizable in a Michigan court but is presently unable to bring it or cause it to be brought and the reasons why;

(b) the subject matter of the expected action and the petitioner's interest in it;

(c) the facts sought to be established by the proposed testimony and the reasons for desiring to perpetuate it;

(d) the names or a description of the persons that the petitioner expects will be adverse parties and their addresses so far as known; and

(e) the names and addresses of the persons to be examined and the substance of the testimony that the petitioner expects to elicit from each.

The petition must ask for an order authorizing the petitioner to take the depositions of the persons to be examined named in the petition for the purpose of perpetuating their testimony.

(2) *Notice and Service.* The petitioner shall serve a notice on each person named in the petition as an expected adverse party, together with a copy of the petition, stating that the petitioner will apply to the court, at a specified time and place, for the order described in the petition. At least 21 days before the date of hearing, the notice must be served in the manner provided in MCR 2.105 for service of summons. If service cannot be made on an expected adverse party with due diligence, the court may issue an order as is just for service by publication or otherwise, and shall appoint, for persons not served in the manner provided in MCR 2.105, an attorney to represent them, and to cross-examine the deponent. If an expected adverse party is a minor or an incompetent person, the law relating to minors and incompetents, including MCR 2.201(E), applies.

(3) *Order and Examination.* If the court is satisfied that the perpetuation of the testimony may prevent a failure or delay of justice, it shall issue an order designating or describing the persons whose depositions may be taken and specifying the subject matter of the examination and whether the depositions are to be taken on oral examination or written interrogatories. The depositions may then be taken in accordance with these rules. In addition the court may issue orders of the character provided for by MCR 2.310 and 2.311.

(4) *Use of Deposition.*

(a) If a deposition to perpetuate testimony is taken under these rules, it may be used in an action involving the same subject matter subsequently brought in a Michigan court, in accordance with MCR 2.308.

(b) If a deposition to perpetuate testimony has been taken under the Federal Rules of Civil Procedure, or the rules of another state, the court may, if it finds that the deposition was taken in substantial compliance with these rules, allow the deposition to be used as if it had been taken under these rules.

(B) Pending Appeal. If an appeal has been taken from a judgment of a trial court, or before the taking of an appeal if the time for appeal has not expired, the court in which the judgment was rendered may allow the taking of the depositions of witnesses to perpetuate their testimony for use if there are further proceedings in that court. The party who wishes to perpetuate the testimony may move for leave to take the depositions, with the same notice and service of the motion as if the action were then pending in the trial court. The motion must show

(1) the names and addresses of the persons to be examined and the substance of the testimony that the party expects to elicit from each; and

(2) the reasons for perpetuating their testimony.

If the court finds that the perpetuation of testimony is proper to avoid a failure or delay of justice, it may issue an order allowing the depositions to be taken and may issue orders of the character provided for by MCR 2.310 and 2.311. The depositions may then be taken and used in the same manner and under the same conditions prescribed in these rules for depositions taken in actions pending before the court.

[Effective March 1, 1985.]

1985 Staff Comment

MCR 2.303 is similar to GCR 1963, 303, which was virtually identical to FR Civ P 27.

Under subrule (A)(4)(b), the fact that a deposition was taken in conformity with the rules of another jurisdiction does not necessarily make the deposition admissible. The rule merely puts such a deposition on the same footing as one taken under these rules.

RULE 2.304 PERSONS BEFORE WHOM DEPOSITIONS MAY BE TAKEN

(A) **Within the United States.** Within the United States or within a territory or insular possession subject to the dominion of the United States, depositions may be taken

(1) before a person authorized to administer oaths by the laws of Michigan, the United States, or the place where the examination is held;

(2) before a person appointed by the court in which the action is pending; or

(3) before a person on whom the parties agree by stipulation under MCR 2.302(F)(1).

A person acting under subrule (A)(2) or (3) has the power to administer oaths, take testimony, and do all other acts necessary to take a deposition.

(B) **In Foreign Countries.** In a foreign country, depositions may be taken

(1) on notice before a person authorized to administer oaths in the place in which the examination is held, by either the law of that place or of the United States; or

(2) before a person commissioned by the court, and a person so commissioned has the power by virtue of

the commission to administer a necessary oath and take testimony; or

(3) pursuant to a letter rogatory.

A commission or a letter rogatory may be issued on motion and notice and on terms that are just and appropriate. It is not requisite to the issuance of a commission or a letter rogatory that the taking of the deposition in another manner is impracticable or inconvenient; both a commission and a letter rogatory may be issued in a proper case. A notice or commission may designate the person before whom the deposition is to be taken either by name or descriptive title. A letter rogatory may be addressed "To the Appropriate Authority in [*name of country*]." Evidence obtained in response to a letter rogatory need not be excluded merely because it is not a verbatim transcript or the testimony was not taken under oath, or because of a similar departure from the requirements for depositions taken within the United States under these rules.

(C) **Disqualification for Interest.** Unless the parties agree otherwise by stipulation in writing or on the record, a deposition may not be taken before a person who is

(1) a relative or employee of or an attorney for a party,

(2) a relative or employee of an attorney for a party, or

(3) financially interested in the action.

[Effective March 1, 1985.]

1985 Staff Comment

MCR 2.304 is comparable to GCR 1963, 304. However, subrule (B), regarding the taking of depositions in foreign countries, is changed to more closely parallel FR Civ P 28(b). Compare GCR 1963, 304.2.

RULE 2.305 SUBPOENA FOR TAKING DEPOSITION

(A) **General Provisions.**

(1) After serving the notice provided for in MCR 2.303(A)(2), 2.306(B), or 2.307(A)(2), a party may have a subpoena issued in the manner provided by MCR 2.506 for the person named or described in the notice. Service on a party or a party's attorney of notice of the taking of the deposition of a party, or of a director, trustee, officer, or employee of a corporate party, is sufficient to require the appearance of the deponent; a subpoena need not be issued.

(2) The subpoena may command the person to whom it is directed to produce and permit inspection and copying of designated documents or other tangible things relevant to the subject matter of the pending action and within the scope of discovery under MCR 2.302(B). The procedures in MCR 2.310 apply to a party deponent.

(3) A deposition notice and a subpoena under this rule may provide that the deposition is solely for producing documents or other tangible things for inspection and copying, and that the party does not intend to examine the deponent.

(4) A subpoena issued under this rule is subject to the provisions of MCR 2.302(C), and the court in which the action is pending, on timely motion made before the time specified in the subpoena for compliance, may

(a) quash or modify the subpoena if it is unreasonable or oppressive;

(b) enter an order permitted by MCR 2.302(C); or

(c) condition denial of the motion on prepayment by the person on whose behalf the subpoena is issued of the reasonable cost of producing books, papers, documents, or other tangible things.

(5) Service of a subpoena on the deponent must be made as provided in MCR 2.506. A copy of the subpoena must be served on all other parties in the same manner as the deposition notice.

(B) Inspection and Copying of Documents. A subpoena issued under subrule (A) may command production of documents or other tangible things, but the following rules apply:

(1) The subpoena must be served at least 14 days before the time for production. The subpoenaed person may, not later than the time specified in the subpoena for compliance, serve on the party serving the subpoena written objection to inspection or copying of some or all of the designated materials.

(2) If objection is made, the party serving the subpoena is not entitled to inspect and copy the materials without an order of the court in which the action is pending.

(3) The party serving the subpoena may, with notice to the deponent, move for an order compelling production of the designated materials. MCR 2.313(A)(5) applies to motions brought under this subrule.

(C) Place of Examination.

(1) A deponent may be required to attend an examination in the county where the deponent resides, is employed, or transacts business in person, or at another convenient place specified by order of the court.

(2) In an action pending in Michigan, the court may order a nonresident plaintiff or an officer or managing agent of the plaintiff to appear for a deposition at a designated place in Michigan or elsewhere on terms and conditions that are just, including payment by the defendant of the reasonable expenses of travel, meals, and lodging incurred by the deponent in attending.

(3) If it is shown that the deposition of a nonresident defendant cannot be taken in the state where the defendant resides, the court may order the defendant or an officer or managing agent of the defendant to appear for a deposition at a designated place in Michigan or elsewhere on terms and conditions that are just, including payment by the plaintiff of the reasonable expenses of travel, meals, and lodging incurred by the deponent in attending.

(D) Petition to Courts Outside Michigan to Compel Testimony. When the place of examination is in another state, territory, or country, the party desiring to take the deposition may petition a court of that state, territory, or country for a subpoena or equivalent process to require the deponent to attend the examination.

(E) Action Pending in Another State, Territory, or Country. An officer or a person authorized by the laws of another state, territory, or country to take a deposition in Michigan, with or without a commission, in an action pending in a court of that state, territory, or country may petition a court of record in the county in which the deponent resides, is employed, transacts business in person, or is found, for a subpoena to compel the deponent to give testimony. The court may hear and act on the petition with or without notice, as the court directs.

[Effective March 1, 1985; amended effective December 1, 1998.]

1985 Staff Comment

MCR 2.305 is based on GCR 1963, 305.

The main substantive change is the addition of subrule (B) covering the subject of subpoenas directing the production of documents or other tangible things. When such a subpoena is directed to a party deponent, the procedures of MCR 2.310, regarding requests to produce, apply.

In addition, in subrule (A)(1), the reference to the subpoena being issued by the clerk is deleted in view of the change in MCR 2.506, which permits subpoenas to be signed by the attorney for a party.

Staff Comment to 1998 Amendment

The December 1, 1998 [effective date], amendments of Rules 2.305, 2.310, and 2.506 were suggested by the Representative Assembly of the State Bar of Michigan. The changes made clear that nonparty records-only discovery subpoenas are authorized. The normal procedure for noticing a deposition applies to records-only subpoenas, and the procedure in MCR 2.310 still pertains to requests to a nonparty for entry on land or production of items for testing or sampling. The time for responding to a document subpoena or a document request under Rule 2.305(B)(1) was changed from seven to fourteen days. The time for responding under Rule 2.310(C)(2) was changed from twenty-eight to fourteen days. The amendments also made nonsubstantive changes to clarify and simplify language.

RULE 2.306   DEPOSITIONS ON ORAL EXAMINATION

(A) When Depositions May Be Taken.

(1) After commencement of the action, a party may take the testimony of a person, including a party, by

deposition on oral examination. Leave of court, granted with or without notice, must be obtained only if the plaintiff seeks to take a deposition before the defendant has had a reasonable time to obtain an attorney. A reasonable time is deemed to have elapsed if:

(a) the defendant has filed an answer;

(b) the defendant's attorney has filed an appearance;

(c) the defendant has served notice of the taking of a deposition or has taken other action seeking discovery;

(d) the defendant has filed a motion under MCR 2.116; or

(e) 28 days have expired after service of the summons and complaint on a defendant or after service made under MCR 2.106.

(2) The deposition of a person confined in prison or of a patient in a state home, institution, or hospital for the mentally ill or mentally handicapped, or any other state hospital, home, or institution, may be taken only by leave of court on terms as the court provides.

(B) Notice of Examination; Subpoena; Production of Documents and Things.

(1) A party desiring to take the deposition of a person on oral examination must give reasonable notice in writing to every other party to the action. The notice must state

(a) the time and place for taking the deposition, and

(b) the name and address of each person to be examined, if known, or, if the name is not known, a general description sufficient to identify the person or the particular class or group to which the person belongs.

If the subpoena to be served directs the deponent to produce documents or other tangible things, the designation of the materials to be produced as set forth in the subpoena must be attached to or included in the notice.

(2) On motion for good cause, the court may extend or shorten the time for taking the deposition. The court may regulate the time and order of taking depositions to best serve the convenience of the parties and witnesses and the interests of justice.

(3) The attendance of witnesses may be compelled by subpoena as provided in MCR 2.305.

(4) The notice to a party deponent may be accompanied by a request for the production of documents and tangible things at the taking of the deposition. MCR 2.310 applies to the request.

(5) In a notice and subpoena, a party may name as the deponent a public or private corporation, partnership, association, or governmental agency and describe with reasonable particularity the matters on which examination is requested. The organization named must designate one or more officers, directors, or managing agents, or other persons, who consent to testify on its behalf, and may set forth, for each person designated, the matters on which the person will testify. A subpoena must advise a nonparty organization of its duty to make the designation. The persons designated shall testify to matters known or reasonably available to the organization. This subrule does not preclude taking a deposition by another procedure authorized in these rules.

(C) Conduct of Deposition; Examination and Cross-Examination; Manner of Recording; Objections.

(1) The person before whom the deposition is to be taken must put the witness on oath. Examination and cross-examination of the witness shall proceed as permitted at a trial under the Michigan Rules of Evidence. In lieu of participating in the oral examination, a party may send written questions to the person conducting the examination, who shall propound them to the witness and record the witness' answers.

(2) The person before whom the deposition is taken shall personally, or by someone acting under his or her direction and in his or her presence, record the testimony of the witness.

(a) The testimony must be taken stenographically or recorded by other means in accordance with this subrule. The testimony need not be transcribed unless requested by one of the parties.

(b) While the testimony is being taken, a party, as a matter of right, may also make a record of it by nonsecret mechanical or electronic means, except that video recording is governed by MCR 2.315. Any use of the recording in court is within the discretion of the court. A person making such a record must furnish a duplicate of the record to another party at the request and expense of the other party.

(3) The court may order, or the parties may stipulate, that the testimony at a deposition be recorded by other than stenographic means.

(a) The order or stipulation must designate the manner of recording and preserving the deposition, and may include other provisions to assure that the recorded testimony will be accurate and trustworthy. A deposition in the form of a recording may be filed with the court as are other depositions.

(b) If a deposition is taken by other than stenographic means on order of the court, a party may nevertheless arrange to have a stenographic transcription made at that party's own expense.

(c) Before a deposition taken by other than stenographic means may be used in court it must be transcribed unless the court enters an order waiving transcription. The costs of transcription are borne by the parties as determined by the court.

(d) Subrule (C)(3) does not apply to video depositions, which are governed by MCR 2.315.

(4) All objections made at the deposition, including objections to

(a) the qualifications of the person taking the deposition,

(b) the manner of taking it,

(c) the evidence presented, or

(d) the conduct of a party,

must be noted on the record by the person before whom the deposition is taken.

Subject to limitations imposed by an order under MCR 2.302(C) or subrule (D) of this rule, evidence objected to on grounds other than privilege shall be taken subject to the objections.

(D) Motion to Terminate or Limit Examination.

(1) At any time during the taking of the deposition, on motion of a party or of the deponent and on a showing that the examination is being conducted in bad faith or in a manner unreasonably to annoy, embarrass, or oppress the deponent or party, or that the matter inquired about is privileged, a court in which the action is pending or the court in the county or district where the deposition is being taken may order the person conducting the examination to cease taking the deposition, or may limit the scope and manner of the taking of the deposition as provided in MCR 2.302(C). If the order entered terminates the examination, it may resume only on order of the court in which the action is pending.

(2) On demand of the objecting party or deponent, the taking of the deposition must be suspended for the time necessary to move for an order. MCR 2.313(A)(5) applies to the award of expenses incurred in relation to the motion.

(3) If a party knows before the time scheduled for the taking of a deposition that he or she will assert that the matter to be inquired about is privileged, the party must move to prevent the taking of the deposition before its occurrence or be subject to costs under subrule (G).

(4) A party who has a privilege regarding part or all of the testimony of a deponent must either assert the privilege at the deposition or lose the privilege as to that testimony for purposes of the action. A party who claims a privilege at a deposition may not at the trial offer the testimony of the deponent pertaining to the evidence objected to at the deposition. A party who asserts a privilege regarding medical information is subject to the provisions of MCR 2.314(B).

(E) Exhibits. Documents and things produced for inspection during the examination of the witness must, on the request of a party, be marked for identification and annexed to the deposition, if practicable, and may be inspected and copied by a party, except as follows:

(1) The person producing the materials may substitute copies to be marked for identification, if he or she affords to all parties fair opportunity to verify the copies by comparison with the originals.

(2) If the person producing the materials requests their return, the person conducting the examination or the stenographer must mark them, give each party an opportunity to inspect and copy them, and return them to the person producing them, and the materials may then be used in the same manner as if annexed to the deposition. A party may move for an order that the original be annexed to and filed with the deposition, pending final disposition of the action.

(F) Certification and Transcription; Filing; Copies.

(1) If transcription is requested by a party, the person conducting the examination or the stenographer must certify on the deposition that the witness was duly sworn and that the deposition is a true record of the testimony given by the witness. A deposition transcribed and certified in accordance with subrule (F) need not be submitted to the witness for examination and signature.

(2) On payment of reasonable charges, the person conducting the examination shall furnish a copy of the deposition to a party or to the deponent. Where transcription is requested by a party other than the party requesting the deposition, the court may order, or the parties may stipulate, that the expense of transcription or a portion of it be paid by the party making the request.

(3) Except as provided in subrule (C)(3) or in MCR 2.315(E), a deposition may not be filed with the court unless it has first been transcribed. If a party requests that the transcript be filed, the person conducting the examination or the stenographer shall, after transcription and certification:

(a) securely seal the transcript in an envelope endorsed with the title and file number of the action and marked "Deposition of [*name of witness*]", and promptly file it with the court in which the action is pending or send it by registered or certified mail to the clerk of that court for filing;

(b) give prompt notice of its filing to all other parties, unless the parties agree otherwise by stipulation in writing or on the record.

(G) Failure to Attend or to Serve Subpoena; Expenses.

(1) If the party giving the notice of the taking of a deposition fails to attend and proceed with the deposition and another party attends in person or by attorney pursuant to the notice, the court may order the party giving the notice to pay to the other party the reasonable expenses incurred in attending, including reasonable attorney fees.

(2) If the party giving the notice of the taking of a deposition of a witness fails to serve a subpoena on the witness, and the witness because of the failure does not attend, and if another party attends in person or by attorney because he or she expects the deposition of that witness to be taken, the court may order the party giving the notice to pay to the other party the reasonable expenses incurred in attending, including reasonable attorney fees.

[Effective March 1, 1985; amended effective September 1, 1994.]

1985 Staff Comment

MCR 2.306 contains the basic deposition procedures drawn from GCR 1963, 302 and 306 and FR Civ P 30.

Subrule (A) covers when depositions may be taken. The only limitation is on depositions taken by the plaintiff. GCR 1963, 302.1 simply provided that they could be taken after commencement of the action, and FR Civ P 30(a) permits a plaintiff to take a deposition 30 days after service of the summons and complaint. Subrule (A)(1) lists the events that trigger the plaintiff's right to take a deposition.

Subrule (A)(2) carries forward the requirement of GCR 1963, 302.2(2) that the deposition of a person confined in a prison or state institution may be taken only by leave of the court.

Subrule (B) contains the various notice provisions, some of which were covered by GCR 1963, 306.1. Subrules (B)(4) and (5) are comparable to FR Civ P 30(b)(5) and (6), and were not found in the former Michigan rules.

Subrule (C) brings together various provisions regarding the conduct and recording of depositions, found in GCR 1963, 302.3 and 306.4, and FR Civ P 30(b)(4) and (c).

Subrule (D) is comparable to GCR 1963, 306.4. Subrule (D)(3) is new. A deponent who knows that he or she will assert a privilege at the deposition is required to raise the matter by motion in advance or be subject to costs.

Subrule (E) adds the substance of FR Civ P 30(f), regarding the annexing of documents and things produced for inspection at a deposition.

Subrule (F) includes the provisions on certification, transcription, and filing of depositions, the subject formerly covered by GCR 1963, 306.6. The filing provisions are modified in light of MCR 2.302(H). Subrule (F)(1) eliminates the requirement, previously found in GCR 1963, 306.5 (and FR Civ P 30[b][4]), that the deposition transcript be submitted to the witness for review and signing. Parties would not be prohibited from doing so, however.

Subrule (G) is substantially the same as GCR 1963, 306.7 (and FR Civ P 30[g]).

Staff Comment to 1994 Amendment

[Under the September 1, 1994 amendment,] the language of former MCR 2.302(B)(1)(b) is moved to the deposition rule as new MCR 2.306(D)(4), and a cross reference to MCR 2.314 is added.

RULE 2.307 DEPOSITIONS ON WRITTEN QUESTIONS

(A) Serving Questions; Notice.

(1) Under the same circumstances as set out in MCR 2.306(A), a party may take the testimony of a person, including a party, by deposition on written questions. The attendance of the witnesses may be compelled by the use of a subpoena as provided in MCR 2.305. A deposition on written questions may be taken of a public or private corporation or partnership or association or governmental agency in accordance with the provisions of MCR 2.306(B)(5).

(2) A party desiring to take a deposition on written questions shall serve them on every other party with a notice stating

(a) the name and address of the person who is to answer them, if known, and, if the name is not known, a general description sufficient to identify the person or the particular class or group to which the person belongs; and

(b) the name or descriptive title and address of the person before whom the deposition is to be taken.

(3) Within 14 days after the notice and written questions are served, a party may serve cross-questions on all other parties. Within 7 days after being served with cross-questions, a party may serve redirect questions on all other parties. Within 7 days after being served with redirect questions, a party may serve recross-questions on all other parties. The parties, by stipulation in writing, or the court, for cause shown, may extend or shorten the time requirements.

(B) Taking of Responses and Preparation of Record. A copy of the notice, any stipulation, and copies of all questions served must be delivered by the party who proposed the deposition to the person before whom the deposition will be taken as stated in the notice. The person before whom the deposition is to be taken must proceed promptly to take the testimony of the witness in response to the questions, and, if requested, to transcribe, certify, and file the deposition in the manner provided by MCR 2.306(C), (E), and (F), attaching the copy of the notice, the questions, and any stipulations of the parties.

[Effective March 1, 1985.]

1985 Staff Comment

MCR 2.307 is comparable to GCR 1963, 307.

The rule is modified (including the deletion of former GCR 1963, 307.3) because of the change in the rules regarding filing of discovery materials. See MCR 2.302(H).

The language of former GCR 1963, 307.4 is deleted; the subject of protective orders is covered by the general discovery provisions in MCR 2.302(C).

RULE 2.308 USE OF DEPOSITIONS IN COURT PROCEEDINGS

(A) In General. Depositions or parts thereof shall be admissible at trial or on the hearing of a motion or in an interlocutory proceeding only as provided in the Michigan Rules of Evidence.

(B) Objections to Admissibility. Subject to the provisions of subrule (C) and MCR 2.306(C)(4), objection may be made at the trial or hearing to receiving in evidence a deposition or part of a deposition for any reason that would require the exclusion of the evidence.

(C) Effect of Errors or Irregularities in Depositions.

(1) *Notice.* Errors or irregularities in the notice for taking a deposition are waived unless written objection is promptly served on the party giving notice.

(2) *Disqualification of Person Before Whom Taken.* Objection to taking a deposition because of disqualification of the person before whom it is to be taken is waived unless made before the taking of the deposition begins or as soon thereafter as the disqualification becomes known or could be discovered with reasonable diligence.

(3) *Taking of Deposition.*

(a) Objections to the competency of a witness or to the competency, relevancy, or materiality of testimony are not waived by failure to make them before or during the taking of a deposition, unless the ground of the objection is one which might have been obviated or removed if presented at that time.

(b) Errors and irregularities occurring at the deposition in the manner of taking the deposition, in the form of the questions or answers, in the oath or affirmation, or in the conduct of parties and errors of any other kind which might be cured if promptly presented, are waived unless seasonable objection is made at the taking of the deposition.

(c) Objections to the form of written questions submitted under MCR 2.307 are waived unless served in writing on the party propounding them within the time allowed for serving the succeeding cross-questions or other questions and within 7 days after service of the last questions authorized.

(d) On motion and notice a party may request a ruling by the court on an objection in advance of the trial.

(4) *Certification, Transcription, and Filing of Deposition.* Errors and irregularities in the manner in which the testimony is transcribed or the deposition is prepared, signed, certified, sealed, endorsed, transmitted, filed, or otherwise dealt with by the person before whom it was taken are waived unless a motion objecting to the deposition is filed within a reasonable time.

(5) *Harmless Error.* None of the foregoing errors or irregularities, even when not waived, or any others, preclude or restrict the use of the deposition, except insofar as the court finds that the errors substantially destroy the value of the deposition as evidence or render its use unfair or prejudicial.

[Effective March 1, 1985; amended effective December 1, 1989.]

1985 Staff Comment

MCR 2.308 brings together the various provisions on use of depositions in court proceedings previously found in GCR 1963, 302.4, 302.5, and 308. It is very similar to FR Civ P 32. The federal rule, however, does not include the harmless error provision found in subrule (C)(5) (and GCR 1963, 308.5).

The rule does not include the language previously found in GCR 1963, 302.4(4), providing that when a party introduces only part of a deposition, another party may introduce other parts. That subject is now covered by MRE 106.

Staff Comment to 1989 Amendment

Former subrule (A) mostly duplicated provisions in the Michigan Rules of Evidence. See, e.g., MRE 106, 803(18), and 804. The [December 1, 1989] amendment eliminates the overlap, and the possibility of conflict, by explicitly deferring to the MRE provisions. MRE 804(b) [was] amended concurrently.

RULE 2.309   INTERROGATORIES TO PARTIES

(A) Availability; Procedure for Service. A party may serve on another party written interrogatories to be answered by the party served or, if the party served is a public or private corporation, partnership, association, or governmental agency, by an officer or agent. Interrogatories may, without leave of court, be served:

(1) on the plaintiff after commencement of the action;

(2) on a defendant with or after the service of the summons and complaint on that defendant.

(B) Answers and Objections.

(1) Each interrogatory must be answered separately and fully in writing under oath. The answers must include such information as is available to the party served or that the party could obtain from his or her employees, agents, representatives, sureties, or indemnitors. If the answering party objects to an interrogatory, the reasons for the objection must be stated in lieu of an answer.

(2) The answering party shall repeat each interrogatory or subquestion immediately before the answer to it.

(3) The answers must be signed by the person making them and the objections signed by the attorney or an unrepresented party making them.

(4) The party on whom the interrogatories are served must serve the answers and objections, if any, on all other parties within 28 days after the interrogatories are served, except that a defendant may serve answers within 42 days after being served with the

summons and complaint. The court may allow a longer or shorter time and, for good cause shown, may excuse service on parties other than the party who served the interrogatories.

(C) Motion to Compel Answers. The party submitting the interrogatories may move for an order under MCR 2.313(A) with respect to an objection to or other failure to answer an interrogatory. If the motion is based on the failure to serve answers, proof of service of the interrogatories must be filed with the motion. The motion must state that the movant has in good faith conferred or attempted to confer with the party not making the disclosure in an effort to secure the disclosure without court action.

(D) Scope; Use at Trial.

(1) An interrogatory may relate to matters that can be inquired into under MCR 2.302(B).

(2) An interrogatory otherwise proper is not necessarily objectionable merely because an answer to the interrogatory involves an opinion or contention that relates to fact or the application of law to fact, but the court may order that an interrogatory need not be answered until after designated discovery has been completed or until a pretrial conference or other later time.

(3) The answer to an interrogatory may be used to the extent permitted by the rules of evidence.

(E) Option to Produce Business Records. Where the answer to an interrogatory may be derived from

(1) the business records of the party on whom the interrogatory has been served,

(2) an examination, audit, or inspection of business records, or

(3) a compilation, abstract, or summary based on such records,

and the burden of deriving the answer is substantially the same for the party serving the interrogatory as for the party served, it is a sufficient answer to the interrogatory to specify the records from which the answer may be derived and to afford to the party serving the interrogatory reasonable opportunity to examine, audit, or inspect the records and to make copies, compilations, abstracts, or summaries. A specification shall be in sufficient detail to permit the interrogating party to identify, as readily as can the party served, the records from which the answer may be derived.

[Effective March 1, 1985; amended effective January 1, 2003.]

1985 Staff Comment

MCR 2.309 is drawn from GCR 1963, 309 and FR CIV P 33.

The time provisions are changed to roughly coincide with those of FR Civ P 33(a): the party served has 28 days to answer (versus 15 days in GCR 1963, 309.2). The defendant may answer within 42 days after being served with the summons and complaint, if the interrogatories are served with or soon after the summons and complaint. There was a related provision in GCR 1963, 309.1—the plaintiff must wait 10 days after commencing the action before serving interrogatories.

Subrule (B)(3) adds a requirement that the answering party repeat the interrogatory immediately before the answer.

The burden of bringing disputes regarding interrogatories to the attention of the court by motion is placed on the party submitting the interrogatories, rather than the answering party. Compare subrule (C) with GCR 1963, 309.3.

Consistent with the other provisions on the scope of discovery, subrule (D)(2) adopts language from FR Civ P 33(b) providing that interrogatories may seek answers that involve opinions or application of law to fact.

Under subrule (D)(3) use of interrogatories is governed by the rules of evidence. GCR 1963, 309.4 incorporated the rule regarding use of depositions.

Subrule (E) adopts the substance of FR Civ P 33(c), giving the answering party the option to produce business records in certain circumstances.

Staff Comment to 2002 Amendment

The July 16, 2002 amendments of subrules 2.309(C), 2.310(C)(3), and 2.312(3), effective January 1, 2003, require that discovery motions include a statement that the movant has in good faith conferred or attempted to confer with the party not making the disclosure in an effort to secure the disclosure without court action. Subrule 2.310(C)(6) was added to clarify the respective responsibilities for the costs of discovery.

The staff comment is published only for the benefit of the bench and bar and is not an authoritative construction by the Court.

RULE 2.310 REQUESTS FOR PRODUCTION OF DOCUMENTS AND OTHER THINGS; ENTRY ON LAND FOR INSPECTION AND OTHER PURPOSES

(A) Definitions. For the purpose of this rule,

(1) "Documents" includes writings, drawings, graphs, charts, photographs, phono records, and other data compilations from which information can be obtained, translated, if necessary, by the respondent through detection devices into reasonably usable form.

(2) "Entry on land" means entry upon designated land or other property in the possession or control of the person on whom the request is served for the purpose of inspecting, measuring, surveying, photographing, testing, or sampling the property or a designated object or operation on the property, within the scope of MCR 2.302(B).

(B) Scope.

(1) A party may serve on another party a request

(a) to produce and permit the requesting party, or someone acting for that party,

(i) to inspect and copy designated documents or

(ii) to inspect and copy, test, or sample other tangible things

that constitute or contain matters within the scope of MCR 2.302(B) and that are in the possession, custody, or control of the party on whom the request is served; or

(b) to permit entry on land.

(2) A party may serve on a nonparty a request

(a) to produce and permit the requesting party or someone acting for that party to inspect and test or sample tangible things that constitute or contain matters within the scope of MCR 2.302(B) and that are in the possession, custody, or control of the person on whom the request is served; or

(b) to permit entry on land.

(C) Request to Party.

(1) The request may, without leave of court, be served on the plaintiff after commencement of the action and on the defendant with or after the service of the summons and complaint on that defendant. The request must list the items to be inspected, either by individual item or by category, and describe each item and category with reasonable particularity. The request must specify a reasonable time, place, and manner of making the inspection and performing the related acts.

(2) The party on whom the request is served must serve a written response within 28 days after service of the request, except that a defendant may serve a response within 42 days after being served with the summons and complaint. The court may allow a longer or shorter time. With respect to each item or category, the response must state that inspection and related activities will be permitted as requested or that the request is objected to, in which event the reasons for objection must be stated. If objection is made to part of an item or category, the part must be specified.

(3) The party submitting the request may move for an order under MCR 2.313(A) with respect to an objection to or a failure to respond to the request or a part of it, or failure to permit inspection as requested. If the motion is based on a failure to respond to a request, proof of service of the request must be filed with the motion. The motion must state the movant has in good faith conferred or attempted to confer with the party not making the disclosure in an effort to secure the disclosure without court action.

(4) The party to whom the request is submitted may seek a protective order under MCR 2.302(C).

(5) A party who produces documents for inspection shall produce them as they are kept in the usual course of business or shall organize and label them to correspond with the categories in the request.

(6) Unless otherwise ordered by the court for good cause, the party producing items for inspection shall bear the cost of assembling them and the party requesting the items shall bear any copying costs.

(D) Request to Nonparty.

(1) A request to a nonparty may be served at any time, except that leave of the court is required if the plaintiff seeks to serve a request before the occurrence of one of the events stated in MCR 2.306(A)(1).

(2) The request must be served on the person to whom it is directed in the manner provided in MCR 2.105, and a copy must be served on the other parties.

(3) The request must

(a) list the items to be inspected and tested or sampled, either by individual item or by category, and describe each item and category with reasonable particularity,

(b) specify a reasonable time, place, and manner of making the inspection and performing the related acts, and

(c) inform the person to whom it is directed that unless he or she agrees to allow the inspection or entry at a reasonable time and on reasonable conditions, a motion may be filed seeking a court order to require the inspection or entry.

(4) If the person to whom the request is directed does not permit the inspection or entry within 14 days after service of the request (or a shorter time if the court directs), the party seeking the inspection or entry may file a motion to compel the inspection or entry under MCR 2.313(A). The motion must include a copy of the request and proof of service of the request. The movant must serve the motion on the person from whom discovery is sought as provided in MCR 2.105.

(5) The court may order the party seeking discovery to pay the reasonable expenses incurred in complying with the request by the person from whom discovery is sought.

(6) This rule does not preclude an independent action against a nonparty for production of documents and other things and permission to enter on land or a subpoena to a nonparty under MCR 2.305.

(7) This rule does not preclude an independent action against a nonparty for production of documents and things and permission to enter on land.

[Effective March 1, 1985; amended effective December 1, 1998; September 1, 2000; January 1, 2003.]

1985 Staff Comment

MCR 2.310 is based on FR Civ P 34.

The rule adopts the federal formulation of requiring a party to serve a request for production of documents or things or permission to enter land before seeking a court order as was required by GCR 1963, 310.1. The time provisions are similar to those of FR Civ P 34(b)—the party served with the request has 28 days to respond (except that a defendant has at least 42 days after being served with the summons and complaint).

In subrule (C) a new procedure is created for serving a request to produce or permit entry on land on a nonparty. Both the former Michigan rule (GCR 1963, 310) and FR Civ P 34 limit the procedure to requests to parties, although they leave open the possibility of independent actions against nonparties. The procedure parallels that for requests to parties, although service of both the request and of any subsequent motion must be made in the manner provided by MCR 2.105. Subrule (C)(5) permits the court to order the party seeking discovery to pay reasonable expenses incurred by the person complying with the request.

The [March 1, 1985] amendment of MCR 2.310(C)(1) makes more specific the cross-reference to MCR 2.306.

Staff Comment to 1998 Amendment

The December 1, 1998 [effective date], amendments of Rules 2.305, 2.310, and 2.506 were suggested by the Representative Assembly of the State Bar of Michigan. The changes made clear that nonparty records-only discovery subpoenas are authorized. The normal procedure for noticing a deposition applies to records-only subpoenas, and the procedure in MCR 2.310 still pertains to requests to a nonparty for entry on land or production of items for testing or sampling. The time for responding to a document subpoena or a document request under Rule 2.305(B)(1) was changed from seven to fourteen days. The time for responding under Rule 2.310(C)(2) was changed from twenty-eight to fourteen days. The amendments also made nonsubstantive changes to clarify and simplify language.

Staff Comment to 2000 Amendment

The June 21, 2000 amendment of MCR 2.310(C)(2), effective September 1, 2000, increased from 14 to 28 days the time for a party to respond to a request under the court rule. The change was recommended by the Representative Assembly of the State Bar of Michigan.

Staff Comment to 2002 Amendment

The July 16, 2002 amendments of subrules 2.309(C), 2.310(C)(3), and 2.312(3), effective January 1, 2003, require that discovery motions include a statement that the movant has in good faith conferred or attempted to confer with the party not making the disclosure in an effort to secure the disclosure without court action. Subrule 2.310(C)(6) was added to clarify the respective responsibilities for the costs of discovery.

The staff comment is published only for the benefit of the bench and bar and is not an authoritative construction by the Court.

RULE 2.311   PHYSICAL AND MENTAL EXAMINATION OF PERSONS

(A) Order for Examination. When the mental or physical condition (including the blood group) of a party, or of a person in the custody or under the legal control of a party, is in controversy, the court in which the action is pending may order the party to submit to a physical or mental or blood examination by a physician (or other appropriate professional) or to produce for examination the person in the party's custody or legal control. The order may be entered only on motion for good cause with notice to the person to be examined and to all parties. The order must specify the time, place, manner, conditions, and scope of the examination and the person or persons by whom it is to be made, and may provide that the attorney for the person to be examined may be present at the examination.

(B) Report of Examining Physician.

(1) If requested by the party against whom an order is entered under subrule (A) or by the person examined, the party causing the examination to be made must deliver to the requesting person a copy of a detailed written report of the examining physician setting out the findings, including results of all tests made, diagnosis, and conclusions, together with like reports on all earlier examinations of the same condition, and must make available for inspection and examination X-rays, cardiograms, and other diagnostic aids.

(2) After delivery of the report, the party causing the examination to be made is entitled on request to receive from the party against whom the order is made a similar report of any examination previously or thereafter made of the same condition, and to a similar inspection of all diagnostic aids unless, in the case of a report on the examination of a nonparty, the party shows that he or she is unable to obtain it.

(3) If either party or a person examined refuses to deliver a report, the court on motion and notice may enter an order requiring delivery on terms as are just, and if a physician refuses or fails to comply with this rule, the court may order the physician to appear for a discovery deposition.

(4) By requesting and obtaining a report on the examination ordered under this rule, or by taking the deposition of the examiner, the person examined waives any privilege he or she may have in that action, or another action involving the same controversy, regarding the testimony of every other person who has examined or may thereafter examine the person as to the same mental or physical condition.

(5) Subrule (B) applies to examinations made by agreement of the parties, unless the agreement expressly provides otherwise.

(6) Subrule (B) does not preclude discovery of a report of an examining physician or the taking of a deposition of the physician under any other rule.

[Effective March 1, 1985.]

1985 Staff Comment

MCR 2.311 is based on GCR 1963, 311 and FR Civ P 35.

In the last sentence of subrule (A), the word "must" is changed to "may", allowing the trial court to direct that the examination take place without the attorney for the party being examined present.

New subrule (B)(5) is added to make clear that the provisions also apply to examinations conducted by agreement of the parties, unless the agreement provides otherwise.

RULE 2.312   REQUEST FOR ADMISSION

(A) Availability; Scope. Within the time for completion of discovery, a party may serve on another party a written request for the admission of the truth of a matter within the scope of MCR 2.302(B) stated in the request that relates to statements or opinions of fact or the application of law to fact, including the genuineness of documents described in the request. Copies of the documents must be served with the request unless they have been or are otherwise furnished or made available for inspection and copying. Each matter of which an admission is requested must be stated separately.

(B) Answer; Objection.

(1) Each matter as to which a request is made is deemed admitted unless, within 28 days after service of the request, or within a shorter or longer time as the court may allow, the party to whom the request is directed serves on the party requesting the admission a written answer or objection addressed to the matter. Unless the court orders a shorter time a defendant may serve an answer or objection within 42 days after being served with the summons and complaint.

(2) The answer must specifically deny the matter or state in detail the reasons why the answering party cannot truthfully admit or deny it. A denial must fairly meet the substance of the request, and when good faith requires that a party qualify an answer or deny only part of the matter of which an admission is requested, the party must specify the parts that are admitted and denied.

(3) An answering party may not give lack of information or knowledge as a reason for failure to admit or deny unless the party states that he or she has made reasonable inquiry and that the information known or readily obtainable is insufficient to enable the party to admit or deny.

(4) If an objection is made, the reasons must be stated. A party who considers that a matter of which an admission has been requested presents a genuine issue for trial may not, on that ground alone, object to the request. The party may, subject to the provisions of MCR 2.313(C), deny the matter or state reasons why he or she cannot admit or deny it.

(C) Motion Regarding Answer or Objection. The party who has requested the admission may move to determine the sufficiency of the answer or objection. The motion must state that the movant has in good faith conferred or attempted to confer with the party not making the disclosure in an effort to secure the disclosure without court action. Unless the court determines that an objection is justified, it shall order that an answer be served. If the court determines that an answer does not comply with the requirements of the rule, it may order either that the matter is admitted, or that an amended answer be served. The court may, in lieu of one of these orders, determine that final disposition of the request be made at a pretrial conference or at a designated time before trial. The provisions of MCR 2.313(A)(5) apply to the award of expenses incurred in relation to the motion.

(D) Effect of Admission.

(1) A matter admitted under this rule is conclusively established unless the court on motion permits withdrawal or amendment of an admission. For good cause the court may allow a party to amend or withdraw an admission. The court may condition amendment or withdrawal of the admission on terms that are just.

(2) An admission made by a party under this rule is for the purpose of the pending action only and is not an admission for another purpose, nor may it be used against the party in another proceeding.

(E) Public Records.

(1) A party intending to use as evidence

    (a) a record that a public official is required by federal, state, or municipal authority to receive for filing or recording or is given custody of by law, or

    (b) a memorial of a public official,

may prepare a copy, synopsis, or abstract of the record, insofar as it is to be used, and serve it on the adverse party sufficiently in advance of trial to allow the adverse party a reasonable opportunity to determine its accuracy.

(2) The copy, synopsis, or abstract is then admissible in evidence as admitted facts in the action, if otherwise admissible, except insofar as its inaccuracy is pointed out by the adverse party in an affidavit filed and served within a reasonable time before trial.

(F) Filing With Court. Requests and responses under this rule must be filed with the court either before service or within a reasonable time thereafter.

[Effective March 1, 1985; amended effective January 1, 2003.]

1985 Staff Comment

MCR 2.312 is drawn from GCR 1963, 312 and FR Civ P 36.

Subrule (A) adopts the federal formulation of the scope of requests for admission, allowing a request to ask for admissions regarding the application of law to fact. Compare GCR 1963, 312.1 with FR Civ P 36(a).

The time for response is the same as for interrogatories and requests to produce, and is comparable to that in FR Civ P 36(a) (28 days; as to a defendant, at least 42 days after service of the summons and complaint). GCR 1963, 312.1 required a response within 10 days.

As in the interrogatory rule, MCR 2.309(C), subrule (C) adopts the federal practice of placing the burden of filing a motion on the requesting party if there is a dispute. Compare FR Civ P 36(a) with GCR 1963, 312.1.

Subrule (F) excepts requests for admission from the general rule regarding filing of discovery materials. See MCR 2.302(H).

Staff Comment to 2002 Amendment

The July 16, 2002 amendments of subrules 2.309(C), 2.310(C)(3), and 2.312(3), effective January 1, 2003, require that discovery motions include a statement that the movant has in good faith conferred or attempted to confer with the party not making the disclosure in an effort to secure the disclosure without court action. Subrule 2.310(C)(6) was added to clarify the respective responsibilities for the costs of discovery.

The staff comment is published only for the benefit of the bench and bar and is not an authoritative construction by the Court.

RULE 2.313 FAILURE TO PROVIDE OR TO PERMIT DISCOVERY; SANCTIONS

(A) Motion for Order Compelling Discovery. A party, on reasonable notice to other parties and all persons affected, may apply for an order compelling discovery as follows:

(1) *Appropriate Court.* A motion for an order under this rule may be made to the court in which the action is pending, or, as to a matter relating to a deposition, to a court in the county or district where the deposition is being taken.

(2) *Motion.* If

(a) a deponent fails to answer a question propounded or submitted under MCR 2.306 or 2.307,

(b) a corporation or other entity fails to make a designation under MCR 2.306(B)(5) or 2.307(A)(1),

(c) a party fails to answer an interrogatory submitted under MCR 2.309, or

(d) in response to a request for inspection submitted under MCR 2.310, a person fails to respond that inspection will be permitted as requested,

the party seeking discovery may move for an order compelling an answer, a designation, or inspection in accordance with the request. When taking a deposition on oral examination, the proponent of the question may complete or adjourn the examination before applying for an order.

(3) *Ruling; Protective Order.* If the court denies the motion in whole or in part, it may enter a protective order that it could have entered on motion made under MCR 2.302(C).

(4) *Evasive or Incomplete Answer.* For purposes of this subrule an evasive or incomplete answer is to be treated as a failure to answer.

(5) *Award of Expenses of Motion.*

(a) If the motion is granted, the court shall, after opportunity for hearing, require the party or deponent whose conduct necessitated the motion or the party or attorney advising such conduct, or both, to pay to the moving party the reasonable expenses incurred in obtaining the order, including attorney fees, unless the court finds that the opposition to the motion was substantially justified or that other circumstances made an award of expenses unjust.

(b) If the motion is denied, the court shall, after opportunity for hearing, require the moving party or the attorney advising the motion, or both, to pay to the person who opposed the motion the reasonable expenses incurred in opposing the motion, including attorney fees, unless the court finds that the making of the motion was substantially justified or that other circumstances make an award of expenses unjust.

(c) If the motion is granted in part and denied in part, the court may apportion the reasonable expenses incurred in relation to the motion among the parties and other persons in a just manner.

(B) Failure to Comply With Order.

(1) *Sanctions by Court Where Deposition Is Taken.* If a deponent fails to be sworn or to answer a question after being directed to do so by a court in the county or district in which the deposition is being taken, the failure may be considered a contempt of that court.

(2) *Sanctions by Court in Which Action Is Pending.* If a party or an officer, director, or managing agent of a party, or a person designated under MCR 2.306(B)(5) or 2.307(A)(1) to testify on behalf of a party, fails to obey an order to provide or permit discovery, including an order entered under subrule (A) of this rule or under MCR 2.311, the court in which the action is pending may order such sanctions as are just, including, but not limited to the following:

(a) an order that the matters regarding which the order was entered or other designated facts may be taken to be established for the purposes of the action in accordance with the claim of the party obtaining the order;

(b) an order refusing to allow the disobedient party to support or oppose designated claims or defenses, or prohibiting the party from introducing designated matters into evidence;

(c) an order striking pleadings or parts of pleadings, staying further proceedings until the order is obeyed, dismissing the action or proceeding or a part of it, or rendering a judgment by default against the disobedient party;

(d) in lieu of or in addition to the foregoing orders, an order treating as a contempt of court the failure to obey an order, except an order to submit to a physical or mental examination;

(e) where a party has failed to comply with an order under MCR 2.311(A) requiring the party to produce another for examination, such orders as are listed in subrules (B)(2)(a), (b), and (c), unless the party failing to comply shows that he or she is unable to produce such person for examination.

In lieu of or in addition to the foregoing orders, the court shall require the party failing to obey the order or the attorney advising the party, or both, to pay the reasonable expenses, including attorney fees, caused by the failure, unless the court finds that the failure was substantially justified or that other circumstances make an award of expenses unjust.

(C) Expenses on Failure to Admit. If a party denies the genuineness of a document, or the truth of a matter as requested under MCR 2.312, and if the party requesting the admission later proves the genuineness of the document or the truth of the matter, the requesting party may move for an order requiring the other party to pay the expenses incurred in making that proof, including attorney fees. The court shall enter the order unless it finds that

(1) the request was held objectionable pursuant to MCR 2.312,

(2) the admission sought was of no substantial importance,

(3) the party failing to admit had reasonable ground to believe that he or she might prevail on the matter, or

(4) there was other good reason for the failure to admit.

(D) Failure of Party to Attend at Own Deposition, to Serve Answers to Interrogatories, or to Respond to Request for Inspection.

(1) If a party; an officer, director, or managing agent of a party; or a person designated under MCR 2.306(B)(5) or 2.307(A)(1) to testify on behalf of a party fails

(a) to appear before the person who is to take his or her deposition, after being served with a proper notice;

(b) to serve answers or objections to interrogatories submitted under MCR 2.309, after proper service of the interrogatories; or

(c) to serve a written response to a request for inspection submitted under MCR 2.310, after proper service of the request,

on motion, the court in which the action is pending may order such sanctions as are just. Among others, it may take an action authorized under subrule (B)(2)(a), (b), and (c).

(2) In lieu of or in addition to an order, the court shall require the party failing to act or the attorney advising the party, or both, to pay the reasonable expenses, including attorney fees, caused by the failure, unless the court finds that the failure was substantially justified or that other circumstances make an award of expenses unjust.

(3) A failure to act described in this subrule may not be excused on the ground that the discovery sought is objectionable unless the party failing to act has moved for a protective order as provided by MCR 2.302(C).

[Effective March 1, 1985.]

1985 Staff Comment

MCR 2.313 is based on GCR 1963, 313 and FR Civ P 37. The rule follows the structure of the federal rule but does not require that a motion regarding a deposition be brought in the county where the deposition is held. This is consistent with the practice under GCR 1963, 313.1(1).

The rule provides greater detail regarding award of costs than did GCR 1963, 313. Compare subrules (A)(5), (B)(2), and (D)(2) with GCR 1963, 313.1(3) and (4). As under the corresponding federal provisions, the cost sanctions may be imposed on an attorney for a party as well as on the party. See FR Civ P 37(a)(4), 37(b)(2), 37(d).

RULE 2.314 DISCOVERY OF MEDICAL INFORMATION CONCERNING PARTY

(A) Scope of Rule.

(1) When a mental or physical condition of a party is in controversy, medical information about the condition is subject to discovery under these rules to the extent that

(a) the information is otherwise discoverable under MCR 2.302(B), and

(b) the party does not assert that the information is subject to a valid privilege.

(2) Medical information subject to discovery includes, but is not limited to, medical records in the possession or control of a physician, hospital, or other custodian, and medical knowledge discoverable by deposition or interrogatories.

(3) For purposes of this rule, medical information about a mental or physical condition of a party is within the control of the party, even if the information is not in the party's immediate physical possession.

(B) Privilege; Assertion; Waiver; Effects.

(1) A party who has a valid privilege may assert the privilege and prevent discovery of medical information relating to his or her mental or physical condition. The privilege must be asserted in the party's written response to a request for production of documents under MCR 2.310, in answers to interrogatories under MCR 2.309(B), before or during the taking of a deposition, or by moving for a protective order under MCR 2.302(C). A privilege not timely asserted is waived in that action, but is not waived for the purposes of any other action.

(2) Unless the court orders otherwise, if a party asserts that the medical information is subject to a privilege and the assertion has the effect of preventing discovery of medical information otherwise discover-

able under MCR 2.302(B), the party may not thereafter present or introduce any physical, documentary, or testimonial evidence relating to the party's medical history or mental or physical condition.

(C) Response by Party to Request for Medical Information.

(1) A party who is served with a request for production of medical information under MCR 2.310 must either:

(a) make the information available for inspection and copying as requested;

(b) assert that the information is privileged;

(c) object to the request as permitted by MCR 2.310(B)(2); or

(d) furnish the requesting party with signed authorizations in the form approved by the state court administrator sufficient in number to enable the requesting party to obtain the information requested from persons, institutions, hospitals, and other custodians in actual possession of the information requested.

(2) A party responding to a request for medical information as permitted by subrule (C)(1)(d) must also inform the adverse party of the physical location of the information requested.

(D) Release of Medical Information by Custodian.

(1) A physician, hospital, or other custodian of medical information (referred to in this rule as the "custodian") shall comply with a properly authorized request for the medical information within 28 days after the receipt of the request, or, if at the time the request is made the patient is hospitalized for the mental or physical condition for which the medical information is sought, within 28 days after the patient's discharge or release. The court may extend or shorten these time limits for good cause.

(2) In responding to a request for medical information under this rule, the custodian will be deemed to have complied with the request if the custodian

(a) makes the information reasonably available for inspection and copying; or

(b) delivers to the requesting party the original information or a true and exact copy of the original information accompanied by a sworn certificate in the form approved by the state court administrator, signed by the custodian verifying that the copy is a true and complete reproduction of the original information.

(3) If it is essential that an original document be examined when the authenticity of the document, questions of interpretation of handwriting, or similar questions arise, the custodian must permit reasonable inspection of the original document by the requesting party and by experts retained to examine the information.

(4) If x-rays or other records incapable of reproduction are requested, the custodian may inform the requesting party that these records exist, but have not been delivered pursuant to subrule (D)(2). Delivery of the records may be conditioned on the requesting party or the party's agent signing a receipt that includes a promise that the records will be returned to the custodian after a reasonable time for inspection purposes has elapsed.

(5) In complying with subrule (D)(2), the custodian is entitled to receive reasonable reimbursement in advance for expenses of compliance.

(6) If a custodian does not respond within the time permitted by subrule (D)(1) to a party's authorized request for medical information, a subpoena may be issued under MCR 2.305(A)(2), directing that the custodian present the information for examination and copying at the time and place stated in the subpoena.

(E) Persons Not Parties. Medical information concerning persons not parties to the action is not discoverable under this rule.

[Effective March 1, 1985; amended effective September 1, 1994.]

1985 Staff Comment

MCR 2.314 is largely new and covers discovery of medical records of a party via a request for production under MCR 2.310. There were related provisions in GCR 1963, 506.7 regarding subpoenas for production of hospital records.

Subrule (B) covers privileges regarding medical information and in general requires a party to decide whether or not to assert the privilege at the discovery stage. Under subrule (B)(1), if the party does not assert the privilege in response to a request to produce, it is waived. Under subrule (B)(2) if the party asserts the privilege and thereby prevents discovery of the information, the party is precluded from introducing testimony at trial relating to the party's medical history or condition. However, the court may modify this procedure.

Under subrule (C), when a party is served with a request for production of his or her medical records, the party must make the records available, assert they are privileged, object to the request, or furnish authorization forms that will enable the adverse party to obtain the records from medical records custodians.

The provisions regarding compliance by custodians of medical records are in subrule (D). The state court administrator is to approve forms for use in connection with this procedure.

Subrule (E) makes clear that the rule does not preclude discovery of medical records in other ways permitted by these rules.

Staff Comment to 1994 Amendment

Several changes are made in MCR 2.314, the rule regarding discovery of medical information. As amended [effective September 1, 1994], the rule applies the preclusive effect of subrule (B)(1) to a party who asserts a privilege as to medical information in connection with depositions and interrogatories as well as to requests for production of documents. See *Gibson* v. *Bronson Methodist Hosp,* 445 Mich. 331, 517 N.W.2d 736 (Mich. 1994).

RULE 2.315   VIDEO DEPOSITIONS

(A) When Permitted. Depositions authorized under MCR 2.303 and 2.306 may be taken by means of simultaneous audio and visual electronic recording without leave of the court or stipulation of the parties, provided the deposition is taken in accordance with this rule.

(B) Rules Governing. Except as provided in this rule, the taking of video depositions is governed by the rules governing the taking of other depositions unless the nature of the video deposition makes compliance impossible or unnecessary.

(C) Procedure.

(1) A notice of the taking of a video deposition and a subpoena for attendance at the deposition must state that the deposition is to be visually recorded.

(2) A video deposition must be timed by means of a digital clock or clocks capable of displaying the hours, minutes, and seconds. The clock or clocks must be in the picture at all times during the taking of the deposition.

(3) A video deposition must begin with a statement on camera of the date, time, and place at which the recording is being made, the title of the action, and the identification of the attorneys.

(4) The person being deposed must be sworn as a witness on camera by an authorized person.

(5) More than one camera may be used, in sequence or simultaneously.

(6) The parties may make audio recordings while the video deposition is being taken.

(7) At the conclusion of the deposition a statement must be made on camera that the deposition is completed.

(D) Custody of Tape and Copies.

(1) The person making the video recording must retain possession of it. The video recording must be securely sealed and marked for identification purposes.

(2) The parties may purchase audio or audio-visual copies of the recording from the operator.

(E) Filing; Notice of Filing. If a party requests that the deposition be filed, the person who made the recording shall

(1) file the recording with the court under MCR 2.306(F)(3), together with an affidavit identifying the recording, stating the total elapsed time, and attesting that no alterations, additions, or deletions other than those ordered by the court have been made;

(2) give the notice required by MCR 2.306(F)(3), and

(3) serve copies of the recording on all parties who have requested them under MCR 2.315(D)(2).

(F) Use as Evidence; Objections.

(1) A video deposition may not be used in a court proceeding unless it has been filed with the court.

(2) Except as modified by this rule, the use of video depositions in court proceedings is governed by MCR 2.308.

(3) A party who seeks to use a video deposition at trial must provide the court with either

(a) a transcript of the deposition, which shall be used for ruling on any objections, or

(b) a stipulation by all parties that there are no objections to the deposition and that the recording (or an agreed portion of it) may be played.

(4) When a video deposition is used in a court proceeding, the court must indicate on the record what portions of the recording have been played. The court reporter or recorder need not make a record of the statements in the recording.

(G) Custody of Video Deposition After Filing. After filing, a video deposition shall remain in the custody of the court unless the court orders the recording stored elsewhere for technical reasons or because of special storage problems. The order directing the storage must direct the custodian to keep the recordings sealed until the further order of the court. Video depositions filed with the court shall have the same status as other depositions and documents filed with the court, and may be reproduced, preserved, destroyed, or salvaged as directed by order of the court.

(H) Appeal. On appeal the recording remains part of the record and shall be transmitted with it. A party may request that the appellate court view portions of the video deposition. If a transcript was not provided to the court under subrule (F)(3), the appellant must arrange and pay for the preparation of a transcript to be included in the record on appeal.

(I) Costs. The costs of taking a video deposition and the cost for its use in evidence may be taxed as costs as provided by MCR 2.625 in the same manner as depositions recorded in other ways.

[Effective March 1, 1985.]

1985 Staff Comment

MCR 2.315 is based on GCR 1963, 315.

Subrule (E) modifies the filing and notice of filing provisions to be consistent with the general deposition provisions of MCR 2.306(F). The video recording need only be filed if requested by a party, and the person who made the recording, rather than the clerk, is responsible for giving notice of the filing. Compare GCR 1963, 315.5.

Subrule (F) revises the provisions regarding the use of a video deposition as evidence and the procedure for objections to material in the deposition. GCR 1963, 315.6(2) directed the judge to rule on objections after viewing the video tape. Under subrule (F)(3), the party seeking to introduce the recording must either provide a transcript for use in ruling on objections, or obtain the stipulation of all parties that there is no objection to the deposition and that all or part of it may be played. The court reporter or recorder need not make a record of the playing of the deposition. However, the court must indicate on the record what portions have been played.

There are related provisions regarding video depositions on appeal in subrule (H). The recording itself is part of the record, and may be viewed by the appellate court. In addition, if a transcript was not provided for use by the trial court in ruling on objections, the appellant must have the deposition transcribed for the appeal.

RULE 2.316 REMOVAL OF DISCOVERY MATERIALS FROM FILE

(A) Definition. For the purpose of this rule, "discovery material" means deposition transcripts, audio or video recordings of depositions, interrogatories, and answers to interrogatories and requests to admit.

(B) Removal From File. In civil actions, discovery materials may be removed from files and destroyed in the manner provided in this rule.

(1) *By Stipulation.* If the parties stipulate to the removal of discovery materials from the file, the clerk may remove the materials and dispose of them in the manner provided in the stipulation.

(2) *By the Clerk.*

(a) The clerk may initiate the removal of discovery materials from the file in the following circumstances.

(i) If an appeal has not been taken, 18 months after entry of judgment on the merits or dismissal of the action.

(ii) If an appeal has been taken, 91 days after the appellate proceedings are concluded, unless the action is remanded for further proceedings in the trial court.

(b) The clerk shall notify the parties and counsel of record, when possible, that discovery materials will be removed from the file of the action and destroyed on a specified date at least 28 days after the notice is served unless within that time

(i) the party who filed the discovery materials retrieves them from the clerk's office, or

(ii) a party files a written objection to removal of discovery materials from the file.

If an objection to removal of discovery materials is filed, the discovery materials may not be removed unless the court so orders after notice and opportunity for the objecting party to be heard. The clerk shall schedule a hearing and give notice to the parties. The rules governing motion practice apply.

(3) *By Order.* On motion of a party, or on its own initiative after notice and hearing, the court may order discovery materials removed at any other time on a finding that the materials are no longer necessary. However, no discovery materials may be destroyed by court personnel or the clerk until the periods set forth in subrule (2)(a)(i) or (2)(a)(ii) have passed.

[Adopted effective June 1, 1989.]

1989 Staff Comment

The Michigan Judges Association recommended adoption of this rule to reduce costs and lessen the physical burden of maintaining voluminous discovery materials that cannot or will not be utilized in the trial of civil cases.

SUBCHAPTER 2.400 PRETRIAL PROCEDURE; ALTERNATIVE DISPUTE RESOLUTION; OFFERS OF JUDGMENT; SETTLEMENTS

RULE 2.401 PRETRIAL PROCEDURES; CONFERENCES; SCHEDULING ORDERS

(A) Time; Discretion of Court. At any time after the commencement of the action, on its own initiative or the request of a party, the court may direct that the attorneys for the parties, alone or with the parties, appear for a conference. The court shall give reasonable notice of the scheduling of a conference. More than one conference may be held in an action.

(B) Early Scheduling Conference and Order.

(1) *Early Scheduling Conference.* The court may direct that an early scheduling conference be held. In addition to those considerations enumerated in subrule (C)(1), during this conference the court should consider:

(a) whether jurisdiction and venue are proper or whether the case is frivolous,

(b) whether to refer the case to an alternative dispute resolution procedure under MCR 2.410, and

(c) the complexity of a particular case and enter a scheduling order setting time limitations for the processing of the case and establishing dates when future actions should begin or be completed in the case.

(2) *Scheduling Order.*

(a) At an early scheduling conference under subrule (B)(1), a pretrial conference under subrule (C), or at such other time as the court concludes that such an order would facilitate the progress of the case, the court shall establish times for events the court deems appropriate, including

(i) the initiation or completion of an ADR process,

(ii) the amendment of pleadings, adding of parties, or filing of motions,

(iii) the completion of discovery,

(iv) the exchange of witness lists under subrule (I), and

(v) the scheduling of a pretrial conference, a settlement conference, or trial.

More than one such order may be entered in a case.

(b) The scheduling of events under this subrule shall take into consideration the nature and complexity of the case, including the issues involved, the number and location of parties and potential witnesses, including experts, the extent of expected and necessary discovery, and the availability of reasonably certain trial dates.

(c) Whenever reasonably practical, the scheduling of events under this subrule shall be made after meaningful consultation with all counsel of record.

(i) If a scheduling order is entered under this subrule in a manner that does not permit meaningful advance consultation with counsel, within 14 days after entry of the order, a party may file and serve a written request for amendment of the order detailing the reasons why the order should be amended.

(ii) Upon receiving such a written request, the court shall reconsider the order in light of the objections raised by the parties. Whether the reconsideration occurs at a conference or in some other manner, the court must either enter a new scheduling order or notify the parties in writing that the court declines to amend the order. The court must schedule a conference, enter the new order, or send the written notice, within 14 days after receiving the request.

(iii) The submission of a request pursuant to this subrule, or the failure to submit such a request, does not preclude a party from filing a motion to modify a scheduling order.

(C) Pretrial Conference; Scope.

(1) At a conference under this subrule, in addition to the matters listed in subrule (B)(1), the court and the attorneys for the parties may consider any matters that will facilitate the fair and expeditious disposition of the action, including:

(a) the simplification of the issues;

(b) the amount of time necessary for discovery;

(c) the necessity or desirability of amendments to the pleadings;

(d) the possibility of obtaining admissions of fact and of documents to avoid unnecessary proof;

(e) the limitation of the number of expert witnesses;

(f) the consolidation of actions for trial, the separation of issues, and the order of trial when some issues are to be tried by a jury and some by the court;

(g) the possibility of settlement;

(h) whether mediation, case evaluation, or some other form of alternative dispute resolution would be appropriate for the case, and what mechanisms are available to provide such services;

(i) the identity of the witnesses to testify at trial;

(j) the estimated length of trial;

(k) whether all claims arising out of the transaction or occurrence that is the subject matter of the action have been joined as required by MCR 2.203(A);

(*l*) other matters that may aid in the disposition of the action.

(2) *Conference Order.* If appropriate, the court shall enter an order incorporating agreements reached and decisions made at the conference.

(D) Order for Trial Briefs. The court may direct the attorneys to furnish trial briefs as to any or all of the issues involved in the action.

(E) Appearance of Counsel. The attorneys attending the conference shall be thoroughly familiar with the case and have the authority necessary to fully participate in the conference. The court may direct that the attorneys who intend to try the case attend the conference.

(F) Presence of Parties at Conference. In the case of a conference at which meaningful discussion of settlement is anticipated, the court may direct that persons with authority to settle the case, including the parties to the action, agents of parties, representatives of lien holders, or representatives of insurance carriers:

(1) be present at the conference; or

(2) be immediately available at the time of the conference. The court's order may specify whether the availability is to be in person or by telephone.

This subrule does not apply to an early scheduling conference held pursuant to subrule (B).

(G) Failure To Attend; Default; Dismissal.

(1) Failure of a party or the party's attorney to attend a scheduled conference, as directed by the court, constitutes a default to which MCR 2.603 is applicable or grounds for dismissal under MCR 2.504(B).

(2) The court shall excuse the failure of a party or the party's attorney to attend a conference, and enter an order other than one of default or dismissal, if the court finds that

(a) entry of an order of default or dismissal would cause manifest injustice; or

(b) the failure to attend was not due to the culpable negligence of the party or the attorney.

The court may condition the order on the payment by the offending party or attorney of reasonable expenses as provided in MCR 2.313(B)(2).

(H) Conference After Discovery. If the court finds at a pretrial conference held after the completion of discovery that due to a lack of reasonable diligence by a party the action is not ready for trial, the court may enter an appropriate order to facilitate preparation of the action for trial and may require the offending party to pay the reasonable expenses, including attorney fees, caused by the lack of diligence.

(I) Witness Lists.

(1) No later than the time directed by the court under subrule (B)(2)(a), the parties shall file and serve witness lists. The witness list must include:

(a) the name of each witness, and the witness's address, if known; however, records custodians whose testimony would be limited to providing the foundation for the admission of records may be identified generally;

(b) whether the witness is an expert, and the field of expertise.

(2) The court may order that any witness not listed in accordance with this rule will be prohibited from testifying at trial except upon good cause shown.

(3) This subrule does not prevent a party from obtaining an earlier disclosure of witness information by other discovery means as provided in these rules.

[Effective March 1, 1985; amended effective October 1, 1991; August 1, 2000.]

1985 Staff Comment

MCR 2.401 is comparable to GCR 1963, 301.

Subrule (A) makes the holding of a pretrial conference optional. Under GCR 1963, 301.1 such conferences were required, although Wayne circuit local rule 301.1 made them optional in that court and GCR 1963, 301.8 permitted the parties to waive the pretrial conference in other counties. Despite the general rule that the holding of a conference is optional, under subrule (A)(2) one must be held if requested by a party within 182 days after the filing of an answer, if that would not delay the trial.

Subrule (B) covers the matters that may be considered at the pretrial conference. Added to the list found in GCR 1963, 301.1 are the necessity for additional time for discovery (see MCR 2.301), and the appropriateness of mediation under MCR 2.403.

Under subrule (C) the court may direct the attorneys to prepare the summary of the results of the conference.

Subrule (C)(3) differs slightly from GCR 1963, 301.3. The latter said that a party is not to be deprived of the right to present evidence on issues raised by the pleadings unless they were waived at the pretrial conference. Subrule (C)(3) takes account of the fact that some issues need not be pleaded in order to be preserved for trial, but rather may be preserved by motion. See MCR 2.111(F)(2)(a).

Subrule (E) retains the provision of GCR 1963, 301.5 allowing the court to require the parties to be present or available at the conference. There is a new, related provision in MCR 2.506(A)(2), which also applies to insurance representatives.

New language is added in subrule (F) regarding sanctions for failure to appear at a conference. Dismissal is added as a possible sanction. In addition, the court may excuse the failure to appear under certain circumstances.

The protracted litigation provision of GCR 1963, 301.6 is omitted.

Staff Comment to 1991 Amendment

There are extensive revisions of MCR 2.401 [effective October 1, 1991], governing pretrial procedure and conferences. In addition to adjustments in a number of the other subrules, new provisions are added regarding scheduling orders [subrule (B)(2)], attendance of attorneys at conferences [subrule (E)], and service of witness lists [subrule (I)].

Staff Comment to 2000 Amendment

The May 8, 2000, amendments [effective August 1, 2000] are based on the recommendations of the Michigan Supreme Court Dispute Resolution Task Force, which were published for comment on May 10, 1999 [see 459 Mich 1251], and were the subject of a series of public hearings across the state.

The Task Force report, issued in January 1999, and its Addendum report, issued in January 2000 after receipt of comments, should be consulted for the background and details of the amendments. Basically, the changes are as follows:

The amendments of MCR 2.403, 2.404, 2.405, 2.501, 2.502 and 2.503 are mainly to change terminology, replacing "mediation," as used in current MCR 2.403, with the term "case evaluation." "Mediation" will be used to describe the facilitative process established in MCR 2.411, in keeping with the generally accepted usage of the term.

MCR 2.401 is amended to direct consideration of alternative dispute resolution processes at scheduling and pretrial conferences.

New MCR 2.410 has general provisions governing referral of cases to alternative dispute resolution processes. Local courts wishing to use ADR techniques are to adopt ADR plans within the framework provided by the rule.

The one ADR process that is specifically established by the rules is mediation under new MCR 2.411. Among other things, the rule establishes general standards for mediator qualifications, and procedures for selection of mediators.

MCR 3.216, the domestic relations mediation rule, is substantially revised, to be more comparable to the mediation process in MCR 2.411.

MCR 5.143, regarding use of alternative dispute resolution processes in probate court, is amended to conform to the other rule changes.

Dissenting Statement of Justice Kelly to 2000 Amendment

I support the expanded use of alternative dispute resolution by our courts. However, I cannot cast a vote favoring the proposed Dispute Resolution Court Rules for two reasons: 1) they authorize judges to compel parties to submit to mediation and 2) they include nonlawyers as mediators and other ADR providers.

Regarding the mandatory nature of the new rules, I believe that mediation is, by its very nature, a process that works only when the parties enter into it voluntarily. I would support rules that permit courts to order parties to a session at which the merits of ADR are explored, but not that mandate mediation.

It is my fear that mandatory mediation will present insurmountable financial obstacles to low income litigants and could even provoke challenges based on a violation of due process principles. I am concerned that, in some heavily burdened courts, judges may use the new rules, not as an option for the parties, but as a docket control mechanism for the court. Also, I find no limit in the rules to the number of times a party could be ordered to an ADR process.

Mediation should not become yet another hurdle to a just resolution of disputes. Parties should not feel pressed to settle against their best interests, or involuntarily to expend financial resources in excess of the normal costs of trial. Litigation, without the new rules, is already too costly.

I agree with the Board of Commissioners of the State Bar of Michigan that, absent agreement of the parties, only licensed lawyers should be allowed to serve as ADR providers. Mediation and other types of ADR typically involve complex legal matters requiring skilled ADR providers. Yet, no system has been developed to ensure the training and accountability of nonlawyers who participate.

Finally, I agree with the Open Justice Commission's recommendations that chief judges should be required to report the race, ethnicity, and gender of case evaluators and other ADR providers that they appoint. I view this as a vital step toward ensuring persons wishing to function as ADR providers will not be passed over solely on the basis of their race, gender, ethnic background, or similar factors.

RULE 2.402   USE OF COMMUNICATION EQUIPMENT

(A) Definition. "Communication equipment" means a conference telephone or other electronic device that permits all those appearing or participating to hear and speak to each other.

(B) Use. A court may, on its own initiative or on the written request of a party, direct that communication equipment be used for a motion hearing, pretrial conference, scheduling conference, or status conference. The court must give notice to the parties before directing on its own initiative that communication equipment be used. A party wanting to use communication equipment must submit a written request to the court at least 7 days before the day on which such equipment is sought to be used, and serve a copy on the other parties, unless good cause is shown to waive this requirement. The requesting party also must provide a copy of the request to the office of the judge to whom the request is directed. The court may, with the consent of all parties or for good cause, direct that the testimony of a witness be taken through communication equipment. A verbatim record of the proceeding must still be made.

(C) Burden of Expense. The party who initiates the use of communication equipment shall pay the cost

for its use, unless the court otherwise directs. If the use of communication equipment is initiated by the court, the cost for its use is to be shared equally, unless the court otherwise directs.

[Effective March 1, 1985; amended effective September 1, 1998; September 1, 2000.]

1985 Staff Comment

MCR 2.402 is substantially the same as GCR 1963, 918.

Staff Comment to 1998 Amendment

The June 1998 amendment of MCR 2.402(B), effective September 1, 1998, was suggested by the Michigan Judges Association. The amendment permits a court to arrange for a witness to testify through communication equipment "for good cause," as well as if all parties consent.

Staff Comment to 2000 Amendment

The June 21, 2000 amendments of MCR 2.402 (B) and (C), effective September 1, 2000, added a scheduling conference to the list of proceedings for which communication equipment may be used, allowed discretion for late requests, required that a copy of the request be provided to the office of the judge to whom it is directed, and assigned the cost for using communication equipment to the requesting party.

RULE 2.403   CASE EVALUATION

(A) Scope and Applicability of Rule.

(1) A court may submit to case evaluation any civil action in which the relief sought is primarily money damages or division of property.

(2) Case evaluation of tort cases filed in circuit court is mandatory beginning with actions filed after the effective dates of Chapters 49 and 49A of the Revised Judicature Act, as added by 1986 PA 178; however, the court may except an action from case evaluation on motion for good cause shown if it finds that case evaluation of that action would be inappropriate.

(3) Cases filed in district court may be submitted to case evaluation under this rule. The time periods set forth in subrules (B)(1), (G)(1), (L)(1) and (L)(2) may be shortened at the discretion of the district judge to whom the case is assigned.

(B) Selection of Cases.

(1) The judge to whom an action is assigned or the chief judge may select it for case evaluation by written order no earlier than 91 days after the filing of the answer

   (a) on written stipulation by the parties,

   (b) on written motion by a party, or

   (c) on the judge's own initiative.

(2) Selection of an action for case evaluation has no effect on the normal progress of the action toward trial.

(C) Objections to Case Evaluation.

(1) To object to case evaluation, a party must file a written motion to remove from case evaluation and a notice of hearing of the motion and serve a copy on the attorneys of record and the ADR clerk within 14 days after notice of the order assigning the action to case evaluation. The motion must be set for hearing within 14 days after it is filed, unless the court orders otherwise.

(2) A timely motion must be heard before the case is submitted to case evaluation.

(D) Case Evaluation Panel.

(1) Case evaluation panels shall be composed of 3 persons.

(2) The procedure for selecting case evaluation panels is as provided in MCR 2.404.

(3) A judge may be selected as a member of a case evaluation panel, but may not preside at the trial of any action in which he or she served as a case evaluator.

(4) A case evaluator may not be called as a witness at trial.

(E) Disqualification of Case Evaluators. The rule for disqualification of a case evaluator is the same as that provided in MCR 2.003 for the disqualification of a judge.

(F) ADR Clerk. The court shall designate the ADR clerk specified under MCR 2.410, or some other person, to administer the case evaluation program. In this rule and MCR 2.404, "ADR clerk" refers to the person so designated.

(G) Scheduling Case Evaluation Hearing.

(1) The ADR clerk shall set a time and place for the hearing and send notice to the case evaluators and the attorneys at least 42 days before the date set.

(2) Adjournments may be granted only for good cause, in accordance with MCR 2.503.

(H) Fees.

(1) Within 14 days after the mailing of the notice of the case evaluation hearing, unless otherwise ordered by the court, each party must send to the ADR clerk a check for $75 made payable in the manner specified in the notice of the case evaluation hearing. However, if a judge is a member of the panel, the fee is $50. The ADR clerk shall arrange payment to the case evaluators. Except by stipulation and court order, the parties may not make any other payment of fees or expenses to the case evaluators than that provided in this subrule.

(2) Only a single fee is required of each party, even where there are counterclaims, cross-claims, or third-party claims.

(3) If one claim is derivative of another (e.g., husband-wife, parent-child) they must be treated as a single claim, with one fee to be paid and a single award made by the case evaluators.

(4) In the case of multiple injuries to members of a single family, the plaintiffs may elect to treat the action as involving one claim, with the payment of one fee and the rendering of one lump sum award to be accepted or rejected. If no such election is made, a separate fee must be paid for each plaintiff, and the case evaluation panel will then make separate awards for each claim, which may be individually accepted or rejected.

(5) Fees paid pursuant to subrule (H) shall be refunded to the parties if

(a) the court sets aside the order submitting the case to case evaluation or on its own initiative adjourns the case evaluation hearing, or

(b) the parties notify the ADR clerk in writing at least 14 days before the case evaluation hearing of the settlement, dismissal, or entry of judgment disposing of the action, or of an order of adjournment on stipulation or the motion of a party.

In the case of an adjournment, the fees shall not be refunded if the adjournment order sets a new date for case evaluation. If case evaluation is rescheduled at a later time, the fee provisions of subrule (H) apply regardless of whether previously paid fees have been refunded. Penalties for late filing of papers under subrule (I)(2) are not to be refunded.

(I) Submission of Documents.

(1) At least 14 days before the hearing, each party shall file with the ADR clerk 3 copies of documents pertaining to the issues to be mediated and 3 copies of a concise summary setting forth that party's factual and legal position on issues presented by the action, and shall serve one copy of the documents and summary on each attorney of record. A copy of a proof of service must be attached to the copies filed with the ADR clerk.

(2) Failure to file the required materials with the ADR clerk or to serve copies on each attorney of record by the required date subjects the offending attorney or party to a $150 penalty to be paid in the manner specified in the notice of the case evaluation hearing. An offending attorney shall not charge the penalty to the client, unless the client agreed in writing to be responsible for the penalty.

(J) Conduct of Hearing.

(1) A party has the right, but is not required, to attend a case evaluation hearing. If scars, disfigurement, or other unusual conditions exist, they may be demonstrated to the panel by a personal appearance; however, no testimony will be taken or permitted of any party.

(2) The rules of evidence do not apply before the case evaluation panel. Factual information having a

bearing on damages or liability must be supported by documentary evidence, if possible.

(3) Oral presentation shall be limited to 15 minutes per side unless multiple parties or unusual circumstances warrant additional time. Information on applicable insurance policy limits and settlement negotiations shall be disclosed at the request of the case evaluation panel.

(4) Statements by the attorneys and the briefs or summaries are not admissible in any court or evidentiary proceeding.

(5) Counsel or the parties may not engage in ex parte communications with the case evaluators concerning the action prior to the hearing. After the evaluation, the case evaluators need not respond to inquiries by the parties or counsel regarding the proceeding or the evaluation.

(K) Decision.

(1) Within 14 days after the hearing, the panel will make an evaluation and notify the attorney for each party of its evaluation in writing. If an award is not unanimous, the evaluation must so indicate.

(2) The evaluation must include a separate award as to the plaintiff's claim against each defendant and as to each cross-claim, counterclaim, or third-party claim that has been filed in the action. For the purpose of this subrule, all such claims filed by any one party against any other party shall be treated as a single claim.

(3) The evaluation may not include a separate award on any claim for equitable relief, but the panel may consider such claims in determining the amount of an award.

(4) In a tort case to which MCL 600.4915(2); MSA 27A.4915(2) or MCL 600.4963(2); MSA 27A.4963(2) applies, if the panel unanimously finds that a party's action or defense as to any other party is frivolous, the panel shall so indicate on the evaluation. For the purpose of this rule, an action or defense is "frivolous" if, as to all of a plaintiff's claims or all of a defendant's defenses to liability, at least 1 of the following conditions is met:

(a) The party's primary purpose in initiating the action or asserting the defense was to harass, embarrass, or injure the opposing party.

(b) The party had no reasonable basis to believe that the facts underlying that party's legal position were in fact true.

(c) The party's legal position was devoid of arguable legal merit.

(5) In an action alleging medical malpractice to which MCL 600.4915; MSA 27A.4915 applies, the evaluation must include a specific finding that

(a) there has been a breach of the applicable standard of care,

(b) there has not been a breach of the applicable standard of care, or

(c) reasonable minds could differ as to whether there has been a breach of the applicable standard of care.

(L) Acceptance or Rejection of Evaluation.

(1) Each party shall file a written acceptance or rejection of the panel's evaluation with the ADR clerk within 28 days after service of the panel's evaluation. Even if there are separate awards on multiple claims, the party must either accept or reject the evaluation in its entirety as to a particular opposing party. The failure to file a written acceptance or rejection within 28 days constitutes rejection.

(2) There may be no disclosure of a party's acceptance or rejection of the panel's evaluation until the expiration of the 28–day period, at which time the ADR clerk shall send a notice indicating each party's acceptance or rejection of the panel's evaluation.

(3) In case evaluations involving multiple parties the following rules apply:

(a) Each party has the option of accepting all of the awards covering the claims by or against that party or of accepting some and rejecting others. However, as to any particular opposing party, the party must either accept or reject the evaluation in its entirety.

(b) A party who accepts all of the awards may specifically indicate that he or she intends the acceptance to be effective only if

(i) all opposing parties accept, and/or

(ii) the opposing parties accept as to specified coparties.

If such a limitation is not included in the acceptance, an accepting party is deemed to have agreed to entry of judgment, or dismissal as provided in subrule (M)(1), as to that party and those of the opposing parties who accept, with the action to continue between the accepting party and those opposing parties who reject.

(c) If a party makes a limited acceptance under subrule (L)(3)(b) and some of the opposing parties accept and others reject, for the purposes of the cost provisions of subrule (O) the party who made the limited acceptance is deemed to have rejected as to those opposing parties who accept.

(M) Effect of Acceptance of Evaluation.

(1) If all the parties accept the panel's evaluation, judgment will be entered in accordance with the evaluation, unless the amount of the award is paid within 28 days after notification of the acceptances, in which case the court shall dismiss the action with prejudice. The judgment or dismissal shall be deemed to dispose of all claims in the action and includes all fees, costs, and interest to the date it is entered.

(2) In a case involving multiple parties, judgment, or dismissal as provided in subrule (1), shall be entered as to those opposing parties who have accepted the portions of the evaluation that apply to them.

(N) Proceedings After Rejection.

(1) If all or part of the evaluation of the case evaluation panel is rejected, the action proceeds to trial in the normal fashion.

(2) If a party's claim or defense was found to be frivolous under subrule (K)(4), that party may request that the court review the panel's finding by filing a motion within 14 days after the ADR clerk sends notice of the rejection of the case evaluation award.

(a) The motion shall be submitted to the court on the case evaluation summaries and documents that were considered by the case evaluation panel. No other exhibits or testimony may be submitted. However, oral argument on the motion shall be permitted.

(b) After reviewing the materials submitted, the court shall determine whether the action or defense is frivolous.

(c) If the court agrees with the panel's determination, the provisions of subrule (N)(3) apply, except that the bond must be filed within 28 days after the entry of the court's order determining the action or defense to be frivolous.

(d) The judge who hears a motion under this subrule may not preside at a nonjury trial of the action.

(3) Except as provided in subrule (2), if a party's claim or defense was found to be frivolous under subrule (K)(4), that party shall post a cash or surety bond, pursuant to MCR 3.604, in the amount of $5,000 for each party against whom the action or defense was determined to be frivolous.

(a) The bond must be posted within 56 days after the case evaluation hearing or at least 14 days before trial, whichever is earlier.

(b) If a surety bond is filed, an insurance company that insures the defendant against a claim made in the action may not act as the surety.

(c) If the bond is not posted as required by this rule, the court shall dismiss a claim found to have been frivolous, and enter the default of a defendant whose defense was found to be frivolous. The action shall proceed to trial as to the remaining claims and parties, and as to the amount of damages against a defendant in default.

(d) If judgment is entered against the party who posted the bond, the bond shall be used to pay any costs awarded against that party by the court under any applicable law or court rule. MCR 3.604 applies to proceedings to enforce the bond.

(4) The ADR clerk shall place a copy of the case evaluation and the parties' acceptances and rejections in a sealed envelope for filing with the clerk of the court. In a nonjury action, the envelope may not be opened and the parties may not reveal the amount of the evaluation until the judge has rendered judgment.

(O) Rejecting Party's Liability for Costs.

(1) If a party has rejected an evaluation and the action proceeds to verdict, that party must pay the opposing party's actual costs unless the verdict is more favorable to the rejecting party than the case evaluation. However, if the opposing party has also rejected the evaluation, a party is entitled to costs only if the verdict is more favorable to that party than the case evaluation.

(2) For the purpose of this rule "verdict" includes,

(a) a jury verdict,

(b) a judgment by the court after a nonjury trial,

(c) a judgment entered as a result of a ruling on a motion after rejection of the case evaluation.

(3) For the purpose of subrule (O)(1), a verdict must be adjusted by adding to it assessable costs and interest on the amount of the verdict from the filing of the complaint to the date of the case evaluation, and, if applicable, by making the adjustment of future damages as provided by MCL 600.6306; MSA 27A.6306. After this adjustment, the verdict is considered more favorable to a defendant if it is more than 10 percent below the evaluation, and is considered more favorable to the plaintiff if it is more than 10 percent above the evaluation. If the evaluation was zero, a verdict finding that a defendant is not liable to the plaintiff shall be deemed more favorable to the defendant.

(4) In cases involving multiple parties, the following rules apply:

(a) Except as provided in subrule (O)(4)(b), in determining whether the verdict is more favorable to a party than the case evaluation, the court shall consider only the amount of the evaluation and verdict as to the particular pair of parties, rather than the aggregate evaluation or verdict as to all parties. However, costs may not be imposed on a plaintiff who obtains an aggregate verdict more favorable to the plaintiff than the aggregate evaluation.

(b) If the verdict against more than one defendant is based on their joint and several liability, the plaintiff may not recover costs unless the verdict is more favorable to the plaintiff than the total case evaluation as to those defendants, and a defendant may not recover costs unless the verdict is more favorable to that defendant than the case evaluation as to that defendant.

(c) Except as provided by subrule (O)(10), in a personal injury action, for the purpose of subrule (O)(1), the verdict against a particular defendant shall not be adjusted by applying that defendant's proportion of fault as determined under MCL 600.6304(1)-(2); MSA 27A.6304(1)-(2).

(5) If the verdict awards equitable relief, costs may be awarded if the court determines that

(a) taking into account both monetary relief (adjusted as provided in subrule [O][3]) and equitable relief, the verdict is not more favorable to the rejecting party than the evaluation, and

(b) it is fair to award costs under all of the circumstances.

(6) For the purpose of this rule, actual costs are

(a) those costs taxable in any civil action, and

(b) a reasonable attorney fee based on a reasonable hourly or daily rate as determined by the trial judge for services necessitated by the rejection of the case evaluation.

For the purpose of determining taxable costs under this subrule and under MCR 2.625, the party entitled to recover actual costs under this rule shall be considered the prevailing party.

(7) Costs shall not be awarded if the case evaluation award was not unanimous.

(8) A request for costs under this subrule must be filed and served within 28 days after the entry of the judgment or entry of an order denying a timely motion for a new trial or to set aside the judgment.

(9) In an action under MCL 436.22; MSA 18.993, if the plaintiff rejects the award against the minor or alleged intoxicated person, or is deemed to have rejected such an award under subrule (L)(3)(c), the court shall not award costs against the plaintiff in favor of the minor or alleged intoxicated person unless it finds that the rejection was not motivated by the need to comply with MCL 436.22(6); MSA 18.993(6).

(10) In an action filed on or after March 28, 1996, for the purpose of subrule (O)(1), a verdict awarding damages for personal injury, property damage, or wrongful death shall be adjusted for relative fault as provided by MCL 600.6304; MSA 27A.6304.

(11) If the "verdict" is the result of a motion as provided by subrule (O)(2)(c), the court may, in the interest of justice, refuse to award actual costs.

[Effective March 1, 1985; amended January 22, 1987 to apply to mediation hearings conducted and removal orders entered on or after April 1, 1987; amended effective October 1, 1987; December 1, 1987; January 1, 1988; March 31, 1990; July 2, 1991; February 1, 1995; February 1, 1997; October 1, 1997; August 1, 2000.]

1985 Staff Comment

MCR 2.403 corresponds to GCR 1963, 316. There are a number of revisions.

Subrule (A) deletes the authorization for a separate procedure for the Third Judicial Circuit. However, one of the key features of the third circuit rule is adopted for statewide use. Under subrule (L)(1), failure to file an acceptance or rejection of a mediation award within the time provided constitutes acceptance of the award, unlike the practice under GCR 1963, 316.6(H)(1), which made failure to file an acceptance the equivalent of rejection. The time for accepting or rejecting the award is set at 28 days.

Subrule (C)(2) is changed from the corresponding language of GCR 1963, 316.3(B). Under the latter provision, a motion to remove a case from mediation stayed mediation proceedings. Subrule (C)(2) does not include the stay provision, but says instead that such a motion must be heard before the case is submitted to mediation.

Subrules (F)–(O) are reorganized and rewritten, although only a few substantive changes are included.

First, subrule (H)(1) does not direct that the checks by which the parties pay the mediation fee are to be payable to the attorney mediators, as had GCR 1963, 316.6(C)(1). Rather, the checks are to be made payable in the manner specified in the mediation notice. In some courts the mediation program might be arranged so that it is more convenient to have the checks payable to the mediation clerk or the court clerk.

Subrule (I) not only requires that the parties submit documents relating to the issues to be mediated, but also that they supply briefs or summaries setting forth their legal or factual positions on the issues. Failure to submit either document to the mediation clerk at least 7 days before the hearing date subjects the party to the cost penalty imposed by subrule (I)(2). Under the corresponding provision, GCR 1963, 316.6(E), the penalty provisions applied only to the documents. Submission of the brief or summary was optional.

Under GCR 1963, 316.6(F)(3), the mediators were not permitted to inquire into settlement negotiations. Subrule (J)(3) modifies the prohibition. The mediators may inquire unless a party objects. This is similar to the provision of the former third circuit local rule 403.12.

Several provisions of the rule are modified to deal with the situation in which there is more than one party on a side. Subrule (H)(1) makes clear that only a single fee is required of each party even where there are counterclaims, cross-claims, or third-party claims. Second, subrule (K)(2) specifies that the evaluation must include a separate award as to each cross-claim, counterclaim, or third-party claim, although all claims between any two parties are treated as a single claim. Finally, under subrule (L)(3), parties are permitted to accept some, but less than all, of the individual awards. Judgment will be entered as to those pairs of parties who have accepted. See subrule (M)(2). However, a party has the option of making a "conditional" acceptance of the entire award, specifying that if fewer than all of the opposing parties accept, the party making the conditional acceptance should be taken as rejecting as to all of them. A party may be willing to accept the award in its entirety if that has the effect of eliminating the need for a trial. However, if the case is going to be tried anyway, the party may prefer to have a trial as to all opposing parties. For the purpose of applying the cost provisions, a party making a conditional acceptance is treated as having rejected the award as to those opposing parties who accepted it. See subrule (L)(3)(c).

Subrule (N)(2) provides that in a nonjury case not only must the evaluation itself be sealed until the judge has entered judgment, but the parties are forbidden to tell the judge about the mediation award. Compare GCR 1963, 316.6(H)(2).

The [March 1, 1985] amendment of MCR 2.403(N)(2) deletes the requirement that the mediation clerk return copies of mediation documents to the attorney who submitted them.

The [March 1, 1985] amendment of MCR 2.403(O)(1) revises the language regarding the liability for costs of a party who rejects a mediation evaluation, correcting an unintended change from GCR 316.7(b). The rejecting party is liable for costs unless that party improves its position by at least 10 percent (unless the other party has rejected, in which case a party is liable for costs only if the opponent improves its position by at least 10 percent).

Finally, subrule (O)(4) adopts the principle, found in the third circuit local rule 403.15, that where the mediation panel's award is not unanimous, costs are not to be awarded against a rejecting party. Subrule (K)(1) requires that if the award is not unanimous, it must so indicate.

Staff Comment to April, 1987 Amendment

The [April 1, 1987] amendments of MCR 2.403(K) and (N) and 4.003(A) deal with the relationship between mediation and removal of cases from circuit to district court under MCL 600.641; MSA 27A.641. The language adopted is that recommended by a committee appointed to evaluate the mediation process. See Volume 426B of Michigan Reports.

New MCR 2.403(K) provides that if a mediation award does not exceed the jurisdictional limitation on the district court, the mediators must include a statement as to whether the damages sustained, without regard to liability questions, exceed the district court jurisdictional limit.

A corresponding amendment of MCR 2.403(N) requires that this statement be provided to the circuit judge when the judge is informed that the award does not exceed the district court jurisdictional limit.

Staff Comment to October, 1987 Amendment

The August 12, 1987, amendment of subrule (A) relates to the adoption of the new domestic relations mediation rule, MCR 3.211, effective October 1, 1987.

Staff Comment to December, 1987 Amendment

The September 25, 1987, amendments of MCR 2.403 [effective December 1, 1987] grew out of the work of the Mediation Evaluation Committee appointed on April 4, 1986. A detailed explanation of its proposals can be found in the Committee's report, which was published as Volume 426B of Michigan Reports. Several other parts of the Committee's recommendations had been acted upon in previous orders amending MCR 2.403, 428 Mich cxlvii, MCR 4.003, 428 Mich clix, and adopting new MCR 3.211, 428 Mich cxlix.

The amendment of subrule (A)(1) emphasizes that mediation is intended for use in cases involving money damages and division of property, but leaves open the possibility of submitting cases in which other kinds of relief are sought. There are related changes in subrules (K)(3) and (O)(5) dealing with the form of mediation evaluations and the awarding of costs.

New subrule (A)(2) deals with probate proceedings, permitting submission to mediation of portions of such proceedings.

Subrule (I)(1) is amended to require that a proof of service on the opposing party be submitted with the other mediation documents.

The amendment to subrule (K)(2) clarifies that a separate award must be made as to plaintiff's claim against each defendant.

There are a series of changes in subrule (O), which concerns the award of costs following rejection of a mediation evaluation.

New subrule (O)(2) defines "verdict."

Language is added to subrule (O)(3) [formerly (O)(2)] to provide that a verdict is considered "more favorable" to a defendant than a mediation award when both the award and the verdict are zero.

New subrule (O)(4) adds several provisions for determining liability for costs in cases involving multiple parties.

Subrule (O)(6) [formerly (O)(3)] is amended to provide that the attorney fee component of costs awarded under the rule is to be computed on a reasonable hourly or daily rate.

Several other recommendations of the Mediation Evaluation Committee remain under study. In addition, other provisions of the proposal published for comment [see 65 Michigan Bar Journal 1157 (November, 1986)] relate to the mediation provisions of 1986 PA 178, which are being considered by a separate committee appointed to study the mediation of medical malpractice actions.

Staff Comment to 1988 Amendment

The October 23, 1987, amendments to MCR 2.403 [effective January 1, 1988] relate to the mediation provisions of 1986 PA 178, MCL 600.4901–600.4969; MSA 27A.4901–27A.4969. The amendments are effective January 1, 1988. Although a number of subrules are unaffected by the amendments, the text of the entire rule is set forth to avoid confusion in light of the September 25, 1987, amendments to the rule, which take effect on December 1, 1987.

New subrule (A)(2) implements the requirements of MCL 600.4903; MSA 27A.4903 and MCL 600.4951; MSA 27A.4951, which direct that all tort cases be mediated. The trial court may except a case on motion for good cause.

New subrule (D)(4) implements MCL 600.4905; MSA 27A.4905, which directs that in medical malpractice cases the mediation panel include two health care professionals. The new provision spells out the procedure for making designations of health care professionals, including provisions dealing with cases in which there is more than one party on a side or in which the defendants have different specialties or fields of practice. Subrule (D)(4)(c) provides that the mediation hearing is to proceed with fewer than five mediators if a party fails to make a designation or a designated person does not appear at the hearing.

New subrule (D)(5) prohibits the calling of a mediator as a witness at trial.

Subrule (G)(1) is amended to provide that the notice of the mediation hearing must be given 56 days in advance, in order to give the parties time to locate and designate health care professionals to serve on the mediation panel.

In subrule (H), the fee is increased to $125 in medical malpractice cases, since there are two additional mediators. The rule also expressly provides that the parties may not make any payments to mediators other than as provided in the rule.

Subrule (I)(1) is amended to require five copies of mediation documents in medical malpractice cases.

There is a minor change in subrule (I)(2) regarding payment of penalties to mediators to take account of the possibility of non-lawyers serving as mediators.

Subrule (K)(5) is added and subrule (N)(1) is amended to implement the provisions of MCL 600.4915(2); MSA 27A.4915(2) and MCL 600.4963(2); MSA 27A.4963(2), which require the posting of a bond by a party whose claim or defense the mediation panel unanimously finds to be frivolous.

New subrule (K)(6) implements MCL 600.4915(1); MSA 27A.4915(1), which requires that the evaluation in medical malpractice cases include a specific finding on the applicable standard of care.

Staff Comment to 1989 Amendment

On May 3, 1989, the Court ordered published for comment several proposals regarding the mediation rule, MCR 2.403, and the offer of judgment rule, MCR 2.405. See 68 Michigan Bar Journal 558 (June, 1989). The January 3, 1990, order [effective March 31, 1990] adopts several of those changes, some with modifications. Other proposed amendments to MCR 2.403(H)(1), (I)(2), and (J), giving trial courts greater flexibility in the use of mediation fees, increasing penalties for late filing of mediation documents with each day that they are late, and requiring attorneys and unrepresented parties to attend mediation sessions, remain under consideration.

MCR 2.403(G)(1) and (I)(1) are amended to lengthen the time for giving notice of the mediation hearing and for submitting mediation summaries.

There is a minor change in MCR 2.403(H)(1) to give courts flexibility in setting the time when mediation fees are to be paid.

New MCR 2.403(H)(5) covers the refunding of fees when the mediation hearing is not held.

There are three minor amendments to MCR 2.403(I)(1). First, the language is changed to direct the parties to "file," rather than "submit," mediation documents. Second, the amended rule refers to a mediation "summary" rather than "summary or brief." The summary must include both the party's factual and legal arguments. Third, there is a change in the language regarding the filing of a proof of service of mediation documents. There is a corresponding change in subrule (I)(2), making the failure to serve opposing counsel grounds for imposing the late filing penalty.

In MCR 2.403(I)(2), new language provides that attorneys may not charge late filing penalties to their clients unless the clients have agreed to be responsible for the penalties.

MCR 2.403(L)(1) is amended to provide that the failure to file an acceptance or rejection is considered a rejection, as had been the case under former GCR 1963, 316.6(h)(1).

The revision of MCR 2.403(M) would clarify that the entry of a judgment following acceptance of an award disposes of the entire case, even if the case includes equitable claims on which the mediation panel is not permitted to make an award.

There are several changes in MCR 2.403(O)(6) to clarify what costs are recoverable.

In both MCR 2.403(O)(8) and MCR 2.405(D), there is new language setting the time within which a party must seek to recover costs under the mediation and offer of judgment rules.

Staff Comment to 1991 Amendment

The July 2, 1991, amendment of MCR 2.403(O) adds a new subrule (9), in light of the decision in *Shay v JohnKAL, Inc*, 437 Mich 394, 471 NW2d 551 (decided July 2, 1991).

Staff Comment to 1995 Amendment

Former subrule 2.403(A)(3) is deleted [effective February 1, 1995]. The mediation for probate proceedings is covered in MCR 5.403. Mediation for civil actions in probate court remains under this rule. See MCR 5.101(C).

Staff Comment to February, 1997 Amendment

The November 6 amendments of MCR 2.112, 2.222, 2.223, and 2.403, and the repeal of MCR 2.224, effective February 1, 1997, relate to statutory changes made by 1995 PA 161 and 1995 PA 249.

The [November 6, 1997] amendment of MCR 2.403 [effective February 1, 1997] adds a new subrule (O)(10) to the mediation rule. It requires the adjusting of verdicts for relative fault as required by MCL 600.6304; MSA 2 7A.6304.

Staff Comment to October, 1997 Amendment

The May 8, 1997, order repeals MCR 4.003, which governed removal of cases from circuit to district court, effective July 1, 1997. This reinstates the February 28, 1997, repeal of the rule, which was suspended on March 13, 1997.

In addition, the order postpones the effective date of earlier amendments of MCR 2.403, 2.405, and 3.216, and new MCR 2.404, affecting mediation procedure, to October 1, 1997. The order also makes adjustments in MCR 2.403(K) and (N) in light of the repeal of MCR 4.003. The text of MCR 2.403, 2.404, 2.405 and 3.216 is the same as that adopted in the Court's March 5, 1997, order dealing with those rules.

Staff Comment to 2000 Amendment

The May 8, 2000, amendments [effective August 1, 2000] are based on the recommendations of the Michigan Supreme Court Dispute Resolution Task Force, which were published for comment on May 10, 1999 [see 459 Mich 1251], and were the subject of a series of public hearings across the state.

The Task Force report, issued in January 1999, and its Addendum report, issued in January 2000 after receipt of comments, should be consulted for the background and details of the amendments. Basically, the changes are as follows:

The amendments of MCR 2.403, 2.404, 2.405, 2.501, 2.502 and 2.503 are mainly to change terminology, replacing "mediation," as used in current MCR 2.403, with the term "case evaluation." "Mediation" will be used to describe the facilitative process established in MCR 2.411, in keeping with the generally accepted usage of the term.

MCR 2.401 is amended to direct consideration of alternative dispute resolution processes at scheduling and pretrial conferences.

New MCR 2.410 has general provisions governing referral of cases to alternative dispute resolution processes. Local courts wishing to use ADR techniques are to adopt ADR plans within the framework provided by the rule.

The one ADR process that is specifically established by the rules is mediation under new MCR 2.411. Among other things, the rule establishes general standards for mediator qualifications, and procedures for selection of mediators.

MCR 3.216, the domestic relations mediation rule, is substantially revised, to be more comparable to the mediation process in MCR 2.411.

MCR 5.143, regarding use of alternative dispute resolution processes in probate court, is amended to conform to the other rule changes.

Dissenting Statement of Justice Kelly to 2000 Amendment

I support the expanded use of alternative dispute resolution by our courts. However, I cannot cast a vote favoring the proposed Dispute Resolution Court Rules for two reasons: 1) they authorize judges to compel parties to submit to mediation and 2) they include nonlawyers as mediators and other ADR providers.

Regarding the mandatory nature of the new rules, I believe that mediation is, by its very nature, a process that works only when the parties enter into it voluntarily. I would support rules that permit courts to order parties to a session at which the merits of ADR are explored, but not that mandate mediation.

It is my fear that mandatory mediation will present insurmountable financial obstacles to low income litigants and could even provoke challenges based on a violation of due process principles. I am concerned that, in some heavily burdened courts, judges may use the new rules, not as an option for the parties, but as a docket control mechanism for the court. Also, I find no limit in the rules to the number of times a party could be ordered to an ADR process.

Mediation should not become yet another hurdle to a just resolution of disputes. Parties should not feel pressed to settle against their best interests, or involuntarily to expend financial resources in excess of the normal costs of trial. Litigation, without the new rules, is already too costly.

I agree with the Board of Commissioners of the State Bar of Michigan that, absent agreement of the parties, only licensed lawyers should be allowed to serve as ADR providers. Mediation and other types of ADR typically involve complex legal matters requiring skilled ADR providers. Yet, no system has been developed to ensure the training and accountability of nonlawyers who participate.

Finally, I agree with the Open Justice Commission's recommendations that chief judges should be required to report the race, ethnicity, and gender of case evaluators and other ADR providers that they appoint. I view this as a vital step toward ensuring persons wishing to function as ADR providers will not be passed over solely on the basis of their race, gender, ethnic background, or similar factors.

RULE 2.404   SELECTION OF CASE EVALUATION PANELS

(A) Case Evaluator Selection Plans.

(1) *Requirement.* Each trial court that submits cases to case evaluation under MCR 2.403 shall adopt by local administrative order a plan to maintain a list of persons available to serve as case evaluators and to assign case evaluators from the list to panels. The plan must be in writing and available to the public in the ADR clerk's office.

(2) *Alternative Plans.*

(a) A plan adopted by a district or probate court may use the list of case evaluators and appointment procedure of the circuit court for the circuit in which the court is located.

(b) Courts in adjoining circuits or districts may jointly adopt and administer a case evaluation plan.

(c) If it is not feasible for a court to adopt its own plan because of the low volume of cases to be submitted or because of inadequate numbers of available case evaluators, the court may enter into an agreement with a neighboring court to refer cases for case evaluation under the other court's system. The agreement may provide for payment by the referring court to cover the cost of administering case evaluation. However, fees and costs may not be assessed against the parties to actions evaluated except as provided by MCR 2.403.

(d) Other alternative plans must be submitted as local court rules under MCR 8.112(A).

(B) Lists of Case Evaluators.

(1) *Application.* An eligible person desiring to serve as a case evaluator may apply to the ADR clerk to be placed on the list of case evaluators. Application forms shall be available in the office of the ADR clerk. The form shall include an optional section identifying the applicant's gender and racial/ethnic background. The form shall include a certification that

(a) the case evaluator meets the requirements for service under the court's selection plan, and

(b) the case evaluator will not discriminate against parties, attorneys, or other case evaluators on the basis of race, ethnic origin, gender, or other protected personal characteristic.

(2) *Eligibility.* To be eligible to serve as a case evaluator, a person must meet the qualifications provided by this subrule.

(a) The applicant must have been a practicing lawyer for at least 5 years and be a member in good standing of the State Bar of Michigan. The plan may not require membership in any other organization as a qualification for service as a case evaluator.

(b) An applicant must reside, maintain an office, or have an active practice in the jurisdiction for which the list of case evaluators is compiled.

(c) An applicant must demonstrate that a substantial portion of the applicant's practice for the last 5 years has been devoted to civil litigation matters, including investigation, discovery, motion practice, case evaluation, settlement, trial preparation, and/or trial.

(d) If separate sublists are maintained for specific types of cases, the applicant must have had an active practice in the practice area for which the case evaluator is listed for at least the last 3 years.

If there are insufficient numbers of potential case evaluators meeting the qualifications stated in this rule, the plan may provide for consideration of alternative qualifications.

(3) *Review of Applications.* The plan shall provide for a person or committee to review applications annually, or more frequently if appropriate, and compile one or more lists of qualified case evaluators. Persons meeting the qualifications specified in this rule shall be placed on the list of approved case evaluators. Selections shall be made without regard to race, ethnic origin, or gender.

(a) If an individual performs this review function, the person must be an employee of the court.

(b) If a committee performs this review function, the following provisions apply.

(i) The committee must have at least three members.

(ii) The selection of committee members shall be designed to assure that the goals stated in subrule (D)(2) will be met.

(iii) A person may not serve on the committee more than 3 years in any 9 year period.

(c) Applicants who are not placed on the case evaluator list or lists shall be notified of that decision. The plan shall provide a procedure by which such an applicant may seek reconsideration of the decision by some other person or committee. The plan need not provide for a hearing of any kind as part of the reconsideration process. Documents considered in the initial review process shall be retained for at least the period of time during which the applicant can seek reconsideration of the original decision.

(4) *Specialized Lists.* If the number and qualifications of available case evaluators makes it practicable to do so, the ADR clerk shall maintain

(a) separate lists for various types of cases, and,

(b) where appropriate for the type of cases, separate sublists of case evaluators who primarily represent plaintiffs, primarily represent defendants, and neutral cases evaluators whose practices are not identifiable as representing primarily plaintiffs or defendants.

(5) *Reapplication.* Persons shall be placed on the list of case evaluators for a fixed period of time, not to exceed 5 years, and must reapply at the end of that time in the same manner as persons seeking to be added to the list.

(6) *Availability of Lists.* The list of case evaluators must be available to the public in the ADR clerk's office.

(7) *Removal from List.* The plan must include a procedure for removal from the list of case evaluators who have demonstrated incompetency, bias, made themselves consistently unavailable to serve as a case evaluator, or for other just cause.

(8) The court may require case evaluators to attend orientation or training sessions or provide written materials explaining the case evaluation process and the operation of the court's case evaluation program. However, case evaluators may not be charged any fees or costs for such programs or materials.

(C) Assignments to Panels.

(1) *Method of Assignment.* The ADR clerk shall assign case evaluators to panels in a random or rotating manner that assures as nearly as possible that each case evaluator on a list or sublist is assigned approximately the same number of cases over a period of time. If a substitute case evaluator must be assigned, the same or similar assignment procedure shall be used to select the substitute. The ADR clerk shall maintain records of service of case evaluators on panels and shall make those records available on request.

(2) *Assignment from Sublists.* If sublists of plaintiff, defense, and neutral case evaluators are maintained for a particular type of case, the panel shall include one case evaluator who primarily represents plaintiffs, one case evaluator who primarily represents defendants, and one neutral case evaluator. If a judge is assigned to a panel as permitted by MCR 2.403(D)(3), the judge shall serve as the neutral case evaluator if sublists are maintained for that class of cases.

(3) *Special Panels.* On stipulation of the parties, the court may appoint a panel selected by the parties. In such a case, the qualification requirements of subrule (B)(2) do not apply, and the parties may agree to modification of the procedures for conduct of case evaluation. Nothing in this rule or MCR 2.403 precludes parties from stipulating to other ADR procedures that may aid in resolution of the case.

(D) Supervision of Selection Process.

(1) The chief judge shall exercise general supervision over the implementation of this rule and shall review the operation of the court's case evaluation plan at least annually to assure compliance with this rule. In the event of non-compliance, the court shall take such action as is needed. This action may include recruiting persons to serve as case evaluators or changing the court's case evaluation plan. The court shall submit an annual report to the State Court Administrator on the operation of the court's case evaluation program on a form provided by the State Court Administrator.

(2) In implementing the selection plan, the court, court employees, and attorneys involved in the procedure shall take all steps necessary to assure that as far as reasonably possible the list of case evaluators fairly reflects the racial, ethnic, and gender diversity of the members of the state bar in the jurisdiction for

which the list is compiled who are eligible to serve as case evaluators.

[Adopted effective October 1, 1997; amended effective August 1, 2000.]

1997 Staff Comment

The May 8, 1997, order repeals MCR 4.003, which governed removal of cases from circuit to district court, effective July 1, 1997. This reinstates the February 28, 1997, repeal of the rule, which was suspended on March 13, 1997.

In addition, the order postpones the effective date of earlier amendments of MCR 2.403, 2.405, and 3.216, and new MCR 2.404, affecting mediation procedure, to October 1, 1997. The order also makes adjustments in MCR 2.403(K) and (N) in light of the repeal of MCR 4.003. The text of MCR 2.403, 2.404, 2.405 and 3.216 is the same as that adopted in the Court's March 5, 1997, order dealing with those rules.

Staff Comment to 2000 Amendment

The May 8, 2000, amendments [effective August 1, 2000] are based on the recommendations of the Michigan Supreme Court Dispute Resolution Task Force, which were published for comment on May 10, 1999 [see 459 Mich 1251], and were the subject of a series of public hearings across the state.

The Task Force report, issued in January 1999, and its Addendum report, issued in January 2000 after receipt of comments, should be consulted for the background and details of the amendments. Basically, the changes are as follows:

The amendments of MCR 2.403, 2.404, 2.405, 2.501, 2.502 and 2.503 are mainly to change terminology, replacing "mediation," as used in current MCR 2.403, with the term "case evaluation." "Mediation" will be used to describe the facilitative process established in MCR 2.411, in keeping with the generally accepted usage of the term.

MCR 2.401 is amended to direct consideration of alternative dispute resolution processes at scheduling and pretrial conferences.

New MCR 2.410 has general provisions governing referral of cases to alternative dispute resolution processes. Local courts wishing to use ADR techniques are to adopt ADR plans within the framework provided by the rule.

The one ADR process that is specifically established by the rules is mediation under new MCR 2.411. Among other things, the rule establishes general standards for mediator qualifications, and procedures for selection of mediators.

MCR 3.216, the domestic relations mediation rule, is substantially revised, to be more comparable to the mediation process in MCR 2.411.

MCR 5.143, regarding use of alternative dispute resolution processes in probate court, is amended to conform to the other rule changes.

Dissenting Statement of Justice Kelly to 2000 Amendment

I support the expanded use of alternative dispute resolution by our courts. However, I cannot cast a vote favoring the proposed Dispute Resolution Court Rules for two reasons: 1) they authorize judges to compel parties to submit to mediation and 2) they include nonlawyers as mediators and other ADR providers.

Regarding the mandatory nature of the new rules, I believe that mediation is, by its very nature, a process that works only when the parties enter into it voluntarily. I would support rules that permit courts to order parties to a session at which the merits of ADR are explored, but not that mandate mediation.

It is my fear that mandatory mediation will present insurmountable financial obstacles to low income litigants and could even provoke challenges based on a violation of due process principles. I am concerned that, in some heavily burdened courts, judges may use the new rules, not as an option for the parties, but as a docket control mechanism for the court. Also, I find no limit in the rules to the number of times a party could be ordered to an ADR process.

Mediation should not become yet another hurdle to a just resolution of disputes. Parties should not feel pressed to settle against their best interests, or involuntarily to expend financial resources in excess of the normal costs of trial. Litigation, without the new rules, is already too costly.

I agree with the Board of Commissioners of the State Bar of Michigan that, absent agreement of the parties, only licensed lawyers should be allowed to serve as ADR providers. Mediation and other types of ADR typically involve complex legal matters requiring skilled ADR providers. Yet, no system has been developed to ensure the training and accountability of nonlawyers who participate.

Finally, I agree with the Open Justice Commission's recommendations that chief judges should be required to report the race, ethnicity, and gender of case evaluators and other ADR providers that they appoint. I view this as a vital step toward ensuring persons wishing to function as ADR providers will not be passed over solely on the basis of their race, gender, ethnic background, or similar factors.

RULE 2.405 OFFERS TO STIPULATE TO ENTRY OF JUDGMENT

(A) Definitions. As used in this rule:

(1) "Offer" means a written notification to an adverse party of the offeror's willingness to stipulate to the entry of a judgment in a sum certain, which is deemed to include all costs and interest then accrued. If a party has made more than one offer, the most recent offer controls for the purposes of this rule.

(2) "Counteroffer" means a written reply to an offer, served within 21 days after service of the offer, in which a party rejects an offer of the adverse party and makes his or her own offer.

(3) "Average offer" means the sum of an offer and a counteroffer, divided by two. If no counteroffer is made, the offer shall be used as the average offer.

(4) "Verdict" includes,

    (a) a jury verdict,

    (b) a judgment by the court after a nonjury trial,

    (c) a judgment entered as a result of a ruling on a motion after rejection of the offer of judgment.

(5) "Adjusted verdict" means the verdict plus interest and costs from the filing of the complaint through the date of the offer.

(6) "Actual costs" means the costs and fees taxable in a civil action and a reasonable attorney fee for services necessitated by the failure to stipulate to the entry of judgment.

(B) Offer. Until 28 days before trial, a party may serve on the adverse party a written offer to stipulate to the entry of a judgment for the whole or part of the claim, including interest and costs then accrued.

(C) Acceptance or Rejection of Offer.

(1) To accept, the adverse party, within 21 days after service of the offer, must serve on the other parties a written notice of agreement to stipulate to the entry of the judgment offered, and file the offer, the notice of acceptance, and proof of service of the notice with the court. The court shall enter a judgment according to the terms of the stipulation.

(2) An offer is rejected if the offeree

(a) expressly rejects it in writing, or

(b) does not accept it as provided by subrule (C)(1).

A rejection does not preclude a later offer by either party.

(3) A counteroffer may be accepted or rejected in the same manner as an offer.

(D) Imposition of Costs Following Rejection of Offer. If an offer is rejected, costs are payable as follows:

(1) If the adjusted verdict is more favorable to the offeror than the average offer, the offeree must pay to the offeror the offeror's actual costs incurred in the prosecution or defense of the action.

(2) If the adjusted verdict is more favorable to the offeree than the average offer, the offeror must pay to the offeree the offeree's actual costs incurred in the prosecution or defense of the action. However, an offeree who has not made a counteroffer may not recover actual costs unless the offer was made less than 42 days before trial.

(3) The court shall determine the actual costs incurred. The court may, in the interest of justice, refuse to award an attorney fee under this rule.

(4) Evidence of an offer is admissible only in a proceeding to determine costs.

(5) Proceedings under this rule do not affect a contract or relationship between a party and his or her attorney.

A request for costs under this subrule must be filed and served within 28 days after the entry of the judgment or entry of an order denying a timely motion for a new trial or to set aside the judgment.

(E) Relationship to Case Evaluation. Costs may not be awarded under this rule in a case that has been submitted to case evaluation under MCR 2.403 unless the case evaluation award was not unanimous.

[Effective March 1, 1985; amended effective March 31, 1990; October 1, 1997; August 1, 2000.]

1985 Staff Comment

MCR 2.405 substantially revises the offer of judgment procedure found in GCR 1963, 519, under which only a party defending against a claim could invoke the procedure. Under MCR 2.405 either the claimant or the defending party may do so. Additional details regarding the procedure are added.

A party may offer to stipulate to entry of judgment in a specified amount. If an offer is accepted, judgment will be entered for that amount; if rejected, the case proceeds in the usual fashion. A party who has failed to accept an opposing party's offer of judgment may be subjected to payment of the opposing party's costs necessitated by the failure to accept if the verdict is less favorable to the rejecting party than the rejected offer. If each side has made an offer, the average of the two becomes the triggering value for determination of potential liability for costs.

As with the mediation rule, in determining whether a verdict has been more or less favorable to a party, it is to be adjusted by adding interest and costs. Compare MCR 2.403(O)(2), with subrule (A)(5).

The court has discretion not to include an attorney fee in the award of costs. See subrule (D)(3).

Finally, subrule (E) explains the relationship of this rule to mediation. In a case in which both procedures have been used, the cost provisions of the rule under which the later rejection occurred will be used.

Staff Comment to 1989 Amendment

On May 3, 1989, the Court ordered published for comment several proposals regarding the mediation rule, MCR 2.403, and the offer of judgment rule, MCR 2.405. See 68 Michigan Bar Journal 558 (June 1989). The January 3, 1990, order adopts several of those changes, some with modifications. Other proposed amendments to MCR 2.403(H)(1), (I)(2), and (J), giving trial courts greater flexibility in the use of mediation fees, increasing penalties for late filing of mediation documents with each day that they are late, and requiring attorneys and unrepresented parties to attend mediation sessions, remain under consideration.

In both MCR 2.403(8) and MCR 2.405(D), there is new language setting the time within which a party must seek to recover costs under the mediation and offer of judgment rules.

New language is added to MCR 2.405(A)(2) to specify when a counteroffer must be served.

The amendment to MCR 2.405(E) modifies the relationship between the cost provisions of the mediation and offer of judgment rules.

Staff Comment to 1997 Amendment

The May 8, 1997, order repeals MCR 4.003, which governed removal of cases from circuit to district court, effective July 1, 1997. This reinstates the February 28, 1997, repeal of the rule, which was suspended on March 13, 1997.

In addition, the order postpones the effective date of earlier amendments of MCR 2.403, 2.405, and 3.216, and new MCR 2.404, affecting mediation procedure, to October 1, 1997. The order also makes adjustments in MCR 2.403(K) and (N) in light of the repeal of MCR 4.003. The text of MCR 2.403, 2.404, 2.405 and 3.216 is the same as that adopted in the Court's March 5, 1997, order dealing with those rules.

Staff Comment to 2000 Amendment

The May 8, 2000, amendments [effective August 1, 2000] are based on the recommendations of the Michigan Supreme Court Dispute Resolution Task Force, which were published for comment on May 10, 1999 [see 459 Mich 1251], and were the subject of a series of public hearings across the state.

The Task Force report, issued in January 1999, and its Addendum report, issued in January 2000 after receipt of comments, should be consulted for the background and details of the amendments. Basically, the changes are as follows:

The amendments of MCR 2.403, 2.404, 2.405, 2.501, 2.502 and 2.503 are mainly to change terminology, replacing "mediation," as used in current MCR 2.403, with the term "case evaluation." "Mediation" will be used to describe the facilitative process established in MCR 2.411, in keeping with the generally accepted usage of the term.

MCR 2.401 is amended to direct consideration of alternative dispute resolution processes at scheduling and pretrial conferences.

New MCR 2.410 has general provisions governing referral of cases to alternative dispute resolution processes. Local courts wishing to use ADR techniques are to adopt ADR plans within the framework provided by the rule.

The one ADR process that is specifically established by the rules is mediation under new MCR 2.411. Among other things, the rule establishes general standards for mediator qualifications, and procedures for selection of mediators.

MCR 3.216, the domestic relations mediation rule, is substantially revised, to be more comparable to the mediation process in MCR 2.411.

MCR 5.143, regarding use of alternative dispute resolution processes in probate court, is amended to conform to the other rule changes.

Dissenting Statement of Justice Kelly to 2000 Amendment

I support the expanded use of alternative dispute resolution by our courts. However, I cannot cast a vote favoring the proposed Dispute Resolution Court Rules for two reasons: 1) they authorize judges to compel parties to submit to mediation and 2) they include nonlawyers as mediators and other ADR providers.

Regarding the mandatory nature of the new rules, I believe that mediation is, by its very nature, a process that works only when the parties enter into it voluntarily. I would support rules that permit courts to order parties to a session at which the merits of ADR are explored, but not that mandate mediation.

It is my fear that mandatory mediation will present insurmountable financial obstacles to low income litigants and could even provoke challenges based on a violation of due process principles. I am concerned that, in some heavily burdened courts, judges may use the new rules, not as an option for the parties, but as a docket control mechanism for the court. Also, I find no limit in the rules to the number of times a party could be ordered to an ADR process.

Mediation should not become yet another hurdle to a just resolution of disputes. Parties should not feel pressed to settle against their best interests, or involuntarily to expend financial resources in excess of the normal costs of trial. Litigation, without the new rules, is already too costly.

I agree with the Board of Commissioners of the State Bar of Michigan that, absent agreement of the parties, only licensed lawyers should be allowed to serve as ADR providers. Mediation and other types of ADR typically involve complex legal matters requiring skilled ADR providers. Yet, no system has been developed to ensure the training and accountability of nonlawyers who participate.

Finally, I agree with the Open Justice Commission's recommendations that chief judges should be required to report the race, ethnicity, and gender of case evaluators and other ADR providers that they appoint. I view this as a vital step toward ensuring persons wishing to function as ADR providers will not be passed over solely on the basis of their race, gender, ethnic background, or similar factors.

RULE 2.410   ALTERNATIVE DISPUTE RESOLUTION

(A) Scope and Applicability of Rule; Definitions.

(1) All civil cases are subject to alternative dispute resolution processes unless otherwise provided by statute or court rule.

(2) For the purposes of this rule, alternative dispute resolution (ADR) means any process designed to resolve a legal dispute in the place of court adjudication, and includes settlement conferences ordered under MCR 2.401; case evaluation under MCR 2.403; mediation under MCR 2.411; domestic relations mediation under MCR 3.216; and other procedures provided by local court rule or ordered on stipulation of the parties.

(B) ADR Plan.

(1) Each trial court that submits cases to ADR processes under this rule shall adopt an ADR plan by local administrative order. The plan must be in writing and available to the public in the ADR clerk's office.

(2) At a minimum, the ADR plan must:

(a) designate an ADR clerk, who may be the clerk of the court, the court administrator, the assignment clerk, or some other person;

(b) if the court refers cases to mediation under MCR 2.411, specify how the list of persons available to serve as mediators will be maintained and the system by which mediators will be assigned from the list under MCR 2.411(B)(3);

(c) include provisions for disseminating information about the operation of the court's ADR program to litigants and the public; and

(d) specify how access to ADR processes will be provided for indigent persons. If a party qualifies for waiver of filing fees under MCR 2.002 or the court determines on other grounds that the party is unable to pay the full cost of an ADR provider's services, and free or low-cost dispute resolution services are not available, the court shall not order that party to participate in an ADR process.

(3) The plan may also provide for referral relationships with local dispute resolution centers, including those affiliated with the Community Dispute Resolution Program.

(4) Courts in adjoining circuits or districts may jointly adopt and administer an ADR plan.

(C) Order for ADR.

(1) At any time, after consultation with the parties, the court may order that a case be submitted to an appropriate ADR process. More than one such order may be entered in a case.

(2) Unless the specific rule under which the case is referred provides otherwise, in addition to other provisions the court considers appropriate, the order shall

(a) specify, or make provision for selection of, the ADR provider;

(b) provide time limits for initiation and completion of the ADR process; and

(c) make provision for the payment of the ADR provider.

(3) The order may require attendance at ADR proceedings as provided in subrule (D).

(D) Attendance at ADR Proceedings.

(1) *Appearance of Counsel.* The attorneys attending an ADR proceeding shall be thoroughly familiar with the case and have the authority necessary to fully participate in the proceeding. The court may direct that the attorneys who intend to try the case attend ADR proceedings.

(2) *Presence of Parties.* The court may direct that persons with authority to settle a case, including the parties to the action, agents of parties, representatives of lien holders, or representatives of insurance carriers:

(a) be present at the ADR proceeding;

(b) be immediately available at the time of the proceeding.

The court's order may specify whether the availability is to be in person or by telephone.

(3) *Failure to Attend; Default; Dismissal.*

(a) Failure of a party or the party's attorney to attend a scheduled ADR proceeding, as directed by the court, constitutes a default to which MCR 2.603 is applicable or grounds for dismissal under MCR 2.504(B).

(b) The court shall excuse the failure of a party or the party's attorney to attend an ADR proceeding, and enter an order other than one of default or dismissal, if the court finds that

(i) entry of an order of default or dismissal would cause manifest injustice; or

(ii) the failure to attend was not due to the culpable negligence of the party or the attorney.

The court may condition the order on the payment by the offending party or attorney of reasonable expenses as provided in MCR 2.313(B)(2).

(E) Objections to ADR. Within 14 days after entry of an order referring a case to an ADR process, a party may move to set aside or modify the order. A timely motion must be decided before the case is submitted to the ADR process.

(F) Supervision of ADR Plan. The chief judge shall exercise general supervision over the implementation of this rule and shall review the operation of the court's ADR plan at least annually to assure compliance with this rule. In the event of noncompliance, the court shall take such action as is needed. This action may include recruiting persons to serve as ADR providers or changing the court's ADR plan.

[Adopted effective August 1, 2000.]

2000 Staff Comment

The May 8, 2000, amendments [effective August 1, 2000] are based on the recommendations of the Michigan Supreme Court Dispute Resolution Task Force, which were published for comment on May 10, 1999 [see 459 Mich 1251], and were the subject of a series of public hearings across the state.

The Task Force report, issued in January 1999, and its Addendum report, issued in January 2000 after receipt of comments, should be consulted for the background and details of the amendments. Basically, the changes are as follows:

The amendments of MCR 2.403, 2.404, 2.405, 2.501, 2.502 and 2.503 are mainly to change terminology, replacing "mediation," as used in current MCR 2.403, with the term "case evaluation." "Mediation" will be used to describe the facilitative process established in MCR 2.411, in keeping with the generally accepted usage of the term.

MCR 2.401 is amended to direct consideration of alternative dispute resolution processes at scheduling and pretrial conferences.

New MCR 2.410 has general provisions governing referral of cases to alternative dispute resolution processes. Local courts wishing to use ADR techniques are to adopt ADR plans within the framework provided by the rule.

The one ADR process that is specifically established by the rules is mediation under new MCR 2.411. Among other things, the rule establishes general standards for mediator qualifications, and procedures for selection of mediators.

MCR 3.216, the domestic relations mediation rule, is substantially revised, to be more comparable to the mediation process in MCR 2.411.

MCR 5.143, regarding use of alternative dispute resolution processes in probate court, is amended to conform to the other rule changes.

Dissenting Statement of Justice Kelly to 2000 Adoption

I support the expanded use of alternative dispute resolution by our courts. However, I cannot cast a vote favoring the proposed Dispute Resolution Court Rules for two reasons: 1) they authorize judges to compel parties to submit to mediation and 2) they include nonlawyers as mediators and other ADR providers.

Regarding the mandatory nature of the new rules, I believe that mediation is, by its very nature, a process that works only when the parties enter into it voluntarily. I would support rules that permit courts to order parties to a session at which the merits of ADR are explored, but not that mandate mediation.

It is my fear that mandatory mediation will present insurmountable financial obstacles to low income litigants and could even provoke challenges based on a violation of due process principles. I am concerned that, in some heavily burdened courts, judges may use the new rules, not as an option for the parties, but as a docket control mechanism for the court. Also, I find no limit in the rules to the number of times a party could be ordered to an ADR process.

Mediation should not become yet another hurdle to a just resolution of disputes. Parties should not feel pressed to settle against their best interests, or involuntarily to expend financial resources in excess of the normal costs of trial. Litigation, without the new rules, is already too costly.

I agree with the Board of Commissioners of the State Bar of Michigan that, absent agreement of the parties, only licensed lawyers should be allowed to serve as ADR providers. Mediation and other types of ADR typically involve complex legal matters requiring skilled ADR providers. Yet, no system has been developed to ensure the training and accountability of nonlawyers who participate.

Finally, I agree with the Open Justice Commission's recommendations that chief judges should be required to report the race, ethnicity, and gender of case evaluators and other ADR providers that they appoint. I view this as a vital step toward ensuring persons wishing to function as ADR providers will not be passed over solely on the basis of their race, gender, ethnic background, or similar factors.

RULE 2.411 MEDIATION

(A) Scope and Applicability of Rule; Definitions.

(1) This rule applies to cases that the court refers to mediation as provided in MCR 2.410. MCR 3.216 governs mediation of domestic relations cases.

(2) "Mediation" is a process in which a neutral third party facilitates communication between parties, assists in identifying issues, and helps explore solutions to promote a mutually acceptable settlement. A mediator has no authoritative decision-making power.

(B) Selection of Mediator.

(1) The parties may stipulate to the selection of a mediator. A mediator selected by agreement of the parties need not meet the qualifications set forth in subrule (F). The court must appoint a mediator stipulated to by the parties, provided the mediator is willing to serve within a period that would not interfere with the court's scheduling of the case for trial.

(2) If the order referring the case to mediation does not specify a mediator, the order shall set the date by which the parties are to have conferred on the selection of a mediator. If the parties do not advise the ADR clerk of the mediator agreed upon by that date,

the court shall appoint one as provided in subrule (B)(3).

(3) The procedure for selecting a mediator from the approved list of mediators must be established by local ADR plan adopted under MCR 2.410(B). The ADR clerk shall assign mediators in a rotational manner that assures as nearly as possible that each mediator on list is assigned approximately the same number of cases over a period of time. If a substitute mediator must be assigned, the same or similar assignment procedure shall be used to select the substitute.

(4) The rule for disqualification of a mediator is the same as that provided in MCR 2.003 for the disqualification of a judge. The mediator must promptly disclose any potential basis for disqualification.

(C) Scheduling and Conduct of Mediation.

(1) *Scheduling.* The order referring the case for mediation shall specify the time within which the mediation is to be completed. The ADR clerk shall send a copy of the order to each party and the mediator selected. Upon receipt of the court's order, the mediator shall promptly confer with the parties to schedule mediation in accordance with the order. Factors that may be considered in arranging the process may include the need for limited discovery before mediation, the number of parties and issues, and the necessity for multiple sessions. The mediator may direct the parties to submit in advance, or bring to the mediation, documents or summaries providing information about the case.

(2) *Conduct of Mediation.* The mediator shall meet with counsel and the parties, explain the mediation process, and then proceed with the process. The mediator shall discuss with the parties and counsel, if any, the facts and issues involved. The mediation will continue until a settlement is reached, the mediator determines that a settlement is not likely to be reached, the end of the first mediation session, or until a time agreed to by the parties. Additional sessions may be held as long as it appears that the process may result in settlement of the case.

(3) *Completion of Mediation.* Within 7 days after the completion of the ADR process, the mediator shall so advise the court, stating only the date of completion of the process, who participated in the mediation, whether settlement was reached, and whether further ADR proceedings are contemplated.

(4) *Settlement.* If the case is settled through mediation, within 21 days the attorneys shall prepare and submit to the court the appropriate documents to conclude the case.

(5) *Confidentiality.* Statements made during the mediation, including statements made in written submissions, may not be used in any other proceedings, including trial. Any communications between the parties or counsel and the mediator relating to a mediation are confidential and shall not be disclosed without

the written consent of all parties. This prohibition does not apply to

(a) the report of the mediator under subrule (C)(3),

(b) information reasonably required by court personnel to administer and evaluate the mediation program,

(c) information necessary for the court to resolve disputes regarding the mediator's fee, or

(d) information necessary for the court to consider issues raised under MCR 2.410(D)(3).

(D) Fees.

(1) A mediator is entitled to reasonable compensation based on an hourly rate commensurate with the mediator's experience and usual charges for services performed.

(2) The costs of mediation shall be divided between the parties on a pro-rata basis unless otherwise agreed by the parties or ordered by the court. The mediator's fee shall be paid no later than

(a) 42 days after the mediation process is concluded, or

(b) the entry of judgment, or

(c) the dismissal of the action,

whichever occurs first.

(3) If acceptable to the mediator, the court may order an arrangement for the payment of the mediator's fee other than that provided in subrule (D)(2).

(4) The mediator's fee is deemed a cost of the action, and the court may make an appropriate order to enforce the payment of the fee.

(5) If a party objects to the total fee of the mediator, the matter may be scheduled before the trial judge for determination of the reasonableness of the fee.

(E) List of Mediators.

(1) *Application.* An eligible person desiring to serve as a mediator may apply to the ADR clerk to be placed on the court's list of mediators. Application forms shall be available in the office of the ADR clerk.

(a) The form shall include a certification that

(i) the applicant meets the requirements for service under the court's selection plan;

(ii) the applicant will not discriminate against parties or attorneys on the basis of race, ethnic origin, gender, or other protected personal characteristic; and

(iii) the mediator will comply with the court's ADR plan, orders of the court regarding cases submitted to mediation, and the standards of conduct adopted by the State Court Administrator under subrule (G).

(b) On the form the applicant shall indicate the applicant's hourly rate for providing mediation services.

(c) The form shall include an optional section identifying the applicant's gender and racial/ethnic background.

(2) *Review of Applications.* The court's ADR plan shall provide for a person or committee to review applications annually, or more frequently if appropriate, and compile a list of qualified mediators.

(a) Persons meeting the qualifications specified in this rule shall be placed on the list of approved mediators. Approved mediators shall be placed on the list for a fixed period, not to exceed 5 years, and must reapply at the end of that time in the same manner as persons seeking to be added to the list.

(b) Selections shall be made without regard to race, ethnic origin, or gender. Residency or principal place of business may not be a qualification.

(c) The approved list and the applications of approved mediators, except for the optional section identifying the applicant's gender and racial/ethnic background, shall be available to the public in the office of the ADR clerk.

(3) *Rejection; Reconsideration.* Applicants who are not placed on the list shall be notified of that decision. Within 21 days of notification of the decision to reject an application, the applicant may seek reconsideration of the ADR clerk's decision by the Chief Judge. The court does not need to provide a hearing. Documents considered in the initial review process shall be retained for at least the period during which the applicant can seek reconsideration of the original decision.

(4) *Removal from List.* The ADR clerk may remove from the list mediators who have demonstrated incompetence, bias, made themselves consistently unavailable to serve as a mediator, or for other just cause. Within 21 days of notification of the decision to remove a mediator from the list, the mediator may seek reconsideration of the ADR clerk's decision by the Chief Judge. The court does not need to provide a hearing.

(F) Qualification of Mediators.

(1) *Small Claims Mediation.* District courts may develop individual plans to establish qualifications for persons serving as mediators in small claims cases.

(2) *General Civil Mediation.* To be eligible to serve as a general civil mediator, a person must meet the following minimum qualifications:

(a) Complete a training program approved by the State Court Administrator providing the generally accepted components of mediation skills;

(b) Have one or more of the following:

(i) Juris doctor degree or graduate degree in conflict resolution; or

(ii) 40 hours of mediation experience over two years, including mediation, co-mediation, observation, and role-playing in the context of mediation.

(c) Observe two general civil mediation proceedings conducted by an approved mediator, and conduct one general civil mediation to conclusion under the supervision and observation of an approved mediator.

(3) An applicant who has specialized experience or training, but does not meet the specific requirements of subrule (F)(2), may apply to the ADR clerk for special approval. The ADR clerk shall make the determination on the basis of criteria provided by the State Court Administrator. Service as a case evaluator under MCR 2.403 does not constitute a qualification for serving as a mediator under this section.

(4) Approved mediators are required to obtain 8 hours of advanced mediation training during each 2–year period. Failure to submit documentation establishing compliance is ground for removal from the list under subrule(E)(4).

(5) Additional qualifications may not be imposed upon mediators.

(G) Standards of Conduct for Mediators. The State Court Administrator shall develop and approve standards of conduct for mediators designed to promote honesty, integrity, and impartiality in providing court-connected dispute resolution services. These standards shall be made a part of all training and educational requirements for court-connected programs, shall be provided to all mediators involved in court-connected programs, and shall be available to the public.

[Adopted effective August 1, 2000.]

2000 Staff Comment

The May 8, 2000, amendments [effective August 1, 2000] are based on the recommendations of the Michigan Supreme Court Dispute Resolution Task Force, which were published for comment on May 10, 1999 [see 459 Mich 1251], and were the subject of a series of public hearings across the state.

The Task Force report, issued in January 1999, and its Addendum report, issued in January 2000 after receipt of comments, should be consulted for the background and details of the amendments. Basically, the changes are as follows:

The amendments of MCR 2.403, 2.404, 2.405, 2.501, 2.502 and 2.503 are mainly to change terminology, replacing "mediation," as used in current MCR 2.403, with the term "case evaluation." "Mediation" will be used to describe the facilitative process established in MCR 2.411, in keeping with the generally accepted usage of the term.

MCR 2.401 is amended to direct consideration of alternative dispute resolution processes at scheduling and pretrial conferences.

New MCR 2.410 has general provisions governing referral of cases to alternative dispute resolution processes. Local courts wishing to use ADR techniques are to adopt ADR plans within the framework provided by the rule.

The one ADR process that is specifically established by the rules is mediation under new MCR 2.411. Among other things, the rule establishes general standards for mediator qualifications, and procedures for selection of mediators.

MCR 3.216, the domestic relations mediation rule, is substantially revised, to be more comparable to the mediation process in MCR 2.411.

MCR 5.143, regarding use of alternative dispute resolution processes in probate court, is amended to conform to the other rule changes.

Dissenting Statement of Justice Kelly to 2000 Adoption

I support the expanded use of alternative dispute resolution by our courts. However, I cannot cast a vote favoring the proposed Dispute Resolution Court Rules for two reasons: 1) they authorize judges to compel parties to submit to mediation and 2) they include nonlawyers as mediators and other ADR providers.

Regarding the mandatory nature of the new rules, I believe that mediation is, by its very nature, a process that works only when the parties enter into it voluntarily. I would support rules that permit courts to order parties to a session at which the merits of ADR are explored, but not that mandate mediation.

It is my fear that mandatory mediation will present insurmountable financial obstacles to low income litigants and could even provoke challenges based on a violation of due process principles. I am concerned that, in some heavily burdened courts, judges may use the new rules, not as an option for the parties, but as a docket control mechanism for the court. Also, I find no limit in the rules to the number of times a party could be ordered to an ADR process.

Mediation should not become yet another hurdle to a just resolution of disputes. Parties should not feel pressed to settle against their best interests, or involuntarily to expend financial resources in excess of the normal costs of trial. Litigation, without the new rules, is already too costly.

I agree with the Board of Commissioners of the State Bar of Michigan that, absent agreement of the parties, only licensed lawyers should be allowed to serve as ADR providers. Mediation and other types of ADR typically involve complex legal matters requiring skilled ADR providers. Yet, no system has been developed to ensure the training and accountability of nonlawyers who participate.

Finally, I agree with the Open Justice Commission's recommendations that chief judges should be required to report the race, ethnicity, and gender of case evaluators and other ADR providers that they appoint. I view this as a vital step toward ensuring persons wishing to function as ADR providers will not be passed over solely on the basis of their race, gender, ethnic background, or similar factors.

RULE 2.420 SETTLEMENTS AND JUDGMENTS FOR MINORS AND LEGALLY INCAPACITATED INDIVIDUALS

(A) Applicability. This rule governs the procedure to be followed for the entry of a consent judgment, a settlement, or a dismissal pursuant to settlement in an action brought for a minor or a legally incapacitated individual by a next friend, guardian, or conservator or where a minor or a legally incapacitated individual is to receive a distribution from a wrongful death claim. Before an action is commenced, the settlement of a claim on behalf of a minor or a legally incapacitated individual is governed by the Estates and Protected Individuals Code.

(B) Procedure. In actions covered by this rule, a proposed consent judgment, settlement, or dismissal pursuant to settlement must be brought before the judge to whom the action is assigned and the judge shall pass on the fairness of the proposal.

(1) If the claim is for damages because of personal injury to the minor or legally incapacitated individual,

(a) the minor or legally incapacitated individual shall appear in court personally to allow the judge an opportunity to observe the nature of the injury unless, for good cause, the judge excuses the minor's or legally incapacitated individual's presence, and

(b) the judge may require medical testimony, by deposition or in court, if not satisfied of the extent of the injury.

(2) If the next friend, guardian, or conservator is a person who has made a claim in the same action and will share in the settlement or judgment of the minor or legally incapacitated individual, then a guardian ad litem for the minor or legally incapacitated individual must be appointed by the judge before whom the action is pending to approve the settlement or judgment.

(3) If a next friend, guardian or conservator for the minor or legally incapacitated individual has been appointed by a probate court, the terms of the proposed settlement or judgment may be approved by the court in which the action is pending upon a finding that the payment arrangement is in the best interests of the minor or legally incapacitated individual, but no judgment or dismissal may enter until the court receives written verification from the probate court that it has passed on the sufficiency of the bond and the bond, if any, has been filed with the probate court.

(4) The following provisions apply to settlements for minors.

(a) If the settlement or judgment requires payment of more than $5,000 to the minor either immediately, or if the settlement or judgment is payable in installments in any single year during minority, a

conservator must be appointed by the probate court before the entry of the judgment or dismissal.

(b) If the settlement or judgment does not require payment of more than $5,000 to the minor in any single year, the money may be paid in accordance with the provisions of MCL 700.5102.

(5) If a settlement or judgment provides for the creation of a trust for the minor or legally incapacitated individual, the circuit court shall determine the amount to be paid to the trust, but the trust shall not be funded without prior approval of the trust by the probate court pursuant to notice to all interested persons and a hearing.

[Effective March 1, 1985; amended effective May 1, 1998; January 1, 2002.]

1985 Staff Comment

MCR 2.420 is a new rule based on third circuit local court rule 6.7. It creates procedures for approval of a consent judgment or dismissal pursuant to settlement in an action brought on behalf of a minor.

The rule has two additional features designed to clarify the relative authority of the probate court and the court in which the action is pending. Subrule (A) provides that before an action is commenced, the settlement of the claim is governed by the Revised Probate Code. Second, subrule (B)(2) provides that after an action has been commenced, the settlement is to be approved by the court in which the action is pending. In that circumstance the only role of the probate court is to consider the sufficiency of the bond filed by the conservator, if one has been appointed.

Staff Comment to 1998 Amendment

The May 1998 amendment of MCR 2.420 was based on a recommendation from the Michigan Judges Association to resolve the potential conflict that arises when a spouse serves as guardian or conservator for an incompetent person and settles a personal-injury lawsuit with a consortium claim. In such a circumstance, the rule requires that a guardian *ad litem* be appointed. A like change was made with regard to the settlement of lawsuits involving minors.

Staff Comment to 2002 Amendment

In evaluating whether the payment arrangement of a structured settlement is in the best interests of a minor or legally incapacitated individual, the court should consider the age and life expectancy and current and anticipated financial needs of the minor or individual, any income and estate tax implications, any impact on eligibility for government benefits and the present value of the proposed payment arrangement.

SUBCHAPTER 2.500　TRIALS; SUBPOENAS; JURIES

RULE 2.501　SCHEDULING TRIALS; COURT CALENDARS

(A) Scheduling Conferences or Trial.

(1) Unless the further processing of the action is already governed by a scheduling order under MCR 2.401(B)(2), the court shall

(a) schedule a pretrial conference under MCR 2.401,

(b) schedule the action for an alternative dispute resolution process,

(c) schedule the action for trial, or

(d) enter another appropriate order to facilitate preparation of the action for trial.

(2) A court may adopt a trial calendar or other method for scheduling trials without the request of a party.

(B) Expedited Trials.

(1) On its own initiative, the motion of a party, or the stipulations of all parties, the court may shorten the time in which an action will be scheduled for trial, subject to the notice provisions of subrule (C).

(2) In scheduling trials, the court shall give precedence to actions involving a contest over the custody of minor children and to other actions afforded precedence by statute or court rule.

(C) Notice of Trial. Attorneys and parties must be given 28 days' notice of trial assignments, unless

(1) a rule or statute provides otherwise as to a particular type of action,

(2) the adjournment is of a previously scheduled trial, or

(3) the court otherwise directs for good cause.

Notice may be given orally if the party is before the court when the matter is scheduled, or by mailing or delivering copies of the notice or calendar to attorneys of record and to any party who appears on his or her own behalf.

(D) Attorney Scheduling Conflicts.

(1) The court and counsel shall make every attempt to avoid conflicts in the scheduling of trials.

(2) When conflicts in scheduled trial dates do occur, it is the responsibility of counsel to notify the court as soon as the potential conflict becomes evident. In such cases, the courts and counsel involved shall make every attempt to resolve the conflict in an equitable manner, with due regard for the priorities and time constraints provided by statute and court rule. When counsel cannot resolve conflicts through consultation with the individual courts, the judges shall consult directly to resolve the conflict.

(3) Except where a statute, court rule, or other special circumstance dictates otherwise, priority for trial shall be given to the case in which the pending trial date was set first.

[Effective March 1, 1985; amended effective October 1, 1991; August 1, 2000.]

1985 Staff Comment

MCR 2.501 governs the matter of scheduling actions for trial, as did GCR 1963, 501.

Under subrule (A), following the completion of discovery the court must either schedule the case for trial, for a pretrial conference, or for mediation.

Subrule (B) expressly allows expediting trial on motion or stipulation or when an action is given precedence by statute or court rule.

As to the notice provision, unlike GCR 1963, 501.4, subrule (C) would not permit published notice of the trial calendar to substitute for individual notice, although, of course, a court could publish notice in addition to giving individual notice. The rule specifies that the parties are entitled to 28 days' notice of trial assignment, although for good cause the court may shorten the time.

The [March 1, 1985] amendment of MCR 2.501(C)(2) makes clear that parties need not be given 28 days' notice of trial assignment when a previously scheduled trial is being adjourned.

Staff Comment to 1991 Amendment

There are two changes [effective October 1, 1991] in MCR 2.501. Subrule (A) is modified in light of the related changes regarding scheduling in MCR 2.301 and 2.401. Second, subrule (D) is added covering attorney schedule conflicts.

Staff Comment to 2000 Amendment

The May 8, 2000, amendments [effective August 1, 2000] are based on the recommendations of the Michigan Supreme Court Dispute Resolution Task Force, which were published for comment on May 10, 1999 [see 459 Mich 1251], and were the subject of a series of public hearings across the state.

The Task Force report, issued in January 1999, and its Addendum report, issued in January 2000 after receipt of comments, should be consulted for the background and details of the amendments. Basically, the changes are as follows:

The amendments of MCR 2.403, 2.404, 2.405, 2.501, 2.502 and 2.503 are mainly to change terminology, replacing "mediation," as used in current MCR 2.403, with the term "case evaluation." "Mediation" will be used to describe the facilitative process established in MCR 2.411, in keeping with the generally accepted usage of the term.

MCR 2.401 is amended to direct consideration of alternative dispute resolution processes at scheduling and pretrial conferences.

New MCR 2.410 has general provisions governing referral of cases to alternative dispute resolution processes. Local courts wishing to use ADR techniques are to adopt ADR plans within the framework provided by the rule.

The one ADR process that is specifically established by the rules is mediation under new MCR 2.411. Among other things, the rule establishes general standards for mediator qualifications, and procedures for selection of mediators.

MCR 3.216, the domestic relations mediation rule, is substantially revised, to be more comparable to the mediation process in MCR 2.411.

MCR 5.143, regarding use of alternative dispute resolution processes in probate court, is amended to conform to the other rule changes.

Dissenting Statement of Justice Kelly to 2000 Amendment

I support the expanded use of alternative dispute resolution by our courts. However, I cannot cast a vote favoring the proposed Dispute Resolution Court Rules for two reasons: 1) they authorize judges to compel parties to submit to mediation and 2) they include nonlawyers as mediators and other ADR providers.

Regarding the mandatory nature of the new rules, I believe that mediation is, by its very nature, a process that works only when the parties enter into it voluntarily. I would support rules that permit courts to order parties to a session at which the merits of ADR are explored, but not that mandate mediation.

It is my fear that mandatory mediation will present insurmountable financial obstacles to low income litigants and could even provoke challenges based on a violation of due process principles. I am concerned that, in some heavily burdened courts, judges may use the new rules, not as an option for the parties, but as a docket control mechanism for the court. Also, I find no limit in the rules to the number of times a party could be ordered to an ADR process.

Mediation should not become yet another hurdle to a just resolution of disputes. Parties should not feel pressed to settle against their best interests, or involuntarily to expend financial resources in excess of the normal costs of trial. Litigation, without the new rules, is already too costly.

I agree with the Board of Commissioners of the State Bar of Michigan that, absent agreement of the parties, only licensed lawyers should be allowed to serve as ADR providers. Mediation and other types of ADR typically involve complex legal matters requiring skilled ADR providers. Yet, no system has been developed to ensure the training and accountability of nonlawyers who participate.

Finally, I agree with the Open Justice Commission's recommendations that chief judges should be required to report the race, ethnicity, and gender of case evaluators and other ADR providers that they appoint. I view this as a vital step toward ensuring persons wishing to function as ADR providers will not be passed over solely on the basis of their race, gender, ethnic background, or similar factors.

RULE 2.502 DISMISSAL FOR LACK OF PROGRESS

(A) Notice of Proposed Dismissal.

(1) The court may notify the parties in those actions in which no steps or proceedings appear to have been taken within 91 days that the action will be dismissed for lack of progress unless the parties show that progress is in fact being made or that the failure to prosecute is not due to the fault or lack or reasonable diligence of the party seeking affirmative relief.

(2) A notice of proposed dismissal may not be sent with regard to a case

(a) in which a scheduling order has been entered under MCR 2.401(B)(2) and the times for completion of the scheduled events have not expired,

(b) which is set for a conference, an alternative dispute resolution process, hearing, or trial.

(3) The notice shall be given in the manner provided in MCR 2.501(C) for notice of trial.

(B) Action by Court.

(1) If a party does not make the required showing, the court may direct the clerk to dismiss the action for lack of progress. Such a dismissal is without prejudice unless the court specifies otherwise.

(2) If an action is not dismissed under this rule, the court shall enter orders to facilitate the prompt and just disposition of the action.

(C) Reinstatement of Dismissed Action. On motion for good cause, the court may reinstate an action dismissed for lack of progress on terms the court deems just. On reinstating an action, the court shall enter orders to facilitate the prompt and just disposition of the action.

[Effective March 1, 1985; amended effective October 1, 1991; August 1, 2000.]

1985 Staff Comment

MCR 2.502 deals with the subject of dismissal for lack of progress, which was covered by GCR 1963, 501.3. Subrule (A) retains the shorter time limit in district court than in circuit court (182 days versus 1 year). Compare GCR 1963, 501.3, with DCR 501.3. The parties be given notice in the same manner as provided by MCR 2.501(C) for notices of trial.

Subrule (B)(1) adds language expressly providing that a dismissal under this rule is without prejudice unless the court specifies otherwise.

Subrule (B)(2) provides that an action may not be dismissed for lack of progress before the time for completion of discovery or if it is set for trial or pretrial conference.

Subrule (C) adds an express provision allowing reinstatement of an action that has been dismissed for lack of progress.

Staff Comment to 1991 Amendment

The rule governing dismissals for lack of progress, MCR 2.502, is restructured [effective October 1, 1991], and the time period that triggers the sending of a notice is reduced from one year (182 days in district court) to 91 days.

Staff Comment to 2000 Amendment

The May 8, 2000, amendments [effective August 1, 2000] are based on the recommendations of the Michigan Supreme Court Dispute Resolution Task Force, which were published for comment on May 10, 1999 [see 459 Mich 1251], and were the subject of a series of public hearings across the state.

The Task Force report, issued in January 1999, and its Addendum report, issued in January 2000 after receipt of comments, should be consulted for the background and details of the amendments. Basically, the changes are as follows:

The amendments of MCR 2.403, 2.404, 2.405, 2.501, 2.502 and 2.503 are mainly to change terminology, replacing "mediation," as used in current MCR 2.403, with the term "case evaluation." "Mediation" will be used to describe the facilitative process established in MCR 2.411, in keeping with the generally accepted usage of the term.

MCR 2.401 is amended to direct consideration of alternative dispute resolution processes at scheduling and pretrial conferences.

New MCR 2.410 has general provisions governing referral of cases to alternative dispute resolution processes. Local courts wishing to use ADR techniques are to adopt ADR plans within the framework provided by the rule.

The one ADR process that is specifically established by the rules is mediation under new MCR 2.411. Among other things, the rule establishes general standards for mediator qualifications, and procedures for selection of mediators.

MCR 3.216, the domestic relations mediation rule, is substantially revised, to be more comparable to the mediation process in MCR 2.411.

MCR 5.143, regarding use of alternative dispute resolution processes in probate court, is amended to conform to the other rule changes.

Dissenting Statement of Justice Kelly to 2000 Amendment

I support the expanded use of alternative dispute resolution by our courts. However, I cannot cast a vote favoring the proposed Dispute Resolution Court Rules for two reasons: 1) they authorize judges to compel parties to submit to mediation and 2) they include nonlawyers as mediators and other ADR providers.

Regarding the mandatory nature of the new rules, I believe that mediation is, by its very nature, a process that works only when the parties enter into it voluntarily. I would support rules that permit courts to order parties to a session at which the merits of ADR are explored, but not that mandate mediation.

It is my fear that mandatory mediation will present insurmountable financial obstacles to low income litigants and could even provoke challenges based on a violation of due process principles. I am concerned that, in some heavily burdened courts, judges may use the new rules, not as an option for the parties, but as a docket control mechanism for the court. Also, I find no limit in the rules to the number of times a party could be ordered to an ADR process.

Mediation should not become yet another hurdle to a just resolution of disputes. Parties should not feel pressed to settle against their best interests, or involuntarily to expend financial resources in excess of the normal costs of trial. Litigation, without the new rules, is already too costly.

I agree with the Board of Commissioners of the State Bar of Michigan that, absent agreement of the parties, only licensed lawyers should be allowed to serve as ADR providers. Mediation and other types of ADR typically involve complex legal matters requiring skilled ADR providers. Yet, no system has been developed to ensure the training and accountability of nonlawyers who participate.

Finally, I agree with the Open Justice Commission's recommendations that chief judges should be required to report the race, ethnicity, and gender of case evaluators and other ADR providers that they appoint. I view this as a vital step toward ensuring persons wishing to function as ADR providers will not be passed over solely on the basis of their race, gender, ethnic background, or similar factors.

RULE 2.503 ADJOURNMENTS

(A) Applicability. This rule applies to adjournments of trials, alternative dispute resolution processes, pretrial conferences, and all motion hearings.

(B) Motion or Stipulation for Adjournment.

(1) Unless the court allows otherwise, a request for an adjournment must be by motion or stipulation made in writing or orally in open court based on good cause.

(2) A motion or stipulation for adjournment must state

(a) which party is requesting the adjournment,

(b) the reason for it, and

(c) whether other adjournments have been granted in the proceeding and, if so, the number granted.

(3) The entitlement of a motion or stipulation for adjournment must specify whether it is the first or a later request, e.g., "Plaintiff's Request for Third Adjournment".

(C) Absence of Witness or Evidence.

(1) A motion to adjourn a proceeding because of the unavailability of a witness or evidence must be made as soon as possible after ascertaining the facts.

(2) An adjournment may be granted on the ground of unavailability of a witness or evidence only if the court finds that the evidence is material and that diligent efforts have been made to produce the witness or evidence.

(3) If the testimony or the evidence would be admissible in the proceeding, and the adverse party stipulates in writing or on the record that it is to be considered as actually given in the proceeding, there may be no adjournment unless the court deems an adjournment necessary.

(D) Order for Adjournment; Costs and Conditions.

(1) In its discretion the court may grant an adjournment to promote the cause of justice. An adjournment may be entered by order of the court either in writing or on the record in open court, and the order must state the reason for the adjournment.

(2) In granting an adjournment, the court may impose costs and conditions. When an adjournment is granted conditioned on payment of costs, the costs may be taxed summarily to be paid on demand of the adverse party or the adverse party's attorney, and the adjournment may be vacated if nonpayment is shown by affidavit.

(E) Rescheduling.

(1) Except as provided in subrule (E)(2), at the time the proceeding is adjourned under this rule, or as soon thereafter as possible, the proceeding must be rescheduled for a specific date and time.

(2) A court may place the matter on a specified list of actions or other matters which will automatically reappear before the court on the first available date.

(F) Death or Change of Status of Attorney. If the court finds that an attorney

(1) has died or is physically or mentally unable to continue to act as an attorney for a party,

(2) has been disbarred,

(3) has been suspended,

(4) has been placed on inactive status, or

(5) has resigned from active membership in the bar,

the court shall adjourn a proceeding in which the attorney was acting for a party. The party is entitled to 28 days' notice that he or she must obtain a substitute attorney or advise the court in writing that the party intends to appear on his or her own behalf. See MCR 9.119.

[Effective March 1, 1985; amended effective August 1, 2000.]

1985 Staff Comment

MCR 2.503 is based on GCR 1963, 503. The term "continuance" is changed to "adjournment" throughout.

Subrule (A) is a new provision making clear that the adjournment procedure applies to pretrial conferences, mediations, and motion hearings, as well as to trials.

Subrule (D)(1) specifies that when it grants an adjournment, the court is to do so either in writing or on the record, stating the reasons for granting the adjournment.

Subrule (E) is new, requiring rescheduling when a case is adjourned, or as soon thereafter as possible.

The [March 1, 1985] amendment of MCR 2.503(E) reorganizes the section to make clear that the only exception to the requirement of rescheduling to a specific date is the provision of subrule (E)(2)—placement of the matter on a specified list of actions that appear automatically on the next available date. The court is permitted to delay the rescheduling briefly (for example, to ascertain available dates), but a specific date and time must be set.

Subrule (F) includes the provisions found in GCR 1963, 909 regarding adjournment on the death or disability of an attorney for a party.

Staff Comment to 2000 Amendment

The May 8, 2000, amendments [effective August 1, 2000] are based on the recommendations of the Michigan Supreme Court Dispute Resolution Task Force, which were published for comment on May 10, 1999 [see 459 Mich 1251], and were the subject of a series of public hearings across the state.

The Task Force report, issued in January 1999, and its Addendum report, issued in January 2000 after receipt of comments, should be consulted for the background and details of the amendments. Basically, the changes are as follows:

The amendments of MCR 2.403, 2.404, 2.405, 2.501, 2.502 and 2.503 are mainly to change terminology, replacing "mediation," as used in current MCR 2.403, with the term "case evaluation." "Mediation" will be used to describe the facilitative process established in MCR 2.411, in keeping with the generally accepted usage of the term.

MCR 2.401 is amended to direct consideration of alternative dispute resolution processes at scheduling and pretrial conferences.

New MCR 2.410 has general provisions governing referral of cases to alternative dispute resolution processes. Local courts wishing to use ADR techniques are to adopt ADR plans within the framework provided by the rule.

The one ADR process that is specifically established by the rules is mediation under new MCR 2.411. Among other things, the rule establishes general standards for mediator qualifications, and procedures for selection of mediators.

MCR 3.216, the domestic relations mediation rule, is substantially revised, to be more comparable to the mediation process in MCR 2.411.

MCR 5.143, regarding use of alternative dispute resolution processes in probate court, is amended to conform to the other rule changes.

Dissenting Statement of Justice Kelly to 2000 Amendment

I support the expanded use of alternative dispute resolution by our courts. However, I cannot cast a vote favoring the proposed Dispute Resolution Court Rules for two reasons: 1) they authorize judges to compel parties to submit to mediation and 2) they include nonlawyers as mediators and other ADR providers.

Regarding the mandatory nature of the new rules, I believe that mediation is, by its very nature, a process that works only when the parties enter into it voluntarily. I would support rules that permit courts to order parties to a session at which the merits of ADR are explored, but not that mandate mediation.

It is my fear that mandatory mediation will present insurmountable financial obstacles to low income litigants and could even provoke challenges based on a violation of due process principles. I am concerned that, in some heavily burdened courts, judges may use the new rules, not as an option for the parties, but as a docket control mechanism for the court. Also, I find no limit in the rules to the number of times a party could be ordered to an ADR process.

Mediation should not become yet another hurdle to a just resolution of disputes. Parties should not feel pressed to settle against their best interests, or involuntarily to expend financial resources in excess of the normal costs of trial. Litigation, without the new rules, is already too costly.

I agree with the Board of Commissioners of the State Bar of Michigan that, absent agreement of the parties, only licensed lawyers should be allowed to serve as ADR providers. Mediation and other types of ADR typically involve complex legal matters requiring skilled ADR providers. Yet, no system has been developed to ensure the training and accountability of nonlawyers who participate.

Finally, I agree with the Open Justice Commission's recommendations that chief judges should be required to report the race, ethnicity, and gender of case evaluators and other ADR providers that they appoint. I view this as a vital step toward ensuring persons wishing to function as ADR providers will not be passed over solely on the basis of their race, gender, ethnic background, or similar factors.

RULE 2.504   DISMISSAL OF ACTIONS

(A) Voluntary Dismissal; Effect.

(1) *By Plaintiff; by Stipulation.* Subject to the provisions of MCR 2.420 and MCR 3.501(E), an action may be dismissed by the plaintiff without an order of the court and on the payment of costs

(a) by filing a notice of dismissal before service by the adverse party of an answer or of a motion under MCR 2.116, whichever first occurs; or

(b) by filing a stipulation of dismissal signed by all the parties.

Unless otherwise stated in the notice of dismissal or stipulation, the dismissal is without prejudice, except that a dismissal under subrule (A)(1)(a) operates as an adjudication on the merits when filed by a plaintiff who has previously dismissed an action in any court based on or including the same claim.

(2) *By Order of Court.* Except as provided in subrule (A)(1), an action may not be dismissed at the plaintiff's request except by order of the court on terms and conditions the court deems proper.

(a) If a defendant has pleaded a counterclaim before being served with the plaintiff's motion to dismiss, the court shall not dismiss the action over the defendant's objection unless the counterclaim can remain pending for independent adjudication by the court.

(b) Unless the order specifies otherwise, a dismissal under subrule (A)(2) is without prejudice.

(B) Involuntary Dismissal; Effect.

(1) If the plaintiff fails to comply with these rules or a court order, a defendant may move for dismissal of an action or a claim against that defendant.

(2) In an action tried without a jury, after the presentation of the plaintiff's evidence the defendant, without waiving the right to offer evidence if the motion is not granted, may move for dismissal on the ground that on the facts and the law the plaintiff has shown no right to relief. The court may then determine the facts and render judgment against the plaintiff, or may decline to render judgment until the close of all the evidence. If the court renders judgment on the merits against the plaintiff, the court shall make findings as provided in MCR 2.517.

(3) Unless the court otherwise specifies in its order for dismissal, a dismissal under this subrule or a dismissal not provided for in this rule, other than a dismissal for lack of jurisdiction or for failure to join a party under MCR 2.205, operates as an adjudication on the merits.

(C) Dismissal of Counterclaim, Cross-Claim, or Third-Party Claim. This rule applies to the dismissal of a counterclaim, cross-claim, or third-party claim. A voluntary dismissal by the claimant alone, pursuant to subrule (A)(1), must be made before service by the adverse party of a responsive pleading or a motion under MCR 2.116, or, if no pleading or motion is filed, before the introduction of evidence at the trial.

(D) Costs of Previously Dismissed Action. If a plaintiff who has once dismissed an action in any court commences an action based on or including the same claim against the same defendant, the court may order the payment of such costs of the action previously dismissed as it deems proper and may stay proceedings until the plaintiff has complied with the order.

(E) Dismissal for Failure to Serve Defendant. An action may be dismissed as to a defendant under MCR 2.102(E).

[Effective March 1, 1985.]

1985 Staff Comment

MCR 2.504 is based on GCR 1963, 504.

Subrule (B)(3) is made consistent with FR Civ P 41(b): Dismissals for failure to join a necessary party under MCR 2.205 are added to the category of dismissals that do not operate as an adjudication on the merits.

RULE 2.505 CONSOLIDATION; SEPARATE TRIALS

(A) Consolidation. When actions involving a substantial and controlling common question of law or fact are pending before the court, it may

(1) order a joint hearing or trial of any or all the matters in issue in the actions;

(2) order the actions consolidated; and

(3) enter orders concerning the proceedings to avoid unnecessary costs or delay.

(B) Separate Trials. For convenience or to avoid prejudice, or when separate trials will be conducive to expedition and economy, the court may order a separate trial of one or more claims, cross-claims, counterclaims, third-party claims, or issues.

[Effective March 1, 1985.]

1985 Staff Comment

MCR 2.505 is based on GCR 1963, 505.

In subrule (B), an additional ground is added for ordering separate trials—where separate trials would be conducive to expedition and economy.

RULE 2.506 SUBPOENA; ORDER TO ATTEND

(A) Attendance of Party or Witness.

(1) The court in which a matter is pending may by order or subpoena command a party or witness to appear for the purpose of testifying in open court on a date and time certain and from time to time and day to day thereafter until excused by the court, and to produce notes, records, documents, photographs, or other portable tangible things as specified.

(2) The court may require a party and a representative of an insurance carrier for a party with authority to settle to be present or immediately available at trial.

(3) A subpoena may be issued only in accordance with this rule or MCR 2.305, 2.621(C), 9.112(D), 9.115(I)(1), or 9.212.

(B) Authorized Signatures.

(1) A subpoena signed by an attorney of record in the action or by the clerk of the court in which the matter is pending has the force and effect of an order signed by the judge of that court.

(2) For the purpose of this subrule, an authorized signature includes but is not limited to signatures

written by hand, printed, stamped, typewritten, engraved, photographed, or lithographed.

(C) Notice to Witness of Required Attendance.

(1) The signer of a subpoena must issue it for service on the witness sufficiently in advance of the trial or hearing to give the witness reasonable notice of the date and time the witness is to appear. Unless the court orders otherwise, the subpoena must be served at least 2 days before the witness is to appear.

(2) The party having the subpoena issued must take reasonable steps to keep the witness informed of adjournments of the scheduled trial or hearing.

(3) If the served witness notifies the party that it is impossible for the witness to be present in court as directed, the party must either excuse the witness from attendance at that time or notify the witness that a special hearing may be held to adjudicate the issue.

(D) Form of Subpoena. A subpoena must:

(1) be entitled in the name of the People of the State of Michigan;

(2) be imprinted with the seal of the Supreme Court of Michigan;

(3) have typed or printed on it the name of the court in which the matter is pending;

(4) state the place where the trial or hearing is scheduled;

(5) state the title of the action in which the person is expected to testify;

(6) state the file designation assigned by the court; and

(7) state that failure to obey the commands of the subpoena or reasonable directions of the signer as to time and place to appear may subject the person to whom it is directed to penalties for contempt of court.

The state court administrator shall develop and approve a subpoena form for statewide use.

(E) Refusal of Witness to Attend or to Testify; Contempt.

(1) If a person fails to comply with a subpoena served in accordance with this rule or with a notice under subrule (C)(2), the failure may be considered a contempt of court by the court in which the action is pending.

(2) If a person refuses to be sworn or to testify regarding a matter not privileged after being ordered to do so by the court, the refusal may be considered a contempt of court.

(F) Failure of Party to Attend. If a party or an officer, director, or managing agent of a party fails to attend or produce documents or other tangible evidence pursuant to a subpoena or an order to attend, the court may:

(1) stay further proceedings until the order is obeyed;

(2) tax costs to the other party or parties to the action;

(3) strike all or a part of the pleadings of that party;

(4) refuse to allow that party to support or oppose designated claims and defenses;

(5) dismiss the action or any part of it; or

(6) enter judgment by default against that party.

(G) Service of Subpoena and Order to Attend; Fees.

(1) A subpoena may be served anywhere in Michigan in the manner provided by MCR 2.105. The fee for attendance and mileage provided by law must be tendered to the person on whom the subpoena is served at the time of service. Tender must be made in cash, by money order, by cashier's check, or by a check drawn on the account of an attorney of record in the action or the attorney's authorized agent.

(2) A subpoena may also be served by mailing to a witness a copy of the subpoena and a postage-paid card acknowledging service and addressed to the party requesting service. The fees for attendance and mileage provided by law are to be given to the witness after the witness appears at the court, and the acknowledgment card must so indicate. If the card is not returned, the subpoena must be served in the manner provided in subrule (G)(1).

(3) A subpoena or order to attend directed to a party, or to an officer, director, or managing agent of a party, may be served in the manner provided by MCR 2.107, and fees and mileage need not be paid.

(H) Hearing on Subpoena or Order.

(1) A person served with a subpoena or order to attend may appear before the court in person or by writing to explain why the person should not be compelled to comply with the subpoena, order to attend, or directions of the party having it issued.

(2) The court may direct that a special hearing be held to adjudicate the issue.

(3) For good cause with or without a hearing, the court may excuse a witness from compliance with a subpoena, the directions of the party having it issued, or an order to attend.

(4) A person must comply with the command of a subpoena unless relieved by order of the court or written direction of the person who had the subpoena issued.

(I) Subpoena for Production of Hospital Medical Records.

(1) Except as provided in subrule (I)(5), a hospital may comply with a subpoena calling for production of medical records belonging to the hospital in the man-

ner provided in this subrule. This subrule does not apply to X-ray films or to other portions of a medical record that are not susceptible to photostatic reproduction.

(a) The hospital may deliver or mail to the clerk of the court in which the action is pending, without cost to the parties, a complete and accurate copy of the original record.

(b) The copy of the record must be accompanied by a sworn certificate, in the form approved by the state court administrator, signed by the medical record librarian or another authorized official of the hospital, verifying that it is a complete and accurate reproduction of the original record.

(c) The envelope or other container in which the record is delivered to the court shall be clearly marked to identify its contents. If the hospital wishes the record returned when it is no longer needed in the action, that fact must be stated on the container, and, with the record, the hospital must provide the clerk with a self-addressed, stamped envelope that the clerk may use to return the record.

(d) The hospital shall promptly notify the attorney for the party who caused the subpoena to be issued that the documents involved have been delivered or mailed to the court in accordance with subrule (I)(1).

(2) The clerk shall keep the copies sealed in the container in which they were supplied by the hospital. The container shall be clearly marked to identify the contents, the name of the patient, and the title and number of the action. The container shall not be opened except at the direction of the court.

(3) If the hospital has requested that the record be returned, the clerk shall return the record to the hospital when 42 days have passed after a final order terminating the action, unless an appeal has been taken. In the event of an appeal, the record shall be returned when 42 days have passed after a final order terminating the appeal. If the hospital did not request that the record be returned as provided in subrule (I)(1)(c), the clerk may destroy the record after the time provided in this subrule.

(4) The admissibility of the contents of medical records produced under this rule or under MCR 2.314 is not affected or altered by these procedures and remains subject to the same objections as if the original records were personally produced by the custodian at the trial or hearing.

(5) A party may have a subpoena issued directing that an original record of a person be produced at the trial or hearing by the custodian of the record. The subpoena must specifically state that the original records, not copies, are required. A party may also require, by subpoena, the attendance of the custodian without the records.

[Effective March 1, 1985; amended effective September 4, 1985; October 1, 1991; December 1, 1998.]

1985 Staff Comment

MCR 2.506 substantially revises the provisions of GCR 1963, 506 governing subpoenas and orders to attend.

Subrule (A) permits issuance of a subpoena that commands the witness to appear at a specified day and time and also from day to day thereafter until excused. Subrule (C) requires the party who had the subpoena issued to keep the witness informed of adjournments.

Subrule (A)(2) includes a new provision based on former third circuit local rule 13.1 permitting the trial court to require a party and the representative of an insurance carrier to be present or immediately available at trial or a settlement conference.

Subrule (B) permits the attorney of record in an action to sign a subpoena with the same force as if it were issued by the clerk, as was required under GCR 1963, 506.2.

Subrule (C)(1) requires the party having the subpoena issued to have it served on the witness a reasonable time before the witness is to appear. It specifies that, unless the court otherwise orders, at least 2 days' notice is required.

Subrule (D) specifies in greater detail than did former GCR 1963, 506.4 the information that must be included in the subpoena. It also directs the state court administrator to develop and approve a subpoena form for statewide use.

Subrule (F) modifies the provisions of former GCR 1963, 506.6(2) to make the sanctions available against a party also applicable if an officer, director, or managing agent of the party fails to appear in response to a subpoena or order to attend.

Subrule (G) provides more detail regarding the manner of service of subpoenas and orders to attend than did the corresponding GCR 1963, 506.5. When directed to a party (or officer, director, or managing agent), the subpoena or order may be served in the manner provided by MCR 2.107.

In addition, new subrule (G)(2) permits the service of subpoenas by mail, accompanied by a postage-paid card acknowledging service. This provision was formerly found only in the district court rules regarding criminal cases and civil infractions. See DCR 506.5(b).

Subrule (H) creates a procedure for a hearing on a witness's objection to a subpoena or order.

The [March 1, 1985] amendment of MCR 2.506 adds a new subrule (I) covering the subject of subpoenaing hospital medical records for trial. It carries forward a simplified version of former GCR 1963, 506.7, and incorporates language previously found in MCR 2.314(F).

Staff Comment to 1985 Amendment

The [September 4, 1985] amendment of MCR 2.506(B) permits the "signing" of subpoenas by methods other than a handwritten signature.

Staff Comment to 1991 Amendment

Language regarding requiring the presence of parties at trial is deleted from MCR 2.506 [effective October 1, 1991]. That subject is now covered by MCR 2.401(F).

Staff Comment to 1998 Amendment

The December 1, 1998 [effective date], amendments of Rules 2.305, 2.310, and 2.506 were suggested by the Representative Assembly of the State Bar of Michigan. The changes made clear that nonparty records-only discovery subpoenas are authorized. The normal procedure for noticing a deposition applies to records-only subpoenas, and the procedure in MCR 2.310 still pertains to requests to a nonparty for entry on land or production of items for testing or sampling. The time for responding to a document subpoena or a document request under Rule 2.305(B)(1) was changed from seven to fourteen days. The time for responding under Rule 2.310(C)(2) was changed from twenty-eight to fourteen days. The amendments also made nonsubstantive changes to clarify and simplify language.

RULE 2.507   CONDUCT OF TRIALS

(A) **Opening Statements.** Before the introduction of evidence, the attorney for the party who is to commence the evidence must make a full and fair statement of that party's case and the facts the party intends to prove. Immediately thereafter or immediately before the introduction of evidence by the adverse party, the attorney for the adverse party must make a like statement. Opening statements may be waived with the consent of the court and the opposing attorney.

(B) **Opening the Evidence.** Unless otherwise ordered by the court, the plaintiff must first present the evidence in support of the plaintiff's case. However, the defendant must first present the evidence in support of his or her case, if

(1) the defendant's answer has admitted facts and allegations of the plaintiff's complaint to the extent that, in the absence of further statement on the defendant's behalf, judgment should be entered on the pleadings for the plaintiff, and

(2) the defendant has asserted a defense on which the defendant has the burden of proof, either as a counterclaim or as an affirmative defense.

(C) **Examination and Cross-Examination of Witnesses.** Unless otherwise ordered by the court, no more than one attorney for a party may examine or cross-examine a witness.

(D) **Interpreters.** The court may appoint an interpreter of its own selection and may set reasonable compensation for the interpreter. The compensation is to be paid out of funds provided by law or by one or more of the parties, as the court directs, and may be taxed as costs, in the discretion of the court.

(E) **Final Arguments.** After the close of all the evidence, the parties may rest their cases with or without final arguments. The party who commenced the evidence is entitled to open the argument and, if the opposing party makes an argument, to make a rebuttal argument not beyond the issues raised in the preceding arguments.

(F) **Time Allowed for Opening Statements and Final Arguments.** The court may limit the time allowed each party for opening statements and final arguments. It shall give the parties adequate time for argument, having due regard for the complexity of the action, and may make separate time allowances for co-parties whose interests are adverse.

(G) **Deposit of Fees.** Proofs may not be taken in the trial of a civil action unless the trial fee and judgment fee provided by law have been deposited with the clerk of the court.

(H) **Agreements to Be in Writing.** An agreement or consent between the parties or their attorneys respecting the proceedings in an action, subsequently denied by either party, is not binding unless it was made in open court, or unless evidence of the agreement is in writing, subscribed by the party against whom the agreement is offered or by that party's attorney.

[Effective March 1, 1985.]

1985 Staff Comment

MCR 2.507 is based on GCR 1963, 507. GCR 1963, 507.4 (parties as witnesses) and 507.5 (exceptions unnecessary) are omitted.

Subrule (D) adds provisions regarding appointment of an interpreter.

RULE 2.508   JURY TRIAL OF RIGHT

(A) **Right Preserved.** The right of trial by jury as declared by the constitution must be preserved to the parties inviolate.

(B) **Demand for Jury.**

(1) A party may demand a trial by jury of an issue as to which there is a right to trial by jury by filing a written demand for a jury trial within 28 days after the filing of the answer or a timely reply. A party may include the demand in a pleading if notice of the demand is included in the caption of the pleading. The jury fee provided by law must be paid at the time the demand is filed.

(2) If a party appealing to the circuit court from a municipal court desires a trial by jury of an issue triable of right, demand for jury must be included in the claim of appeal. If another party desires trial by jury of an issue triable of right, the demand must be included in the party's notice of appearance.

(3)(a) If a case is entirely removed from circuit court to district court, or is entirely removed or transferred from district court to circuit court, a timely demand for a trial by jury in the court from which the case is removed or transferred remains effective in the court to which the case is removed or transferred. If a case is entirely removed or transferred from district court to circuit court, and if the amount paid to the district court for the jury fee is less than the circuit court jury fee, then the party requesting the jury shall pay the difference to the circuit court. If a case is entirely removed from circuit court to district court, no additional jury fee is to be paid to the district court nor is there to be a refund of any amount by which the circuit court jury fee exceeds the district court jury fee.

(b) If part of a case is removed from circuit court to district court, or part of a case is removed or transferred from district court to circuit court, but a portion of the case remains in the court from which the case is removed or transferred, then a demand for a trial by jury in the court from which the case is removed or transferred is not effective in the court to which the case is removed or transferred. A party who seeks a trial by jury in the court to which the case is partially removed or transferred must file a written demand for a trial by jury within 21 days of the removal or transfer order, and must pay the jury fee provided by law, even if the jury fee was paid in the court from which the case is removed or transferred.

(c) The absence of a timely demand for a trial by jury in the court from which a case is entirely or partially removed or transferred does not preclude filing a demand for a trial by jury in the court to which the case is removed or transferred. A party who seeks a trial by jury in the court to which the case is removed or transferred must file a written demand for a trial by jury within 21 days of the removal or transfer order, and must pay the jury fee provided by law.

(d) A party who is added to a case after it has been removed or transferred may demand trial by jury in accordance with paragraph (B)(1).

(C) Specifications of Issues.

(1) In a demand for jury trial, a party may specify the issues the party wishes so tried; otherwise, the party is deemed to have demanded trial by jury of all the issues so triable.

(2) If a party has demanded trial by jury of only some of the issues, another party, within 14 days after service of a copy of the demand or within less time as the court may order, may serve a demand for trial by jury of another or all the issues of fact in the action.

(D) Waiver; Withdrawal.

(1) A party who fails to file a demand or pay the jury fee as required by this rule waives trial by jury.

(2) Waiver of trial by jury is not revoked by an amendment of a pleading asserting only a claim or defense arising out of the conduct, transaction, or occurrence stated, or attempted to be stated, in the original pleading.

(3) A demand for trial by jury may not be withdrawn without the consent, expressed in writing or on the record, of the parties or their attorneys.

[Effective March 1, 1985; amended effective January 1, 1995.]

1985 Staff Comment

MCR 2.508 is based on GCR 1963, 508, and DCR 508.

The [March 1, 1985] amendment of MCR 2.508(B)(1) requires that the jury fee be paid at the time the jury demand is filed.

Staff Comment to 1995 Amendment

MCR 2.508(B)(3) took effect in 1995, as did an amendment of MCR 4.002(C). These changes were to address the procedural issue that arose in *Adamski v Cole*, 197 Mich App 124, 494 NW2d 794 (1992), *lv den* 445 Mich 863 (1994).

RULE 2.509 TRIAL BY JURY OR BY COURT

(A) By Jury. If a jury has been demanded as provided in MCR 2.508, the action or appeal must be designated in the court records as a jury action. The trial of all issues so demanded must be by jury unless

(1) the parties agree otherwise by stipulation in writing or on the record, or

(2) the court on motion or on its own initiative finds that there is no right to trial by jury of some or all of those issues.

(B) By Court. Issues for which a trial by jury has not been demanded as provided in MCR 2.508 will be tried by the court. In the absence of a demand for a jury trial of an issue as to which a jury demand might have been made of right, the court in its discretion may order a trial by jury of any or all issues.

(C) Sequence of Trial. In an action in which some issues are to be tried by jury and others by the court, or in which a number of claims, cross-claims, defenses, counterclaims, or third-party claims involve a common issue, the court may determine the sequence of trial of the issues, preserving the constitutional right to trial by jury according to the basic nature of every issue for which a demand for jury trial has been made under MCR 2.508.

(D) Advisory Jury and Trial by Consent. In appeals to circuit court from a municipal court and in actions involving issues not triable of right by a jury because of the basic nature of the issue, the court on motion or on its own initiative may

(1) try the issues with an advisory jury; or

(2) with the consent of all parties, order a trial with a jury whose verdict has the same effect as if trial by jury had been a matter of right.

[Effective March 1, 1985.]

1985 Staff Comment

MCR 2.509 is substantially the same as GCR 1963, 509.

RULE 2.510 JUROR PERSONAL HISTORY QUESTIONNAIRE

(A) Form. The state court administrator shall adopt a juror personal history questionnaire.

(B) Completion of Questionnaire.

(1) The court clerk or the jury board, as directed by the chief judge, shall supply each juror drawn for jury service with a questionnaire in the form adopted pursuant to subrule (A). The court clerk or the jury board shall direct the juror to complete the questionnaire in the juror's own handwriting before the juror is called for service.

(2) Refusal to answer the questions on the questionnaire, or answering the questionnaire falsely, is contempt of court.

(C) Filing the Questionnaire.

(1) On completion, the questionnaire shall be filed with the court clerk or the jury board, as designated under subrule (B)(1). The only persons allowed to examine the questionnaire are:

(a) the judges of the court;

(b) the court clerk and deputy clerks;

(c) parties to actions in which the juror is called to serve and their attorneys; and

(d) persons authorized access by court rule or by court order.

(2) The attorneys must be given a reasonable opportunity to examine the questionnaires before being called on to challenge for cause.

(a) The State Court Administrator shall develop model procedures for providing attorneys and parties reasonable access to juror questionnaires.

(b) Each court shall select and implement one of these procedures by local administrative order adopted pursuant to MCR 8.112(B). If the State Court Administrator determines that, given the circumstances existing in an individual court, the procedure selected does not provide reasonable access, the State Court Administrator may direct the court to implement one of the other model procedures.

(c) If the procedure selected allows attorneys or parties to receive copies of juror questionnaires, an attorney or party may not release them to any person who would not be entitled to examine them under subrule (C)(1).

(3) The questionnaires must be kept on file for 3 years from the time they are filled out.

(D) Summoning Jurors for Court Attendance. The court clerk, the court administrator, the sheriff, or the jury board, as designated by the chief judge, shall summon jurors for court attendance at the time and in the manner directed by the chief judge, the presiding judge, or the judge to whom the action in which jurors are being called for service is assigned. For a juror's first required court appearance, service must be by written notice addressed to the juror at his or her residence as shown by the records of the clerk or jury board. The notice may be by ordinary mail or by personal service. For later service, notice may be in the manner directed by the court. The person giving notice to jurors shall keep a record of the notice and make a return if directed by the court. The return is presumptive evidence of the fact of service.

[Effective March 1, 1985; amended effective April 1, 1987.]

1985 Staff Comment

MCR 2.510 corresponds to GCR 1963, 510.

The form of jury questionnaire is deleted from the rule, and a jury questionnaire form will be approved by the state court administrator. See subrule (A).

Staff Comment to 1987 Amendment

The [April 1, 1987] amendment to MCR 2.510(C)(2) provides for development of model procedures for providing access to juror personal history questionnaires. Corresponding Administrative Order 1987–1 requires courts to select and implement one of the model plans within two months after the State Court Administrator issues them.

RULE 2.511   IMPANELING THE JURY

(A) Selection of Jurors.

(1) Persons who have not been discharged or excused as prospective jurors by the court are subject to selection for the action or actions to be tried during their term of service as provided by law.

(2) In an action that is to be tried before a jury, the names or corresponding numbers of the prospective jurors shall be deposited in a container, and the prospective jurors must be selected for examination by a random blind draw from the container.

(3) The court may provide for random selection of prospective jurors for examination from less than all of the prospective jurors not discharged or excused.

(4) Prospective jurors may be selected by any other fair and impartial method directed by the court or agreed to by the parties.

(B) Alternate Jurors. The court may direct that 7 or more jurors be impaneled to sit. After the instructions to the jury have been given and the action is ready to be submitted, unless the parties have stipulated that all the jurors may deliberate, the names of the jurors must be placed in a container and names drawn to reduce the number of jurors to 6, who shall constitute the jury. The court may retain the alternate jurors during deliberations. If the court does so, it shall instruct the alternate jurors not to discuss the case with any other person until the jury completes its deliberations and is discharged. If an alternate juror replaces a juror after the jury retires to consider its verdict, the court shall instruct the jury to begin its deliberations anew.

(C) Examination of Jurors. The court may conduct the examination of prospective jurors or may permit the attorneys to do so.

(D) Challenges for Cause. The parties may challenge jurors for cause, and the court shall rule on each challenge. A juror challenged for cause may be directed to answer questions pertinent to the inquiry. It is grounds for a challenge for cause that the person:

(1) is not qualified to be a juror;

(2) has been convicted of a felony;

(3) is biased for or against a party or attorney;

(4) shows a state of mind that will prevent the person from rendering a just verdict, or has formed a positive opinion on the facts of the case or on what the outcome should be;

(5) has opinions or conscientious scruples that would improperly influence the person's verdict;

(6) has been subpoenaed as a witness in the action;

(7) has already sat on a trial of the same issue;

(8) has served as a grand or petit juror in a criminal case based on the same transaction;

(9) is related within the ninth degree (civil law) of consanguinity or affinity to one of the parties or attorneys;

(10) is the guardian, conservator, ward, landlord, tenant, employer, employee, partner, or client of a party or attorney;

(11) is or has been a party adverse to the challenging party or attorney in a civil action, or has complained of or has been accused by that party in a criminal prosecution;

(12) has a financial interest other than that of a taxpayer in the outcome of the action;

(13) is interested in a question like the issue to be tried.

Exemption from jury service is the privilege of the person exempt, not a ground for challenge.

(E) Peremptory Challenges.

(1) A juror peremptorily challenged is excused without cause.

(2) Each party may peremptorily challenge three jurors. Two or more parties on the same side are considered a single party for purposes of peremptory challenges. However, when multiple parties having adverse interests are aligned on the same side, three peremptory challenges are allowed to each party represented by a different attorney, and the court may allow the opposite side a total number of peremptory challenges not exceeding the total number of peremptory challenges allowed to the multiple parties.

(3) Peremptory challenges must be exercised in the following manner:

(a) First the plaintiff and then the defendant may exercise one or more peremptory challenges until each party successively waives further peremptory challenges or all the challenges have been exercised, at which point jury selection is complete.

(b) A "pass" is not counted as a challenge but is a waiver of further challenge to the panel as constituted at that time.

(c) If a party has exhausted all peremptory challenges and another party has remaining challenges, that party may continue to exercise his or her remaining peremptory challenges until they are exhausted.

(F) Replacement of Challenged Jurors. After the jurors have been seated in the jurors' box and a challenge for cause is sustained or a peremptory challenge exercised, another juror must be selected and examined before further challenges are made. This juror is subject to challenge as are other jurors.

(G) Oath of Jurors. The jury must be sworn by the clerk substantially as follows:

"Each of you do solemnly swear (or affirm) that, in this action now before the court, you will justly decide the questions submitted to you, that, unless you are discharged by the court from further deliberation, you will render a true verdict, and that you will render your verdict only on the evidence introduced and in accordance with the instructions of the court, so help you God."

[Effective March 1, 1985; amended effective September 1, 2001.]

1985 Staff Comment

MCR 2.511 corresponds to GCR 1963, 511.

Subrule (A) removes some of the detail of GCR 1963, 511.1. It preserves the principle of random selection of jurors from those available.

The language regarding alternate jurors in subrule (B) is modified to be consistent with the provision found in MCR 2.512(A)(3), allowing the parties to stipulate that all of the jurors impaneled (including alternates) may deliberate.

Subrule (D) deletes language (from GCR 1963, 511.4) that had restricted challenges for cause by requiring that they be made after the jurors have been questioned. It may be possible to excuse some jurors in advance based on the questionnaires.

Subrule (E) differs from GCR 1963, 511.5 in that the later provision said that peremptory challenges are to be made after all challenges for cause are completed. Peremptory challenges may be exercised at a time when only the jurors who have been selected from the panel and seated in the jury box have been questioned so as to permit challenges for cause. If a juror is peremptorily challenged and a new one called from the panel and questioned, the parties should be able to challenge that juror for cause.

Subrule (E)(3) makes clear that while a "pass" is not counted as a challenge, it does constitute a waiver of further challenge to the jury panel as then constituted. If the other parties also pass, jury selection is complete.

The oath of the jurors in subrule (G) is taken from PCR 511.7.

The provisions of GCR 1963, 511 and DCR 511 that were specifically applicable to criminal cases have been moved to chapter 6. See MCR 6.102, 6.202.

Staff Comment to 2001 Amendment

The June 26, 2001 amendments of MCR 2.511(B), MCR 6.411, and MCR 6.620(A), effective September 1, 2001, were based on a proposal from the Michigan Judges Association. Consistent with the December 1999 amendment of the Federal Rules of Criminal Procedure for the United States District Courts, the amendments allow courts to retain alternate jurors during deliberations.

RULE 2.512   RENDERING VERDICT

(A) Majority Verdict; Stipulations Regarding Number of Jurors and Verdict. The parties may stipulate in writing or on the record that

(1) the jury will consist of any number less than 6,

(2) a verdict or a finding of a stated majority of the jurors will be taken as the verdict or finding of the jury, or

(3) if more than six jurors were impaneled, all of the jurors may deliberate.

Except as provided in MCR 5.512, in the absence of such stipulation, a verdict in a civil action tried by 6 jurors will be received when 5 jurors agree.

(B) Return; Poll.

(1) The jury must return its verdict in open court.

(2) A party may require a poll to be taken by the court asking each juror if it is his or her verdict.

(3) If the number of jurors agreeing is less than required, the jury must be sent out for further deliberation; otherwise the verdict is complete, and the court shall discharge the jury.

(C) Discharge From Action; New Jury. The court may discharge a jury from the action:

(1) because of an accident or calamity requiring it;

(2) by consent of all the parties;

(3) whenever an adjournment or mistrial is declared;

(4) whenever the jurors have deliberated until it appears that they cannot agree.

The court may order another jury to be drawn, and the same proceedings may be had before the new jury as might have been had before the jury discharged.

(D) Responsibility of Officers.

(1) All court officers, including trial attorneys, must attend during the trial of an action until the verdict of the jury is announced.

(2) A trial attorney may, on request, be released by the court from further attendance, or the attorney may designate an associate or other attorney to act for him or her during the deliberations of the jury.

[Effective March 1, 1985; amended effective September 1, 2000.]

1985 Staff Comment

MCR 2.512 corresponds to GCR 1963, 512. The language of GCR 1963, 512.1 that was specifically applicable to criminal cases is omitted.

Subrule (A)(3) is a new provision expressly allowing the parties to stipulate that all of the jurors impaneled (including alternates) may deliberate.

Staff Comment to 2000 Amendment

The June 21, 2000 amendment, effective September 1, 2000, changed MCR 2.512(B)(1) to read the same as MCR 6.420(A), as recommended by the Michigan Judges Association.

RULE 2.513   VIEW

(A) By Jury. On motion of either party or on its own initiative, the court may order an officer to take the jury as a whole to view property or a place where a material event occurred. During the view, no person other than the officer designated by the court may speak to the jury concerning a subject connected with the trial. The court may order the party requesting a jury view to pay the expenses of the view.

(B) By Court. On application of either party or on its own initiative, the court sitting as trier of fact without a jury may view property or a place where a material event occurred.

[Effective March 1, 1985.]

1985 Staff Comment

MCR 2.513 corresponds to GCR 1963, 513.

New subrule (B) is added, making clear that the judge trying a case without a jury may also view property or a place where a material event occurred.

RULE 2.514   SPECIAL VERDICTS

(A) Use of Special Verdicts; Form. The court may require the jury to return a special verdict in the form of a written finding on each issue of fact, rather than a general verdict. If a special verdict is required, the court shall, in advance of argument and in the absence of the jury, advise the attorneys of this fact and, on the record or in writing, settle the form of the verdict. The court may submit to the jury:

(1) written questions that may be answered categorically and briefly;

(2) written forms of the several special findings that might properly be made under the pleadings and evidence; or

(3) the issues by another method, and require the written findings it deems most appropriate.

The court shall give to the jury the necessary explanation and instruction concerning the matter submitted to enable the jury to make its findings on each issue.

(B) Judgment. After a special verdict is returned, the court shall enter judgment in accordance with the jury's findings.

(C) Failure to Submit Question; Waiver; Findings by Court. If the court omits from the special verdict form an issue of fact raised by the pleadings or the evidence, a party waives the right to a trial by jury of the issue omitted unless before the jury retires the party demands its submission to the jury. The court may make a finding as to an issue omitted without a demand; or, if the court fails to do so, it is deemed to have made a finding in accord with the judgment on the special verdict.

[Effective March 1, 1985.]

1985 Staff Comment

MCR 2.514 is substantially the same as GCR 1963, 514.

RULE 2.515 MOTION FOR DIRECTED VERDICT

A party may move for a directed verdict at the close of the evidence offered by an opponent. The motion must state specific grounds in support of the motion. If the motion is not granted, the moving party may offer evidence without having reserved the right to do so, as if the motion had not been made. A motion for a directed verdict that is not granted is not a waiver of trial by jury, even though all parties to the action have moved for directed verdicts.

[Effective March 1, 1985.]

1985 Staff Comment

MCR 2.515 includes the part of GCR 1963, 515.1 that dealt with motions for a directed verdict. The remaining provisions of GCR 1963, 515 are relocated in the post-trial subchapter. See MCR 2.610.

RULE 2.516 INSTRUCTIONS TO JURY

(A) Request for Instructions.

(1) At a time the court reasonably directs, the parties must file written requests that the court instruct the jury on the law as stated in the requests. In the absence of a direction from the court, a party may file a written request for jury instructions at or before the close of the evidence.

(2) In addition to requests for instructions submitted under subrule (A)(1), after the close of the evidence each party shall submit in writing to the court a statement of the issues and may submit the party's theory of the case as to each issue. The statement must be concise, be narrative in form, and set forth as issues only those disputed propositions of fact which are supported by the evidence. The theory may include those claims supported by the evidence or admitted.

(3) A copy of the requested instructions must be served on the adverse parties in accordance with MCR 2.107.

(4) The court shall inform the attorneys of its proposed action on the requests before their arguments to the jury.

(5) The court need not give the statements of issues or theories of the case in the form submitted if the court presents to the jury the material substance of the issues and theories of each party.

(B) Instructing the Jury.

(1) After the jury is sworn and before evidence is taken, the court shall give such preliminary instructions regarding the duties of the jury, trial procedure, and the law applicable to the case as are reasonably necessary to enable the jury to understand the proceedings and the evidence. MCR 2.516(D)(2) does not apply to such preliminary instructions.

(2) At any time during the trial, the court may, with or without request, instruct the jury on a point of law if the instruction will materially aid the jury to understand the proceedings and arrive at a just verdict.

(3) Before or after arguments or at both times, as the court elects, the court shall instruct the jury on the applicable law, the issues presented by the case, and, if a party requests as provided in subrule (A)(2), that party's theory of the case. The court, at its discretion, may also comment on the evidence, the testimony, and the character of the witnesses, as the interests of justice require.

(4) While the jury is deliberating, the court may further instruct the jury in the presence of or after reasonable notice to the parties.

(5) Either on the request of a party or on the court's own motion, the court may provide the jury with

(a) a full set of written instructions,

(b) a full set of electronically recorded instructions, or

(c) a partial set of written or recorded instructions if the jury asks for clarification or restatement of a particular instruction or instructions or if the parties agree that a partial set may be provided and agree on the portions to be provided.

If it does so, the court must ensure that such instructions are made a part of the record.

(C) Objections. A party may assign as error the giving of or the failure to give an instruction only if the party objects on the record before the jury retires to consider the verdict (or, in the case of instructions given after deliberations have begun, before the jury resumes deliberations), stating specifically the matter to which the party objects and the grounds for the objection. Opportunity must be given to make the objection out of the hearing of the jury.

(D) Model Civil Jury Instructions.

(1) The Committee on Model Civil Jury Instructions appointed by the Supreme Court has the author-

ity to adopt model civil jury instructions M Civ JI) and to amend or repeal those instructions approved by the predecessor committee. Before adopting, amending, or repealing an instruction, the committee shall publish notice of the committee's intent, together with the text of the instruction to be adopted, or the amendment to be made, or a reference to the instruction to be repealed, in the manner provided in MCR 1.201. The notice shall specify the time and manner for commenting on the proposal. The committee shall thereafter publish notice of its final action on the proposed change, including, if appropriate, the effective date of the adoption, amendment, or repeal. A model civil jury instruction does not have the force and effect of a court rule.

(2) Pertinent portions of the instructions approved by the Committee on Model Civil Jury Instructions or its predecessor committee must be given in each action in which jury instructions are given if

(a) they are applicable,

(b) they accurately state the applicable law, and

(c) they are requested by a party.

(3) Whenever the committee recommends that no instruction be given on a particular matter, the court shall not give an instruction unless it specifically finds for reasons stated on the record that

(a) the instruction is necessary to state the applicable law accurately, and

(b) the matter is not adequately covered by other pertinent model civil jury instructions.

(4) This subrule does not limit the power of the court to give additional instructions on applicable law not covered by the model instructions . Additional instructions when given must be patterned as nearly as practicable after the style of the model instructions, and must be concise, understandable, conversational, unslanted, and nonargumentative.

[Effective March 1, 1985; amended effective June 1, 1989; September 1, 1998; May 1, 2002.]

1985 Staff Comment

MCR 2.516 corresponds to GCR 1963, 516. The rule is reorganized and, in addition, has several substantive changes.

The provision on "preliminary" instructions, previously found in GCR 1963, 516.3, is modified in subrule (B)(1). The trial court is directed to give instructions after the selection of the jury and before taking of evidence. These instructions could include instructions on the law applicable to the case in much the same form as the traditional closing instructions.

The [March 1, 1985] amendment of MCR 2.516(B)(1) excepts preliminary instructions from the requirement that Standard Jury Instructions be given when applicable and requested.

Subrule (C) makes the provisions of GCR 1963, 516.2 regarding objections to instructions applicable to all instructions. The special provisions regarding objections to preliminary instructions (failure to give such instructions cannot be assigned as error, GCR 1963, 516.3) and additional instruc-

tions (objection to be made in motion for new trial, GCR 1963, 516.4) are omitted.

In subrule (B)(5), in addition to the authority to submit full or partial sets of written instructions to the jury as had been provided by GCR 1963, 516.1, a trial court may provide the jury with a full or partial (on stipulation) set of electronically recorded instructions.

The [March 1, 1985] amendment of MCR 2.516(D)(1) corrects an inadvertent failure to carry forward the 1980 amendment of GCR 1963, 516.6(1) regarding the operation of the Standard Jury Instruction Committee.

Former GCR 1963, 516.5, regarding condemnation proceedings, is omitted. Under MCL 213.62(1); MSA 8.265(12)(1), jury procedure in condemnation cases is governed by the same rules as are other civil actions.

Staff Comment to 1989 Amendment

The 1989 amendment of MCR 2.516(B)(3) permits the court to elect to instruct the jury prior to final arguments, after final arguments, or at both times. The previous rule provided that instructions were to follow final arguments.

Staff Comment to 1998 Amendment

The June 1998 amendment of MCR 2.516(B)(5)(c), effective September 1, 1998, was suggested by the Michigan Judges Association. The amendment allows the trial court to provide the jury with a partial set of instructions if the jury asks for clarification or restatement of a particular instruction or instructions. Previously, a partial set of instructions could be provided only if the parties agreed. The amendment also added to MCR 2.516 (B)(5) the final sentence in MCR 6.414(G), to ensure that all instructions are made a part of the record.

Staff Comment to 2002 Amendment

The December 18, 2001 amendment of subrule (D), effective May 1, 2002, is consistent with the Supreme Court's adoption of Administrative Order 2001–6, which established the membership and terms for the new Committee on Model Civil Jury Instructions.

The staff comment is published only for the benefit of the bench and bar and is not an authoritative construction by the Court.

RULE 2.517   FINDINGS BY COURT

(A) Requirements.

(1) In actions tried on the facts without a jury or with an advisory jury, the court shall find the facts specially, state separately its conclusions of law, and direct entry of the appropriate judgment.

(2) Brief, definite, and pertinent findings and conclusions on the contested matters are sufficient, without overelaboration of detail or particularization of facts.

(3) The court may state the findings and conclusions on the record or include them in a written opinion.

(4) Findings of fact and conclusions of law are unnecessary in decisions on motions unless findings are required by a particular rule. See, e.g., MCR 2.504(B).

(5) The clerk shall notify the attorneys for the parties of the findings of the court.

(6) Requests for findings are not necessary for purposes of review.

(7) No exception need be taken to a finding or decision.

(B) Amendment. On motion of a party made within 21 days after entry of judgment, the court may amend its findings or make additional findings, and may amend the judgment accordingly. The motion may be made with a motion for new trial pursuant to MCR 2.611. When findings of fact are made in an action tried by the court without a jury, the question of the sufficiency of the evidence to support the findings may thereafter be raised whether the party raising the question has objected to the findings or has moved to amend them or for judgment.

[Effective March 1, 1985.]

1985 Staff Comment

MCR 2.517 corresponds to GCR 1963, 517.

Subrule (A)(3) makes clear that the judge may either write an opinion setting forth the findings or may state them on the record.

The language of GCR 1963, 517.1 that findings are not to be set aside unless clearly erroneous is moved to MCR 2.613.

RULE 2.518   RECEIPT AND RETURN OR DISPOSAL OF EXHIBITS

(A) Receipt of Exhibits. Exhibits introduced into evidence at or during court proceedings shall be received and maintained as provided by Michigan Supreme Court trial court case file management standards.

(B) Return Or Disposal of Exhibits. At the conclusion of a trial or hearing, exhibits should be retrieved by the parties submitting them except that any weapons and drugs shall be returned to the confiscating agency for proper disposition. If the exhibits are not retrieved by the parties within 56 days after conclusion of the trial or hearing, the court may properly dispose of the exhibits without notice to the parties.

[Adopted effective November 30, 1999.]

1999 Staff Comment

The amendments of MCR 2.113, 5.113, 5.901, 7.210, 8.105, 8.110, 8.116, 8.203, 8.205, and 8.302 [effective November 30, 1999] and the addition of MCR 2.518 and 8.119 [effective November 30, 1999] are to accommodate statewide records standards applicable to all courts and all clerks of the courts as developed and recommended by the Michigan Trial Court Case File Management Standards Committee.

SUBCHAPTER 2.600   JUDGMENTS AND ORDERS; POSTJUDGMENT PROCEEDINGS

RULE 2.601   JUDGMENTS

(A) Relief Available. Except as provided in subrule (B), every final judgment may grant the relief to which the party in whose favor it is rendered is entitled, even if the party has not demanded that relief in his or her pleadings.

(B) Default Judgment. A judgment by default may not be different in kind from, nor exceed in amount, the relief demanded in the pleading, unless notice has been given pursuant to MCR 2.603(B)(1).

[Effective March 1, 1985.]

1985 Staff Comment

MCR 2.601 includes the provisions previously found in GCR 1963, 518.3. The portions of that rule regarding judgments in actions involving multiple claims and parties are relocated in a separate rule (MCR 2.604). The references to decrees and exceptions found in GCR 1963, 518.1 and 518.4 are deleted.

In subrule (A) the word "shall" is changed to "may", authorizing but not requiring the granting of relief in excess of that demanded.

Subrule (B) adds a reference to the procedure for giving notice of a request for a default judgment found in MCR 2.603(B)(1).

RULE 2.602   ENTRY OF JUDGMENTS AND ORDERS

(A) Signing; Statement; Date of Entry.

(1) Except as provided in this rule and in MCR 2.603, all judgments and orders must be in writing, signed by the court and dated with the date they are signed.

(2) The date of signing an order or judgment is the date of entry.

(3) Each judgment must state, immediately preceding the judge's signature, whether it resolves the last pending claim and closes the case. Such a statement must also appear on any other order that disposes of the last pending claim and closes the case.

(B) Procedure of Entry of Judgments and Orders. An order or judgment shall be entered by one of the following methods:

(1) The court may sign the judgment or order at the time it grants the relief provided by the judgment or order.

(2) The court shall sign the judgment or order when its form is approved by all the parties and if, in the court's determination, it comports with the court's decision.

(3) Within 7 days after the granting of the judgment or order, or later if the court allows, a party may serve a copy of the proposed judgment or order on the other parties, with a notice to them that it will be submitted to the court for signing if no written objections to its accuracy or completeness are filed with the court clerk within 7 days after service of the notice. The party must file with the court clerk the original of the proposed judgment or order and proof of its service on the other parties.

(a) If no written objections are filed within 7 days, the clerk shall submit the judgment or order to the court, and the court shall then sign it if, in the court's determination, it comports with the court's decision. If the proposed judgment or order does not comport with the decision, the court shall direct the clerk to notify the parties to appear before the court on a specified date for settlement of the matter.

(b) Objections regarding the accuracy or completeness of the judgment or order must state with specificity the inaccuracy or omission.

(c) The party filing the objections must serve them on all parties as required by MCR 2.107, together with a notice of hearing and an alternate proposed judgment or order.

(4) A party may prepare a proposed judgment or order and notice it for settlement before the court.

(C) Filing. The original of the judgment or order must be placed in the file.

(D) Service.

(1) The party securing the signing of the judgment or order shall serve a copy, within 7 days after it has been signed, on all other parties, and file proof of service with the court clerk.

(2) If a judgment for liquidated damages is entered pursuant to MCL 314.14(a); MSA 13.1363(1), the clerk shall mail a copy of the judgment to the Department of Natural Resources. The judgment may be enforced as a civil judgment.

[Effective March 1, 1985; amended effective December 1, 1998; January 1, 2002.]

1985 Staff Comment

MCR 2.602 corresponds to GCR 1963, 522.

The language of subrule (A) is modified to require that the judgment or order be dated the date it is signed by the judge, prohibiting the backdating of judgments and orders.

Under GCR 1963, 522.1(1), a judgment or order approved as to form by all parties could only be entered by the court within the 10 days after the decision. Subrule (B)(2) deletes the 10-day limitation.

Subrule (B)(3) slightly modifies former GCR 1963, 522.1(2), which provided a procedure for entry of an order by serving a copy of a proposed order. The court may allow such a proposed order to be served after the time specified in the rule (7 days). Further, the rule specifies the event that

begins the time within which the opposing party can object—service of the proposed order.

GCR 1963, 522.3 regarding the clerk's recording of proceedings in a "journal" are omitted. The rules governing the records to be kept by the clerk are placed in the administrative rules chapter. See MCR 8.105, 8.203.

Subrule (D)(2) is taken from DCR 522.1, covering certain Game Law violations.

Staff Comment to 1998 Amendment

The December 1, 1998 amendment of MCR 2.602(A) requires that all judgments designate whether they resolve the last pending claim and close a case. The requirement also pertains to other orders that dispose of all pending claims and close a case, *i.e.*, an order that does not decide the merits of a last pending claim but rather dismisses the claim for reasons such as lack of jurisdiction or a discovery violation. The goal of the amendment, which stemmed from a proposal of the Michigan Judges Association, is to facilitate docket management.

Staff Comment to 2002 Amendment

The September 12, 2001 amendment of MCR 2.602(B)(3), effective January 1, 2002, was based on a recommendation from the Michigan Judges Association to eliminate delay and unnecessary work caused by nonspecific and meaningless objections. The amendment shifted some of the burden of going forward from the proponent of the order to the objector and clarified the objection procedure.

The staff comment is published only for the benefit of the bench and bar and is not an authoritative construction by the Court.

RULE 2.603   DEFAULT AND DEFAULT JUDGMENT

(A) Entry; Notice; Effect.

(1) If a party against whom a judgment for affirmative relief is sought has failed to plead or otherwise defend as provided by these rules, and that fact is made to appear by affidavit or otherwise, the clerk must enter the default of that party.

(2) Notice of the entry must be sent to all parties who have appeared and to the defaulted party. If the defaulted party has not appeared, the notice to the defaulted party may be served by personal service, by ordinary first-class mail at his or her last known address or the place of service, or as otherwise directed by the court.

(a) In the district court, the court clerk shall send the notice.

(b) In all other courts, the notice must be sent by the party who sought entry of the default. Proof of service and a copy of the notice must be filed with the court.

(3) Once the default of a party has been entered, that party may not proceed with the action until the default has been set aside by the court in accordance with subrule (D) or MCR 2.612.

(B) Default Judgment.

(1) *Notice of Request for Judgment.*

(a) A party seeking a default judgment must give notice of the request for judgment to the defaulted party

(i) if the party against whom the judgment is sought has appeared in the action;

(ii) if the request for entry of judgment seeks relief different in kind from, or greater in amount than, that stated in the pleadings; or

(iii) if the pleadings do not state a specific amount demanded.

(b) The notice required by this subrule must be served at least 7 days before entry of the requested judgment.

(c) If the defaulted party has appeared, the notice may be given in the manner provided by MCR 2.107. If the defaulted party has not appeared, the notice may be served by personal service, by ordinary first-class mail at the defaulted party's last known address or the place of service, or as otherwise directed by the court.

(d) If the default is entered for failure to appear for a scheduled trial, notice under this subrule is not required.

(2) *Default Judgment Entered by Clerk.* On request of the plaintiff supported by an affidavit as to the amount due, the clerk may sign and enter judgment for that amount and costs against the defendant, if

(a) the plaintiff's claim against a defendant is for a sum certain or for a sum that can by computation be made certain,

(b) the default was entered because the defendant failed to appear, and

(c) the defaulted defendant is not an infant or incompetent person.

The clerk may not enter or record a judgment based on a note or other written evidence of indebtedness until the note or writing is filed with the clerk for cancellation, except by special order of the court.

(3) *Default Judgment Entered by Court.* In all other cases the party entitled to a judgment by default must apply to the court for the judgment.

(a) A judgment by default may not be entered against a minor or an incompetent person unless the person is represented in the action by a conservator, guardian ad litem, or other representative.

(b) If, in order for the court to enter judgment or to carry it into effect, it is necessary to

(i) take an account,

(ii) determine the amount of damages,

(iii) establish the truth of an allegation by evidence, or

(iv) investigate any other matter,

the court may conduct hearings or order references it deems necessary and proper, and shall accord a right of trial by jury to the parties to the extent required by the constitution.

(4) *Notice of Entry of Judgment.* The court clerk must promptly mail notice of entry of a default judgment to all parties. The notice to the defendant shall be mailed to the defendant's last known address or the address of the place of service. The clerk must keep a record that notice was given.

(C) Nonmilitary Affidavit. Nonmilitary affidavits required by law must be filed before judgment is entered in actions in which the defendant has failed to appear.

(D) Setting Aside Default.

(1) A motion to set aside a default or a default judgment, except when grounded on lack of jurisdiction over the defendant, shall be granted only if good cause is shown and an affidavit of facts showing a meritorious defense is filed.

(2) Except as provided in MCR 2.612, if personal service was made on the party against whom the default was taken, the default, and default judgment if one has been entered, may only be set aside if the motion is filed

(a) before entry of judgment, or

(b) if judgment has been entered, within 21 days after the default was entered.

(3) In addition, the court may set aside an entry of default and a judgment by default in accordance with MCR 2.612.

(4) An order setting aside the default must be conditioned on the party against whom the default was taken paying the taxable costs incurred by the other party in reliance on the default, except as prescribed in MCR 2.625(D). The order may also impose other conditions the court deems proper, including a reasonable attorney fee.

(E) Application to Parties Other Than Plaintiff. The provisions of this rule apply whether the party entitled to the judgment by default is a plaintiff or a party who pleaded a cross-claim or counterclaim. In all cases a judgment by default is subject to the limitations of MCR 2.601(B).

[Effective March 1, 1985; amended effective January 1, 1995.]

1985 Staff Comment

MCR 2.603 corresponds to GCR 1963, 520 and DCR 520.

Subrule (A)(2) retains the distinction between circuit and district court practice regarding notice of the entry of default. In the district court, the clerk sends the notice (see DCR 520.1); in all other courts, the party who sought entry of the default does so (see GCR 1963, 520.1). In addition, a defaulted party—even one who has not filed an appearance—is to be given notice of the entry of default. This notice may be mailed to the defaulted defendant's last known address or the place of service.

Similarly, subrule (B)(1) requires the sending of notice to the defaulted party if the request for judgment seeks relief of a different kind or a greater amount than that stated in the pleadings. See MCR 2.601(B).

The provisions of subrules (B)(2) and (3), regarding entry of default judgment by the clerk and by the court, are substantially the same as the provisions of both GCR 1963, 520.2 and DCR 520.2(1) and (2) (although the requirement of notice to a defaulted defendant who has appeared is moved to subrule (B)[1]).

Subrule (B)(4) adopts the district court rule (DCR 520.2[3]) requiring that the clerk give notice to all parties (including the defendant in default) of the entry of the default judgment.

Subrule (D) changes the time within which a defendant who was actually served must move to set aside a default judgment on grounds other than those provided in MCR 2.612. Under GCR 1963, 520.4 the motion was required to be filed before entry of judgment or within 4 months after entry of the default, whichever was later. Under subrule (D)(2), the motion must be filed before entry of judgment or, if judgment has been entered, within 21 days after entry of the default. If the motion is not filed within this time, the party must proceed under MCR 2.612.

The form of default found in GCR 1963, 520.7 is omitted.

Staff Comment to 1995 Amendment

The November 1994 amendment of paragraph (D) [effective January 1, 1995] clarified that attorney fees may be included among the taxable costs upon which an order setting aside a default must be conditioned. The Court of Appeals held to the contrary in *Webb v. Watts (On Remand)*, 194 Mich App 529 (1992). The Supreme Court vacated the judgment of the Court of Appeals and dismissed the appeal in *Webb* for lack of a proper party defendant. 443 Mich 862 (1993).

RULE 2.604   JUDGMENT IN ACTIONS INVOLVING MULTIPLE CLAIMS OR MULTIPLE PARTIES

(A) Except as provided in subrule (B), an order or other form of decision adjudicating fewer than all the claims, or the rights and liabilities of fewer than all the parties, does not terminate the action as to any of the claims or parties, and the order is subject to revision before entry of final judgment adjudicating all the claims and the rights and liabilities of all the parties. Such an order or other form of decision is not appealable as of right before entry of final judgment. A party may file an application for leave to appeal from such an order.

(B) In receivership and similar actions, the court may direct that an order entered before adjudication of all of the claims and rights and liabilities of all the parties constitutes a final order on an express determination that there is no just reason for delay.

[Effective March 1, 1985; amended effective July 1, 1995; September 19, 1995.]

1985 Staff Comment

MCR 2.604 contains the provisions regarding judgments in actions involving multiple claims or parties previously found in GCR 1963, 518.2.

Staff Comment to July, 1995 Amendment

The amendment of MCR 2.604 eliminates the procedure under which a trial court could direct entry of final judgment on an order disposing of fewer than all the claims or parties, permitting an immediate appeal of right from such orders.

Staff Comment to September, 1995 Amendment

The September 19, 1995, amendment of MCR 2.604 permits a trial court to direct entry of final judgment on an order disposing of fewer than all the claims or parties in receivership and similar actions.

RULE 2.605   DECLARATORY JUDGMENTS

(A) Power to Enter Declaratory Judgment.

(1) In a case of actual controversy within its jurisdiction, a Michigan court of record may declare the rights and other legal relations of an interested party seeking a declaratory judgment, whether or not other relief is or could be sought or granted.

(2) For the purpose of this rule, an action is considered within the jurisdiction of a court if the court would have jurisdiction of an action on the same claim or claims in which the plaintiff sought relief other than a declaratory judgment.

(B) Procedure. The procedure for obtaining declaratory relief is in accordance with these rules, and the right to trial by jury may be demanded under the circumstances and in the manner provided in the constitution, statutes, and court rules of the State of Michigan.

(C) Other Adequate Remedy. The existence of another adequate remedy does not preclude a judgment for declaratory relief in an appropriate case.

(D) Hearing. The court may order a speedy hearing of an action for declaratory relief and may advance it on the calendar.

(E) Effect; Review. Declaratory judgments have the force and effect of, and are reviewable as, final judgments.

(F) Other Relief. Further necessary or proper relief based on a declaratory judgment may be granted, after reasonable notice and hearing, against a party whose rights have been determined by the declaratory judgment.

[Effective March 1, 1985.]

1985 Staff Comment

MCR 2.605 is comparable to GCR 1963, 521. The District Court Rules did not include such a provision.

Additional language is included in subrule (A) expressly stating that while any court of record has the power to enter a declaratory judgment, it may do so only in a case of which it otherwise would have jurisdiction.

RULE 2.610 MOTION FOR JUDGMENT NOTWITHSTANDING THE VERDICT

(A) Motion.

(1) Within 21 days after entry of judgment, a party may move to have the verdict and judgment set aside, and to have judgment entered in the moving party's favor. The motion may be joined with a motion for a new trial, or a new trial may be requested in the alternative.

(2) If a verdict was not returned, a party may move for judgment within 21 days after the jury is discharged.

(3) A motion to set aside or otherwise nullify a verdict or a motion for a new trial is deemed to include a motion for judgment notwithstanding the verdict as an alternative.

(B) Ruling.

(1) If a verdict was returned, the court may allow the judgment to stand or may reopen the judgment and either order a new trial or direct the entry of judgment as requested in the motion.

(2) If a verdict was not returned, the court may direct the entry of judgment as requested in the motion or order a new trial.

(3) In ruling on a motion under this rule, the court must give a concise statement of the reasons for the ruling, either in a signed order or opinion filed in the action, or on the record.

(C) Conditional Ruling on Motion for New Trial.

(1) If the motion for judgment notwithstanding the verdict under subrule (A) is granted, the court shall also conditionally rule on any motion for a new trial, determining whether it should be granted if the judgment is vacated or reversed, and shall specify the grounds for granting or denying the motion for a new trial.

(2) A conditional ruling under this subrule has the following effects:

(a) If the motion for a new trial is conditionally granted, that ruling does not affect the finality of the judgment.

(b) If the motion for a new trial is conditionally granted and the judgment is reversed on appeal, the new trial proceeds unless the appellate court orders otherwise.

(c) If the motion for a new trial is conditionally denied, on appeal the appellee may assert error in that denial. If the judgment is reversed on appeal, subsequent proceedings are in accordance with the order of the appellate court.

(D) Motion for New Trial After Ruling.

The party whose verdict has been set aside on a motion for judgment notwithstanding the verdict may serve and file a motion for a new trial pursuant to MCR 2.611 within 14 days after entry of judgment. A party who fails to move for a new trial as provided in this subrule has waived the right to move for a new trial.

(E) Appeal After Denial of Motion.

(1) If the motion for judgment notwithstanding the verdict is denied, the party who prevailed on that motion may, as appellee, assert grounds entitling that party to a new trial if the appellate court concludes that the trial court erred in denying the motion for judgment notwithstanding the verdict.

(2) If the appellate court reverses the judgment, nothing in this rule precludes it from determining that the appellee is entitled to a new trial, or from directing the trial court to determine whether a new trial should be granted.

[Effective March 1, 1985.]

1985 Staff Comment

MCR 2.610 is based on GCR 1963, 515.2, 515.3, and 812.8, concerning motions for judgment notwithstanding the verdict.

Subrule (A) does not include the requirement of GCR 1963, 515.2 that a party move for directed verdict as a condition of the right to move for judgment notwithstanding the verdict.

RULE 2.611 NEW TRIALS; AMENDMENT OF JUDGMENTS

(A) Grounds.

(1) A new trial may be granted to all or some of the parties, on all or some of the issues, whenever their substantial rights are materially affected, for any of the following reasons:

(a) Irregularity in the proceedings of the court, jury, or prevailing party, or an order of the court or abuse of discretion which denied the moving party a fair trial.

(b) Misconduct of the jury or of the prevailing party.

(c) Excessive or inadequate damages appearing to have been influenced by passion or prejudice.

(d) A verdict clearly or grossly inadequate or excessive.

(e) A verdict or decision against the great weight of the evidence or contrary to law.

(f) Material evidence, newly discovered, which could not with reasonable diligence have been discovered and produced at trial.

(g) Error of law occurring in the proceedings, or mistake of fact by the court.

(h) A ground listed in MCR 2.612 warranting a new trial.

(2) On a motion for a new trial in an action tried without a jury, the court may

(a) set aside the judgment if one has been entered,

(b) take additional testimony,

(c) amend findings of fact and conclusions of law, or

(d) make new findings and conclusions and direct the entry of a new judgment.

(B) Time for Motion. A motion for a new trial made under this rule or a motion to alter or amend a judgment must be filed and served within 21 days after entry of the judgment.

(C) On Initiative of Court. Within 21 days after entry of a judgment, the court on its own initiative may order a new trial for a reason for which it might have granted a new trial on motion of a party. The order must specify the grounds on which it is based.

(D) Affidavits.

(1) If the facts stated in the motion for a new trial or to amend the judgment do not appear on the record of the action, the motion must be supported by affidavit, which must be filed and served with the motion.

(2) The opposing party has 21 days after service within which to file and serve opposing affidavits. The period may be extended by the parties by written stipulation for 21 additional days, or may be extended or shortened by the court for good cause shown.

(3) The court may permit reply affidavits and may call and examine witnesses.

(E) Remittitur and Additur.

(1) If the court finds that the only error in the trial is the inadequacy or excessiveness of the verdict, it may deny a motion for new trial on condition that within 14 days the nonmoving party consent in writing to the entry of judgment in an amount found by the court to be the lowest (if the verdict was inadequate) or highest (if the verdict was excessive) amount the evidence will support.

(2) If the moving party appeals, the agreement in no way prejudices the nonmoving party's argument on appeal that the original verdict was correct. If the nonmoving party prevails, the original verdict may be reinstated by the appellate court.

(F) Ruling on Motion. In ruling on a motion for a new trial or a motion to amend the judgment, the court shall give a concise statement of the reasons for the ruling, either in an order or opinion filed in the action or on the record.

(G) Notice of Decision. The clerk must notify the parties of the decision on the motion for a new trial, unless the decision is made on the record while the parties are present.

[Effective March 1, 1985.]

1985 Staff Comment

MCR 2.611 is substantially the same as GCR 1963, 527.

RULE 2.612   RELIEF FROM JUDGMENT OR ORDER

(A) Clerical Mistakes.

(1) Clerical mistakes in judgments, orders, or other parts of the record and errors arising from oversight or omission may be corrected by the court at any time on its own initiative or on motion of a party and after notice, if the court orders it.

(2) If a claim of appeal is filed or an appellate court grants leave to appeal, the trial court may correct errors as provided in MCR 7.208(A) and (B).

(B) Defendant Not Personally Notified. A defendant over whom personal jurisdiction was necessary and acquired, but who did not in fact have knowledge of the pendency of the action, may enter an appearance within 1 year after final judgment, and if the defendant shows reason justifying relief from the judgment and innocent third persons will not be prejudiced, the court may relieve the defendant from the judgment, order, or proceedings for which personal jurisdiction was necessary, on payment of costs or on conditions the court deems just.

(C) Grounds for Relief From Judgment.

(1) On motion and on just terms, the court may relieve a party or the legal representative of a party from a final judgment, order, or proceeding on the following grounds:

(a) Mistake, inadvertence, surprise, or excusable neglect.

(b) Newly discovered evidence which by due diligence could not have been discovered in time to move for a new trial under MCR 2.611(B).

(c) Fraud (intrinsic or extrinsic), misrepresentation, or other misconduct of an adverse party.

(d) The judgment is void.

(e) The judgment has been satisfied, released, or discharged; a prior judgment on which it is based has been reversed or otherwise vacated; or it is no longer equitable that the judgment should have prospective application.

(f) Any other reason justifying relief from the operation of the judgment.

(2) The motion must be made within a reasonable time, and, for the grounds stated in subrules (C)(1)(a), (b), and (c), within one year after the judgment, order, or proceeding was entered or taken. A motion under this subrule does not affect the finality of a judgment or suspend its operation.

(3) This subrule does not limit the power of a court to entertain an independent action to relieve a party from a judgment, order, or proceeding; to grant relief

to a defendant not actually personally notified as provided in subrule (B); or to set aside a judgment for fraud on the court.

[Effective March 1, 1985.]

1985 Staff Comment

MCR 2.612 is comparable to GCR 1963, 528.

Subrule (A)(2) refers to MCR 7.208, which changes the time when the trial court's authority to correct the record ends after an appeal is taken. The trial court may do so until the record is sent to the appellate court. However, after a claim of appeal is filed or the appellate court has granted leave to appeal, notice to the parties is required before such a correction is made.

In subrule (B) the word "conditions" is substituted for "creditors" used in GCR 1963, 528.2.

RULE 2.613 LIMITATIONS ON CORRECTIONS OF ERROR

(A) Harmless Error. An error in the admission or the exclusion of evidence, an error in a ruling or order, or an error or defect in anything done or omitted by the court or by the parties is not ground for granting a new trial, for setting aside a verdict, or for vacating, modifying, or otherwise disturbing a judgment or order, unless refusal to take this action appears to the court inconsistent with substantial justice.

(B) Correction of Error by Other Judges. A judgment or order may be set aside or vacated, and a proceeding under a judgment or order may be stayed, only by the judge who entered the judgment or order, unless that judge is absent or unable to act. If the judge who entered the judgment or order is absent or unable to act, an order vacating or setting aside the judgment or order or staying proceedings under the judgment or order may be entered by a judge otherwise empowered to rule in the matter.

(C) Review of Findings by Trial Court. Findings of fact by the trial court may not be set aside unless clearly erroneous. In the application of this principle, regard shall be given to the special opportunity of the trial court to judge the credibility of the witnesses who appeared before it.

[Effective March 1, 1985.]

1985 Staff Comment

MCR 2.613 includes the provisions of GCR 1963, 529, and the language from GCR 1963, 517.1 that the trial court's findings are not to be set aside unless clearly erroneous.

RULE 2.614 STAY OF PROCEEDINGS TO ENFORCE JUDGMENT

(A) Automatic Stay; Exceptions: Injunctions, Receiverships, and Family Litigation.

(1) Except as provided in this rule, execution may not issue on a judgment and proceedings may not be taken for its enforcement until the expiration of 21 days after its entry. If a motion for new trial, a motion to alter or amend the judgment, a motion for judgment notwithstanding the verdict, or a motion to amend or for additional findings of the court is filed and served within 21 days after entry of the judgment, execution may not issue on the judgment and proceedings may not be taken for its enforcement until the expiration of 21 days after the entry of the order on the motion, unless otherwise ordered by the court on motion for good cause. Nothing in this rule prohibits the court from enjoining the transfer or disposition of property during the 21-day period.

(2) The following orders may be enforced immediately after entry unless the court orders otherwise on motion for good cause:

(a) A temporary restraining order.

(b) A preliminary injunction.

(c) Injunctive relief included in a final judgment.

(d) An interlocutory order in a receivership action.

(e) In a domestic relations action, an order before judgment concerning the custody, control, and management of property; for temporary alimony; or for support or custody of minor children and expenses.

(3) Subrule (C) governs the suspending, modifying, restoring, or granting of an injunction during the pendency of an appeal.

(B) Stay on Motion for Relief From Judgment. In its discretion and on proper conditions for the security of the adverse party, the court may stay the execution of, or proceedings to enforce, a judgment pending the disposition of a motion for relief from a judgment or order under MCR 2.612.

(C) Injunction Pending Appeal. If an appeal is taken from an interlocutory or final judgment granting, dissolving, or denying an injunction, the court may suspend, modify, restore, or grant an injunction during the pendency of the appeal on terms as to bond or otherwise that are proper for the security of the adverse party's rights.

(D) Stay on Appeal. Stay on appeal is governed by MCR 7.101(H), 7.209, and 7.302(G).

(E) Stay in Favor of Governmental Party. In an action or proceeding in which the state, an authorized state officer, a corporate body in charge of a state institution, or a municipal corporation, is a party, bond may not be required of that party as a prerequisite to taking an appeal or making an order staying proceedings.

(F) Power of Appellate Court Not Limited. This rule does not limit the power of the Court of Appeals or the Supreme Court to

(1) stay proceedings during the pendency of an appeal before them;

(2) suspend, modify, restore, or grant an injunction during the pendency of the appeal; or

(3) enter an order appropriate to preserve the status quo or effectiveness of the judgment to be entered.

(G) Stay of Judgment on Multiple Claims. When a court has ordered a final judgment on some, but not all, of the claims presented in the action under the conditions stated in MCR 2.604(B), the court may

(1) stay enforcement of the judgment until the entry of a later judgment or judgments, and

(2) prescribe conditions necessary to secure the benefit of the judgment to the party in whose favor it was entered.

[Effective March 1, 1985; amended effective September 19, 1995.]

1985 Staff Comment

MCR 2.614 is based on GCR 1963, 530.

Language is added to subrule (A)(1) to make clear that the trial court has the authority to enjoin the transfer of property during the automatic stay.

In subrule (A)(2) final injunctive orders are added to the list of orders which are not automatically stayed during the time for taking an appeal of right.

The provisions of GCR 1963, 530.4 regarding stays on appeal are replaced with a cross-reference to the appropriate provisions in the rules governing appeals. See subrule (D).

The references to the granting of a stay of proceedings by a single judge of the Court of Appeals or the Supreme Court, found in GCR 1963, 530.6, are omitted. See subrule (F).

Staff Comment to 1995 Amendment

The amendments of MCR 2.116(J)(1), 2.119(F)(1), 2.204(A)(4), and 2.614(G) correct cross-references to MCR 2.604 that were no longer correct after MCR 2.604 was amended on May 16, 1995, and further amended on September 19, 1995.

RULE 2.615 ENFORCEMENT OF TRIBAL JUDGMENTS

(A) The judgments, decrees, orders, warrants, subpoenas, records, and other judicial acts of a tribal court of a federally recognized Indian tribe are recognized, and have the same effect and are subject to the same procedures, defenses, and proceedings as judgments, decrees, orders, warrants, subpoenas, records, and other judicial acts of any court of record in this state, subject to the provisions of this rule.

(B) The recognition described in subrule (A) applies only if the tribe or tribal court

(1) enacts an ordinance, court rule, or other binding measure that obligates the tribal court to enforce the judgments, decrees, orders, warrants, subpoenas, records, and judicial acts of the courts of this state, and

(2) transmits the ordinance, court rule or other measure to the State Court Administrative Office. The State Court Administrative Office shall make available to state courts the material received pursuant to paragraph (B)(1).

(C) A judgment, decree, order, warrant, subpoena, record, or other judicial act of a tribal court of a federally recognized Indian tribe that has taken the actions described in subrule (B) is presumed to be valid. To overcome that presumption, an objecting party must demonstrate that

(1) the tribal court lacked personal or subject-matter jurisdiction, or

(2) the judgment, decree, order, warrant, subpoena, record, or other judicial act of the tribal court

(a) was obtained by fraud, duress, or coercion,

(b) was obtained without fair notice or a fair hearing,

(c) is repugnant to the public policy of the State of Michigan, or

(d) is not final under the laws and procedures of the tribal court.

(D) This rule does not apply to judgments or orders that federal law requires be given full faith and credit.

[Adopted effective July 1, 1996.]

1996 Staff Comment

The 1996 amendment of MCR 2.112(G) and (J) and the 1996 promulgation of MCR 2.615 were prompted by proposals from the Indian Tribal Court/State Trial Court Forum and from the State Bar of Michigan. The adopted rules reflect a synthesis of those sources, of a corresponding rule of the North Dakota Supreme Court, and of the model rules generated by the Michigan Indian Judicial Association.

RULE 2.620 SATISFACTION OF JUDGMENT

A judgment may be shown satisfied of record in whole or in part by:

(1) filing with the clerk a satisfaction signed and acknowledged by the party or parties in whose favor the judgment was rendered, or their attorneys of record;

(2) payment to the clerk of the judgment, interest, and costs, if it is a money judgment only; or

(3) filing a motion for entry of an order that the judgment has been satisfied.

The court shall hear proofs to determine whether the order should be entered.

The clerk must, in each instance, indicate in the court records that the judgment is satisfied in whole or in part.

[Effective March 1, 1985.]

1985 Staff Comment

MCR 2.620 is substantially the same as GCR 1963, 524.

RULE 2.621 PROCEEDINGS SUPPLEMENTARY TO JUDGMENT

(A) Relief Under These Rules. When a party to a civil action obtains a money judgment, that party may, by motion in that action or by a separate civil action:

(1) obtain the relief formerly obtainable by a creditor's bill;

(2) obtain relief supplementary to judgment under MCL 600.6101–600.6143; MSA 27A.6101–27A.6143; and

(3) obtain other relief in aid of execution authorized by statute or court rule.

(B) Pleading.

(1) If the motion or complaint seeks to reach an equitable interest of a debtor, it must be verified, and

 (a) state the amount due the creditor on the judgment, over and above all just claims of the debtor by way of setoff or otherwise, and

 (b) show that the debtor has equitable interests exceeding $100 in value.

(2) The judgment creditor may obtain relief under MCL 600.6110; MSA 27A.6110, and discovery under subchapter 2.300 of these rules.

(C) Subpoenas and Orders. A subpoena or order to enjoin the transfer of assets pursuant to MCL 600.6119; MSA 27A.6119 must be served under MCR 2.105. The subpoena must specify the amount claimed by the judgment creditor. The court shall endorse its approval of the issuance of the subpoena on the original subpoena, which must be filed in the action. The subrule does not apply to subpoenas for ordinary witnesses.

(D) Order Directing Delivery of Property or Money.

(1) When a court orders the payment of money or delivery of personal property to an officer who has possession of the writ of execution, the order may be entered on notice the court deems just, or without notice.

(2) If a receiver has been appointed, or a receivership has been extended to the supplementary proceeding, the order may direct the payment of money or delivery of property to the receiver.

(E) Receivers. When necessary to protect the rights of a judgment creditor, the court may appoint a receiver in a proceeding under subrule (A)(2), pending the determination of the proceeding.

(F) Violation of Injunction. The court may punish for contempt a person who violates the restraining provision of an order or subpoena or, if the person is not the judgment debtor, may enter judgment against the person in the amount of the unpaid portion of the judgment and costs allowed by law or these rules or in the amount of the value of the property transferred, whichever is less.

(G) New Proceeding. If there has been a prior supplementary proceeding with respect to the same judgment against the party, whether the judgment debtor or another person, further proceedings may be commenced against that party only by leave of court. Leave may be granted on ex parte motion of the judgment creditor, but only on a finding by the court, based on affidavit of the judgment creditor or another person having personal knowledge of the facts, other than the attorney of the judgment creditor. The affidavit must state that

(1) there is reason to believe that the party against whom the proceeding is sought to be commenced has property or income the creditor is entitled to reach, or, if a third party, is indebted to the judgment debtor;

(2) the existence of the property, income, or indebtedness was not known to the judgment creditor during the pendency of a prior supplementary proceeding; and

(3) the additional supplementary proceeding is sought in good faith to discover assets and not to harass the judgment debtor or third party.

(H) Appeal; Procedure; Bonds. A final order entered in a supplementary proceeding may be appealed in the usual manner. The appeal is governed by the provisions of chapter 7 of these rules except as modified by this subrule.

(1) The appellant must give a bond to the effect that he or she will pay all costs and damages that may be awarded against him or her on the appeal. If the appeal is by the judgment creditor, the amount of the bond may not exceed $200, and subrules (H)(2)–(4) do not apply. If the appeal is by a party other than the judgment creditor, subrules (H)(2)–(4) apply.

(2) If the order appealed from is for the payment of money or the delivery of property, the bond of the appellant must be in an amount at least double the amount of the money or property ordered to be paid or delivered. The bond must be on the condition that if the order appealed from is affirmed in whole or in part the appellant will

 (a) pay the amount directed to be paid or deliver the property in as good condition as it is at the time of the appeal, and

 (b) pay all damages and costs that may be awarded against the appellant.

(3) If the order appealed from directs the assignment or delivery of papers or documents by the appellant, the papers must be delivered to the clerk of

the court in which the proceeding is pending or placed in the hands of an officer or receiver, as the judge who entered the order directs, to await the appeal, subject to the order of the appellate courts.

(4) If the order appealed from directs the sale of real estate of the appellant or delivery of possession by the appellant, the appeal bond must also provide that during the possession of the property by the appellant, or any person holding under the appellant, he or she will not commit or suffer any waste of the property, and that if the order is affirmed he or she will pay the value of the use of the property from the time of appeal until the delivery of possession.

[Effective March 1, 1985.]

1985 Staff Comment

MCR 2.621 is substantially the same as GCR 1963, 741.

Subrule (C) allows subpoenas and orders under the rule to be served by any of the methods specified in MCR 2.105. Compare GCR 1963, 741.3, which did not allow substituted service under GCR 1963, 105.2.

RULE 2.622 RECEIVERS IN SUPPLEMENTARY PROCEEDINGS

(A) Powers and Duties.

(1) A receiver of the property of a debtor appointed pursuant to MCL 600.6104(4); MSA 27A.6104(4) has, unless restricted by special order of the court, general power and authority to sue for and collect all the debts, demands, and rents belonging to the debtor, and to compromise and settle those that are unsafe and of doubtful character.

(2) A receiver may sue in the name of the debtor when it is necessary or proper to do so, and may apply for an order directing the tenants of real estate belonging to the debtor, or of which the debtor is entitled to the rents, to pay their rents to the receiver.

(3) A receiver may make leases as may be necessary, for terms not exceeding one year.

(4) A receiver may convert the personal property into money, but may not sell real estate of the debtor without a special order of the court.

(5) A receiver is not allowed the costs of a suit brought by the receiver against an insolvent person from whom the receiver is unable to collect the costs, unless the suit is brought by order of the court or by consent of all persons interested in the funds in the receiver's hands.

(6) A receiver may sell doubtful debts and doubtful claims to personal property at public auction, giving at least 7 days' notice of the time and place of the sale.

(7) A receiver must give security to cover the property of the debtor that may come into the receiver's hands, and must hold the property for the benefit of all creditors who have commenced, or will commence, similar proceedings during the continuance of the receivership.

(8) A receiver may not pay the funds in his or her hands to the parties or to another person without an order of the court.

(9) A receiver may only be discharged from the trust on order of the court.

(B) Notice When Other Action or Proceeding Pending; Appointment.

(1) The court shall ascertain, if practicable, by the oath of the judgment debtor or otherwise, whether another action or motion under MCR 2.621 is pending against the judgment debtor.

(2) If another action or motion under MCR 2.621 is pending and a receiver has not been appointed in that proceeding, notice of the application for the appointment of a receiver and of all subsequent proceedings respecting the receivership must be given, as directed by the court, to the judgment creditor prosecuting the other action or motion.

(3) If several actions or motions under MCR 2.621 are filed by different creditors against the same debtor, only one receiver may be appointed, unless the first appointment was obtained by fraud or collusion, or the receiver is an improper person to execute the trust.

(4) If another proceeding is commenced after the appointment of a receiver, the same person may be appointed receiver in the subsequent proceeding, and must give further security as the court directs. The receiver must keep a separate account of the property of the debtor acquired since the commencement of the first proceeding, and of the property acquired under the appointment in the later proceeding.

(C) Claim of Adverse Interest in Property.

(1) If a person brought before the court by the judgment creditor under MCR 2.621 claims an interest in the property adverse to the judgment debtor, and a receiver has been appointed, the interest may be recovered only in an action by the receiver.

(2) The court may by order forbid a transfer or other disposition of the interest until the receiver has sufficient opportunity to commence the action.

(3) The receiver may bring an action only at the request of the judgment creditor and at the judgment creditor's expense in case of failure. The receiver may require reasonable security against all costs before commencing the action.

(D) Expenses in Certain Cases. When there are no funds in the hands of the receiver at the termination of the receivership, the court, on application of the receiver, may set the receiver's compensation and the fees of the receiver's attorney for the services rendered, and may direct the party who moved for the appointment of the receiver to pay these sums in

addition to the necessary expenditures of the receiver. If more than one creditor sought the appointment of a receiver, the court may allocate the costs among them.

[Effective March 1, 1985.]

1985 Staff Comment

MCR 2.622 is substantially the same as GCR 1963, 742.

Subrule (D) adds language expressly authorizing the court to allocate expenses among multiple creditors.

RULE 2.625 TAXATION OF COSTS

(A) Right to Costs.

(1) *In General.* Costs will be allowed to the prevailing party in an action, unless prohibited by statute or by these rules or unless the court directs otherwise, for reasons stated in writing and filed in the action.

(2) *Frivolous Claims and Defenses.* In an action filed on or after October 1, 1986, if the court finds on motion of a party that an action or defense was frivolous, costs shall be awarded as provided by MCL 600.2591; MSA 27A.2591.

(B) Rules for Determining Prevailing Party.

(1) *Actions With Several Judgments.* If separate judgments are entered under MCR 2.116 or 2.505(A) and the plaintiff prevails in one judgment in an amount and under circumstances which would entitle the plaintiff to costs, he or she is deemed the prevailing party. Costs common to more than one judgment may be allowed only once.

(2) *Actions With Several Issues or Counts.* In an action involving several issues or counts that state different causes of action or different defenses, the party prevailing on each issue or count may be allowed costs for that issue or count. If there is a single cause of action alleged, the party who prevails on the entire record is deemed the prevailing party.

(3) *Actions With Several Defendants.* If there are several defendants in one action, and judgment for or dismissal of one or more of them is entered, those defendants are deemed prevailing parties, even though the plaintiff ultimately prevails over the remaining defendants.

(4) *Costs on Review in Circuit Court.* An appellant in the circuit court who improves his or her position on appeal is deemed the prevailing party.

(C) Costs in Certain Trivial Actions.
In an action brought for damages in contract or tort in which the plaintiff recovers less than $100 (unless the recovery is reduced below $100 by a counterclaim), the plaintiff may recover costs no greater than the amount of damages.

(D) Costs When Default or Default Judgment Set Aside.
The following provisions apply to an order setting aside a default or a default judgment:

(1) If personal jurisdiction was acquired over the defendant, the order must be conditioned on the defendant's paying or securing payment to the party seeking affirmative relief the taxable costs incurred in procuring the default or the default judgment and acting in reliance on it;

(2) If jurisdiction was acquired by publication, the order may be conditioned on the defendant's paying or securing payment to the party seeking affirmative relief all or a part of the costs as the court may direct;

(3) If jurisdiction was in fact not acquired, costs may not be imposed.

(E) Costs in Garnishment Proceedings.
Costs in garnishment proceedings are allowed as in civil actions. Costs may be awarded to the garnishee defendant as follows:

(1) The court may award the garnishee defendant as costs against the plaintiff reasonable attorney fees and other necessary expenses the garnishee defendant incurred in filing the disclosure, if the issue of the garnishee defendant's liability to the principal defendant is not brought to trial.

(2) The court may award the garnishee defendant, against the plaintiff, the total costs of the garnishee defendant's defense, including all necessary expenses and reasonable attorney fees, if the issue of the garnishee defendant's liability to the principal defendant is tried and

    (a) the garnishee defendant is held liable in a sum no greater than that admitted in disclosure, or

    (b) the plaintiff fails to recover judgment against the principal defendant.

In either (a) or (b), the garnishee defendant may withhold from the amount due the principal defendant the sum awarded for costs, and is chargeable only for the balance.

(F) Procedure for Taxing Costs.

(1) Costs may be taxed by the court on signing the judgment, or may be taxed by the clerk as provided in this subrule.

(2) When costs are to be taxed by the clerk, the party entitled to costs must present to the clerk, within 28 days after the judgment is signed, or within 28 days after entry of an order denying a motion for new trial, a motion to set aside the judgment, or a motion for other postjudgment relief except a motion under MCR 2.612(C),

    (a) a bill of costs conforming to subrule (G),

    (b) a copy of the bill of costs for each other party, and

    (c) a list of the names and addresses of the attorneys for each party or of parties not represented by attorneys.

In addition, the party presenting the bill of costs shall immediately serve a copy of the bill and any accompanying affidavits on the other parties. Failure to present a bill of costs within the time prescribed constitutes a waiver of the right to costs.

(3) Within 14 days after service of the bill of costs, another party may file objections to it, accompanied by affidavits if appropriate. After the time for filing objections, the clerk must promptly examine the bill and any objections or affidavits submitted and allow only those items that appear to be correct, striking all charges for services that in the clerk's judgment were not necessary. The clerk shall notify the parties in the manner provided in MCR 2.107.

(4) The action of the clerk is reviewable by the court on motion of any affected party filed within 7 days from the date that notice of the taxing of costs was sent, but on review only those affidavits or objections that were presented to the clerk may be considered by the court.

(G) Bill of Costs; Supporting Affidavits.

(1) Each item claimed in the bill of costs, except fees of officers for services rendered, must be specified particularly.

(2) The bill of costs must be verified and must contain a statement that

(a) each item of cost or disbursement claimed is correct and has been necessarily incurred in the action, and

(b) the services for which fees have been charged were actually performed.

(3) If witness fees are claimed, an affidavit in support of the bill of costs must state the distance traveled and the days actually attended. If fees are claimed for a party as a witness, the affidavit must state that the party actually testified as a witness on the days listed.

(H) Taxation of Fees on Settlement. Unless otherwise specified a settlement is deemed to include the payment of any costs that might have been taxable.

(I) Special Costs or Damages.

(1) In an action in which the plaintiff's claim is reduced by a counterclaim, or another fact appears that would entitle either party to costs, to multiple costs, or to special damages for delay or otherwise, the court shall, on the application of either party, have that fact entered in the records of the court. A taxing officer may receive no evidence of the matter other than a certified copy of the court records or the certificate of the judge who entered the judgment.

(2) Whenever multiple costs are awarded to a party, they belong to the party. Officers, witnesses, jurors, or other persons claiming fees for services rendered in the action are entitled only to the amount prescribed by law.

(3) A judgment for multiple damages under a statute entitles the prevailing party to single costs only, except as otherwise specially provided by statute or by these rules.

[Effective March 1, 1985; amended effective December 12, 1986; July 1, 2001.]

1985 Staff Comment

MCR 2.625 is comparable to GCR 1963, 526.

Subrule (C) would make the provision of GCR 1963, 526.6, limiting the availability of costs when less than $100 is recovered, applicable to all courts. Compare DCR 526.6.

Subrule (D)(3) slightly modifies the language previously found in GCR 1963, 526.8(3). The former provision said that if jurisdiction had not been acquired over the defendant, an order setting aside the default judgment was to be "without condition" as to costs. The new rule provides that in such a circumstance costs may not be imposed.

Subrule (F) includes several modifications regarding the taxing of costs by the clerk. The party submitting the bill of costs is to provide a copy for each other party, along with the addresses of their attorneys (or of parties not represented by attorneys). Subrule (F)(2) expressly requires service of the bill of costs. Subrule (F)(3) adds specific requirements that the clerk examine objections or affidavits that have been submitted and that the clerk notify the parties of the taxing of costs. In subrule (F)(4) the time for seeking review of the clerk's action by the court is modified. The time begins to run not from the date of taxing of costs, but from the date notice of the taxing was sent. Compare GCR 1963, 526.10(3).

The [March 1, 1985] amendment of MCR 2.625(F)(3) clarifies the time within which objections to a proposed bill of costs may be filed. The opposing party has 14 days within which to serve objections, and the clerk is to examine the bill promptly thereafter.

Subrule (H) is new, and provides that when a claim is settled, the settlement is deemed to include the payment of all taxable costs.

The language in subrule (I)(1) is modified to make clear that when the clerk taxes the costs, the notice is to be given by the party entitled to costs, not by the clerk.

The provisions found in GCR 1963, 526.7 and 526.14, regarding summary judgment and bond costs, are omitted. Those matters are covered by MCR 2.116(F) and by statute. See MCL 600.2405, 600.2441(2); MSA 27A.2405, 27A.2441(2).

Staff Comment to 2001 Amendment

The April 3, 2001 amendment of MCR 2.625(F)(2), effective July 1, 2001, expanded the categories of postjudgment motions that extend the initial 28-day deadline for presenting a bill of costs. An exception is a motion under MCR 2.612(C), which does not extend the deadline.

RULE 2.626   Attorney Fees

An award of attorney fees may include an award for the time and labor of any legal assistant who contributed nonclerical, legal support under the supervision of an attorney, provided the legal assistant meets the criteria set forth in Article 1, § 6 of the Bylaws of the State Bar of Michigan.

[Adopted effective January 1, 2001.]

The October 24, 2000, adoption of MCR 2.626, effective January 1, 2001, was based on a proposal from the Representative Assembly of the State Bar of Michigan, in response to *Joerger v Gordon Food Service Inc*, 224 Mich App 167 (1997).

RULE 2.630 DISABILITY OF JUDGE

If, after a verdict is returned or findings of fact and conclusions of law are filed, the judge before whom an action has been tried is unable to perform the duties prescribed by these rules because of death, illness, or other disability, another judge regularly sitting in or assigned to the court in which the action was tried may perform those duties. However, if the substitute judge is not satisfied that he or she can do so, the substitute judge may grant a new trial.

[Effective March 1, 1985.]

MCR 2.630 is substantially the same as GCR 1963, 531.

CHAPTER 3. SPECIAL PROCEEDINGS AND ACTIONS

Effective March 1, 1985

[For Table of Rules, see page 1 et seq.]

SUBCHAPTER 3.000   GENERAL PROVISIONS

RULE 3.001   APPLICABILITY

The rules in this chapter apply in circuit court and in other courts as provided by law or by these rules. [Effective March 1, 1985.]

1985 Staff Comment

MCR 3.001 is new.

The rules in chapter 3 govern various special proceedings that were provided for by the General Court Rules, generally in the GCR 1963, 700 series. Some of these proceedings are available only in circuit court; others can be brought in other courts, at least in some circumstances.

SUBCHAPTER 3.100   DEBTOR–CREDITOR

RULE 3.101   GARNISHMENT AFTER JUDGMENT

(A) Definitions. In this rule,

(1) "plaintiff" refers to any judgment creditor,

(2) "defendant" refers to any judgment debtor,

(3) "garnishee" refers to the garnishee defendant,

(4) "periodic payments" includes but is not limited to, wages, salary, commissions, bonuses, and other income paid to the defendant during the period of the writ; land contract payments; rent; and other periodic debt or contract payments. Interest payments and other payments listed in MCL 600.4012(4)(a)–(d); MSA 27A.4012(4)(a)–(d) are not periodic payments.

(B) Postjudgment Garnishments.

(1) Periodic garnishments are garnishments of periodic payments, as provided in this rule.

(a) Unless otherwise ordered by the court, a writ of periodic garnishment served on a garnishee who is obligated to make periodic payments to the defendant is effective until the first to occur of the following events:

(i) the amount withheld pursuant to the writ equals the amount of the unpaid judgment, interest, and costs stated in the verified statement in support of the writ;

(ii) the expiration of 91 days after the date the writ was issued;

(iii) the plaintiff files and serves on the defendant and the garnishee a notice that the amount withheld exceeds the remaining unpaid judgment, interest, and costs, or that the judgment has otherwise been satisfied.

(b) The plaintiff may not obtain the issuance of a second writ of garnishment on a garnishee who is obligated to make periodic payments to the defendant while a prior writ served on that garnishee remains in effect relating to the same judgment. The plaintiff may seek a second writ after the first writ expires under subrule (B)(1)(a).

(c) If a writ of periodic garnishment is served on a garnishee who is obligated to make periodic payments to the defendant while another order that has priority under MCL 600.4012(2); MSA 27A.4012(2) is in effect, or if a writ or order with higher priority is served on the garnishee while another writ is in effect, the garnishee is not obligated to withhold payments pursuant to the lower priority writ until the expiration of the higher priority one. However, in the case of garnishment of earnings, the garnishee shall withhold pursuant to the lower priority writ to the extent that the amount being withheld pursuant to the higher priority order is less than the maximum that could be withheld by law pursuant to the lower priority writ (see, e.g., 15 USC 1673). Upon the expiration of the higher priority writ, the lower priority one becomes effective until it would otherwise have expired under subrule (B)(1)(a). The garnishee shall notify the plaintiff of receipt of any higher priority writ or order and provide the information required by subrule (H)(2)(c).

(2) Nonperiodic garnishments are garnishments of property or obligations other than periodic payments.

(C) Forms. The state court administrator shall publish approved forms for use in garnishment proceedings. Separate forms shall be used for periodic and nonperiodic garnishments. The verified statement, writ, and disclosure filed in garnishment proceedings must be substantially in the form approved by the state court administrator.

(D) Request for and Issuance of Writ. The clerk of the court that entered the judgment shall issue a writ of garnishment if the plaintiff, or someone on the plaintiff's behalf, makes and files a statement verified in the manner provided in MCR 2.114(A) stating:

(1) that a judgment has been entered against the defendant and remains unsatisfied;

(2) the amount of the judgment and the amount remaining unpaid;

(3) that the person signing the verified statement knows or has good reason to believe that

(a) a named person has control of property belonging to the defendant,

(b) a named person is indebted to the defendant, or

(c) a named person is obligated to make periodic payments to the defendant.

(E) Writ of Garnishment.

(1) The writ of garnishment must have attached or must include a copy of the verified statement requesting issuance of the writ, and must include information that will permit the garnishee to identify the defendant, such as the defendant's address, social security number, employee identification number, federal tax identification number, employer number, or account number, if known.

(2) Upon issuance of the writ, it shall be served upon the garnishee as provided in subrule (F)(1). The writ shall include the date on which it was issued and the last day by which it must be served to be valid, which is 91 days after it was issued.

(3) The writ shall direct the garnishee to:

(a) serve a copy of the writ on the defendant as provided in subrule (F)(2);

(b) within 14 days after the service of the writ, file with the court clerk a verified disclosure indicating the garnishee's liability (as specified in subrule [G][1]) to the defendant and mail or deliver a copy to the plaintiff and the defendant;

(c) deliver no tangible or intangible property to the defendant, unless allowed by statute or court rule;

(d) pay no obligation to the defendant, unless allowed by statute or court rule; and

(e) in the discretion of the court and in accordance with subrule (J), order the garnishee either to

(i) make all payments directly to the plaintiff or

(ii) send the funds to the court in the manner specified in the writ.

(4) The writ shall direct the defendant to refrain from disposing of

(a) any negotiable instrument representing a debt of the garnishee (except the earnings of the defendant), or

(b) any negotiable instrument of title representing property in which the defendant claims an interest held in the possession or control of the garnishee.

(5) The writ shall inform the defendant that unless the defendant files objections within 14 days after the service of the writ on the defendant,

(a) without further notice the property or debt held pursuant to the garnishment may be applied to the satisfaction of the plaintiff's judgment, and

(b) periodic payments due to the defendant may be withheld for as long as 91 days after the issuance of the writ and in the discretion of the court paid directly to the plaintiff.

(6) The writ shall direct the plaintiff to serve the garnishee as provided in subrule (F)(1), and to file a proof of service.

(F) Service of Writ.

(1) The plaintiff shall serve the writ of garnishment, a copy of the writ for the defendant, the disclosure form, and any applicable fees, on the garnishee within 91 days after the date the writ was issued in the manner provided for the service of a summons and complaint in MCR 2.105.

(2) The garnishee shall within 7 days after being served with the writ deliver a copy of the writ to the defendant or mail a copy to the defendant at the defendant's last known address by first class mail.

(G) Liability of Garnishee.

(1) Subject to the provisions of the garnishment statute and any setoff permitted by law or these rules, the garnishee is liable for

(a) all tangible or intangible property belonging to the defendant in the garnishee's possession or control when the writ is served on the garnishee, unless the property is represented by a negotiable document of title held by a bona fide purchaser for value other than the defendant;

(b) all negotiable documents of title and all goods represented by negotiable documents of title belonging to the defendant if the documents of title are in the garnishee's possession when the writ is served on the garnishee;

(c) all corporate share certificates belonging to the defendant in the garnishee's possession or control when the writ is served on the garnishee;

(d) all debts, whether or not due, owing by the garnishee to the defendant when the writ is served on the garnishee, except for debts evidenced by negotiable instruments or representing the earnings of the defendant;

(e) all debts owing by the garnishee evidenced by negotiable instruments held or owned by the defendant when the writ of garnishment is served on the defendant, as long as the instruments are brought before the court before their negotiation to a bona fide purchaser for value;

(f) the portion of the defendant's earnings that are not protected from garnishment by law (see, e.g., 15 USC 1673) as provided in subrule (B);

(g) all judgments in favor of the defendant against the garnishee in force when the writ is served on the garnishee;

(h) all tangible or intangible property of the defendant that, when the writ is served on the garnishee, the garnishee holds by conveyance, transfer, or title that is void as to creditors of the defendant, whether or not the defendant could maintain an action against the garnishee to recover the property; and

(i) the value of all tangible or intangible property of the defendant that, before the writ is served on the garnishee, the garnishee received or held by conveyance, transfer, or title that was void as to creditors of the defendant, but that the garnishee no longer held at the time the writ was served, whether or not the defendant could maintain an action against the garnishee for the value of the property.

(2) The garnishee is liable for no more than the amount of the unpaid judgment, interest, and costs as stated in the verified statement requesting the writ of garnishment. Property or debts exceeding that amount may be delivered or paid to the defendant notwithstanding the garnishment.

(H) Disclosure. The garnishee shall mail or deliver to the court, the plaintiff, and the defendant, a verified disclosure within 14 days after being served with the writ.

(1) *Nonperiodic Garnishments.*

(a) If indebted to the defendant, the garnishee shall file a disclosure revealing the garnishee's liability to the defendant as specified in subrule (G)(1) and claiming any setoff that the garnishee would have against the defendant, except for claims for unliquidated damages for wrongs or injuries.

(b) If not indebted to the defendant, the garnishee shall file a disclosure so indicating.

(2) *Periodic Garnishments.*

(a) If not obligated to make periodic payments to the defendant, the disclosure shall so indicate, and the garnishment shall be considered to have expired.

(b) If obligated to make periodic payments to the defendant, the disclosure shall indicate the nature and frequency of the garnishee's obligation. The information must be disclosed even if money is not owing at the time of the service of the writ.

(c) If a writ or order with a higher priority is in effect, in the disclosure the garnishee shall specify the court that issued the writ or order, the file number of the case in which it was issued, the date it was issued, and the date it was served.

(I) Withholding. This subrule applies only if the garnishee is indebted to or obligated to make periodic payments to the defendant.

(1) Except as otherwise provided in this subrule, the writ shall be effective as to obligations owed and property held by the garnishee as of the time the writ is served on the garnishee.

(2) In the case of periodic earnings, withholding shall commence according to the following provisions:

(a) For garnishees with weekly, biweekly, or semimonthly pay periods, withholding shall commence with the first full pay period after the writ was served.

(b) For garnishees with monthly pay periods, if the writ is served on the garnishee within the first 14 days of the pay period, withholding shall commence on the date the writ is served. If the writ is served on the garnishee on or after the 15th day of the pay period, withholding shall commence the first full pay period after the writ was served.

(3) In the case of periodic earnings, withholding shall cease according to the following provisions:

(a) For garnishees with weekly, biweekly, or semimonthly pay periods, withholding shall cease upon the end of the last full pay period prior to the expiration of the writ.

(b) For garnishees with monthly pay periods, withholding shall continue until the writ expires.

(4) At the time that a periodic payment is withheld, the garnishee shall provide the following information to the plaintiff and defendant:

(a) the name of the parties;

(b) the case number;

(c) the date and amount withheld;

(d) the balance due on the writ.

The information shall also be provided to the court if funds are sent to the court.

(5) If funds have not been withheld because a higher priority writ or order was in effect, and the higher priority writ ceases to be effective before expiration of the lower priority one, the garnishee shall begin withholding pursuant to the lower priority writ as of the date of the expiration of the higher priority writ.

(J) Payment.

(1) After 28 days from the date of the service of the writ on the garnishee, the garnishee shall transmit all withheld funds to the plaintiff or the court as directed by the court pursuant to subrule (E)(3)(e) unless notified that objections have been filed.

(2) For periodic garnishments, all future payments shall be paid as they become due as directed by the court pursuant to subrule (E)(3)(e) until expiration of the garnishment.

(3) Upon receipt of proceeds from the writ, the court shall forward such proceeds to the plaintiff.

(4) Payment to the plaintiff may not exceed the amount of the unpaid judgment, interest, and costs stated in the verified statement requesting the writ of garnishment. If the plaintiff claims to be entitled to a larger amount, the plaintiff must proceed by motion with notice to the defendant.

(5) In the case of earnings, the garnishee shall maintain a record of all payment calculations and shall make such information available for review by the plaintiff, the defendant, or the court, upon request.

(6) For periodic garnishments, within 14 days after the expiration of the writ or after the garnishee is no longer obligated to make periodic payments, the garnishee shall file with the court and mail or deliver to the plaintiff and the defendant, a final statement of the total amount paid on the writ. If the garnishee is the defendant's employer, the statement is to be filed within 14 days after the expiration of the writ, regardless of changes in employment status during the time that the writ was in effect. The statement shall include the following information:

(a) the names of the parties and the court in which the case is pending;

(b) the case number;

(c) the date of the statement;

(d) the total amount withheld;

(e) the difference between the amount stated in the verified statement requesting the writ and the amount withheld.

(7) If the disclosure states that the garnishee holds property other than money belonging to the defendant, the plaintiff must proceed by motion (with notice to the defendant and the garnishee) to seek an appropriate order regarding application of the property to satisfaction of the judgment. If there are no pending objections to the garnishment, and the plaintiff has not filed such a motion within 56 days after the filing of the disclosure, the garnishment is dissolved and the garnishee may release the property to the defendant.

(K) Objections.

(1) Objections shall be filed with the court within 14 days of the date of service of the writ on the defendant. Objections may be filed after the time provided in this subrule but do not suspend payment pursuant to subrule (J) unless ordered by the court. Objections may only be based on defects in or the invalidity of the garnishment proceeding itself, and may not be used to challenge the validity of the judgment previously entered.

(2) Objections shall be based on one or more of the following:

(a) the funds or property are exempt from garnishment by law;

(b) garnishment is precluded by the pendency of bankruptcy proceedings;

(c) garnishment is barred by an installment payment order;

(d) garnishment is precluded because the maximum amount permitted by law is being withheld pursuant to a higher priority garnishment or order;

(e) the judgment has been paid;

(f) the garnishment was not properly issued or is otherwise invalid.

(3) Within 7 days of the filing of objections, notice of the date of hearing on the objections shall be sent to the plaintiff, the defendant, and the garnishee. The hearing date shall be within 21 days of the date the objections are filed. In district court, notice shall be sent by the court. In circuit and probate court, notice shall be sent by the objecting party.

(4) The court shall notify the plaintiff, the defendant, and the garnishee of the court's decision.

(L) Steps After Disclosure; Third Parties; Interpleader; Discovery.

(1) Within 14 days after service of the disclosure, the plaintiff may serve the garnishee with written interrogatories or notice the deposition of the garnishee. The answers to the interrogatories or the deposition testimony becomes part of the disclosure.

(2) If the garnishee's disclosure declares that a named person other than the defendant and the plaintiff claims all or part of the disclosed indebtedness or property, the court may order that the claimant be added as a defendant in the garnishment action under MCR 2.207. The garnishee may proceed under MCR 3.603 as in interpleader actions, and other claimants may move to intervene under MCR 2.209.

(3) The discovery rules apply to garnishment proceedings.

(4) The filing of a disclosure, the filing of answers to interrogatories, or the personal appearance by or on behalf of the garnishee at a deposition does not waive the garnishee's right to question the court's jurisdiction, the validity of the proceeding, or the plaintiff's right to judgment.

(M) Determination of Garnishee's Liability.

(1) If there is a dispute regarding the garnishee's liability or if another person claims an interest in the garnishee's property or obligation, the issue shall be tried in the same manner as other civil actions.

(2) The verified statement acts as the plaintiff's complaint against the garnishee, and the disclosure serves as the answer. The facts stated in the disclosure must be accepted as true unless the plaintiff has served interrogatories or noticed a deposition within the time allowed by subrule (L)(1) or another party has filed a pleading or motion denying the accuracy of the disclosure. Except as the facts stated in the verified statement are admitted by the disclosure, they are denied. Admissions have the effect of admissions in responsive pleadings. The defendant and other claimants added under subrule (L)(2) may plead their claims and defenses as in other civil actions. The garnishee's liability to the plaintiff shall be tried on the issues thus framed.

(3) Even if the amount of the garnishee's liability is disputed, the plaintiff may move for judgment against the garnishee to the extent of the admissions in the disclosure. The general motion practice rules govern notice (including notice to the garnishee and the defendant) and hearing on the motion.

(4) The issues between the plaintiff and the garnishee will be tried by the court unless a party files a demand for a jury trial within 7 days after the filing of the disclosure, answers to interrogatories, or deposition transcript, whichever is filed last. The defendant or a third party waives any right to a jury trial unless a demand for a jury is filed with the pleading stating the claim.

(5) On the trial of the garnishee's liability, the plaintiff may offer the record of the garnishment proceeding and other evidence. The garnishee may offer evidence not controverting the disclosure, or in the discretion of the court, may show error or mistakes in the disclosure.

(6) If the court determines that the garnishee is indebted to the defendant, but the time for payment has not arrived, a judgment may not be entered until after the time of maturity stated in the verdict or finding.

(N) Orders for Installment Payments.

(1) An order for installment payments under MCL 600.6201 et seq.; MSA 27A.6201 et seq., suspends the effectiveness of a writ of garnishment of periodic payments for work and labor performed by the defendant from the time the order is served on the garnishee. An order for installment payments does not suspend the effectiveness of a writ of garnishment of nonperiodic payments or of an income tax refund or credit.

(2) If an order terminating the installment payment order is entered and served on the garnishee, the writ again becomes effective and remains in force until it would have expired if the installment payment order had never been entered.

(O) Judgment and Execution.

(1) Judgment may be entered against the garnishee for the payment of money or the delivery of specific property as the facts warrant. A money judgment against the garnishee may not be entered in an amount greater than the amount of the unpaid judgment, interest, and costs as stated in the verified statement requesting the writ of garnishment. Judgment for specific property may be enforced only to the extent necessary to satisfy the judgment against the defendant.

(2) The judgment against the garnishee discharges the garnishee from all demands by the defendant for the money paid or property delivered in satisfaction of the judgment. If the garnishee is sued by the defendant for anything done under the provisions of these garnishment rules, the garnishee may introduce as evidence the judgment and the satisfaction.

(3) If the garnishee is chargeable for specific property that the garnishee holds for or is bound to deliver to the defendant, judgment may be entered and execution issued against the interest of the defendant in the property for no more than is necessary to satisfy the judgment against the defendant. The garnishee must deliver the property to the officer serving the execution, who shall sell, apply, and account as in other executions.

(4) If the garnishee is found to be under contract for the delivery of specific property to the defendant, judgment may be entered and execution issued against the interest of the defendant in the property for no more than is necessary to satisfy the judgment against the defendant. The garnishee must deliver the property to the officer serving the execution according to the terms of the contract. The officer shall sell, apply, and account as in ordinary execution.

(5) If the garnishee is chargeable for specific property and refuses to expose it so that execution may be levied on it, the court may order the garnishee to show cause why general execution should not issue against the garnishee. Unless sufficient cause is shown to the contrary, the court may order that an execution be issued against the garnishee in an amount not to exceed twice the value of the specifically chargeable property.

(6) The court may issue execution against the defendant for the full amount due the plaintiff on the judgment against the defendant. Execution against the garnishee may not be ordered by separate writ, but must always be ordered by endorsement on or by incorporation within the writ of execution against the defendant. The court may order additional execution to satisfy the plaintiff's judgment as justice requires.

(7) Satisfaction of all or part of the judgment against the garnishee constitutes satisfaction of a judgment to the same extent against the defendant.

(P) Appeals. A judgment or order in a garnishment proceeding may be set aside or appealed in the same manner and with the same effect as judgments or orders in other civil actions.

(Q) Receivership.

(1) If on disclosure or trial of a garnishee's liability, it appears that when the writ was served the garnishee possessed,

(a) a written promise for the payment of money or the delivery of property belonging to the defendant, or

(b) personal property belonging to the defendant,

the court may order the garnishee to deliver it to a person appointed as receiver.

(2) The receiver must

(a) collect the written promise for payment of money or for the delivery of property and apply the proceeds on any judgment in favor of the plaintiff against the garnishee and pay any surplus to the garnishee, and

(b) dispose of the property in an amount greater than any encumbrance on it can be obtained, and after paying the amount of the encumbrance, apply the balance to the plaintiff's judgment against the garnishee and pay any surplus to the garnishee.

(3) If the garnishee refuses to comply with the delivery order, the garnishee is liable for the amount of the written promise for the payment of money, the value of the promise for the delivery of property, or the value of the defendant's interest in the encumbered personal property. The facts of the refusal and the valuation must be included in the receiver's report to the court.

(4) The receiver shall report all actions pertaining to the promise or property to the court. The report must include a description and valuation of any property, with the valuation to be ascertained by appraisal on oath or in a manner the court may direct.

(R) Costs and Fees.

(1) Costs and fees are as provided by law or these rules.

(2) If the garnishee is not indebted to the defendant, does not hold any property subject to garnishment, and is not the defendant's employer, the plaintiff is not entitled to recover the costs of that garnishment.

(S) Failure to Disclose or to Do Other Acts; Default; Contempt.

(1) If the garnishee fails to disclose or do a required act within the time limit imposed, a default may be taken as in other civil actions. A default judgment

against a garnishee may not exceed the amount of the garnishee's liability as provided in subrule (G)(2).

(2) If the garnishee fails to comply with the court order, the garnishee may be adjudged in contempt of court.

(3) In addition to other actions permitted by law or these rules, the court may impose costs on a garnishee whose default or contempt results in expense to other parties. Costs imposed shall include reasonable attorney fees and shall not be less than $100.

(T) Judicial Discretion. On motion the court may by order extend the time for:

(1) the garnishee's disclosure;

(2) the plaintiff's filing of written interrogatories;

(3) the plaintiff's filing of a demand for oral examination of the garnishee;

(4) the garnishee's answer to written interrogatories;

(5) the garnishee's appearance for oral examination; and

(6) the demand for jury trial.

The order must be filed with the court and served on the other parties.

[Effective March 1, 1985; amended effective December 31, 1991; April 1, 1994; September 1, 1997.]

Staff Comment to 1994 Amendment

The October 26, 1993, amendment of MCR 3.101, effective April 1, 1994, makes a number of changes in the rule governing garnishment after judgment. In addition to changes in terminology and reorganization, the amendment makes significant adjustments in garnishment procedure, particularly regarding garnishments of periodic payments under 1991 PA 67.

The statute recognizes several levels of priority among garnishments and similar orders. Under subrule (B)(1)(c), the amendment clarifies that even if a higher priority writ or order is in effect, the lower priority one may nonetheless be given effect if the amount being withheld pursuant to the higher priority writ or order is less than the maximum that could be withheld by law.

As under the former rule, the State Court Administrator is to publish forms for use in garnishment proceedings. Under subrule (C) as amended, separate forms are to be used for periodic and nonperiodic garnishments.

Under the former rule, it was implicit that a writ of periodic garnishment had to be served within 91 days after it was issued, since that was the latest date that it could expire. The rule contained no provision for expiration of a nonperiodic writ. The amendment sets the same 91 days for nonperiodic garnishments, corresponding to the 91-day life of a summons. MCR 2.102(D). The writ form is to include the last day by which it must be served to be valid. See subrule (E)(2).

The amendment adjusts the time limits within which various actions must be taken. The garnishee is to serve a copy of the writ on the defendant within 7 days after the garnishee was served. Subrule (F)(2). The garnishee's disclosure must be filed and served within 14 days after the garnishee was served with the writ. Subrule (H). The defendant has 14 days after being served to file objections. Subrule (K)(1). Subrule (K) lists the grounds on which objections may be made, and provides that the objections may not be used as a challenge to the validity of the previously entered judgment. If objections are filed, within 7 days the court is to send notice of a date of hearing on the objections, with the hearing to be scheduled within 21 days of the date the objections were filed. Subrule (K)(3).

The amendment significantly modifies the former rule regarding the withholding of periodic payment of earnings, and as to payment by the garnishee to the court or the plaintiff. Under subrule (I)(2), withholding of earnings commences with the first full pay period after the writ was served as to garnishees with weekly, biweekly, or semimonthly pay periods. As to garnishees with monthly pay periods, if the writ is served within the first 14 days of a pay period, withholding commences on the date the writ is served. If service is after the 14th day of the pay period, withholding commences with the first full pay period after service. There are corresponding provisions regarding cessation of withholding in subrule (I)(3). As to weekly, biweekly, and semimonthly pay periods, withholding ceases at the end of the last full pay period before the expiration of the writ. As to monthly pay periods, withholding ceases at the expiration of the writ. Thus, the only circumstances in which a garnishee must compute the amount to be withheld for less than a full pay period is in the case of monthly pay periods.

Subrule (J) covers payment by the garnishee. Under the former rule, the garnishee had the option of sending withheld funds to the court or retaining them until receiving an order to pay. The amended rule requires the garnishee to hold the funds and, if not notified of objections to the garnishment within 28 days, to send the withheld amount to either the court or the plaintiff (or plaintiff's attorney) as specified in the writ. Under subrule (E)(3)(e), in issuing the writ, the court will include a direction as to whom payment is to be made. As to periodic garnishments, as successive payments become due, the garnishee is to make payment as directed by the writ. The garnishee would not be required to file an additional disclosure, but only to provide a statement with each payment including the information specified in subrule (I)(4), which is to be sent to the plaintiff and the defendant, and, if the funds are sent to the court, to the court as well. Within 14 days after the expiration of the writ, the garnishee is to file a final statement containing the information specified in subrule (J)(6).

In situations where the garnishee holds property belonging to the defendant, the garnishee is not to transfer the property until the court enters an order on motion by the plaintiff. If the plaintiff does not seek such an order within 56 days after filing of the disclosure, the garnishment is dissolved, and the garnishee may release the property. Subrule (J)(7).

Former MCR 3.101(S), regarding the procedure when the state is garnishee, is deleted by the amendment.

Staff Comment to 1997 Amendment

May 14, 1997, amendments [effective September 1, 1997] of the rules governing garnishment and installment payment orders are based on suggestions received from several sources following the major revisions of the garnishment rule effective April 1, 1994.

The amendment of MCR 3.101(A)(4) [effective September 1, 1997] modifies the definition of "periodic payments" in

light of uncertainties caused by the current rule and the amendment of MCL 600.4012(4); MSA 27A.4012(4).

The amendment of MCR 3.101(K)(3) [effective September 1, 1997] requires the moving party, rather than the court, to send the notice of hearing on objections to garnishment in circuit and probate court actions.

The changes in MCR 3.101(N) and MCR 3.104 [effective September 1, 1997] relate to installment payment orders under MCL 600.6201 et seq.; MSA 27A.6201 et seq.

The remaining amendments to MCR 3.101 and MCR 3.102 [effective September 1, 1997] are technical corrections in terminology and cross references.

RULE 3.102 GARNISHMENT BEFORE JUDGMENT

(A) Availability of Prejudgment Garnishment.

(1) After commencing an action on a contract, the plaintiff may obtain a prejudgment writ of garnishment under the circumstances and by the procedures provided in this rule.

(2) Except as provided in subrule (A)(3), a prejudgment garnishment may not be used

(a) unless the defendant is subject to the jurisdiction of the court under chapter 7 of the Revised Judicature Act, MCL 600.701 et seq.; MSA 27A.701 et seq.;

(b) to garnish a defendant's earnings; or

(c) to garnish property held or an obligation owed by the state or a governmental unit of the state.

(3) This rule also applies to a prejudgment garnishment in an action brought to enforce a foreign judgment. However, the following provisions apply:

(a) The defendant need not be subject to the court's jurisdiction;

(b) The request for garnishment must show that

(i) the defendant is indebted to the plaintiff on a foreign judgment in a stated amount in excess of all setoffs;

(ii) the defendant is not subject to the jurisdiction of the state, or that after diligent effort the plaintiff cannot serve the defendant with process; and

(iii) the person making the request knows or has good reason to believe that a named person

(A) has control of property belonging to the defendant, or

(B) is indebted to the defendant.

(c) Subrule (H) does not apply.

(B) Request for Garnishment. After commencing an action, the plaintiff may seek a writ of garnishment by filing an ex parte motion supported by a verified statement setting forth specific facts showing that:

(1) the defendant is indebted to the plaintiff on a contract in a stated amount in excess of all setoffs;

(2) the defendant is subject to the jurisdiction of the state;

(3) after diligent effort the plaintiff cannot serve the defendant with process; and

(4) the person signing the statement knows or has good reason to believe that a named person

(a) has control of property belonging to the defendant, or

(b) is indebted to the defendant.

On a finding that the writ is available under this rule and that the verified statement states a sufficient basis for issuance of the writ, the judge to whom the action is assigned may issue the writ.

(C) Writ of Garnishment. The writ of garnishment must have attached or include a copy of the verified statement, and must:

(1) direct the garnishee to:

(a) file with the court clerk within 14 days after the service of the writ on him or her a verified disclosure indicating his or her liability (as specified in subrule [E]) to the defendant;

(b) deliver no tangible or intangible property to the defendant, unless allowed by statute or court rule;

(c) pay no obligation to the defendant, unless allowed by statute or court rule; and

(d) promptly provide the defendant with a copy of the writ and verified statement by personal delivery or by first class mail directed to the defendant's last known address;

(2) direct the defendant to refrain from disposing of any negotiable instrument representing a debt of the garnishee or of any negotiable instrument of title representing property in which he or she claims an interest held in the possession or control of the garnishee;

(3) inform the defendant that unless the defendant files objections within 14 days after service of the writ on the defendant, or appears and submits to the jurisdiction of the court, an order may enter requiring the garnishee to deliver the garnished property or pay the obligation to be applied to the satisfaction of the plaintiff's claim; and

(4) command the process server to serve the writ and to file a proof of service.

(D) Service of Writ. MCR 3.101(F) applies to prejudgment garnishment.

(E) Liability of Garnishee. MCR 3.101(G) applies to prejudgment garnishment except that the earnings of the defendant may not be garnished before judgment.

(F) Disclosure. The garnishee shall file and serve a disclosure as provided in MCR 3.101(H).

(G) Payment or Deposit Into Court. MCR 3.101(I) and (J) apply to prejudgment garnishment, except that payment may not be made to the plaintiff until after entry of judgment, as provided in subrule (I).

(H) Objection; Dissolution of Prejudgment Garnishment. Objections to and dissolution of a prejudgment garnishment are governed by MCR 3.101(K) and MCR 3.103(H).

(I) Proceedings After Judgment.

(1) If the garnishment remains in effect until entry of judgment in favor of the plaintiff against the defendant, the garnished property or obligation may be applied to the satisfaction of the judgment in the manner provided in MCR 3.101(I), (J), (M), and (O).

(2) MCR 3.101(P) and (Q) and MCR 3.103(I)(2) apply to prejudgment garnishment.

(J) Costs and Fees; Default; Contempt; Judicial Discretion. MCR 3.101(R), (S), and (T) apply to prejudgment garnishment.

[Effective March 1, 1985; amended effective September 1, 1997.]

1985 Staff Comment

MCR 3.102 contains the provisions of the garnishment rules regarding prejudgment garnishment procedure. Given the language of the Michigan prejudgment garnishment statute, MCL 600.4011(3); MSA 27A.4011(3), and the United States Supreme Court decision in *Shaffer v. Heitner*, 433 U.S. 186, 97 S.Ct. 2569, 53 L.Ed.2d 683 (1977), prejudgment garnishment has a very limited role.

Subrules (A)(2)(b) and (c) prohibit prejudgment garnishment of the earnings of a defendant or of obligations owed by a governmental entity. See MCL 600.4011(4), (5); MSA 27A.4011(4), (5).

Subrule (A)(3) modifies the rule as to "prejudgment" garnishment in an action brought on a foreign judgment. Such actions are not subject to the same jurisdictional problems as other prejudgment garnishments. See *Shaffer v. Heitner*, supra, 433 U.S. 210–211, fn. 36.

In subrule (B)(2), the requirement that the defendant be subject to the jurisdiction of the state is added. See *Shaffer v. Heitner*, supra. In addition, the judge, rather than the clerk, must issue the prejudgment writ of garnishment.

The provisions of subrule (C) regarding the writ of garnishment are virtually identical to the comparable provisions regarding a postjudgment writ of garnishment. See the note following MCR 3.101.

Most of the remainder of the rule makes various provisions of the postjudgment garnishment (MCR 3.101) and attachment (MCR 3.103) rules applicable to prejudgment garnishment procedure.

Staff Comment to 1997 Amendment

May 14, 1997, amendments [effective September 1, 1997] of the rules governing garnishment and installment payment orders are based on suggestions received from several sources following the major revisions of the garnishment rule effective April 1, 1994.

The remaining amendments to MCR 3.101 and MCR 3.102 [effective September 1, 1997] are technical corrections in terminology and cross references.

RULE 3.103   ATTACHMENT

(A) Availability of Writ. After commencing an action, the plaintiff may obtain a writ of attachment under the circumstances and by the procedures provided in this rule. Except in an action brought on a foreign judgment, attachment may not be used unless the defendant is subject to the jurisdiction of the court under chapter 7 of the Revised Judicature Act. MCL 600.701 et seq.; MSA 27A.701 et seq.

(B) Motion for Writ.

(1) The plaintiff may seek a writ of attachment by filing an ex parte motion supported by an affidavit setting forth specific facts showing that

(a) at the time of the execution of the affidavit the defendant is indebted to the plaintiff in a stated amount on a contract in excess of all setoffs,

(b) the defendant is subject to the judicial jurisdiction of the state, and

(c) after diligent effort the plaintiff cannot serve the defendant with process.

In an action brought on a tort claim or a foreign judgment, subrules (B)(2) and (3), respectively, apply.

(2) In a tort action the following provisions apply:

(a) Instead of the allegations required by subrule (B)(1)(a), the affidavit in support of the motion must describe the injury claimed and state that the affiant in good faith believes that the defendant is liable to the plaintiff in a stated amount. The other requirements of subrule (B)(1) apply.

(b) If the writ is issued the court shall specify the amount or value of property to be attached.

(3) In an action brought on a foreign judgment, instead of the allegations required by subrule (B)(1), the affidavit in support of the motion must show that

(a) the defendant is indebted to the plaintiff on a foreign judgment in a stated amount in excess of all setoffs,

(b) the defendant is not subject to the jurisdiction of the state or that after diligent effort the plaintiff cannot serve the defendant with process.

(C) Issuance of Writ.

(1) On a finding that the writ is available under this rule and that the affidavit states a sufficient basis for issuance of the writ, the judge to whom the action is assigned may issue the writ.

(2) The judge's order shall specify what further steps, if any, must be taken by the plaintiff to notify the defendant of the action and the attachment.

(D) Contents of Writ. The writ of attachment must command the sheriff or other officer to whom it is directed

(1) to attach so much of the defendant's real and personal property not exempt from execution as is necessary to satisfy the plaintiff's demand and costs, and

(2) to keep the property in a secure place to satisfy any judgment that may be recovered by the plaintiff in the action until further order of the court.

(E) Execution of Writ; Subsequent Attachments.

(1) The sheriff or other officer to whom a writ of attachment is directed shall execute the writ by seizing and holding so much of the defendant's property not exempt from execution, wherever found within the county, as is necessary to satisfy the plaintiff's demand and costs. If insufficient property is seized, then the officer shall seize other property of the defendant not exempt from execution, wherever found within Michigan, as is necessary when added to that already seized, to satisfy the plaintiff's demand and costs. The property seized must be inventoried by the officer and appraised by two disinterested residents of the county in which the property was seized. After being sworn under oath to make a true appraisal, the appraisers shall make and sign an appraisal. The inventory and appraisal must be filed and a copy served on the parties under MCR 2.107.

(2) In subsequent attachments of the same property while in the hands of the officer, the original inventory and appraisal satisfy the requirement of subrule (E)(1).

(F) Attachment of Realty; Stock.

(1) The officer may seize an interest in real estate by depositing a certified copy of the writ of attachment, including a description of the land affected, with the register of deeds for the county in which the land is located. It is not necessary that the officer enter on the land or be within view of it.

(2) Shares of stock or the interest of a stockholder in a domestic corporation must be seized in the manner provided for the seizure of that property on execution.

(G) Animals or Perishable Property; Sale; Distribution of Proceeds.

(1) When any of the property attached consists of animals or perishable property, the court may order the property sold and the money from the sale brought into court, to await the order of the court.

(2) After the order for a sale is entered, the officer having the property shall advertise and sell it in the manner that personal property of like character is required to be advertised and sold on execution. The officer shall deposit the proceeds with the clerk of the court in which the action is pending.

(3) If the plaintiff recovers judgment, the court may order the money paid to the plaintiff. If the judgment is entered against the plaintiff or the suit is dismissed or the attachment is dissolved, the court shall order the money paid to the defendant or other person entitled to it.

(H) Dissolution of Attachment.

(1) Except in an action brought on a foreign judgment, if the defendant submits to the jurisdiction of the court, the court shall dissolve the attachment.

(2) A person who owns, possesses, or has an interest in attached property may move at any time to dissolve the attachment. The defendant may move to dissolve the attachment without submitting to the jurisdiction of the court.

(a) When a motion for dissolution of attachment is filed, the court shall enter an order setting a time and place for hearing the motion, and may issue subpoenas to compel witnesses to attend.

(b) The plaintiff must be served with notice under MCR 2.107 at least 3 days before the hearing unless the court's order prescribes a different notice requirement.

(c) At the hearing, the proofs are heard in the same manner as in a nonjury trial. If the court decides that the defendant was not subject to the jurisdiction of the state or that the property was not subject to or was exempt from attachment, it shall dissolve the attachment and restore the property to the defendant, and the attachment may be dissolved for any other sufficient reason. The court may order the losing party to pay the costs of the dissolution proceeding.

(3) If the action is dismissed or judgment is entered for the defendant, the attachment is dissolved.

(I) Satisfaction of Judgment.

(1) If the attachment remains in effect until the entry of judgment against the defendant, the attached property may be applied to the satisfaction of the judgment, including interest and costs, in the same manner as in the case of an execution.

(2) If the court does not acquire personal jurisdiction over the defendant, either by service or by the defendant's appearance, a judgment against the defendant is not binding beyond the value of the attached property.

[Effective March 1, 1985.]

1985 Staff Comment

MCR 3.103 covers attachment, and corresponds to GCR 1963, 735. The changes in this rule are similar to those in the prejudgment garnishment provisions. The attachment statute, MCL 600.4001; MSA 27A.4001, and United States Supreme Court decisions have similarly limited the availability of attachment.

Subrule (B) is changed to require that the defendant be subject to the jurisdiction of the state, and to require the

judge, rather than the clerk, to issue the writ. However, this jurisdictional requirement does not apply in an action brought on a foreign judgment.

Subrule (B)(2) covers special requirements regarding tort actions, in which the amount of damages are likely to be uncertain. Compare GCR 1963, 735.4.

One of the conditions for the issuance of the writ is that the plaintiff had exercised diligent efforts to serve the defendant. Subrule (B)(1)(c). Accordingly, rather than simply requiring that the writ be served on the defendant (see GCR 1963, 735.7[1]), subrule (B)(5) requires the judge to specify what further steps must be taken to notify the defendant of the action and the application. Similarly, in subrules (D) and (E), as in subrule (B)(5), service requirements are omitted, since the very issuance of the writ depends on a showing that the defendant cannot be served.

The provisions of GCR 1963, 735.10, 735.11, and 735.12 are deleted.

Subrule (H) differs from the corresponding provision (GCR 1963, 735.13) in several respects. Subrule (H)(1) dissolves the attachment if the defendant submits to jurisdiction. Under subrule (H)(2) the defendant may move to dissolve the attachment without submitting to the court's jurisdiction. Subrule (H)(3) makes clear that the attachment is dissolved if the action is dismissed or judgment is entered for the defendant.

Subrule (I) is new and contains provisions consistent with the attachment statute regarding satisfaction of a judgment against the defendant.

RULE 3.104   INSTALLMENT PAYMENT ORDERS

(A) Motion for Installment Payment Order. A party against whom a money judgment has been entered may move for entry of an order permitting the judgment to be paid in installments in accordance with MCL 600.6201 et seq.; MSA 27A.6201 et seq. A copy of the motion must be served on the plaintiff, by the clerk of the court in district court and by the party who filed the objection in circuit or probate court.

(B) Consideration of Motion. The motion will be granted without further hearing unless the plaintiff files, and serves on the defendant, written objections within 14 days after the service date of the defendant's motion. If objections are filed, the clerk must promptly present the motion and objections to the court. The court will decide the motion based on the papers filed or notify the parties that a hearing will be required. Unless the court schedules the hearing, the moving party is responsible for noticing the motion for hearing.

(C) Failure to Comply with Installment Order. If the defendant fails to make payments pursuant to the order for installment payments, the plaintiff may file and serve on the defendant a motion to set aside the order for installment payments. Unless a hearing is requested within 14 days after service of the motion, the order to set aside the order for installment payments will be entered.

(D) Request After Failure to Comply with Previous Order. If the defendant moves for an order for installment payments within 91 days after a previous installment order has been set aside, unless good cause is shown the court shall assess costs against the defendant as a condition of entry of the new order.

[Effective March 1, 1985; amended effective September 1, 1997.]

1985 Staff Comment

MCR 3.104 corresponds to GCR 1963, 523. Most of the substantive provisions are omitted and replaced with a reference to the statutory procedures for installment judgments.

Staff Comment to 1997 Amendment

May 14, 1997, amendments [effective September 1, 1997] of the rules governing garnishment and installment payment orders are based on suggestions received from several sources following the major revisions of the garnishment rule effective April 1, 1994.

The changes in MCR 3.101(N) and MCR 3.104 [effective September 1, 1997] relate to installment payment orders under MCL 600.6201 et seq.; MSA 27A.6201 et seq.

RULE 3.105   CLAIM AND DELIVERY

(A) Nature of Action; Replevin. Claim and delivery is a civil action to recover

(1) possession of goods or chattels which have been unlawfully taken or unlawfully detained, and

(2) damages sustained by the unlawful taking or unlawful detention.

A statutory reference to the action of replevin is to be construed as a reference to the action of claim and delivery.

(B) Rules Applicable. A claim and delivery action is governed by the rules applicable to other civil actions, except as provided in MCL 600.2920; MSA 27A.2920, and this rule.

(C) Complaint; Joinder of Claims; Interim Payments. A claim and delivery complaint must:

(1) specifically describe the property claimed;

(2) state the value of the property claimed (which will be used only to set the amount of bond and not as an admission of value);

(3) state if the property claimed is an independent piece of property or a portion of divisible property of uniform kind, quality, and value; and

(4) specifically describe the nature of the claim and the basis for the judgment requested.

If the action is based on a security agreement, a claim for the debt may be joined as a separate count in the complaint. If the plaintiff, while the action is pending, receives interim payments equal to the amount originally claimed, the action must be dismissed.

(D) Answer. An answer to a claim and delivery complaint may concede the claim for possession and yet contest any other claim.

(E) Possession Pending Final Judgment.

(1) *Motion for Possession Pending Final Judgment.* After the complaint is filed, the plaintiff may file a verified motion requesting possession pending final judgment. The motion must

(a) describe the property to be seized, and

(b) state sufficient facts to show that the property described will be damaged, destroyed, concealed, disposed of, or used so as to substantially impair its value, before final judgment unless the property is taken into custody by court order.

(2) *Court Order Pending Hearing.* After a motion for possession pending final judgment is filed, the court, if good cause is shown, must order the defendant to

(a) refrain from damaging, destroying, concealing, disposing of, or using so as to substantially impair its value, the property until further order of the court; and

(b) appear before the court at a specified time to answer the motion.

(3) *Hearing on Motion for Possession Pending Final Judgment.*

(a) At least 7 days before a hearing on a motion filed under this subrule, the defendant must be served with

(i) a copy of the motion; and

(ii) an order entered under subrule (E)(2).

(b) At the hearing, each party may present proofs. To obtain possession before judgment, the plaintiff must establish

(i) that the plaintiff's right to possession is probably valid; and

(ii) that the property will be damaged, destroyed, concealed, disposed of, or used so as to substantially impair its value, before trial.

(c) Adjournment. A court may not

(i) grant an adjournment of this hearing on the basis that a defendant has not yet answered the complaint or the motion filed under this subrule; or

(ii) allow a hearing on this motion if the hearing date has been adjourned more than 56 days with the assent of the plaintiff, unless the plaintiff files a new motion which includes recitations of any payments made by the defendant after the original motion was filed.

(4) *Order for Custody Pending Final Judgment.* After proofs have been taken on the plaintiff's motion for possession pending final judgment, the court may

order whatever relief the evidence requires. This includes:

(a) denying the motion;

(b) leaving the defendant in possession of the property and restraining the defendant from damaging, destroying, concealing, or disposing of the property. The court may condition the defendant's continued possession by requiring the defendant to

(i) furnish a penalty bond, payable to the plaintiff, of not less than $100 and at least twice the value of the property stated in the complaint; and

(ii) agree that he or she will surrender the property to the person adjudged entitled to possession and will pay any money that may be recovered against him or her in the action;

(c) ordering the sheriff or court officer to seize the property within 21 days and either hold it or deliver it to the plaintiff. The court may condition the plaintiff's possession by requiring the plaintiff to

(i) furnish a penalty bond payable to the defendant, and to the sheriff or court officer, of not less than $100 and at least twice the value of the property stated in the complaint; and

(ii) agree that he or she will surrender the property to the person adjudged entitled to possession, diligently prosecute the suit to final judgment, and pay any money that may be recovered against him or her in the action.

A bond required in a claim and delivery action must be approved by and filed with the court within the time the order provides.

(F) Seizure. A copy of an order issued under subrule (E)(4)(c) must be delivered to the sheriff or court officer, who must

(1) seize the property described in the order;

(2) serve a copy of the order on the defendant, under MCR 2.107; and

(3) file a return with the court showing seizure and service.

(G) Custody; Delivery. After seizing the property, the sheriff or court officer shall keep it in a secure place and deliver it in accordance with the court order. The sheriff or court officer is entitled to receive the lawful fees for seizing the property and the necessary expenses for seizing and keeping it.

(H) Judgment.

(1) The judgment must determine

(a) the party entitled to possession of the property,

(b) the value of the property,

(c) the amount of any unpaid debt, and

(d) any damages to be awarded.

(2) If the property is not in the possession of the party who is entitled to possession, a judgment must order the property to be immediately delivered to that party.

(3) If the action is tried on the merits, the value of the property and the damages are determined by the trier of fact.

(4) If the defendant has been deprived of the property by a prejudgment order and the main action is dismissed, the defendant may apply to the court for default judgment under MCR 2.603.

(5) If the plaintiff takes a default judgment, the value of the property and the damages are determined under MCR 2.603. A defendant who appeared at a show-cause proceeding is deemed to have filed an appearance.

(6) The party adjudged entitled to possession of the property described may elect to take judgment for the value of the property instead of possession. The judgment value may not exceed the unpaid debt, if any, secured by such property.

(7) The liability of a surety on a bond given under this rule may be determined on motion under MCR 3.604.

(I) Costs. Costs may be taxed in the discretion of the court. Costs may include the cost of a bond required by the court, and the costs of seizing and keeping the property.

(J) Execution.

(1) The execution issued on a judgment in a claim and delivery action must command the sheriff or court officer

(a) to levy the prevailing party's damages and costs on the property of the opposite party, as in other executions against property; and

(b) if the property described in the judgment is found in the possession of the defendant, to seize the property described in the judgment and deliver it to the prevailing party; or, if the property is not found in the possession of the defendant, to levy the value of it. The value may not exceed the total of the unpaid debt, costs, and damages.

(2) Execution may not issue on a judgment in a claim and delivery action if more than 28 days have passed from the signing of the judgment, unless

(a) the plaintiff files a motion for execution which must include, if money has been paid on the judgment, the amount paid and the conditions under which it was accepted; and

(b) a hearing is held after the defendant has been given notice and an opportunity to appear.

[Effective March 1, 1985.]

1985 Staff Comment

MCR 3.105 is substantially the same as GCR 1963, 757.

RULE 3.106 PROCEDURES REGARDING ORDERS FOR THE SEIZURE OF PROPERTY AND ORDERS OF EVICTION

(A) Scope of Rule. This rule applies to orders for the seizure of property and orders of eviction.

(B) Persons Who May Seize Property or Conduct Evictions. The persons who may seize property or conduct evictions are those persons named in MCR 2. 103(B), and they are subject to the provisions of this rule unless a provision or a statute specifies otherwise.

(1) A court may provide that property shall be seized and evictions conducted only by

(a) court officers and bailiffs serving that court;

(b) sheriffs and deputy sheriffs;

(c) officers of the Department of State Police in an action in which the state is a party; and

(d) police officers of an incorporated city or village in an action in which the city or village is a party.

(2) Each court must post, in a public place at the court, a list of those persons who are serving as court officers or bailiffs. The court must provide the State Court Administrative Office with a copy of the list, and must notify the State Court Administrative Office of any changes.

(C) Appointment of Court Officers. Court officers may be appointed by a court for a term not to exceed 2 years.

(1) The appointment shall be made by the chief judge. Two or more chief judges may jointly appoint court officers for their respective courts.

(2) The appointing court must specify the nature of the court officer's employment relationship at the time of appointment.

(3) The appointing court must maintain a copy of each court officer's application, as required by the State Court Administrative Office.

(4) The State Court Administrative Office shall develop a procedure for the appointment and supervision of court officers, including a model application form. Considerations shall include, but are not limited to, an applicant's character, experience, and references.

(D) Conditions of Service as a Court Officer or Bailiff. Court officers and bailiffs must

(1) post a surety bond pursuant to MCR 8.204;

(2) provide the names and addresses of all financial institutions in which they deposit funds obtained under this rule, and the respective account numbers; and

(3) provide the names and address of those persons who regularly provide services to them in the seizure of property or evictions.

(E) Forms. The State Court Administrative Office shall publish forms approved for use with regard to the procedures described in this rule.

(F) Procedures Generally.

(1) All persons specified in MCR 2.103(B) must carry and display identification authorized by the court or the agency that they serve.

(2) A copy of the order for seizure of property or eviction shall be served on the defendant or the defendant's agent, or left or posted on the premises in a conspicuous place. If property is seized from any other location, a copy of the order shall be mailed to the defendant's last known address.

(G) Procedures Regarding Orders for Seizure of Property.

(1) Orders for seizure of property shall be issued pursuant to statute and endorsed upon receipt.

(2) No funds may be collected pursuant to an order for seizure of property prior to service under subrule (F)(2).

(3) An inventory and receipt shall be prepared upon seizure of property or payment of funds.

(a) The original shall be filed with the court within 7 days of the seizure or payment.

(b) A copy shall be

(i) provided to the parties or their respective attorneys or agents and posted on the premises in a conspicuous place; if the property is seized from any other location, a copy shall be mailed to the nonprevailing party's last known address, and

(ii) retained by the person who seized the property.

(4) Property seized shall be disposed of according to law.

(5) Within 21 days, and as directed by the court, any money that is received shall be paid to the court or deposited in a trust account for payment to the prevailing party or that party's attorney.

(6) Costs allowed by statute shall be paid according to law.

(a) Copies of all bills and receipts for service shall be retained for one year by the person serving the order.

(b) Statutory collection fees shall be paid in proportion to the amount received.

(c) There shall be no payment except as provided by law.

(7) Within 14 days after the expiration of the order or satisfaction of judgment, whichever is first, the following shall be filed with the court and a copy provided to the prevailing party or that party's attorney:

(a) a report summarizing collection activities, including an accounting of all money or property collected,

(b) a report that collection activities will continue pursuant to statute, if applicable, or

(c) a report that no collection activity occurred.

(H) Procedures Regarding Orders of Eviction. Copies of all bills and receipts for services shall be retained by the person serving the order for one year.

[Adopted effective May 1, 2002.]

Staff Comment to 2002 Addition

The September 12, 2001 addition of MCR 3.106, effective May 1, 2002, was recommended by an ad hoc committee of judges, court administrators, court clerks, attorneys, and court officers. The rule incorporated existing practice while protecting against abuses. The September 12, 2001 amendments of MCR 4.201 and 4.202, effective May 1, 2002, made changes consistent with new MCR 3.106.

The staff comment is published only for the benefit of the bench and bar and is not an authoritative construction by the Court.

RULE 3.110 STOCKHOLDERS' LIABILITY PROCEEDINGS

(A) Scope of Rule. This rule applies to actions brought under MCL 600.2909; MSA 27A.2909.

(B) When Action May Be Brought. An action against stockholders in which it is claimed that they are individually liable for debts of a corporation may not be brought until:

(1) a judgment has been recovered against the corporation for the indebtedness;

(2) an execution on the judgment has been issued to the county in which the corporation has its principal office or carries on its business; and

(3) the execution has been returned unsatisfied in whole or in part.

(C) Order for List of Stockholders. When the conditions set out in subrule (B) are met, the plaintiff may apply to the court that entered the judgment to order a list of stockholders. The court shall enter an order to be served on the secretary or other proper officer of the corporation, requiring the officer, within the time provided in the order, to file a statement under oath listing the names and addresses of all persons who appear by the corporation books to have been, or who the officer has reason to believe were, stockholders when the debt accrued, and the amount of stock held by each of them.

(D) Commencement of Action; Complaint. An action against the stockholders to impose personal liability on them for the debt of the corporation may be commenced and carried on as other civil actions under these rules. The complaint must, among other things, state:

(1) that the plaintiff has obtained a judgment against the corporation and the amount;

(2) that execution has been issued and returned unsatisfied in whole or in part, and the amount remaining unpaid;

(3) that the persons named as defendants are the persons listed in the statement filed by the officer of the corporation under subrule (C);

(4) the amount of stock held by each defendant, or that the plaintiff could not, with reasonable diligence, ascertain the amounts;

(5) the consideration received by the corporation for the debt on which judgment was rendered;

(6) a request for judgment against the stockholders in favor of the plaintiff for the amount alleged to be due from the corporation.

(E) Judgment Against Corporation as Evidence. At the trial the judgment against the corporation and the amount remaining unpaid are prima facie evidence of the amount due to the plaintiff but are not evidence that the debt on which the judgment was rendered is one for which the defendants are personally liable.

(F) Entry of Judgment Against Defendant. If a defendant admits the facts set forth in the complaint or defaults by failing to answer, or if the issues are determined against the defendant, judgment may be entered against him or her for the amount of the judgment against the corporation remaining unpaid, on proof that the debt is one for which that defendant is personally liable as a stockholder.

(G) Order of Apportionment; Execution. After judgment has been entered against all or some of the defendants, the court may apportion among these defendants the sum for which they have been adjudged liable pro rata according to the stock held by each. If any defendant fails to pay the amount apportioned against that defendant within 21 days, execution may issue as in other civil actions.

(H) Reapportionment. If execution is returned unsatisfied in whole or in part against any of the defendants as to whom apportionment has been made, the court has the power and the duty on application by the plaintiff to reapportion the sum remaining uncollected on the basis of subrule (G) among the remaining defendants adjudged liable. Execution may issue for the collection of these amounts.

(I) Contribution Among Stockholders. A stockholder who has been compelled to pay more than his or her pro rata share of the debts of the corporation, according to the amount of stock held, is entitled to contribution from other stockholders who are also liable for the debt and who have not paid their portions.

[Effective March 1, 1985.]

SUBCHAPTER 3.200   DOMESTIC RELATIONS ACTIONS

RULE 3.201   APPLICABILITY OF RULES

(A) Subchapter 3.200 applies to

(1) actions for divorce, separate maintenance, the annulment of marriage, the affirmation of marriage, paternity, family support under MCL 552.451 et seq.; MSA 25.222(1) et seq., the custody of minors under MCL 722.21 et seq.; MSA 25.312(1) et seq., and visitation with minors under MCL 722.27b; MSA 25.312(7b), and to

(2) proceedings that are ancillary or subsequent to the actions listed in subrule (A)(1) and that relate to

(a) the custody of minors,

(b) visitation with minors, or

(c) the support of minors and spouses or former spouses.

(B) As used in this subchapter with regard to child support, the terms "minor" or "child" may include children who have reached the age of majority, in the circumstances where the legislature has so provided.

(C) Except as otherwise provided in this subchapter, practice and procedure in domestic relations actions is governed by other applicable provisions of the Michigan Court Rules.

(D) When used in this subchapter, unless the context otherwise indicates:

(1) "Case" means an action initiated in the family division of the circuit court by:

(a) submission of an original complaint, petition, or citation;

(b) acceptance of transfer of an action from another court or tribunal; or

(c) filing or registration of a foreign judgment or order.

(2) "File" means the repository for collection of the pleadings and other documents and materials related to a case. A file may include more than one case involving a family.

(3) "Jurisdiction" means the authority of the court to hear cases and make decisions and enter orders on cases.

[Adopted effective May 1, 1993; amended effective September 1, 1997; January 1, 2003.]

relations actions, such as paternity, injunctive relief under MCL 600.2950; MSA 27A.2950, family support under MCL 552.451 et seq.; MSA 25.222(1) et seq., the custody of minors under MCL 722.21 et seq.; MSA 25.312(1) et seq., and visitation with minors under MCL 722.27b; MSA 25.312(7b).

RULE 3.202   CAPACITY TO SUE

(A) Minors and Incompetent Persons. Except as provided in subrule (B), minors and incompetent persons may sue and be sued as provided in MCR 2.201.

(B) Emancipated Minors. An emancipated minor may sue and be sued in the minor's own name, as provided in MCL 722.4e(1)(b); MSA 25.244(4e)(1)(b).

[Adopted effective May 1, 1993.]

RULE 3.203   PROCESS

(A) Except as otherwise allowed by this rule, process must be served as provided in MCR 2.105.

(B) Notice to Friend of the Court. If a child of the parties or a child born during the marriage is under the age of 18, or if a party is pregnant, or if child support or spousal support is requested, the parties must provide the friend of the court with a copy of all pleadings and other papers filed in the action. The copy must be marked "friend of the court" and submitted to the court clerk at the time of filing. The court clerk must send the copy to the friend of the court.

(C) Notice to Prosecuting Attorney. In an action for divorce or separate maintenance in which a child of the parties or a child born during the marriage is under the age of 18, or if a party is pregnant, the plaintiff must serve a copy of the summons and complaint on the prosecuting attorney when required by law. Service must be made at the time of filing by providing the court clerk with an additional copy marked "prosecuting attorney." The court clerk must send the copy to the prosecuting attorney.

(D) Service of Informational Pamphlet. If a child of the parties or a child born during the marriage is under the age of 18, or if a party is pregnant, or if child support or spousal support is requested, the plaintiff must serve with the complaint a copy of the friend of the court informational pamphlet required by MCL 552.505(a); MSA 25.176(5)(a). The proof of service must state that service of the informational pamphlet has been made.

[Adopted effective May 1, 1993.]

1993 Staff Comment

Former Rule 3.203 has been revised substantially [effective May 1, 1993]. Parts of former subrule 3.203(C) have been moved to Rule 3.207. The provision that governs service on the prosecuting attorney has been changed to require submittal of a designated copy of pleadings and other papers at the time of filing. To insure that litigants receive the friend of the court informational pamphlet, a subrule has been added to require proof of service of the pamphlet.

RULE 3.204 PROCEEDINGS AFFECTING MINORS

(A) Unless otherwise provided by statute, original actions under MCL 722.21 et seq.; MSA 25.312(1) et seq. that are not ancillary to any other action must be filed in the circuit court for the county in which the minor resides.

(B) If an action is pending in circuit court for the support or custody of a minor, or for visitation with a minor, or the circuit court has continuing jurisdiction over such matters because of a prior action, a subsequent action for support, custody, or visitation with regard to that minor must be initiated as an ancillary proceeding.

(C) If a new action for support is filed in a circuit court in which a party has an existing or pending support obligation, the new case must be assigned to the same judge to whom the other case is assigned, pursuant to MCR 8.111(D).

(D) In a case involving a dispute regarding the custody of a minor child, the court may, on motion of a party or on its own initiative, for good cause shown, appoint a guardian ad litem to represent the child and assess the costs and reasonable fees against the parties involved in full or in part.

[Adopted effective May 1, 1993; amended effective January 1, 2003.]

1993 Staff Comment

This rule is new [effective May 1, 1993]. Subrule (A) clarifies the proper jurisdiction for original actions under the Child Custody Act, and subrule (B) makes clear that a subsequent action for support, custody, or visitation must be brought as an ancillary proceeding if a court has continuing jurisdiction because of a prior action. Where there is an existing or pending support obligation, subrule (C) requires that new actions for support be assigned to the same judge to whom the prior case is assigned.

Staff Comment to 2002 Amendment

The September 11, 2002, amendments of MCR 3.201 and 3.204, effective January 1, 2003, are based on proposals by the Family Division Joint Rules Committee. New MCR 3.201(D) defines several terms, and new MCR 3.204(D) states the authority of the court to appoint a guardian ad litem for a minor child in a case in which child custody is disputed.

The staff comment is published only for the benefit of the bench and bar and is not an authoritative construction by the Court.

RULE 3.205 PRIOR AND SUBSEQUENT ORDERS AND JUDGMENTS AFFECTING MINORS

(A) Jurisdiction. If an order or judgment has provided for continuing jurisdiction of a minor and proceedings are commenced in another Michigan court having separate jurisdictional grounds for an action affecting that minor, a waiver or transfer of jurisdiction is not required for the full and valid exercise of jurisdiction by the subsequent court.

(B) Notice to Prior Court, Friend of the Court, Juvenile Officer, and Prosecuting Attorney.

(1) As used in this rule, "appropriate official" means the friend of the court, juvenile officer, or prosecuting attorney, depending on the nature of the prior or subsequent court action and the court involved.

(2) If a minor is known to be subject to the prior continuing jurisdiction of a Michigan court, the plaintiff or other initiating party must mail written notice of proceedings in the subsequent court to the attention of

(a) the clerk or register of the prior court, and

(b) the appropriate official of the prior court.

(3) The notice must be mailed at least 21 days before the date set for hearing. If the fact of continuing jurisdiction is not then known, notice must be given immediately when it becomes known.

(4) The notice requirement of this subrule is not jurisdictional and does not preclude the subsequent court from entering interim orders before the expiration of the 21-day period, if required by the best interests of the minor.

(C) Prior Orders.

(1) Each provision of a prior order remains in effect until the provision is superseded, changed, or terminated by a subsequent order.

(2) A subsequent court must give due consideration to prior continuing orders of other courts, and may not enter orders contrary to or inconsistent with such orders, except as provided by law.

(D) Duties of Officials of Prior and Subsequent Courts.

(1) Upon receipt of the notice required by subrule (B), the appropriate official of the prior court

(a) must provide the subsequent court with copies of all relevant orders then in effect and copies of relevant records and reports, and

(b) may appear in person at proceedings in the subsequent court, as the welfare of the minor and the interests of justice require.

(2) Upon request of the prior court, the appropriate official of the subsequent court

(a) must notify the appropriate official of the prior court of all proceedings in the subsequent court, and

(b) must send copies of all orders entered in the subsequent court to the attention of the clerk or register and the appropriate official of the prior court.

(3) If a circuit court awards custody of a minor pursuant to MCL 722.26b; MSA 25.312(6b), the clerk of the circuit court must send a copy of the judgment or order of disposition to the probate court that has prior or continuing jurisdiction of the minor as a result of the guardianship proceedings, regardless whether there is a request.

(4) Upon receipt of an order from the subsequent court, the appropriate official of the prior court must take the steps necessary to implement the order in the prior court.

[Adopted effective May 1, 1993.]

1993 Staff Comment

Former Rule 3.205 has been rewritten [effective May 1, 1993] to clarify the relative responsibilities when two courts have asserted jurisdiction. The pleading requirement in former Rule 3.205 has been moved to Rule 3.206.

RULE 3.206 PLEADING

(A) Information in Complaint.

(1) Except for matters considered confidential by statute or court rule, in all domestic relations actions, the complaint must state

(a) the allegations required by applicable statutes;

(b) the residence information required by statute;

(c) the complete names of all parties; and

(d) the complete names and dates of birth of any minors involved in the action, including all minor children of the parties and all minor children born during the marriage.

(2) In a case that involves a minor, or if child support is requested, the complaint also must state whether any Michigan court has prior continuing jurisdiction of the minor. If so, the complaint must specify the court and the file number.

(3) In a case in which the custody of a minor is to be determined, the complaint or an affidavit attached to the complaint also must state the information required by MCL 722.1209.

(4) The caption of the complaint must also contain either (a) or (b) as a statement of the attorney for the plaintiff or petitioner, or of a plaintiff or petitioner appearing without an attorney:

(a) There is no other pending or resolved action within the jurisdiction of the family division of the circuit court involving the family or family members of the person[s] who [is/are] the subject of the complaint or petition.

(b) An action within the jurisdiction of the family division of the circuit court involving the family or family members of the person[s] who [is/are] the subject of the complaint or petition has been previously filed in [this court]/[_____ Court], where it was given docket number _____ and was assigned to Judge _____. The action [remains]/[is no longer] pending.

(5) In an action for divorce, separate maintenance, annulment of marriage, or affirmation of marriage, regardless of the contentions of the parties with respect to the existence or validity of the marriage, the complaint also must state

(a) the names of the parties before the marriage;

(b) whether there are minor children of the parties or minor children born during the marriage;

(c) whether a party is pregnant;

(d) the factual grounds for the action, except that in an action for divorce or separate maintenance the grounds must be stated in the statutory language, without further particulars; and

(e) whether there is property to be divided.

(6) A party who requests spousal support in an action for divorce, separate maintenance, annulment, affirmation of marriage, or spousal support, must allege facts sufficient to show a need for such support and that the other party is able to pay.

(7) A party who requests an order for personal protection or for the protection of property, including but not limited to restraining orders and injunctions against domestic violence, must allege facts sufficient to support the relief requested.

(B) Verified Statement.

(1) In an action involving a minor, or if child support or spousal support is requested, the party seeking relief must attach a verified statement to the copies of the papers served on the other party and provided to the friend of the court, stating

(a) the last known telephone number, post office address, residence address, and business address of each party;

(b) the social security number and occupation of each party;

(c) the name and address of each party's employer;

(d) the estimated weekly gross income of each party;

(e) the driver's license number and physical description of each party, including eye color, hair color, height, weight, race, gender, and identifying marks;

(f) any other names by which the parties are or have been known;

(g) the name, age, birth date, social security number, and residence address of each minor involved in the action, as well as of any other minor child of either party;

(h) the name and address of any person, other than the parties, who may have custody of a minor during the pendency of the action;

(i) the kind of public assistance, if any, that has been applied for or is being received by either party or on behalf of a minor, and the AFDC and recipient identification numbers; if public assistance has not been requested or received, that fact must be stated; and

(j) the health care coverage, if any, that is available for each minor child; the name of the policyholder; the name of the insurance company, health care organization, or health maintenance organization; and the policy, certificate, or contract number.

(2) The information in the verified statement is confidential, and is not to be released other than to the court, the parties, or the attorneys for the parties, except on court order. For good cause, the addresses of a party and minors may be omitted from the copy of the statement that is served on the other party.

(3) If any of the information required to be in the verified statement is omitted, the party seeking relief must explain the omission in a sworn affidavit, to be filed with the court.

(C) Attorney Fees and Expenses.

(1) A party may, at any time, request that the court order the other party to pay all or part of the attorney fees and expenses related to the action.

(2) A party who requests attorney fees and expenses must allege facts sufficient to show that the party is unable to bear the expense of the action, and that the other party is able to pay.

[Adopted effective May 1, 1993; amended effective January 1, 1998; September 11, 2002.]

1993 Staff Comment

Former subrule 3.204(A) has been rewritten [effective May 1, 1993] as subrule 3.206(A) to clarify the pleading requirements for different types of domestic relations actions. Subrule (B) is similar to former subrule 3.204(B), except that the term "alimony" has been replaced by the term "spousal support," and there are several additions to the information that must be provided. For instance, it is now necessary to include in the verified statement the driver's license number and physical description of each party, any other names by which a party is known, and information about health care coverage. Also, the verified statement must now disclose the estimated weekly gross income of each party instead of the estimated after-tax income, and there must be a sworn affidavit identifying the reason for any omissions in the verified statement. Former subrule 3.204(C) has been eliminated; Rule 3.209 governs actions to be taken when parties reconcile. Subrule (C) governs attorney fees and expenses.

Staff Comment to 1998 Amendments

The October 1, 1997, amendments of MCR 3.206, 5.931, and 5.961 [effective January 1, 1998] relate to statutory changes made by 1996 PA 388, which created the family division of the circuit court. The amendments are effective January 1, 1998.

New MCR 3.206(A)(4) creates a requirement for identifying pending or prior family division actions involving members of the same family. References to that provision are included in MCR 5.931(B)(8), governing delinquency proceedings, and MCR 5.961(B)(7), governing child protective proceedings.

The December 19, 1997, amendments to Rule 3.206 and subchapter 5.900 of the Michigan Court Rules [effective January 1, 1998] implement recent statutory changes which have created a family division of the circuit court. These amendments will remain in effect until further order of the court.

Staff Comment to 2002 Amendment

The September 11, 2002, amendments of MCR 3.206, 3.214, 3.705, 3.706, 3.708, 5.982, and 8.119, which were given immediate effect, are related to the group of domestic violence statutes enacted in December 2001 that took effect April 1, 2002.

The changes in MCR 3.206 and 3.214 are related to 2001 PA 195, which adopted the Uniform Child–Custody Jurisdiction and Enforcement Act, MCL 722.1101 *et seq.* There is also some nonsubstantive reorganization of MCR 3.214.

The amendment of MCR 3.705 implements the statutory provisions regarding the statement of reasons for granting or denying personal protection orders. See 2001 PA 196.

The amendment of MCR 3.706 incorporates the statutory provisions regarding enforceability of Michigan personal protection orders in other jurisdictions. See 2001 PA 200 and 201.

MCR 3.708 and 5.982 are amended to include foreign protection orders, which are made enforceable in Michigan by 2001 PA 197.

MCR 8.119(F) is amended to conform to 2001 PA 205, which directs that when a motion to seal court records involves allegations of domestic violence, the court is to consider the safety of the potential victim in ruling on the motion.

The staff comment is published only for the benefit of the bench and bar and is not an authoritative construction by the Court.

RULE 3.207   EX PARTE, TEMPORARY, AND PROTECTIVE ORDERS

(A) Scope of Relief. The court may issue ex parte and temporary orders with regard to any matter within its jurisdiction, and may issue protective orders against domestic violence as provided in subchapter 3.700.

(B) Ex Parte Orders.

(1) Pending the entry of a temporary order, the court may enter an ex parte order if the court is satisfied by specific facts set forth in an affidavit or verified pleading that irreparable injury, loss, or damage will result from the delay required to effect notice, or that notice itself will precipitate adverse action before an order can be issued.

(2) The moving party must arrange for the service of true copies of the ex parte order on the friend of the court and the other party.

(3) An ex parte order is effective upon entry and enforceable upon service.

(4) An ex parte order remains in effect until modified or superseded by a temporary or final order.

(5) An ex parte order providing for child support, custody, or visitation pursuant to MCL 722.27a; MSA 25.312(7a), must include the following notice:

"NOTICE:

"1. You may file a written objection to this order or a motion to modify or rescind this order. You must file the written objection or motion with the clerk of the court within 14 days after you were served with this order. You must serve a true copy of the objection or motion on the friend of the court and the party who obtained the order.

"2. If you file a written objection, the friend of the court must try to resolve the dispute. If the friend of the court cannot resolve the dispute and if you wish to bring the matter before the court without the assistance of counsel, the friend of the court must provide you with form pleadings and written instructions and must schedule a hearing with the court.

"3. The ex parte order will automatically become a temporary order if you do not file a written objection or motion to modify or rescind the ex parte order and a request for a hearing. Even if an objection is filed, the ex parte order will remain in effect and must be obeyed unless changed by a later court order."

(6) In all other cases, the ex parte order must state that it will automatically become a temporary order if the other party does not file a written objection or motion to modify or rescind the ex parte order and a request for a hearing. The written objection or motion and the request for a hearing must be filed with the clerk of the court, and a true copy provided to the friend of the court and the other party, within 14 days after the order is served.

(a) If there is a timely objection or motion and a request for a hearing, the hearing must be held within 21 days after the objection or motion and request are filed.

(b) A change that occurs after the hearing may be made retroactive to the date the ex parte order was entered.

(7) The provisions of MCR 3.310 apply to temporary restraining orders in domestic relations cases.

(C) Temporary Orders.

(1) A request for a temporary order may be made at any time during the pendency of the case by filing a verified motion that sets forth facts sufficient to support the relief requested.

(2) A temporary order may not be issued without a hearing, unless the parties agree otherwise or fail to file a written objection or motion as provided in subrules (B)(5) and (6).

(3) A temporary order may be modified at any time during the pendency of the case, following a hearing and upon a showing of good cause.

(4) A temporary order must state its effective date and whether its provisions may be modified retroactively by a subsequent order.

(5) A temporary order remains in effect until modified or until the entry of the final judgment or order.

(6) A temporary order not yet satisfied is vacated by the entry of the final judgment or order, unless specifically continued or preserved. This does not apply to support arrearages that have been assigned to the state, which are preserved unless specifically waived or reduced by the final judgment or order.

[Adopted effective May 1, 1993; amended effective April 1, 1996; September 1, 1997.]

1993 Staff Comment

Parts of revised Rule 3.207 [effective May 1, 1993] come from former Rule 3.206, but much of it is new. The revised rule clarifies and makes consistent existing practice. The terms "ex parte" and "temporary" are continued, but the term "interim" has been eliminated. "Hearing" in the context of subrule (C)(2) does not imply a full evidentiary hearing. Subrule (C)(3) permits modification of a temporary order on the basis of a showing of good cause, whereas former subrule 3.206(D)(3) permitted modification of a temporary order upon a change of circumstance. "Good cause" includes the prior entry of a temporary order without an evidentiary hearing. Subrule (D) emphasizes the availability of protective orders, as a matter of public concern and policy.

Staff Comment to 1996 Amendment

The 1996 amendment of MCR 3.207(B)(5) extended the mandatory notice provision in visitation cases to child support and custody cases. Other changes were made to reflect the November 1993 amendment of MCL 722.27a(13); MSA 25.312(7a)(13).

Staff Comment to 1997 Amendment

The amendments of MCR 3.201, 3.207, and 8.117 and addition of subchapter 3.700 [effective September 1, 1997], are designed to implement the statutes providing for the issuance of personal protection orders. See MCL 600.2950; MSA 27A.2950, MCL 600.2950a; MSA 27A.29501(1).

RULE 3.208   FRIEND OF THE COURT

(A) General. The friend of the court has the powers and duties prescribed by statute, including those duties in the Friend of the Court Act, MCL 552.501 et seq.; MSA 25.176(1) et seq., and the Support and Visitation Enforcement Act, MCL 552.601 et seq.; MSA 25.164(1) et seq.

(B) Enforcement. The friend of the court is responsible for initiating proceedings to enforce an order or judgment for support, visitation, or custody.

(1) If a party has failed to comply with an order or judgment, the friend of the court may petition for an order to show cause why the party should not be held in contempt.

(2) The order to show cause must be served personally or by ordinary mail at the party's last known address.

(3) The hearing on the order to show cause may be held no sooner than seven days after the order is served on the party. If service is by ordinary mail, the hearing may be held no sooner than nine days after the order is mailed.

(4) If the party fails to appear in response to the order to show cause, the court may issue an order for arrest.

(5) The relief available under this rule is in addition to any other relief available by statute.

(6) The friend of the court may petition for an order of arrest at any time, if immediate action is necessary.

(C) Allocation and Distribution of Payments.

(1) Except as otherwise provided in this subrule, all payments shall be allocated and distributed as required by the guidelines established by the state court administrator for that purpose.

(2) If the court determines that following the guidelines established by the state court administrator would produce an unjust result in a particular case, the court may order that payments be made in a different manner. The order must include specific findings of fact that set forth the basis for the court's decision, and must direct the payer to designate with each payment the name of the payer and the payee, the case number, the amount, and the date of the order that allows the special payment.

(3) If a payer with multiple cases makes a payment directly to the friend of the court rather than through income withholding, the payment shall be allocated among all the cases unless the payer requests a different allocation in writing at the time of payment and provides the following information about each case for which payment is intended:

(a) the name of the payer,

(b) the name of the payee,

(c) the case number, and

(d) the amount designated for that case.

(4) A notice of income withholding may not be used by the friend of the court or the state disbursement unit to determine the specific allocation or distribution of payments.

(D) Notice to Attorneys.

(1) Copies of notices required to be given to the parties also must be sent to the attorneys of record.

(2) The notice requirement of this subrule remains in effect until 21 days after judgment is entered or until postjudgment matters are concluded, whichever is later.

[Adopted effective May 1, 1993; interim amendment effective January 1, 2001; amended effective April 3, 2001.]

1993 Staff Comment

Former Rule 3.207 has been renumbered and modified [effective May 1, 1993] to eliminate provisions that have been superseded by statute and provisions that impose duties on the friend of the court that are impractical or unrealistic. Consistent with provisions of the federal child support enforcement program, subrule (C) prohibits the deduction of statutory fees from support money. The notice requirement in subrule (D) ends when the attorney's duty ends.

Staff Comment to January 2001 Amendment

The amendment of MCR 3.208(C) on an interim basis [interim effect January 1, 2001] makes the court rule consistent with the requirements of the federal child support enforcement program, and establishes uniform allocation and distribution procedures among the various circuit courts.

Staff Comment to April 2001 Amendment

The permanent adoption on April 3, 2001 of the interim amendments of MCR 3.208(C), which took effect January 1, 2001, kept the court rule consistent with the requirements of the federal child support enforcement program, and established uniform allocation and distribution procedures in the circuit courts.

RULE 3.209   SUSPENSION OF ENFORCEMENT AND DISMISSAL

(A) Suspension of Enforcement.

(1) Because of a reconciliation or for any other reason, a party may file a motion to suspend the automatic enforcement of a support obligation by the friend of the court. Such a motion may be filed before or after the entry of a judgment.

(2) A support obligation cannot be suspended except by court order.

(B) Dismissal. Unless the order of dismissal specifies otherwise, dismissal of an action under MCR 2.502 or MCR 2.504 cancels past-due child support, except for that owed to the State of Michigan.

[Adopted effective May 1, 1993.]

1993 Staff Comment

Subrule (A) of this new rule [effective May 1, 1993] takes into account recent statutory changes and clarifies the steps that a party may take to suspend automatic enforcement of a support obligation. Subrule (B) protects the interests of the state when an action is dismissed.

RULE 3.210   HEARINGS AND TRIALS

(A) In General.

(1) Proofs or testimony may not be taken in an action for divorce or separate maintenance until the expiration of the time prescribed by the applicable statute, except as otherwise provided by this rule.

(2) In cases of unusual hardship or compelling necessity, the court may, upon motion and proper showing, take testimony and render judgment at any time 60 days after the filing of the complaint.

(3) Testimony may be taken conditionally at any time for the purpose of perpetuating it.

(4) Testimony must be taken in person, except that the court may allow testimony to be taken by telephone or other electronically reliable means, in extraordinary circumstances.

(B) Default Cases.

(1) Default cases are governed by MCR 2.603.

(2) A judgment of divorce, separate maintenance, or annulment may not be entered as a matter of course on the default of the defendant because of failure to appear at the hearing or by consent. Every case must be heard in open court on proofs taken, except as otherwise provided by statute or court rule.

(3) If a party is in default, proofs may not be taken unless the judgment fee has been deposited with the court clerk and the proposed judgment has been given to the court.

(4) If the court determines that the proposed judgment is inappropriate, the party who prepared it must, within 14 days, present a modified judgment in conformity with the court's opinion.

(5) If the court determines not to enter the judgment, the court must direct that the judgment fee be returned to the person who deposited it.

(C) Custody of a Minor.

(1) When the custody of a minor is contested, a hearing on the matter must be held within 56 days

    (a) after the court orders, or

    (b) after the filing of notice that a custody hearing is requested,

unless both parties agree to mediation under MCL 552.513; MSA 25.176(13) and mediation is unsuccessful, in which event the hearing must be held within 56 days after the final mediation session.

(2) If a custody action is assigned to a probate judge pursuant to MCL 722.26b; MSA 25.312(6b), a hearing on the matter must be held by the probate judge within 56 days after the case is assigned.

(3) The court must enter a decision within 28 days after the hearing.

(4) The notice required by this subrule may be filed as a separate document, or may be included in another paper filed in the action if the notice is mentioned in the caption.

(5) If a report has been submitted by the friend of the court, the court must give the parties an opportunity to review the report and to file objections before a decision is entered.

(6) The court may extend for good cause the time within which a hearing must be held and a decision rendered under this subrule.

(7) In deciding whether an evidentiary hearing is necessary with regard to a postjudgment motion to change custody, the court must determine, by requiring an offer of proof or otherwise, whether there are contested factual issues that must be resolved in order for the court to make an informed decision on the motion.

(D) The court must make findings of fact as provided in MCR 2.517, except that

(1) findings of fact and conclusions of law are required on contested postjudgment motions to modify a final judgment or order, and

(2) the court may distribute pension, retirement, and other deferred compensation rights with a qualified domestic relations order, without first making a finding with regard to the value of those rights.

[Adopted effective May 1, 1993; amended effective July 1, 2001.]

1993 Staff Comment

Subrule (A) [effective May 1, 1993] expands the authority of the court to render judgment in certain cases after 60 days, which reflects current practice and perceived public concern. It also expressly permits the taking of testimony by electronic means, but only in extraordinary circumstances. Subrule (C) is similar to former subrule 3.206(F), with the addition of a provision for timely hearing if mediation is unsuccessful, and a provision about custody actions pursuant to MCL 722.26b; MSA 25.312(6b).

Staff Comment to 2001 Amendment

The April 3, 2001 amendment of Rule 3.210, effective July 1, 2001, was based on a recommendation from the Michigan Judges Association and made clear that, in deciding whether an evidentiary hearing is necessary, the court must first determine whether there are contested factual issues that must be resolved in order to make an informed decision.

RULE 3.211 JUDGMENTS AND ORDERS

(A) Each separate subject in a judgment or order must be set forth in a separate paragraph that is prefaced by an appropriate heading.

(B) A judgment of divorce, separate maintenance, or annulment must include

(1) the insurance and dower provisions required by MCL 552.101; MSA 25.131;

(2) a determination of the rights of the parties in pension, annuity, and retirement benefits, as required by MCL 552.101(4); MSA 25.131(4);

(3) a determination of the property rights of the parties; and

(4) a provision reserving or denying spousal support, if spousal support is not granted; a judgment silent with regard to spousal support reserves it.

(C) A judgment or order awarding custody of a minor must provide that

(1) the domicile or residence of the minor may not be moved from Michigan without the approval of the judge who awarded custody or the judge's successor, and

(2) the person awarded custody must promptly notify the friend of the court in writing when the minor is moved to another address.

(D) A judgment or order awarding child support or spousal support must

(1) provide for income withholding as required by MCL 552.604; MSA 25.164(4), and state the payer's source of income and the source's address, if known;

(2) set forth the parties' residence addresses, and require parties over whom the court has obtained jurisdiction to inform the friend of the court of any subsequent change of address or employment;

(3) provide for the payment of statutory fees, if child support is to be paid through the office of the friend of the court; and

(4) provide that the support be paid through the office of the friend of the court, unless otherwise stated in the judgment or order; if an order is silent as to method of payment, support must be paid through the office of the friend of the court.

(E) A judgment or order awarding child support also must

(1) specify the amount of support both at the time of judgment and as the number of children for whom there is a support obligation decreases;

(2) provide for payment until the child reaches the age of 18, and may provide for payment after the age of 18, as allowed by law;

(3) provide for health care coverage as required by MCL 722.27; MSA 25.312(7) and MCL 722.3; MSA 25.244(3);

(4) provide for the preservation of child support arrearages owing to the state on the date of the entry of the judgment, whether the arrearages arose under a temporary child support order or under a separate judgment entered pursuant to MCL 552.451 et seq.; MSA 25.222(1) et seq.; and

(5) contain the following provision regarding non-retroactive support, as required by MCL 552.603(10); MSA 25.164(3)(10):

"Except as otherwise provided in section 3 of the support and visitation enforcement act, Act No. 295 of the Public Acts of 1982, being section 552.603 of the Michigan Compiled Laws, a support order that is part of a judgment or is an order in a domestic relations matter as that term is defined in section 31 of the friend of the court act, Act No. 294 of the Public Acts of 1982, being section 552.531 of the Michigan Compiled Laws, is a judgment on and after the date each support payment is due, with the full force, effect, and attributes of a judgment of this state, and is not, on and after the date it is due, subject to retroactive modification."

(F) Unless otherwise ordered, all support arrearages owing to the state are preserved upon entry of a final order or judgment. Upon a showing of good cause and notice to the friend of the court, the prosecuting attorney, and other interested parties, the court may waive or reduce such arrearages.

(G) Within 21 days after the court renders an opinion or the settlement agreement is placed on the record, the moving party must submit a judgment, order, or a motion to settle the judgment or order, unless the court has granted an extension.

(H) Friend of the Court Review. For all judgments and orders containing provisions identified in subrules (C), (D), (E), and (F), the court may require that the judgment or order be submitted to the friend of the court for review.

(I) Service of Judgment or Order.

(1) When a judgment or order is obtained for temporary or permanent spousal support, child support, or separate maintenance, the prevailing party must

immediately deliver one copy to the court clerk. The court clerk must write or stamp "true copy" on the order or judgment and file it with the friend of the court.

(2) The party securing entry of a judgment or order that provides for child support or spousal support must serve a copy on the party ordered to pay the support, as provided in MCR 2.602(D)(1), even if that party is in default.

(3) The record of divorce and annulment required by MCL 333.2864; MSA 14.15(2864) must be filed at the time of the filing of the judgment.

[Adopted effective May 1, 1993.]

1993 Staff Comment

Rule 3.211 [effective May 1, 1993] is a reorganization and expansion of former Rule 3.209, consistent with statutory provisions and the provisions of the Michigan Child Support Guidelines. Subrule (E) takes into account the statutory changes that provide for support beyond age 18 in certain circumstances. Subrules (F), (G) and (H) are new. Subrule (F) requires notice to the friend of the court, the prosecuting attorney, and other interested parties, as well as a showing of good cause, before arrearages owing to the state may be waived or reduced. The prosecutor is included, as legal representative of the state, to insure that the court is adequately advised of such arrearages. Subrule (G) requires the moving party to submit a judgment or order within 21 days after the court issues an opinion or the settlement agreement is put on the record. Subrule (H) provides for the review of judgments and orders by the friend of the court, at the option of the court. There is a new requirement in subrule (I) regarding the filing of the record of divorce and annulment. The term "alimony" has been replaced by the term "spousal support" throughout the rule.

RULE 3.212 POSTJUDGMENT TRANSFER OF DOMESTIC RELATIONS CASES

(A) Motion.

(1) A party, court-ordered custodian, or friend of the court may move for the postjudgment transfer of a domestic relations action in accordance with this rule, or the court may transfer such an action on its own motion. A transfer includes a change of venue and a transfer of all friend of the court responsibilities. The court may enter a consent order transferring a postjudgment domestic relations action, provided the conditions under subrule (B) are met.

(2) The postjudgment transfer of an action initiated pursuant to MCL 780.151 et seq.; MSA 25.225(1) et seq., is controlled by MCR 3.214.

(B) Conditions.

(1) A motion filed by a party or court-ordered custodian may be granted only if all of the following conditions are met:

(a) the transfer of the action is requested on the basis of the residence and convenience of the par-

ties, or other good cause consistent with the best interests of the minor;

(b) neither party nor the court-ordered custodian has resided in the county of current jurisdiction for at least 6 months prior to the filing of the motion;

(c) at least one party or the court-ordered custodian has resided in the county to which the transfer is requested for at least 6 months prior to the filing of the motion; and

(d) the county to which the transfer is requested is not contiguous to the county of current jurisdiction.

(2) When the court or the friend of the court initiates a transfer, the conditions stated in subrule (B)(1) do not apply.

(C) Transfer Order.

(1) The court ordering a postjudgment transfer must enter all necessary orders pertaining to the certification and transfer of the action. The transferring court must send to the receiving court all court files and friend of the court files, ledgers, records, and documents that pertain to the action. Such materials may be used in the receiving jurisdiction in the same manner as in the transferring jurisdiction.

(2) The court may order that any past-due fees and costs be paid to the transferring friend of the court office at the time of transfer.

(3) The court may order that one or both of the parties or the court-ordered custodian pay the cost of the transfer.

(D) Filing Fee. An order transferring a case under this rule must provide that the party who moved for the transfer pay the statutory filing fee applicable to the court to which the action is transferred, except where MCR 2.002 applies. If the parties stipulate to the transfer of a case, they must share equally the cost of transfer unless the court orders otherwise. In either event, the transferring court must submit the filing fee to the court to which the action is transferred, at the time of transfer. If the court or the friend of the court initiates the transfer, the statutory filing fee is waived.

(E) Physical Transfer of Files. Court and friend of the court files must be transferred by registered or certified mail, return receipt requested, or by another secure method of transfer.

[Adopted effective May 1, 1993.]

1993 Staff Comment

Former Rule 3.213 has been changed [effective May 1, 1993] to provide for the transfer of a case at the initiation of the court or the friend of the court, in the event that the court or the friend of the court is disqualified or for other reason believes that a transfer is necessary. Subrule (D) clarifies that the filing fee is to accompany the physical transfer of a case.

RULE 3.213   POSTJUDGMENT MOTIONS AND ENFORCEMENT

Postjudgment motions in domestic relations actions are governed by MCR 2.119.

[Adopted effective May 1, 1993.]

1993 Staff Comment

This is a new rule [effective May 1, 1993]. There previously was no specific rule for postjudgment motions in domestic relations cases.

RULE 3.214.   ACTIONS UNDER UNIFORM ACTS

(A) Governing Rules.   Actions under the Revised Uniform Reciprocal Enforcement of Support Act (RURESA), MCL 780.151 *et seq.*, the Uniform Interstate Family Support Act (UIFSA), MCL 552.1101 *et seq.*, and the Uniform Child–Custody Jurisdiction and Enforcement Act (UCCJEA), MCL 722.1101 *et seq.*, are governed by the rules applicable to other civil actions, except as otherwise provided by those acts and this rule.

(B) RURESA Actions.

(1) Definition. As used in this subrule, "support order" is defined by MCL 780.153b(8).

(2) Transfer; Initiating and Responding RURESA Cases.

(a) If a Michigan court initiates a RURESA action and there exists in another Michigan court a prior valid support order, the initiating court must transfer to that other court any RURESA order entered in a responding state. The initiating court must inform the responding court of the transfer.

(b) If a court in another state initiates a RURESA action and there exists in Michigan a prior valid support order, the responsive proceeding should be commenced in the court that issued the prior valid support order. If the responsive proceeding is commenced erroneously in any other Michigan court and a RURESA order enters, that court, upon learning of the error, must transfer the RURESA order to the court that issued the prior valid support order. The transferring court must inform the initiating court of the transfer.

(c) A court ordering a transfer must send to the court that issued the prior valid support order all pertinent papers, including all court files and friend of the court files, ledgers, records, and documents.

(d) Court files and friend of the court files must be transferred by registered or certified mail, return receipt requested, or by other secure method.

(e) The friend of the court office that issued the prior valid support order must receive and disburse immediately all payments made by the obligor or sent by a responding state.

(C) Sending Notices in UIFSA Cases.   The friend of the court office shall send all notices and copies of orders required to be sent by the tribunal under MCL 552.1101 *et seq.*

(D) Registration of Child Custody Determinations Under UCCJEA.   The procedure for registration and enforcement of a child custody determination by the court of another state is as provided in MCL 722.1304. There is no fee for the registration of such a determination.

[Adopted effective May 1, 1993; amended effective June 1, 1997; September 11, 2002.]

1993 Staff Comment

The revised rule [effective May 1, 1993] is essentially the same as former Rule 3.210.

Staff Comment to 1997 Amendment

May 20, 1997, these amendments [effective June 1, 1997] are made to provide for the implementation of the Uniform Interstate Family Support Act, which is effective June 1, 1997. This Act was adopted so that Michigan would be in compliance with the federal Personal Responsibility and Work Opportunity Act of 1996.

The amendment to MCR 3.214 [effective June 1, 1997] makes it clear that the circuit court friend of the court office is responsible for sending various notices required by the Uniform Interstate Family Support Act. The amendment to MCR 8.117 provides new case classification codes for actions filed pursuant to this Act.

Staff Comment to 2002 Amendment

The September 11, 2002, amendments of MCR 3.206, 3.214, 3.705, 3.706, 3.708, 5.982, and 8.119, which were given immediate effect, are related to the group of domestic violence statutes enacted in December 2001 that took effect April 1, 2002.

The changes in MCR 3.206 and 3.214 are related to 2001 PA 195, which adopted the Uniform Child–Custody Jurisdiction and Enforcement Act, MCL 722.1101 *et seq.* There is also some nonsubstantive reorganization of MCR 3.214.

The amendment of MCR 3.705 implements the statutory provisions regarding the statement of reasons for granting or denying personal protection orders. See 2001 PA 196.

The amendment of MCR 3.706 incorporates the statutory provisions regarding enforceability of Michigan personal protection orders in other jurisdictions. See 2001 PA 200 and 201.

MCR 3.708 and 5.982 are amended to include foreign protection orders, which are made enforceable in Michigan by 2001 PA 197.

MCR 8.119(F) is amended to conform to 2001 PA 205, which directs that when a motion to seal court records involves allegations of domestic violence, the court is to consider the safety of the potential victim in ruling on the motion.

The staff comment is published only for the benefit of the bench and bar and is not an authoritative construction by the Court.

RULE 3.215　DOMESTIC RELATIONS REFEREES

(A) Qualifications of Referees. A referee appointed by the chief judge of the circuit pursuant to MCL 552.507(1); MSA 25.176(7)(1) must be a member in good standing of the State Bar of Michigan. A friend of the court who is not a lawyer, but who is serving as a referee at the time of adoption of this rule, may continue to serve. A successor must meet the qualifications established by this rule.

(B) Referrals to the Referee.

(1) The chief judge may refer motions of a particular kind to a referee, by administrative order.

(2) To the extent allowed by law, the judge to whom an action is assigned may refer other motions to a referee

(a) on written stipulation of the parties,

(b) on written motion by a party, or

(c) on the judge's own initiative.

(C) Scheduling of the Referee Hearing.

(1) Within 14 days after receiving a motion under subrule (B)(1) or a referral under subrule (B)(2), the referee must schedule the matter for hearing.

(2) The referee must serve a notice of hearing on the attorneys for the parties, or on the parties if they are not represented by counsel. The notice of hearing must clearly state that the matter will be heard by a referee.

(D) Conduct of Hearings.

(1) The Michigan Rules of Evidence apply to referee hearings.

(2) A referee must provide the parties with notice of the right to request a judicial hearing by giving

(a) oral notice during the hearing, and

(b) written notice in the recommendation for an order.

(3) Testimony must be taken in person, except that a referee may allow testimony to be taken by telephone or other electronically reliable means, in extraordinary circumstances.

(4) An electronic or stenographic record must be kept of all hearings.

(E) Posthearing Procedures.

(1) Within 21 days after a hearing, except for a hearing on income withholding, the referee must either make a statement of findings on the record or submit a written, signed report containing a summary of testimony and a statement of findings. In either event, the referee must make a recommendation for an order and arrange for it to be submitted to the court and the attorneys for the parties, or the parties if they are not represented by counsel. A proof of service must be filed with the court. If the recommendation for an order is approved by the court and no written objection is filed with the court clerk within 21 days after the recommendation is served on the attorneys for the parties, or the parties if they are not represented by counsel, the order will take effect.

(2) If the hearing concerns income withholding, the referee must arrange for a recommended order to be submitted to the court forthwith. If the recommended order is approved by the court, it must be given immediate effect pursuant to MCL 552.607(4); MSA 25.164(7)(4).

(3) A party may obtain a judicial hearing on any matter that has been the subject of a referee hearing by filing

(a) a written objection and notice of hearing within 14 days after the referee's recommended order is served on the attorneys for the parties, or the parties if they are not represented by counsel, if the order is for income withholding, or

(b) a written objection and notice of hearing within 21 days after the referee's recommendation for an order is served on the attorneys for the parties, or the parties if they are not represented by counsel, if the order concerns any other matter.

(4) The party who requests a judicial hearing must serve the objection and notice of hearing on the opposing party or counsel in the manner provided in MCR 2.119(C).

(F) Judicial Hearings.

(1) The judicial hearing must be held within 21 days after the written objection is filed, unless the time is extended by the court for good cause.

(2) If both parties consent, the judicial hearing may be based solely on the record of the referee hearing.

(3) If the court determines that an objection is frivolous or has been interposed for the purpose of delay, the court may assess reasonable costs and attorney fees.

[Adopted effective May 1, 1993.]

1993 Staff Comment

There have been discrepancies among the circuits regarding domestic relations referees. This new rule [effective May 1, 1993] brings consistency to the system. Subrule (A) provides that referees must be members of the state bar. A grandfather clause permits a nonlawyer friend of the court to continue to serve as referee. Subrules (B) and (C) provide for timely scheduling and notice. Subrule (D) clarifies that an electronic or stenographic record of referee hearings is required, and permits a referee to take testimony by electronic means, in extraordinary circumstances. Subrule (E) explains procedures for requesting a judicial hearing. Subrule (F) provides that the judicial hearing may be based solely on the record of the referee hearing, if the parties consent.

RULE 3.216 DOMESTIC RELATIONS MEDIATION

(A) Scope and Applicability of Rule, Definitions.

(1) All domestic relations cases, as defined in MCL 552.502(h); MSA 25.176(2)(h), are subject to mediation under this rule, unless otherwise provided by statute or court rule.

(2) Domestic relations mediation is a nonbinding process in which a neutral third party facilitates communication between parties to promote settlement. If the parties so request, and the mediator agrees to do so, the mediator may provide a written recommendation for settlement of any issues that remain unresolved at the conclusion of a mediation proceeding. This procedure, known as evaluative mediation, is governed by subrule (I).

(3) This rule does not restrict the Friend of the Court from enforcing custody, parenting time, and support orders.

(4) The court may order, on stipulation of the parties, the use of other settlement procedures.

(B) Mediation Plan. Each trial court that submits domestic relations cases to mediation under this rule shall include in its alternative dispute resolution plan adopted under MCR 2.410(B) provisions governing selection of domestic relations mediators, and for providing parties with information about mediation in the family division as soon as reasonably practical.

(C) Referral to Mediation.

(1) On written stipulation of the parties, on written motion of a party, or on the court's initiative, the court may submit to mediation by written order any contested issue in a domestic relations case, including postjudgment matters.

(2) The court may not submit contested issues to evaluative mediation unless all parties so request.

(3) Parties who are subject to a personal protection order or who are involved in a child abuse and neglect proceeding may not be referred to mediation without a hearing to determine whether mediation is appropriate.

(D) Objections to Referral to Mediation.

(1) To object to mediation, a party must file a written motion to remove the case from mediation and a notice of hearing of the motion, and serve a copy on the attorneys of record within 14 days after receiving notice of the order assigning the action to mediation. The motion must be set for hearing within 14 days after it is filed, unless the hearing is adjourned by agreement of counsel or unless the court orders otherwise.

(2) A timely motion must be heard before the case is mediated.

(3) Cases may be exempt from mediation on the basis of the following:

(a) child abuse or neglect;

(b) domestic abuse, unless attorneys for both parties will be present at the mediation session;

(c) inability of one or both parties to negotiate for themselves at the mediation, unless attorneys for both parties will be present at the mediation session;

(d) reason to believe that one or both parties' health or safety would be endangered by mediation; or

(e) for other good cause shown.

(E) Selection of Mediator.

(1) Domestic relations mediation will be conducted by a mediator selected as provided in this subrule.

(2) The parties may stipulate to the selection of a mediator. A mediator selected by agreement of the parties need not meet the qualifications set forth in subrule (G). The court must appoint a mediator stipulated to by the parties, provided the mediator is willing to serve within a period that would not interfere with the court's scheduling of the case for trial.

(3) If the parties have not stipulated to a mediator, the parties must indicate whether they prefer a mediator who is willing conduct evaluative mediation. Failure to indicate a preference will be treated as not requesting evaluative mediation.

(4) If the parties have not stipulated to a mediator, the judge may recommend, but not appoint one. If the judge does not make a recommendation, or if the recommendation is not accepted by the parties, the ADR clerk will assign a mediator from the list of qualified mediators maintained under subrule (F). The assignment shall be made on a rotational basis, except that if the parties have requested evaluative mediation, only a mediator who is willing to provide an evaluation may be assigned.

(5) The rule for disqualification of a mediator is the same as that provided in MCR 2.003 for the disqualification of a judge. The mediator must promptly disclose any potential basis for disqualification.

(F) List of Mediators.

(1) *Application.* An eligible person desiring to serve as a domestic relations mediator may apply to the ADR clerk to be placed on the court's list of mediators. Application forms shall be available in the office of the ADR clerk.

(a) The form shall include a certification that

(i) the applicant meets the requirements for service under the court's selection plan;

(ii) the applicant will not discriminate against parties or attorneys on the basis of race, ethnic origin, gender, or other protected personal characteristic; and

(iii) the mediator will comply with the court's ADR plan, orders of the court regarding cases submitted to mediation, and the standards of conduct adopted by the State Court Administrator under subrule (K).

(b) The applicant shall indicate on the form whether the applicant is willing to offer evaluative mediation, and the applicant's hourly rate for providing mediation services.

(c) The form shall include an optional section identifying the applicant's gender and racial/ethnic background; however, this section shall not be made available to the public.

(2) *Review of Applications.* The court's ADR plan shall provide for a person or committee to review applications annually, or more frequently if appropriate, and compile a list of qualified mediators.

(a) Persons meeting the qualifications specified in this rule shall be placed on the list of approved mediators. Approved mediators shall be placed on the list for a fixed period, not to exceed 5 years, and must reapply at the end of that time in the same manner as persons seeking to be added to the list.

(b) Selections shall be made without regard to race, ethnic origin, or gender. Residency or principal place of business may not be a qualification.

(c) The approved list and the applications of approved mediators, except for the optional section identifying the applicant's gender and racial/ethnic background, shall be available to the public in the office of the ADR clerk.

(3) *Rejection; Reconsideration.* Applicants who are not placed on the list shall be notified of that decision. Within 21 days of notification of the decision to reject an application, the applicant may seek reconsideration of the ADR clerk's decision by the presiding judge of the family division. The court does not need to provide a hearing. Documents considered in the initial review process shall be retained for at least the period during which the applicant can seek reconsideration of the original decision.

(4) *Removal from List.* The ADR clerk may remove from the list mediators who have demonstrated incompetence, bias, made themselves consistently unavailable to serve as a mediator, or for other just cause. Within 21 days of notification of the decision to remove a mediator from the list, the mediator may seek reconsideration of the ADR clerk's decision by the presiding judge of the family division. The court does not need to provide a hearing.

(G) Qualification of Mediators.

(1) To be eligible to serve as a domestic relations mediator under this rule, a applicant must meet the following minimum qualifications:

(a) The applicant must

(i) be a licensed attorney, a licensed or limited licensed psychologist, a licensed professional counselor, or a licensed marriage and family therapist;

(ii) have a masters degree in counseling, social work, or marriage and family therapy;

(iii) have a graduate degree in a behavioral science; or

(iv) have 5 years experience in family counseling.

(b) The applicant must have completed a training program approved by the State Court Administrator providing the generally accepted components of domestic relations mediation skills.

(c) The applicant must have observed two domestic relations mediation proceedings conducted by an approved mediator, and have conducted one domestic relations mediation to conclusion under the supervision and observation of an approved mediator.

(2) An applicant who has specialized experience or training, but does not meet the specific requirements of subrule (G)(1), may apply to the ADR clerk for special approval. The ADR clerk shall make the determination on the basis of criteria provided by the State Court Administrator.

(3) Approved mediators are required to obtain 8 hours of advanced mediation training during each 2-year period. Failure to submit documentation establishing compliance is grounds for removal from the list under subrule(F)(4).

(4) Additional qualifications may not be imposed upon mediators.

(H) Mediation Procedure.

(1) The mediator must schedule a mediation session within a reasonable time at a location accessible by the parties.

(2) A mediator may require that no later than 3 business days before the mediation session, each party submit to the mediator, and serve on the opposing party, a mediation summary that provides the following information, where relevant:

(a) the facts and circumstances of the case;

(b) the issues in dispute;

(c) a description of the marital assets and their estimated value, where such information is appropriate and reasonably ascertainable;

(d) the income and expenses of the parties;

(e) a proposed settlement; and

(f) such documentary evidence as may be available to substantiate information contained in the summary.

Failure to submit these materials to the mediator within the designated time may subject the offending party to sanctions imposed by the court.

(3) The parties must attend the mediation session in person unless excused by the mediator.

(4) Except for legal counsel, the parties may not bring other persons to the mediation session, whether expert or lay witnesses, unless permission is first obtained from the mediator, after notice to opposing counsel. If the mediator believes it would be helpful to the settlement of the case, the mediator may request information or assistance from third persons at the time of the mediation session.

(5) The mediator shall discuss with the parties and counsel, if any, the facts and issues involved. The mediation will continue until a settlement is reached, the mediator determines that a settlement is not likely to be reached, the end of the first mediation session, or until a time agreed to by the parties.

(6) Within 7 days of the completion of mediation, the mediator shall so advise the court, stating only the date of completion of the process, who participated in the mediation, whether settlement was reached, and whether further ADR proceedings are contemplated. If an evaluation will be made under subrule (I), the mediator may delay reporting to the court until completion of the evaluation process.

(7) If a settlement is reached as a result of the mediation, to be binding, the terms of that settlement must be reduced to a signed writing by the parties or acknowledged by the parties on an audio or video recording. After a settlement has been reached, the parties shall take steps necessary to enter judgment as in the case of other settlements.

(8) Statements made during the mediation, including statements made in written submissions, may not be used in any other proceedings, including trial. Any communications between the parties or counsel and the mediator relating to a mediation are confidential and shall not be disclosed without the written consent of all parties. This prohibition does not apply to

(a) the report of the mediator under subrule (H)(6),

(b) information reasonably required by court personnel to administer and evaluate the mediation program,

(c) information necessary for the court to resolve disputes regarding the mediator's fee, or

(d) information necessary for the court to consider issues raised under MCR 2.410(D)(3) or 3.216(H)(2).

(I) Evaluative Mediation.

(1) This subrule applies if the parties requested evaluative mediation, or if they do so at the conclusion of mediation and the mediator is willing to provide an evaluation.

(2) If a settlement is not reached during mediation, the mediator, within a reasonable period after the conclusion of mediation shall prepare a written report to the parties setting forth the mediator's proposed recommendation for settlement purposes only. The mediator's recommendation shall be submitted to the parties of record only and may not be submitted or made available to the court.

(3) If both parties accept the mediator's recommendation in full, the attorneys shall proceed to have a judgment entered in conformity with the recommendation.

(4) If the mediator's recommendation is not accepted in full by both parties and the parties are unable to reach an agreement as to the remaining contested issues, mediator shall report to the court under subrule (H)(6), and the case shall proceed toward trial.

(5) A court may not impose sanctions against either party for rejecting the mediator's recommendation. The court may not inquire and neither the parties nor the mediator may inform the court of the identity of the party or parties who rejected the mediator's recommendation.

(6) The mediator's report and recommendation may not be read by the court and may not be admitted into evidence or relied upon by the court as evidence of any of the information contained in it without the consent of both parties. The court shall not request the parties' consent to read the mediator's recommendation.

(J) Fees.

(1) A mediator is entitled to reasonable compensation based on an hourly rate commensurate with the mediator's experience and usual charges for services performed.

(2) Before mediation, the parties shall agree in writing that each shall pay one-half of the mediator's fee no later than:

(a) 42 days after the mediation process is concluded or the service of the mediator's report and recommendation under subrule (I)(2), or

(b) the entry of judgment, or

(c) the dismissal of the action,

whichever occurs first. If the court finds that some other allocation of fees is appropriate, given the economic circumstances of the parties, the court may order that one of the parties pay more than one-half of the fee.

(3) If acceptable to the mediator, the court may order an arrangement for the payment of the mediator's fee other than that provided in subrule (J)(2).

(4) The mediator's fee is deemed a cost of the action, and the court may make an appropriate judgment under MCL 552.13(l); MSA 25.93(l) to enforce the payment of the fee.

(5) In the event either party objects to the total fee of the mediator, the matter may be scheduled before the trial judge for determination of the reasonableness of the fee.

(K) Standards of Conduct. The State Court Administrator shall develop and approve standards of conduct for domestic relations mediators designed to promote honesty, integrity, and impartiality in providing court-connected dispute resolution services. These standards shall be made a part of all training and educational requirements for court-connected programs, shall be provided to all mediators involved in court-connected programs, and shall be available to the public.

[Adopted effective May 1, 1993; amended effective October 1, 1997; August 1, 2000.]

1993 Staff Comment

Former MCR 3.211 was approved by the Supreme Court effective October 1, 1987, for a one-year period. Local rules and administrative orders relating to domestic relations mediation were suspended in the interim. The Court extended the rule on July 8, 1988, until further order. Pending a full review, the rule again has been extended, as renumbered [effective May 1, 1993], with only minor changes for grammar and style, until further order of the Court.

Staff Comment to 1997 Amendment

The May 8, 1997 [effective October 1, 1997], order repeals MCR 4.003, which governed removal of cases from circuit to district court, effective July 1, 1997. This reinstates the February 28, 1997, repeal of the rule, which was suspended on March 13, 1997.

In addition, the order postpones the effective date of earlier amendments of MCR 2.403, 2.405, and 3.216, and new MCR 2.404, affecting mediation procedure, to October 1, 1997. The order also makes adjustments in MCR 2.403(K) and (N) in light of the repeal of MCR 4.003. The text of MCR 2.403, 2.404, 2.405 and 3.216 is the same as that adopted in the Court's March 5, 1997, order dealing with those rules.

Staff Comment to 2000 Amendment

The May 8, 2000, amendments [effective August 1, 2000] are based on the recommendations of the Michigan Supreme Court Dispute Resolution Task Force, which were published for comment on May 10, 1999 [see 459 Mich 1251], and were the subject of a series of public hearings across the state.

The Task Force report, issued in January 1999, and its Addendum report, issued in January 2000 after receipt of comments, should be consulted for the background and details of the amendments. Basically, the changes are as follows:

The amendments of MCR 2.403, 2.404, 2.405, 2.501, 2.502 and 2.503 are mainly to change terminology, replacing "mediation," as used in current MCR 2.403, with the term "case evaluation." "Mediation" will be used to describe the facilitative process established in MCR 2.411, in keeping with the generally accepted usage of the term.

MCR 2.401 is amended to direct consideration of alternative dispute resolution processes at scheduling and pretrial conferences.

New MCR 2.410 has general provisions governing referral of cases to alternative dispute resolution processes. Local courts wishing to use ADR techniques are to adopt ADR plans within the framework provided by the rule.

The one ADR process that is specifically established by the rules is mediation under new MCR 2.411. Among other things, the rule establishes general standards for mediator qualifications, and procedures for selection of mediators.

MCR 3.216, the domestic relations mediation rule, is substantially revised, to be more comparable to the mediation process in MCR 2.411.

MCR 5.143, regarding use of alternative dispute resolution processes in probate court, is amended to conform to the other rule changes.

Dissenting Statement of Justice Kelly to 2000 Amendment

I support the expanded use of alternative dispute resolution by our courts. However, I cannot cast a vote favoring the proposed Dispute Resolution Court Rules for two reasons: 1) they authorize judges to compel parties to submit to mediation and 2) they include nonlawyers as mediators and other ADR providers.

Regarding the mandatory nature of the new rules, I believe that mediation is, by its very nature, a process that works only when the parties enter into it voluntarily. I would support rules that permit courts to order parties to a session at which the merits of ADR are explored, but not that mandate mediation.

It is my fear that mandatory mediation will present insurmountable financial obstacles to low income litigants and could even provoke challenges based on a violation of due process principles. I am concerned that, in some heavily burdened courts, judges may use the new rules, not as an option for the parties, but as a docket control mechanism for the court. Also, I find no limit in the rules to the number of times a party could be ordered to an ADR process.

Mediation should not become yet another hurdle to a just resolution of disputes. Parties should not feel pressed to settle against their best interests, or involuntarily to expend financial resources in excess of the normal costs of trial. Litigation, without the new rules, is already too costly.

I agree with the Board of Commissioners of the State Bar of Michigan that, absent agreement of the parties, only licensed lawyers should be allowed to serve as ADR providers. Mediation and other types of ADR typically involve complex legal matters requiring skilled ADR providers. Yet, no system has been developed to ensure the training and accountability of nonlawyers who participate.

Finally, I agree with the Open Justice Commission's recommendations that chief judges should be required to report the race, ethnicity, and gender of case evaluators and other ADR providers that they appoint. I view this as a vital step toward ensuring persons wishing to function as ADR providers will not be passed over solely on the basis of their race, gender, ethnic background, or similar factors.

RULE 3.217 ACTIONS UNDER THE PATERNITY ACT

(A) Governing Law. Procedure in actions under the Paternity Act, MCL 722.711 et seq.; MSA 25.491 et seq., is governed by the rules applicable to other civil actions except as otherwise provided by this rule and the act.

(B) Jury Demand. In an action brought under the Paternity Act, either the mother or the alleged father may demand a trial by jury. MCR 2.508 governs the demand for and waiver of trial by jury.

(C) Blood or Tissue Typing Tests. A petition for blood or tissue typing tests under MCL 722.716; MSA 25.496 must be filed at or before the pretrial conference or, if a pretrial conference is not held, within the time specified by the court. Failure to timely petition waives the right to such tests, unless the court, in the interest of justice, permits a petition at a later time.

(D) Advice Regarding Right to an Attorney.

(1) The summons issued under MCL 722.714; MSA 25.494 must include a form advising the alleged father of the right to an attorney as described in subrule (D)(2), and the procedure for requesting the appointment of an attorney. The form must be served with the summons and the complaint, and the proof of service must so indicate.

(2) If the alleged father appears in court following the issuance of a summons under MCL 722.714; MSA 25.494, the court must personally advise him that he is entitled to the assistance of an attorney, and that the court will appoint an attorney at public expense, at his request, if he is financially unable to retain an attorney of his choice.

(3) If the alleged father indicates that he wants to proceed without an attorney, the record must affirmatively show that he was given the advice required by subrule (D)(2) and that he waived the right to counsel.

(4) If the alleged father does not appear in court following the issuance of a summons under MCL 722.714; MSA 25.494, subrule (D)(3) does not apply.

(E) Visitation Rights of Noncustodial Parent.

(1) On the petition of either party, the court may provide in the order of filiation for such reasonable visitation by the noncustodial parent as the court deems justified and in the best interests of the child.

(2) Absent a petition from either party, the right of reasonable visitation is reserved.

[Adopted effective May 1, 1993.]

1993 Staff Comment

The revised rule [effective May 1, 1993] is similar to former Rule 3.212. Because of statutory changes, subrule (D) has been modified to eliminate the provision for appearance following issuance of a summons.

RULE 3.218 ACCESS TO FRIEND OF THE COURT RECORDS

(A) General Definitions. When used in this subrule, unless the context indicates otherwise,

(1) "records" means paper files, computer files, microfilm, microfiche, audio tape, video tape, and photographs;

(2) "access" means inspection of records, obtaining copies of records upon receipt of payment for costs of reproduction, and oral transmission by staff of information contained in friend of the court records;

(3) "confidential information" means

(a) staff notes from investigations, mediation sessions, and settlement conferences;

(b) Family Independence Agency protective services reports;

(c) formal mediation records;

(d) communications from minors;

(e) friend of the court grievances filed by the opposing party and the responses;

(f) a party's address or any other information if release is prohibited by a court order;

(g) except as provided in MCR 3.219, any information for which a privilege could be claimed, or that was provided by a governmental agency subject to the express written condition that it remain confidential; and

(h) all information classified as confidential by the laws and regulations of title IV, part D of the Social Security Act, 42 USC 651 *et seq*.

(B) A party, third-party custodian, guardian, guardian ad litem or counsel for a minor, lawyer-guardian ad litem, and an attorney of record must be given access to friend of the court records related to the case, other than confidential information.

(C) A citizen advisory committee established under the Friend of the Court Act, MCL 552.501 *et seq*.; MSA 25.176(1) *et seq*.,

(1) shall be given access to a grievance filed with the friend of the court, and to information related to the case, other than confidential information;

(2) may be given access to confidential information related to a grievance if the court so orders, upon clear demonstration by the committee that the information is necessary to the performance of its duties and that the release will not impair the rights of a party or the well-being of a child involved in the case.

When a citizen advisory committee requests information that may be confidential, the friend of the court shall notify the parties of the request and that they have 14 days from the date the notice was mailed to file a written response with the court. If the court grants access to the information, it may impose such terms and conditions as it determines are appropriate to protect the rights of a party or the well-being of a child.

(D) Protective services personnel from the Family Independence Agency must be given access to friend of the court records related to the investigation of alleged abuse and neglect.

(E) The prosecuting attorney and personnel from the Office of Child Support and the Family Independence Agency must be given access to friend of the court records required to perform the functions required by title IV, part D of the Social Security Act, 42 USC 651 *et seq.*

(F) Auditors from state and federal agencies must be given access to friend of the court records required to perform their audit functions.

(G) Any person who is denied access to friend of the court records or confidential information may file a motion for an order of access with the judge assigned to the case or, if none, the chief judge.

(H) A court, by administrative order adopted pursuant to MCR 8.112(B), may make reasonable regulations necessary to protect friend of the court records and to prevent excessive and unreasonable interference with the discharge of friend of the court functions.

[Adopted effective May 1, 1993; amended effective April 1, 2001.]

1993 Staff Comment

This new rule [effective May 1, 1993] insures that there will be reasonable access to friend of the court files.

Staff Comment to 2000 Amendment

The December 7, 2000 amendments of MCR 3.218, effective April 1, 2001, are consistent with changes made effective March 1, 1999, to the Child Custody Act, MCL 722.21 *et seq.*; MSA 25.312(1) *et seq.*, and the Friend of the Court Act, MCL 552.501 *et seq.*; MSA 25.176(1) *et seq.*

RULE 3.219 DISSEMINATION OF A PROFESSIONAL REPORT

If there is a dispute involving custody, visitation, or change of domicile, and the court uses a community resource to assist its determination, the court must assure that copies of the written findings and recommendations of the resource are provided to the friend of the court and to the attorneys of record for the parties, or the parties if they are not represented by counsel. The attorneys for the parties, or the parties if they are not represented by counsel, may file objections to the report before a decision is made.

[Adopted effective May 1, 1993.]

1993 Staff Comment

This is a new rule [effective May 1, 1993]. It recognizes the circuit court's ability to use community resources in resolving disputes under the Child Custody Act.

RULE 3.220 INCARCERATED PARTIES [RENUMBERED]

[Renumbered as rule 2.004 and amended effective January 1, 2003.]

SUBCHAPTER 3.300 EXTRAORDINARY WRITS

RULE 3.301 EXTRAORDINARY WRITS IN GENERAL

(A) Applicability and Scope of Rules.

(1) A civil action or appropriate motion in a pending action may be brought to obtain

(a) superintending control,

(b) habeas corpus,

(c) mandamus, or

(d) quo warranto.

Unless a particular rule or statute specifically provides otherwise, an original action may not be commenced in the Supreme Court or the Court of Appeals if the circuit court would have jurisdiction of an action seeking that relief.

(2) These special rules govern the procedure for seeking the writs or relief formerly obtained by the writs, whether the right to relief is created by statute or common law. If the right to relief is created by statute, the limitations on relief in the statute apply, as well as the limitations on relief in these rules.

(3) The general rules of procedure apply except as otherwise provided in this subchapter.

(B) Joinder of Claims. More than one kind of writ may be sought in an action either as an independent claim or as an alternative claim. Subject to MCR 2.203, other claims may be joined in an action for a writ or writs.

(C) Process; Service of Writs. Process must be issued and served as in other civil actions. However, if a writ, order, or order to show cause is issued before service of process, then service of the writ, order, or order to show cause in the manner prescribed in MCR 2.105, accompanied by a copy of the complaint, makes service of other process unnecessary.

(D) Assignment for Trial. Actions brought under these special rules may be given precedence under MCR 2.501(B).

(E) Records. The action taken on applications for writs or orders to show cause must be noted in court records in the same manner as actions taken in other civil actions.

(F) No Automatic Stay. The automatic stay provisions of MCR 2.614(A) do not apply to judgments in actions brought under this subchapter.

(G) Procedure Where Relief Is Sought in Supreme Court or Court of Appeals.

(1) MCR 7.304 applies to original proceedings brought in the Supreme Court to obtain relief under this subchapter.

(2) MCR 7.206 applies to original proceedings brought in the Court of Appeals to obtain relief under this subchapter.

[Effective March 1, 1985.]

1985 Staff Comment

MCR 3.301 is comparable to GCR 1963, 710.

The [March 1, 1985] amendment of MCR 3.301(A)(1) adds language comparable to that found in GCR 1963, 710.1(3), providing that original actions are not to be brought in the Supreme Court or Court of Appeals if the circuit court would have jurisdiction.

GCR 1963, 710.7, regarding the procedures to be followed in the Court of Appeals, is replaced with cross-references to the provisions of chapter 7 governing original proceedings in the Supreme Court and the Court of Appeals.

RULE 3.302 SUPERINTENDING CONTROL

(A) Scope. A superintending control order enforces the superintending control power of a court over lower courts or tribunals.

(B) Policy Concerning Use. If another adequate remedy is available to the party seeking the order, a complaint for superintending control may not be filed. See subrule (D)(2), and MCR 7.101(A)(2), and 7.304(A).

(C) Writs Superseded. A superintending control order replaces the writs of certiorari and prohibition and the writ of mandamus when directed to a lower court or tribunal.

(D) Jurisdiction.

(1) The Supreme Court, the Court of Appeals, and the circuit court have jurisdiction to issue superintending control orders to lower courts or tribunals. In this rule the term "circuit court" includes the Recorder's Court of the City of Detroit as to superintending control actions of which that court has jurisdiction.

(2) When an appeal in the Supreme Court, the Court of Appeals, the circuit court, or the recorder's court is available, that method of review must be used. If superintending control is sought and an appeal is available, the complaint for superintending control must be dismissed.

(E) Procedure for Superintending Control in Circuit Court.

(1) *Complaint.* A person seeking superintending control in the circuit court must file a complaint with the court. Only the plaintiff's name may appear in the title of the action (for example, *In re Smith*). The plaintiff must serve a copy of the complaint on the court or tribunal over which superintending control is sought. If the superintending control action arises out of a particular action, a copy of the complaint must also be served on each other party to the proceeding in that court or tribunal.

(2) *Answer.* Anyone served under subrule (E)(1) may file an answer within 21 days after the complaint is served.

(3) *Issuance of Order; Dismissal.*

(a) After the filing of a complaint and answer or, if no answer is filed, after expiration of the time for filing an answer, the court may

(i) issue an order to show cause why the order requested should not be issued,

(ii) issue the order requested, or

(iii) dismiss the complaint.

(b) If a need for immediate action is shown, the court may enter an order before an answer is filed.

(c) The court may require in an order to show cause that additional records and papers be filed.

(d) An order to show cause must specify the date for hearing the complaint.

[Effective March 1, 1985.]

1985 Staff Comment

MCR 3.302 is substantially the same as GCR 1963, 711.

Subrule (D) is modified (from GCR 1963, 711.4) to take account of the superintending control and appellate jurisdiction of the Recorder's Court of the City of Detroit. See MCL 725.10b; MSA 27.3950(2); MCL 770.3(1)(c); MSA 28.1100(1)(c).

RULE 3.303 HABEAS CORPUS TO INQUIRE INTO CAUSE OF DETENTION

(A) Jurisdiction and Venue; Persons Detained on Criminal Charges.

(1) An action for habeas corpus to inquire into the cause of detention of a person may be brought in any court of record except the probate court.

(2) The action must be brought in the county in which the prisoner is detained. If it is shown that there is no judge in that county empowered and available to issue the writ or that the judicial circuit for that county has refused to issue the writ, the action may be brought in the Court of Appeals.

(3) A prisoner detained in a county jail for a criminal charge, who has not been sentenced to detention by a court of competent jurisdiction, may be removed from detention by a writ of habeas corpus to inquire into the cause of detention only if the writ is issued by the court in which the prisoner would next appear if the criminal process against the prisoner continued, or by the judicial circuit for the county in which the

prisoner is detained. This subrule does not limit the power of the Court of Appeals or Supreme Court to issue the writ.

(B) Who May Bring. An action for habeas corpus may be brought by the prisoner or by another person on the prisoner's behalf.

(C) Complaint. The complaint must state:

(1) that the person on whose behalf the writ is applied for (the prisoner) is restrained of his or her liberty;

(2) the name, if known, or the description of the prisoner;

(3) the name, if known, or the description of the officer or person by whom the prisoner is restrained;

(4) the place of restraint, if known;

(5) that the action for habeas corpus by or on behalf of the prisoner is not prohibited;

(6) the cause or pretense of the restraint, according to the plaintiff's best knowledge and belief; and

(7) why the restraint is illegal.

(D) Issuance of the Writ or Order to Show Cause.

(1) On the filing of the complaint, the court may issue

(a) a writ of habeas corpus directed to the person having custody of the prisoner, or that person's superior, ordering him or her to bring the prisoner before the court forthwith; or

(b) an order to show cause why the writ should not be issued,

unless it appears that the prisoner is not entitled to relief.

(2) On the showing required by MCL 600.4337; MSA 27A.4337, the court may issue a warrant in lieu of habeas corpus.

(3) Duplicate original writs may be issued.

(E) Certification of Record. When proceedings in another court or agency are pertinent to a determination of the issue raised in a habeas corpus action, the court may order the transcript of the record and proceedings certified to the court within a specified time. The order must identify the records to be certified with sufficient specificity to allow them to be located.

(F) Issuance Without Application or Before Filing.

(1) A judge of a court of record, except the probate court, may issue a writ of habeas corpus or order to show cause if

(a) the judge learns that a person within the judge's jurisdiction is illegally restrained, or

(b) an application is presented to the judge before or after normal court hours.

(2) If the prisoner is being held on criminal charges, the writ or order may only be issued by a judge of a court authorized to issue a writ of habeas corpus under subrule (A)(3).

(3) If a complaint is presented to a judge under the provisions of subrule (F)(1)(b), it need not be filed with the court before the issuance of a writ of habeas corpus. The complaint must subsequently be filed with the court whether or not the writ is granted.

(G) Endorsement of Allowance of Writ. Every writ issued must be endorsed with a certificate of its allowance and the date of the allowance. The endorsement must be signed by the judge issuing the writ, or, if the writ is issued by a panel of more than 1 judge, by a judge of the court.

(H) Form of Writ. A writ of habeas corpus must be substantially in the form approved by the state court administrator.

(I) Service of Writ.

(1) *Person to Be Served.* The writ or order to show cause must be served on the defendant in the manner prescribed in MCR 2.105. If the defendant cannot be found, or if the defendant does not have the prisoner in custody, the writ or order to show cause may be served on anyone having the prisoner in custody or that person's superior, in the manner and with the same effect as if that person had been made a defendant in the action.

(2) *Tender of Fees.* If the Attorney General or a prosecuting attorney brings the action, or if a judge issues the writ on his or her own initiative, there is no fee. In other actions, to make the service of a writ of habeas corpus effective, the person making service must give the fee provided by law or this rule to the person having custody of the prisoner or to that person's superior.

(a) If the prisoner is in the custody of a sheriff, coroner, constable, or marshal, the fee is that allowed by law to a sheriff for bringing up a prisoner.

(b) If the prisoner is in the custody of another person, the fee is that, if any, allowed by the court issuing the writ, not exceeding the fee allowed by law to a sheriff for similar services.

(J) Sufficiency of Writ. The writ or order to show cause may not be disobeyed because of a defect in form. The writ or order to show cause is sufficient if the prisoner is designated by name, if known, or by a description sufficient to permit identification. The writ or order may designate the person to whom it is directed as the person having custody of the prisoner. Anyone served with the writ or order is deemed the person to whom it is directed and is considered a defendant in the action.

(K) Time for Answer and Hearing.

(1) If the writ is to be answered and the hearing held on a specified day and hour, the answer must be made and the prisoner produced at the time and place specified in the writ.

(2) If an order to show cause is issued, it must be answered as provided in subrule (N), and the hearing must be held at the time and place specified in the order.

(L) Notice of Hearing Before Discharge.

(1) When the answer states that the prisoner is in custody on process under which another person has an interest in continuing the custody, an order of discharge may not be issued unless the interested person or that person's attorney has had at least 4 days' notice of the time and place of the hearing.

(2) When the answer states that the prisoner is detained on a criminal charge, the prisoner may not be discharged until sufficient notice of the time and place of the hearing is given to the prosecuting attorney of the county within which the prisoner is detained or, if there is no prosecuting attorney within the county, to the Attorney General.

(M) Habeas Corpus to Obtain Custody of Child.

(1) A complaint seeking a writ of habeas corpus to inquire into a child's custody must be presented to the judicial circuit for the county in which the child resides or is found.

(2) An order to show cause, not a writ of habeas corpus, must be issued initially if the action is brought by a parent, foster parent, or other relative of the child, to obtain custody of a child under the age of 16 years from a parent, foster parent, or other relative of the child. The court may direct the friend of the court to investigate the circumstances of the child's custody.

(N) Answer.

(1) *Contents of Answer; Contempt.* The defendant or person served must obey the writ or order to show cause or show good cause for not doing so, and must answer the writ or order to show cause within the time allowed. Failure to file an answer is contempt. The answer must state plainly and unequivocally

(a) whether the defendant then has, or at any time has had, the prisoner under his or her control and, if so, the reason; and

(b) if the prisoner has been transferred, to whom, when the transfer was made, and the reason or authority for the transfer.

(2) *Exhibits.* If the prisoner is detained because of a writ, warrant, or other written authority, a copy must be attached to the answer as an exhibit, and the original must be produced at the hearing. If an order under subrule (E) requires it, the answer must be

accompanied by the certified transcript of the record and proceedings.

(3) *Verification.* The answer must be signed by the person answering, and, except when the person is a sworn public officer and answers in his or her official capacity, it must be verified by oath.

(O) Answer May Be Controverted. In a reply or at a hearing, the plaintiff or the prisoner may controvert the answer under oath, to show either that the restraint is unlawful or that the prisoner is entitled to discharge.

(P) Prisoner; When Bailed. Because a habeas corpus action must be decided promptly with no more than the brief delay provided by subrule (Q)(2), release of a prisoner on bail will not normally be considered until after determination that legal cause exists for the detention. Thereafter, if the prisoner is entitled to bail, the court issuing the writ or order may set bail.

(Q) Hearing and Judgment.

(1) The court shall proceed promptly to hear the matter in a summary manner and enter judgment.

(2) In response to the writ of habeas corpus or order to show cause, the defendant may request adjournment of the hearing. Adjournment may be granted only for the brief delay necessary to permit the defendant

(a) to prepare a written answer (unless waived by the plaintiff); or

(b) to present to the court or judge issuing the writ or order testimonial or documentary evidence to establish the cause of detention at the time for answer.

(3) In the defendant's presence, the court shall inform the prisoner that he or she has the right to an attorney and the right to remain silent.

(4) From the time the prisoner is produced in response to the writ or order until judgment is entered, the judge who issued the writ or order has custody of the prisoner and shall make certain that the prisoner's full constitutional rights are protected.

(5) The hearing on the return to a writ of habeas corpus or an order to show cause must be recorded verbatim, unless a court reporter or recorder is not available. If the hearing is conducted without a verbatim record being made, as soon as possible the judge shall prepare and certify a narrative written report. The original report is part of the official record in the action, and copies must be sent forthwith to the parties or their attorneys.

(6) If the prisoner is restrained because of mental disease, the court shall consider the question of the prisoner's mental condition at the time of the hearing,

rather than merely the legality of the original detention.

[Effective March 1, 1985.]

1985 Staff Comment

MCR 3.303 is comparable to GCR 1963, 712.

Subrule (A)(1) is rewritten to remove the authority of a single judge of the Court of Appeals to entertain an action for habeas corpus. The rule does not list the courts in which the action may be brought, as did GCR 1963, 712.1(1), but rather provides that it may be brought in any court of record except the probate court. See MCL 600.4304; MSA 27A.4304.

Subrule (A)(2) is revised. If there is no judge in the county empowered and available to issue the writ, or the circuit court of a county has refused to issue it, the action can be brought in the Court of Appeals, rather than in an adjoining county as was provided in GCR 1963, 712.1(2).

Subrule (A)(3) is revised with regard to prisoners detained pending criminal proceedings. In addition to the circuit court in that county, the court in which the prisoner would next appear if the criminal process continued (e.g., the Recorder's Court of the City of Detroit or the district court) may do so.

Subrule (B) is a new provision explicitly stating that the action may be brought on behalf of a prisoner by another person. See MCL 600.4307; MSA 27A.4307.

Subrule (C) omits the requirement of GCR 1963, 712.3(2) that a copy of the warrant or process by which the prisoner is being held be attached to the complaint.

Subrule (D)(2) limits the circumstances in which a warrant in lieu of habeas corpus may be issued by citing the controlling statute.

Subrule (F) adds additional detail as to the procedure when a writ of habeas corpus is sought after court hours or when a judge issues the writ without a complaint being filed. Compare GCR 1963, 712.7.

Subrule (M), regarding habeas corpus to obtain custody of a child, limits the bringing of such actions to the circuit court. Compare GCR 1963, 712.14.

The form for a writ of habeas corpus, found in GCR 1963, 712.9, is omitted. Such forms will be approved by the state court administrator.

RULE 3.304 HABEAS CORPUS TO BRING PRISONER TO TESTIFY OR FOR PROSECUTION

(A) Jurisdiction; When Available. A court of record may issue a writ of habeas corpus directing that a prisoner in a jail or prison in Michigan be brought to testify

(1) on the court's own initiative; or

(2) on the ex parte motion of a party in an action before a court or an officer or body authorized to examine witnesses.

A writ of habeas corpus may also be issued to bring a prisoner to court for prosecution. Subrules (C)–(G) apply to such a writ.

(B) Contents of Motion. The motion must be verified by the party and must state

(1) the title and nature of the action in which the testimony of the prisoner is desired; and

(2) that the testimony of the prisoner is relevant and necessary to the party in that proceeding.

(C) Direction to Surrender Custody for Transportation. The writ may direct that the prisoner be placed in the custody of a designated officer for transportation to the place where the hearing or trial is to be held, rather than requiring the custodian to bring the prisoner to that place.

(D) Form of Writ. A writ of habeas corpus to produce a prisoner to testify or for prosecution must be substantially in the form approved by the state court administrator.

(E) Answer and Hearing. If the prisoner is produced or delivered to the custody of a designated officer as ordered, the person served with the writ need not answer the writ, and a hearing on the writ is unnecessary.

(F) Remand. When a prisoner is brought on a writ of habeas corpus to testify or for prosecution, the prisoner must be returned to the original custodian after testifying or prosecution.

(G) Applicability of Other Rules. MCR 3.303(G), (I), (J), and (K)(1) apply to habeas corpus to produce a prisoner to testify or for prosecution.

[Effective March 1, 1985.]

1985 Staff Comment

MCR 3.304 corresponds to GCR 1963, 713. The rule is expanded to allow its procedures to be used to bring a prisoner for prosecution as well as to testify.

Subrule (B)(2) modifies the provisions of GCR 1963, 713.2(2) by eliminating the requirement that the verified motion state that the party's attorney has advised that the witness is necessary.

Subrule (C) provides that the writ may direct that the prisoner be placed in the custody of a designated officer for transportation to the hearing, rather than requiring the custodian to transport the prisoner.

RULE 3.305 MANDAMUS

(A) Jurisdiction.

(1) An action for mandamus against a state officer may be brought in the Court of Appeals or the circuit court.

(2) All other actions for mandamus must be brought in the circuit court unless a statute or rule requires or allows the action to be brought in another court.

(B) Venue.

(1) The general venue statutes and rules apply to actions for mandamus unless a specific statute or rule contains a special venue provision.

(2) In addition to any other county in which venue is proper, an action for mandamus against a state officer may be brought in Ingham County.

(C) Order to Show Cause. On ex parte motion and a showing of the necessity for immediate action, the court may issue an order to show cause. The motion may be made in the complaint. The court shall indicate in the order when the defendant must answer the order.

(D) Answer. If necessity for immediate action is not shown, and the action is not dismissed, the defendant must answer the complaint as in an ordinary civil action.

(E) Exhibits. A party may attach to the pleadings, as exhibits, certified or authenticated copies of record evidence on which the party relies.

(F) Hearings in Circuit Court. The court may hear the matter or may allow the issues to be tried by a jury.

(G) Writ Contained in Judgment. If the judgment awards a writ of mandamus, the writ may be contained in the judgment in the form of an order, and a separate writ need not be issued or served.

[Effective March 1, 1985.]

1985 Staff Comment

MCR 3.305 is comparable to GCR 1963, 714.

Subrule (A)(1) permits actions against state officers to be brought in either the Court of Appeals or the circuit court. See MCL 600.4401; MSA 27.4401.

In subrule (A)(2) the list of other categories of mandamus defendants is replaced with a reference to "all other" mandamus actions. Compare GCR 1963, 714.1(2).

The venue provisions of subrule (B) are new.

RULE 3.306   QUO WARRANTO

(A) Jurisdiction.

(1) An action for quo warranto against a person who usurps, intrudes into, or unlawfully holds or exercises a state office, or against a state officer who does or suffers an act that by law works a forfeiture of the office, must be brought in the Court of Appeals.

(2) All other actions for quo warranto must be brought in the circuit court.

(B) Parties.

(1) *Actions by Attorney General.* An action for quo warranto is to be brought by the Attorney General when the action is against:

  (a) a person specified in subrule (A)(1);

  (b) a person who usurps, intrudes into, or wrongfully holds or exercises an office in a public corporation created by this state's authority;

  (c) an association, or number of persons, acting as a corporation in Michigan without being legally incorporated;

  (d) a corporation that is in violation of a provision of the act or acts creating, offering, or renewing the corporation;

  (e) a corporation that has violated the provisions of a law under which the corporation forfeits its charter by misuse;

  (f) a corporation that has forfeited its privileges and franchises by nonuse;

  (g) a corporation that has committed or omitted acts that amount to a surrender of its corporate rights, privileges, and franchises, or has exercised a franchise or privilege not conferred on it by law.

(2) *Actions by Prosecutor or Citizen.* Other actions for quo warranto may be brought by the prosecuting attorney of the proper county, without leave of court, or by a citizen of the county by special leave of the court.

(3) *Application to Attorney General.*

  (a) A person may apply to the Attorney General to have the Attorney General bring an action specified in subrule (B)(1). The Attorney General may require the person to give security to indemnify the state against all costs and expenses of the action. The person making the application, and any other person having the proper interest, may be joined as parties plaintiff.

  (b) If, on proper application and offer of security, the Attorney General refuses to bring the action, the person may apply to the appropriate court for leave to bring the action himself or herself.

(C) Person Alleged to Be Entitled to Office. If the action is brought against the defendant for usurping an office, the complaint may name the person rightfully entitled to the office, with an allegation of his or her right to it, and that person may be made a party.

(D) Venue. The general venue statutes and rules apply to actions for quo warranto, unless a specific statute or rule contains a special venue provision applicable to an action for quo warranto.

(E) Hearing. The court may hear the matter or may allow the issues to be tried by a jury.

[Effective March 1, 1985.]

1985 Staff Comment

MCR 3.306 is comparable to GCR 1963, 715.

The venue provisions are stated in somewhat more detail in subrule (D) than in GCR 1963, 715.4.

RULE 3.310   INJUNCTIONS

(A) Preliminary Injunctions.

(1) Except as otherwise provided by statute or these rules, an injunction may not be granted before a hearing on a motion for a preliminary injunction or on an order to show cause why a preliminary injunction should not be issued.

(2) Before or after the commencement of the hearing on a motion for a preliminary injunction, the court may order the trial of the action on the merits to be advanced and consolidated with the hearing on the motion. Even when consolidation is not ordered, evidence received at the hearing for a preliminary injunction that would be admissible at the trial on the merits becomes part of the trial record and need not be repeated at the trial. This provision may not be used to deny the parties any rights they may have to trial by jury.

(3) A motion for a preliminary injunction must be filed and noticed for hearing in compliance with the rules governing other motions unless the court orders otherwise on a showing of good cause.

(4) At the hearing on an order to show cause why a preliminary injunction should not issue, the party seeking injunctive relief has the burden of establishing that a preliminary injunction should be issued, whether or not a temporary restraining order has been issued.

(5) If a preliminary injunction is granted, the court shall promptly schedule a pretrial conference. The trial of the action on the merits must be held within 6 months after the injunction is granted, unless good cause is shown or the parties stipulate to a longer period. The court shall issue its decision on the merits within 56 days after the trial is completed.

(B) Temporary Restraining Orders.

(1) A temporary restraining order may be granted without written or oral notice to the adverse party or the adverse party's attorney only if

(a) it clearly appears from specific facts shown by affidavit or by a verified complaint that immediate and irreparable injury, loss, or damage will result to the applicant from the delay required to effect notice or from the risk that notice will itself precipitate adverse action before an order can be issued;

(b) the applicant's attorney certifies to the court in writing the efforts, if any, that have been made to give the notice and the reasons supporting the claim that notice should not be required; and

(c) a permanent record or memorandum is made of any nonwritten evidence, argument, or other representations made in support of the application.

(2) A temporary restraining order granted without notice must:

(a) be endorsed with the date and time of issuance;

(b) describe the injury and state why it is irreparable and why the order was granted without notice;

(c) except in domestic relations actions, set a date for hearing at the earliest possible time on the motion for a preliminary injunction or order to show

cause why a preliminary injunction should not be issued.

(3) Except in domestic relations actions, a temporary restraining order granted without notice expires by its terms within such time after entry, not to exceed 14 days, as the court sets unless within the time so fixed the order, for good cause shown, is extended for a like period or unless the party against whom the order is directed consents that it may be extended for a longer period. The reasons for the extension must be stated on the record or in a document filed in the action.

(4) A temporary restraining order granted without notice must be filed forthwith in the clerk's office and entered in the court records.

(5) A motion to dissolve a temporary restraining order granted without notice takes precedence over all matters except older matters of the same character, and may be heard on 24 hours' notice. For good cause shown, the court may order the motion heard on shorter notice. The court may set the time for the hearing at the time the restraining order is granted, without waiting for the filing of a motion to dissolve it, and may order that the hearing on a motion to dissolve a restraining order granted without notice be consolidated with the hearing on a motion for a preliminary injunction or an order to show cause why a preliminary injunction should not be issued. At a hearing on a motion to dissolve a restraining order granted without notice, the burden of justifying continuation of the order is on the applicant for the restraining order whether or not the hearing has been consolidated with a hearing on a motion for a preliminary injunction or an order to show cause.

(C) Form and Scope of Injunction. An order granting an injunction or restraining order

(1) must set forth the reasons for its issuance;

(2) must be specific in terms;

(3) must describe in reasonable detail, and not by reference to the complaint or other document, the acts restrained; and

(4) is binding only on the parties to the action, their officers, agents, servants, employees, and attorneys, and on those persons in active concert or participation with them who receive actual notice of the order by personal service or otherwise.

(D) Security.

(1) Before granting a preliminary injunction or temporary restraining order, the court may require the applicant to give security, in the amount the court deems proper, for the payment of costs and damages that may be incurred or suffered by a party who is found to have been wrongfully enjoined or restrained.

(2) Security is not required of the state or of a Michigan county or municipal corporation or its officer or agency acting in an official capacity. As to other parties, if security is not required the order must state the reason.

(3) If the party enjoined deems the security insufficient and has had no prior opportunity to be heard, the party may object to the sufficiency of the surety in the manner provided in MCR 3.604(E). The procedures provided in MCR 3.604(F) apply to the objection.

(4) When a bond is required before the issuance of an injunction or temporary restraining order, the bond must be filed with the clerk before the sealing and delivery of the injunction or restraining order.

(E) Stay of Action. An injunction or temporary restraining order may not be granted in one action to stay proceedings in another action pending in another court if the relief requested could be sought in the other pending action.

(F) Denial of Application. When an application for a preliminary injunction or temporary restraining order is denied, but an order is not signed, an endorsement of the denial must be made on the complaint or affidavit, and the complaint or affidavit filed.

(G) Later Application After Denial of Injunction.

(1) If a circuit judge has denied an application for an injunction or temporary restraining order, in whole or in part, or has granted it conditionally or on terms, later application for the same purpose and in relation to the same matter may not be made to another circuit judge.

(2) If an order is entered on an application in violation of subrule (G)(1), it is void and must be revoked by the judge who entered it, on due proof of the facts. A person making the later application contrary to this rule is subject to punishment for contempt.

(H) Motion for Injunction in Pending Actions. An injunction may also be granted before or in connection with final judgment on a motion filed after an action is commenced.

(I) Application to Special Actions. This rule applies to a special statutory action for an injunction only to the extent that it does not conflict with special procedures prescribed by the statute or the rules governing the special action.

[Effective March 1, 1985; amended effective September 1, 2002.]

1985 Staff Comment

MCR 3.310 is a substantial revision of GCR 1963, 718. In general, the rule makes Michigan practice much more like that under FR Civ P 65.

The rule adopts the terminology used in the federal rule, distinguishing between temporary restraining orders, which are entered without notice, and preliminary injunctions, which are granted with notice and after hearing.

Subrule (A)(2) adopts the principle of FR Civ P 65(a)(2), which permits the trial of the action to be consolidated with the hearing on the motion for preliminary injunction.

New subrules (A)(3) and (4) emphasize that at a hearing on a motion for a preliminary injunction or on an order to show cause, the burden of proof is on the party seeking the injunction, even though a temporary restraining order may have been issued. Subrule (B)(5) includes a related provision: At a hearing on a motion to dissolve a temporary restraining order granted without notice, the party seeking continuation of the restraining order has the burden of proving that he or she is entitled to that relief.

Subrule (B)(1)(a) makes it a ground for a temporary restraining order that there is a risk that notice itself will precipitate adverse action before an order can be entered.

Subrule (B)(1)(c) requires that a record be kept of any evidence, argument, or representations made to the court in support of an application for a temporary restraining order.

Subrule (B)(2)(c) requires that a temporary restraining order set a date for hearing on the question of issuance of a preliminary injunction. This is consistent with FR Civ P 65(b). Domestic relations actions are excepted from that provision.

Subrule (B)(3) adopts the formulation of FR Civ P 65(b) that a temporary restraining order expires automatically after a specified time (14 days in subrule [B][3]) unless the court extends it for good cause or on the consent of the enjoined party. Again, domestic relations actions are excepted.

Although there is some reorganization, subrules (C)–(I) essentially carry forward the provisions of GCR 1963, 718.3–718.11.

2002 Staff Comment

The March 12, 2002 amendments of Rules 3.310, 7.208, and 7.213, effective September 1, 2002, require trial courts to expeditiously decide actions in which preliminary injunctions have been granted, and allow them to proceed even if the Court of Appeals has granted interlocutory leave to appeal. Similarly, if the Court of Appeals grants leave to review entry of a preliminary injunction on an interlocutory basis, that Court is required to give priority to resolution of the appeal. See *Michigan Coalition of State Employee Unions v Michigan Civil Service Comm*, 465 Mich 212, 214, n 1 (2001).

The staff comment is published only for the benefit of the bench and bar and is not an authoritative construction by the Court.

SUBCHAPTER 3.400 PROCEEDINGS
INVOLVING REAL PROPERTY

RULE 3.401 PARTITION

(A) Matters to Be Determined by Court. On the hearing of an action or proceeding for partition, the court shall determine

(1) whether the premises can be partitioned without great prejudice to the parties;

(2) the value of the use of the premises and of improvements made to the premises; and

(3) other matters the court considers pertinent.

(B) Partition or Sale in Lieu of Partition. If the court determines that the premises can be partitioned, MCR 3.402 governs further proceedings. If the court determines that the premises cannot be partitioned without undue prejudice to the owners, it may order the premises sold in lieu of partition under MCR 3.403.

(C) Joinder of Lienholders. A creditor having a lien on all or part of the premises, by judgment, mortgage, or otherwise, need not be made a party to the partition proceedings. However, the plaintiff may join every creditor having a specific lien on the undivided interest or estate of a party. If the creditors are made parties, the complaint must state the nature of every lien or encumbrance.

[Effective March 1, 1985.]

1985 Staff Comment

MCR 3.401, 3.402, and 3.403 cover the same subject matter as GCR 1963, 748, 749, 750, and 751. There is some reorganization, with the general provisions being placed in MCR 3.401, the procedure for partitioning in 3.402, and the procedure for sale in lieu of partition in 3.403.

MCR 3.401 includes the substance of GCR 1963, 748 and 751, as well as a new subrule (B), which refers to the other two partition rules.

RULE 3.402 PARTITION PROCEDURE

(A) Determination of Parties' Interests. In ordering partition the court shall determine the rights and interests of the parties in the premises, and describe parts or shares that are to remain undivided for owners whose interests are unknown or not ascertained.

(B) Appointment of Partition Commissioner.

(1) The court shall appoint a disinterested person as partition commissioner to make the partition according to the court's determination of the rights and interests of the parties. If the parties agree, three commissioners may be appointed who shall meet together to perform their duties and act by majority vote.

(2) The partition commissioner must be sworn before an officer authorized to administer oaths to honestly and impartially partition the property as directed by the court. The oath must be filed with the clerk of the court.

(3) If the partition commissioner dies, resigns, or neglects to serve, the court may appoint a replacement.

(C) Proceedings Before Partition Commissioner.

(1) The partition commissioner

(a) may apply to the court for instructions;

(b) must give notice of the meeting to consider the problems of the partition to the parties so that they may be heard if they wish to be; and

(c) may take evidence at the meeting concerning the problems of partition.

(2) The partition commissioner shall divide the premises and allot the respective shares according to the terms in the court's judgment or separate order, and shall designate the several shares and portions by reference to a plat or survey prepared by a land surveyor or engineer licensed by the state.

(3) The partition commissioner must report to the court, specifying the procedures followed, describing the land divided and the shares allotted to each party, and listing the commissioner's charges. The parties shall not be present during the preparation of the report or during the deliberations of a panel of three commissioners. A copy of the report must be sent to each party who has appeared in the action.

(D) Setting Aside, Modification, or Confirmation of Partition Commissioner's Report.

(1) The court may modify or set aside the report and may refer the action to either the same or a newly appointed partition commissioner as often as necessary.

(2) On confirming the report, the court shall enter a judgment binding and conclusive on:

(a) all parties named in the action who

(i) have an interest in the partitioned premises as owners in fee or tenants for years,

(ii) are entitled to the reversion, remainder, or inheritance of the premises after the termination of a particular estate in the premises,

(iii) are or will become entitled to a beneficial interest in the premises, or

(iv) have an interest in an undivided share of the premises as tenants for years, for life, or in dower;

(b) the legal representatives of the parties listed in subrule (D)(2)(a);

(c) all persons interested in the premises who were unknown at the time the action was commenced and were given sufficient notice either by publication or personally; and

(d) all other persons claiming from any of the above parties or persons.

(3) The judgment and partition do not affect persons who have claims as tenants in dower or for life to the entire premises subject to the partition; nor do they preclude a person, except those specified in subrule (D)(2), from claiming title to the premises in question or from controverting the title or interest of the parties among whom the partition was made.

(4) An authenticated copy of the report, the judgment confirming it, and any incorporated surveys may be recorded with the register of deeds of the county in which the land is located. Copies of subdivision plats already of record need not be recorded.

(E) Expenses and Costs. The court may order that the expenses and costs, including attorney fees, be paid by the parties in accordance with their respective rights and equities in the premises. An order requiring a party to pay expenses and costs may be enforced in the same manner as a judgment.

(F) Setting Off of Interests in Special Cases.

(1) The court may by order set off the interest that belonged to a deceased party, without subdivision, to those claiming under that party when it is expedient to do so. Those legally entitled under or through the deceased party must be mentioned by name in the judgment.

(2) If the original parties in interest were fully known, but death, legal proceedings, or other operation of law has caused uncertainty about the identity of the present parties in interest, the interests originally owned by known parties but now owned by unknown persons may be separated as provided in this rule, instead of being left undivided. The division and judgment operate to convey the title to the persons claiming under the known party, according to their legal rights.

(3) If an interest in the premises belongs to known or unknown parties who have not appeared in the action, the court shall order partition of the ascertained interests of the known parties who have appeared in the action. The residue of the premises remains for the parties whose interests have not been ascertained, subject to future division.

[Effective March 1, 1985.]

1985 Staff Comment

MCR 3.402 is comparable to GCR 1963, 749.

Subrule (B)(1) changes the current provision of GCR 1963, 749.1, by permitting appointment of only a single partition commissioner. Compare MCL 700.208; MSA 27.5208, which provides for only one commissioner in partition proceedings in probate court.

In subrule (C)(2) the requirements for the description of the shares of the premises are stated in terms of a plat or survey, rather than the language of GCR 1963, 749.2(2), which spoke of "posts, stones, or other permanent monuments".

New subrule (D)(4) adds a requirement that a copy of the report and the judgment confirming it may be recorded with the register of deeds.

Subrule (E) simplifies the language of GCR 1963, 749.4 regarding expenses and costs.

RULE 3.403 SALE OF PREMISES AND DIVISION OF PROCEEDS AS SUBSTITUTE FOR PARTITION

(A) Order of Sale.

(1) If a party has a dower interest or life estate in all or a part of the premises at the time of the order for sale, the court shall determine whether, under all the circumstances and with regard for the interests of all the parties, that interest should be excepted from the sale or be sold with the premises. If the court orders that the sale include that party's interest, the sale conveys that interest.

(2) In the order of sale the court shall designate:

(a) which premises are to be sold;

(b) whether the premises are to be sold in separate parcels or together;

(c) whether there is a minimum price at which the premises may be sold;

(d) the terms of credit to be allowed and the security to be required; and

(e) how much of the proceeds will be invested, as required by this rule, for the benefit of unknown owners, infants, parties outside Michigan, and parties who have dower interests or life estates.

(B) Specific Procedures and Requirements of Sale.

(1) The person appointed by the court to conduct the sale shall give notice of the sale, including the terms. Notice must be given in the same manner as required by MCL 600.6052; MSA 27A.6052.

(2) Neither the person conducting the sale nor anyone acting in his or her behalf may directly or indirectly purchase or be interested in the purchase of the premises sold. The conservator of a minor or legally incapacitated individual may not purchase or be interested in the purchase of lands that are the subject of the proceedings, except for the benefit of the ward. Sales made contrary to this provision are voidable, except as provided by MCL 700.5421.

(3) The part of the price for which credit is allowed must be secured at interest by a mortgage of the

premises sold, a note of the purchaser, and other security the court prescribes.

(a) The person conducting the sale may take separate mortgages and other securities in the name of the clerk of the court and the clerk's successors for the shares of the purchase money the court directs to be invested, and in the name of a known owner, 18 years of age or older, who desires to have his or her share so invested.

(b) When the sale is confirmed, the person conducting the sale must deliver the mortgages and other securities to the clerk of the court, or to the known owners whose shares are invested.

(4) After completing the sale, the person conducting the sale shall file a report with the court, stating

(a) the name of each purchaser,

(b) a description of the parcels of land sold to each purchaser, and

(c) the price paid for each parcel.

A copy of the report must be sent to each party who has appeared in the action.

(5) If the court confirms the sale, it shall enter an order authorizing and directing the person conducting the sale to execute conveyances pursuant to the sale.

(6) Conveyances executed according to these rules shall be recorded in the county where the land is located. These conveyances are a bar against

(a) all interested persons who were made parties to the proceedings;

(b) all unknown parties who were ordered to appear and answer by proper publication or personal service of notice;

(c) all persons claiming through parties listed in subrules (B)(6)(a) and (b);

(d) all persons who have specific liens on an undivided share or interest in the premises, if they were made parties to the proceedings.

(7) If the court confirms the sale, and the successful bidder fails to purchase under the terms of the sale, the court may order that the premises be resold at that bidder's risk. That bidder is liable to pay the amount of his or her bid minus the amount received on resale.

(C) Costs and Expenses of the Proceeding. The person conducting the sale shall deduct the costs and expenses of the proceeding, including the plaintiff's reasonable attorney fees as determined by the court, from the proceeds of the sale and pay them to the plaintiff or the plaintiff's attorney.

(D) Distribution of Proceeds of Sale.

(1) When premises that include a dower interest or life estate are sold, the owner of the dower interest or life estate shall be compensated as provided in this subrule.

(a) Unless the owner consents to the alternative compensation provided in subrule (D)(1)(b), the court shall order that the following amount be invested in interest-bearing accounts insured by an agency of the United States government, with the interest paid annually for life to the owner of the dower interest or life estate:

(i) in the case of a dower interest, one-third of the proceeds of the sale of the premises or of the undivided share of the premises on which the claim of dower existed, after deduction of the owner's share of the expenses of the proceeding;

(ii) in the case of a life estate, the entire proceeds of the sale of the premises, or undivided share of the premises in which the life estate existed, after deduction of the proportion of the owner's share of the expenses of the proceeding.

If the owner of the dower interest or life estate is unknown, the court shall order the protection of the person's rights in the same manner, as far as possible, as if he or she were known and had appeared.

(b) If, before the person conducting the sale files the report of sale, the owner of the dower interest or life estate consents, the court shall direct that the owner be paid an amount that, on the principles of law applicable to annuities, is reasonable compensation for the interest or estate. To be effective the consent must be by a written instrument witnessed and acknowledged in the manner required to make a deed eligible for recording.

(2) If there are encumbrances on the estate or interest in the premises of a party to the proceeding, the person conducting the sale must pay to the clerk the portion of the proceeds attributable to the sale of that estate or interest, after deducting the share of the costs, charges, and expenses for which it is liable. The party who owned that estate or interest may apply to the court for payment of his or her claim out of these proceeds. The application must be accompanied by

(a) an affidavit stating the amount due on each encumbrance and the name and address of the owner of each encumbrance, as far as known; and

(b) proof by affidavit that notice was served on each owner of an encumbrance, in the manner prescribed in MCR 2.107.

The court shall hear the proofs, determine the rights of the parties, and direct who must pay the costs of the trial.

After ascertaining the amount of existing encumbrances, the court shall order the distribution of the money held by the clerk among the creditors having encumbrances, according to their priority. When paying an encumbrance the clerk must procure satisfaction of the encumbrance, acknowledged in the form required by law, and must record the satisfaction of the encumbrance. The clerk may pay the expenses of these services out of the portion of the money in court that belongs to the party by whom the encumbrance was payable.

The proceedings under this subrule to ascertain and settle the amounts of encumbrances do not affect other parties to the proceedings for partition and do not delay the payment to a party whose estate in the premises is not subject to an encumbrance or the investing of the money for the benefit of such a person.

(3) The proceeds of a sale, after deducting the costs, must be divided among the parties whose rights and interests have been sold, in proportion to their respective rights in the premises.

(a) The shares of the parties who are 18 years of age or older must be paid to them or to their legal representatives (or brought into court for their use) by the person conducting the sale.

(b) The court may direct that the share of a minor or legally incapacitated individual be paid to his or her conservator or be invested in interest-bearing accounts insured by an agency of the United States government in the name and for the benefit of the minor or legally incapacitated individual.

(c) If a party whose interest has been sold is absent from the state and has no legal representative in the state or is not known or named in the proceedings, the court shall direct that his or her share be invested in interest-bearing accounts insured by the United States government for the party's benefit until claimed.

(4) The court may require that before receiving a share of the proceeds of a sale a party give a note to secure refund of the share, with interest, if the party is later found not entitled to it.

(5) When the court directs that security be given or investments be made, or the person conducting the sale takes security on the sale of real estate, the bonds, notes, and investments must be taken in the name of the clerk of the court and the clerk's successors in office, unless provision is made to take them in the name of a known owner.

The clerk must hold them and deliver them to his or her successor, and must receive the interest and principal as they become due and apply or reinvest them, as the court directs. The clerk shall annually give to the court a written, sworn account of the money received and the disposition of it.

A security, bond, note, mortgage, or other evidence of the investment may not be discharged, transferred, or impaired by an act of the clerk without the order of the court. A person interested in an investment, with the leave of the court, may prosecute it in the name of the existing clerk, and an action is not abated by the death, removal from office, or resignation of the clerk

to whom the instruments were executed or the clerk's successors.

[Effective March 1, 1985; amended effective May 1, 2002.]

1985 Staff Comment

MCR 3.403 is comparable to GCR 1963, 750.

The language of subrule (B)(2) is modified from that in GCR 1963, 750.3(2) in accordance with the terms of the Revised Probate Code.

Subrule (B)(7) deletes the language found in GCR 1963, 750.3(7) that entitled a defaulting purchaser to the amount by which the proceeds of the resale exceeds his or her bid.

In subrule (D)(3), the terminology is changed to conform to the Revised Probate Code. Compare GCR 1963, 750.5(4).

The provisions of GCR 1963, 750.5(6) regarding investment of the proceeds of sale by the clerk are modified in subrule (D). The clerk's authority to invest in mortgages is deleted and replaced with a provision that the proceeds are to be invested in accounts insured by an agency of the United States government.

Staff Comment to 2002 Amendment

The December 18, 2001 amendments, effective May 1, 2002, updated various rules in light of the Estates and Protected Individuals Code (EPIC), MCL 700.1101 et seq., and revisions made to EPIC by 2000 PA 312, 313, and 469.

The staff comment is published only for the benefit of the bench and bar and is not an authoritative construction by the Court.

RULE 3.410 FORECLOSURE OF MORTGAGES AND LAND CONTRACTS

(A) **Rules Applicable.** Except as prescribed in this rule, the general rules of procedure apply to actions to foreclose mortgages and land contracts.

(B) **Pleading.**

(1) A plaintiff seeking foreclosure or satisfaction of a mortgage on real estate or a land contract must state in the complaint whether an action has ever been brought to recover all or part of the debt secured by the mortgage or land contract and whether part of the debt has been collected or paid.

(2) In a complaint for foreclosure or satisfaction of a mortgage or a land contract, it is not necessary to set out in detail the rights and interests of the defendants who are purchasers of, or who have liens on, the premises, subsequent to the recording of the mortgage or land contract. It is sufficient for the plaintiff, after setting out his or her own interest in the premises, to state generally that the defendants have or claim some interest in the premises as subsequent purchasers, encumbrancers, or otherwise.

(C) **Time for Sale.** A sale under a judgment of foreclosure may not be ordered on less than 42 days' notice. Publication may not begin until the time set by the judgment for payment has expired, and

(1) until 6 months after an action to foreclose a mortgage is begun;

(2) until 3 months after an action to foreclose a land contract is begun.

(D) Disposition of Surplus. When there is money remaining from a foreclosure sale after paying the amount due the plaintiff, a party to the action may move for the disposition of the surplus in accordance with the rights of the parties entitled to it.

(E) Administration of Mortgage Trusts in Equity.

(1) Proceedings of the kind described in MCL 600.3170; MSA 27A.3170 are governed by the procedures prescribed by MCL 451.401–451.405; MSA 27.1281–27.1285, except as modified by this subrule.

(2) A bond, other obligation, or beneficial interest held by or for the benefit of the mortgagor or the mortgagor's successor in estate, or subject to an agreement or option by which the mortgagor or the mortgagor's successor in estate may acquire it or an interest in it, may not be considered in determining a majority of such obligations or beneficial interests, either as part of the majority or as part of the whole number of which the majority is required.

[Effective March 1, 1985.]

1985 Staff Comment

MCR 3.410 is comparable to GCR 1963, 745.

Most of the procedures regarding foreclosure of mortgage trusts, found in GCR 1963, 745.5, are deleted and replaced in subrule (E) with a reference to statutory procedures.

RULE 3.411 CIVIL ACTION TO DETERMINE INTERESTS IN LAND

(A) This rule applies to actions to determine interests in land under MCL 600.2932; MSA 27A.2932. It does not apply to summary proceedings to recover possession of premises under MCL 600.5701–600.5759; MSA 27A.5701–27A.5759.

(B) Complaint.

(1) The complaint must describe the land in question with reasonable certainty by stating

(a) the section, township, and range of the premises;

(b) the number of the block and lot of the premises; or

(c) another description of the premises sufficiently clear so that the premises may be identified.

(2) The complaint must allege

(a) the interest the plaintiff claims in the premises;

(b) the interest the defendant claims in the premises; and

(c) the facts establishing the superiority of the plaintiff's claim.

(C) Written Evidence of Title to Be Referred to in Pleadings.

(1) Written evidence of title may not be introduced at trial unless it has been sufficiently referred to in the pleadings in accordance with this rule.

(2) The plaintiff must attach to the complaint, and the defendant must attach to the answer, a statement of the title on which the pleader relies, showing from whom the title was obtained and the page and book where it appears of record.

(3) Within a reasonable time after demand for it, a party must furnish to the adverse party a copy of an unrecorded conveyance on which he or she relies or give a satisfactory reason for not doing so.

(4) References to title may be amended or made more specific in accordance with the general rules regarding amendments and motions for more definite statement.

(D) Findings as to Rights in and Title to Premises.

(1) After evidence has been taken, the court shall make findings determining the disputed rights in and title to the premises.

(2) If a party not in possession of the premises is found to have had a right to possession at the time the action was commenced, but that right expired before the trial, that party must prove the damages sustained because the premises were wrongfully withheld, and the court shall enter judgment in the amount proved.

(E) Claim for Reasonable Value of Use of Premises.

(1) Within 28 days after the finding of title, the party found to have title to the premises may file a claim against the party who withheld possession of the premises for the reasonable value of the use of the premises during the period the premises were withheld, beginning 6 years before the action was commenced.

(2) The court shall hear evidence and make findings, determining the value of the use of the premises.

(a) The findings must be based on the value of the use of the premises in their condition at the time the withholding party, or those through whom that party claims, first went into possession. The use of the buildings or improvements put on the land by the party who withheld possession may not be considered.

(b) The findings must be based on the general value of the use of the premises, not on a peculiar value the use of the premises had to the party who withheld possession or might have had to the party who had title.

(F) Claim for Value of Buildings Erected and Improvements Made on Premises.

(1) Within 28 days after the finding of title, a party may file a claim against the party found to have title to the premises for the amount that the present value of the premises has been increased by the erection of buildings or the making of improvements by the party making the claim or those through whom he or she claims.

(2) The court shall hear evidence as to the value of the buildings erected and the improvements made on the premises, and the value the premises would have if they had not been improved or built upon. The court shall determine the amount the premises would be worth at the time of the claim had the premises not been improved, and the amount the value of the premises was increased at the time of the claim by the buildings erected and improvements made.

(3) The party claiming the value of the improvements may not recover their value if they were made in bad faith.

(G) Election by Party in Title.

(1) The person found to have title to the premises may elect to abandon them to the party claiming the value of the improvements and to take a judgment against that party for the value the premises would have had at the time of the trial if they had not been improved. The election must be filed with the court within 28 days after the findings on the claim for improvements. The judgment for the value of the premises is a lien against the premises.

(2) If the person found to have title does not elect to abandon the premises under subrule (G)(1), the judgment will provide that he or she recover the premises and pay the value of the improvements to the clerk of the court within the time set in the judgment.

(a) The person found to have title must pay the amount, plus accrued interest, before taking possession of the premises under the judgment, if that person is not already in possession.

(b) If the person found to have title fails to pay the amount of the judgment and the accrued interest within the time set in the judgment, he or she is deemed to have abandoned all claim of title to the premises to the parties in whose favor the judgment for the value of the improvements runs.

(H) Judgment Binding Only on Parties to Action. The judgment determining a claim to title, equitable title, right to possession, or other interests in lands under this rule, determines only the rights and interests of the known and unknown persons who are parties to the action, and of persons claiming through those parties by title accruing after the commencement of the action.

(I) Possession Under Judgment Not to Be Affected by Vacation of Judgment Alone. When the judgment in an action under these rules determines that a party is entitled to possession of the premises in dispute, that party's right to possession is not affected by vacation of the judgment and the granting of a new trial, until a contrary judgment is rendered as a result of the new trial.

[Effective March 1, 1985.]

1985 Staff Comment

MCR 3.411 is comparable to GCR 1963, 754.

New subrule (A) states the applicability of the rule.

Subrule (G)(1) states more specifically than did GCR 1963, 754.6(1) the manner in which the party found to have title may exercise the election to abandon the premises and take a judgment for the value of the premises before improvement.

RULE 3.412   CONSTRUCTION LIENS

In an action to enforce a lien under MCL 570.1101 et seq.; MSA 26.316(101) et seq., or other similar law, if the plaintiff has joined others holding liens or others have filed notice of intention to claim liens against the same property, it is not necessary for the plaintiff to answer the counterclaim or cross-claim of another lien claimant, nor for the other lien claimants to answer the plaintiff's complaint or the cross-claim of another lien claimant, unless one of them disputes the validity or amount of the lien sought to be enforced. If no issue has been raised between lien claimants as to the validity or amount of a lien, the action is ready for hearing when at issue between the lien claimants and the owners, part owners, or lessees of the property.

[Effective March 1, 1985.]

1985 Staff Comment

MCR 3.412 is substantially the same as GCR 1963, 793. The current statute uses the term "construction" lien, rather than "mechanics'" lien. See MCL 570.1101; MSA 26.316(101).

SUBCHAPTER 3.500   REPRESENTATIVE ACTIONS

RULE 3.501   CLASS ACTIONS

(A) Nature of Class Action.

(1) One or more members of a class may sue or be sued as representative parties on behalf of all members in a class action only if:

(a) the class is so numerous that joinder of all members is impracticable;

(b) there are questions of law or fact common to the members of the class that predominate over questions affecting only individual members;

(c) the claims or defenses of the representative parties are typical of the claims or defenses of the class;

(d) the representative parties will fairly and adequately assert and protect the interests of the class; and

(e) the maintenance of the action as a class action will be superior to other available methods of adjudication in promoting the convenient administration of justice.

(2) In determining whether the maintenance of the action as a class action will be superior to other available methods of adjudication in promoting the convenient administration of justice, the court shall consider among other matters the following factors:

(a) whether the prosecution of separate actions by or against individual members of the class would create a risk of

(i) inconsistent or varying adjudications with respect to individual members of the class that would confront the party opposing the class with incompatible standards of conduct; or

(ii) adjudications with respect to individual members of the class that would as a practical matter be dispositive of the interests of other members not parties to the adjudications or substantially impair or impede their ability to protect their interests;

(b) whether final equitable or declaratory relief might be appropriate with respect to the class;

(c) whether the action will be manageable as a class action;

(d) whether in view of the complexity of the issues or the expense of litigation the separate claims of individual class members are insufficient in amount to support separate actions;

(e) whether it is probable that the amount which may be recovered by individual class members will be large enough in relation to the expense and effort of administering the action to justify a class action; and

(f) whether members of the class have a significant interest in controlling the prosecution or defense of separate actions.

(3) Class members shall have the right to be excluded from the action in the manner provided in this rule, subject to the authority of the court to order them made parties to the action pursuant to other applicable court rules.

(4) Class members have the right to intervene in the action, subject to the authority of the court to regulate the orderly course of the action.

(5) An action for a penalty or minimum amount of recovery without regard to actual damages imposed or authorized by statute may not be maintained as a class action unless the statute specifically authorizes its recovery in a class action.

(B) Procedure for Certification of Class Action.

(1) *Motion.*

(a) Within 91 days after the filing of a complaint that includes class action allegations, the plaintiff must move for certification that the action may be maintained as a class action.

(b) The time for filing the motion may be extended by order on stipulation of the parties or on motion for cause shown.

(2) *Effect of Failure to File Motion.* If the plaintiff fails to file a certification motion within the time allowed by subrule (B)(1), the defendant may file a notice of the failure. On the filing of such a notice, the class action allegations are deemed stricken, and the action continues by or against the named parties alone. The class action allegations may be reinstated only if the plaintiff shows that the failure was due to excusable neglect.

(3) *Action by Court.*

(a) Except on motion for good cause, the court shall not proceed with consideration of the motion to certify until service of the summons and complaint on all named defendants or until the expiration of any unserved summons under MCR 2.102(D).

(b) The court may allow the action to be maintained as a class action, may deny the motion, or may order that a ruling be postponed pending discovery or other preliminary procedures.

(c) In an order certifying a class action, the court shall set forth a description of the class.

(d) When appropriate the court may order that

(i) the action be maintained as a class action limited to particular issues or forms of relief, or

(ii) a proposed class be divided into separate classes with each treated as a class for purposes of certifying, denying certification, or revoking a certification.

(e) If certification is denied or revoked, the action shall continue by or against the named parties alone.

(C) Notice to Class Members.

(1) *Notice Requirement.* Notice shall be given as provided in this subrule to persons who are included in a class action by certification or amendment of a prior certification, and to persons who were included in a class action by a prior certification but who are to be excluded from the class by amendment or revocation of the certification.

(2) *Proposals Regarding Notice.* The plaintiff shall include in the motion for certification a proposal regarding notice covering the matters that must be determined by the court under subrule (C)(3). In lieu

of such a proposal, the plaintiff may state reasons why a determination of these matters cannot then be made and offer a proposal as to when such a determination should be made. Such a proposal must also be included in a motion to revoke or amend certification.

(3) *Action by Court.* As soon as practicable, the court shall determine how, when, by whom, and to whom the notice shall be given; the content of the notice; and to whom the response to the notice is to be sent. The court may postpone the notice determination until after the parties have had an opportunity for discovery, which the court may limit to matters relevant to the notice determination.

(4) *Manner of Giving Notice.*

(a) Reasonable notice of the action shall be given to the class in such manner as the court directs.

(b) The court may require individual written notice to all members who can be identified with reasonable effort. In lieu of or in addition to individual notice, the court may require notice to be given through another method reasonably calculated to reach the members of the class. Such methods may include using publication in a newspaper or magazine; broadcasting on television or radio; posting; or distribution through a trade or professional association, union, or public interest group.

(c) In determining the manner of notice, the court shall consider, among other factors,

(i) the extent and nature of the class,

(ii) the relief requested,

(iii) the cost of notifying the members,

(iv) the resources of the plaintiff, and

(v) the possible prejudice to be suffered by members of the class or by others if notice is not received.

(5) *Content of Notice.* The notice shall include:

(a) a general description of the action, including the relief sought, and the names and addresses of the representative parties;

(b) a statement of the right of a member of the class to be excluded from the action by submitting an election to be excluded, including the manner and time for exercising the election;

(c) a description of possible financial consequences for the class;

(d) a general description of any counterclaim or notice of intent to assert a counterclaim by or against members of the class, including the relief sought;

(e) a statement that the judgment, whether favorable or not, will bind all members of the class who are not excluded from the action;

(f) a statement that any member of the class may intervene in the action;

(g) the address of counsel to whom inquiries may be directed; and

(h) other information the court deems appropriate.

(6) *Cost of Notice.*

(a) The plaintiff shall bear the expense of the notification required by subrule (C)(1). The court may require the defendant to cooperate in the notice process, but any additional costs incurred by the defendant in doing so shall be paid by the plaintiff.

(b) Upon termination of the action, the court may allow as taxable costs the expenses of notification incurred by the prevailing party.

(c) Subrules (C)(6)(a) and (b) shall not apply when a statute provides for a different allocation of the cost of notice in a particular class of actions.

(7) *Additional Notices.* In addition to the notice required by subrule (C)(1), during the course of the action the court may require that notice of any other matter be given in such manner as the court directs to some or all of the members of the class.

(D) **Judgment.**

(1) The judgment shall describe the parties bound.

(2) A judgment entered before certification of a class binds only the named parties.

(3) A motion for judgment (including partial judgment) under MCR 2.116 may be filed and decided before the decision on the question of class certification. A judgment entered before certification in favor of a named party does not preclude that party from representing the class in the action if that is otherwise appropriate.

(4) A complaint that does not include class action allegations may not be amended to include such allegations after the granting of judgment or partial judgment under MCR 2.116.

(5) A judgment entered in an action certified as a class action binds all members of the class who have not submitted an election to be excluded, except as otherwise directed by the court.

(E) **Dismissal or Compromise.** An action certified as a class action may not be dismissed or compromised without the approval of the court, and notice of the proposed dismissal or compromise shall be given to the class in such manner as the court directs.

(F) **Statute of Limitations.**

(1) The statute of limitations is tolled as to all persons within the class described in the complaint on the commencement of an action asserting a class action.

(2) The statute of limitations resumes running against class members other than representative parties and intervenors:

(a) on the filing of a notice of the plaintiff's failure to move for class certification under subrule (B)(2);

(b) 28 days after notice has been made under subrule (C)(1) of the entry, amendment, or revocation of an order of certification eliminating the person from the class;

(c) on entry of an order denying certification of the action as a class action;

(d) on submission of an election to be excluded;

(e) on final disposition of the action.

(3) If the circumstance that brought about the resumption of the running of the statute is superseded by a further order of the trial court, by reversal on appeal, or otherwise, the statute of limitations shall be deemed to have been tolled continuously from the commencement of the action.

(G) Discovery. Representative parties and intervenors are subject to discovery in the same manner as parties in other civil actions. Other class members are subject to discovery in the same manner as persons who are not parties, and may be required to submit to discovery procedures applicable to parties to the extent ordered by the court.

(H) Counterclaims.

(1) *Right to File Counterclaims.* A party to a class action may file counterclaims as in any other action, including counterclaims by or against a class or an individual class member.

(2) *Notice of Intent to File Counterclaims.* The defendant may file notice of intent to assert counterclaims against absent class members before notice of certification is given under subrule (C)(1), identifying or describing the persons against whom counterclaims may be filed and describing the nature of the counterclaims.

(3) *Time to File.* A counterclaim against a class member other than a representative party must be filed and served within 56 days after the class member intervenes or submits a claim for distribution of a share of any award recovered in the action, whichever is earlier, or within such further time as the court allows.

(4) *Notice to Class Members.* If the notice of certification given under subrule (C)(1) did not notify potential class members of the counterclaim, each class member against whom a counterclaim is asserted shall be permitted to elect to be excluded from the action. Notice of this right shall be served with the counterclaim.

(5) *Control of Action.* The court shall take such steps as are necessary to prevent the pendency of counterclaims from making the action unmanageable as a class action. Such steps include but are not limited to severing counterclaims for separate trial under MCR 2.505(B) or ordering that consideration of the counterclaims be deferred until after determination of the issue of the defendant's liability, at which time the court may hear the counterclaims, remove them to a lower court, change venue, dismiss them without prejudice, or take other appropriate action.

(I) Defendant Classes.

(1) An action that seeks to recover money from individual members of a defendant class may not be maintained as a class action.

(2) A representative of a defendant class, other than a public body or a public officer, may decline to defend the action in a representative capacity unless the court finds that the convenient administration of justice otherwise requires.

[Effective March 1, 1985.]

1985 Staff Comment

MCR 3.501 is substantially the same as GCR 1963, 208.

RULE 3.502   SECONDARY ACTION BY SHAREHOLDERS

(A) Pleading. In an action brought by one or more shareholders in an incorporated or unincorporated association because the association has refused or failed to enforce rights which may properly be asserted by it, the complaint shall set forth under oath and with particularity the efforts of the plaintiff to secure from the managing directors or trustees the action the plaintiff desires and the reasons for the failure to obtain such action, or the reasons for not making such an effort.

(B) Security. At any stage of an action under this subrule the court may require such security and impose such terms as shall fairly and adequately protect the interests of the class or association in whose behalf the action is brought or defended.

(C) Notice. The court may order that notice be given, in the manner and to the persons it directs,

(1) of the right of absent persons to appear and present claims and defenses;

(2) of the pendency of the action;

(3) of a proposed settlement;

(4) of entry of judgment; or

(5) of any other proceedings in the action.

(D) Inadequate Representation. Whenever the representation appears to the court inadequate to protect the interests of absent persons who may be bound by the judgment, the court may at any time prior to judgment order an amendment of the pleadings to eliminate references to representation of absent persons, and the court shall enter judgment in such form as to affect only the parties to the action and those adequately represented.

[Effective March 1, 1985.]

1985 Staff Comment

MCR 3.502 is substantially the same as GCR 1963, 211.1.

RULE 3.503   ACTION BY FIDUCIARY

(A) Court Order. When a proceeding is instituted by a fiduciary seeking instruction or authorization with respect to fiduciary duties or the trust property, and it appears that it is impracticable to bring all of the beneficiaries before the court, the court shall enter an order:

(1) setting forth the form of and manner for giving notice of the proceedings to the beneficiaries, and

(2) selecting representatives of the beneficiaries to act as representatives of the class.

(B) Notice. The contents of the notice shall fairly state the purpose of the proceedings and shall specify the time and place of hearing. Where an applicable statute provides for notice, the court may dispense with other notice.

[Effective March 1, 1985.]

1985 Staff Comment

MCR 3.503 is substantially the same as GCR 1963, 211.2.

SUBCHAPTER 3.600   MISCELLANEOUS PROCEEDINGS

RULE 3.601   PUBLIC NUISANCES

(A) Procedure to Abate Public Nuisance. Actions to abate public nuisances are governed by the general rules of procedure and evidence applicable to nonjury actions, except as provided by the statutes covering public nuisances and by this rule.

(B) Default; Hearing; Notice and Time. If a defendant fails to answer within the time provided, his or her default may be taken. On answer of a defendant or entry of a defendant's default, a party other than a defendant in default may notice the action for hearing on 7 days' notice. Hearings in actions under this rule take precedence over actions that are not entitled to priority by statute or rule and may be held at the time they are noticed without further pretrial proceedings.

(C) Motions; Hearing. Motions by the defendant filed and served with the answer are heard on the day of the hearing of the action.

(D) Entry of Order or Judgment; Preliminary Injunction.

(1) On the day noticed for hearing, the court shall hear and determine the disputed issues and enter a proper order and judgment.

(2) If the hearing is adjourned at the defendant's request, and the court is satisfied by affidavit or otherwise that the allegations in the complaint are true and that the plaintiff is entitled to relief, an injunction as requested may be granted, to be binding until further order.

(3) If service is not obtained on all of the defendants named in the complaint, the court has jurisdiction to hear the action and enter a proper order of abatement and judgment against those defendants who have been served. The order and judgment may not adversely affect the interests of the defendants who have not been served.

(E) Temporary Restraining Order. If a preliminary injunction is requested in the complaint and the court is satisfied by affidavit or otherwise that the material allegations are true, and that the plaintiff is entitled to relief, it may issue a temporary restraining order in accordance with MCR 3.310(B), restraining the defendant from conducting, maintaining, and permitting the continuance of the nuisance and from removing or permitting the removal of the liquor, furniture, fixtures, vehicles, or other things used in the maintenance of the nuisance, until the final hearing and determination on the complaint or further order.

(F) Substitution for Complaining Party. The court may substitute the Attorney General or prosecuting attorney for the complaining party and direct the substituted officer to prosecute the action to judgment.

(G) Further Orders of Court. The court may enter other orders consistent with equity and not inconsistent with the provisions of the statute and this rule.

[Effective March 1, 1985.]

1985 Staff Comment

MCR 3.601 is comparable to GCR 1963, 782.

The provision of GCR 1963, 782.2 regarding service of process is deleted. The same methods of service would be available under MCR 2.105.

Subrule (B) modifies the language of GCR 1963, 782.3 to make clear that any party not in default may notice the action for hearing.

Subrule (D)(3) modifies the language of GCR 1963, 782.4 to make clear that an order or judgment may not adversely affect the interests of defendants who have not been served.

In subrule (E), an additional requirement for the issuance of a temporary restraining order is added: Not only must the court be satisfied that the allegations are true, but also it must find that those allegations justify the relief sought. The rule also incorporates the provisions of MCR 3.310 regarding temporary restraining orders.

In several places, the word "shall" is changed to "may" to emphasize the judge's discretion in entering orders. See subrules (D)(2) and (E).

RULE 3.602 ARBITRATION

(A) Applicability of Rule. This rule governs statutory arbitration under MCL 600.5001–600.5035; MSA 27A.5001–27A.5035. Subrules (I)–(N) apply to proceedings under the malpractice arbitration act. MCL 600.5040–600.5065; MSA 27A.5040–27A.5065.

(B) Proceedings to Compel or to Stay Arbitration.

(1) In a pending action an application to the court for an order under this rule must be by motion, which shall be heard in the manner and on the notice provided by these rules for motions. An initial application for an order under this rule, other than in a pending action, must be made by filing a complaint as in other civil actions.

(2) On application of a party showing an agreement to arbitrate that conforms to the arbitration statute, and the opposing party's refusal to arbitrate, the court may order the parties to proceed with arbitration and to take other steps necessary to carry out the arbitration agreement and the arbitration statute. If the opposing party denies the existence of an agreement to arbitrate, the court shall summarily determine the issues and may order arbitration or deny the application.

(3) On application, the court may stay an arbitration proceeding commenced or threatened on a showing that there is no agreement to arbitrate. If there is a substantial and good-faith dispute, the court shall summarily try the issue and may enter a stay or direct the parties to proceed to arbitration.

(4) An application to compel arbitration may not be denied on the ground that the claim sought to be arbitrated lacks merit or is not filed in good faith, or because fault or grounds for the claim have not been shown.

(C) Action Involving Issues Subject to Arbitration; Stay. Subject to MCR 3.310(E), an action or proceeding involving an issue subject to arbitration must be stayed if an order for arbitration or an application for such an order has been made under this rule. If the issue subject to arbitration is severable, the stay may be limited to that issue. If an application for an order compelling arbitration is made in the action or proceeding in which the issue is raised, an order for arbitration must include a stay.

(D) Hearing; Time; Place; Adjournment.

(1) The arbitrator shall set the time and place for the hearing, and may adjourn it as necessary.

(2) On a party's request for good cause, the arbitrator may postpone the hearing to a time not later than the day set for rendering the award.

(E) Oath of Arbitrator and Witnesses.

(1) Before hearing testimony, the arbitrator must be sworn to hear and fairly consider the matters submitted and to make a just award according to his or her best understanding.

(2) The arbitrator has the power to administer oaths to the witnesses.

(F) Subpoena; Depositions.

(1) MCR 2.506 applies to arbitration hearings.

(2) On a party's request, the arbitrator may permit the taking of a deposition, for use as evidence, of a witness who cannot be subpoenaed or is unable to attend the hearing. The arbitrator may designate the manner of and the terms for taking the deposition.

(G) Representation by Attorney. A party has the right to be represented by an attorney at a proceeding or hearing under this rule. A waiver of the right before the proceeding or hearing is ineffective.

(H) Award by Majority; Absence of Arbitrator. If the arbitration is by a panel of arbitrators, the hearing shall be conducted by all of them, but a majority may decide any question and render a final award unless the concurrence of all of the arbitrators is expressly required by the agreement to submit to arbitration. If, during the course of the hearing, an arbitrator ceases to act for any reason, the remaining arbitrator or arbitrators may continue with the hearing and determine the controversy.

(I) Award; Confirmation by Court. An arbitration award filed with the clerk of the court designated in the agreement or statute within one year after the award was rendered may be confirmed by the court, unless it is vacated, corrected, or modified, or a decision is postponed, as provided in this rule.

(J) Vacating Award.

(1) On application of a party, the court shall vacate an award if:

(a) the award was procured by corruption, fraud, or other undue means;

(b) there was evident partiality by an arbitrator appointed as a neutral, corruption of an arbitrator, or misconduct prejudicing a party's rights;

(c) the arbitrator exceeded his or her powers; or

(d) the arbitrator refused to postpone the hearing on a showing of sufficient cause, refused to hear evidence material to the controversy, or otherwise conducted the hearing to prejudice substantially a party's rights.

The fact that the relief could not or would not be granted by a court of law or equity is not ground for vacating or refusing to confirm the award.

(2) An application to vacate an award must be made within 21 days after delivery of a copy of the award to the applicant, except that if it is predicated on corruption, fraud, or other undue means, it must be made within 21 days after the grounds are known or should have been known.

(3) In vacating the award, the court may order a rehearing before a new arbitrator chosen as provided in the agreement, or, if there is no such provision, by the court. If the award is vacated on grounds stated in subrule (J)(1)(c) or (d), the court may order a rehearing before the arbitrator who made the award. The time within which the agreement requires the award to be made is applicable to the rehearing and commences from the date of the order.

(4) If the application to vacate is denied and there is no motion to modify or correct the award pending, the court shall confirm the award.

(K) Modification or Correction of Award.

(1) On application made within 21 days after delivery of a copy of the award to the applicant, the court shall modify or correct the award if:

(a) there is an evident miscalculation of figures or an evident mistake in the description of a person, a thing, or property referred to in the award;

(b) the arbitrator has awarded on a matter not submitted to the arbitrator, and the award may be corrected without affecting the merits of the decision on the issues submitted; or

(c) the award is imperfect in a matter of form, not affecting the merits of the controversy.

(2) If the application is granted, the court shall modify and correct the award to effect its intent and shall confirm the award as modified and corrected. Otherwise, the court shall confirm the award as made.

(3) An application to modify or correct an award may be joined in the alternative with an application to vacate the award.

(L) Judgment. The court shall render judgment giving effect to the award as corrected, confirmed, or modified. The judgment has the same force and effect, and may be enforced in the same manner, as other judgments.

(M) Costs. The costs of the proceedings may be taxed as in civil actions, and, if provision for the fees and expenses of the arbitrator has not been made in the award, the court may allow compensation for the arbitrator's services as it deems just. The arbitrator's compensation is a taxable cost in the action.

(N) Appeals. Appeals may be taken as from orders or judgments in other civil actions.

[Effective March 1, 1985.]

1985 Staff Comment

MCR 3.602 is comparable to GCR 1963, 769.

Subrule (A) clarifies the applicability of the arbitration rule to arbitrations under the medical malpractice provisions of MCL 600.5040–600.5065; MSA 27A.5040–27A.5065.

Subrule (B)(1) requires that a request to invoke court jurisdiction in an arbitration matter is to be made by filing a civil action, unless the matter arises in a pending action, in which case a motion may be used.

The references to the "judgment roll" in GCR 1963, 769.13(1) are omitted from subrule (L).

Subrule (M) modifies the provision on fees and costs. GCR 1963, 769.12 referred to costs provided by law in the case of references. However, the relevant statute had been repealed.

RULE 3.603   INTERPLEADER

(A) Availability.

(1) Persons having claims against the plaintiff may be joined as defendants and required to interplead when their claims are such that the plaintiff is or may be exposed to double or multiple liability. It is not a ground for objection to the joinder that the claims of the several claimants or the titles on which their claims depend do not have a common origin or are not identical, but are adverse to and independent of one another, or that the plaintiff denies liability to any or all of the claimants in whole or in part.

(2) A defendant exposed to liability as described in subrule (A)(1), may obtain interpleader by counterclaim or cross-claim. A claimant not already before the court may be joined as defendant, as provided in MCR 2.207 or MCR 2.209.

(3) If one or more actions concerning the subject matter of the interpleader action have already been filed, the interpleader action must be filed in the court where the first action was filed.

(B) Procedure.

(1) The court may order the property or the amount of money as to which the plaintiff admits liability to be deposited with the court or otherwise preserved, or to be secured by a bond in an amount sufficient to assure payment of the liability admitted.

(2) The court may thereafter enjoin the parties before it from commencing or prosecuting another action regarding the subject matter of the interpleader action.

(3) On hearing, the court may order the plaintiff discharged from liability as to property deposited or secured before determining the rights of the claimants.

(C) Rule Not Exclusive. The provisions of this rule supplement and do not in any way limit the joinder of parties permitted by MCR 2.206.

(D) Disposition of Earlier Action. If another action concerning the subject matter of the interpleader action has previously been filed, the court in which the earlier action was filed may:

(1) transfer the action, entirely or in part, to the court in which the interpleader action is pending,

(2) hold the action entirely or partially in abeyance, pending resolution of the interpleader action,

(3) dismiss the action, entirely or in part, or

(4) upon a showing of good cause, proceed with the action, explaining on the record the basis of the decision to proceed.

(E) Actual Costs. The court may award actual costs to an interpleader plaintiff. For the purposes of this rule, actual costs are those costs taxable in any civil action, and a reasonable attorney fee as determined by the trial court.

(1) The court may order that the plaintiff's actual costs of filing the interpleader request, tendering the disputed property to the court, and participating in the case as a disinterested stakeholder be paid from the disputed property or by another party.

(2) If the plaintiff incurs actual costs other than those described in subrule (1) due to another party's unreasonable litigation posture, the court may order that the other party pay those additional actual costs.

(3) An award made pursuant to this rule may not include reimbursement for the actual costs of asserting the plaintiff's own claim to the disputed property, or of supporting or opposing another party's claim.

[Effective March 1, 1985; amended effective December 1, 1996; January 1, 2003.]

1985 Staff Comment

MCR 3.603 is comparable to GCR 1963, 210.

Staff Comment to 1996 Amendment

The 1996 amendment of MCR 3.603 added paragraph (A)(3) and subrule (D). These changes were made to address the situation discussed in *Marsh* v. *Foremost Ins Co*, 451 Mich 62; 544 NW2d 646 (1996).

Staff Comment to 2002 Amendment

The August 1, 2002, amendment, effective January 1, 2003, added subrule (E). It authorizes courts to award actual costs, including a reasonable attorney fee, to an interpleader plaintiff. Depending on the circumstances, the court may order that the money be paid either from the disputed property or by another party. See *Terra Energy, Ltd v Michigan*, 241 Mich App 393 (2000), lv den 463 Mich 994 (2001).

The staff comment is published only for the benefit of the bench and bar and is not an authoritative construction by the Court.

RULE 3.604 BONDS

(A) Scope of Rule. This rule applies to bonds given under the Michigan Court Rules and the Revised Judicature Act, unless a rule or statute clearly indicates that a different procedure is to be followed.

(B) Submission to Jurisdiction of Court by Surety. A surety on a bond or undertaking given under the Michigan Court Rules or the Revised Judicature Act submits to the jurisdiction of the court and consents that further proceedings affecting the surety's liability on the bond or undertaking may be conducted under this rule.

(C) Death of Party; Substitution of Surety. If the only plaintiff or the only defendant dies during the pendency of an action, in addition to the parties substituted under MCR 2.202, each surety on a bond given by the deceased party shall be made a party to the action, on notice to the surety in the manner prescribed in MCR 2.107.

(D) Affidavit of Surety; Notice of Bond.

(1) A surety on a bond, except for a surety company authorized to do business in Michigan, must execute an affidavit that he or she has pecuniary responsibility and attach the affidavit to the bond.

(2) In alleging pecuniary responsibility, a surety must affirm that he or she owns assets not exempt from execution having a fair market value exceeding his or her liabilities by at least twice the amount of the bond.

(3) A copy of a bond and the accompanying affidavit must be promptly served on the party for whose benefit it is given in the manner prescribed in MCR 2.107. Proof of service must be filed promptly with the court in which the bond has been filed.

(4) In an action alleging medical malpractice filed on or after October 1, 1986, notice of the filing of security for costs or the affidavit in lieu of such security, required by MCL 600.2912d, 600.2912e; MSA 27A.2912(4), 27A.2912(5), shall be given as provided in MCR 2.109(B).

(E) Objections to Surety. A party for whose benefit a bond is given may, within 7 days after receipt of a copy of the bond, serve on the officer taking the bond and the party giving the bond a notice that the party objects to the sufficiency of the surety. Failure to do so waives all objections to the surety.

(F) Hearing on Objections to Surety. Notice of objection to a surety must be filed as a motion for hearing on objections to the bond.

(1) On demand of the objecting party, the surety must appear at the hearing of the motion and be subject to examination as to the surety's pecuniary responsibility or the validity of the execution of the bond.

(2) After the hearing, the court may approve or reject the bond as filed or require an amended, substitute, or additional bond, as the circumstances warrant.

(3) In an appeal to the circuit court from a lower court or tribunal, an objection to the surety is heard in the circuit court.

(G) Surety Company Bond. A surety company certified by the Commissioner of Insurance as authorized to do business in Michigan may act as surety on a bond.

(H) Assignment or Delivery of Bond. If the condition of a bond is broken, or the circumstances require, the court shall direct the delivery or assignment of the bond for prosecution to the person for whose benefit it was given. Proceedings to enforce the bond may be taken in the action pursuant to subrule (I).

(I) Judgment Against Surety.

(1) *Judgment on Motion.* In an action in which a bond or other security has been posted, judgment may be entered directly against the surety or the security on motion without the necessity of an independent action on a showing that the condition has occurred giving rise to the liability on the bond or to the forfeiture of the security.

(2) *Notice.* Notice of the hearing on the motion for judgment must be given to the surety or the owner of the security in the manner prescribed in MCR 2.107. The notice may be mailed to the address stated in the bond or stated when the security was furnished unless the surety or owner has given notice of a change of address.

(3) *Restitution.* If in later proceedings in the action, on appeal or otherwise, it is determined that the surety is not liable or that the security should not have been forfeited, the court may order restitution of money paid or security forfeited.

(J) Application to Another Judge After Supersedeas Refused.

(1) If a circuit judge has denied an application for supersedeas in whole or in part, or has granted it conditionally or on terms, a later application for the same purpose and in the same matter may not be made to another circuit judge if the first judge is available.

(2) If an order is entered contrary to the provisions of subrule (J)(1), it is void and must be revoked by the judge who entered it, on proof of the facts. A person making a later application contrary to this rule is subject to punishment for contempt.

(K) Cash or Securities Bond. The furnishing of a cash or securities bond under MCL 600.2631; MSA 27A.2631 is deemed compliance with these rules.

(L) Stay of Proceedings Without Bond. If a party required to give a bond under these rules for supersedeas, appeal, or otherwise is unable to give the bond by reason of poverty, the court may, on proof of the inability, limit or eliminate the requirement for surety on the bond on appropriate conditions and for a reasonable time.

[Effective March 1, 1985; amended effective December 12, 1986.]

1985 Staff Comment

MCR 3.604 brings together the various provisions regarding bonds found in GCR 1963, 525 and 763.

Subrule (B) does not include the language of GCR 1963, 763.1 making the clerk the surety's agent for service of papers.

Subrule (J)(1) omits the language of GCR 1963, 736.9(1), which referred to persons other than a judge authorized to grant bonds.

RULE 3.605 COLLECTION OF PENALTIES, FINES, FORFEITURES, AND FORFEITED RECOGNIZANCES

(A) Definition. The term "penalty", as used in this rule, includes fines, forfeitures, and forfeited recognizances, unless otherwise provided in this rule.

(B) Parties. The civil action for a pecuniary penalty incurred for the violation of an ordinance of a city or village must be brought in the name of the city or village. Other actions to recover penalties must be brought in the name of the people of the State of Michigan.

(C) Judgment on Penalty. In an action against a party liable for a penalty, judgment may be rendered directly against the party and in favor of the other party on motion and showing that the condition has occurred giving rise to the penalty. This subrule does not apply to forfeited civil recognizances under MCR 3.604 or to forfeited criminal recognizances under MCL 765.28; MSA 28.915.

(D) Remission of Penalty. An application for the remission of a penalty, including a bond forfeiture, may be made to the judge who imposed the penalty or ordered the forfeiture. The application may not be heard until reasonable notice has been given to the prosecuting attorney (or municipal attorney) and he or she has had an opportunity to examine the matter and prepare to resist the application. The application may not be granted without payment of the costs and expenses incurred in the proceedings for the collection of the penalty.

(E) Duty of Clerk When Fine Without Order for Commitment; Duty of Prosecutor. When a fine is imposed by a court on a person, without an order for the immediate commitment of the person until the fine is paid, the clerk of the court shall deliver a copy of the order imposing the fine to the prosecuting attorney of the county in which the court is held, or the municipal attorney in the case of a fine that is payable to a municipality. The prosecuting attorney (or municipal attorney) shall obtain execution to collect the fine.

[Effective March 1, 1985.]

1985 Staff Comment

MCR 3.605 is comparable to GCR 1963, 772.

In subrules (D) and (E), the references to the "prosecuting attorney" are changed to references to prosecuting attorney "or municipal attorney" to take account of the application of the rule to the district court. See DCR 772.4.

RULE 3.606 CONTEMPTS OUTSIDE IMMEDIATE PRESENCE OF COURT

(A) Initiation of Proceeding. For a contempt committed outside the immediate view and presence of the court, on a proper showing on ex parte motion supported by affidavits, the court shall either

(1) order the accused person to show cause, at a reasonable time specified in the order, why that person should not be punished for the alleged misconduct; or

(2) issue a bench warrant for the arrest of the person.

(B) Writ of Habeas Corpus. A writ of habeas corpus to bring up a prisoner to testify may be used to bring before the court a person charged with misconduct under this rule. The court may enter an appropriate order for the disposition of the person.

(C) Bond for Appearance.

(1) The court may allow the giving of a bond in lieu of arrest, prescribing in the bench warrant the penalty of the bond and the return day for the defendant.

(2) The defendant is discharged from arrest on executing and delivering to the arresting officer a bond

(a) in the penalty endorsed on the bench warrant to the officer and the officer's successors,

(b) with two sufficient sureties, and

(c) with a condition that the defendant appear on the return day and await the order and judgment of the court.

(3) *Return of Bond.* On returning a bench warrant, the officer executing it must return the bond of the defendant, if one was taken. The bond must be filed with the bench warrant.

(D) Assignment of Bond; Damages. The court may order assignment of the bond to an aggrieved party who is authorized by the court to prosecute the bond under MCR 3.604(H). The measure of the damages to be assessed in an action on the bond is the extent of the loss or injury sustained by the aggrieved party because of the misconduct for which the order for arrest was issued, and that party's costs and expenses in securing the order. The remainder of the penalty of the bond is paid into the treasury of the county in which the bond was taken, to the credit of the general fund.

(E) Prosecution on Bond by Attorney General or Prosecutor. If the court does not order an assignment as provided in (D), it shall order the breach prosecuted by the Attorney General or by the prosecuting attorney for the county in which the bond was taken, under MCR 3.604. The penalty recovered is to be paid into the treasury of the county in which the bond was taken, to the credit of the general fund.

[Effective March 1, 1985.]

1985 Staff Comment

MCR 3.606 is substantially the same as GCR 1963, 760.

RULE 3.607 PROCEEDINGS TO RESTORE LOST RECORDS OR PAPERS IN COURTS OF RECORD

(A) Application for Order. When a record or paper relating to an action or proceeding pending or determined in a Michigan court of record is lost, a person having an interest in its recovery may apply to the court having jurisdiction of the action or the record for an order that a duplicate of the lost record or paper be prepared and filed in the court.

(B) Manner of Proceeding; Notice to Interested Parties. The party making the application must show to the satisfaction of the court that the record or paper once existed and has been lost, without the fault or connivance, directly or indirectly, of the applicant. On that showing, the court shall direct the manner of proceeding to replace the lost item, and the notice to be given to parties interested in the application.

(C) Witnesses; Interrogatories. The court before which the application is pending may issue subpoenas for and compel the attendance of witnesses, or may compel witnesses to submit to examination on interrogatories and to establish facts relevant to the proceeding.

(D) Order; Effect of Duplicate. If the court is satisfied that the record or paper proposed as a substitute for the lost one exhibits all the material facts of the original, the court shall enter an order providing that the substitute record or paper be filed or recorded with the officer who had custody of the original. During the continuance of the loss, the substituted record or paper has the same effect in all respects and in all places as the original.

[Effective March 1, 1985.]

1985 Staff Comment

MCR 3.607 is substantially the same as GCR 1963, 766.

RULE 3.611 VOLUNTARY DISSOLUTION OF CORPORATIONS

(A) Scope; Rules Applicable. This rule governs actions to dissolve corporations brought under MCL 600.3501; MSA 27A.3501. The general rules of procedure apply to these actions, except as provided in this rule and in MCL 600.3501–600.3515; MSA 27A.3501–27A.3515.

(B) Contents of Complaint; Statements Attached. A complaint seeking voluntary dissolution of a corporation must state why the plaintiff desires a dissolution of the corporation, and there must be attached:

(1) an inventory of all the corporation's property;

(2) a statement of all encumbrances on the corporation's property;

(3) an account of the corporation's capital stock, specifying the names of the stockholders, their addresses, if known, the number of shares belonging to each, the amount paid in on the shares, and the amount still due on them;

(4) an account of all the corporation's creditors and the contracts entered into by the corporation that may not have been fully satisfied and canceled, specifying:

(a) the address of each creditor and of every known person with whom the contracts were made, if known, and if not known, that fact to be stated;

(b) the amount owing to each creditor;

(c) the nature of each debt, demand, or obligation; and

(d) the basis of and consideration for each debt, demand, or obligation; and

(5) the affidavit of the plaintiff that the facts stated in the complaint, accounts, inventories, and statements are complete and true, so far as the plaintiff knows or has the means of knowing.

(C) **Notice of Action.** Process may be served as in other actions, or, on the filing of the complaint, the court may order all persons interested in the corporation to show cause why the corporation should not be dissolved, at a time and place to be specified in the order, but at least 28 days after the date of the order. Notice of the contents of the order must be served by mail on all creditors and stockholders at least 28 days before the hearing date, and must be published once each week for 3 successive weeks in a newspaper designated by the court.

(D) **Hearing.** At a hearing ordered under subrule (C), the court shall hear the allegations and proofs of the parties and take testimony relating to the property, debts, credits, engagements, and condition of the corporation. After the hearing, the court may dismiss the action, order the corporation dissolved, appoint a receiver, schedule further proceedings, or enter another appropriate order.

(E) **Suits by Receiver.** An action may be brought by the receiver in his or her own name and may be continued by the receiver's successor or co-receiver. An action commenced by or against the corporation before the filing of the complaint for dissolution is not abated by the complaint or by the judgment of dissolution, but may be prosecuted or defended by the receiver. The court in which an action is pending may on motion order substitution of parties or enter another necessary order.

[Effective March 1, 1985.]

1985 Staff Comment

MCR 3.611 is comparable to GCR 1963, 778. New subrule (A) specifies the applicability of the rule.

RULE 3.612 WINDING UP OF CORPORATION WHOSE TERM OR CHARTER HAS EXPIRED

(A) **Scope; Rules Applicable.** This rule applies to actions under MCL 600.3520; MSA 27A.3520. The general rules of procedure apply to these actions, except as provided in this rule and in MCL 600.3520; MSA 27A.3520.

(B) **Contents of Complaint.** The complaint must include:

(1) the nature of the plaintiff's interest in the corporation or its property, the date of organization of the corporation, the title and the date of approval of the special act under which the corporation is organized, if appropriate, and the term of corporate existence;

(2) whether any of the corporation's stockholders are unknown to the plaintiff;

(3) that the complaint is filed on behalf of the plaintiff and all other persons interested in the property of the corporation as stockholders, creditors, or otherwise who may choose to join as parties plaintiff and share the expense of the action;

(4) an incorporation by reference of the statements required by subrule (C);

(5) other appropriate allegations; and

(6) a demand for appropriate relief, which may include that the affairs of the corporation be wound up and its assets disposed of and distributed and that a receiver of its property be appointed.

(C) **Statements Attached to Complaint.** The complaint must have attached:

(1) a copy of the corporation's articles of incorporation, if they are on file with the Department of Commerce, and, if the corporation is organized by special act, a copy of the act;

(2) a statement of the corporation's assets, so far as known to the plaintiff;

(3) a statement of the amount of capital stock and of the amount paid in, as far as known, from the last report of the corporation on file with the Department of Commerce or, if none has been filed, from the articles of incorporation on file with the Department of Commerce, or the special legislative act organizing the corporation;

(4) if the corporation's stock records are accessible to the plaintiff, a list of the stockholders' names and addresses and the number of shares held by each, insofar as shown in the records;

(5) a statement of all encumbrances on the corporation's property, and all claims against the corporation,

and the names and addresses of the encumbrancers and claimants, so far as known to the plaintiff; and

(6) a statement of the corporation's debts, the names and addresses of the creditors, and the nature of the consideration for each debt, so far as known to the plaintiff.

(D) Parties Defendant. The corporation must be made a defendant. All persons claiming encumbrances on the property may be made defendants. It is not necessary to make a stockholder or creditor of the corporation a defendant.

(E) Process and Order for Appearance; Publication.

(1) Process must be issued and served as in other civil actions or, on the filing of the complaint, the court may order the appearance and answer of the corporation, its stockholders, and creditors at least 28 days after the date of the order.

(2) The order for appearance must be published in the manner prescribed in MCR 2.106.

(3) When proof of the publication is filed and the time specified in the order for the appearance of the corporation, stockholders, and creditors has expired, an order may be entered taking the complaint as confessed by those who have not appeared.

(F) Appearance by Defendants.

(1) Within the time the order for appearance sets, the following persons may appear and defend the suit as the corporation might have:

(a) a stockholder in the corporation while it existed and who still retains rights in its property by owning stock;

(b) an assignee, purchaser, heir, devisee, or personal representative of a stockholder; or

(c) a creditor of the corporation, whose claim is not barred by the statute of limitations.

(2) All persons so appearing must defend in the name of the corporation.

(3) If a person other than the corporation has been named as a defendant in the complaint, that person must be served with process as in other civil actions.

(G) Subsequent Proceedings. So far as applicable, the procedures established in MCR 3.611 govern hearings and later proceedings in an action under this rule.

(H) Continuation of Proceeding for Benefit of Stockholder or Creditor. If the plaintiff fails to establish that he or she is a stockholder or creditor of the corporation, the action may be continued by another stockholder or creditor who has appeared in the action.

[Effective March 1, 1985.]

1985 Staff Comment

MCR 3.612 is comparable to GCR 1963, 779.

New subrule (A) states the applicability of the rule.

There are changes in terminology to take account of statutory changes regarding corporate filings. Compare, for example, subrules (C)(1) and (3) with GCR 1963, 779.2(1) and (3).

RULE 3.613   CHANGE OF NAME

(A) Published Notice, Contents. A published notice of a proceeding to change a name shall include the name of the petitioner; the current name of the subject of the petition; the proposed name; and the time, date and place of the hearing.

(B) Minor's Signature. A petition for a change of name by a minor need not be signed in the presence of a judge.

(C) Notice to Noncustodial Parent. Service on a noncustodial parent of a minor who is the subject of a petition for change of name shall be made in the following manner.

(1) *Address Known.* If the noncustodial parent's address or whereabouts is known, that parent shall be served with a copy of the petition and a notice of hearing.

(2) *Address Unknown.* If the noncustodial parent's address or whereabouts is not known and cannot be ascertained after diligent inquiry, that parent shall be served with a notice of hearing by publishing in a newspaper and filing a proof of service as provided by MCR 2.106(F) and (G). The notice must be published one time at least 14 days before the date of the hearing, must include the name of the noncustodial parent and a statement that the result of the hearing may be to bar or affect the noncustodial parent's interest in the matter, and that publication must be in the county where the court is located unless a different county is specified by statute, court rule, or order of the court. A notice published under this subrule need not set out the contents of the petition if it contains the information required under subrule (A). A single publication may be used to notify the general public and the noncustodial parent whose address cannot be ascertained if the notice contains the noncustodial parent's name.

(D) Consultation With Minor, Presumption. A child 7 years of age and under is presumed not of sufficient age to be consulted concerning a preference on change of name.

(E) Confidential Records. In cases where the court orders that records are to be confidential and that no publication is to take place, records are to be maintained in a sealed envelope marked confidential and placed in a private file. Except as otherwise ordered by the court, only the original petitioner may gain access to confidential files, and no information relating to a confidential record, including whether the record exists, shall be accessible to the general public.

[Formerly Rule 5.781, adopted effective April 1, 1991. Renumbered 3.613, and amended effective May 1, 2002.]

Staff Comment to 2002 Renumber and Amendment

The amendment and renumbering of MCR 5.750–5.756 and 5.781–5.783 as MCR 3.800–3.806 and 3.613–3.615, effective May 1, 2002, were proposed by the Family Division Joint Rules Committee. The statute creating the family division of circuit court gave it jurisdiction of a number of types of proceedings formerly heard in the probate court. See MCL 600.1021. The amendments move the rules governing adoptions, change of name, Parental Rights Restoration Act proceedings, and proceedings regarding persons who pose health threats to others, from Chapter 5, which contains probate court provisions, to Chapter 3. In addition, there are several modifications of the rules. The change-of-name rule will use the circuit court publication procedure. MCR 3.613(C)(2). A provision on confidentiality of records is added to the change-of-name rule. MCR 3.613(E). New subrule MCR 3.614(C) will specify the interested parties in a petition for treatment of infectious disease. (File No. 99–55.)

The staff comment is published only for the benefit of the bench and bar and is not an authoritative construction by the Court.

RULE 3.614   HEALTH THREATS TO OTHERS

(A) Public Health Code, Application. Except as modified by this rule, proceedings relating to carriers of contagious diseases who pose threats to the health of others under part 52 of the public health code are governed by the rules generally applicable to civil proceedings.

(B) Service of Papers. The moving party is responsible for service when service is required.

(C) Interested Parties. The interested parties in a petition for treatment of infectious disease are the petitioner and the respondent.

(D) Commitment Review Panel.

(1) *Appointment.* On receipt of a petition for treatment of infectious disease which requests that the individual be committed to an appropriate facility, the Court shall forthwith appoint a Commitment Review Panel from a list of physicians prepared by the Department of Public Health.

(2) *Respondent's Choice of Physician.* On motion of the respondent requesting that a specific physician be appointed to the Commitment Review Panel, the Court shall appoint the physician so requested, unless the physician refuses. If the individual is unable to pay such physician, the court shall pay such physician a reasonable fee comparable with fees paid to other court appointed experts. On appointment of the requested physician, the Court shall discharge one of the initially appointed physicians.

(3) The Commitment Review Panel shall make written recommendations to the Court prior to the date of hearing on the petition. The recommendations shall be substantially in a form approved by the State Court Administrator.

(E) Commitment to Facility.

(1) *Renewal of Order of Commitment.* A motion for continuing commitment shall be filed at least 14 days prior to the expiration of the order of commitment. The motion shall be made by the director of the commitment facility or the director's designee. The court shall conduct a hearing on the motion prior to the expiration of the existing order of commitment. Notice shall be given as on the initial petition and to the local department of public health. The court shall reconvene the respondent's Commitment Review Panel. At the hearing, the petitioner must show good cause for continued commitment in the facility. No order of commitment shall exceed 6 months in length.

(2) *Reevaluation at Request of Respondent.* Once within any six-month period or more often by leave of the court, an individual committed to a facility for treatment of an infectious disease may file in the court a petition for a new Commitment Review Panel recommendation on whether the patient's commitment should be terminated. Within 14 days after receipt of the report of the reconvened Commitment Review Panel, the court shall review the panel's report and enter an order. The court may modify, continue or terminate its order of commitment without a hearing.

[Formerly Rule 5.782, adopted effective July 1, 1991. Renumbered 3.614, and amended effective May 1, 2002.]

1991 Probate Rules Committee Comment

This is a new rule. The reevaluation provided in subrule (D)(2) is the "appeal" provided in subsection 5205(6) of the public health code, MCL 333.5205(6); MSA 14.15(5205)(6).

Staff Comment to 2002 Renumber and Amendment

The amendment and renumbering of MCR 5.750–5.756 and 5.781–5.783 as MCR 3.800–3.806 and 3.613–3.615, effective May 1, 2002, were proposed by the Family Division Joint Rules Committee. The statute creating the family division of circuit court gave it jurisdiction of a number of types of proceedings formerly heard in the probate court. See MCL 600.1021. The amendments move the rules governing adoptions, change of name, Parental Rights Restoration Act proceedings, and proceedings regarding persons who pose health threats to others, from Chapter 5, which contains probate court provisions, to Chapter 3. In addition, there are several modifications of the rules. The change-of-name rule will use the circuit court publication procedure. MCR 3.613(C)(2). A provision on confidentiality of records is added to the change-of-name rule. MCR 3.613(E). New subrule MCR 3.614(C) will specify the interested parties in a petition for treatment of infectious disease. (File No. 99–55.)

The staff comment is published only for the benefit of the bench and bar and is not an authoritative construction by the Court.

RULE 3.615 PARENTAL RIGHTS RESTORATION ACT PROCEEDINGS

(A) Applicable Rules. A proceeding by a minor to obtain a waiver of parental consent for an abortion shall be governed by the rules applicable to civil proceedings except as modified by this rule.

(B) Confidentiality, Use of Initials, Private File, Reopening.

(1) The court shall assure the confidentiality of the file, the assistance given the minor by court personnel, and the proceedings.

(2) If requested by the minor, the title of the proceeding shall be by initials or some other means of assuring confidentiality. At the time the petition is filed, the minor shall file a Confidential Information Sheet listing the minor's name, date of birth, permanent residence, title to be used in the proceeding and the method by which the minor may be reached during the pendency of the proceeding. The Confidential Information Sheet and all other documents containing identifying information shall be sealed in an envelope marked confidential on which the case number has been written and placed in a private file. Confidential information shall not be entered into a computer file.

(3) The court shall maintain only one file of all papers for each case. The file shall be inspected only by the judge, specifically authorized court personnel, the minor, her attorney, her next friend, the guardian ad litem, and any other person authorized by the minor. After the proceedings are completed, the file may be opened only by order of the court for good cause shown and only for a purpose specified in the order of the court.

(4) The file of a completed case shall not be destroyed until two years after the minor has reached the age of majority. The court shall not microfilm or otherwise copy the file.

(C) Advice of Rights, Method of Contact.

(1) If a minor seeking a waiver of parental consent makes first contact with the court by personal visit to the court, the court shall provide a written notice of rights and forms for a petition for waiver of parental consent, a confidential information sheet, and a request for appointment of an attorney, each substantially in the form approved by the state court administrator.

(2) If a minor seeking a waiver of parental consent makes first contact with the court by telephone, the court shall tell the minor that she can receive a notice of rights and forms for a petition, a confidential information sheet, and a request for appointment of an attorney by coming to the court or that the court will mail such forms to the minor. If the minor requests that the court mail the forms, the court shall mail the

forms within 24 hours of the telephone contact to an address specified by the minor.

(3) Any person on personal visit to the court shall be given, on request, a copy of the notice of rights or any other form.

(D) Assistance With Preparation of Petition. On request of the minor or next friend, the court shall provide the minor with assistance in preparing and filing of a petition, confidential information sheet and request for appointment of an attorney, each substantially in the form approved by the state court administrator.

(E) Next Friend. If the minor proceeds through a next friend, the petitioner shall certify that the next friend is not disqualified by statute and that the next friend is an adult. The next friend may act on behalf of the minor without prior appointment of the court and is not responsible for the costs of the action.

(F) Attorney, Request, Appointment, Duties.

(1) At the request of the minor or next friend before or after filing the petition, the court shall immediately appoint an attorney to represent the minor. The request shall be in writing in substantially the form approved by the state court administrator. Except for good cause stated on the record, the court shall appoint an attorney selected by the minor if the minor has secured the attorney's agreement to represent her or the attorney has previously indicated to the court a willingness to be appointed.

(2) If it deems necessary, the court may appoint an attorney to represent the minor at any time.

(3) The minor shall contact the court appointed attorney within 24 hours of such appointment. The court shall advise the minor of this requirement.

(4) If an attorney is appointed to represent a minor prior to filing a petition, the attorney shall consult with the minor within 48 hours of appointment.

(G) Guardian ad Litem, Appointment, Duties.

(1) *Request of Minor.* The court shall immediately appoint a guardian ad litem to represent the minor at the request of the minor or next friend before or after filing the petition.

(2) *Appointment on Court's Motion.*

(a) At any time if it deems necessary, the court may appoint a guardian ad litem to assist the court.

(b) The guardian ad litem may obtain information by contacting the minor and other persons with the consent of the minor, provided the confidentiality of the proceedings is not violated.

(H) Filing Petition, Setting Hearing, Notice of Hearing.

(1) The petition shall be filed in person by the minor, attorney or next friend.

(2) The court shall set a time and place for a hearing and notify the filer at the time the petition is filed. The court shall give notice of the hearing only to the minor, the minor's attorney, next friend and guardian ad litem. Notice of hearing may be oral or written and may be given at any time prior to the hearing. The hearing may be scheduled to commence immediately if the minor and her attorney, if any, are ready to proceed.

(3) Insofar as practical, at the minor's request the hearing shall be scheduled at a time and place that will not interfere with the minor's school attendance.

(I) Venue, Transfer. Venue is in the county of the minor's residence or where the minor is found at the time of the filing of the petition. Transfer of venue properly laid shall not be made without consent of the minor.

(J) Hearing.

(1) *Burden and Standard of Proof.* The petitioner has the burden of proof by preponderance of the evidence and must establish the statutory criteria at a hearing.

(2) *Closed Hearing.* The hearing shall be closed to the public. The court shall limit attendance at the hearing to the minor, the minor's attorney, the next friend, the guardian ad litem, persons who are called to testify by the minor or with the minor's consent, necessary court personnel and one support person who would not be disqualified as a next friend by MCL 722.902(d); MSA 25.248(102)(d).

(3) All relevant and material evidence may be received.

(4) The hearing may be conducted informally in the chambers of a judge.

(5) The hearing shall commence and be concluded within 72 hours, excluding Sundays and holidays, of the filing of the petition, unless the minor consents to an adjournment. The order of the court shall be issued within 48 hours, excluding Sundays and holidays, of the conclusion of the hearing.

(K) Order.

(1) *Order Granting Waiver, Duration, Effect.* If the petition is granted, the court immediately shall provide the minor with two certified copies of the order granting waiver of parental consent. The order shall be valid for 90 days from the date of entry. Nothing in the order shall require or permit an abortion that is otherwise prohibited by law.

(2) *Order Denying Waiver, Notice of Appeal, Appointment of Counsel, Preparation of Transcript.* If the order denies relief, the court shall endorse the time and date on the order. The order shall be served on the minor's attorney or, if none, the minor along with

(a) a unified appellate document substantially in the form approved by the state court administrator which may be used as notice of appeal, claim of appeal, request for appointment of an attorney and order of transcript, and

(b) a notice that, if the minor desires to appeal, the minor must file the notice of appeal with the court within 24 hours.

(3) *Appeal.*

(a) Upon receipt of a timely notice of appeal, the court must appoint counsel and order that the transcript be prepared immediately and two copies filed within 72 hours. If the minor was represented by counsel in the court proceedings, the court must reappoint the same attorney unless there is good cause for a different appointment. As soon as the transcript is filed, the court shall forward the file to the Court of Appeals.

(b) Time for Filing Notice.

(1) If the order was entered at the conclusion of the hearing or at any other time when the minor's attorney or, if none, the minor was in attendance at court, the minor must file the notice of appeal within 24 hours of the date and time stamped on the order, or

(2) If the order was entered at any other time, the minor must file the notice of appeal within 24 hours of the time when the order was received by the minor's attorney or, if none, the minor.

(c) If a court in which a document is to be filed is closed for business at the end of a filing period, the document will be filed on a timely basis if filed during the morning of the next day when the court is open for business.

(d) Perfection of Appeal. The minor's attorney must perfect the appeal by filing in the Court of Appeals a claim of appeal and a copy of the order denying waiver. The appeal must be perfected within 72 hours, excluding Sundays and holidays, of the filing of the notice of appeal.

(e) Brief. The minor's attorney shall file at the time of perfecting appeal five copies of the brief on appeal. The brief need not contain citations to the transcript.

(f) Oral Argument. There will be no oral argument, unless ordered by the Court of Appeals.

[Formerly Rule 5.783, adopted effective April 1, 1991. Renumbered 3.615, and amended effective May 1, 2002.]

Publisher's Note

The Michigan Supreme Court Order which adopted Rule 5.783, entered March 28, 1991, contained the following language:

"In adopting these rules, the Court should not be understood as foreclosing consideration of a challenge to the wisdom, validity or meaning of a rule when a question is brought to the Court judicially or by a proposal for a change in a rule. See, e.g., *Meek v Centre County Banking Co,* 268

US 426; 45 SCt 560; 69 LEd 1028 (1925), and *Mississippi Publishing Corp v Murphree*, 326 US 438; 66 SCt 242; 90 LEd 185 (1946). While these rules are binding on Michigan courts, the Court does not intend to preclude objection in the trial court based on a challenge to the wisdom, validity or meaning of a rule and development of a separate record so as to properly present the challenge for review by this Court."

Staff Comment to 2002 Renumber and Amendment

The amendment and renumbering of MCR 5.750–5.756 and 5.781–5.783 as MCR 3.800–3.806 and 3.613–3.615, effective May 1, 2002, were proposed by the Family Division Joint Rules Committee. The statute creating the family division of circuit court gave it jurisdiction of a number of types of proceedings formerly heard in the probate court. See MCL 600.1021. The amendments move the rules governing adoptions, change of name, Parental Rights Restoration Act proceedings, and proceedings regarding persons who pose health threats to others, from Chapter 5, which contains probate court provisions, to Chapter 3. In addition, there are several modifications of the rules. The change-of-name rule will use the circuit court publication procedure. MCR 3.613(C)(2). A provision on confidentiality of records is added to the change-of-name rule. MCR 3.613(E). New subrule MCR 3.614(C) will specify the interested parties in a petition for treatment of infectious disease. (File No. 99–55.)

The staff comment is published only for the benefit of the bench and bar and is not an authoritative construction by the Court.

SUBCHAPTER 3.700   PERSONAL PROTECTION PROCEEDINGS

RULE 3.701   APPLICABILITY OF RULES; FORMS

(A) Scope. Except as provided by this subchapter of rules and the provisions of MCL 600.2950 and 600.2950a, actions for personal protection for relief against domestic violence or stalking are governed by the Michigan Court Rules. Procedure related to personal protection orders against adults is governed by this subchapter. Procedure related to personal protection orders against minors is governed by subchapter 5.900, except as noted in MCR 5.981.

(B) Forms. The state court administrator shall approve forms for use in personal protection act proceedings. The forms shall be made available for public distribution by the clerk of the circuit court.

[Adopted effective September 1, 1997; amended effective January 10, 2000; September 1, 2001.]

1997 Staff Comment

The amendments of MCR 3.201, 3.207, and 8.117 and addition of subchapter 3.700 [effective September 1, 1997], are designed to implement the statutes providing for the issuance of personal protection orders. See MCL 600.2950; MSA 27A.2950, MCL 600.2950a; MSA 27A.29501(1).

Staff Comment to 1999 Amendment

These rules [effective January 10, 2000] clarify the procedure applicable to the new minor personal protection orders ("minor PPOs") created in 1998 PA 474–477, which went into effect March 1, 1999. Because the new statutes do not make clear whether existing PPO procedural rules apply or rules for Juvenile Code proceedings apply, these rules are promulgated to assure consistency in the processing of minor PPOs in Michigan's Circuit Court Family Divisions. Immediate adoption has been ordered to provide needed procedural guidance for courts already facing minor PPO cases.

Staff Comment to 2001 Amendment

The June 1, 2001 amendments of MCR 3.701, MCR 3.702, 3.703, 3.704, 3.706, 3.707, and 3.708, effective September 1, 2001, are designed, in part, to clarify the court rule provisions adopted effective September 1, 1997. 456 Mich clxxxiv (1997).

RULE 3.702   DEFINITIONS

When used in this subchapter, unless the context otherwise indicates:

(1) "personal protection order" means a protection order as described under MCL 600.2950 and 600.2950a;

(2) "petition" refers to a pleading for commencing an independent action for personal protection and is not considered a motion as defined in MCR 2.119;

(3) "petitioner" refers to the party seeking protection;

(4) "respondent" refers to the party to be restrained;

(5) "existing action" means an action in this court or any other court in which both the petitioner and the respondent are parties; existing actions include, but are not limited to, pending and completed domestic relations actions, criminal actions, other actions for personal protection orders.

(6) "minor" means a person under the age of 18.

(7) "minor personal protection order" means a personal protection order issued by a court against a minor and under jurisdiction granted by MCL 712A.2(h).

[Adopted effective September 1, 1997; amended effective January 10, 2000; September 1, 2001.]

1997 Staff Comment

The amendments of MCR 3.201, 3.207, and 8.117 and addition of subchapter 3.700 [effective September 1, 1997], are designed to implement the statutes providing for the issuance of personal protection orders. See MCL 600.2950; MSA 27A.2950, MCL 600.2950a; MSA 27A.29501(1).

Staff Comment to 1999 Amendment

These rules [effective January 10, 2000] clarify the procedure applicable to the new minor personal protection orders ("minor PPOs") created in 1998 PA 474–477, which went into effect March 1, 1999. Because the new statutes do not make clear whether existing PPO procedural rules apply or rules for Juvenile Code proceedings apply, these rules are promulgated to assure consistency in the processing of minor PPOs in Michigan's Circuit Court Family Divisions. Immediate adoption has been ordered to provide needed procedural guidance for courts already facing minor PPO cases.

Staff Comment to 2001 Amendment

The June 1, 2001 amendments of MCR 3.701, MCR 3.702, 3.703, 3.704, 3.706, 3.707, and 3.708, effective September 1, 2001, are designed, in part, to clarify the court rule provisions adopted effective September 1, 1997. 456 Mich clxxxiv (1997).

RULE 3.703　COMMENCING A PERSONAL PROTECTION ACTION

(A) Filing. A personal protection action is an independent action commenced by filing a petition with a court. There are no fees for filing a personal protection action and no summons is issued. A personal protection action may not be commenced by filing a motion in an existing case or by joining a claim to an action.

(B) Petition in General. The petition must

(1) be in writing;

(2) state with particularity the facts on which it is based;

(3) state the relief sought and the conduct to be restrained;

(4) state whether an ex parte order is being sought;

(5) state whether a personal protection order action involving the same parties has been commenced in another jurisdiction; and

(6) be signed by the party or attorney as provided in MCR 2.114. The petitioner may omit his or her residence address from the documents filed with the court, but must provide the court with a mailing address.

(C) Petition Against a Minor. In addition to the requirements outlined in (B), a petition against a minor must list:

(1) the minor's name, address, and either age or date of birth; and

(2) if known or can be easily ascertained, the names and addresses of the minor's parent or parents, guardian, or custodian.

(D) Other Pending Actions; Order, Judgments.

(1) The petition must specify whether there are any other pending actions in this or any other court, or orders or judgments already entered by this or any other court affecting the parties, including the name of the court and the case number, if known.

(a) If the petition is filed in the same court as a pending action or where an order or judgment has

already been entered by that court affecting the parties, it shall be assigned to the same judge.

(b) If there are pending actions in another court or orders or judgments already entered by another court affecting the parties, the court should contact the court where the pending actions were filed or orders or judgments were entered, if practicable, to determine any relevant information.

(2) If the prior action resulted in an order providing for continuing jurisdiction of a minor, and the new action requests relief with regard to the minor, the court must comply with MCR 3.205.

(E) Venue.

(1) If the respondent is an adult, the petitioner may file a personal protection action in any county in Michigan regardless of residency.

(2) If the respondent is a minor, the petitioner may file a personal protection order in either the petitioner's or respondent's county of residence. If the respondent does not live in this state, venue for the action is proper in the petitioner's county of residence.

(F) Minor or Legally Incapacitated Individual as Petitioner.

(1) If the petitioner is a minor or a legally incapacitated individual, the petitioner shall proceed through a next friend. The petitioner shall certify that the next friend is not disqualified by statute and that the next friend is an adult.

(2) Unless the court determines appointment is necessary, the next friend may act on behalf of the minor or legally incapacitated person without appointment. However, the court shall appoint a next friend if the minor is less than 14 years of age. The next friend is not responsible for the costs of the action.

(G) Request for Ex Parte Order.

If the petition requests an ex parte order, the petition must set forth specific facts showing that immediate and irreparable injury, loss, or damage will result to the petitioner from the delay required to effect notice or from the risk that notice will itself precipitate adverse action before an order can be issued.

[Adopted effective September 1, 1997; amended effective January 10, 2000; September 1, 2001.]

1997 Staff Comment

The amendments of MCR 3.201, 3.207, and 8.117 and addition of subchapter 3.700 [effective September 1, 1997], are designed to implement the statutes providing for the issuance of personal protection orders. See MCL 600.2950; MSA 27A.2950, MCL 600.2950a; MSA 27A.29501(1).

Staff Comment to 1999 Amendment

These rules [effective January 10, 2000] clarify the procedure applicable to the new minor personal protection orders ("minor PPOs") created in 1998 PA 474–477, which went into effect March 1, 1999. Because the new statutes do not make clear whether existing PPO procedural rules apply or rules

commodate the conditions of the personal protection order.

(a) If the respondent or petitioner wants the existing custody or parenting time order modified, the respondent or petitioner must file a motion with the court having jurisdiction of the custody or parenting time order and request a hearing. The hearing must be held within 21 days after the motion is filed.

(b) Proceedings to modify custody and parenting time orders are subject to subchapter 3.200.

(D) Service. The petitioner shall serve the order on the respondent as provided in MCR 2.105(A). If the respondent is a minor, and the whereabouts of the respondent's parent or parents, guardian, or custodian is known, the petitioner shall also in the same manner serve the order on the respondent's parent or parents, guardian, or custodian. On an appropriate showing, the court may allow service in another manner as provided in MCR 2.105(I). Failure to serve the order does not affect its validity or effectiveness.

(E) Oral Notice. If oral notice of the order is made by a law enforcement officer as described in MCL 600.2950(22) or 600.2950a(19), proof of the notification must be filed with the court by the law enforcement officer.

[Adopted effective September 1, 1997; amended effective January 10, 2000; September 1, 2001; September 11, 2002.]

1997 Staff Comment

The amendments of MCR 3.201, 3.207, and 8.117 and addition of subchapter 3.700 [effective September 1, 1997], are designed to implement the statutes providing for the issuance of personal protection orders. See MCL 600.2950; MSA 27A.2950, MCL 600.2950a; MSA 27A.29501(1).

Staff Comment to 1999 Amendment

These rules [effective January 10, 2000] clarify the procedure applicable to the new minor personal protection orders ("minor PPOs") created in 1998 PA 474–477, which went into effect March 1, 1999. Because the new statutes do not make clear whether existing PPO procedural rules apply or rules for Juvenile Code proceedings apply, these rules are promulgated to assure consistency in the processing of minor PPOs in Michigan's Circuit Court Family Divisions. Immediate adoption has been ordered to provide needed procedural guidance for courts already facing minor PPO cases.

Staff Comment to 2001 Amendment

The June 1, 2001 amendments of MCR 3.701, MCR 3.702, 3.703, 3.704, 3.706, 3.707, and 3.708, effective September 1, 2001, are designed, in part, to clarify the court rule provisions adopted effective September 1, 1997. 456 Mich clxxxiv (1997).

Staff Comment to 2002 Amendment

The September 11, 2002, amendments of MCR 3.206, 3.214, 3.705, 3.706, 3.708, 5.982, and 8.119, which were given immediate effect, are related to the group of domestic violence statutes enacted in December 2001 that took effect April 1, 2002.

The changes in MCR 3.206 and 3.214 are related to 2001 PA 195, which adopted the Uniform Child–Custody Jurisdiction and Enforcement Act, MCL 722.1101 *et seq.* There is also some nonsubstantive reorganization of MCR 3.214.

The amendment of MCR 3.705 implements the statutory provisions regarding the statement of reasons for granting or denying personal protection orders. See 2001 PA 196.

The amendment of MCR 3.706 incorporates the statutory provisions regarding enforceability of Michigan personal protection orders in other jurisdictions. See 2001 PA 200 and 201.

MCR 3.708 and 5.982 are amended to include foreign protection orders, which are made enforceable in Michigan by 2001 PA 197.

MCR 8.119(F) is amended to conform to 2001 PA 205, which directs that when a motion to seal court records involves allegations of domestic violence, the court is to consider the safety of the potential victim in ruling on the motion.

The staff comment is published only for the benefit of the bench and bar and is not an authoritative construction by the Court.

RULE 3.707 MODIFICATION, TERMINATION, OR EXTENSION OF ORDER

(A) Modification or Termination.

(1) *Time for Filing and Service.*

(a) The petitioner may file a motion to modify or terminate the personal protection order and request a hearing at any time after the personal protection order is issued.

(b) The respondent may file a motion to modify or terminate the personal protection order and request a hearing within 14 days after being served with, or receiving actual notice of, the order unless good cause is shown for filing the motion after the 14 days have elapsed.

(c) The moving party shall serve the motion to modify or terminate the order and the notice of hearing at least 7 days before the hearing date as provided in MCR 2.105(A)(2) at the mailing address or addresses provided to the court. On an appropriate showing, the court may allow service in another manner as provided in MCR 2.105(I). If the moving party is a respondent who is issued a license to carry a concealed weapon and is required to carry a weapon as a condition of employment, a police officer certified by the Michigan law enforcement training council act of 1965, 1965 PA 203, MCL 28.601 to 28.616, a sheriff, a deputy sheriff or a member of the Michigan department of state police, a local corrections officer, department of corrections employee, or a federal law enforcement officer who carries a firearm during the normal course of employment, providing notice one day before the hearing is deemed as sufficient notice to the petitioner.

(2) *Hearing on the Motion.* The court must schedule and hold a hearing on a motion to modify or terminate a personal protection order within 14 days of the filing of the motion, except that if the respondent is a person described in MCL 600.2950(2) or 600.2950a(2), the court shall schedule the hearing on the motion within 5 days after the filing of the motion.

(3) *Notice of Modification or Termination.* If a personal protection order is modified or terminated, the clerk must immediately notify the law enforcement agency specified in the personal protection order of the change. A modified or terminated order must be served as provided in MCR 2.107.

(B) Extension of Order.

(1) *Time for Filing.* The petitioner may file an ex parte motion to extend the effectiveness of the order, without hearing, by requesting a new expiration date. The motion must be filed with the court that issued the personal protection order no later than 3 days before the order is to expire. The court must act on the motion within 3 days after it is filed. Failure to timely file a motion to extend the effectiveness of the order does not preclude the petitioner from commencing a new personal protection action regarding the same respondent, as provided in MCR 3.703.

(2) *Notice of Extension.* If the expiration date on a personal protection order is extended, an amended order must be entered. The clerk must immediately notify the law enforcement agency specified in the personal protection order of the change. The order must be served on the respondent as provided in MCR 2.107.

(C) Minors and Legally Incapacitated Individuals. Petitioners or respondents who are minors or legally incapacitated individuals must proceed through a next friend, as provided in MCR 3.703(F).

(D) Fees. There are no motion fees for modifying, terminating, or extending a personal protection order.

[Adopted effective September 1, 1997; amended effective January 10, 2000; September 1, 2001.]

1997 Staff Comment

The amendments of MCR 3.201, 3.207, and 8.117 and addition of subchapter 3.700 [effective September 1, 1997], are designed to implement the statutes providing for the issuance of personal protection orders. See MCL 600.2950; MSA 27A.2950, MCL 600.2950a; MSA 27A.29501(1).

Staff Comment to 1999 Amendment

These rules [effective January 10, 2000] clarify the procedure applicable to the new minor personal protection orders ("minor PPOs") created in 1998 PA 474–477, which went into effect March 1, 1999. Because the new statutes do not make clear whether existing PPO procedural rules apply or rules for Juvenile Code proceedings apply, these rules are promulgated to assure consistency in the processing of minor PPOs in Michigan's Circuit Court Family Divisions. Immediate adoption has been ordered to provide needed procedural guidance for courts already facing minor PPO cases.

Staff Comment to 2001 Amendment

The June 1, 2001 amendments of MCR 3.701, MCR 3.702, 3.703, 3.704, 3.706, 3.707, and 3.708, effective September 1, 2001, are designed, in part, to clarify the court rule provisions adopted effective September 1, 1997. 456 Mich clxxxiv (1997).

RULE 3.708 CONTEMPT PROCEEDINGS FOR VIOLATION OF PERSONAL PROTECTION ORDERS

(A) In General.

(1) A personal protection order is enforceable under MCL 600.2950(23) and (25), MCL 600.2950a(20) and (22), MCL 764.15b, and MCL 600.1701 *et seq.* For the purpose of this rule, "personal protection order" includes a foreign protection order enforceable in Michigan under MCL 600.2950*l.*

(2) Proceedings to enforce a minor personal protection order where the respondent is under 18 are governed by subchapter 5.900. Proceedings to enforce a personal protection order issued against an adult, or to enforce a minor personal protection order still in effect when the respondent is 18 or older, are governed by this rule.

(B) Motion to Show Cause.

(1) *Filing.* If the respondent violates the personal protection order, the petitioner may file a motion, supported by appropriate affidavit, to have the respondent found in contempt. There is no fee for such a motion. If the petitioner's motion and affidavit establish a basis for a finding of contempt, the court shall either:

(a) order the respondent to appear at a specified time to answer the contempt charge; or

(b) issue a bench warrant for the arrest of the respondent.

(2) *Service.* The petitioner shall serve the motion to show cause and the order on the respondent by personal service at least 7 days before the show cause hearing.

(C) Arrest.

(1) If the respondent is arrested for violation of a personal protection order as provided in MCL 764.15b(1), the court in the county where the arrest is made shall proceed as provided in MCL 764.15b(2)-(5), except as provided in this rule.

(2) A contempt proceeding brought in a court other than the one that issued the personal protection order shall be entitled "In the Matter of Contempt of [Respondent]." The clerk shall provide a copy of any documents pertaining to the contempt proceeding to the court that issued the personal protection order.

(3) If it appears that a circuit judge will not be available within 24 hours after arrest, the respondent shall be taken, within that time, before a district court,

which shall set bond and order the respondent to appear for arraignment before the family division of the circuit court in that county.

(D) Appearance or Arraignment; Advice to Respondent. At the respondent's first appearance before the circuit court, whether for arraignment under MCL 764.15b, enforcement under MCL 600.2950, 600.2950a, or 600.1701, or otherwise, the court must:

(1) advise the respondent of the alleged violation,

(2) advise the respondent of the right to contest the charge at a contempt hearing,

(3) advise the respondent that he or she is entitled to a lawyer's assistance at the hearing and, if the court determines it might sentence the respondent to jail, that the court will appoint a lawyer at public expense if the individual wants one and is financially unable to retain one,

(4) if requested and appropriate, appoint a lawyer,

(5) set a reasonable bond pending a hearing of the alleged violation.

(6) take a guilty plea as provided in subrule (E) or schedule a hearing as provided in subrule (F).

(E) Pleas of Guilty. The respondent may plead guilty to the violation. Before accepting a guilty plea, the court, speaking directly to the respondent and receiving the respondent's response, must

(1) advise the respondent that by pleading guilty the respondent is giving up the right to a contested hearing and, if the respondent is proceeding without legal representation, the right to a lawyer's assistance as set forth in subrule (D)(3).

(2) advise the respondent of the maximum possible jail sentence for the violation,

(3) ascertain that the plea is understandingly, voluntarily, and knowingly made, and

(4) establish factual support for a finding that the respondent is guilty of the alleged violation.

(F) Scheduling or Postponing Hearing. Following the respondent's appearance or arraignment, the court shall do the following:

(1) Set a date for the hearing at the earliest practicable time except as required under MCL 764.15b.

(a) The hearing of a respondent being held in custody for an alleged violation of a personal protection order must be held within 72 hours after the arrest, unless extended by the court on the motion of the arrested individual or the prosecuting attorney. The court must set a reasonable bond pending the hearing unless the court determines that release will not reasonably ensure the safety of the individuals named in the personal protection order.

(b) If a respondent is released on bond pending the hearing, the bond may include any condition specified in MCR 6.106(D) necessary to reasonably ensure the safety of the individuals named in the personal protection order, including continued compliance with the personal protection order. The release order shall also comply with MCL 765.6b.

(c) If the alleged violation is based on a criminal offense that is a basis for a separate criminal prosecution, upon motion of the prosecutor, the court may postpone the hearing for the outcome of that prosecution.

(2) Notify the prosecuting attorney of a criminal contempt proceeding.

(3) Notify the petitioner and his or her attorney, if any, of the contempt proceeding and direct the party to appear at the hearing and give evidence on the charge of contempt.

(G) Prosecution After Arrest. In a criminal contempt proceeding commenced under MCL 764.15b, the prosecuting attorney shall prosecute the proceeding unless the petitioner retains his or her own attorney for the criminal contempt proceeding.

(H) The Violation Hearing.

(1) *Jury.* There is no right to a jury trial.

(2) *Conduct of the Hearing.* The respondent has the right to be present at the hearing, to present evidence, and to examine and cross-examine witnesses.

(3) *Evidence; Burden of Proof.* The rules of evidence apply to both criminal and civil contempt proceedings. The petitioner or the prosecuting attorney has the burden of proving the respondent's guilt of criminal contempt beyond a reasonable doubt and the respondent's guilt of civil contempt by clear and convincing evidence.

(4) *Judicial Findings.* At the conclusion of the hearing, the court must find the facts specially, state separately its conclusions of law, and direct entry of the appropriate judgment. The court must state its findings and conclusions on the record or in a written opinion made a part of the record.

(5) *Sentencing.*

(a) if the respondent pleads or is found guilty of criminal contempt, the court shall impose a sentence of incarceration for no more than 93 days and may impose a fine of not more than $500.00.

(b) If the respondent pleads or is found guilty of civil contempt, the court shall impose a fine or imprisonment as specified in MCL 600.1715 and MCL 600.1721.

In addition to such a sentence, the court may impose other conditions to the personal protection order.

[Adopted effective September 1, 1997; amended effective January 10, 2000; September 1, 2001; September 11, 2002.]

1997 Staff Comment

The amendments of MCR 3.201, 3.207, and 8.117 and addition of subchapter 3.700 [effective September 1, 1997], are designed to implement the statutes providing for the issuance of personal protection orders. See MCL 600.2950; MSA 27A.2950, MCL 600.2950a; MSA 27A.29501(1).

Staff Comment to 1999 Amendment

These rules [effective January 10, 2000] clarify the procedure applicable to the new minor personal protection orders ("minor PPOs") created in 1998 PA 474–477, which went into effect March 1, 1999. Because the new statutes do not make clear whether existing PPO procedural rules apply or rules for Juvenile Code proceedings apply, these rules are promulgated to assure consistency in the processing of minor PPOs in Michigan's Circuit Court Family Divisions. Immediate adoption has been ordered to provide needed procedural guidance for courts already facing minor PPO cases.

Staff Comment to 2001 Amendment

The June 1, 2001 amendments of MCR 3.701, MCR 3.702, 3.703, 3.704, 3.706, 3.707, and 3.708, effective September 1, 2001, are designed, in part, to clarify the court rule provisions adopted effective September 1, 1997. 456 Mich clxxxiv (1997).

Staff Comment to 2002 Amendment

The September 11, 2002, amendments of MCR 3.206, 3.214, 3.705, 3.706, 3.708, 5.982, and 8.119, which were given immediate effect, are related to the group of domestic violence statutes enacted in December 2001 that took effect April 1, 2002.

The changes in MCR 3.206 and 3.214 are related to 2001 PA 195, which adopted the Uniform Child–Custody Jurisdiction and Enforcement Act, MCL 722.1101 et seq. There is also some nonsubstantive reorganization of MCR 3.214.

The amendment of MCR 3.705 implements the statutory provisions regarding the statement of reasons for granting or denying personal protection orders. See 2001 PA 196.

The amendment of MCR 3.706 incorporates the statutory provisions regarding enforceability of Michigan personal protection orders in other jurisdictions. See 2001 PA 200 and 201.

MCR 3.708 and 5.982 are amended to include foreign protection orders, which are made enforceable in Michigan by 2001 PA 197.

MCR 8.119(F) is amended to conform to 2001 PA 205, which directs that when a motion to seal court records involves allegations of domestic violence, the court is to consider the safety of the potential victim in ruling on the motion.

The staff comment is published only for the benefit of the bench and bar and is not an authoritative construction by the Court.

RULE 3.709　APPEALS

(A) Rules Applicable. Except as provided by this rule, appeals involving personal protection order matters must comply with subchapter 7.200. Appeals involving minor personal protection actions under the Juvenile Code must additionally comply with MCR 5.993.

(B) From Entry of Personal Protection Order.

(1) Either party has an appeal of right from

(a) an order granting or denying a personal protection order after a hearing under subrule 3.705(B)(6), or

(b) the ruling on respondent's first motion to rescind or modify the order if an ex parte order was entered.

(2) Appeals of all other orders are by leave to appeal.

(C) From Finding after Violation Hearing.

(1) The respondent has an appeal of right from a sentence for criminal contempt entered after a contested hearing.

(2) All other appeals concerning violation proceedings are by application for leave.

[Adopted effective September 1, 1997; amended effective January 10, 2000.]

1997 Staff Comment

The amendments of MCR 3.201, 3.207, and 8.117 and addition of subchapter 3.700 [effective September 1, 1997], are designed to implement the statutes providing for the issuance of personal protection orders. See MCL 600.2950; MSA 27A.2950, MCL 600.2950a; MSA 27A.29501(1).

Staff Comment to 1999 Amendment

These rules [effective January 10, 2000] clarify the procedure applicable to the new minor personal protection orders ("minor PPOs") created in 1998 PA 474–477, which went into effect March 1, 1999. Because the new statutes do not make clear whether existing PPO procedural rules apply or rules for Juvenile Code proceedings apply, these rules are promulgated to assure consistency in the processing of minor PPOs in Michigan's Circuit Court Family Divisions. Immediate adoption has been ordered to provide needed procedural guidance for courts already facing minor PPO cases.

SUBCHAPTER 3.800　ADOPTION

RULE 3.800　APPLICABLE RULES

Except as modified by MCR 3.801–3.806, adoption proceedings are governed by the rules generally applicable to civil proceedings.

[Formerly Rule 5.750, effective March 1, 1985. Renumbered 3.800 and amended, effective May 1, 2002.]

1985 Staff Comment

MCR 5.750 is substantially the same as PCR 750.

Staff Comment to 2002 Renumber and Amendment

The amendment and renumbering of MCR 5.750–5.756 and 5.781–5.783 as MCR 3.800–3.806 and 3.613–3.615, effective May 1, 2002, were proposed by the Family Division Joint Rules Committee. The statute creating the family division of circuit court gave it jurisdiction of a number of types of proceedings formerly heard in the probate court. See MCL 600.1021. The amendments move the rules governing adoptions, change of name, Parental Rights Restoration Act proceedings, and proceedings regarding persons who pose health threats to others, from Chapter 5, which contains probate court provisions, to Chapter 3. In addition, there are several modifications of the rules. The change-of-name rule will use the circuit court publication procedure. MCR 3.613(C)(2). A provision on confidentiality of records is added to the change-of-name rule. MCR 3.613(E). New subrule MCR 3.614(C) will specify the interested parties in a petition for treatment of infectious disease. (File No. 99–55.)

The staff comment is published only for the benefit of the bench and bar and is not an authoritative construction by the Court.

RULE 3.801   PAPERS, EXECUTION

(A) A waiver, affirmation, or disclaimer to be executed by the father of a child born out of wedlock may be executed any time after the conception of the child.

(B) A release or consent is valid if executed in accordance with the law at the time of execution.

[Formerly Rule 5.751, effective March 1, 1985; amended effective September 1, 1997. Renumbered 3.801 and amended, effective May 1, 2002.]

1985 Staff Comment

MCR 5.751 is substantially the same as PCR 751.

Staff Comment to 1997 Amendment

Former subrule (A) is deleted as redundant in light of subchapter 5.100. Former subrule (B) is deleted because it is unnecessary. Subrule (C)(1) is deleted as covered in MCL 710.34; MSA 27.3178(555.34). Subrule (C)(2) is deleted because it is not required by law. Former subrule (D)(1) is deleted because it dilutes the requirements of statute. The remaining portions of subrule (D) are redesignated as (A) and (B). Former subrule (E) is deleted.

Staff Comment to 2002 Renumber and Amendment

The amendment and renumbering of MCR 5.750–5.756 and 5.781–5.783 as MCR 3.800–3.806 and 3.613–3.615, effective May 1, 2002, were proposed by the Family Division Joint Rules Committee. The statute creating the family division of circuit court gave it jurisdiction of a number of types of proceedings formerly heard in the probate court. See MCL 600.1021. The amendments move the rules governing adoptions, change of name, Parental Rights Restoration Act proceedings, and proceedings regarding persons who pose health threats to others, from Chapter 5, which contains probate court provisions, to Chapter 3. In addition, there are several modifications of the rules. The change-of-name rule will use the circuit court publication procedure. MCR 3.613(C)(2). A provision on confidentiality of records is added to the change-of-name rule. MCR 3.613(E). New subrule MCR 3.614(C) will specify the interested parties in a petition for treatment of infectious disease. (File No. 99–55.)

The staff comment is published only for the benefit of the bench and bar and is not an authoritative construction by the Court.

RULE 3.802   MANNER AND METHOD OF SERVICE

(A) Service of Papers.

(1) A notice of intent to release or consent pursuant to MCL 710.34(1) may only be served by personal service by a peace officer or a person authorized by the court.

(2) Notice of a petition to identify a putative father and to determine or terminate his rights, or a petition to terminate the rights of a noncustodial parent, must be served on the individual or the individual's attorney in the manner provided in MCR 5.105(B)(1)(a) or (b).

(3) Except as provided in subrules (B) and (C), all other papers may be served by mail under MCR 2.107(C)(3).

(B) Service When Identity or Whereabouts of Father is Unascertainable.

(1) If service cannot be made under subrule (A)(2)(a) because the identity of the father of a child born out of wedlock or the whereabouts of the identified father has not been ascertained after diligent inquiry, the petitioner must file proof, by affidavit or by declaration under MCR 2.114(B)(2), of the attempt to identify or locate the father. No further service is necessary before the hearing to identify the father and to determine or terminate his rights.

(2) At the hearing, the court shall take evidence concerning the attempt to identify or locate the father. If the court finds that a reasonable attempt was made, the court shall proceed under MCL 710.37(2); MSA 27.3178(555.37)(2). If the court finds that a reasonable attempt was not made, the court shall adjourn the hearing under MCL 710.36(7); MSA 27.3178(555.36)(7) and shall

    (a) order a further attempt to identify or locate the father so that service can be made under subrule (A)(2)(a), or

    (b) direct any manner of substituted service of the notice of hearing except service by publication.

(C) Service When Whereabouts of Noncustodial Parent is Unascertainable. If service of a petition to terminate the parental rights of a noncustodial parent pursuant to MCL 710.51(6) cannot be made under subrule (A)(2)(b) because the whereabouts of the noncustodial parent has not been ascertained after diligent inquiry, the petitioner must file proof, by affidavit or by declaration under MCR 2.114(B)(2), of the attempt to locate the noncustodial parent. If the court finds, on reviewing the affidavit or declaration, that service cannot be made because the whereabouts of the person has not been determined after reasonable effort, the court may direct any manner of substituted service of the notice of hearing, including service by publication.

[Formerly Rule 5.752, effective March 1, 1985; amended effective September 1, 1997. Renumbered 5.752 and amended effective May 1, 2002.]

1985 Staff Comment

MCR 5.752 corresponds to PCR 752.

Subrule (A)(1) limits the requirement of personal service to notices under MCL 710.34(1); MSA 27.3178(555.34[1]), as to which the statute requires personal service.

New subrule (C) creates a procedure for notice of a petition to terminate the parental rights of a noncustodial parent when that person's identity or whereabouts is unknown. If the court concludes that reasonable efforts have been made to locate the parent, it may direct an appropriate method of substituted service.

Staff Comment to 1997 Amendment

Subrule (A) is amended to add the requirement that the putative father and noncustodial parent must be served with certain papers by personal service or by certified mail, return receipt requested. Subrule (B) applies only to putative fathers described in MCL 710.39(1); MSA 27.3178(555.39)(1), while subrule (C) applies only to a noncustodial parent described in MCL 710.51; MSA 27.3178(555.51). Subrule (C) is amended to more precisely delineate the criteria for the court's ruling.

Staff Comment to 2002 Renumber and Amendment

The amendment and renumbering of MCR 5.750–5.756 and 5.781–5.783 as MCR 3.800–3.806 and 3.613–3.615, effective May 1, 2002, were proposed by the Family Division Joint Rules Committee. The statute creating the family division of circuit court gave it jurisdiction of a number of types of proceedings formerly heard in the probate court. See MCL 600.1021. The amendments move the rules governing adoptions, change of name, Parental Rights Restoration Act proceedings, and proceedings regarding persons who pose health threats to others, from Chapter 5, which contains probate court provisions, to Chapter 3. In addition, there are several modifications of the rules. The change-of-name rule will use the circuit court publication procedure. MCR 3.613(C)(2). A provision on confidentiality of records is added to the change-of-name rule. MCR 3.613(E). New subrule MCR 3.614(C) will specify the interested parties in a petition for treatment of infectious disease. (File No. 99–55.)

The staff comment is published only for the benefit of the bench and bar and is not an authoritative construction by the Court.

RULE 3.803   FINANCIAL REPORTS, SUBSEQUENT ORDERS

(A) Updated Accountings and Statements.

(1) The update of the accounting filed pursuant to MCL 710.54(8); MSA 27.3178(555.54)(8) may include by reference the total expenses itemized in the accounting required by MCL 710.54(7); MSA 27.3178(555.54)(7).

(2) Any verified statement filed pursuant to MCL 710.54(7); MSA 27.3178(555.54)(7) need not be filed again unless, at the time of the update required by MCL 710.54(8); MSA 27.3178(555.54)(8), any such statement does not reflect the facts at that time.

(B) Subsequent Orders.

(1) Only one order approving fees disclosed in the financial reports required by MCL 710.54(7); MSA 27.3178(555.54)(7) need be entered, and it must be

entered after the filing required by MCL 710.54(8); MSA 27.3178(555.54)(8).

(2) The order placing the child may be entered before the elapse of the 7–day period required by MCL 710.54(7); MSA 27.3178(555.54)(7).

(3) The final order of adoption may be entered before the elapse of the 21–day period required by MCL 710.54(8); MSA 27.3178(555.54)(8).

[Adopted effective September 1, 1997. Formerly Rule 5.753. Renumbered 3.803, and amended effective May 1, 2002.]

1997 Staff Comment

This rule is new. Subrules (A) and (B) eliminate the potential for redundancies in the updating requirements of MCL 710.54(7) and (8); MSA 27.3178(555.54)(7) and (8). Subrules (B)(2) and (3) allow a court to reduce the time for review of the statutorily required documents.

Staff Comment to 2002 Renumber and Amendment

The amendment and renumbering of MCR 5.750–5.756 and 5.781–5.783 as MCR 3.800–3.806 and 3.613–3.615, effective May 1, 2002, were proposed by the Family Division Joint Rules Committee. The statute creating the family division of circuit court gave it jurisdiction of a number of types of proceedings formerly heard in the probate court. See MCL 600.1021. The amendments move the rules governing adoptions, change of name, Parental Rights Restoration Act proceedings, and proceedings regarding persons who pose health threats to others, from Chapter 5, which contains probate court provisions, to Chapter 3. In addition, there are several modifications of the rules. The change-of-name rule will use the circuit court publication procedure. MCR 3.613(C)(2). A provision on confidentiality of records is added to the change-of-name rule. MCR 3.613(E). New subrule MCR 3.614(C) will specify the interested parties in a petition for treatment of infectious disease. (File No. 99–55.)

The staff comment is published only for the benefit of the bench and bar and is not an authoritative construction by the Court.

RULE 3.804   CONSENT HEARING

The consent hearing required by MCL 710.44(1); MSA 27.3178(555.44)(1) must be promptly scheduled by the court after the court examines and approves the report of the investigation or foster family study filed pursuant to MCL 710.46; MSA 27.3178(555.46). If an interested party has requested a consent hearing, the hearing shall be held within 7 days of the filing of the report or foster family study.

[Formerly Rule 5.754, adopted effective September 1, 1997. Renumbered 3.804, and amended effective May 1, 2002.]

1997 Staff Comment

This rule is new.

Staff Comment to 2002 Renumber and Amendment

The amendment and renumbering of MCR 5.750–5.756 and 5.781–5.783 as MCR 3.800–3.806 and 3.613–3.615, effective May 1, 2002, were proposed by the Family Division Joint Rules Committee. The statute creating the family division of circuit court gave it jurisdiction of a number of types of proceedings formerly heard in the probate court. See MCL

600.1021. The amendments move the rules governing adoptions, change of name, Parental Rights Restoration Act proceedings, and proceedings regarding persons who pose health threats to others, from Chapter 5, which contains probate court provisions, to Chapter 3. In addition, there are several modifications of the rules. The change-of-name rule will use the circuit court publication procedure. MCR 3.613(C)(2). A provision on confidentiality of records is added to the change-of-name rule. MCR 3.613(E). New subrule MCR 3.614(C) will specify the interested parties in a petition for treatment of infectious disease. (File No. 99–55.)

The staff comment is published only for the benefit of the bench and bar and is not an authoritative construction by the Court.

RULE 3.805 TEMPORARY PLACEMENTS, TIME FOR SERVICE OF NOTICE OF HEARING TO DETERMINE DISPOSITION OF CHILD

(A) Time for Personal Service. Personal service of notice of hearing on a petition for disposition of a child pursuant to MCL 710.23e(1); MSA 27.3178(555.23e)(1) must be served at least 3 days before the date set for hearing.

(B) Time for Service by Mail. Service by mail must be made at least 7 days before the date set for hearing.

(C) Interested Party, Whereabouts Unknown. If the whereabouts of an interested party, other than the putative father who did not join in the temporary placement, is unknown, service on that interested party will be sufficient if personal service or service by mail is attempted at the last known address of the interested party.

(D) Putative Father, Identity or Whereabouts Unknown. If the identity of the putative father is unknown or the whereabouts of a putative father who did not join in the temporary placement is unknown, he need not be served notice of the hearing.

[Formerly Rule 5.755, adopted effective September 1, 1997. Renumbered 3.805, and amended effective May 1, 2002.]

1997 Staff Comment

This rule is new. It deals with service of notice of the hearing mandated by MCL 710.23e(1); MSA 27.3178(555.23e)(1).

Staff Comment to 2002 Renumber and Amendment

The amendment and renumbering of MCR 5.750–5.756 and 5.781–5.783 as MCR 3.800–3.806 and 3.613–3.615, effective May 1, 2002, were proposed by the Family Division Joint Rules Committee. The statute creating the family division of circuit court gave it jurisdiction of a number of types of proceedings formerly heard in the probate court. See MCL 600.1021. The amendments move the rules governing adoptions, change of name, Parental Rights Restoration Act proceedings, and proceedings regarding persons who pose health threats to others, from Chapter 5, which contains probate court provisions, to Chapter 3. In addition, there are several modifications of the rules. The change-of-name rule will use the circuit court publication procedure. MCR

3.613(C)(2). A provision on confidentiality of records is added to the change-of-name rule. MCR 3.613(E). New subrule MCR 3.614(C) will specify the interested parties in a petition for treatment of infectious disease. (File No. 99–55.)

The staff comment is published only for the benefit of the bench and bar and is not an authoritative construction by the Court.

RULE 3.806 REHEARINGS

(A) Filing, Notice and Response. A party may seek rehearing under MCL 710.64(1); MSA 27.3178(555.64)(1) by timely filing a petition stating the basis for rehearing. Immediately upon filing the petition, the petitioner must give all interested parties notice of its filing in accordance with MCR 5.105. Any interested party may file a response within 7 days of the date of service of notice on the interested party.

(B) Procedure for Determining Whether to Grant a Rehearing. The court must base a decision on whether to grant a rehearing on the record, the pleading filed, or a hearing on the petition. The court may grant a rehearing only for good cause. The reasons for its decision must be in writing or stated on the record.

(C) Procedure if Rehearing Granted. If the court grants a rehearing, the court may, after notice, take new evidence on the record. It may affirm, modify, or vacate its prior decision in whole or in part. The court must state the reasons for its action in writing or on the record.

(D) Stay. Pending a ruling on the petition for rehearing, the court may stay any order, or enter another order in the best interest of the minor.

[Former MCR 5.755 effective March 1, 1985; redesignated as MCR 5.756 effective September 1, 1997. Renumbered 3.806, and amended effective May 1, 2002.]

1997 Staff Comment

This rule has been redesignated from 5.755. It has been rewritten to provide more specific guidance.

Staff Comment to 2002 Renumber and Amendment

The amendment and renumbering of MCR 5.750–5.756 and 5.781–5.783 as MCR 3.800–3.806 and 3.613–3.615, effective May 1, 2002, were proposed by the Family Division Joint Rules Committee. The statute creating the family division of circuit court gave it jurisdiction of a number of types of proceedings formerly heard in the probate court. See MCL 600.1021. The amendments move the rules governing adoptions, change of name, Parental Rights Restoration Act proceedings, and proceedings regarding persons who pose health threats to others, from Chapter 5, which contains probate court provisions, to Chapter 3. In addition, there are several modifications of the rules. The change-of-name rule will use the circuit court publication procedure. MCR 3.613(C)(2). A provision on confidentiality of records is added to the change-of-name rule. MCR 3.613(E). New subrule MCR 3.614(C) will specify the interested parties in a petition for treatment of infectious disease. (File No. 99–55.)

The staff comment is published only for the benefit of the bench and bar and is not an authoritative construction by the Court.

CHAPTER 4. DISTRICT COURT

Effective March 1, 1985

[For Table of Rules, see page 1 et seq.]

SUBCHAPTER 4.000 GENERAL PROVISIONS

RULE 4.001 APPLICABILITY

Procedure in the district and municipal courts is governed by the rules applicable to other actions. The rules in this chapter apply to the specific types of proceedings within the jurisdiction of the district and municipal courts.

[Effective March 1, 1985.]

1985 Staff Comment

MCR 4.001 is a new provision indicating the applicability of the rules in chapter 4. The chapter title refers only to the district court; however, the few remaining municipal courts are subject to the same rules because MCL 600.6502; MSA 27A.6502 provides that absent some provision to the contrary, the municipal courts are governed by the rules and statutes applicable to the district court.

RULE 4.002 TRANSFER OF ACTIONS FROM DISTRICT COURT TO CIRCUIT COURT

(A) Counterclaim or Cross-Claim in Excess of Jurisdiction.

(1) If a defendant asserts a counterclaim or cross-claim seeking relief of an amount or nature beyond the jurisdiction or power of the district court in which the action is pending, and accompanies the notice of the claim with an affidavit stating that the defendant is justly entitled to the relief demanded, the clerk shall record the pleading and affidavit and present them to the judge to whom the action is assigned. The judge shall either order the action transferred to the circuit court to which appeal of the action would ordinarily lie or inform the defendant that transfer will not be ordered without a motion and notice to the other parties.

(2) MCR 4.201(G)(2) and 4.202(I)(4) govern transfer of summary proceedings to recover possession of premises.

(B) Change in Conditions.

(1) A party may, at any time, file a motion with the district court in which an action is pending, requesting that the action be transferred to circuit court. The motion must be supported by an affidavit stating that

(a) due to a change in condition or circumstance, or

(b) due to facts not known by the party at the time the action was commenced,

the party wishes to seek relief of an amount or nature that is beyond the jurisdiction or power of the court to grant.

(2) If the district court finds that the party filing the motion may be entitled to the relief the party now seeks to claim and that the delay in making the claim is excusable, the court shall order the action transferred to the circuit court to which an appeal of the action would ordinarily lie.

(C) Conditions Precedent to Transfer. The action may not be transferred under this rule until the party seeking transfer pays to the opposing parties the costs they have reasonably incurred up to that time that would not have been incurred if the action had originally been brought in circuit court, and pays the statutory circuit court filing fee to the clerk of the court from which the action is to be transferred. If a case is entirely transferred from district court to circuit court and the jury fee was paid in the district court, the district court clerk shall forward the fee to the circuit court with the papers and filing fee under subrule (D). If the amount paid to the district court for the jury fee is less than the circuit court jury fee, then the party requesting the jury shall pay the difference to the circuit court.

(D) Filing in Circuit Court. After the court has ordered transfer and the costs and fees required by subrule (C) have been paid, the clerk of the court from which the action is transferred shall forward to the clerk of the circuit court the original papers in the action and the circuit court filing fee.

(E) Procedure After Transfer. After transfer no further proceedings may be conducted in the district court, and the action shall proceed in the circuit court. The circuit court may order further pleadings and set the time when they must be filed.

[Effective March 1, 1985; amended effective January 1, 1995.]

1985 Staff Comment

MCR 4.002 is based on DCR 203.5 and GCR 1963, 704. The rule uses the term "transfer" to distinguish the procedure from the statutory "removal" from the circuit to the district court under MCL 600.641; MSA 27A.641.

Subrule (A) is changed to make clear that only the court may transfer the case. The clerk is to present the counter-claim or cross-claim and the affidavit to the judge to whom the case is assigned, and the judge shall either order the case transferred or inform the defendant that a motion is required.

New subrule (A)(2) is added excepting from the operation of this rule transfer of summary proceedings to recover possession of premises. The rules governing those proceedings include their own transfer provisions. MCR 4.201(G)(2), 4.202(I)(4).

Subrule (B) is new. It would permit transfer of a case on a motion of any party, including the plaintiff, if changed conditions or facts not known at the time the action was commenced justify relief beyond the jurisdiction or power of the court in which the case is pending. The court may order transfer on findings that the moving party may be entitled to the relief sought and that the delay in seeking the relief was excusable.

Subrule (C) slightly modifies the cost provisions previously found in DCR 203.5(2). The party seeking transfer need pay only the opposing party's costs that would not have been incurred had the action originally been brought in the circuit court.

The [March 1, 1985] amendment of MCR 4.002(C) provides that if the jury fee has been paid in the district court before transfer of the action to circuit court, the fee is to be forwarded to the circuit court by the clerk.

Subrule (E) also includes provisions previously found in GCR 1963, 704. However, the circuit court is not required to order further pleadings after transfer, but may do so.

Staff Comment to 1995 Amendment

MCR 2.508(B)(3) took effect in 1995, as did an amendment of MCR 4.002(C). These changes were to address the procedural issue that arose in *Adamski* v *Cole*, 197 Mich App 124; 494 NW2d 794 (1992), lv den 445 Mich 863 (1994).

RULE 4.003 REMOVAL OF ACTIONS FROM CIRCUIT COURT TO DISTRICT COURT [REPEALED]

[Repealed effective July 1, 1997.]

1997 Staff Comment

The May 8, 1997, order repeals MCR 4.003, which governed removal of cases from circuit to district court, effective July 1, 1997. This reinstates the February 28, 1997, repeal of the rule, which was suspended on March 13, 1997.

In addition, the order postpones the effective date of earlier amendments of MCR 2.403, 2.405, and 3.216, and new MCR 2.404, affecting mediation procedure, to October 1, 1997. The order also makes adjustments in MCR 2.403(K) and (N) in light of the repeal of MCR 4.003. The text of MCR 2.403, 2.404, 2.405 and 3.216 is the same as that adopted in the Court's March 5, 1997, order dealing with those rules.

SUBCHAPTER 4.100 CIVIL INFRACTION ACTIONS

RULE 4.101 CIVIL INFRACTION ACTIONS

(A) Citation; Complaint; Summons; Warrant.

(1) Except as otherwise provided by court rule or statute, a civil infraction action may be initiated by a law enforcement officer serving a written citation on the alleged violator, and filing the citation in the district court.

(a) If the infraction is a parking violation, the action may be initiated by an authorized person placing a citation securely on the vehicle or mailing a citation to the registered owner of the vehicle. In either event, the citation must be filed in the district court.

(b) If the infraction is a municipal civil infraction, the action may be initiated by an authorized local official serving a written citation on the alleged violator. If the infraction involves the use or occupancy of land or a building or other structure, service may be accomplished by posting the citation at the site and sending a copy to the owner by first-class mail.

The citation serves as the complaint in a civil infraction action, and may be filed either on paper or electronically.

(2) The citation serves as a summons to command

(a) the initial appearance of the defendant; and

(b) a response from the defendant as to his or her responsibility for the alleged violation.

(3) A single citation may not allege both a misdemeanor and a civil infraction.

(4) A warrant may not be issued for a civil infraction unless permitted by statute.

(B) Appearances; Failure to Appear; Default Judgment.

(1) Depending on the nature of the violation and on the procedure appropriate to the violation, a defendant may appear in person, by representation, or by mail.

(2) A defendant may not appear by making a telephone call to the court, but a defendant may telephone the court to obtain a date to appear.

(3) A clerk of the court may enter a default after certifying, on a form to be furnished by the court, that the defendant has not made a scheduled appearance, or has not answered a citation within the time allowed by statute.

(4) If a defendant fails to appear or otherwise to respond to any matter pending relative to a civil infraction action, the court:

(a) must enter a default against the defendant;

(b) must make a determination of responsibility, if the complaint is sufficient;

(c) must impose a sanction by entering a default judgment;

(d) must send the defendant a notice of the entry of the default judgment and the sanctions imposed; and

(e) may retain the driver's license of a nonresident as permitted by statute, if the court has received that license pursuant to statute. The court need not retain the license past its expiration date.

(5) If a defendant fails to appear or otherwise to respond to any matter pending relative to a traffic civil infraction, the court

(a) must notify the secretary of state of the entry of the default judgment, as required by MCL 257.732; MSA 9.2432, and

(b) must initiate the procedures required by MCL 257.321a; MSA 9.2021(1).

(6) If a defendant fails to appear or otherwise to respond to any matter pending relative to a state civil infraction, the court must initiate the procedures required by MCL 257.321a; MSA 9.2021(1).

(C) Motion to Set Aside Default Judgment.

(1) A defendant may move to set aside a default judgment within 14 days after the court sends notice of the judgment to the defendant. The motion

(a) may be informal,

(b) may be either written or presented to the court in person,

(c) must explain the reason for the nonappearance of the defendant,

(d) must state that the defendant wants to offer a defense to or an explanation of the complaint, and

(e) must be accompanied by a cash bond equal to the fine and costs due at the time the motion is filed.

(2) For good cause, the court may

(a) set aside the default and direct that a hearing on the complaint take place, or

(b) schedule a hearing on the motion to set aside the default judgment.

(3) A defendant who does not file this motion on time may use the procedure set forth in MCR 2.603(D).

(D) Response.

(1) Except as provided in subrule (4), an admission without explanation may be offered to and accepted by

(a) a district judge;

(b) a district court magistrate as authorized by the chief judge, the presiding judge, or the only judge of the district; or

(c) other district court personnel as authorized by a judge of the district.

(2) Except as provided in subrule (4), an admission with explanation may be written or offered orally to a judge or district court magistrate, as authorized by the district judge.

(3) Except as provided in subrule (4), a denial of responsibility must be made by the defendant appearing at a time set either by the citation or as the result of a communication with the court.

(4) If the violation is a trailway municipal civil infraction, and there has been damage to property or a vehicle has been impounded, the defendant's response must be made at a formal hearing.

(E) Contested Actions; Notice; Defaults.

(1) A contested action may not be heard until a citation is filed with the court. If the citation is filed electronically, the court may decline to hear the matter until the citation is signed by the officer or official who issued it, and is filed on paper. A citation that is not signed and filed on paper, when required by the court, will be dismissed with prejudice.

(2) An informal hearing will be held unless

(a) a party expressly requests a formal hearing, or

(b) the violation is a trailway municipal civil infraction which requires a formal hearing pursuant to MCL 600.8717(4); MSA 27A.8717(4).

(3) The provisions of MCR 2.501(C) regarding the length of notice of trial assignment do not apply in civil infraction actions.

(4) A defendant who obtains a hearing date other than the date specified in the citation, but who does not appear to explain or contest responsibility, is in default, and the procedures established by subrules (B)(4)-(6) apply.

(F) Post-determination Orders; Sanctions, Fines, and Costs; Schedules.

(1) A court may not increase a scheduled civil fine because the defendant has requested a hearing.

(2) Upon a finding of responsibility in a traffic civil infraction action, the court:

(a) must inform the secretary of state of the finding, as required by MCL 257.732; MSA 9.2432; and

(b) must initiate the procedures required by MCL 257.321a; MSA 9.2021(1), if the defendant fails to pay a fine or to comply with an order or judgment of the court.

(3) Upon a finding of responsibility in a state civil infraction action, the court must initiate the procedures required by MCL 257.321a(1); MSA 9.2021(1), if the defendant fails to pay a fine or to comply with an order or judgment of the court.

(4) The court may waive fines, costs and fees, pursuant to statute or court rule, or to correct clerical error.

(G) Appeal; Bond.

(1) An appeal following a formal hearing is a matter of right. Except as otherwise provided in this rule, the appeal is governed by subchapter 7.100.

(a) A defendant who appeals must post with the district court, at the time the appeal is taken, a bond equal to the fine and costs imposed. A defendant who has paid the fine and costs is not required to post a bond.

(b) If a defendant who has posted a bond fails to comply with the requirements of MCR 7.101(C)(2) or (F)(1), the appeal may be considered abandoned, and the district court may dismiss the appeal on 7 days' notice to the parties pursuant to MCR 7.101(G). The court clerk must promptly notify the circuit court of a dismissal and the circuit court shall dismiss the claim of appeal. If the appeal is dismissed or the judgment is affirmed, the district court may apply the bond to the fine and costs.

(c) A plaintiff's appeal must be asserted by the prosecuting authority of the political unit that provided the plaintiff's attorney for the formal hearing. A bond is not required.

(2) An appeal following an informal hearing is a matter of right, and must be asserted in writing, within 7 days after the decision, on a form to be provided by the court. The appeal will result in a de novo formal hearing.

(a) A defendant who appeals must post a bond as provided in subrule (1)(a). If a defendant who has posted a bond defaults by failing to appear at the formal hearing, or if the appeal is dismissed or the judgment is affirmed, the bond may be applied to the fine and costs.

(b) A plaintiff's appeal must be asserted by the prosecuting authority of the political unit that is responsible for providing the plaintiff's attorney for the formal hearing. A bond is not required.

(3) There is no appeal of right from an admission of responsibility. However, within 14 days after the admission, a defendant may file with the district court a written request to withdraw the admission, and must post a bond as provided in subrule (1)(a). If the court grants the request, the case will be scheduled for either a formal hearing or an informal hearing, as

ordered by the court. If the court denies the request, the bond may be applied to the fine and costs.

[Effective March 1, 1985; amended effective June 1, 1989; July 1, 1989; September 2, 1997.]

1985 Staff Comment

MCR 4.101 is based on DCR 2011. There is some reorganization and several slight modifications.

In subrule (A)(4), the prohibition on issuing a warrant for a civil infraction is qualified where issuance of a warrant is permitted by statute.

Under DCR 2011.3(A)(3), in order to enter a default, the clerk was required to certify that the defendant had not answered the citation. Subrule (B)(3)(b) adds the words "within the time allowed by statute".

In subrule (E)(1) the reference to a "sworn" complaint is removed. Under MCL 257.727c(3); MSA 9.2427(3)(3), the citation is treated as sworn to if it includes the declaration provided by that statute.

The [March 1, 1985] amendment of MCR 4.101(E) excepts civil infraction actions from the requirement of MCR 2.501(C) that the parties be given at least 28 days' notice of trial.

Subrule (G)(2) provides that if a defendant who has posted a bond in order to appeal fails to appear at the formal hearing, the bond may be applied to the fine and costs imposed.

Staff Comment to June, 1989 Amendment

The March 23, 1989 [amendment to MCR 4.101, effective June 1, 1989, makes] several changes in the procedures for appealing to the circuit court.

MCR 4.101(G)(4) is amended to clarify the bond requirement when a defendant appeals to circuit court in a civil infraction action.

Staff Comment to July, 1989 Amendment

The May 3, 1989 amendments to MCR 4.101(B) and (F), 4.102(B) and 8.105(G) [effective July 1, 1989], suggested by the Task Force on Reporting Traffic–Related Offenses, are intended to implement recent statutory changes.

Staff Comment to 1997 Amendment

The September 1997 amendments of MCR 4.101, 4.401, and 6.615, and the addition of MCR 8.125, [effective September 2, 1997] were adopted at the request of the Michigan District Judges Association because of recent statutory changes that created new categories of civil infractions, and the availability of electronic filing. In addition, the amendment of MCR 4.401(G) was made to clarify the procedure for challenging a civil infraction judgment.

RULE 4.102 MISDEMEANOR CASES [DELETED]

[Deleted effective October 1, 1989.]

1989 Staff Comment

Former MCR 4.102, covering misdemeanor traffic cases, has been moved to the district court subchapter of the Rules of Criminal Procedure. See MCR 6.615.

SUBCHAPTER 4.200   LANDLORD–TENANT PROCEEDINGS; LAND CONTRACT FORFEITURE

RULE 4.201   SUMMARY PROCEEDINGS TO RECOVER POSSESSION OF PREMISES

(A) Applicable Rules; Forms. Except as provided by this rule and MCL 600.5701 et seq.; MSA 27A.5701 et seq., a summary proceeding to recover possession of premises from a person in possession as described in MCL 600.5714; MSA 27A.5714 is governed by the Michigan Court Rules. Forms available for public distribution at the court clerk's office may be used in the proceeding.

(B) Complaint.

(1) *In General.* The complaint must

(a) comply with the general pleading requirements;

(b) have attached to it a copy of any written instrument on which occupancy was or is based;

(c) have attached to it copies of any notice to quit and any demand for possession (the copies must show when and how they were served);

(d) describe the premises or the defendant's holding if it is less than the entire premises;

(e) show the plaintiff's right to possession and indicate why the defendant's possession is improper or unauthorized; and

(f) demand a jury trial, if the plaintiff wishes one. The jury trial fee must be paid when the demand is made.

(2) *Specific Requirements.*

(a) If rent or other money is due and unpaid, the complaint must show

(i) the rental period and rate;

(ii) the amount due and unpaid when the complaint was filed; and

(iii) the date or dates the payments became due.

(b) If the tenancy involves housing operated by or under the rules of a governmental unit, the complaint must contain specific reference to the rules or law establishing the basis for ending the tenancy.

(c) If the tenancy is of residential premises, the complaint must allege that the lessor or licensor has performed his or her covenants to keep the premises fit for the use intended and in reasonable repair during the term of the lease or license, unless the parties to the lease or license have modified those obligations.

(d) If possession is claimed for a serious and continuing health hazard or for extensive and continuing physical injury to the premises pursuant to MCL 600.5714(1)(c); MSA 27A.5714(1)(c), the complaint must

(i) describe the nature and the seriousness or extent of the condition on which the complaint is based, and

(ii) state the period of time for which the property owner has been aware of the condition.

(e) If possession is sought for trespass pursuant to MCL 600.5714(1)(d); MSA 27A.5714(1)(d), the complaint must describe, when known by the plaintiff, the conditions under which possession was unlawfully taken or is unlawfully held and allege that no lawful tenancy of the premises has existed between the parties since defendant took possession.

(C) Summons.

(1) The summons must comply with MCR 2.102, except that it must command the defendant to appear for trial in accord with MCL 600.5735(2); MSA 27A.5735(2), unless by local court rule the provisions of MCL 600.5735(4); MSA 27A.5735(4) have been made applicable.

(2) The summons must also include the following advice to the defendant:

(a) The defendant has the right to employ an attorney to assist in answering the complaint and in preparing defenses.

(b) If the defendant does not have an attorney but does have money to retain one, he or she might locate an attorney through the State Bar of Michigan or a local lawyer referral service.

(c) If the defendant does not have an attorney and cannot pay for legal help, he or she might qualify for assistance through a local legal aid office.

(d) The defendant has a right to a jury trial which will be lost unless it is demanded in the first defense response, written or oral. The jury trial fee must be paid when the demand is made, unless payment of fees is waived or suspended under MCR 2.002.

(D) Service of Process. A copy of the summons and complaint and all attachments must be served on the defendant by mail. Unless the court does the mailing and keeps a record, the plaintiff must perfect the mail service by attaching a postal receipt to the proof of service. In addition to mailing, the defendant must be served in one of the following ways:

(1) By a method provided in MCR 2.105;

(2) By delivering the papers at the premises to a member of the defendant's household who is

    (a) of suitable age,

    (b) informed of the contents, and

    (c) asked to deliver the papers to the defendant; or

(3) After diligent attempts at personal service have been made, by securely attaching the papers to the main entrance of the tenant's dwelling unit. A return of service made under subrule (D)(3) must list the attempts at personal service. Service under subrule (D)(3) is effective only if a return of service is filed showing that, after diligent attempts, personal service could not be made. An officer who files proof that service was made under subrule (D)(3) is entitled to the regular personal service fee.

(E) Recording. All landlord-tenant summary proceedings conducted in open court must be recorded by stenographic or mechanical means, and only a reporter or recorder certified under MCR 8.108(G) may file a transcript of the record in a Michigan court.

(F) Appearance and Answer; Default.

(1) *Appearance and Answer.* The defendant or the defendant's attorney must appear and answer the complaint by the date on the summons. Appearance and answer may be made as follows:

    (a) By filing a written answer or a motion under MCR 2.115 or 2.116 and serving a copy on the plaintiff or the plaintiff's attorney. If proof of the service is not filed before the hearing, the defendant or the defendant's attorney may attest to service on the record.

    (b) By orally answering each allegation in the complaint at the hearing. The answers must be recorded or noted on the complaint.

(2) *Right to an Attorney.* If either party appears in person without an attorney, the court must inform that party of the right to retain an attorney. The court must also inform the party about legal aid assistance when it is available.

(3) *Jury Demand.* If the defendant wants a jury trial, he or she must demand it in the first response, written or oral. The jury trial fee must be paid when the demand is made.

(4) *Default.*

    (a) If the defendant fails to appear, the court, on the plaintiff's motion, may enter a default and may hear the plaintiff's proofs in support of judgment. If satisfied that the complaint is accurate, the court must enter a default judgment under MCL 600.5741; MSA 27A.5741, and in accord with subrule (K). The default judgment must be mailed to the defendant by the court clerk and must inform the defendant that (if applicable)

        (i) he or she may be evicted from the premises;

        (ii) he or she may be liable for a money judgment.

    (b) If the plaintiff fails to appear, a default judgment as to costs under MCL 600.5747; MSA 27A.5747 may be entered.

    (c) If a party fails to appear, the court may adjourn the hearing for up to 7 days. If the hearing is adjourned, the court must mail notice of the new date to the party who failed to appear.

(5) *Trial Fee.* If both parties appear without demanding a jury trial, the court must determine that a true issue of fact or law exists before ordering payment of the trial fee.

(G) Claims and Counterclaims.

(1) *Joinder.*

    (a) A party may join:

        (i) A money claim or counterclaim described by MCL 600.5739; MSA 27A.5739. A money claim must be separately stated in the complaint. A money counterclaim must be labeled and separately stated in a written answer.

        (ii) A claim or counterclaim for equitable relief.

    (b) If personal jurisdiction over the defendant was not obtained, a money claim must be

        (i) dismissed without prejudice if the defendant does not answer or appear, or

        (ii) adjourned until personal jurisdiction over the defendant is obtained.

    (c) A court with a territorial jurisdiction which has a population of more than 1,000,000 may provide, by local rule, that a money claim or counterclaim must be tried separately from a claim for possession unless joinder is allowed by leave of the court pursuant to subrule (G)(1)(e).

    (d) If trial of a money claim or counterclaim

        (i) might substantially delay trial of the possession claim, or

        (ii) requires that the premises be returned before damages can be determined, the court must adjourn the trial of the money claim or counterclaim to a date no later than 28 days after the time expires for issuing an order of eviction. A party may file and serve supplemental pleadings no later than 7 days before trial, except by leave of the court.

    (e) If adjudication of a money counterclaim will affect the amount the defendant must pay to prevent issuance of an order of eviction, that counterclaim must be tried at the same time as the claim for possession, subrules (G)(1)(c) and (d) notwithstanding, unless it appears to the court that the counterclaim is without merit.

(2) *Removal.*

(a) A summary proceedings action need not be removed from the court in which it is filed because an equitable defense or counterclaim is interposed.

(b) If a money claim or counterclaim exceeding the court's jurisdiction is introduced, the court, on motion of either party or on its own initiative, shall order removal of that portion of the action to the circuit court, if the money claim or counterclaim is sufficiently shown to exceed the court's jurisdictional limit.

(H) Interim Orders. On motion of either party, or by stipulation, for good cause, a court may issue such interim orders as are necessary, including, but not limited to the following:

(1) *Injunctions.* The interim order may award injunctive relief

(a) to prevent the person in possession from damaging the property; or

(b) to prevent the person seeking possession from rendering the premises untenantable or from suffering the premises to remain untenantable.

(2) *Escrow Orders.*

(a) If trial is adjourned more than 7 days and the plaintiff shows a clear need for protection, the court may order the defendant to pay a reasonable rent for the premises from the date the escrow order is entered, including a pro rata amount per day between the date of the order and the next date rent ordinarily would be due. In determining a reasonable rent, the court should consider evidence offered concerning the condition of the premises or other relevant factors. The order must provide that:

(i) payments be made to the court clerk within 7 days of the date of entry of the order, and thereafter within 7 days of the date or dates each month when rent would ordinarily be due, until the right to possession is determined;

(ii) the plaintiff must not interfere with the obligation of the defendant to comply with the escrow order; and

(iii) if the defendant does not comply with the order, the defendant waives the right to a jury trial only as to the possession issue, and the plaintiff is entitled to an immediate trial within 14 days which may be by jury if a party requests it and if, in the court's discretion, the court's schedule permits it. The 14-day limit need not be rigidly adhered to if the plaintiff is responsible for a delay.

(b) Only the court may order the disbursement of money collected under an escrow order. The court must consider the defendant's defenses. If trial was postponed to permit the premises to be repaired, the court may condition disbursement by requiring that the repairs be completed by a certain time. Otherwise, the court may condition disbursement as justice requires.

(I) Consent Judgment When Party Is Not Represented. The following procedures apply to consent judgments and orders entered when either party is not represented by an attorney.

(1) The judgment or order may not be enforced until 3 regular court business days have elapsed after the judgment or order was entered. The judge shall review, in court, a proposed consent judgment or order with the parties, and shall notify them of the delay required by this subrule at the time the terms of the consent judgment or order are placed on the record.

(2) A party who was not represented by an attorney at the time of the consent proceedings may move to set aside the consent judgment or order within the 3-day period. Such a motion stays the judgment or order until the court decides the motion or dismisses it after notice to the moving party.

(3) The court shall set aside a consent judgment or order on a satisfactory showing that the moving party misunderstood the basis for, or the rights which were being relinquished in, the judgment or order.

(J) Trial.

(1) *Time.* When the defendant appears, the court may try the action, or, if good cause is shown, may adjourn trial up to 56 days. If the court adjourns trial for more than 7 days, an escrow order may be entered pursuant to subrule (H)(2). The parties may adjourn trial by stipulation in writing or on the record, subject to the approval of the court.

(2) *Pretrial Action.* At trial, the court must first decide pretrial motions and determine if there is a triable issue. If there is no triable issue, the court must enter judgment.

(3) *Government Reports.* If the defendant claims that the plaintiff failed to comply with an ordinance or statute, the court may admit an authenticated copy of any relevant government employee's report filed with a government agency. Objections to the report affect the weight given it, not its admissibility.

(4) *Payment or Acceptance of Money.* The payment or the acceptance of money by a party before trial does not necessarily prevent or delay the proceedings.

(K) Judgment.

(1) *Requirements.* A judgment for the plaintiff must

(a) comply with MCL 600.5741; MSA 27A.5741;

(b) state when, and under what conditions, if any, an order of eviction will issue;

(c) separately state possession and money awards; and

(d) advise the defendant of the right to appeal or file a postjudgment motion within 10 days.

If the judgment is in favor of the defendant, it must comply with MCL 600.5747; MSA 27A.5747.

(2) *Injunctions.* The judgment may award injunctive relief

(a) to prevent the person in possession from damaging the property; or

(b) to prevent the person seeking possession from rendering the premises untenantable, or from suffering the premises to remain untenantable.

(3) *Partial Payment.* The judgment may provide that acceptance of partial payment of an amount due under the judgment will not prevent issuance of an order of eviction.

(4) *Costs.* Only those costs permitted by MCL 600.5759; MSA 27A.5759 may be awarded.

(5) *Notice.* The court must mail or deliver a copy of the judgment to the parties. The time period for applying for the order of eviction does not begin to run until the judgment is mailed or delivered.

(L) Order of Eviction.

(1) *Request.* When the time stated in the judgment expires, a party awarded possession may apply for an order of eviction. The application must:

(a) be written;

(b) be verified by a person having knowledge of the facts stated;

(c) if any money has been paid after entry of the judgment, show the conditions under which it was accepted; and

(d) state whether the party awarded judgment has complied with its terms.

(2) *Issuance of Order of Eviction and Delivery of Order.* Subject to the provisions of subrule (L)(4), the order of eviction shall be delivered to the person serving the order for service within 7 days after the order is filed.

(3) *Issuance Immediately on Judgment.* The court may issue an order immediately on entering judgment if

(a) the court is convinced the statutory requirements are satisfied, and

(b) the defendant was given notice, before the judgment, of a request for immediate issuance of the order.

The court may condition the order to protect the defendant's interest.

(4) *Limitations on Time for Issuance and Execution.* Unless a hearing is held after the defendant has been given notice and an opportunity to appear, an order of eviction may not

(a) be issued later than 56 days after judgment is entered,

(b) be executed later than 56 days after it is issued.

(5) *Acceptance of Partial Payment.* An order of eviction may not be issued if any part of the amount due under the judgment has been paid, unless

(a) a hearing is held after the defendant has been given notice and an opportunity to appear, or

(b) the judgment provides that acceptance of partial payment of the amount due under the judgment will not prevent issuance of an order of eviction.

(M) Postjudgment Motions. Except as provided in MCR 2.612, any postjudgment motion must be filed no later than 10 days after judgment enters.

(1) If the motion challenges a judgment for possession, the court may not grant a stay unless

(a) the motion is accompanied by an escrow deposit of 1 month's rent, or

(b) the court is satisfied that there are grounds for relief under MCR 2.612(C), and issues an order that waives payment of the escrow; such an order may be ex parte.

If a stay is granted, a hearing shall be held within 14 days after it is issued.

(2) If the judgment does not include an award of possession, the filing of the motion stays proceedings, but the plaintiff may move for an order requiring a bond to secure the stay. If the initial escrow deposit is believed inadequate, the plaintiff may apply for continuing adequate escrow payments in accord with subrule (H)(2). The filing of a postjudgment motion together with a bond, bond order, or escrow deposit stays all proceedings, including an order of eviction issued but not executed.

(N) Appeals From Possessory Judgments.

(1) *Rules Applicable.* Except as provided by this rule, appeals must comply with MCR 7.101, 7.102, and 7.103.

(2) *Time.* An appeal of right must be filed within 10 days after the entry of judgment.

(3) *Stay of Order of Eviction.*

(a) Unless a stay is ordered by the trial court, an order of eviction must issue as provided in subrule (L).

(b) The filing of a claim of appeal together with a bond or escrow order of the court stays all proceedings, including an order of eviction issued but not executed.

(4) *Appeal Bond; Escrow.*

(a) A plaintiff who appeals must file a bond providing that if the plaintiff loses he or she will pay the appeal costs.

(b) A defendant who appeals must file a bond providing that if the defendant loses, he or she will pay

(i) the appeal costs,

(ii) the amount due stated in the judgment, and

(iii) damages from the time of forcible entry, the detainer, the notice to quit, or the demand for possession.

The court may waive the bond requirement of subrule (N)(4)(b)(i) on the grounds stated in MCR 2.002(C) or (D).

(c) If the plaintiff won a possession judgment, the court shall enter an escrow order under subrule (H)(2) and require the defendant to make payments while the appeal is pending. This escrow order may not be retroactive as to arrearages preceding the date of the post-trial escrow order unless there was a pretrial escrow order entered under subrule (H)(2), in which case the total escrow amount may include the amount accrued between the time of the original escrow order and the filing of the appeal.

(d) If it is established that an appellant cannot obtain sureties or make a sufficient cash deposit, the court must permit the appellant to comply with an escrow order.

(O) Objections to Fees Covered by Statute for Orders of Eviction. Objections shall be by motion. The fee to be paid shall be reasonable in light of all the circumstances. In determining the reasonableness of a fee, the court shall consider all issues bearing on reasonableness, including but not limited to

(1) the time of travel to the premises,

(2) the time necessary to execute the order,

(3) the amount and weight of the personal property removed from the premises,

(4) who removed the personal property from the premises,

(5) the distance that the personal property was moved from the premises, and

(6) the actual expenses incurred in executing the order of eviction.

[Effective March 1, 1985; amended effective May 1, 2002.]

1985 Staff Comment

MCR 4.201 is based on DCR 754. There are several minor changes.

DCR 754.2(8) required that the complaint include certain additional information when the housing involved is operated by a local governmental unit. Subrule (B)(2)(b) deletes the limitation to local units, and also covers housing operated under the rules of a governmental unit as well as housing operated by the governmental unit.

In subrule (C)(2)(d), regarding payment of the jury fee, a cross-reference is added to MCR 2.002, governing waiver or suspension of fees for indigent persons.

Subrule (K)(5) permits the court to deliver a copy of the judgment to the parties rather than to mail it. Compare DCR 754.11(e).

Subrule (L)(4) modifies the language of DCR 754.12(c)(3) by adding an exception to the requirement that there must be a hearing before issuance of a writ of restitution when there has been partial payment of the amount due under the judgment. A hearing is not required if the judgment includes the provision permitted by subrule (K)(3)—that partial payment does not prevent the issuance of a writ of restitution.

Staff Comment to 2002 Amendment

The September 12, 2001 addition of MCR 3.106, effective May 1, 2002, was recommended by an ad hoc committee of judges, court administrators, court clerks, attorneys, and court officers. The rule incorporated existing practice while protecting against abuses. The September 12, 2001 amendments of MCR 4.201 and 4.202, effective May 1, 2002, made changes consistent with new MCR 3.106.

The staff comment is published only for the benefit of the bench and bar and is not an authoritative construction by the Court.

RULE 4.202 SUMMARY PROCEEDINGS; LAND CONTRACT FORFEITURE

(A) Applicable Rules. Except as provided by this rule and MCL 600.5701 et seq.; MSA 27A.5701 et seq., a summary proceeding to recover possession of premises after forfeiture of an executory contract for the purchase of premises as described in MCL 600.5726; MSA 27A.5726 is governed by the Michigan Court Rules.

(B) Jurisdiction.

(1) *Status of Premises.* The proceeding may be brought when the premises are vacant or are in the possession of

(a) the vendee,

(b) a party to the contract,

(c) an assignee of the contract, or

(d) a third party.

(2) *Powers of Court.* The court may do all things necessary to hear and resolve the proceeding, including but not limited to

(a) hearing and deciding all issues,

(b) ordering joinder of additional parties,

(c) ordering or permitting amendments or additional pleadings, and

(d) making and enforcing writs and orders.

(C) Necessary Parties. The plaintiff must join as defendants

(1) the vendee named in the contract,

(2) any person known to the plaintiff to be claiming an interest in the premises under the contract, and

(3) any person in possession of the premises, unless that party has been released from liability.

(D) Complaint. The complaint must:

(1) comply with the general pleading requirements;

(2) allege

(a) the original selling price,

(b) the principal balance due, and

(c) the amount in arrears under the contract;

(3) state with particularity any other material breach claimed as a basis for forfeiture; and

(4) have attached to it a copy of the notice of forfeiture, showing when and how it was served on each named defendant.

(E) Summons. The summons must comply with MCR 2.102 and MCL 600.5735; MSA 27A.5735, and command the defendant to appear and answer or take other action permitted by law within the time permitted by statute after service of the summons on the defendant.

(F) Service of Process. The defendant must be served with a copy of the complaint and summons under MCR 2.105.

(G) Recording. All executory contract summary proceedings conducted in open court must be recorded by stenographic or mechanical means, and only a reporter or recorder certified under MCR 8.108(G) may file a transcript of the record in a Michigan court.

(H) Answer; Default.

(1) *Answer.* The answer must comply with general pleading requirements and allege those matters on which the defendant intends to rely to defeat the claim or any part of it.

(2) *Default.*

(a) If the defendant fails to appear, the court, on the plaintiff's motion, may enter a default and may hear the plaintiff's proofs in support of judgment. If satisfied that the complaint is accurate, the court must enter a default judgment under MCL 600.5741; MSA 27A.5741, and in accord with subrule (J). The default judgment must be mailed to the defendant by the court clerk and must inform the defendant that (if applicable)

(i) he or she may be evicted from the premises;

(ii) he or she may be liable for a money judgment.

(b) If the plaintiff fails to appear, a default and judgment as to costs under MCL 600.5747; MSA 27A.5747 may be entered.

(c) If a party fails to appear, the court may adjourn the hearing for up to 7 days. If the hearing is adjourned, the court must mail notice of the new date to the party who failed to appear.

(3) *Trial Fee.* If both parties appear without demanding a jury trial, the court must determine that a true issue of fact or law exists before ordering payment of the trial fee.

(I) Joinder; Removal.

(1) A party may join a claim or counterclaim for equitable relief or a money claim or counterclaim described by MCL 600.5739; MSA 27A.5739. A money claim must be separately stated in the complaint. A money counterclaim must be labeled and separately stated in a written answer. If such a joinder is made, the court may order separate summary disposition of the claim for possession, as described by MCL 600.5739; MSA 27A.5739.

(2) A court with a territorial jurisdiction which has a population of more than 1,000,000 may provide, by local rule, that a money claim or counterclaim must be tried separately from a claim for possession unless joinder is allowed by leave of the court pursuant to subrule (I)(3).

(3) If adjudication of a money counterclaim will affect the amount the defendant must pay to prevent the issuance of a writ of restitution, the counterclaim must be tried at the same time as the claim for possession, subrules (I)(1) and (2) notwithstanding, unless it appears to the court that the counterclaim is without merit.

(4) If a money claim or counterclaim exceeding the court's jurisdiction is introduced, the court, on motion of either party or on its own initiative, shall order removal of that portion of the action, if the money claim or counterclaim is sufficiently shown to exceed the court's jurisdictional limit.

(J) Judgment. The judgment

(1) must comply with MCL 600.5741; MSA 27A.5741;

(2) must state when, and under what conditions, if any, a writ of restitution will issue;

(3) must state that an appeal or postjudgment motion to challenge the judgment may be filed within 10 days;

(4) may contain such other terms and conditions as the nature of the action and the rights of the parties require; and

(5) must be mailed or delivered by the court to the parties. The time period for applying for the writ of restitution does not begin to run until the judgment is mailed or delivered.

(K) Order of Eviction.

(1) *Request.* When the time stated in the judgment expires, a party awarded possession may apply for an order of eviction. The application must:

(a) be written;

(b) be verified by a person having knowledge of the facts stated;

(c) if any money due under the judgment has been paid, show the conditions under which it was accepted; and

(d) state whether the party awarded judgment has complied with its terms.

(2) Hearing Required if Part of Judgment Has Been Paid. An order of eviction may not be issued if any part of the amount due under the judgment has been paid unless a hearing has been held after the defendant has been given notice and an opportunity to appear.

(L) Appeal. Except as provided by this rule or by law, the rules applicable to other appeals to circuit court (see MCR 7.101–7.103) apply to appeals from judgments in land contract forfeiture cases. However, in such cases the time limit for filing a claim of appeal under MCR 7.101(B)(1) is 10 days.

[Effective March 1, 1985; amended effective May 1, 2002.]

1985 Staff Comment

MCR 4.202 is substantially the same as DCR 755.

Subrule (J)(5) permits the court to deliver a copy of the judgment to the parties as a substitute for mailing.

The [March 1, 1985] amendment of MCR 4.202 adds a new subrule (L) expressly incorporating the rules applicable to other appeals from district to circuit court (MCR 7.101–7.103), except that the time for taking an appeal of a land contract forfeiture judgment is 10 days.

Staff Comment to 2002 Amendment

The September 12, 2001 addition of MCR 3.106, effective May 1, 2002, was recommended by an ad hoc committee of judges, court administrators, court clerks, attorneys, and court officers. The rule incorporated existing practice while protecting against abuses. The September 12, 2001 amendments of MCR 4.201 and 4.202, effective May 1, 2002, made changes consistent with new MCR 3.106.

The staff comment is published only for the benefit of the bench and bar and is not an authoritative construction by the Court.

SUBCHAPTER 4.300   SMALL CLAIMS ACTIONS

RULE 4.301   APPLICABILITY OF RULES

Actions in a small claims division are governed by the procedural provisions of Chapter 84 of the Revised Judicature Act, MCL 600.8401 et seq.; MSA 27A.8401 et seq., and by this subchapter of the rules. After judgment, other applicable Michigan Court Rules govern actions that were brought in a small claims division.

[Effective March 1, 1985.]

1985 Staff Comment

MCR 4.301 is comparable to DCR 5001. The substance of DCR 4005.10 is added, making clear that after entry of judgment the rules applicable to other actions apply to actions that were brought in the small claims division.

The [March 1, 1985] amendment of MCR 4.301 modifies the reference to the small claims chapter of the Revised Judicature Act, to be consistent with 1984 PA 278, which was effective January 1, 1985.

RULE 4.302   STATEMENT OF CLAIM

(A) Contents. The statement of the claim must be in an affidavit in substantially the form approved by the state court administrator. Affidavit forms shall be available at the clerk's office. The nature and amount of the claim must be stated in concise, nontechnical language, and the affidavit must state the date or dates when the claim arose.

(B) Affidavit; Signature.

(1) If the plaintiff is an individual, the affidavit must be signed by the plaintiff, or the plaintiff's guardian, conservator, or next friend.

(2) If the plaintiff is a sole proprietorship, a partnership, or a corporation, the affidavit must be signed by a person authorized to file the claim by MCL 600.8407(3); MSA 27A.8407(3).

(C) Names.

(1) The affidavit must state the full and correct name of the plaintiff and whether the plaintiff is a corporation or a partnership. If the plaintiff was acting under an assumed name when the claim arose, the assumed name must be given.

(2) The defendant may be identified as permitted by MCL 600.8426; MSA 27A.8426, or as is proper in other civil actions.

(D) Claims in Excess of Statutory Limitation. If the amount of the plaintiff's claim exceeds the statutory limitation, the actual amount of the claim must be stated. The claim must state that by commencing the action the plaintiff waives any claim to the excess over the statutory limitation, and that the amount equal to the statutory limitation, exclusive of costs, is claimed by the action. A judgment on the claim is a bar to a later action in any court to recover the excess.

[Effective March 1, 1985.]

1985 Staff Comment

MCR 4.302 is comparable to DCR 5002.

Under subrule (A) affidavit forms are to be available at the clerk's office. See MCL 600.8403; MSA 27A.8403.

Subrule (B)(2) modifies the provisions of DCR 5002.2 to take account of the 1978 amendment of MCL 600.8407(3); MSA 27A.8407(3), as to who may sign the complaint on behalf of certain parties.

Subrule (C) is changed (from DCR 5002.3) to refer to the statute applicable to the names of the parties.

RULE 4.303   NOTICE

(A) Contents. The notice to the defendant must meet the requirements of MCL 600.8404; MSA 27A.8404. The court clerk shall notify the plaintiff to appear at the time and place specified with the books, papers, and witnesses necessary to prove the claim, and that if the plaintiff fails to appear, the claim will be dismissed.

(B) Certified Mail. If the defendant is a corporation or a partnership, the certified mail described in MCL 600.8405; MSA 27A.8405 need not be deliverable to the addressee only, but may be deliverable to and signed for by an agent of the addressee.

(C) Notice Not Served. If it appears that notice was not received by the defendant at least 7 days before the appearance date and the defendant does not appear, the clerk must, at the plaintiff's request, issue further notice without additional cost to the plaintiff, setting the hearing for a future date. The notice may be served as provided in MCR 2.105.

[Effective March 1, 1985.]

1985 Staff Comment

MCR 4.303 is comparable to DCR 5003.

Unlike DCR 5003.1, subrule (A) does not include the provision regarding notice that the defendant may arrange terms of payment. That requirement was included in the 1978 amendment of MCL 600.8404; MSA 27A.8404, which is incorporated in subrule (A).

RULE 4.304   CONDUCT OF TRIAL

(A) Appearance. If the parties appear, the court shall hear the claim as provided in MCL 600.8411; MSA 27A.8411. The trial may be adjourned to a later date for good cause.

(B) Nonappearance.

(1) If a defendant fails to appear, judgment may be entered by default if the claim is liquidated, or on the ex parte proofs the court requires if the claim is unliquidated.

(2) If the plaintiff fails to appear, the claim may be dismissed for want of prosecution, the defendant may proceed to trial on the merits, or the action may be adjourned, as the court directs.

(3) If all parties fail to appear, the claim may be dismissed for want of prosecution or the court may order another disposition, as justice requires.

[Effective March 1, 1985.]

1985 Staff Comment

MCR 4.304 is substantially the same as DCR 5004.

RULE 4.305   JUDGMENTS

(A) Entry of Judgments. A judgment must be entered at the time of the entry of the court's findings, and must contain the payment and stay provisions required by MCL 600.8410(2); MSA 27A.8410(2).

(B) Modification; Vacation. A judgment of the small claims division may be modified or vacated in the same manner as judgments in other civil actions, except that an appeal may not be taken.

(C) Garnishment. A writ of garnishment may not be issued to enforce the judgment until the expiration of 21 days after it was entered. If a judgment had been ordered to be paid by installments, an affidavit for a writ of garnishment must so state and must state that the order has been set aside or vacated.

[Effective March 1, 1985.]

1985 Staff Comment

MCR 4.305 is comparable to DCR 5005.

The provisions of DCR 5005.2 regarding installment payments are omitted. Language is added to subrule (A) to incorporate the 1978 statutory amendment regarding installment payments and stays. MCL 600.8410(2); MSA 27A.8410(2).

Language is added to subrule (B) to make clear that, while the district court may modify a judgment as in other actions, an appeal is not available.

The garnishment provisions of subrule (C) are modified with the addition of a prohibition on garnishment for 21 days after entry of the judgment. In a sense, this corresponds to the automatic stay provisions of other civil actions. See MCR 2.614(A).

RULE 4.306   REMOVAL TO TRIAL COURT

(A) Demand. A party may demand that the action be removed from the small claims division to the trial court for further proceedings by

(1) signing a written demand for removal and filing it with the clerk at or before the time set for hearing; or

(2) appearing before the court at the time and place set for hearing and demanding removal.

(B) Order; Fee. On receiving a demand for removal, the court shall, by a written order filed in the action, direct removal to the trial court for further proceedings.

(1) The order must direct a defendant to file a written answer and serve it as provided in MCR 2.107 within 14 days after the date of the order.

(2) A copy of the order must be mailed to each party by the clerk.

(3) There is no fee for the removal, order, or mailing.

(C) Motion for More Definite Statement. After removal, the affidavit is deemed to be a sufficient statement of the plaintiff's claim unless a defendant, within the time permitted for answer, files a motion for a more definite statement.

(1) The motion must state the information sought and must be supported by an affidavit that the defendant

(a) does not have the information and cannot secure it with the exercise of reasonable diligence, and

(b) is unable to answer the plaintiff's claim without it.

(2) The court may decide the motion without a hearing on just and reasonable terms or may direct that a hearing be held after notice to both parties at a time set by the court.

(3) If the plaintiff fails to file a more definite statement after having been ordered to do so, the clerk shall dismiss the claim for want of prosecution.

(D) Default. On removal, if the defendant fails to file an answer or motion within the time permitted, the clerk shall enter the default of the defendant. MCR 2.603 governs further proceedings.

(E) Procedure After Removal. Except as provided in this rule, further proceedings in actions removed to the trial court are governed by the rules applicable to other civil actions.

[Effective March 1, 1985.]

1985 Staff Comment

MCR 4.306 is comparable to DCR 5006.

Subrule (C)(2) allows the denial, as well as the granting, of a motion for a more definite statement without a hearing. Compare DCR 5006.3. This is consistent with the general motion practice rule. See MCR 2.119(E)(3).

Subrule (E) modifies the language of DCR 5006.5. After removal to the trial court, all provisions governing other cases in district court apply, not only those applicable to trials.

SUBCHAPTER 4.400 MAGISTRATES

RULE 4.401 MAGISTRATES

(A) Procedure. Proceedings involving magistrates must be in accordance with relevant statutes and rules.

(B) Duties. Notwithstanding statutory provisions to the contrary, magistrates exercise only those duties expressly authorized by the chief judge of the district or division.

(C) Control of Magisterial Action. An action taken by a magistrate may be superseded, without formal appeal, by order of a district judge in the district in which the magistrate serves.

(D) Appeals. Appeals of right may be taken from a decision of the magistrate to the district court in the district in which the magistrate serves by filing a written claim of appeal in substantially the form provided by MCR 7.101(C) within 7 days of the entry of the decision of the magistrate. No fee is required on the filing of the appeal, except as otherwise provided by statute or court rule. The action is heard de novo by the district court.

[Effective March 1, 1985; amended effective September 2, 1997; January 1, 2002.]

1985 Staff Comment

MCR 4.401 includes the provisions of DCR 3001.1–3001.4. The remaining provisions of DCR 3001, covering administrative matters, are placed in MCR 8.205.

Staff Comment to 1997 Amendment

The September 1997 amendments of MCR 4.101, 4.401, and 6.615, and the addition of MCR 8.125, [effective September 2, 1997] were adopted at the request of the Michigan District Judges Association because of recent statutory changes that created new categories of civil infractions, and the availability of electronic filing. In addition, the amendment of MCR 4.401(G) was made to clarify the procedure for challenging a civil infraction judgment.

Staff Comment to 2002 Amendment

The November 26, 2001 amendments of MCR 4.401(D), 7.210(H), 7.212(C), 7.213(A), and 7.302(C), effective January 1, 2002, recognized numbering changes in other rules and the elimination of the "parallel citation" requirement from the Michigan Uniform System of Citation (Supreme Court AO 2001-5).

The staff comment is published only for the benefit of the bench and bar and is not an authoritative construction by the Court.

CHAPTER 5. PROBATE COURT

Effective March 1, 1985

Probate Rules Committee Comment to 2000 Amendment

The Estates and Protected Individuals Code (EPIC), MCL 700.1101 *et seq.*; MSA 27.11101 *et seq.*, effective April 1, 2000, changes many of the procedures and much terminology relating to estates, trusts and protected individuals. The Probate Rules Committee of the Probate and Estate Planning Section of the State Bar of Michigan reviewed subchapters 5.000 through 5.780 of the Michigan Court rules and made proposals to harmonize the rules with EPIC. The committee has drafted comments to many of the rules, briefly summarizing the purpose of the changes and pointing the reader to the relevant provisions in EPIC.

In general, EPIC significantly reduces court involvement in trusts and estates. Most estates will be administered by personal representatives without court involvement except at the opening and closing of the estate. EPIC does not provide terminology for this regular, unsupervised administration and these comments will use the term "unsupervised administration." Under EPIC, unsupervised administration may commence either through informal probate and appointment proceedings involving filing certain papers to be reviewed by the probate register, MCL 700.3301 through 700.3311; MSA 27.13301 through 27.13311 or through formal testacy and appointment proceedings, resulting in orders from the judge of probate, MCL 700.3401 through 700.3414; MSA 27.13401 through 27.13414. Similarly, closing unsupervised administration may be through filing a closing statement and register's certificate, MCL 700.3954 and 700.3958; MSA 27.13954 and 27.13958 or through formal proceedings resulting in orders of the court, MCL 700.3952 and 700.3953; MSA 27.13952 and 27.13953. EPIC provides for requests to the court for rulings on matters which may arise during the administration, MCL 700.3415; MSA 27.13415. EPIC also contains provisions allowing administration under continuing court supervision, MCL 700.3501 through 700.3505; MSA 27.13501 through 27.13505, but that will be the exception.

The proposed amendments affect every rule in chapter 5 except for subchapters 5.000 (applicability), 5.730 (mental health rules), 5.750 (adoption), and 5.900 (proceedings in juvenile division). Rules formerly in subchapters 5.200 through 5.600 have been renumbered and placed in subchapter 5.100 (general rules of pleading and practice). To the maximum extent possible, these rules have been renumbered so that the last two digits of the new rule number match the prior subchapter number and final digit. Thus, new MCR 5.121 deals with the subject matter of prior MCR 5.201; new MCR 5.125, with the subject matter of prior MCR 5.205 and so forth. Other renumbering is as follows: subchapter 5.715 (provisions common to multiple types of fiduciaries is moved to subchapter 5.200; subchapter 5.700 (proceedings in decedent estates), to subchapter 5.300; subchapter 5.760 (guardianship, conservatorship, and protective order proceedings), to subchapter 5.400; and subchapter 5.720 (trust proceedings), to subchapter 5.500. Miscellaneous proceedings remain as subchapter 5.780; and appeals as subchapter 5.800. Where a new rule substantially duplicates an old rule, the changes are shown in the order of the Supreme Court publishing the proposals for comment. Prior rules so shown are to be amended as shown. All other prior rules in the affected subchapters are repealed.

Probate Rules Committee Comment to 2002 Amendment

The Estates and Protected Individuals Code (EPIC), MCL 700.1101 *et seq.*, effective April 1, 2000, changed many of the procedures and much terminology relating to estates, trusts and protected individuals. The Probate Rules Committee of the Probate and Estate Planning Section of the State Bar of Michigan, assisted by the Probate Rules Committee of the Michigan Probate Judges Association, reviewed subchapters 5.000 through 5.780 of the Michigan Court rules and made proposals to harmonize the rules with EPIC [effective January 1, 2002]. The committee drafted comments to many of the rules, briefly summarizing the purpose of the changes and pointing the reader to the relevant provisions in EPIC.

[For Table of Rules, see page 1 et seq.]

SUBCHAPTER 5.000   GENERAL PROVISIONS

RULE 5.001   APPLICABILITY

(A) Applicability of Rules. Procedure in probate court is governed by the rules applicable to other civil proceedings, except as modified by the rules in this chapter.

(B) Terminology.

(1) References to the "clerk" in the Michigan Court Rules also apply to the register in probate court proceedings.

(2) References to "pleadings" in the Michigan Court Rules also apply to petitions, objections, and claims in probate court proceedings.

[Effective March 1, 1985.]

MCR 5.001 corresponds to PCR 11.

Under the Michigan Court Rules, proceedings in probate court are subject to the same rules as other actions, except as provided in chapter 5. New subrule (B) makes clear that these provisions apply regardless of the differences in terminology used in probate proceedings. A separate subchapter, 5.900, covers proceedings in the juvenile division of the probate court.

In view of the application of the other rules to probate court, many of the provisions of the Probate Court Rules have been eliminated because they were very similar or identical to the provisions in chapter 2. The remaining rules in chapter 5 have been given numbers to correspond to the related subjects in chapter 2.

Subchapter 5.700 contains the rules governing the various types of proceedings that are peculiar to probate court.

SUBCHAPTER 5.100 GENERAL RULES OF PLEADING AND PRACTICE

RULE 5.101 FORM AND COMMENCEMENT OF ACTION

(A) Form of Action. There are two forms of action, a "proceeding" and a "civil action."

(B) Commencement of Proceeding. A proceeding is commenced by filing an application or a petition with the court.

(C) Civil Actions, Commencement, Governing Rules. The following actions, must be titled civil actions, commenced by filing a complaint and governed by the rules which are applicable to civil actions in circuit court:

(1) Any action against another filed by a fiduciary, and

(2) Any action filed by a claimant after notice that the claim has been disallowed.

[Effective March 1, 1985; amended effective April 1, 1992; interim amendment effective April 1, 2000; amended effective January 1, 2002.]

1985 Staff Comment

MCR 5.101 includes the provisions of PCR 12 and 101.1.

Probate Rules Committee Comment to 1992 Amendment

Subrule (C) [effective April 1, 1992] is a new provision to deal with cases brought under the expanded jurisdiction of the Probate Court granted by 1989 PA 69.

RULE 5.102 NOTICE OF HEARING

A petitioner, fiduciary, or other moving party must cause to be prepared, served, and filed, a notice of hearing for all matters requiring notification of interested persons. It must state the time and date, the place, and the nature of the hearing. Hearings must be noticed for and held at times previously approved by the court.

[Effective March 1, 1985; amended effective April 1, 1992; interim amendment effective April 1, 2000.]

1985 Staff Comment

MCR 5.102 corresponds to PCR 102.

The language of PCR 102.1 regarding a court order for service or order for publication is omitted because the statute to which that language related has been repealed.

Probate Rules Committee Comment to 1992 Amendment

[Effective April 1, 1992,] former subrule (B) has been deleted because it duplicates MCR 5.113(A)(1)(c). The provisions of former subrule (C) have been moved to MCR 5.118 where they more logically belong. The provisions of former subrule (D) have been moved to MCR 5.104(A) where they more logically belong. The remainder of the rule has been reorganized for clarity. The final sentence of the rule has been relocated from former MCR 5.119(B).

RULE 5.103 WHO MAY SERVE

(A) Qualifications. Service may be made by any adult or emancipated minor, including an interested person.

(B) Service in a Governmental Institution. Personal service on a person in a governmental institution, hospital, or home must be made by the person in charge of the institution or a person designated by that person.

[Effective March 1, 1985; amended effective April 1, 1992; interim amendment effective April 1, 2000.]

1985 Staff Comment

MCR 5.103 corresponds to PCR 103.

The language in subrule (B) regarding service on patients in state institutions is modified to correspond to MCR 2.103(C).

Former PCR 103.3 is omitted because the statutes that required the court to serve foreign consul and the Attorney General have been repealed. The current provisions place that responsibility on the parties. See MCL 700.180, 700.181, 700.316; MSA 27.5180, 27.5181, 27.5316.

Probate Rules Committee Comment to 1992 Amendment

Subrule (A) is amended [effective April 1, 1992] to indicate that an emancipated minor may serve process. Other changes are to make the style of the rule correspond to similar rules in chapter 2. The requirement of service on the Attorney General formerly in subrule (B) is deleted as antiquated. The adjective "government" in subrule (B) modifies the entire list, "institution, hospital or home."

RULE 5.104   PROOF OF SERVICE; WAIVER AND CONSENT; UNOPPOSED PETITION

(A) Proof of Service.

(1) Whenever service is required by statute or court rule, a proof of service must be filed promptly and at the latest before a hearing to which the paper relates or at the time the paper is required to be filed with the court if the paper does not relate to a hearing. The proof of service must include a description of the papers served, the date of service, the manner and method of service and the person or persons served.

(2) Except as otherwise provided by rule, proof of service of a paper required or permitted to be served may be by

(a) a copy of the notice of hearing, if any;

(b) copies of other papers served with the notice of hearing, with a description of the papers in the proof of service;

(c) authentication under MCR 5.114(B) of the person making service.

(3) Subrule (A)(1) notwithstanding, in decedent estates, no proof of service need be filed in connection with informal proceedings or unsupervised administration unless required by court rule.

(4) In unsupervised administration of a trust, subrule (A)(1) notwithstanding, no proof of service need be filed unless required by court rule.

(B) Waiver and Consent.

(1) *Waiver.* The right to notice of hearing may be waived. The waiver must

(a) be stated on the record at the hearing, or

(b) be in a writing, which is dated and signed by the interested person or someone authorized to consent on the interested person's behalf and specifies the hearing to which it applies.

(2) *Consent.* The relief requested in an application, petition or motion may be granted by consent. An interested person who consents to an application, petition or motion does not have to be served with or waive notice of hearing on the application, petition or motion. The consent must

(a) be stated on the record at the hearing, or

(b) be in a writing which is dated and signed by the interested person or someone authorized to consent on the interested person's behalf and must contain a declaration that the person signing has received a copy of the application, petition or motion.

(3) *Who May Waive and Consent.* A waiver and a consent may be made

(a) by a legally competent interested person;

(b) by a person designated in these rules as eligible to be served on behalf of an interested person who is a legally disabled person; or

(c) on behalf of an interested person whether competent or legally disabled, by an attorney who has previously filed a written appearance.

However, a guardian, conservator, or trustee cannot waive or consent with regard to petitions, motions, accounts, or reports made by that person as guardian, conservator or trustee.

(4) *Order.* If all interested persons have consented, the order may be entered immediately.

(C) Unopposed Petition. If a petition is unopposed at the time set for the hearing, the court may either grant the petition on the basis of the recitations in the petition or conduct a hearing. However, an order determining heirs based on an uncontested petition to determine heirs may only be entered on the basis of sworn testimony or a sworn testimony form. An order granting a petition to appoint a guardian may only be entered on the basis of testimony at a hearing.

[Effective March 1, 1985; amended effective April 1, 1992; February 1, 1995; interim amendment effective April 1, 2000; amended effective January 1, 2002; May 1, 2002.]

1985 Staff Comment

MCR 5.104 is substantially the same as PCR 104.

Probate Rules Committee Comment to 1992 Amendment

The requirement of former subrule (A)(2)(b) that a copy of papers served must be attached to a proof of service has been deleted [effective April 1, 1992] to avoid duplication of filing where copies have already been filed. A proof of service may no longer be filed at the hearing to which the papers relate, former subrule (A)(4). The other provisions of subrule (A) have been reorganized for clarity.

The provisions of subrule (B) have been modified to clarify the distinction between waiver and consent. A party may no longer waive receipt of papers, except for notices of hearing, but parties may consent to granting of petitions. An emancipated minor is legally competent to waive and consent within this subrule. The provision that a waiver might be combined with a consent is deleted as unnecessary. The provision of subrule (B)(1) regarding waiver of receipt of documents is more restrictive than Revised Probate Code, § 34, MCL 700.34; MSA 27.5034.

Probate Rules Committee Comment to 2000 Amendment

Subrule (A)(3) is new [effective April 1, 2000]. It indicates that proofs of service are not required in unsupervised administration except where a rule specifically requires it. See, for instance, MCR 8.303. The last clause of subrule (B)(4) is deleted. See MCR 5.308(B)(1). New subrule (C) creates a procedure for granting unopposed petitions without a hearing.

Probate Rules Committee Comment to 2002 Amendment

Subrule (A)(3) is new [effective January 1, 2002]. It indicates that proofs of service are not required in unsupervised administration except where a rule specifically requires it. See, for instance, MCR 5.309(C)(3). The last clause of subrule (B)(4) is deleted. See MCR 5.308(B)(1). New subrule (C) creates a procedure for granting unopposed petitions without a hearing.

Staff Comment to 2002 Amendment

The December 18, 2001 amendments, effective May 1, 2002, updated various rules in light of the Estates and Protected Individuals Code (EPIC), MCL 700.1101 *et seq.*, and revisions made to EPIC by 2000 PA 312, 313, and 469.

The staff comment is published only for the benefit of the bench and bar and is not an authoritative construction by the Court.

RULE 5.105   MANNER AND METHOD OF SERVICE

(A) Manner of Service.

(1) Service on an interested person may be by personal service within or without the State of Michigan.

(2) Unless another method of service is required by statute, court rule, or special order of a probate court, service may be made to the current address of an interested person by registered, certified, or ordinary first-class mail. Foreign consul and the Attorney General may be served by mail.

(3) An interested person whose address or whereabouts is not known may be served by publication, if an affidavit or declaration under MCR 5.114(B) is filed with the court, showing that the address or whereabouts of the interested person could not be ascertained on diligent inquiry. Except in proceedings seeking a determination of a presumption of death based on absence pursuant to MCL 700.1208(2), after an interested person has once been served by publication, notice is only required on an interested person whose address is known or becomes known during the proceedings.

(4) The court, for good cause on ex parte petition, may direct the manner of service if

(a) no statute or court rule provides for the manner of service on an interested person, or

(b) service cannot otherwise reasonably be made.

(B) Method of Service.

(1) *Personal Service.*

(a) On an Attorney. Personal service of a paper on an attorney must be made by

(i) handing it to the attorney personally;

(ii) leaving it at the attorney's office with a clerk or with some person in charge or, if no one is in charge or present, by leaving it in some conspicuous place there, or by electronically delivering a facsimile to the attorney's office;

(iii) if the office is closed or the attorney has no office, by leaving it at the attorney's usual residence with some person of suitable age and discretion residing there; or

(iv) sending the paper by registered mail or certified mail, return receipt requested, and delivery restricted to the addressee; but service is not made for purpose of this subrule until the attorney receives the paper.

(b) On Other Individuals. Personal service of a paper on an individual other than an attorney must be made by

(i) handing it to the individual personally;

(ii) leaving it at the person's usual residence with some person of suitable age and discretion residing there; or

(iii) sending the paper by registered mail or certified mail, return receipt requested, and delivery restricted to the addressee; but service is not made for purpose of this subrule until the individual receives the paper.

(c) On Persons Other Than Individuals. Service on an interested person other than an individual must be made in the manner provided in MCR 2.105(C)-(G).

(2) *Mailing.* Mailing of a copy under this rule means enclosing it in a sealed envelope with first-class postage fully prepaid, addressed to the person to be served, and depositing the envelope and its contents in the United States mail. Service by mail is complete at the time of mailing.

(3) *Publication.* Service by publication must be made in the manner provided in MCR 5.106.

(C) Petitioner, Service Not Required. For service of notice of hearing on a petition, the petitioner, although otherwise an interested person, is presumed to have waived notice and consented to the petition, unless the petition expressly indicates that the petitioner does not waive notice and does not consent to the granting of the requested prayers without a hearing. Although a petitioner or a fiduciary may in fact be an interested person, the petitioner need not indicate, either by written waiver or proof of service, that the petitioner has received a copy of any paper required by these rules to be served on interested persons.

(D) Service on Persons Under Legal Disability or Otherwise Legally Represented. In a guardianship or conservatorship proceeding, a petition or notice of hearing asking for an order that affects the ward or protected individual must be served on that ward or protected individual. In all other matters, service on an interested person under legal disability or otherwise legally represented may be made instead on the following:

(1) The guardian of an adult, conservator, or guardian ad litem of a minor or other legally disabled person, except with respect to:

(a) a petition for commitment or

(b) a petition, account, inventory or report made as the guardian, conservator, or guardian ad litem.

(2) The trustee of a trust with respect to a beneficiary of the trust, except that the trustee may not be served on behalf of the beneficiary on petitions, accounts, or reports made by the trustee as trustee or as personal representative of the settlor's estate.

(3) The guardian ad litem of any unascertained or unborn person.

(4) A parent of a minor with whom the minor resides, provided the interest of the parent in the outcome of the hearing is not in conflict with the interest of the minor and provided the parent has filed an appearance on behalf of the minor.

(5) The attorney for an interested person who has filed a written appearance in the proceeding. If the appearance is in the name of the office of the United States attorney, the counsel for the Veterans' Administration, the Attorney General, the prosecuting attorney, or the county or municipal corporation counsel, by a specifically designated attorney, service must be directed to the attention of the designated attorney at the address stated in the written appearance.

(6) The agent of an interested person under an unrevoked power of attorney filed with the court. A power of attorney is deemed unrevoked until written revocation is filed or it is revoked by operation of law.

For purposes of service, an emancipated minor without a guardian or conservator is not deemed to be under legal disability.

(E) Service on Beneficiaries of Future Interests. A notice that must be served on unborn or unascertained interested persons not represented by a fiduciary or guardian ad litem is considered served on the unborn or unascertained interested persons if it is served as provided in this subrule.

(1) If an interest is limited to persons in being and the same interest is further limited to the happening of a future event to unascertained or unborn persons, notice and papers must be served on the persons to whom the interest is first limited.

(2) If an interest is limited to persons whose existence as a class is conditioned on some future event, notice and papers must be served on the persons in being who would comprise the class if the required event had taken place immediately before the time when the papers are served.

(3) If a case is not covered by subrule (E)(1) or (2), notice and papers must be served on all known persons whose interests are substantially identical to those of the unascertained or unborn interested persons.

[Effective March 1, 1985; amended effective April 1, 1992; interim amendment effective April 1, 2000; amended effective January 1, 2002.]

1985 Staff Comment

MCR 5.105 is a rewritten version of PCR 105 covering the manner of service of notices in probate proceedings.

Essentially, the rule provides the following: Personal service is always permitted; Service by mail is permitted unless a statute, rule, or order requires another method; Service by publication is permitted when the whereabouts of an interested party is unknown; The court may order another method.

The rule also includes the details of how these methods of service are to be carried out, as well as retaining the provisions of PCR 105.3 and 105.6–105.8 as subrules (C)–(E).

Probate Rules Committee Comment to 1992 Amendment

The rule has been changed [effective April 1, 1992] to be applicable to all papers where service is required. Subrule (B)(1) has been changed to allow service of a paper on an attorney by facsimile machine and on attorneys and other individuals by registered mail and certified mail, return receipt requested and delivery restricted to addressee. Subrule (E) has been changed to affirmatively state methods of service on unborn or unascertained persons. The change in subrule (E) does not affect the requirements of MCL 700.814; MSA 27.5814.

Probate Rules Committee Comment to 2000 Amendment

Notice of a petition to appoint a guardian or conservator must be served on the prospective ward or individual to be protected [effective April 1, 2000]. In addition, MCL 700.5219(2) and 700.5405(2); MSA 27.15219(2) and 27.15405(2) require service on a minor ward or a protected individual of petitions or orders after the fiduciary's appointment. However, the fiduciary may be served on behalf of these individuals under MCR 2.105(B)(3) in a civil action or a proceeding other than the protective proceeding relating to that individual.

Probate Rules Committee Comment to 2002 Amendment

Notice of a petition to appoint a guardian or conservator must be served on the prospective ward or individual to be protected [effective January 1, 2002]. In addition, MCL 700.5219(2) and 700.5405(2) require service on a minor ward or a protected individual of petitions or orders after the fiduciary's appointment. However, the fiduciary may be served on behalf of these individuals under MCR 2.105(B)(3) in a civil action or a proceeding other than the protective proceeding relating to that individual.

RULE 5.106 PUBLICATION OF NOTICE OF HEARING

(A) Requirements. A notice of hearing or other notice required to be made by publication must be published in a newspaper as defined by MCR 2.106(F) one time at least 14 days before the date of the hearing, except that publication of a notice seeking a determination of a presumption of death based on absence pursuant to MCL 700.1208(2) must be made once a month for 4 consecutive months before the hearing.

(B) Contents of Published Notice. If notice is given to a person by publication because the person's address or whereabouts is not known and cannot be ascertained after diligent inquiry, the published notice must include the name of the person to whom the notice is given and a statement that the result of the hearing may be to bar or affect the person's interest in the matter.

(C) Affidavit of Publication. The person who orders the publication must cause to be filed with the court a copy of the publication notice and the publisher's affidavit stating

(1) the facts that establish the qualifications of the newspaper, and

(2) the date or dates the notice was published.

(D) Service of Notice. A copy of the notice:

(1) must be mailed to an interested person at his or her last known address if the person's present address is not known and cannot be ascertained by diligent inquiry;

(2) need not be mailed to an interested person if an address cannot be ascertained by diligent inquiry.

(E) Location of Publication. Publication must be in the county where the court is located unless a different county is specified by statute, court rule, or order of the court.

[Effective March 1, 1985; amended effective January 1, 1989; April 1, 1992; interim amendment effective April 1, 2000; amended effective January 1, 2002.]

Staff Comment

MCR 5.106 is substantially the same as PCR 106.

Staff Comment to 1989 Amendment

[See "Staff Comment to January 1, 1989 Amendments," set forth following Rule 5.993.]

Probate Rules Committee Comment to 1992 Amendment

The exception in subrule (A) to the requirement of a single publication [effective April 1, 1992] refers to proceedings under MCL 700.492, 700.493; MSA 27.5492, 27.5493. New subrule (E) specifies the place of publication.

Probate Rules Committee Comment to 2002 Amendment

An example of the other notice referred to in subrule (A) [effective January 1, 2002] is found in MCR 5.309(C)(2).

RULE 5.107   OTHER PAPERS REQUIRED TO BE SERVED

(A) Other Papers to be Served. The person filing a petition, an application, a sworn testimony form, supplemental sworn testimony form, a motion, a response or objection, an instrument offered or admitted to probate, an accounting or a sworn closing statement with the court must serve a copy of that document on interested persons. The person who obtains an order from the court must serve a copy of the order on interested persons.

(B) Exceptions.

(1) Service of the papers listed in subrule (A) is not required to be made on an interested person whose address or whereabouts, on diligent inquiry, is unknown, or on an unascertained or unborn person. The court may excuse service on an interested person for good cause.

(2) Service is not required for a small estate filed under MCL 700.3982.

[Effective March 1, 1985; amended effective April 1, 1992; interim amendment effective April 1, 2000; amended effective January 1, 2002.]

1985 Staff Comment

MCR 5.107 is substantially the same as PCR 107.

RULE 5.108   TIME OF SERVICE

(A) Personal. Personal service of a petition or motion must be made at least 7 days before the date set for hearing, or an adjourned date, unless a different period is provided or permitted by court rule. This subrule applies regardless of conflicting statutory provisions.

(B) Mail. Service by mail of a petition or motion must be made at least 14 days before the date set for hearing, or an adjourned date.

(C) Exception: Foreign Consul. This rule does not affect the manner and time for service on foreign consul provided by law.

(D) Computation of Time. MCR 1.108 governs computation of time in probate proceedings.

(E) Responses. A written response or objection may be served at any time before the hearing or at a time set by the court.

[Effective March 1, 1985. Interim amendment effective April 1, 2000; amended effective January 1, 2002.]

1985 Staff Comment

MCR 5.108 corresponds to PCR 108.

The time for service is changed to 7 days in advance of the hearing for personal service and 14 days for service by mail. The computation of time provisions of PCR 108.4 are replaced with a cross-reference to MCR 1.108, which includes some provisions from PCR 108.

RULE 5.112   PRIOR PROCEEDINGS AFFECTING THE PERSON OF A MINOR

Proceedings affecting the person of a minor subject to the prior continuing jurisdiction of another court of record are governed by MCR 3.205, including the requirement that petitions in such proceedings must contain allegations with respect to the prior proceedings.

[Effective March 1, 1985.]

1985 Staff Comment

MCR 5.112 is substantially the same as PCR 111.2.

RULE 5.113   PAPERS; FORM AND FILING

(A) Form of Papers Generally.

(1) An application, petition, motion, inventory, report, account, or other paper in a proceeding must

(a) be legibly typewritten or printed in ink in the English language, and

(b) include the

(i) name of the court and title of the proceeding in which it is filed;

(ii) case number, if any, including a prefix of the year filed and a two-letter suffix for the case-type code (see MCR 8.117) according to the principal subject matter of the proceeding, and if the case is filed under the juvenile code, the petition number which also includes a prefix of the year filed and a two-letter suffix for the case-type code;

(iii) character of the paper; and

(iv) name, address, and telephone number of the attorney, if any, appearing for the person filing the paper, and

(c) be substantially in the form approved by the State Court Administrator, if a form has been approved for the use.

(2) A judge or register shall not receive and file a nonconforming paper.

(B) Contents of Petitions.

(1) A petition must include allegations and representations sufficient to justify the relief sought and must:

(a) identify the petitioner, and the petitioner's interest in proceedings, and qualification to petition;

(b) include allegations as to residence, domicile, or property situs essential to establishing court jurisdiction;

(c) identify and incorporate, directly or by reference, any documents to be admitted, construed, or interpreted;

(d) include any additional allegations required by law or court rule;

(e) except when ex parte relief is sought, include a current list of interested persons, indicate the existence and form of incapacity of any of them, the mailing addresses of the persons or their representatives, the nature of representation and the need, if any, for special representation.

(2) The petition may incorporate by reference papers and lists of interested persons previously filed with the court if changes in the papers or lists are set forth in the incorporating petition.

(C) Filing by Registered Mail. Any document required by law to be filed in or delivered to the court by registered mail, may be filed or delivered by certified mail, return receipt requested.

(D) Filing Additional Papers. The court in its discretion may receive for filing a paper not required to be filed.

[Effective March 1, 1985; amended effective April 1, 1992; November 30, 1999; interim amendment effective April 1, 2000; amended effective May 23, 2000; May 1, 2002.]

1985 Staff Comment

MCR 5.113 includes the provisions of PCR 110.1 and 111.1.

The [March 1, 1985] amendment of MCR 5.113(A)(1)(b)(ii) adds a requirement that case-type codes be used in probate court proceedings.

Probate Rules Committee Comment to 1992 Amendment

Former subrule (B)(3) has been deleted [effective April 1, 1992] as unnecessary. Portions of former subrule (C) have been incorporated into MCR 5.602. This rule does not apply to informal letters under § 637 of the Mental Health Code, MCL 330.1637; MSA 14.800(637) and § 447 of the Revised Probate Code, MCL 700.447; MSA 27.5447.

Staff Comment to 1999 Amendment

The amendments of MCR 2.113, 5.113, 5.901, 7.210, 8.105, 8.110, 8.116, 8.203, 8.205, and 8.302 [effective November 30, 1999] and the addition of MCR 2.518 and 8.119 [effective November 30, 1999] are to accommodate statewide records standards applicable to all courts and all clerks of the courts as developed and recommended by the Michigan Trial Court Case File Management Standards Committee.

Probate Rules Committee Comment to 2000 Amendment

Former subrule (C) is deleted because the matter is covered in MCR 8.119(C). New subrule (C) [effective April 1, 2000] allows a person otherwise required to file a document with the court by registered mail, to use certified mail, return receipt requested. New subrule (D) gives the court discretion to regulate the practice of filing papers in addition to those required to be filed.

Staff Comment to 2000 Amendment

These amendments [effective May 23, 2000] are made to allow for flexibility in making changes to case classification codes. Case classification codes are used principally for administrative purposes by trial courts and the State Court Administrator for collecting management information regarding case and for identifying the administrative processing of cases.

The notice requirements of MCR 1.201 were dispensed with in order that several changes in case classification codes required with the implementation of the Estates and Protected Individuals Code, MCL 700.1101 et seq.; MSA 27.11101 et seq. could be implemented immediately by the State Court Administrator. The Estates and Protected Individuals Code became effective April 1, 2000. This matter will be included on the Court's future public hearing agenda for the purpose of receiving comments.

The State Court Administrator will incorporate case classification codes in the Case File Management Standards maintained by that office. The State Court Administrator will publish a revised case classification code schedule immediately, and will periodically publish case classification codes for the benefit of the public and the bar.

Staff Comment to 2002 Amendment

The December 18, 2001 amendments, effective May 1, 2002, updated various rules in light of the Estates and

Protected Individuals Code (EPIC), MCL 700.1101 *et seq.*, and revisions made to EPIC by 2000 PA 312, 313, and 469.

The staff comment is published only for the benefit of the bench and bar and is not an authoritative construction by the Court.

RULE 5.114 SIGNING AND AUTHENTICATION OF PAPERS

(A) Signing of Papers.

(1) The provisions of MCR 2.114 regarding the signing of papers apply in probate proceedings except as provided in this subrule.

(2) When a person is represented by an attorney, the signature of the attorney is required on any paper filed in a form approved by the State Court Administrator only if the form includes a place for a signature.

(3) An application, petition or other paper may be signed by the attorney for the petitioner, except that an inventory, account, acceptance of appointment, and sworn closing statement must be signed by the fiduciary or trustee. A receipt for assets must be signed by the person entitled to the assets.

(B) Authentication by Verification or Declaration.

(1) An application, petition, inventory, accounting, proof of claim, or proof of service must be either authenticated by verification under oath by the person making it, or, in the alternative, contain a statement immediately above the date and signature of the maker: "I declare under the penalties of perjury that this _____ has been examined by me and that its contents are true to the best of my information, knowledge, and belief." Any requirement of law that a document filed with the court must be sworn may be met by this declaration.

(2) In addition to the sanctions provided by MCR 2.114(E), a person who knowingly makes a false declaration under subrule (B)(1) is in contempt of court.

[Effective March 1, 1985; amended effective April 1, 1992; interim amendment effective April 1, 2000; amended effective January 1, 2002.]

1985 Staff Comment

MCR 5.114 includes the provisions of PCR 110.2 and 111.3. In addition, the rule incorporates the provisions of MCR 2.114 regarding the signing of papers and the sanctions for violation of those requirements.

Probate Rules Committee Comment to 1992 Amendment

Former subrule (A)(1) (now [A][3]) has been amended [effective April 1, 1992] to allow a person filing a paper on a form approved by the State Court Administrator to rely on the lack of a signature block on the form. The provision of former subrule (A)(2) on signing of papers by a minor in a proceeding to change a name has been moved to MCR 5.781.

Probate Rules Committee Comment to 2000 Amendment

Subrule (B)(1) is amended [effective April 1, 2000] to correspond with MCR 600.852; MSA 27A.852.

Probate Rules Committee Comment to 2002 Amendment

Subrule (B)(1) is amended [effective January 1, 2002] to correspond with MCL 600.852.

RULE 5.117 APPEARANCES BY ATTORNEYS

(A) Representation of Fiduciary. An attorney filing an appearance on behalf of a fiduciary shall represent the fiduciary.

(B) Appearance.

(1) *In General.* An attorney may appear by an act indicating that the attorney represents an interested person in the proceeding. An appearance by an attorney for an interested person is deemed an appearance by the interested person. Unless a particular rule indicates otherwise, any act required to be performed by an interested person may be performed by the attorney representing the interested person.

(2) *Notice of Appearance.* If an appearance is made in a manner not involving the filing of a paper served with the court or if the appearance is made by filing a paper which is not served on the interested persons, the attorney must promptly file a written appearance and serve it on the interested persons whose addresses are known and on the fiduciary. The attorney's address and telephone number must be included in the appearance.

(3) *Appearance by Law Firm.*

(a) A pleading, appearance, motion, or other paper filed by a law firm on behalf of a client is deemed the appearance of the individual attorney first filing a paper in the action. All notices required by these rules may be served on that individual. That attorney's appearance continues until an order of substitution or withdrawal is entered. This subrule is not intended to prohibit other attorneys in the law firm from appearing in the action on behalf of the client.

(b) The appearance of an attorney is deemed to be the appearance of every member of the law firm. Any attorney in the firm may be required by the court to conduct a court-ordered conference or trial.

(C) Duration of Appearance by Attorney.

(1) *In General.* Unless otherwise stated in the appearance or ordered by the court, an attorney's appearance applies only in the court in which it is made or to which the action is transferred and only for the proceeding in which it is filed.

(2) *Appearance on Behalf of Fiduciary.* An appearance on behalf of a fiduciary applies until the proceedings are completed, the client is discharged, or an order terminating the appearance is entered.

(3) *Termination of Appearance on Behalf of Personal Representative.* In unsupervised administration, the probate register may enter an order terminating an appearance on behalf of personal representative if the personal representative consents in writing to the termination.

(4) *Other Appearance.* An appearance on behalf of a client other than a fiduciary applies until a final order is entered disposing of all claims by or against the client, or an order terminating the appearance is entered.

(5) *Substitution of Attorneys.* In the case of a substitution of attorneys, the court in a supervised administration or the probate register in unsupervised administration may enter an order permitting the substitution without prior notice to the interested persons or fiduciary. If the order is entered, the substituted attorney must give notice of the substitution to all interested persons and the fiduciary.

(D) Right to Determination of Compensation. An attorney whose services are terminated retains the right to have compensation determined before the proceeding is closed.

[Effective March 1, 1985; amended effective April 1, 1992; February 1, 1995; interim amendment effective April 1, 2000.]

1985 Staff Comment

MCR 5.117 includes the provisions of PCR 908.1 and 908.2.

Probate Rules Committee Comment to 1992 Amendment

Subrule A [as amended effective April 1, 1992] clarifies that the attorney represents the fiduciary or trustee and not the estate.

Staff Comment to 1995 Amendment

A new subrule (C)(3) is added [effective February 1, 1995] to permit withdrawal of an attorney for an independent personal representative without hearing or supervision if the independent personal representative consents in writing.

RULE 5.118 AMENDING OR SUPPLEMENTING PAPERS

(A) Papers Subject to Hearing. A person who has filed a paper that is subject to a hearing may amend or supplement the paper

(1) before a hearing if notice is given pursuant to these rules, or

(2) at the hearing without new notice of hearing if the court determines that material prejudice would not result to the substantial rights of the person to whom the notice should have been directed.

(B) Papers not Subject to Hearing. A person who has filed a paper that is not subject to a hearing may amend or supplement the paper if service is made pursuant to these rules.

[Effective March 1, 1985; amended effective April 1, 1992; February 1, 1995; interim amendment effective April 1, 2000.]

1985 Staff Comment

MCR 5.118 is taken from PCR 110.3.

Probate Rules Committee Comment to 1992 Amendment

Former MCR 5.102(C) has been incorporated into this rule as subrule (B) [effective April 1, 1992].

RULE 5.119 ADDITIONAL PETITIONS; OBJECTIONS; HEARING PRACTICES

(A) Right to Hearing, New Matter. An interested person may, within the period allowed by law or these rules, file a petition and obtain a hearing with respect to the petition. The petitioner must serve copies of the petition and notice of hearing on the fiduciary and other interested persons whose addresses are known.

(B) Objection to Pending Matter. An interested person may object to a pending petition orally at the hearing or by filing and serving a paper which conforms with MCR 5.113. The court may adjourn a hearing based on an oral objection and require that a proper written objection be filed and served.

(C) Adjournment. A petition that is not heard on the day for which it is noticed, in the absence of a special order, stands adjourned from day to day or until a day certain.

(D) Briefs; Argument. The court may require that briefs of law and fact and proposed orders be filed as a condition precedent to oral argument. The court may limit oral argument.

[Effective March 1, 1985; amended effective April 1, 1992; interim amendment effective April 1, 2000.]

1985 Staff Comment

MCR 5.119 includes the provisions of PCR 112 and 113.

Probate Rules Committee Comment to 1992 Amendment

[Effective April 1, 1992,] subrule (A) has been divided into two subrules to deal with the differing situations in which an interested party might object to a pending matter, new subrule (B), or might obtain a hearing on a matter not currently pending in a proceeding, subrule (A). Former subrules (B) and (C) are redesignated as subrules (C) and (D), respectively. The first sentence of former subrule (B) is moved to MCR 5.102. The second sentence of former subrule (B) is deleted.

RULE 5.120 ACTION BY FIDUCIARY IN CONTESTED MATTER; NOTICE TO INTERESTED PERSONS; FAILURE TO INTERVENE.

The fiduciary represents the interested persons in a contested matter. The fiduciary must give notice to all interested persons whose addresses are known that a contested matter has been commenced and must keep such interested persons reasonably informed of the fiduciary's actions concerning the matter. The fiduciary must inform the interested persons that they may file a petition to intervene in the matter and that failure to intervene shall result in their being bound by the actions of the fiduciary. The interested person shall be bound by the actions of the fiduciary after such notice and until the interested person notifies the fiduciary that the interested person has filed with the court a petition to intervene.

[Adopted effective April 1, 1992. Interim amendment effective April 1, 2000.]

1992 Probate Rules Committee Comment

This is a new rule, designed to give finality to actions of fiduciaries and trustees. The rule does not apply to the personal representative of an estate who has authority to settle claims without consent of all interested parties, MCL 700.743; MSA 27.5743.

RULE 5.121   GUARDIAN AD LITEM; VISITOR

(A) Appointment.

(1) *Guardian Ad Litem.* The court shall appoint a guardian ad litem when required by law. If it deems necessary, the court may appoint a guardian ad litem to appear for and represent the interests of any person in any proceeding. The court shall state the purpose of the appointment in the order of appointment. The order may be entered with or without notice.

(2) *Visitor.* The court may appoint a visitor when authorized by law.

(B) Revocation. If it deems necessary, the court may revoke the appointment and appoint another guardian ad litem or visitor.

(C) Duties. Before the date set for hearing, the guardian ad litem or visitor shall conduct an investigation and shall make a report in open court or file a written report of the investigation and recommendations. The guardian ad litem or visitor need not appear personally at the hearing unless required by law or directed by the court. Any written report must be filed with the court at least 24 hours before the hearing or such other time specified by the court.

(D) Evidence.

(1) *Reports, Admission Into Evidence.* Oral and written reports of a guardian ad litem or visitor may be received by the court and may be relied on to the extent of their probative value, even though such evidence may not be admissible under the Michigan Rules of Evidence.

(2) *Reports, Review and Cross–Examination.*

(a) Any interested person shall be afforded an opportunity to examine and controvert reports received into evidence.

(b) The person who is the subject of a report received under subrule (D)(1) shall be permitted to cross-examine the individual making the report if the person requests such an opportunity.

(c) Other interested persons may cross-examine the individual making a report on the contents of the report, if the individual is reasonably available. The court may limit cross-examination for good cause.

(E) Attorney–Client Privilege.

(1) *During Appointment of Guardian Ad Litem.* When the guardian ad litem appointed to represent the interest of a person is an attorney, that appointment does not create an attorney-client relationship. Communications between that person and the guardian ad litem are not subject to the attorney-client privilege. The guardian ad litem must inform the person whose interests are represented of this lack of privilege as soon as practicable after appointment. The guardian ad litem may report or testify about any communication with the person whose interests are represented.

(2) *Later Appointment as Attorney.* If the appointment of the guardian ad litem is terminated and the same individual is appointed attorney, the appointment as attorney creates an attorney-client relationship. The attorney client privilege relates back to the date of the appointment of the guardian ad litem.

[Formerly Rule 5.201, effective March 1, 1985. Amended effective April 1, 1992; January 1, 1994. Renumbered Rule 5.121 as interim amendment effective April 1, 2000.]

Probate Rules Committee Comment to 2000 Amendment

This rule was MCR 5.201 [renumbered rule 5.121 effective April 1, 2000]. Subrule (C) is amended by adding a requirement that a guardian ad litem file any written report with the court 24 hours before a hearing. This will provide the court and interested persons with some notice of the contents of the report. Any more notice would often be impractical. The 24 hour provision contains an exception that the court might specify another time for filing a report in an emergency.

RULE 5.125   INTERESTED PERSONS DEFINED

(A) Special Persons. In addition to persons named in subrule (C) with respect to specific proceedings, the following persons must be served:

(1) The Attorney General must be served if required by law or court rule. The Attorney General must be served in the specific proceedings enumerated in subrule (C) when the decedent is not survived by any known heirs, or the protected person has no known presumptive heirs.

(2) A foreign consul must be served if required by MCL 700.1401(4) or court rule. An attorney who has filed an appearance for a foreign consul must be served when required by subrule (A)(5).

(3) On a petition for the appointment of a guardian or conservator of a person on whose account benefits are payable by the Veterans' Administration, the Administrator of Veterans' Affairs must be served through the administrator's Michigan district counsel.

(4) A guardian, conservator, or guardian ad litem of a person must be served with notice of proceedings as to which the represented person is an interested person, except as provided by MCR 5.105(D)(1).

(5) An attorney who has filed an appearance must be served notice of proceedings concerning which the attorney's client is an interested person.

(6) A special fiduciary appointed under MCL 700.1309.

(7) A person who filed a demand for notice under MCL 700.3205 or a request for notice under MCL 700.5104 if the demand or request has not been withdrawn, expired, or terminated by court order.

(B) Special Conditions for Interested Persons.

(1) *Claimant.* Only a claimant who files a claim with the court, with a personal representative, or with a trustee of a trust required to give notice to creditors pursuant to MCL 700.7504, and whose claim remains undetermined or unpaid need be notified of specific proceedings under subrule (C).

(2) *Devisee.* Only a devisee whose devise remains unsatisfied need be notified of specific proceedings under subrule (C).

(3) *Trust as Devisee.* If either a trust or a trustee is a devisee, the trustee is the interested person. If no trustee has qualified, the interested persons are the current trust beneficiaries and the nominated trustee, if any.

(4) *Father of a Child Born out of Wedlock.* Except as otherwise provided by law, the natural father of a child born out of wedlock need not be served notice of proceedings in which the child's parents are interested persons unless his paternity has been determined in a manner provided by law.

(C) Specific Proceedings. Subject to subrules (A) and (B) and MCR 5.105(E), the following provisions apply. When a single petition requests multiple forms of relief, the petitioner must give notice to all persons interested in each type of relief:

(1) The persons interested in an application or a petition to probate a will are the

(a) devisees,

(b) nominated trustee and current trust beneficiaries of a trust under the will,

(c) heirs,

(d) nominated personal representative, and

(e) trustee of a revocable trust described in MCL 700.7501(1).

(2) The persons interested in an application or a petition to appoint a personal representative, other than a special personal representative, of an intestate estate are the

(a) heirs,

(b) nominated personal representative, and

(c) trustee of a revocable trust described in MCL 700.7501(1).

(3) The persons interested in a petition to determine the heirs of a decedent are the heirs.

(4) The persons interested in a petition of surety for discharge from further liability are the

(a) principal on the bond,

(b) co-surety,

(c) devisees of a testate estate,

(d) heirs of an intestate estate,

(e) protected person and presumptive heirs of the protected person in a conservatorship, and

(f) claimants.

(5) The persons interested in a proceeding for spouse's allowance are the

(a) devisees of a testate estate,

(b) heirs of an intestate estate,

(c) claimants,

(d) spouse, and

(e) the personal representative, if the spouse is not the personal representative.

(6) The persons interested in a proceeding for examination of an account of a fiduciary are the

(a) devisees of a testate estate, and if one of the devisees is a trustee or a trust, the persons referred to in MCR 5.125(B)(3),

(b) heirs of an intestate estate,

(c) protected person and presumptive heirs of the protected person in a conservatorship,

(d) claimants, and

(e) current trust beneficiaries in a trust accounting.

(7) The persons interested in a proceeding for partial distribution of the estate of a decedent are the

(a) devisees of a testate estate entitled to share in the residue,

(b) heirs of an intestate estate,

(c) claimants, and

(d) any other person whose unsatisfied interests in the estate may be affected by such assignment.

(8) The persons interested in a petition for an order of complete estate settlement under MCL 700.3952 or a petition for discharge under MCR 5.311(B)(3) are the

    (a) devisees of a testate estate,

    (b) heirs unless there has been an adjudication that decedent died testate,

    (c) claimants, and

    (d) such other persons whose interests are affected by the relief requested.

(9) The persons interested in a proceeding for an estate settlement order pursuant to MCL 700.3953 are the

    (a) personal representative,

    (b) devisees,

    (c) claimants, and

    (d) such other persons whose interests are affected by the relief requested.

(10) The persons interested in a proceeding for assignment and distribution of the share of an absent apparent heir or devisee in the estate of a decedent are the

    (a) devisees of the will of the decedent,

    (b) heirs of the decedent if the decedent did not leave a will,

    (c) devisees of the will of the absent person, and

    (d) presumptive heirs of the absent person.

(11) The persons interested in a petition for supervised administration after an estate has been commenced are the

    (a) devisees, unless the court has previously found decedent died intestate,

    (b) heirs, unless the court has previously found decedent died testate,

    (c) personal representative, and

    (d) claimants.

(12) The persons interested in an independent request for adjudication under MCL 700.3415 and a petition for an interim order under MCL 700.3505 are the

    (a) personal representative, and

    (b) other persons who will be affected by the adjudication.

(13) The persons interested in a petition for settlement of a wrongful-death action or distribution of wrongful-death proceeds are the

    (a) heirs of the decedent,

    (b) other persons who may be entitled to distribution of wrongful-death proceeds, and

    (c) claimants whose interests are affected.

(14) The persons interested in a will contest settlement proceeding are the

    (a) heirs of the decedent and

    (b) devisees affected by settlement.

(15) The persons interested in a partition proceeding where the property has not been assigned to a trust under the will are the

    (a) heirs in an intestate estate or

    (b) devisees affected by partition.

(16) The persons interested in a partition proceeding where the property has been assigned to a trust under the will are the

    (a) trustee and

    (b) beneficiaries affected by the partition.

(17) The persons interested in a petition to establish the cause and date of death in an accident or disaster case under MCL 700.1208 are the heirs of the presumed decedent.

(18) The persons interested in a proceeding under the Mental Health Code that may result in an individual receiving involuntary mental health treatment or judicial admission of an individual with a developmental disability to a center are the

    (a) individual,

    (b) individual's attorney,

    (c) petitioner,

    (d) prosecuting attorney or petitioner's attorney,

    (e) director of any hospital or center to which the individual has been admitted,

    (f) the individual's spouse, if the spouse's whereabouts are known,

    (g) the individual's guardian, if any,

    (h) in a proceeding for judicial admission to a center, the community mental health program, and

    (i) such other relatives or persons as the court may determine.

(19) The persons interested in a petition for appointment of a guardian for a minor are:

    (a) the minor, if 14 years of age or older;

    (b) if known by the petitioner, each person who had the principal care and custody of the minor during the 63 days preceding the filing of the petition;

    (c) the parents of the minor or, if neither of them is living, any grandparents and the adult presumptive heirs of the minor, and

    (d) the nominated guardian.

(20) The persons interested in the acceptance of parental appointment of the guardian of a minor under MCL 700.5202 are:

    (a) the minor, if 14 years of age or older,

(b) the person having the minor's care, and

(c) each grandparent and the adult presumptive heirs of the minor.

(21) The persons interested in a 7–day notice of acceptance of appointment as guardian of an incapacitated individual under MCL 700.5301 are the

(a) incapacitated individual,

(b) person having the care of the incapacitated individual, and

(c) presumptive heirs of the incapacitated individual.

(22) The persons interested in a petition for appointment of a guardian of an alleged incapacitated individual are

(a) the alleged incapacitated individual,

(b) if known, a person named as attorney in fact under a durable power of attorney,

(c) the alleged incapacitated individual's spouse,

(d) the alleged incapacitated individual's children or, if no adult child is living, the individual's parents,

(e) if no spouse, child, or parent is living, the presumptive heirs of the individual,

(f) the person who has the care and custody of the alleged incapacitated individual, and

(g) the nominated guardian.

(23) The persons interested in receiving a copy of the report of a guardian of a legally incapacitated individual on the condition of a ward are:

(a) the ward,

(b) the person who has principal care and custody of the ward, and

(c) the spouse and adult children or, if no adult children are living, the presumptive heirs of the individual.

(24) The persons interested in a petition for the appointment of a conservator or for a protective order are:

(a) the individual to be protected if 14 years of age or older,

(b) the presumptive heirs of the individual to be protected,

(c) if known, a person named as attorney in fact under a durable power of attorney,

(d) the nominated conservator, and

(e) a governmental agency paying benefits to the individual to be protected or before which an application for benefits is pending.

(25) The persons interested in a petition for the modification or termination of a guardianship or conservatorship or for the removal of a guardian or a conservator are

(a) those interested in a petition for appointment under subrule (C)(19), (21), (22), or (23) as the case may be, and

(b) the guardian or conservator.

(26) The persons interested in a petition by a conservator for instructions or approval of sale of real estate or other asset are

(a) the protected individual and

(b) those persons listed in subrule (C)(23) who will be affected by the instructions or order.

(27) The persons interested in receiving a copy of an inventory or account of a conservator or of a guardian are:

(a) the protected individual or ward, if 14 years of age or older and can be located,

(b) the presumptive heirs of the protected individual or ward and

(c) claimants.

(28) The persons interested in a petition for approval of a trust under MCR 2.420 are

(a) the protected individual if 14 years of age or older,

(b) the presumptive heirs of the protected individual,

(c) if there is no conservator, a person named as attorney in fact under a durable power of attorney,

(d) the nominated trustee, and

(e) a governmental agency paying benefits to the individual to be protected or before which an application for benefits is pending.

(29) The persons interested in a petition for treatment of infectious disease are

(a) the petitioner and

(b) the respondent.

(30) The persons interested in a petition for emancipation of a minor are

(a) the minor,

(b) parents of the minor,

(c) the affiant on an affidavit supporting emancipation, and

(d) any guardian or conservator.

(31) Interested persons for any proceeding concerning a durable power of attorney for health care are:

(a) the patient;

(b) the patient's advocate;

(c) the patient's spouse;

(d) the patient's adult children;

(e) the patient's parents if the patient has no adult children;

(f) if the patient has no spouse, adult children or parents, the patient's minor children, or, if there are none, the presumptive heirs whose addresses are known;

(g) the patient's guardian and conservator, if any; and

(h) the patient's guardian ad litem.

(32) The persons interested in various adoption proceedings are as found at MCL 710.24a except as follows:

Petition to terminate rights of a noncustodial parent. The interested persons in a petition to terminate the rights of the noncustodial parent pursuant to MCL 710.51(6) are:

(a) the petitioner;

(b) the adoptee, if over 14 years of age; and

(c) the noncustodial parent.

(33) Persons interested in a proceeding to require, hear, or settle an accounting of an agent under a power of attorney are:

(a) the principal,

(b) the attorney in fact or agent,

(c) any fiduciary of the principal,

(d) the principal's guardian ad litem or attorney, if any, and

(e) the principal's presumptive heirs.

(D) The court shall make a specific determination of the interested persons if they are not defined by statute or court rule.

(E) In the interest of justice, the court may require additional persons be served.

[Formerly Rule 5.205, effective March 1, 1985. Amended effective September 1, 1990; April 1, 1991; April 1, 1992; January 1, 1994; September 1, 1997. Renumbered Rule 5.125 as interim amendment effective April 1, 2000; amended effective January 1, 2002; May 1, 2002.]

Probate Rules Committee Comment to 2000 Amendment

This rule was MCR 5.205 [renumbered rule 5.125 effective April 1, 2000]. The proceedings described in subrules (C)(27), (28), and (30) have been transferred to the exclusive jurisdiction of the family division of the circuit court. However, the subrules are left in place temporarily until development of rules for family division.

Staff Comment to 2002 Amendment

The December 18, 2001 amendments, effective May 1, 2002, updated various rules in light of the Estates and Protected Individuals Code (EPIC), MCL 700.1101 *et seq.*, and revisions made to EPIC by 2000 PA 312, 313, and 469.

The staff comment is published only for the benefit of the bench and bar and is not an authoritative construction by the Court.

RULE 5.126   DEMAND OR REQUEST FOR NOTICE

(A) Applicability. For purposes of this rule "demand" means a demand or request. This rule governs

the procedures to be followed regarding a person who files a demand for notice pursuant to MCL 700.3205 or MCL 700.5104. This person under both sections is referred to as a "demandant."

(B) Procedure.

(1) *Obligation to Provide Notice or Copies of Documents.* Except in small estates under MCL 700.3982 and MCL 700.3983, the person responsible for serving a paper in a decedent estate, guardianship, or conservatorship in which a demand for notice is filed is responsible for providing copies of any orders and filings pertaining to the proceeding in which the demandant has requested notification. If no proceeding is pending at the time the demand is filed, the court must notify the petitioner or applicant at the time of filing that a demand for notice has been filed and of the responsibility to provide notice to the demandant.

(2) *Rights and Obligations of Demandant.*

(a) The demandant must serve on interested persons a copy of a demand for notice filed after a proceeding has been commenced.

(b) Unless the demand for notice is limited to a specified class of papers, the demandant is entitled to receive copies of all orders and filings subsequent to the filing of the demand. The copies must be mailed to the address specified in the demand. If the address becomes invalid and the demandant does not provide a new address, no further copies of papers need be provided to the demandant.

(C) Termination, Withdrawal.

(1) *Termination on Disqualification of Demandant.* The fiduciary or an interested person may petition the court to determine that a person who filed a demand for notice does not meet the requirements of statute or court rule to receive notification. The court on its own motion may require the demandant to show cause why the demand should not be stricken.

(2) *Expiration of Demand When no Proceeding is Opened.* If a proceeding is not opened, the demand expires three years from the date the demand is filed.

(3) *Withdrawal.* The demandant may withdraw the demand at any time by communicating the withdrawal in writing to the fiduciary.

[Interim adoption effective April 1, 2000. Amended effective January 1, 2002.]

2000 Probate Rules Committee Comment

This rule is new [effective April 1, 2000]. It deals with the demand for notice provided for in MCL 700.3205; MSA 27.13205 and MCL 700.5104; MSA 27.15104.

Probate Rules Committee Comment to 2002 Amendment

This rule is new. It deals with the demand for notice in MCL 700.3205 and the request for notice in MCL 700.5104.

RULE 5.127　VENUE OF CERTAIN ACTIONS

(A) Defendant Found Incompetent to Stand Trial. When a criminal defendant is found mentally incompetent to stand trial and is referred to the probate court for admission to a treating facility,

(1) if the defendant is a Michigan resident, venue is proper in the county where the defendant resides;

(2) if the defendant is not a Michigan resident, venue is proper in the county of the referring criminal court.

(B) Guardian of Property of Nonresident with a Developmental Disability. If an individual with a developmental disability is a nonresident of Michigan and needs a guardian for Michigan property under the Mental Health Code, venue is proper in the probate court of the county where any of the property is located.

(C) Guardian of Individual With a Developmental Disability Who is in a Facility. If venue for a proceeding to appoint a guardian for an individual with a developmental disability who is in a facility is questioned, and it appears that the convenience of the individual with a developmental disability or guardian would not be served by proceeding in the county where the individual with a developmental disability was found, venue is proper in the county where the individual with a developmental disability most likely would reside if not disabled. In making its decision, the court shall consider the situs of the property of the individual with a developmental disability and the residence of relatives or others who have provided care.

[Formerly Rule 5.220, effective March 1, 1985. Amended effective January 1, 1994. Renumbered Rule 5.127 as interim amendment effective April 1, 2000.]

Probate Rules Committee Comment to 2000 Amendment

This rule was MCR 5.220 [renumbered rule 5.127 effective April 1, 2000].

RULE 5.128　CHANGE OF VENUE

(A) Reasons for Change. On petition by an interested person or on the court's own initiative, the venue of a proceeding may be changed to another county by court order for the convenience of the parties and witnesses, for convenience of the attorneys, or if an impartial trial cannot be had in the county where the action is pending.

(B) Procedure. If venue is changed

(1) the court must send to the transferee court, without charge, copies of necessary documents on file as requested by the parties or the transferee court and the original of an unadmitted will or a certified copy of an admitted will; and

(2) except as provided in MCR 5.306(A) or unless the court directs otherwise, notices required to be published must be published in the county to which venue was changed.

[Formerly Rule 5.221, effective March 1, 1985. Amended effective January 1, 1994. Renumbered Rule 5.128 as interim amendment effective April 1, 2000; amended effective January 1, 2002.]

Probate Rules Committee Comment to 2000 Amendment

This rule was MCR 5.221 [renumbered rule 5.128 effective April 1, 2000].

RULE 5.131　DISCOVERY GENERALLY

(A) The general discovery rules apply in probate proceedings.

(B) Scope of Discovery in Probate Proceedings. Discovery in a probate proceeding is limited to matters raised in any petitions or objections pending before the court. Discovery for civil actions in probate court is governed by subchapter 2.300.

[Formerly Rule 5.301, effective March 1, 1985. Renumbered Rule 5.131 as interim amendment effective April 1, 2000.]

Probate Rules Committee Comment to 2000 Amendment

This rule was MCR 5.301 [renumbered rule 5.131 effective April 1, 2000]. New subrule (B) clarifies that discovery in a probate proceeding is not available for the subject matter of a prospective civil action before the filing of such an action.

RULE 5.132　PROOF OF WILLS

(A) Deposition of Witness to Will. If no written objection has been filed to the admission to probate of a document purporting to be the will of a decedent, the deposition of a witness to the will or of other witnesses competent to testify at a proceeding for the probate of the will may be taken and filed without notice. However, the deposition is not admissible in evidence if at the hearing on the petition for probate of the will an interested person who was not given notice of the taking of the deposition as provided by MCR 2.306(B) objects to its use.

(B) Use of Copy of Will. When proof of a will is required and a deposition is to be taken, a copy of the original will or other document made by photographic or similar process may be used at the deposition.

[Formerly Rule 5.302, effective March 1, 1985. Renumbered Rule 5.132 as interim amendment effective April 1, 2000.]

Probate Rules Committee Comment to 2000 Amendment

This rule was MCR 5.302 [renumbered as rule 5.132 effective April 1, 2000].

RULE 5.141　PRETRIAL PROCEDURES; CONFERENCES; SCHEDULING ORDERS

The procedures of MCR 2.401 shall apply in a contested proceeding.

[Formerly Rule 5.401, effective March 1, 1985. Amended effective January 1, 1994. Renumbered Rule 5.141 as interim amendment effective April 1, 2000.]

Probate Rules Committee Comment to 2000 Amendment

This rule was MCR 5.401 [renumbered rule 5.141 effective April 1, 2000].

RULE 5.142   PRETRIAL MOTIONS IN CONTESTED PROCEEDINGS

In a contested proceeding, pretrial motions are governed by the rules that are applicable in civil actions in circuit court.

[Formerly Rule 5.402, adopted effective January 1, 1994. Renumbered Rule 5.142 as interim amendment effective April 1, 2000.]

Probate Rules Committee Comment to 2000 Amendment

This rule was MCR 5.402 [renumbered rule 5.142 effective April 1, 2000].

RULE 5.143   ALTERNATIVE DISPUTE RESOLUTION

(A) The court may submit to mediation, case evaluation, or other alternative dispute resolution process one or more requests for relief in any contested proceeding. MCR 2.410 applies to the extent feasible.

(B) If a dispute is submitted to case evaluation, MCR 2.403 and 2.404 shall apply to the extent feasible, except that sanctions must not be awarded unless the subject matter of the case evaluation involves money damages or division of property.

[Formerly Rule 5.403, adopted effective February 1, 1995. Renumbered Rule 5.143 as interim amendment effective April 1, 2000; amended effective August 1, 2000.]

Probate Rules Committee Comment to 2000 Amendment

This rule was MCR 5.403 [renumbered rule 5.143 effective April 1, 2000].

Staff Comment to 2000 Amendment

The May 8, 2000, amendments [effective August 1, 2000] are based on the recommendations of the Michigan Supreme Court Dispute Resolution Task Force, which were published for comment on May 10, 1999 [see 459 Mich 1251], and were the subject of a series of public hearings across the state.

The Task Force report, issued in January 1999, and its Addendum report, issued in January 2000 after receipt of comments, should be consulted for the background and details of the amendments. Basically, the changes are as follows:

The amendments of MCR 2.403, 2.404, 2.405, 2.501, 2.502 and 2.503 are mainly to change terminology, replacing "mediation," as used in current MCR 2.403, with the term "case evaluation." "Mediation" will be used to describe the facilitative process established in MCR 2.411, in keeping with the generally accepted usage of the term.

MCR 2.401 is amended to direct consideration of alternative dispute resolution processes at scheduling and pretrial conferences.

New MCR 2.410 has general provisions governing referral of cases to alternative dispute resolution processes. Local courts wishing to use ADR techniques are to adopt ADR plans within the framework provided by the rule.

The one ADR process that is specifically established by the rules is mediation under new MCR 2.411. Among other things, the rule establishes general standards for mediator qualifications, and procedures for selection of mediators.

MCR 3.216, the domestic relations mediation rule, is substantially revised, to be more comparable to the mediation process in MCR 2.411.

MCR 5.143, regarding use of alternative dispute resolution processes in probate court, is amended to conform to the other rule changes.

Dissenting Statement of Justice Kelly to 2000 Amendment

I support the expanded use of alternative dispute resolution by our courts. However, I cannot cast a vote favoring the proposed Dispute Resolution Court Rules for two reasons: 1) they authorize judges to compel parties to submit to mediation and 2) they include nonlawyers as mediators and other ADR providers.

Regarding the mandatory nature of the new rules, I believe that mediation is, by its very nature, a process that works only when the parties enter into it voluntarily. I would support rules that permit courts to order parties to a session at which the merits of ADR are explored, but not that mandate mediation.

It is my fear that mandatory mediation will present insurmountable financial obstacles to low income litigants and could even provoke challenges based on a violation of due process principles. I am concerned that, in some heavily burdened courts, judges may use the new rules, not as an option for the parties, but as a docket control mechanism for the court. Also, I find no limit in the rules to the number of times a party could be ordered to an ADR process.

Mediation should not become yet another hurdle to a just resolution of disputes. Parties should not feel pressed to settle against their best interests, or involuntarily to expend financial resources in excess of the normal costs of trial. Litigation, without the new rules, is already too costly.

I agree with the Board of Commissioners of the State Bar of Michigan that, absent agreement of the parties, only licensed lawyers should be allowed to serve as ADR providers. Mediation and other types of ADR typically involve complex legal matters requiring skilled ADR providers. Yet, no system has been developed to ensure the training and accountability of nonlawyers who participate.

Finally, I agree with the Open Justice Commission's recommendations that chief judges should be required to report the race, ethnicity, and gender of case evaluators and other ADR providers that they appoint. I view this as a vital step toward ensuring persons wishing to function as ADR providers will not be passed over solely on the basis of their race, gender, ethnic background, or similar factors.

RULE 5.144   ADMINISTRATIVELY CLOSED FILE

(A) Administrative Closing. The court may administratively close a file

(1) for failure to file a notice of continuing administration as provided by MCL 700.3951(3) or

(2) for other reasons as provided by MCR 5.203(D) or, after notice and hearing, upon a finding of good cause.

(B) Reopening Administratively Closed Estate. Upon petition by an interested person, with or without notice as the court directs, the court may order an administratively closed estate reopened. The court may appoint the previously appointed fiduciary, a successor fiduciary, a special fiduciary, or a special personal representative, or the court may order completion of the administration without appointing a fiduciary. In a decedent estate, the court may order supervised administration if it finds that supervised administration is necessary under the circumstances.

[Interim adoption effective April 1, 2000. Amended effective January 1, 2002.]

2000 Probate Rules Committee Comment

This rule is new [effective April 1, 2000].

RULE 5.151 JURY TRIAL, APPLICABLE RULES

Jury trials in probate proceedings shall be governed by MCR 2.508 through 2.516 except as modified by this subchapter or MCR 5.740 for mental health proceedings and MCR 5.911 for juvenile proceedings.

[Formerly Rule 5.501, adopted effective February 1, 1995. Renumbered Rule 5.151 as interim amendment effective April 1, 2000.]

Probate Rules Committee Comment to 2000 Amendment

This rule was MCR 5.501 [renumbered rule 5.151 effective April 1, 2000].

RULE 5.158 JURY TRIAL OF RIGHT IN CONTESTED PROCEEDINGS

(A) Demand. A party may demand a trial by jury of an issue for which there is a right to trial by jury by filing in a manner provided by these rules a written demand for a jury trial within 28 days after an issue is contested. However, if trial is conducted within 28 days of the issue being joined, the jury demand must be filed at least 4 days before trial. party who was not served with notice of the hearing at least 7 days before the hearing or trial may demand a jury trial at any time before the time set for the hearing. The court may adjourn the hearing in order to impanel the jury. A party may include the demand in a pleading if notice of the demand is included in the caption of the pleading. The jury fee provided by law must be paid at the time the demand is filed.

(B) Waiver. A party who fails to file a demand or pay the jury fee as required by this rule waives trial by jury. A jury is waived if trial or hearing is commenced without a demand being filed.

[Formerly Rule 5.508, effective March 1, 1985. Amended effective February 1, 1995; September 1, 1997. Renumbered Rule 5.158 as interim amendment effective April 1, 2000.]

Probate Rules Committee Comment to 2000 Amendment

This rule was MCR 5.508 [renumbered rule 5.158 effective April 1, 2000]. It covers how a party with a right to a jury trial may exercise that right. It does not purport to grant a right to a jury trial where none exists otherwise. Any such right is limited to a participant at the trial.

RULE 5.162 FORM AND SIGNING OF JUDGMENTS AND ORDERS

(A) Form of Judgments and Orders. A proposed judgment or order must include the name, address, and telephone number of the attorney or party who prepared it. All judgments and orders of the court must be typewritten or legibly printed in ink and signed by the judge to whom the proceeding is assigned.

(B) Procedure for Entry of Judgments and Orders. In a contested matter, the procedure for entry of judgments and orders is as provided in MCR 2.602(B).

[Formerly Rule 5.602, effective March 1, 1985. Amended effective April 1, 1992; February 1, 1995. Renumbered Rule 5.162 as interim amendment effective April 1, 2000.]

Probate Rules Committee Comment to 2000 Amendment

This rule was MCR 5.602 [renumbered rule 5.162 effective April 1, 2000].

SUBCHAPTER 5.200 PROVISIONS COMMON TO MULTIPLE TYPES OF FIDUCIARIES

RULE 5.201 APPLICABILITY *

Rules in this subchapter contain requirements applicable to all fiduciaries except trustees and apply to all estates except trusts.

[Interim adoption effective April 1, 2000. Amended effective January 1, 2002.]

* The contents of former MCR 5.201 have been moved to MCR 5.121, pursuant to the Supreme Court Orders dated January 14, 2000 and March 24, 2000, with interim effect of April 1, 2000.

2000 Probate Rules Committee Comment

This rule is new [effective April 1, 2000]. It address the matters formerly covered in MCR 5.715. The use of the term fiduciary in this subchapter differs from that in the Estates and Protected Individuals Code by excluding trustee. That exclusion is only for convenience of this subchapter which does not apply to trusts or trustees.

RULE 5.202 LETTERS OF AUTHORITY

(A) Issuance. Letters of authority shall be issued after the appointment and qualification of the fiduciary. Unless ordered by the court, letters of authority will not have an expiration date.

(B) Restrictions and Limitations. The court may restrict or limit the powers of a fiduciary. The restrictions and limitations imposed must appear on the letters of authority. The court may modify or remove the restrictions and limitations with or without a hearing.

(C) Certification. A certification of the letters of authority and a statement that on a given date the letters are in full force and effect may appear on the face of copies furnished to the fiduciary or interested persons.

[Formerly Rule 5.716, adopted effective February 1, 1995. Renumbered Rule 5.202 as interim amendment effective April 1, 2000. Amended effective January 1, 2002; May 1, 2002.]

Probate Rules Committee Comment to 2000 Amendment

This rule was MCR 5.716 [renumbered rule 5.202 effective April 1, 2000]. Former subrule (B) is deleted because the subject matter is covered in MCL 700.3951; MSA 27.13951. The remaining subrules are redesignated. The register may not impose restrictions in the letters of authority. One of the restrictions imposed by the court may be a limit on the length of time that the letters are effective. These rules use only the term "letters of authority" but the Estates and Protected Individuals Code uses other terms. See MCL 700.3504; MSA 27.13504 and MCL 700.7504; MSA 27.17504.

Probate Rules Committee Comment to 2002 Amendment

This rule was MCR 5.716. Former subrule (B) is deleted because the subject matter is covered in MCL 700.3951. The remaining subrules are redesignated. The register may not impose restrictions in the letters of authority. One of the restrictions imposed by the court may be a limit on the length of time that the letters are effective. These rules use only the term "letters of authority" but the Estates and Protected Individuals Code uses other terms. See MCL 700.3504 and MCL 700.7504 [effective January 1, 2002].

Staff Comment to 2002 Amendment

The December 18, 2001 amendments, effective May 1, 2002, updated various rules in light of the Estates and Protected Individuals Code (EPIC), MCL 700.1101 *et seq.*, and revisions made to EPIC by 2000 PA 312, 313, and 469.

The staff comment is published only for the benefit of the bench and bar and is not an authoritative construction by the Court.

RULE 5.203　FOLLOW–UP PROCEDURES

Except in the instance of a personal representative who fails to timely comply with the requirements of MCL 700.3951(1), if it appears to the court that the fiduciary is not properly administering the estate, the court shall proceed as follows:

(A) Notice of Deficiency. The court must notify the fiduciary, the attorney for the fiduciary, if any, and each of the sureties for the fiduciary of the nature of the deficiency, together with a notice to correct the deficiency within 28 days, or, in the alternative, to appear before the court or an officer designated by it at a time specified within 28 days for a conference concerning the deficiency. Service is complete on mailing to the last known address of the fiduciary.

(B) Conference, Memorandum. If a conference is held, the court must prepare a written memorandum setting forth the date of the conference, the persons present, and any steps required to be taken to correct the deficiency. The steps must be taken within the time set by the court but not to exceed 28 days from the date of the conference. A copy of the memorandum must be given to those present at the conference and, if the fiduciary is not present at the conference, mailed to the fiduciary at the last known address.

(C) Extension of Time. For good cause, the court may extend the time for performance of required duties for a further reasonable period or periods, but any extended period may not exceed 28 days and shall only be extended to a day certain. The total period as extended may not exceed 56 days.

(D) Suspension of Fiduciary, Appointment of Special Fiduciary. If the fiduciary fails to perform the duties required within the time allowed, the court may do any of the following: suspend the powers of the dilatory fiduciary, appoint a special fiduciary, and close the estate administration. If the court suspends the powers of the dilatory fiduciary or closes the estate administration, the court must notify the dilatory fiduciary, the attorney of record for the dilatory fiduciary, the sureties on any bond of the dilatory fiduciary that has been filed, and the interested persons at their addresses shown in the court file. This rule does not preclude contempt proceedings as provided by law.

(E) Reports on the Status of Estates. The chief judge of each probate court must file with the state court administrator, on forms provided by the state court administrative office, any reports on the status of estates required by the state court administrator.

[Formerly Rule 5.717, adopted effective February 1, 1995. Renumbered Rule 5.203 as interim amendment effective April 1, 2000; amended effective April 1, 2000; January 1, 2002.]

Probate Rules Committee Comment to the January 2000 Amendment

This rule was MCR 5.717 [renumbered rule 5.203 effective April 1, 2000]. It applies to any potential improper administration of an estate, including a failure under MCL 700.3951; MSA 27.13951. The provisions concerning reports to the state court administrator are stricken because MCR 8.119(G) provides sufficient authority to require reports.

Probate Rules Committee Comment to 2002 Amendment

This rule was MCR 5.717. It applies to any potential improper administration of an estate, except for a failure to timely file a notice of continuing administration which is covered by MCL 700.3951 [effective January 1, 2002].

RULE 5.204 APPOINTMENT OF SPECIAL FIDUCIARY

(A) Appointment. The court may appoint a special fiduciary or enjoin a person subject to the court's jurisdiction under MCL 700.1309; MSA 27.11309 on its own initiative, on the notice it directs or without notice in its discretion.

(B) Duties and Powers. The special fiduciary has all the duties and powers specified in the order of the court appointing the special fiduciary. Appointment of a special fiduciary suspends the powers of the general fiduciary unless the order of appointment provides otherwise. The appointment may be for a specified time and the special fiduciary is an interested person for all purposes in the proceeding until the appointment terminates.

[Formerly Rule 5.718, adopted effective February 1, 1995. Renumbered Rule 5.204 as interim amendment effective April 1, 2000.]

Probate Rules Committee Comment to 2000 Amendment

This rule was MCR 5.718 [renumbered 5.204 effective April 1, 2000]. It is amended to give the court maximum flexibility to use a special fiduciary to respond to reports of problems concerning a general fiduciary. See MCL 500.1309. This rule does not apply to a special personal representative under MCL 700.3614.

RULE 5.205 ADDRESS OF FIDUCIARY *

A fiduciary must keep the court and the interested persons informed in writing within 7 days of any change in the fiduciary's address. Any notice sent to the fiduciary by the court by ordinary mail to the last address on file shall be notice to the fiduciary.

[Interim adoption effective April 1, 2000.]

* The contents of former MCR 5.205 have been moved to MCR 5.125, pursuant to the Supreme Court Orders dated January 14, 2000 and March 24, 2000, with interim effect of April 1, 2000.

2000 Probate Rules Committee Comment

This rule is new [effective April 1, 2000]. The substance was formerly in MCR 5.707(B).

RULE 5.206 DUTY TO COMPLETE ADMINISTRATION

A fiduciary and an attorney for a fiduciary must take all actions reasonably necessary to regularly close administration of an estate. If the fiduciary or the attorney fails to take such actions, the court may act to regularly close the estate and assess costs against the fiduciary or attorney personally.

[Effective January 1, 2002.]

Probate Rules Committee Comments to 2002 Adoption and Deletion

This rule is new [effective January 1, 2002].

Former interim rule 5.206 is deleted [effective January 1, 2002].

RULE 5.207 SALE OF REAL ESTATE

(A) Petition. Any petition to approve the sale of real estate must contain the following:

(1) the terms and purpose of the sale,

(2) the legal description of the property, and

(3) the financial condition of the estate before the sale.

(B) Bond. The court may require a bond before approving a sale of real estate in an amount sufficient to protect the estate.

[Interim adoption effective April 1, 2000. Amended effective January 1, 2002.]

2000 Probate Rules Committee Comment

This rule is new [effective April 1, 2000]. It permits, but does not require, obtaining prior approval of a decision to sell.

Probate Rules Committee Comment to 2002 Amendment

This rule is new (effective January 1, 2002). Interested persons to be served notice of hearing on a sale of real estate are listed in MCR 5.125(C)(12) and (26) for decedent estates and conservatorships, respectively.

RULE 5.220 VENUE OF CERTAIN ACTIONS [RENUMBERED] *

[Renumbered effective April 1, 2000.]

* MCR 5.220 was renumbered pursuant to the Supreme Court Orders dated January 14, 2000 and March 24, 2000, with interim effect of April 1, 2000. The contents of MCR 5.220 have been moved to MCR 5.127. See the Probate Rules Committee Comment preceding Subchapter 5.000, ante.

RULE 5.221 CHANGE OF VENUE [RENUMBERED] *

[Renumbered effective April 1, 2000.]

* MCR 5.221 was renumbered pursuant to the Supreme Court Orders dated January 14, 2000 and March 24, 2000, with interim effect of April 1, 2000. The contents of MCR 5.221 have been moved to MCR 5.128. See the Probate Rules Committee Comment preceding Subchapter 5.000, ante.

SUBCHAPTER 5.300   PROCEEDINGS IN DECEDENT ESTATES

RULE 5.301   APPLICABILITY *

The rules in this subchapter apply to decedent estate proceedings other than proceedings provided by law for small estates under MCL 700.3982.

[Formerly Rule 5.701, effective March 1, 1985. Amended effective February 1, 1995. Renumbered Rule 5.301 as interim amendment effective April 1, 2000. Amended effective January 1, 2002.]

* The contents of former MCR 5.301 have been moved to MCR 5.131, pursuant to the Supreme Court Orders dated January 14, 2000 and March 24, 2000, with interim effect of April 1, 2000.

Probate Rules Committee Comment to 2000 Amendment

This rule was MCR 5.701 [renumbered rule 5.301 effective April 1, 2000]. Former subrule (B) is deleted because the term "temporary personal representative" has been replaced in the Estates and Protected Individuals Code (EPIC) by "special personal representative". The code defines special personal representative. MCL 700.1107(e).

RULE 5.302   COMMENCEMENT OF DECEDENT ESTATES *

(A) Methods of Commencement. A decedent estate may be commenced by filing an application for an informal proceeding or a petition for a formal testacy proceeding. A request for supervised administration may be made in a petition for a formal testacy proceeding.

(B) Sworn Testimony Form. A sworn testimony form sufficient to establish the identity of interested persons must be submitted with the application or petition that commences proceedings. The form must be executed before a person authorized to administer oaths.

(C) Preservation of Testimony. If a hearing is held, proofs included as part of the record are deemed preserved for further administration purposes.

(D) Petition by Parent of Minor. In the interest of justice, the court may allow a custodial parent who has filed an appearance to file a petition to commence proceedings in a decedent estate on behalf of a minor child where the child is an interested person in the estate.

[Interim adoption effective April 1, 2000. Amended effective May 1, 2002.]

* The contents of former MCR 5.302 have been moved to MCR 5.132, pursuant to the Supreme Court Orders dated January 14, 2000 and March 24, 2000, with interim effect of April 1, 2000.

2000 Probate Rules Committee Comment

This rule is new [effective April 1, 2000]. It incorporates part of former MCR 5.702(A). See MCL 700.3301 for commencing an informal proceeding by application and MCL 700.3401 for commencing a formal testacy proceeding by petition. Provision for multiple requests in one petition are found in MCL 700.3107(1)(b) and 700.3502(1). For matters covered by former MCR 5.702(B), see MCL 700.3614–700.3618. The term "informal proceedings" is defined in MCL 700.1105(b). These rules use the term "formal proceeding" to refer to both a formal testacy proceeding defined in MCL 700.3401 and an independent request to the court authorized by MCL 700.3415.

Staff Comment to 2002 Amendment

The December 18, 2001 amendments, effective May 1, 2002, updated various rules in light of the Estates and Protected Individuals Code (EPIC), MCL 700.1101 *et seq.*, and revisions made to EPIC by 2000 PA 312, 313, and 469.

The staff comment is published only for the benefit of the bench and bar and is not an authoritative construction by the Court.

RULE 5.304   NOTICE OF APPOINTMENT

(A) Notice of Appointment. The personal representative must, not later than 14 days after appointment, serve notice of appointment as provided in MCL 700.3705 and the agreement and notice relating to attorney fees required by MCR 5.313(D). No notice of appointment need be served if the person serving as personal representative is the only person to whom notice must be given.

(B) Publication of Notice. If the address or identity of a person who is to receive notice of appointment is not known and cannot be ascertained with reasonable diligence, the notice of appointment must be published one time in a newspaper, as defined in MCR 2.106(F), in the county in which a resident decedent was domiciled or in the county in which the proceedings with respect to a nonresident were initiated. The published notice of appointment is sufficient if it includes:

(1) statements that estate proceedings have been commenced, giving the name and address of the court, and, if applicable, that a will has been admitted to probate,

(2) the name of any interested person whose name is known but whose address cannot be ascertained after diligent inquiry, and a statement that the result of the administration may be to bar or affect that person's interest in the estate, and

(3) the name and address of the person appointed personal representative, and the name and address of the court.

(C) Prior Publication. After an interested person has once been served by publication, notice of appointment is only required if that person's address is known or becomes known during the proceedings.

[Interim adoption effective April 1, 2000. Amended effective January 1, 2002.]

This rule is new [effective April 1, 2000]. It and the two succeeding rules deal with all the notices that a personal representative must give at the commencement of administration, in addition to notice of hearing. Subrule (C) limits the requirement to serve an interested person by publication to the first such notice. Thus, the publication required under subrule (B) will not have to be made in formal proceedings if the notice of the petition for formal testacy or appointment proceedings was already published.

RULE 5.305 NOTICE TO SPOUSE; ELECTION

(A) Notice to Spouse. In the estate of a decedent who was domiciled in the state of Michigan at the time of death, the personal representative, except a special personal representative, must serve notice of the rights of election under part 2 of article II of the Estates and Protected Individuals Code, including the time for making the election and the rights to exempt property and allowances under part 4 of article II of the code, on the surviving spouse of the decedent within 28 days after the personal representative's appointment. An election as provided in subrule (C) may be filed in lieu of the notice. No notice need be given if the surviving spouse is the personal representative or one of several personal representatives or if there is a waiver under MCL 700.2205.

(B) Proof of Service. The personal representative is not required to file a proof of service of the notice of the rights of election.

(C) Spouse's Election. If the surviving spouse exercises the right of election, the spouse must serve a copy of the election on the personal representative personally or by mail. The election must be made within 63 days after the date for presentment of claims or within 63 days after the service of the inventory upon the surviving spouse, whichever is later. The election may be filed with the court.

(D) Assignment of Dower. A petition for the assignment of dower under MCL 558.1–558.29 must include:

(1) a full and accurate description of the land in Michigan owned by a deceased husband and of which he died seized, from which the petitioner asks to have the dower assigned;

(2) the name, age, and address of the widow and the names and addresses of the other heirs;

(3) the date on which the husband died and his domicile on the date of his death; and

(4) the fact that the widow's right to dower has not been barred and that she or some other person interested in the land wishes it set apart.

If there is a minor or other person other than the widow under legal disability having no legal guardian or conservator, there may not be a hearing on the petition until after the appointment of a guardian ad litem for such person.

[Interim adoption effective April 1, 2000. Amended effective January 1, 2002.]

This rule is new [effective April 1, 2000]. The topic was treated in former MCR 5.707(A)(2). See MCL 700.3705(5); MSA 27.13705(5) on the duty of the personal representative to provide the notice and MCL 700.2202; MSA 27.12202 on the time and manner for making the election. Subrule (B) overrides MCL 700.2202(3); MSA 27.12202(3). Subrule (D) was former MCR 5.707(C).

This rule is new. The topic was treated in former MCR 5.707(A)(2). See MCL 700.3705(5) on the duty of the personal representative to provide the notice and MCL 700.2202 on the time and manner for making the election. Subrule (B) overrides MCL 700.2202(4). Subrule (D) was former MCR 5.707(C).

RULE 5.306 NOTICE TO CREDITORS, PRESENTMENT OF CLAIMS

(A) Publication of Notice to Creditors; Contents. Unless the notice has already been given, the personal representative must publish, and a special personal representative may publish, in a newspaper, as defined by MCR 2.106(F), in a county in which a resident decedent was domiciled or in which the proceeding as to a nonresident was initiated, a notice to creditors as provided in MCL 700.3801. The notice must include:

(1) The name, and, if known, last known address, date of death, and date of birth of the decedent;

(2) The name and address of the personal representative;

(3) The name and address of the court where proceedings are filed; and

(4) A statement that claims will be forever barred unless presented to the personal representative, or to both the court and the personal representative within 4 months after the publication of the notice.

(B) Notice to Known Creditors and Trustee. A personal representative who has published notice must cause a copy of the published notice or a similar notice to be served personally or by mail on each known creditor of the estate and to the trustee of a trust of which the decedent is settlor, as defined in MCL 700.7501(1). Notice need not be served on the trustee if the personal representative is the trustee.

(1) Within the time limits prescribed by law, the personal representative must cause a copy of the published notice or a similar notice to be served personally or by mail on each creditor of the estate whose identity at the time of publication or during the 4 months following publication is known to, or can be

reasonably ascertained by, the personal representative.

(2) If, at the time of publication, the address of a creditor is unknown and cannot be ascertained after diligent inquiry, the name of the creditor must be included in the published notice.

(C) No Notice to Creditors. No notice need be given to creditors in the following situations:

(1) The estate has no assets;

(2) The estate qualifies and is administered under MCL 700.3982, MCL 700.3983 or MCL 700.3987;

(3) The decedent has been dead for more than 3 years;

(4) Notice has previously been given under MCL 700.7504 in the county where the decedent was domiciled in Michigan.

Notice need not be given to a creditor whose claim has been presented or paid.

(D) Presentment of Claims. A claim may be presented to the personal representative by mailing or delivering the claim to the personal representative's attorney. A claim is presented

(1) on mailing, if addressed to the personal representative, the personal representative's attorney or the court, or

(2) in all other cases, when received by the personal representative or the court.

For purposes of this subrule, personal representative includes a proposed personal representative.

[Formerly Rule 5.706, effective March 1, 1985. Amended effective January 1, 1989; February 1, 1995. Renumbered Rule 5.306 as interim amendment effective April 1, 2000. Amended effective January 1, 2002.]

Probate Rules Committee Comment to 2000 Amendment

This rule was MCR 5.706 [renumbered rule 5.306 effective April 1, 2000]. The changes in the rule are to comply with the provisions of the Estates and Protected Individuals Code. The trust referred to in subrule (B) is a trust described in MCL 700.7501(1); MSA 27.17501(1), see MCL 700.3801(1); MSA 27.13801(1).

Probate Rules Committee Comment to 2002 Amendment

This rule was MCR 5.706. The changes in the rule are to comply with the provisions of the Estates and Protected Individuals Code. The trust referred to in subrule (B) is a trust described in MCL 700.7501(1), see MCL 700.3801(1). If a claimant presents a claim by filing with the court, the claimant must deliver or mail a copy of the claim to the personal representative, MCL 700.3804(1)(a). Subrule (D) modifies MCL 700.3804 by allowing the timing of presentment to be the date of mailing to the personal representative or the personal representative's attorney. Otherwise, timing of presentment is as provided in MCL 700.3804.

RULE 5.307 REQUIREMENTS APPLICABLE TO ALL DECEDENT ESTATES

(A) Inventory Fee. Within 91 days of the date of the letters of authority, the personal representative must submit to the court the information necessary for computation of the probate inventory fee. The inventory fee must be paid no later than the filing of the petition for an order of complete estate settlement under MCL 700.3952, the petition for settlement order under MCL 700.3953, or the sworn statement under MCL 700.3954, or one year after appointment, whichever is earlier.

(B) Notice to Personal Representative. At the time of appointment, the court must provide the personal representative with written notice of information to be provided to the court. The notice should be substantially in the following form or in the form specified by MCR 5.310(E), if applicable:

"Inventory Information: Within 91 days of the date of the letters of authority, you must submit to the court the information necessary for computation of the probate inventory fee.

"Change of Address: You must keep the court and all interested persons informed in writing within 7 days of any change in your address.

"Notice of Continued Administration: If you are unable to complete the administration of the estate within one year of your original appointment, you must file with the court and all interested persons a notice that the estate remains under administration, specifying the reason for the continuation of the administration. You must give this notice within 28 days of the first anniversary of your appointment and all subsequent anniversaries during which the administration remains uncompleted.

"Duty to Complete Administration of Estate: You must complete the administration of the estate and file appropriate closing papers with the court. Failure to do so may result in personal assessment of costs."

(C) Claim by Personal Representative. A claim by a personal representative against the estate for an obligation that arose before the death of the decedent shall only be allowed in a formal proceeding by order of the court.

(D) Requiring or Filing of Additional Papers. Except in formal proceedings and supervised administration, the court may not require the filing of any papers other than those required to be filed by statute or court rule. However, additional papers may be filed under MCR 5.113(D).

[Interim adoption effective April 1, 2000. Amended effective January 1, 2002; May 1, 2002.]

2000 Probate Rules Committee Comment

This rule is new [effective April 1, 2000]. It deals with matters addressed in former MCR 5.707, but substantially changed to comply with the new provisions of the Estates and Protected Individuals Code. Since the normal process occurs without court supervision or monitoring, most of the provisions of the former rule have been omitted or moved to the rules on supervised administration or formal proceedings. Former MCR 5.707(C) on assignment of dower has been moved to MCR 5.305(D). Subrule (C) supersedes the notice and objection procedure of MCL 700.3804(3); MSA 27.13804(3).

Probate Rules Committee Comment to 2002 Amendment

This rule is new. It deals with matters addressed in former MCR 5.707, but it is substantially changed to comply with the new provisions of the Estates and Protected Individuals Code. Since the normal process occurs without court supervision or monitoring, most of the provisions of the former rule have been omitted or moved to the rules on supervised administration or formal proceedings. Former MCR 5.707(C) on assignment of dower has been moved to MCR 5.305(D). Subrule (C) supersedes the notice and objection procedure of MCL 700.3804(3).

Staff Comment to 2002 Amendment

The December 18, 2001 amendments, effective May 1, 2002, updated various rules in light of the Estates and Protected Individuals Code (EPIC), MCL 700.1101 *et seq.*, and revisions made to EPIC by 2000 PA 312, 313, and 469.

The staff comment is published only for the benefit of the bench and bar and is not an authoritative construction by the Court.

RULE 5.308   FORMAL PROCEEDINGS

(A) Accounts. Any account filed with the court must be in the form required by MCR 5.310(C)(2)(c).

(B) Determination of Heirs.

(1) *Determination During Estate Administration.* Every petition for formal probate of a will or for adjudication of intestacy shall include a request for a determination of heirs unless heirs were previously determined. Determination of heirs is also required whenever supervised administration is requested. No other petition for a formal proceeding, including a petition to appoint a personal representative which does not request formal probate of a will or adjudication of intestacy, need contain a request for determination of heirs. The personal representative or an interested person may at any time file a petition for determination of heirs. Heirs may only be determined in a formal hearing.

(2) *Determination Without Estate Administration.*

(a) Petition and Testimony Form. Any person may initiate a formal proceeding to determine intestacy and heirs without appointment of a personal representative by filing a petition and a sworn testimony form, executed before a person authorized to administer oaths, sufficient to establish the domicile of the decedent at the time of death and the identity of the interested persons.

(b) Notice, Publication. The petitioner must serve notice of hearing on all interested persons. If an interested person's address or whereabouts is not known, the petitioner shall serve notice on that person by publication as provided in MCR 5.105(A)(3). The court may require other publication if it deems necessary.

(c) Order. If notice and proofs are sufficient, the court must enter an order determining the date of death, the domicile of the decedent at the time of death, whether the decedent died intestate, and the names of the heirs.

(d) Closing File. If there are no further requests for relief and no appeal, the court may close its file.

[Interim adoption effective April 1, 2000; amended effective May 1, 2002.]

2000 Probate Rules Committee Comment

This rule is new [effective April 1, 2000]. Subrule (B) deals with the matter covered by former MCR 5.708. Subrule (B)(1) summarizes the requirements of the Estates and Protected Individuals Code on when a petition for formal proceedings must include a request for determination of heirs. Subrule (B)(2) changes the provisions of the previous rule in light of the revision in the statutory authorization for a court to determine heirs without further proceedings, now found at MCL 700.3106 and 700.3402(2)(c).

Staff Comment to 2002 Amendment

The December 18, 2001 amendments, effective May 1, 2002, updated various rules in light of the Estates and Protected Individuals Code (EPIC), MCL 700.1101 *et seq.*, and revisions made to EPIC by 2000 PA 312, 313, and 469.

The staff comment is published only for the benefit of the bench and bar and is not an authoritative construction by the Court.

RULE 5.309   INFORMAL PROCEEDINGS

(A) Denial of Application. If the probate register denies the application for informal probate or informal appointment, the applicant may file a petition for a formal proceeding, which may include a request for supervised administration.

(B) Effect of Form of Administration in Another State or Country. The fact that any particular form of administration has been initiated in the estate of a decedent in another state or country does not preclude any other form of proceedings with respect to that decedent in Michigan without regard to the form of the proceeding in the other state or country.

(C) Notice of Intent to Seek Informal Appointment as Personal Representative.

(1) A person who desires to be appointed personal representative in informal proceedings must give notice of intent to seek appointment and a copy of the application to each person having a prior or equal right to appointment who does not waive this right in writing before the appointment is made.

(2) Service of notice of intent to seek appointment and a copy of the application must be made at least 14 days by mail or 7 days by personal service before

appointment as personal representative. If the address of one or more of the persons having a prior or equal right to appointment is unknown and cannot be ascertained after diligent inquiry, notice of the intent to file the application must be published pursuant to MCR 5.106 at least 14 days prior to the appointment, but a copy of the application need not be published.

(3) Proof of service must be filed with the court along with the application for informal appointment as personal representative.

(D) Publication. If the address of an heir, devisee, or other interested person entitled to the information on the informal probate under MCL 700.3306 is unknown and cannot be ascertained after diligent inquiry, the information in MCL 700.3306(2) must be provided by publication pursuant to MCR 5.106. Publication of notice under this rule is not required if a personal representative has been appointed and provided notice under MCR 5.304.

[Interim adoption effective April 1, 2000. Amended effective January 1, 2002.]

2000 Probate Rules Committee Comment

This rule is new [effective April 1, 2000]. Subrule (B) allows use of any of the various forms of proceedings or administration-informal or formal, unsupervised or supervised-in this state without regard to the form which may have been used is another state or country in the administration of the estate of the same decedent. Subrule (C) deals with the notice of intent requirement of MCL 700.3310; MSA 27.13310. See also MCL 700.1401; MSA 27.11401.

Probate Rules Committee Comment to 2002 Amendment

This rule is new. Subrule (B) allows use of any of the various forms of proceedings or administration-informal or formal, unsupervised or supervised-in this state without regard to the form which may have been used in another state or country in the administration of the estate of the same decedent. Subrule (C) deals with the notice of intent requirement of MCL 700.3310. See also MCL 700.1401.

RULE 5.310 SUPERVISED ADMINISTRATION

(A) Applicability. The other rules applicable to decedent estates apply to supervised administration unless they conflict with this rule.

(B) Commencement of Supervised Administration. A request for supervised administration in a decedent estate may be made in the petition for formal testacy and appointment proceedings. A petition for formal testacy and appointment proceedings including a request for supervised administration may be filed at any time during the estate proceedings if testacy has not previously been adjudicated. If testacy and appointment have been previously adjudicated, a separate petition for supervised administration may be filed at any time during administration of the estate. Whenever supervised administration is requested, the court must determine heirs unless heirs were previously determined, even if supervised administration is denied.

(C) Filing Papers With the Court. The personal representative must file the following additional papers with the court and serve copies on the interested persons:

(1) *Inventory.*

(a) Administration Commenced Supervised. If supervised administration is ordered at the commencement of the estate administration, the personal representative must file the inventory within 91 days of the date of the letters of authority.

(b) Administration Commenced Without Supervision. If supervised administration is ordered after a personal representative has been appointed, the court must specify in the order a time for that personal representative to file the inventory.

(2) *Accountings.*

(a) Time for Filing. Unless the court designates a shorter period, the personal representative must file accountings within 56 days after the end of the accounting period. A final account must be filed when the estate is ready for closing or on removal of a personal representative. The court may order an interim accounting at any time the court deems necessary.

(b) Accounting Period. The accounting period ends on the anniversary date of the issuance of the letters of authority or, if applicable, on the anniversary date of the close of the last period covered by an accounting. The personal representative may elect to change the accounting period so that it ends on a different date. If the personal representative elects to make such a change, the first accounting period thereafter shall not be more than a year. A notice of the change must be filed with the court.

(c) Contents. All accountings must be itemized, showing in detail receipts and disbursements during the accounting period, unless itemization is waived by all interested persons. A written description of services performed must be included or appended regarding compensation sought by a personal representative. This description need not be duplicated in the order. The accounting must include notice that (i) objections concerning the accounting must be brought to the court's attention by an interested person because the court does not normally review the accounting without an objection; (ii) interested persons have a right to review proofs of income and disbursements at a time reasonably convenient to the personal representative and the interested person; (iii) interested persons may object to all or part of an accounting by filing an objection with the court before allowance of the accounting; and (iv) if an objection is filed and not otherwise resolved, the court will hear and determine the objection.

(d) Proof of Income and Disbursements. After filing and before the allowance of an accounting, the personal representative must make proofs of income and disbursements reasonably available for examination by any interested person who requests to see them or as required by the court. An interested person, with or without examination of the proofs of income and disbursements, may file an objection to an accounting with the court. If an interested person files an objection without examining the proofs and the court concludes that such an examination would help resolve the objection, the court may order the interested person to examine the proofs before the court hears the objection.

(e) Deferral of Hearings on Accountings. Hearing on each accounting may be deferred in the discretion of the court. The court in any case at any time may require a hearing on an accounting with or without a request by an interested person.

(3) Notice of appointment.

(4) Fees notice pursuant to MCR 8.303.

(5) Notice to spouse.

(6) Affidavit of any required publication.

(7) Such other papers as are ordered by the court.

(D) **Tax Information.** The personal representative must file with the court

(1) in the case of a decedent dying before October 1, 1993, proof that all Michigan inheritance taxes have been paid or

(2) in the case of an estate of a decedent dying after September 30, 1993, either

(a) if a federal estate tax return was required to be filed for the decedent, proof from the Michigan Department of Treasury that all Michigan estate taxes have been paid, or

(b) if no federal estate tax return was required to be filed for the decedent, a statement that no Michigan estate tax is due.

(E) **Notice to Personal Representative.** When supervised administration is ordered, the court must serve a written notice of duties on the personal representative. The notice must be substantially as follows:

"Inventories: You are required to file an inventory of the assets of the estate within 91 days of the date of your letters of authority or as ordered by the court. The inventory must list in reasonable detail all the property owned by the decedent at the time of death, indicating, for each listed item, the fair market value at the time of decedent's death and the type and amount of any encumbrance. If the value of any item has been obtained through an appraiser, the inventory should include the appraiser's name and address with the item or items appraised by that appraiser.

"Accountings: You are required to file annually, or more often if the court directs, a complete itemized accounting of your administration of the estate, showing in detail all the receipts and disbursements and the property remaining in your hands together with the form of the property. When the estate is ready for closing, you are required to file a final accounting and an itemized and complete list of all properties remaining. Subsequent annual and final accountings must be filed within 56 days after the close of the accounting period.

"Change of Address: You are required to keep the court and interested persons informed in writing within 7 days of any change in your address.

"Notice of Continued Administration: If you are unable to complete the administration of the estate within one year of your original appointment, you must file with the court and all interested persons a notice that the estate remains under administration, specifying the reason for the continuation of the administration. You must give this notice within 28 days of the first anniversary of your appointment and all subsequent anniversaries during which the administration remains uncompleted.

"Duty to Complete Administration of Estate: You must complete the administration of the estate and file appropriate closing papers with the court. Failure to do so may result in personal assessment of costs."

(F) **Changing from Supervised to Unsupervised Administration.** At any time during supervised administration, any interested person or the personal representative may petition the court to terminate supervision of administration. The court may terminate supervision unless the court finds that proceeding with supervision is necessary under the circumstances. Termination of supervision does not discharge the personal representative.

(G) Approval of compensation of an attorney must be sought pursuant to MCR 5.313.

(H) **Order of Complete Estate Settlement.** An estate being administered in supervised administration must be closed under MCL 700.3952, using the procedures specified in MCR 5.311(B)(1).

[Interim adoption effective April 1, 2000. Amended effective January 1, 2002; May 1, 2002.]

2000 Probate Rules Committee Comment

This rule is new [effective April 1, 2000], but the contents are modeled on the former provisions of MCR 5.707. Papers required to be served on interested persons are subject to MCR 5.104. Requirements regarding the inventory are in MCL 700.3706; MSA 27.13706 and MCL 700.3707; MSA 27.13707. Requirements regarding accountings are in MCL 700.3703(4); MSA 27.13703(4). Subrule (F) is modeled on former MCR 5.709(H) and permits moving from supervised administration to unsupervised administration. Determination of whether continuing supervision is necessary should be guided by MCL 700.3502(2), (3); MSA 27.13502(2), (3).

Probate Rules Committee Comment to 2002 Amendment

This rule is new, but the contents are modeled on the former provisions of MCR 5.707. Papers required to be served on interested persons are subject to MCR 5.104. Requirements regarding the inventory are in MCL 700.3706 and MCL 700.3707. Requirements regarding accountings are in MCL 700.3703(4). Subrule (C) lists only those papers not required to be filed by some other rule or statute. The reader should not rely on subrule (C) as a complete list of papers which the personal representative must file with the court. Subrule (F) is modeled on former MCR 5.709(H) and permits moving from supervised administration to unsupervised administration. Determination of whether continuing supervision is necessary should be guided by MCL 700.3502(2) and (3).

Staff Comment to 2002 Amendment

The December 18, 2001 amendments, effective May 1, 2002, updated various rules in light of the Estates and Protected Individuals Code (EPIC), MCL 700.1101 *et seq.*, and revisions made to EPIC by 2000 PA 312, 313, and 469.

The staff comment is published only for the benefit of the bench and bar and is not an authoritative construction by the Court.

RULE 5.311 CLOSING ESTATE

(A) Closing by Sworn Statement. In unsupervised administration, a personal representative may close an estate by filing a sworn closing statement under MCL 700.3954 or MCL 700.3988.

(B) Formal Proceedings.

(1) *Requirements for Order of Complete Estate Settlement under MCL 700.3952.* An estate being administered in supervised administration must be closed by an order for complete estate settlement under MCL 700.3952. All other estates may be closed under that provision. A petition for complete estate settlement must state the relief requested. If the petitioner requests a determination of testacy, the petitioner must comply with the requirements of the statute and court rules dealing with a determination of testacy in a formal proceeding.

(2) *Requirements for Settlement Order under MCL 700.3953.* A personal representative or a devisee may file a petition for a settlement order under MCL 700.3953; only in an estate being administered under a will admitted to probate in an informal proceeding. The petition may not contain a request for a determination of the decedent testacy status in a formal proceeding.

(3) *Discharge.* A personal representative may petition for discharge from liability with notice to the interested persons. A personal representative who files such a petition with the court must also file the papers described in MCR 5.310(C) and (D), as applicable, proofs of service of those papers that are required to be served on interested persons, and such other papers as the court may require. The court may order the personal representative discharged if the court is satisfied that the personal representative has properly administered the estate.

(4) *Other Requests for Relief.* With respect to other requests for relief, the petitioner must file appropriate papers to support the request for relief.

(5) *Order.* If the estate administration is completed, the order entered under MCL 700.3952 or MCL 700.3953 shall, in addition to any other relief, terminate the personal representative's authority and close the estate.

(C) Closing of Reopened Estate. After completion of the reopened estate administration, the personal representative shall proceed to close the estate by filing a petition under MCL 700.3952 or MCL 700.3953 or a supplemental closing statement under MCL 700.3954. If a supplemental closing statement is filed, the personal representative must serve a copy on each interested person. If an objection is not filed within 28 days, the personal representative is entitled to receive a supplemental certificate of completion.

[Interim adoption effective April 1, 2000. Amended effective January 1, 2002; May 1, 2002.]

2000 Probate Rules Committee Comment

This rule is new [effective April 1, 2000].

Probate Rules Committee Comment to 2002 Amendment

This rule is new. Use of a sworn statement to close an estate is limited to situations specified in MCL 700.3954 and MCL 700.3988.

Staff Comment to 2002 Amendment

The December 18, 2001 amendments, effective May 1, 2002, updated various rules in light of the Estates and Protected Individuals Code (EPIC), MCL 700.1101 *et seq.*, and revisions made to EPIC by 2000 PA 312, 313, and 469.

The staff comment is published only for the benefit of the bench and bar and is not an authoritative construction by the Court.

RULE 5.312 REOPENING DECEDENT ESTATE

(A) Reopening by Application. If there is good cause to reopen a previously administered estate, other than an estate that was terminated in supervised administration, any interested person may apply to the register to reopen the estate and appoint the former personal representative or another person who has priority. For good cause and without notice, the register may reopen the estate, appoint the former personal representative or a person who has priority, and issue letters of authority with a specified termination date.

(B) Reopening by Petition. The previously appointed personal representative or an interested person may file a petition with the court to reopen the estate and appoint a personal representative under MCL 700.3959.

(C) Calculation of Due Dates. For purposes of determining when the inventory fee calculation, the inventory filing, the inventory fee payment, and the notice of continued administration are due, a reopened decedent estate is to be treated as a new case.

[Interim adoption effective April 1, 2000. Amended effective January 1, 2002; May 1, 2002.]

2000 Probate Rules Committee Comment

This rule is new [effective April 1, 2000]. It is adapted from former MCR 5.709(J). It deals with reopening an estate after administration has been closed. Note that in estates closed by closing statement under MCL 700.3954; MSA 27.13954, the appointment of the personal representative continues for one year. In such estates, the personal representative would have authority to act during that period without being reappointed. There is no restriction, other than with regard to supervised administration, against using informal proceedings to reopen an estate that had been closed by order.

Probate Rules Committee Comment to 2002 Amendment

This rule is new. It is adapted from former MCR 5.709(J). It deals with reopening an estate after administration has been closed. Note that in estates closed by closing statement under MCL 700.3954, the appointment of the personal representative continues for one year. In such estates, the personal representative would have authority to act during that period without being reappointed. There is no restriction, other than with regard to supervised administration, against using informal proceedings to reopen an estate that had been closed by order.

Staff Comment to 2002 Amendment

The December 18, 2001 amendments, effective May 1, 2002, updated various rules in light of the Estates and Protected Individuals Code (EPIC), MCL 700.1101 *et seq.*, and revisions made to EPIC by 2000 PA 312, 313, and 469.

The staff comment is published only for the benefit of the bench and bar and is not an authoritative construction by the Court.

RULE 5.313 COMPENSATION OF ATTORNEYS

(A) Reasonable Fees and Costs. An attorney is entitled to receive reasonable compensation for legal services rendered on behalf of a personal representative, and to reimbursement for costs incurred in rendering those services. In determining the reasonableness of fees, the court must consider the factors listed in MRPC 1.5(a). The court may also take into account the failure to comply with this rule.

(B) Written Fee Agreement. At the commencement of the representation, the attorney and the personal representative or the proposed personal representative must enter into a written fee agreement signed by them. A copy of the agreement must be provided to the personal representative.

(C) Records. Regardless of the fee agreement, every attorney who represents a personal representative must maintain time records for services that must reflect the following information: the identity of the person performing the services, the date the services are performed, the amount of time expended in performing the services, and a brief description of the services.

(D) Notice to Interested Persons. Within 14 days after the appointment of a personal representative or the retention of an attorney by a personal representative, whichever is later, the personal representative must mail to the interested persons whose interests will be affected by the payment of attorney fees, a notice in the form substantially approved by the State Court Administrator and a copy of the written fee agreement. The notice must state:

(1) the anticipated frequency of payment,

(2) that the person is entitled to a copy of each statement for services or costs upon request,

(3) that the person may object to the fees at any time prior to the allowance of fees by the court,

(4) that an objection may be made in writing or at a hearing and that a written objection must be filed with the court and a copy served on the personal representative or attorney.

(E) Payment of Fees. A personal representative may make, and an attorney may accept, payments for services and costs, on a periodic basis without prior court approval if prior to the time of payment

(1) the attorney and personal representative have entered a written fee agreement;

(2) copies of the fee agreement and the notice required by subrule (D) have been sent to all interested persons who are affected;

(3) a statement for services and costs (containing the information required by subrule [C]) has been sent to the personal representative and each interested person who has requested a copy of such statement; and

(4) no written, unresolved objection to the fees, current or past, has been served on the attorney and personal representative.

In all other instances, attorney fees must be approved by the court prior to payment. Costs may be paid without prior court approval. Attorney fees and costs paid without prior court approval remain subject to review by the court.

(F) Claims for Compensation, Required Information. Except when the compensation is consented to by all the parties affected, the personal representative must append to an accounting, petition, or motion in which compensation is claimed a statement containing the information required by subrule (D).

(G) Contingent Fee Agreements under MCR 8.121. Subrules (C), (E) and (F) of this rule do not apply to a contingent fee agreement between a personal representative and an attorney under MCR 8.121.

[Formerly Rule 8.303, effective March 1, 1985; amended effective January 1, 1994; interim amendment effective April 1, 2000. Renumbered Rule 5.313 as amended effective January 1, 2002.]

Probate Rules Committee Comment to 1994 Amendment

This rule governs compensation of attorneys representing fiduciaries. It is substantially revised [effective January 1, 1994] to provide grounds for resolving disputes, subrule (A); written fee agreements, subrule (B); record keeping, subrule (C), appropriate to the fiduciary status; notice to interested parties who might be affected, subrule (D); and periodic payments, subrule (E).

Subrule (A) directs a court determining reasonableness of fees to consider the factors listed in MRPC 1.5(a). The requirement of subrule (C) on keeping records of time spent, identity of provider, and nature of services facilitates this review.

Subrule (B) mandates compliance with the recommendation of MRPC 1.5(b), because of the fiduciary status of the client.

Subrule (D) requires only that the notice be sent to those interested parties who are affected by the payment of fees. For example, in a solvent estate where there are specific devises and all expenses are payable out of the residue, only the residuary devisees must receive the notice. This notice requirement applies to independent probate as well as supervised probate. The term "interested parties" does not include creditors, MCL 700.7; MSA 27.5007.

Subrule (F) defines "fiduciary" in a manner consistent with MCL 700.5; MSA 27.5005 with the exception that there is no restriction on the inclusion of a testamentary trustee.

Probate Rules Committee Comment to 2000 Amendment

This rule is amended [effective April 1, 2000] to limit its applicability to attorneys representing personal representatives and to reflect changes in practice and terminology by the Estates and Protected Individuals Code, MCL 700.1101 et seq.; MSA 27.11101 et seq. The rule is not intended to dictate the terms of a fee agreement. It requires that any fee be reasonable and fairly disclosed to the fiduciary and interested persons.

Probate Rules Committee Comment to 2002 Amendment

This rule was MCR 8.303 [renumbered rule 5.313 effective January 1, 2002]. It is amended to limit its applicability to attorneys representing personal representatives and to reflect changes in practice and terminology by the Estates and Protected Individuals Code, MCL 700.1101 et seq. The rule is not intended to dictate the terms of a fee agreement. It requires that any fee be reasonable and fairly disclosed to the personal representative and interested persons.

SUBCHAPTER 5.400 GUARDIANSHIP, CONSERVATOR-SHIP AND PROTECTIVE ORDER PROCEEDINGS

RULE 5.401 GENERAL PROVISIONS *

This subchapter governs guardianships, conservatorships, and protective order proceedings. The other rules in chapter 5 also apply to these proceedings unless they conflict with rules in this subchapter. Except as modified in this subchapter, proceedings for guardianships of adults and minors, conservatorships and protective orders shall be in accordance with the Estates and Protected Individuals Code, 1998 PA 386 and, where applicable, the Mental Health Code, 1974 PA 258, as amended.

[Formerly Rule 5.761, adopted effective September 1, 1990. Renumbered Rule 5.401 as interim amendment effective April 1, 2000.]

* The contents of former MCR 5.401 have been moved to MCR 5.141, pursuant to the Supreme Court Orders dated January 14, 2000 and March 24, 2000, with interim effect of April 1, 2000.

Probate Rules Committee Comment to 2000 Amendment

This rule was MCR 5.761 [renumbered rule 5.401 effective April 1, 2000].

RULE 5.402 COMMON PROVISIONS *

(A) Petition; Multiple Prayers. A petition for the appointment of a guardian or a conservator or for a protective order may contain multiple prayers for relief.

(B) Petition by Minor. A petition and a nomination for the appointment of a guardian or conservator of a minor may be executed and made by a minor 14 years of age or older.

(C) Responsibility for Giving Notice; Manner of Service. The petitioner is responsible for giving notice of hearing. Regardless of statutory provisions, an interested person may be served by mail, by personal service, or by publication when necessary; however, if the person who is the subject of the petition is 14 years of age or older, notice of the initial hearing must be served on the person personally unless another method of service is specifically permitted in the circumstances.

(D) Letters of Authority. On the filing of the acceptance of appointment or bond required by the order appointing a fiduciary, the court shall issue letters of authority on a form approved by the state court administrator. Any restriction or limitation of the powers of a guardian or conservator must be set forth in the letters of authority.

[Formerly Rule 5.762, adopted effective September 1, 1990. Renumbered Rule 5.402 as interim amendment effective April 1, 2000. Amended effective January 1, 2002.]

* The contents of former MCR 5.402 have been moved to MCR 5.142, pursuant to the Supreme Court Orders dated January 14, 2000 and March 24, 2000, with interim effect of April 1, 2000.

Probate Rules Committee Comment to 2000 Amendment

This rule was MCR 5.762 [renumbered rule 5.402 effective April 1, 2000]. MCR 5.104(C) excludes a petition to appoint a guardian from the unopposed petition procedure of that subrule.

RULE 5.403 PROCEEDINGS ON TEMPORARY GUARDIANSHIP *

(A) Limitation. The court may appoint a temporary guardian only in the course of a proceeding for permanent guardianship.

(B) Notice of Hearing, Minor. For good cause, the court may shorten the period for notice of hearing or may dispense with notice of a hearing for the appointment of a temporary guardian of a minor, except that the minor shall always receive notice if the minor is 14 years of age or older.

(C) Temporary Guardian for Incapacitated Individual Where no Current Appointment; Guardian Ad Litem. For the purpose of an emergency hearing for appointment of a temporary guardian of an alleged incapacitated individual, the court shall appoint a guardian ad litem unless such appointment would cause delay and the alleged incapacitated individual would likely suffer serious harm if immediate action is not taken. The duties of the guardian ad litem are to visit the alleged incapacitated individual, report to the court and take such other action as directed by the court. The requirement of MCL 700.5312(1) that the court hold the fully noticed hearing within 28 days applies only when the court grants temporary relief.

(D) Temporary Guardian for Minor.

(1) *Prior to Appointment of Guardian.* If necessary during proceedings for the appointment of a guardian for a minor, the court may appoint a temporary guardian after a hearing at which testimony is taken. Where a petition for appointment of a limited guardian has been filed, the court, before the appointment of a temporary guardian, shall take into consideration the limited guardianship placement plan in determining the powers and duties of the parties during the temporary guardianship.

(2) *When Guardian Previously Appointed.* If it comes to the attention of the court that a guardian of a minor is not properly performing the duties of a guardian, the court, after a hearing at which testimony is taken, may appoint a temporary guardian for a period not to exceed 6 months. The temporary guardian shall have the authority of the previously appointed guardian whose powers are suspended during the term of the temporary guardianship. The temporary guardian shall determine whether a petition to remove the guardian should be filed. If such a petition is not filed, the temporary guardian shall report to court with recommendations for action that the court should take in order to protect the minor upon expiration of the term of the temporary guardian. The report shall be filed within 1 month of the date of the expiration of the temporary guardianship.

[Formerly Rule 5.763, adopted effective September 1, 1990. Amended effective April 1, 1992; September 1, 1997. Renumbered Rule 5.403 as interim amendment effective April 1, 2000. Amended effective January 1, 2002.]

*The contents of former MCR 5.403 have been moved to MCR 5.143, pursuant to the Supreme Court Orders dated January 14, 2000 and March 24, 2000, with interim effect of April 1, 2000.

Probate Rules Committee Comment to 2000 Amendment

This rule was MCR 5.763 [renumbered rule 5.403 effective April 1, 2000].

RULE 5.404 GUARDIANSHIP OF MINOR

(A) Limited Guardianship.

(1) *Modification of Placement Plan.*

(a) The parties to a limited guardianship placement plan may file a proposed modification of the plan without filing a petition. The proposed modification shall be substantially in the form approved by the state court administrator.

(b) The court shall examine the proposed modified plan and take further action under subrules (c) and (d) within 14 days of the filing of the proposed modified plan.

(c) If the court approves the proposed modified plan, the court shall endorse the modified plan and notify the interested persons of its approval.

(d) If the court does not approve the modification, the court either shall set the proposed modification plan for a hearing or notify the parties of the objections of the court and that they may schedule a hearing or submit another proposed modified plan.

(2) *Limited Guardianship of the Child of a Minor.* On the filing of a petition for appointment of a limited guardian for a child whose parent is an unemancipated minor, the court shall appoint a guardian ad litem to represent the minor parent. A limited guardianship placement plan is not binding on the minor parent until consented to by the guardian ad litem.

(B) Limited Guardianship Placement Plans and Court–Structured Plans.

(1) All limited guardianship placement plans and court-structured plans shall at least include provisions concerning all of the following:

(a) visitation and contact with the minor by the parent or parents sufficient to maintain a parent and child relationship;

(b) the duration of the guardianship;

(c) financial support for the minor; and

(d) in a limited guardianship, the reason why the parent or parents are requesting the court to appoint a limited guardian for the minor.

(2) All limited guardianship placement plans and court-structured plans may include the following:

(a) a schedule of services to be followed by the parent or parents, child, and guardian and

(b) any other provisions that the court deems necessary for the welfare of the child.

(C) Evidence.

(1) *Reports, Admission into Evidence.* At any hearing concerning a guardianship of a minor, all relevant and material evidence, including written reports, may be received by the court and may be relied on to the extent of their probative value, even though such evidence may not be admissible under the Michigan Rules of Evidence.

(2) *Written Reports, Review and Cross–Examination.* Interested persons shall be afforded an opportunity to examine and controvert written reports so received and, in the court's discretion, may be allowed to cross-examine individuals making reports when such individuals are reasonably available.

(3) *Privilege, Abrogation.* No assertion of an evidentiary privilege, other than the privilege between attorney and client, shall prevent the receipt and use of materials prepared pursuant to a court-ordered examination, interview, or course of treatment.

(D) Review of Guardianship for Minor.

(1) *Periodic Review.* The court shall conduct a review of a guardianship of a minor annually in each case where the minor is under age 6 as of the anniversary of the qualification of the guardian. The review shall be commenced within 63 days after the anniversary date of the qualification of the guardian. The court may at any time conduct a review of a guardianship as it deems necessary.

(2) *Investigation.* The court shall appoint the Family Independence Agency or any other person to conduct an investigation of the guardianship of a minor. The investigator shall file a written report with the court within 28 days of such appointment. The report shall include a recommendation regarding whether the guardianship should be continued or modified and whether a hearing should be scheduled. If the report recommends modification, the report shall state the nature of the modification.

(3) *Judicial Action.* After informal review of the report, the court shall enter an order continuing the guardianship or set a date for a hearing to be held within 28 days. If a hearing is set, an attorney may be appointed to represent the minor.

(E) Termination of Guardianship.

(1) *Necessity of Order.* A guardianship may terminate without order of the court on the minor's death, adoption, marriage, or attainment of majority. No full, testamentary, or limited guardianship shall otherwise terminate without an order of the court.

(2) *Continuation of Guardianship.* When a court has continued a guardianship for a period not exceeding one year, the court shall hold the final hearing not less than 28 days before the expiration of the period of continuance.

(3) *Petition for Family Division of Circuit Court to Take Jurisdiction.* If the court appoints an attorney or the Family Independence Agency to investigate whether to file a petition with the family division of circuit court to take jurisdiction of the minor, the attorney or Family Independence Agency shall, within 21 days, report to the court that a petition has been filed or why a petition has not been filed.

(a) If a petition is not filed with the family division, the court shall take such further action as is warranted, except the guardianship may not be continued for more than one year after the hearing on the petition to terminate.

(b) If a petition is filed with the family division, the guardianship shall terminate when the family division authorizes the petition under MCL 712A.11, unless the family division determines that continuation of such guardianship pending disposition is necessary for the well-being of the child.

(4) *Resignation of Limited Guardian.* A petition by a limited guardian to resign shall be treated as a petition for termination of the limited guardianship. The parents or the sole parent with the right to custody may file a petition for a new limited guardianship. If the court does not approve the new limited guardianship or if no petition is filed, the court may proceed in the manner for termination of a guardianship under section 5209 or 5219 of the Estates and Protected Individuals Code, MCL 700.5209 or MCL 700.5219.

(5) *Petition for Termination by a Party Other than a Parent.* If a petition for termination is filed by other than a parent, the court may proceed in the manner for termination of a guardianship under section 5209 of the Estates and Protected Individuals Code, MCL 700.5209.

[Formerly Rule 5.764, adopted effective April 1, 1992. Renumbered Rule 5.404 as interim amendment effective April 1, 2000. Amended effective January 1, 2002; May 1, 2002.]

Probate Rules Committee Comment to 2000 Amendment

This rule was MCR 5.764 [renumbered rule 5.404 effective April 1, 2000].

Staff Comment to 2002 Amendment

The December 18, 2001 amendments, effective May 1, 2002, updated various rules in light of the Estates and Protected Individuals Code (EPIC), MCL 700.1101 *et seq.*, and revisions made to EPIC by 2000 PA 312, 313, and 469.

The staff comment is published only for the benefit of the bench and bar and is not an authoritative construction by the Court.

RULE 5.405　PROCEEDINGS ON GUARDIANSHIP OF INCAPACITATED INDIVIDUAL

(A) Examination by Physician or Mental Health Professional.

(1) *Admission of Report.* The court may receive into evidence without testimony a written report of a physician or mental health professional who examined an individual alleged to be incapacitated, provided that a copy of the report is filed with the court five days before the hearing and that the report is substantially in the form required by the state court administrator. A party offering a report must promptly inform the parties that the report is filed and available. The court may issue on its own initiative, or any party may secure, a subpoena to compel the preparer of the report to testify.

(2) *Abrogation of Privilege.* A report ordered by the court may be used in guardianship proceedings without regard to any privilege. Any privilege regarding a report made as part of an independent evaluation at the request of a respondent is waived if the respondent seeks to have the report considered in the proceedings.

(3) *Determination of Fee.* As a condition of receiving payment, the physician or mental health professional shall submit an itemized statement of services and expenses for approval. In reviewing a statement, the court shall consider the time required for examination, evaluation, preparation of reports and court appearances; the examiner's experience and training; and the local fee for similar services.

(B) Hearings at Site Other Than Courtroom. When hearings are not held in the courtroom where the court ordinarily sits, the court shall ensure a quiet and dignified setting that permits an undisturbed proceeding and inspires the participants' confidence in the integrity of the judicial process.

(C) Guardian of Incapacitated Individual Appointed by Will or Other Writing.

(1) *Appointment.* A guardian appointed by will or other writing under MCL 700.5301 may qualify after the death or adjudicated incapacity of a parent or spouse who had been the guardian of an incapacitated individual by filing an acceptance of appointment with the court that has jurisdiction over the guardianship . Unless the court finds the person unsuitable or incompetent for the trust, the court shall issue to the nominated guardian letters of guardianship equivalent to those that had been issued to the deceased guardian.

(2) *Notice, Revocation.* The testamentary guardian shall notify the court in which the testamentary instrument has been or will be filed of the appointment as guardian. The probating court shall notify the court having jurisdiction over the guardianship if the will is denied probate, and the court having the guardianship jurisdiction shall immediately revoke the letters of guardianship.

[Formerly Rule 5.765, adopted effective September 1, 1990. Renumbered Rule 5.405 as interim amendment effective April 1, 2000. Amended effective January 1, 2002.]

Probate Rules Committee Comment to 2000 Amendment

This rule was MCR 5.765 [renumbered rule 5.405 effective April 1, 2000].

Probate Rules Committee Comment to 2002 Amendment

This rule was MCR 5.765. Subrule (C) is changed [effective January 1, 2002] to reflect the nomination of a guardian by a writing other than a will in MCL 700.5301. If there is a difference between the court designated by the rule for filing the acceptance of appointment and that designated by the statute, the nominated guardian should file in both courts.

RULE 5.406 TESTAMENTARY GUARDIAN OF INDIVIDUAL WITH DEVELOPMENTAL DISABILITIES

(A) Appointment. If the court has not appointed a standby guardian, a testamentary guardian may qualify after the death of a parent who had been the guardian of an individual with developmental disabilities by filing an acceptance of appointment with the court that appointed the deceased parent as guardian. If the nominated person is to act as guardian of the estate of the ward, the guardian should also file a bond in the amount last required of the deceased guardian. Unless the court finds the person unsuitable or incompetent for the appointment, the court shall issue to the testamentary guardian letters of authority equivalent to those that had been issued to the deceased guardian.

(B) Notice, Revocation. The testamentary guardian must notify the court in which the testamentary instrument has been or will be filed of the appointment as guardian. The probating court shall notify the court having jurisdiction over the guardianship if the will is denied probate, and the court having the guardianship jurisdiction shall immediately revoke the letters of authority.

[Formerly Rule 5.766, adopted effective September 1, 1990. Renumbered Rule 5.406 as interim amendment effective April 1, 2000. Amended effective January 1, 2002.]

Probate Rules Committee Comment to 2000 Amendment

This rule was MCR 5.766 [renumbered rule 5.406 effective April 1, 2000].

RULE 5.407 CONSERVATORSHIP; SETTLEMENTS

A conservator may not enter into a settlement in any court on behalf of the protected person if the conservator will share in the settlement unless a guardian ad litem has been appointed to represent the protected person's interest and has consented to such settlement in writing or on the record or the court approves the settlement over any objection.

[Formerly Rule 5.767, adopted effective September 1, 1990. Amended effective September 1, 1997. Renumbered Rule 5.407 as interim amendment effective April 1, 2000. Amended effective May 1, 2002.]

Probate Rules Committee Comment to 2000 Amendment

This rule was MCR 5.767 [renumbered rule 5.407 effective April 1, 2000].

Staff Comment to 2002 Amendment

The December 18, 2001 amendments, effective May 1, 2002, updated various rules in light of the Estates and Protected Individuals Code (EPIC), MCL 700.1101 *et seq.*, and revisions made to EPIC by 2000 PA 312, 313, and 469.

The staff comment is published only for the benefit of the bench and bar and is not an authoritative construction by the Court.

RULE 5.408 REVIEW AND MODIFICATION OF GUARDIANSHIPS OF LEGALLY INCAPACITATED INDIVIDUALS

(A) Periodic Review of Guardianship.

(1) *Periodic Review.* The court shall commence a review of a guardianship of a legally incapacitated individual not later than 1 year after the appointment of the guardian and not later than every 3 years thereafter.

(2) *Investigation.* The court shall appoint a person to investigate the guardianship and report to the court by a date set by the court. The person appointed must visit the legally incapacitated individual or include in the report to the court an explanation why a visit was not practical. The report shall include a recommendation on whether the guardianship should be modified.

(3) *Judicial Action.* After informal review of the report, the court shall enter an order continuing the guardianship, or enter an order appointing an attorney to represent the legally incapacitated individual for the purpose of filing a petition for modification of guardianship. In either case, the court shall send a copy of the report and the order to the legally incapacitated individual and the guardian.

(4) *Petition for Modification.* If an attorney is appointed under subrule (A)(3), the attorney shall file proper pleadings with the court within 14 days of the date of appointment.

(B) Petition for Modification; Appointment of Attorney or Guardian Ad Litem.

(1) *Petition by Legally Incapacitated Individual.* If a petition for modification or written request for modification comes from the legally incapacitated individual and that individual does not have an attorney, the court shall immediately appoint an attorney.

(2) *Petition by Person Other Than Legally Incapacitated Individual.* If a petition for modification or written request for modification comes from some other party, the court shall appoint a guardian ad litem. If the guardian ad litem ascertains that the legally incapacitated individual contests the relief requested, the court shall appoint an attorney for the legally incapacitated individual and terminate the appointment of the guardian ad litem.

[Formerly Rule 5.768, adopted effective September 1, 1990. Renumbered Rule 5.408 as interim amendment effective April 1, 2000. Amended effective January 1, 2002.]

Probate Rules Committee Comment to 2000 Amendment

This rule was MCR 5.768 [renumbered rule 5.408 effective April 1, 2000].

RULE 5.409 REPORT OF GUARDIAN; INVENTORIES AND ACCOUNTS OF CONSERVATORS

(A) Reports. A guardian shall file a written report annually within 56 days after the anniversary of appointment and at other times as the court may order. Reports must be substantially in the form approved by the state court administrator. The guardian must serve the report on the persons listed in MCR 5.125(C)(23).

(B) Inventories.

(1) *Guardian.* At the time of appointing a guardian, the court shall determine whether there would be sufficient assets under the control of the guardian to require the guardian to file an inventory. If the court determines that there are sufficient assets, the court shall order the guardian to file an inventory.

(2) *Filing and Service.* Within 56 days after appointment, a conservator or, if ordered to do so, a guardian shall file with the court a verified inventory of the estate of the protected person, serve copies on the persons required by law or court rule to be served, and file proof of service with the court.

(C) Accounts.

(1) *Filing, Service.* A conservator must file an annual account unless ordered not to by the court. A guardian must file an annual account if ordered by the court. The copy of the account served on interested persons must include a notice that any objections to the account should be filed with the court and noticed for hearing. When required, an accounting must be filed within 56 days after the end of the accounting period.

(2) *Accounting Period.* The accounting period ends on the anniversary date of the issuance of the letters of authority, unless the conservator selects another accounting period or unless the court orders otherwise. If the conservator selects another accounting period, notice of that selection shall be filed with the court. The accounting period may be a calendar year or a fiscal year ending on the last day of a month. The conservator may use the same accounting period as that used for income tax reporting, and the first accounting period may be less than a year but not longer than a year.

(3) *Hearing.* On filing, the account may be set for hearing or the hearing may be deferred to a later time.

(4) *Exception, Conservatorship of Minor.* Unless otherwise ordered by the court, no accounting is required in a minor conservatorship where the assets are restricted or in a conservatorship where no assets have been received by the conservator.

(5) *Contents.* The accounting is subject to the provisions of MCR 5.310(C)(2)(c) and (d), except that references to a personal representative shall be to a conservator.

(6) *Periodic Review.* Unless accounts have been allowed, the court shall review the accounts no less often than once every three years.

(D) Service and Notice. A copy of the account must be sent to the interested persons as provided by these rules. Notice of hearing to approve the account must be given to interested persons as provided in subchapter 5.100 of these rules.

(E) Procedures. The procedures prescribed in MCR 5.203, 5.204 and 5.310(E) apply to guardianship and conservatorship proceedings, except that references to a personal representative shall be to a guardian or conservator, as the situation dictates.

(F) Death of Ward. If an individual who is subject to a guardianship or conservatorship dies, the guardian or conservator must give written notification to the court within 14 days of the individual's date of death. If accounts are required to be filed with the court, a final account must be filed within 56 days of the date of death.

[Formerly Rule 5.769, adopted effective September 1, 1990. Amended effective February 1, 1995. Renumbered Rule 5.409 as interim amendment effective April 1, 2000. Amended effective January 1, 2002; May 1, 2002.]

Probate Rules Committee Comment to 2000 Amendment

This rule was MCR 5.769 [renumbered rule 5.409 effective April 1, 2000]. Subrule (C) is amended to reflect that MCL 700.5418; MSA 27.15418 requires annual accounting. Two exceptions are added for situations where no purpose would be served by an accounting.

Probate Rules Committee Comment to 2002 Amendment

This rule was MCR 5.769. Subrule (C) is amended to reflect that MCL 700.5418 requires annual accounting. Two exceptions are added in subrule (C)(4) for situations where no purpose would be served by an accounting. New subrule (C)(6) [effective January 1, 2002] requires court review of accounts no less often than once every three years. The scope of the review is not defined, so as to allow the court flexibility in choosing among methods such as staff review, appointment of a guardian ad litem and other methods which may be appropriate for specific files. However, minimum levels of review should be consistent with standards to be set by the State Court Administrator.

Staff Comment to 2002 Amendment

The December 18, 2001 amendments, effective May 1, 2002, updated various rules in light of the Estates and Protected Individuals Code (EPIC), MCL 700.1101 *et seq.*, and revisions made to EPIC by 2000 PA 312, 313, and 469.

The staff comment is published only for the benefit of the bench and bar and is not an authoritative construction by the Court.

SUBCHAPTER 5.500   TRUST PROCEEDINGS

RULE 5.501   TRUST PROCEEDINGS IN GENERAL *

(A) Applicability. This subchapter applies to all trusts as defined in MCL 700.1107(m), including a trust established under a will and a trust created by court order or a separate document.

(B) Unsupervised Administration of Trusts. Unless an interested person invokes court jurisdiction, the administration of a trust shall proceed expeditiously, consistent with the terms of the trust, free of judicial intervention and without court order, approval, or other court action. Neither registration nor a proceeding concerning a trust results in continued supervisory proceedings.

(C) Commencement of Trust Proceedings. A proceeding concerning a trust is commenced by filing a petition in the court where the trust is or could be properly registered. Registration of the trust is not required for filing a petition.

(D) Appointment of Trustee not Named in Creating Document. An interested person may petition the court for appointment of a trustee when the order, will, or other document creating a trust does not name a trustee or when the person named in the creating document is either not available or cannot be qualified as trustee. The petitioner must give notice of hearing on the petition to the interested persons. The court may issue an order appointing as trustee the person nominated in the petition or another person. The order must state whether the trustee must file a bond or execute an acceptance.

(E) Qualification of Trustee. A trustee appointed by an order of the court, nominated as a trustee in a will that has been admitted to probate or nominated as a successor in a document other than a will that created a trust shall qualify by executing an acceptance indicating the nominee's willingness to serve. The trustee must serve the acceptance and order, if any, on the then known current trust beneficiaries and, in the case of a testamentary trustee, on the personal representative of the decedent estate, if one has been appointed. No letters of trusteeship shall be issued by the court. The trustee or the attorney for the trustee may establish the trustee's incumbency by executing an affidavit to that effect, identifying the trustee and the trust document and indicating that any required bond has been filed with the court and is in force.

(F) Transitional Rule. A trustee of a trust under the jurisdiction of the court before April 1, 2000, may request an order of the court closing court supervision and the file. On request by the trustee or on its own initiative, the court may order the closing of supervision of the trust and close the file. The trustee must give notice of the order to all current trust beneficiaries. Closing supervision does not preclude any interested trust beneficiary from later petitioning the court for supervision. Without regard to whether the court file is closed, all letters of authority for existing trusts are canceled as of April 1, 2000, and the trustee's incumbency may be established in the manner provided in subrule (E).

[Interim adoption effective April 1, 2000. Amended effective January 1, 2002; May 1, 2002.]

   * The contents of former MCR 5.501 have been moved to MCR 5.151, pursuant to the Supreme Court Orders dated January 14, 2000 and March 24, 2000, with interim effect of April 1, 2000.

2000 Probate Rules Committee Comment

This rule is new [effective April 1, 2000]. The Estates and Protected Individuals Code provides that courts do not generally supervise trusts. MCL 700.7201(2). Subrule (F) applies to trusts under court supervision as of April 1, 2000, including those under former MCR 5.722(E).

Staff Comment to 2002 Amendment

The December 18, 2001 amendments, effective May 1, 2002, updated various rules in light of the Estates and Protected Individuals Code (EPIC), MCL 700.1101 *et seq.*, and revisions made to EPIC by 2000 PA 312, 313, and 469.

The staff comment is published only for the benefit of the bench and bar and is not an authoritative construction by the Court.

RULE 5.502 SUPERVISION OF TRUSTS

If, during a trust proceeding, the court orders supervision of the trust, the court shall specify the terms of the supervision.

[Interim adoption effective April 1, 2000.]

2000 Probate Rules Committee Comment

This rule is new [effective April 1, 2000].

RULE 5.503 NOTICE TO CREDITORS BY TRUSTEE OF REVOCABLE INTER VIVOS TRUST

(A) Place of Publication, Proof. A notice that must be published under MCL 700.7504 must be published in a newspaper as defined by MCR 2.106(F) in the county in which the settlor was domiciled at the time of death. No proof of publication need be filed in connection with unsupervised administration of a trust.

(B) When Notice is not Required. The trustee of a revocable inter vivos trust is not required to give notice to creditors in the following situations:

(1) The costs of trust administration equal or exceed the value of the trust estate, or

(2) The settlor has been dead for more that 3 years.

[Interim adoption effective April 1, 2000. Amended effective May 1, 2002.]

2000 Probate Rules Committee Comment

This rule is new [effective April 1, 2000]. The provisions on when a trustee of a revocable inter vivos trust must give notice to creditors are found at MCL 700.7504.

Staff Comment to 2002 Amendment

The December 18, 2001 amendments, effective May 1, 2002, updated various rules in light of the Estates and Protected Individuals Code (EPIC), MCL 700.1101 *et seq.*, and revisions made to EPIC by 2000 PA 312, 313, and 469.

The staff comment is published only for the benefit of the bench and bar and is not an authoritative construction by the Court.

RULE 5.505 TRIAL OF CLAIMS AGAINST ESTATES [DELETED]

[Deleted effective February 1, 1995.]

1995 Staff Comment

Consolidation and severance of claims will be handled under the rules applicable to civil cases.

RULE 5.508 JURY TRIAL OF RIGHT IN CONTESTED PROCEEDINGS [RENUMBERED] *

[Renumbered effective April 1, 2000.]

   * MCR 5.508 was renumbered pursuant to the Supreme Court Orders dated January 14, 2000 and March 24, 2000, with interim effect of April 1, 2000. The contents of MCR 5.508 have been moved to MCR 5.158. See the Probate Rules Committee Comment preceding Subchapter 5.000, ante.

RULE 5.510 JUROR PERSONAL HISTORY QUESTIONNAIRE [DELETED]

[Deleted effective February 1, 1995.]

1995 Staff Comment

MCR 5.510 is deleted. The topic is governed by MCR 2.510.

RULE 5.512 VERDICT IN COMMITMENT PROCEEDINGS [DELETED]

[Deleted effective February 1, 1995.]

1995 Staff Comment

This rule has been moved to MCR 5.740(C).

SUBCHAPTER 5.600   JUDGMENTS AND ORDERS IN PROCEEDINGS

RULE 5.602   FORM AND SIGNING OF JUDGMENTS AND ORDERS [RENUMBERED] *

[Renumbered effective April 1, 2000.]

* MCR 5.602 was renumbered pursuant to the Supreme Court Orders dated January 14, 2000 and March 24, 2000, with interim effect of April 1, 2000. The contents of MCR 5.602 have been moved to MCR 5.162. See the Probate Rules Committee Comment preceding Subchapter 5.000, ante.

SUBCHAPTER 5.700   PROCEEDINGS IN DECEDENTS' ESTATES

RULE 5.701   APPLICATION; DEFINITION [RENUMBERED] *

[Renumbered effective April 1, 2000.]

* MCR 5.701 was renumbered pursuant to the Supreme Court Orders dated January 14, 2000 and March 24, 2000, with interim effect of April 1, 2000. The contents of MCR 5.701 have been moved to MCR 5.301. See the Probate Rules Committee Comment preceding Subchapter 5.000, ante.

RULE 5.702   COMMENCEMENT OF ESTATE PROCEEDINGS; TEMPORARY PERSONAL REPRESENTATIVE [REPEALED] *

[Repealed effective April 1, 2000.]

* MCR 5.702 was repealed pursuant to the Supreme Court Orders dated January 14, 2000 and March 24, 2000, with interim effect of April 1, 2000. See the Probate Rules Committee Comment preceding Subchapter 5.000, ante.

RULE 5.703   INITIAL HEARING [REPEALED] *

[Repealed effective April 1, 2000.]

* MCR 5.703 was repealed pursuant to the Supreme Court Orders dated January 14, 2000 and March 24, 2000, with interim effect of April 1, 2000. See the Probate Rules Committee Comment preceding Subchapter 5.000, ante.

RULE 5.704   BOND OF FIDUCIARIES [DELETED]

[Deleted effective February 1, 1995.]

1995 Staff Comment

Former MCR 5.704(A) and (B) are stricken because they needlessly duplicate the provisions of MCL 700.502; MCL 27.5502. Former MCR 5.704(C) is stricken because it is redundant in light of MCR 5.113(A)(1)(c).

RULE 5.705   LETTERS OF AUTHORITY [DELETED]

[Deleted effective February 1, 1995.]

1995 Staff Comment

The provisions of this rule have been moved to new MCR 5.716.

RULE 5.706   PUBLICATION AND CLAIMS [RENUMBERED] *

[Renumbered effective April 1, 2000.]

* MCR 5.706 was renumbered pursuant to the Supreme Court Orders dated January 14, 2000 and March 24, 2000, with interim effect of April 1, 2000. The contents of MCR 5.706 have been moved to MCR 5.306. See the Probate Rules Committee Comment preceding Subchapter 5.000, ante.

RULE 5.707   ADMINISTRATION OF ESTATES; REPORTING REQUIREMENTS; CLOSING [REPEALED] *

[Repealed effective April 1, 2000.]

* MCR 5.707 was repealed pursuant to the Supreme Court Orders dated January 14, 2000 and March 24, 2000, with interim effect of April 1, 2000. See the Probate Rules Committee Comment preceding Subchapter 5.000, ante.

RULE 5.708   DETERMINATION OF HEIRS [REPEALED] *

[Repealed effective April 1, 2000.]

* MCR 5.708 was repealed pursuant to the Supreme Court Orders dated January 14, 2000 and March 24, 2000, with interim effect of April 1, 2000. See the Probate Rules Committee Comment preceding Subchapter 5.000, ante.

RULE 5.709   INDEPENDENT PROBATE [REPEALED] *

[Repealed effective April 1, 2000.]

* MCR 5.709 was repealed pursuant to the Supreme Court Orders dated January 14, 2000 and March 24, 2000, with interim effect of April 1, 2000. See the Probate Rules Committee Comment preceding Subchapter 5.000, ante.

SUBCHAPTER 5.715   PROVISIONS COMMON TO MULTIPLE TYPES OF FIDUCIARIES

RULE 5.715   APPLICATION; DEFINITION [REPEALED] *

[Repealed effective April 1, 2000.]

* MCR 5.715 was repealed pursuant to the Supreme Court Orders dated January 14, 2000 and March 24, 2000, with interim effect of April 1, 2000. See the Probate Rules Committee Comment preceding Subchapter 5.000, ante.

RULE 5.716   LETTERS OF AUTHORITY [RENUMBERED] *

[Renumbered effective April 1, 2000.]

* MCR 5.716 was renumbered pursuant to the Supreme Court Orders dated January 14, 2000 and March 24, 2000, with interim effect of April 1, 2000. The contents of MCR 5.716 have been moved to MCR 5.202. See the Probate Rules Committee Comment preceding Subchapter 5.000, ante.

RULE 5.717   FOLLOW-UP PROCEDURES [RENUMBERED] *

[Renumbered effective April 1, 2000.]

* MCR 5.717 was renumbered pursuant to the Supreme Court Orders dated January 14, 2000 and March 24, 2000, with interim effect of April 1, 2000. The contents of MCR 5.717 have been moved to MCR 5.203. See the Probate Rules Committee Comment preceding Subchapter 5.000, ante.

RULE 5.718   APPOINTMENT OF SPECIAL FIDUCIARY [RENUMBERED] *

[Renumbered effective April 1, 2000.]

* MCR 5.718 was renumbered pursuant to the Supreme Court Orders dated January 14, 2000 and March 24, 2000, with interim effect of April 1, 2000. The contents of MCR 5.718 have been moved to MCR 5.204. See the Probate Rules Committee Comment preceding Subchapter 5.000, ante.

SUBCHAPTER 5.720   TRUST PROCEEDINGS

RULE 5.720   TRUST ESTATES; LETTERS; INVENTORY [REPEAL] *

[Repealed effective April 1, 2000.]

* MCR 5.720 was repealed pursuant to the Supreme Court Orders dated January 14, 2000 and March 24, 2000, with interim effect of April 1, 2000. See the Probate Rules Committee Comment preceding Subchapter 5.000, ante.

RULE 5.721   TRUST ESTATES; COURT APPROVAL OF PROCEEDINGS; HEARINGS; NOTICE [REPEALED] *

[Repealed effective April 1, 2000.]

* MCR 5.721 was repealed pursuant to the Supreme Court Orders dated January 14, 2000 and March 24, 2000, with interim effect of

April 1, 2000. See the Probate Rules Committee Comment preceding Subchapter 5.000, ante.

RULE 5.722   TRUSTEE ACCOUNTING; FOLLOW–UP PROCEDURES [REPEALED] *

[Repealed effective April 1, 2000.]

* MCR 5.722 was repealed pursuant to the Supreme Court Orders dated January 14, 2000 and March 24, 2000, with interim effect of April 1, 2000. See the Probate Rules Committee Comment preceding Subchapter 5.000, ante.

SUBCHAPTER 5.730   MENTAL HEALTH RULES

RULE 5.730   MENTAL HEALTH CODE; APPLICATION

Except as modified by this subchapter, civil admission and discharge proceedings under the Mental Health Code are governed by the rules generally applicable to probate court.

[Effective March 1, 1985; amended effective September 1, 1997.]

1985 Staff Comment

MCR 5.730 is substantially the same as PCR 730.

RULE 5.731   DEFINITIONS [DELETED]

[Deleted effective September 1, 1997.]

1997 Staff Comment

The rule is deleted because the terms no longer reflect current statutory usage.

RULE 5.732   ATTORNEYS

(A) Continuing Appointment of Attorney. The attorney of record must represent the individual in all probate court proceedings under the Mental Health Code until the attorney is discharged by court order or another attorney has filed an appearance on the individual's behalf.

(B) Duties. The attorney must serve as an advocate for the individual's preferred position. If the individual does not express a preference, the attorney must advocate for the position that the attorney believes is in the individual's best interest.

(C) Waiver; Appointment of Guardian Ad Litem.
The individual may waive an attorney only in open
court and after consultation with an attorney. The
court may not accept the waiver if it appears that the
waiver is not voluntarily and understandingly made.
If an attorney is waived, the court may appoint a
guardian ad litem for the individual.

[Effective March 1, 1985; amended effective September 1,
1997.]

1985 Staff Comment

MCR 5.732 is substantially the same as PCR 732.

Staff Comment to 1997 Amendment

Subrule (B)(1) is struck because the topic is covered by
§ 455(2) of the Mental Health Code, MCL 330.1455(2); MSA
14.800(455)(2). Subrule (B) is further amended to require
the attorney to advocate for the disposition that is in the
individual's best interest, if the individual does not express a
preference for a disposition. Former subrule (C) is deleted
as no longer necessary. Former subrule (D) is redesignated
as (C).

RULE 5.733 APPOINTMENT OF INDE-PENDENT EXAMINER; DETERMINA-TION OF FEES AND EXPENSES

(A) Appointment. When an indigent individual requests an independent clinical evaluation, the court
must appoint the physician, psychiatrist, or licensed
psychologist chosen by the individual, unless the person chosen refuses to examine the individual or the
requested appointment would require unreasonable
expense.

(B) Determination of Fee. In its order of appointment, a court must direct the independent examiner to submit an itemized statement of services and
expenses for approval. In reviewing a fee, the court
must consider:

(1) the time required for examination, evaluation,
preparation of reports, and court appearances;

(2) the examiner's experience and training; and

(3) the local fee for similar services.

[Effective March 1, 1985; amended effective September 1,
1997.]

1985 Staff Comment

MCR 5.733 is based on PCR 733.

Language is added in subrule (A) to allow an adjournment
of up to 7 days when the demand for an independent medical
examination is made less than 7 days before the hearing.

Staff Comment to 1997 Amendment

The final sentence of subrule (A) has been deleted. See
MCL 330.1462; MSA 14.800(462), as amended by 1995 PA
290.

RULE 5.734 SERVICE OF PAPERS; NOTICE OF SUBSEQUENT PETITIONS; TIME FOR SERVICE

(A) Service of Papers. When required by the
Mental Health Code, the court must have the necessary papers served. The individual must be served
personally. The individual's attorney also must be
served.

(B) Notice of Subsequent Petitions. The court
must serve a copy of a petition for the second or
continuing order of involuntary mental health treatment or petition for discharge and the notice of hearing on all persons required to be served with notice of
hearing on the initial petition or application for hospitalization .

(C) Time for Service.

(1) A notice of hearing must be served on the
individual and the individual's attorney

(a) at least 2 days before the time of a hearing
that is scheduled by the court to be held within 7
days or less; or

(b) at least 5 days before the time scheduled for
other hearings.

(2) A notice of hearing must be served on other
interested parties

(a) by personal service, at least 2 days before the
time of a hearing that is scheduled by the court to
be held within 7 days or less; or

(b) by personal service or by mail, at least 5 days
before the time scheduled for other hearings.

The court may permit service of a notice of hearing
on the individual , the individual's attorney, or other
interested parties within a shorter period of time with
the consent of the individual and the individual's attorney.

[Effective March 1, 1985; amended effective September 1,
1997.]

1985 Staff Comment

MCR 5.734 is substantially the same as PCR 734.

Staff Comment to 1997 Amendment

Former subrule (C) is struck as redundant to subchapter
5.100. Former subrule (D) is redesignated as (C).

RULE 5.735 ADJOURNMENT

A hearing may be adjourned only for good cause.
The reason for an adjournment must be submitted in
writing to the court and to the opposing attorney or
stated on the record.

[Effective March 1, 1985.]

1985 Staff Comment

MCR 5.735 is substantially the same as PCR 735.

RULE 5.736   PRESENCE AT HEARINGS; WAIVER; EXCLUSION [DELETED]

[Deleted effective September 1, 1997.]

1997 Staff Comment

The rule is struck because its topic is covered in § 455(1) of the Mental Health Code, MCL 330.1455(1); MSA 14.800(455)(1).

RULE 5.737   WAIVER OF RIGHTS

Unless a statute or court rule requires that a waiver be made by the individual personally and on the record, a waiver may be in writing signed by the individual, witnessed by the individual's attorney, and filed with the court.

[Effective March 1, 1985; amended effective September 1, 1997.]

1985 Staff Comment

MCR 5.737 corresponds to PCR 737, although it is written from a different perspective. The former rule said that where a statute or rule requires a specific waiver, the respondent is to waive the rights personally and on the record. MCR 5.737 says that unless a particular provision requires a special kind of waiver, rights can be waived in a writing signed by the respondent and witnessed by the respondent's attorney.

RULE 5.738   CONDITIONS AT HEARINGS

(A) Hearings at Hospitals. When hearings are not held in the courtroom where the court ordinarily sits, the court shall ensure a quiet and dignified setting that permits an undisturbed proceeding and inspires the participants' confidence in the integrity of the judicial process.

(B) Clothing. The individual may attend a hearing in personal clothing.

(C) Restraints at Hearing. At a court hearing, the individual may not be handcuffed or otherwise restrained, except

(1) on the prior approval of the court, based on the individual's immediate past conduct indicating the individual is reasonably likely to try to escape or to inflict physical harm on himself or herself or others; or

(2) after an incident occurring during transportation in which the individual has attempted to escape or inflict physical harm on himself or herself or others.

[Effective March 1, 1985; amended effective September 1, 1997.]

1985 Staff Comment

MCR 5.738 is substantially the same as PCR 738.

RULE 5.739   PRELIMINARY HEARINGS [DELETED]

[Deleted effective September 1, 1997.]

1997 Staff Comment

The rule is struck as unnecessary because the Legislature repealed former § 450 of the Mental Health Code, former MCL 330.1450; MSA 14.800(450).

RULE 5.740   JURY TRIAL

(A) Persons Permitted to Demand Jury Trial. Notwithstanding MCR 5.158(A), only an individual alleged to be in need of involuntary mental health treatment or an individual with mental retardation alleged to meet the criteria for judicial admission may demand a jury trial in a civil admission proceeding.

(B) Time for Demand. An individual may demand a jury trial any time before testimony is received at the hearing for which the jury is sought.

(C) Verdict in Commitment Proceedings. In proceedings involving possible commitment to a hospital or facility under the Mental Health Code, or to a correctional or training facility under the juvenile code, the jury's verdict must be unanimous.

(D) Fee. A jury fee is not required from a party demanding a jury trial under the Mental Health Code.

[Effective March 1, 1985; amended effective February 1, 1995; September 1, 1997; May 1, 2002.]

1985 Staff Comment

MCR 5.740 is substantially the same as PCR 740.

Staff Comment to 1995 Amendment

Subrule (C) is former MCR 5.512. New subrule (D) is taken from former MCR 5.508(A)(4).

Staff Comment to 1997 Amendment

The last sentence in subrule (B) has been deleted. See MCL 330.1462; MSA 14.800(462), as amended by 1995 PA 290.

Staff Comment to 2002 Amendment

The December 18, 2001 amendments, effective May 1, 2002, updated various rules in light of the Estates and Protected Individuals Code (EPIC), MCL 700.1101 *et seq.*, and revisions made to EPIC by 2000 PA 312, 313, and 469.

The staff comment is published only for the benefit of the bench and bar and is not an authoritative construction by the Court.

RULE 5.741   INQUIRY INTO ADEQUACY OF TREATMENT

(A) Written Report or Testimony Required. Before ordering a course of involuntary mental health treatment or of care and treatment at a center, the court must receive a written report or oral testimony describing the type and extent of treatment that will be provided to the individual and the appropriateness and adequacy of this treatment.

(B) Use of Written Report; Notice. The court may receive a written report in evidence without accompanying testimony if a copy is filed with the court before the hearing. At the time of filing the report with the court, the preparer of the report must promptly provide the individual's attorney with a copy of the report. The attorney may subpoena the preparer of the report to testify.

[Effective March 1, 1985; amended effective September 1, 1997.]

1985 Staff Comment

MCR 5.741 is substantially the same as PCR 741.

Staff Comment to 1997 Amendment

Subrule (B) is amended [effective September 1, 1997] to require the preparer of the report to serve it on the individual's attorney. Subrule (C) is deleted.

RULE 5.742 OBJECTIONS TO FORMAL VOLUNTARY OR ADMINISTRATIVE ADMISSIONS [DELETED]

[Deleted effective September 1, 1997.]

1997 Staff Comment

This rule is struck because the material is covered in statute. See MCL 330.1469a; MSA 14.800(469a) and MCL 330.1511; MSA 14.800(511).

RULE 5.743 APPEAL BY INDIVIDUAL RECEIVING INVOLUNTARY MENTAL HEALTH TREATMENT WHO IS RETURNED TO HOSPITAL AFTER AUTHORIZED LEAVE

(A) Applicability. This rule applies to an individual receiving involuntary mental health treatment who has been returned to a hospital following an authorized leave.

(B) Notifications. When an individual receiving involuntary mental health treatment has been returned to a hospital from an authorized leave in excess of 10 days, the director of the hospital must, within 24 hours, notify the court of the return and notify the individual of the right to appeal the return and have a hearing to determine the appeal. The court must notify the individual's attorney or appoint a new attorney to consult with the individual and determine whether the individual desires a hearing.

(C) Request and Time for Hearing. An individual who wishes to appeal must request a hearing in writing within 7 days of the notice to the individual under subrule (B). The court must schedule a requested hearing to be held within 7 days of the court's receipt of the request.

(D) Reports Filed With Court. At least 3 days before the hearing, the director of the hospital must deliver to the court, the individual, and the individual's attorney, copies of a clinical certificate and a current alternative treatment report

(E) Conduct of Hearing. At the hearing, the director of the hospital must show that the individual requires treatment in a hospital. The clinical certificate may be admitted in evidence without accompanying testimony by the preparer. However, the individual's attorney may subpoena the preparer of the clinical certificate to testify.

(F) Order After Hearing. If the court finds that the individual requires treatment at a hospital, it must dismiss the appeal and order the individual returned to the hospital. If the court finds that the director lacked an adequate basis for concluding that the individual requires further treatment in the hospital, it must do one of the following:

(1) order the individual returned to authorized leave status; or

(2) order treatment through an alternative to hospitalization

(a) (if the individual was under an order of hospitalization of up to 60 days), for a period not to exceed the difference between 90 days and the combined time the individual has been hospitalized and on authorized leave status, or

(b) (if the individual was under an order of hospitalization of up to 90 days or under a continuing order), for a period not to exceed the difference between 1 year and the combined time the individual has been hospitalized and on authorized leave status

[Effective March 1, 1985; amended effective September 1, 1997.]

1985 Staff Comment

MCR 5.743 is substantially the same as PCR 743.

Staff Comment to 1997 Amendment

Some terminology is changed throughout the rule to reflect current statutory usage. New subrule (A) specifies the topic of the rule. Subrule (C), formerly (B), is rewritten for clarity. Subrule (D), formerly (C) is modified to require that the court be provided with available, current information for its review of the decision to return the individual to the hospital. Subrules (E) and (F) are modified to eliminate the suggestion that appeal rehears the decision to require involuntary mental health treatment including hospitalization. The appeal only reviews the return of the individual to the hospital for up to the remainder of the period previously authorized. Former subrule (E)(4) is deleted because it referred to individuals with mental retardation, now under MCR 5.743a and 5.743b. Former subrule (F) is deleted because voluntary admissions are no longer subject to return procedures under § 408 of the Mental Health Code, MCL 330.1408; MSA 14.800(408).

RULE 5.743a APPEAL BY ADMINISTRATIVELY ADMITTED INDIVIDUAL RETURNED TO CENTER AFTER AUTHORIZED LEAVE

(A) Applicability. This rule applies to an individual with a developmental disability who was admitted to a center by an administrative admission and who has been returned to a center following an authorized leave.

(B) Notifications. When an administratively admitted individual has been returned to a center from an authorized leave in excess of 10 days, the director of the center must, within 24 hours, notify the court of the return and notify the individual of the right to appeal the return. The court must notify the individual's guardian, if any, and the parents of an individual who is a minor of the return and the right to appeal the return and have a hearing to determine the appeal.

(C) Request for Hearing. An individual who wishes to appeal that individual's return must request a hearing in writing within 7 days of the notice to the individual under subrule (B). If the individual is less than 13 years of age, the request may be made by the individual's parent or guardian. The court must schedule a requested hearing to be held within 7 days of the court's receipt of the request.

(D) Statement Filed With Court. At least 3 days before the hearing, the director of the center must deliver to the court, the individual, the individual's parents or guardian, if applicable, and the individual's attorney a statement setting forth:

(1) the reason for the individual's return to the center;

(2) the reason the individual is believed to need care and treatment at the center; and

(3) the plan for further care and treatment.

(E) Conduct of Hearing. The hearing shall proceed as provided in § 511(4) of the Mental Health Code, MCL 330.1511; MSA 14.800(511). At the hearing, the director of the center must show that the individual needs care and treatment at the center and that no alternative to the care and treatment provided at the center is available and adequate to meet the individual's needs.

(F) Order After Hearing. If the court finds the individual requires care and treatment at the center, it must dismiss the appeal and order the individual to remain at the center. If the court finds the director did not sustain the burden of proof, it must order the individual returned to authorized leave status.

[Adopted effective September 1, 1997.]

1997 Staff Comment

This rule is new. See § 537 of the Mental Health Code, MCL 330.1537; MSA 14.800(537).

RULE 5.743b APPEAL BY JUDICIALLY ADMITTED INDIVIDUAL RETURNED TO CENTER AFTER AUTHORIZED LEAVE

(A) Applicability. This rule applies to an individual with mental retardation who has been admitted to a center by judicial order, and who has been on authorized leave for a continuous period of less than 1 year.

(B) Notifications. When a judicially admitted individual has been returned to a center from an authorized leave in excess of 10 days, the director of the center must, within 24 hours, notify the court of the return and notify the individual of the right to appeal the return and have a hearing to determine the appeal. The court must notify the individual's attorney or appoint a new attorney to consult with the individual and to determine whether the individual desires a hearing.

(C) Request for Hearing. An individual who wishes to appeal the return must request a hearing in writing within 7 days of the notice to the individual under subrule (B). The court must schedule a requested hearing to be held within 7 days of the court's receipt of the request.

(D) Statement Filed With Court. At least 3 days before the hearing, the director of the center must deliver to the court, the individual, and the individual's attorney a statement setting forth:

(1) the reason for the individual's return to the center;

(2) the reason the individual is believed to need care and treatment at the center; and

(3) the plan for further care and treatment.

(E) Report. The court may order an examination of the individual and the preparation and filing with the court of a report that contains such information as the court deems necessary.

(F) Conduct of Hearing. The court shall proceed as provided in § 511(4) of the Mental Health Code, MCL 330.1511(4); MSA 14.800(511)(4). At the hearing, the director of the center must show that the individual needs care and treatment at the center, and that no alternative to the care and treatment provided at the center is available and adequate to meet the individual's needs.

(G) Order After Hearing. If the court finds the individual requires care and treatment at the center, it must dismiss the appeal and order the individual to remain at the center. If the court finds the director did not sustain the burden of proof, it must do one of the following:

(1) order the individual returned to authorized leave status; or

(2) order the individual to undergo a program of care and treatment for up to one year as an alternative to remaining at the center.

[Adopted effective September 1, 1997.]

1997 Staff Comment

This rule is new. See MCL 330.1537; MSA 14.800(537).

RULE 5.744 PROCEEDINGS REGARDING THE MODIFICATION OF AN ORDER THAT PROVIDED FOR AN ALTERNATIVE TREATMENT PROGRAM

(A) Scope of Rule. This rule applies to any proceeding that results in a modification of an order without a hearing and the rights of an individual transferred to a hospital as a result of such a modification.

(B) Notification. The notification requesting an order of hospitalization or of change in an alternative treatment program must be in writing.

(C) Service of Papers. If the court enters a new order without a hearing, the court must serve the individual with a copy of that order. If the order includes hospitalization, the court must also serve the individual with notice of the right to object and demand a hearing.

(D) Objection; Scheduling Hearing. An individual hospitalized without a hearing, either by order of the court or by a psychiatrist's order, may file an objection to the order not later than 7 days after receipt of notice of the right to object. The court must schedule a hearing to be held within 10 days after receiving the objection.

(E) Conduct of Hearing. A hearing convened under this rule is without a jury. At the hearing the party seeking hospitalization of the individual must present evidence that hospitalization is necessary.

[Effective March 1, 1985; amended effective September 1, 1997.]

1985 Staff Comment

MCR 5.744 is substantially the same as PCR 744.

Staff Comment to 1997 Amendment

This rule has been substantially rewritten to reflect the changes in §§ 475 and 475a of the Mental Health Code, MCL 330.1475 and 1475a; MSA 14.800(475) and (475a), that only provide a right to a hearing when the individual is placed in a hospital, not when there is a change in alternate treatment programs. The psychiatrist's order mentioned in subrule (D) is the order of hospitalization found in MCL 330.1474a; MSA 14.800(474a).

RULE 5.744a PROCEEDINGS REGARDING AN INDIVIDUAL SUBJECT TO JUDICIAL ADMISSION WHO IS TRANSFERRED TO A CENTER FROM ALTERNATIVE SETTING

(A) Applicability. This rule applies to an individual with mental retardation under court order to undergo a program of care and treatment as an alternative to admission to a center.

(B) Immediate Transfer. After the court receives written notification concerning the need to transfer a judicially admitted individual receiving alternative care and treatment, the court may direct the filing of additional information and may do one of the following:

(1) modify its original order and direct the individual's transfer to another program of alternative care and treatment for the remainder of the 1–year period;

(2) enter a new order directing the individual's admission to either

    (a) a center recommended by the community mental health services program; or

    (b) a licensed hospital requested by the individual or the individual's family if private funds are to be used; or

(3) set a date for a hearing.

(C) Investigation Report. On receipt of notification, the court must promptly obtain from the community mental health services program or other appropriate agency a report stating

(1) the reason for concern about the adequacy of the care and treatment being received at the time of the notification;

(2) the continued suitability of that care and treatment; and

(3) the adequacy of care and treatment available at another alternative or at a center or licensed hospital.

(D) Service of Papers. If the court enters a new order without a hearing, it must serve the interested parties with a copy of that order and a copy of the investigation report when it becomes available. If the order includes transfer of the individual to a center, the court must also serve the interested parties with written notification of the individual's right to object and demand a hearing.

(E) Hearing. If within 7 days of service under subrule (D) the court receives a written objection from the individual or the individual's attorney, guardian, or presumptive heir, the court must schedule a hearing to be held within 10 days of the court's receipt of the objection.

(F) Conduct of Hearing. A hearing convened under this rule is without a jury. At the hearing, the person seeking transfer of the individual to a center must present evidence that the individual had not complied with the applicable order or that the order is not sufficient to prevent the individual from inflicting harm or injuries on himself, herself or others. The evidence must support a finding that transfer to another alternative, a center or a licensed hospital is necessary.

(G) Order After Hearing. The court may affirm or rescind the order issued under subrule (B), order a new program of care and treatment, or order discharge. The court may not place the individual in a center without inquiring into the adequacy of care and treatment for that individual at that center.

[Adopted effective September 1, 1997.]

1997 Staff Comment

This rule is new. See MCL 330.1519(4); MSA 14.800(519)(4).

RULE 5.745 MULTIPLE PROCEEDINGS

(A) New Proceedings Not Prohibited. The admission of an individual under the Mental Health Code may not be invalidated because the individual is already subject to a court order as a result of a prior admission proceeding.

(B) Procedure. On being informed that an individual is subject to a previous court order, the court must:

(1) if it was the court issuing the previous order, dismiss the new proceeding and determine the proper disposition of the individual under its previous order or vacate the previous order and proceed under the new petition; or

(2) if the previous order was issued by another court, continue the new proceeding and issue an appropriate order. After entry of the order, the court with the new proceeding must consult with the court with the prior proceeding to determine if the best interests of the individual will be served by changing venue of the prior proceeding to the county where the new proceeding has been initiated. If not, the court with the new proceeding must transfer the matter to the other court.

(C) Disposition. The court may treat a petition or certificate filed in connection with the more recent proceeding as "notification" under MCR 5.743 or 5.744 and proceed with disposition under those rules.

[Effective March 1, 1985; amended effective September 1, 1997.]

1985 Staff Comment

MCR 5.745 is substantially the same as PCR 745.

Staff Comment to 1997 Amendment

Subrule (B) is modified [effective September 1, 1997] to make clear that the preference is for the matter to proceed with the court already familiar with the patient, unless it is in the best interest of the patient for a new court to start a new proceeding.

RULE 5.746 PLACEMENT OF INDIVIDUAL WITH A DEVELOPMENTAL DISABILITY IN A FACILITY

(A) Petition for Authorization. If placement in a facility of an individual with a developmental disability has not been authorized or if permission is sought for authorization to place the individual in a more restrictive setting than previously ordered, a guardian of the individual must petition the court for authorization to place the individual in a facility or in a more restricted setting.

(B) Order. If the court grants the petition for authorization, it may order that:

(1) the guardian may execute an application for the individual's administrative admission to a specific center;

(2) the guardian may request the individual's temporary admission to a center for a period not to exceed 30 days for each admission; or

(3) the guardian may place the individual in a specific facility or class of facility as defined in MCL 330.1600; MSA 14.800(600).

(C) Notice of Hearing. Notice of hearing on a petition for authorization to place an individual must be given to those persons required to be served with notice of hearing for the appointment of a guardian.

[Effective March 1, 1985; amended effective September 1, 1997.]

1985 Staff Comment

MCR 5.746 is substantially the same as PCR 746.

Staff Comment to 1997 Amendment

This rule refers to the initial authorization for a guardian to place in any facility an individual with a developmental disability, MCL 330.1623; MSA 14.800(623) and a modification of that authorization, MCL 330.1637; MSA 14.800(637). Subrule (C) refers to the notice required by MCL 330.1614; MSA 14.800(614). Provisions of the former rule which duplicate statutory requirements have been removed.

RULE 5.747 PETITION FOR DISCHARGE OF INDIVIDUAL

At a hearing on a petition for discharge of an individual, the burden is on the person who seeks to prevent discharge to show that the individual is a person requiring treatment.

[Effective March 1, 1985; amended effective September 1, 1997.]

1985 Staff Comment

MCR 5.747 is a new rule, covering the burden of proof with regard to petitions seeking discharge of a patient. See MCL 330.1484, 330.1485; MSA 14.800(484), 14.800(485). The burden is on the person seeking to prevent discharge. See *In re Wagstaff*, 93 MichApp 755 (1979).

RULE 5.748 TRANSITIONAL PROVISION ON TERMINATION OF INDEFINITE ORDERS OF HOSPITALIZATION

If on March 27, 1996, any individual is subject to any order that may result in the individual's hospitalization for a period beyond March 27, 1997, a petition for a determination that the individual continues to require involuntary mental health treatment must be filed on or before the time set for the second periodic review after March 27, 1996. The petition may be for involuntary health treatment for a period of not more than one year. This rule expires on March 28, 1997.

[Adopted effective June 1, 1996.]

1996 Staff Comment

This new provision deals with the effect of §§ 469 and 472 of the Mental Health Code, MCL 330.1469; MSA 14.800(469) and MCL 330.1472; MSA 14.800(472), which limit the term of orders of involuntary treatment to one year. The treatment options are described in §§ 469(11) and 472(3), MCL 330.1469(11); MSA 14.800(469)(11) and MCL 330.1472(3); MSA 14.800(472)(3).

SUBCHAPTER 5.750 ADOPTION

Probate Rules Committee Comment to 2000 Amendment

The proceedings described in this subchapter have been transferred to the exclusive jurisdiction of the family division of the circuit court. However, the subchapter is left in place temporarily until development of rules for family division.

RULE 5.750 APPLICABLE RULES [RENUMBERED]

[Renumbered 3.800, and amended effective May 1, 2002.]

RULE 5.751 PAPERS, EXECUTION [RENUMBERED]

[Renumbered 3.801, effective May 1, 2002.]

RULE 5.752 MANNER AND METHOD OF SERVICE [RENUMBERED]

[Renumbered 3.802, and amended effective May 1, 2002.]

RULE 5.753 FINANCIAL REPORTS, SUBSEQUENT ORDERS [RENUMBERED] *

[Renumbered 3.803, effective May 1, 2002.]

* The contents of former MCR 5.753 have been moved to MCR 5.205(C)(31) pursuant to Supreme Court Order dated June 17, 1997, effective September 1, 1997.

RULE 5.754 CONSENT HEARING [RENUMBERED] *

[Renumbered 3.804, effective May 1, 2002.]

*The contents of former MCR 5.754 have been stricken, pursuant to Supreme Court Order dated June 17, 1997, effective September 1, 1997. For the subject matter of Subrule (A) of former MCR 5.754, see Administrative Order 1995–2. For the subject matter of Subrule (B) of former MCR 5.754, see MCL 710.54(7) and (8).

RULE 5.755 TEMPORARY PLACEMENTS, TIME FOR SERVICE OF NOTICE OF HEARING TO DETERMINE DISPOSITION OF CHILD [RENUMBERED] *

[Renumbered 3.805, effective May 1, 2002.]

* The contents of former MCR 5.755 have been redesignated as MCR 5.756.

RULE 5.756 REHEARINGS [RENUMBERED]

[Renumbered 3.806 effective May 1, 2002.]

SUBCHAPTER 5.760 GUARDIANSHIP, CONSERVATOR-SHIP AND PROTECTIVE ORDER PROCEEDINGS

RULE 5.761 GENERAL PROVISIONS [RENUMBERED] *

[Renumbered effective April 1, 2000.]

* MCR 5.761 was renumbered pursuant to the Supreme Court Orders dated January 14, 2000 and March 24, 2000, with interim effect of April 1, 2000. The contents of MCR 5.761 have been moved to MCR 5.401. See the Probate Rules Committee Comment preceding Subchapter 5.000, ante.

RULE 5.762 COMMON PROVISIONS [RENUMBERED] *

[Renumbered effective April 1, 2000.]

* MCR 5.762 was renumbered pursuant to the Supreme Court Orders dated January 14, 2000 and March 24, 2000, with interim effect of April 1, 2000. The contents of MCR 5.762 have been moved to MCR 5.402. See the Probate Rules Committee Comment preceding Subchapter 5.000, ante.

RULE 5.763 PROCEEDINGS ON TEMPORARY GUARDIANSHIP [RENUMBERED] *

[Renumbered effective April 1, 2000.]

* MCR 5.763 was renumbered pursuant to the Supreme Court Orders dated January 14, 2000 and March 24, 2000, with interim effect of April 1, 2000. The contents of MCR 5.763 have been moved to MCR 5.403. See the Probate Rules Committee Comment preceding Subchapter 5.000, ante.

RULE 5.764 GUARDIANSHIP OF MINOR [RENUMBERED] *

[Renumbered effective April 1, 2000.]

* MCR 5.764 was renumbered pursuant to the Supreme Court Orders dated January 14, 2000 and March 24, 2000, with interim effect of April 1, 2000. The contents of MCR 5.764 have been moved to MCR 5.404. See the Probate Rules Committee Comment preceding Subchapter 5.000, ante.

RULE 5.765 PROCEEDINGS ON GUARDIANSHIP OF LEGALLY INCAPACITATED PERSON [RENUMBERED] *

[Renumbered effective April 1, 2000.]

* MCR 5.765 was renumbered pursuant to the Supreme Court Orders dated January 14, 2000 and March 24, 2000, with interim effect of April 1, 2000. The contents of MCR 5.765 have been moved to MCR 5.405. See the Probate Rules Committee Comment preceding Subchapter 5.000, ante.

RULE 5.766 TESTAMENTARY GUARDIAN OF DEVELOPMENTALLY DISABLED PERSON [RENUMBERED] *

[Renumbered effective April 1, 2000.]

* MCR 5.766 was renumbered pursuant to the Supreme Court Orders dated January 14, 2000 and March 24, 2000, with interim effect of April 1, 2000. The contents of MCR 5.766 have been moved to MCR 5.406. See the Probate Rules Committee Comment preceding Subchapter 5.000, ante.

RULE 5.767 CONSERVATORSHIP; CONFIRMATION OF SALE OF REAL ESTATE SETTLEMENTS [RENUMBERED] *

[Renumbered effective April 1, 2000.]

* MCR 5.767 was renumbered pursuant to the Supreme Court Orders dated January 14, 2000 and March 24, 2000, with interim

effect of April 1, 2000. The contents of MCR 5.767 have been moved to MCR 5.407. See the Probate Rules Committee Comment preceding Subchapter 5.000, ante.

RULE 5.768 REVIEW AND MODIFICATION OF GUARDIANSHIPS OF LEGALLY INCAPACITATED PERSONS [RENUMBERED] *

[Renumbered effective April 1, 2000.]

* MCR 5.768 was renumbered pursuant to the Supreme Court Orders dated January 14, 2000 and March 24, 2000, with interim effect of April 1, 2000. The contents of MCR 5.768 have been moved to MCR 5.408. See the Probate Rules Committee Comment preceding Subchapter 5.000, ante.

RULE 5.769 REPORT OF GUARDIAN; INVENTORIES AND ACCOUNTS OF CONSERVATORS [RENUMBERED] *

[Renumbered effective April 1, 2000.]

* MCR 5.769 was renumbered pursuant to the Supreme Court Orders dated January 14, 2000 and March 24, 2000, with interim effect of April 1, 2000. The contents of MCR 5.769 have been moved to MCR 5.409. See the Probate Rules Committee Comment preceding Subchapter 5.000, ante.

SUBCHAPTER 5.780 MISCELLANEOUS PROCEEDINGS

RULE 5.781 CHANGE OF NAME [RENUMBERED]

[Renumbered 3.613, and amended effective May 1, 2002.]

RULE 5.782 HEALTH THREATS TO OTHERS [RENUMBERED]

[Renumbered 3.614, and amended effective May 1, 2002.]

RULE 5.783 PARENTAL RIGHTS RESTORATION ACT PROCEEDINGS [RENUMBERED]

[Renumbered 3.615, and amended effective May 1, 2002.]

RULE 5.784 PROCEEDINGS ON A DURABLE POWER OF ATTORNEY FOR HEALTH CARE

(A) Petition, Who Shall File. The petition concerning a durable power of attorney for health care must be filed by any interested party or the patient's attending physician.

(B) Venue. Venue for any proceeding concerning a durable power of attorney for health care is proper in the county in which the patient resides or the county where the patient is found.

(C) Notice of Hearing, Service, Manner and Time.

(1) *Manner of Service.* If the address of an interested party is known or can be learned by diligent inquiry, notice must be by mail or personal service, but service by mail must be supplemented by facsimile or telephone contact within the period for timely service when the hearing is an expedited hearing or a hearing on the initial determination regarding whether the patient is unable to participate in medical treatment decisions.

(2) *Waiving Service.* At an expedited hearing or a hearing on an initial determination regarding whether the patient is unable to participate in medical treatment decisions, the court may dispense with notice of the hearing on those interested parties who could not be contacted after diligent effort by the petitioner.

(3) *Time of Service.* Notice of hearing must be served at least 2 days before the time of a hearing on an initial determination regarding whether the patient is unable to participate in medical treatment decisions. Notice of an expedited hearing must be served at such time as directed by the court. Notice of other hearings must be served at such time as directed by MCR 5.108.

(D) Hearings.

(1) *Time.* Hearings on a petition for an initial determination regarding whether a patient is unable

to participate in a medical treatment decision must be held within 7 days of the filing of the petition. The court may order an expedited hearing on any petition concerning a durable power of attorney for health care decisions on a showing of good cause to expedite the proceedings. A showing of good cause to expedite proceedings may be made ex parte.

(2) *Trial.* Disputes concerning durable powers of attorney for health care decisions are tried by the court without a jury.

(3) *Proof.* The petitioner has the burden of proof by a preponderance of evidence on all contested issues except that the standard is by clear and convincing evidence on an issue whether a patient has authorized the patient advocate to decide to withhold or withdraw treatment, which decision could or would result in the patient's death.

(4) *Privilege, Waiver.* The physician-patient privilege must not be asserted.

(E) Temporary Relief. On a sufficient showing of need, the court may issue a temporary restraining order pursuant to MCR 3.310 pending a hearing on any petition concerning a durable power of attorney for health care.

[Adopted effective April 1, 1992.]

1992 Probate Rules Committee Comment

The rule addresses proceedings under § 496 of the Revised Probate Code, MCL 700.496: MSA 27.5496.

SUBCHAPTER 5.800 APPEALS

RULE 5.801 APPEALS TO OTHER COURTS

(A) Right to Appeal. An interested person aggrieved by an order of the probate court may appeal as provided by this rule.

(B) Orders Appealable to Court of Appeals. Orders appealable of right to the Court of Appeals are defined as and limited to the following:

(1) a final order affecting the rights or interests of an interested person in a decedent estate, the estate of a person who has disappeared or is missing, a conservatorship or other protective proceeding, the estate of an individual with developmental disabilities, or an inter vivos or testamentary trust. These are defined as and limited to orders resolving the following matters:

    (a) appointing or removing a personal representative, conservator, or trustee, or denying such an appointment or removal;

    (b) admitting or denying to probate of a will, codicil, or other testamentary instrument;

    (c) interpreting or construing a testamentary instrument or inter vivos trust;

    (d) approving a settlement of a contest relating to an inter vivos trust or a testamentary instrument;

    (e) discharging a surety on a bond from further liability;

    (f) allowing or rejecting claims;

    (g) assigning, selling, leasing, or encumbering any of the assets of an estate or trust;

    (h) authorizing or denying the continuation of a business;

    (i) determining special allowances in a decedent's estate such as a homestead allowance, an exempt property allowance, a family allowance, or right to remain in a dwelling;

    (j) authorizing or denying rights of election;

    (k) determining heirs or devisees;

    (*l*) determining title or claims to property;

    (m) authorizing or denying partition of property;

    (n) authorizing or denying specific performance;

    (*o*) ascertaining survivorship of parties;

    (p) granting or denying a petition to bar a mentally incompetent or minor wife from dower in the property of her living husband;

    (q) granting or denying a petition to determine cy pres;

    (r) directing or denying repayment of distributions;

    (s) determining or denying a constructive trust;

    (t) determining or denying an oral contract relating to a will;

    (u) allowing or disallowing an account, fees, or administration expenses;

    (v) surcharging or refusing to surcharge a fiduciary;

    (w) authorizing federal estate tax apportionment;

    (x) distributing proceeds recovered for wrongful death under MCL 600.2922; MSA 27A.2922;

    (y) determining or directing payment of inheritance taxes;

    (z) assigning residue;

    (aa) granting or denying a petition for instructions;

    (bb) authorizing disclaimers.

(2) other appeals as may be hereafter provided by statute.

(C) Final Orders Appealable to Circuit Court. All final orders not enumerated in subrule (B) are appealable of right to the circuit court. These include, but are not limited to:

(1) a final order affecting the rights and interests of an adult or a minor in a guardianship proceeding;

(2) a final order affecting the rights or interests of a person under the Mental Health Code, except for a final order affecting the rights or interests of a person in the estate of an individual with developmental disabilities.

(D) Interlocutory Orders. An interlocutory order, such as an order regarding discovery; ruling on evidence; appointing a guardian ad litem; or suspending a fiduciary for failure to give a new bond, to file an inventory, or to render an account, may be appealed only to the circuit court and only by leave of that court. The circuit court shall pay particular attention to an application for leave to appeal an interlocutory order if the probate court has certified that the order involves a controlling question of law as to which there is substantial ground for difference of opinion and that an immediate appeal may materially advance the termination of the litigation.

(E) Transfer of Appeals From Court of Appeals to Circuit Court. If an appeal of right within the jurisdiction of the circuit court is filed in the Court of Appeals, the Court of Appeals may transfer the appeal to the circuit court, which shall hear the appeal as if it had been filed in the circuit court.

(F) Appeals to Court of Appeals on Certification by Probate Court. Instead of appealing to the circuit court, a party may appeal directly to the Court of Appeals if the probate court certifies that the order involves a controlling question of law as to which there is substantial ground for difference of opinion and that an appeal directly to the Court of Appeals may materially advance the ultimate termination of the litigation. An appeal to the Court of Appeals under this subrule is by leave only under the provisions of MCR 7.205. In lieu of granting leave to appeal, the Court

of Appeals may remand the appeal to the circuit court for consideration as on leave granted.

[Effective March 1, 1985. Interim amendment effective April 1, 2000.]

1985 Staff Comment

MCR 5.801 is substantially the same as PCR 801.

A new category of final order appealable to the Court of Appeals is added to subrule 5.801(B)(3): an order surcharging or refusing to surcharge a fiduciary.

RULE 5.802   APPELLATE PROCEDURE; STAYS PENDING APPEAL

(A) Procedure. Except as modified by this subchapter, chapter 7 of these rules governs appeals from the probate court.

(B) Record.

(1) An appeal from the probate court is on the papers filed and a written transcript of the proceedings in the probate court or on a record settled and agreed to by the parties and approved by the court. The appeal is not de novo.

(2) The probate register may transmit certified copies of the necessary documents and papers in the file if the original papers are needed for further proceedings in the probate court. The parties shall not be required to pay for the copies as costs or otherwise.

(C) Stays Pending Appeals. An order removing a fiduciary; appointing a special personal representative or a special fiduciary; granting a new trial or rehearing; granting an allowance to the spouse or children of a decedent; granting permission to sue on a fiduciary's bond; or suspending a fiduciary and appointing a special fiduciary, is not stayed pending appeal unless ordered by the court on motion for good cause.

[Effective March 1, 1985. Interim amendment effective April 1, 2000. Amended effective January 1, 2002.]

1985 Staff Comment

MCR 5.802 is comparable to PCR 802.

Subrule (B)(2) includes a new provision prohibiting the charging of fees to the parties when certified copies of documents are sent to the appellate court in lieu of the originals as part of the record on appeal.

SUBCHAPTER 5.900   PROCEEDINGS IN THE JUVENILE DIVISION

RULE 5.901   APPLICABILITY OF RULES

(A) Scope. The rules in this subchapter, in subchapter 1.100 and in rule 5.113, govern practice and procedure in the family division of the circuit court in all cases filed under the Juvenile Code. Other Michigan Court Rules apply to such juvenile cases in the family division of the circuit court only when this subchapter specifically provides.

(B) Application. Unless the context otherwise indicates:

(1) MCR 5.901–5.927, 5.980 and 5.991–5.993 apply to delinquency proceedings and child protective proceedings;

(2) MCR 5.931–5.950 apply only to delinquency proceedings;

(3) MCR 5.951–5.956 apply only to designated proceedings;

(4) MCR 5.961–5.974 apply only to child protective proceedings;

(5) MCR 5.981–5.989 apply only to minor personal protection order proceedings.

[Adopted effective January 1, 1988; amended effective May 15, 1997; January 1, 1998; November 30, 1999; January 10, 2000.]

[See 1988 Staff Comment following Rule 5.993.]

Staff Comment to 1997 Amendment

The April 8, 1997, amendments of subchapter 5.900 of the Michigan Court Rules [effective May 15, 1997] implement recent statutory changes applicable to the juvenile division of the probate court. See, e.g., 1996 PA 247, 1996 PA 248, 1996 PA 255, 1996 PA 259, and 1996 PA 262. The amendments are based on proposals submitted by the Juvenile Court Rules Committee of the Probate Judges Association. These temporary amendments will remain in effect until further order of the court, and will be reconsidered after receipt of comments.

Staff Comment to 1998 Amendment

The December 19, 1997, amendments to Rule 3.206 and subchapter 5.900 of the Michigan Court Rules [effective January 1, 1998] implement recent statutory changes which have created a family division of the circuit court. These amendments will remain in effect until further order of the court.

Staff Comment to November 1999 Amendment

The amendments of MCR 2.113, 5.113, 5.901, 7.210, 8.105, 8.110, 8.116, 8.203, 8.205, and 8.302 [effective November 30, 1999] and the addition of MCR 2.518 and 8.119 [effective November 30, 1999] are to accommodate statewide records standards applicable to all courts and all clerks of the courts as developed and recommended by the Michigan Trial Court Case File Management Standards Committee.

Staff Comment to December 1999 Amendment

These rules [effective January 10, 2000] clarify the procedure applicable to the new minor personal protection orders ("minor PPOs") created in 1998 PA 474–477, which went into effect March 1, 1999. Because the new statutes do not make clear whether existing PPO procedural rules apply or rules for Juvenile Code proceedings apply, these rules are promulgated to assure consistency in the processing of minor PPOs in Michigan's Circuit Court Family Divisions. Immediate adoption has been ordered to provide needed procedural guidance for courts already facing minor PPO cases.

RULE 5.902   CONSTRUCTION

(A) **In General.** The rules are to be construed to secure fairness, flexibility, and simplicity. The court shall proceed in a manner that safeguards the rights and proper interests of the parties. Limitations on corrections of error are governed by MCR 2.613.

(B) **Philosophy.** The rules must be interpreted and applied in keeping with the philosophy expressed in the Juvenile Code. The court shall ensure that each minor coming within the jurisdiction of the court shall:

(1) receive the care, guidance, and control, preferably in the minor's own home, that is conducive to the minor's welfare and the best interests of the public; and

(2) when removed from parental control, be placed in care as nearly as possible equivalent to the care that the minor's parents should have given the minor.

[Adopted effective January 1, 1988; amended effective April 1, 1989.]

[See "1988 Staff Comment" and "Staff Comment to April 1, 1989 Amendments," set forth following Rule 5.993.]

RULE 5.903   DEFINITIONS

(A) **General Definitions.** When used in this subchapter, unless the context otherwise indicates:

(1) "Child born out of wedlock" means a child conceived and born to a woman who is unmarried from the conception to the birth of the child, or a child determined by judicial notice or otherwise to have been conceived or born during a marriage but who is not the issue of that marriage.

(2) "Child protective proceeding" means a proceeding concerning an offense against a child.

(3) "Delinquency proceeding" means a proceeding concerning an offense by a juvenile.

(4) "Father" means:

(a) a man married to the mother at any time from a minor's conception to the minor's birth unless the minor is determined to be a child born out of wedlock;

(b) a man who legally adopts the minor;

(c) a man who was named on a Michigan birth certificate for a minor born after July 20, 1993, as provided by MCL 333.21532; MSA 14.15(21532); or

(d) a man whose paternity is established in one of the following ways within time limits, when applicable, set by the court pursuant to this subchapter:

(i) the man and the mother of the minor acknowledge that he is the minor's father by completing and filing an acknowledgement of paternity. The man and mother shall each sign the acknowledgement of paternity in the presence of 2 witnesses, who shall also sign the acknowledgement, and in the presence of a judge, clerk of the court, or notary public appointed in this state. The acknowledgement shall be filed at either the time of birth or another time during the child's lifetime with the probate court in the mother's county of residence or, if the mother is not a resident of this state when the acknowledgement is executed, in the county of the child's birth.

(ii) the man and the mother file a joint written request for a correction of the certificate of birth pertaining to the minor that results in issuance of a substituted certificate recording the birth;

(iii) the man acknowledges that he is the minor's father by completing and filing an acknowledgement of paternity, without the mother joining in the acknowledgment if she is disqualified from signing the acknowledgement by reason of mental incapacity, death, or any other reason satisfactory to the probate judge of the county of the mother's residence or, if the mother is not a resident of this state, when the man signs the acknowledgement, of the county of the minor's birth.

(iv) a man who by order of filiation or by judgment of paternity is determined judicially to be the father of the minor.

(5) An authorized petition is deemed "filed" when it is delivered to, and accepted by, the register or clerk of the court.

(6) "Formal calendar" means the judicial phases other than a delinquency proceeding on the consent calendar, a preliminary inquiry, or a preliminary hearing of a delinquency or child protective proceeding.

(7) "Juvenile Code" means 1944 (1st Ex Sess) PA 54, MCL 712A.1 et seq.; MSA 27.3178(598.1) et seq., as amended.

(8) "Juvenile court" or "court" means the family division of the circuit court.

(9) "Records" means the pleadings, motions, authorized petition, notices, memoranda, briefs, exhibits, available transcripts, findings of the court, and court orders.

(10) "Minor" means a person under the age of 18, and may include a person of age 18 or older concerning whom proceedings are commenced in the juvenile court and over whom the juvenile court has continuing jurisdiction pursuant to MCL 712A.2; MSA 27.3178(598.2).

(11) "Officer" means a government official with the power to arrest or any other person designated and directed by the court to apprehend, detain, or place a minor.

(12) "Parent" means a person who is legally responsible for the control and care of the minor, including a mother, father, guardian, or custodian, other than a custodian of a state facility, a guardian ad litem, or a juvenile court-ordered custodian.

(13) "Party" includes the

(a) petitioner, juvenile, or parent in a delinquency proceeding; and

(b) petitioner, child, respondent parent, or other parent or guardian in a protective proceeding.

(14) "Petition" means a complaint or other written accusation, verified in the manner provided in MCR 2.114(A), that a parent has harmed or failed to properly care for a child, or that a juvenile has committed an offense.

(15) "Petition authorized to be filed" refers to written permission given by a judge or a referee to file the petition containing the formal allegations against the juvenile or respondent with the register or clerk of the court.

(16) "Petitioner" means the person or agency who requests the court to take action against a juvenile or on behalf of a child.

(17) "Preliminary inquiry" means informal review by the court to determine appropriate action on a petition.

(18) "Confidential files" means all materials made confidential by statute or court rule including but not limited to the diversion record of a minor pursuant to the Juvenile Diversion Act, 1988 PA 13, MCL 722.821 et seq.; MSA 25.243(51) et seq.; the separate statement about known victims of juvenile offenses, as required by 1988 PA 22, MCL 780.781 et seq.; MSA 28.1287(781) et seq.; the testimony taken during a closed proceeding pursuant to MCR 5.925(A)(2) and § 17 of the Juvenile Code, MCL 712A.17; MSA 27.3178(598.17); the dispositional reports pursuant to MCR 5.943(C)(3) and MCR 5.973(A)(4)(c); fingerprinting material required to be maintained for reportable juvenile offenses pursuant to MCL 28.243 et seq.; MSA 4.463 et seq., as amended by 1988 PA 40; reports of sexually motivated crimes, MCL 28.247; MSA 4.467(1); test results of those charged with certain sexual offenses or substance abuse offenses, MCL 333.5129; MSA 14.15(5129); and court materials or records that the court has determined to be confidential.

(19) "Trial" means the fact-finding adjudication of a case on the formal calendar on a charge contained in an authorized petition to determine if the minor comes within the jurisdiction of the court.

(20) "Designated proceeding" means a proceeding in which the prosecuting attorney has designated, or has requested the court to designate, the case for trial in juvenile court in the same manner as an adult.

(B) Delinquency Proceeding(s). When used in delinquency proceedings, unless the context otherwise indicates:

(1) "Detention" means court-ordered control of a juvenile including court-approved removal of a juvenile from parental custody, pending trial, disposition, commitment, or further order.

(2) "Juvenile" means a minor defendant alleged or found to be within the jurisdiction of the court because of having committed an offense.

(3) "Major offense" means an offense by a juvenile which would be a felony if committed by an adult.

(4) "Offense by a juvenile" means an act which violates a criminal statute, a criminal ordinance, an act which violates MCL 712A.2(a) or (d); MSA 27.3178(598.2)(a) or (d), or an act which violates a traffic law other than an offense designated as a civil infraction.

(5) "Prosecuting attorney" means the prosecuting attorney for a county, an assistant prosecuting attorney for a county, the attorney general, the deputy attorney general, an assistant attorney general, a special prosecuting attorney, and, in connection with the prosecution of an ordinance violation, an attorney for the political subdivision or governmental entity which enacted the ordinance, charter, rule, or regulation upon which the ordinance violation is based.

(6) "Reportable juvenile offense" means any offense or attempted offense that would constitute a crime as designated below:

(a) burning of a dwelling house, MCL 750.72; MSA 28.267;

(b) assault with intent to commit murder, MCL 750.83; MSA 28.278;

(c) assault with intent to do great bodily harm less than murder, MCL 750.84; MSA 28.279;

(d) assault with intent to maim, MCL 750.86; MSA 28.281;

(e) assault with intent to rob—unarmed, MCL 750.88; MSA 28.283;

(f) assault with intent to rob—armed, MCL 750.89; MSA 28.284;

(g) attempted murder, MCL 750.91; MSA 28.286;

(h) breaking and entering, MCL 750.110; MSA 28.305;

(i) home invasion in the first degree, MCL 750.110a(2); MSA 28.305(a)(2);

(j) escape from a juvenile facility, MCL 750.186a; MSA 28.383a;

(k) first-degree murder, MCL 750.316; MSA 28.548;

(*l*) second-degree murder, MCL 750.317; MSA 28.549;

(m) kidnapping, MCL 750.349; MSA 28.581;

(n) larceny in a building, MCL 750.360; MSA 28.592;

(o) unlawfully driving away an automobile, MCL 750.413; MSA 28.645;

(p) first-degree criminal sexual conduct, MCL 750.520b; MSA 28.788(2);

(q) second-degree criminal sexual conduct, MCL 750.520c; MSA 28.788(3);

(r) third-degree criminal sexual conduct, MCL 750.520d; MSA 28.788(4);

(s) assault with intent to commit criminal sexual conduct, MCL 750.520g; MSA 28.788(7);

(t) armed robbery, MCL 750.529; MSA 28.797;

(u) carjacking, MCL 750.529a; MSA 28.797(a);

(v) unarmed robbery, MCL 750.530; MSA 28.798; and

(w) bank, safe or vault robbery, MCL 750.531; MSA 28.799;

(x) possession of or manufacture, delivery, or possession with intent to manufacture or deliver 650 grams or more of any schedule 1 or 2 controlled substance, MCL 333.7401; MSA 14.15(7401) and MCL 333.7403; MSA 14.15(7403).

(C) **Child Protective Proceedings.** When used in child protective proceedings, unless the context otherwise indicates,

(1) "Agency" means a public or private organization, institution, or facility responsible pursuant to court order or contractual arrangement for the care and supervision of a child.

(2) "Child" means a minor alleged or found to be within the jurisdiction of the court on grounds of abuse, dependency, or neglect.

(3) "Concerned person" means a foster parent with whom the child is living or has lived who has specific knowledge of behavior by the parent constituting grounds for termination under MCL 712A.19b(3)(b) or (g); MSA 27.3178(598.19b)(3)(b) or (g), and who has contacted the department of social services, the prosecuting attorney, the child's attorney, and the child's guardian ad litem, if any, and is satisfied that none of these persons intends to file a petition to terminate parental rights.

(4) "Foster care" means care provided to a child in a foster family home, foster family group home, or child caring institution licensed or approved under MCL 722.111 et seq.; MSA 25.358(11) et seq., or care provided to a child in a relative's home pursuant to an order of the court.

(5) "Offense against a child" means an act or omission by a person other than the child asserted as grounds for bringing the child within the jurisdiction of the court pursuant to the Juvenile Code.

(6) "Placement" means court-approved removal of a child from the parental home and placement in foster care, in a shelter home, in a hospital, or with a private treatment agency.

(7) "Prosecutor" or "prosecuting attorney" means the prosecuting attorney of the county in which the court has its principal office or an assistant to the prosecuting attorney.

(8) "Respondent" means the parent who is alleged to have committed an offense against a child or as defined in MCR 5.974(B).

(D) **Designated Proceedings.**

(1) "Arraignment" means the first hearing in a designated case at which the juvenile is informed of the allegations, the juvenile's rights, and the potential consequences of the proceeding; the matter is set for a probable cause or designation hearing; and, if the juvenile is in custody or custody is requested pending

trial, a decision is made regarding custody pursuant to MCR 5.935(D).

(2) "Court-designated case" means a case in which the court, pursuant to a request by the prosecuting attorney, has decided according to the factors set forth in MCR 5.952(C)(3) that the juvenile is to be tried in juvenile court in the same manner as an adult for an offense other than a specified juvenile violation.

(3) "Designated case" means either a prosecutor-designated case or a court-designated case.

(4) "Designation hearing" means a hearing on the prosecuting attorney's request that the court designate the case for trial in juvenile court in the same manner as an adult.

(5) "Preliminary examination" means a probable cause hearing in which the court determines whether there is probable cause to believe that the specified juvenile violation or alleged offense occurred and whether there is probable cause to believe that the juvenile committed the specified juvenile violation or alleged offense.

(6) "Prosecutor-designated case" means a case in which the prosecuting attorney has endorsed a petition charging a juvenile with a "specified juvenile violation" with the designation that the juvenile is to be tried in juvenile court in the same manner as an adult.

(7) "Sentencing" means the imposition of any sanction on a juvenile that could be imposed on an adult convicted of the offense for which the juvenile was convicted or the decision to delay the imposition of such a sanction.

(8) "Specified juvenile violation" means any offense, attempted offense, conspiracy to commit an offense, or solicitation to commit an offense that would constitute a violation of any of the following:

    a. burning of a dwelling house, MCL 750.72; MSA 28.267;

    b. assault with intent to commit murder, MCL 750.83; MSA 28.278;

    c. assault with intent to maim, MCL 750.86; MSA 28.281;

    d. assault with intent to rob—armed, MCL 750.89; MSA 28.284;

    e. attempted murder, MCL 750.91; MSA 28.286;

    f. first-degree murder, MCL 750.316; MSA 28.548;

    g. second-degree murder, MCL 750.317; MSA 28.549;

    h. kidnaping, MCL 750.349; MSA 28.581;

    i. first-degree criminal sexual conduct, MCL 750.520b; MSA 28.788(2);

    j. armed robbery, MCL 750.529; MSA 28.797;

    k. carjacking, MCL 750.529a; MSA 28.797(a);

    l. robbery of a bank, safe or vault, MCL 750.531; MSA 28.799;

    m. possession of or manufacture, delivery, or possession with intent to manufacture or deliver 650 grams or more of any schedule one or two controlled substance, MCL 333.7401–333.7403; MSA 14.15(7401)–14.15 (7403);

    n. assault with intent to do great bodily harm less than murder, MCL 750.84; MSA 28.279, if armed with a dangerous weapon as defined by MCL 712A.2d(9)(b); MSA 27.3178(598.2d)(9)(b);

    o. first-degree home invasion, MCL 750.110a(2); MSA 28.305(a)(2), if armed with a dangerous weapon as defined by MCL 712A.2d(9)(b); MSA 27.3178(598.2d)(9)(b);

    p. escape or attempted escape from a medium security or high security facility operated by the Family Independence Agency or a high-security facility operated by a private agency under contract with the Family Independence Agency, MCL 750.186a; MSA 28.383a.

    q. any lesser-included offense of an offense described in (a) through (p) above, if the juvenile was alleged in the petition to have violated an offense described in (a) through (p), above.

    r. any offense arising out of the same transaction as an offense described in (a) through (p) if the juvenile was alleged in the petition to have violated an offense described in (a) through (p), above.

(9) "Tried in the same manner as an adult" means a trial in which the juvenile is afforded all the legal and procedural protections that an adult would be given if charged with the same offense in a court of general criminal jurisdiction.

(E) Minor Personal Protection Order Proceedings. When used in minor personal protection order proceedings, unless the context otherwise indicates:

(1) "minor personal protection order" means a personal protection order issued by a court against a minor and under jurisdiction granted by MCL 712A.2(h); MSA 27.3178(598.2)(h).

(2) "original petitioner" means, in the context of minor personal protection order enforcement proceedings, the person who originally petitioned for the minor personal protection order.

[Adopted effective January 1, 1988; amended effective June 1, 1988; April 1, 1989; July 1, 1989; October 1, 1995; May 15, 1997; January 1, 1998; January 10, 2000.]

1988 and 1989 Staff Comments

[See "1988 Staff Comment," "Staff Comment to April 1, 1989 Amendments," and "Staff Comment to July 1, 1989 Amendments," all set forth following Rule 5.993.]

Staff Comment to 1995 Amendment

The August 22, 1995 amendments of MCR 5.903, 5.915, 5.920, 5.921, 5.973, and 5.974 were adopted in response to the enactment of 1994 PA 264, which amended parts of Chapter XIIA of 1939 PA 288.

Staff Comment to 1997 Amendment

The April 8, 1997, amendments of subchapter 5.900 of the Michigan Court Rules [effective May 15, 1997] implement recent statutory changes applicable to the juvenile division of the probate court. See, e.g., 1996 PA 247, 1996 PA 248, 1996 PA 255, 1996 PA 259, and 1996 PA 262. The amendments are based on proposals submitted by the Juvenile Court Rules Committee of the Probate Judges Association. These temporary amendments will remain in effect until further order of the court, and will be reconsidered after receipt of comments.

Staff Comment to 1998 Amendment

The December 19, 1997, amendments to Rule 3.206 and subchapter 5.900 of the Michigan Court Rules [effective January 1, 1998] implement recent statutory changes which have created a family division of the circuit court. These amendments will remain in effect until further order of the court.

Staff Comment to 1999 Amendment

These rules [effective January 10, 2000] clarify the procedure applicable to the new minor personal protection orders ("minor PPOs") created in 1998 PA 474–477, which went into effect March 1, 1999. Because the new statutes do not make clear whether existing PPO procedural rules apply or rules for Juvenile Code proceedings apply, these rules are promulgated to assure consistency in the processing of minor PPOs in Michigan's Circuit Court Family Divisions. Immediate adoption has been ordered to provide needed procedural guidance for courts already facing minor PPO cases.

RULE 5.911 JURY

(A) Right. The right to a jury in juvenile court exists only at the trial.

(B) Jury Demand. A party who is entitled to a trial by jury may demand a jury by filing a written demand with the court within:

(1) 14 days after the court gives notice of the right to jury trial, or

(2) 14 days after the filing of appearance of counsel,

whichever is later, but no later than 7 days before trial. The court may excuse a late filing in the interest of justice.

(C) Jury Procedure. Jury procedure in the juvenile court is governed by MCR 2.510–2.516, except as provided in this subrule.

(1) In a delinquency proceeding,

  (a) each party is entitled to 5 peremptory challenges, and

  (b) the verdict must be unanimous.

(2) In a child protective proceeding,

  (a) each party is entitled to 5 peremptory challenges, and the child is to be considered a separate party, and

  (b) a verdict in a case tried by 6 jurors will be received when 5 jurors agree.

(3) Two or more parties on the same side, other than a child in a child protective proceeding, are considered a single party for purposes of peremptory challenges.

  (a) When two or more parties are aligned on the same side and have adverse interests, the court shall allow each such party represented by a different attorney 3 peremptory challenges.

  (b) When multiple parties are allowed more than 5 peremptory challenges under this subrule, the court may allow the opposite side a total number of peremptory challenges not to exceed the number allowed to the multiple parties.

(4) In a designated case, jury procedure is governed by MCR 6.401–6.420.

[Adopted and amended effective January 1, 1988; amended effective May 15, 1997.]

1988 Staff Comment

See 1988 Staff Comment following Rule 5.993.

Staff Comment to 1997 Amendment

The April 8, 1997, amendments of subchapter 5.900 of the Michigan Court Rules [effective May 15, 1997] implement recent statutory changes applicable to the juvenile division of the probate court. See, e.g., 1996 PA 247, 1996 PA 248, 1996 PA 255, 1996 PA 259, and 1996 PA 262. The amendments are based on proposals submitted by the Juvenile Court Rules Committee of the Probate Judges Association. These temporary amendments will remain in effect until further order of the court, and will be reconsidered after receipt of comments.

RULE 5.912 JUDGE

(A) Right. The parties have the right to a judge at a hearing on the formal calendar.

(1) A judge must preside at:

  (a) a trial by jury,

  (b) a nonjury trial in a designated case,

  (c) a preliminary examination in a designated case,

  (d) a sentencing in a designated case, and

  (e) a waiver proceeding pursuant to MCR 5.950.

(2) The judge who presides at the preliminary examination may not preside at the trial of the same designated case unless a determination of probable cause is waived. The judge who presides at a preliminary examination may accept a plea in the designated case.

(3) The juvenile has the right to demand that the same judge who accepted the plea or presided at the trial of a designated case preside at sentencing or delayed imposition of sentence, but not at a juvenile disposition of the designated case.

(B) Demand. A party may demand that a judge rather than a referee serve as factfinder at a nonjury trial by filing a written demand with the court within:

(1) 14 days after the court gives notice of the right to a judge, or

(2) within 14 days after the filing of appearance of counsel,

whichever is later, but no later than 7 days before trial. The court may excuse a late filing in the interest of justice.

(C) Disqualification of Judge. The disqualification of a juvenile court judge is governed by MCR 2.003.

[Adopted effective January 1, 1988; amended effective May 15, 1997.]

1988 Staff Comment

See 1988 Staff Comment following Rule 5.993.

Staff Comment to 1997 Amendment

The April 8, 1997, amendments of subchapter 5.900 of the Michigan Court Rules [effective May 15, 1997] implement recent statutory changes applicable to the juvenile division of the probate court. See, e.g., 1996 PA 247, 1996 PA 248, 1996 PA 255, 1996 PA 259, and 1996 PA 262. The amendments are based on proposals submitted by the Juvenile Court Rules Committee of the Probate Judges Association. These temporary amendments will remain in effect until further order of the court, and will be reconsidered after receipt of comments.

RULE 5.913 REFEREES

(A) Assignment of Matters to Referees.

(1) *General.* Subject to the limitation set forth in subrules (A)(2) and (A)(3), the court may assign a referee to conduct a preliminary inquiry or to preside at a hearing other than: (a) a jury trial; (b) a waiver proceeding pursuant to MCR 5.950; (c) a preliminary examination, trial or sentencing of a designated case; or (d) a proceeding on the issuance, modification, or termination of a minor personal protection order, and to make recommended findings and conclusions.

(2) *Delinquency Proceedings.* Except as otherwise provided by MCL 712A.10; MSA 27.3178(598.10), only a person licensed to practice law in Michigan may serve as a referee at a delinquency proceeding other than a preliminary inquiry or preliminary hearing, if the juvenile is before the court under MCL 712A.2(a)(1); MSA 27.3178(598.2)(a)(1).

(3) *Child Protective Proceedings.* Only a person licensed to practice law in Michigan may serve as a referee at a child protective proceeding other than a preliminary inquiry, preliminary hearing, or a progress review under MCR 5.973(D).

(4) *Designated Cases.* A referee licensed to practice law in Michigan may preside at a hearing to designate a case or to amend a petition to designate a case and to make recommended findings and conclusions.

(5) *Minor Personal Protection Actions.* Only a referee licensed to practice law in Michigan may preside at a hearing for the enforcement of a minor personal protection order, including preliminary hearings, violation hearings, dispositional phases, and supplemental disposition hearings.

(B) Duration of Assignment. Unless a party has demanded trial by jury or by a judge, pursuant to MCR 5.911 and 5.912, a referee may conduct the trial and further proceedings through the dispositional phase.

(C) Advise of Right to Appeal. At the conclusion of the dispositional hearing, the referee must inform the minor, the parent, and the respondent of the right to file a request for review of the referee's recommended findings and conclusions as provided in MCR 5.991(B).

[Adopted and amended effective January 1, 1988; amended effective June 1, 1988; April 1, 1989; May 15, 1997; January 10, 2000.]

1988 and 1989 Staff Comments

[See "1988 Staff Comment" and "Staff Comment to April 1, 1989 Amendments," set forth following Rule 5.993.]

Staff Comment to 1997 Amendment

The April 8, 1997, amendments of subchapter 5.900 of the Michigan Court Rules [effective May 15, 1997] implement recent statutory changes applicable to the juvenile division of the probate court. See, e.g., 1996 PA 247, 1996 PA 248, 1996 PA 255, 1996 PA 259, and 1996 PA 262. The amendments are based on proposals submitted by the Juvenile Court Rules Committee of the Probate Judges Association. These temporary amendments will remain in effect until further order of the court, and will be reconsidered after receipt of comments.

Staff Comment to 1999 Amendment

These rules [effective January 10, 2000] clarify the procedure applicable to the new minor personal protection orders ("minor PPOs") created in 1998 PA 474–477, which went into effect March 1, 1999. Because the new statutes do not make clear whether existing PPO procedural rules apply or rules for Juvenile Code proceedings apply, these rules are promulgated to assure consistency in the processing of minor PPOs in Michigan's Circuit Court Family Divisions. Immediate adoption has been ordered to provide needed procedural guidance for courts already facing minor PPO cases.

RULE 5.914 PROSECUTING ATTORNEY

(A) General. On request of the court, the prosecuting attorney shall review the petition for legal sufficiency and shall appear at any child protective proceeding or any delinquency proceeding.

(B) Delinquency Proceeding.

(1) *Petition Approval.* Only the prosecuting attorney may request the court to take jurisdiction of a

juvenile under MCL 712A.2(a)(1); MSA 27.3178(598.2)(a)(1).

(2) *Appearance.* The prosecuting attorney shall participate in every delinquency proceeding under MCL 712A.2(a)(1); MSA 27.3178(598.2)(a)(1) that requires a hearing and the taking of testimony.

(C) Child Protective Proceedings.

(1) *Legal Consultant to Department.* On request of the Michigan department of social services or of an agent under contract with the department, the prosecuting attorney must serve as a legal consultant to the department of social services or agent under contract with the department at all stages of a child protective proceeding.

(2) *Appearance.* In a child protective proceeding the department may retain legal representation of its choice when the prosecuting attorney does not appear on behalf of the department or on behalf of an agent under contract with the department.

(D) Designated Proceedings.

(1) *Prosecutor Designation.* Only the prosecuting attorney may designate a case in which the petition alleges a specified juvenile violation.

(2) *Leave to Designate.* Only the prosecuting attorney may request leave of court to amend a petition to designate a case in which the petition alleges a specified juvenile violation.

(3) *Court Designation.* Only the prosecuting attorney may request the court to designate a case involving a petition that alleges an offense other than the specified juvenile violation.

[Adopted effective January 1, 1988; amended effective June 1, 1988; April 1, 1989; May 15, 1997.]

1988 and 1989 Staff Comments

[See "1988 Staff Comment" and "Staff Comment to April 1, 1989 Amendments," set forth following Rule 5.993.]

Staff Comment to 1997 Amendment

The April 8, 1997, amendments of subchapter 5.900 of the Michigan Court Rules [effective May 15, 1997] implement recent statutory changes applicable to the juvenile division of the probate court. See, e.g., 1996 PA 247, 1996 PA 248, 1996 PA 255, 1996 PA 259, and 1996 PA 262. The amendments are based on proposals submitted by the Juvenile Court Rules Committee of the Probate Judges Association. These temporary amendments will remain in effect until further order of the court, and will be reconsidered after receipt of comments.

RULE 5.915 ASSISTANCE OF ATTORNEY

(A) Delinquency Proceedings.

(1) *Advice.* If the juvenile is not represented by an attorney, the court shall advise the juvenile of the right to the assistance of an attorney at each stage of the proceedings on the formal calendar, including trial, plea of admission, and disposition.

(2) *Appointment of an Attorney.* The court shall appoint an attorney to represent the juvenile in a delinquency proceeding if:

(a) the parent refuses or fails to appear and participate in the proceedings,

(b) the parent is the complainant or victim,

(c) the juvenile and those responsible for the support of the juvenile are found financially unable to retain an attorney and the juvenile does not waive an attorney,

(d) those responsible for the support of the juvenile refuse or neglect to retain an attorney for the juvenile and the juvenile does not waive an attorney, or

(e) the court determines that the best interests of the juvenile or the public require appointment.

(3) *Waiver of Attorney.* The juvenile may waive the assistance of an attorney except where a parent or guardian ad litem objects or when the appointment is based on subrule (A)(2)(e). The waiver by a juvenile must be made in open court to the judge or referee, who shall find and place on the record that the waiver was voluntarily and understandingly made.

(B) Child Protective Proceedings.

(1) *Respondent.*

(a) At respondent's first court appearance, the court shall advise the respondent of the right to retain an attorney to represent the respondent at any hearing conducted pursuant to these rules and that

(i) the respondent has the right to a court-appointed attorney if the respondent is financially unable to retain counsel, and,

(ii) if the respondent is not represented by an attorney, that the respondent may request and receive a court-appointed attorney at any later hearing.

(b) When it appears to the court, following an examination of the record, through written financial statements, or through other means that the respondent is financially unable to retain an attorney and the respondent desires an attorney, the court shall appoint one to represent the respondent at any hearing conducted pursuant to these rules.

(c) The respondent may waive the right to an attorney, except that the court shall not accept the waiver by a respondent who is a minor when a parent or guardian ad litem objects to the waiver.

(2) *Child.* The court must appoint an attorney to represent the child at every hearing, including the preliminary hearing. The child may not waive the assistance of an attorney.

(a) The attorney for the child must be present at every hearing for which the attorney receives notice.

(b) The appointed attorney shall observe and, dependent upon the child's age and capability, interview the child.

(c) If the child is placed in foster care, the attorney shall, before representing the child in each proceeding or hearing subsequent to a preliminary hearing or emergency removal hearing, review the agency case file and consult with the foster parents and the caseworker.

(d) The court may permit another attorney to temporarily substitute for the child's attorney at a hearing, if that would prevent the hearing from being adjourned, or for other good cause. An attorney who temporarily substitutes for the child's attorney must be familiarized with the case and, for hearings other than a preliminary hearing or emergency removal hearing, must review the agency case file and consult with the foster parents and caseworker prior to the hearing unless the child's attorney has done so and communicated that information to the substitute attorney. The court shall inquire on the record whether the attorneys have complied with the requirements of this subrule.

(e) The attorney appointed to represent the child must receive compensation as determined by the court, including compensation for all out-of-court consultations as required by statute or court rule.

(C) Appearance. The appearance of an attorney is governed by MCR 2.117(B).

(D) Costs. When an attorney is appointed for a party under this rule, the court may enter an order assessing costs of the representation against the party or against a person responsible for the support of that party, which order may be enforced through contempt proceedings.

(E) Discharge. An attorney appointed by the court to represent a party shall serve until discharged by the court.

[Adopted and amended effective January 1, 1988; amended effective April 1, 1989; October 1, 1995; April 1, 1998.]

1988 and 1989 Staff Comments

[See "1988 Staff Comment" and "Staff Comment to April 1, 1989 Amendments," set forth following Rule 5.993.]

Staff Comment to 1995 Amendment

The August 22, 1995 amendments of MCR 5.903, 5.915, 5.920, 5.921, 5.973, and 5.974 were adopted in response to the enactment of 1994 PA 264, which amended parts of Chapter XIIA of 1939 PA 288.

Staff Comment to 1998 Amendment

The January 16, 1998, amendments of MCR 5.915, 5.923, 5.963, 5.965 and 5.974 [effective April 1, 1998] relate to recommendations made by the Binsfeld Children's Commission in its July 1996 report regarding children (Recommendations 36, 70, 71, 76, 77, 107, 111, and 121). The amendments are effective April 1, 1998, to coincide with

the implementation of legislation enacted pursuant to recommendations of the commission.

RULE 5.916   GUARDIAN AD LITEM

(A) General. The court may appoint a guardian ad litem for a party if the court finds that the welfare of the party requires it.

(B) Appearance. The appearance of a guardian ad litem must be in writing and in a manner and form designated by the court. The appearance shall contain a statement as to the existence of any interest which the guardian ad litem holds in relation to the minor, the minor's family, or any other person in the proceeding before the court or in other matters.

(C) Access to Information. The appearance entitles the guardian ad litem to be furnished copies of all petitions, motions, and orders filed or entered, and to consult with the attorney of the party for whom the guardian ad litem has been appointed.

(D) Costs. The court may assess the cost of providing a guardian ad litem against the party or a person responsible for the support of the party, and may enforce the order of reimbursement through contempt proceedings.

[Adopted effective January 1, 1988.]

1988 Staff Comment

See 1988 Staff Comment following Rule 5.993.

RULE 5.920   SERVICE OF PROCESS

(A) General. Unless a party must be summoned as provided in subrule (B), a party shall be given notice of a proceeding in juvenile court in any manner authorized by the rules in this subchapter.

(B) Summons.

(1) *In General.* A summons may be issued and served on a party before any proceeding in juvenile court.

(2) *When Required.* Except as otherwise provided in these rules, the court shall direct the service of a summons in the following circumstances:

(a) In a juvenile court proceeding, the summons must be issued and served on the parent or person with whom the minor resides, other than a court-ordered custodian, directing such person to appear with the minor for trial. If the person summoned is not the parent, the parent shall be notified by service as provided in subrule (B)(4). The court may direct that the child's appearance in court is unnecessary.

(b) In a delinquency proceeding, the juvenile shall be summoned and personally served to appear for trial.

(c) In a child protective proceeding, the summons must be issued and served on the parent or person with whom the child resides, other than a court-ordered custodian, for a hearing on a petition seeking the termination of parental rights. The court may direct that the child's appearance in court is unnecessary. If the person summoned is not the respondent, respondent shall be notified by service as provided in subrule (B)(4).

(3) *Content.* The summons shall direct the person to whom it is addressed to appear with the minor (unless the minor's appearance has been excused under subrule [B][2]) at a time and place specified by the court and must:

(a) identify the nature of hearing;

(b) explain the right to an attorney and the right to trial by judge or jury;

(c) if the summons is for a child protective proceeding, include a prominent notice that the hearings could result in termination of parental rights; and

(d) have a copy of the petition attached to the summons.

(4) *Manner of Serving Summons.*

(a) Except as provided in subrules (B)(4)(b) and (c), a summons required under subrule (B)(2) must be served by delivering the summons to the party personally.

(b) If personal service of the summons is impracticable or cannot be achieved, the court may direct that it be served by registered or certified mail addressed to the last known address of the party, return receipt requested.

(c) If the court finds service cannot be made because the whereabouts of the person to be summoned has not been determined after reasonable effort, the court may direct any manner of substituted service, including publication.

(d) If personal service of a summons is unnecessary, the court may direct that it be served in a manner reasonably calculated to provide notice.

(5) *Time of Service.*

(a) A summons shall be personally served at least:

(i) 14 days before hearing on a petition that seeks to terminate parental rights or 14 days before a permanency planning hearing,

(ii) 7 days before trial or 7 days before a child protective dispositional review hearing,

(iii) 3 days before any other hearing.

(b) If the summons is served by registered mail, it must be sent at least 7 days earlier than subrule (a) requires for personal service of a summons if the party to be served resides in Michigan, or 14 days earlier than required by subrule (a) if the party to whom the summons is addressed resides outside Michigan.

(c) If service is by publication, the published notice, which does not require publication of the petition itself, shall appear in a newspaper in the county where the party resides if known, and, if not, in the county where the action is pending. The published notice must appear one or more times 21 days before a hearing as set forth in subrule (a)(i), 14 days before trial or hearing as set forth in subrule (a)(ii), or 7 days before any other hearing.

(C) Notice of Hearing.

(1) *General.* Notice of a hearing must be given in writing or on the record at least 7 days prior to the hearing except as provided in subrules (C)(2) and (C)(3), or as otherwise provided in the rules.

(2) *Preliminary Hearing; Emergency Removal Hearing.*

(a) When a juvenile is detained, notice of the preliminary hearing shall be given to the juvenile and to the parent of the juvenile as soon as the hearing is scheduled, and the notice may be in person, in writing, on the record, or by telephone.

(b) When a child is placed, notice of the preliminary hearing or an emergency removal hearing under MCR 5.973(E)(3) shall be given to the parent of the child as soon as the hearing is scheduled, and the notice may be in person, in writing, on the record, or by telephone.

(3) *Permanency Planning Hearing; Termination Proceedings.*

(a) Notice of a permanency planning hearing must be given in writing at least 14 days before the hearing.

(b) Notice of a hearing on a petition requesting to terminate parental rights in a child protective proceeding must be given in writing at least 14 days before the hearing.

(4) When a party fails to appear in response to a notice of hearing, the court may order the party's appearance by summons or subpoena.

(D) Subpoenas.

(1) The attorney for a party or the court on its own motion may cause a subpoena to be served upon a person whose testimony or appearance is desired.

(2) It is not necessary to tender advance fees to the person served a subpoena in order to compel attendance.

(3) Except as otherwise stated in this subrule, service of a subpoena is to be as provided by MCR 2.506.

(E) Waiver of Service. A person may waive notice of hearing or service of process. The waiver shall be in writing. When a party waives service of a summons required by subrule (B), the party must be advised as set forth in (B)(3).

(F) Subsequent Notices. After a party's first appearance before the court, subsequent notice of proceedings and pleadings shall be served on that party or, if the party has an attorney, on the attorney for the party, except that a summons must be served before trial or termination hearing as provided in subrule (B) unless a prior court appearance of the party in the case was in response to service by summons.

[Adopted and amended effective January 1, 1988; amended effective April 1, 1989; January 1, 1993; October 1, 1995.]

1988 Staff Comment

[See 1988 Staff Comment following Rule 5.993.]

[Under the January 1, 1988 amendment,] MCR 5.920(4)(b) now permits service of a summons by certified as well as registered mail in certain cases. See MCL 8.11; MSA 2.220, and MCR 2.105(K).

Staff Comment to 1989 Amendment

[See "Staff Comment to April 1, 1989 Amendment," set forth following Rule 5.993.]

Staff Comment to 1995 Amendment

The August 22, 1995 amendments of MCR 5.903, 5.915, 5.920, 5.921, 5.973, and 5.974 were adopted in response to the enactment of 1994 PA 264, which amended parts of Chapter XIIA of 1939 PA 288.

RULE 5.921   PERSONS ENTITLED TO NOTICE

(A) Delinquency Proceeding. In a delinquency proceeding, the court shall direct that the following persons be notified of each hearing:

(1) the juvenile,

(2) the parent of the juvenile,

(3) the guardian ad litem of a party appointed pursuant to these rules, and

(4) the attorney retained or appointed to represent the juvenile.

The petitioner must be notified of the first hearing on the petition.

(B) Protective Proceedings.

(1) *General.* In a child protective proceeding other than a dispositional review hearing concerning a child in foster care, other than a permanency planning hearing, and other than a hearing on a petition requesting the termination of parental rights, the court shall ensure that the following persons are notified of each hearing:

(a) the respondent,

(b) the attorney for the respondent,

(c) the child or the attorney for the child,

(d) a parent or guardian, if any, other than the respondent,

(e) the petitioner,

(f) the guardian ad litem or a party appointed pursuant to these rules, and

(g) any other person the court may direct to be notified.

(2) *Dispositional Review Hearings and Permanency Planning Hearings.* Prior to a dispositional review hearing or a permanency planning hearing, the court shall ensure that the following persons are notified in writing of each hearing:

(a) the agency responsible for the care and supervision of the child,

(b) the foster parent or custodian of the child,

(c) the parents of the child and the attorney for the respondent parent unless parental rights have been terminated,

(d) the guardian of the child,

(e) the guardian ad litem for the child,

(f) the attorney for the child,

(g) the attorneys for each party,

(h) the prosecuting attorney if the prosecuting attorney has appeared in the case,

(i) the child, if 11 years or older,

(j) any tribal leader if there is an Indian tribe affiliation, and

(k) any other person the court may direct to be notified.

(3) *Termination of Parental Rights.* Written notice of a hearing to determine if the parental rights to a child shall be terminated must be given to those appropriate persons or entities listed in subrule (B)(2).

(C) Mother or Father Without Physical Custody. A mother or father of the minor, who, at the time the minor comes to court, does not otherwise fall within the definition of parent or party in MCR 5.903(A)(12), (13), and whose parental rights over the minor have not been terminated, must be notified of the first hearing on the petition in either a delinquency or protective proceeding. Subsequent notice need only be given when this person requests further notice.

(D) Putative Fathers. If, at any time during the pendency of a proceeding, the court determines that the minor has no father as defined in MCR 5.903(A)(4), the court may, in its discretion, take appropriate action as described in this subrule.

(1) The court may take initial testimony on the tentative identity and address of the natural father. If the court finds probable cause to believe that an identifiable person is the natural father of the minor, the court shall direct that notice be served on that person in the manner as provided in MCR 5.920. The notice shall include the following information:

(a) that a petition has been filed with the court;

(b) the time and place of hearing at which the natural father is to appear to express his interest, if any, in the minor; and

(c) a statement that failure to attend the hearing will constitute a denial of interest in the minor, a waiver of notice for all subsequent hearings, a waiver of a right to appointment of an attorney, and could result in termination of any parental rights.

(2) After notice to the putative father as provided in subrule (D)(1), the court may conduct a hearing and determine that:

(a) the putative father has been personally served or served in some other manner which the court finds to be reasonably calculated to provide notice to the putative father. If so, the court may proceed in the absence of the putative father.

(b) a preponderance of the evidence establishes that the putative father is the natural father of the minor and justice requires that he be allowed 14 days to establish his relationship according to MCR 5.903(A)(4); provided that if the court decides the interests of justice so require, it shall not be necessary for the mother of the minor to join in an acknowledgment. The court may extend the time for good cause shown.

(c) there is probable cause to believe that another identifiable person is the natural father of the minor. If so, the court shall proceed with respect to the other person in accord with subrule (D).

(d) after diligent inquiry, the identity of the natural father cannot be determined. If so, the court may proceed without further notice or court-appointed attorney for the unidentified person.

(3) The court may find that the natural father waives all rights to further notice, including the right to notice of termination of parental rights, and the right to legal counsel if:

(a) he fails to appear after proper notice, or

(b) he appears, but fails to establish paternity within the time set by the court.

(E) Failure to Appear; Notice by Publication. When persons whose whereabouts are unknown fail to appear in response to notice by publication or otherwise, the court need not give further notice by publication of subsequent hearings except a hearing on the termination of parental rights.

[Adopted and amended effective January 1, 1988; amended effective April 1, 1989; October 1, 1995.]

1988 and 1989 Staff Comments

[See "1988 Staff Comment" and "Staff Comment to April 1, 1989 Amendments," set forth following Rule 5.993.]

Staff Comment to 1995 Amendment

The August 22, 1995 amendments of MCR 5.903, 5.915, 5.920, 5.921, 5.973, and 5.974 were adopted in response to the enactment of 1994 PA 264, which amended parts of Chapter XIIA of 1939 PA 288.

RULE 5.922 PRETRIAL PROCEDURES IN DELINQUENCY AND CHILD PROTECTION PROCEEDINGS

(A) Discovery.

(1) The following materials are discoverable as of right in all proceedings provided they are requested no later than 21 days before trial:

(a) all written or recorded statements and notes of statements made by the juvenile or respondent which are in possession or control of petitioner or a law enforcement agency, including oral statements if they have been reduced to writing;

(b) all written or recorded nonconfidential statements made by any person with knowledge of the events in possession or control of petitioner or a law enforcement agency, including police reports;

(c) the names of prospective witnesses;

(d) a list of all physical or tangible objects which are prospective evidence;

(e) the results of all scientific, medical, or other expert tests or experiments, including the reports or findings of all experts, which are prospective evidence in the matter;

(f) the results of any lineups or showups, including written reports or lineup sheets; and

(g) all search warrants issued in connection with the matter, including applications for such warrants, affidavits, and returns or inventories.

(2) On motion of a party, the court may permit discovery of any other materials and evidence, including untimely requested materials and evidence that would have been discoverable of right under subrule (A)(1) if timely requested. Absent manifest injustice, no motion for discovery will be granted unless the moving party has requested and has not been provided the materials or evidence sought through an order of discovery.

(B) Notice of Defenses; Rebuttal.

(1) Within 21 days after the juvenile has been given notice of the date of trial, but no later than 7 days before the trial date, the juvenile or the juvenile's attorney must file a written notice with the court and prosecuting attorney of the intent to rely on a defense of alibi, insanity, or diminished capacity, or a defense of mental illness negating an element of the alleged offense. The notice shall include a list of the names and addresses of defense witnesses.

(2) Within 7 days after receipt of notice, but no later than 2 days before the trial date, the prosecutor shall provide written notice to the court and defense of an intent to offer rebuttal to the above-listed defenses. The notice shall include names and addresses of rebuttal witnesses.

(3) Failure to comply with subrules (1) and (2) may result in the sanctions set forth in MCL 768.21; MSA 28.1044.

(C) Motion Practice. Motion practice in juvenile court is governed by MCR 2.119, except that a motion to suppress evidence must be filed at least 7 days before trial or, within the court's discretion, at trial.

(D) Pretrial Conference. The court may direct the parties to appear at a pretrial conference to settle all pretrial matters. Except as otherwise provided in or unless inconsistent with the rules of this subchapter, the scope and effect of a pretrial conference are governed by MCR 2.401.

[Adopted and amended effective January 1, 1988; amended effective January 1, 1993; May 15, 1997.]

1988 Staff Comment

[See 1988 Staff Comment following Rule 5.993.]

Staff Comment to 1997 Amendment

The April 8, 1997, amendments of subchapter 5.900 of the Michigan Court Rules [effective May 15, 1997] implement recent statutory changes applicable to the juvenile division of the probate court. See, e.g., 1996 PA 247, 1996 PA 248, 1996 PA 255, 1996 PA 259, and 1996 PA 262. The amendments are based on proposals submitted by the Juvenile Court Rules Committee of the Probate Judges Association. These temporary amendments will remain in effect until further order of the court, and will be reconsidered after receipt of comments.

RULE 5.923   MISCELLANEOUS HEARING PROCEDURES

(A) Additional Evidence. If at any time the court believes that the evidence has not been fully developed, it may

(1) examine a witness,

(2) call a witness, or

(3) adjourn the matter before the court, and

   (a) cause service of process on additional witnesses, or

   (b) order production of other evidence.

(B) Examination or Evaluation. The court may order that a minor or parent be examined or evaluated by a physician, dentist, psychologist, or psychiatrist.

(C) Fingerprinting and Photographing. The court may permit fingerprinting or photographing or both of a minor when the minor is in court custody. Fingerprints and photographs must be placed in the confidential files, capable of being located and destroyed on court order.

(D) Lineup. If a complaint or petition is filed against a juvenile alleging violation of a criminal law or ordinance, the court may, at the request of the prosecuting attorney, order the juvenile to appear at a place and time designated by the court for identification by another person, including a corporeal lineup pursuant to MCL 712A.32; MSA 27.3178(598.30b). If the court orders the juvenile to appear for such an identification proceeding, the court must notify the juvenile and the juvenile's parent, guardian or legal custodian that the juvenile has the right to consult with an attorney and have an attorney present during the identification proceeding and that if the juvenile and the juvenile's parent, guardian or legal custodian cannot afford an attorney, the court will appoint an attorney for the juvenile if requested on the record or in writing by the juvenile or the juvenile's parent, guardian or legal custodian.

(E) Electronic Equipment; Support Person. The court may allow the use of closed-circuit television, speaker telephone, or other similar electronic equipment to facilitate hearings or to protect the parties. The court may allow the use of videotaped statements and depositions, anatomical dolls, support persons, and take other measures to protect the child witness as authorized by, and enumerated in, 1987 PA 45, MCL 712A.17b; MSA 27.3178(598.17b).

(F) Impartial Questioner. The court may appoint an impartial psychologist or psychiatrist to ask questions of a child witness at a hearing.

(G) Adjournments. At each stage of a child protective proceeding, the court shall adhere to the time limits specified in these rules. Adjournments or continuances of trials or hearings in child protective proceedings shall be granted only:

(1) on written motion of a party filed no later than 14 days prior to the hearing, or

(2) on motion of the court for good cause, for a period not to exceed 28 days, taking into consideration the best interests of the child.

[Adopted and amended effective January 1, 1988; amended effective April 1, 1989; May 15, 1997; April 1, 1998.]

1988 Staff Comment

[See 1988 Staff Comment following Rule 5.993.]

[Under January 1, 1988 amendment,] MCR 5.923 incorporates by reference the legislation concerning child witnesses. See 1987 PA 45.

Staff Comment to 1989 Amendment

[See "Staff Comment to April 1, 1989 Amendment," following Rule 5.993.]

Staff Comment to 1997 Amendment

The April 8, 1997, amendments of subchapter 5.900 of the Michigan Court Rules [effective May 15, 1997] implement recent statutory changes applicable to the juvenile division of the probate court. See, e.g., 1996 PA 247, 1996 PA 248, 1996 PA 255, 1996 PA 259, and 1996 PA 262. The amendments are based on proposals submitted by the Juvenile Court Rules Committee of the Probate Judges Association. These temporary amendments will remain in effect until further order of the court, and will be reconsidered after receipt of comments.

Staff Comment to January, 1998 Amendment

The January 16, 1998, amendments of MCR 5.915, 5.923, 5.963, 5.965 and 5.974 [effective April 1, 1998] relate to recommendations made by the Binsfeld Children's Commission in its July 1996 report regarding children (Recommendations 36, 70, 71, 76, 77, 107, 111, and 121). The amendments are effective April 1, 1998, to coincide with the implementation of legislation enacted pursuant to recommendations of the commission.

Staff Comment to February, 1998 Amendment

The order of February 24, 1998 [effective April 1, 1998], modifies MCR 5.923, which had been amended by order of January 16, 1998, to be effective April 1, 1998. The amendment eliminates reference to adjournments in delinquency proceedings and corrects the numbering of the subrule governing adjournments.

RULE 5.924 INFORMATION FURNISHED ON REQUEST BY COURT

Persons or agencies providing testimony, reports, or other information relevant and material to the proceedings following authorization of a petition, and at the request of the court, are immune from any subsequent legal action with respect to furnishing the information to the court.

[Adopted effective January 1, 1988.]

1988 Staff Comment

[See 1988 Staff Comment following Rule 5.993.]

RULE 5.925 OPEN PROCEEDINGS; JUDGMENTS AND ORDERS; RECORDS CONFIDENTIALITY; EXPUNGEMENT

(A) Open Proceedings.

(1) *General.* Except as provided in subrule (A)(2), juvenile court proceedings on the formal calendar and preliminary hearings shall be open to the public.

(2) *Closed Proceedings; Criteria.* The court, on motion of a party or a victim, may close the proceedings to the public during the testimony of a child or during the testimony of the victim to protect the welfare of either. In making such a determination, the court shall consider the nature of the proceedings, the age and maturity of the witness and the preference of the witness, and the preference of a parent if the witness is a child, that the proceedings be open or closed. The court may not close the proceedings to the public during the testimony of the juvenile if jurisdiction is requested under MCL 712A.2(a)(1); MSA 27.3178(598.2)(a)(1).

(B) Record of Proceedings. A record of the proceedings on the formal calendar must be made and preserved by stenographic recording or by mechanical or electronic recording as provided by statute or MCR 8.108. Unless otherwise provided in this subchapter, a record of other hearings may be made and preserved by a written memorandum executed by the judge or referee setting forth findings and procedures followed.

(C) Judgments and Orders. The form and signing of judgments are governed by subchapter 5.600.

(D) Public Access to Records; Confidential File.

(1) *General.* Records of the juvenile court other than confidential files shall be open to the general public.

(2) *Confidential Files.* Only persons who are found by the court to have a legitimate interest may be allowed access to the confidential files. In determining whether a person has a legitimate interest, the court shall consider the nature of the proceedings, the welfare and safety of the public, and the interest of the minor.

(E) Expunging Court Records; Setting Aside Adjudications.

(1) *Definitions.* When used in this subrule, unless the context otherwise indicates:

(a) "expunge" means to obliterate or destroy;

(b) "set aside" means to negate or rescind.

(2) *Court Files and Records.*

(a) General. The court may at any time for good cause expunge its own files and records pertaining to an offense by or against a minor other than an adjudicated offense described in subrule (E)(3)(a) and (b).

(b) Delinquency Files and Records. The court must expunge the diversion record of a juvenile within 28 days after the juvenile becomes 17 years of age. The court must expunge the files and records pertaining to a person's juvenile offenses, other than any adjudicated offense described in subrule (E)(3)(a) and (b), when the person becomes 30 years of age.

(c) Child Protective Files and Records. The court shall expunge child protective proceeding files and records pertaining to the minor 25 years after the jurisdiction over the last child in the family ends.

(3) *Setting Aside Adjudications.*

(a) Life Offenses and Criminal Traffic Violations. The court may not set aside an adjudication of an offense which if committed by an adult would be a felony for which the maximum punishment is life imprisonment, or an offense which if committed by an adult would be a criminal traffic violation.

(b) The court may only set aside an adjudication of a reportable juvenile offense pursuant to the procedures of MCL 712A.18e; MSA 27.3178(598.18e).

(c) Upon the entry of an order setting aside an adjudication, the court shall:

(i) send a copy of the order to the Central Records Division of the Department of State Police and to the law enforcement agency involved in the apprehension of the juvenile; and

(ii) expunge its own files and records pertaining to the offense by the juvenile.

(4) *Setting Aside Convictions.* The court may only set aside a conviction pursuant to MCL 780.621; MSA 28.1274(101).

(F) Access to Juvenile Offense Record of Convicted Adults. When the juvenile offense record of an adult convicted of a crime is made available to the appropriate agency, as provided in MCL 791.228(1); MSA 28.2298(1), the record must state whether, as to each adjudication, the juvenile had counsel or voluntarily waived counsel.

[Adopted and amended effective January 1, 1988; amended effective June 1, 1988; March 1, 1989; May 15, 1997.]

1988 Staff Comment

[See 1988 Staff Comment following Rule 5.993.]

Staff Comment to 1997 Amendment

The April 8, 1997, amendments of subchapter 5.900 of the Michigan Court Rules [effective May 15, 1997] implement recent statutory changes applicable to the juvenile division of the probate court. See, e.g., 1996 PA 247, 1996 PA 248, 1996 PA 255, 1996 PA 259, and 1996 PA 262. The amendments are based on proposals submitted by the Juvenile Court Rules Committee of the Probate Judges Association. These temporary amendments will remain in effect until further order of the court, and will be reconsidered after receipt of comments.

RULE 5.926 TRANSFER OF JURISDICTION; CHANGE OF VENUE

(A) As used in MCL 712A.2; MSA 27.3178(598.2), a child is "found within the county" where the offense against the child occurred, where the offense committed by the juvenile occurred, or where the minor is physically present.

(B) Transfer to County of Residence. When a minor is brought before a juvenile court in a county other than where the minor resides, the court may transfer the case to the court in the county of residence prior to trial.

(C) Costs. When a juvenile court other than the court in a county where the minor resides orders disposition, it will be responsible for any costs incurred in connection with such order unless:

(1) the court in the county where the minor resides agrees to pay the costs of such disposition, or

(2) the minor is made a state ward pursuant to the youth rehabilitation services act, 1974 PA 150, MCL 803.301 et seq.; MSA 25.399(51) et seq., and the county of residence withholds consent to a transfer of the case.

(D) Change of Venue; Grounds. The court, on motion of a party, may order a case to be heard before a juvenile court in another county:

(1) for the convenience of the parties and witnesses, provided that a judge of the other court agrees to hear the case; or

(2) when an impartial trial cannot be had where the case is pending.

All costs of the proceeding in another county are to be borne by the juvenile court ordering the change of venue.

(E) Transfer of Records. The court entering an order of transfer or change of venue shall send the original pleadings and documents, or certified copies of pleadings and documents, to the receiving court without charge.

(F) Designated Cases. Designated cases are to be filed in the juvenile court of the county in which the offense is alleged to have occurred. Other than a change of venue for the purpose of trial, a designated case may not be transferred to any other county, except, after conviction, a designated case may be transferred to the juvenile's county of residence for entry of a juvenile disposition only. Sentencing of a juvenile, including delayed imposition of sentence, may only be done in the county in which the offense occurred.

[Adopted and amended effective January 1, 1988; amended effective April 1, 1989; January 1, 1993; May 15, 1997; January 1, 1998.]

1988 and 1989 Staff Comments

[See "1988 Staff Comment" and "Staff Comment to April 1, 1989 Amendments," set forth following Rule 5.993.]

Staff Comment to 1997 Amendment

The April 8, 1997, amendments of subchapter 5.900 of the Michigan Court Rules [effective May 15, 1997] implement recent statutory changes applicable to the juvenile division of the probate court. See, e.g., 1996 PA 247, 1996 PA 248, 1996 PA 255, 1996 PA 259, and 1996 PA 262. The amendments are based on proposals submitted by the Juvenile Court Rules Committee of the Probate Judges Association. These temporary amendments will remain in effect until further order of the court, and will be reconsidered after receipt of comments.

Staff Comment to 1998 Amendment

The December 19, 1997, amendments to Rule 3.206 and subchapter 5.900 of the Michigan Court Rules [effective January 1, 1998] implement recent statutory changes which have created a family division of the circuit court. These amendments will remain in effect until further order of the court.

RULE 5.927 PRIOR COURT ORDERS

In a juvenile court proceeding involving a minor who is subject to a prior order of another Michigan court, the manner of notice to the other court and the authority of the juvenile court to proceed are governed by MCR 3.205.

[Adopted effective January 1, 1988.]

1988 Staff Comment

[See 1988 Staff Comment following Rule 5.993.]

RULE 5.928 CONTEMPT OF COURT; ATTENDANCE; CONTEMPT

If a parent or guardian of a juvenile who is within the court's jurisdiction under MCL 712A.2(a)(1); MSA 27.3178(598.2)(a)(1) fails to attend a hearing before a judge or referee after having received a summons earlier in the proceedings and, subsequently, been given notice of the hearing by the court, the parent or guardian may be held in contempt of court and fined, although not jailed, as provided in MCL 600.1715; MSA 27A.1715 unless the court had, before the hearing, excused the parent's attendance or unless, at a hearing to consider the issue of contempt, the parent or guardian shows good cause for failure to attend the juvenile's hearing. The parent or guardian is entitled to a due process hearing. The contempt shall be considered criminal in nature. If the parent or guardian fails to pay the fine within a reasonable time set by the court, proceedings to enforce the fine may be either civil or criminal in nature and may include jail as provided in MCL 600.1715; MSA 27A.1715.

[Adopted effective May 15, 1997.]

1997 Staff Comment

The April 8, 1997, amendments of subchapter 5.900 of the Michigan Court Rules [effective May 15, 1997] implement recent statutory changes applicable to the juvenile division of the probate court. See, e.g., 1996 PA 247, 1996 PA 248, 1996 PA 255, 1996 PA 259, and 1996 PA 262. The amendments are based on proposals submitted by the Juvenile Court Rules Committee of the Probate Judges Association. These temporary amendments will remain in effect until further order of the court, and will be reconsidered after receipt of comments.

RULE 5.931 INITIATING DELINQUENCY PROCEEDINGS

(A) **Commencement of Proceeding.** Any request for court action against a juvenile must be in writing by means of a petition.

(B) **Content of Petition.** A petition must contain the following information, if known:

(1) the juvenile's name, address, and date of birth;

(2) the names and addresses of

(a) the juvenile's mother and father,

(b) the parent or person with whom the juvenile is in custody, if other than a mother or father,

(c) the nearest known relative of the juvenile, if no parent can be found, and

(d) any court with prior continuing jurisdiction;

(3) the essential facts which constitute an offense by the juvenile;

(4) a citation to the section of the Juvenile Code relied upon for jurisdiction;

(5) a citation to the federal, state, or local law or ordinance allegedly violated by the juvenile;

(6) the court action requested;

(7) if applicable, the notice required by MCL 257.732(7); MSA 9.2432(7), and the juvenile's Michigan driver's license number; and

(8) information required by MCR 3.206(A)(4), identifying whether a family division matter involving members of the same family is or was pending.

(C) **Citation or Appearance Ticket.** A citation or appearance ticket which conforms to the requirements for valid issuance to an adult may serve as a petition as to an offense other than a major offense when presented to the court. A citation or appearance ticket shall not serve as a basis for pretrial detention.

(D) **Motor Vehicle Violations; Appearances; Failure to Appear.** If the juvenile is a Michigan resident and fails to appear or otherwise to respond to any matter pending relative to a motor vehicle violation, the court:

(1) must initiate the procedure required by MCL 257.321a; MSA 9.2021(1) for the failure to answer a citation;

(2) may issue an order to apprehend the juvenile after a petition is filed with the court.

[Adopted and amended effective January 1, 1988; amended effective November 1, 1989; January 1, 1998.]

1988 Staff Comment

[See 1988 Staff Comment following Rule 5.993.]

Staff Comment to 1989 Amendment

The September 1989 amendments to MCR 5.931(B) and (D) [effective November 1, 1989] were suggested by the Task Force on Reporting Traffic–Related Offenses, and implement recent statutory changes.

Staff Comment to 1998 Amendment

The October 1, 1997, amendments of MCR 3.206, 5.931, and 5.961 [effective January 1, 1998] relate to statutory changes made by 1996 PA 388, which created the family division of the circuit court. The amendments are effective January 1, 1998.

New MCR 3.206(A)(4) creates a requirement for identifying pending or prior family division actions involving members of the same family. References to that provision are included in MCR 5.931(B)(8), governing delinquency proceedings, and MCR 5.961(B)(7), governing child protective proceedings.

RULE 5.932 SUMMARY INITIAL PROCEEDINGS

(A) **Preliminary Inquiry.** When a petition is not accompanied by a request for detention of the juvenile, the court, at a preliminary inquiry, may, in the interest of the juvenile and the public:

(1) deny authorization of the petition;

(2) refer the matter to a public or private agency providing available services pursuant to the Juvenile Diversion Act, 1988 PA 13, MCL 722.821 et seq.; MSA 25.243(51) et seq.;

(3) direct that the juvenile and parent be notified to appear for further informal inquiry on the petition;

(4) proceed on the consent calendar as provided in subrule (B); or

(5) place the matter on the formal calendar as provided in subrule (C).

(B) Consent Calendar. If it appears that protective and supportive action by the court will serve the best interests of the juvenile and the public, the court may, on authorizing the filing of a petition or on receipt of a citation or appearance ticket, and with consent of the juvenile and parent, proceed informally to hear the matter on the consent calendar in the manner provided in this subrule.

(1) *Notice.* Formal notice is not required.

(2) *Limited Disposition.* If, after hearing, the court finds the accusation is true, it may dispose of the matter pursuant to MCL 712A.18; MSA 27.3178(598.18), except that the juvenile shall not be removed from the custody of the parent. If, after hearing, the court finds that the juvenile has violated the Michigan Vehicle Code, MCL 257.1 et seq.; MSA 9.1801 et seq., the court must fulfill the reporting requirements imposed by MCL 712A.2b(d), 257.732; MSA 27.3178(598.2b)(d), 9.2432.

(3) *Transfer to Formal Calendar.* Failure to appear or violation of conditions of a disposition under subrule (B)(2) may result in transfer of the case from the consent calendar to the formal calendar on the charges contained in the authorized petition. Upon transfer, the court shall inform the juvenile of the rights, when applicable, as set forth in MCR 5.935(B)(4). Statements made by the juvenile during the informal proceeding pursuant to this subrule may not be used against the juvenile at a trial on the formal calendar based upon the same charge.

(C) Formal Calendar. The court may authorize a petition to be filed and docketed on the formal calendar if it appears to the court that formal court action is in the best interest of the juvenile and the public. The court shall not authorize an original petition that requests the court to take jurisdiction of a juvenile under MCL 712A.2(a)(1); MSA 27.3178(598.2)(a)(1), unless the prosecuting attorney has approved submitting the petition to the court.

[Adopted and amended effective January 1, 1988; amended effective June 1, 1988; January 1, 1993.]

1988 Staff Comment

[See 1988 Staff Comment following Rule 5.993.]

RULE 5.933 ACQUIRING PHYSICAL CONTROL OF JUVENILE

(A) Custody Without Court Order. When an officer apprehends a juvenile for an offense without court order and does not warn and release the juvenile, does not refer the juvenile to a diversion program, or does not have authorization from the prosecuting attorney to file a complaint and warrant charging the juvenile with an offense as though an adult pursuant to MCL 764.1f; MSA 28.860(6), the officer may:

(1) issue a citation or ticket to appear at a date and time to be set by the court and release the juvenile;

(2) accept a written promise of the parent to bring the juvenile to court, if requested, at a date and time to be set by the court, and release the juvenile to the parent; or

(3) take the juvenile into custody and submit a petition, if:

(a) the officer has reason to believe that due to the nature of the offense, the interest of the juvenile or the interest of the public would not be protected by release of the juvenile, or

(b) a parent cannot be located or the parent refuses to take custody of the juvenile.

(B) Custody With Court Order. When a petition is presented to the court, and probable cause exists to believe that a juvenile has committed an offense, the court may issue an order to apprehend the juvenile. The order may include authorization to:

(1) enter specified premises as required for the purpose of bringing the juvenile before the court, and

(2) detain the juvenile pending preliminary hearing.

(C) Notification of Court. The officer who apprehends a juvenile must immediately contact the court when:

(1) the officer detains the juvenile,

(2) the officer is unable to reach a parent who will appear promptly to accept custody of the juvenile, or

(3) the parent will not agree to bring the juvenile to court as provided in subrule (A)(2).

(D) Separate Custody of Juvenile. While awaiting arrival of the parent, appearance before the court, or otherwise, the juvenile must be maintained separately from adult prisoners to prevent any verbal, visual, or physical contact with an adult prisoner.

[Adopted and amended effective January 1, 1988; amended effective July 1, 1989.]

1988 and 1989 Staff Comments

[See "1988 Staff Comment" and "Staff Comment to July 1, 1989 Amendments," set forth following Rule 5.993.]

RULE 5.934 ARRANGING COURT APPEARANCE; DETAINED JUVENILE

(A) General. Unless the prosecuting attorney has authorized a complaint and warrant charging the juvenile with an offense as though an adult pursuant to MCL 764.1f; MSA 28.860(6), when a juvenile is apprehended and not released, the officer shall:

(1) forthwith take the juvenile

(a) before the court for a preliminary hearing, or

(b) to a place designated by the court pending the scheduling of a preliminary hearing;

(2) ensure that the petition is prepared and presented to the court;

(3) notify the parent of the detaining of the juvenile, and of the need for the presence of the parent at the preliminary hearing;

(4) prepare a custody statement for submission to the court including:

(a) the grounds for and the time and location of detention, and

(b) the names of persons notified and the times of notification, or the reason for failure to notify.

(B) Temporary Detention; Court Not Open.

(1) *Grounds.* A juvenile apprehended without court order when the court is not open may be detained pending preliminary hearing if the offense or the juvenile meets a circumstance set forth in MCR 5.935(D)(2), or if no parent can be located.

(2) *Designated Court Person.* The court must designate a judge, referee or other person who may be contacted by the officer taking a juvenile into custody when the court is not open. In each county there must be a designated facility open at all times at which an officer may obtain the name of the person to be contacted for permission to detain the juvenile pending preliminary hearing.

[Adopted effective January 1, 1988; amended effective July 1, 1989.]

1988 and 1989 Staff Comments

[See "1988 Staff Comment" and "Staff Comment to July 1, 1989 Amendments," set forth following Rule 5.993.]

RULE 5.935 PRELIMINARY HEARING

(A) Time.

(1) *Commencement; Preliminary Hearing.* The preliminary hearing must commence no later than 24 hours after the juvenile has been taken into court custody, excluding Sundays and holidays, or the juvenile must be released.

(2) *General Adjournment.* The court may adjourn the hearing for up to 14 days:

(a) to secure the attendance of the juvenile's parents or witnesses, or

(b) for other good cause shown.

(3) *Special Adjournment; Life Offense.* This subrule shall apply to a juvenile accused of an offense that allegedly was committed between the 15th and 17th birthdate of the juvenile and which, if committed by an adult, would constitute a life offense as specifically listed in MCL 712A.2(a)(1); MSA 27.3178(598.2)(a)(1). On request of a prosecuting attorney who has approved the submission of a petition with the court, conditioned on the opportunity to withdraw it within 5 days if the prosecuting attorney authorizes the filing of a complaint and warrant with a magistrate, the court shall comply with subrules (3)(a) through (c).

(a) The court shall adjourn the preliminary hearing for up to 5 days to give the prosecuting attorney the opportunity to determine whether to authorize the filing of a criminal complaint and warrant charging the juvenile with an offense as though an adult pursuant to MCL 764.1f; MSA 28.860(6), instead of unconditionally approving the filing of a petition with the court.

(b) The court, during the special adjournment under subrule 3(a), must defer a decision as to whether to authorize the filing of the petition.

(c) The court, during the special adjournment under subrule 3(a), must release the juvenile pursuant to MCR 5.935(C) or detain the juvenile pursuant to MCR 5.935(D).

If, at the resumption of the preliminary hearing following special adjournment, the prosecuting attorney has not authorized the filing of a criminal complaint and warrant on the charge with a magistrate concerning the juvenile, approval of the petition by the prosecuting attorney shall no longer be deemed conditional and the court shall proceed with the preliminary hearing and decide whether to authorize the petition to be filed. This rule shall not preclude the prosecuting attorney from moving for a waiver of jurisdiction over the juvenile under MCR 5.950.

(B) Procedure.

(1) The court shall determine whether the parent has been notified and is present. The preliminary hearing may be conducted without a parent provided a guardian ad litem or attorney appears with the juvenile.

(2) The court shall read the allegations in the petition.

(3) The court shall determine whether the petition should be dismissed, whether the matter should be referred to alternate services pursuant to the Juvenile Diversion Act, 1988 PA 13, MCL 722.821 et seq.; MSA 25.243(51) et seq., whether the matter should be heard on the consent calendar as provided by MCR

255

5.932(B), or whether it shall continue with the preliminary hearing.

(4) If the hearing is to continue, the court shall advise the juvenile on the record in plain language of:

(a) the right to an attorney pursuant to MCR 5.915(A)(2);

(b) the right to trial by judge or jury on the allegations in the petition and that a referee may be assigned to hear the case unless demand for a jury or judge is filed pursuant to MCR 5.911 or 5.912; and

(c) the privilege against self-incrimination, and that any statement by the juvenile may be used against the juvenile.

(5) If the charge is a violation of MCL 712A.2(a)(2)–(6) or (d); MSA 27.3178(598.2)(a)(2)–(6) or (d), the court shall inquire if the juvenile or the parent is a registered member of any American Indian tribe or band, or if the juvenile is eligible for such membership. If so, determine and notify the tribe or band and follow the procedures set forth in MCR 5.980.

(6) The juvenile must be allowed an opportunity to deny or otherwise plead to the allegations.

(7) Unless the preliminary hearing is adjourned, the court must decide whether to authorize the petition to be filed pursuant to MCR 5.932(C). If it authorizes the filing of the petition, the court must:

(a) release the juvenile pursuant to subrule (C), or

(b) order detention of the juvenile as provided in subrule (D); and

(c) determine if fingerprints must be taken as provided by MCR 5.936.

(C) **Release of Juvenile.** The court may release a juvenile to a parent pending the resumption of the preliminary hearing, pending trial, or until further order without conditions, or may release a juvenile on the basis of any lawful conditions, including the requirement that bail be posted.

(1) *Factors.* A juvenile may be released and conditions set after the court considers available information on

(a) family ties and relationships,

(b) the juvenile's prior delinquency record,

(c) the juvenile's record of appearance or nonappearance at court proceedings,

(d) the violent nature of the alleged offense,

(e) the juvenile's prior history of committing acts that resulted in bodily injury to others,

(f) the juvenile's character and mental condition,

(g) the court's ability to supervise the juvenile if placed with a parent or relative, and

(h) any other factor indicating the juvenile's ties to the community, the risk of nonappearance, and the danger to the juvenile or the public if the juvenile is released.

(2) *Cash or Surety Bond.* In addition to any other conditions of release, the court may require a parent to post a surety bond or cash in the full amount of the bail, at the parent's option. Except as otherwise provided by this rule, MCR 3.604 applies to bonds posted under this rule.

(3) *Option to Deposit Cash or 10 Percent of Bail.* Unless the court requires a surety bond or cash as provided in subrule (C)(2), the court shall advise the parent of the option to satisfy the monetary requirement of bail by:

(a) posting cash in the full amount of bail set by the court or a surety bond written by a person or company licensed to write surety bonds, or

(b) depositing with the register, clerk, or cashier of the court currency equal to 10 percent of the bail, but at least $10.

(4) *Findings.* The court must state the reasons for its decision to grant or deny release on the record or in a written memorandum. The court's statement need not include a finding on each of the enumerated factors.

(5) *Revocation or Modification.* The court may modify or revoke the bail for good cause after providing the parties notice and an opportunity to be heard.

(6) *Return of Bail.* If the conditions of bail are met, the court shall discharge any surety.

(a) If disposition imposes reimbursement or costs, the bail money posted by the parent must first be applied to the amount of reimbursement and costs, and the balance, if any, returned.

(b) If the juvenile is discharged from all obligations in the case, the court shall return the cash posted, or return 90 percent and retain 10 percent if the amount posted represented 10 percent of the bail.

(7) *Forfeiture.* If the conditions of bail are not met, the court may issue a writ for the apprehension of the juvenile and enter an order declaring the bail money, if any, forfeited.

(a) The court must immediately mail notice of the forfeiture order to the parent at the last known address and to any surety.

(b) If the juvenile does not appear and surrender to the court within 28 days from the forfeiture date, or does not within the period satisfy the court that the juvenile is not at fault, the court may enter judgment against the parent and surety, if any, for the entire amount of the bail and, when allowed, costs of the court proceedings.

(D) Pretrial Detention. A juvenile shall not be removed from the parent pending trial or further court order unless:

(1) probable cause exists to believe the juvenile committed an offense, and

(2) the court finds one or more of the following circumstances to be present:

(a) the offense alleged to have been committed by the juvenile is so serious that release would endanger the public safety;

(b) the juvenile charged with a major offense will likely commit another offense pending trial, if released, and

(i) another petition is pending against the juvenile,

(ii) the juvenile is on probation, or

(iii) the juvenile has a prior adjudication but is not under the court's jurisdiction at the time of apprehension;

(c) there is a substantial likelihood that if the juvenile is released to the parent, with or without conditions, the juvenile will fail to appear at the next court proceeding;

(d) pretrial detention is otherwise specifically authorized by law.

(3) *Waiver.* A juvenile in custody may waive the probable cause phase of a detention determination only if the juvenile is represented by an attorney.

(4) *Evidence; Findings.* The juvenile may contest the sufficiency of evidence to support detention by cross-examination of witnesses, presentation of defense witnesses, or by other evidence. The court shall permit the use of subpoena power to secure attendance of defense witnesses. A finding of probable cause under subrule (D)(1) may be based on hearsay evidence which possesses adequate guarantees of trustworthiness. The findings of the court to support detention of the juvenile shall be in writing or placed on the record.

(5) *Type of Detention.* The detained juvenile must be placed in the least restrictive environment that will meet the needs of the juvenile and the public, and that will conform to the requirements of 1987 PA 72, MCL 712A.15, 712A.16; MSA 27.3178(598.15), 27.3178(598.16).

[Adopted and amended effective January 1, 1988; amended effective June 1, 1988; July 1, 1989.]

1988 Staff Comment

[See 1988 Staff Comment following Rule 5.993.]

[Under the January 1, 1988 amendment,] MCR 5.935 becomes consistent with 1987 PA 72, MCL 712A.15, 712A.16; MSA 27.3178(598.15), 27.3178(598.16).

Staff Comment to 1989 Amendment

[See "Staff Comment to July 1, 1989 Amendments," following Rule 5.993.]

RULE 5.936 FINGERPRINTING

(A) General. The court must permit fingerprinting of a juvenile pursuant to MCL 712A.11, 712A.18; MSA 27.3178(598.11), 27.3178(598.18), and as provided in this rule. Notice of fingerprinting retained by the court is confidential.

(B) Order for Fingerprints. At the time that the court authorizes the filing of a petition alleging a reportable juvenile offense and before the court enters an order of disposition on a reportable juvenile offense, the court shall examine the confidential files and verify that the juvenile has been fingerprinted. If it appears to the court that the juvenile has not been fingerprinted, the court must:

(1) direct the juvenile to go to the law enforcement agency involved in the apprehension of the juvenile, or to the sheriff's department, so fingerprints may be taken; or

(2) issue an order to the sheriff's department to apprehend the juvenile and to take the fingerprints of the juvenile.

(C) Notice of Disposition. The court shall notify the Central Records Division of the Department of State Police in writing:

(1) of any juvenile who had been fingerprinted for a reportable juvenile offense and who was found not to be within the jurisdiction of the juvenile court under MCL 712A.2(a)(1); MSA 27.3178(598.2)(a)(1); or

(2) that the court took jurisdiction of a juvenile under MCL 712A.2(a)(1); MSA 27.3178(598.2)(a)(1), who was fingerprinted for a reportable juvenile offense specifying the nature of the adjudicated offense, the method of adjudication, and the disposition ordered.

(D) Order for Return of Fingerprints. If a juvenile is fingerprinted for a juvenile offense, and if no petition on the offense is submitted to the court, if the court does not authorize the petition, or if the court does not take jurisdiction of the juvenile under MCL 712A.2(a)(1); MSA 27.3178(598.2)(a)(1), the court, on motion filed pursuant to MCL 28.243(5); MSA 4.463(5), shall:

(1) issue a peremptory order directing the Central Records Division of the Department of State Police to return the fingerprints, arrest card, and description of the juvenile pertaining to the offense other than an offense as listed in MCL 28.243(8)(a); MSA 4.463(8)(a), as amended by 1988 PA 40; and

(2) direct that fingerprint information in the court file pertaining to the offense be expunged.

[Adopted effective June 1, 1988.]

1988 Staff Comment

[See 1988 Staff Comment following Rule 5.993.]

RULE 5.939   CASE TRANSFERRED FROM DISTRICT COURT PURSUANT TO SUBCHAPTER 6.900

(A) General Procedure. Except as provided in subrule (B), the court shall hear and dispose of a case transferred pursuant to MCL 766.14; MSA 28.932 in the same manner as if the case had commenced in the juvenile court. A petition that has been approved by the prosecuting attorney must be submitted to the court.

(B) Probable Cause Finding of Magistrate. The court may use the probable cause finding of the magistrate made at the preliminary examination to satisfy the requisite probable cause in MCR 5.935(D).

[Adopted effective August 23, 1989.]

1989 Staff Comment

Under recent legislation, a prosecuting official may authorize the filing of a complaint and warrant criminally charging a 15- or 16-year-old juvenile with one or more of nine enumerated life offenses instead of filing a petition in the juvenile court. MCL 600.606; MSA 27A.606 as added by 1988 PA 52; MCL 725.10a(1)(c); MSA 27.3950(1)(c) as amended by 1988 PA 51; MCL 764.1f; MSA 28.860(6) as added by 1988 PA 67. Under this approach there is no requirement that the juvenile court waive its jurisdiction. MCL 712A.2(a)(1); MSA 27.3178(598.2)(a)(1) as amended by 1988 PA 53. Should the district court magistrate fail to find that a juvenile has committed one or more of the enumerated life offenses, the magistrate is required to determine if the juvenile has committed any nonenumerated offense. MCL 766.14; MSA 28.932 as added by 1988 PA 67. The magistrate must transfer the case to the juvenile court for further proceedings if there is probable cause to believe that the juvenile has committed any nonenumerated offense. Under Rule 5.939, the juvenile court essentially must begin the case anew. This includes the requirement that a petition be submitted for authorization by the court.

RULE 5.941   PLEAS OF ADMISSION OR NO CONTEST

(A) Capacity. A juvenile may offer a plea of admission or of no contest to an offense with the consent of the court. The court shall not accept a plea to an offense unless the court is satisfied that the plea is accurate, voluntary, and understanding.

(B) Qualified Pleas. The court may accept a plea of admission or of no contest conditioned on preservation of an issue for appellate review.

(C) Plea Procedure. Before accepting a plea of admission or of no contest, the court must personally address the juvenile and must comply with subrules (1)–(4).

(1) *An Understanding Plea.* The court shall tell the juvenile:

(a) the name of the offense charged,

(b) the possible dispositions,

(c) that if the plea is accepted, the juvenile will not have a trial of any kind, so the juvenile gives up the rights that would be present at trial, including the right:

(i) to trial by jury,

(ii) to trial by the judge if the juvenile does not want trial by jury,

(iii) to be presumed innocent until proven guilty,

(iv) to have the petitioner or prosecutor prove guilt beyond a reasonable doubt,

(v) to have witnesses against the juvenile appear at the trial,

(vi) to question the witnesses against the juvenile,

(vii) to have the court order any witnesses for the juvenile's defense to appear at the trial,

(viii) to remain silent and not have the juvenile's silence used against the juvenile, and

(ix) to testify at trial, if the juvenile wants to testify.

(2) *A Voluntary Plea.*

(a) The court shall confirm any plea agreement on the record.

(b) The court shall ask the juvenile if any promises have been made beyond those in a plea agreement or whether anyone has threatened the juvenile.

(3) *An Accurate Plea.* The court may not accept a plea of admission or of no contest without establishing support for a finding that the juvenile committed the offense:

(a) either by questioning the juvenile or by other means when the plea is a plea of admission, or

(b) by means other than questioning the juvenile when the juvenile pleads no contest. The court shall also state why a plea of no contest is appropriate.

(4) *Parental Support for Plea.* The court shall inquire of the parent or guardian ad litem whether the parent or guardian ad litem knows of any reason why the court should not accept the plea tendered by the juvenile. Agreement or objection by the parent or guardian ad litem to a plea of admission or of no contest by a juvenile must be placed on the record if the parent or guardian ad litem is present.

(D) Plea Withdrawal. The court may take a plea of admission or of no contest under advisement. Before the court accepts the plea, the juvenile may withdraw the plea offer by right. After the court accepts the plea, the court has discretion to allow the juvenile to withdraw a plea.

[Adopted effective January 1, 1988.]

1988 Staff Comment

[See 1988 Staff Comment following Rule 5.993.]

RULE 5.942   TRIAL

(A) Time. In all cases the trial must be held within 6 months after the filing of the petition, unless adjourned for good cause. If the juvenile is detained, the trial has not started within 63 days after the juvenile is taken into custody, and the delay in starting the trial is not attributable to the defense, the court shall forthwith order the juvenile released pending trial without requiring that bail be posted unless the juvenile is being detained on another matter.

(B) Preliminary Matters.

(1) The court shall determine whether all parties are present.

(a) The juvenile has the right to be present at the trial along with parents, guardian ad litem, and attorney.

(b) The court may proceed in the absence of a parent properly noticed to appear.

(c) The victim has the right to be present at trial as provided by MCL 780.751 et seq.; MSA 28.1287(751) et seq., as added by 1988 PA 22.

(2) The court shall read the allegations contained in the petition, unless waived.

(3) The court shall inform the juvenile of the right to the assistance of an attorney pursuant to MCR 5.915 unless legal counsel appears with the juvenile. If the juvenile requests to proceed without the assistance of counsel, the court must advise the juvenile of the dangers and disadvantages of self-representation and make sure the juvenile is competent to conduct the defense and literate.

(C) Evidence; Standard of Proof. The Michigan Rules of Evidence and the standard of proof beyond a reasonable doubt apply at trial.

[Adopted and amended effective January 1, 1988; amended effective June 1, 1988; January 1, 1991; May 15, 1997.]

1988 Staff Comment

[See 1988 Staff Comment following Rule 5.993.]

[Under the January 1, 1988 amendment,] MCR 5.942 is changed to provide that a detained juvenile need not be released when the trial has not started in 42 days if the delay is attributable to the defense. MCR 5.943 and MCR 5.973 mean that when the probate court orders a person to be examined by a physician, psychiatrist, social worker, etc., that professional's interview and opinion cannot be prevented from being used at the disposition on a theory that it is privileged information.

Staff Comment to 1997 Amendment

The April 8, 1997, amendments of subchapter 5.900 of the Michigan Court Rules [effective May 15, 1997] implement recent statutory changes applicable to the juvenile division of the probate court. See, e.g., 1996 PA 247, 1996 PA 248, 1996 PA 255, 1996 PA 259, and 1996 PA 262. The amendments are based on proposals submitted by the Juvenile Court Rules Committee of the Probate Judges Association. These temporary amendments will remain in effect until further order of the court, and will be reconsidered after receipt of comments.

RULE 5.943   DISPOSITIONAL PHASE

(A) General. A dispositional hearing is conducted to determine what measures the court will take concerning the juvenile who is properly found within the jurisdiction of the court, and, when applicable, against any adult.

(B) Time. The interval between the plea of admission or trial and disposition, if any, is within the court's discretion. When the juvenile is detained, the interval may not be more than 35 days, except for good cause.

(C) Evidence.

(1) At the dispositional hearing all relevant and material evidence, including oral and written reports, may be received by the court and may be relied upon to the extent of its probative value, even though such evidence may not be admissible at trial.

(2) The juvenile, or the juvenile's attorney, and the petitioner shall be afforded an opportunity to examine and controvert written reports so received and, in the court's discretion, may be allowed to cross-examine individuals making reports when such individuals are reasonably available.

(3) No assertion of an evidentiary privilege, other than the privilege between attorney and client, shall prevent the receipt and use, at the dispositional phase, of materials prepared pursuant to a court-ordered examination, interview, or course of treatment.

(D) Presence of Juvenile and Victim.

(1) The juvenile may be excused from part of the dispositional hearing for good cause shown, but the juvenile must be present when the disposition is announced.

(2) The victim has the right to be present at the dispositional hearing as provided by MCL 780.751 et seq.; MSA 28.1287(751) et seq.; as added by 1988 PA 22.

(E) Dispositions.

(1) If the juvenile has been found to have committed an offense, the court may enter an order of disposition as provided by MCL 712A.18; MSA 27.3178(598.18).

(2) Before a juvenile is placed in an institution outside the state of Michigan as a disposition, the court must find:

(a) institutional care is in the best interests of the juvenile,

(b) equivalent facilities to meet the juvenile's needs are not available within Michigan, and

(c) the placement will not cause undue hardship.

(3) The court shall not enter an order of disposition for a reportable juvenile offense until the court verifies that the juvenile has been fingerprinted. If the juvenile has not been fingerprinted, the court shall proceed as provided by MCR 5.936.

(4) *Mandatory Detention for Use of a Firearm.*

(a) In addition to any other disposition, a juvenile, other than a juvenile sentenced in the same manner as an adult under MCL 712A.18(1)(n); MSA 27.3178(598.18)(1)(n) shall be committed under MCL 712A.18(1)(e); MSA 27.3178(598.18)(1)(e) to a detention facility for a specified time if all the following circumstances exist:

(i) the juvenile is under the jurisdiction of the juvenile division under MCL 712A.2(a)(1); MSA 27.3178(598.2)(a)(1),

(ii) the juvenile was adjudicated or convicted of violating a criminal municipal ordinance or law of this state or of the United States, and

(iii) the juvenile was found to have used a firearm during the offense.

(b) The length of the commitment to a detention facility shall not exceed the length of the sentence that could have been imposed if the juvenile had been sentenced as an adult.

(c) "Firearm" means any weapon from which a dangerous projectile may be propelled by using explosives, gas or air as a means of propulsion, except any smoothbore rifle or hand gun designed and manufactured exclusively for propelling BB's not exceeding.177 caliber by means of spring, gas or air.

[Adopted and amended effective January 1, 1988; amended effective June 1, 1988; May 15, 1997.]

1988 Staff Comment

[See 1988 Staff Comment following Rule 5.993.]

Staff Comment to 1997 Amendment

The April 8, 1997, amendments of subchapter 5.900 of the Michigan Court Rules [effective May 15, 1997] implement recent statutory changes applicable to the juvenile division of the probate court. See, e.g., 1996 PA 247, 1996 PA 248, 1996 PA 255, 1996 PA 259, and 1996 PA 262. The amendments are based on proposals submitted by the Juvenile Court Rules Committee of the Probate Judges Association. These temporary amendments will remain in effect until further order of the court, and will be reconsidered after receipt of comments.

RULE 5.944 SUPPLEMENTAL DISPOSITIONS; DISPOSITIONAL REHEARINGS

(A) **Probation Violation Hearings.**

(1) When it is alleged that a juvenile has violated a condition of probation the court may:

(a) authorize preparation and filing of a supplemental petition; and

(b) direct that the juvenile be notified pursuant to MCR 5.920 to appear for a hearing on the alleged violation, or order that the juvenile be apprehended and brought to the court for a preliminary hearing as provided in MCR 5.935.

(2) At a preliminary appearance on the alleged violation or in the notice to appear for the probation violation hearing, the juvenile shall be provided a copy of the supplemental petition and advised of the right:

(a) to have witnesses against the juvenile appear at a hearing and to question the witnesses;

(b) to have the court order any witnesses for the juvenile's defense to appear at the hearing;

(c) to remain silent and to not have the juvenile's silence used against the juvenile;

(d) to an attorney as provided in MCR 5.915.

(3) The juvenile may admit the violation.

(4) If the juvenile denies the allegation, the court shall schedule a probation violation hearing within 42 days after the filing of the supplemental petition.

(5) The juvenile shall have the right to appear, present evidence, and cross-examine witnesses at the hearing. The standard of proof for establishing the violation of probation is a preponderance of the evidence. The rules of evidence, other than those with respect to privileges, do not apply. There is no right to a jury.

(6) If the court finds that a violation has occurred, the court may make a supplemental disposition including revoking probation and committing the juvenile.

(B) **Juveniles on Conditional Release.** The procedures set forth in subrule (A) apply to juveniles committed under MCL 712A.18; MSA 27.3178(598.18) who have allegedly violated a condition of release after being returned to the community on release from a public institution. The court need not conduct such a hearing when there will be an administrative hearing by the agency to which the juvenile is committed provided the court has not retained jurisdiction.

(C) **Progress Review of Court-Committed Juveniles.**

(1) *General.* The court shall review the progress of a juvenile it has committed to a facility or institution under MCL 712A.18(1)(e); MSA 27.3178(598.18)(1)(e) when the court has retained jurisdiction over the juvenile as required by law.

(2) *Time.* The court must conduct the progress review no later than 182 days after entry of the order of commitment, and semiannually thereafter, so long as the juvenile remains in placement.

(3) *Review Report.* The court shall examine the report prepared by the department of social services

covering placement, services being provided the juvenile, and the progress of the juvenile.

(4) *No Restrictive Placement Change Without Hearing.* If not specified in its order, the court may not order a more physically restrictive level of placement of the juvenile or order more restrictive treatment absent a hearing as provided in subrule (D)(4).

(D) Commitment Review Hearings.

(1) *General.* The objectives of the commitment review hearing include deciding whether to release a court-committed juvenile, whether to continue jurisdiction over the court-committed juvenile until age 21 pursuant to MCL 712A.18d; MSA 27.3178(598.18d) and to give the juvenile an opportunity to be heard before moving a juvenile to a more physically restrictive level of placement or ordering more restrictive treatment.

(2) *Notice.* Notice of the hearing must be given to the prosecuting attorney, the agency or the superintendent of the facility to which the juvenile has been committed, the juvenile, and the parent of the juvenile if the parent's address or whereabouts are known, at least 14 days prior to the hearing.

(3) *Required Commitment Review Hearing.* When a juvenile has been placed in a facility or institution under MCL 712A.18(1)(e); MSA 27.3178(598.18)(1)(e) for having committed, after October 1, 1988, a reportable juvenile offense other than (h), (n) and (o) of MCR 5.903(B)(6), the court shall schedule a commitment review hearing to be held within 42 days before the juvenile attains age 19 unless adjourned for good cause.

(a) Notice. Notice of the required hearing must clearly indicate that the court may extend jurisdiction over the juvenile until age 21 years. The notice shall include advice to the juvenile and the parent of the juvenile that the juvenile has the right to an attorney.

(b) Appointment of an Attorney. The court must appoint an attorney to represent the juvenile at the required review hearing unless legal counsel has been retained.

(c) Burden of Proof; Evidence; Criteria. The juvenile has the burden of proving by a preponderance of the evidence that the juvenile has been rehabilitated and that the juvenile does not present a serious risk to public safety. Evidence shall be received under the rules applicable to a dispositional hearing pursuant to MCR 5.943(C). In making the determination, the court must consider the following factors:

(i) the extent and nature of the juvenile's participation in education, counseling, or work programs;

(ii) the juvenile's willingness to accept responsibility for prior behavior;

(iii) the juvenile's behavior in the current placement;

(iv) the prior record and character of the juvenile and physical and mental maturity;

(v) the juvenile's potential for violent conduct as demonstrated by prior behavior;

(vi) the recommendations of the institution, agency, or facility charged with the juvenile's care for the juvenile's release or continued custody; and

(vii) any other information the prosecuting attorney or the juvenile may submit.

(4) *Other Commitment Review Hearings.* The court, on motion of the institution, agency, or facility to which the juvenile is committed, may at any time discharge a juvenile upon a showing by a preponderance of evidence that the juvenile has been rehabilitated and is not a risk to public safety. The notice provisions and criteria in subrule (3) shall apply. Evidence shall be received under the same rules as applicable to a dispositional hearing pursuant to MCR 5.943(C). The court must appoint an attorney to represent the juvenile at the hearing unless legal counsel has been retained. The court, upon notice and opportunity to be heard, may order the juvenile moved to a more physically restrictive level of placement or may order more restrictive treatment.

(E) Dispositional Review Hearings. An order entered in any delinquency case may be supplemented or amended in accordance with MCL 712A.18; MSA 27.3178(598.18), as long as the juvenile remains under the jurisdiction of the court. If not specified in the order of the court, the juvenile shall not be moved to a more physically restrictive level of placement absent a hearing and further order of the court, or absent the consent of the juvenile. If the juvenile is in foster care, the court shall hold a dispositional review hearing no later than every 182 days as provided in MCL 712A.19(2); MSA 27.3178(598.19)(2).

[Adopted and amended effective January 1, 1988; amended effective July 1, 1989; May 15, 1997.]

1988 and 1989 Staff Comments

[See "1988 Staff Comment" and "Staff Comment to July 1, 1989 Amendments," set forth following Rule 5.993.]

Staff Comment to 1997 Amendment

The April 8, 1997, amendments of subchapter 5.900 of the Michigan Court Rules [effective May 15, 1997] implement recent statutory changes applicable to the juvenile division of the probate court. See, e.g., 1996 PA 247, 1996 PA 248, 1996 PA 255, 1996 PA 259, and 1996 PA 262. The amendments are based on proposals submitted by the Juvenile Court Rules Committee of the Probate Judges Association. These temporary amendments will remain in effect until further order of the court, and will be reconsidered after receipt of comments.

RULE 5.950　WAIVER OF JURISDICTION

(A) Motion by Prosecuting Attorney. A motion by the prosecuting attorney requesting that the juvenile court waive its jurisdiction to a court of general criminal jurisdiction must be in writing and must clearly indicate the charges and that if the motion is granted the juvenile will be prosecuted as though an adult.

(1) A motion to waive jurisdiction of the juvenile must be filed within 14 days after the filing of the petition. Absent a timely motion and good cause shown, the juvenile shall no longer be subject to waiver of jurisdiction on the charges.

(2) A copy of the motion seeking waiver shall be personally served on the juvenile and the parent of the juvenile, if their addresses or whereabouts are known or can be determined by the exercise of due diligence.

(B) Hearing Procedure. The waiver hearing shall consist of two phases. Notice of the date, time, and place of the hearings may be given either on the record directly to the juvenile or to the attorney for the juvenile, the prosecuting attorney, and all other parties, or in writing, served on each individual.

(1) *First Phase.* The first-phase hearing is to determine whether there is probable cause that an offense has been committed which if committed by an adult would be a felony, and that there is probable cause that the juvenile who is 14 years of age or older committed the offense.

(a) The probable cause hearing shall be commenced within 28 days after the filing of the petition unless adjourned for good cause.

(b) At the hearing, the prosecuting attorney has the burden to present legally admissible evidence to establish each element of the offense and to establish probable cause that the juvenile committed the offense.

(c) The court need not conduct the first phase of the waiver hearing, if:

(i) the court has found the requisite probable cause at a hearing under MCR 5.935(D)(1), provided that at the earlier hearing only legally admissible evidence was used to establish probable cause that the offense was committed and probable cause that the juvenile committed the offense; or

(ii) the juvenile, after being informed by the court on the record that the probable cause hearing is equivalent to and held in place of preliminary examination in district court, waives the hearing. The court must determine that the waiver of hearing is freely, voluntarily, and understandingly given and that the juvenile knows there will be no preliminary examination in district court if the court waives jurisdiction.

(2) *Second Phase.* If the court finds the requisite probable cause at the first-phase hearing, or if there is no hearing pursuant to subrule (B)(1)(c), the second-phase hearing shall be held to determine whether the interests of the juvenile and the public would best be served by granting the motion, unless the juvenile has previously been subject to the general criminal jurisdiction of the circuit court under MCL 712A.4; MSA 27.3178(598.4) or MCL 600.606; MSA 27A.606, or the Recorder's Court of the City of Detroit under MCL 712A.4; MSA 27.3178(598.4) or MCL 725.10a; MSA 27.3950(1). If the juvenile has been subject to the general criminal jurisdiction of either the circuit court or Recorder's Court under MCL 712A.4, MCL 600.606 or MCL 725.10a, the court shall waive jurisdiction of the juvenile to the court of general criminal jurisdiction without holding the second-phase hearing.

(a) The Michigan Rules of Evidence, other than those with respect to privileges, do not apply to the second phase of the waiver hearing.

(b) The second-phase hearing shall be commenced within 28 days after the conclusion of the first phase or within 35 days after the filing of the petition if there was no hearing pursuant to subrule (B)(1)(c), unless adjourned for good cause.

(c) The prosecuting attorney has the burden of establishing by a preponderance of the evidence that the best interests of the juvenile and the public would be served by waiver.

(d) The court, in determining whether to waive the juvenile to the court having general criminal jurisdiction, shall consider and make findings on the following criteria, giving greater weight to the seriousness of the alleged offense and the juvenile's prior record of delinquency and to other criteria:

(i) the seriousness of the alleged offense in terms of community protection, including, but not limited to, the existence of any aggravating factors recognized by the sentencing guidelines, the use of a firearm or other dangerous weapon, and the effect on any victim;

(ii) the culpability of the juvenile in committing the alleged offense, including, but not limited to, the level of the juvenile's participation in planning and carrying out the offense and the existence of any aggravating or mitigating factors recognized by the sentencing guidelines;

(iii) the juvenile's prior record of delinquency including, but not limited to, any record of detention, any police record, any school record, or any other evidence indicating prior delinquent behavior;

(iv) the juvenile's programming history, including, but not limited to, the juvenile's past willingness to participate meaningfully in available programming;

(v) the adequacy of the punishment or programming available in the juvenile justice system;

(vi) the dispositional options available for the juvenile.

(e) The court, in determining whether to waive the juvenile to the court having general criminal jurisdiction, may also consider any stipulation by the defense to a finding that the best interests of the juvenile and the public support a waiver.

(C) Grant of Waiver Motion.

(1) If the court determines that it is in the best interests of the juvenile and public to waive jurisdiction over the juvenile, the court must:

(a) enter a written order granting the motion to waive jurisdiction and transferring the matter to the appropriate court having general criminal jurisdiction for arraignment of the juvenile on an information.

(b) make findings of fact and conclusions of law forming the basis for entry of the waiver order. The findings and conclusions may be incorporated in a written opinion or stated on the record.

(c) advise the juvenile, orally or in writing, that

(i) the juvenile is entitled to appellate review of its decision to waive jurisdiction,

(ii) the juvenile must seek review of the decision in the Court of Appeals within 21 days of the order to preserve the appeal of right, and

(iii) if the juvenile is financially unable to retain a lawyer, the court will appoint a lawyer to represent the juvenile on appeal.

(d) The court shall send, without cost, a copy of the order and a copy of the written opinion or transcript of the findings and conclusions of the court, to the court having general criminal jurisdiction.

(2) Upon the grant of a waiver motion, a juvenile shall be transferred to the adult criminal justice system and shall be subject to the same procedures used for adult criminal defendants. Juveniles waived pursuant to this rule are not required to be kept separate and apart from adult prisoners.

(D) Denial of Waiver Motion. If the waiver motion is denied, the court shall make written findings or place them on the record. A transcript of the court's findings or, if a written opinion is prepared, a copy of the written opinion shall be sent to the prosecuting attorney, juvenile, or juvenile's attorney upon request. If the juvenile is detained and the trial of the matter in juvenile court has not started within 28 days after entry of the order denying the waiver motion and the delay is not attributable to the defense, the court shall forthwith order the juvenile released pending trial without requiring that bail be posted unless the juvenile is being detained on another matter.

(E) Psychiatric Testimony.

(1) A psychiatrist, psychologist, or certified social worker who conducts a court-ordered examination for purposes of a waiver hearing may not testify at a subsequent criminal proceeding involving the juvenile without the juvenile's written consent.

(2) The juvenile's consent may only be given:

(a) in the presence of an attorney representing the juvenile or, if no legal counsel represents the juvenile, in the presence of a parent;

(b) after the juvenile has had an opportunity to read the report of the psychiatrist, psychologist, or certified social worker; and

(c) after the waiver decision is rendered.

(3) Consent to testimony by the psychiatrist, psychologist, or certified social worker shall not waive the juvenile's privilege against self-incrimination.

(F) As used in this rule, "felony" means an offense punishable by imprisonment for more than one year or an offense designated by law as a felony.

[Adopted and amended effective January 1, 1988; amended effective July 1, 1989; May 15, 1997; January 1, 1998.]

1988 and 1989 Staff Comments

[See "1988 Staff Comment" and "Staff Comment to July 1, 1989 Amendments," set forth following Rule 5.993.]

Staff Comment to 1997 Amendment

The April 8, 1997, amendments of subchapter 5.900 of the Michigan Court Rules [effective May 15, 1997] implement recent statutory changes applicable to the juvenile division of the probate court. See, e.g., 1996 PA 247, 1996 PA 248, 1996 PA 255, 1996 PA 259, and 1996 PA 262. The amendments are based on proposals submitted by the Juvenile Court Rules Committee of the Probate Judges Association. These temporary amendments will remain in effect until further order of the court, and will be reconsidered after receipt of comments.

Staff Comment to 1998 Amendment

The December 19, 1997, amendments to Rule 3.206 and subchapter 5.900 of the Michigan Court Rules [effective January 1, 1998] implement recent statutory changes which have created a family division of the circuit court. These amendments will remain in effect until further order of the court.

RULE 5.951   INITIATING DESIGNATED PROCEEDINGS

(A) Prosecutor–Designated Cases.

(1) *Juvenile in Custody or Custody Requested.*

(a) If the prosecuting attorney submits a petition designating the case for trial in the same manner as an adult, the arraignment must commence no later than 24 hours after the juvenile has been taken into court custody, excluding Sundays and holidays as defined by MCR 8.110(D)(2), or the juvenile must be released.

(b) General Adjournment. The court may adjourn the arraignment for up to 7 days:

(i) to secure the attendance of the juvenile's parent, guardian, or legal custodian or of a witness, or

(ii) for other good cause shown.

(c) Procedure.

(i) The court shall determine whether the juvenile's parent, guardian, or legal custodian has been notified and is present. The arraignment may be conducted without a parent, guardian, or legal custodian, provided a guardian ad litem or attorney appears with the juvenile.

(ii) The court shall read the allegations in the petition.

(iii) The court shall advise the juvenile on the record in plain language:

a. of the right to an attorney pursuant to MCR 5.915(A)(2);

b. of the right to trial by judge or jury on the allegations in the petition;

c. of the right to remain silent and that any statement made by the juvenile may be used against the juvenile;

d. of the right to have a preliminary examination within 14 days;

e. that the case has been designated for trial in the same manner as an adult and if the prosecuting attorney proves that there is probable cause to believe an offense was committed and there is probable cause to believe that the juvenile committed the offense, the juvenile will be afforded all the rights of an adult charged with the same crime and that upon conviction the juvenile may be sentenced as an adult;

f. of the maximum possible prison sentence and any mandatory minimum sentence required by law.

(iv) Unless the arraignment is adjourned, the court must decide whether to authorize the petition to be filed. If it authorizes the filing of the petition, the court must:

a. determine if fingerprints must be taken as provided by MCR 5.936; and

b. determine if conditions warrant detention pursuant to MCR 5.935(D), or

c. release the juvenile pursuant to MCR 5.935(C).

(v) A juvenile may be detained pending the completion of the arraignment if it appears to the court that one of the circumstances in MCR 5.935(D)(2) is present.

(vi) If the petition is authorized for filing, the court must schedule a preliminary examination within 14 days before a judge other than the judge who would conduct the trial.

(2) *Juvenile Not in Custody; Custody Not Requested.*

(a) If the prosecuting attorney submits a petition designating the case for trial in the same manner as an adult, the juvenile shall be brought before the court for an arraignment as soon as the juvenile's attendance can be secured.

(b) Procedure.

(i) The court shall determine whether the juvenile's parent, guardian, or legal custodian has been notified and is present. The arraignment may be conducted without a parent, guardian, or legal custodian, provided a guardian ad litem or attorney appears with the juvenile.

(ii) The court shall read the allegations in the petition.

(iii) The court shall advise the juvenile on the record in plain language:

a. of the right to an attorney pursuant to MCR 5.915(A)(2);

b. of the right to trial by judge or jury on the allegations in the petition;

c. of the right to remain silent and that any statement made by the juvenile may be used against the juvenile;

d. of the right to have a preliminary examination within 14 days;

e. that the case has been designated for trial in the same manner as an adult and if the prosecuting attorney proves that there is probable cause to believe an offense was committed and there is probable cause to believe that the juvenile committed the offense, the juvenile will be afforded all the rights of an adult charged with the same crime and that upon conviction the juvenile may be sentenced as an adult;

f. of the maximum possible prison sentence and any mandatory minimum sentence required by law.

(iv) Unless the arraignment is adjourned, the court must decide whether to authorize the petition to be filed. If it authorizes the filing of the petition, the court must determine if fingerprints must be taken as provided by MCR 5.936.

(v) If the petition is authorized for filing, the court must schedule a preliminary examination within 14 days before a judge other than the judge who would conduct the trial.

(3) If a petition submitted by the prosecuting attorney alleging a specified juvenile violation did not include a designation of the case for trial as an adult:

(a) the prosecuting attorney may, by right, amend the petition to designate the case during the preliminary hearing, or

(b) the prosecuting attorney may request leave of the court to amend the petition to designate the case no later than the pretrial hearing or, if there is no pretrial hearing, at least 21 days before trial, absent good cause for further delay. The court may permit the prosecuting attorney to amend the petition to designate the case as the interests of justice require.

(B) Court–Designated Cases.

(1) *Juvenile in Custody or Custody Requested.*

(a) If the prosecuting attorney submits a petition charging an offense other than a specified juvenile violation and requests the court to designate the case for trial in the same manner as an adult, arraignment must commence no later than 24 hours after the juvenile has been taken into court custody, excluding Sundays and holidays as defined by MCR 8.110(D)(2), or the juvenile must be released.

(b) General adjournment. The court may adjourn the arraignment for up to 7 days:

(i) to secure the attendance of the juvenile's parent, guardian, or legal custodian or of a witness, or

(ii) for other good cause shown.

(c) Procedure.

(i) The court shall determine whether the juvenile's parent, guardian, or legal custodian has been notified and is present. The arraignment may be conducted without a parent, guardian, or legal custodian, provided a guardian ad litem or attorney appears with the juvenile.

(ii) The court shall read the allegations in the petition.

(iii) The court shall advise the juvenile on the record in plain language:

a. of the right to an attorney pursuant to MCR 5.915(A)(2);

b. of the right to trial by judge or jury on the allegations in the petition;

c. of the right to remain silent and that any statement made by the juvenile may be used against the juvenile;

d. of the right to have a designation hearing within 14 days;

e. of the right to have a preliminary examination within 14 days after the case is designated if the juvenile is charged with a felony or offense for which an adult could be imprisoned for more than one year;

f. that if the case is designated by the court for trial in the same manner as an adult and, if a preliminary examination is required by law, the prosecuting attorney proves that there is probable cause to believe that an offense was committed and there is probable cause to believe that the juvenile committed the offense, the juvenile will be afforded all the rights of an adult charged with the same crime and that upon conviction the juvenile may be sentenced as an adult;

g. of the maximum possible prison sentence and any mandatory minimum sentence required by law.

(iv) Unless the arraignment is adjourned, the court must decide whether to authorize the petition to be filed. If it authorizes the filing of the petition, the court must:

a. determine if fingerprints must be taken as provided by MCR 5.936; and

b. determine if conditions warrant detention pursuant to MCR 5.935(D), or

c. release the juvenile pursuant to MCR 5.935(C).

(v) A juvenile may be detained pending the completion of the arraignment if it appears to the court that one of the circumstances in MCR 5.935(D)(2) is present.

(vi) If the petition is authorized for filing, the court must schedule a designation hearing within 14 days.

(2) *Juvenile Not in Custody; Custody Not Requested.*

(a) If the prosecuting attorney submits a petition alleging an offense other than a specified juvenile violation and requests the court to designate the case for trial in the same manner as an adult, the juvenile shall be brought before the court for an arraignment as soon as the juvenile's attendance can be secured.

(b) Procedure.

(i) The court shall determine whether the juvenile's parent, guardian, or legal custodian has been notified and is present. The arraignment may be conducted without a parent, guardian, or legal custodian, provided a guardian ad litem or attorney appears with the juvenile.

(ii) The court shall read the allegations in the petition.

(iii) The court shall advise the juvenile on the record in plain language:

a. of the right to an attorney pursuant to MCR 5.915(A)(2);

b. of the right to trial by judge or jury on the allegations in the petition;

c. of the right to remain silent and that any statement made by the juvenile may be used against the juvenile;

d. of the right to have a designation hearing within 14 days,

e. of the right to have a preliminary examination within 14 days after the case is designated if the juvenile is charged with a felony or offense for which an adult could be imprisoned for more than one year;

f. that if the case is designated by the court for trial in the same manner as an adult and, if a preliminary examination is required by law, the prosecuting attorney proves that there is probable cause to believe an offense was committed and there is probable cause to believe that the juvenile committed the offense, the juvenile will be afforded all the rights of an adult charged with the same crime and that upon conviction the juvenile may be sentenced as an adult;

g. of the maximum possible prison sentence and any mandatory minimum sentence required by law.

(iv) Unless the arraignment is adjourned, the court must decide whether to authorize the petition to be filed. If it authorizes the filing of the petition, the court must determine if fingerprints must be taken as provided by MCR 5.936; and

(v) If the petition is authorized for filing, the court must schedule a designation hearing within 14 days.

(3) If a petition submitted by the prosecuting attorney alleging an offense other than a specified juvenile violation did not include a request that the court designate the case for trial as an adult,

(a) The prosecuting attorney may, by right, amend the petition to request the court to designate the case during the preliminary hearing, or

(b) The prosecuting attorney may request leave of the court to amend the petition to request the court to designate the case no later than the pretrial hearing or, if there is no pretrial hearing, at least 21 days before trial, absent good cause for further delay. The court may permit the prosecuting attorney to amend the petition to request the court to designate the case as the interests of justice require.

[Adopted effective May 15, 1997.]

1997 Staff Comment

The April 8, 1997, amendments of subchapter 5.900 of the Michigan Court Rules [effective May 15, 1997] implement recent statutory changes applicable to the juvenile division of the probate court. See, e.g., 1996 PA 247, 1996 PA 248, 1996 PA 255, 1996 PA 259, and 1996 PA 262. The amendments are based on proposals submitted by the Juvenile Court Rules Committee of the Probate Judges Association. These temporary amendments will remain in effect until further order of the court, and will be reconsidered after receipt of comments.

RULE 5.952 DESIGNATION HEARING

(A) Time. The designation hearing shall be commenced within 14 days after the arraignment, unless adjourned for good cause.

(B) Notice.

(1) A copy of the petition or a copy of the petition and separate written request for court designation shall be personally served on the juvenile and the juvenile's parent, guardian, or legal custodian, if the address or whereabouts of the juvenile's parent, guardian, or custodian is known or can be determined by the exercise of due diligence.

(2) Notice of the date, time, and place of the designation hearing may be given either orally on the record to the juvenile, the juvenile's parent, guardian, or legal custodian, and the attorney for the juvenile, if any, and the prosecuting attorney, or in writing, served on each individual by mail or other manner reasonably calculated to provide notice.

(C) Hearing procedure.

(1) *Evidence.* The Michigan Rules of Evidence, other than those with respect to privileges, do not apply.

(2) The prosecuting attorney has the burden of proving by a preponderance of the evidence that the best interests of the juvenile and the public would be served by designation.

(3) The court, in determining whether to designate the case for trial in the same manner as an adult, shall consider all the following factors, giving greater weight to the seriousness of the alleged offense and the juvenile's prior delinquency record than to the other factors:

(a) the seriousness of the alleged offense in terms of community protection, including, but not limited to, the existence of any aggravating factors recognized by the sentencing guidelines, the use of a firearm or other dangerous weapon, and the effect on any victim;

(b) the culpability of the juvenile in committing the alleged offense, including, but not limited to, the level of the juvenile's participation in planning and carrying out the offense and the existence of any aggravating or mitigating factors recognized by the sentencing guidelines;

(c) the juvenile's prior record of delinquency, including, but not limited to, any record of detention, any police record, any school record, or any other evidence indicating prior delinquent behavior;

(d) the juvenile's programming history, including, but not limited to, the juvenile's past willingness to participate meaningfully in available programming;

(e) the adequacy of the punishment or programming available in the juvenile justice system; and

(f) the dispositional options available for the juvenile.

(D) Grant of Request for Court Designation.

(1) If the court determines that it is in the best interests of the juvenile and the public that the juvenile be tried in the same manner as an adult in the juvenile court, the court must:

(a) enter a written order granting the request for court designation and

(i) schedule a preliminary examination within 14 days if the juvenile is charged with a felony or an offense for which an adult could be imprisoned for more than one year, or

(ii) schedule the matter for trial or pretrial hearing if the juvenile is charged with a misdemeanor.

(b) make findings of fact and conclusions of law forming the basis for entry of the order designating the petition. The findings and conclusions may be incorporated in a written opinion or stated on the record.

(E) Denial of Request for Designation. If the request for court designation is denied, the court shall make written findings or place them on the record. Trial shall be scheduled pursuant to MCR 5.941–5.944.

[Adopted and amended effective May 15, 1997.]

1997 Staff Comment

The April 8, 1997, amendments of subchapter 5.900 of the Michigan Court Rules [effective May 15, 1997] implement recent statutory changes applicable to the juvenile division of the probate court. See, e.g., 1996 PA 247, 1996 PA 248, 1996 PA 255, 1996 PA 259, and 1996 PA 262. The amendments are based on proposals submitted by the Juvenile Court Rules Committee of the Probate Judges Association. These temporary amendments will remain in effect until further order of the court, and will be reconsidered after receipt of comments.

Staff Comment to May, 1997 Amendment

The May 9, 1997, order amends MCR 5.952(C)(3) [effective May 15, 1997], which was adopted on April 8, 1997, to be effective May 15, 1997, as part of a substantial revision of the rules affecting the juvenile division of probate court.

RULE 5.953 PRELIMINARY EXAMINATION IN DESIGNATED CASES

(A) Requirement. A preliminary examination must be held only in designated cases in which the juvenile is alleged to have committed a felony or an offense for which an adult could be imprisoned for more than one year.

(B) Waiver. The juvenile may waive the preliminary examination if the juvenile is represented by an attorney and the waiver is made and signed by the juvenile in open court. The judge shall find and place on the record that the waiver was freely, understandingly, and voluntarily given.

(C) Combined Hearing. The preliminary examination may be combined with a designation hearing provided that the Michigan Rules of Evidence, except as otherwise provided by law, apply only to the preliminary examination phase of the combined hearing.

(D) Time. The preliminary examination must commence within 14 days of the arraignment in a prosecutor-designated case or within 14 days after court-ordered designation of a petition, unless the preliminary examination was combined with the designation hearing.

(E) Procedure. The preliminary examination must be conducted in accordance with MCR 6.110.

(F) Findings.

(1) If the court finds there is probable cause to believe that the alleged offense was committed and probable cause to believe the juvenile committed the offense, the court may schedule the matter for trial or a pretrial hearing.

(2) If the court does not find there is probable cause to believe that the alleged offense was committed or does not find there is probable cause to believe the juvenile committed the offense, the court shall dismiss the petition, unless the court finds there is probable cause to believe that a lesser-included offense was committed and probable cause to believe the juvenile committed that offense.

(3) If the court finds there is probable cause to believe that a lesser-included offense was committed and probable cause to believe the juvenile committed that offense, the court may, as provided in MCR 5.952, further determine whether the case should be designated as a case in which the juvenile should be tried in the same manner as an adult. If the court designates the case following the determination of probable cause under this subsection, the court may schedule the matter for trial or a pretrial hearing.

(G) Confinement. If the court has designated the case and finds probable cause that a felony or an offense for which an adult could be imprisoned for more than one year has been committed and probable cause that the juvenile committed the offense, the judge may confine the juvenile in the county jail pending trial. If the juvenile is under 17 years of age, the juvenile may be confined in jail only if the juvenile can be separated by sight and sound from adult prisoners and if the sheriff has approved the confinement.

[Adopted effective May 15, 1997.]

1997 Staff Comment

The April 8, 1997, amendments of subchapter 5.900 of the Michigan Court Rules [effective May 15, 1997] implement recent statutory changes applicable to the juvenile division of the probate court. See, e.g., 1996 PA 247, 1996 PA 248, 1996 PA 255, 1996 PA 259, and 1996 PA 262. The amendments are based on proposals submitted by the Juvenile Court Rules Committee of the Probate Judges Association. These temporary amendments will remain in effect until further order of the court, and will be reconsidered after receipt of comments.

RULE 5.954   TRIAL OF DESIGNATED CASES

Trials of designated cases are governed by subchapter 6.400 of the Michigan Court Rules except for MCR 6.402(A). The court may not accept a waiver of trial by jury until after the juvenile has been offered an opportunity to consult with a lawyer.

[Adopted effective May 15, 1997.]

1997 Staff Comment

The April 8, 1997, amendments of subchapter 5.900 of the Michigan Court Rules [effective May 15, 1997] implement recent statutory changes applicable to the juvenile division of the probate court. See, e.g., 1996 PA 247, 1996 PA 248, 1996 PA 255, 1996 PA 259, and 1996 PA 262. The amendments are based on proposals submitted by the Juvenile Court Rules Committee of the Probate Judges Association. These temporary amendments will remain in effect until further order of the court, and will be reconsidered after receipt of comments.

RULE 5.955   SENTENCING OR DISPOSITION IN DESIGNATED CASES

(A) If a juvenile is convicted under MCL 712A.2d; MSA 27.3178(598.2d), sentencing or disposition shall be made as provided in MCL 712A.18(l)(n); MSA 27.3178(598.18)(1)(n). In deciding whether to enter an order of disposition, or impose or delay imposition of sentence, the court shall consider all the following factors, giving greater weight to the seriousness of the offense and the juvenile's prior record:

(1) the seriousness of the alleged offense in terms of community protection, including but not limited to, the existence of any aggravating factors recognized by the sentencing guidelines, the use of a firearm or other dangerous weapon, and the effect on any victim;

(2) the culpability of the juvenile in committing the alleged offense, including, but not limited to, the level of the juvenile's participation in planning and carrying out the offense and the existence of any aggravating or mitigating factors recognized by the sentencing guidelines;

(3) the juvenile's prior record of delinquency including, but not limited to, any record of detention, any police record, any school record, or any other evidence indicating prior delinquent behavior;

(4) the juvenile's programming history, including, but not limited to, the juvenile's past willingness to participate meaningfully in available programming;

(5) the adequacy of the punishment or programming available in the juvenile justice system;

(6) the dispositional options available for the juvenile.

(B) The court shall enter an order of disposition unless the court determines that the best interests of the public would be served by sentencing the juvenile as an adult. The prosecuting attorney has the burden of proving by a preponderance of the evidence that, on the basis of the criteria in subsection (A), it would be in the best interests of the public to sentence the juvenile as an adult.

(C) **Sentencing.** If the court determines that the juvenile should be sentenced as an adult, either initially or following a delayed imposition of sentence, the sentencing hearing shall be held in accordance with the procedures set forth in MCR 6.425.

(D) **Delayed Imposition of Sentence.** If the court determines that the juvenile should be sentenced as an adult, the court may, in its discretion, enter an order of disposition delaying imposition of sentence and placing the juvenile on probation on such terms and conditions as it considers appropriate, including ordering any disposition under MCL 712A.18; MSA 27.3178(598.18). A delayed sentence may be imposed in accordance with MCR 5.956.

(E) **Disposition.** If the court does not determine that the juvenile should be sentenced as an adult, the court shall hold a dispositional hearing and comply with the procedures set forth in MCR 5.943.

[Adopted effective May 15, 1997.]

1997 Staff Comment

The April 8, 1997, amendments of subchapter 5.900 of the Michigan Court Rules [effective May 15, 1997] implement recent statutory changes applicable to the juvenile division of the probate court. See, e.g., 1996 PA 247, 1996 PA 248, 1996 PA 255, 1996 PA 259, and 1996 PA 262. The amendments are based on proposals submitted by the Juvenile Court Rules Committee of the Probate Judges Association. These temporary amendments will remain in effect until further order of the court, and will be reconsidered after receipt of comments.

RULE 5.956   REVIEW HEARINGS; PROBATION VIOLATION

(A) **Review Hearings in Delayed Imposition of Sentence Cases.**

(1) *When Required.* If the court entered an order of disposition delaying imposition of sentence, the court shall conduct a review hearing to determine whether the juvenile has been rehabilitated and whether the juvenile presents a serious risk to public safety.

(a) Time of Hearing.

(i) Annual Review. The court shall conduct an annual review of the probation, including, but not limited to, the services being provided to the juvenile, the juvenile's placement, and the juvenile's progress in placement. In conducting the review, the court must examine any report prepared under MCL 803.223; MSA 25.399(223) and any report prepared by the officer or agency supervising probation. The court may order changes in the juvenile's probation on the basis of the review including, but not limited to, imposition of sentence.

(ii) *Periodic Review.* If an institution or agency to which the juvenile was committed believes that the juvenile has been rehabilitated and that the juvenile does not present a serious risk to public safety, the institution or agency may petition the court to conduct a review hearing at any time before the juvenile becomes 19 years of age or if the court has extended jurisdiction, any time before the juvenile becomes 21 years of age.

(iii) *Mandatory Review.* The court shall schedule a review hearing to be held within 42 days before the juvenile attains age 19, unless adjourned for good cause.

(iv) *Final Review.* The court shall conduct a final review of the juvenile's probation not less than 91 days before the end of the probation period.

(b) *Notice of Hearing.* Notice of the hearing must be given to the prosecuting attorney, the agency, or the superintendent of the institution or facility to which the juvenile has been committed, the juvenile, and, if the address or whereabouts are known, the parent, guardian, or legal custodian of the juvenile, at least 14 days before the hearing. The notice shall clearly indicate that the court may extend jurisdiction over the juvenile or impose sentence and shall advise the juvenile and the parent, guardian, or legal custodian of the juvenile that the juvenile has a right to an attorney.

(2) *Appointment of Attorney.* The court shall appoint an attorney to represent the juvenile unless an attorney has been retained. The court may assess the cost of providing an attorney as costs against the juvenile or those responsible for the juvenile's support, or both, if the persons to be assessed are financially able to comply.

(3) *Evidence; Commitment Report.* The court may consider the commitment report prepared as provided in MCL 803.225; MSA 25.399(225) and any report prepared upon the court's order by the officer or agency supervising probation.

(4) *Burden of Proof; Findings.*

(a) Before the court may continue jurisdiction over the juvenile or impose sentence, the prosecuting attorney must demonstrate by a preponderance of the evidence that the juvenile has not been rehabilitated or that the juvenile presents a serious risk to public safety. The Michigan Rules of Evidence, other than those with respect to privileges, do not apply. In making the determination, the court must consider the following factors:

(i) the extent and nature of the juvenile's participation in education, counseling, or work programs;

(ii) the juvenile's willingness to accept responsibility for prior behavior;

(iii) the juvenile's behavior in the current placement;

(iv) the juvenile's prior record, character, and physical and mental maturity;

(v) the juvenile's potential for violent conduct as demonstrated by prior behavior;

(vi) the recommendation of the institution, agency, or facility charged with the juvenile's care for the juvenile's release or continued custody;

(vii) any other information the prosecuting attorney or the juvenile may submit.

(b) Before the court may impose a sentence at the final review hearing, the court must determine that the best interests of the public would be served by the imposition of a sentence provided by law for an adult offender. In making the determination, the court must consider the following factors, in addition to the criteria specified in subrule (4)(a):

(i) the effect of treatment on the juvenile's rehabilitation;

(ii) whether the juvenile is likely to be dangerous to the public if released;

(iii) the best interests of the public welfare and the protection of public security.

(5) *Sentencing Credit.* If a sentence of imprisonment is imposed, the juvenile shall receive credit for the time served on probation.

(B) Violation of Probation in Delayed Imposition of Sentence Cases.

(1) *Subsequent Conviction.* If a juvenile placed on probation under an order of disposition delaying imposition of sentence is found by the court to have violated probation by being convicted of a felony or a misdemeanor punishable by imprisonment for more than 1 year, or adjudicated as responsible for an offense that if committed by an adult would be a felony or a misdemeanor punishable by imprisonment for more than 1 year, the court shall revoke probation and sentence the juvenile to imprisonment for a term that does not exceed the penalty that could have been imposed for the offense for which the juvenile was originally convicted and placed on probation.

(2) *Other Violations of Probation.* If a juvenile placed on probation under an order of disposition delaying imposition of sentence is found by the court to have violated probation other than as provided in subrule (B)(1), the court may impose sentence or may order any of the following for the juvenile:

(a) a change in placement;

(b) community service;

(c) substance abuse counseling;

(d) mental health counseling;

(e) participation in a vocational-technical program;

(f) incarceration in the county jail for not more than 30 days if the present county jail facility would meet all requirements under federal law and regulations for housing juveniles and if the court has consulted with the sheriff to determine when the sentence will begin to ensure that space will be available for the juvenile. If the juvenile is under 17 years of age, the juvenile must be placed in a room or ward out of sight and sound from adult prisoners;

(g) other participation or performance as the court considers necessary.

(3) *Hearing.* The probation violation hearing must be conducted pursuant to MCR 5.944(C).

(4) *Sentencing Credit.* If a sentence of imprisonment is imposed, the juvenile must receive credit for the time served on probation.

[Adopted effective May 15, 1997.]

1997 Staff Comment

The April 8, 1997, amendments of subchapter 5.900 of the Michigan Court Rules [effective May 15, 1997] implement recent statutory changes applicable to the juvenile division of the probate court. See, e.g., 1996 PA 247, 1996 PA 248, 1996 PA 255, 1996 PA 259, and 1996 PA 262. The amendments are based on proposals submitted by the Juvenile Court Rules Committee of the Probate Judges Association. These temporary amendments will remain in effect until further order of the court, and will be reconsidered after receipt of comments.

RULE 5.961   INITIATING CHILD PROTECTIVE PROCEEDINGS

(A) **Form.** Absent exigent circumstances, a request for court action to protect a child must be in the form of a petition.

(B) **Content of Petition.** A petition must contain the following information, if known:

(1) the child's name, address, and date of birth;

(2) the names and addresses of:

(a) the child's mother and father,

(b) the parent or person who has custody of the child, if other than a mother or father,

(c) the nearest known relative of the child, if no parent can be found, and

(d) any court with prior continuing jurisdiction;

(3) the essential facts which constitute an offense against the child under the Juvenile Code;

(4) a citation to the section of the Juvenile Code relied upon for jurisdiction;

(5) the child's membership or eligibility for membership in an American Indian tribe or band, if any, and the identity of the tribe;

(6) the type of relief requested, including whether temporary or permanent custody is sought; and

(7) information required by MCR 3.206(A)(4), identifying whether a family division matter involving members of the same family is or was pending.

[Adopted and amended effective January 1, 1988; amended effective April 1, 1989; January 1, 1998.]

1988 and 1989 Staff Comments

[See "1988 Staff Comment" and "Staff Comment to April 1, 1989 Amendments," set forth following Rule 5.993.]

Staff Comment to 1998 Amendment

The October 1, 1997, amendments of MCR 3.206, 5.931, and 5.961 [effective January 1, 1998] relate to statutory changes made by 1996 PA 388, which created the family division of the circuit court. The amendments are effective January 1, 1998.

New MCR 3.206(A)(4) creates a requirement for identifying pending or prior family division actions involving members of the same family. References to that provision are included in MCR 5.931(B)(8), governing delinquency proceedings, and MCR 5.961(B)(7), governing child protective proceedings.

RULE 5.962   PRELIMINARY INQUIRY

(A) **Purpose.** When a petition is not accompanied by a request for placement of the child and the child is not in temporary custody, the court may conduct a preliminary inquiry to determine the appropriate action to be taken on a petition.

(B) **Action by Court.** At the preliminary inquiry, the court may:

(1) dismiss the complaint or deny authorization of the petition,

(2) refer the matter to alternative services, or

(3) authorize the filing of a petition upon a showing of probable cause that 1 or more of the allegations in the petition are true and fall within MCL 712A.2(b); MSA 27.3178(598.2)(b).

When used in this subrule, a showing of probable cause may be established with such information and in such a manner as the court deems sufficient.

[Adopted effective January 1, 1988; amended effective April 1, 1989.]

1988 and 1989 Staff Comments

[See "1988 Staff Comment" and "Staff Comment to April 1, 1989 Amendments," set forth following Rule 5.993.]

RULE 5.963   ACQUIRING PHYSICAL CUSTODY OF CHILD

(A) **Taking Custody Without Court Order.** An officer may without court order remove a child from the child's surroundings and take the child into temporary custody if, after investigation, the officer has reasonable grounds to conclude that the health, safety, or welfare of the child is endangered.

(B) Court-Ordered Custody. The court may order an officer or other person to immediately take a child into custody when, after presentment to the court of a petition, a judge or referee has reasonable grounds to believe that conditions or surroundings under which the child is found are such as would endanger the health, safety, or welfare of the child. The court shall inquire whether a member of the child's immediate or extended family is available to take custody of the child pending preliminary hearing and whether there has been a central registry clearance and whether a criminal history check has been initiated. The court may include in such an order:

(1) an authorization to enter specified premises to remove the child, and

(2) a directive to place the child in protective custody pending preliminary hearing.

(C) Arranging for Court Appearance. An officer who takes a child into custody must:

(1) immediately attempt to notify the child's parent of the custody;

(2) inform the parent of the date, time, and place of the preliminary hearing scheduled by the court;

(3) immediately bring the child to the court for preliminary hearing, or immediately contact the court for instruction as to placement pending preliminary hearing;

(4) if the court is not open, contact the person designated under MCR 5.934(B)(2) for permission to place or release the child pending preliminary hearing;

(5) ensure that the petition is prepared and submitted to the court;

(6) prepare a custody statement similar to the statement required for detention of a juvenile as provided in MCR 5.934(A)(4) and submit it to the court or leave it at the placement facility.

[Adopted effective January 1, 1988; amended effective April 1, 1989; April 1, 1998.]

1888 and 1989 Staff Comments

[See "1988 Staff Comment" and "Staff Comment to April 1, 1989 Amendments," set forth following Rule 5.993.]

Staff Comment to 1998 Amendment

The January 16, 1998, amendments of MCR 5.915, 5.923, 5.963, 5.965 and 5.974 [effective April 1, 1998] relate to recommendations made by the Binsfeld Children's Commission in its July 1996 report regarding children (Recommendations 36, 70, 71, 76, 77, 107, 111, and 121). The amendments are effective April 1, 1998, to coincide with the implementation of legislation enacted pursuant to recommendations of the commission.

RULE 5.965   PRELIMINARY HEARING

(A) Time for Preliminary Hearing of Child in Custody. The preliminary hearing must commence no later than 24 hours after the child has been taken into court custody, excluding Sundays and holidays, unless adjourned for good cause shown, or the child must be released.

(B) Procedure.

(1) The court shall determine if the parent has been notified and, if the parent is not present, direct that an attempt be made to secure the presence of the parent. The preliminary hearing may be adjourned for the purpose of securing the appearance of a parent or may be conducted in the parent's absence.

(2) The child's attorney shall be present to represent the child at the preliminary hearing. The court may make temporary orders for the protection of the child pending the appearance of counsel or pending the completion of the preliminary hearing.

(3) The court shall read the allegations in the petition in open court, unless waived.

(4) The court shall determine if the petition should be dismissed or the matter referred to alternate services. If so, release the child and, if not, continue with the hearing.

(5) The court shall advise the respondent of the right to the assistance of an attorney pursuant to MCR 5.915.

(6) The court shall advise the respondent of the right to trial on the allegations in the petition and that the trial may be before a referee unless the required demand for a judge or jury is filed pursuant to MCR 5.912 or 5.913.

(7) The court shall inquire if the child or parent is a registered member of any American Indian tribe or band, or if the child is eligible for such membership. If so, determine and notify the tribe or band and follow the procedures set forth in MCR 5.980.

(8) The court shall allow the respondent an opportunity to deny or admit the allegations and make a statement of explanation.

(9) Unless the preliminary hearing is adjourned, the court shall decide whether to authorize the filing of the petition. The court may authorize the filing of the petition upon a showing of probable cause, unless waived, that one or more of the allegations in the petition are true and fall within MCL 712A.2(b); MSA 27.3178(598.2)(b). The court shall indicate whether temporary or permanent custody is sought, and must direct that the respondent and the attorney for the child receive a copy of the petition authorized to be filed.

(10) If the court authorizes the filing of the petition as provided in subrule (B)(9), the court may release the child to a parent or the court may place the child

with someone other than a parent as provided in subrule (C). Release of the child to a parent following the authorization of a petition may be accompanied by reasonable terms and conditions believed necessary to protect the physical health or mental well being of the child.

(C) Pretrial Placement.

(1) *Placement; Proofs.* If the child was not released under subrule (B), the court shall receive evidence to establish that the criteria for placement set forth in MCR 5.965(C)(2) are present. The respondent shall be given an opportunity to cross-examine witnesses, to subpoena witnesses, and to offer proof to counter the allegations against respondent. The court may permit the respondent to waive the probable cause determination or the court may adjourn the hearing for up to 14 days to secure the attendance of witnesses or for other good cause shown.

(2) *Criteria.* The court may place the child with someone other than the parent pending trial or further court order if the court determines that all of the following conditions exist:

(a) custody of the child with the parent presents a substantial risk of harm to the life, physical health, or mental well being of the child;

(b) no provision of service or other arrangement except removal of the child is reasonably available to adequately safeguard the child from the risk as described in subrule (C)(2)(a); and

(c) conditions of child custody away from the parent are adequate to safeguard the health and welfare of the child.

(3) *Findings.* If placement is ordered, the court must make a written statement of findings or place them on the record. The findings may be on the basis of hearsay evidence that possesses an adequate degree of trustworthiness.

(4) *Type of Placement.* If the child is not released, the child must be placed in the most family-like setting consistent with the needs of the child. The court shall inquire whether a member of the child's immediate or extended family is available to take custody of the child, whether there has been a central registry clearance and whether a criminal history check has been initiated.

(5) *No Right to Bail.* The respondent shall not have the right to post bail in a protective proceeding for the release of a child in custody of the court.

(6) *Advice, Initial Service Plan.* If placement is ordered, the court must, orally or in writing, inform the parties:

(a) that the agency designated to care and supervise the child will prepare an initial service plan no later than 30 days of the placement;

(b) that participation in the initial service plan is voluntary unless otherwise ordered by the court; and

(c) that the general elements of an initial service plan include:

(i) the background of the child and the family;

(ii) an evaluation of the experiences and problems of the child;

(iii) a projection of the expected length of stay in foster care; and

(iv) an identification of specific goals and projected time frames for meeting the goals.

(7) *Visitation.* The court shall ensure that the parent is allowed frequent visitation of a child in placement unless visitation, even if supervised, would be harmful to the child.

(8) *Review of Placement Order and Initial Service Plan.* On motion of a party, the court must review the custody order, placement order, or the initial service plan, and may modify those orders and plan if it is in the best interest of the child.

[Adopted and amended effective January 1, 1988; amended effective April 1, 1989; April 1, 1998.]

1988 Staff Comment

[See 1988 Staff Comment following Rule 5.993.]

[Under the January 1, 1988 amendment,] MCR 5.965(B)(2) manifests that if the preliminary hearing is adjourned, the court may still make a temporary placement decision pending further hearing on the basis of available information.

Staff Comment to 1989 Amendment

[See "Staff Comment to April 1, 1989 Amendments," set forth following Rule 5.993.]

Staff Comment to 1998 Amendment

The January 16, 1998, amendments of MCR 5.915, 5.923, 5.963, 5.965 and 5.974 [effective April 1, 1998] relate to recommendations made by the Binsfeld Children's Commission in its July 1996 report regarding children (Recommendations 36, 70, 71, 76, 77, 107, 111, and 121). The amendments are effective April 1, 1998, to coincide with the implementation of legislation enacted pursuant to recommendations of the commission.

RULE 5.971 PLEAS OF ADMISSION OR NO CONTEST

(A) General. A respondent may make a plea of admission or of no contest to the original charge in the petition. The court has discretion to allow a respondent to enter a plea of admission or a plea of no contest to an amended petition. The plea may be taken at any time after the filing of the petition provided that the petitioner and the attorney of the child have been notified of a plea offer to an amended petition and have been given the opportunity to object before the plea is accepted.

(B) Advice of Rights and Possible Disposition. Before accepting a plea of admission or plea of no contest, the court must advise the respondent on the record or in a writing that is made a part of the file:

(1) of the allegations in the petition;

(2) of the right to an attorney, if respondent is without counsel;

(3) that if the court accepts the plea the respondent will give up the rights to

(a) trial by a judge or trial by a jury,

(b) have the petitioner prove the allegations in the petition by a preponderance of the evidence,

(c) have witnesses against the respondent appear and testify under oath at the trial,

(d) cross-examine witnesses,

(e) have the court subpoena any witnesses the respondent believes could give testimony in the respondent's favor;

(4) of the consequences of the plea including that the plea can later be used to terminate parental rights.

(C) Voluntary, Accurate Plea.

(1) *Voluntary Plea.* The court shall not accept a plea of admission or of no contest without satisfying itself that the plea is knowingly, understandingly, and voluntarily made.

(2) *Accurate Plea.* The court shall not accept a plea of admission or of no contest without establishing support for a finding that the child comes within the jurisdiction of the court, preferably by questioning the respondent unless the offer is to plead no contest. If the plea is no contest, the court shall not question the respondent, but, by some other means, shall obtain support for a finding that the respondent committed the offense against the child. The court shall state why a plea of no contest is appropriate.

[Adopted and amended effective January 1, 1988; amended effective April 1, 1989.]

1988 and 1989 Staff Comments

[See "1988 Staff Comment" and "Staff Comment to April 1, 1989 Amendments," set forth following Rule 5.993.]

RULE 5.972   TRIAL

(A) Time. If the child is not in placement, the trial must be held within 6 months after the filing of the petition. If the child is in placement, the trial must commence as soon as possible but not later than 63 days after the child is placed by the court unless the trial is postponed:

(1) upon stipulation of the parties;

(2) where process cannot be completed; or

(3) the court finds that the testimony of a presently unavailable witness is needed.

When trial is postponed pursuant to subrule (2) or (3), the court shall release the child to the parent unless the court finds that returning the child to the custody of the parent will likely result in physical harm or serious emotional damage to the child.

(B) Preliminary Proceedings.

(1) The court shall determine that the proper parties are present. The respondent has the right to be present, but the court may proceed in the absence of the respondent provided notice has been served on the respondent. The child may be excused as the court determines the child's interests require.

(2) The court shall read the allegations in the petition, unless waived, and explain the nature of the proceedings.

(C) Evidence; Standard of Proof.

(1) Except as otherwise provided in these rules, the rules of evidence for a civil proceeding and the standard of proof by a preponderance of evidence apply at the trial, notwithstanding that the petition contains a request to terminate parental rights.

(2) A statement made by a child under ten years of age describing an act of child abuse as defined in section 2(c) of the child protection law, MCL 722.622(c); MSA 25.248(2)(c), performed with or on the child, not otherwise admissible under an exception to the hearsay rule, may be admitted into evidence at the trial if the court has found, in a hearing held prior to trial, that the nature and circumstances surrounding the giving of the statement provide adequate indicia of trustworthiness, and that there is sufficient corroborative evidence of the act.

[Adopted effective January 1, 1988; amended effective April 1, 1989; January 1, 1991.]

1988 and 1989 Staff Comments

[See "1988 Staff Comment" and "Staff Comment to April 1, 1989 Amendments," set forth following Rule 5.993.]

RULE 5.973   DISPOSITIONAL PHASE

(A) General. A dispositional hearing is conducted to determine measures to be taken by the court with respect to the child properly within its jurisdiction and, when applicable, against any adult, once the court has determined following trial, plea of admission, or plea of no contest that the child comes within its jurisdiction.

(1) *Notice.* Unless the dispositional hearing is held immediately after the trial, notice of hearing may be given by scheduling it on the record in the presence of the parties or in accordance with MCR 5.920.

(2) *Time.* The interval, if any, between the trial and the dispositional hearing is within the discretion of the court. When the child is in placement, the interval may not be more than 35 days, except for good cause.

(3) *Presence of Parties.*

(a) The child may be excused from the dispositional hearing as the interests of the child require provided that the child's guardian ad litem or attorney is present at the hearing.

(b) The respondent has the right to be present or may appear through legal counsel.

(c) The court may proceed in the absence of parties provided that proper notice has been given.

(4) *Evidence.*

(a) The Michigan Rules of Evidence do not apply at the initial dispositional hearing. All relevant and material evidence, including oral and written reports may be received and may be relied on to the extent of its probative value, even though such evidence may not be admissible at trial. The court shall consider the case service plan and any written or oral information concerning the child from the child's parent, guardian, custodian, foster parent, child caring institution, or relative with whom the child is placed. If the agency responsible for the care and supervision of the child recommends not placing the child with the parent, the agency shall report in writing what efforts were made to prevent removal, or to rectify conditions that caused removal, of the child from the home.

(b) The parties shall be given an opportunity to examine and controvert written reports so received and may be allowed to cross-examine individuals making reports when such individuals are reasonably available.

(c) Written reports, other than those portions made confidential by law, case service plans, and court orders, including all updates and revisions, shall be available to the foster parent, child caring institution, or relative with whom the child is placed. The foster parents, child caring institution, or relative with whom the child is placed shall not have the right to cross-examine individuals making such reports or the right to controvert such reports beyond the making of a written or oral statement concerning the child as provided in subsection (A)(4)(a).

(d) No assertion of an evidentiary privilege, other than the privilege between attorney and client, shall prevent the receipt and use, at the dispositional phase, of materials prepared pursuant to a court-ordered examination, interview, or course of treatment.

(5) *Dispositional Orders.*

(a) The court shall enter an order of disposition as provided in the Juvenile Code and the rules.

(b) The court shall not enter an order of disposition until it has examined the case service plan as provided in MCL 712A.18f; MSA 27.3178(598.18f). The court may order compliance with all or part of the case service plan and may enter such orders as it considers necessary in the interest of the child.

(c) The court, on consideration of the written report prepared by the agency responsible for the care and supervision of the child pursuant to MCL 712A.18f(1); MSA 27.3178(598.18f)(1), shall, when appropriate, include a statement in the order of disposition as to whether reasonable efforts were made:

(i) to prevent the child's removal from home, or

(ii) to rectify the conditions that caused the child to be removed from the child's home.

(B) Dispositional Review Hearings.

(1) *General.* The main objectives of a dispositional review hearing are:

(a) court review of the progress made to comply with any order of disposition and with the case service plan prepared pursuant to MCL 712A.18f; MSA 27.3178(598.18f); and

(b) court evaluation of the continued need and appropriateness for the child to be in foster care.

(2) *Time.* The court must conduct dispositional review hearings at intervals as follows, so long as the child remains in foster care:

(a) no later than every 91 days for the first year following entry of the original order of disposition;

(b) no later than every 182 days after the first year following entry of the original order of disposition (the calculation to commence from the date of the first permanency planning hearing); and

(c) no later than every 91 days for the first year after placement of a child in foster care following a dispositional review hearing or a hearing under MCR 5.973(E), and every 182 days thereafter.

(3) *Irregularly Scheduled Hearings.* At the initial dispositional hearing and at every regularly scheduled dispositional review hearing, the court must decide whether it will conduct the next dispositional review hearing before what would otherwise be the next regularly scheduled dispositional review hearing as provided in subrule (2). In deciding whether to shorten the interval between review hearings, the court shall, among other factors, consider:

(a) the ability and motivation of the parent to make changes needed to provide the child a suitable home environment;

(b) the reasonable likelihood that the child will be ready to return home earlier than the next scheduled dispositional review hearing.

(4) *Notice.* The court shall ensure that written notice of a dispositional review hearing is given to the appropriate persons in accordance with MCR 5.920 and MCR 5.921(B)(2).

(5) *Procedure.* Dispositional review hearings shall be conducted in accordance with the procedures and rules of evidence applicable to the initial dispositional hearing. The report of the agency that is filed with

the court must be accessible to the parties and offered into evidence. The court shall consider any written or oral information concerning the child from the child's parent, guardian, custodian, foster parent, child caring institution, or relative with whom a child is placed, in addition to any other evidence at the hearing. The court, on request of a party or on its own motion, may accelerate the hearing to consider any element of a case service plan.

(6) *Criteria.*

(a) Review of Case Service Plan. The court, in reviewing the progress toward compliance with the case service plan, must consider:

(i) the services provided or offered to the child and parent of the child;

(ii) whether the parent has benefited from the services provided or offered;

(iii) the extent of parental visitation, including a determination as to why visitation was not frequent or never occurred;

(iv) the extent to which the parent complied with each provision of the case service plan, prior court orders, and any agreement between the parent and the agency;

(v) likely harm to the child if the child continues to be separated from his or her parent, guardian, or custodian; and

(vi) likely harm to the child if the child is returned to his or her parent, guardian, or custodian.

(b) Progress Toward Return Home of the Child. The court must decide the extent of the progress made toward alleviating or mitigating conditions that caused the child to be, and to remain, in foster care.

(7) *Supplemental Orders.*

(a) General. The court, following a dispositional review hearing, may:

(i) order the return of the child home,

(ii) modify the dispositional order,

(iii) modify any part of the case service plan,

(iv) enter a new dispositional order, or

(v) continue the prior dispositional order.

(b) Return Home of Child Without Dispositional Review Hearing. Unless waived, if not less than 7 days written notice is given to all parties prior to the return of a child to the home, and if no party requests a hearing within the 7 days, the court may issue an order without a hearing permitting the agency to return the child home.

(C) **Permanency Planning Hearing.**

(1) *Purpose.* When a child who is within the jurisdiction of the court under MCL 712A.2(b); MSA 27.3178(598.2)(b) remains in foster care for an extended time and without parental rights to the child having been terminated, the court shall conduct a post-disposition permanency planning hearing. At the hearing the court may determine that the child is to return home, that the child is to continue in foster care for a limited specified time or on a long-term basis, or that the agency failed to demonstrate that initiating the termination of parental rights to the child is clearly not in the best interest of the child.

(2) *Time.* The court must conduct the permanency planning hearing no later than 364 days after entry of the original order of disposition. The interval between permanency planning hearings shall be no later than every 364 days while the child remains in foster care. The court may combine the permanency planning hearing with a dispositional review hearing.

(3) *Notice.* Written notice of a permanency planning hearing shall be given as provided in MCR 5.920 and MCR 5.921(B)(2). The notice must include a brief statement of the purpose of the hearing, such as to review the status of the child, the progress made toward returning the child home, or why the child should not be placed in permanent custody of the court and must include a notice that the hearing may result in further proceedings to terminate parental rights.

(4) *Hearing Procedure; Options.*

(a) Evidence. At the permanency planning hearing all relevant and material evidence, including oral and written reports, may be received by the court and may be relied upon to the extent of its probative value, even though such evidence may not be admissible at trial. The court shall consider any written or oral information concerning the child from the child's parent, guardian, custodian, foster parent, child caring institution, or relative with whom the child is placed, in addition to any other evidence offered at the hearing. The parties shall be afforded an opportunity to examine and controvert written reports so received and may be allowed to cross-examine individuals who made the reports when those individuals are reasonably available.

(b) Determine Whether to Return Child Home. At the conclusion of the permanency planning hearing, the court must order the child returned home unless it determines that the return would cause a substantial risk of harm to the life, the physical health, or the mental well being of the child. Failure to substantially comply with the case service plan is evidence that return of the child to the parent may cause a substantial risk of harm to the child's life, physical health, or mental well being. In addition, the court shall consider any condition or circumstance of the child that may be evidence that a return to the parent would cause a substantial risk of harm to the child's life, physical health or mental well-being.

(c) Continue Foster Care Pending Determination on Termination of Parental Rights. If the court determines that the child will not be returned home, it shall order continuation of foster care, and shall order the agency to initiate proceedings to terminate parental rights, no later than 42 days after the permanency planning hearing, unless the agency demonstrates to the court that it is clearly not in the best interest of the child to presently begin proceedings to terminate parental rights.

(d) Other Placement Plans. If the court does not return the child to the parent and if the agency demonstrates that termination of parental rights is not in the best interest of the child, the court shall either:

(i) continue the placement of the child in foster care for a limited period to be set by the court; or

(ii) place the child in foster care on a long-term basis.

(D) Review of Child's Progress at Home.

(1) *General.* The court shall periodically review the progress of a child not in foster care over whom it has retained jurisdiction.

(2) *Time.* The progress of the child must be reviewed no later than 182 days after entry of the original order of disposition if the child remained at home following the initial dispositional hearing. The review shall occur no later than 182 days after the child returns home when the child is no longer in foster care. The court may not order a change in the placement of a child solely on the basis of a progress review.

(E) Child at Home; Change in Placement; Hearing Required.

(1) *General.* If the child, over whom the court has retained jurisdiction, remains at home following the initial dispositional hearing or has otherwise returned home from foster care, the court must conduct a hearing before it may order the placement of the child.

(2) *Notice.* The court shall ensure that the parties are given notice of the hearing as provided in MCR 5.920 and MCR 5.921.

(3) *Emergency Removal Hearing.* If the court orders removal of the child from the parent to protect the child's health, safety, or welfare, the court must conduct an emergency removal hearing no later than 24 hours after the child has been taken into custody, excluding Sundays and holidays. Unless the child is returned to the parent pending the dispositional review, the court must make a determination that the criteria for placement as listed in MCR 5.965(C)(2) are satisfied.

(a) At the emergency removal hearing, the respondent parent shall receive a written statement of the reasons for removal. The respondent parent shall also be advised of his or her rights

(i) to be represented by counsel pursuant to MCR 5.915, unless the parent is already represented;

(ii) to contest the continuing placement at a subsequent hearing within 14 days; and

(iii) to compulsory process to obtain witnesses.

(b) At an emergency removal hearing, the parent shall be given an opportunity to state why the child should be returned to the parent's custody pending further hearings.

(4) *Review Hearing; Procedure.* If the child is in placement pursuant to subrule (E)(3), the hearing must commence no later than 14 days after the child is placed by the court, except for good cause shown. The hearing shall be conducted in accordance with the procedures and rules of evidence applicable to the dispositional review hearing.

[Adopted and amended effective January 1, 1988; amended effective April 1, 1989; January 1, 1993; October 1, 1995.]

1988 and 1989 Staff Comments

[See "1988 Staff Comment" and "Staff Comment to April 1, 1989 Amendments," set forth following Rule 5.993.]

Staff Comment to 1993 Amendment

The 1992 amendments, which took effect January 1, 1993, originated with proposals from the Juvenile Rules Committee of the Michigan Probate Judges Association.

Staff Comment to 1995 Amendment

The August 22, 1995 amendments of MCR 5.903, 5.915, 5.920, 5.921, 5.973, and 5.974 were adopted in response to the enactment of 1994 PA 264, which amended parts of Chapter XIIA of 1939 PA 288.

RULE 5.974   PARENTAL RIGHTS; TERMINATION

(A) General.

(1) This rule applies to all proceedings in which termination of parental rights is sought except those which involve an Indian child as defined by 25 USC § 1901 et seq. Proceedings for termination of parental rights involving an Indian child are to be governed by MCR 5.980.

(2) Parental rights of the respondent over the child may not be terminated unless termination was requested in an original, amended, or supplemental petition made by the agency, the child, the guardian, custodian or representative of the child, a concerned person as defined in MCR 5.903(C)(3), the state children's ombudsman, or the prosecuting attorney, whether or not the prosecuting attorney is representing or acting as a legal consultant to the agency or any other party.

(3) The burden of proof is on the party seeking by court order to terminate the rights of the respondent

over the child. There is no right to a jury determination.

(B) Definition. When used in this rule, unless the context otherwise indicates, "respondent" includes

(1) the natural or adoptive mother of the child, and/or

(2) the father of the child as defined by MCR 5.903(A)(4).

"Respondent" shall not include other persons to whom legal custody has been given by court order, persons who are acting in the place of the mother or father, or other persons responsible for the control, care, and welfare of the child.

(C) Notice. Notice must be given as provided in MCR 5.920 and MCR 5.921(B)(3).

(D) Termination of Parental Rights at the Initial Disposition. The court shall order termination of the parental rights of a respondent at the initial dispositional hearing held pursuant to MCR 5.973(A), and shall order that additional efforts for reunification of the child with the respondent shall not be made, if

(1) the original, or amended, petition contains a request for termination;

(2) the trier of fact found by a preponderance of the evidence that the child comes under the jurisdiction of the court on the basis of MCL 712A.2(b); MSA 27.3178(598.2)(b);

(3) the court finds on the basis of clear and convincing legally admissible evidence introduced at the trial, or at plea proceedings, on the issue of assumption of court jurisdiction, that one or more facts alleged in the petition:

(a) are true,

(b) justify terminating parental rights at the initial dispositional hearing, and

(c) fall under MCL 712A.19b(3); MSA 27.3178(598.19b)(3);

unless the court finds, in accordance with the rules of evidence as provided in subrule (F)(2), that termination of parental rights is clearly not in the best interest of the child.

(E) Termination of Parental Rights on the Basis of Changed Circumstances. The court may take action on a supplemental petition that seeks to terminate the parental rights of a respondent over a child already within the jurisdiction of the court on the basis of one or more circumstances new or different from the offense that led the court to take jurisdiction. The new or different circumstance must fall within MCL 712A.19b(3); MSA 27.3178(598.19b)(3), and must be sufficient to warrant termination of parental rights.

(1) *Factfinding Step.* Legally admissible evidence must be used to establish the factual basis of parental unfitness sufficient to warrant termination of parental

rights. Except as provided in MCR 5.980, the proofs must be clear and convincing.

(2) *Best Interest Step.* Once it is established that one or more grounds exist under MCL 712A.19b(3); MSA 27.3178(598.19b)(3), to terminate the parental rights of respondent over the child, the court shall order termination of the respondent's parental rights and order that additional efforts for reunification of the child with the respondent shall not be made, unless the court finds in accordance with the rules of evidence as provided in subrule (F)(2) that termination is clearly not in the best interest of the child.

(F) Termination of Parental Rights; Child in Foster Care. If the parental rights of the respondent over the child are not terminated at the initial dispositional hearing, and the child is in foster care in the temporary custody of the court, the court following a dispositional review hearing or a permanency planning hearing under MCR 5.973 may take action on a supplemental petition that seeks to terminate the parental rights of respondent over the child on the basis of one or more grounds listed in MCL 712A.19b; MSA 27.3178(598.19b).

(1) *Time.*

(a) Filing Petition. The supplemental petition for termination of parental rights shall be filed no later than 42 days after a dispositional review hearing or permanency planning hearing where the court has initially determined that the child should not be returned to the parent and the agency has failed to demonstrate that initiating termination proceedings is not clearly in the child's best interest.

(b) Hearing on Petition. The hearing on a supplemental petition for termination of parental rights under this subrule must be held within 42 days after the filing of the supplemental petition. The court may, for good cause shown, extend the time period for an additional 21 days.

(2) *Evidence.* At the hearing all relevant and material evidence, including oral and written reports, may be received by the court and may be relied upon to the extent of its probative value, even though such evidence may not be admissible at trial. The respondent and the petitioner shall be afforded an opportunity to examine and controvert written reports so received and shall be allowed to cross-examine individuals who made the reports when those individuals are reasonably available.

(3) *Standard of Proof.* Except as provided in MCR 5.980, the proofs must be clear and convincing that one or more grounds exist under MCL 712A.19b(3); MSA 27.3178(598.19b)(3) sufficient to warrant termination of parental rights. If the court finds that the requisite factual basis of parental unfitness exists, the court shall order termination of the respondent's parental rights and order that additional efforts for reunification of the child with the respondent shall not

be made, unless the court finds that termination of parental rights to the child is clearly not in the best interest of the child.

(G) Findings.

(1) *General.* The court shall state on the record or in writing its findings of fact and conclusions of law. Brief, definite, and pertinent findings and conclusions on contested matters are sufficient. If the court does not issue a decision on the record following hearing, it shall file its decision within 28 days after the taking of final proofs, but no later than 70 days after the commencement of the hearing to terminate parental rights.

(2) *Denial of Termination.* If the court finds that the parental rights of respondent should not be terminated, the court must make findings of fact and conclusions of law.

(3) *Order of Termination.* An order terminating parental rights under the juvenile code may not be entered unless the court makes findings of fact, states its conclusions of law, and includes the statutory basis for the order.

(H) Advice of Right: to Appeal, to an Attorney, to Transcripts; About Identifying Information.

(1) *Advice.* Immediately after entry of an order terminating parental rights, the court shall advise the respondent parent orally or in writing that

(a) respondent is entitled to appellate review of the order;

(b) if respondent is financially unable to provide an attorney to perfect an appeal, the court will appoint an attorney and furnish the attorney with the portions of the transcript and record the attorney requires to appeal;

(c) a request for the assistance of an attorney must be made within 21 days after notice of the order is given. The court must then give a form to the respondent with the instructions (to be repeated on the form) that if respondent desires the appointment of an attorney, the form must be returned to the court within the required period of time (to be stated on the form); and

(d) respondent has the right to file a denial of release of identifying information, a revocation of a denial of release, and to keep current the respondent's name and address as provided in MCL 710.27; MSA 27.3178(555.27), as amended.

(2) *Appointment of Attorney.* If a request is timely filed and the court finds that the respondent is financially unable to provide his or her own attorney, the court shall enter an order appointing an attorney. In the interest of justice, the court may appoint an attorney where the request is filed untimely.

(3) *Transcripts.* If the court finds that the respondent is financially unable to pay for the preparation of transcripts for appeal, the court may, on motion or its own initiative, order transcripts prepared at public expense.

(I) Review Standard. The clearly erroneous standard shall be used in reviewing the findings of the juvenile court on appeal from an order terminating parental rights.

(J) Post-termination Review Hearing. If a child remains in foster care following the termination of parental rights to the child, the court shall conduct a review hearing, at least every 182 days, as required by MCL 712A.19c; MSA 27.3178(598.19c) to review the progress toward permanent placement of the child. The court shall make findings on whether reasonable efforts have been made to establish permanent placement for the child, and may enter such orders as it considers necessary in the best interest of the child.

[Adopted and amended effective January 1, 1988; amended effective April 1, 1989; October 1, 1995; April 1, 1998.]

1988 Staff Comment

[See 1988 Staff Comment following Rule 5.993.]

[Under the January 1, 1988 amendment,] MCR 5.974 now includes the term "compelling" to describe the type of grounds which would justify a termination at the initial disposition.

MCR 5.974(H) authorizes transcripts at public expense to indigent respondents in protective proceedings when their parental rights have been severed. See *Reist v Bay County Circuit Judge,* 396 Mich 326 (1976). The latest time to file a delayed appeal from an order terminating parental rights in the Court of Appeals is now 63 days from the relevant order. The names of child abuse and neglect victims will no longer be used in published opinions.

Staff Comment to 1989 Amendment

[See "Staff Comment to April 1, 1989 Amendments," set forth following Rule 5.993.]

Staff Comment to 1995 Amendment

The August 22, 1995 amendments of MCR 5.903, 5.915, 5.920, 5.921, 5.973, and 5.974 were adopted in response to the enactment of 1994 PA 264, which amended parts of Chapter XIIA of 1939 PA 288.

Staff Comment to 1998 Amendment

The January 16, 1998, amendments of MCR 5.915, 5.923, 5.963, 5.965 and 5.974 [effective April 1, 1998] relate to recommendations made by the Binsfeld Children's Commission in its July 1996 report regarding children (Recommendations 36, 70, 71, 76, 77, 107, 111, and 121). The amendments are effective April 1, 1998, to coincide with the implementation of legislation enacted pursuant to recommendations of the commission.

RULE 5.980　CHILD CUSTODY PROCEEDING CONCERNING AMERICAN INDIAN CHILD

(A) Notice; Transfer. If any Indian child as defined by the Indian Child Welfare Act, 25 USC 1901 et seq. is the subject of a protective proceeding or is charged with an offense in violation of MCL

712A.2(a)(2)–(4) or (d); MSA 27.3178(598.2)(a)(2)–(4) or (d), the following procedures shall be used:

(1) If the Indian child resides on a reservation or is under tribal court jurisdiction at the time of referral, the matter shall be transferred to the tribal court having jurisdiction.

(2) If the child does not reside on a reservation, the court shall ensure that the petitioner has given notice of the proceedings to the child's tribe and the child's parents or Indian custodian and, if the tribe is unknown, to the Secretary of the Interior.

(3) If the tribe exercises its right to appear in the proceeding and requests that the proceeding be transferred to tribal court, the court shall transfer the case to the tribal court unless either parent objects to the transfer of the case to tribal court jurisdiction or the court finds good cause not to transfer. The perceived adequacy of the tribal court or tribal services shall not be good cause to refuse to transfer the case.

(B) Emergency Removal. An Indian child who resides or is domiciled on a reservation, but temporarily located off the reservation, shall not be removed from a parent or Indian custodian unless the removal is to prevent immediate physical harm to the child. An Indian child not residing or domiciled on a reservation may be temporarily removed if the child's health, safety, or welfare is endangered.

(C) Placement.

(1) Except in cases of emergency removal, an Indian child shall not be removed from the home unless there is clear and convincing evidence, including testimony by qualified expert witnesses, that services designed to prevent the break-up of the Indian family have been furnished to the family and that continual custody of the child by the parent or Indian custodian is likely to result in serious emotional or physical damage to the child.

(2) The Indian child, if removed from his or her home, shall be placed, in descending order of preference, with:

(a) a member of the child's extended family,

(b) a foster home licensed, approved, or specified by the child's tribe,

(c) an Indian foster family licensed or approved by a non-Indian licensing authority,

(d) an institution for children approved by an Indian tribe or operated by an Indian organization which has a program suitable to meet the child's needs.

The court may order another placement for good cause shown.

(D) Termination of Parental Rights. The parental rights of a parent of an Indian child shall not be terminated unless there is evidence beyond a reasonable doubt, including testimony of qualified expert witnesses, that parental rights should be terminated

because continued custody of the child by the parent or Indian custodian will likely result in serious emotional or physical damage to the child.

[Adopted and amended effective January 1, 1988; amended effective April 1, 1989.]

1988 and 1989 Staff Comments

[See "1988 Staff Comment" and "Staff Comment to April 1, 1989 Amendments," set forth following Rule 5.993.]

RULE 5.981 MINOR PERSONAL PROTECTION ORDERS; ISSUANCE; MODIFICATION; RECISION; APPEAL

Procedure on the issuance, dismissal, modification, or recision of minor personal protection orders is pursuant to subchapter 3.700. Procedure on appeals related to minor personal protection orders is pursuant to MCR 3.709 and MCR 5.993.

[Adopted effective January 10, 2000]

1999 Staff Comment

These rules [effective January 10, 2000] clarify the procedure applicable to the new minor personal protection orders ("minor PPOs") created in 1998 PA 474–477, which went into effect March 1, 1999. Because the new statutes do not make clear whether existing PPO procedural rules apply or rules for Juvenile Code proceedings apply, these rules are promulgated to assure consistency in the processing of minor PPOs in Michigan's Circuit Court Family Divisions. Immediate adoption has been ordered to provide needed procedural guidance for courts already facing minor PPO cases.

RULE 5.982 ENFORCEMENT OF MINOR PERSONAL PROTECTION ORDERS

(A) In General. A minor personal protection order is enforceable under MCL 600.2950(22), (25), MCL 600.2950a(19), (22), MCL 764.15b, and MCL 600.1701 *et seq.* For the purpose of MCR 5.981–5.989, "minor personal protection order" includes a foreign protection order against a minor respondent enforceable in Michigan under MCL 600.2950*l*.

(B) Procedure. Unless indicated otherwise in these rules, contempt proceedings for the enforcement of minor personal protection orders where the respondent is under 18 years of age are governed by MCR 5.982–5.989.

(C) Supplemental Petition.

(1) Any request for court action against a minor for purposes of enforcing a minor personal protection order must be in writing by means of a supplemental petition. The supplemental petition must contain a specific description of the facts constituting a violation of the personal protection order.

(2) The supplemental petition may be submitted only by the original petitioner, a law enforcement officer, a prosecuting attorney, a probation officer, or a caseworker.

(D) Form of Proceeding. A contempt proceeding brought in a court other than the one that issued the minor personal protection order shall be entitled "In the Matter of Contempt of [Respondent], a minor". The clerk shall provide a copy of the contempt proceeding to the court that issued the minor personal protection order.

[Adopted effective January 10, 2000; amended effective September 11, 2002.]

1999 Staff Comment

These rules [effective January 10, 2000] clarify the procedure applicable to the new minor personal protection orders ("minor PPOs") created in 1998 PA 474–477, which went into effect March 1, 1999. Because the new statutes do not make clear whether existing PPO procedural rules apply or rules for Juvenile Code proceedings apply, these rules are promulgated to assure consistency in the processing of minor PPOs in Michigan's Circuit Court Family Divisions. Immediate adoption has been ordered to provide needed procedural guidance for courts already facing minor PPO cases.

Staff Comment to 2002 Amendment

The September 11, 2002, amendments of MCR 3.206, 3.214, 3.705, 3.706, 3.708, 5.982, and 8.119, which were given immediate effect, are related to the group of domestic violence statutes enacted in December 2001 that took effect April 1, 2002.

The changes in MCR 3.206 and 3.214 are related to 2001 PA 195, which adopted the Uniform Child–Custody Jurisdiction and Enforcement Act, MCL 722.1101 *et seq.* There is also some nonsubstantive reorganization of MCR 3.214.

The amendment of MCR 3.705 implements the statutory provisions regarding the statement of reasons for granting or denying personal protection orders. See 2001 PA 196.

The amendment of MCR 3.706 incorporates the statutory provisions regarding enforceability of Michigan personal protection orders in other jurisdictions. See 2001 PA 200 and 201.

MCR 3.708 and 5.982 are amended to include foreign protection orders, which are made enforceable in Michigan by 2001 PA 197.

MCR 8.119(F) is amended to conform to 2001 PA 205, which directs that when a motion to seal court records involves allegations of domestic violence, the court is to consider the safety of the potential victim in ruling on the motion.

The staff comment is published only for the benefit of the bench and bar and is not an authoritative construction by the Court.

RULE 5.983　INITIATION OF CONTEMPT PROCEEDING BY ORIGINAL PETITIONER

(A) Filing; Scheduling. If a respondent allegedly violates a minor personal protection order, the original petitioner may submit a supplemental petition to have the respondent found in contempt. Upon receiving the supplemental petition, the court shall either:

(1) set a date for a preliminary hearing on the supplemental petition, to be held as soon as practicable, and issue a summons to appear; or

(2) issue an order authorizing a peace officer or other person designated by the court to apprehend the respondent.

(B) Service. If the court sets a date for a preliminary hearing upon receiving the supplemental petition, the petitioner shall, at least 7 days before the preliminary hearing, serve, as provided in MCR 5.920, the supplemental petition and summons on the respondent and, if the relevant address or addresses is or are known or easily ascertainable, on the parent or parents, guardian, or custodian.

(C) Order To Apprehend.

(1) The court order to apprehend the respondent may include authorization to:

(a) enter specified premises as required for the purpose of bringing the minor before the court, and

(b) detain the minor pending preliminary hearing if it appears there is a substantial likelihood of retaliation or continued violation.

(2) Upon apprehending a minor respondent under a court order, the officer shall comply with MCR 5.984(B),(C).

[Adopted effective January 10, 2000.]

1999 Staff Comment

These rules [effective January 10, 2000] clarify the procedure applicable to the new minor personal protection orders ("minor PPOs") created in 1998 PA 474–477, which went into effect March 1, 1999. Because the new statutes do not make clear whether existing PPO procedural rules apply or rules for Juvenile Code proceedings apply, these rules are promulgated to assure consistency in the processing of minor PPOs in Michigan's Circuit Court Family Divisions. Immediate adoption has been ordered to provide needed procedural guidance for courts already facing minor PPO cases.

RULE 5.984　APPREHENSION OF ALLEGED VIOLATOR

(A) Apprehension; Release to Parent, Guardian, or Custodian. When an officer apprehends a minor for violation of a minor personal protection order without a court order for apprehension and does not warn and release the minor, the officer may accept a written promise of the minor's parent(s), guardian, or custodian to bring the minor to court, and release the minor to the parent(s), guardian, or custodian.

(B) Custody; Detention. When, pursuant to a court order, an officer apprehends a minor in relation to a minor personal protection order and the court order specifies that the minor is to be brought directly to court, or when, without a court order, an officer apprehends a minor for an alleged violation of a minor personal protection order and either the officer has failed to get a written promise from the minor's parent(s), guardian, or custodian to bring the minor to court, or it appears to the officer that there is a substantial likelihood of retaliation or violation by the minor, the officer shall immediately:

(1) if the whereabouts of the minor's parent or parents, guardian, or custodian is known, inform the minor's parent or parents, guardian, or custodian of the minor's apprehension and of the minor's whereabouts and of the need for the parent or parents, guardian, or custodian to be present at the preliminary hearing;

(2) take the minor

(a) before the court for a preliminary hearing, or

(b) to a place designated by the court pending the scheduling of a preliminary hearing;

(3) prepare a custody statement for submission to the court including:

(a) the grounds for and the time and location of detention, and

(b) the names of persons notified and the times of notification, or the reason for failure to notify.

(4) ensure that a supplemental petition is prepared and filed with the court.

(C) Separate Custody. While awaiting arrival of the parent(s), guardian, or custodian, appearance before the court, or otherwise, a minor under 17 years of age must be maintained separately from adult prisoners to prevent any verbal, visual, or physical contact with an adult prisoner.

(D) Designated Court Person. The court must designate a judge, referee or other person who may be contacted by the officer taking a minor under 17 into custody when the court is not open. In each county there must be a designated facility open at all times at which an officer may obtain the name of the person to be contacted for permission to detain the minor pending preliminary hearing.

(E) Out-of-County Violation. Subject to MCR 5.985(H), if a minor is apprehended for violation of a minor personal protection order in a jurisdiction other than the jurisdiction where the minor personal protection order was issued, the apprehending jurisdiction may notify the issuing jurisdiction that it may request that the respondent be returned to the issuing jurisdiction for enforcement proceedings.

[Adopted effective January 10, 2000.]

1999 Staff Comment

These rules [effective January 10, 2000] clarify the procedure applicable to the new minor personal protection orders ("minor PPOs") created in 1998 PA 474–477, which went into effect March 1, 1999. Because the new statutes do not make clear whether existing PPO procedural rules apply or rules for Juvenile Code proceedings apply, these rules are promulgated to assure consistency in the processing of minor PPOs in Michigan's Circuit Court Family Divisions. Immediate

adoption has been ordered to provide needed procedural guidance for courts already facing minor PPO cases.

RULE 5.985   PRELIMINARY HEARING

(A) Time.

(1) *Commencement.* If the respondent was apprehended or arrested for violation of a minor personal protection order or was apprehended or arrested under a court order, and the respondent is taken into court custody or is jailed, the preliminary hearing must commence no later than 24 hours after the minor was apprehended or arrested, excluding Sundays and holidays, or the minor must be released. Otherwise, the preliminary hearing must commence as soon as practicable after the apprehension or arrest, or submission of a supplemental petition by the original petitioner.

(2) *General Adjournment.* The court may adjourn the hearing for up to 14 days:

(a) to secure the attendance of witnesses or the minor's parent, guardian, or custodian, or

(b) for other good cause shown.

(B) Procedure.

(1) The court shall determine whether the parent, guardian, or custodian has been notified and is present. The preliminary hearing may be conducted without a parent, guardian, or custodian provided a guardian ad litem or attorney appears with the minor.

(2) Unless waived by the respondent, the court shall read the allegations in the supplemental petition, and ensure that the respondent has received written notice of the alleged violation.

(3) Immediately after the reading of the allegations, the court shall advise the respondent on the record in plain language of the right to:

(a) contest the allegations at a violation hearing;

(b) an attorney at every stage in the proceedings, and, if the court determines it might sentence the respondent to jail or place the respondent in secure detention, the fact that the court will appoint a lawyer at public expense if the respondent wants one and is financially unable to retain one;

(c) a nonjury trial and that a referee may be assigned to hear the case unless demand for a judge is filed pursuant to MCR 5.912;

(d) have witnesses against the respondent appear at a violation hearing and to question the witnesses;

(e) have the court order any witnesses for the respondent's defense to appear at the hearing; and

(f) remain silent and to not have the respondent's silence used against the respondent, and that any statement by the respondent may be used against him or her.

(4) The court must decide whether to authorize the filing of the supplemental petition and proceed formally, or dismiss the supplemental petition.

(5) The respondent must be allowed an opportunity to deny or otherwise plead to the allegations. If the respondent wishes to enter a plea of admission or of nolo contendere, the court shall follow MCR 5.986.

(6) If the court authorizes the filing of the supplemental petition, the court must:

(a) set a date and time for the violation hearing, or, following a plea, either enter a dispositional order or set the matter for dispositional hearing; and

(b) either release the respondent pursuant to subrule (E) or order detention of the respondent as provided in subrule (F).

(C) Notification. Following the preliminary hearing, if the respondent denies the allegations in the supplemental petition, the court must:

(1) notify the prosecuting attorney of the scheduled violation hearing;

(2) notify the respondent, his or her attorney, if any, and his or her parent(s), guardian, or custodian of the scheduled violation hearing and direct the parties to appear at the hearing and give evidence on the charge of contempt;

(3) cause notice of hearing to be given by personal service or ordinary mail at least 7 days before the violation hearing, unless the respondent is detained, in which case notice of hearing is to be served at least 24 hours prior to the hearing.

(D) Absence of Respondent. If the respondent was notified of the preliminary hearing and fails to appear for the preliminary hearing, the court may issue an order in accordance with MCR 5.983(C) authorizing a peace officer or other person designated by the court to apprehend the respondent. If the respondent is under 17 years of age, the court may order the respondent detained pending a hearing on the apprehension order; if the court releases the respondent it may set bond for the respondent's appearance at the violation hearing. If the respondent is 17 years of age, the court may order the respondent confined to jail pending a hearing on the apprehension order; if the court releases the respondent it must set bond for the respondent's appearance at the violation hearing.

(E) Release of Respondent.

(1) Subject to the conditions set forth in subrule (F), the respondent may be released, with conditions, to a parent, guardian, or custodian pending the resumption of the preliminary hearing or pending the violation hearing after the court considers available information on

(a) family ties and relationships,

(b) the minor's prior juvenile delinquency or minor personal protection order record, if any,

(c) the minor's record of appearance or nonappearance at court proceedings,

(d) the violent nature of the alleged violation,

(e) the minor's prior history of committing acts that resulted in bodily injury to others,

(f) the minor's character and mental condition,

(g) the court's ability to supervise the minor if placed with a parent or relative,

(h) the likelihood of retaliation or violation of the order by the respondent, and

(i) any other factor indicating the minor's ties to the community, the risk of nonappearance, and the danger to the respondent or the original petitioner if the respondent is released.

(2) Bail procedure is pursuant to MCR 5.935(C)(2)-(3), (5)-(7).

(F) Detention Pending Violation Hearing.

(1) *Conditions.* A minor shall not be removed from the parent, guardian, or custodian pending violation hearing or further court order unless:

(a) probable cause exists to believe the minor violated the minor personal protection order; and

(b) at the preliminary hearing the court finds one or more of the following circumstances to be present:

(i) there is a substantial likelihood of retaliation or continued violation by the minor who allegedly violated the minor personal protection order;

(ii) there is a substantial likelihood that if the minor is released to the parent, with or without conditions, the minor will fail to appear at the next court proceeding; or

(iii) detention pending violation hearing is otherwise specifically authorized by law.

(2) *Waiver.* A minor respondent in custody may waive the probable cause phase of a detention determination only if the minor is represented by an attorney.

(3) *Evidence; Findings.* At the preliminary hearing the minor respondent may contest the sufficiency of evidence to support detention by cross-examination of witnesses, presentation of defense witnesses, or by other evidence. The court shall permit the use of subpoena power to secure attendance of defense witnesses. A finding of probable cause under subsection (1)(a) may be based on hearsay evidence which possesses adequate guarantees of trustworthiness.

(4) *Type of Detention.* The detained minor must be placed in the least restrictive environment that will meet the needs of the minor and the public, and that will conform to the requirements of MCL 712A.15, 712A.16; MSA 27.3178(598.15), 27.3178(598.16).

(G) Findings. At the preliminary hearing the court must state the reasons for its decision to release the minor, or to detain the minor, on the record or in a written memorandum.

(H) Out-of-County Violation. If a minor is apprehended for violation of a minor personal protection order in a jurisdiction other than the jurisdiction where the minor personal protection order was issued, and the apprehending jurisdiction conducts the preliminary hearing, and the apprehending jurisdiction has not already notified the issuing jurisdiction that it may request that the respondent be returned to the issuing jurisdiction for enforcement proceedings, the apprehending jurisdiction shall so notify the issuing jurisdiction immediately following the preliminary hearing.

[Adopted effective January 10, 2000.]

1999 Staff Comment

These rules [effective January 10, 2000] clarify the procedure applicable to the new minor personal protection orders ("minor PPOs") created in 1998 PA 474–477, which went into effect March 1, 1999. Because the new statutes do not make clear whether existing PPO procedural rules apply or rules for Juvenile Code proceedings apply, these rules are promulgated to assure consistency in the processing of minor PPOs in Michigan's Circuit Court Family Divisions. Immediate adoption has been ordered to provide needed procedural guidance for courts already facing minor PPO cases.

RULE 5.986   PLEAS OF ADMISSION OR NO CONTEST

(A) Capacity. A minor may offer a plea of admission or of no contest to the violation of a minor personal protection order with the consent of the court. The court shall not accept a plea to a violation unless the court is satisfied that the plea is accurate, voluntary, and understanding.

(B) Qualified Pleas. The court may accept a plea of admission or of no contest conditioned on preservation of an issue for appellate review.

(C) Support of Plea by Parent, Guardian, Custodian. The court shall inquire of the parent(s), guardian, custodian, or guardian ad litem whether he or she knows of any reason why the court should not accept the plea tendered by the minor. Agreement or objection by the parent, guardian, custodian, or guardian ad litem to a plea of admission or of no contest by a minor must be placed on the record if he or she is present.

(D) Plea Withdrawal. The court may take a plea of admission or of no contest under advisement. Before the court accepts the plea, the minor may withdraw the plea offer by right. After the court accepts the plea, the court has discretion to allow the minor to withdraw a plea.

[Adopted effective January 10, 2000]

1999 Staff Comment

These rules [effective January 10, 2000] clarify the procedure applicable to the new minor personal protection orders ("minor PPOs") created in 1998 PA 474–477, which went into effect March 1, 1999. Because the new statutes do not make clear whether existing PPO procedural rules apply or rules for Juvenile Code proceedings apply, these rules are promulgated to assure consistency in the processing of minor PPOs in Michigan's Circuit Court Family Divisions. Immediate adoption has been ordered to provide needed procedural guidance for courts already facing minor PPO cases.

RULE 5.987   VIOLATION HEARING

(A) Time. Upon completion of the preliminary hearing the court shall set a date and time for the violation hearing if the respondent denies the allegations in the supplemental petition. The violation hearing must be held within 72 hours of apprehension, excluding Sundays and holidays, if the respondent is detained. If the respondent is not detained the hearing must be held within 21 days.

(B) Prosecution After Apprehension. If a criminal contempt proceeding is commenced under MCL 764.15b; MSA 28.874(2), the prosecuting attorney shall prosecute the proceeding unless the petitioner retains an attorney to prosecute the criminal contempt proceeding.

(C) Preliminary Matters. The court shall

(1) determine whether all parties have been notified and are present.

    (a) The respondent has the right to be present at the violation hearing along with parents, guardian, or custodian, and guardian ad litem and attorney.

    (b) The court may proceed in the absence of a parent properly noticed to appear, provided the respondent is represented by an attorney.

    (c) The original petitioner has the right to be present at the violation hearing.

(2) read the allegations contained in the supplemental petition, unless waived.

(3) inform the minor of the right to the assistance of an attorney unless legal counsel appears with the minor, and inform the minor that if the court determines it might sentence the respondent to jail or place the respondent in secure detention then the court will appoint a lawyer at public expense if the respondent wants one and is financially unable to retain one. If the juvenile requests to proceed without the assistance of counsel, the court must advise the minor of the dangers and disadvantages of self-representation and make sure the minor is competent to conduct the defense and is literate.

(D) Jury. There is no right to a jury trial.

(E) Conduct of the Hearing. The respondent has the right to be present at the hearing, to present evidence, and to examine and cross-examine witnesses.

(F) Evidence; Burden of Proof. The rules of evidence apply to both criminal and civil contempt proceedings. The petitioner or the prosecuting attorney has the burden of proving the respondent's guilt of criminal contempt beyond a reasonable doubt and the respondent's guilt of civil contempt by a preponderance of the evidence.

(G) Judicial Findings. At the conclusion of the hearing, the court must make specific findings of fact, state separately its conclusions of law, and direct entry of the appropriate judgment. The court must state its findings and conclusions on the record or in a written opinion made a part of the record.

[Adopted effective January 10, 2000.]

1999 Staff Comment

These rules [effective January 10, 2000] clarify the procedure applicable to the new minor personal protection orders ("minor PPOs") created in 1998 PA 474–477, which went into effect March 1, 1999. Because the new statutes do not make clear whether existing PPO procedural rules apply or rules for Juvenile Code proceedings apply, these rules are promulgated to assure consistency in the processing of minor PPOs in Michigan's Circuit Court Family Divisions. Immediate adoption has been ordered to provide needed procedural guidance for courts already facing minor PPO cases.

RULE 5.988 DISPOSITIONAL PHASE

(A) Time. The time interval between the entry of judgment finding a violation of a minor personal protection order and disposition, if any, is within the court's discretion, but may not be more than 35 days. When the minor is detained, the interval may not be more than 14 days, except for good cause.

(B) Presence of Respondent and Petitioner.

(1) The respondent may be excused from part of the dispositional hearing for good cause, but the respondent must be present when the disposition is announced.

(2) The petitioner has the right to be present at the dispositional hearing.

(C) Evidence.

(1) At the dispositional hearing all relevant and material evidence, including oral and written reports, may be received by the court and may be relied upon to the extent of its probative value, even though such evidence may not be admissible at the violation hearing.

(2) The respondent, or the respondent's attorney, and the petitioner shall be afforded an opportunity to examine and controvert written reports so received and, in the court's discretion, may be allowed to cross-examine individuals making reports when such individuals are reasonably available.

(3) No assertion of an evidentiary privilege, other than the privilege between attorney and client, shall prevent the receipt and use, at the dispositional phase, of materials prepared pursuant to a court-ordered examination, interview, or course of treatment.

(D) Dispositions.

(1) If a minor respondent at least 17 years of age pleads or is found guilty of criminal contempt, the court may impose a sentence of incarceration of up to 93 days and may impose a fine of not more than $500.

(2) If a minor respondent pleads or is found guilty of civil contempt, the court shall

(a) impose a fine or imprisonment as specified in MCL 600.1715 and 600.1721; MSA 27A.1715 and 27A.1721, if the respondent is at least 17 years of age.

(b) subject the respondent to the dispositional alternatives listed in MCL 712A.18; MSA 27.3178(598.18), if the respondent is under 17 years of age.

(3) In addition to the sentence, the court may impose other conditions to the minor personal protection order.

[Adopted effective January 10, 2000.]

1999 Staff Comment

These rules [effective January 10, 2000] clarify the procedure applicable to the new minor personal protection orders ("minor PPOs") created in 1998 PA 474–477, which went into effect March 1, 1999. Because the new statutes do not make clear whether existing PPO procedural rules apply or rules for Juvenile Code proceedings apply, these rules are promulgated to assure consistency in the processing of minor PPOs in Michigan's Circuit Court Family Divisions. Immediate adoption has been ordered to provide needed procedural guidance for courts already facing minor PPO cases.

RULE 5.989 SUPPLEMENTAL DISPOSITIONS

When it is alleged that a minor placed on probation for the violation of a minor personal protection order has violated a condition of probation, the court shall follow the procedures for supplemental disposition as outlined in MCR 5.944.

[Adopted effective January 10, 2000.]

1999 Staff Comment

These rules [effective January 10, 2000] clarify the procedure applicable to the new minor personal protection orders ("minor PPOs") created in 1998 PA 474–477, which went into effect March 1, 1999. Because the new statutes do not make clear whether existing PPO procedural rules apply or rules for Juvenile Code proceedings apply, these rules are promulgated to assure consistency in the processing of minor PPOs in Michigan's Circuit Court Family Divisions. Immediate adoption has been ordered to provide needed procedural guidance for courts already facing minor PPO cases.

RULE 5.991 REVIEW OF REFEREE RECOMMENDATIONS

(A) General. A judge of the court shall review a referee's recommended findings and conclusion when requested

(1) by a party in a case on the formal calendar heard by a referee,

(2) by a juvenile or petitioner from a determination as to bail or probable cause to support detention,

(3) by a party from a determination as to placement, or

(4) to avoid manifest injustice in any case.

(B) Form of Request; Time. The request for review of either a referee recommendation or an order based on a referee recommendation must:

(1) be in writing,

(2) state the grounds for review, and

(3) be filed with the court within 7 days after the conclusion of the disposition if the basis for review is as stated in subrule (A)(1), or within 7 days after the conclusion of the hearing which resulted in the recommendation if the basis for review is as provided in subrule (A)(2) or (A)(3). A party may file a written response within 7 days after the filing of the request for review.

(C) Prompt Review; No Party Appearance Required. Absent good cause for delay, the judge shall consider the request within 21 days after it is filed if the minor is in placement or detention. The judge need not schedule a hearing to rule on a request for review of a referee's recommendations.

(D) Review Standard. The judge shall deny the request for review unless:

(1) the judge would have reached a different result had he or she heard the case; or

(2) the referee committed a clear error of law, which

 (a) likely would have affected the outcome, or

 (b) cannot otherwise be considered harmless.

(E) Remedy. The judge may affirm, modify, or deny the recommendation of the referee in whole or in part, on the basis of the record and the memoranda prepared, or may conduct a hearing, whichever the court in its discretion finds appropriate for the case.

(F) Stay. The court may stay any order, or grant bail to a detained juvenile, pending its decision on review of the referee's recommendation.

[Adopted and amended effective January 1, 1988.]

1988 Staff Comment

[See 1988 Staff Comment following Rule 5.993.]

RULE 5.992 REHEARINGS

(A) Time and Grounds. Except for the case of a juvenile tried as an adult in the juvenile court for a criminal offense, a party may seek a rehearing or new trial by filing a written motion stating the basis for the relief sought within 21 days after decision of disposition or supplemental disposition. The court may entertain an untimely motion for good cause shown. A motion will not be considered unless it presents a matter not previously presented to the court, or presented but not previously considered by the court, which, if true, would cause the court to reconsider the case.

(B) Notice. All parties must be given notice of the motion in accordance with Rule 5.920.

(C) Response by Parties. Any response by parties must be in writing and filed with the court and opposing parties within 7 days after notice of the motion.

(D) Procedure. The judge may affirm, modify, or vacate the decision previously made in whole or in part, on the basis of the record, the memoranda prepared, or a hearing on the motion, whichever the court in its discretion finds appropriate for the case.

(E) Hearings. The court need not hold a hearing before ruling on a motion. Any hearing conducted shall be in accordance with the rules for dispositional hearings and, at the discretion of the court, may be assigned to the person who conducted the hearing. The court shall state the reasons for its decision on the motion on the record or in writing.

(F) Stay. The court may stay any order, or grant bail to a detained juvenile, pending a ruling on the motion.

[Adopted effective January 1, 1988; amended effective May 15, 1997; January 1, 1998.]

1988 Staff Comment

[See 1988 Staff Comment following Rule 5.993.]

Staff Comment to 1997 Amendment

The April 8, 1997, amendments of subchapter 5.900 of the Michigan Court Rules [effective May 15, 1997] implement recent statutory changes applicable to the juvenile division of the probate court. See, e.g., 1996 PA 247, 1996 PA 248, 1996 PA 255, 1996 PA 259, and 1996 PA 262. The amendments are based on proposals submitted by the Juvenile Court Rules Committee of the Probate Judges Association. These temporary amendments will remain in effect until further order of the court, and will be reconsidered after receipt of comments.

Staff Comment to 1998 Amendment

The December 19, 1997, amendments to Rule 3.206 and subchapter 5.900 of the Michigan Court Rules [effective January 1, 1998] implement recent statutory changes which have created a family division of the circuit court. These amendments will remain in effect until further order of the court.

RULE 5.993 APPEALS

(A) The following orders are appealable to the Court of Appeals by right:

(1) an order of disposition placing a minor under the supervision of the court or removing the minor from the home,

(2) an order terminating parental rights,

(3) any order required by law to be appealed to the Court of Appeals, and

(4) any final order.

(B) All orders not listed in subrule (A) are appealable to the Court of Appeals by leave.

(C) Procedure; Delayed Appeals. Except as modified by this rule, Chapter 7 of the Michigan Court Rules governs appeals from the juvenile court.

(1) The Court of Appeals may not grant an application for leave to appeal an order of the juvenile court terminating parental rights if filed more than 63 days after entry of an order of judgment on the merits, or if filed more than 63 days after entry of an order denying reconsideration or rehearing.

(2) *Use of Minor's Initials in Published Opinions.* On appeal from a judgment of the juvenile court in a child protective proceeding, the Supreme Court Reporter shall delete the full name of the minor and replace the name with the minor's initials before the Court of Appeals or Supreme Court opinion is published.

[Adopted and amended effective January 1, 1988; amended effective January 1, 1998.]

1988 Staff Comment

The rules recognize separate practice and procedure for juvenile delinquency proceedings and child protective proceedings in the juvenile division of the probate court. MCR 5.901 through MCR 5.927, MCR 5.980, and MCR 5.991–5.993 are applicable to both.

Under MCR 5.901, other subchapters of the Michigan Court Rules which pertain to practice and procedure are inapplicable to the juvenile division of the probate court unless they are expressly incorporated. Since subchapter 8.100 relates to administrative matters rather than practice and procedure, that subchapter continues to apply to the juvenile court. The following rules from other subchapters have been incorporated by reference:

MCR 2.613 on correcting error,

MCR 2.114 on verified pleadings,

MCR 2.510–2.516 on jury procedure,

MCR 2.003 on disqualification of a judge,

MCR 2.117(B) relative to appearance of an attorney,

MCR 2.506 relative to the manner of serving a subpoena,

MCR 2.119 on motion practice,

MCR 2.401 on pretrial conference,

MCR 8.108 on recording of proceedings,

MCR 5.602 on the form of signing judgment and orders,

MCR 3.205 pertaining to the transfer of cases from other courts,

MCR 3.604 on surety bonds, and

subchapter 7.100 on appeals.

The decision not to carry forward the rule authorizing automatic exclusion of a custodial confession of a juvenile unless counsel is waived with the concurrence of a parent does not authorize the police to obtain a waiver of counsel from the juvenile in the absence of a parent before interrogation. The presence or absence of the parent is to be considered a factor among many in determining the voluntariness of the confession under a totality of circumstance standard. See *Fare* v *Michael C,* 442 US 707, 724–725; 99 S Ct 2560; 61 L Ed 2d 197 (1979).

There are elaborate definitions in MCR 5.903. "Juvenile" refers to the minor defendant in a delinquency proceeding. "Child" refers to the minor "victim" in a child protective proceeding. The definition of "minor" comes from section 2a(2) of the Juvenile Code. MCL 712A.2a; MSA 27.3178(598.2a). It is used in the rules to cover both the juvenile and child. Note a reference is made to "dependency" in defining child. Const 1963, art 6, § 15, provides that the court "shall have original jurisdiction in all cases of juvenile delinquents and dependents".

The term "child born out of wedlock" comes from MCL 710.22(d); MSA 27.3178(555.22)(d). The term "father" is based in part on MCL 700.111(4)(a) and (b); MSA 27.5111(4)(a) and (b).

The definition of "parent" focuses on the person who is vested, naturally or otherwise, with the right of physical custody as well as the duty to provide food, shelter, clothing, medical care, and to assure that the minor is educated, disciplined, protected and nurtured. For purposes of termination of parental rights, however, "parent" or "respondent" refers only to a natural or adoptive mother or father. See MCR 5.974. The court need not "terminate parental rights" before entering an order of permanent wardship in other "parent-child" relationships. Respondent is the parent or parents whose act or inaction brought the matter of the child to the court's attention. The rules seem to allow the court to terminate only one of the parent's rights under certain circumstances. See *In re Arntz,* 418 Mich 941; 344 NW2d 1 (1984).

The petition describes the initial complaint of wrongdoing on the part of the juvenile defendant or a respondent parent, and refers to the charging document filed with the court register after authorization by the judge or referee. The filing of the authorized petition, as opposed to submission of an *unauthorized* petition, signals the start of the formal calendar proceeding which includes the plea of admission or of no contest, trial, and disposition. It is often the point of reference from which to calculate the time frame for conducting proceedings.

The rules reflect the practice of separating confidential material from nonconfidential material by defining legal and social file. The "legal file" is generally open for public inspection when the juvenile court proceeding is open to the public. Access to materials in other instances will be judged individually, on the basis of whether the moving party establishes a legitimate interest. See MCL 712A.28; MSA 27.3178(598.28).

In a delinquency proceeding, "detention" is defined broadly to cover the pretrial removal of the juvenile from the parent. It does not just mean court-ordered custody in a secure facility. "Placement" is also broadly defined. What is least restrictive detention placement before or after trial depends on the circumstances of the case. The unavailability of a parent would not justify secure detention, for example.

Rules 5.911 through 5.916 list the important functionaries in the juvenile justice system, including jury, judge, referee, prosecutor, defense attorney, and guardian ad litem. A referee may be assigned to hear a case other than a waiver hearing when there is no demand for a judge or jury. The party who seeks to exercise the statutory right to a jury, pursuant to MCL 712A.17; MSA 27.3178(598.17), must file a written demand under MCR 5.911. Under MCR 5.912 the same method is used to request a judge. The demand for a jury is to be made 14 days after the court gives notice of the right, 14 days after counsel files an appearance, or 7 days before trial. The court may excuse a late filing in the interest of justice. This can be read to allow a party to request that a judge preside at a difficult dispositional hearing even if the trial was presided over by a referee. The notice of rights, such as the right to a jury, is not always going to be interchangeable with service of a summons in order to obtain jurisdiction over a party which, under MCR 5.920 and § 13 of the Juvenile Code, may be served as few as 7 days before trial or three days before hearing. MCL 712A.13; MSA 27.3178(598.13).

Under MCR 5.913 a referee may not preside at a jury trial, and only the referee who has been admitted to the practice of law in this state may now hear a neglect case past the preliminary hearing stage, or conduct formal calendar proceedings in a delinquency case on an authorized petition charging a major offense. Since "major offense" is defined as a felony if it had been committed by an adult, the nonlawyer referee may act as a factfinder and dispose of matters involving a truant, runaway, undisciplined minor or a juvenile who committed an offense which, if committed by an adult would be a misdemeanor. See *People* v *Smith*, 423 Mich 427; 378 NW2d 384 (1985).

Under MCR 5.915, the court must advise the respondent parent at his or her first court appearance of the right to an attorney, and to appointed counsel if the parent is indigent. A respondent parent who initially decides not to be represented by counsel may request and obtain a court-appointed attorney at any later proceeding. Respondent is understood to mean any natural or adoptive father or mother when the proceeding involves termination of that person's parental rights, which is virtually every proceeding in light of the continuous nature of the child protective proceedings. The court must appoint an attorney for a child in all child protective proceedings. In a delinquency proceeding, the court must not accept a waiver of counsel except on the record. If the juvenile desires to try his own case, the court must be assured that he is able to do so and tell the juvenile of the dangers and disadvantages of self-representation. MCR 5.942.

The relative importance of the guardian ad litem may have diminished since the child protective law was enacted, requiring that the child be represented by an attorney. Presumably the attorney can serve the function traditionally assigned to the guardian, which is "to promote and protect the interests of a child involved in a judicial proceeding through assuring representation of those interests in the courts and throughout the social service and ancillary service systems."

Deardurff, *Representing the interests of the abused and neglected child: The guardian ad litem and access to confidential information*, 11 U Day L R 649 n 3 (1986), quoting Davidson, *The Guardian Ad Litem in Protecting Children Through the Legal System*, 835, 843 (1981). Under the rule, the court may appoint a guardian ad litem on behalf of any party, not just a minor.

Rule 5.920 is both consistent with the legislative intent manifested in the Juvenile Code that delivery of a summons is the preferred manner and form for service of process over the minor and the parent, and at the same time practical in that the rule contemplates a one-time service of a summons, unless otherwise waived, on the juvenile or parent in order to bring them within the jurisdiction of the court. MCL 712A.12, 712A.13 and 712A.20; MSA 27.3178(598.12), 27.3178(598.13), 27.3178(598.20). Unless waived, a juvenile is to be personally summoned to appear at trial. A form of summons is also to be used to insure that the parent appears with the minor for trial in a child protective proceeding. The child may be excused, however. The respondent parent must also be served with a summons on a petition or supplemental petition seeking to terminate parental rights unless respondent's prior court appearance in the case was in response to service of a summons. When that is the case, other forms of notice such as service of summons by mail may be used. The summons has to give the place and time of the trial or hearing, the nature of the proceeding, tell about the right to an attorney and to trial by judge or jury, and have a copy of the petition attached. The parties may be notified of hearings in writing or on the record or, if the party has an attorney, by service on the attorney. In a delinquency proceeding, notice of hearing is to be served on the juvenile, the parents, any guardian ad litem, and the attorney of the juvenile. The petitioner and the mother or father of the juvenile who does not possess legal or physical custody because of divorce or legal separation must be notified of the first hearing. If the person with whom the juvenile resides at the time of trial is not the parent, the parent must be notified of the trial, unless waived, by notice equivalent to the service of a summons. In a child protective proceeding, the parents, the child or the attorney of the child, the petitioner, any guardian ad litem, and the attorney for the parent are to be notified of all hearings. The notice or summons regarding a termination hearing must contain language that the hearing could result in the termination of parental rights.

MCR 5.912(D) describes procedures to follow when determining whether a person is a natural father. The provisions are similar to those in the Adoption Code, where the court holds a hearing to identify the father and determine or terminate his rights. See MCL 710.36 et seq.; MSA 27.3178(555.36) et seq. Under the rule, if the court determines that the interest of justice so requires, it is unnecessary for the mother of a child to join in the acknowledgement with the father to establish legal paternity.

MCR 5.922 lists materials discoverable as of right by a party in a juvenile court proceeding. The party seeking discovery must file the request 21 days before trial. All other materials are discoverable by leave. The court may also order discovery on its own initiative. MCR 5.923.

In a delinquency proceeding the juvenile must give notice of a defense, such as insanity, no later than 7 days before trial. The notice would include providing a list of witnesses expected to be called. The prosecutor would also have to provide a list of rebuttal witnesses. The rule is applicable independent of the discovery rule. Further, under MCR 5.923(B), the court is granted authority to order psychiatric examination. See also MCR 5.935(D)(2)(d) and MCR 5.965(C)(2)(b). Motions to suppress evidence should be filed no later than seven days before trial. A provision is made to protect a witness of tender years by permitting the court to use electronic equipment and appoint an impartial psychologist or psychiatrist to question the young witness. MCR 5.923(D) and (E).

MCR 5.924 carries forward former rule 5.907(B)(6) that judicial immunity extends to those who furnish reports on court request. *Dabkowski v Davis*, 364 Mich 429; 111 NW2d 68 (1961). But see *Bolton v Jones*, 156 Mich App 642; 401 NW2d 894 (1986).

Juvenile delinquency proceedings, other than those involving status offenders, are to be open to the public except for good cause shown. Child protective proceedings, and those proceedings involving status offenders, are to be closed unless opened for good cause. News cameras are forbidden. When the proceedings are open, the legal file shall be also available for public inspection. MCR 5.925(A) and (D). The rule appears consistent with the Juvenile Code provision that authorizes the court to decide whether the general public is to be excluded. MCL 712A.17(1); MSA 27.3178(598.17).

A person must now reach age 30 before expungement of the person's delinquency records becomes automatic. The court has discretion to expunge a juvenile delinquent's records before age 30 if two years have elapsed since the final discharge of the youth or the date of the adjudication and there are no criminal or juvenile delinquency proceedings pending against the person. The juvenile's motor vehicle violations must be expunged at age 19. Although no definition of expungement appears in the rule, it is common practice to actually obliterate or destroy the records. The rule no longer expressly authorizes the juvenile court to order expungement of law enforcement files and records. When the records of an adult convict have not been expunged and are requested by the Department of Corrections, the court under MCL 5.925(F) will have to designate whether the adjudications were obtained when the then-juvenile was represented by an attorney or waived counsel.

MCR 5.926(A) is consistent with § 2 of the Juvenile Code in allowing transfer of the case to the county of the minor's residence prior to trial. MCR 712A.2(d); MSA 27.3178(598.2)(d). MCR 5.926(C) permits change of venue for convenience of the parties or witnesses or when an impartial trial cannot be had and is consistent generally with MCR 2.221–2.226.

MCR 5.927 recognizes the authority of the juvenile court to act when a child is the subject of a prior or continuing order of another court. See 1986 PA 203, amending MCL 712A.2; MSA 27.3178(598.2); *Krajewski v Krajewski*, 420 Mich 729; 362 NW2d 230 (1984).

MCR 5.931 through MCR 5.950 only apply to juvenile delinquency proceedings. The request to authorize the filing of a petition or to take other action begins the juvenile delinquency proceeding. MCR 5.931. The petition has to conform to the requirements of the Juvenile Code. MCL 712A.11; MSA 27.3178(598.11). In addition, the petition must contain a citation to the Juvenile Code section and any general law, allegedly violated by the juvenile. If the petitioner is not requesting pretrial detention, an appearance ticket may be used in lieu of a petition. The court may also authorize the filing of a petition after a preliminary inquiry, which does not require an actual hearing. The inquiry

serves as a screening device and is to be used when the juvenile is not in custody. A decision to notify the parents and juvenile for "further formal inquiry" should be made when limited disposition is anticipated.

If a juvenile is apprehended and the officer does not decide to release the youth, the juvenile must be taken forthwith to the juvenile court for a preliminary hearing. MCR 5.934. If the court is not open, the officer must contact the person who has been designated by the court to decide whether the juvenile may be detained overnight in a facility pending the holding of a preliminary hearing. If the court is open, the preliminary hearing must start as soon as possible, but no later than 24 hours after custody or the juvenile is to be released. MCR 5.935. Court custody would appear to vary depending on the circumstances. For example, if the court is not open, it would appear to be at the point the designated person approves temporary detention. If the custody is pursuant to an order of apprehension, it is at the point that the officer apprehends the juvenile. Sundays and holidays are excluded in the calculation of the 24 hours and adjournment is allowed for good cause. The time to complete a preliminary hearing is now 14, rather than 10 days. When no preliminary hearing is held, advice of right may be accomplished when the summons is served or other notice is given, MCR 5.920(B)(2). At the preliminary hearing, the court must advise the juvenile and his or her parents of the juvenile's rights to jury and attorney, and the privilege against self-incrimination. There must be a determination whether there is probable cause to believe that the juvenile committed the offense. The court determines whether to authorize a petition and to detain the youth. A principal reason for the preliminary hearing is to determine if there is to be pretrial detention. Under MCR 5.935(D)(3), the probable cause determination may be waived only if the juvenile has an attorney. It contemplates waiver only after advice from counsel. Generally, the court is to release the juvenile with or without conditions after considering the factors listed in MCR 5.935(C). A juvenile may be detained if there is probable cause to believe that the juvenile committed the offense as alleged and one or more circumstances listed in MCR 5.935(D)(2) are present. Circumstances justifying detention include: where the offense is so serious that it would endanger the youth or the public to release the juvenile or the court finds the juvenile is a "habitual offender" who will likely commit further offenses if released. See *Schall v Martin*, 467 US 253; 104 S Ct 2403; 81 L Ed 2d 207 (1984). Note MCR 5.935(D)(2)(d) is taken from the Juvenile Code. MCL 712A.15(d); MSA 27.3187(598.15)(d). The referee or judge may use hearsay evidence at the preliminary hearing to support the finding of probable cause for pretrial detention so long as the evidence is trustworthy. MCR 5.935(D)(4). At a preliminary inquiry or the preliminary hearing, the court may determine to divert the case to alternate services or, once the petition is authorized, place the matter on the consent calendar. MCR 5.932; MCR 5.935(B)(3). The rule would permit the court to transfer a case from the consent calendar to the formal calendar when the juvenile fails to meet conditions of the consent agreement. MCR 5.932(B)(3).

A case typically is placed on the formal calendar once the authorized petition is filed with the juvenile court register. If the juvenile is in detention, the trial must be held within 42 days after the juvenile is taken into custody or the juvenile must be released on his or her own recognizance. The same type of automatic release is contemplated when the trial of a juvenile, who was not waived over to a court of general criminal jurisdiction, has not started within 28 days after the denial of waiver.

The rule allows for a plea of admission or no contest to an offense with the consent of the court. MCR 5.941(A). A juvenile may tender a qualified plea of guilty. This will allow the juvenile to raise a nonjurisdictional issue on appeal despite the plea.

Once the case is placed on the formal calendar and the juvenile does not tender a plea of admission or of no contest, the juvenile is tried, and the trier of fact must find beyond a reasonable doubt that the juvenile committed the offense as alleged in the petition. The Michigan Rules of Evidence apply at the trial. MCR 5.942(C). The order of proceedings, although not spelled out, is intended to be similar to that in criminal proceedings. The court would allow the parties to deliver an opening statement. The petitioner would make his or her opening statement first. The petitioner would offer evidence in support of the petition and then the juvenile would be allowed to offer evidence in defense. The petitioner may offer evidence in rebuttal of the juvenile's evidence, and the juvenile may then offer evidence in rebuttal of the petitioner's evidence. In the interest of justice, the court may allow the parties to offer further rebuttal or surrebuttal evidence. At the conclusion of the evidence, the petitioner, followed by the juvenile, has the right to deliver a closing argument. The petitioner would then have the right to deliver a rebuttal closing argument.

If the court determines to take jurisdiction over the juvenile, it may enter any number of dispositional alternatives under § 18 of the Juvenile Code, MCL 712A.18; MSA 27.3178(598.18). A dispositional hearing may be held anytime after the plea of admission or trial up to 35 days unless adjourned further for good cause shown. In MCR 5.943(B), the extension from 28 to 35 days is to insure that psychiatric reports are received before disposition. MCR 5.943(E)(2) is consistent with the Interstate Compact on the Placement of Children, MCL 3.711 et seq.; MSA 4.146(11) et seq.

MCR 5.944 represents the procedures used to act on an alleged violation of a juvenile's probation. The rule is patterned after the probation revocation proceedings for adults charged with violating conditions of probation. MCR 6.111. There must be a supplemental petition authorized and filed and the juvenile served with process pursuant to MCR 5.920 unless an order of apprehension is issued by the court. If the juvenile who is alleged to have violated his probation is detained, he or she must be brought for a preliminary hearing, and the probation violation hearing must be held no later than 42 days after the filing of the supplemental petition. MCR 5.944(A)(1)(b) and (A)(4). The burden of proof to establish a violation is preponderance of the evidence; the Michigan Rules of Evidence do not apply.

Under MCR 5.950, the juvenile shall no longer be subject to waiver of jurisdiction to stand trial as an adult if the prosecutor fails to move to waive jurisdiction within 14 days after the filing of the authorized petition unless good cause is shown for the delay. There are two phases to the waiver hearing as provided by the former court rule: the probable cause phase and the phase where the court determines it is in the best interests of the juvenile and the public to waive the juvenile over to stand trial as an adult. The probable cause phase may be waived by the juvenile or it need not be held if the requisite probable cause was found at the preliminary hearing conducted by a judge solely on that basis of legally admissible evidence. MCR 5.950(B). The juvenile may not waive the second phase of a waiver hearing. In addition to the criteria set forth in the Juvenile Code to determine whether the interest of the juvenile and the public would be best served by waiving the juvenile over to stand trial as an adult, MCL 712A.4(1); MSA 27.3178(598.4)(1), MCR 5.950(B)(2), the court may consider whether the youth has previously been waived over to a court of general criminal jurisdiction, and may consider any stipulation by the defense counsel that it would be in the best interests of the juvenile and public to waive the juvenile over to stand trial as an adult. MCR 5.950(B)(2)(c). Note that now a certified social worker's testimony, as well as that of a psychiatrist and psychologist, may not be used at subsequent criminal proceedings involving a juvenile without the juvenile's consent. MCR 5.950(E). The court must make findings on an order of denial of waiver, as well as an order granting waiver, to a court of general criminal jurisdiction.

MCR 5.961 through MCR 5.974 govern matters of practice and procedure in child protective proceedings in the juvenile court. As in the delinquency proceeding, a preliminary hearing is used when the child is in custody or the petitioner seeks to have the child removed from the parents pending a determination as to whether the court will assume jurisdiction over the child. Otherwise a preliminary inquiry is used to act on an unauthorized petition. The juvenile court retains the discretion to proceed informally on a case despite objection from the petitioner. The "exigent circumstance" exception in MCR 5.961 appears to have modified the requirement that a request for court action be in writing. Compare *Oversmith* v *Lake*, 295 Mich 627; 295 NW 339 (1940). The child may be placed with a relative or in foster care, etc., if at the preliminary hearing the court finds that the child's surroundings are such as to endanger the child's health, safety or welfare and the allegations in the petition are supported by reasonable grounds. MCR 5.963, 5.965. A preliminary hearing must commence no later than 24 hours after the child has been taken into custody, excluding Sundays and holidays. The rule requires due diligence on the part of the petitioner in trying to secure the parent's presence at the hearing. MCR 5.963(C) and MCR 5.965(B). There is no consent calendar for child protective proceedings and no right to post bail to obtain the release of the child. MCR 5.965(C)(5). The court may accept a plea of no contest as well as a plea of admission under MCR 5.971. Under the one continuous proceeding approach to child protection proceedings, the provision in MCR 5.971 requiring the court to tell the respondent parent that a plea may later be used in part to terminate parental rights and the need for thorough fact finding to support an order terminating parental rights, MCR 5.974(G), are of great importance.

Under MCR 5.972(A), all trials in child protective proceedings must be held within six months after the filing of the petition. Trial must start 42 days after the child has been placed unless there is a stipulation of the parties, a material witness is unavailable, or service of process cannot be completed. The child must still be returned to the parent, even if delay is based on an excused circumstance justifying postponement other than stipulation, unless the child will be physically or seriously emotionally harmed if returned to the parent. MCR 5.972 contains a new exception to the hearsay rule akin to the tender years exception. In a child protective trial, a hearsay statement by a child under ten years of age which describes an act of child abuse as defined by the child protection law, may be admitted into evidence to corroborate the testimony of the child, provided that at a pretrial hearing the court finds that the nature and circumstances surrounding the giving of the statement indicate adequate indicia of trustworthiness and that there is sufficient corroborative evidence of the act.

Once the court determines to assume jurisdiction over the child following trial or plea, it must hold a dispositional hearing no later than 35 days after the original trial or plea of admission, except when adjourned for good cause shown. MCR 5.973(A). The Michigan Rules of Evidence do not apply at the dispositional hearing. Only relevant and material evidence is permitted. However, the party is given an opportunity to examine and controvert any written reports received as a basis for the dispositional order. The party is not permitted to assert an evidentiary privilege other than the attorney-client privilege to prevent the receipt and use of court-ordered materials at the dispositional phase. If the child is placed other than with the parent, the statutory review hearings must be held every 6 months. Cf. MCL 712A.19; MSA 27.3178(598.19).

Because of the fundamental liberty interest which a natural or adoptive parent has in the care and custody of his or her child, parental rights may not be terminated unless the petitioner proves by clear and convincing evidence that grounds exist under the Juvenile Code to warrant termination. *Santosky* v *Kramer*, 455 US 745; 102 S Ct 1388; 71 L Ed 2d 599 (1982). MCR 5.974 continues to treat the matter of termination of parental rights as basically dispositional. *In re Mathers*, 371 Mich 516; 124 NW2d 878 (1963). However, MCR 5.974 should be applied with the philosophy of the Juvenile Code concerning preserving family integrity in perspective. See MCL 712A.1; MSA 27.3178(598.1); *In re Mathers*. Although the reason for the juvenile court's existence pertains to the interest of the child, MCR 5.974 makes it clear that the statutory grounds for termination of parental rights must be established before the court considers whether it is in the best custodial interest of the child to actually terminate the rights of the parent. *Fritts* v *Krugh*, 354 Mich 97; 92 NW2d 604 (1958).

MCR 5.974 recognizes that circumstances may justify the court taking permanent custody of the child at the initial disposition, and that in such instance the court is not limited to the grounds listed in § 19a of the Juvenile Code, MCL 712A.19a; MSA 27.3178(598.19a); *In re Kidder*, 393 Mich 819 (1975); *In re Sharpe*, 68 Mich App 619; 243 NW2d 696 (1976). Only legally admissible evidence may be used to establish the grounds to support termination at the initial disposition. Relevant and material evidence may be used to decide whether it is in the best custodial interest of the child to terminate once the grounds for termination are established.

If the court assumes jurisdiction over the child and does not terminate parental rights at the initial disposition, MCR 5.974 provides that a later request (supplemental petition) to terminate parental rights must be based on the grounds as set forth in § 19a of the Code, except where there exists a new or changed circumstance. A hearing on the supplemental petition under § 19a of the Juvenile Code must be held within 42 days after the petition is filed unless good cause is shown. In no case should the time period be extended past an additional 21 days. The basis for termination under § 19a may be established by material and relevant evidence only. However, the parties are to be given a chance to examine and controvert written reports, and the court in its discretion may permit cross-examination of individuals who furnish the report if they are reasonably available. The rule contemplates an instance where parental rights may be terminated other than at the initial disposition or pursuant to

§ 19a of the Code. If, for example, a child in foster care is seriously harmed by a parent during a visit, the court may authorize a new petition alleging that the misconduct warrants termination of parental rights. Under those circumstances, proofs must establish by clear and convincing legally admissible evidence that the misconduct warrants termination of parental rights. If so, and if it is in the best custodial interest of the child, the court may terminate. The rule requires that the court issue findings of fact and conclusions of law when it determines to terminate parental rights. It requires that the decision be made within 28 days after the taking of final proofs. It requires that the court advise a person whose parental rights have been terminated that he or she has the right to an appeal and the right to the appointment of an attorney to represent the party on appeal if indigent. *Reist* v *Bay County Circuit Judge*, 396 Mich 326; 241 NW2d 55 (1976).

The provision indicating that the standard of review on appeal from the termination of parental rights is the clearly erroneous test comes from the Court decision in *In re Cornet*, 422 Mich 274; 373 NW2d 536 (1985).

MCR 5.980 concerns custody proceedings involving Indian children, consistent with the Indian Child Welfare Act, 25 USC 1901 et seq. "Indian child" is a person who is either a registered member of an Indian tribe or band or has at least one biological parent who is a member of the tribe or band, with the child being eligible for tribal membership. Each tribe determines its own eligibility for membership. The Indian Child Welfare Act does not apply to offenses by juveniles other than status offenses. When proceedings involve an Indian child, notice to the tribe is necessary. MCR 5.980(A)(2). The burden of proof concerning the termination of parental rights over an Indian child is evidence beyond a reasonable doubt based on qualified expert witness testimony that the continued custody of the child with the parent will likely result in serious emotional or physical damage to the child.

MCR 5.991 sets forth the procedure for reviewing the recommended findings and conclusions of a referee. The rule is not to be read as giving the petitioner the right to request a review of findings and orders issued after jeopardy attaches in a delinquency proceeding. In other words, the petitioner would not be entitled to file a request to review a not guilty verdict rendered by a referee following trial in a delinquency proceeding. The respondent parent should be able to appeal a referee's probable cause decision under MCR 5.991(A)(3).

Note that review of a referee's decision following trial may be filed sooner than 7 days after the disposition "to avoid a manifest injustice." MCR 5.991 requires the judge to promptly handle the review request when the minor is in placement or detention. The standard of review de novo, rather than the clearly erroneous standard, is consistent with the authority given a judge to delegate duties to the referee under the Juvenile Code: "to administer oaths and examine witnesses, hearing and taking of testimony [and] make a written signed report to the judge containing a summary of the testimony taken and a recommendation for the court's findings and disposition of such matters." MCL 712A.10; MSA 27.3178(598.10). The terms "memoranda prepared" in MCR 5.991(E) refers to records of proceedings at the preliminary stages if not preserved by stenographic, mechanical or electronic recording. See MCR 5.925(B).

MCR 5.993 incorporates chapter 7 on appellate procedure by reference. It is consistent with MCL 600.861; MSA

27A.861. There is no appeal of right to the Court of Appeals from an order denying termination of parental rights. "If the State initially fails to win termination it always can try once again to cut off the parents' rights after gathering more or better evidence." *Santosky* v *Kramer*, 455 US 745, 764; 102 S Ct 1388; 71 L Ed 2d 599 (1982). *In re Youmans (Dept of Social Services* v *Youmans)*, 428 Mich 870 (1987).

Staff Comment to June 1, 1988 Amendments

Legislation in the area of juvenile justice takes effect on June 1, 1988. Specifically the new acts deal with fingerprinting of juveniles, lawyer referees in delinquency proceedings, open juvenile court proceedings, diversion of juveniles from formal court proceedings, the role of the prosecuting attorney in delinquency proceedings, confidential files, expungement of records, and restitution. See 1988 PA 13, 22, 40, 71, 72, 91, and 92. The Court adopted revisions proposed by the Juvenile Rules Committee in response to the new legislation.

One should become familiar with the terms "reportable juvenile offense", "juvenile offense under § 2(a)(1) of the Juvenile Code, MCL 712A.2a(1); MSA 27.3178(598.2)(a)(1)" and "records". A juvenile offense under § 2(a)(1) of the Juvenile Code is essentially what would be a crime if committed by an adult. A § 2(a)(1) offense does not include status offenses, such as truancy, incorrigibility, and running away from home. The § 2(a)(1) offense is a focal point for many of the new rules. It sets the stage for involvement by the prosecuting attorney without request by the court. It determines whether the referee must be a lawyer to serve past the preliminary hearing stage in a delinquency proceeding. A § 2(a)(1) offense determines whether the procedures in the juvenile diversion act must be followed and whether a child witness who is the juvenile defendant will be allowed to move to close the proceedings during the taking of his or her testimony.

The term "reportable juvenile offense" as defined in the rules is taken from the definition in the new law requiring the Central Records Division of the Department of State Police to keep track of serious juvenile offenders. 1988 PA 40. The term becomes important when the court orders a juvenile fingerprinted and when the juvenile court expunges records.

Section 10 of the Juvenile Code, prior to recent amendment, did not require that a person had to be a lawyer to serve as a juvenile court referee. On November 17, 1987, the Court adopted then MCR 5.913 to take effect July 1, 1988. It required that a person had to be admitted to the practice of law to serve as a referee in child protective proceeding past the preliminary hearing stage. The Legislature has now amended § 10 of the Juvenile Code, effective June 1, 1988, to provide that a person must be licensed to practice law in Michigan to serve as a referee in a delinquency proceeding under § 2(a)(1) of the Juvenile Code. The statutory provision grandfathers in nonlawyers who served as referees before January 1, 1988. It also permits the nonlawyer referee to conduct the preliminary inquiry or preliminary hearing. See 1988 PA 92. The new rule on lawyer referee implements the statutory requirement for delinquency proceedings. It also moves from July 1, 1988, to June 1, 1988, the requirement that a referee be a lawyer to serve in a child protective proceeding past the preliminary hearing stage. It therefore supersedes the November 17, 1987, order of the Court. There is no grandfather clause for nonlawyer referees in child protective proceedings.

Section 17 of the Juvenile Code formerly provided in pertinent part that: "The prosecuting attorney shall appear for the people when requested by the court". MCL 712A.17; MSA 27.3178(598.17). That section served as the source for MCR 5.914, as adopted by the Court in June, 1987. The Legislature has now amended § 17 of the Juvenile Code to provide not only that the prosecutor must appear on court request, but must also appear automatically in any juvenile delinquency proceeding under § 2(a)(1) if the proceeding requires "a hearing and the taking of testimony". 1988 PA 92.

The Legislature has also amended § 11 of the Juvenile Code to provide that: "Only the prosecuting attorney may file a petition requesting the court to take jurisdiction of a child allegedly within section 2(a)(1)". 1988 PA 92. In light of these legislative changes, the Court has amended MCR 5.914, 5.932(C), and 5.935(B)(7) to require the prosecutor to approve the submission of any petition with the court that requests the court to take jurisdiction of the juvenile under § 2(a)(1) of the Juvenile Code as a condition precedent to the court authorizing the filing of the petition. Furthermore, the prosecutor will have to participate in all contested matters and evidentiary hearings in delinquency proceedings under § 2(a)(1). Finally, the definition of prosecuting attorney makes it clear that a city attorney will be unable to request the court to take jurisdiction of a juvenile under § 2(a)(1) without approval of the county prosecutor.

The Legislature has now deleted language from § 17 of the Juvenile Code, which authorized the court to close proceedings. Effective June 1, 1988, the following is stricken from the Code: "In the hearing of any case the general public may be excluded and only those persons admitted as have a direct interest in the case". Under a new § 17, as added by 1988 PA 91, the court may only close proceedings to the general public while a child witness or a victim testifies, to protect the welfare of either.

The Legislature has not only opened proceedings in the juvenile court to the public, but has also authorized public access to nonconfidential court records. Confidential files, such as the juvenile diversion record, will not be accessible to the general public. Only those individuals with a legitimate interest may be allowed access to materials that the court has determined to be confidential. In short, in light of the legislative change, the new rule opens juvenile court proceedings on the formal calendar and the preliminary hearing to the public and permits general public access to nonconfidential records. See MCR 5.903(A)(9), (18), 5.925(A) and (D).

New MCR 5.925(E) follows the legislation which added a new § (18)(e) to the Juvenile Code. See 1988 PA 72. This amendment has provided new categories of a more limited form of expungement, setting aside an adjudication. The juvenile court is prohibited from setting aside or otherwise expunging life offenses and criminal traffic offenses. Reportable juvenile offenses, as specifically defined in the rule, other than life offenses, may be set aside only by following the procedures set forth in new § 18(e) of the Juvenile Code. If the juvenile court sets aside a reportable offense, it must expunge its own record pertaining to that offense and it must give notice to Central Records Division of the Department of State Police.

If the adjudicated offense is neither a life offense, traffic offense, or reportable juvenile offense under § 2(a)(1) of the Juvenile Code (i.e., a less serious type felony or misdemeanor if committed by an adult), the court will effectively set aside the adjudication by expunging the record. Should the juvenile court expunge the record of a juvenile adjudicated on a nonreportable offense, the court must still notify the Central

Records Division of the Department of State Police if the original petition authorized to be filed alleged a reportable offense.

Rule 5.936 on fingerprinting is new. It is intended to bring the court rule into conformity with the new legislation on fingerprinting serious juvenile offenders. See 1988 PA 40. The rule complies with new § 11 of the Juvenile Code, as amended by 1988 PA 72, requiring the court to examine its files at the time of the authorization of the petition alleging a reportable juvenile offense and before it enters a disposition on a reportable juvenile offense to verify if the juvenile has been fingerprinted. If not, the court must order the juvenile to voluntarily submit to the arresting agency or direct that the juvenile be picked up by the sheriff's department and fingerprinted. The rule also provides for notification of the Central Records Division of the Department of State Police, provides a separate definition of reportable juvenile offense listing the actual charges that require fingerprinting, and provide an avenue for return of fingerprints by court order if necessary, when for example the proceedings against the juvenile are discontinued or the juvenile is found not to come within the jurisdiction of the juvenile court under § 2(a)(1) of the Juvenile Code.

Finally, MCR 5.942 and MCR 5.943 have been amended to recognize the right of the victim of a juvenile offense to be present at trial or dispositional hearing, as provided in the victim's right legislation. See MCL 780.751 et seq.; MSA 28.1287(751) et seq., as added by 1988 PA 22.

Staff Comment to January 1, 1989 Amendments

The October 27, 1988, amendments [effective January 1, 1989] to several rules in Subchapter 5 of the Michigan Court Rules are to take account of the new provisions regarding claims against estates found in 1988 PA 222.

The amendments, which are based on recommendations by the State Bar Probate and Estate Planning Section, were made without publication for comment because of the January 1, 1989, effective date of the Act. However, the order adopting the amendments invited prompt comments from interested persons.

In MCR 5.106(A) the provision regarding the time for making claims is deleted in view of the statutory provision setting the time at four months after the published notice. MCL 700.703(1); MSA 27.5703(1).

New MCR 5.505 contains the provision on severance and consolidation of claims that was formerly found in MCR 5.509. The remaining provisions of MCR 5.509 are deleted in view of the repeal of the statutory authorization for using referees to hear claims.

Former MCR 5.702(B) is deleted and a revised version placed in MCR 5.706(A). MCR 5.706 is significantly revised in light of the new statute. Subrule (C) covers the subject of giving notice to known creditors. Subrule (D) makes clear that the notice requirements do not apply if the estate qualifies as a small estate under the Revised Probate Code.

In accord with the provisions of the statute applying the same notice requirements in independent probate proceedings as in supervised ones, several changes are made in MCR 5.709, deleting the former provisions covering notice in independent probate proceedings and referring to the MCR 5.706 notice rules, with minor variations.

Staff Comment to April 1, 1989 Amendments

General Background

On July 1, 1987, the Supreme Court adopted new rules governing practice and procedure in juvenile division of the probate court which were to take effect on January 1, 1988. See Advance Sheet 428B Mich 1 (August 10, 1987). These newly adopted rules were further revised before their effective date by orders of November 17 and 18, 1987. See Advance Sheet 429A Mich 1 (December 11, 1987).

In the early part of 1988 the Legislature enacted several new statutes dealing with juvenile law, including 1988 PA 13, 22, 40, 71, 72, 91, and 92. Most of this legislation took effect on June 1, 1988. The Court, by order of May 26, 1988, responded to the legislation on the recommendation of the Juvenile Court Rules Committee, by adopting several revisions to Subchapter 5.900 believed to be consistent with the legislative changes. See 430 Mich cvi through cxviii (1988). By October 1, 1988, further legislation dealing with serious juvenile offenders became the law. See 1988 PA 51 through 54, 64, 67, 73, 75–78, and 182. The Court responded on September 20, 1988, to this legislation by issuing Administrative Order No. 1988–5, which is still pending. See 431 Mich xix–lix (1988).

On July 1, 1988, Enrolled House Bills commonly known as the Coleman Commission legislation, were signed into law to take effect April 1, 1989. See 1988 PA 223–225. This legislation is the topic of the current responsive rules submitted to the Court by the Juvenile Court Rules Committee; published for comment in January, 1989; and adopted effective April 1, 1989.

Philosophy

The legislative philosophy evinced by 1988 PA 224 is to keep a child in the home if possible, avoid prolonged faulty parent-child relationships when termination of parental rights is inevitable, and make reasonable efforts to find the child a permanent place after termination. The Legislature has determined to phase out court-supervised foster care of children brought under the jurisdiction of the court on the basis of abuse and neglect. See § 16(1)(a), (5), and (6) of the Juvenile Code.

The juvenile court may assume jurisdiction over a 17–year–old minor who is a victim of abuse and neglect. The prosecuting attorney becomes legal consultant to the Department of Social Services or an agency thereof in a child protective proceeding. Should the prosecuting attorney fail to appear on behalf of the department or agency, then the department may retain the attorney of its choice.

Pretrial Placement

The new criteria for placement of a child pending trial in a protective proceeding are specified in § 13a of the Juvenile Code and in Rule 5.965(C). To protect the child's well being, the court may, for example, release the child to the parent pending trial on the condition that the parent not pressure the child to testify differently or not at all.

If, pending trial on the question of assumption of court jurisdiction over the child under Section 2(b)(1), the child is placed with someone other than the parent, the court is to encourage the parent to visit the child frequently unless the visitation would be harmful even if it were supervised. Moreover, placement of the child pending trial should be in the most *family-like setting* available and it is hoped in proximity to the parents.

Case Service Plan

The agency with supervision and control of a child in foster care plays a pivotal role as preparer of the case service plan. It is unclear whether the Legislature intended to authorize the court to order parents to comply with the "initial service plan" at the pretrial stage. Traditionally, a court would not order the parent to comply with a case service plan before it has assumed jurisdiction over the child.

The new legislation and court rule indicate that a parent's failure to comply with the case service plan is evidence that a return of the child home following a permanency planning hearing would be a risk. Presumably this inference would not arise if the court orders the parent, as a part of disposition, to take action contrary to the case service plan. The court may order the case service plan be modified.

Termination of Parental Rights

The Legislature has now expressly authorized the juvenile court to terminate parental rights at the initial disposition. See § 19b(4) of the Juvenile Code, as amended. The grounds for terminating parental rights at the initial disposition, on the basis of changed circumstances, or following a permanency planning hearing or dispositional review hearing, are limited to those listed in § 19b(3). Court decisions that indicate a juvenile court is not limited to the grounds set forth in § 19 of the Juvenile Code as a basis for terminating parental rights no longer appear to be the law. See *In re Kidder*, 393 Mich 819 (1975); *In re Sharpe*, 68 Mich App 619 (1976). The proposed court rule continues to require that the evidence received to establish the grounds to terminate parental rights at the initial disposition, or when based on new or different circumstances, must be legally admissible evidence. See MCR 5.974(D) and (E).

To avoid confusing the standard of proof required in making the dispositional decision to terminate parental rights (clear and convincing evidence), with the trial standard required to assume jurisdiction (a preponderance of evidence), MCR 5.972(A) provides that the standard of proof is preponderance of the evidence for taking jurisdiction over the child even if the petition also requests termination of parental rights.

MCR 5.974(H) requires the court to advise a respondent whose parental rights were terminated of the rights concerning identifying information in 1988 PA 505.

Dispositional Hearings, Progress Review

Most procedural requirements in the new legislation relate to the dispositional phase of the child protective proceeding. The rules follow the legislation concerning notice, time for holding hearings, criteria, and available options at the dispositional review hearing and permanency planning hearing.

To complement the dispositional review hearing when the child is in foster care, MCR 5.973(D) requires a semi-annual progress review of children not in foster care over whom the court has taken jurisdiction. Because the progress review is not a hearing and no change in placement may occur without a hearing following the progress review, there appears no need for the appointment of counsel. A nonlawyer referee may handle the progress review.

MCR 5.973(E) is new. It requires an initial hearing following an emergency removal of a child already within the jurisdiction of the court, but it is less formal than the preliminary hearing. However, placement pending dispositional review hearing in such a case is conditioned on meeting the criteria of § 13a of the Juvenile Code and MCR 5.965(C).

Others

Other changes include deleting the requirements that a court explain to a respondent at a plea proceeding that the child protective proceeding is continuous and that the court advise the respondent at the preliminary hearing that termination of parental rights may occur if the court takes formal action. The advice about possible termination of parental rights is included in the petition and summons, and must be given before a respondent enters a plea of admission or no contest. The decision to omit requiring that the court advise the parent at a plea proceeding about the doctrine of a continuous proceeding should not be taken as a signal that the Court is abandoning the underlying legal principle of continuous proceeding. The deletion of "by respondent" from MCR 5.972 will broaden the "tender years" exception to the hearsay rule. Note that under the exception a child need not testify at trial as a condition to the admission of the child's statement.

The revised rule would make it clear, as required by the federal legislation on Indian children, that MCR 5.980 would not authorize going onto the reservation and taking an Indian child unless the removal is to prevent immediate physical harm.

Staff Comment to July 1, 1989 Amendments

The comment at the end of Administrative Order 1988–5 continues to reflect, in general and when applicable, the import of these rule changes. See 431 Mich xlvi–lix (1988). *[Publisher's Note: An edited version of the Administrative Order 1988–5 comment appears under the caption "Staff Comment to Subchapter 6.900", following Rule 6.937, infra.]* Nevertheless, the following differences between the published rules and the rules adopted are worth notation. The progress review must occur every 182 days rather than annually. MCR 5.944(C)(2). When the juvenile is in foster care following adjudication, the court must hold a dispositional review hearing no later than every 182 days. At the first phase of the hearing on whether to waive juvenile court jurisdiction so the juvenile may be prosecuted as though an adult, the probable cause standard applies to the showing that an offense was committed, not just the showing that the juvenile committed it. MCR 5.950(B)(1).

The circuit or the recorder's court need not request a copy of the opinion in support of the waiver order. The juvenile court must automatically send it without charge.

The juvenile court will now advise the juvenile over whom it has waived jurisdiction of the right of appellate review in circuit court. MCR 5.950(C)(3).

Staff Comment to 1998 Amendment

The December 19, 1997, amendments to Rule 3.206 and subchapter 5.900 of the Michigan Court Rules [effective January 1, 1998] implement recent statutory changes which have created a family division of the circuit court. These amendments will remain in effect until further order of the court.

CHAPTER 6. CRIMINAL PROCEDURE

Effective October 1, 1989

[For Table of Rules, see page 1 et seq.]

SUBCHAPTER 6.000 GENERAL PROVISIONS

RULE 6.001 SCOPE; APPLICABILITY OF CIVIL RULES; SUPERSEDED RULES AND STATUTES

(A) Felony Cases. The rules in subchapters 6.000–6.500 govern matters of procedure in criminal cases cognizable in the circuit courts and in courts of equivalent criminal jurisdiction.

(B) Misdemeanor Cases. MCR 6.001–6.004, 6.106, 6.125, 6.427, 6.445, and the rules in subchapters 6.600–6.800 govern matters of procedure in criminal cases cognizable in the district courts.

(C) Juvenile Cases. The rules in subchapter 6.900 govern matters of procedure in the district courts and in circuit courts and courts of equivalent criminal jurisdiction in cases involving juveniles against whom the prosecutor has authorized the filing of a criminal complaint as provided in MCL 764.1f; MSA 28.860(6).

(D) Civil Rules Applicable. The provisions of the rules of civil procedure apply to cases governed by this chapter, except

(1) as otherwise provided by rule or statute,

(2) when it clearly appears that they apply to civil actions only, or

(3) when a statute or court rule provides a like or different procedure.

Depositions and other discovery proceedings under subchapter 2.300 may not be taken for the purposes of discovery in cases governed by this chapter. The provisions of MCR 2.501(C) regarding the length of notice of trial assignment do not apply in cases governed by this chapter.

(E) Rules and Statutes Superseded. The rules in this chapter supersede all prior court rules in this chapter and any statutory procedure pertaining to and inconsistent with a procedure provided by a rule in this chapter.

[Adopted effective October 1, 1989; amended effective January 1, 1991.]

1989 Staff Comment

MCR 6.001 is a new rule but includes a modified version of former 6.001 pertaining to the applicability of the rules of civil procedure.

Although the rules that have been developed and incorporated in this chapter are relatively comprehensive, criminal procedure is such a diverse and pervasive area of the law that a substantial portion of criminal procedure will continue to be regulated by statutes, the civil court rules, and case-law prescribed procedures. Subrules (D) and (E) provide standards for identifying what civil rule and statutory procedures will continue to be applicable.

Furthermore, although the rules in this chapter attempt to comply with state and federal constitutional requirements, they avoid, to the extent that it is practical, codification of constitutional requirements and standards. As with the other Michigan court rules, constitutional requirements apply independently of these rules and, in the event of any conflict, prevail over the requirements of these rules.

Subrule (A) identifies the subchapters in which the rules governing procedure in felony cases will be found.

Subrule (B) similarly identifies the subchapters in which the rules governing procedure in misdemeanor cases will be found.

With one exception, the former rules in this chapter applicable to misdemeanor proceedings in district court have been amended with new numbers for placement in the appropriate subchapters. Former 6.201, entitled "Criminal Procedure Generally," has been renumbered 6.610. Former 6.202, entitled "Impaneling The Jury," has been renumbered 6.620. Former 6.205, entitled "Other Rules Applicable," has not been renumbered, but rather, its provisions have been incorporated in the instant subrule. Consequently, it has been superseded.

One other change pertinent to this subrule is noteworthy. MCR 4.102, entitled "Misdemeanor Cases," has been retitled "Misdemeanor Traffic Cases," and renumbered 6.615 for placement with the other misdemeanor rules.

Subrule (C) designates subchapter 6.900 as the subchapter in which will be found the rules governing criminal prosecution of juveniles as provided in MCL 764.1f; MSA 28.860(6).

Subrule (D) is a slightly modified version of former 6.001. This subrule makes the provisions of the rules of civil procedure applicable generally in criminal cases and then sets forth exceptions. The only substantive modification this subrule makes is in the exception described in subrule (D)(3). The former rule described this exception as "when a statute or court rule provides a different procedure." In this subrule language has been added so this exception now provides: "when a statute or court provides a *like* or different procedure." This change reflects that the rules of criminal procedure that have been adopted now set forth procedures not only that are "different," but also, similar or identical to the procedures set forth in the civil rules. Since the rules in this chapter govern criminal procedure, it follows that civil rules providing "like" procedures should no longer be applicable. Likewise, it follows that statutes prescribing criminal procedures take precedence over, and should render inapplicable, civil rules providing like procedures.

Subrule (E) declares that all of the prior rules in this chapter not readopted in this version of the rules are superseded. It also declares that the rules supersede certain undetermined statutory procedures and sets forth a test for determining what those statutory procedures are. A statutory procedure is superseded if it "pertain[s] to and is inconsistent with a procedure provided by a rule in this chapter." Some superseded statutory procedures are discussed in the commentary to the rules. See, for example, 6.402 setting forth an oral waiver of jury trial procedure that supersedes the statutory procedure having the added requirement of a written waiver. Like the court rule the statutory procedure pertains to waiver of jury trial. It is inconsistent with the court rule procedure because, if applicable, it would render invalid waivers complying with the court rule requirements.

Staff Comment to 1991 Amendment

The [January 1, 1991] amendment of MCR 6.001(B) makes the probation revocation procedure set forth in MCR 6.445 applicable to all probation revocation proceedings in district court regardless of the seriousness of the misdemeanor conviction that led to probation. The proposal for such an amendment of this subrule was submitted by the Michigan District Judges Association.

RULE 6.002 PURPOSE AND CONSTRUCTION

These rules are intended to promote a just determination of every criminal proceeding. They are to be construed to secure simplicity in procedure, fairness in administration, and the elimination of unjustifiable expense and delay.

[Adopted effective October 1, 1989.]

1989 Staff Comment

MCR 6.002 is a new rule patterned after Federal Rules of Criminal Procedure, Rule 2.

RULE 6.003 DEFINITIONS

For purposes of subchapters 6.000–6.800:

(1) "Party" includes the lawyer representing the party.

(2) "Defendant's lawyer" includes a self-represented defendant proceeding without a lawyer.

(3) "Prosecutor" includes any lawyer prosecuting the case.

(4) "Court" or "judicial officer" includes a judge, a magistrate, or a district court magistrate authorized in accordance with the law to perform the functions of a magistrate.

(5) "Court clerk" includes a deputy clerk.

(6) "Court reporter" includes a court recorder.

[Adopted effective October 1, 1989.]

1989 Staff Comment

MCR 6.003 is a new rule. The scope rule, 6.001, makes the definitions in this rule applicable to the rules found in Subchapters 6.000–6.800.

Subrule (4), which defines a "court" or "judicial officer," recognizes a statutory distinction between a "magistrate" and a "district court magistrate" set forth in MCL 761.1(f); MSA 28.843(f). The "functions of a magistrate" that a district court magistrate may be authorized to perform are set forth in MCL 600.8501 et seq.; MSA 27A.8501 et seq., and subject to MCR 4.401(B).

RULE 6.004 SPEEDY TRIAL

(A) **Right to Speedy Trial.** The defendant and the people are entitled to a speedy trial and to a speedy resolution of all matters before the court.

(B) **Priorities in Scheduling Criminal Cases.** The trial court has the responsibility to establish and control a trial calendar. In assigning cases to the calendar, and insofar as it is practicable,

(1) the trial of criminal cases must be given preference over the trial of civil cases, and

(2) the trial of defendants in custody and of defendants whose pretrial liberty presents unusual risks must be given preference over other criminal cases.

(C) **Delay in Felony and Misdemeanor Cases; Recognizance Release.** In a felony case in which the defendant has been incarcerated for a period of 6 months or more to answer for the same crime or a crime based on the same conduct or arising from the same criminal episode, or in a misdemeanor case in which the defendant has been incarcerated for a period of 28 days or more to answer for the same crime or a crime based on the same conduct or arising from the same criminal episode, the defendant must be released on personal recognizance. In computing the 28–day and 6–month periods, the court is to exclude

(1) periods of delay resulting from other proceedings concerning the defendant, including but not limited to competency and criminal responsibility proceedings, pretrial motions, interlocutory appeals, and the trial of other charges,

(2) the period of delay during which the defendant is not competent to stand trial,

(3) the period of delay resulting from an adjournment requested or consented to by the defendant's lawyer,

(4) the period of delay resulting from an adjournment requested by the prosecutor, but only if the prosecutor demonstrates on the record either

(a) the unavailability, despite the exercise of due diligence, of material evidence that the prosecutor has reasonable cause to believe will be available at a later date; or

(b) exceptional circumstances justifying the need for more time to prepare the state's case,

(5) a reasonable period of delay when the defendant is joined for trial with a codefendant as to whom the time for trial has not run, but only if good cause exists for not granting the defendant a severance so as to enable trial within the time limits applicable, and

(6) any other periods of delay that in the court's judgment are justified by good cause, but not including delay caused by docket congestion.

(D) Untried Charges Against State Prisoner.

(1) *The 180–Day Rule.* Except for crimes exempted by MCL 780.131(2); MSA 28.969(1)(2), the prosecutor must make a good faith effort to bring a criminal charge to trial within 180 days of either of the following:

(a) the time from which the prosecutor knows that the person charged with the offense is incarcerated in a state prison or is detained in a local facility awaiting incarceration in a state prison, or

(b) the time from which the Department of Corrections knows or has reason to know that a criminal charge is pending against a defendant incarcerated in a state prison or detained in a local facility awaiting incarceration in a state prison.

For purposes of this subrule, a person is charged with a criminal offense if a warrant, complaint, or indictment has been issued against the person.

(2) *Remedy.* In cases covered by subrule (1)(a), the defendant is entitled to have the charge dismissed with prejudice if the prosecutor fails to make a good faith effort to bring the charge to trial within the 180–day period. When, in cases covered by subrule (1)(b), the prosecutor's failure to bring the charge to trial is attributable to lack of notice from the Department of Corrections, the defendant is entitled to sentence credit for the period of delay. Whenever the defendant's constitutional right to a speedy trial is violated, the defendant is entitled to dismissal of the charge with prejudice.

[Adopted effective October 1, 1989.]

1989 Staff Comment

MCR 6.004 is a modified version of the former speedy trial rule, 6.109.

Subrule (A) is not new. It restates the dual entitlements to speedy trial described in the speedy trial statute, MCL 768.1; MSA 28.1024. Former 6.109(A), pertaining to scheduling of criminal cases, made reference to these entitlements in more general language ("the right of the accused to a speedy trial and the interest of the public in prompt disposition of criminal cases"). Of course, in addition to the statutory right to a speedy trial, the defendant has a constitutional right. See Const 1963, art 1, § 20; US Const, Am VI.

Subrule (B) is a stylistically improved version of former 6.109(A) except for its first sentence, which is based on the first sentence of former 6.109(C). Former 6.109(C), describing the Chief Judge's duty to report delays of trials, and former 6.109(D), describing the State Court Administrator's duty to investigate the delays reported, have been removed from this rule and from this chapter and reincorporated respectively in 8.110(E), the "chief judge rule," and 8.103, the "state court administrator rule."

Subrule (C) is a stylistically improved version of former 6.109(B) except for two substantive changes.

Subrule (C)(3) is based on former 6.109(B)(2), but eliminates the latter's requirements for the defendant's concurrence "on the record" and after "he or she has been advised by the court of his or her right to a speedy trial and the effect of concurrence."

Subrule (C)(4)(b) substitutes a more restrictive standard ("exceptional circumstances justifying the need for more time to prepare the state's case") for exclusion of delay resulting from an adjournment requested by the prosecutor in place of the standard of former 6.109(B)(3)(b) ("the adjournment is granted for good cause on the record to allow the prosecutor additional time to prepare the state's case"). The new standard is based on 2 ABA Standards for Criminal Justice (2d ed), Standard 12–2.3(d)(ii) ("additional time is justified because of the exceptional circumstances of the case").

Subrule (D) is new. It incorporates the requirements of the statutory 180–day rule set forth in MCL 780.131 et seq.; MSA 28.969(1) et seq. As the rule reflects, a statutory amendment has exempted from the requirements of the 180–day rule certain criminal offenses (those committed by an inmate of a state correctional facility "while incarcerated in the correctional facility" or "after the inmate has escaped from the correctional facility and before he or she has been returned to the custody of the Department of Corrections"). 1988 PA 400. MCL 780.131(2); MSA 28.969(1)(2).

Subrule (D) incorporates the court's interpretation of the 180–day rule statute in *People* v *Hendershot*, 357 Mich 300 (1959) (construing the statute as requiring "good faith action" on the part of the prosecutor within the 180–day period to ready the case for trial) and, with one significant exception, the rules adopted by the Court in *People* v *Hill*, 402 Mich 272 (1978), to effectuate the purpose of the statute. *Hill* held that the 180–day period begins to run not only from when the prosecutor "knows or should know" that a charge is pending against the state prison inmate, but also from when "the Department of Corrections knows or should know" of such a charge. The statutory remedy of dismissal was held applicable in both situations. Subrule (D) modifies *Hill* by changing the remedy, when the 180–day rule is violated due to "lack of notice from the Department of Corrections," from dismissal to "sentence credit for the period of delay."

RULE 6.005 RIGHT TO ASSISTANCE OF LAWYER; ADVICE; APPOINTMENT FOR INDIGENTS; WAIVER; JOINT REPRESENTATION; GRAND JURY PROCEEDINGS

Text of rule eff. until Jan. 1, 2004

(A) Advice of Right. At the arraignment on the warrant or complaint, the court must advise the defendant

(1) of entitlement to a lawyer's assistance at all subsequent court proceedings, and

(2) that the court will appoint a lawyer at public expense if the defendant wants one and is financially unable to retain one.

The court must question the defendant to determine whether the defendant wants a lawyer and, if so, whether the defendant is financially unable to retain one.

(B) Questioning Defendant About Indigency. If the defendant requests a lawyer and claims financial inability to retain one, the court must determine whether the defendant is indigent. The determination of indigency must be guided by the following factors:

(1) present employment, earning capacity and living expenses;

(2) outstanding debts and liabilities, secured and unsecured;

(3) whether the defendant has qualified for and is receiving any form of public assistance;

(4) availability and convertibility, without undue financial hardship to the defendant and the defendant's dependents, of any personal or real property owned; and

(5) any other circumstances that would impair the ability to pay a lawyer's fee as would ordinarily be required to retain competent counsel.

The ability to post bond for pretrial release does not make the defendant ineligible for appointment of a lawyer.

(C) Partial Indigency. If a defendant is able to pay part of the cost of a lawyer, the court may require contribution to the cost of providing a lawyer and may establish a plan for collecting the contribution.

(D) Appointment or Waiver of a Lawyer. If the court determines that the defendant is financially unable to retain a lawyer, it must promptly appoint a lawyer and promptly notify the lawyer of the appointment. The court may not permit the defendant to make an initial waiver of the right to be represented by a lawyer without first

(1) advising the defendant of the charge, the maximum possible prison sentence for the offense, any mandatory minimum sentence required by law, and the risk involved in self-representation, and

(2) offering the defendant the opportunity to consult with a retained lawyer or, if the defendant is indigent, the opportunity to consult with an appointed lawyer.

(E) Advice at Subsequent Proceedings. If a defendant has waived the assistance of a lawyer, the record of each subsequent proceeding (e.g., preliminary examination, arraignment, proceedings leading to possible revocation of youthful trainee status, hearings, trial or sentencing) need show only that the court advised the defendant of the continuing right to a lawyer's assistance (at public expense if the defendant is indigent) and that the defendant waived that right. Before the court begins such proceedings,

(1) the defendant must reaffirm that a lawyer's assistance is not wanted; or

(2) if the defendant requests a lawyer and is financially unable to retain one, the court must appoint one; or

(3) if the defendant wants to retain a lawyer and has the financial ability to do so, the court must allow the defendant a reasonable opportunity to retain one.

(F) Multiple Representation. When two or more indigent defendants are jointly charged with an offense or offenses or their cases are otherwise joined, the court must appoint separate lawyers unassociated in the practice of law for each defendant. Whenever two or more defendants who have been jointly charged or whose cases have been joined are represented by the same retained lawyer or lawyers associated in the practice of law, the court must inquire into the potential for a conflict of interest that might jeopardize the right of each defendant to the undivided loyalty of the lawyer. The court may not permit the joint representation unless:

(1) the lawyer or lawyers state on the record the reasons for believing that joint representation in all probability will not cause a conflict of interests;

(2) the defendants state on the record after the court's inquiry and the lawyer's statement, that they desire to proceed with the same lawyer; and

(3) the court finds on the record that joint representation in all probability will not cause a conflict of interest and states its reasons for the finding.

(G) Unanticipated Conflict of Interest. If, in a case of joint representation, a conflict of interest arises at any time, including trial, the lawyer must immediately inform the court. If the court agrees that a conflict has arisen, it must afford one or more of the defendants the opportunity to retain separate lawyers. The court should on its own initiative inquire into any potential conflict that becomes apparent, and take such action as the interests of justice require.

(H) Scope of Trial Lawyer's Responsibilities. The responsibilities of the trial lawyer appointed to represent the defendant include

(1) representing the defendant in all trial court proceedings including sentencing and proceedings leading to possible revocation of youthful trainee status,

(2) filing of interlocutory appeals the lawyer deems appropriate,

(3) responding to any preconviction appeals by the prosecutor, and

(4) unless an appellate lawyer has been appointed, filing of postconviction motions the lawyer deems appropriate, including motions for new trial, for a directed verdict of acquittal, to withdraw plea, or for resentencing.

(I) Plan for Appointment. In each county, the court with trial jurisdiction over felony cases must adopt and publish a plan to govern the process of selecting and appointing lawyers to represent indigent defendants and file it with the supreme court clerk and the state court administrator under MCR 8.112(B)(3).

(J) Assistance of Lawyer at Grand Jury Proceedings.

(1) A witness called before a grand jury or a grand juror is entitled to have a lawyer present in the hearing room while the witness gives testimony. A witness may not refuse to appear for reasons of unavailability of the lawyer for that witness. Except as otherwise provided by law, the lawyer may not participate in the proceedings other than to advise the witness.

(2) The prosecutor assisting the grand jury is responsible for ensuring that a witness is informed of the right to a lawyer's assistance during examination by written notice accompanying the subpoena to the witness and by personal advice immediately before the examination. The notice must include language informing the witness that if the witness is financially unable to retain a lawyer, the chief judge in the circuit court in which the grand jury is convened will on request appoint one for the witness at public expense.

[Adopted effective October 1, 1989; amended effective January 1, 1996.]

Publisher's Note

For text of rule eff. Jan. 1, 2004, see rule 6.005, post.

1989 Staff Comment

MCR 6.005 is a modified version of former 6.101(C).

Subrule (A) is a stylistically improved version of former 6.101(C)(1). The title of the "arraignment on the complaint *and* warrant" found in former 6.101(C)(1) has been changed in subrule (A) to "arraignment on the warrant *or* complaint" corresponding to the title of Rule 6.104 and its recognition that an arraignment on a complaint without the issuance of a warrant is statutorily authorized. See MCL 764.1c; MSA 28.860(3).

Subrule (B) is new. It incorporates the indigency standard and criteria set forth in Administrative Order No. 1972–4, 387 Mich xxx (1972). The last sentence of this subrule is based on 1 ABA Standards for Criminal Justice (2d ed), Standard 5–6.1 ("[c]ounsel should not be denied merely ... because bond has been or can be posted").

Subrule (C) is new. It is based on 1 ABA Standards for Criminal Justice (2d ed), Standard 5–6.2 ("[t]he ability to pay part of the cost of adequate representation should not preclude eligibility"). This subrule pertains to contribution and should not be construed as authorizing subsequent reimbursement.

The first sentence of subrule (D), dealing with appointment, is a modified version of the first sentence of former 6.101(C)(2) (requiring the appointment to be made "promptly"), adding the requirement that the court "promptly notify the lawyer of the appointment." The remainder of subrule (D) pertains to the defendant's *initial* waiver of the right to be represented by a lawyer and addresses the defendant's constitutional right to self-representation. See *Faretta* v *California*, 422 US 806; 95 SCt 2525; 45 LEd2d 562 (1975). The requirements of subrules (1) and (2) are intended to ensure that the defendant's decision to waive the right to representation and to proceed without a lawyer is an informed and voluntary one. Subrule (2) does not require that the defendant actually consult with a lawyer, but rather, that the defendant be "offer[ed] ... the opportunity" to consult with one.

Subrule (E) is a stylistically improved version of former 6.101(C)(3).

Subrule (F) substantially changes former 6.101(C)(4). The former rule permitted joint representation regardless of whether the lawyer was appointed or retained. The rule as changed requires the appointment of "separate lawyers unassociated in the practice of law" for each defendant. This change avoids conflict of interest problems that arose despite the procedure set forth in the former rule (and repeated in this rule as to retained counsel) to protect against such problems. The latter procedure is kept in retained counsel cases in recognition of a defendant's right to choose joint representation, at least where no conflict of interest is apparent.

Subrule (G) is a slightly modified version of the last part of former 6.101(C)(4). The former rule required a lawyer representing joined defendants to immediately inform the court of a conflict of interest that "occurs during trial." The modified rule expands the lawyer's duty by requiring the lawyer to immediately inform the court of a conflict of interest that "arises at any time, including trial." This expansion recognizes that a conflict of interest may arise before, during, or after trial. Furthermore, the duty of the court to inquire into potential conflicts is now directive ("should") rather than permissive ("may").

Subrule (H) expands the scope of an appointed trial lawyer's responsibilities set forth in former 6.101(C)(2). The former rule made no reference to an appointed trial attorney's ability to file "postconviction motions the lawyer deems appropriate." Clearly, there are circumstances when it is more appropriate for the trial attorney to seek postconviction relief for his client than to await the appointment of appellate counsel. Under the scheme of the rules, however, a defendant should have only one appointed lawyer representing him at any time, and consequently, the appointment of appellate counsel should act as an end to the responsibilities of the trial attorney under the appointment order.

The language change in subrule (3) is significant. Former 6.101(C)(2)(c) authorized the appointed attorney to "respond to prosecutor appeals to the Court of Appeals, either interlocutory or as of right." The substituted language in subrule (H)(3) gives the appointed trial lawyer responsibility for "responding to any preconviction appeals by the prosecutor." This latter language indicates that the appointed lawyer is responsible for responding to any appeals by the prosecutor, whether by leave or by right, that are "preconviction." This would include a prosecutor's appeal taken from the trial court grant of a defense motion resulting in a new trial. The language of the former rule, making the appointed trial lawyer responsible for any appeals by the prosecutor "as of right," is now too broad in light of the statutory amendment that has expanded the prosecutor's right to appeal to include postconviction appeals. 1988 PA 66, MCL 770.12; MSA 28.1109.

Subrule (I) is new.

Subrule (J) repeats, with minor stylistic changes, former 6.107(C), dealing with the right of a witness to the assistance of a lawyer at grand jury proceedings.

Staff Comment to 1996 Amendment

The 1996 amendment of MCR 6.005(D) emphasized that the advice in subrules (D)(1) and (D)(2) pertains only to the defendant's *initial* waiver of the right to the assistance of a lawyer. The amendment of subrule (E) clarified that when a defendant has waived the assistance of a lawyer, the record of subsequent proceedings need only show that the court advised the defendant of the continuing right to a lawyer's assistance, and that the defendant waived that right.

RULE 6.005 RIGHT TO ASSISTANCE OF LAWYER; ADVICE; APPOINTMENT FOR INDIGENTS; WAIVER; JOINT REPRESENTATION; GRAND JURY PROCEEDINGS

Text of rule eff. Jan. 1, 2004

(A) Advice of Right. At the arraignment on the warrant or complaint, the court must advise the defendant

(1) of entitlement to a lawyer's assistance at all subsequent court proceedings, and

(2) that the court will appoint a lawyer at public expense if the defendant wants one and is financially unable to retain one.

The court must question the defendant to determine whether the defendant wants a lawyer and, if so, whether the defendant is financially unable to retain one.

(B) Questioning Defendant About Indigency. If the defendant requests a lawyer and claims financial inability to retain one, the court must determine whether the defendant is indigent. The determination of indigency must be guided by the following factors:

(1) present employment, earning capacity and living expenses;

(2) outstanding debts and liabilities, secured and unsecured;

(3) whether the defendant has qualified for and is receiving any form of public assistance;

(4) availability and convertibility, without undue financial hardship to the defendant and the defendant's dependents, of any personal or real property owned; and

(5) any other circumstances that would impair the ability to pay a lawyer's fee as would ordinarily be required to retain competent counsel.

The ability to post bond for pretrial release does not make the defendant ineligible for appointment of a lawyer.

(C) Partial Indigency. If a defendant is able to pay part of the cost of a lawyer, the court may require contribution to the cost of providing a lawyer and may establish a plan for collecting the contribution.

(D) Appointment or Waiver of a Lawyer. If the court determines that the defendant is financially unable to retain a lawyer, it must promptly appoint a lawyer and promptly notify the lawyer of the appointment. The court may not permit the defendant to make an initial waiver of the right to be represented by a lawyer without first

(1) advising the defendant of the charge, the maximum possible prison sentence for the offense, any mandatory minimum sentence required by law, and the risk involved in self-representation, and

(2) offering the defendant the opportunity to consult with a retained lawyer or, if the defendant is indigent, the opportunity to consult with an appointed lawyer.

(E) Advice at Subsequent Proceedings. If a defendant has waived the assistance of a lawyer, the record of each subsequent proceeding (e.g., preliminary examination, arraignment, proceedings leading to possible revocation of youthful trainee status, hearings, trial or sentencing) need show only that the court advised the defendant of the continuing right to a lawyer's assistance (at public expense if the defendant is indigent) and that the defendant waived that right. Before the court begins such proceedings,

(1) the defendant must reaffirm that a lawyer's assistance is not wanted; or

(2) if the defendant requests a lawyer and is financially unable to retain one, the court must appoint one; or

(3) if the defendant wants to retain a lawyer and has the financial ability to do so, the court must allow the defendant a reasonable opportunity to retain one.

(F) Multiple Representation. When two or more indigent defendants are jointly charged with an offense or offenses or their cases are otherwise joined, the court must appoint separate lawyers unassociated in the practice of law for each defendant. Whenever two or more defendants who have been jointly charged or whose cases have been joined are represented by the same retained lawyer or lawyers associated in the practice of law, the court must inquire into the potential for a conflict of interest that might jeopardize the right of each defendant to the undivided loyalty of the lawyer. The court may not permit the joint representation unless:

(1) the lawyer or lawyers state on the record the reasons for believing that joint representation in all probability will not cause a conflict of interests;

(2) the defendants state on the record after the court's inquiry and the lawyer's statement, that they desire to proceed with the same lawyer; and

(3) the court finds on the record that joint representation in all probability will not cause a conflict of interest and states its reasons for the finding.

(G) Unanticipated Conflict of Interest. If, in a case of joint representation, a conflict of interest arises at any time, including trial, the lawyer must immediately inform the court. If the court agrees that a conflict has arisen, it must afford one or more of the defendants the opportunity to retain separate lawyers. The court should on its own initiative inquire into any potential conflict that becomes apparent, and take such action as the interests of justice require.

(H) Scope of Trial Lawyer's Responsibilities. The responsibilities of the trial lawyer appointed to represent the defendant include

(1) representing the defendant in all trial court proceedings including sentencing and proceedings leading to possible revocation of youthful trainee status,

(2) filing of interlocutory appeals the lawyer deems appropriate,

(3) responding to any preconviction appeals by the prosecutor, and

(4) unless an appellate lawyer has been appointed, filing of postconviction motions the lawyer deems appropriate, including motions for new trial, for a directed verdict of acquittal, to withdraw plea, or for resentencing.

(I) Assistance of Lawyer at Grand Jury Proceedings.

(1) A witness called before a grand jury or a grand juror is entitled to have a lawyer present in the hearing room while the witness gives testimony. A witness may not refuse to appear for reasons of unavailability of the lawyer for that witness. Except as otherwise provided by law, the lawyer may not participate in the proceedings other than to advise the witness.

(2) The prosecutor assisting the grand jury is responsible for ensuring that a witness is informed of the right to a lawyer's assistance during examination by written notice accompanying the subpoena to the witness and by personal advice immediately before the examination. The notice must include language informing the witness that if the witness is financially unable to retain a lawyer, the chief judge in the circuit court in which the grand jury is convened will on request appoint one for the witness at public expense.

[Adopted effective October 1, 1989; amended effective January 1, 1996; January 1, 2004.]

Publisher's Note

For text of rule eff. until Jan. 1, 2004, see rule 6.005, ante.

1989 Staff Comment

MCR 6.005 is a modified version of former 6.101(C).

Subrule (A) is a stylistically improved version of former 6.101(C)(1). The title of the "arraignment on the complaint *and* warrant" found in former 6.101(C)(1) has been changed in subrule (A) to "arraignment on the warrant *or* complaint" corresponding to the title of Rule 6.104 and its recognition that an arraignment on a complaint without the issuance of a warrant is statutorily authorized. See MCL 764.1c; MSA 28.860(3).

Subrule (B) is new. It incorporates the indigency standard and criteria set forth in Administrative Order No. 1972–4, 387 Mich xxx (1972). The last sentence of this subrule is based on 1 ABA Standards for Criminal Justice (2d ed), Standard 5–6.1 ("[c]ounsel should not be denied merely ... because bond has been or can be posted").

Subrule (C) is new. It is based on 1 ABA Standards for Criminal Justice (2d ed), Standard 5–6.2 ("[t]he ability to pay part of the cost of adequate representation should not preclude eligibility"). This subrule pertains to contribution and should not be construed as authorizing subsequent reimbursement.

The first sentence of subrule (D), dealing with appointment, is a modified version of the first sentence of former 6.101(C)(2) (requiring the appointment to be made "promptly"), adding the requirement that the court "promptly notify the lawyer of the appointment." The remainder of subrule (D) pertains to the defendant's *initial* waiver of the right to be represented by a lawyer and addresses the defendant's constitutional right to self-representation. See *Faretta* v *California*, 422 US 806; 95 SCt 2525; 45 LEd2d 562 (1975). The requirements of subrules (1) and (2) are intended to ensure that the defendant's decision to waive the right to representation and to proceed without a lawyer is an informed and voluntary one. Subrule (2) does not require that the defendant actually consult with a lawyer, but rather, that the defendant be "offer[ed] ... the opportunity" to consult with one.

Subrule (E) is a stylistically improved version of former 6.101(C)(3).

Subrule (F) substantially changes former 6.101(C)(4). The former rule permitted joint representation regardless of whether the lawyer was appointed or retained. The rule as changed requires the appointment of "separate lawyers unassociated in the practice of law" for each defendant. This change avoids conflict of interest problems that arose despite the procedure set forth in the former rule (and repeated in this rule as to retained counsel) to protect against such problems. The latter procedure is kept in retained counsel cases in recognition of a defendant's right to choose joint representation, at least where no conflict of interest is apparent.

Subrule (G) is a slightly modified version of the last part of former 6.101(C)(4). The former rule required a lawyer representing joined defendants to immediately inform the court of a conflict of interest that "occurs during trial." The modified rule expands the lawyer's duty by requiring the lawyer to immediately inform the court of a conflict of interest that "arises at any time, including trial." This expansion recognizes that a conflict of interest may arise before, during, or after trial. Furthermore, the duty of the court to inquire into potential conflicts is now directive ("should") rather than permissive ("may").

Subrule (H) expands the scope of an appointed trial lawyer's responsibilities set forth in former 6.101(C)(2). The former rule made no reference to an appointed trial attorney's ability to file "postconviction motions the lawyer deems appropriate." Clearly, there are circumstances when it is more appropriate for the trial attorney to seek postconviction relief for his client than to await the appointment of appellate counsel. Under the scheme of the rules, however, a defendant should have only one appointed lawyer representing him at any time, and consequently, the appointment of appellate counsel should act as an end to the responsibilities of the trial attorney under the appointment order.

The language change in subrule (3) is significant. Former 6.101(C)(2)(c) authorized the appointed attorney to "respond to prosecutor appeals to the Court of Appeals, either interlocutory or as of right." The substituted language in subrule (H)(3) gives the appointed trial lawyer responsibility for "responding to any preconviction appeals by the prosecutor." This latter language indicates that the appointed lawyer is responsible for responding to any appeals by the prosecutor, whether by leave or by right, that are "preconviction." This would include a prosecutor's appeal taken from the trial court grant of a defense motion resulting in a new trial. The language of the former rule, making the appointed trial lawyer responsible for any appeals by the prosecutor "as of right," is now too broad in light of the statutory amendment that has expanded the prosecutor's right to appeal to include postconviction appeals. 1988 PA 66, MCL 770.12; MSA 28.1109.

Subrule (I) is new.

Subrule (J) repeats, with minor stylistic changes, former 6.107(C), dealing with the right of a witness to the assistance of a lawyer at grand jury proceedings.

Staff Comment to 1996 Amendment

The 1996 amendment of MCR 6.005(D) emphasized that the advice in subrules (D)(1) and (D)(2) pertains only to the defendant's *initial* waiver of the right to the assistance of a lawyer. The amendment of subrule (E) clarified that when a defendant has waived the assistance of a lawyer, the record of subsequent proceedings need only show that the court advised the defendant of the continuing right to a lawyer's assistance, and that the defendant waived that right.

Staff Comment to 2002 Amendment

MCR 8.123 was adopted on December 13, 2002, effective January 1, 2004. Subrule (B) requires trial courts to standardize their procedures for selecting and compensating appointed counsel. Subrule (D) requires the courts to maintain records of appointments and compensation. Subrule (E) requires that the records be public records.

The staff comment is published only for the benefit of the bench and bar and is not an authoritative construction by the Court.

SUBCHAPTER 6.100 PRELIMINARY PROCEEDINGS

RULE 6.101 THE COMPLAINT

(A) Definition and Form. A complaint is a written accusation that a named or described person has committed a specified criminal offense. The complaint must include the substance of the accusation against the accused and the name and statutory citation of the offense.

(B) Signature and Oath. The complaint must be signed and sworn to before a judicial officer or court clerk.

(C) Prosecutor's Approval or Posting of Security. A complaint may not be filed without a prosecutor's written approval endorsed on the complaint or attached to it, or unless security for costs is filed with the court.

[Adopted effective October 1, 1989.]

1989 Staff Comment

MCR 6.101 is a new rule. Subrules (A) and (B) state the statutory requirements for a complaint set forth in MCL 764.1a(1); MSA 28.860(1)(1) and MCL 764.1d; MSA 28.860(4). Additionally, subrule (A) incorporates, for efficiency purposes, the requirement that the complaint include "the name and statutory citation of the offense." Subrule (C) implements the statutory provisions of MCL 764.1(1); MSA 28.860(1), including the procedure permitting a private citizen to file a complaint when "security for costs is filed with the magistrate."

Like the cited statutes, this rule does not apply to prosecutions arising as a result of grand jury proceedings. See *People v O'Hara*, 278 Mich 281, 293 (1936).

RULE 6.102 ARREST ON A WARRANT

(A) Issuance of Warrant. A court must issue an arrest warrant, or a summons in accordance with MCR 6.103, if presented with a proper complaint and if the court finds probable cause to believe that the accused committed the alleged offense.

(B) Probable Cause Determination. A finding of probable cause may be based on hearsay evidence and rely on factual allegations in the complaint, affidavits from the complainant or others, the testimony of a sworn witness adequately preserved to permit review, or any combination of these sources.

(C) Contents of Warrant; Court's Subscription. A warrant must

(1) contain the accused's name, if known, or an identifying name or description;

(2) describe the offense charged in the complaint;

(3) command a peace officer or other person authorized by law to arrest and bring the accused before a judicial officer of the judicial district in which the offense allegedly was committed or some other designated court; and

(4) be signed by the court.

(D) Warrant Specification of Interim Bail. The court may specify on the warrant the bail that an accused may post to obtain release before arraignment on the warrant and, if the court deems it appropriate, include as a bail condition that the arrest of the accused occur on or before a specified date or within a specified period of time after issuance of the warrant.

(E) Execution and Return of Warrant. Only a peace officer or other person authorized by law may execute an arrest warrant. On execution or attempted execution of the warrant, the officer must make a return on the warrant and deliver it to the court before which the arrested person is to be taken.

(F) Release on Interim Bail. If an accused has been arrested pursuant to a warrant that includes an interim bail provision, the accused must either be arraigned promptly or released pursuant to the interim bail provision. The accused may obtain release by posting the bail on the warrant and by submitting a recognizance to appear before a specified court at a specified date and time, provided that

(1) the accused is arrested prior to the expiration date, if any, of the bail provision;

(2) the accused is arrested in the county in which the warrant was issued, or in which the accused resides or is employed, and the accused is not wanted on another charge;

(3) the accused is not under the influence of liquor or controlled substance; and

(4) the condition of the accused or the circumstances at the time of arrest do not otherwise suggest a need for judicial review of the original specification of bail.

[Adopted effective October 1, 1989.]

1989 Staff Comment

MCR 6.102 is a new rule.

Subrule (A) states the requirements for issuance of a warrant set forth in MCL 764.1a; MSA 28.860(1) except that it substitutes "probable cause" for "reasonable cause." These terms are viewed as equivalent, with "probable cause" being preferable because it is a familiar and recognized standard.

Subrule (B) is consistent with the requirements of MCL 764.1a(2); MSA 28.860(1)(2). Additionally, this subrule imposes the requirement that any sworn testimony relied on in making the probable cause determination be "adequately preserved to permit review." An objective of this subrule is to ensure that there is a reviewable record in the event that the probable cause determination is subsequently challenged. Accordingly, if any oral testimony is relied on, it must be preserved adequately in some fashion to permit a review of its sufficiency to support the probable cause determination. An electronically recorded or verbatim written record obviously satisfies this requirement. A written or recorded oral summary of the testimony sufficiently contemporaneous to be reliable, and certified as accurate by the judicial officer, may also satisfy this requirement.

Subrule (C) sets forth the requirements of MCL 764.1b; MSA 28.860(2).

Subrule (D) sets forth a new procedure. It authorizes in felony cases the specification on the warrant of interim bail similar to the procedure currently authorized by statute in misdemeanor cases. See MCL 780.582; MSA 28.872(2) and MCL 780.585; MSA 28.872(5). Subrule (D) further authorizes the court, in its discretion, to include an expiration date for the interim bail provision. This option permits the court to set a cut-off date, beyond which release may not be obtained, to prevent the release of a person who may be avoiding arrest. However, setting of an expiration date may also defeat the purpose of the interim bail provision if it is too short or is used in cases where the arrest of the defendant is sought solely in a passive fashion such as awaiting the defendant's stop for a traffic offense.

Subrule (E) implements MCL 764.1b; MSA 28.860(2).

Subrule (F) is new and sets forth a procedure applicable when an accused is arrested on a warrant containing an interim bail provision. The arresting agency has the option of either releasing the accused on the interim bail or immediately taking the accused to be arraigned if the arraignment can be conducted promptly. This subrule also lists conditions that must be met in order for an accused to be eligible for release on interim bail. Subrule (2) requires that the accused be arrested in the county in which the warrant was issued or in which the accused resides or is employed. The purpose of this limitation is to preclude the availability of interim bail to a person who may be avoiding arrest. Subrule (3) does not preclude interim bail release of an accused who was under the influence of liquor at the time of arrest but who is no longer in that condition. Subrule (4) is a catch-all provision and should be applied in good faith. Implicit in subrule (F) is the condition that the accused be satisfactorily identified as the person named in the warrant. Additionally, the rule does not preclude the police agency from requiring the accused to submit to photographing and fingerprinting before being released.

RULE 6.103   SUMMONS INSTEAD OF ARREST

(A) Issuance of Summons. If the prosecutor so requests, the court may issue a summons instead of an arrest warrant. If an accused fails to appear in response to a summons, the court, on request, must issue an arrest warrant.

(B) Form. A summons must contain the same information as an arrest warrant, except that it should summon the accused to appear before a designated court at a stated time and place.

(C) Service and Return of Summons. A summons may be served by

(1) delivering a copy to the named individual; or

(2) leaving a copy with a person of suitable age and discretion at the individual's home or usual place of abode; or

(3) mailing a copy to the individual's last known address.

Service should be made promptly to give the accused adequate notice of the appearance date. The person serving the summons must make a return to the court before which the person is summoned to appear.

[Adopted effective October 1, 1989.]

1989 Staff Comment

MCR 6.103 is a new rule based on Federal Rule of Criminal Procedure 4.

Subrule (A) is a variation of Federal Rule 4(a), which provides in part:

"Upon the request of the attorney for the government a summons instead of a warrant shall issue."

Under subrule (A) a summons may not be issued except on the request of the prosecutor, but the court retains the discretion ("may") to decline the request and issue an arrest warrant instead. The second sentence of subrule (A) also varies from the federal rule, which provides:

"If a defendant fails to appear in response to the summons, a warrant shall issue."

Under subrule (A) issuance of the arrest warrant for failure to appear in response to a summons is not automatic, and is required only on the request of the prosecutor. A prosecutor's "request" made under this rule should be in writing.

Subrule (B) is based on Federal Rule 4(c)(2).

Subrule (C) is based on provisions in Federal Rule 4(d)(3) and (4).

RULE 6.104 ARRAIGNMENT ON THE WARRANT OR COMPLAINT

(A) Arraignment Without Unnecessary Delay. Unless released beforehand, an arrested person must be taken without unnecessary delay before a court for arraignment in accordance with the provisions of this rule.

(B) Place of Arraignment. An accused arrested pursuant to a warrant must be taken to a court specified in the warrant. An accused arrested without a warrant must be taken to a court in the judicial district in which the offense allegedly occurred. If the arrest occurs outside the county in which these courts are located, the arresting agency must make arrangements with the authorities in the demanding county to have the accused promptly transported to the latter county for arraignment in accordance with the provisions of this rule. If prompt transportation cannot be arranged, the accused must be taken without unnecessary delay before the nearest available court for preliminary appearance in accordance with subrule (C).

(C) Preliminary Appearance Outside County of Offense. When, under subrule (B), an accused is taken before a court outside the county of the alleged offense, the court must advise the accused of the rights specified in subrule (E)(2) and determine what form of pretrial release, if any, is appropriate. To be released, the accused must submit a recognizance for appearance within the next 14 days before a court specified in the arrest warrant or, in a case involving an arrest without a warrant, before either a court in the judicial district in which the offense allegedly occurred or some other court designated by that court. The court must certify the recognizance and have it delivered or sent without delay to the appropriate court. If the accused is not released, the arresting agency must arrange prompt transportation to the judicial district of the offense. In all cases, the arraignment is then to continue under subrule (D), if applicable, and subrule (E) either in the judicial district of the alleged offense or in such court as otherwise is designated.

(D) Arrest Without Warrant. If an accused is arrested without a warrant, a complaint complying with MCR 6.101 must be filed at or before the time of arraignment. On receiving the complaint and on finding probable cause, the court must either issue a warrant or endorse the complaint as provided in MCL 764.1c; MSA 28.860(3). Arraignment of the accused may then proceed in accordance with subrule (E).

(E) Arraignment Procedure; Judicial Responsibilities. The court at the arraignment must

(1) inform the accused of the nature of the offense charged, and its maximum possible prison sentence and any mandatory minimum sentence required by law;

(2) if the accused is not represented by a lawyer at the arraignment, advise the accused that

(a) the accused has a right to remain silent,

(b) anything the accused says orally or in writing can be used against the accused in court,

(c) the accused has a right to have a lawyer present during any questioning consented to, and

(d) if the accused does not have the money to hire a lawyer, the court will appoint a lawyer for the accused;

(3) advise the accused of the right to a lawyer at all subsequent court proceedings and, if appropriate, appoint a lawyer;

(4) set a date within the next 14 days for the accused's preliminary examination and inform the accused of the date;

(5) determine what form of pretrial release, if any, is appropriate; and

(6) ensure that the accused has been fingerprinted as required by law.

The court may not question the accused about the alleged offense or request that the accused enter a plea.

(F) Arraignment Procedure; Recording. A verbatim record must be made of the arraignment.

(G) Plan for Judicial Availability. In each county, the court with trial jurisdiction over felony cases must adopt and file with the state court administrator a plan for judicial availability. The plan shall

(1) make a judicial officer available for arraignments each day of the year, or

(2) make a judicial officer available for setting bail for every person arrested for commission of a felony each day of the year conditioned upon

(a) the judicial officer being presented a proper complaint and finding probable cause pursuant to MCR 6.102(A), and

(b) the judicial officer having available information to set bail.

This portion of the plan must provide that the judicial officer shall order the arresting officials to arrange prompt transportation of any accused unable to post bond to the judicial district of the offense for arraignment not later than the next regular business day.

[Adopted effective October 1, 1989; amended effective April 1, 1990; October 1, 1994.]

1989 Staff Comment

MCR 6.104 is a new rule.

Subrule (A) implements the requirement for prompt arraignment of a person arrested with a warrant, MCL 764.26; MSA 28.885, or without a warrant, MCL 764.13; MSA 28.871(1). The rule recognizes, however, that prompt arraignment is not required if an arrested person is "released beforehand." This may occur as a result of outright release of an arrested person by the police agency because of the decision not to file a complaint, or because the defendant was released on a secured or unsecured recognizance issued by a judge or magistrate in lieu of prompt arraignment. When a delay becomes "unnecessary" and what its effect is on the admissibility of evidence are left to case law. See, for example, *People* v *Cipriano*, 431 Mich 315 (1988).

Subrule (B) makes some modifications in existing law. With regard to an accused arrested *without a warrant* in the county outside the alleged offense occurred, it implements the requirement of MCL 764.13; MSA 28.871(1) that the accused be taken "before a magistrate of the judicial district in which the offense is charged to have been committed." With regard to an accused arrested *with a warrant* in the county in which the alleged offense occurred, the rule requires that the accused be taken before "a court specified in the warrant." MCR 6.102(C) permits the warrant to command a peace officer to bring the accused before a magistrate of the judicial district in which the offense is charged to have been committed "or some other designated court." These latter quoted provisions accommodate the requirement for prompt arraignments, including weekends, by allowing specification in the warrant of another court, such as one shared by the judicial districts for the purpose of conducting weekend or nonbusiness-hour arraignments. This does not imply, however, that an accused arrested without a warrant may not be taken before a court that is not in the judicial district in which the offense occurred but that is authorized to conduct weekend or nonbusiness-hour arraignments for that court.

The remainder of the procedure described in this subrule, setting forth responsibilities pertaining to an accused arrested in a county outside the one in which the offense occurred, is new. The rule provides that on the arrest of an accused in such a county, the arresting agency "must make arrangements with the authorities in the demanding county" to have the accused promptly transported to that county for arraignment as required by this rule. This does not imply that it is the arresting agency's responsibility to transport the accused to the demanding county if the authorities in the demanding county refuse to provide such transportation. In such a situation, the arresting agency has the option of itself providing the transportation or taking the accused to a local court for a "preliminary appearance" as provided in subrule (C).

Subrule (C) sets forth the procedure that the local court must follow in conducting a preliminary appearance occurring outside the county of the offense and the duty of the arresting agency if the accused is not released as a result of that appearance. At that appearance the court's duty is solely to advise the unrepresented accused of *Miranda* rights and decide if the accused may be released on a secured or unsecured recognizance to appear "within the next 14 days" before a court in the judicial district in which the offense occurred. The recognizance promptly must be delivered or mailed to the appropriate court. If the accused is not released, the arresting agency has no option other than to "arrange prompt transportation" of the accused to the judicial district of the offense. Accordingly, if the police agency in the demanding county still declines to provide prompt transportation of the accused, that responsibility will fall on the arresting agency.

Subrule (D) repeats the procedure set forth in MCL 764.1c; MSA 28.860(3). The rule's substitution of the terminology "probable cause" for the statutory terminology "reasonable cause" does not indicate a substantive difference.

Subrule (E) sets forth the arraignment procedure that must be followed by a court authorized to perform the arraignment of the accused. The procedure has some requirements extending beyond current practice. Requiring the arraigning court to give *Miranda* rights to an unrepresented accused is new and addresses Fifth and Sixth Amendment concerns. Subrule (E)(6) implements a statutory requirement for the arraigning court to ensure that the accused has been fingerprinted. MCL 764.29; MSA 28.887(1). The last sentence of subrule (E) prohibits the court from questioning the accused "about the alleged offense" but does not preclude other questioning pertinent to the court's performance of its arraignment functions.

Subrule (F) is new but does not state a new requirement.

Staff Comment to 1990 Amendment

The February 9, 1990 amendment of MCR 6.104(G) [effective April 1, 1990] is a slightly altered version of a proposal made by the Michigan District Judges Association.

Staff Comment to 1994 Amendment

In 1994, MCR 6.104(E)(4) and MCR 6.907(C)(2) were amended to reflect the change made by 1994 PA 167, which extended from 12 to 14 days the period within which a preliminary examination must be conducted. MCL 766.4; MSA 28.922. A similar change was also made in MCR 6.445(C), concerning the timing of a probation revocation hearing.

RULE 6.106　PRETRIAL RELEASE

(A) In General. At the defendant's first appearance before a court, unless an order in accordance with this rule was issued beforehand, the court must order that, pending trial, the defendant be

(1) held in custody as provided in subrule (B);

(2) released on personal recognizance or an unsecured appearance bond; or

(3) released conditionally, with or without money bail (ten percent, cash or surety).

(B) Pretrial Release/Custody Order Under Const 1963, Art 1, § 15.

(1) The court may deny pretrial release to

(a) a defendant charged with

(i) murder or treason, or

(ii) committing a violent felony and

[A] at the time of the commission of the violent felony, the defendant was on probation, parole, or released pending trial for another violent felony, or

[B] during the 15 years preceding the commission of the violent felony, the defendant had been convicted of 2 or more violent felonies under the laws of this state or substantially similar laws of the United States or another state arising out of separate incidents,

if the court finds that proof of the defendant's guilt is evident or the presumption great;

(b) a defendant charged with criminal sexual conduct in the first degree, armed robbery, or kidnapping with the intent to extort money or other valuable thing thereby, if the court finds that proof of the defendant's guilt is evident or the presumption great, unless the court finds by clear and convincing evidence that the defendant is not likely to flee or present a danger to any other person.

(2) A "violent felony" within the meaning of subrule (B)(1) is a felony, an element of which involves a violent act or threat of a violent act against any other person.

(3) If the court determines as provided in subrule (B)(1) that the defendant may not be released, the court must order the defendant held in custody for a period not to exceed 90 days after the date of the order, excluding delays attributable to the defense, within which trial must begin or the court must immediately schedule a hearing and set the amount of bail.

(4) The court must state the reasons for an order of custody on the record and on a form approved by the State Court Administrator's Office entitled "Custody Order." The completed form must be placed in the court file.

(C) Release on Personal Recognizance. If the defendant is not ordered held in custody pursuant to subrule (B), the court must order the pretrial release of the defendant on personal recognizance, or on an unsecured appearance bond, subject to the conditions that the defendant will appear as required, will not leave the state without permission of the court, and will not commit any crime while released, unless the court determines that such release will not reasonably ensure the appearance of the defendant as required, or that such release will present a danger to the public.

(D) Conditional Release. If the court determines that the release described in subrule (C) will not reasonably ensure the appearance of the defendant as required, or will not reasonably ensure the safety of the public, the court may order the pretrial release of the defendant on the condition or combination of conditions that the court determines are appropriate including

(1) that the defendant will appear as required, will not leave the state without permission of the court, and will not commit any crime while released, and

(2) subject to any condition or conditions the court determines are reasonably necessary to ensure the appearance of the defendant as required and the safety of the public, which may include requiring the defendant to

(a) make reports to a court agency as are specified by the court or the agency;

(b) not use alcohol or illicitly use any controlled substance;

(c) participate in a substance abuse testing or monitoring program;

(d) participate in a specified treatment program for any physical or mental condition, including substance abuse;

(e) comply with restrictions on personal associations, place of residence, place of employment, or travel;

(f) surrender driver's license or passport;

(g) comply with a specified curfew;

(h) continue to seek employment;

(i) continue or begin an educational program;

(j) remain in the custody of a responsible member of the community who agrees to monitor the defendant and report any violation of any release condition to the court;

(k) not possess a firearm or other dangerous weapon;

(*l*) not enter specified premises or areas and not assault, beat, molest or wound a named person or persons;

(m) satisfy any injunctive order made a condition of release; or

(n) comply with any other condition, including the requirement of money bail as described in subrule (E), reasonably necessary to ensure the defendant's appearance as required and the safety of the public.

(E) Money Bail. If the court determines for reasons it states on the record that the defendant's appearance or the protection of the public cannot otherwise be assured, money bail, with or without conditions described in subrule (D), may be required.

(1) The court may require the defendant to

(a) post a bond that, at the defendant's option, is executed

(i) by a surety approved by the court, or

(ii) by the defendant, or by another who is not a licensed surety, and secured by

[A] a cash deposit, or its equivalent, for the full bond amount, or

[B] a cash deposit of 10 percent of the bond amount, or, with the court's consent,

[C] designated real property; or

(b) post a bond that, at the defendant's option, is executed

(i) by a surety approved by the court, or

(ii) by the defendant, or by another who is not a licensed surety, and secured by

[A] a cash deposit, or its equivalent, for the full bond amount, or, with the court's consent,

[B] designated real property.

(2) The court may require satisfactory proof of value and interest in property if the court consents to the posting of a bond secured by designated real property.

(F) Decision; Statement of Reasons.

(1) In deciding which release to use and what terms and conditions to impose, the court is to consider relevant information, including

(a) defendant's prior criminal record, including juvenile offenses;

(b) defendant's record of appearance or nonappearance at court proceedings or flight to avoid prosecution;

(c) defendant's history of substance abuse or addiction;

(d) defendant's mental condition, including character and reputation for dangerousness;

(e) the seriousness of the offense charged, the presence or absence of threats, and the probability of conviction and likely sentence;

(f) defendant's employment status and history and financial history insofar as these factors relate to the ability to post money bail;

(g) the availability of responsible members of the community who would vouch for or monitor the defendant;

(h) facts indicating the defendant's ties to the community, including family ties and relationships, and length of residence, and

(i) any other facts bearing on the risk of nonappearance or danger to the public.

(2) If the court orders the defendant held in custody pursuant to subrule (B) or released on conditions in subrule (D) that include money bail, the court must state the reasons for its decision on the record. The court need not make a finding on each of the enumerated factors.

(3) Nothing in subrules (C) through (F) may be construed to sanction pretrial detention nor to sanction the determination of pretrial release on the basis of race, religion, gender, economic status, or other impermissible criteria.

(G) Custody Hearing.

(1) *Entitlement to Hearing.* A court having jurisdiction of a defendant may conduct a custody hearing if the defendant is being held in custody pursuant to subrule (B) and the defendant requests a custody hearing. The purpose of the hearing is to permit the parties to litigate all of the issues relevant to challenging or supporting a custody decision pursuant to subrule (B).

(2) *Hearing Procedure.*

(a) At the custody hearing, the defendant is entitled to be present and to be represented by a lawyer, and the defendant and the prosecutor are entitled to present witnesses and evidence, to proffer information, and to cross-examine each other's witnesses.

(b) The rules of evidence, except those pertaining to privilege, are not applicable. Unless the court makes the findings required to enter an order under subrule (B)(1), the defendant must be ordered released under subrule (C) or (D). A verbatim record of the hearing must be made.

(H) Appeals; Modification of Release Decision.

(1) *Appeals.* A party seeking review of a release decision may file a motion in the court having appellate jurisdiction over the court that made the release decision. There is no fee for filing the motion. The reviewing court may not stay, vacate, modify, or reverse the release decision except on finding an abuse of discretion.

(2) *Modification of Release Decision.*

(a) Prior to Arraignment on the Information. Prior to the defendant's arraignment on the information, any court before which proceedings against the defendant are pending may, on the motion of a party or its own initiative and on finding that there is a substantial reason for doing so, modify a prior release decision or reopen a prior custody hearing.

(b) Arraignment on Information and Afterwards. At the defendant's arraignment on the information and afterwards, the court having jurisdiction of the defendant may, on the motion of a party or its own initiative, make a de novo determination and modify a prior release decision or reopen a prior custody hearing.

(c) Burden of Going Forward. The party seeking modification of a release decision has the burden of going forward.

(3) *Emergency Release.* If a defendant being held in pretrial custody under this rule is ordered released from custody as a result of a court order or law requiring the release of prisoners to relieve jail conditions, the court ordering the defendant's release may, if appropriate, impose conditions of release in accordance with this rule to ensure the appearance of the defendant as required and to protect the public. If such conditions of release are imposed, the court must inform the defendant of the conditions on the record or by furnishing to the defendant or the defendant's lawyer a copy of the release order setting forth the conditions.

(I) Termination of Release Order.

(1) If the conditions of the release order are met and the defendant is discharged from all obligations in the case, the court must vacate the release order, discharge anyone who has posted bond, and return the cash (or its equivalent) posted in the full amount of a bond, or, if there has been a deposit of 10 percent of the bond amount, return 90 percent of the deposited money and retain 10 percent.

(2) If the defendant has failed to comply with the conditions of release, the court may issue a warrant for the arrest of the defendant and enter an order revoking the release order and declaring the bail money deposited or the surety bond, if any, forfeited.

(a) The court must mail notice of any revocation order immediately to the defendant at the defendant's last known address and, if forfeiture of bond has been ordered, to anyone who posted bond.

(b) If the defendant does not appear and surrender to the court within 28 days after the revocation date or does not within the period satisfy the court that there was compliance with the conditions of release or that compliance was impossible through no fault of the defendant, the court may continue the revocation order and enter judgment for the state or local unit of government against the defendant and anyone who posted bond for the entire amount of the bond and costs of the court proceedings.

(c) The 10 percent bond deposit made under subrule (E)(1)(a)(ii)[B] must be applied to the costs and, if any remains, to the balance of the judgment. The amount applied to the judgment must be transferred to the county treasury for a circuit court or recorder's court case, to the treasuries of the governments contributing to the district control unit for a district court case, or to the treasury of the appropriate municipal government for a municipal court case. The balance of the judgment may be enforced and collected as a judgment entered in a civil case.

(3) If money was deposited on a bond executed by the defendant, the money must be first applied to the amount of any fine, costs, or statutory assessments imposed and any balance returned, subject to subrule (I)(1).

[Adopted effective October 1, 1989; amended effective June 1, 1992.]

1989 Staff Comment

MCR 6.106 repeats former MCR 6.110. A court-appointed committee is developing a proposed revision of this rule.

Staff Comments to 1992 Amendment

Revised MCR 6.106 [effective June 1, 1992] is based on a proposed revision of the pretrial release rule submitted by a committee appointed by the Court to study the need for updating the former rule. The revised rule contains many of the changes recommended by the committee to improve the pretrial release procedure, and modifications made by the Court after consideration of comments received following publication.

The May 21, 1992 amendments of revised MCR 6.106, which is to take effect on June 1, 1992, make several technical changes.

RULE 6.107 GRAND JURY PROCEEDINGS

(A) Right to Grand Jury Records. Whenever an indictment is returned by a grand jury or a grand juror, the person accused in the indictment is entitled to the part of the record, including a transcript of the part of the testimony of all witnesses appearing before the grand jury or grand juror, that touches on the guilt or innocence of the accused of the charge contained in the indictment.

(B) Procedure to Obtain Records.

(1) To obtain the part of the record and transcripts specified in subrule (A), a motion must be addressed to the chief judge of the circuit court in the county in which the grand jury issuing the indictment was convened, or, if the grand jury convened on the order of the Recorder's Court for the City of Detroit, then to the chief judge of that court.

(2) The motion must be filed within 14 days after arraignment on the indictment or at a reasonable time thereafter as the court may permit on a showing of good cause and a finding that the interests of justice will be served.

(3) On receipt of the motion, the chief judge shall order the entire record and transcript of testimony taken before the grand jury to be delivered to him or her by the person having custody of it for an in camera inspection by the chief judge.

(4) Following the in camera inspection, the chief judge shall certify the parts of the record, including the testimony of all grand jury witnesses that touches on the guilt or innocence of the accused, as being all of the evidence bearing on that issue contained in the record, and have two copies of it prepared, one to be

delivered to the attorney for the accused, or to the accused if not represented by an attorney, and one to the attorney charged with the responsibility for prosecuting the indictment.

(5) The chief judge shall then have the record and transcript of all testimony of grand jury witnesses returned to the person from whom it was received for disposition according to law.

[Adopted effective October 1, 1989.]

1989 Staff Comment

MCR 6.107(A) and (B), governing the right to obtain and procedure for obtaining grand jury records, are unchanged from the former rule. Former MCR 6.107(C), which covered the right to counsel at grand jury proceedings, is relocated to MCR 6.005(J).

RULE 6.110　THE PRELIMINARY EXAMINATION

(A) Right to Preliminary Examination. The people and the defendant are entitled to a prompt preliminary examination. If the court permits the defendant to waive the preliminary examination, it must bind the defendant over for trial on the charge set forth in the complaint or indictment.

(B) Time of Examination; Remedy.

(1) Unless adjourned by the court, the preliminary examination must be held on the date specified by the court at the arraignment on the warrant or complaint. The court may not adjourn a preliminary examination unless it makes a finding on the record of good cause shown for the adjournment.

(2) The issues whether the preliminary examination was timely held or the requisite record showing for delay was made must be raised, if at all, in a written or oral motion no later than immediately before the commencement of the preliminary examination. To challenge the denial of a timely motion, the defendant must before the trial either file a timely application for leave to appeal with the trial court or, within 21 days after the filing of the information in the trial court, file a motion to dismiss in the trial court. If relief is denied by the trial court, a defendant who wishes to obtain further review must file a timely application with the Court of Appeals, and, if relief is denied by the Court of Appeals, a further timely application with the Supreme Court. A defendant may not after conviction seek relief on the basis of a violation of subrule (B)(1).

(C) Conduct of Examination. Each party may subpoena witnesses, offer proofs, and examine and cross-examine witnesses at the preliminary examination. Except as otherwise provided by law, the court must conduct the examination in accordance with the rules of evidence. A verbatim record must be made of the preliminary examination.

(D) Exclusionary Rules. If, during the preliminary examination, the court determines that evidence being offered is excludable, it must, on motion or objection, exclude the evidence. If, however, there has been a preliminary showing that the evidence is admissible, the court need not hold a separate evidentiary hearing on the question of whether the evidence should be excluded. The decision to admit or exclude evidence, with or without an evidentiary hearing, does not preclude a party from moving for and obtaining a determination of the question in the trial court on the basis of

(1) a prior evidentiary hearing, or

(2) a prior evidentiary hearing supplemented with a hearing before the trial court, or

(3) if there was no prior evidentiary hearing, a new evidentiary hearing.

(E) Probable Cause Finding. If, after considering the evidence, the court determines that probable cause exists to believe both that an offense not cognizable by the district court has been committed and that the defendant committed it, the court must bind the defendant over for trial. If the court finds probable cause to believe that the defendant has committed an offense cognizable by the district court, it must proceed thereafter as if the defendant initially had been charged with that offense.

(F) Discharge of Defendant. If, after considering the evidence, the court determines that probable cause does not exist to believe either that an offense has been committed or that the defendant committed it, the court must discharge the defendant without prejudice to the prosecutor initiating a subsequent prosecution for the same offense. Except as provided in MCR 8.111(C), the subsequent preliminary examination must be held before the same judicial officer and the prosecutor must present additional evidence to support the charge.

(G) Return of Examination. Immediately on concluding the examination, the court must certify and transmit to the court before which the defendant is bound to appear the prosecutor's authorization for a warrant application, the complaint, a copy of the register of actions, the examination return, and any recognizances received.

(H) Motion to Dismiss. If, on proper motion, the trial court finds a violation of subrule (C), (D), (E), or (F), it must either dismiss the information or remand the case to the district court for further proceedings.

(I) Scheduling the Arraignment. Unless the trial court does the scheduling of the arraignment on the information, the district court must do so in accordance with the administrative orders of the trial court.

[Adopted effective October 1, 1989.]

Publisher's Note—Validity

Partial invalidity of this rule, see People v. Glass, 464 Mich. 266, 627 N.W.2d 261 (2001).

1989 Staff Comment

MCR 6.110 is a new rule except for subrule (A).

The first sentence of subrule (A) revises the language of former MCR 6.108, by more closely following the language of the statutory description of the right of the state and the defendant to "a prompt examination" found in MCL 766.1; MSA 28.919. The remainder of this subrule is new. The defendant's right to a preliminary examination following the filing of a complaint, and the waiver procedure found in the second sentence of subrule (A), are set forth in MCL 767.42; MSA 28.982. The defendant's right to a preliminary examination following indictment by a grand jury was recognized in *People* v *Duncan,* 388 Mich 489 (1972).

Subrule (B)(1) implements the statutory 12–day rule set forth in MCL 766.4; MSA 28.922 and the statutory adjournment procedure set forth in MCL 766.7; MSA 28.925 as interpreted in *People* v *Crawford,* 429 Mich 151 (1987).

Subrule (B)(2) incorporates with minor revisions the procedural remedy adopted in *Crawford,* 429 Mich 161–162, for violations of the 12–day rule or of the statutory adjournment procedure. This rule varies from *Crawford* by changing from 20 to 21 days the time after the filing of the information in which a motion to dismiss may be filed, and by expressly prohibiting the defendant from seeking postconviction relief on the basis of a violation of subrule (B)(1).

Subrule (C) implements existing law. MCL 766.11; MSA 28.929, MCL 766.12; MSA 28.930. See MCL 600.2167; MSA 27A.2167 expressly authorizing admission at a preliminary examination of a report made by a state technician.

Subrule (D) reflects existing law and practice.

Subrules (E) and (F) implement MCL 766.13; MSA 28.931. Although the language the rules use in describing the bindover and discharge standards is different than that used in the statute, no substantive difference is intended. The other provisions in these subrules are also consistent with existing law.

Subrule (G) is consistent with the procedure set forth in MCL 766.15(1); MSA 28.933(1).

Subrule (H) is consistent with current practice. This subrule does not address, and leaves to case law, what effect a violation of these rules or an error in ruling on a motion filed in the trial court may have when raised following conviction.

Subrule (I) reflects current practice.

RULE 6.112　THE INFORMATION OR INDICTMENT

(A) Informations and Indictments; Similar Treatment. Except as otherwise provided in these rules or elsewhere, the law and rules that apply to informations and prosecutions on informations apply to indictments and prosecutions on indictments.

(B) Use of Information or Indictment. A prosecution must be based on an information or an indictment. Unless the defendant is a fugitive from justice, the prosecutor may not file an information until the defendant has had or waives a preliminary examina-

tion. An indictment may be returned and filed before a defendant's preliminary examination. When this occurs, the indictment may substitute for the complaint and commence judicial proceedings.

(C) Time of Filing Information or Indictment. The prosecutor must file the information on or before the date set for the arraignment.

(D) Information; Nature and Contents; Attachments. The information must set forth the substance of the accusation against the defendant and the name, statutory citation, and penalty of the offense allegedly committed. If applicable, the information must also set forth the notice required by MCL 767.45; MSA 28.985, and the defendant's Michigan driver's license number. To the extent possible, the information should specify the time and place of the alleged offense. Allegations relating to conduct, the method of committing the offense, mental state, and the consequences of conduct may be stated in the alternative. A list must be attached to the information of all witnesses known to the prosecutor who might be called at trial and all res gestae witnesses known to the prosecutor or investigating law enforcement officers. A prosecutor must sign the information.

(E) Bill of Particulars. The court, on motion, may order the prosecutor to provide the defendant a bill of particulars describing the essential facts of the alleged offense.

(F) Notice of Intent to Seek Enhanced Sentence. A notice of intent to seek an enhanced sentence pursuant to MCL 769.13; MSA 28.1085 must list the prior convictions that may be relied upon for purposes of sentence enhancement. The notice must be filed within 21 days after the defendant is arraigned or has waived arraignment on the information charging the underlying felony, or before trial begins, if the defendant is tried within the 21–day period.

(G) Harmless Error. Absent a timely objection and a showing of prejudice, a court may not dismiss an information or reverse a conviction because of an untimely filing or because of an incorrectly cited statute or a variance between the information and proof regarding time, place, the manner in which the offense was committed, or other factual detail relating to the alleged offense. This provision does not apply to the untimely filing of a notice of intent to seek an enhanced sentence.

(H) Amendment of Information. The court before, during, or after trial may permit the prosecutor to amend the information unless the proposed amendment would unfairly surprise or prejudice the defendant. On motion, the court must strike unnecessary allegations from the information.

[Adopted effective October 1, 1989; amended effective October 3, 2000.]

Publisher's Note—Validity

Partial invalidity of this rule, see People v. Glass, 464 Mich. 266, 627 N.W.2d 261 (2001).

1989 Staff Comment

MCR 6.112 is new.

Subrules (A) and (B) implement existing law. See MCL 767.1; MSA 28.941, MCL 767.2; MSA 28.942 and MCL 767.42; MSA 28.982.

Subrule (C) sets forth a new requirement. It mandates that the information be filed on or before the date set for the arraignment. This represents a change from the past practice under which it was permissible for an information to be filed after the date set for the arraignment.

The second sentence of subrule (C) merely restates the rule announced in *People v Shelton*, 412 Mich 565 (1982).

Subrule (D) implements existing law. See MCL 767.45; MSA 28.985, MCL 767.44; MSA 28.984, MCL 767.51; MSA 28.991, MCL 767.40; MSA 28.980, and MCL 767.40a(1); MSA 28.980(1)(1).

Subrule (E) reflects current law and practice. See MCL 767.44; MSA 28.984 and MCL 767.51; MSA 28.991.

Subrule (G) sets forth a harmless error rule consistent with current law. See MCL 767.45; MSA 28.985, MCL 767.51; MSA 28.991, and MCL 767.76; MSA 28.1016.

Subrule (G) implements existing law. MCL 767.76; MSA 28.1016. What type of amendment may or may not "unfairly surprise or prejudice the defendant" is left to case law.

Staff Comment to 2000 Amendment

The October 3, 2000, amendment of MCR 6.112 made the court rule consistent with MCL 769.13; MSA 28.1085.

RULE 6.113   THE ARRAIGNMENT ON THE INDICTMENT OR INFORMATION

(A) Time of Conducting. Unless the defendant waives arraignment or the court for good cause orders a delay, the court with trial jurisdiction must arraign the defendant on the scheduled date. The court may hold the arraignment before the preliminary examination transcript has been prepared and filed. Unless the defendant demonstrates actual prejudice, failure to hold the arraignment on the scheduled date is to be deemed harmless error.

(B) Arraignment Procedure. The prosecutor must give a copy of the information to the defendant before the defendant is asked to plead. Unless waived by the defendant, the court must either state to the defendant the substance of the charge contained in the information or require the information to be read to the defendant. If the defendant has waived legal representation, the court must advise the defendant of the pleading options. If the defendant offers a plea other than not guilty, the court must proceed in accordance with the rules in subchapter 6.300. Otherwise, the court must enter a plea of not guilty on the record. A verbatim record must be made of the arraignment.

(C) Waiver. A defendant represented by a lawyer may, as a matter of right, enter a plea of not guilty or stand mute without arraignment by filing, at or before the time set for the arraignment, a written statement signed by the defendant and the defendant's lawyer acknowledging that the defendant has received a copy of the information, has read or had it read or explained, understands the substance of the charge, waives arraignment in open court, and pleads not guilty to the charge or stands mute.

(D) Preliminary Examination Transcript. Unless the defendant pleads guilty at the arraignment or the parties otherwise agree, the court must order the court reporter to transcribe and file the record of the preliminary examination. The order must also provide for the payment of the reporter's fees.

[Adopted effective October 1, 1989.]

1989 Staff Comment

MCR 6.113 is new, except for subrules (B) and (C).

Subrule (A) corresponds to current practice. The procedure for scheduling of the arraignment date is set forth in MCR 6.110(I).

Subrule (B) incorporates a revised version of former MCR 6.101(D)(1). The former rule required the indictment or information to "be read to the defendant unless expressly waived by the defendant or his or her attorney." Subrule (B) gives the court the option of stating to the defendant "the substance of the charge contained in the information" in lieu of having it read to the defendant. This subrule also sets forth the subsequent procedure that must be followed at the arraignment of eliciting the defendant's plea. If the defendant is proceeding in propria persona, the court must advise the defendant of the pleading options. Those options are set forth in MCR 6.301.

Subrule (C) repeats former rule 6.101(D)(2) with stylistic changes.

Subrule (D) sets forth a procedure that differs from the statutory procedure set forth in MCL 766.15(2), (3); MSA 28.933(2), (3). The statute permits a party to file a written request for the preparation and filing of a preliminary examination transcript "if filed within 2 weeks following the arraignment on the information or indictment." Subrule (D) provides that if at the time of the arraignment the transcript has not been requested and the parties are unable to agree either that it will not be needed or to postpone their decision to a later date (for example, because of plea negotiations), the court must order the transcript prepared. The objective of this requirement is to accelerate necessary transcript preparation and not to have unnecessary transcripts prepared. Accordingly, proper implementation of this rule to avoid waste requires the parties and the court at the arraignment to resolve whether the transcript is needed or whether that decision should be postponed to a later date when that need can be determined. The subrule further provides that the court may specify in its order how the reporter's fees will be paid. If the order is the result of a request or demand by a nonindigent defendant, the order should provide for the reporter's fees to be paid by the defendant. If the order is based on the demand or request of the prosecutor, or on the court's own initiative, the appropriate funding unit may be specified.

RULE 6.120   JOINDER AND SEVERANCE; SINGLE DEFENDANT

(A) Permissive Joinder. An information or indictment may charge a single defendant with any two or more offenses. Each offense must be stated in a separate count. Two or more informations or indictments against a single defendant may be consolidated for a single trial.

(B) Right of Severance; Unrelated Offenses. On the defendant's motion, the court must sever unrelated offenses for separate trials. For purposes of this rule, two offenses are related if they are based on

(1) the same conduct, or

(2) a series of connected acts or acts constituting part of a single scheme or plan.

(C) Other Joinder or Severance. On the motion of either party, except as to offenses severed under subrule (B), the court may join or sever offenses on the ground that joinder or severance is appropriate to promote fairness to the parties and a fair determination of the defendant's guilt or innocence of each offense. Relevant factors include the timeliness of the motion, the drain on the parties' resources, the potential for confusion or prejudice stemming from either the number of charges or the complexity or nature of the evidence, the potential for harassment, the convenience of witnesses, and the parties' readiness for trial. Subject to an objection by either party, the court may sever offenses on its own initiative.

[Adopted effective October 1, 1989.]

1989 Staff Comment

MCR 6.120 is a new rule. It sets forth the procedure for joining or severing charges against a single defendant.

Subrule (A) is patterned after 2 ABA Standards for Criminal Justice (2d ed), Standard 13–2.1, and permits joinder in the charging instrument of charges, related or unrelated, against a single defendant. This provision is consistent with Michigan law. See *People v Tobey*, 401 Mich 141 (1977), and *People v Thompson*, 410 Mich 66 (1980). This subrule does not address the issue of joinder of charges that may be required because of double jeopardy considerations. See, for example, *People v White*, 390 Mich 245 (1973).

Subrule (B) pertains to the defendant's unqualified right to severance of unrelated offenses. This provision varies from ABA Standard 13–3.1 which entitles both the defendant *and the prosecutor* to severance of unrelated offenses.

The standard in subrule (B), defining when two offenses "are related," is derived from ABA Standard 13–1.2, and a predecessor standard, ABA Project on Minimum Standards for Criminal Justice, Standards Relating to Joinder and Severance (Approved Draft, 1968), Standard 1.1. Elaboration on this standard may be found in *People v Tobey*, 401 Mich 141 (1977).

Subrule (C) relates to the procedure for joining or severing charges other than those that have been severed pursuant to the defendant's right to severance under subrule (B). On the motion of either party, the court may allow the joinder or severance of charges on determining that the joinder or severance "is appropriate to promote fairness to the parties *and* a fair determination of the defendant's guilt or innocence of each offense." This standard combines "fairness to the parties" with ABA Standard 13–3.1(b)(i). Some of the factors relevant to the two prongs of this standard are listed in this rule. The rule further permits the court to "sever" offenses on its own initiative, but subject to the considerations of this rule if there is an objection. This subrule does not address constitutional considerations (e.g., double jeopardy), which independently may require or preclude joinder or severance depending on the circumstances.

RULE 6.121   JOINDER AND SEVERANCE; MULTIPLE DEFENDANTS

(A) Permissive Joinder. An information or indictment may charge two or more defendants with the same offense. It may charge two or more defendants with two or more offenses when

(1) each defendant is charged with accountability for each offense, or

(2) the offenses are related as defined in MCR 6.120(B).

When more than one offense is alleged, each offense must be stated in a separate count. Two or more informations or indictments against different defendants may be consolidated for a single trial whenever the defendants could be charged in the same information or indictment under this rule.

(B) Right of Severance; Unrelated Offenses. On a defendant's motion, the court must sever offenses that are not related as defined in MCR 6.120(B).

(C) Right of Severance; Related Offenses. On a defendant's motion, the court must sever the trial of defendants on related offenses on a showing that severance is necessary to avoid prejudice to substantial rights of the defendant.

(D) Discretionary Severance. On the motion of any party, the court may sever the trial of defendants on the ground that severance is appropriate to promote fairness to the parties and a fair determination of the guilt or innocence of one or more of the defendants. Relevant factors include the timeliness of the motion, the drain on the parties' resources, the potential for confusion or prejudice stemming from either the number of defendants or the complexity or nature of the evidence, the convenience of witnesses, and the parties' readiness for trial.

[Adopted effective October 1, 1989.]

1989 Staff Comment

MCR 6.121 is a new rule. It sets forth procedure for joining or severing the cases of multiple defendants.

Subrule (A) relates to the permissive joinder of the charges against two or more defendants either as a result of being placed in the same charging instrument or as a result of consolidation of the defendants' cases for trial. A joinder of cases for trial may be based on a prosecution or defense motion. The standard for permitting joinder is patterned after 2 ABA Standards for Criminal Justice (2d ed), Standard 13–2.2(a).

Subrule (B) incorporates by reference a defendant's right to severance of unrelated offenses as provided in MCR 6.120(B). The effect of such a severance in multiple defendant cases will depend on the circumstances.

Subrule (C) sets forth a defendant's entitlement to a separate trial, if not obtainable pursuant to subrule (B), on a showing that it "is necessary to avoid prejudice to substantial rights of the defendant." This standard is taken from *People v Schram*, 378 Mich 145, 156 (1966), and *People v Carroll*, 396 Mich 408, 414 (1976). It is said to reflect a strong policy in favor of joint trials set forth in MCL 768.5; MSA 28.1028 and found in case law. The right of a defendant to a fair trial and other substantial rights, however, may necessitate severance. See, for example, *People v Hurst*, 396 Mich 1, 4 (1976), stating that a defendant is entitled to a separate trial if it appears that a codefendant "may testify to exculpate himself and incriminate the defendant seeking a separate trial."

Subrule (D) is similar to MCR 6.120(C) but pertains only to severance. It provides that "any party" may invoke the court's discretion to grant separate trials on the ground that it will "promote fairness to the parties and a fair determination of the guilt or innocence of one or more of the defendants." Like MCR 6.120(C), this rule does not address constitutional considerations, such as double jeopardy, that may in some cases preclude severance.

RULE 6.125 MENTAL COMPETENCY HEARING

(A) Applicable Provisions. Except as provided in these rules, a mental competency hearing in a criminal case is governed by MCL 330.2020 et seq.; MSA 14.800(1020) et seq.

(B) Time and Form of Motion. The issue of the defendant's competence to stand trial or to participate in other criminal proceedings may be raised at any time during the proceedings against the defendant. The issue may be raised by the court before which such proceedings are pending or being held, or by motion of a party. Unless the issue of defendant's competence arises during the course of proceedings, a motion raising the issue of defendant's competence must be in writing. If the competency issue arises during the course of proceedings, the court may adjourn the proceeding or, if the proceeding is defendant's trial, the court may, consonant with double jeopardy considerations, declare a mistrial.

(C) Order for Examination.

(1) On a showing that the defendant may be incompetent to stand trial, the court must order the defendant to undergo an examination by a certified or licensed examiner of the center for forensic psychiatry or other facility officially certified by the department of mental health to perform examinations relating to the issue of competence to stand trial.

(2) The defendant must appear for the examination as required by the court.

(3) If the defendant is held in detention pending trial, the examination may be performed in the place of detention or the defendant may be transported by the sheriff to the diagnostic facility for examination.

(4) The court may order commitment to a diagnostic facility for examination if the defendant fails to appear for the examination as required or if commitment is necessary for the performance of the examination.

(5) The defendant must be released from the facility on completion of the examination and, if (3) is applicable, returned to the place of detention.

(D) Independent Examination. On a showing of good cause by either party, the court may order an independent examination of the defendant relating to the issue of competence to stand trial.

(E) Hearing. A competency hearing must be held within 5 days of receipt of the report required by MCL 330.2028; MSA 14.800(1028) or on conclusion of the proceedings then before the court, whichever is sooner, unless the court, on a showing of good cause, grants an adjournment.

(F) Motions; Testimony.

(1) A motion made while a defendant is incompetent to stand trial must be heard and decided if the presence of the defendant is not essential for a fair hearing and decision on the motion.

(2) Testimony may be presented on a pretrial defense motion if the defendant's presence could not assist the defense.

[Adopted effective October 1, 1989.]

1989 Staff Comment

With three exceptions, MCR 6.125 is a stylistically revised version of former MCR 6.106.

Subrule (B) dealing with when and how the issue of defendant's competence may be raised is substantially expanded to allow the issue to be raised "at any time during the proceedings against the defendant," thus including proceedings in the district court, or subsequent to trial, such as sentencing. Furthermore, it may be raised by *any* court before which such proceedings "are pending or being held." The party's motion raising this issue must be in writing unless the issue manifests itself during the course of court proceedings, in which event the court, on its own initiative or on the motion of a party, may adjourn the proceedings and issue an order for examination under this rule. Of course, if the competency issue arises during the course of the defendant's trial, double jeopardy considerations must be accommodated.

In addition to the foregoing expansion in subrule (B), this rule incorporates a new provision in subrule (D) giving the trial court discretion, "on a showing of good cause by either party," to order an independent examination of the defendant's competency to stand trial. Because of a presumption that the Center for Forensic Psychiatry or other facility officially certified by the Department of Mental Health will properly perform their functions, "good cause" justifying an independent competency examination should arise only in exceptional cases.

The only other substantive change in this rule is in subrule (E), which changes the provision in the former rule requiring the competency hearing to be held within 7 days of receipt of the psychiatric report, to 5 days. This change has been made to make the court rule consistent with the statute, MCL 330.2030; MSA 14.800(1030), which mandates the competency hearing to be held "within 5 days" of receipt of the psychiatric report or at the conclusion of the proceedings then before the court, "whichever is sooner."

SUBCHAPTER 6.200 DISCOVERY

RULE 6.201 DISCOVERY

(A) Mandatory Disclosure. In addition to disclosures required by provisions of law other than MCL 767.94a; MSA 28.1023(194a), a party upon request must provide all other parties:

(1) the names and addresses of all lay and expert witnesses whom the party intends to call at trial;

(2) any written or recorded statement by a lay witness whom the party intends to call at trial, except that a defendant is not obliged to provide the defendant's own statement;

(3) any report of any kind produced by or for an expert witness whom the party intends to call at trial;

(4) any criminal record that the party intends to use at trial to impeach a witness;

(5) any document, photograph, or other paper that the party intends to introduce at trial; and

(6) a description of and an opportunity to inspect any tangible physical evidence that the party intends to introduce at trial. On good cause shown, the court may order that a party be given the opportunity to test without destruction such tangible physical evidence.

(B) Discovery of Information Known to the Prosecuting Attorney. Upon request, the prosecuting attorney must provide each defendant:

(1) any exculpatory information or evidence known to the prosecuting attorney;

(2) any police report concerning the case, except so much of a report as concerns a continuing investigation;

(3) any written or recorded statements by a defendant, codefendant, or accomplice, even if that person is not a prospective witness at trial;

(4) any affidavit, warrant, and return pertaining to a search or seizure in connection with the case; and

(5) any plea agreement, grant of immunity, or other agreement for testimony in connection with the case.

(C) Prohibited Discovery.

(1) Notwithstanding any other provision of this rule, there is no right to discover information or evidence that is protected from disclosure by constitution, statute, or privilege, including information or evidence protected by a defendant's right against self-incrimination, except as provided in subrule (2).

(2) If a defendant demonstrates a good-faith belief, grounded in articulable fact, that there is a reasonable probability that records protected by privilege are likely to contain material information necessary to the defense, the trial court shall conduct an in-camera inspection of the records.

(a) If the privilege is absolute, and the privilege holder refuses to waive the privilege to permit an in-camera inspection, the trial court shall suppress or strike the privilege holder's testimony.

(b) If the court is satisfied, following an in-camera inspection, that the records reveal evidence necessary to the defense, the court shall direct that such evidence as is necessary to the defense be made available to defense counsel. If the privilege is absolute and the privilege holder refuses to waive the privilege to permit disclosure, the trial court shall suppress or strike the privilege holder's testimony.

(c) Regardless of whether the court determines that the records should be made available to the defense, the court shall make findings sufficient to facilitate meaningful appellate review.

(d) The court shall seal and preserve the records for review in the event of an appeal

(i) by the defendant, on an interlocutory basis or following conviction, if the court determines that the records should not be made available to the defense, or

(ii) by the prosecution, on an interlocutory basis, if the court determines that the records should be made available to the defense.

(e) Records disclosed under this rule shall remain in the exclusive custody of counsel for the parties, shall be used only for the limited purpose approved by the court, and shall be subject to such other terms and conditions as the court may provide.

(D) Excision. When some parts of material or information are discoverable and other parts are not discoverable, the party must disclose the discoverable parts and may excise the remainder. The party must inform the other party that nondiscoverable information has been excised and withheld. On motion, the court must conduct a hearing in camera to determine whether the reasons for excision are justifiable. If the court upholds the excision, it must seal and preserve the record of the hearing for review in the event of an appeal.

(E) Protective Orders. On motion and a showing of good cause, the court may enter an appropriate protective order. In considering whether good cause exists, the court shall consider the parties' interests in a fair trial; the risk to any person of harm, undue annoyance, intimidation, or threats; the risk that evidence will be fabricated; and the need for secrecy regarding the identity of informants or other law enforcement matters. On motion, with notice to the other party, the court may permit the showing of good cause for a protective order to be made in camera. If the court grants a protective order, it must seal and preserve the record of the hearing for review in the event of an appeal.

(F) Timing of Discovery. Unless otherwise ordered by the court, the prosecuting attorney must comply with the requirements of this rule within 7 days of a request under this rule and a defendant must comply with the requirements of this rule within 14 days of a request under this rule.

(G) Copies. Except as ordered by the court on good cause shown, a party's obligation to provide a photograph or paper of any kind is satisfied by providing a clear copy.

(H) Continuing Duty to Disclose. If at any time a party discovers additional information or material subject to disclosure under this rule, the party, without further request, must promptly notify the other party.

(I) Modification. On good cause shown, the court may order a modification of the requirements and prohibitions of this rule.

(J) Violation. If a party fails to comply with this rule, the court, in its discretion, may order that testimony or evidence be excluded, or may order another remedy.

[Adopted effective January 1, 1995; amended effective July 1, 1996; January 1, 1998.]

1995 Staff Comment

MCR 6.201 took effect January 1, 1995. It followed the Court's decision in *People v Lemcool*, 445 Mich 491; 518 NW2d 437 (1994) and the enactment of 1994 PA 113, MCL 767.94a; MSA 28.1023(194a). Pursuant to Administrative Order 1994–10, discovery in criminal cases is governed by this court rule, and not by MCL 767.94a; MSA 28.1023(194a).

Staff Comment to 1996 Amendment

Consistent with *People v Stanaway*, 446 Mich 643 (1994), the addition of subrule (C)(2) in 1996 provided for the in-camera inspection of confidential records protected by privilege, and subsequent appellate review.

Staff Comment to 1998 Amendment

The January 1, 1998 amendment of MCR 6.201 added subrule (H), at the recommendation of the Michigan Judges Association, and redesignated former subrules (H) and (I) to be (I) and (J), respectively. New subrule (H) imposes a continuing obligation of disclosure similar to the obligation that exists in civil cases.

SUBCHAPTER 6.300   PLEAS

RULE 6.301   AVAILABLE PLEAS

(A) Possible Pleas. Subject to the rules in this subchapter, a defendant may plead not guilty, guilty, nolo contendere, guilty but mentally ill, or not guilty by reason of insanity. If the defendant refuses to plead or stands mute, or the court, pursuant to the rules, refuses to accept the defendant's plea, the court must enter a not guilty plea on the record. A plea of not guilty places in issue every material allegation in the information and permits the defendant to raise any defense not otherwise waived.

(B) Pleas That Require the Court's Consent. A defendant may enter a plea of nolo contendere only with the consent of the court.

(C) Pleas That Require the Consent of the Court and the Prosecutor. A defendant may enter the following pleas only with the consent of the court and the prosecutor:

(1) A defendant who has asserted an insanity defense may enter a plea of guilty but mentally ill or a plea of not guilty by reason of insanity. Before such a plea may be entered, the defendant must comply with the examination required by law.

(2) A defendant may enter a conditional plea of guilty, nolo contendere, guilty but mentally ill, or not guilty by reason of insanity. A conditional plea preserves for appeal a specified pretrial ruling or rulings notwithstanding the plea-based judgment and entitles the defendant to withdraw the plea if a specified pretrial ruling is overturned on appeal. The ruling or rulings as to which the defendant reserves the right to appeal must be specified orally on the record or in a writing made a part of the record. The appeal is by application for leave to appeal only.

(D) Pleas to Lesser Charges. The court may not accept a plea to an offense other than the one charged without the consent of the prosecutor.

[Adopted effective October 1, 1989; amended December 30, 1994, applicable to all crimes committed on or after December 27, 1994 as provided by 1994 PA 374 and 1994 PA 375, effective until further order of the Court after consideration of comments and legislative action, if any, or until April 1, 1995; by Order of March 31, 1995, December 30, 1994 amendment ordered to remain in effect until June 30, 1995; by Order of June 19, 1995, December 30, 1994 amendment ordered to remain in effect until October 15, 1995; by Order of October 13, 1995, December 30, 1994 amendment ordered to remain in effect until August 15, 1996; by Order of July 16, 1996, December 30, 1994 amendment ordered to remain in effect until September 1, 1997; by Order of July 25, 1997, December 30, 1994 amendment ordered to remain in effect until further order of the Court.]

1989 Staff Comment

MCR 6.301 is a new rule, but incorporates elements of former 6.101.

Subrule (A) describes the various pleas available to a defendant under the rules in this subchapter. In addition to the pleas of not guilty, guilty, and nolo contendere described in the former rule, the rules in this subchapter add the pleas of guilty but mentally ill and not guilty by reason of insanity. A plea of guilty but mentally ill was created by statute. MCL 768.36(2); MSA 28.1059(2). A plea of not guilty by reason of insanity is created by these rules. See subrule (C)(1) and 6.304. The second sentence of subrule (A) is a modified version of former 6.101(E)(1). It allows a court to refuse to accept a defendant's plea, but only "pursuant to the rules." The quoted phrase refers to pleas that can be refused (1) because they require the court's consent [pleas in nolo contendere and the pleas described in subrule (C)] or (2) because they fail to comply with a requirement of the rules in this subchapter. The last sentence of subrule (A) is a stylistically revised version of former 6.101(E)(2).

Subrule (B) is a modification of a provision in former 6.101(F). The former rule provided that the court's consent was required before a defendant would be permitted to plead guilty or nolo contendere. Subrule (B) has deleted the requirement for the court's consent to a plea of guilty. The consent provision in the former rule has been construed as giving the trial court the discretion to refuse to accept a guilty plea because of disagreement with the plea bargain agreed to by the prosecutor and the defendant. See *People v Ott*, 144 MichApp 76 (1985). Accordingly, deletion of the consent provision indicates that the trial court may not refuse to accept a guilty plea based solely on disagreement with the wisdom of the plea, of the charge, or of the plea bargain, unless the bargain is conditioned on the court's agreement to some provision, such as sentence disposition. See 6.302(C)(3). As is noted in subrule (A), however, the court may refuse to accept a plea based on noncompliance with a requirement in these rules.

As indicated, subrule (B) retains the discretion of the court, subject to the requirements of these rules, to accept or reject a plea of nolo contendere. Rule 6.302(D)(2)(a) requires the court to state on the record "why a plea of nolo contendere is appropriate."

Subrule (C) is new. It describes two categories of pleas requiring the consent of both the court and the prosecutor. Subrule (C)(1) describes the pleas of guilty but mentally ill and not guilty by reason of insanity. A plea of guilty but mentally ill was created by statute, MCL 768.36(2); MSA 28.1059(2), and is now implemented in these rules. See subrule (A) above and 6.303. The statute conditions entry of such a plea on the consent of the prosecutor and the trial court, and on the defendant having asserted a defense of insanity and having complied with the examination requirements of the insanity defense statute. MCL 768.20a; MSA 28.1043(1).

The plea of not guilty by reason of insanity is new and is recognized for the first time in these rules. See subrule (A) above and 6.304. Not guilty by reason of insanity has existed however, as a defense assertable at trial. In cases in which prosecutors chose not to contest this defense, the practice was followed by which the parties, with the court's consent, agreed to entry of a judgment of not guilty by reason of insanity following a pro forma bench trial. The rules take advantage of the benefits of this past practice while providing a structured plea procedure allowing elimination of an unnecessary pro forma trial.

Subrule (C)(2) incorporates and expands the conditional plea procedure authorized in *People v Reid*, 420 Mich 326 (1984), by which a defendant, with the agreement of the prosecutor and the court, may enter a plea of guilty while preserving, for appeal purposes, a challenge to a pretrial ruling that might otherwise be waived by the plea. This subrule expands the availability of the conditional plea procedure to the other forms of plea available under these rules. It also permits a conditional plea to be used to preserve challenges to one or more pretrial rulings and places no limitation on the type of ruling that may be preserved. Consistent with *Reid*, however, it requires that the defendant be permitted to withdraw the plea if any ruling preserved by this procedure is overturned on appeal. Furthermore, the subrule requires that any challenged ruling being preserved for appeal be "specified orally on the record or in a writing made a part of the record." The availability of this procedure, however, should not be construed as precluding a defendant from raising on appeal issues that are not waived by entry of a plea. The question of what issues are not waived by a plea is addressed by case law. See, for example, *People v New*, 427 Mich 482 (1986).

Subrule (D) is new and sets forth the settled principle stated in *Genesee Prosecutor v Genesee Circuit Judge*, 391 Mich 115 (1974).

Staff Comment to 1994 Amendment

The December 30, 1994 amendments of MCR 6.301, 6.302, 6.311, 6.425, 7.203, 7.204 and 7.205 modified procedure regarding appeals in criminal cases in light of the amendment of Const 1963, art 1, § 20 at the November 1994 general election and the legislation implementing the constitutional amendment. Changes will remain in effect until April 1, 1995 and will be reconsidered by the Court in light of comments received and any further legislation.

RULE 6.302   PLEAS OF GUILTY
AND NOLO CONTENDERE

(A) Plea Requirements. The court may not accept a plea of guilty or nolo contendere unless it is convinced that the plea is understanding, voluntary, and accurate. Before accepting a plea of guilty or nolo contendere, the court must place the defendant under oath and personally carry out subrules (B)–(E).

(B) An Understanding Plea. Speaking directly to the defendant, the court must advise the defendant and determine that the defendant understands:

(1) the name of the offense to which the defendant is pleading; the court is not obliged to explain the elements of the offense, or possible defenses;

(2) the maximum possible prison sentence for the offense and any mandatory minimum sentence required by law;

(3) if the plea is accepted, the defendant will not have a trial of any kind, and so gives up the rights the defendant would have at a trial, including the right:

(a) to be tried by a jury;

(b) to be tried by the court without a jury, if the defendant chooses and the prosecutor and court consent;

(c) to be presumed innocent until proved guilty;

(d) to have the prosecutor prove beyond a reasonable doubt that the defendant is guilty;

(e) to have the witnesses against the defendant appear at the trial;

(f) to question the witnesses against the defendant;

(g) to have the court order any witnesses the defendant has for the defense to appear at the trial;

(h) to remain silent during the trial;

(i) to not have that silence used against the defendant; and

(j) to testify at the trial if the defendant wants to testify.

(4) if the plea is accepted, the defendant will be giving up any claim that the plea was the result of promises or threats that were not disclosed to the court at the plea proceeding, or that it was not the defendant's own choice to enter the plea;

(5) any appeal from the conviction and sentence pursuant to the plea will be by application for leave to appeal and not by right;

(6) if the plea is accepted, the defendant is not entitled to have counsel appointed at public expense to assist in filing an application for leave to appeal or to assist with other postconviction remedies unless the defendant is financially unable to retain counsel and

(a) the defendant's sentence exceeds the guidelines,

(b) the plea is a conditional plea under MCR 6.301(C)(2),

(c) the prosecuting attorney seeks leave to appeal, or

(d) the Court of Appeals or the Supreme Court grants leave to appeal.

(C) A Voluntary Plea.

(1) The court must ask the prosecutor and the defendant's lawyer whether they have made a plea agreement.

(2) If there is a plea agreement, the court must ask the prosecutor or the defendant's lawyer what the terms of the agreement are and confirm the terms of the agreement with the other lawyer and the defendant.

(3) If there is a plea agreement and its terms provide for the defendant's plea to be made in exchange for a specific sentence disposition or a prosecutorial sentence recommendation, the court may

(a) reject the agreement; or

(b) accept the agreement after having considered the presentence report, in which event it must sentence the defendant to the sentence agreed to or recommended by the prosecutor; or

(c) accept the agreement without having considered the presentence report; or

(d) take the plea agreement under advisement.

If the court accepts the agreement without having considered the presentence report or takes the plea agreement under advisement, it must explain to the defendant that the court is not bound to follow the sentence disposition or recommendation agreed to by the prosecutor, and that if the court chooses not to follow it, the defendant will be allowed to withdraw from the plea agreement.

(4) The court must ask the defendant:

(a) (if there is no plea agreement) whether anyone has promised the defendant anything, or (if there is a plea agreement) whether anyone has promised anything beyond what is in the plea agreement;

(b) whether anyone has threatened the defendant; and

(c) whether it is the defendant's own choice to plead guilty.

(D) An Accurate Plea.

(1) If the defendant pleads guilty, the court, by questioning the defendant, must establish support for a finding that the defendant is guilty of the offense charged or the offense to which the defendant is pleading.

(2) If the defendant pleads nolo contendere, the court may not question the defendant about participation in the crime. The court must:

(a) state why a plea of nolo contendere is appropriate; and

(b) hold a hearing, unless there has been one, that establishes support for a finding that the defendant is guilty of the offense charged or the offense to which the defendant is pleading.

(E) Additional Inquiries. On completing the colloquy with the defendant, the court must ask the prosecutor and the defendant's lawyer whether either is aware of any promises, threats, or inducements other than those already disclosed on the record, and whether the court has complied with subrules (B)–(D). If it appears to the court that it has failed to comply with subrules (B)–(D), the court may not accept the defendant's plea until the deficiency is corrected.

(F) Plea Under Advisement; Plea Record. The court may take the plea under advisement. A verbatim record must be made of the plea proceeding.

[Adopted effective October 1, 1989; amended December 30, 1994, applicable to all crimes committee on or after December 27, 1994 as provided by 1994 PA 374 and 1994 PA 375, effective until further order of the Court after consideration of comments and legislative action, if any, or until April 1, 1995; amended effective March 1, 1995; by Order of March 31, 1995, December 30, 1994 amendment ordered to remain in effect until June 30, 1995; by Order of June 19, 1995, December 30, 1994 amendment ordered to remain in effect until October 15, 1995; by Order of October 13, 1995, December 30, 1994 amendment ordered to remain in effect until August 15, 1996; by Order of July 16, 1996, December 30, 1994 amendment ordered to remain in effect until September 1, 1997; by Order of July 25, 1997, December 30, 1994 amendment ordered to remain in effect until further order of the Court; amended effective April 1, 2000; September 1, 2002.]

1989 Staff Comment

With a few modifications, MCR 6.302 repeats former 6.101(F)(1)–(6).

The first sentence of subrule (A) repeats former 6.101(5) except that it limits the applicability of this rule to a plea of guilty or nolo contendere. Pertinent provisions of this rule, however, are incorporated by reference in the rules applicable to the plea of guilty but mentally ill, 6.303, and the plea of not guilty by reason of insanity, 6.304. The second sentence of subrule (A) repeats a provision in former 6.101(F).

Subrule (B) is a stylistically improved version of former 6.101(F)(1) and incorporates two substantive changes.

Subrule (B)(2) enlarges former 6.101(F)(1)(b) (requiring the court to advise the defendant of "the maximum possible prison sentence for the offense") by adding the requirement that the court also advise the defendant of "any mandatory minimum sentence required by law."

Subrule (B)(3)(b) changes the advice required by former 6.101(F)(1)(c)(ii) ("to trial by the court if the defendant does not want trial by a jury") to reflect that the consent of the prosecutor and the court is also required. This change corresponds to the legislative amendment conditioning the defendant's statutory right to a bench trial on obtaining the consent of the prosecutor and the court. 1988 PA 89, MCL 763.3; MSA 28.856. See 6.401.

Subrules (C)(1) and (2) repeat former 6.101(F)(2)(a) and (b).

Subrule (C)(3) is new. It incorporates and clarifies the sentence-bargaining procedures set forth in *People* v *Killebrew*, 416 Mich 189, 206–212 (1982). Subrule (3)(b) recognizes that frequently trial courts have access to a presentence report at the time of the plea proceeding and are in a position to make a final acceptance of the agreement. In such a case the court is bound to comply with the sentence agreement, be it for a specific disposition or recommended disposition. If the court does not have a presentence report or chooses not to consider it at that time, the court's options are to accept the agreement conditionally, (3)(c), or take the plea agreement under advisement, (3)(d). A conditionally accepted agreement is binding on the defendant unless the court chooses not to follow the sentence disposition or recommendation. If, however, the court takes a plea agreement under advisement, the plea is not accepted and the defendant has the right under 6.310(A) to withdraw the plea "until the court accepts it on the record." If the court accepts the agreement conditionally or takes the plea agreement under advisement, it must inform the defendant that the court is not bound to follow the sentence agreement, but that the defendant will be allowed to withdraw the plea in the event that the court does not follow it.

Subrule (C)(4) repeats, with stylistic changes, former 6.101(F)(2)(c).

Subrule (D) repeats, with stylistic changes, the procedure for establishing the factual basis for the plea set forth in former 6.101(F)(3).

Subrule (E) is a stylistically revised version of former 6.101(F)(4)(a). Former 6.101(F)(4)(b), requiring the court to state whether it has agreed to any plea or sentence bargaining, has been eliminated from this subrule because it is now covered in subrule (C)(3).

The first sentence of subrule (F) repeats the provision in former 6.101(F)(6). The last sentence of subrule (F) repeats the record requirement found in former 6.101(H).

Staff Comment to 1994 Amendment

The December 30, 1994 amendments of MCR 6.301, 6.302, 6.311, 6.425, 7.203, 7.204 and 7.205 modified procedure regarding appeals in criminal cases in light of the amendment of Const 1963, art 1, § 20 at the November 1994 general election and the legislation implementing the constitutional amendment. Changes will remain in effect until April 1, 1995 and will be reconsidered by the Court in light of comments received and any further legislation.

Staff Comment to March, 1995 Amendment

The 1995 amendment of MCR 6.302(A) [effective March 1, 1995] requires the court to place a defendant under oath before accepting a plea of guilty or nolo contendere. The amendment of subrule (B) requires the court to inform the defendant that, by pleading guilty or nolo contendere, the defendant gives up any claim that the plea was the result of promises or threats that were not disclosed to the court at the plea proceeding, or that it was not the defendant's own choice to enter the plea. The amendment of subrule (E) requires the court to inquire whether either the prosecutor or the defendant's lawyer is aware of any promises, threats, or inducements other than those already disclosed on the record.

Staff Comment to 2000 Amendment

The March 28, 2000 amendment of Rules 6.302, 6.425, and 6.615, and the adoption of new Rule 6.625, were made in light of 1999 PA 200, MCL 770.3a; MSA 28.1100a, and were effective as to pleas taken on or after April 1, 2000.

Dissent to 2002 Amendment

Cavanagh, J. (dissenting). This amendment is ill-advised and, at the least, premature in light of the pending Sixth Circuit Court of Appeals' review of this issue in Tesmer v Granholm, Docket Nos. 00–1824 and 00–1845.

Kelly, J. I join in the dissenting statement of Justice Cavanagh.

Staff Comment to 2002 Amendment

The April 23, 2002 amendment of MCR 6.302(B), effective September 1, 2002, shortens the advice given at plea proceedings regarding an "understanding plea" by eliminating the requirement that the court list the circumstances in which it has discretion to appoint counsel at public expense. That advice remains in MCR 6.425(E)(2)(c).

The staff comment is published only for the benefit of the bench and bar and is not an authoritative construction by the Court.

RULE 6.303　PLEA OF GUILTY BUT MENTALLY ILL

Before accepting a plea of guilty but mentally ill, the court must comply with the requirements of MCR 6.302. In addition to establishing a factual basis for the plea pursuant to MCR 6.302(D)(1) or (D)(2)(b), the court must examine the psychiatric reports prepared and hold a hearing that establishes support for a finding that the defendant was mentally ill, but not insane, at the time of the offense to which the plea is entered. The reports must be made a part of the record.

[Adopted effective October 1, 1989.]

1989 Staff Comment

MCR 6.303 is a new rule. The availability of the plea of guilty but mentally ill is noted in 6.301(A). The statutory authorization for the plea is found in MCL 768.36(2); MSA 28.1059(2). The statute sets forth some procedural prerequisites to the plea, including that the defendant have asserted the defense of insanity and undergone psychiatric examination as provided in the insanity defense statute. These requirements are incorporated in 6.301(C)(1). Additionally, before acceptance of the plea, the court is required to examine the psychiatric reports and hold a hearing to establish that the defendant was mentally ill at the time of the offense. In *People* v *Booth*, 414 Mich 343 (1982), the Court determined that the latter statutory procedure was intended as an adjunct to the traditional plea procedure. Accordingly, it fashioned a procedure combining the court rule plea procedure relating to the issue of criminal liability and the statutory procedure relating to the issue of mental illness.

The rule is consistent with the procedure adopted in *Booth*. The court must comply with the requirements of the guilty plea rule, including the advice requirements and establishing a factual basis for the criminal liability either by direct questioning as provided in 6.302(D)(1), or the nolo contendere procedure provided in (D)(2)(b). Additionally, as to the issue of mental illness, the court must follow the statutory requirements of examining the psychiatric reports prepared and holding a hearing to establish that the defendant was mentally ill, "but not insane," at the time of the offense. Of course, "hearing" implies that the parties are entitled to present evidence at the hearing. The court rule also incorporates the statutory requirement for the psychiatric reports to be made a part of the record.

RULE 6.304　PLEA OF NOT GUILTY BY REASON OF INSANITY

(A) Advice to Defendant. Before accepting a plea of not guilty by reason of insanity, the court must comply with the requirements of MCR 6.302 except that subrule (C) of this rule, rather than MCR 6.302(D), governs the manner of determining the accuracy of the plea.

(B) Additional Advice Required. After complying with the applicable requirements of MCR 6.302, the court must advise the defendant, and determine whether the defendant understands, that the plea will result in the defendant's commitment for diagnostic examination at the center of forensic psychiatry for up to 60 days, and that after the examination, the probate court may order the defendant to be committed for an indefinite period of time.

(C) Factual Basis. Before accepting a plea of not guilty by reason of insanity, the court must examine the psychiatric reports prepared and hold a hearing that establishes support for findings that

(1) the defendant committed the acts charged, and

(2) a reasonable doubt exists about the defendant's legal sanity at the time of the offense.

(D) Report of Plea. After accepting the defendant's plea, the court must forward to the center for forensic psychiatry a full report, in the form of a settled record, of the facts concerning the crime to which the defendant pleaded and the defendant's mental state at the time of the crime.

[Adopted effective October 1, 1989.]

1989 Staff Comment

MCR 6.304 is a new rule. It sets forth the procedure for the new plea of not guilty by reason of insanity. It is similar to the procedure in 6.303 providing for a plea of guilty but mentally ill. It incorporates additional procedural steps, however, requiring additional advice because of the consequences of the plea, and a hearing and reporting procedure corresponding to the statutory requirements relating to a person acquitted of criminal charges by reason of insanity. MCL 330.2050; MSA 14.800(1050). The statute requires a person acquitted of criminal charges by reason of insanity to be committed to the center for forensic psychiatry for a period not to exceed 60 days. It further requires the court to forward to the center "a full report, in the form of a settled record, of the facts concerning the crime which the patient was found to have committed but of which he was acquitted by reason of insanity." This latter requirement necessitates a more elaborate fact finding than is required to establish a factual basis for a guilty plea or a plea of guilty but mentally ill.

Subrule (A) requires the trial court to comply with the requirements of the guilty plea rule, 6.302, except that the factual basis for the plea is to be governed by the procedures set forth in subrule (C).

Subrule (B) requires the court to give the defendant additional advice concerning the unique consequences of this plea to ensure that the defendant's plea is made voluntarily and understandingly. The court must advise the defendant that the plea will result in the defendant's commitment for a diagnostic examination that may last up to 60 days and that afterwards the defendant may be committed for an indefinite period of time.

The procedure for establishing a factual basis for this plea differs from the other plea procedures because of the greater likelihood that the defendant will not be able to supply a factual basis establishing that the crime was committed, and also because of the more elaborate report requirement that the court is statutorily required to make to the center for forensic psychiatry. This does not preclude the court, however, from considering statements and testimony elicited from the defendant or from relying on other information admitted during the course of the hearing. Additionally, the court must consider the psychiatric reports prepared and such other evidence presented at the hearing that establishes a reasonable doubt concerning the defendant's sanity at the time of the offense.

Subrule (D) implements the statutory reporting requirement applicable to a person acquitted by reason of insanity. Since the plea procedure has the same effect as an acquittal following a trial, the same subsequent examination and commitment procedure must be followed.

RULE 6.310 WITHDRAWAL OR VACATION OF PLEA BEFORE ACCEPTANCE OR SENTENCE

(A) Withdrawal Before Acceptance. The defendant has a right to withdraw any plea until the court accepts it on the record.

(B) Withdrawal Before Sentence. On the defendant's motion or with the defendant's consent, the court in the interest of justice may permit an accepted plea to be withdrawn before sentence is imposed unless withdrawal of the plea would substantially prejudice the prosecutor because of reliance on the plea. If the defendant's motion is based on an error in the plea proceeding, the court must permit the defendant to withdraw the plea if it would be required by MCR 6.311(B).

(C) Vacation of Plea Before Sentence. On the prosecutor's motion, the court may vacate a plea before sentence is imposed if the defendant has failed to comply with the terms of a plea agreement.

[Adopted effective October 1, 1989.]

1989 Staff Comment

With the exception of subrule (A), MCR 6.310 substantially modifies prior rules and law.

Subrule (A) is a modified version of Rule 6.101(F)(6)(a). The rule states the defendant's right to withdraw "any plea" until it is accepted on the record. The terminology "any plea" is used to make it clear that this rule applies to any of the forms of plea described in these rules.

Subrule (B) sets forth the procedure for withdrawing a plea after it has been accepted but before the sentence has been imposed. The former rule, 6.101(F)(6)(b), did not place any limits on the court's discretion to set aside an accepted plea ("the court may set it aside"). Case law indicated that the trial judge's discretion "should be exercised with great liberality" when the defendant's request was made before sentencing. *People* v *Zaleski*, 375 Mich 71, 79 (1965). Subrule (B) states a new standard. It permits the court to allow a plea to be withdrawn before sentencing if it is "in the interest of justice" *and* if withdrawal of the plea would not "substantially prejudice the prosecutor because of reliance on the plea." The new standard has similarities to Federal Rule of Criminal Procedure 32(d) ("upon a showing by the defendant of any fair and just reason") and ABA Standard, 14–2.1(a) ("for any fair and just reason unless the prosecution has been substantially prejudiced by reliance upon the defendant's plea.").

The foregoing portion of subrule (B) pertains to discretionary withdrawals of pleas. The last portion of subrule (B) deals with withdrawals that are not discretionary, but rather, mandatory because of a defect in the plea or the plea proceeding entitling the defendant to withdraw the plea

regardless of whether the motion is made before or after sentencing. The latter bases for withdrawal are discussed in 6.311(B).

Subrule (C) is a new rule authorizing the court to vacate a plea before sentencing on the basis of the prosecutor's motion and showing that the defendant has failed to comply with the terms of a plea agreement. Because the trial court's authority is discretionary ("may vacate"), the court is not required to vacate a plea if it finds that the breach was insignificant.

RULE 6.311 CHALLENGING PLEA AFTER SENTENCE

(A) Motion to Withdraw Plea. The defendant may file a motion to withdraw the plea within the time for filing an application for leave to appeal. After the time for filing an application for leave, the defendant may seek relief in accordance with the procedure set forth in subchapter 6.500.

(B) Remedy. If the trial court determines that there was an error in the plea proceeding that would entitle the defendant to have the plea set aside, the court must give the advice or make the inquiries necessary to rectify the error and then give the defendant the opportunity to elect to allow the plea and sentence to stand or to withdraw the plea. If the defendant elects to allow the plea and sentence to stand, the additional advice given and inquiries made become part of the plea proceeding for the purposes of further proceedings, including appeals.

(C) Preservation of Issues. A defendant convicted on the basis of a plea may not raise on appeal any claim of noncompliance with the requirements of the rules in this subchapter, or any other claim that the plea was not an understanding, voluntary, or accurate one, unless the defendant has moved to withdraw the plea in the trial court, raising as a basis for withdrawal the claim sought to be raised on appeal.

[Adopted effective October 1, 1989; amended December 30, 1994, applicable to all crimes committee on or after December 27, 1994 as provided by 1994 PA 374 and 1994 PA 375, effective until further order of the Court after consideration of comments and legislative action, if any, or until April 1, 1995; by Order of March 31, 1995, December 30, 1994 amendment ordered to remain in effect until June 30, 1995; by Order of June 19, 1995, December 30, 1994 amendment ordered to remain in effect until October 15, 1995; by Order of October 13, 1995, December 30, 1994 amendment ordered to remain in effect until August 15, 1996; by Order of July 16, 1996, December 30, 1994 amendment ordered to remain in effect until September 1, 1997; by Order of July 25, 1997, December 30, 1994 amendment ordered to remain in effect until further order of the Court.]

1989 Staff Comment

Except for subrule (A), MCR 6.311 repeats provisions in former 6.101.

Subrule (A) sets the times within which a motion to withdraw a plea may be filed.

Subrule (A)(1) sets the basic time at 42 days after the entry of judgment. Such a timely motion extends the time for filing the claim of appeal. See MCR 7.204(A)(2)(d). The remaining subrules follow the filing of later motions that do not have the effect of extending the time for taking an appeal of right.

Under subrule (A)(2), if a claim of appeal has been filed, typically as a result of the appointment of appellate counsel [see MCR 6.425(F)(3)], the motion must be made in the manner provided in MCR 7.208(B) or by seeking an order of the Court of Appeals remanding the case to the trial court under MCR 7.211(C)(1).

Subrule (A)(3) provides that if a defendant fails to file a timely claim of appeal, the motion to withdraw the plea may be filed at any time before expiration of the time for filing an application for leave to appeal.

Finally, under subrule (A)(4), a defendant who is not entitled to appeal by right or by leave, either because the defendant has had an appeal or because the 18–month time limit has expired [see MCR 7.204(F)(3)], may only seek relief under the procedure provided by subchapter 6.500.

The rules governing motions for judgment of acquittal [MCR 6.419(B)], for resentencing [MCR 6.429(B)], and for new trial [MCR 6.431(A)] have similar time limits.

Subrule (B) repeats the provisions in former 6.101(F)(7)(b) and (c). The language "an error in the plea proceeding that would entitle the defendant to have the plea set aside" is significant because it incorporates by reference case law, principally *Guilty Plea Cases*, 395 Mich 96 (1975), and subsequent cases, determining on a case-by-case basis what type of defect in a plea or departure from a court rule requirement will or will not require a plea to be set aside. This body of law and case law approach have been retained in these rules. While these rules set forth a number of new requirements, as was stated in *Guilty Plea Cases*, whether a particular departure will entitle a defendant to have the plea set aside "will depend on the nature of the noncompliance."

Subrules (B) and (C) retain the requirement of former 6.101(F)(7) for a challenge to a plea based on noncompliance with the rules or any other nonjurisdictional defect to be raised in the trial court as a prerequisite to being raised on appeal. This permits the trial court to rule on the claim and rectify the error according to the procedure set forth in subrule (B).

It should be noted that subrule (C) expands the applicability of this provision to any plea set forth in these rules whereas the former provision was limited to "a plea of guilty or nolo contendere". Additionally, subrule (C) is made applicable to "any claim of noncompliance with the requirements of the rules in this subchapter" whereas the former rule was applicable to "any alleged noncompliance with the requirements of subrules (F)(1)–(4)". Accordingly, under subrule (C), a defendant seeking to set aside any type of plea set forth in these rules on the basis of noncompliance with any requirement of these rules must, as a precondition to preserving that claim for appeal, first raise it in the trial court in a motion to withdraw the plea. Subrule (A) sets forth the various procedures available to a defendant to have a claim heard in the trial court before presenting it on appeal.

Staff Comment to 1994 Amendment

The December 30, 1994 amendments of MCR 6.301, 6.302, 6.311, 6.425, 7.203, 7.204 and 7.205 modified procedure regarding appeals in criminal cases in light of the amendment of Const 1963, art 1, § 20 at the November 1994 general election and the legislation implementing the constitutional amendment. Changes will remain in effect until April 1, 1995 and will be reconsidered by the Court in light of comments received and any further legislation.

RULE 6.312   EFFECT OF WITHDRAWAL OR VACATION OF PLEA

If a plea is withdrawn by the defendant or vacated by the trial court or an appellate court, the case may proceed to trial on any charges that had been brought or that could have been brought against the defendant if the plea had not been entered.

[Adopted effective October 1, 1989.]

1989 Staff Comment

MCR 6.312 is a modified version of former 6.101(F)(7)(d). *People* v *McMiller*, 389 Mich 425 (1973), and *People* v *Thornton*, 403 Mich 389 (1978), held that when a plea-based conviction was reversed on appeal or set aside by the trial court for violation of plea-taking rules, the defendant could not be reprosecuted on a higher charge arising out of the same transaction. Former MCR 6.101(F)(7)(d) removed that prohibition as to pleas set aside by the trial court. The new provision allows prosecution on higher charges regardless of whether the plea is withdrawn by the defendant or vacated by the trial court or an appellate court.

SUBCHAPTER 6.400   TRIALS

RULE 6.401   RIGHT TO TRIAL BY JURY OR BY THE COURT

The defendant has the right to be tried by a jury, or may, with the consent of the prosecutor and approval by the court, elect to waive that right and be tried before the court without a jury.

[Adopted effective October 1, 1989.]

1989 Staff Comment

MCR 6.401 is a new rule. It states the statutory right of a defendant to elect waiver of a jury trial in favor of trial by the court. A 1988 legislative amendment has conditioned the defendant's right by requiring "the consent of the prosecutor and approval by the court." 1988 PA 89, MCL 763.3; MSA 28.856.

RULE 6.402   WAIVER OF JURY TRIAL BY THE DEFENDANT

(A) Time of Waiver. The court may not accept a waiver of trial by jury until after the defendant has had or waived an arraignment on the information and has been offered an opportunity to consult with a lawyer.

(B) Waiver and Record Requirements. Before accepting a waiver, the court must advise the defendant in open court of the constitutional right to trial by jury. The court must also ascertain, by addressing the defendant personally, that the defendant understands the right and that the defendant voluntarily chooses to give up that right and to be tried by the court. A verbatim record must be made of the waiver proceeding.

[Adopted effective October 1, 1989.]

1989 Staff Comment

MCR 6.402 is a new rule. It sets forth a procedure for waiver of jury trial that differs substantially from the requirements set forth in MCL 763.3; MSA 28.856 and the procedure implementing those requirements adopted in *People v Pasley*, 419 Mich 297 (1984).

Subrule (A) is consistent with the requirements of subsection (2) of the statute, permitting the waiver "after the defendant has been arraigned and has had the opportunity to consult with legal counsel." The rule uses the terminology "*offered* an opportunity to consult with a lawyer" to clarify that actual consultation with a lawyer is not required so long as a defendant has been offered the opportunity and declined it.

The waiver procedure set forth in subrule (B) differs from the statute and the procedure adopted in *Pasley* because it eliminates the written waiver requirement and replaces it with an oral waiver procedure consistent with the waiver procedure applicable at plea proceedings. See 6.302(B)(3). The statutory procedure is superseded by the court rule procedure. See 6.001(E).

RULE 6.403   TRIAL BY THE JUDGE IN WAIVER CASES

When trial by jury has been waived, the court with jurisdiction must proceed with the trial. The court must find the facts specially, state separately its conclusions of law, and direct entry of the appropriate judgment. The court must state its findings and conclusions on the record or in a written opinion made a part of the record.

[Adopted effective October 1, 1989.]

1989 Staff Comment

MCR 6.403 is a new rule, but incorporates existing law. The first sentence of the rule describes the judge's duty set forth in MCL 763.4; MSA 28.857. The second sentence incorporates the special fact finding requirements of MCR 2.517(A)(1), made applicable to criminal cases by *People v Jackson*, 390 Mich 621, 627 (1973). Since this rule adopts an existing rule, it also implicitly incorporates the existing body of decisional law beginning with *Jackson* addressing issues such as the sufficiency of fact findings and the appropriate remedy when findings are insufficient.

The applicability of special fact finding at bench trials, however, should not be construed as implying that it is not required in relation to other evidentiary hearings at which the court must decide a contested factual issue. See, for example, *People v LaBate*, 122 MichApp 644 (1983), holding the special fact-finding requirement applicable at an entrapment hearing.

RULE 6.410   JURY TRIAL; NUMBER OF JURORS; UNANIMOUS VERDICT

(A) Number of Jurors. Except as provided in this rule, a jury that decides a case must consist of 12 jurors. At any time before a verdict is returned, the parties may stipulate with the court's consent to have the case decided by a jury consisting of a specified number of jurors less than 12. On being informed of the parties' willingness to stipulate, the court must personally advise the defendant of the right to have the case decided by a jury consisting of 12 jurors. By addressing the defendant personally, the court must ascertain that the defendant understands the right and that the defendant voluntarily chooses to give up that right as provided in the stipulation. If the court finds that the requirements for a valid waiver have been satisfied, the court may accept the stipulation. Even if the requirements for a valid waiver have been satisfied, the court may, in the interest of justice, refuse to accept a stipulation, but it must state its reasons for doing so on the record. The stipulation and procedure described in this subrule must take place in open court and a verbatim record must be made.

(B) Unanimous Verdicts. A jury verdict must be unanimous.

[Adopted effective October 1, 1989; amended effective March 1, 1995.]

1989 Staff Comment

MCR 6.410 is a new rule. Its provisions modify and change existing law.

Subrule (A) sets forth a procedure by which a defendant charged with a felony may waive the constitutional right to have the case decided by twelve jurors. See Const 1963, art 1, § 20. Waiver of this right was held permissible in *Attorney General v Montgomery*, 275 Mich 504 (1936), and a waiver procedure was subsequently incorporated in former GCR 1963, 512.1, allowing the parties to stipulate orally or in writing to a jury of less than twelve. This provision, however, was deleted from MCR 2.512 as part of a general excision of criminal provisions from the civil rules.

Subrule (A) recognizes that a defendant may waive the right to trial by twelve jurors. To ensure, however, that the waiver is voluntary and not the product of coercion, the rule restricts the availability of stipulation and waiver until after the jury is impaneled. Additionally, the subrule sets forth a stipulation and oral waiver procedure to ensure that the waiver is an informed and voluntary one. The rule permits the court, however, to decline to accept the stipulation if the court determines, and states the reasons why, it is not in the interest of justice.

GCR 1963, 512.1 also authorized the parties in a criminal case to stipulate to a less than unanimous verdict. In *People v Miller*, 121 MichApp 691 (1982), it was held that under existing law a defendant may waive the constitutional right to a unanimous jury verdict. Subrule (B) changes the law by mandating that a jury verdict in a criminal case governed by these rules be unanimous. This mandate implicitly prohibits a stipulation or waiver to a less than unanimous verdict.

Staff Comment to 1994 Amendment

Consistent with *People v Champion*, 442 Mich 874 (1993), the March 1995 amendment of subrule (A) permits the parties to stipulate, with the court's consent and at any time before a verdict is returned, to proceed with fewer than 12 jurors.

RULE 6.411   ADDITIONAL JURORS

The court may impanel more than 12 jurors. If more than the number of jurors required to decide the case are left on the jury before deliberations are to begin, the names of the jurors must be placed in a container and names drawn from it to reduce the number of jurors to the number required to decide the case. The court may retain the alternate jurors during deliberations. If the court does so, it shall instruct the alternate jurors not to discuss the case with any other person until the jury completes its deliberations and is discharged. If an alternate juror replaces a juror after the jury retires to consider its verdict, the court shall instruct the jury to begin its deliberations anew.

[Adopted effective October 1, 1989; amended effective September 1, 2001.]

1989 Staff Comment

MCR 6.411 restates former 6.102(A), permitting the impaneling of more than 12 jurors, but with a modification providing for the number of jurors to be reduced prior to deliberations to the number "required to decide the case." This modification accommodates the possibility that there has been a stipulation to a jury of less than twelve as provided in Rule 6.410(A).

Staff Comment to 2001 Amendment

The June 26, 2001 amendments of MCR 2.511(B), MCR 6.411, and MCR 6.620(A), effective September 1, 2001, were based on a proposal from the Michigan Judges Association. Consistent with the December 1999 amendment of the Federal Rules of Criminal Procedure for the United States District Courts, the amendments allow courts to retain alternate jurors during deliberations.

RULE 6.412   SELECTION OF THE JURY

(A) Selecting and Impaneling the Jury. Except as otherwise provided by the rules in this subchapter, MCR 2.510 and 2.511 govern the procedure for selecting and impaneling the jury.

(B) Instructions and Oath Before Selection. Before beginning the jury selection process, the court should give the prospective jurors appropriate preliminary instructions and must have them sworn.

(C) Voir Dire of Prospective Jurors.

(1) *Scope and Purpose.* The scope of voir dire examination of prospective jurors is within the discretion of the court. It should be conducted for the purposes of discovering grounds for challenges for cause and of gaining knowledge to facilitate an intelligent exercise of peremptory challenges. The court should confine the examination to these purposes and prevent abuse of the examination process.

(2) *Conduct of the Examination.* The court may conduct the examination of prospective jurors or permit the lawyers to do so. If the court conducts the examination, it may permit the lawyers to supplement the examination by direct questioning or by submitting questions for the court to ask. On its own initiative or on the motion of a party, the court may provide for a prospective juror or jurors to be questioned out of the presence of the other jurors.

(D) Challenges for Cause.

(1) *Grounds.* A prospective juror is subject to challenge for cause on any ground set forth in MCR 2.511(D) or for any other reason recognized by law.

(2) *Procedure.* If, after the examination of any juror, the court finds that a ground for challenging a juror for cause is present, the court on its own initiative should, or on motion of either party must, excuse the juror from the panel.

(E) Peremptory Challenges.

(1) *Challenges by Right.* Each defendant is entitled to 5 peremptory challenges unless an offense charged is punishable by life imprisonment, in which case a defendant being tried alone is entitled to 12 peremptory challenges, 2 defendants being tried jointly are each entitled to 10 peremptory challenges, 3 defendants being tried jointly are each entitled to 9 peremptory challenges, 4 defendants being tried jointly are each entitled to 8 peremptory challenges, and 5 or more defendants being tried jointly are each entitled to 7 peremptory challenges. The prosecutor is entitled to the same number of peremptory challenges as a defendant being tried alone, or, in the case of jointly tried defendants, the total number of peremptory challenges to which all the defendants are entitled.

(2) *Additional Challenges.* On a showing of good cause, the court may grant one or more of the parties an increased number of peremptory challenges. The additional challenges granted by the court need not be equal for each party.

(F) Instructions and Oath After Selection. After the jury is selected and before trial begins, the court must have the jurors sworn and should give them appropriate pretrial instructions.

[Adopted effective October 1, 1989.]

1989 Staff Comment

MCR 6.412 is a new rule.

Subrule (A) incorporates by reference the jury selection procedure set forth in the civil rules.

Subrule (B) is consistent with existing practice. Appropriate preliminary instructions and an appropriate oath may be found in the Michigan Criminal Jury Instructions.

The provisions in subrule (C)(1) pertaining to voir dire of perspective jurors reflects existing law. See *People v Har-*

rell, 398 Mich 384, 388 (1976). The provision in the last sentence of subrule (C)(1) is new and states the trial court's responsibility to confine voir dire examination to its proper purposes.

The provisions in subrule (C)(2) are consistent with existing law. See *Harrell*, supra. The "or" in the first sentence is used in its conjunctive sense, indicating that voir dire examination may be conducted by the court, by the lawyers, or by both.

Subrule (D)(1) is consistent with existing law and incorporates by reference the grounds for challenge for cause set forth in MCR 2.511(D). Subrule (D)(2) also reflects the existing law. It provides, however, that the court's duty to discharge a juror for cause sua sponte is directive ("should") rather than mandatory or permissive.

Subrule (E)(1) substantially changes existing law. By statute, MCL 768.13; MSA 28.1036, and pursuant to former 6.102(B), every defendant charged with a capital offense was entitled to 20 peremptory challenges, whether tried separately or jointly, and the prosecutor was entitled to 15 peremptory challenges for each defendant. Subrule (B) reduces the entitlement to peremptory challenges in such cases to 12 for individually charged defendants, and a progressively reduced number for each defendant in multiple defendant cases to a minimum of seven challenges per defendant. Subrule (B) also changes the prosecutor's entitlement to peremptory challenges by making it equal to the total number of peremptory challenges available to the defendants in a case. The peremptory challenge entitlement applicable in noncapital cases is unchanged. See former 6.102(B) and MCL 768.12; MSA 28.1035.

Subrule (E)(2) is a new provision that gives the court discretion, "on a showing of good cause," to allow a party or the parties additional peremptory challenges. It is based on 3 ABA Standards for Criminal Justice (2d ed), Standard 15–2.6(a), which indicates that such additional challenges should be allowed "when special circumstances justify doing so."

Subrule (F) is consistent with current practice. The Michigan Criminal Jury Instructions set forth an appropriate oath and appropriate jury instructions.

RULE 6.414   CONDUCT OF JURY TRIAL

(A) Court's Responsibility. The trial court must control the proceedings during trial, limit the evidence and arguments to relevant and proper matters, and take appropriate steps to ensure that the jurors will not be exposed to information or influences that might affect their ability to render an impartial verdict on the evidence presented in court. The court may not communicate with the jury or any juror pertaining to the case without notifying the parties and permitting them to be present. The court must ensure that all communications pertaining to the case between the court and the jury or any juror are made a part of the record.

(B) Opening Statements. Unless the parties and the court agree otherwise, the prosecutor, before presenting evidence, must make a full and fair statement of the prosecutor's case and the facts the prosecutor intends to prove. Immediately thereafter, or immediately before presenting evidence, the defendant may make a like statement. The court may impose reasonable limits on the opening statements.

(C) Note Taking by Jurors. The court may permit the jurors to take notes regarding the evidence presented in court. If the court permits note taking, it must instruct the jurors that they need not take notes and that they should not permit note taking to interfere with their attentiveness. The court also must instruct the jurors both to keep their notes confidential except as to other jurors and to destroy their notes when the trial is concluded.

(D) View. The court may order a jury view of property or of a place where a material event occurred. The parties are entitled to be present at the jury view. During the view, no person other than the officer designated by the court may speak to the jury concerning a subject connected with the trial.

(E) Closing Arguments. After the close of all the evidence, the parties may make closing arguments. The prosecutor is entitled to make the first closing argument. If the defendant makes an argument, the prosecutor may offer a rebuttal limited to the issues raised in the defendant's argument. The court may impose reasonable limits on the closing arguments.

(F) Instructions to the Jury. Before closing arguments, the court must give the parties a reasonable opportunity to submit written requests for jury instructions. Each party must serve a copy of the written requests on all other parties. The court must inform the parties of its proposed action on the requests before their closing arguments. After closing arguments are made or waived, the court must instruct the jury as required and appropriate, but with the parties' consent, the court may instruct the jury before the parties make closing arguments. After jury deliberations begin, the court may give additional instructions that are appropriate.

(G) Materials in Jury Room. The court may permit the jury, on retiring to deliberate, to take into the jury room a writing, other than the charging document, setting forth the elements of the charges against the defendant and any exhibits and writings admitted into evidence. On the request of a party or on its own initiative, the court may provide the jury with a full set of written instructions, a full set of electronically recorded instructions, or a partial set of written or recorded instructions if the jury asks for clarification or restatement of a particular instruction or instructions or if the parties agree that a partial set may be provided and agree on the portions to be provided. If it does so, the court must ensure that such instructions are made a part of the record.

(H) Review of Evidence. If, after beginning deliberation, the jury requests a review of certain testimony or evidence, the court must exercise its discretion to ensure fairness and to refuse unreasonable requests, but it may not refuse a reasonable request. The court may order the jury to deliberate further without the requested review, so long as the possibility of having the testimony or evidence reviewed at a later time is not foreclosed.

[Adopted effective October 1, 1989; amended effective September 1, 1998.]

1989 Staff Comment

MCR 6.414 is a new rule.

The first sentence of subrule (A) combines the directives found in MCL 768.29; MSA 28.1052 and a directive derived from 3 ABA Standards of Criminal Justice (2d ed), Standard 15–3.7(a) ("take appropriate steps . . . to ensure that the jurors will not be exposed to sources of information or opinion, or subject to influences, which might tend to affect their ability to render an impartial verdict on the evidence presented in court"). To the extent that existing law prohibits the court from having any ex parte communications with the jury, it is modified by the second sentence of the subrule, prohibiting only communications "pertaining to the case." This modification recognizes that communications that are not related to the case such as those pertaining to administrative or "house-keeping" functions have no tendency to be harmful, are necessary and should be permitted. The requirement in this rule for a record to be kept of other communications between the court and the jury is consistent with existing law.

Subrule (B) is a stylistically revised version of MCR 2.507(A). The last sentence is consistent with MCR 2.507(F).

Subrule (C) is consistent with current practice. See *People* v *Young,* 146 MichApp 337, 339–341 (1985).

Subrule (D) incorporates pertinent provisions from MCR 2.513(A).

Subrule (E) is a stylistically revised version of MCR 2.507(E). The last sentence is consistent with MCR 2.507(F).

Subrule (F) incorporates provisions from MCL 768.29; MSA 28.1052, MCR 2.516, and Federal Rule of Criminal Procedure 30. Unlike MCR 2.516(A)(3), which requires a party to serve requested instructions "on the adverse parties," this subrule follows the federal rule, which requires service on "all other parties." Additionally, the subrule incorporates a provision based on a provision in the federal rule permitting the court to instruct the jury before or after closing arguments. Unlike the federal rule, however, the subrule requires the consent of the parties in order for the court to instruct the jury before the parties make their closing arguments. Implicit in this provision is the option, if consented to by the parties, of instructing the jury both before and after closing arguments.

Subrule (G) is consistent with existing practice, however, it expressly prohibits the charging document from being sent into the jury room. This prohibition is based on the fact the charging documents generally contain extraneous information, such as reference to penalty, that is not an appropriate jury consideration. The provisions in this rule relating to the various forms of instructions that may be sent into the jury room are taken from MCR 2.516(B)(5). A record requirement has been added, however, to permit review.

Subrule (H) incorporates the procedure governing jury requests for review adopted in *People* v *Howe,* 392 Mich 670 (1974).

Staff Comment to 1998 Amendment

The June 1998 amendment of MCR 6.414(G), effective September 1, 1998, was suggested by the Michigan Judges Association. The amendment allows the trial court to provide the jury with a partial set of instructions if the jury asks for clarification or restatement of a particular instruction or instructions. Previously, a partial set of instructions could be provided only if the parties agreed.

RULE 6.416　PRESENTATION OF EVIDENCE

Subject to the rules in this chapter and to the Michigan rules of evidence, each party has discretion in deciding what witnesses and evidence to present.

[Adopted effective October 1, 1989.]

1989 Staff Comment

MCR 6.416 is a new rule. It is consistent with a 1986 legislative amendment abrogating the prosecutor's duty to endorse and produce res gestae witnesses. See 1986 PA 46, MCL 767.40; MSA 28.980. Although this rule gives each party the right to decide what witnesses and evidence to present, that right is made subject to the requirements of the rules of criminal procedure and the Michigan Rules of Evidence.

RULE 6.419　MOTION FOR DIRECTED VERDICT OF ACQUITTAL

(A) Before Submission to Jury. After the prosecutor has rested the prosecution's case in chief and before the defendant presents proofs, the court on its own initiative may, or on the defendant's motion must, direct a verdict of acquittal on any charged offense as to which the evidence is insufficient to support conviction. The court may not reserve decision on the defendant's motion. If the defendant's motion is made after the defendant presents proofs, the court may reserve decision on the motion, submit the case to the jury, and decide the motion before or after the jury has completed its deliberations.

(B) After Jury Verdict. After a jury verdict, the defendant may file an original or renewed motion for directed verdict of acquittal in the same manner as provided by MCR 6.431(A) for filing a motion for a new trial.

(C) Conditional New Trial Ruling. If the court grants a directed verdict of acquittal after the jury has returned a guilty verdict, it must also conditionally rule on any motion for a new trial by determining whether it would grant the motion if the directed verdict of acquittal is vacated or reversed.

(D) Explanation of Rulings on Record. The court must state orally on the record or in a written ruling made a part of the record its reasons for granting or denying a motion for a directed verdict of acquittal and for conditionally granting or denying a motion for a new trial.

[Adopted effective October 1, 1989.]

1989 Staff Comment

MCR 6.419 is a new rule.

Subrule (A) is based on 3 ABA Standards for Criminal Justice (2d ed), Standard 15–3.5(b) and is consistent with existing practice except for the provision prohibiting the court from reserving decision on a defense motion for directed verdict made at the close of the prosecution's proofs. This rule does not state the standard of proof that the court must apply in determining the sufficiency of the evidence. The standard is constitutional and it is therefore left to case law. See *People v Hampton*, 407 Mich. 354 (1979).

Subrule (B) pertains to motions for directed verdict of acquittal made after the jury verdict. It incorporates by reference the same postconviction procedures that a defendant may use to move for a new trial. This rule does not impose any time limits on a motion for directed verdict of acquittal in the event that the jury does not reach a verdict and is discharged.

Subrule (C) is derived from MCR 2.610(C), which requires the court to rule conditionally on any motion for new trial in the event that it grants a motion for judgment notwithstanding the verdict.

Subrule (D) is derived from the provisions in MCR 2.610(B)(3) and (C)(1) requiring the court to place on the record the reasons for its rulings.

RULE 6.420   VERDICT

(A) Return. The jury must return its verdict in open court.

(B) Several Defendants. If two or more defendants are jointly on trial, the jury at any time during its deliberations may return a verdict with respect to any defendant as to whom it has agreed. If the jury cannot reach a verdict with respect to any other defendant, the court may declare a mistrial as to that defendant.

(C) Poll of Jury. Before the jury is discharged, the court on its own initiative may, or on the motion of a party must, have each juror polled in open court as to whether the verdict announced is that juror's verdict. If polling discloses the jurors are not in agreement, the court may (1) discontinue the poll and order the jury to retire for further deliberations, or (2) either (a) with the defendant's consent, or (b) after determining that the jury is deadlocked or that some other manifest necessity exists, declare a mistrial and discharge the jury.

[Adopted effective October 1, 1989.]

1989 Staff Comment

MCR 6.420 is a new rule.

Subrules (A) and (B) are consistent with existing practice and are based on Federal Rules of Criminal Procedure 31(a) and (b).

Subrule (C) is consistent with the jury polling procedure set forth in MCR 2.512, but is modified to address constitutional concerns applicable in criminal jury trials. See *People v Hall*, 396 Mich 650, 654–655 (1976).

The option in subrule (C) permitting the court to "discontinue the poll and order the jury to retire for further deliberations" requires the court to cut off the polling as soon as disagreement is disclosed. The court should not allow the polling to continue because of its potentially coercive effect. Nor, for the same reason, should the court question the jury to determine where the jury stands numerically. See *People v Wilson*, 390 Mich 689 (1973).

RULE 6.425   SENTENCING; APPOINTMENT OF APPELLATE COUNSEL

(A) Presentence Report; Contents. Prior to sentencing, the probation officer must investigate the defendant's background and character, verify material information, and report in writing the results of the investigation to the court. The report must be succinct and, depending on the circumstances, include:

(1) a description of the defendant's prior criminal convictions and juvenile adjudications,

(2) a complete description of the offense and the circumstances surrounding it,

(3) a brief description of the defendant's vocational background and work history, including military record and present employment status,

(4) a brief social history of the defendant, including marital status, financial status, length of residence in the community, educational background, and other pertinent data,

(5) the defendant's medical history, substance abuse history, if any, and, if indicated, a current psychological or psychiatric report,

(6) information concerning the financial, social, psychological, or physical harm suffered by any victim of the offense, including the restitution needs of the victim,

(7) if provided and requested by the victim, a written victim's impact statement as provided by law,

(8) any statement the defendant wishes to make,

(9) a statement prepared by the prosecutor on the applicability of any consecutive sentencing provision,

(10) an evaluation of and prognosis for the defendant's adjustment in the community based on factual information in the report,

(11) a specific recommendation for disposition, and

(12) any other information that may aid the court in sentencing.

Regardless of the sentence imposed, the court must have a copy of the presentence report and of any psychiatric report sent to the Department of Corrections. If the defendant is sentenced to prison, the copies must be sent with the commitment papers.

(B) Presentence Report; Disclosure Before Sentencing. The court must permit the prosecutor, the defendant's lawyer, and the defendant to review the presentence report at a reasonable time before the day of sentencing. The court may exempt from disclosure information or diagnostic opinion that might seriously disrupt a program of rehabilitation and sources of information that have been obtained on a promise of confidentiality. When part of the report is not disclosed, the court must inform the parties that information has not been disclosed and state on the record the reasons for nondisclosure. To the extent it can do so without defeating the purpose of nondisclosure, the court also must provide the parties with a written or oral summary of the nondisclosed information and give them an opportunity to comment on it. The court must have the information exempted from disclosure specifically noted in the report. The court's decision to exempt part of the report from disclosure is subject to appellate review.

(C) Presentence Report; Disclosure After Sentencing. After sentencing, the court, on written request, must provide the prosecutor, the defendant's lawyer, or the defendant not represented by a lawyer, with a copy of the presentence report and any attachments to it. The court must exempt from disclosure any information the sentencing court exempted from disclosure pursuant to subrule (B).

(D) Imposition of Sentence.

(1) *Sentencing Guidelines.* The court must use the sentencing guidelines, as provided by law. Not later than the date of sentencing, the court must complete a sentencing information report on a form to be prescribed by and returned to the state court administrator.

(2) *Sentencing Procedure.* The court must sentence the defendant within a reasonably prompt time after the plea or verdict unless the court delays sentencing as provided by law. At sentencing the court, complying on the record, must:

(a) determine that the defendant, the defendant's lawyer, and the prosecutor have had an opportunity to read and discuss the presentence report,

(b) give each party an opportunity to explain, or challenge the accuracy or relevancy of, any information in the presentence report, and resolve any challenges in accordance with the procedure set forth in subrule (D)(3),

(c) give the defendant, the defendant's lawyer, the prosecutor, and the victim an opportunity to advise the court of any circumstances they believe the court should consider in imposing sentence,

(d) state the sentence being imposed, including the minimum and maximum sentence if applicable, together with any credit for time served to which the defendant is entitled,

(e) articulate its reasons for imposing the sentence given, and

(f) if a victim of the crime has suffered harm and the court does not order restitution as provided by law or orders only partial restitution, state the reasons for its action.

(3) *Resolution of Challenges.* If any information in the presentence report is challenged, the court must make a finding with respect to the challenge or determine that a finding is unnecessary because it will not take the challenged information into account in sentencing. If the court finds merit in the challenge or determines that it will not take the challenged information into account in sentencing, it must direct the probation officer to

(a) correct or delete the challenged information in the report, whichever is appropriate, and

(b) provide defendant's lawyer with an opportunity to review the corrected report before it is sent to the Department of Corrections.

(E) Advice Concerning the Right to Appeal; Appointment of Counsel.

(1) In a case involving a conviction following a trial, immediately after imposing sentence, the court must advise the defendant, on the record, that

(a) the defendant is entitled to appellate review of the conviction and sentence,

(b) if the defendant is financially unable to retain a lawyer, the court will appoint a lawyer to represent the defendant on appeal, and

(c) the request for a lawyer must be made within 42 days after sentencing.

(2) In a case involving a conviction following a plea of guilty or nolo contendere, immediately after imposing sentence, the court must advise the defendant, on the record, that

(a) the defendant is entitled to file an application for leave to appeal;

(b) if the defendant is financially unable to retain a lawyer, the court must appoint a lawyer to represent the defendant on appeal if

(i) the defendant's sentence exceeds the upper limit of the minimum sentence range of the applicable sentencing guidelines,

(ii) the defendant seeks leave to appeal a conditional plea under MCR 6.301(C)(2),

(iii) the prosecuting attorney seeks leave to appeal, or

(iv) the Court of Appeals or the Supreme Court grants the defendant's application for leave to appeal;

(c) if the defendant is financially unable to retain a lawyer, the court, in its discretion, may appoint a lawyer to represent the defendant on appeal if all the following apply:

[i] the defendant seeks leave to appeal on the basis of an alleged improper scoring of an offense variable or a prior record variable,

[ii] the defendant objected to the scoring or otherwise preserved the matter for appeal, and

[iii] the sentence constitutes an upward departure from the upper limit of the minimum sentence range that the defendant alleges should have been scored; and

(d) the request for a lawyer must be made within 42 days after sentencing, unless the entitlement to counsel arises under (b)(iii) or (iv).

With regard to paragraphs (b) and (c), the court is required to give only the advice that is applicable to the particular circumstances.

Upon sentencing, the court shall give the defendant a form developed by the State Court Administrative Office that the defendant may complete and file as an application for leave to appeal.

(3) The court also must give the defendant a request for counsel form containing an instruction informing the defendant that the form must be completed and returned to the court within 42 days after sentencing if the defendant wants the court to appoint a lawyer. The 42–day time limit does not apply if the entitlement to counsel arises under subrule (2)(b)(iii) or (iv).

(4) When imposing sentence in a case in which sentencing guidelines enacted in 1998 PA 317, MCL 777.1 *et seq.*; MSA 28.1274(11), *et seq.*, are applicable, if the court imposes a minimum sentence that is longer or more severe than the range provided by the sentencing guidelines, the court must advise the defendant on the record and in writing that the defendant may seek appellate review of the sentence, by right if the conviction followed trial or by application if the conviction entered by plea, on the ground that it is longer or more severe than the range provided by the sentencing guidelines.

(F) Appointment of Lawyer; Trial Court Responsibilities in Connection with Appeal.

(1) *Appointment of Lawyer.*

(a) Unless there is a postjudgment motion pending, the court must rule on a defendant's request for a lawyer within 14 days after receiving it. If there is a postjudgment motion pending, the court must rule on the request after the court's disposition of the pending motion and within 14 days after that disposition.

(b) In a case involving a conviction following a trial, if the defendant is indigent, the court must enter an order appointing a lawyer if the request is filed within 42 days after sentencing or within the time for filing an appeal of right. The court should liberally grant an untimely request as long as the defendant may file an application for leave to appeal.

(c) Scope of Appellate Lawyer's Responsibilities. The responsibilities of the appellate lawyer appointed to represent the defendant include representing the defendant

(i) in available postconviction proceedings in the trial court the lawyer deems appropriate,

(ii) in postconviction proceedings in the Court of Appeals,

(iii) in available proceedings in the trial court the lawyer deems appropriate under MCR 7.208(B) or 7.211(C)(1), and

(iv) as appellee in relation to any postconviction appeal taken by the prosecutor.

(2) *Order to Prepare Transcript.* The appointment order also must

(a) direct the court reporter to prepare and file, within the time limits specified in MCR 7.210,

(i) the trial or plea proceeding transcript,

(ii) the sentencing transcript, and

(iii) such transcripts of other proceedings, not previously transcribed, that the court directs or the parties request, and

(b) provide for the payment of the reporter's fees.

The court must promptly serve a copy of the order on the prosecutor, the defendant, the appointed lawyer, the court reporter, and the Michigan Appellate Assigned Counsel System.

(3) *Order as Claim of Appeal; Trial Cases.* In a case involving a conviction following a trial, if the defendant's request for a lawyer, timely or not, was made within the time for filing a claim of appeal, the order described in (F)(1) and (2) must be entered on a form approved by the State Court Administrator's Office, entitled "Claim of Appeal and Appointment of Counsel," and the court must immediately send to the Court of Appeals a copy of the order and a copy of the judgment being appealed. The court also must file in the Court of Appeals proof of having made service of the order as required in subrule (F)(2). Entry of the order by the trial court pursuant to this subrule constitutes a timely filed claim of appeal for the purposes of MCR 7.204.

[Adopted effective October 1, 1989; amended effective July 1, 1994; amended December 30, 1994, applicable to all crimes committed on or after December 27, 1994 as provided by 1994 PA 374 and 1994 PA 375, effective until further order of the Court after consideration of comments and legislative action, if any, or until April 1, 1995; by Order of March 31, 1995, December 30, 1994 amendment ordered to remain in effect until June 30, 1995; by Order of June 19, 1995, December 30, 1994 amendment ordered to remain in effect until October 15, 1995; by Order of October 13, 1995, December 30, 1994 amendment ordered to remain in effect until August 15, 1996; by Order of July 16, 1996, December 30, 1994 amendment ordered to remain in effect until September 1, 1997; by Order of July 25, 1997, December 30, 1994 amendment ordered to remain in effect until further order of the Court; amended effective May 6, 1998; January 1, 1999; April 1, 2000.]

1989 Staff Comment

MCR 6.425 is a new rule but incorporates elements of former 6.101.

Subrule (A) is based on MCL 771.14; MSA 28.1144 which sets forth the duties of a probation officer in relation to preparation of presentence reports and prescribes the contents of such reports. This subrule expands the content requirements by including information relevant to sentencing traditionally included in presentence reports. The content of the victim's impact statement described in subrule (A)(7) is set forth in MCL 780.763; MSA 28.1287(763). The last paragraph of the subrule implements the statutory requirement set forth in MCL 771.14(7); MSA 28.1144(7).

Subrule (B) is a stylistically revised version of former 6.101(K) except for three substantive modifications. The provision in the former rule requiring the court to give the parties an opportunity to review the presentence report "prior to sentencing" has been modified in this subrule to require the review opportunity to be given "at a reasonable time before the day of sentencing." This rule also modifies the portion of the rule setting forth the procedure for withholding disclosure of confidential or sensitive information in the presentence report. The rule adds the requirements that (1) "[t]o the extent it can do so without defeating the purpose of nondisclosure, the court also must provide the parties with a written or oral summary of the nondisclosed information and give them an opportunity to comment on it," and (2) the "court must have the information exempted from disclosure specifically noted in the report." The procedure requiring, if feasible, the summarizing of nondisclosed information is new. The procedure of specifically noting in the report information withheld from disclosure is not new, but rather, reflects the statutory requirement set forth in MCL 771.14(3); MSA 28.1144(3).

Subrule (C) is based on, but substantially modifies the procedure set forth in former 6.101(K) for furnishing, after sentencing, a copy of the presentence report to the parties. The former rule required the court to furnish a copy of the report to the parties "[o]n the filing of the defendant's first claim of appeal or application for leave to appeal." Subrule (C) deletes the precondition that a claim of appeal or application be filed and replaces it with the simple requirement of a written request made "after sentencing." A party's right to obtain a copy of the presentence report should not be conditioned on the existence of an appeal since a common objective of obtaining a copy of the report is to determine whether it discloses a ground for appeal. For the same reason, language in the former rule requiring provision of a copy of the report to "the defendant if proceeding without an attorney" has been replaced with "the defendant not represented by a lawyer." This latter language describes an unrepresented defendant who has not yet filed any sort of appeal. A defendant who has filed an appeal and is proceeding in propria persona falls within the definition of "defendant's lawyer." See 6.003(2).

Subrule (D)(1) is new. It incorporates the requirements and procedure for use of the Sentencing Guidelines set forth in Supreme Court administrative orders. The reference to "applicable Sentencing Guidelines" reflects that the guidelines have gone through revisions and that the duty to apply refers to the guidelines version applicable at the time the defendant was sentenced. The language describing the procedure that must be followed is taken verbatim from Administrative Order No. 1988–4.

Subrule (D)(2), setting forth the sentencing procedure, is a substantially modified version of former 6.101(G). It contains a new provision requiring the court to sentence the defendant "within a reasonably prompt time after the plea or verdict unless the court delays sentencing as provided by law." Reasonably prompt sentencing is consistent with existing practice and its inclusion in the rule does not indicate a change in procedure. This provision also takes into account, however, that statutory provisions may authorize the court to delay sentencing. See, for example, MCL 771.1; MSA 28.1131 authorizing in certain cases the court to delay sentencing for a period of up to one year.

Subrule (D)(2)(a) is new but is consistent with current practice and implements the requirement in subrule (B) for the parties to be given an opportunity to review the presentence report before sentencing.

Subrule (D)(2)(b) is new to this rule, but incorporates the requirement in former 6.101(K) for the parties to "be given an opportunity at the time of sentencing to explain or controvert any factual representations in the presentence report."

Subrules (D)(2)(c) and (d) are stylistically revised versions of former 6.101(G)(2) and (3).

Subrule (D)(2)(e) is new and incorporates the articulation requirement adopted in *People* v *Coles*, 417 Mich 523, 549 (1983).

Subrule (D)(2)(f) is new and implements a requirement in the Crime Victim's Rights Act. MCL 780.766; MSA 28.1287(766). See also Const 1963, art 1, § 24.

The provision found in former 6.101(G) declaring that a failure to comply with the provisions of that subrule "shall require resentencing" has been deleted from this subrule. Whether failure to comply with a provision in this subrule will entitle a defendant to resentencing depends on the nature of the noncompliance and must be determined by reference to past case law or on an individual case basis.

Subrule (D)(3) is new but sets forth a procedure consistent with the requirements of MCL 771.14(5); MSA 28.1144(5) and the procedure prescribed in *People* v *Fleming*, 428 Mich 408, 418 (1987). The procedural requirements of the rule, however, are expanded to require that when, as a result of a challenge, information in the presentence report is deleted or corrected, the defendant's lawyer must be given "an opportunity to review the corrected report before it is sent to the Department of Corrections."

Subrule (E), concerning appellate rights advice at sentencing, is a modified version of former 6.101(J)(1).

Subrule (E)(1) requires the court to advise the defendant of the right to appellate review of both the "conviction and sentence." The advice in the former rule referred to the right to appellate review of the "conviction," but made no mention of the sentence.

Subrule (E)(2) deletes the advice required by the former rule relating to furnishing the appointed lawyer with portions of the transcript and record required to perfect an appeal. There is no need for reference to this right in light of the provisions in these rules fully setting forth the defendant's rights to transcript and record.

Subrule (E)(3) requires the defendant to be advised that the request for an appellate lawyer must be made within 42 days of sentencing. The former rule provided that the request must be made within 56 days.

The last paragraph of subrule (E) is a stylistically revised version of the provision in the former rule requiring the defendant to be provided with a request for counsel form containing pertinent instructions. This provision implements MCL 771.14(7); MSA 28.1144(7).

Subrule (F) is new but incorporates elements of former 6.101(J)(2).

Subrule (F)(1)(a) sets forth a new requirement for the court to rule on a defendant's request for appellate lawyer "within 14 days after receiving it," unless there is a post-judgment motion pending, in which event the ruling must be made after, but within 14 days of, the disposition of the motion. This provision avoids delay in the appointment of an appellate lawyer, but also avoids dual representation and appointment of an appellate lawyer that may not be necessary if the court grants the defendant relief pursuant to a pending postconviction motion.

Subrule (F)(1)(b) is new but is consistent with general practice. The policy view underlying this provision is that every defendant should have one appeal, either by right or by leave, and it should be with legal representation, particularly in cases that may have arguable appellate issues or involve conviction of a serious offense. In certain cases, the filing of a postjudgment motion will result in the time for requesting appellate counsel [42 days after entry of judgment, see MCR 6.425(E)] expiring while the defendant still has the right to file a claim of appeal [42 days after decision on the motion, MCR 7.204(A)(2)(3)]. In that situation, the court must appoint counsel (assuming the defendant is indigent) if the request is filed while an appeal of right is available.

Subrule (F)(1)(c) is a substantially revised version of former 6.101(J)(2)(a). The rule parallels the like rule pertaining to the "responsibilities" of an appointed trial lawyer, 6.005(H). This subrule reflects the various types of postconviction proceedings available under the scheme of the rules. Subrule (F)(1)(c)(i) refers to "available postconviction proceedings in the trial court" because such proceedings are not available to an appointed appellate lawyer if the appointment order acted as a claim of appeal. See subrule (F)(3). In that event the lawyer may only use the procedures set forth in 7.208(B) or 7.211(C)(1). See, for example, 6.429(B)(2). A lawyer appointed after the claim of appeal period has expired, however, may file a postconviction motion in the trial court before filing an application for leave to appeal. See, for example, 6.429(B)(3). Likewise, a lawyer appointed without a claim of appeal having been filed may not proceed under 7.208(B). Accordingly, subrule (iii) also includes the modifier "available."

Regardless of whether the appointment order acted as a claim of appeal, the appointed lawyer is responsible for representing a defendant in postconviction proceedings in the Court of Appeals (ii) and as appellee in relation to any postconviction appeal taken by the prosecutor (iv). This latter provision reflects the legislatively enlarged right of the prosecutor to appeal by right, and the corresponding responsibility of the appointed appellate lawyer to respond to any appeals, including applications to the Supreme Court, taken by the prosecutor.

Subrules (i) and (iii) recognize that the decision to proceed in the trial court prior to an appeal is within the lawyer's discretion ("the lawyer deems appropriate").

Subrule (F)(2) is a substantially revised version of former 6.101(J)(2) and (3). The appointment order, regardless of whether it also acts as a claim of appeal pursuant to subrule (F)(3), must include directions to the court reporter to prepare and file the trial or plea transcript, the sentencing transcript and whatever other transcripts of recorded proceedings, not previously transcribed, that the court or parties request. The former rule merely provided for the order to authorize the reporter to prepare transcripts requested by the attorney. This new provision will substantially accelerate the preparation of necessary transcripts.

The appointment order must also provide for payment of the reporter's fees. A copy of the order must be served "promptly" on the parties, the court reporter, and the Michigan Appellate Assigned Counsel System. This rule applies only to an order appointing a lawyer to represent a defendant on an appeal of right or by leave.

Subrule (F)(3) is a new rule. It is designed to substantially accelerate the commencement of appeals by having the appointment order also act as a claim of appeal in cases in which the defendant's request for a lawyer was timely, or, if not timely, was made within the time for filing a timely claim of appeal. The subrule further provides that the State Court Administrator's Office is to approve a form for use by the trial courts that will act as a combination order of appointment and claim of appeal. The completed form and a copy of the judgment being appealed from must be sent "immediately" to the Court of Appeals. Copies of the order must also be served as provided in subrule (F)(2) and a proof of such service filed in the Court of Appeals. The last sentence of this rule clarifies that entry of the order by the trial court pursuant to this subrule constitutes the filing of a claim of appeal for jurisdictional purposes under MCR 7.204. The defense need not file anything further in the Court of Appeals to perfect the filing of the claim. Any defects in the filings in the Court of Appeals required by this subrule must be corrected by the trial court but do not affect the validity of the claim of appeal, effectively filed on entry of the appointment order.

Staff Comment to July 1994 Amendment

The May 2, 1994 amendment of subrule (F)(2)(a)(i), effective July 1, 1994, was based on a proposal from the Michigan Judges Association. The amendment specifies that the court reporter shall not be directed to transcribe the jury voir dire unless certain conditions are met.

Staff Comment to December 1994 Amendment

The December 30, 1994 amendments of MCR 6.301, 6.302, 6.311, 6.425, 7.203, 7.204 and 7.205 modified procedure regarding appeals in criminal cases in light of the amendment of Const 1963, art 1, § 20 at the November 1994 general election and the legislation implementing the constitutional amendment. Changes will remain in effect until April 1, 1995 and will be reconsidered by the Court in light of comments received and any further legislation.

Staff Comment to May 1998 Amendment

The May 6, 1998, amendment [effective May 6, 1998] of subrule F(2)(a)(i) removed the limitations on transcription of the jury voir dire that took effect July 1, 1994.

Staff Comment to September 1998 Amendment

MCR 6.425(D)(1) was amended in 1998 [effective January 1, 1999] in response to the enactment of the sentencing guidelines. 1998 PA 317, MCL ___ et seq.; MSA ___ et seq.

Staff Comment to December 1998 Amendment

MCR 6.425(E)(4) was added in 1998 [effective January 1, 1999] in response to the enactment of the sentencing guidelines. See MCL 769.34(7); MSA 28.1097(3.4)(7), as amended by 1998 PA 317.

Staff Comment to 2000 Amendment

The March 28, 2000 amendment of Rules 6.302, 6.425, and 6.615, and the adoption of new Rule 6.625, were made in light of 1999 PA 200, MCL 770.3a; MSA 28.1100a, and were effective as to pleas taken on or after April 1, 2000.

RULE 6.427   JUDGMENT

Within 7 days after sentencing, the court must date and sign a written judgment of sentence that includes:

(1) the title and file number of the case;

(2) the defendant's name;

(3) the crime for which the defendant was convicted;

(4) the defendant's plea;

(5) the name of the defendant's attorney if one appeared;

(6) the jury's verdict or the finding of guilt by the court;

(7) the term of the sentence;

(8) the place of detention;

(9) the conditions incident to the sentence; and

(10) whether the conviction is reportable to the Secretary of State pursuant to MCL 257.732; MSA 9.2432 and, if so, the defendant's Michigan driver's license number.

If the defendant was found not guilty or for any other reason is entitled to be discharged, the court must enter judgment accordingly. The date a judgment is signed is its entry date.

[Adopted effective October 1, 1989.]

1989 Staff Comment

MCR 6.427 restates the former judgment rule, 6.103, and adds two provisions. Subrule (10) is added to accommodate the recording and reporting requirements set forth in MCL 257.732; MSA 9.2432. The second addition is the penultimate sentence in the rule, which reflects that entry of judgment is also required in the event that the defendant is entitled to discharge.

RULE 6.429   CORRECTION AND APPEAL OF SENTENCE

(A) Authority to Modify Sentence. The court may correct an invalid sentence, but the court may not modify a valid sentence after it has been imposed except as provided by law.

(B) Time for Filing Motion.

(1) A motion for resentencing may be filed within 42 days after entry of the judgment.

(2) If a claim of appeal has been filed, a motion for resentencing may only be filed in accordance with the procedure set forth in MCR 7.208(B) or the remand procedure set forth in MCR 7.211(C)(1).

(3) If the defendant fails to file a timely claim of appeal, the defendant may file a motion for resentencing within the time for filing an application for leave to appeal.

(4) If the defendant is no longer entitled to appeal by right or by leave, the defendant may seek relief pursuant to the procedure set forth in subchapter 6.500.

(C) Preservation of Issues Concerning Presentence Report and Sentencing Guidelines. A party may not raise on appeal an issue challenging the accuracy of the presentence report or the scoring of the sentencing guidelines unless the party has raised the issue at or before sentencing or demonstrates that the challenge was brought as soon as the inaccuracy could reasonably have been discovered. Any other challenge may be brought only by motion for relief from judgment under subchapter 6.500.

[Adopted effective October 1, 1989; amended effective April 1, 1996.]

1989 Staff Comment

MCR 6.429 is a new rule.

Subrule (A) states the settled principle in this jurisdiction that the trial court may not modify a valid sentence after it has been imposed. See *People* v *Barfield*, 411 Mich 700 (1981). The Legislature, however, has authorized trial courts to modify some types of sentences. See, for example, MCL 801.257; MSA 28.1747(7) authorizing trial courts to reduce the sentence of jail inmates by one-quarter for good conduct.

Although the trial court may not modify a valid sentence, it may correct an invalid sentence after it has been imposed. See *People* v *Whalen*, 412 Mich 166 (1981). Invalid sentence refers to any error or defect in the sentence or sentencing procedure that entitles a defendant to be resentenced or to have the sentence changed.

Subrule (B) sets the times within which a motion for resentencing may be filed.

Subrule (B)(1) sets the basic time at 42 days after the entry of the judgment. Such a timely motion extends the time for filing a claim of appeal. See MCR 7.204(A)(2)(d). The remaining subrules follow the filing of later motions that do not have the effect of extending the time for taking an appeal of right.

Under subrule (B)(2), if a claim of appeal has been filed, typically as a result of the appointment of appellate counsel [see MCR 6.425(F)(3)], the motion must be made in the manner provided in MCR 7.208(B) or by seeking an order of the Court of Appeals remanding the case to the trial court under MCR 7.211(C)(1).

Subrule (B)(3) provides that if a defendant fails to file a timely claim of appeal, the motion for resentencing may be filed at any time before expiration of the time for filing an application for leave to appeal.

Finally, under subrule (B)(4), a defendant who is not entitled to appeal by right or by leave, either because the defendant has had an appeal or because the 18–month time limit has expired [see MCR 7.205(F)(3)], may only seek relief under the procedure provided by Subchapter 6.500.

The rules governing motions for judgment of acquittal [MCR 6.419(B)], to withdraw a plea [MCR 6.311(A)], and for new trial [MCR 6.431(A)], have similar time limits.

Subrule (C) incorporates the issue preservation requirement adopted in *People* v *Walker*, 428 Mich 261, 266 (1987), for challenges to Sentencing Guidelines scoring. The rule provides that a defendant who wishes to challenge the scoring of Sentencing Guidelines must make the challenge in the trial court before raising it on the defendant's initial appeal, whether that appeal is by right or by leave. The rule further sets forth the various methods by which the defendant may raise the issue in the trial court.

Staff Comment to 1996 Amendment

The amendment of MCR 6.429(C) modifies the rule governing preservation of issues regarding sentence guideline scoring and presentence report information. Such challenges must be made at or before sentencing unless the party demonstrates that the challenge was brought as soon as the inaccuracy could reasonably have been discovered.

RULE 6.431   NEW TRIAL

(A) Time for Making Motion.

(1) A motion for a new trial may be filed within 42 days after entry of the judgment.

(2) If a claim of appeal has been filed, a motion for a new trial may only be filed in accordance with the procedure set forth in MCR 7.208(B) or the remand procedure set forth in MCR 7.211(C)(1).

(3) If the defendant fails to file a timely claim of appeal, the defendant may file a motion for a new trial within the time for filing an application for leave to appeal.

(4) If the defendant is no longer entitled to appeal by right or by leave, the defendant may seek relief pursuant to the procedure set forth in subchapter 6.500.

(B) Reasons for Granting. On the defendant's motion, the court may order a new trial on any ground that would support appellate reversal of the conviction or because it believes that the verdict has resulted in a miscarriage of justice. The court must state its reasons for granting or denying a new trial orally on the record or in a written ruling made a part of the record.

(C) Trial Without Jury. If the court tried the case without a jury, it may, on granting a new trial and with the defendant's consent, vacate any judgment it has entered, take additional testimony, amend its findings of fact and conclusions of law, and order the entry of a new judgment.

(D) Inclusion of Motion for Judgment of Acquittal. The court must consider a motion for a new trial challenging the weight or sufficiency of the evidence as including a motion for a directed verdict of acquittal.

[Adopted effective October 1, 1989.]

1989 Staff Comment

MCR 6.431 is a new rule.

Subrule (A) sets the time limits within which a motion for new trial may be filed.

Subrule (A)(1) sets the basic time at 42 days after the entry of judgment. Such a timely motion extends the time for filing the claim of appeal. See MCR 7.204(A)(2)(d). The remaining subrules follow the filing of later motions that do not have the effect of extending the time for taking an appeal of right.

Under subrule (A)(2), if a claim of appeal has been filed, typically as a result of the appointment of appellate counsel [see MCR 6.425(F)(3)], the motion must be made in the manner provided in MCR 7.208(B) or by seeking an order of the Court of Appeals remanding the case to the trial court under MCR 7.211(C)(1).

Subrule (A)(3) provides that if a defendant fails to file a timely claim of appeal, the motion to withdraw the plea may be filed at any time before expiration of the time for filing an application for leave to appeal.

Finally, under subrule (A)(4), a defendant who is not entitled to appeal by right or by leave, either because the defendant has had an appeal or because the 18–month time limit has expired [see MCR 7.205(F)(3)], may only seek relief under the procedure provided by Subchapter 6.500.

The rules governing motions for judgment of acquittal [MCR 6.419(B)], to withdraw a plea [MCR 6.311(A)], and for resentencing [MCR 6.429(B)], have similar time limits.

Subrule (B) substantially modifies the statutory standards for granting a new trial set forth in MCL 770.1; MSA 28.1098 and applied by the courts. See *People* v *Hampton*, 407 Mich 354, 372–373 (1979). The statute provides that the trial court may grant a new trial (1) "for any cause for which by law a new trial may be granted," or (2) "when it appears to the court that justice has not been done." Although the court rule repeats in stylistically revised language the first standard, it substitutes a new second standard: "Because [the trial court] believes the verdict has resulted in a miscarriage of justice." What substantive difference, if any, exists between the new standard and the former standard is left to be addressed by case law.

Subrule (C) incorporates the provisions in MCR 2.611(A)(2) and adds a condition found in the Uniform Rules of Criminal Procedure, Rule 552(a), requiring "the defendant's consent."

Subrule (D) is derived from MCR 2.610(A)(3), which requires a motion for new trial to be "deemed to include a motion for judgment notwithstanding the verdict as an alternative." Subrule (D), however, limits its own applicability to a motion for new trial "challenging the weight or sufficiency of the evidence." When making findings pursuant to this rule the trial court should clearly distinguish on the record and in its order its disposition of the two motions. See 6.419(D).

RULE 6.433　DOCUMENTS FOR POST-CONVICTION PROCEEDINGS; INDIGENT DEFENDANT

(A) Appeals of Right. An indigent defendant may file a written request with the sentencing court for specified court documents or transcripts, indicating that they are required to pursue an appeal of right. The court must order the clerk to provide the defendant with copies of documents without cost to the defendant, and, unless the transcript has already been ordered as provided in MCR 6.425(F)(2), must order the preparation of the transcript.

(B) Appeals by Leave. An indigent defendant who may file an application for leave to appeal may obtain copies of transcripts and other documents as provided in this subrule.

(1) The defendant must make a written request to the sentencing court for specified documents or transcripts indicating that they are required to prepare an application for leave to appeal.

(2) If the requested materials have been filed with the court and not provided previously to the defendant, the court clerk must provide a copy to the defendant. If the requested materials have been provided previously to the defendant, on defendant's showing of good cause to the court, the clerk must provide the defendant with another copy.

(3) If the request includes the transcript of a proceeding that has not been transcribed, the court must order the materials transcribed and filed with court. After the transcript has been prepared, court clerk must provide a copy to the defendant.

(C) Other Postconviction Proceedings. An indigent defendant who is not eligible to file an appeal of right or an application for leave to appeal may obtain records and documents as provided in this subrule.

(1) The defendant must make a written request to the sentencing court for specific court documents or transcripts indicating that the materials are required to pursue postconviction remedies in a state or federal court and are not otherwise available to the defendant.

(2) If the documents or transcripts have been filed with the court, the clerk must provide the defendant with copies of such materials without cost to the defendant.

(3) The court may order the transcription of additional proceedings if it finds that there is good cause for doing so. After such a transcript has been prepared, the clerk must provide a copy to the defendant.

(4) Nothing in this rule precludes the court from ordering materials to be supplied to the defendant in a proceeding under subchapter 6.500.

[Adopted effective October 1, 1989; amended effective July 1, 1994; May 6, 1998.]

1989 Staff Comment

MCR 6.433 covers the subject of providing copies of court documents and transcripts to indigent defendants for use on appeal or in other postconviction proceedings. It covers the subject in more detail than the corresponding provision of the former rule, MCR 6.101(L). The new rule is structured around the various types of postconviction procedures available.

Subrule (A) deals with the provision of documents for use in appeals of right. At this stage, the defendant has the broadest right of access to free copies of documents and transcripts.

Subrule (B) deals with a defendant who is eligible to file an application for leave to appeal—i.e., a defendant who has not previously appealed of right or sought leave to appeal and as to whom the 18–month time limit on applications has not expired. See MCR 7.205(F)(3). Such a defendant is entitled to copies of materials that have not been previously furnished to the defendant. As to materials that have been previously furnished, the defendant must show good cause to be entitled to a new copy. If proceedings have not been transcribed, the court is to order preparation of the transcript.

Subrule (C) deals with defendants who are not eligible to appeal by right or to apply for leave to appeal. Such defendants have more restricted rights to documents. There is a threshold requirement that the documents are not otherwise available to the defendant. If that standard is met, documents or transcripts that had been filed with the court are to be supplied to the defendant. The court has discretion as to whether to order transcription of additional proceedings on a finding of good cause.

Staff Comment to 1994 Amendment

The May 2, 1994 amendment, which added subrule (D), effective July 1, 1994, was based on a proposal from the Michigan Judges Association. The amendment specifies that the court shall not order the transcript of the jury voir dire unless certain conditions are met.

Staff Comment to 1998 Amendment

The May 6, 1998, deletion subrule D removed the limitations on transcription of the jury voir dire that took effect July 1, 1994.

RULE 6.435　CORRECTING MISTAKES

(A) Clerical Mistakes. Clerical mistakes in judgments, orders, or other parts of the record and errors arising from oversight or omission may be corrected by the court at any time on its own initiative or on motion of a party, and after notice if the court orders it.

(B) Substantive Mistakes. After giving the parties an opportunity to be heard, and provided it has not yet entered judgment in the case, the court may reconsider and modify, correct, or rescind any order it concludes was erroneous.

(C) Correction of Record. If a dispute arises as to whether the record accurately reflects what occurred in the trial court, the court, after giving the parties the opportunity to be heard, must resolve the dispute and, if necessary, order the record to be corrected.

(D) Correction During Appeal. If a claim of appeal has been filed or leave to appeal granted in the case, corrections under this rule are subject to MCR 7.208(A) and (B).

[Adopted effective October 1, 1989.]

1989 Staff Comment

MCR 6.435 is a new rule that combines former court rule provisions with a new provision.

Subrule (A) repeats verbatim the civil clerical mistakes rule, MCR 2.612(A)(1). Under this rule the court may correct an inadvertent error or omission in the record, or in an order or judgment. The correction can be made by the court at any time subject to the limitation in subrule (D) pertaining to cases on appeal. The court, in its discretion, may give the parties prior notice.

Subrule (B) is new and pertains to mistakes relating not to the accuracy of the record, but rather, to the correctness of the conclusions and decisions reflected in the record. Substantive mistake refers to a conclusion or decision that is erroneous because it was based on a mistaken belief in the facts or the applicable law. Unlike clerical mistakes under subrule (A), the court's ability to correct substantive mistakes pursuant to subrule (B) ends with the entry of the judgment. See 6.427. This limitation does not, however, prohibit a party aggrieved by a substantive mistake from obtaining relief by using available postconviction procedures.

The following examples illustrate the distinction between the two foregoing provisions. A prison sentence entered on a judgment that is erroneous because the judge misspoke or the clerk made a typing error is correctable under subrule (A). A prison sentence entered on a judgment that is erroneous because the judge relied on mistaken facts (for example, confused codefendants) or made a mistake of law (for example, unintentionally imposed a sentence in violation of the *Tanner* rule) is a substantive mistake and is correctable by the judge under subrule (B) until the judge signs the judgment, but not afterwards. In the latter event, however, the defendant may obtain relief by filing a postconviction motion. See 6.429.

Subrule (C) is consistent with MCR 7.208(B)(2) but it is patterned stylistically after Federal Rule of Appellate Procedure 10(e).

Subrule (D) repeats the limitation in MCR 2.612(A)(2) applicable to corrections under subrule (A) when a case is on appeal but expands it to reflect that this limitation is applicable as well to corrections of the record under subrule (C). See 7.208(B).

RULE 6.440 DISABILITY OF JUDGE

(A) During Jury Trial. If, by reason of death, sickness, or other disability, the judge before whom a jury trial has commenced is unable to continue with the trial, another judge regularly sitting in or assigned to the court, on certification of having become familiar with the record of the trial, may proceed with and complete the trial.

(B) During Bench Trial. If a judge becomes disabled during a trial without a jury, another judge may be substituted for the disabled judge, but only if

(1) both parties consent in writing to the substitution, and

(2) the judge certifies having become familiar with the record of the trial, including the testimony previously given.

(C) After Verdict. If, after a verdict is returned or findings of fact and conclusions of law are filed, the trial judge because of disability becomes unable to perform the remaining duties the court must perform, another judge regularly sitting in or assigned to the court may perform those duties; but if that judge is not satisfied of an ability to perform those duties because of not having presided at the trial or determines that it is appropriate for any other reason, the judge may grant the defendant a new trial.

[Adopted effective October 1, 1989.]

1989 Staff Comment

MCR 6.440 is a new rule.

Subrule (A) is based on Federal Rule of Criminal Procedure 25(a) and substantially changes existing law. Under MCR 2.630 substitution of a judge due to disability in a jury trial case is limited to "after a verdict is returned." Under subrule (A), substitution is permissible during a jury trial provided the substitute judge has certified "having become familiar with the record of the trial."

Subrule (B) is based on Rule 741(e) of the Uniform Rules of Criminal Procedure and likewise substantially changes existing law. Substitution of a judge presiding over a bench trial is limited by MCR 2.630 to after the "findings of fact and conclusions of law are filed." Under subrule (B) substitution is permissible during a bench trial if the parties give their consent in writing *and* if the substitute judge has certified "having become familiar with the record of the trial, including the testimony previously given."

Subrule (C) is a modified version of MCR 2.630 that adds a provision from Federal Rule of Criminal Procedure 25(b) allowing a substitute judge to grant a new trial not only if the judge is not satisfied of having the ability to perform the remaining duties, but also if the judge determines that a new trial is "appropriate for any other reason."

RULE 6.445 PROBATION REVOCATION

(A) Issuance of Summons; Warrant. On finding probable cause to believe that a probationer has violated a condition of probation, the court may

(1) issue a summons in accordance with MCR 6.103(B) and (C) for the probationer to appear for arraignment on the alleged violation, or

(2) issue a warrant for the arrest of the probationer.

An arrested probationer must promptly be brought before the court for arraignment on the alleged violation.

(B) Arraignment on the Charge. At the arraignment on the alleged probation violation, the court must

(1) ensure that the probationer receives written notice of the alleged violation,

(2) advise the probationer that

(a) the probationer has a right to contest the charge at a hearing, and

(b) the probationer is entitled to a lawyer's assistance at the hearing and at all subsequent court proceedings, and that the court will appoint a lawyer at public expense if the probationer wants one and is financially unable to retain one,

(3) if requested and appropriate, appoint a lawyer,

(4) determine what form of release, if any, is appropriate, and

(5) subject to subrule (C), set a reasonably prompt hearing date or postpone the hearing.

(C) Scheduling or Postponement of Hearing. The hearing of a probationer being held in custody for an alleged probation violation must be held within 14 days after the arraignment or the court must order the probationer released from that custody pending the hearing. If the alleged violation is based on a criminal offense that is a basis for a separate criminal prosecution, the court may postpone the hearing for the outcome of that prosecution.

(D) Continuing Duty to Advise of Right to Assistance of Lawyer. Even though a probationer charged with probation violation has waived the assistance of a lawyer, at each subsequent proceeding the court must comply with the advice and waiver procedure in MCR 6.005(E).

(E) The Violation Hearing.

(1) *Conduct of the Hearing.* The evidence against the probationer must be disclosed to the probationer. The probationer has the right to be present at the hearing, to present evidence, and to examine and cross-examine witnesses. The court may consider only evidence that is relevant to the violation alleged, but it need not apply the rules of evidence except those pertaining to privileges. The state has the burden of proving a violation by a preponderance of the evidence.

(2) *Judicial Findings.* At the conclusion of the hearing, the court must make findings in accordance with MCR 6.403.

(F) Pleas of Guilty. With the consent of the court that granted probation, the probationer may, at the arraignment or afterward, plead guilty to the violation. Before accepting a guilty plea, the court, speaking directly to the probationer and receiving the probationer's response, must

(1) advise the probationer that by pleading guilty the probationer is giving up the right to a contested hearing and, if the probationer is proceeding without legal representation, the right to a lawyer's assistance as set forth in subrule (B)(2)(b),

(2) advise the probationer of the maximum possible jail or prison sentence for the offense,

(3) ascertain that the plea is understandingly, voluntarily, and knowingly made, and

(4) establish factual support for a finding that the probationer is guilty of the alleged violation.

(G) Sentencing. If the court finds that the probationer has violated a condition of probation, or if the probationer pleads guilty to a violation, the court may continue probation, modify the conditions of probation, extend the probation period, or revoke probation and impose a sentence of incarceration. The court may not sentence the probationer to prison without having considered a current presentence report and having complied with the provisions set forth in MCR 6.425(B), (D)(2), and (D)(3).

(H) Review.

(1) In a case involving a sentence of incarceration under subrule (G), the court must advise the probationer on the record, immediately after imposing sentence, that

(a) the probationer has a right to appeal, if the conviction occurred at a contested hearing, or

(b) the probationer is entitled to file an application for leave to appeal, if the conviction was the result of a plea of guilty.

(2) In a case that involves a sentence other than incarceration under subrule (G), the court must advise the probationer on the record, immediately after imposing sentence, that the probationer is entitled to file an application for leave to appeal.

[Adopted effective October 1, 1989; amended effective October 1, 1994; January 1, 1999.]

1989 Staff Comment

MCR 6.445 is a stylistically improved version of the former probation revocation rule, 6.111, but incorporates a number of substantive changes.

Subrule (A)(1) substitutes an expanded summons option. The former rule, 6.111(A)(1)(a), restricted the use of summons to an alleged probation violation "other than a criminal offense." The expanded option in subrule (A)(1) gives the court discretion to issue a summons for any alleged probation violation. This is similar to the summons option in 6.103, available when a defendant is charged with a felony. Unlike that summons procedure, however, issuance of a summons under this rule is not conditioned on being requested by the prosecutor. It is, however, required to comply with the form requirements of 6.103(B) and the service and return provisions of 6.103(C).

Subrule (B) is a substantially revised version of former 6.111(B), conforming more closely with the procedure and advice provisions in the arraignment rule, 6.104. The requirement for the court to advise a probationer of the ability to ask for bail in former 6.111(B)(2) is replaced with the provision in subrule (B)(4) requiring only that the court make a bail decision. The requirement to advise the probationer that the court will set a date for a hearing in former 6.111(B)(4) is replaced with the provision in subrule (B)(5) requiring the court to set a reasonably prompt hearing date. The requirement to advise the probationer of the right to be released from custody if the revocation hearing is not held within fourteen days is replaced with the provision in subrule (C) requiring the hearing of a probationer in custody to be held within twelve days or the court must order the probationer released. The change from fourteen to twelve days in this latter provision is made to be consistent with the twelve-day rule for preliminary examinations on which this provision is based.

Subrule (C) is new but incorporates stylistically revised versions of the provisions in former 6.111(B)(5) (discussed above) and in former (D)(2), allowing postponement of the hearing to await the outcome of the criminal prosecution on which a probation violation may be based.

Subrule (D) incorporates by reference the continuing advice requirement relating to legal representation set forth in 6.005(E) rather than repeating it verbatim as did former 6.111(C).

Subrule (E) is a stylistically revised version of the former revocation hearing rule, 6.111(D). Additionally, subrule (E)(1) adds a new provision consistent with existing law recognizing that, in addition to relevance, the only other limitation on the evidence that the court may consider at the hearing is that it conform with the admissibility requirements of privilege law.

Subrule (E)(2) makes a modification by referring to the special fact-finding requirements of 6.403 in place of the reference in former 6.111(D)(4) to the like provision in the civil rules, MCR 2.517(A).

Subrule (F) is a stylistically revised version of former 6.111(E). The only significant change is in language in subrule (F)(2) which substitutes "maximum possible jail or prison sentence" for the former language "maximum possible sentence." This change clarifies that this advice requirement pertains only to maximum possible incarceration and not to other consequences such as maximum possible fine. Additionally, the term "jail" is added to accommodate the use of the procedure in this rule in misdemeanor cases.

Subrule (G) is a stylistically revised version of former 6.111(F). Additionally, this subrule expands the court's duties, when imposing a "prison sentence," to conforming with the presentence report disclosure procedure, 6.425(B), sentencing procedure, 6.425(D)(2), and presentence report challenge procedure, 6.425(D)(3), applicable to felony sentencing.

Subrule (H) is a stylistically improved version of former 6.111(G).

Staff Comment to 1994 Amendment

In 1994, MCR 6.104(E)(4) and MCR 6.907(C)(2) were amended to reflect the change made by 1994 PA 167, which extended from 12 to 14 days the period within which a preliminary examination must be conducted. MCL 766.4; MSA 28.922. A similar change was also made in MCR 6.445(C), concerning the timing of a probation revocation hearing.

Staff Comment to 1998 Amendment

The September 1998 amendment of MCR 6.445(H), effective January 1, 1999, was proposed by the Michigan Judges Association, in light of the 1994 amendment of Const 1963, art 1, § 20, and the related amendment of MCR 6.425.

SUBCHAPTER 6.500 POSTAPPEAL RELIEF

RULE 6.501 SCOPE OF SUBCHAPTER

Unless otherwise specified by these rules, a judgment of conviction and sentence entered by the circuit court or the Recorder's Court for the City of Detroit not subject to appellate review under subchapters 7.200 or 7.300 may be reviewed only in accordance with the provisions of this subchapter.

[Adopted effective October 1, 1989.]

1989 Staff Comment

New Subchapter 6.500 establishes a procedure for postappeal proceedings challenging criminal convictions. It provides the exclusive means to challenge convictions in Michigan courts for a defendant who has had an appeal by right or by leave, who has unsuccessfully sought leave to appeal, or who is unable to file an application for leave to appeal to the Court of Appeals because 18 months have elapsed since the judgment. See MCR 7.205(F)(3). The rules are similar in structure to the federal rules governing proceedings under 28 USC 2255, though there are a number of differences in substance and language.

RULE 6.502 MOTION FOR RELIEF FROM JUDGMENT

(A) Nature of Motion. The request for relief under this subchapter must be in the form of a motion to set aside or modify the judgment. The motion must specify all of the grounds for relief which are available to the defendant and of which the defendant has, or by the exercise of due diligence, should have knowledge.

(B) Limitations on Motion. A motion may seek relief from one judgment only. If the defendant desires to challenge the validity of additional judgments, the defendant must do so by separate motions. For the purpose of this rule, multiple convictions resulting from a single trial or plea proceeding shall be treated as a single judgment.

(C) Form of Motion. The motion must be typed or legibly handwritten and include a verification by the defendant or defendant's lawyer in accordance with MCR 2.114. The motion must be substantially in the form approved by the State Court Administrator, and must include:

(1) The name of the defendant;

(2) The name of the court in which the defendant was convicted and the file number of the defendant's case;

(3) The place where the defendant is confined, or, if not confined, the defendant's current address;

(4) The offenses for which the defendant was convicted and sentenced;

(5) The date on which the defendant was sentenced;

(6) Whether the defendant was convicted by a jury, by a judge without jury, or on a plea of guilty, guilty but mentally ill, or nolo contendere;

(7) The sentence imposed (probation, fine, and/or imprisonment), the length of the sentence imposed, and whether the defendant is now serving that sentence;

(8) The name of the judge who presided at trial and imposed sentence;

(9) The court, title, and file number of any proceeding (including appeals and federal court proceedings) instituted by the defendant to obtain relief from conviction or sentence, specifying whether a proceeding is pending or has been completed;

(10) The name of each lawyer who represented the defendant at any time after arrest, and the stage of the case at which each represented the defendant;

(11) The relief requested;

(12) The grounds for the relief requested;

(13) The facts supporting each ground, stated in summary form;

(14) Whether any of the grounds for the relief requested were raised before; if so, at what stage of the case, and, if not, the reasons they were not raised;

(15) Whether the defendant requests the appointment of counsel, and, if so, information necessary for the court to determine whether the defendant is entitled to appointment of counsel at public expense.

Upon request, the clerk of each court with trial level jurisdiction over felony cases shall make available blank motion forms without charge to any person desiring to file such a motion.

(D) Return of Insufficient Motion. If a motion does not substantially comply with the requirements of these rules, the court may direct that it be returned to the defendant with a statement of the reasons for its return. The clerk of the court shall retain a copy of the motion.

(E) Attachments to Motion. The defendant may attach to the motion any affidavit, document, evidence, or memorandum of law to support the relief requested.

(F) Amendment and Supplementation of Motion. The court may permit the defendant to amend or supplement the motion at any time.

(G) Successive Motions.

(1) Except as provided in subrule (G)(2), regardless of whether a defendant has previously filed a motion for relief from judgment, after August 1, 1995, one and only one motion for relief from judgment may be filed with regard to a conviction. The court shall return without filing any successive motions for relief

from judgment. A defendant may not appeal the denial or rejection of a successive motion.

(2) A defendant may file a second or subsequent motion based on a retroactive change in law that occurred after the first motion for relief from judgment or a claim of new evidence that was not discovered before the first such motion. The clerk shall refer a successive motion that asserts that one of these exceptions is applicable to the judge to whom the case is assigned for a determination whether the motion is within one of the exceptions.

[Adopted effective October 1, 1989; amended effective August 1, 1995.]

1989 Staff Comment

The defendant initiates proceedings under Subchapter 6.500 by filing a motion for relief from judgment. The motion is to list all grounds for relief of which defendant has knowledge or with reasonable diligence should have knowledge. The motion is to be limited to a single judgment, although multiple convictions resulting from a single trial or plea proceeding are treated as if they were a single judgment and may be included in the same motion. Subrule (C) spells out the required contents of the motion, which is to be in substantially the form approved by the State Court Administrator. The defendant is permitted to attach affidavits, evidentiary material, or a memorandum of law to the motion. If the motion does not comply with the requirements of the rule, the court may direct that it be returned to the defendant with a statement of the reasons for its rejection.

Staff Comment to 1995 Amendment

New MCR 6.502(G) limits criminal defendants to filing one motion for relief from judgment with respect to a conviction, except where the motion is based on a retroactive change in the law or on newly discovered evidence.

RULE 6.503   FILING AND SERVICE OF MOTION

(A) Filing; Copies.

(1) A defendant seeking relief under this subchapter must file a motion, together with two copies, with the clerk of the court in which the defendant was convicted and sentenced.

(2) Upon receipt of a motion, the clerk shall file it under the same number as the original conviction.

(B) Service. The clerk shall serve a copy of the motion and notice of its filing on the prosecuting attorney. Unless so ordered by the court as provided in this subchapter, the filing and service of the motion does not require a response by the prosecutor.

[Adopted effective October 1, 1989.]

1989 Staff Comment

The defendant is to file the original and two copies of the motion with the court, and the clerk will serve it on the prosecuting attorney. The prosecutor is not required to respond unless directed by the court.

RULE 6.504 ASSIGNMENT; PRELIMINARY CONSIDERATION BY JUDGE; SUMMARY DENIAL

(A) Assignment to Judge. The motion shall be presented to the judge to whom the case was assigned at the time of the defendant's conviction. If the appropriate judge is not available, the motion must be assigned to another judge in accordance with the court's procedure for the re-assignment of cases.

(B) Initial Consideration by Court.

(1) The court shall promptly examine the motion, together with all the files, records, transcripts, and correspondence relating to the judgment under attack. The court may request that the prosecutor provide copies of transcripts, briefs, or other records.

(2) If it plainly appears from the face of the materials described in subrule (B)(1) that the defendant is not entitled to relief, the court shall deny the motion without directing further proceedings. The order must include a concise statement of the reasons for the denial. The clerk shall serve a copy of the order on the defendant and the prosecutor. The court may dismiss some requests for relief or grounds for relief and direct further proceedings as to others.

(3) If the motion is summarily dismissed under subrule (B)(2), the defendant may move for reconsideration of the dismissal within 21 days after the clerk serves the order. The motion must concisely state why the court's decision was based on a clear error and that a different decision must result from correction of the error. A motion which merely presents the same matters that were considered by the court will not be granted.

(4) If the entire motion is not dismissed under subrule (B)(2), the court shall order the prosecuting attorney to file a response as provided in MCR 6.506, and shall conduct further proceedings as provided in MCR 6.505–6.508.

[Adopted effective October 1, 1989.]

1989 Staff Comment

The motion is to be assigned to the judge to whom the case was assigned at the time of the conviction. The usual procedures for using a substitute judge are to be followed where that judge is not available. The judge is to examine the motion together with the court's records regarding the case. The court may request that the prosecutor provide copies of other materials.

The court may summarily dismiss the motion if it "plainly appears" from the materials that the defendant is not entitled to relief. The provision outlining the grounds for relief is found in MCR 6.508(D). The "plainly appears" standard is taken from the corresponding federal rule implementing 28 USC 2255. Rule 4 of the Rules Governing Proceedings in the United States District Courts Under § 2255 of Title 28, United States Code. The court can summarily dismiss some claims, while directing further proceedings on others. Subrule (B)(3) provides a procedure by which the defendant may request reconsideration of a summary dismissal.

If the entire motion is not summarily dismissed, the court is to direct the prosecutor to file a response and to conduct further proceedings.

RULE 6.505 RIGHT TO LEGAL ASSISTANCE

(A) Appointment of Counsel. If the defendant has requested appointment of counsel, and the court has determined that the defendant is indigent, the court may appoint counsel for the defendant at any time during the proceedings under this subchapter. Counsel must be appointed if the court directs that oral argument or an evidentiary hearing be held.

(B) Opportunity to Supplement the Motion. If the court appoints counsel to represent the defendant, it shall afford counsel 56 days to amend or supplement the motion. The court may extend the time on a showing that a necessary transcript or record is not available to counsel.

[Adopted effective October 1, 1989.]

1989 Staff Comment

The matter of appointment of counsel for a defendant is covered by MCR 6.505. The court may appoint counsel at any time, and is required to do so if it directs that oral argument or an evidentiary hearing be held. If counsel is appointed, the court is to allow counsel time to amend or supplement the motion.

RULE 6.506 RESPONSE BY PROSECUTOR

(A) Contents of Response. On direction of the court pursuant to MCR 6.504(B)(4), the prosecutor shall respond in writing to the allegations in the motion. If the response refers to transcripts or briefs that are not in the court's file, the prosecutor shall submit copies of those items with the response.

(B) Filing and Service. The prosecutor shall file the response and one copy with the clerk of the court and serve one copy on the defendant.

[Adopted effective October 1, 1989.]

1989 Staff Comment

If the court does not summarily dismiss the motion under MCR 6.504, it is to direct the prosecutor to file a response. MCR 6.506 has several provisions regarding filing and service of the response. The prosecutor is to supply copies of transcripts or briefs to which the response refers that are not in the court's file.

RULE 6.507 EXPANSION OF RECORD

(A) Order to Expand Record. If the court does not deny the motion pursuant to MCR 6.504(B)(2), it may direct the parties to expand the record by including any additional materials it deems relevant to the decision on the merits of the motion. The expanded record may include letters, affidavits, documents, exhibits, and answers under oath to interrogatories propounded by the court.

(B) Submission to Opposing Party. Whenever a party submits items to expand the record, the party shall serve copies of the items to the opposing party. The court shall afford the opposing party an opportunity to admit or deny the correctness of the items.

(C) Authentication. The court may require the authentication of any item submitted under this rule.

[Adopted effective October 1, 1989.]

1989 Staff Comment

The court is given considerable discretion in the matter of expanding the record if further information is necessary to decide the motion.

RULE 6.508 PROCEDURE; EVIDENTIARY HEARING; DETERMINATION

(A) Procedure Generally. If the rules in this subchapter do not prescribe the applicable procedure, the court may proceed in any lawful manner. The court may apply the rules applicable to civil or criminal proceedings, as it deems appropriate.

(B) Decision Without Evidentiary Hearing. After reviewing the motion and response, the record, and the expanded record, if any, the court shall determine whether an evidentiary hearing is required. If the court decides that an evidentiary hearing is not required, it may rule on the motion or, in its discretion, afford the parties an opportunity for oral argument.

(C) Evidentiary Hearing. If the court decides that an evidentiary hearing is required, it shall schedule and conduct the hearing as promptly as practicable. At the hearing, the rules of evidence other than those with respect to privilege do not apply. The court shall assure that a verbatim record is made of the hearing.

(D) Entitlement to Relief. The defendant has the burden of establishing entitlement to the relief requested. The court may not grant relief to the defendant if the motion

(1) seeks relief from a judgment of conviction and sentence that still is subject to challenge on appeal pursuant to subchapter 7.200 or subchapter 7.300;

(2) alleges grounds for relief which were decided against the defendant in a prior appeal or proceeding under this subchapter, unless the defendant establishes that a retroactive change in the law has undermined the prior decision;

(3) alleges grounds for relief, other than jurisdictional defects, which could have been raised on appeal from the conviction and sentence or in a prior motion under this subchapter, unless the defendant demonstrates

(a) good cause for failure to raise such grounds on appeal or in the prior motion, and

(b) actual prejudice from the alleged irregularities that support the claim for relief. As used in this subrule, "actual prejudice" means that,

(i) in a conviction following a trial, but for the alleged error, the defendant would have had a reasonably likely chance of acquittal;

(ii) in a conviction entered on a plea of guilty, guilty but mentally ill, or nolo contendere, the defect in the proceedings was such that it renders the plea an involuntary one to a degree that it would be manifestly unjust to allow the conviction to stand;

(iii) in any case, the irregularity was so offensive to the maintenance of a sound judicial process that the conviction should not be allowed to stand regardless of its effect on the outcome of the case;

(iv) in the case of a challenge to the sentence, the sentence is invalid.

The court may waive the "good cause" requirement of subrule (D)(3)(a) if it concludes that there is a significant possibility that the defendant is innocent of the crime.

(E) Ruling. The court, either orally or in writing, shall set forth in the record its findings of fact and its conclusions of law, and enter an appropriate order disposing of the motion.

[Adopted effective October 1, 1989.]

1989 Staff Comment

Most of the provisions on governing hearings and decision on the motion are found in MCR 6.508. Where no particular provision of Subchapter 6.500 prescribes a procedure, the court has discretion to select appropriate procedures. The court is to determine whether the case can be decided on the motion and response, the court records, and the expanded record, if any. If it decides that an evidentiary hearing is not required, it is to rule on the motion, with or without hearing oral argument. If an evidentiary hearing is ordered, the rules of evidence, other than those with respect to privilege, do not apply. Compare MRE 1101(b)(3). A verbatim record is to be made of any evidentiary hearing.

MCR 6.508(D) covers the standard for entitlement to relief. There are three basic provisions.

First, the motion is to be denied if it seeks relief from a conviction that is still subject to challenge on appeal.

Second, if the issues raised were previously decided against the defendant in an appeal or a proceeding under Subchapter 6.500, relief is to be denied unless there has been a retroactive change in the law that undermines the prior decision.

Third, relief is not to be granted where the defendant could have raised the issue in a prior appeal or motion under Subchapter 6.500, unless defendant demonstrates both good cause for failure to raise the issue previously and actual prejudice from the alleged error. These standards are based on several decisions of the United States Supreme Court.

See *Wainright* v *Sykes*, 433 US 72; 97 S Ct 2497; 53 L Ed 2d 594 (1977) (habeas corpus action by state prisoner); *United States* v *Frady*, 456 US 152; 102 S Ct 1584; 71 L Ed 2d 816 (1982) (under 28 USC 2255).

Actual prejudice is defined in subrule (D)(3)(b). In the case of a trial, it means that but for the error the defendant would have had a reasonably likely chance of acquittal. In the case of a plea-based conviction, the defect must be such that the plea is rendered involuntary to a degree that it would be manifestly unjust to allow the conviction to stand. In any case, actual prejudice can be shown if the irregularity was so offensive to the maintenance of a sound judicial process that the conviction should not be allowed to stand regardless of its effect on the outcome of the case. Finally, where the challenge is to the sentence, actual prejudice requires that the sentence be invalid.

The court is allowed to waive the good cause requirement if it concludes that there is a significant possibility that the defendant is innocent.

The court is to make findings of fact and conclusions of law either in writing or orally on the record, followed by entry of an appropriate order.

RULE 6.509 APPEAL

(A) Availability of Appeal. Appeals from decisions under this subchapter are by application for leave to appeal to the Court of Appeals pursuant to MCR 7.205. The 12–month time limit provided by MCR 7.205(F)(3), runs from the decision under this subchapter. Nothing in this subchapter shall be construed as extending the time to appeal from the original judgment.

(B) Responsibility of Appointed Counsel. If the trial court has appointed counsel for the defendant during the proceeding, that appointment authorizes the attorney to represent the defendant in connection with an application for leave to appeal to the Court of Appeals.

[Adopted effective October 1, 1989; amended effective November 1, 1995.]

1989 Staff Comment

Appeals from decisions under Subchapter 6.500 are by application for leave to appeal to the Court of Appeals. The rule does not extend the time to appeal from the original judgment. If the trial court appointed counsel for the defendant during the proceeding, that appointment authorizes the attorney to represent the defendant in connection with an application for leave to appeal to the Court of Appeals.

Staff Comment to 1995 Amendment

In MCR 6.509(A), the reference to the time for filing an application for leave to appeal is changed to 12 months to conform to the March 3, 1995, amendment of MCR 7.205(F)(3).

SUBCHAPTER 6.600   CRIMINAL PROCEDURE IN DISTRICT COURT

RULE 6.610 CRIMINAL PROCEDURE GENERALLY

(A) Precedence. Criminal cases have precedence over civil actions.

(B) Pretrial. The court, on its own initiative or on motion of either party, may direct the prosecutor and the defendant or the defendant's attorney to appear for a pretrial conference. The court may require collateral matters and pretrial motions to be filed and argued no later than this conference.

(C) Record. Unless a writing is permitted, a verbatim record of the proceedings before a court under subrules (D)–(F) must be made.

(D) Arraignment; District Court Offenses.

(1) Whenever a defendant is arraigned on an offense over which the district court has jurisdiction, he or she must be informed of

(a) the name of the offense;

(b) the maximum sentence permitted by law; and

(c) the defendant's right

(i) to the assistance of an attorney and to a trial;

(ii) (if subrule [D][2] applies) to an appointed attorney; and

(iii) (unless he or she is charged under an ordinance that does not correspond to a criminal statute or permit a jail sentence) to a trial by jury.

The information may be given in a writing that is made a part of the file or by the court on the record.

(2) An indigent defendant has a right to an appointed attorney whenever

(a) the offense charged requires on conviction a minimum term in jail, or

(b) the court determines that it might sentence the defendant to jail.

If an indigent defendant is without an attorney and has not waived the right to an appointed attorney, the court may not sentence the defendant to jail.

(3) The right to the assistance of an attorney, to an appointed attorney, or to a trial by jury is not waived unless the defendant

(a) has been informed of the right; and

(b) has waived it in a writing that is made a part of the file or orally on the record.

(4) The court may allow a defendant to enter a plea of not guilty or to stand mute without formal arraignment by filing a written statement signed by the defendant and any defense attorney of record, reciting

the general nature of the charge, the maximum possible sentence, the rights of the defendant at arraignment, and the plea to be entered. The court may require that an appropriate bond be executed and filed and appropriate and reasonable sureties posted or continued as a condition precedent to allowing the defendant to be arraigned without personally appearing before the court.

(E) Pleas of Guilty and No Contest. Before accepting a plea of guilty or no contest the court shall in all cases comply with this rule.

(1) The court shall determine that the plea is understanding, voluntary, and accurate. In determining the accuracy of the plea,

(a) if the defendant pleads guilty, the court, by questioning him or her, shall establish support for a finding that defendant is guilty of the offense charged or the offense to which he or she is pleading, or

(b) if the defendant pleads nolo contendere, the court shall not question him or her about his or her participation in the crime, but shall make the determination on the basis of other available information.

(2) The court shall inform the defendant of the right to the assistance of an attorney. If

(a) the offense charged requires on conviction a minimum term in jail, or

(b) the court determines that it might sentence the defendant to jail,

the court shall inform the defendant that if the defendant is indigent he or she has the right to an appointed attorney.

A subsequent charge or sentence may not be enhanced because of this conviction unless a defendant who is entitled to appointed counsel is represented by an attorney or waives the right to an attorney.

(3) The court shall advise the defendant of the following:

(a) the mandatory minimum jail sentence, if any, and the maximum possible penalty for the offense,

(b) that if the plea is accepted he or she will not have a trial of any kind and that he or she gives up the following rights that he or she would have at trial:

(i) the right to have witnesses called for his or her defense at trial,

(ii) the right to cross-examine all witnesses called against him or her,

(iii) the right to testify or to remain silent without an inference being drawn from said silence,

(iv) the presumption of innocence and the requirement that his or her guilt be proven beyond a reasonable doubt.

(4) A defendant may be informed of the trial rights listed in subrule (3)(b) as follows:

(a) on the record,

(b) in a writing made part of the file, or

(c) in a writing referred to on the record.

If the court uses a writing pursuant to subrule (E)(4)(b) or (c), the court shall address the defendant and obtain from him or her orally on the record, a statement that the rights were read and understood and a waiver of those rights. The waiver may be obtained without repeating the individual rights.

(5) The court shall make the plea agreement a part of the record and determine that the parties agree on all the terms of that agreement. The court shall accept, reject or indicate on what basis it accepts the plea.

(6) A plea of guilty or no contest in writing is permissible without a personal appearance of the defendant if

(a) the court decides that the combination of the circumstances and the range of possible sentences makes the situation proper for a plea of guilty or no contest;

(b) the court notifies the defendant in writing, in advance of a plea, of the following:

(i) the sentence to be imposed in the particular case, and

(ii) the rights enumerated in subrule (3)(b); and

(c) the defendant acknowledges guilt or no contest, and the sentence to be imposed, in a writing to be placed in the district court file.

(7) The following provisions apply where a defendant seeks to challenge the plea.

(a) A defendant may not challenge a plea on appeal unless the defendant moved in the trial court to withdraw the plea for noncompliance with these rules. Such a motion may be made either before or after sentence has been imposed. After imposition of sentence, the defendant may file a motion to withdraw the plea within the time for filing an application for leave to appeal under MCR 7.103(B)(6).

(b) If the trial court determines that a deviation affecting substantial rights occurred, it shall correct the deviation and give the defendant the option of permitting the plea to stand or of withdrawing the plea. If the trial court determines either a deviation did not occur, or that the deviation did not affect substantial rights, it may permit the defendant to withdraw the plea only if it does not cause substantial prejudice to the people because of reliance on the plea.

(c) If a deviation is corrected, any appeal will be on the whole record including the subsequent advice and inquiries.

(8) The state court administrator shall develop and approve forms to be used under subrules (E)(4)(b) and (c) and (E)(6)(b) and (c).

(F) Sentencing. At the sentencing, the court shall:

(1) require the presence of the defendant's attorney, unless the defendant does not have one or has waived the attorney's presence;

(2) give the defendant's attorney or, if the defendant is not represented by an attorney, the defendant an opportunity to review the presentence report, if any, and to advise the court of circumstances defendant believes should be considered in imposing sentence;

(3) inform the defendant of credit to be given for time served, if any.

(G) Arraignment; Circuit Court Offenses. In a prosecution in which a defendant is charged with a felony or a misdemeanor not cognizable by the district court, the court shall

(1) read the complaint or warrant into the record;

(2) inform the defendant of

(a) the right to a preliminary examination;

(b) the right to an attorney, if the defendant is not represented by an attorney at the arraignment;

(c) the right to have an attorney appointed at public expense if the defendant is indigent; and

(d) the right to be released on bond.

If a defendant not represented by an attorney waives the preliminary examination, the court shall ascertain that the waiver is freely, understandingly, and voluntarily given before accepting it.

(H) Motion for New Trial. A motion for a new trial must be filed within 21 days after the entry of judgment. However, if an appeal has not been taken, a delayed motion may be filed within the time for filing an application for leave to appeal.

[Adopted effective October 1, 1989; amended effective October 1, 1999; September 1, 2000; April 1, 2001.]

1989 Staff Comment

MCR 6.610 contains the provisions formerly found in MCR 6.201.

Staff Comment to 1999 Amendment

The July 1999 amendment of subrules (D) and (E), effective October 1, 1999, was based on a recommendation from the Prosecuting Attorneys Association of Michigan, in light of statutory changes effected by 1998 PA 341, 1998 PA 342, and 1998 PA 350.

Staff Comment to September 2000 Amendment

The amendment of MCR 6.610(E)(7) [effective September 1, 2000] establishes time limits for moving to withdraw pleas in district court criminal cases, comparable to those in circuit court cases. See MCR 6.311. New MCR 6.610(H) sets time limits for filing a motion for a new trial in district court criminal cases.

The amendment of MCR 7.103(B)(6) [effective September 1, 2000] places a 6-month time limit on applications for leave to appeal to circuit court, corresponding to the 12-month limit applicable in appeals to the Court of Appeals. See MCR 7.205(F)(3). As to judgments entered before the effective date of the amendment, the 6-month period specified in MCR 7.103(B)(6) begins on the effective date, September 1, 2000.

Staff Comment to December 2000 Amendment

The December 21, 2000 amendment of subrules (D)(2) and (E)(2), effective April 1, 2001, was recommended by the Prosecuting Attorneys Association of Michigan, in light of the holding in *People v Reichenbach*, 459 Mich 109, 120 (1998), that, under both the United States and the Michigan Constitutions, a defendant accused of a misdemeanor is entitled to appointed trial counsel only if "actually imprisoned."

RULE 6.615   MISDEMEANOR TRAFFIC CASES

(A) Citation; Complaint; Summons; Warrant.

(1) A misdemeanor traffic case may be begun by one of the following procedures:

(a) Service by a law enforcement officer on the defendant of a written citation, and the filing of the citation in the district court.

(b) The filing of a sworn complaint in the district court and the issuance of an arrest warrant. A citation may serve as the sworn complaint and as the basis for a misdemeanor warrant.

(c) Other special procedures authorized by statute.

(2) The citation serves as a summons to command

(a) the initial appearance of the defendant; and

(b) a response from the defendant as to his or her guilt of the violation alleged.

(3) A single citation may not allege both a misdemeanor and a civil infraction.

(B) Appearances; Failure to Appear. If a defendant fails to appear or otherwise to respond to any matter pending relative to a misdemeanor traffic citation, the court shall proceed as provided in this subrule.

(1) If the defendant is a Michigan resident, the court

(a) must initiate the procedures required by MCL 257.321a; MSA 9.2021(1) for the failure to answer a citation; and

(b) may issue a warrant for the defendant's arrest after a sworn complaint is filed with the court.

(2) If the defendant is not a Michigan resident,

(a) the court may mail a notice to appear to the defendant at the address in the citation;

(b) the court may issue a warrant for the defendant's arrest after a sworn complaint is filed with the court; and

(c) if the court has received the driver's license of a nonresident, pursuant to statute, it may retain the license as allowed by statute. The court need not retain the license past its expiration date.

(C) Arraignment. An arraignment in a misdemeanor traffic case may be conducted by

(1) a judge of the district, or

(2) a district court magistrate as authorized by statute and by the judges of the district.

(D) Contested Cases.

(1) A contested case may not be heard until a citation is filed with the court. If the citation is filed electronically, the court may decline to hear the matter until the citation is signed by the officer or official who issued it, and is filed on paper. A citation that is not signed and filed on paper, when required by the court, will be dismissed with prejudice.

(2) A misdemeanor traffic case must be conducted in compliance with the constitutional and statutory procedures and safeguards applicable to misdemeanors cognizable by the district court.

(E) Appeal. An appeal from a misdemeanor trial is governed by subchapter 7.100.

[Adopted effective October 1, 1989; amended effective September 2, 1997.]

1989 Staff Comment

MCR 6.615 is the rule governing misdemeanor traffic cases, formerly found in MCR 4.102.

Staff Comment to 1997 Amendment

The September 1997 amendments of MCR 4.101, 4.401, and 6.615, and the addition of MCR 8.125, [effective September 2, 1997] were adopted at the request of the Michigan District Judges Association because of recent statutory changes that created new categories of civil infractions, and the availability of electronic filing. In addition, the amendment of MCR 4.401(G) was made to clarify the procedure for challenging a civil infraction judgment.

RULE 6.620   IMPANELING THE JURY

(A) Alternate Jurors. The court may direct that 7 or more jurors be impaneled to sit in a criminal case. After the instructions to the jury have been given and the case submitted, the names of the jurors must be placed in a container and names drawn to reduce the number of jurors to 6, who shall constitute the jury. The court may retain the alternate jurors during deliberations. If the court does so, it shall instruct the alternate jurors not to discuss the case with any other person until the jury completed its deliberations and is discharged. If an alternate juror replaces a juror after the jury retires to consider its verdict, the court shall instruct the jury to begin its deliberations anew.

(B) Peremptory Challenges. Each party in a criminal case is entitled to three peremptory challenges. In a case involving two or more jointly tried defendants, each defendant is entitled to three peremptory challenges.

[Adopted effective October 1, 1989; amended effective September 1, 2001.]

1989 Staff Comment

MCR 6.620 contains the jury selection procedures formerly found in 6.202.

Staff Comment to 2001 Amendment

The June 26, 2001 amendments of MCR 2.511(B), MCR 6.411, and MCR 6.620(A), effective September 1, 2001, were based on a proposal from the Michigan Judges Association. Consistent with the December 1999 amendment of the Federal Rules of Criminal Procedure for the United States District Courts, the amendments allow courts to retain alternate jurors during deliberations.

RULE 6.625   APPEAL; APPOINTMENT OF LAWYER

An appeal from a misdemeanor case is governed by subchapter 7.100. An indigent defendant who pleads guilty, guilty but mentally ill, or nolo contendere is entitled to the assistance of assigned appellate counsel at public expense if the prosecution seeks leave to appeal or the Court or Appeals or the Supreme Court grants the defendant's application for leave to appeal.

[Adopted effective April 1, 2000]

2000 Staff Comment

The March 28, 2000 amendment of Rules 6.302, 6.425, and 6.615, and the adoption of new Rule 6.625, were made in light of 1999 PA 200, MCL 770.3a; MSA 28.1100a, and were effective as to pleas taken on or after April 1, 2000.

SUBCHAPTER 6.900   RULES APPLICABLE TO JUVENILES CHARGED WITH LIFE OFFENSES SUBJECT TO THE JURISDICTION OF DISTRICT, CIRCUIT AND RECORDER'S COURT

RULE 6.901   APPLICABILITY

(A) Precedence. The rules in this subchapter take precedence over, but are not exclusive of, the rules of procedure applicable to criminal actions against adult offenders.

(B) Scope. The rules apply to proceedings in the district court, the circuit court, and the recorder's court concerning a juvenile against whom the prosecuting attorney has authorized the filing of a criminal complaint and warrant charging an enumerated life offense instead of approving the filing of a petition in the juvenile court. The rules do not apply to a person charged solely with an offense in which the juvenile court has waived jurisdiction pursuant to MCL 712A.4; MSA 27.3178(598.4).

[Adopted effective October 1, 1989.]

RULE 6.903   DEFINITIONS

When used in this subchapter, unless the context otherwise indicates:

(A) "Commitment review hearing" includes a hearing as required by MCL 769.1; MSA 28.1072, as added by 1988 PA 78, to decide whether the jurisdiction of the court shall continue over a juvenile who was placed on juvenile probation and committed to state wardship.

(B) "Commitment review report" means a report on a juvenile committed to state wardship for use at a commitment review hearing prepared by the department of social services pursuant to section 5 of the Juvenile Facilities Act, 1988 PA 73, MCL 803.225; MSA 25.399(225).

(C) "Court" means the circuit court and the Recorder's Court for the City of Detroit as provided in MCL 600.606; MSA 27A.606, and MCL 725.10a(1)(c); MSA 27.3950(1)(1)(c).

(D) "Juvenile" means a person 15 years of age or older who is subject to the jurisdiction of the court for having allegedly committed a life offense on or after the person's 15th birthday and before the person's 17th birthday.

(E) "Juvenile court" means the juvenile division of the probate court.

(F) "Juvenile sentencing hearing" means a hearing conducted by the court following a criminal conviction to determine whether the best interests of the juvenile and of the public would be served:

(1) by retaining jurisdiction over the juvenile, placing the juvenile on juvenile probation, and committing the juvenile to a state institution or agency as a state ward, as provided in MCL 769.1; MSA 28.1072; or

(2) by imposing sentence as provided by law for an adult offender.

(G) "Juvenile facility" means an institution or facility operated by the juvenile division of the probate court, or a state institution or agency described in the Youth Rehabilitation Services Act, 1974 PA 150, MCL 803.301 et seq.; MSA 25.399(51) et seq., or a county facility or institution operated as an agency of the county other than a facility designed or used to incarcerate adults.

(H) "Life offense" means one or more of the following offenses allegedly committed by a juvenile in which the prosecuting attorney has authorized the filing of a criminal complaint and warrant instead of proceeding in the juvenile court:

(1) assault with intent to commit murder, MCL 750.83; MSA 28.278;

(2) assault with intent to rob while armed, MCL 750.89; MSA 28.284;

(3) attempted murder, MCL 750.91; MSA 28.286;

(4) first-degree murder, MCL 750.316; MSA 28.548;

(5) second-degree murder, MCL 750.317; MSA 28.549;

(6) first-degree criminal sexual conduct, MCL 750.520b; MSA 28.788(2);

(7) armed robbery, MCL 750.529; MSA 28.797; or

(8) possession of or manufacture, delivery, or possession with intent to manufacture or deliver 650 grams or more of any schedule I or II controlled substance, MCL 333.7401–333.7403; MSA 14.15(7401)–14.15(7403).

(I) "Magistrate" means the district court or a municipal court as defined in MCL 761.1(f); MSA 28.843(f).

(J) "Progress report" means the report on a juvenile in state wardship prepared by the department of social services for the court as required by section 3 of the Juvenile Facilities Act, 1988 PA 73, MCL 803.223; MSA 25.399(223) and by these rules.

(K) "Social report" means the written report on a juvenile for use at the juvenile sentencing hearing prepared by the department of social services as required by section 4 of the Juvenile Facilities Act, 1988 PA 73, MCL 803.224; MSA 25.399(224).

(L) "State wardship" means care and control of a juvenile for up to the 21st birthday of the juvenile by an institution or agency within or under the supervision of the department of social services as provided in the Youth Rehabilitation Services Act, MCL 803.301 et seq.; MSA 25.399(51) et seq., as amended by 1988 PA 76, while the juvenile remains under the jurisdiction of the court on the basis of a court order of juvenile probation and commitment as provided in MCL 769.1; MSA 28.1072.

[Adopted effective October 1, 1989.]

RULE 6.905 ASSISTANCE OF ATTORNEY

(A) Advice of Right. If the juvenile is not represented by an attorney, the magistrate or court shall advise the juvenile at each stage of the criminal proceedings of the right to the assistance of an attorney. If the juvenile has waived the right to an attorney, the court at later proceedings must reaffirm that the juvenile continues to not want an attorney to represent the juvenile.

(B) Court Appointed Attorney. Unless the juvenile has a retained attorney, or has waived the right to an attorney, the magistrate or the court must appoint an attorney to represent the juvenile.

(C) Waiver of Attorney. The magistrate or court may permit a juvenile to waive representation by an attorney if:

(1) an attorney is appointed to give the juvenile advice on the question of waiver;

(2) the magistrate or the court finds that the juvenile is literate and is competent to conduct a defense;

(3) the magistrate or the court advises the juvenile of the dangers and of the disadvantages of self-representation;

(4) the magistrate or the court finds on the record that the waiver is voluntarily and understandingly made; and

(5) the court appoints standby counsel to assist the juvenile at trial and at the juvenile sentencing hearing.

(D) Cost. The court may assess cost of legal representation, or part thereof, against the juvenile or against a person responsible for the support of the juvenile, or both. The order assessing cost shall not be binding on a person responsible for the support of the juvenile unless an opportunity for a hearing has been given and until a copy of the order is served on the person, personally or by first class mail, to the person's last known address.

[Adopted effective October 1, 1989.]

RULE 6.907 ARRAIGNMENT ON COMPLAINT AND WARRANT

(A) Time. When the prosecuting attorney authorizes the filing of a complaint and warrant charging a juvenile with a life offense instead of approving the filing of a petition in juvenile court, the juvenile in custody must be taken to the magistrate for arraignment on the charge. The prosecuting attorney must make a good-faith effort to notify the parent of the juvenile of the arraignment. The juvenile must be released if arraignment has not commenced:

(1) within 24 hours of the arrest of the juvenile; or

(2) within 24 hours after the prosecuting attorney authorized the complaint and warrant during special adjournment pursuant to MCR 5.935(A)(3), provided the juvenile is being detained in a juvenile facility.

(B) Temporary Detention Pending Arraignment. If the prosecuting attorney has authorized the filing of a complaint and warrant charging a life offense instead of approving the filing of a petition in juvenile court, a juvenile may, following apprehension, be detained pending arraignment:

(1) in a juvenile facility operated by the county;

(2) in a regional juvenile detention facility operated by the state; or

(3) in a juvenile-court-operated facility with the consent of the juvenile court or an order of a court as defined in these rules.

If no juvenile facility is reasonably available and if it is apparent that the juvenile may not otherwise be safely detained, the magistrate may, without a hearing, authorize that the juvenile be lodged pending arraignment in a facility used to incarcerate adults. The juvenile must be kept separate from adult prisoners as required by law.

(C) Procedure. At the arraignment on the complaint and warrant:

(1) The magistrate shall determine whether a parent, guardian, or an adult relative of the juvenile is present. Arraignment may be conducted without the presence of a parent, guardian, or adult relative provided the magistrate appoints an attorney to appear at arraignment with the juvenile or provided an attorney has been retained and appears with the juvenile.

(2) The magistrate shall set a date for the juvenile's preliminary examination within the next 14 days, less time given and used by the prosecuting attorney under special adjournment pursuant to MCR 5.935(A)(3), up to three days credit. The magistrate shall inform the juvenile and the parent, guardian, or adult relative of the juvenile, if present, of the preliminary examination date. If a parent, guardian, or an adult relative is not present at the arraignment, the court shall direct the attorney of the juvenile to advise

a parent or guardian of the juvenile of the scheduled preliminary examination.

[Adopted effective October 1, 1989; amended effective October 1, 1994.]

Staff Comment to 1994 Amendment

In 1994, MCR 6.104(E)(4) and MCR 6.907(C)(2) were amended to reflect the change made by 1994 PA 167, which extended from 12 to 14 days the period within which a preliminary examination must be conducted. MCL 766.4; MSA 28.922. A similar change was also made in MCR 6.445(C), concerning the timing of a probation revocation hearing.

RULE 6.909 RELEASING OR DETAINING JUVENILES PRIOR TO TRIAL OR JUDGMENT OF SENTENCE

(A) Bail; Detention.

(1) *Bail.* Except as provided in subrule (2) the magistrate or court must advise the juvenile of a right to bail as provided for an adult accused. The magistrate or the court may order a juvenile released to a parent or guardian on the basis of any lawful condition, including that bail be posted.

(2) *Detention Without Bail.* If the proof is evident or if the presumption is great that the juvenile committed the offense, the magistrate or the court may deny bail:

(a) to a juvenile charged with first-degree murder, second-degree murder, or

(b) to a juvenile charged with first-degree criminal sexual conduct, or armed robbery,

(i) who is likely to flee, or

(ii) who clearly presents a danger to others.

(B) Place of Confinement.

(1) *Juvenile Facility.* Except as provided in subrule (B)(2) and in MCR 6.907(B), the juvenile charged with a crime and not released must be placed in a juvenile facility while awaiting trial and, if necessary, sentencing, rather than being placed in a jail or similar facility designed and used to incarcerate adult prisoners.

(2) *Jailing of Juveniles; Restricted.* On motion of a prosecuting attorney or a superintendent of a juvenile facility where the juvenile is detained, the magistrate or court may order the juvenile confined in a jail or similar facility designed and used to incarcerate adult prisoners upon a showing that

(a) the juvenile's habits or conduct are considered a menace to other juveniles; or

(b) the juvenile may not otherwise be safely detained in a juvenile facility.

(3) *Juvenile–Court–Operated Facility.* The juvenile shall not be placed in an institution operated by the juvenile court except with the consent of the

juvenile court or on order of a court as defined in these rules.

(4) *Separate Custody of Juvenile.* The juvenile in custody or detention must be maintained separately from the adult prisoners or adult accused as required by MCL 764.27a; MSA 28.886(1).

(C) Speedy Trial. Within 7 days of the filing of a motion, the court shall release a juvenile who has remained in detention while awaiting trial for more than 91 days to answer for the life offense or unless the trial has commenced. In computing the 91–day period, the court is to exclude delays as provided in MCR 6.004(C)(1) through (6) and the time required to conduct the hearing on the motion.

[Adopted effective October 1, 1989.]

RULE 6.911 PRELIMINARY EXAMINATION

(A) Waiver. The juvenile may waive a preliminary examination if the juvenile is represented by an attorney and the waiver is made and signed by the juvenile in open court. The magistrate shall find and place on the record that the waiver was freely, understandingly, and voluntarily given.

(B) Transfer to Juvenile Court. If the magistrate, following preliminary examination, finds that there is no probable cause that a life offense occurred or that there is no probable cause that the juvenile committed the life offense, but that some other offense occurred that if committed by an adult would constitute a crime, and that there is probable cause to believe that the juvenile committed that offense, the magistrate shall transfer the matter to the juvenile court of the county where the offense is alleged to have been committed for further proceedings. If the court transfers the matter to juvenile court, a transcript of the preliminary examination shall be sent to the juvenile court without charge upon request.

[Adopted effective October 1, 1989.]

RULE 6.931 JUVENILE SENTENCING HEARING

(A) General. After a juvenile has been convicted, the court must conduct a juvenile sentencing hearing unless the hearing is waived as provided in subrule (B).

(B) No Juvenile Sentencing Hearing; Consent. The court need not conduct a juvenile sentencing hearing if the prosecuting attorney, the juvenile, and the attorney of the juvenile, consent that it is not in the best interests of the juvenile and the public to sentence the juvenile as though an adult offender. In the absence of a juvenile sentencing hearing, the court shall not impose a sentence as provided by law for an adult offender. The court must place the juvenile on juvenile probation and commit the juvenile to state wardship.

(C) Notice of Juvenile Sentencing Hearing Following Verdict. The prosecuting attorney, the juvenile, and the attorney of the juvenile must be advised on the record immediately following conviction of the juvenile by a guilty plea or verdict of guilty that a hearing will be conducted at sentencing, unless waived, to determine whether to sentence the juvenile as an adult or to place the juvenile on juvenile probation and commit the juvenile to state wardship as though a delinquent. The court may announce the scheduled date of the hearing. On request, the court shall notify the victim of the juvenile sentencing hearing.

(D) Review of Reports. The court must give the prosecuting attorney, the juvenile, and the attorney of the juvenile, an opportunity to review the presentence report and the social report prior to the juvenile sentencing hearing. The court may exempt information from the reports as provided in MCL 771.14, 771.14a; MSA 28.1144, 28.1144(1).

(E) Juvenile Sentencing Hearing Procedure.

(1) *Evidence.* At the juvenile sentencing hearing all relevant and material evidence may be received by the court and relied upon to the extent of its probative value, even though such evidence may not be admissible at trial. The rules of evidence do not apply. The court shall receive and consider the presentence report prepared by the probation officer and the social report prepared by the department of social services.

(2) *Burden of Proof.* The prosecuting attorney has the burden of establishing by a preponderance of the evidence that the best interests of the juvenile and the public would be served by imposing a sentence against the juvenile as though the juvenile were an adult offender.

(3) *Criteria.* The court shall consider the following criteria in determining whether to impose a sentence against the juvenile as though an adult offender or whether to place the juvenile on juvenile probation and commit the juvenile to state wardship, giving each weight as appropriate to the circumstances:

(a) the juvenile's prior record and character, physical and mental maturity, and pattern of living;

(b) the seriousness and circumstances of the offense;

(c) whether the offense is part of a repetitive pattern of offenses which would lead to the determination:

(i) that the juvenile is not amenable to treatment, or

(ii) that, despite the juvenile's potential for treatment, owing to the nature of the delinquent behavior, the juvenile is likely to disrupt the rehabilitation of others in the treatment program owing to the nature of the delinquent behavior;

(d) whether, despite the juvenile's potential for treatment, the nature of the juvenile's delinquent behavior is likely to render the juvenile dangerous to the public when released at age 21;

(e) whether the juvenile is more likely to be rehabilitated by the services and facilities available in the adult programs and procedures than in the juvenile programs and procedures; and

(f) what is in the best interests of the public welfare and the protection of the public security.

(4) *Findings.* The court must make findings of fact and conclusions of law forming the basis for the juvenile probation and commitment decision or the decision to sentence the juvenile as though an adult offender. The findings and conclusions may be incorporated in a written opinion or stated on the record.

(F) Postjudgment Procedure; Juvenile Probation and Commitment to State Wardship. If the court retains jurisdiction over the juvenile, places the juvenile on juvenile probation, and commits the juvenile to state wardship; the court shall comply with subrules (1) through (11):

(1) The court shall enter a judgment which shall contain a provision for reimbursement by the juvenile or those responsible for the juvenile's support, or both, for the cost of care and services pursuant to MCL 769.1(6); MSA 28.1072(6). An order assessing such cost against a person responsible for the support of the juvenile shall not be binding on the person, unless an opportunity for a hearing has been given and until a copy of the order is served on the person, personally or by first class mail to the person's last known address.

(2) The court shall advise the juvenile at sentencing that if the juvenile, while on juvenile probation, is convicted of a felony or a misdemeanor punishable by more than one year's imprisonment, the court must revoke juvenile probation and sentence the juvenile to a term of years in prison not to exceed the penalty that might have been imposed for the offense for which the juvenile was originally convicted.

(3) The court shall assure that the juvenile receives a copy of the social report.

(4) The court shall send a copy of the order and a copy of the written opinion or transcript of the findings and conclusions of law to the department of social services.

(5) The court shall not place the juvenile on deferred sentencing, as provided in MCL 771.1(2); MSA 28.1131(2).

(6) The court shall not place the juvenile on life probation for conviction of a controlled substance violation, as set forth in MCL 771.1(3); MSA 28.1131(3).

(7) The five-year limit on the term of probation for an adult felony offender shall not apply.

(8) The court shall not require as a condition of juvenile probation that the juvenile report to a department of corrections probation officer.

(9) The court shall not, as a condition of juvenile probation, impose jail time against the juvenile except as provided in MCR 6.933(B)(2).

(10) The court shall not commit the juvenile to the department of corrections for failing to comply with a restitution order.

(11) The court shall not place the juvenile in a department of corrections camp for one year, as otherwise provided in MCL 771.3a(1); MSA 28.1133(1).

[Adopted effective October 1, 1989; amended effective December 1, 1993.]

Staff Comment to 1993 Amendment

The 1993 amendment of MCR 6.931(A) clarified that a sentencing hearing is to take place when a juvenile is convicted (unless the hearing is waived), without regard to whether the conviction enters by plea or following a trial.

RULE 6.933 JUVENILE PROBATION REVOCATION

(A) **General Procedure.** When a juvenile, who was placed on juvenile probation and committed to an institution as a state ward, is alleged to have violated juvenile probation, the court shall proceed as provided in MCR 6.445(A) through (F).

(B) **Disposition.**

(1) *Certain Criminal Offense Violations.* If the court finds that the juvenile has violated juvenile probation by being convicted of a felony or a misdemeanor punishable by more than one year's imprisonment, the court must revoke the probation of the juvenile and order the juvenile committed to the department of corrections for a term of years not to exceed the penalty that could have been imposed for the offense that led to the probation. The court in imposing sentence shall grant credit against the sentence as required by law.

(2) *Other Violations.* If the court finds that the juvenile has violated juvenile probation, other than as provided in subrule (B)(1), the juvenile must be continued on juvenile probation and remain under state wardship provided that the court may order:

(a) a change of placement,

(b) restitution,

(c) community service,

(d) substance abuse counselling,

(e) mental health counselling,

(f) participation in a vocational-technical education program,

(g) incarceration in a county jail for not more than 30 days, and

(h) any other participation or performance as the court considers necessary.

If the court determines to place the juvenile in jail for up to 30 days, and the juvenile is under 17 years of age, the juvenile must be placed separately from adult prisoners as required by law.

(3) If the court revokes juvenile probation pursuant to subrule (B)(1), the court must receive an updated presentence report and comply with MCR 6.445(G) before it imposes a prison sentence on the juvenile.

(C) **Review.** The juvenile may appeal as of right from the imposition of a sentence of incarceration after a finding of juvenile probation violation.

[Adopted effective October 1, 1989.]

RULE 6.935 SEMIANNUAL PROGRESS REVIEW OF COURT–COMMITTED JUVENILES

(A) **General.** The court shall review the progress of a juvenile it has placed on juvenile probation and committed to state wardship under MCL 769.1; MSA 28.1072.

(B) **Time.** The court must conduct the progress review no later than 182 days after the entry of the order placing the juvenile on juvenile probation and committing the juvenile to state wardship. The review shall be made semiannually thereafter so long as the juvenile remains in state wardship.

(C) **Progress Review Report.** The court shall examine the progress review report prepared by the department of social services covering placement and services being provided the juvenile, and the progress of the juvenile.

(D) The court may not order a more physically restrictive change in the level of placement of the juvenile or order more restrictive treatment absent a hearing as provided in MCR 6.937.

[Adopted effective October 1, 1989.]

RULE 6.937 COMMITMENT REVIEW HEARING

(A) **Required Hearing.** When a juvenile has been placed on probation and committed to state wardship, the court must schedule a commitment review hearing to be held within 42 days before the juvenile attains age 19 unless adjourned for good cause.

(1) *Notice.* The department of social services or agency, facility, or institution to which the juvenile is committed, shall advise the court at least 91 days before the juvenile attains age 19 of the need to schedule a commitment review hearing. Notice of the hearing must be given to the prosecuting attorney, the agency or the superintendent of the facility to which

the juvenile has been committed, the juvenile, and the parent of the juvenile if the parent's address or whereabouts are known, at least 14 days prior to the hearing. Notice must clearly indicate that the court may extend jurisdiction over the juvenile until age 21. The notice shall include advice to the juvenile and the parent of the juvenile that the juvenile has the right to an attorney.

(2) *Appointment of an Attorney.* The court must appoint an attorney to represent the juvenile at the hearing unless legal counsel has been retained or is waived pursuant to MCR 6.905(C).

(3) *Findings; Criteria.* Before the court continues the jurisdiction over the juvenile until age 21, the prosecutor must demonstrate by a preponderance of the evidence that the juvenile has not been rehabilitated or that the juvenile presents a serious risk to public safety. The rules of evidence shall not apply. In making the determination, the court must consider the following factors:

(a) the extent and nature of the juvenile's participation in education, counselling, or work programs;

(b) the juvenile's willingness to accept responsibility for prior behavior;

(c) the juvenile's behavior in the current placement;

(d) the prior record and character of the juvenile and physical and mental maturity;

(e) the juvenile's potential for violent conduct as demonstrated by prior behavior;

(f) the recommendations of the state institution or agency charged with the juvenile's care for the juvenile's release or continued custody; and

(g) other information the prosecuting attorney or the juvenile may submit.

(B) Other Commitment Review Hearings. The court, on motion of the institution, agency, or facility to which the juvenile is committed, may release a juvenile at any time upon a showing by a preponderance of evidence that the juvenile has been rehabilitated and is not a risk to public safety. The notice provision in subrule (A), other than the requirement that the court clearly indicate that it may extend jurisdiction over the juvenile until age 21, and the criteria in subrule (A) shall apply. The rules of evidence shall not apply. The court must appoint an attorney to represent the juvenile at the hearing unless legal counsel has been retained or the right to counsel waived. The court, upon notice and opportunity to be heard as provided in this rule, may also move the juvenile to a more restrictive placement or treatment program.

[Adopted effective October 1, 1989.]

1989 Staff Comment to Subchapter 6.900

An edited version of the staff comment relative to Administrative Order 1988–5 is reprinted below because it pertains in large part to the new rules in subchapter 6.900.

The significant differences between the proposed rules and the rules adopted on April 13, 1989 are as follows.

The juvenile in custody must be released if the case is not tried within 91 days excluding delays as provided in MCR 6.004(C). See MCR 6.909(C). The magistrate must deduct the time use by the prosecuting attorney in deciding whether to authorize the filing of a complaint and warrant as provided in MCR 5.935 from the time required to hold the preliminary examination after arraignment. However, the reduction can be no more than three days. MCR 6.907(C)(2). The juvenile is entitled to a lawyer irrespective of indigency. A lawyer must be appointed unless waived or unless a lawyer has been retained.

The subchapter does not apply to the juvenile over whom the juvenile court waived jurisdiction.

The prosecutor must make effort to notify the parent or guardian of the arraignment on the complaint and warrant. A similar duty is placed on the defense attorney if parent or guardian does not show up at the arraignment relative to notification of preliminary examination. MCR 6.907(A); MCR 6.907(C)(2).

The burden of proof is preponderance of the evidence at the commitment review hearing whether it is the automatic hearing at age 19 or a hearing on motion of the institution or facility where the juvenile is committed. MCR 6.937.

The proposed new subchapter 6.900 is responsive to the following public acts: 1988 PA 51, 52, 53, 54, 64, 67, 73, 75, 76, 77, 78, and 182.

Background

Prior to October 1, 1988, the *juvenile court* [1] *had exclusive jurisdiction* over juveniles under 17 years of age charged with offenses that would be criminal if committed by adults.[2] The juvenile who is charged in a petition, and not diverted to a social program, faces adjudication, by trial or plea of admission; the ultimate decision to be made is whether the juvenile court will take jurisdiction over the juvenile. The phrase "take jurisdiction over the juvenile" refers to the authority of the state, in particular the juvenile court, to assume parental authority as guardian of all children within its borders, when the authority of the natural parent or guardian or adoptive parent falters by virtue of juvenile delinquency, child abuse, or child neglect.

The juvenile who is found to come within the jurisdiction of the juvenile court may, as a delinquent, be civilly committed until age 19. If the juvenile is committed as a state ward to a public institution under § 18 of the Juvenile Code,[3] the youth parole and review board has the authority to release the juvenile.[4]

The *juvenile court has authority to waive its exclusive jurisdiction* over juveniles who are alleged to have committed acts while between the age of 15 and 17 years that would constitute felonies if committed by adults.[5] A waiver of jurisdiction hearing is held on the motion of the prosecuting attorney. At the hearing the juvenile court must decide whether the best interests of the juvenile and the public would be served by waiving its exclusive jurisdiction over the juvenile so that the juvenile could be prosecuted as though an adult offender.

Should the juvenile court waive its exclusive jurisdiction, the waived juvenile would be arraigned on a complaint and warrant in district court. Further, the magistrate (district court judge) must, as with an adult offender, conduct a preliminary examination, unless waived, to decide whether the juvenile will stand trial on the charge in circuit court or recorder's court for the city of Detroit.[6] The circuit or recorder's court acquires jurisdiction over the juvenile upon the making of a proper return from the magistrate before whom the juvenile was examined or waived examination.[7] The circuit or recorder's court must impose a sentence provided by law for an adult offender if the juvenile is convicted following trial or a plea of guilty.

New Legislation

A. General. After October 1, 1988, the prosecuting attorney has discretion to criminally charge a juvenile who, at age 15 or 16 allegedly committed one or more of nine enumerated offenses carrying penalties of up to life in prison,[8] including murder, armed robbery, and first-degree criminal sexual conduct. No longer will the prosecuting attorney have to obtain a waiver of the juvenile court's exclusive jurisdiction under § 4 of the Juvenile Code[9] to charge the juvenile as though an adult offender. The exclusive jurisdiction of the juvenile court will depend on the prosecuting attorney's approval of the filing of a petition in the juvenile court instead of authorization of the filing of a criminal complaint and warrant with a magistrate.[10] Once the prosecuting attorney authorizes the filing of a criminal complaint and warrant charging an enumerated life offense, the juvenile becomes *subject to* the jurisdiction of a court having general criminal jurisdiction.[11] On the other hand, the juvenile court's jurisdiction becomes exclusive when the prosecuting attorney unconditionally approves a filing of a petition in juvenile court rather than authorizing the filing of a criminal complaint and warrant with the magistrate.

B. Juvenile Court Jurisdiction—Before Authorization of Criminal Complaint. It is arguable, under the new language in § 2 of the Juvenile Code,[12] that the circuit or recorder's court has jurisdiction over the juvenile at the point following apprehension of a juvenile on an enumerated life offense, but before the prosecuting attorney has decided to prosecute the juvenile as though an adult offender. The Juvenile Court Rules Committee based its proposed rules to the Court on the premise that *an apprehended juvenile under 17 is not to be treated as an adult before it is known whether the prosecuting attorney will exercise the discretion to treat the juvenile as though an adult offender.* This appears to be in keeping with the intent of the Legislature. When the legislation is read as a whole, it manifests the intent that the juvenile be treated as though an adult offender only for purposes of court proceedings until after a conviction and disposition hearing. Owing to the juvenile's minority and to the language in Const 1963, art 6, § 15, providing the juvenile court original jurisdiction over all juvenile delinquents except as otherwise provided by law, the jurisdiction over the juvenile who has been apprehended on a life offense is with the juvenile court unless and until the prosecutor decides to prosecute the juvenile as though an adult offender or until the prosecutor obtains a waiver of the juvenile court's jurisdiction under § 4 of the Juvenile Code.[13]

C. District Court Proceedings. After the prosecuting attorney decides to proceed against a juvenile on a life offense as though an adult offender, the juvenile must be arraigned on an authorized complaint and warrant in district court and is entitled to a preliminary examination. Should the magistrate find at the preliminary examination that the prosecuting attorney has *not* made a prima facie showing that an enumerated life offense has been committed, or that probable cause does not exist that the juvenile committed the life offense, the magistrate may not bind the juvenile over to stand trial as an adult. The magistrate must transfer the case to juvenile court provided it is shown that some criminal offense occurred and that probable cause exists to believe the juvenile committed the offense.[14]

D. Postconviction Proceedings in Circuit or Recorder's Court. A juvenile who is bound over and convicted of an enumerated life offense must be given a special disposition hearing at sentencing unless waived. Following the disposition hearing, the court must decide whether to place the juvenile on probation and commit the juvenile to a public institution as a state ward until age 21, or sooner, or to impose a sentence as provided by law for an adult.[15]

The criteria used at the dispositional hearing to decide whether to civilly commit or criminally punish is similar to the criteria used by the juvenile court when it waives its exclusive jurisdiction over the juvenile under § 4 of the Code. See, infra ["F. New Statutory Procedures for Juvenile Court Waiver of Its Jurisdiction."]

The circuit or recorder's court retains jurisdiction over the juvenile when it places the juvenile on probation and makes the juvenile a state ward under the Youth Rehabilitation Services Act.[16] The court that retains jurisdiction must conduct annual progress reviews of the juvenile and must hold a commitment review hearing before the juvenile reaches age 19. The purpose of the commitment review hearing is to decide whether jurisdiction over the juvenile should continue until the juvenile reaches age 21. The court must retain jurisdiction over the juvenile if at the commitment review hearing it is shown that the juvenile remains a public safety risk or has not been rehabilitated.[17] The Department of Social Services is required by the Juvenile Facilities Act[18] to make written reports to assist the circuit or recorder's court in its effort to decide what to do at the original juvenile disposition hearing, the commitment review hearing, and when the court undertakes its annual progress review.

E. Probation Revocation. The juvenile who commits a felony or misdemeanor punishable by imprisonment for one year or more while under the jurisdiction of the circuit or recorder's court as a state ward must, following a probation violation hearing, be sentenced to "a term of years" not to exceed what an adult offender could have received. Presumably, under the literal language of 1988 PA 78, the juvenile who is civilly committed after conviction for first-degree murder and who is subsequently convicted of committing another felony, may only receive a "term of years" rather than mandatory life. This is not the case, however, with respect to the juvenile who is initially sentenced as an adult following the juvenile disposition hearing. It should be noted that it takes "a conviction" to revoke the probation. This may mean that if the juvenile is still on probation and committed to state wardship when the juvenile commits another felony while still under age 17, the prosecutor will have to obtain a waiver of the juvenile court's jurisdiction under § 4, before obtaining a conviction unless, of course, the offense that is the subject of the probation violation is one of the nine enumerated life offenses.[19]

F. New Statutory Procedures for Juvenile Court Waiver of Its Jurisdiction. The prosecuting attorney, for whatever reason,[20] may decide to move the juvenile court to waive its exclusive jurisdiction over the juvenile even when the juvenile is accused of an enumerated life offense, rather than proceed directly against the juvenile as though an adult offender. After October 1, 1988, the criteria set forth in § 4 of the Juvenile Code for waiving the juvenile over to stand trial as an adult have been refined along the general lines of the decisions in *People v Dunbar*, 423 Mich 380; 377 NW2d 262 (1985), and *People v Schumacher*, 75 Mich App 505, 511–512; 256 NW2d 39 (1977). Nevertheless, the juvenile court at the waiver hearing, as well as the circuit court at the juvenile disposition hearing, may now give more weight to one criterion than another on the basis of legislative language: "consider the following criteria giving each weight as appropriate to the circumstances." [21] The waiver of the juvenile court's exclusive jurisdiction so the juvenile may stand trial as an adult means that the case will now go directly to the circuit or recorder's court for arraignment on an information. There no longer will be an arraignment on the complaint and warrant or a preliminary examination. The first phase of the waiver hearing, the probable cause phase, will serve as the equivalent of the preliminary examination stage.[22] There is, however, an apparent inconsistency in the language in the new legislation concerning the standard for establishing probable cause.

Under § 4 of the Juvenile Code, as amended, the Legislature has provided that the standard for establishing probable cause at the first phase of the waiver hearing to decide whether the juvenile court will waive its jurisdiction is "if there is probable cause to believe that an offense has been committed which if committed by an adult would be a felony and if there is probable cause to believe that the child [juvenile] committed the offense." [23] Under § 14(2) of Chapter VI of the Code of Criminal Procedure, the standard at the preliminary examination involving juveniles is whether an offense took place and probable cause to believe that the juvenile committed it.[24]

G. Keeping the Juvenile in Juvenile Court. In many cases, particularly criminal sexual conduct charges, the prosecuting attorney will approve the filing of the petition in juvenile court without seeking a waiver of jurisdiction or proceeding directly to a court having general criminal jurisdiction. When the juvenile is adjudicated for having committed one or more acts which if committed by an adult would be a felony, and the juvenile court orders the juvenile committed to an institution under § 18(1)(e) of the Juvenile Code,[25] the juvenile court will retain jurisdiction over the juvenile and conduct annual review of the juvenile's progress. Should the juvenile be committed for a specific offense that is more serious than just any felony,[26] the jurisdiction of the juvenile court may be extended over the juvenile who has been committed to a public institution under § 18(1)(e) of the Juvenile Code until age 21. However, there must be an automatic commitment review hearing before the juvenile reaches age 19 to determine if the juvenile remains a public safety risk or is not rehabilitated. It seems the law that extends jurisdiction over the juvenile until age 21 applies only to those juveniles who have committed the offense which subject them to the extended jurisdiction after October 1, 1988.[27] Further, the Youth Parole and Review Board within the Department of Social Services is being phased out.[28]

H. Detention. With limited exceptions, Const 1963, art 1, § 15, gives the individual charged with a crime the right to bail: "[A]ll persons shall, *before conviction*, be bailable by sufficient sureties, except that bail may be denied " (Emphasis added.) The juvenile court delinquency proceeding is not criminal.[29] A juvenile court adjudication is not a criminal

conviction. The traditional purpose of the juvenile court has been for the benefit of the juvenile. Further:

"[J]uveniles, unlike adults, are always in some form of custody. *Lehman* v *Lycoming County Children's Services*, 458 US 502, 510–511 [103 S Ct 3213; 73 L Ed 2d 928] (1982); *In re Gault*, [387 US 1, 17; 87 S Ct 1428; 18 L Ed 2d 527]. Children, by definition, are not assumed to have the capacity to take care of themselves. They are assumed to be subject to the control of their parents, and if parental control falters, the State must play its part as parens patriae. See *State* v *Gleason*, 404 A2d 573, 580 (Me, 1979); *People ex rel Wayburn* v *Schupf*, [39 NY2d 682, 690]; 350 NE2d [906 (1976)]; *Baker* v *Smith*, 477 SW2d 149, 150–151 (Ky App, 1971). In this respect, the juvenile's liberty interest may, in appropriate circumstances, be subordinated to the State's 'parens patriae interest in preserving and promoting the welfare of the child.' *Santosky* v *Kramer*, [455 US 745, 766; 102 S Ct 1388; 71 L Ed 2d 599 (1982)]." [30]

In juvenile court proceedings, the parent may, by statute, post bail to assure that the juvenile is going to appear in court for trial.[31] A juvenile court may order a juvenile detained if there is probable cause to believe that the juvenile committed the offense alleged and the juvenile fits a circumstance, such as that the offense is so serious that release of the juvenile would be a risk to the public. MCR 5.935(D). However, the juvenile court is supposed to detain a juvenile in the least restrictive environment that will meet the needs of the juvenile and public. MCR 5.935(D)(5). Thus, when the juvenile is detained by the juvenile court and placed in a less restrictive environment than a pretrial detention of an adult prisoner, such as foster care, shelter, etc., the juvenile court may not be required to set bail if the grounds exist to detain unless the reason for detention was solely to assure that the juvenile shows up for trial.

Although it is not clear, it seems that when a juvenile is charged with an offense which if committed by an adult would be a crime, and the juvenile is placed in secure detention equivalent to pretrial incarceration of an adult prisoner, the juvenile ought to be given a chance to post bail if an adult could.[32]

When the juvenile is prosecuted as an adult, the state constitutional provision noted above directly applies, limiting the right of the government to detain.

It is clear from the new Public Acts that the Legislature intended that a juvenile under 17, who is criminally prosecuted without a waiver hearing under § 4 of the Juvenile Code, may not be detained in a jail with adult prisoners pending trial, acquittal or conviction, or decision at a juvenile disposition hearing. The Legislature intended that the juvenile who is criminally charged with one or more enumerated life offense without being waived over must be housed in a juvenile facility.[33] The exceptions are if the juvenile is considered to be a menace to other juveniles because of habit or conduct, or may not otherwise be safely detained. In such cases the juvenile may be housed in a jail or similar institution designed to incarcerate adult prisoners, if placed in a room or ward out of sight and sound from the other adults.[34] Note further that the juvenile, from the point of apprehension, must be kept separate from adult prisoners.

The Juvenile Court Rules Committee, when it formulated suggested proposals based on the new legislation, debated the question whether the district court was authorized to place a juvenile in a facility pending trial. The committee found no specific express provision because there is none.

The statutory waiver package, read as a whole, establishes that the Legislature believed that the source of authority to detain a juvenile in a juvenile facility pending trial is § 27a of Chapter IV (arrests) in the Code of Criminal Procedure:

"(1) If a juvenile is taken into custody or detained, the juvenile shall not be confined in a police station, prison, jail, lock-up, or reformatory, or be transported with, or compelled or permitted to associate or mingle with, criminal persons while awaiting trial. However, a juvenile whose habits or conduct are considered to be a menace to other children, or who may not otherwise be safely detained, may be ordered by a court to be placed in a jail or other place of detention for adults, but in a room or ward out of sight and sound from adults.

"(2) If a person is convicted of a crime within this state and has served time in a juvenile facility prior to sentencing because of being denied or being unable to furnish bond for the offense of which he or she is convicted, the trial court in imposing sentence shall specifically grant credit against the sentence for time served in a juvenile facility prior to sentencing." MCL 764.27a; MSA 28.886(1), as added by 1988 PA 67.

It would have been preferable for the Legislature to have expressly stated that the juvenile may be detained in a juvenile facility with court sanction pending trial or disposition. Nevertheless, when a juvenile is apprehended and the prosecutor has authorized the filing of a criminal complaint and warrant, it is believed that the juvenile may be placed in a juvenile facility unless and until the court, including a district court, either orders the juvenile released with or without bail at arraignment, or other hearing, orders the juvenile committed to jail, because the juvenile is a menace to other children or may not otherwise be safely detained, or continues the detention in the juvenile facility. Commitment pending trial, if at all, was clearly intended by the Legislature to be in a juvenile facility. Unlike the juvenile system, which is civil in nature and which requires specific statutory authority in order to hold a juvenile pending adjudication, the accused in the adult criminal system is detained on a charge until arraigned and ordered released, even if arrested without a warrant. The written authority to detain if needed is provided by the complaint and warrant.

Section 27a represents a further limitation on government than just the Fourth Amendment and the like when it comes to juveniles who are to be criminally prosecuted as though adults. But a limitation implies authority that needs limits. The first sentence of § 27a(1) assumes not only that the juvenile has been taken into custody. It also assumes that the juvenile may be subject to detention. This is followed by the limitation that the juvenile not be put with adult prisoners while awaiting trial.

The second sentence of § 27a(1), making provision for the juvenile who may be a menace to other children, assumes that the juvenile will probably be in a facility with children—a juvenile facility. It should be remembered that jail has been defined by the Legislature in the Code of Criminal Procedure to include a juvenile facility for purposes of placement under § 27a. This indicates there is an absolute prohibition against placing a juvenile with adult prisoners in any facility whatsoever. The second sentence of § 27a also indicates that a court may put a juvenile in jail who may not otherwise be safely detained. "Juvenile facility" equates with jail for purposes of placement under § 27a. This may mean that the court that had earlier conditioned release of the juvenile on in-home detention, foster care and the like,

and later finds that the juvenile cannot otherwise be safely detained in such lesser restrictive environment, or is a menace to others, may place that juvenile in secure detention in a juvenile facility or, if necessary, in a jail used to incarcerate adults so long as the juvenile is out of sight and sound from adults. In short, the only apparent thing that a district court cannot do that a circuit court can do concerning juvenile detention pending trial is to order that the juvenile be placed in a *juvenile-court-operated* facility without the consent of the juvenile court.[35] Section 27a is one of the last provisions in the chapter of the Code of Criminal Procedure entitled "Arrest." It is followed by the chapter on bail, the first section of which authorizes a court, including a district court, to release a detained person "brought before the judge or district court magistrate to bail pursuant to section 15 of article 1 of the state constitution of 1963." [36]

Amendments of the Juvenile Court Rules

MCR 5.933 and 5.934 as amended effective July 1, 1989, make it clear that a juvenile will no longer be taken immediately to the *juvenile court* following apprehension on a life offense if the prosecuting attorney has authorized the filing of a criminal complaint and warrant. In that case the juvenile must be taken to the district court for arraignment on the complaint. See MCR 6.905(A). In the absence of an authorization from the prosecuting attorney, however, the juvenile must be brought to juvenile court or to a designated facility if following apprehension the court is not open.

A. Special Adjournment. The Juvenile Court Rules Committee proposes to create a special adjournment at the preliminary hearing stage to allow the prosecutor time to decide whether to criminally prosecute the juvenile or remain in the juvenile court. MCR 5.935(A)(3). The adjournment (for up to five days) must be granted on motion of the prosecuting attorney if the prosecutor has approved submitting a petition in juvenile court conditional on withdrawal within five days if the prosecuting attorney authorizes a criminal complaint and warrant. The juvenile must be released during the adjournment period unless the juvenile court satisfies the requirements for detention in MCR 5.935(D). The juvenile court must not authorize the petition during the special adjournment. If the prosecuting attorney takes no action to authorize a criminal complaint during the five-day adjournment, this acts as an effective bar to the prosecuting attorney from pursuing criminal prosecution, unless a waiver of the juvenile court's exclusive jurisdiction is obtained.

Should the prosecuting attorney authorize the filing of a criminal complaint during the adjournment period, the time used must be deducted from the twelve days given to conduct the preliminary examination following arraignment on the complaint and warrant.

B. Post-commitment Reviews. MCR 5.944 will implement the new procedure for dealing with juveniles who remain under the jurisdiction of the juvenile court after commitment to a public institution pursuant to § 18(1)(e) of the Juvenile Code. No actual hearing is held when the juvenile court undertakes a semi-annual progress review of the committed juvenile. However, the court may not, following progress review, order a juvenile moved to a more restrictive placement without giving the juvenile notice and opportunity to be heard.[37]

At the automatic commitment review hearing held 42 days before the 19th birthday of the juvenile who has been committed to a public institution on a "reportable offense" as defined in the court rules, other than breaking and entering, larceny from a building, and unauthorized driving away of an automobile, the prosecutor has the burden of proof. The prosecutor must show that the juvenile is not rehabilitated or that the juvenile is a public safety risk if released at 19. If the court is satisfied following a hearing that the prosecuting attorney met the burden of proof, the jurisdiction of the court over the juvenile continues until age 21 or further order of the court.

A commitment review hearing may also be held at any time on motion of the institution where the juvenile is committed. There is no provision authorizing the juvenile to personally move for a commitment review hearing. At the nonautomatic commitment review hearing, it is the moving party that has the burden to show that the juvenile is rehabilitated and not a public safety risk. The criteria to decide if the juvenile court will continue jurisdiction past 19 stems from 1988 PA 54.

C. Rule on Waiver Hearing. The Juvenile Court Rules Committee proposes that existing MCR 5.950 on waiver be amended to reflect the changes in § 4 of the Juvenile Code, as amended by 1988 PA 182. The juvenile who wants to waive the probable cause phase of the waiver hearing must be advised that the probable cause phase is the equivalent of and substitute for a preliminary examination in district court.

The Juvenile Court Rules Committee adopts the legislative view that the court's findings on waiver now may be stated on the record as an alternative to incorporating them into a written opinion. The committee proposes that the findings need only be sent to the circuit court along with the order of waiver if the circuit court requests them. Compare MCL 712A.4; MSA 27.3178(598.4), as added by 1988 PA 182. The Court adopted a rule that is consistent with the legislation.

District and Circuit Court Rules Pertaining to Juveniles Charged with Enumerated Life Offenses

A. Scope and Definitions. A new subchapter 6.900 covers the individual over 15 who is criminally charged, without the juvenile court having waived its jurisdiction following hearing, with committing an enumerated life offense between ages 15 and 17.

The definitions in the new subchapter pertaining to juveniles are very detailed, but facilitate organization by giving names to hearings not expressly designated in the legislation, including juvenile disposition hearing, commitment review hearing, and progress report.

B. Pretrial Rules. When a juvenile is apprehended for an offense including a life offense, unless the prosecuting attorney has authorized the filing of a complaint and warrant, the juvenile is to be taken immediately to the juvenile court for preliminary hearing.[38] A similar approach is taken for the juvenile who is apprehended for an enumerated life offense and the prosecutor has authorized the filing of a complaint and warrant except that the juvenile is to be taken forthwith to the district court. The juvenile must be released within 24 hours of the arrest unless the juvenile was first taken to the juvenile court and a special adjournment obtained. In the latter case, the juvenile will be arraigned on the complaint and warrant the same day the prosecuting attorney authorizes the complaint. At the arraignment on the complaint and warrant, the magistrate must appoint counsel to appear at the arraignment when no parent, or relative of the juvenile is present. Further, the time for holding the preliminary examination following arraignment may be as short as seven days, depending on the time given

the prosecuting attorney by a probate court to decide whether to proceed criminally against the juvenile following apprehension. The magistrate or court will have to appoint an attorney for the juvenile virtually in every instance unless waived. This may include appointing an attorney for a juvenile who insists on waiving an attorney and trying the case in pro per. See Const 1963, art 1, § 13, which provides a "suitor in any court in this state has the right to prosecute or defend his suit, either in his own person or by an attorney". On the "dangers and disadvantages" of self-representation, see *People* v *Anderson*, 398 Mich 361; 247 NW2d 857 (1976); *People* v *Riley*, 156 Mich App 396, 399; 401 NW2d 875 (1986). Waiver of an attorney is made difficult because of the age of the juvenile and the seriousness of the charge. Note that the cost of a court-appointed attorney, or a part thereof, may be recovered, even against a third party who is responsible for the juvenile following notice and opportunity to be heard. At the preliminary hearing, if the magistrate does not find the requisite probable cause for bindover on the enumerated life offense, the court must determine whether any other offense has taken place and whether there is probable cause to believe that the juvenile did it. If so, the juvenile must be transferred to the juvenile court in the county where the offense allegedly occurred. See MCR 6.911.

C. Detention. Bail must be set pursuant to MCR 6.110. However, the magistrate or court is not prohibited from looking to the factors used by the juvenile court. MCR 5.935. Furthermore, the rule contemplates some continuity between the courts in lodging the juvenile. If possible, the juvenile who is placed in a juvenile-court-operated detention facility pending decision by the prosecuting attorney on whether to authorize the filing of a criminal complaint and warrant might, with the consent of the juvenile court, remain in that facility, if not released, rather than be transported to another facility simply because the prosecutor chooses to proceed in adult court. On the other hand, unless the juvenile court consents to the magistrate's decision that the juvenile will remain in detention pending arraignment on the information, or unless the circuit court orders the juvenile to remain in the juvenile-court-operated facility while awaiting trial in adult court, the juvenile will likely have to be moved to a non-court-operated facility. The Legislature in adding § 2(f) to the Juvenile Code may have believed that only a court of general criminal jurisdiction should be directing the juvenile court to place a person within its juvenile-court-operated facility when the person is no longer within the jurisdiction of the juvenile court.

The juvenile who is detained in the juvenile court system is entitled to be tried within 42 days after having been taken into custody or released. The rule for the juvenile in detention while awaiting trial in adult court is release after 91 days. MCR 6.909(C).

D. Circuit or Recorder's Court Rules. MCR 6.931 reflects the procedure for a juvenile disposition hearing at sentencing. The purpose is to decide whether the circuit court will put the juvenile on probation and send the juvenile to a public institution or agency under the direction of the department of social services, or to impose a sentence as though the juvenile were an adult. The criteria for deciding whether to make the juvenile a state ward, while still retaining jurisdiction over the juvenile, or imposing a prison sentence is essentially the same criteria used by the juvenile court when it waives its jurisdiction over the juvenile so that the juvenile may stand trial as an adult. See, supra ["F.

New Statutory Procedures for Juvenile Court Waiver of Its Jurisdiction."]

The procedure in the proposed rule on probation revocation is self-explanatory. The prosecuting attorney will probably have to get a waiver of jurisdiction by the juvenile court as well as a conviction before seeking to revoke the juvenile's probation for having committed a felony or a high misdemeanor since the language in the statute requires that there be a conviction. The annual progress review and the commitment review hearings are similar to those proceedings in juvenile court, as explained earlier.

FOOTNOTES

1. The term "juvenile court" refers to the juvenile division of the probate court.

2. MCL 712A.2(a)(1); MSA 27.3178(598.2a)(1).

3. MCL 712A.18(1)(e); MSA 27.3178(598.18)(1)(e).

4. *In re Jackson*, 163 Mich App 105; 414 NW2d 156 (1987), *lv den* 429 Mich 885 (1987).

5. MCL 712A.4; MSA 27.3178(598.4).

6. *People v Dunigan*, 409 Mich 765; 298 NW2d 430 (1980).

7. *People v Curtis*, 389 Mich 698, 707; 209 NW2d 243 (1973).

8. The enumerated life offenses are assault with intent to murder, attempted murder, first-degree murder, second-degree murder, assault with intent to commit armed robbery, armed robbery, first-degree criminal sexual conduct, and possession of or manufacture, delivery, or possession with intent to deliver of 650 grams or more of a schedule 1 or 2 controlled substance.

9. MCL 712A.4; MSA 27.3178(598.4).

10. See MCL 712A.2(a)(1); MSA 27.3187(598.2)(a)(1), as amended by 1988 PA 53; MCL 764.1f; MSA 28.860(6), as added by 1988 PA 67.

11. MCL 600.606; MSA 27A.606, as added by 1988 PA 52; MCL 725.10a(1)(c); MSA 27.3950(1)(1)(c), as amended by 1988 PA 51.

12. MCL 712A.2(a)(1); MSA 27.3178(598.2)(a)(1), as amended by 1988 PA 53 reads:

"The juvenile division of the probate court shall have the following authority and jurisdiction:

"(a) Exclusive original jurisdiction superior to and regardless of the jurisdiction of any other court in proceedings concerning a child under 17 years of age who is found within the county if 1 or more of the following applies:

"(1) Except as otherwise provided in this subparagraph, the child has violated any municipal ordinance or law of the state or of the United States. The juvenile division of the probate court shall have jurisdiction over a child of 15 years of age or older who is charged with a violation of section 83, 89, 91, 316, 317, 520b, or 529 of the Michigan penal code, Act No. 328 of the Public Acts of 1931, being sections 750.83, 750.89, 750.91, 750.316, 750.317, 750.520b, and 750.529 of the Michigan Compiled Laws, or section 7401(2)(a)(i) or 7403(2)(a)(i) of the public health code, Act No. 368 of the Public Acts of 1978, being sections 333.7401 and 333.7403 of the Michigan Compiled Laws, if the prosecuting attorney files a petition in the juvenile court instead of authorizing a complaint and warrant."

It should be noted that the original bill on waiver provided only that the circuit or recorder's court would have authority to hear and determine a violation of one of the enumerated life offenses allegedly committed by a juvenile. The Legislature subsequently amended the provisions to give the prosecuting attorney discretion to authorize the filing of a criminal complaint and warrant or to approve the filing of a petition in juvenile court.

13. At best the jurisdiction of the circuit or recorder's court may be concurrent until the prosecutor decides to proceed in juvenile court. In other words, the exclusive jurisdiction of the juvenile court is conditional on the prosecuting attorney "filing a petition" in juvenile court "*instead* of authorizing" the filing of a complaint and warrant. The language in §§ 2(a)(1) and 11 of the Juvenile Code about the prosecutor "filing" the petition is a term of art meaning approved for filing. It is similar to the authorization to file a criminal complaint.

However, authorization was not used because it is a juvenile court judge or referee that authorizes the filing of a petition.

14. See MCL 766.14; MSA 28.932, as added by 1988 PA 67.

15. MCL 769.1; MSA 28.1072, as added by 1988 PA 78. It appears questionable whether a circuit or recorder's court will lose jurisdiction to the juvenile court if the juvenile is not found guilty of an enumerated life offense (i.e., convicted of a lesser included offense) or the juvenile tenders a plea of guilty to an offense other than an enumerated life offense.

16. See MCL 803.301 et seq.; MSA 25.399(51) et seq., as amended by 1988 PA 76. Under § 2(b)(ii) a state ward includes "a person accepted for care by the department [of social services] who is at least 15 years of age at the time committed to the department by the court of general criminal jurisdiction under section 1 of chapter IX of the code of criminal procedure and if the act for which the youth is committed occurred before his or her seventeenth birthday."

17. MCL 769.1b; MSA 28.1072(1), as added by 1988 PA 78.

18. See 1988 PA 73.

19. Section 7(1) of Chapter XI of the Code of Criminal Procedure, MCL 771.7; MSA 28.1137, as added by 1988 PA 78, provides:

"If a juvenile placed on probation and committed under section 1(3) or (4) of chapter IX to a state institution or agency described in the youth rehabilitation services act, Act No. 150 of the Public Acts of 1974, being sections 803.301 to 803.309 of the Michigan Compiled Laws, is found by the court to have violated probation by being convicted of a felony or a misdemeanor punishable by more than 1 year imprisonment, the court shall revoke probation and order the juvenile committed to the department of corrections for a term of years that shall not exceed the penalty that could have been imposed for the offense for which the juvenile was originally convicted and placed on probation with credit granted against the sentence for the period of time the juvenile served on probation."

20. The prosecuting attorney may believe that the question whether the juvenile should be treated as an adult is close enough to warrant a hearing and to obtain the guidance of the juvenile court. The prosecuting attorney may not want to go to the time and expense of criminal proceedings in circuit or recorder's court only to have the court, after conviction, place the juvenile on probation for a life offense and civilly commit the juvenile to state wardship.

21. See MCL 712A.4; MSA 27.3178(598.4), as amended by 1988 PA 182; and MCL 769.1(3); MSA 28.1072(3), as added by 1988 PA 78.

22. See MCL 712A.4(9); MSA 27.3178(598.4)(9), as added by 1988 PA 182 and MCL 766.4; MSA 28.922, as amended by 1988 PA 64.

23. MCL 712A.4(3); MSA 27.3178(598.4)(3), as added by 1988 PA 182.

24. MCL 766.14(2); MSA 28.932(2), as added by 1988 PA 67.

25. See MCL 712A.18c; MSA 27.3178(598.18c), as added by 1988 PA 54.

26. See MCL 712A.18d; MSA 27.3178(598.18d), as added by 1988 PA 54. A serious offense that may lead to commitment until age 21 is basically a reportable juvenile offense as defined in MCR 5.903(B)(6), as added by court order of May 26, 1988, 430 Mich, part IV, xxxiv, other than the offenses of breaking and entering, unauthorized driving away an automobile and larceny from a building.

27. See *People ex rel Oakland Prosecutor v Bureau of Pardons & Paroles*, and *State Defender v Director of Elections*, 405 Mich 815 (1979).

28. See § 121(1) of the Social Welfare Act, 1939 PA 280, MCL 400.121(1); MSA 16.490(31)(1), as amended by 1988 PA 75, and § 18c of the Juvenile Code, MCL 712A.18c; MSA 27.3178(598.18c), as added by 1988 PA 54.

29. MCL 712A.1; MSA 27.3178(598.1) provides in part: "Proceedings under this chapter shall not be deemed to be criminal proceedings."

30. *Schall v Martin*, 467 US 253, 265; 104 S Ct 2403; 81 L Ed 2d 207 (1984).

31. MCL 712A.15; MSA 27.3178(598.15).

32. A secure detention facility would be one that prevents the juvenile from leaving the premises as a result of restraints stemming from the structure or perhaps regulation of the facility.

33. "Juvenile facility" is defined in MCL 761.1(s); MSA 28.843(s), as added by 1988 PA 67. See, also, MCL 764.27a; MSA 28.886(1), as

added by 1988 PA 67; MCL 400.115d(1); MSA 16.490(25d)(1), as amended by 1988 PA 75. MCL 720.651; MSA 25.398(1), as added by 1988 PA 77. See, also, §§ 2(c) and 4(1) of the Juvenile Facilities Act, 1988 PA 73.

34. See MCL 764.27a; MSA 28.886(1): Jail includes juvenile facility "in which a juvenile has been placed pending trial under section 27a of chapter IV." MCL 761.1(q); MSA 28.843(q), added by 1988 PA 67. Juvenile means a person *subject* to the jurisdiction of

the circuit or recorder's court although the Legislature inartfully used the term "within."

35. See MCL 712A.2(f); MSA 27.3178(598.2)(f), as added by 1988 PA 53.

36. See MCL 765.1(1); MSA 28.888(1).

37. The superintendent of the public institution where the juvenile is committed may be able to move the juvenile without court hearing. See MCL 720.601; MSA 27.3178(598.31), as amended by 1988 PA 74.

38. See MCL 764.27; MSA 28.886.

CHAPTER 7.   APPELLATE RULES

Effective March 1, 1985

[For Table of Rules, see page 1 et seq.]

SUBCHAPTER 7.100   APPEALS TO CIRCUIT COURT

RULE 7.101   PROCEDURE GENERALLY

(A) Applicability; Scope.

(1) This rule applies to appeals to the circuit court from the district court and probate court, each referred to as "trial court" in MCR 7.101 and 7.103. The term "circuit court" includes the Recorder's Court of the City of Detroit as to appeals of which that court has jurisdiction. In appeals from probate court, the term "clerk" refers to the probate register.

(2) An order or judgment of a trial court reviewable in the circuit court may be reviewed only by an appeal.

(3) This rule does not restrict or enlarge the right of review provided by law or make an order or judgment reviewable if it is not otherwise reviewable.

(B) Time for Taking Appeal.

(1) *Appeal of Right.* Except when another time is prescribed by statute or court rule, an appeal of right must be taken within

(a) 21 days after the entry of the order or judgment appealed from; or

(b) 21 days after the entry of an order denying a motion for new trial or judgment notwithstanding the verdict, a motion for rehearing or reconsideration, or a motion for other postjudgment relief, if the motion was filed within the original 21–day period.

A motion for rehearing or reconsideration of a motion mentioned in subrule (B)(1)(b) does not extend the time for filing a claim of appeal, unless the motion for rehearing or reconsideration was itself filed within the 21–day period.

(2) *Appeal by Leave.* When an appeal of right is not available, or the time for taking an appeal of right has passed, the time for filing an application for leave to appeal is governed by MCR 7.103.

(C) Manner of Taking Appeal; Appeal of Right.

(1) *Claim of Appeal.* To appeal of right, within the time for taking an appeal, an appellant must file a claim of appeal with the circuit court clerk and pay the fee, if required by law. The parties are named in the same order as they appeared in the trial court, but with the added designation "appellant" or "appellee". The claim must state:

"*[Name of aggrieved party]* claims an appeal from the *[judgment or order]* entered *[date]* in *[name of the trial court]*."

The appellant or the appellant's attorney must date and sign the claim of appeal and place his or her business address and telephone number under the signature.

(2) *Other Requirements.* In addition to doing the acts required by subrule (C)(1), no later than the time the claim of appeal is filed, the appellant must do the following:

(a) File in the trial court copies of the claim of appeal and of the judgment or order appealed from;

(b) File in the trial court a bond for costs on appeal unless the appellant has filed a stay bond that includes security for costs or unless the appellant is exempt or excused from filing a bond or bond is waived under MCR 3.604(L). This subrule does not, however, apply to civil infraction actions, criminal cases, or summary proceedings for the possession of premises.

(i) The bond must be in the amount of $200, unless the trial court sets another amount.

(ii) The bond must have at least one surety, unless the court excuses this requirement under MCR 3.604(L).

(iii) The bond must be on the condition that the appellant will pay the costs under subrule (O) and the damages under subrule (P) awarded on appeal.

(iv) Objections to the bond or surety are governed by MCR 3.604.

(c) Deliver or deposit money, property, or documents and do other acts required by law.

(d) Order in writing a copy of the full transcript and secure payment for it. On the appellant's motion, with notice to the appellee, the trial court may order that a lesser portion, or none, of the proceedings be transcribed. The appellee may file with the trial court a transcript of a portion of the proceedings not filed by the appellant. Except in appeals that the circuit court hears de novo, if a transcript of relevant proceedings cannot be obtained, the appellant may initiate procedures for preparation of a settled record in the manner provided in MCR 7.210(B)(2).

(e) File in the trial court exhibits in the appellant's possession.

(3) *Notice and Proof of Service.* Within 7 days after the claim of appeal is filed, the appellant must serve on the appellee and on any other person entitled by rule or statute to notice of the appeal:

(a) a copy of the claim of appeal;

(b) a statement specifying

(i) when an appeal bond, if any, was filed, the amount of the bond, and the sureties,

(ii) when the required fees were paid,

(iii) when an act was performed under subrule (C)(2)(c) and the nature of the act;

(c) a copy of the reporter's or recorder's certificate showing that

(i) the transcript has been ordered and payment secured, with the estimated date of completion,

(ii) the transcript has been furnished, or

(iii) there is no record to be transcribed.

Proof of service, the reporter's or recorder's certificate, and the required statement must be filed in the trial court and the circuit court.

(D) Appellee's Appearance; Cross Appeal.

(1) *Notice of Appearance.* Within 14 days after being served with the claim of appeal, the required statement, and the reporter's or recorder's certificate, the appellee must file an appearance in the trial court and circuit court and file exhibits in his or her possession with the trial court clerk.

(2) *Cross Appeal.* The appellee may take a cross appeal by filing a claim of cross appeal with his or her appearance. The provisions of this rule regarding an appeal govern a cross appeal.

(E) Effect of Appeal. The circuit court clerk shall assign a file number to an appeal when it is filed. The trial court retains jurisdiction until the trial court clerk sends the record to the circuit court clerk under subrule (F).

(F) Record on Appeal.

(1) Within 28 days after filing the claim of appeal, the appellant must file with the trial court the transcript or a copy of the reporter's or recorder's certificate and a statement that the transcript is not yet available.

(2) After the appellant makes the filing under subrule (F)(1), the clerk or register of the trial court shall

(a) ensure that the docket entries are correct and ready for transmittal;

(b) ensure that all exhibits have been filed;

(c) ensure that all relevant documents and papers from the court file are ready for transmittal; and

(d) determine that the required fees have been paid and required bond filed.

(3) If the record is ready for transmittal, the court shall sign an order transmitting the record. The trial court may eliminate exhibits from the record.

(4) If the transcript is not yet available, the trial court shall postpone transmittal of the record, enter an order to facilitate the preparation of the record, and notify the circuit court of the postponement and of the estimated date of transmittal.

(5) The trial court clerk must send the record to the circuit court clerk and notify the parties of the transmittal.

(G) Dismissal of an Appeal. If an appellant does not comply with subrule (C)(2) or (F)(1), the appeal may be considered abandoned, and the trial court may dismiss the appeal on 7 days' notice to the parties, unless the trial court or circuit court has granted a motion for further time. The trial court clerk must promptly notify the circuit court of a dismissal, and the circuit court shall dismiss the claim of appeal. Compliance with subrule (F)(1) after the 28-day period does not preclude dismissal of the appeal unless the appellant shows a reasonable excuse for the late compliance.

(H) Stay of Proceedings.

(1) *Civil Actions.*

(a) Unless otherwise provided by rule or ordered by the trial court, an execution may not issue and proceedings may not be taken to enforce an order or judgment until the expiration of the time for taking an appeal under subrule (B).

(b) An appeal does not stay execution unless

(i) the appellant files a stay bond to the opposing party as provided by this rule or by law; or

(ii) the appellant is exempted by law from filing a bond or is excused from filing a bond under MCL 600.2605; MSA 27A.2605 or MCR 3.604(L) and the trial court grants a stay on motion.

(c) The stay bond must be set by the trial court in an amount adequate to protect the opposing party. If the appeal is by a person against whom a money judgment has been entered, it must be not less than 1¼ times the amount of the judgment. The bond must:

(i) recite the names and designations of the parties and the judge in the trial court, identify the parties for whom and against whom judgment was entered, and state the amount recovered;

(ii) contain the conditions that the appellant

(A) will diligently prosecute the appeal to a decision and, if a judgment is rendered against him or her, will pay the amount of the judgment, including costs and interest;

(B) will pay the amount of the judgment, if any, rendered against him or her in the trial court, including costs and interest, if the appeal is dismissed;

(C) will pay any costs assessed against him or her in the circuit court; and

(D) will perform any other act prescribed in the statute authorizing appeal; and

(iii) be executed by the appellant with one or more sufficient sureties as required by MCR 3.604.

If the appeal is from a judgment for the possession of land, the bond must include the conditions provided in MCR 4.201(N)(4).

(d) Unless otherwise provided in this rule, the filing of a bond stays all further proceedings in the trial court under the order or judgment appealed from. If an execution has issued, it is suspended by giving notice of the bond to the officer holding the execution.

(2) *Probate Proceedings.*

(a) The probate court has continuing jurisdiction to decide other matters arising out of a proceeding in which an appeal is filed.

(b) A stay in an appeal from the probate court is governed by MCL 600.867, and MCR 5.802(C).

(3) *Civil Infractions.* An appeal bond and stay in a civil infraction proceeding is governed by MCR 4.101(G).

(4) *Criminal Cases.* Unless a bond pending appeal is filed with the trial court, a criminal judgment may be executed immediately even though the time for taking an appeal has not elapsed. The granting of bond and the amount of it are within the discretion of the trial court, subject to the applicable laws and rules on bonds pending appeals in criminal cases.

(5) *Request for Stay Filed in Circuit Court.* If a request for a stay pending appeal is filed in the circuit court, the court may condition a stay on the filing of a new or higher bond than otherwise required by these rules with appropriate conditions and sureties satisfactory to the court.

(I) Filing and Service of Briefs.

(1) Within 21 days after the trial court clerk notifies the parties that the record on appeal has been sent to the circuit court, the appellant must file a brief in the circuit court and serve it on the appellee. The appellee may file and serve a reply brief within 21 days after the appellant's brief is served on the appellee. The appellant's brief must comply with MCR 7.212(C), and the appellee's brief must comply with MCR 7.212(D).

(2) Before the brief is due, a party may withdraw the transcript and exhibits by giving the clerk a written receipt for them. A party may use them only to prepare the brief and must return them to the clerk when the party is finished. The court may order their return by a specified date.

(J) Dismissal for Failure to File Brief. If an appellant does not file a brief within the time provided by subrule (I)(1) and neither the trial court nor the circuit court has granted a motion for further time, the appeal may be considered abandoned, and the circuit court may dismiss the appeal on 7 days' notice to the parties. The circuit court clerk must promptly notify the trial court of a dismissal. Compliance with subrule (I)(1) after the 21-day period does not preclude dismissal of the appeal unless the appellant shows a reasonable excuse for the late filing.

(K) Oral Argument. A party who has filed a timely brief is entitled to oral argument by writing "ORAL ARGUMENT REQUESTED" in boldface type on the title page of the party's brief.

(L) Setting for Hearing. Within 14 days after the appellee's brief is filed or within 14 days after the time for filing it has expired, the circuit court clerk shall

(1) schedule the case for argument and notify the parties by mail, if a party has requested oral argument; or

(2) if no party has requested oral argument, submit the file to the judge to whom the appeal is assigned for decision.

(M) Judgment in Circuit Court; Process. After the appeal is decided or dismissed, the circuit court clerk shall promptly send to the trial court clerk a copy of the judgment, order, or opinion entered in the circuit court and all documents previously received from the trial court. The trial court issues further process.

(N) Control of Appeal Process.

(1) If the trial court postpones transmittal of the record or transmittal is otherwise delayed, the circuit court may on its own initiative exercise superintending control over the trial court, the court reporter or recorder, or other personnel to prevent delay.

(2) The circuit court may on the appellee's motion or its own initiative issue an order to show cause why the appeal should not be dismissed. An order to show cause is not required for a dismissal under subrules (G) or (J).

(3) A party may obtain interlocutory review of the appellate process by filing a motion in the circuit court under the rules governing motion practice.

(4) The circuit court may accelerate the appellate process on a party's motion.

(O) Costs. Costs in an appeal to the circuit court may be taxed as provided in MCR 2.625. A prevailing party may tax only the reasonable costs incurred in the appeal, including:

(1) the cost of an appeal or stay bond;

(2) the transcript;

(3) documents required for the record on appeal;

(4) fees paid to the clerk or to the trial court clerk incident to the appeal;

(5) taxable costs allowed by law in appeals to the Supreme Court (MCL 600.2441; MSA 27A.2441); and

(6) other expenses taxable under applicable court rules or statutes.

(P) Vexatious Proceedings.

(1) The circuit court may, on its own initiative or the motion of a party, dismiss an appeal, assess actual and punitive damages, or take other disciplinary action when it determines that an appeal or any of the proceedings in an appeal was vexatious because

(a) the appeal was taken for purposes of hindrance or delay or without any reasonable basis for belief that there was a meritorious issue to be determined on appeal; or

(b) a pleading, motion, argument, brief, document, or record filed in the case or any testimony presented in the case was grossly lacking in the requirements of propriety, violated court rules, or grossly disregarded the requirements of a fair presentation of the issues to the court.

(2) Damages may not exceed actual damages and expenses incurred by the opposing party because of the vexatious appeal or proceedings, including reasonable attorney fees, and punitive damages in an added amount not exceeding actual damages.

[Effective March 1, 1985; amended effective June 1, 1989; August 1, 1996; May 1, 2002.]

1985 Staff Comment

MCR 7.101 is based on GCR 1963, 701.

In subrule (A)(1) a reference to the Recorder's Court of the City of Detroit is added in view of that court's jurisdiction over certain appeals. See MCL 770.3(1)(c); MSA 28.1100(1)(c).

The provisions regarding appeal bonds are revised from the corresponding provisions of GCR 1963, 701.5(a)(1) and 701.8. Subrule (C)(2) covers the bond which is required in order to take an appeal, and subrule (H) covers the subject of bond to stay enforcement of a trial court decision. Separate provisions regarding appeals from probate court and of civil infraction actions are added.

The reference to GCR 1963, 120 (which deals with waiver of fees and costs) in GCR 1963, 701.8(a)(2) is replaced with references to the provision regarding excusing bond requirements, MCR 3.604(L). See subrules (C)(2)(a) and (H)(1)(b)(ii).

Subrule (G) corresponds to GCR 1963, 701.7. Language is added to make clear that an appellant's performance of required acts after the specified time, but before an order dismissing the appeal, does not necessarily prevent dismissal.

Subrule (H)(5) is a new provision explicitly covering the possibility that the request for a stay may be made in the circuit court. It is similar to MCR 7.209(D), which deals with the authority of the Court of Appeals with regard to bonds and stays in appeals to that court.

Subrule (J) is new. It covers the authority of the circuit court to dismiss an appeal, a point that was briefly mentioned in GCR 1963, 701.13(b).

Under subrule (K) oral argument may be requested on the title page of a brief, as in the Court of Appeals. See MCR 7.212(C)(1).

New subrules (O) and (P) cover taxation of costs and imposition of penalties for vexatious appeals. The latter provision is similar to the rules applicable to the Court of Appeals (MCR 7.216[C]) and the Supreme Court (7.315[D]).

Staff Comment to 1989 Amendment

The March 23, 1989, amendments to MCR 7.101 [effective June 1, 1989] make several changes in the procedures for appealing to the circuit court.

The requirement of filing a copy of the judgment or order appealed from with the claim of appeal is deleted.

The requirement of filing a copy of the claim of appeal with the trial court is moved to subrule (C)(2)(a), and language is added to that subrule requiring that a copy of the judgment or order appealed from also be filed at that time.

In order to remove a potential conflict with subrule (C)(3), subrule (C)(2) is amended to provide that the acts it requires must be performed no later than the filing of the claim of appeal, rather than within the time allowed for filing the claim.

Language is added in subrule (C)(2)(b) to make clear that the bond is to be filed in the trial court.

Subrule (C)(3) is amended to delete language that appeared to require a second filing of the claim of appeal.

Subrule (G) is amended to authorize the trial court to dismiss the appeal for failure to perform the acts required by subrule (C)(2).

Staff Comment to 1996 Amendment

The June 25, 1996, amendment of MCR 7.101(B)(1), governing the time for filing an appeal of right in the circuit court, makes the rule consistent with the corresponding provision regarding appeals to the Court of Appeals, MCR 7.204(A)(1), by providing that timely motions for rehearing or reconsideration extend the time for taking an appeal.

Staff Comment to 2002 Amendment

The December 18, 2001 amendments, effective May 1, 2002, updated various rules in light of the Estates and Protected Individuals Code (EPIC), MCL 700.1101 *et seq.*, and revisions made to EPIC by 2000 PA 312, 313, and 469.

The staff comment is published only for the benefit of the bench and bar and is not an authoritative construction by the Court.

RULE 7.102 APPEALS FROM MUNICIPAL COURTS

(A) Time for Taking Appeal. To appeal of right from a municipal court, an appellant must comply with MCR 7.101(B) and (C)(1).

(B) Procedure on Appeal. Except when inapplicable because of subrule (C), MCR 7.101 governs procedure on appeal.

(C) Review in Circuit Court. Review in the circuit court is a retrial of the issues on evidence introduced in the circuit court. Depositions in the trial court may be used. The circuit court may render any judgment or enter any order that should have been rendered or entered in the trial court, and may grant other relief as may be required for the just disposition of the appeal.

[Effective March 1, 1985.]

1985 Staff Comment

MCR 7.102 is substantially the same as GCR 1963, 702.

RULE 7.103 APPLICATION FOR LEAVE TO APPEAL

(A) Availability. The circuit court may grant leave to appeal from a trial court or municipal court when

(1) no appeal of right exists, or

(2) the time for taking an appeal under MCR 7.101(B)(1) has expired.

(B) Procedure.

(1) Except when another time is prescribed by statute, an application for leave to appeal must be filed within 21 days after the entry of the judgment or order appealed from.

(2) The application must state the grounds for the appeal and describe the proceedings in the trial court.

(3) A copy of the application must be filed with the trial court and served on the appellee. If service cannot reasonably be accomplished, the appellant may ask the circuit court to prescribe service under MCR 2.107(E).

(4) The application must be noticed for hearing in the circuit court at least 14 days after its filing. The circuit court may shorten the notice period on a showing of a need for immediate consideration.

(5) The circuit court shall consider the merit of the grounds for the appeal and enter an order granting or denying leave to appeal.

(6) An application under subrule (A)(2) or an application that is not timely under subrule (B)(1), must be accompanied by an affidavit explaining the delay. The circuit court may consider the length of and the reasons for the delay in deciding whether to grant the application. A delayed application may not be filed more that 6 months after entry of the order or judgment on the merits.

(C) Leave to Appeal Granted. Immediately after an order granting leave to appeal is entered, the appellant must file a copy with the trial court and serve a copy on the appellee. MCR 7.101 governs further proceedings, except that:

(1) the appellant must perform the acts required by MCR 7.101(C) within 7 days after the entry of the order granting leave to appeal; however, filing and service of a claim of appeal are not required;

(2) an appellee may file a claim of cross appeal within 14 days after service of the order granting leave to appeal; and

(3) the appellant must perform the acts required by MCR 7.101(F)(1) within 28 days after the entry of the order granting leave to appeal.

[Effective March 1, 1985; amended effective September 1, 2000.]

1985 Staff Comment

MCR 7.103 is comparable to GCR 1963, 703.

As in the corresponding rules applicable to the Court of Appeals (MCR 7.205[E]) and the Supreme Court (MCR 7.302[C][3]), subrule (B)(6) does not refer to an affidavit of "nonculpable negligence" (see GCR 1963, 703.2[f]), but rather says that the affidavit must explain the delay and that the appellate court may consider the length of and reason for the delay in deciding whether to grant the application.

Subrule (C) states in more detail than did GCR 1963, 703.3 what actions must be taken after leave to appeal is granted, and when.

Staff Comment to 2000 Amendment

The amendment of MCR 7.103(B)(6) [effective September 1, 2000] places a 6–month time limit on applications for leave to appeal to circuit court, corresponding to the 12–month limit applicable in appeals to the Court of Appeals. See MCR 7.205(F)(3). As to judgments entered before the effective date of the amendment, the 6–month period specified in MCR 7.103(B)(6) begins on the effective date, September 1, 2000.

RULE 7.104 APPEALS FROM ADMINISTRATIVE AGENCIES

(A) Appeals Under MCL 600.631; MSA 27A.631. An appeal in the circuit court under MCL 600.631; MSA 27A.631 is governed by MCR 7.101 and 7.103, except that the bond requirements do not apply.

(B) Appeals Under Michigan Employment Security Act.

(1) To obtain review of an order or decision of the Michigan Employment Security Board of Review, a party must file in the circuit court

(a) a claim of appeal within 30 days after the mailing to the party of the board of review's decision (see MCR 7.101[C][1]); and

(b) proof that a copy was served on the board of review and all interested parties.

The board of review is not an appellee. The timely filing of the claim of appeal constitutes the taking of an appeal. Failure to take any further steps to pursue the appeal is governed by MCR 7.101(G), (J), and (N).

(2) Within 14 days after service of the claim of appeal, the appellee must file an appearance in the circuit court. A cross appeal may be filed with the appearance. See MCR 7.101(D).

(3) Within 42 days after the claim of appeal is served on the board of review or within further time the circuit court allows, the board of review must send to the circuit court clerk a certified copy of the record of proceedings before the referee and the board of review and notify the parties of the transmittal.

(4) The appeal is heard by the circuit court on the certified record. Briefs and oral argument are governed by MCR 7.101(I), (K), and (L).

(5) Claimants under MCL 421.1 et seq.; MSA 17.501 et seq., whose rights to unemployment compensation turn on the provisions of that act constitute a class for appeal to the circuit court under MCL 421.38; MSA 17.540 and any subsequent appeals. One or more claimants who will fairly ensure the adequate representation of all may sue or be sued on behalf of the class in proceedings under this subrule when the character of the rights sought to be enforced for the class is several, and there is a common question of law or fact affecting the several rights and a common relief is sought. Notice in writing, or other notice as the court directs, must be given to every member of the proposed class, setting forth the nature of the proposed class action, and clearly and specifically providing an opportunity to each member of the proposed class to notify in writing the representative that he or she declines to be included in the class. The declination constitutes a reservation of the right to pursue one's own remedies individually and persons so declining may intervene as parties to the suit. MCR 3.501. The judgment in the suit is binding on all members of the class. An organization representing the claimants may pay the costs and fees of the proceedings.

(C) Appeals From Michigan Civil Service Commission. An appeal from a decision of the Michigan Civil Service Commission is governed by the provisions for appeals from administrative agencies in the Administrative Procedures Act. MCL 24.201 et seq.; MSA 3.560(101) et seq.

(D) Appeals From Michigan Parole Board.

(1) *Venue.* An application for leave to appeal a decision of the parole board may be filed only in the circuit court of the sentencing county, pursuant to MCL 791.234(9); MSA 28.2304(9). The prosecutor or the victim shall be designated the "appellant" and the prisoner shall be designated the "appellee." The parole board may intervene as an appellee.

(2) *Procedure.* Except as otherwise provided in this rule, applications for leave to appeal are governed by MCR 7.103(B).

(a) An application for leave to appeal may be filed within 28 days after the parole board mails to the prosecutor and the victim, if the victim has requested notification under MCL 780.771; MSA 28.1287(771), a notice of action granting parole and a copy of any written opinion. Upon request, the prisoner, the prosecutor, and the victim may receive the parole eligibility report and any prior parole eligibility reports that are mentioned, and any parole guidelines that support the action taken. An order of parole shall not be issued under MCL 791.236; MSA 28.2306 until 28 days after the mailing of the notice of action.

(b) A delayed application for leave to appeal may be filed under MCR 7.103(B)(6).

(c) Timely service of an application for leave to appeal must be made on the parole board and the prisoner. When the victim is appealing, timely service of the application also must be made on the prosecutor. When the prosecutor is appealing, timely service of the application also must be made on the victim, if the victim has requested notification under MCL 780.771; MSA 28.1287(771).

(i) The parole board shall be served by sending a copy of the application for leave to appeal and any supporting documents, by registered or certified mail, return receipt requested, to the parole board's office of record. A copy of the return receipt signed by an agent of the parole board must be attached to the proof of service.

(ii) The prosecutor shall be served by sending a copy of the application for leave to appeal and any supporting documents, by registered or certified mail, return receipt requested, to the office of the prosecuting attorney of the sentencing county. A copy of the return receipt signed by an agent of the prosecutor must be attached to the proof of service.

(iii) The prisoner shall be served by sending a copy of the application for leave to appeal and any supporting documents, by registered or certified mail, return receipt requested, to the facility where the prisoner is incarcerated, with instructions to the person in charge of the facility, or a designee, to personally serve the prisoner. A copy of the return of service executed by the appropriate prison official must be filed with the clerk of the court.

In addition to the pleadings, service on the prisoner must include a notice, in a form approved by the State Court Administrative Office, advising the prisoner that

(A) the prisoner may respond to the application for leave to appeal by counsel or in propria persona, although no response is required; and

(B) if an order of parole is issued under MCL 791.236; MSA 28.2306 before completion of appellate proceedings, a stay may be granted in the manner provided by MCR 7.105(G), except that no bond is required.

(3) *Decision to Grant Leave to Appeal.*

(a) The circuit court shall determine promptly whether to grant leave to appeal.

(b) The circuit court must make its determination within 28 days after the application for leave to appeal is filed. If the court does not make a determination within that time, the court shall enter an order to produce the prisoner before the court for a show cause hearing to determine whether the prisoner should be released on parole pending disposition of the appeal.

(4) *Leave to Appeal Granted.* If leave to appeal is granted, the appeal is governed generally by MCR 7.103, except that

(a) no bond is required;

(b) the expense of preparing and serving the parole board's evidentiary materials for the appeal may be taxed to a non-prevailing appellant, except that expenses may not be taxed to an indigent party;

(c) the record on appeal shall consist of the prisoner's central office file at the Department of Corrections, and any other documents considered by the parole board in reaching its decision. Within 14 days after being served with an order granting leave to appeal, the parole board shall send copies of the record to the circuit court and the other parties; and

(d) within 28 days after the parties receive a copy of the record, the appellant must file a brief in the circuit court and serve it on the appellee. The appellee may file and serve a reply brief within 21 days after the appellant's brief is served on the appellee.

(5) *Burden of Proof.* The burden shall be on the appellant to prove that the decision of the parole board was

(a) in violation of the Michigan Constitution, a statute, an administrative rule, or a written agency regulation that is exempted from promulgation pursuant to MCL 24.207; MSA 3.560(107), or

(b) a clear abuse of discretion.

(6) *Appeals to the Court of Appeals.* An appeal of a circuit court decision is by application for leave to appeal to the Court of Appeals pursuant to MCR 7.205. The application shall be filed as an emergency appeal under MCR 7.205(E), and the Court of Appeals shall expedite its consideration of the matter.

(7) *Motion to Remand.* On timely motion by a party, or on the court's own motion, the court may remand the matter to the parole board for an explanation of its decision. The parole board shall hear and decide the matter within 28 days of the date of the order, unless the board determines that an adjourn-

ment is necessary to obtain evidence or that there is other good cause for an adjournment. The time to file briefs on appeal under MCR 7.104(D)(4)(d) is tolled while the matter is pending on remand.

(8) *Parole Board Responsibility After Reversal or Remand.* If a decision of the parole board is reversed or remanded, the board shall review the matter and take action consistent with the circuit court's decision within 28 days. If the circuit court order requires the board to undertake further review of the file or to reevaluate its prior decision, the board shall provide the parties with an opportunity to be heard. An appeal to the Court of Appeals does not affect the board's jurisdiction to act under this subsection.

[Effective March 1, 1985; amended effective April 1, 1996; March 10, 2000.]

1985 Staff Comment

MCR 7.104 is substantially the same as GCR 1963, 706.

Staff Comment to 1996 Amendment

The 1996 addition of MCR 7.104(D) was recommended by the State Bar of Michigan, in light of the passage of 1992 PA 22, which established a procedure by which prosecutors and victims may appeal a decision of the parole board. MCL 791.234(7); MSA 28.2304(7).

Staff Comment to 2000 Amendment

The February 29, 2000 amendment of MCR 7.104(D), effective March 10, 2000, eliminated the references to an appeal of a parole decision by a prisoner. A prisoner's right to appeal such a decision was eliminated by the Legislature in 1999 PA 191, amending MCL 791.234; MSA 28.2304.

RULE 7.105 APPEALS FROM ADMINISTRATIVE AGENCIES IN "CONTESTED CASES"

(A) Definitions. As used in this rule:

(1) "Agency" means a state department, bureau, division, section, board, commission, trustee, authority or officer created by the constitution, statute, or agency action, from whose decision in a contested case an appeal to the circuit court is authorized by law. It does not include an agency in the legislative or judicial branches of government, the Governor, the Bureau of Workmen's Compensation, the Workers' Compensation Appeal Board, a Michigan employment security hearing referee, or the Michigan Employment Security Board of Review.

(2) "Contested case" means a proceeding including but not limited to ratemaking, price fixing, and licensing, in which determination of the legal rights, duties, or privileges of a named party is required by law to be made by an agency after an opportunity for an evidentiary hearing. An appeal of one agency's decision to another agency is a continuous proceeding as though before a single agency.

(3) "Court" means the circuit court.

(4) "Decision" means either a final determination, opinion, or order of an agency in a contested case, or a preliminary, procedural, or intermediate agency action or ruling.

(B) Scope.

(1) This rule governs an appeal to the circuit court from an agency decision in a contested case, except when a statute requires a different procedure. A petitioner intending to rely on a different procedure permitted by statute shall identify the statutory procedure in the petition for review. Failure to do so waives the right to use the different procedure.

(2) The court need not dismiss an action incorrectly initiated under some other rule, if it is timely filed and served as required by this rule and the applicable statute. Instead, leave may be freely given, when justice requires, to amend an appeal and a response to conform to the requirements of this rule and otherwise proceed under this rule.

(C) Form; Content; Attachment of Decision. Judicial review of an agency decision in a contested case is initiated by filing, within the time required by the applicable statute, a document entitled "Petition for Review," conforming to the following form, content, and attachment requirements.

(1) *Form.*

(a) A petition for review is captioned in the circuit court, and shall otherwise conform to the requirements of MCR 2.113.

(b) The person aggrieved by the agency decision is the "petitioner" and is listed first in the caption. A person who seeks to sustain the decision of the agency is the "respondent." If there is no respondent, the caption may read "In re [*name of petitioner or other identification of subject of the case*]," followed by the name of the petitioner. Except when otherwise provided by law, the agency or another party to the contested case may become a respondent by promptly filing an appearance.

(c) The petition for review must state:

"[*Name of aggrieved party*] petitions for review of the decision entered [*date*] by [*name of agency*]."

(d) The petitioner or petitioner's attorney, must date and sign the petition for review and place his or her business address and telephone number under the signature.

(2) *Content.* The petition for review must contain a concise statement of:

(a) the nature of the proceedings as to which review is sought, including the authority under which the proceedings were conducted, and any statutory authority for review;

(b) the facts on which venue is based;

(c) the grounds on which relief is sought, stated in as many separate paragraphs as there are separate grounds alleged;

(d) the relief sought.

(3) *Attachment.* The petitioner shall attach to the petition for review, as an exhibit, a copy of the agency decision of which review is sought, or explain why it is not attached.

(D) Service. Promptly after filing the petition for review, the petitioner shall serve true copies of the petition for review on the agency, the Attorney General, and all other parties to the contested case in the manner provided by MCR 2.107, and promptly file proof of service with the court.

(E) Interlocutory Review. A preliminary procedural or intermediate agency action or ruling is not immediately reviewable, except that a court may grant interlocutory review of a preliminary, procedural, or intermediate decision by an agency only on a showing that review of the final decision would not be an adequate remedy.

(1) A petition for review must be filed with the court within 14 days of the contested decision.

(2) The petition must follow the form, content, and attachment requirements of subrule (C), with the following additional requirements:

(a) the petition must be entitled "Petition for Interlocutory Review";

(b) the grounds for relief must set forth why review of the agency's final decision will not be an adequate remedy;

(c) the relief sought must include a prayer that the court grant leave to the petitioner to file a petition for review.

(3) If the petition is granted by the court, the appeal thereafter proceeds under this rule in the same manner as appeals from final decisions, unless a particular provision of the rule specifically states otherwise.

(F) Answer. A respondent may file an answer to a petition for review. A court may require an answer.

(G) Stay of Enforcement.

(1) The filing of a petition for review does not stay enforcement of the decision or order of which review is sought. The court may order a stay on appropriate terms and conditions only:

(a) after hearing on the written motion for stay that is supported by affidavit and states with particularity the grounds therefor;

(b) on finding:

(i) that the applicant will suffer irreparable injury if a stay is not entered;

(ii) that the applicant has made a strong showing that it is likely to prevail on the merits;

(iii) that the public interest will not be harmed if a stay is granted; and

(iv) that the harm to the applicant in the absence of a stay outweighs the harm to other parties to the proceedings if a stay is granted; and

(c) on the filing by the applicant of a bond in the amount required by any applicable statute authorizing the appeal or, in the absence of a statute, in an amount and with sureties the court may deem adequate to protect the public and other parties, conditioned:

(i) to prosecute the review to a decision and to obey and act in accordance with the decision or order as may be rendered by the court;

(ii) to obey and act in accordance with the order or decision if it is not set aside or revised.

(2) The court may grant a temporary stay of enforcement without written notice to the respondent only if it clearly appears from specific facts shown by affidavit that immediate and irreparable injury will result if a stay is not entered before the respondent can be heard and only if the petitioner's attorney certifies to the court in writing that efforts have been made to contact the respondent and the respondent's attorney, if known, and stating that those efforts were unsuccessful. The court may use an appropriate method to communicate with a respondent regarding an application for stay of enforcement without written notice.

A temporary stay may be granted by the court only until a hearing on a motion or order to show cause required by subrule (G)(1). A hearing on a motion to dissolve a temporary stay will be heard on 24 hours' notice, or less on order of the court for good cause shown, and takes precedence over all matters except previously filed matters of the same character.

(3) An order granting a stay of enforcement is subject to the requirements, procedures, and limitations of MCR 3.310(C), (F), and (G).

(4) For the purpose of subrule (G), the agency shall be considered a respondent, whether or not it has filed an appearance.

(H) Stipulations. The parties may stipulate in writing regarding any matter relevant to the petition for review or the record below or any part of the record if the stipulation is made part of the record and transmitted to the court.

(I) Additional Evidence. An application to present proofs of alleged irregularity in procedure before the agency, or to allow the taking of additional evidence before the agency, is timely only if it is filed with or included in the petition for review. The petitioner shall promptly notice the request for hearing in the manner for notice of hearing of motions. If the court orders the taking of additional evidence, the time for filing briefs is stayed until the taking of the evidence is completed.

(J) Motion to Dismiss or Affirm or for Peremptory Reversal.

(1) In addition to any other relief available under this rule, the respondent may file a motion to dismiss or affirm accompanied by a brief in support of it. When appropriate, a motion to affirm may be joined in the alternative with a motion to dismiss.

(2) A motion to dismiss an appeal may be made by a respondent on the ground that:

(a) the appeal is not within the jurisdiction of the court;

(b) the appeal was not taken or pursued in conformity with the rules, or a special statutory review procedure;

(c) the petitioner has failed to exhaust administrative remedies;

(d) the appeal is moot.

(3) A motion to affirm may be made by a respondent on the ground that:

(a) it is manifest that the question or questions sought to be reviewed on which the decision of the case depends are so unsubstantial as to need no argument or formal submission;

(b) the question or questions sought to be reviewed were not timely or properly raised, if the petitioner is required by law to have raised the question or questions at an earlier time.

(4) The petitioner may file a motion for peremptory reversal on the ground that error requiring reversal is so manifest that an immediate reversal of the judgment or order appealed from should be granted without formal argument or submission.

(5) A party has 14 days after service of a motion to dismiss, to affirm, or for peremptory reversal in which to file a brief opposing the motion.

(6) On the filing of the brief in opposition to a motion to dismiss, to affirm, or for peremptory reversal, or after the expiration of the time for filing the brief, whichever is earlier, the clerk shall submit the motion and briefs for decision by the court. After consideration of the motion, the court shall enter an appropriate order. Unless otherwise ordered by the court, the filing of a motion to dismiss, to affirm, or for peremptory reversal does not extend the time for taking any steps required by this rule.

(K) Briefs and Arguments.

(1) Within 28 days after the record is filed with the court (see MCL 24.304[2]; MSA 3.560[204][2]), the petitioner shall file with the court its brief, in the form provided in MCR 7.212(C), serve a copy on all respondents, and promptly file proof of that service with the court. Within 28 days after petitioner's brief is served, each respondent shall file with the court its

brief, in the form provided in MCR 7.212(D), serve a copy on all other parties, and promptly file proof of that service with the court. The petitioner may file and serve a reply brief within 14 days after service of the respondent's brief. A 28-day extension of the time for filing a brief may be obtained on written stipulation of the parties or by order of the court. Further extension of time for filing of a brief can be obtained only on order of the court on motion for cause shown.

(2) If a party does not timely serve its brief, the court may, after notice and opportunity to respond, enter an appropriate order, including dismissal of a petition for review, or affirmance or reversal of the decision appealed from.

(3) A party who files a timely brief is entitled to oral argument by writing "ORAL ARGUMENT RE-QUESTED" in boldface type on the title page of the party's brief. However, in cases in which a party is incarcerated, the court need not order the production of that party for argument but instead may order the case to be submitted on briefs.

(4) Within 14 days after the filing of the last brief allowed under subrule (K)(1), or within 14 days after the time for filing it has expired, the court clerk must:

    (a) if a party is entitled to oral argument, schedule a hearing and notify the parties by mail; or

    (b) if no party has requested oral argument, submit the file to the judge assigned for decision.

(L) Earlier Filing and Serving. For good cause the court may shorten the time for filing and serving either the petitioner's or the respondent's brief or other documents,

    (1) on its own motion,

    (2) on a motion filed by a party, or

    (3) by stipulation of the parties.

(M) Order, Findings, Relief, and Final Process. On completing review the court shall enter a written order. The court may affirm, reverse, remand, or modify the decision of the agency and may grant the petitioner or the respondent further relief as appropriate based on the record, findings, and conclusions. When the court finds that the decision or order of an agency is not supported by competent, material, and substantial evidence on the whole record, the court shall separately state which finding or findings of the agency are so affected. When the court finds that a decision or order of an agency violates the constitution or a statute, is affected by a material error of law, or is affected by unlawful procedure resulting in material prejudice to a party, the court shall state its findings of fact and conclusions of law and the reasons for its conclusions, and identify those conclusions of law of the agency, if any, that are being reversed.

(N) Vexatious Proceedings; Consequences.

(1) The court may, on its own motion or on the motion of any party, dismiss a petition for review, assess punitive damages, or take other disciplinary action when it determines that an appeal or any proceedings in the appeal were vexatious for any of the reasons set forth in MCR 7.101(P)(1).

(2) Punitive damages may not exceed an amount equivalent to the actual or reasonable costs or expenses of the opposing parties, including the reasonable attorney fees.

(O) Delayed Petition for Review. After expiration of the period for seeking judicial review of an agency decision, if the applicable review statute permits a delayed appeal, the court may on application with the affidavit and brief attached, and an evidentiary hearing, grant leave to file a petition for review of a decision on finding that there is merit in the grounds for the application, that the delay was not due to the petitioner's culpable negligence, that the delay has not resulted in any substantial prejudice to any other party, and that the court retains jurisdiction to grant leave. Any other party may file an opposing statement, affidavits, and briefs. On a grant of leave to file a petition for review, the petitioner shall file a petition for review within 21 days and review shall proceed in accordance with this rule.

[Effective March 1, 1985; amended effective March 19, 1985.]

1985 Staff Comment

MCR 7.105 corresponds to GCR 1963, 705, which was effective February 1, 1984. There are several modifications.

Under GCR 1963, 705.3(1)(b), the agency whose decision was being reviewed was the respondent on appeal. That is changed in subrule (C)(1)(b). The person who seeks to sustain the agency decision is the respondent. The rule contemplates that there may be no such person in a particular case, and explains the way the caption should be arranged in that situation.

The March 19, 1985, amendments of MCR 7.105 clarify the status of the agency in appeals from certain administrative agency decisions. Under subrule (C)(1)(b), the agency may become a respondent by filing an appearance. Under subrule (G), when the petitioner seeks a stay, the agency is deemed a respondent whether or not it has filed an appearance.

Subrules (D) and (K) permit service of papers by any manner permitted in MCR 2.107. This is in contrast to GCR 1963, 705.4 and 705.11, which required mailing.

Subrule (I) adds additional detail, not found in GCR 1963, 705.9, concerning the procedure for taking additional evidence. The request to take additional evidence, before either the court or the agency, must be included in or filed with the petition for review. The appellant is required to notice the request for hearing in the same manner as provided for notice of motions. If the taking of additional evidence is ordered, further proceedings on appeal are stayed until the completion of the taking of the evidence.

In subrule (J) the grounds for motions to dismiss and to affirm are adjusted to conform to the corresponding provisions regarding motions in the Court of Appeals. See MCR 7.211(C)(2) and (3). Compare GCR 1963, 705.10 and 817.5(2).

In addition, under subrule (J)(3)(b) it is a ground for affirmance that the petitioner did not timely or properly raise an issue only if the petitioner was required to raise the matter at an earlier stage. Compare GCR 1963, 705.10(2)(c).

Subrule (K) adds a provision governing the filing of reply briefs. The petitioner has 14 days after the service of the appellee's brief to do so.

The amendment of MCR 7.105(K)(1) [effective March 1, 1985] adds a reference to the statute (MCL 24.304[2]; MSA 3.560[204][2]) that sets the time within which the administrative agency record is to be transferred to the circuit court for use in the appeal.

SUBCHAPTER 7.200 COURT OF APPEALS

RULE 7.201 ORGANIZATION AND OPERATION OF COURT OF APPEALS

(A) Chief Judge and Chief Judge Pro Tempore.

(1) The Supreme Court shall select a judge of the Court of Appeals to serve as chief judge. No later than October 1 of each odd-numbered year, the Court of Appeals may submit the names of no fewer than two judges whom the judges of that court recommend for selection as chief judge.

(2) The chief judge shall select a chief judge pro tempore, who shall fulfill such functions as the chief judge assigns.

(3) The chief judge and chief judge pro tempore shall serve a two-year term beginning on January 1 of each even-numbered year, provided that the chief judge serves at the pleasure of the Supreme Court and the chief judge pro tempore serves at the pleasure of the chief judge.

(B) Court of Appeals Clerk; Place of Filing Papers; Fees.

(1) The court shall appoint a chief clerk who is subject to the requirements imposed on the Supreme Court clerk in MCR 7.319. The clerk's office must be located in Lansing and be operated under the court's direction. With the court's approval, the clerk may appoint assistant and deputy clerks.

(2) Papers to be filed with the court or the clerk must be filed in the clerk's office in Lansing or with a deputy clerk in Detroit, Southfield, or Grand Rapids. Fees paid to a deputy clerk must be forwarded to the clerk's office in Lansing. Claims of appeal, applications, motions, and complaints need not be accepted for filing until all required documents have been filed and the requisite fees have been paid.

(3) If a case is accepted for filing without all of the required documents, transcripts, or fees, the appellant, or the plaintiff in an original action under MCR 7.206, must supply the missing items within 21 days after the date of the clerk's notice of deficiency. The chief judge or another designated judge may dismiss the appeal and assess costs if the deficiency is not remedied within that time.

(C) Sessions of Court. There are 9 regular sessions of the court each year. Except as otherwise required for the efficient administration of the court, each session begins on the first Tuesday during the months of October through June. Each session continues for the number of days necessary to conclude the hearing of cases scheduled for argument. The chief judge may order a special session.

(D) Panels. The court shall sit to hear cases in panels of 3 judges. The decision of a majority of the judges of a panel in attendance at the hearing is the decision of the court. Except as modified by the Supreme Court, a decision of the court is final. The judges must be rotated so that each judge sits with every other judge with equal frequency, consistent with the efficient administration of the court's business. The Supreme Court may assign persons to act as temporary judges of the court, under the constitution and statutes. Only one temporary judge may sit on a 3-judge panel.*

* Publisher's Note: See Administrative Order 1991–9.

(E) Assignments and Presiding Judge. Before the calendar for each session is prepared, the chief judge shall assign the judges to each panel and the cases to be heard by them and designate one of them as presiding judge. A presiding judge presides at a hearing and performs other functions the court or the Supreme Court by rule or special order directs. The chief judge may assign a motion or any other matter to any panel.

(F) Place of Hearing. The court shall sit in Detroit, Lansing, Grand Rapids, and Marquette, or another place the chief judge designates. A calendar case will be assigned for hearing in the city nearest to the court or tribunal from which the appeal was taken or as the parties stipulate, except as otherwise required for the efficient administration of the court's business.

(G) Judicial Conferences. At least once a year and at other times the chief judge finds necessary, the judges shall meet to consider proposals to amend the rules of the court, improve the administration of justice, including the operations of the court, and transact any business which properly comes before them.

(H) Approval of Expenses. The state court administrator shall approve the expenses for operation of the court and the expense accounts of the judges, including attendance at a judicial conference. The state court administrator shall prepare a budget for the court.

[Effective March 1, 1985; amended effective January 1, 1992; February 1, 1994; September 13, 1995; November 6, 1996; September 1, 1999.]

1985 Staff Comment

MCR 7.201 is comparable to GCR 1963, 800.

Staff Comment to 1994 Amendment

MCR 7.201(B)(3) [effective February 1, 1994] is a new provision. It specifies the time for completing a filing and allows the chief judge to dismiss a case or assess costs if a deficiency is not remedied within that time.

Staff Comment to 1995 Amendment

In 1995, MCR 7.201(A) was amended to provide that the Supreme Court would appoint the Chief Judge of the Court of Appeals. In 1995, the Supreme Court also consolidated MCR 8.110(B), (C), and (D) into a new MCR 8.110(B), which likewise provided that the chief judges of the trial courts would be appointed by the Supreme Court. MCR 8.110(G) and (H) were repealed. MCR 8.110 was also amended to require chief judges to meet regularly with other chief judges whose courts are wholly or partially in the same county. As indicated in its 1995 order, the Supreme Court took these steps "to facilitate the Court's exercise of its constitutional responsibility to administer and superintend the courts of this state" and to "enhance the Supreme Court's ability to implement sound policies statewide, and assure a greater degree of responsiveness to the leadership that the constitution requires this Court to exercise."

Staff Comment to 1999 Amendment

This group of amendments [effective September 1, 1999] deal with various matters regarding appellate procedure. The following rules are affected:

MCR 7.201(B), 7.217(A) and (C)—Permit the Chief Judge, or another designated judge, acting alone, to enter certain orders when a party does not proceed in accordance with the rules.

MCR 7.202(6)—Delete the definition of "signed" from the rule.

New MCR 7.203(F)—Permit the chief judge, or another designated judge, acting alone, to dismiss an appeal or original proceeding for lack of jurisdiction, and create a procedure for the appellant or plaintiff to seek reconsideration of that decision.

MCR 7.212(C) and (D)—Clarify the requirement of specific page references to the record in appellate briefs.

MCR 7.215(H)—Modify several provisions in the rule governing resolution of conflicts in Court of Appeals decisions.

RULE 7.202   DEFINITIONS

For purposes of this subchapter:

(1) "clerk" means the Court of Appeals clerk, unless otherwise stated;

(2) "date of filing" means the date of receipt of a document by a court clerk;

(3) "entry" means the placing of an order, judgment, or other document into the file and records of a lower court or the Court of Appeals by the clerk;

(4) "entry fee" means the fee required by law or, in lieu of that fee, a motion to waive fees or a copy of an order appointing an attorney;

(5) "filing" means the delivery of a document to a court clerk and the receipt and acceptance of the document by the clerk with the intent to enter it in the record of the court;

(6) "custody case" means a domestic relations case in which the custody of a minor child is an issue, an adoption case, or a case in which the juvenile division of probate court has entered an order terminating parental rights or an order of disposition removing a child from the child's home;

(7) "final judgment" or "final order" means:

(a) In a civil case,

(i) the first judgment or order that disposes of all the claims and adjudicates the rights and liabilities of all the parties, including such an order entered after reversal of an earlier final judgment or order,

(ii) an order designated as final under MCR 2.604(B),

(iii) in a domestic relations action, a postjudgment order affecting the custody of a minor,

(iv) a postjudgment order awarding or denying attorney fees and costs under MCR 2.403, 2.405, 2.625 or other law or court rule,

(v) An order denying governmental immunity to a governmental party, including a governmental agency, official, or employee;

(b) In a criminal case,

(i) an order dismissing the case;

(ii) the original sentence imposed following conviction;

(iii) a sentence imposed following the granting of a motion for resentencing;

(iv) a sentence imposed, or order entered, by the trial court following a remand from an appellate court in a prior appeal of right; or

(v) a sentence imposed following revocation of probation.

[Effective March 1, 1985; amended effective January 1, 1996; September 1, 1999; April 1, 2001; September 1, 2002.]

1985 Staff Comment

MCR 7.202 is a new provision defining several terms used in the Court of Appeals subchapter.

Staff Comment to 1996 Amendment

The October 19, 1995, amendment of MCR 7.202 [effective January 1, 1996] adds a definition of "final judgment" or "final order". The principal effect would be to eliminate appeals of right from certain postjudgment orders.

Staff Comment to 1999 Amendment

This group of amendments [effective September 1, 1999] deal with various matters regarding appellate procedure. The following rules are affected:

MCR 7.201(B), 7.217(A) and (C)—Permit the Chief Judge, or another designated judge, acting alone, to enter certain orders when a party does not proceed in accordance with the rules.

MCR 7.202(6)—Delete the definition of "signed" from the rule.

New MCR 7.203(F)—Permit the chief judge, or another designated judge, acting alone, to dismiss an appeal or original proceeding for lack of jurisdiction, and create a procedure for the appellant or plaintiff to seek reconsideration of that decision.

MCR 7.212(C) and (D)—Clarify the requirement of specific page references to the record in appellate briefs.

MCR 7.215(H)—Modify several provisions in the rule governing resolution of conflicts in Court of Appeals decisions.

Staff Comment to 2000 Amendment

The December 13, 2000, amendments of MCR 7.202 and 7.215, effective April 1, 2001, make several changes regarding procedure in the Court of Appeals.

The amendment of MCR 7.202(7)(b)(iv) makes certain orders entered by the trial court on remand from an appellate court appealable by right.

The amendment to MCR 7.215(A) permits a single judge of the Court of Appeals panel to designate an opinion for publication.

New MCR 7.215(D) re-establishes a procedure under which a party may request publication of a Court of Appeals opinion that was not initially designated for publication. The former provision was deleted in 1995.

Staff Comment to 2002 Amendment

The June 4, 2002, amendments of MCR 7.202, 7.203, and 7.209, effective September 1, 2002, involve orders appealable by right to the Court of Appeals.

The provisions concerning custody orders in domestic relations cases and orders regarding attorney fees and costs are moved from MCR 7.203(A)(3) and (4) to MCR 7.202(7)(a)(iii) and (iv). There is also a change in the language regarding fees and costs, to refer to "postjudgment" orders.

New MCR 7.202(7)(a)(v) includes as "final" an order denying immunity to a governmental defendant, as is provided in many jurisdictions. See, *e.g.*, *Mitchell* v *Forsyth*, 472 US 511; 105 S Ct 2806; 86 L Ed 2d 411 (1985).

Language is added to MCR 7.203(A) to make clear that an appeal from an order described in MCR 7.202(7)(a)(iii)–(v) is limited to the portion of the order regarding which there is an appeal of right. In addition, obsolete references to the recorder's court are deleted from that subrule.

New MCR 7.209(E)(4) provides for a stay with respect to a governmental party who takes an appeal of right from an order denying immunity.

The staff comment is published only for the benefit of the bench and bar and is not an authoritative construction by the Court.

RULE 7.203 JURISDICTION OF THE COURT OF APPEALS

(A) Appeal of Right. The court has jurisdiction of an appeal of right filed by an aggrieved party from the following:

(1) A final judgment or final order of the circuit court or the court of claims, as defined in MCR 7.202(7), except a judgment or order of the circuit court

(a) on appeal from any other court or tribunal;

(b) in a criminal case in which the conviction is based on a plea of guilty or nolo contendere;

An appeal from an order described in MCR 7.202(7)(a)(iii)–(v) is limited to the portion of the order with respect to which there is an appeal of right.

(2) A judgment or order of a court or tribunal from which appeal of right to the Court of Appeals has been established by law or court rule.

(B) Appeal by Leave. The court may grant leave to appeal from:

(1) a judgment or order of the circuit court, court of claims, and recorder's court which is not a final judgment appealable of right;

(2) a final judgment entered by the circuit court or the recorder's court on appeal from any other court;

(3) a final order of an administrative agency or tribunal which by law is appealable to or reviewable by the Court of Appeals or the Supreme Court;

(4) any other judgment or order appealable to the Court of Appeals by law or rule;

(5) any judgment or order when an appeal of right could have been taken but was not timely filed.

(C) Extraordinary Writs, Original Actions, and Enforcement Actions. The court may entertain an action for:

(1) superintending control over a lower court or a tribunal immediately below it arising out of an action or proceeding which, when concluded, would result in an order appealable to the Court of Appeals;

(2) mandamus against a state officer (see MCL 600.4401; MSA 27A.4401);

(3) habeas corpus (see MCL 600.4304; MSA 27A.4304);

(4) quo warranto involving a state office or officer;

(5) any original action required by law to be filed in the Court of Appeals or Supreme Court;

(6) any action to enforce a final order of an administrative tribunal or agency required by law to be filed in the Court of Appeals or Supreme Court.

(D) Other Appeals and Proceedings. The court has jurisdiction over any other appeal or action established by law.

(E) Appeals by Prosecution. Appeals by the prosecution in criminal cases are governed by MCL 770.12; MSA 28.1109, except as provided by MCL 770.3; MSA 28.1100.

(F) Dismissal.

(1) Except when a motion to dismiss has been filed, the chief judge or another designated judge may, acting alone, dismiss an appeal or original proceeding for lack of jurisdiction.

(2) The appellant or plaintiff may file a motion for reconsideration within 21 days after the date of the order of dismissal. The motion shall be submitted to a panel of 3 judges. No entry fee is required for a motion filed under this subrule.

(3) The clerk will not accept for filing a motion for rehearing of an order issued by a 3–judge panel that denies a motion for reconsideration filed under subrule (2).

[Effective March 1, 1985; amended effective October 1, 1989; February 1, 1994; amended December 30, 1994, applicable to all crimes committed on or after December 27, 1994 as provided by 1994 PA 374 and 1994 PA 375, effective until further order of the Court after consideration of comments and legislative action, if any, or until April 1, 1995; by Order of March 31, 1995, December 30, 1994 amendment ordered to remain in effect until June 30, 1995; by Order of June 19, 1995, December 30, 1994 amendment ordered to remain in effect until October 15, 1995; by Order of October 13, 1995, December 30, 1994 amendment ordered to remain in effect until August 15, 1996; amended effective January 1, 1996; by Order of July 16, 1996, December 30, 1994 amendment ordered to remain in effect until September 1, 1997; by Order of July 25, 1997, December 30, 1994 amendment ordered to remain in effect until further order of the Court; amended effective September 1, 1999; November 30, 1999; February 1, 2000; September 11, 2001; September 1, 2002.]

1985 Staff Comment

MCR 7.203 is drawn from GCR 1963, 801, 806.1, 806.2, and 816.2(2). The provisions of the former rules are rewritten, although their substance is not changed.

In subrule (B)(2) a reference to cases that were appealed to the Recorder's Court of the City of Detroit is added, in view of that court's appellate jurisdiction over the 36th District Court. MCL 770.3(1)(c); MSA 28.1100(1)(c).

The [March 1, 1985] amendment of MCR 7.203(B)(2) corrects an inadvertent addition of the words "or tribunal" at the end of the subrule, which describes the class of cases appealable to the Court of Appeals by leave. This makes the rule consistent with GCR 1963, 806.2(4).

Subrule (B)(3) is new. It limits review of agency decisions to final orders, a principle that had previously been expressed in appellate decisions.

The 18–month time limit on filing an application for leave to appeal in a civil action (see GCR 1963, 806.2) is placed in MCR 7.205(F).

Staff Comment to 1989 Amendment

The [October 1, 1989] amendment of MCR 7.203(E) incorporates the statute governing appeals by the prosecutor. The circumstances in which such appeals can be taken was considerably expanded by 1988 PA 66.

Staff Comment to February 1994 Amendment

The change in MCR 7.203(A)(1) [effective February 1, 1994] eliminates appeals of right as to certain types of judgments or orders. An appeal from a lower court judgment after review of an agency decision will be by leave only. In domestic relations cases, the only postjudgment orders that will be appealable by right are those involving the custody of minors.

Staff Comment to December 1994 Amendment

The December 30, 1994 amendments of MCR 6.301, 6.302, 6.311, 6.425, 7.203, 7.204 and 7.205 modified procedure regarding appeals in criminal cases in light of the amendment of Const 1963, art 1, § 20 at the November 1994 general election and the legislation implementing the constitutional amendment. Changes will remain in effect until April 1, 1995 and will be reconsidered by the Court in light of comments received and any further legislation.

Staff Comment to 1996 Amendment

New MCR 7.203(A)(3) retains an exception, formerly found in MCR 7.203(A)(1), for postjudgment orders in divorce and paternity actions that affect the custody of a minor. MCR 7.203(A)(2) is amended to make clear that appeals of right exist where so provided by court rule, as well as by statute. See, e.g., MCR 5.801(B); MCR 5.993(A).

Staff Comment to September 1999 Amendment

This group of amendments [effective September 1, 1999] deal with various matters regarding appellate procedure. The following rules are affected:

MCR 7.201(B), 7.217(A) and (C)—Permit the Chief Judge, or another designated judge, acting alone, to enter certain orders when a party does not proceed in accordance with the rules.

MCR 7.202(6)—Delete the definition of "signed" from the rule.

New MCR 7.203(F)—Permit the chief judge, or another designated judge, acting alone, to dismiss an appeal or original proceeding for lack of jurisdiction, and create a procedure for the appellant or plaintiff to seek reconsideration of that decision.

MCR 7.212(C) and (D)—Clarify the requirement of specific page references to the record in appellate briefs.

MCR 7.215(H)—Modify several provisions in the rule governing resolution of conflicts in Court of Appeals decisions.

Staff Comment to November 1999 Amendment

The 1999 amendments of MCR 7.203(A)(1) and 7.204(A) [effective November 30, 1999] are explained in *Allied Electric Supply Co v Tenaglia*, [461] Mich [285], ___; [602] NW2d [572] (1999).

Staff Comment to December 1999 Amendment

The amendments to MCR 7.203 and 7.208 [effective February 1, 2000] deal with two issues regarding the relationship of appeals and orders awarding or denying attorney fees and costs.

One amendment concerns the authority of the trial court to rule on requests for sanctions when an appeal has been taken. See *Co-Jo, Inc v Strand*, 226 Mich App 108 (1997). New MCR 7.208(I) provides that the trial court has the authority to rule on such requests despite the pendency of an appeal.

Second, MCR 7.203(A) is amended to make orders awarding or denying sanctions appealable by right.

Staff Comment to 2001 Amendment

The September 11, 2001, amendment of subrule (A)(3) clarified that the provision applies to all domestic relations actions, not just to divorce and paternity actions.

Staff Comment to 2002 Amendment

The June 4, 2002, amendments of MCR 7.202, 7.203, and 7.209, effective September 1, 2002, involve orders appealable by right to the Court of Appeals.

The provisions concerning custody orders in domestic relations cases and orders regarding attorney fees and costs are moved from MCR 7.203(A)(3) and (4) to MCR 7.202(7)(a)(iii) and (iv). There is also a change in the language regarding fees and costs, to refer to "postjudgment" orders.

New MCR 7.202(7)(a)(v) includes as "final" an order denying immunity to a governmental defendant, as is provided in many jurisdictions. See, *e.g., Mitchell* v *Forsyth*, 472 US 511; 105 S Ct 2806; 86 L Ed 2d 411 (1985).

Language is added to MCR 7.203(A) to make clear that an appeal from an order described in MCR 7.202(7)(a)(iii)–(v) is limited to the portion of the order regarding which there is an appeal of right. In addition, obsolete references to the recorder's court are deleted from that subrule.

New MCR 7.209(E)(4) provides for a stay with respect to a governmental party who takes an appeal of right from an order denying immunity.

The staff comment is published only for the benefit of the bench and bar and is not an authoritative construction by the Court.

RULE 7.204   FILING APPEAL OF RIGHT; APPEARANCE

(A) Time Requirements. The time limit for an appeal of right is jurisdictional. See MCR 7.203(A). The provisions of MCR 1.108 regarding computation of time apply.

(1) An appeal of right in a civil action must be taken within

(a) 21 days after entry of the judgment or order appealed from;

(b) 21 days after the entry of an order denying a motion for new trial, a motion for rehearing or reconsideration, or a motion for other postjudgment relief, if the motion was filed within the initial 21–day appeal period or within further time the trial court may have allowed during that 21–day period; or

(c) another time provided by law.

If a party in a civil action is entitled to the appointment of an attorney and requests the appointment within 21 days after the final judgment or order, the 21–day period for the taking of an appeal or the filing of a postjudgment motion begins to run from the entry of an order appointing or denying the appointment of an attorney. If a timely postjudgment motion is filed before a request for appellate counsel, the party may request counsel within 21 days after the decision on the motion.

(2) An appeal of right in a criminal case must be taken

(a) in accordance with MCR 6.425(F)(3);

(b) within 42 days after entry of an order denying a timely motion for the appointment of a lawyer pursuant to MCR 6.425(F)(1);

(c) within 42 days after entry of the judgment or order appealed from; or

(d) within 42 days after the entry of an order denying a motion for a new trial, for judgment of acquittal, or for resentencing, if the motion was filed within the time provided by 6.419(B), 6.429(B)(1), or 6.431(A)(1), as the case may be.

A motion for rehearing or reconsideration of a motion mentioned in subrules (A)(1)(b) or (A)(2)(d) does not extend the time for filing a claim of appeal, unless the motion for rehearing or reconsideration was itself filed within the 21– or 42–day period.

(B) Manner of Filing. To vest the Court of Appeals with jurisdiction in an appeal of right, an appellant shall file with the clerk within the time for taking an appeal

(1) the claim of appeal, and

(2) the entry fee.

(C) Other Documents. With the claim of appeal, the appellant shall file the following documents with the clerk:

(1) a copy of the judgment or order appealed from;

(2) a copy of the certificate of the court reporter or recorder filed under subrule (E)(4), a statement by the attorney that the transcript has been ordered (in which case the certificate of the court reporter or recorder must be filed as soon as possible thereafter), or a statement by the attorney that there is no record to be transcribed;

(3) proof that a copy of the claim of appeal was served on all other parties in the case and on any other person or officer entitled by rule or law to notice of the appeal;

(4) if the appellant has filed a bond, a true copy of the bond;

(5) a copy of the docket or calendar entries; and

(6) a jurisdictional checklist on a form provided by the clerk's office.

(D) Form of Claim of Appeal.

(1) A claim of appeal is entitled "In the Court of Appeals." The parties are named in the same order as they appear in the trial court, with the added designation "appellant" or "appellee" as appropriate. The claim must be substantially in the following form:

[*Name of appellant*], [*plaintiff or defendant*], claims an appeal from the [*judgment or order*] entered [*date of judgment or order or date sentence im-*

posed] in the [*name of court or tribunal from which the appeal is taken*] by [*name of judge or officer who entered the judgment, order, or sentence*].

(2) The claim of appeal must be dated and signed, and must list the appropriate business address and telephone number under the signature.

(3) If the case involves

(a) a contest as to the custody of a minor child, or

(b) a ruling that a provision of the Michigan Constitution, a Michigan statute, a rule or regulation included in the Michigan Administrative Code, or any other action of the legislative or executive branch of state government is invalid,

that fact must be stated in capital letters on the claim of appeal. In an appeal specified in subrule (D)(3)(b), the Court of Appeals shall give expedited consideration to the appeal, and, if the state or an officer or agency of the state is not a party to the appeal, the Court of Appeals shall send copies of the claim of appeal and the judgment or order appealed from to the Attorney General.

(E) Trial Court Filing Requirements. Within the time for taking the appeal, the appellant shall file in the court or the tribunal from which the appeal is taken

(1) a copy of the claim of appeal;

(2) any fee required by law;

(3) any bond required by law as a condition for taking the appeal; and

(4) unless there is no record to be transcribed, the certificate of the court reporter or recorder stating that a transcript has been ordered and payment for it made or secured, and that it will be filed as soon as possible or has already been filed.

(F) Other Requirements. Within the time for taking the appeal, the appellant shall also

(1) make any delivery or deposit of money, property, or documents, and do any other act required by the statute authorizing the appeal, and file with the clerk an affidavit or other evidence of compliance;

(2) serve on all other parties in the case and on any other person or officer entitled by rule or law to notice of the appeal a copy of the claim of appeal and a copy of any bond filed under subrule (C)(4).

(G) Appearance. Within 14 days after being served with the claim of appeal, the appellee shall file an appearance (identifying the individual attorneys of record) in the Court of Appeals and in the court or tribunal from which the appeal is taken. An appellee who does not file a timely appearance is not entitled to notice of further proceedings until an appearance is filed.

(H) Docketing Statement. In all civil appeals within 28 days after the claim of appeal is filed, the appellant must file two copies of a docketing statement with the clerk of the Court of Appeals and serve a copy on the opposing parties.

(1) *Contents.* The docketing statement must contain the information required from time to time by the Court of Appeals through the office of the Chief Clerk on forms provided by the Clerk's office and must set forth:

(a) the nature of the proceeding;

(b) the date of the judgment or order sought to be reviewed, and whether the appeal was timely filed and is within the court's jurisdiction;

(c) a concise, accurate summary of all facts material to consideration of the issues presented, but transcripts are not required at this stage;

(d) the issues presented by the appeal, including a concise summary of how they arose and how they were preserved in the trial court. General conclusory statements such as, "the judgment of the trial court is not supported by the law or the facts," will not be accepted;

(e) a reference to all related or prior appeals, and the appropriate citation, if any.

(2) *Amendment.* The Court of Appeals may, upon motion and good cause shown, allow for the amendment of the docketing statement.

(3) *Cross Appeals.* A party who files a cross appeal shall file a docketing statement in accordance with this rule within 28 days after filing the cross appeal.

(4) *Dismissal.* If the appellant fails to file a timely docketing statement, the chief judge may dismiss the appeal pursuant to MCR 7.217.

[Effective March 1, 1985; amended effective October 1, 1989; February 1, 1994; amended December 30, 1994, applicable to all crimes committed on or after December 27, 1994 as provided by 1994 PA 374 and 1994 PA 375, effective until further order of the Court after consideration of comments and legislative action, if any, or until April 1, 1995; by Order of March 31, 1995, December 30, 1994 amendment ordered to remain in effect until June 30, 1995; amended effective May 1, 1995; by Order of June 19, 1995, December 30, 1994 amendment ordered to remain in effect until October 15, 1995; by Order of October 13, 1995, December 30, 1994 amendment ordered to remain in effect until August 15, 1996; by Order of July 16, 1996, December 30, 1994 amendment ordered to remain in effect until September 1, 1997; by Order of July 25, 1997, December 30, 1994 amendment ordered to remain in effect until further order of the Court; amended effective September 1, 1997; September 1, 1998; November 30, 1999; September 1, 2002.]

1985 Staff Comment

MCR 7.204 is based on GCR 1963, 802.1, 803.1, 803.5, 804.1, and 805. The rule brings together the various provisions on the filing of an appeal of right.

The [March 1, 1985] amendments of MCR 6.101(F)(7)(e) and 7.204(A)(3) have the effect of allowing a criminal defendant to file a motion for resentencing in the trial court before filing a claim of appeal. If the defendant does so, the time for taking an appeal of right runs from the denial of the motion.

Under GCR 1963, 805(3) the appellant was required to file a copy of the court reporter's or recorder's certificate that the transcript had been ordered. GCR 1963, 812.3(1); MCR 7.210(B)(3)(a). Subrule (C)(2) permits as a substitute a statement by the attorney that the transcript has been ordered. In certain circumstances the time required to obtain the certificate itself might delay the taking of an appeal. However, the certificate must be filed as soon as possible thereafter.

Subrule (C)(4) adds a requirement that if a bond was filed a copy of it must be filed in the Court of Appeals with the claim of appeal. A copy must be served on the other parties under subrule (F)(2).

Subrule (G) adds a new requirement that the appellee file an appearance in the Court of Appeals. Under MCR 2.117(C)(1), an appearance by an attorney in the trial court continues only until the entry of final judgment and through the time for taking an appeal of right. Thus, a timely claim of appeal could be served on the attorney for a party. However, the trial court appearance will have expired by the time the appellant's brief is to be served.

The provisions of GCR 1963, 803.6, which halved the time for filing a claim of appeal (among other steps) in certain cases, are omitted.

The checklist of steps on appeal formerly found in GCR 1963, 823 is omitted.

Staff Comment to 1989 Amendment

There are three changes [under the October 1, 1989 amendment] in MCR 7.204(A). The last paragraph of MCR 7.204(A)(1) is amended to adjust the relationship between the times for taking an appeal of right and for requesting appointment of counsel in those situations in which a civil litigant is entitled to such an appointment. Under the prior rule, a party could lose an appeal of right where a post-trial motion was filed but counsel was not requested until more than 21 days after the judgment.

The provisions of subrule (A)(2) on the taking of an appeal of right in criminal cases are modified to take account of the revised procedures in MCR 6.425(E) and (F). The basic time for taking an appeal, or for requesting counsel, is shortened from 56 to 42 days. Former subrule (A)(3), which created a separate procedure in guilty plea cases, is eliminated.

A new concluding paragraph of MCR 7.204(A) is added to make clear that a series of postjudgment motions cannot indefinitely extend the time for taking an appeal. Only motions filed within 21 days after the judgment in civil cases, and 42 days in criminal cases, extend the time for taking an appeal.

Staff Comment to February, 1994 Amendment

MCR 7.204(H) is a new provision [adopted December 15, 1993, effective February 1, 1994]. It requires that a docketing statement be filed in all appeals.

The January 28, 1994 amendment of MCR 7.204(H) [effective February 1, 1994] makes it clear that the requirement that a docketing statement be filed applies only in appeals of civil cases. The Supreme Court is considering, as a separate matter, whether to impose such a requirement in appeals of criminal cases.

Staff Comment to December, 1994 Amendment

The December 30, 1994 amendments of MCR 6.301, 6.302, 6.311, 6.425, 7.203, 7.204 and 7.205 modified procedure regarding appeals in criminal cases in light of the amendment of Const 1963, art 1, § 20 at the November 1994 general election and the legislation implementing the constitutional amendment. Changes will remain in effect until April 1, 1995 and will be reconsidered by the Court in light of comments received and any further legislation.

Staff Comment to 1995 Amendment

MCR 7.204(C)(5) is amended to require a copy of the docket or calendar entries in all appeals of right.

Staff Comment to 1997 Amendment

There are two changes in MCR 7.204(H) regarding the docketing statement that must be filed in the Court of Appeals. Two copies would be required, and the Court of Appeals would be authorized to require that additional information be included on the docketing statement form.

Staff Comment to 1998 Amendment

The June 2, 1998, amendments [effective September 1, 1998] of subchapter 7.200 deal with procedure in the Court of Appeals. The following rules are amended:

MCR 7.204(C). Require a jurisdictional checklist to be filed with the claim of appeal.

MCR 7.205(B) and (C), 7.206(D), 7.211(A) and (B). Eliminate the filing of a notice of hearing, instead specifying the time for response.

MCR 7.211(A)(2). Eliminate the requirement of filing affidavits with motions.

MCR 7.211(B)(2)(a) [former (A)(5)(a)]. Add motions to remand to the list of motions for which the notice period for submission is 21 days.

MCR 7.212(B). Require a party to obtain advance permission to file a brief in excess of the page limit set by the rule.

MCR 7.215(G)(1). Require a copy of the order with a motion for rehearing of the order.

Proposed amendments of MCR 7.212(A)(6) and (F), published for comment at 77 Mich B J 117 (January 1998), which would have prohibited parties represented by counsel from filing briefs or supplemental authority communications in propria persona, were not adopted.

Staff Comment to 1999 Amendment

The 1999 amendments of MCR 7.203(A)(1) and 7.204(A) [effective November 30, 1999] are explained in *Allied Electric Supply Co v Tenaglia*, [461] Mich [285], ___; [602] NW2d [572] (1999).

Staff Comment to 2002 Amendment

The May 17, 2002, amendments of MCR 7.204, 7.212, 7.213, 7.215, and 7.302, which are effective September 1, 2002, relate to appeals in which a Michigan constitutional provision, statute, regulation, or other governmental action has been held to be invalid.

The amendment of MCR 7.204(D)(3) requires that the claim of appeal identify cases involving such a ruling, and directs the Court of Appeals to give expedited treatment to such appeals and to send copies of the claim of appeal and the order appealed from to the Attorney General if the state is not a party.

The staff comment is published only for the benefit of the bench and bar and is not an authoritative construction by the Court.

RULE 7.205 APPLICATION FOR LEAVE TO APPEAL

(A) Time Requirements. An application for leave to appeal must be filed within 21 days after entry of the judgment or order to be appealed from or within other time as allowed by law or rule.

(B) Manner of Filing. To apply for leave to appeal, the appellant shall file with the clerk:

(1) 5 copies of an application for leave to appeal (one signed), stating the date and nature of the judgment or order appealed from; concisely reciting the appellant's allegations of error and the relief sought; setting forth a concise argument, conforming to MCR 7.212(C), in support of the appellant's position on each issue; and, if the order appealed from is interlocutory, setting forth facts showing how the appellant would suffer substantial harm by awaiting final judgment before taking an appeal;

(2) 5 copies of the judgment or order appealed from, of the calendar or docket entries, of the opinion or findings of the lower court, tribunal or agency, and of any opinion or findings reviewed by the lower court, tribunal or agency;

(3) if the appeal is from an administrative tribunal or agency, or from a circuit court on review of an administrative tribunal or agency, evidence that the tribunal or agency has been requested to send its record to the Court of Appeals;

(4) 1 copy of certain transcripts, as follows:

(a) in an appeal relating to the evidence presented at an evidentiary hearing in a civil or criminal case, the transcript of the evidentiary hearing, including the opinion or findings of the court which conducted the hearing;

(b) in an appeal from the circuit court or recorder's court after an appeal from another court, the transcript of proceedings in the court reviewed by the circuit court or recorder's court;

(c) in an appeal challenging jury instructions, the transcript of the entire charge to the jury;

(d) in an appeal from a judgment in a criminal case entered pursuant to a plea of guilty or nolo contendere, the transcripts of the plea and sentence;

(e) in an appeal from an order granting or denying a new trial, such portion of the transcript of the trial as, in relation to the issues raised, permits the court to determine whether the trial court's decision on the motion was for a legally recognized reason and based on arguable support in the record;

(f) in an appeal raising a sentencing issue, the transcript of the sentencing proceeding and the transcript of any hearing on a motion relating to sentencing;

(g) in an appeal raising any other issue, such portion of the transcript as substantiates the existence of the issue, objections or lack thereof, arguments of counsel, and any comment or ruling of the trial judge.

If the transcript is not yet available, or if there is no record to be transcribed, the appellant shall file a copy of the certificate of the court reporter or recorder or a statement by the appellant's attorney as provided in MCR 7.204(C)(2). The appellant must file the transcript with the Court of Appeals as soon as it is available.

(5) if the appeal is from a probate court order, 5 copies of the probate court's certification of the issue, as required by law;

(6) proof that a copy of the filed documents was served on all other parties; and

(7) the entry fee.

(C) Answer. Any other party in the case may file with the clerk, within 21 days of service of the application,

(1) 5 copies of an answer to the application (one signed) conforming to MCR 7.212(D), except that transcript page references are not required unless a transcript has been filed; and

(2) proof that a copy was served on the appellant and any other appellee.

(D) Decision.

(1) There is no oral argument. The application is decided on the documents filed and, in an appeal from an administrative tribunal or agency, the certified record.

(2) The court may grant or deny the application; enter a final decision; grant other relief; request additional material from the record; or require a certified concise statement of proceedings and facts from the court, tribunal, or agency whose order is being appealed. The clerk shall enter the court's order and mail copies to the parties.

(3) If an application is granted, the case proceeds as an appeal of right, except that the filing of a claim of appeal is not required and the time limits for the filing of a cross appeal and for the taking of the other steps in the appeal, including the filing of the docketing statement (28 days), and the filing of the court reporter's or recorder's certificate if the transcript has not been filed (14 days), run from the date the order granting leave is certified.

(4) Unless otherwise ordered, the appeal is limited to the issues raised in the application and supporting brief.

(E) Emergency Appeal..

(1) If the order appealed requires acts or will have consequences within 56 days of the date the application is filed, appellant shall alert the clerk of that fact by prominent notice on the cover sheet or first page of the application, including the date by which action is required.

(2) When an appellant requires a hearing on an application in less than 21 days, the appellant shall file and serve a motion for immediate consideration, concisely stating facts showing why an immediate hearing is required. A notice of hearing of the application and motion or a transcript is not required. An answer may be filed within the time the court directs. If a copy of the application and of the motion for immediate consideration are personally served under MCR 2.107(C)(1) or (2), the application may be submitted to the court immediately on filing. If mail service is used, it may not be submitted until the first Tuesday 7 days after the date of service, unless the party served acknowledges receipt. In all other respects, submission, decision, and further proceedings are as provided in subrule (D).

(F) Late Appeal.

(1) When an appeal of right or an application for leave was not timely filed, the appellant may file an application as prescribed in subrule (B), file 5 copies of a statement of facts explaining the delay, and serve 1 copy on all other parties. The answer may challenge the claimed reasons for delay. The court may consider the length of and the reasons for delay in deciding whether to grant the application. In all other respects, submission, decision, and further proceedings are as provided in subrule (D).

(2) In a criminal case, the defendant may not file an application for leave to appeal from a judgment of conviction and sentence if the defendant has previously taken an appeal from that judgment by right or leave granted or has sought leave to appeal that was denied.

(3) Except as provided in subrule (F)(4), leave to appeal may not be granted if an application for leave to appeal is filed more than 12 months after the later of:

(a) entry of a final judgment or other order that could have been the subject of an appeal of right under MCR 7.203(A), but if a motion described in MCR 7.204(A)(1)(b) was filed within the time prescribed in that rule, then the 12 months are counted from the entry of the order denying that motion; or

(b) entry of the order or judgment to be appealed from, but if a motion for new trial, a motion for rehearing or reconsideration, or a motion for other postjudgment relief was filed within the initial 21-day appeal period or within further time the trial court may have allowed during that 21-day period, then the 12 months are counted from the entry of the order denying that motion.

(4) The limitation provided in subrule (F)(3) does not apply to an application for leave to appeal by a criminal defendant if the defendant files an application for leave to appeal within 21 days after the trial court decides a motion for a new trial, for judgment of acquittal, to withdraw a plea, or for resentencing, if the motion was filed within the 12-month period, or if

(a) the defendant has filed a delayed request for the appointment of counsel pursuant to MCR 6.425(F)(1) within the 12-month period,

(b) the defendant or defendant's lawyer, if one is appointed, has ordered the appropriate transcripts within 28 days of service of the order granting or denying the delayed request for counsel, unless the transcript has already been filed or has been ordered by the court under MCR 6.425(F)(2), and

(c) the application for leave to appeal is filed in accordance with the provisions of this rule within 42 days after the filing of the transcript. If the transcript was filed before the order appointing or denying the appointment of counsel, the 42-day period runs from the date of that order.

A defendant who seeks to rely on one of the exceptions in subrule (F)(4) must file with the application for leave to appeal an affidavit stating the relevant docket entries, a copy of the docket or calendar entries, or other documentation showing that the application is filed within the time allowed.

(G) Certified Concise Statement.

(1) When the Court of Appeals requires a certified concise statement of proceedings and facts, the appellant shall, within 7 days after the order requiring the certified concise statement is certified, serve on all other parties a copy of a proposed concise statement of proceedings and facts, describing the course of proceedings and the facts pertinent to the issues raised in the application, and notice of hearing with the date, time, and place for settlement of the concise statement.

(2) Hearing on the proposed concise statement must be within 14 days after the proposed concise statement and notice is served on the other parties.

(3) Objections to the proposed concise statement must be filed in writing with the trial court and served on the appellant and any other appellee before the time set for settlement.

(4) The trial court shall promptly settle objections to the proposed concise statement and may correct it or add matters of record necessary to present the issues properly. When a court's discretionary act is being reviewed, the trial court may add to the statement its reasons for the act. Within 7 days after the settlement hearing, the trial court shall certify the proposed or a corrected concise statement of proceedings and facts as fairly presenting the factual basis for the questions to be reviewed as directed by the Court of Appeals. Immediately after certification, the trial

court shall send the certified concise statement to the Court of Appeals clerk and serve a copy on each party.

[Effective March 1, 1985; amended effective January 1, 1988; October 1, 1989; February 1, 1994; amended December 30, 1994, applicable to all crimes committed on or after December 27, 1994 as provided by 1994 PA 374 and 1994 PA 375, effective until further order of the Court after consideration of comments and legislative action, if any, or until April 1, 1995; by Order of March 31, 1995, December 30, 1994 amendment ordered to remain in effect until June 30, 1995; by Order of June 19, 1995, December 30, 1994 amendment ordered to remain in effect until October 15, 1995; by Order of October 13, 1995, December 30, 1994 amendment ordered to remain in effect until August 15, 1996; amended effective November 1, 1995; April 1, 1996; by Order of July 16, 1996, December 30, 1994 amendment ordered to remain in effect until September 1, 1997; by Order of July 25, 1997, December 30, 1994 amendment ordered to remain in effect until further order of the Court; amended effective September 1, 1997; September 1, 1998; September 1, 2002.]

1985 Staff Comment

MCR 7.205 is based on GCR 1963, 803.2–803.4 and 806.2–806.7.

Throughout the rule 5 copies of the application and related documents are required, rather than 4 as under GCR 1963, 806.3(4).

GCR 1963, 806.3 required that a concise statement of the proceedings and facts be filed with every timely application. That provision is not included in the new rule. Such a statement is necessary only if the Court of Appeals directs that it be prepared. See subrule (G).

The rule omits the language in GCR 1963, 806.3(1)(a) that required the Court of Appeals to "pay particular attention" to certain grounds for appeal.

Subrule (B) requires additional papers to be filed with the application in certain cases. In appeals from administrative tribunals, proof must be submitted that the tribunal record has been requested. Subrule (B)(4). Transcripts are required in certain appeals. Subrule (B)(5). A certificate of the probate court must be filed when required by law (see MCL 600.863[3]; MSA 27A.863[3]). Subrule (B)(6).

Both subrule (D), covering decision by the Court of Appeals, and subrule (E), governing emergency appeals, include more detailed procedures than the corresponding rules, GCR 1963, 806.7 and 806.5.

The [March 1, 1985] amendment of MCR 7.205(D) subdivides the provision into several paragraphs, and sets 14 days after a Court of Appeals order granting leave to appeal as the time within which the court reporter's or recorder's certificate regarding the transcript must be filed.

Subrule (F), governing late appeals, does not require an affidavit showing that the delay was not due to "culpable negligence". See GCR 1963, 806.4(2). Rather, the affidavit is only required to explain the delay, and the court will consider the length of and reasons for the delay in reaching its decision.

Most of the special provisions of GCR 1963, 806.6 regarding appeals from administrative tribunals are omitted.

Staff Comment to 1989 Amendment

There are several significant changes in MCR 7.205(F) [under the October 1, 1989 amendment]. First, subrule

(F)(2) is added, limiting a criminal defendant to a single appeal. Thereafter, the defendant must utilize the procedure established in Subchapter 6.500.

Second, the 18–month time limit on applications for leave to appeal, formerly applicable only to civil cases, is extended to criminal cases. However, under subrule (F)(4), if a criminal defendant initiates the process by requesting counsel within the 18–month period, and the subsequent steps regarding ordering the transcript and filing the application are taken within specified time limits, the 18–month limitation does not apply. A criminal defendant who seeks to rely on those exceptions must document the facts that make the application a timely one.

Staff Comment to February, 1994 Amendment

MCR 7.205(B) and (C) have been changed [effective February 1, 1994] to require that the application for leave to appeal and the answer to the application include the parties' arguments. Separate briefs no longer will be filed.

Staff Comment to December, 1994 Amendment

The December 30, 1994 amendments of MCR 6.301, 6.302, 6.311, 6.425, 7.203, 7.204 and 7.205 modified procedure regarding appeals in criminal cases in light of the amendment of Const 1963, art 1, § 20 at the November 1994 general election and the legislation implementing the constitutional amendment. Changes will remain in effect until April 1, 1995 and will be reconsidered by the Court in light of comments received and any further legislation.

Staff Comment to November, 1995 Amendment

The amendment of MCR 7.205(F) shortens the limitation on filing late appeals from 18 to 12 months. This amendment is effective November 1, 1995.

Staff Comment to 1996 Amendment

The amendments of MCR 7.205(B)(2) and (3) [effective April 1, 1996] require the filing of additional materials with applications for leave to appeal in certain cases.

On January 26, 1996, MCR 7.205(B)(4) was amended [effective April 1, 1996] to require the filing of transcripts with applications for leave to appeal in additional circumstances. The March 7, 1996, order [effective April 1, 1996] clarifies that if the transcript is not yet available, a court reporter's or recorder's certificate or attorney's statement may be filed, comparable to the procedure in appeals of right. See MCR 7.204(C)(2).

Staff Comment to 1997 Amendment

The amendment of MCR 7.205(E) [effective September 1, 1997] requires an appellant to notify the clerk if the order appealed from requires action or will have consequences within 56 days of the filing of the application.

Staff Comment to 1998 Amendment

The June 2, 1998, amendments [effective September 1, 1998] of subchapter 7.200 deal with procedure in the Court of Appeals. The following rules are amended:

MCR 7.204(C). Require a jurisdictional checklist to be filed with the claim of appeal.

MCR 7.205(B) and (C), 7.206(D), 7.211(A) and (B). Eliminate the filing of a notice of hearing, instead specifying the time for response.

MCR 7.211(A)(2). Eliminate the requirement of filing affidavits with motions.

MCR 7.211(B)(2)(a) [former (A)(5)(a)]. Add motions to remand to the list of motions for which the notice period for submission is 21 days.

MCR 7.212(B). Require a party to obtain advance permission to file a brief in excess of the page limit set by the rule.

MCR 7.215(G)(1). Require a copy of the order with a motion for rehearing of the order.

Proposed amendments of MCR 7.212(A)(6) and (F), published for comment at 77 Mich B J 117 (January 1998), which would have prohibited parties represented by counsel from filing briefs or supplemental authority communications in propria persona, were not adopted.

2002 Staff Comment

The April 23, 2002, amendment of subrule (F)(3), effective September 1, 2002, broadens the instances in which a late application for leave to appeal can be filed in the Court of Appeals.

The staff comment is published only for the benefit of the bench and bar and is not an authoritative construction by the Court.

RULE 7.206 EXTRAORDINARY WRITS, ORIGINAL ACTIONS, AND ENFORCEMENT ACTIONS

(A) General Rules of Pleading. Except as otherwise provided in this rule, the general rules of pleading apply as nearly as practicable. See MCR 2.111–2.114.

(B) Superintending Control, Mandamus, and Habeas Corpus. To the extent that they do not conflict with this rule, the rules in subchapter 3.300 apply to actions for superintending control, mandamus, and habeas corpus.

(C) Quo Warranto. In a quo warranto action, the Attorney General also must be served with a copy of each pleading and document filed in the Court of Appeals. The Attorney General has the right to intervene as a party on either side.

(D) Actions for Extraordinary Writs and Original Actions.

(1) *Filing of Complaint.* To commence an original action, the plaintiff shall file with the clerk:

(a) 5 copies of a complaint (one signed), which may have copies of supporting documents or affidavits attached to each copy;

(b) 5 copies of a supporting brief (one signed) conforming to MCR 7.212(C) to the extent possible;

(c) proof that a copy of each of the filed documents was served on every named defendant and, in a superintending control action, on any other party involved in the case which gave rise to the complaint for superintending control; and

(d) the entry fee.

(2) *Answer.* The defendant or any other interested party must file with the clerk within 21 days of service of the complaint and any supporting documents or affidavits:

(a) 5 copies of an answer to the complaint (one signed), which may have copies of supporting documents or affidavits attached to each copy;

(b) 5 copies of an opposing brief (one signed) conforming to MCR 7.212(D) to the extent possible; and

(c) proof that a copy of each of the filed documents was served on the plaintiff and any other interested party.

(3) *Preliminary Hearing.* There is no oral argument on preliminary hearing of a complaint. The court may deny relief, grant peremptory relief, or allow the parties to proceed to full hearing on the merits in the same manner as an appeal of right either with or without referral to a judicial circuit or tribunal or agency for the taking of proofs and report of factual findings. If the case is ordered to proceed to full hearing, the time for filing a brief by the plaintiff begins to run from the date the order allowing the case to proceed is certified or the date the transcript or report of factual findings on referral is filed, whichever is later. The plaintiff's brief must conform to MCR 7.212(C). An opposing brief must conform to MCR 7.212(D). In a habeas corpus proceeding, the prisoner need not be brought before the Court of Appeals.

(E) Enforcement of Administrative Tribunal or Agency Orders.

(1) *Complaint.* To obtain enforcement of a final order of an administrative tribunal or agency, the plaintiff shall file with the clerk within the time limit provided by law:

(a) 5 copies of a complaint (one signed) concisely stating the basis for relief and the relief sought;

(b) 5 copies of the order sought to be enforced;

(c) 5 copies of a supporting brief (one signed) which conforms to MCR 7.212(C) to the extent possible;

(d) a notice of preliminary hearing on the complaint on the first Tuesday at least 21 days after the complaint and supporting documents are served on the defendant, the agency (unless the agency is the plaintiff), and any other interested party;

(e) proof that a copy of each of the filed documents was served on the defendant, the agency (unless the agency is the plaintiff), and any other interested party;

(f) the certified tribunal or agency record or evidence the plaintiff has requested that the certified record be sent to the Court of Appeals; and

(g) the entry fee.

(2) *Answer.* The defendant must file, and any other interested party may file, with the clerk before the date of the preliminary hearing:

(a) 5 copies of an answer to the complaint (one signed);

(b) 5 copies of an opposing brief (one signed) conforming to MCR 7.212(D) to the extent possible; and

(c) proof that a copy of each of the filed documents was served on the plaintiff, the agency, and any other interested party.

(3) *Preliminary Hearing.* There is no oral argument on preliminary hearing of a complaint. The court may deny relief, grant peremptory relief, or allow the parties to proceed to full hearing on the merits in the same manner as an appeal of right. If the case is ordered to proceed to full hearing, the time for filing of a brief by the plaintiff begins to run from the date the clerk certifies the order allowing the case to proceed. The plaintiff's brief must conform to MCR 7.212(C). An opposing brief must conform to MCR 7.212(D). The case is heard on the certified record transmitted by the tribunal or agency. MCR 7.210(A)(2), regarding the content of the record, applies.

[Effective March 1, 1985; amended effective September 1, 1998.]

1985 Staff Comment

MCR 7.206 corresponds to GCR 1963, 816.2(2). The provisions are rewritten to more precisely prescribe the procedures to be followed.

Five copies of the complaint and other papers are required, rather than four.

The rule incorporates the pleading rules of chapter 2 (see subrule [A]), and the provisions generally governing extraordinary writs in subchapter 3.300 (see subrule [B]).

Subrule (E) is a new provision covering actions to enforce orders of administrative agencies, where statutes provide for such proceedings. E.g., MCL 423.23(d); MSA 17.454(25)(d) (enforcement of decisions of the Michigan Employment Relations Commission).

Staff Comment to 1998 Amendment

The June 2, 1998, amendments [effective September 1, 1998] of subchapter 7.200 deal with procedure in the Court of Appeals. The following rules are amended:

MCR 7.204(C). Require a jurisdictional checklist to be filed with the claim of appeal.

MCR 7.205(B) and (C), 7.206(D), 7.211(A) and (B). Eliminate the filing of a notice of hearing, instead specifying the time for response.

MCR 7.211(A)(2). Eliminate the requirement of filing affidavits with motions.

MCR 7.211(B)(2)(a) [former (A)(5)(a)]. Add motions to remand to the list of motions for which the notice period for submission is 21 days.

MCR 7.212(B). Require a party to obtain advance permission to file a brief in excess of the page limit set by the rule.

MCR 7.215(G)(1). Require a copy of the order with a motion for rehearing of the order.

Proposed amendments of MCR 7.212(A)(6) and (F), published for comment at 77 Mich B J 117 (January 1998), which would have prohibited parties represented by counsel from filing briefs or supplemental authority communications in propria persona, were not adopted.

RULE 7.207　CROSS APPEALS

(A) Right of Cross Appeal.

(1) When an appeal of right is filed or the court grants leave to appeal any appellee may file a cross appeal.

(2) If there is more than 1 party plaintiff or defendant in a civil action and 1 party appeals, any other party, whether on the same or opposite side as the party first appealing, may file a cross appeal against all or any of the other parties to the case as well as against the party who first appealed. If the cross appeal operates against a party not affected by the first appeal or in a manner different from the first appeal, that party may file a further cross appeal as if the cross appeal affecting that party had been the first appeal.

(B) Manner of Filing. To file a cross appeal, the cross appellant shall file with the clerk a claim of cross appeal in the form required by MCR 7.204(D) and the entry fee

(1) within 21 days after the claim of appeal is filed with the Court of Appeals or served on the cross appellant, whichever is later, if the first appeal was of right; or

(2) within 21 days after the clerk certifies the order granting leave to appeal, if the appeal was initiated by application for leave to appeal.

The cross appellant shall file proof that a copy of the claim of cross appeal was served on the cross appellee and any other party in the case. A copy of the judgment or order from which the cross appeal is taken must be filed with the claim.

(C) Additional Requirements. The cross appellant shall perform the steps required by MCR 7.204(E) and (F), except that the cross appellant is not required to order a transcript or file a court reporter's or recorder's certificate unless the initial appeal is abandoned or dismissed. Otherwise the cross appeal proceeds in the same manner as an ordinary appeal.

(D) Abandonment or Dismissal of Appeal. If the appellant abandons the initial appeal or the court dismisses it, the cross appeal may nevertheless be prosecuted to its conclusion. Within 21 days after the clerk certifies the order dismissing the initial appeal, if there is a record to be transcribed, the cross appellant shall file a certificate of the court reporter or recorder that a transcript has been ordered and payment for it made or secured and will be filed as soon as possible or has already been filed.

(E) Delayed Cross Appeal. A party seeking leave to take a delayed cross appeal shall proceed under MCR 7.205.

[Effective March 1, 1985; amended effective November 1, 1998.]

1985 Staff Comment

MCR 7.207 corresponds to GCR 1963, 807. The rule is rewritten but retains most of the substance of the former rule.

The principal change is the extension of the right to cross appeal to criminal cases. Compare subrule (A)(1) with GCR 1963, 807.1.

New subrule (E) expressly provides for delayed cross appeal, directing the cross appellant to proceed under MCR 7.205, the rule governing applications for leave to appeal.

Staff Comment to 1998 Amendment

The September 15, 1998 amendment of MCR 7.207(B), effective November 1, 1998, provided, consistent with *Hall* v *Stewart*, 454 Mich 903 (1997), that a claim of cross appeal is timely if filed within 21 days after a claim of appeal is filed or the claim is served on the cross appellant, whichever is later, if the first appeal was of right.

RULE 7.208   AUTHORITY OF COURT OR TRIBUNAL APPEALED FROM

(A) Limitations. After a claim of appeal is filed or leave to appeal is granted, the trial court or tribunal may not set aside or amend the judgment or order appealed from except

(1) by order of the Court of Appeals,

(2) by stipulation of the parties,

(3) after a decision on the merits in an action in which a preliminary injunction was granted, or

(4) as otherwise provided by law.

> In a criminal case, the filing of the claim of appeal does not preclude the trial court from granting a timely motion under subrule (B).

(B) Postjudgment Motions in Criminal Cases.

(1) No later than 56 days after the commencement of the time for filing the defendant-appellant's brief as provided by MCR 7.212(A)(1)(a)(iii), the defendant may file in the trial court a motion for a new trial, for judgment of acquittal, to withdraw a plea, or for resentencing.

(2) A copy of the motion must be filed with the Court of Appeals and served on the prosecuting attorney.

(3) The trial court shall hear and decide the motion within 28 days of filing, unless the court determines that an adjournment is necessary to secure evidence needed for the decision on the motion or that there is other good cause for an adjournment.

(4) Within 28 days of the trial court's decision, the court reporter or recorder must file with the trial court clerk the transcript of any hearing held.

(5) If the motion is granted in whole or in part,

(a) the defendant must file the appellant's brief or a notice of withdrawal of the appeal within 42 days after the trial court's decision or after the filing of the transcript of any hearing held, whichever is later;

(b) the prosecuting attorney may file a cross appeal in the manner provided by MCR 7.207 within 21 days after the trial court's decision. If the defendant has withdrawn the appeal before the prosecuting attorney has filed a cross appeal, the prosecuting attorney may file a claim of appeal or an application for leave to appeal within the 21–day period.

(6) If the motion is denied, defendant-appellant's brief must be filed within 42 days after the decision by the trial court, or the filing of the transcript of any trial court hearing, whichever is later.

(C) Correction of Defects. Except as otherwise provided by rule and until the record is filed in the Court of Appeals, the trial court or tribunal has jurisdiction

(1) to grant further time to do, properly perform, or correct any act in the trial court or tribunal in connection with the appeal that was omitted or insufficiently done, other than to extend the time for filing a claim of appeal or for paying the entry fee or to allow delayed appeal;

(2) to correct any part of the record to be transmitted to the Court of Appeals, but only after notice to the parties and an opportunity for a hearing on the proposed correction.

After the record is filed in the Court of Appeals, the trial court may correct the record only with leave of the Court of Appeals.

(D) Supervision of Property. When an appeal is filed while property is being held for conservation or management under the order or judgment of the trial court, that court retains jurisdiction over the property pending the outcome of the appeal, except as the Court of Appeals otherwise orders.

(E) Temporary Orders. A trial court order entered before final judgment concerning custody, control, and management of property; temporary alimony, support or custody of a minor child, or expenses in a domestic relations action; or a preliminary injunction, remains in effect and is enforceable in the trial court, pending interlocutory appeal, except as the trial court or the Court of Appeals may otherwise order.

(F) Stays and Bonds. The trial court retains authority over stay and bond matters, except as the Court of Appeals otherwise orders.

(G) Matters Pertaining to Appointment of Attorney. Throughout the pendency of an appeal involving an indigent person, the trial court retains authority to appoint, remove, or replace an attorney except as the Court of Appeals otherwise orders.

(H) Acts by Other Judges. Whenever the trial judge who has heard a case dies, resigns, or vacates office, or is unable to perform any act necessary to an appeal of a case within the time prescribed by law or these rules, another judge of the same court, or if another judge of that court is unavailable, another judge assigned by the state court administrator, may perform the acts necessary to the review process. Whenever a case is heard by a judge assigned from another court, the judicial acts necessary in the preparation of a record for appeal may be performed, with consent of the parties, by a judge of the court in which the case was heard.

(I) Attorney Fees and Costs. The trial court may rule on requests for costs or attorney fees under MCR 2.403, 2.405, 2.625 or other law or court rule, unless the Court of Appeals orders otherwise.

[Effective March 1, 1985; amended effective October 1, 1989; April 1, 1996; February 1, 2000; September 1, 2002.]

1985 Staff Comment

MCR 7.208 is based on GCR 1963, 802 and 812.9.

Subrule (B)(2) gives the court or tribunal from which the appeal is taken the authority to correct the record, after notice to the parties and opportunity for hearing, until the record is sent to the Court of Appeals.

Subrules (E) and (F) explicitly state the authority of the trial court to deal with stays, bonds, and matters relating to attorneys appointed for indigent persons.

Staff Comment to 1989 Amendment

[Under the October 1, 1989 amendment,] MCR 7.208(B) creates a new procedure under which a criminal defendant-appellant may file postjudgment motions in the trial court notwithstanding the fact that the Court of Appeals has jurisdiction of the case because the order appointing appellate counsel serves as the claim of appeal. See MCR 6.425(F)(3). Unlike motions to remand under MCR 7.211(C)(1), leave of the Court of Appeals is not required to take advantage of this procedure. The defendant-appellant may take advantage of this procedure by filing a motion in the trial court within 28 days after the period for filing the appellant's brief has begun to run. The rule sets forth the time limits for processing such a motion in the trial court and for further proceedings in the Court of Appeals following various possible dispositions of the motion by the trial court.

Staff Comment to 1996 Amendment

The March 15, 1996, amendment of MCR 7.208(B)(1) [effective April 1, 1996] extends the time during which a criminal defendant may file postjudgment motions in the trial court, despite the fact that the Court of Appeals has jurisdiction of the case, from 28 days after the commencement of the time for filing the defendant–appellant's brief to 56 days.

Staff Comment to 1999 Amendment

The amendments to MCR 7.203 and 7.208 [effective February 1, 2000] deal with two issues regarding the relationship of appeals and orders awarding or denying attorney fees and costs.

One amendment concerns the authority of the trial court to rule on requests for sanctions when an appeal has been taken. See *Co-Jo, Inc v Strand*, 226 Mich App 108 (1997). New MCR 7.208(I) provides that the trial court has the authority to rule on such requests despite the pendency of an appeal.

Second, MCR 7.203(A) is amended to make orders awarding or denying sanctions appealable by right.

2002 Staff Comment

The March 12, 2002 amendments of Rules 3.310, 7.208, and 7.213, effective September 1, 2002, require trial courts to expeditiously decide actions in which preliminary injunctions have been granted, and allow them to proceed even if the Court of Appeals has granted interlocutory leave to appeal. Similarly, if the Court of Appeals grants leave to review entry of a preliminary injunction on an interlocutory basis, that Court is required to give priority to resolution of the appeal. See *Michigan Coalition of State Employee Unions v Michigan Civil Service Comm*, 465 Mich 212, 214, n 1 (2001).

The staff comment is published only for the benefit of the bench and bar and is not an authoritative construction by the Court.

RULE 7.209　BOND; STAY OF PROCEEDINGS

(A) Effect of Appeal; Prerequisites.

(1) An appeal does not stay the effect or enforceability of a judgment or order of a trial court unless the trial court or the Court of Appeals otherwise orders.

(2) A motion for bond or for a stay pending appeal may not be filed in the Court of Appeals unless such a motion was decided by the trial court.

(3) A motion for bond or a stay pending appeal filed in the Court of Appeals must include a copy of the trial court's opinion and order, and a copy of the transcript of the hearing on the motion in the trial court.

(B) Responsibility for Setting Amount of Bond in Trial Court.

(1) *Civil Actions.* Unless determined by law, the dollar amount of a stay or appeal bond in a civil action must be set by the trial court in an amount adequate to protect the opposite party.

(2) *Criminal Cases.* In a criminal case the granting of bond pending appeal and the amount of it are within the discretion of the trial court, subject to applicable law and rules. Bond must be sufficient to guarantee the appearance of the defendant. Unless bond pending appeal is allowed and a bond is filed with the trial court, a criminal judgment may be executed immediately, even though the time for taking an appeal has not elapsed.

(C) Amendment of Bond. On motion, the trial court may order an additional or different bond, set the amount, and approve or require different sureties.

(D) Review by Court of Appeals. Except as otherwise provided by rule or law, on motion filed in a case pending before it, the Court of Appeals may amend the amount of bond set by the trial court, order an additional or different bond and set the amount, or require different or additional sureties. The Court of Appeals may also refer a bond or bail matter to the court from which the appeal is taken. The Court of Appeals may grant a stay of proceedings in the trial court or stay of effect or enforcement of any judgment or order of a trial court on the terms it deems just.

(E) Stay of Proceedings by Trial Court.

(1) Except as otherwise provided by law or rule, the trial court may order a stay of proceedings, with or without a bond as justice requires.

(a) When the stay is sought before an appeal is filed and a bond is required, the party seeking the stay shall file a bond, with the party in whose favor the judgment or order was entered as the obligee, by which the party promises to

(i) perform and satisfy the judgment or order stayed if it is not set aside or reversed; and

(ii) prosecute to completion any appeal subsequently taken from the judgment or order stayed and perform and satisfy the judgment or order entered by the Court of Appeals or Supreme Court.

(b) If a stay is sought after an appeal is filed, any bond must meet the requirements set forth in subrule 7.209(F).

(2) If a stay bond filed under this subrule substantially meets the requirements of subrule (F), it will be a sufficient bond to stay proceedings pending disposition of an appeal subsequently filed.

(3) The stay order must conform to any condition expressly required by the statute authorizing review.

(4) If a government party files a claim of appeal from an order described in MCR 7.202(7)(a)(v), the trial court shall stay proceedings regarding that party during the pendency of the appeal, unless the Court of Appeals directs otherwise.

(F) Conditions of Appeal Bond.

(1) *Civil Actions.* In a bond filed for stay pending appeal in a civil action, the appellant shall promise in writing:

(a) to prosecute the appeal to decision;

(b) to perform or satisfy a judgment or order of the Court of Appeals or the Supreme Court;

(c) to perform or satisfy the judgment or order appealed from, if the appeal is dismissed;

(d) in an action involving the possession of land or judgment for foreclosure of a mortgage or land contract, to pay the appellee the damages which may result from the stay of proceedings; and

(e) to do any other act which is expressly required in the statute authorizing appeal.

(2) *Criminal Cases.* A criminal defendant for whom bond pending appeal is allowed after conviction shall promise in writing:

(a) to prosecute the appeal to decision;

(b) if the sentence is one of incarceration, to surrender himself or herself to the sheriff of the county in which he or she was convicted or other custodial authority if the sentence is affirmed on appeal or if the appeal is dismissed;

(c) if the judgment or order appealed is other than a sentence of incarceration, to perform and comply with the order of the trial court if it is affirmed on appeal or if the appeal is dismissed;

(d) to appear in the trial court if the case is remanded for retrial or further proceedings or if a conviction is reversed and retrial is allowed;

(e) to remain in Michigan unless the court gives written approval to leave; and

(f) to notify the trial court clerk of a change of address.

(G) Sureties and Filing of Bond. Except as otherwise specifically provided in this rule, MCR 3.604 applies. A bond must be filed with the clerk of the court which entered the order or judgment to be stayed.

(1) *Civil Actions.* A bond in a civil action need not be approved by a court or clerk before filing but is subject to the objection procedure provided in MCR 3.604.

(2) *Criminal Cases.* A criminal defendant filing a bond after conviction shall give notice to the county prosecuting attorney of the time and place the bond will be filed. The bond is subject to the objection procedure provided in MCR 3.604.

(H) Stay of Execution.

(1) If a bond is filed before execution issues, and notice is given to the officer having authority to issue execution, execution is stayed. If the bond is filed after the issuance but before execution, and notice is given to the officer holding it, execution is suspended.

(2) The Court of Appeals may stay or terminate a stay of any order or judgment of a lower court or tribunal on just terms.

(3) When the amount of the judgment is more than $1000 over the insurance policy coverage or surety obligation, then the policy or obligation does not qualify to stay execution under MCL 500.3036; MSA 24.13036 on the portion of the judgment in excess of the policy or bond limits. Stay pending appeal may

be achieved by complying with that statute and by filing a bond in an additional amount adequate to protect the opposite party or by obtaining a trial court or Court of Appeals order waiving the additional bond.

(4) A statute exempting a municipality or other governmental agency from filing a bond to stay execution supersedes the requirements of this rule.

(I) Ex Parte Stay. Whenever an ex parte stay of proceedings is necessary to allow a motion in either the trial court or the Court of Appeals, the court before which the motion will be heard may grant an ex parte stay for that purpose. Service of a copy of the order, with a copy of the motion, any affidavits on which the motion is based, and notice of hearing on the motion, shall operate as a stay of proceedings until the court rules on the motion unless the court supersedes or sets aside the order in the interim. Proceedings may not be stayed for longer than necessary to enable the party to make the motion according to the practice of the court, and if made, until the decision of the court.

[Effective March 1, 1985; amended effective February 1, 1994; September 1, 2002.]

1985 Staff Comment

MCR 7.209 is based on GCR 1963, 808. The provisions are rewritten, but retain the substance of the former rule.

Subrule (F) lists the required conditions of a stay bond in criminal cases in more detail than GCR 1963, 808.1–808.2.

In subrule (H)(3) the language regarding a stay when the judgment exceeds the amount of insurance coverage is modified to more closely conform to the applicable statute. MCL 500.3036; MSA 24.13036.

Subrule (H)(4) adds a new provision recognizing the exemption of certain governmental units from bond requirements. See also MCR 2.614(E).

Staff Comment to 1994 Amendment

MCR 7.209(A) has been amended [effective February 1, 1994] to require that a motion for bond or stay first be decided by the trial court.

Staff Comment to 2002 Amendment

The June 4, 2002, amendments of MCR 7.202, 7.203, and 7.209, effective September 1, 2002, involve orders appealable by right to the Court of Appeals.

The provisions concerning custody orders in domestic relations cases and orders regarding attorney fees and costs are moved from MCR 7.203(A)(3) and (4) to MCR 7.202(7)(a)(iii) and (iv). There is also a change in the language regarding fees and costs, to refer to "postjudgment" orders.

New MCR 7.202(7)(a)(v) includes as "final" an order denying immunity to a governmental defendant, as is provided in many jurisdictions. See, *e.g.*, *Mitchell* v *Forsyth*, 472 US 511; 105 S Ct 2806; 86 L Ed 2d 411 (1985).

Language is added to MCR 7.203(A) to make clear that an appeal from an order described in MCR 7.202(7)(a)(iii)–(v) is limited to the portion of the order regarding which there is an appeal of right. In addition, obsolete references to the recorder's court are deleted from that subrule.

New MCR 7.209(E)(4) provides for a stay with respect to a governmental party who takes an appeal of right from an order denying immunity.

The staff comment is published only for the benefit of the bench and bar and is not an authoritative construction by the Court.

RULE 7.210   RECORD ON APPEAL

(A) Content of Record. Appeals to the Court of Appeals are heard on the original record.

(1) *Appeal From Court.* In an appeal from a lower court, the record consists of the original papers filed in that court or a certified copy, the transcript of any testimony or other proceedings in the case appealed, and the exhibits introduced. In an appeal from probate court in an estate or trust proceeding, only the order appealed from and those petitions, opinions, and other documents pertaining to it need be included.

(2) *Appeal From Tribunal or Agency.* In an appeal from an administrative tribunal or agency, the record includes all documents, files, pleadings, testimony, and opinions and orders of the tribunal, agency, or officer (or a certified copy), except those summarized or omitted in whole or in part by stipulation of the parties. Testimony not transcribed when the certified record is sent for consideration of an application for leave to appeal, and not omitted by stipulation of the parties, must be filed and sent to the court as promptly as possible.

(3) *Excluded Evidence.* The substance or transcript of excluded evidence offered at a trial and the proceedings at the trial in relation to it must be included as part of the record on appeal.

(4) *Stipulations.* The parties in any appeal to the Court of Appeals may stipulate in writing regarding any matters relevant to the lower court or tribunal or agency record if the stipulation is made a part of the record on appeal and sent to the Court of Appeals.

(B) Transcript.

(1) *Appellant's Duties; Orders; Stipulations.*

(a) The appellant is responsible for securing the filing of the transcript as provided in this rule. Except in cases governed by MCR 6.425(F)(2), or as otherwise provided by Court of Appeals order or the remainder of this subrule, the appellant shall order from the court reporter or recorder the full transcript of testimony and other proceedings in the trial court or tribunal. Once an appeal is filed in the Court of Appeals, a party must serve a copy of any request for transcript preparation on opposing counsel and file a copy with the Court of Appeals.

(b) In an appeal from probate court in an estate or trust proceeding, only that portion of the transcript concerning the order appealed from need be filed. The appellee may file additional portions of the transcript.

(c) On the appellant's motion, with notice to the appellee, the trial court or tribunal may order that some portion less than the full transcript (or no transcript at all) be included in the record on appeal. The motion must be filed within the time required for filing an appeal, and, if the motion is granted, the appellee may file any portions of the transcript omitted by the appellant. The filing of the motion extends the time for filing the court reporter's or recorder's certificate until 7 days after entry of the trial court's or tribunal's order on the motion.

(d) The parties may stipulate that some portion less than the full transcript (or none) be filed.

(e) The parties may agree on a statement of facts without procuring the transcript and the statement signed by the parties may be filed with the trial court or tribunal clerk and sent as the record of testimony in the action.

(2) *Transcript Unavailable.* When a transcript of the proceedings in the trial court or tribunal cannot be obtained from the court reporter or recorder, the appellant shall file a settled statement of facts to serve as a substitute for the transcript.

(a) Within 14 days after filing the claim of appeal, the appellant shall file with the trial court or tribunal clerk, and serve on each appellee, a proposed statement of facts. The proposed statement of facts must concisely set forth the substance of the testimony, or the oral proceedings before the trial court or tribunal if no testimony was taken, in sufficient detail to inform the Court of Appeals of the nature of the controversy and of the proceedings in the trial court or tribunal.

(b) The appellant shall notice the proposed statement of facts for prompt settlement before the trial court or tribunal. An amendment or objection to the proposed statement of facts must be in writing, filed in the trial court or tribunal before the time set for settlement, and served on the appellant and any other appellee.

(c) The trial court or tribunal shall settle any controversy and certify a statement of facts as an accurate, fair, and complete statement of the proceedings before it.

(d) The statement of facts and the certifying order must be filed with the trial court or tribunal clerk and a copy of the certifying order must be filed with the Court of Appeals.

(3) *Duties of Court Reporter or Recorder.*

(a) Certificate. Within 7 days after a transcript is ordered by a party or the court, the court reporter or recorder shall furnish a certificate stating that the transcript has been ordered and payment for it made and secured and that it will be filed as soon as possible or has already been filed.

(b) Time for Filing. The court reporter or recorder shall give precedence to transcripts necessary for interlocutory criminal appeals and custody cases. The court reporter or recorder shall file the transcript with the trial court or tribunal clerk within

(i) 14 days after it is ordered for an application for leave to appeal from an order granting or denying a motion to suppress evidence in a criminal case;

(ii) 28 days after it is ordered in an appeal of a criminal conviction based on a plea of guilty, guilty but mentally ill, or nolo contendere;

(iii) 42 days after it is ordered in any other interlocutory criminal appeal or custody case;

(iv) 91 days after it is ordered in other cases.*

The Court of Appeals may extend or shorten these time limits in an appeal pending in the court on motion filed by the court reporter or recorder or a party.

(c) Copies. Additional copies of the transcripts required by the appellant may be ordered from the court reporter or recorder or photocopies may be made of the transcript furnished by the court reporter or recorder.

(d) Form of Transcript. The transcript must be filed in one or more volumes under a hard-surfaced or other suitable cover, stating the title of the action, and prefaced by a table of contents showing the subject matter of the transcript with page references to the significant parts of the trial or proceedings, including the testimony of each witness by name, the arguments of the attorneys, and the jury instructions. The pages of the transcript must be consecutively numbered on the bottom of each page. Transcripts with more than one page, reduced in size, printed on a single page are permitted and encouraged, but a page in that format may not contain more than four reduced pages of transcript.

(e) Notice. Immediately after the transcript is filed, the court reporter or recorder shall notify the Court of Appeals and all parties that it has been filed and file in the Court of Appeals an affidavit of mailing of notice to the parties.

(f) Discipline. A court reporter or recorder failing to comply with the requirements of these rules is subject to disciplinary action by the courts, including punishment for contempt of court, on the court's own initiative or motion of a party.

(g) Responsibility When More Than One Reporter or Recorder. In a case in which portions of the transcript must be prepared by more than one reporter or recorder, unless the court has designated another person, the person who recorded the beginning of the proceeding is responsible for ascertaining that the entire transcript has been prepared, filing it, and giving the notice required by subrule (B)(3)(e).

(C) Exhibits. Within 21 days after the claim of appeal is filed, a party possessing any exhibits offered in evidence, whether admitted or not, shall file them with the trial court or tribunal clerk, unless by stipulation of the parties or order of the trial court or tribunal they are not to be sent, or copies, summaries, or excerpts are to be sent. Xerographic copies of exhibits may be filed in lieu of originals unless the trial court or tribunal orders otherwise. When the record is returned to the trial court or tribunal, the trial court or tribunal clerk shall return the exhibits to the parties who filed them.

(D) Reproduction of Records. Where facilities for the copying or reproduction of records are available to the clerk of the court or tribunal whose action is to be reviewed, the clerk, on a party's request and on deposit of the estimated cost or security for the cost, shall procure for the party as promptly as possible and at the cost to the clerk the requested number of copies of documents, transcripts, and exhibits on file.

(E) Record on Motion. If, before the time the complete record on appeal is sent to the Court of Appeals, a party files a motion that requires the Court of Appeals to have the record, the trial court or tribunal clerk shall, on request of a party or the Court of Appeals, send the Court of Appeals the documents needed.

(F) Service of Record. Within 21 days after the transcript is filed with the trial court clerk, the appellant shall serve a copy of the entire record on appeal, including the transcript and exhibits, on each appellee. However, copies of documents the appellee already possesses need not be served. Proof that the record was served must be promptly filed with the Court of Appeals and the trial court or tribunal clerk. If the filing of a transcript has been excused as provided in subrule (B), the record is to be served within 21 days after the filing of the transcript substitute.

(G) Transmission of Record. Within 21 days after the briefs have been filed or the time for filing the appellee's brief has expired, or when the court requests, the trial court or tribunal clerk shall send to the Court of Appeals the record on appeal in the case pending on appeal, except for those things omitted by written stipulation of the parties. Weapons, drugs, or money are not to be sent unless the Court of Appeals requests. The trial court or tribunal clerk shall append a certificate identifying the name of the case and the papers with reasonable definiteness and shall include as part of the record:

(1) a register of actions in the case;

(2) all opinions, findings, and orders of the court or tribunal; and

(3) the order or judgment appealed from.

Transcripts and all other documents which are part of the record on appeal must be attached in one or more file folders or other suitable hard-surfaced binders showing the name of the trial court or tribunal, the title of the case, and the file number.

(H) Return of Record. After the Court of Appeals disposes of an appeal, the Court of Appeals shall promptly send the original record, together with a certified copy of the opinion, judgment, or order entered by the Court of Appeals

(1) to the Clerk of the Supreme Court if a timely application for leave to appeal is filed in the Supreme Court, or

(2) to the clerk of the court or tribunal from which it was received when

(a) the period for a timely application for leave to appeal to the Supreme Court has expired without the filing of an application, and

(b) there is pending in the Court of Appeals no

(i) timely motion for rehearing,

(ii) timely petition for a special panel under MCR 7.215(I), or

(iii) timely request by a judge of the Court of Appeals for a special panel under MCR 7.215(I),

and the period for such a timely motion, petition, or request has expired.

(I) Notice by Trial Court or Tribunal Clerk. The trial court or tribunal clerk shall promptly notify all parties of the return of the record in order that they may take the appropriate action in the trial court or tribunal under the Court of Appeals mandate.

[Effective March 1, 1985; amended effective October 1, 1989; November 30, 1990; July 1, 1994; April 1, 1996; amended September 27, 1996, effective as to transcripts ordered on or after January 1, 1997, but before November 1, 1997; amended October 21, 1997; amended effective May 6, 1998; November 30, 1999; January 1, 2002.]

* The Michigan Supreme Court Order of October 21, 1997, ordered that the "amendment of MCR 7.210(B)(3)(b)(iv), adopted September 27, 1996, shall remain in effect until further order of the Court."

1985 Staff Comment

MCR 7.210 is based on GCR 1963, 809, 811, 812, and 815.1(2). The provisions are rewritten and are more detailed than the former rules, although the substance is basically the same.

Under subrules (A)(1) and (B)(1)(a), in an appeal from a probate court estate or trust proceeding, only the papers and the portion of the transcript that are relevant to the order appealed from are required.

GCR 1963, 812.3(1) said that a court reporter who fails to file a transcript as required by the rule was subject to punishment for contempt. This provision is modified slightly in subrule (B)(3)(f), which says that the court reporter is subject to discipline for any failure to comply with the duties imposed by the rules.

Subrule (B)(3)(g) is a new provision dealing with the situation in which more than one court reporter or recorder took the testimony in a case. Unless the court designates another person, the reporter or recorder who records the beginning of the proceeding is responsible for ascertaining that the transcript has been prepared, filing it, and giving the required notices. This is consistent with the general rule covering court reporters and recorders, MCR 8.108(B)(2).

Under subrule (H) certain types of exhibits are not to be sent to the Court of Appeals unless that court requests them.

GCR 1963, 812.8 is omitted. Similar provisions are included in MCR 2.610(C)–(E).

Staff Comment to 1989 Amendment

There are three changes [under the October 1, 1989 amendment] in MCR 7.210. MCR 7.210(B)(1)(a) is amended to clarify the relative duties of the appellant and the court reporter with regard to the ordering and filing of transcripts.

In MCR 7.210(B)(3)(b)(iv) the time limit on filing of transcripts in trial cases is reduced from 91 days to 56.

The amendment of MCR 7.210(H) sets 21 days as the time within which the trial court or tribunal clerk is to send the record on appeal to the Court of Appeals after the transcript is filed.

Staff Comment to 1990 Amendment

The [November 30,] 1990 amendment of MCR 7.210(I) permits the Court of Appeals to retain the lower court records until the completion of proceedings under Administrative Order 1990–6.

Staff Comment to 1994 Amendment

The May 2, 1994 amendment of subrule (B)(1)(a), effective July 1, 1994, was based on a proposal from the Michigan Judges Association. The amendment recognizes a change in Rule 6.433 regarding the transcribing of the jury voir dire.

Staff Comment to April, 1996 Amendment

The amendment of MCR 7.210(B)(3)(d) allows transcripts to be prepared with up to four reduced pages of transcript appearing on a single page.

Staff Comment to September, 1996 Amendment

The September 27, 1996, amendment of MCR 7.210(B)(3)(b)(iv) [effective as to transcripts ordered on or after January 1, 1997, but before November 1, 1997] lengthens the time within which the court reporter or recorder must file the transcript in most appeals from 56 to 91 days, which was the time limit before the October 1, 1989, amendment of the rule. The shortened time limits for filing transcripts in appeals from decisions on motions to suppress evidence in criminal cases, appeals of plea-based criminal convictions, other interlocutory criminal appeals, and appeals in custody cases are not affected. The Court will reexamine the need for the increase in time for filing transcripts before November 1, 1997.

Staff Comment to 1997 Amendment

The October 21, 1997, order extends indefinitely the September 27, 1996, amendment of MCR 7.210(B)(3)(b)(iv), which lengthened the time within which the court reporter or recorder must file the transcript in most appeals from 56 to 91 days.

Staff Comment to 1999 Amendment

The amendments of MCR 2.113, 5.113, 5.901, 7.210, 8.105, 8.110, 8.116, 8.203, 8.205, and 8.302 [effective November 30, 1999] and the addition of MCR 2.518 and 8.119 [effective November 30, 1999] are to accommodate statewide records standards applicable to all courts and all clerks of the courts as developed and recommended by the Michigan Trial Court Case File Management Standards Committee.

Staff Comment to 2002 Amendment

The November 26, 2001 amendments of MCR 4.401(D), 7.210(H), 7.212(C), 7.213(A), and 7.302(C), effective January 1, 2002, recognized numbering changes in other rules and the elimination of the "parallel citation" requirement from the Michigan Uniform System of Citation (Supreme Court AO 2001-5).

The staff comment is published only for the benefit of the bench and bar and is not an authoritative construction by the court.

RULE 7.211   MOTIONS IN COURT OF APPEALS

(A) Manner of Making Motion. A motion is made in the Court of Appeals by filing:

(1) 5 copies of a motion (one signed) stating briefly but distinctly the facts and the grounds on which it is based and the relief requested;

(2) the entry fee;

(3) for a motion to dismiss, to affirm, or for peremptory reversal, 5 copies of a supporting brief. A supporting brief may be filed with any other motion. A brief must conform to MCR 7.212(C) as nearly as possible, except that page references to a transcript are not required unless the transcript is relevant to the issue raised in the motion. A brief in conformance with MCR 7.212(C) is not required in support of a motion to affirm when the appellant argues that:

(a) the trial court's findings of fact are clearly erroneous;

(b) the trial court erred in applying established law;

(c) the trial court abused its discretion; or

(d) a sentence which is within the sentencing guidelines is invalid.

Instead of a brief in support of a motion to affirm in such a circumstance, the movant may append those portions of the transcript that are pertinent to the issues raised in the motion; in that case, the motion must include a summary of the movant's position;

(4) a motion for immediate consideration if the party desires a hearing on a date earlier than the applicable date set forth in subrules (B)(2)(a)-(e);

(5) proof that a copy of the motion, the motion for immediate consideration if one has been filed, and any other supporting papers were served on all other parties to the appeal.

(B) Answer.

(1) A party to an appeal may answer a motion by filing:

(a) 5 copies of an answer (one signed); and

(b) proof that a copy of the answer and any other opposing papers were served on all other parties to the appeal.

(2) Unless a motion for immediate consideration has been filed, the answer must be filed within

(a) 21 days after the motion is served on the other parties, for a motion to dismiss, to remand, or to affirm;

(b) 35 days after the motion is served on the appellee, if the motion is for peremptory reversal;

(c) 56 days after the motion is served on the defendant, for a motion to withdraw as the appointed appellate attorney;

(d) 14 days after the motion is served on the other parties, for a motion for rehearing of an opinion or an order;

(e) 7 days after the motion is served on the other parties, for all other motions.

If a motion for immediate consideration has been filed, the answer must be filed before the notice date, if any, or as directed by the Court of Appeals. See subrule (C)(6).

(3) Five copies of an opposing brief may be filed. A brief must conform to MCR 7.212(D) as nearly as possible, except that page references to a transcript are not required unless the transcript is relevant to the issue raised in the motion.

(C) Special Motions. If the record on appeal has not been sent to the Court of Appeals, except as provided in subrule (C)(6), the party making a special motion shall request the clerk of the trial court or tribunal to send the record to the Court of Appeals. A copy of the request must be filed with the motion.

(1) *Motion to Remand.*

(a) Within the time provided for filing the appellant's brief, the appellant may move to remand to the trial court. The motion must identify an issue sought to be reviewed on appeal and show:

(i) that the issue should be initially decided by the trial court; or

(ii) that development of a factual record is required for appellate consideration of the issue. A motion under this subrule must be supported by affidavit or offer of proof regarding the facts to be established at a hearing.

(b) A timely motion must be granted if it is accompanied by a certificate from the trial court that it will grant a motion for new trial.

(c) In a case tried without a jury, the appellant need not file a motion for remand to challenge the great weight of the evidence in order to preserve the issue for appeal.

(d) If a motion to remand is granted, further proceedings in the Court of Appeals are stayed until completion of the proceedings in the trial court

pursuant to the remand, unless the Court of Appeals orders otherwise. Unless the Court of Appeals sets another time, the appellant's brief must be filed within 21 days after the trial court's decision or after the filing of the transcript of any hearing held, whichever is later.

(2) *Motion to Dismiss.* An appellee may file a motion to dismiss an appeal any time before it is placed on a session calendar on the ground that

(a) the appeal is not within the Court of Appeals jurisdiction;

(b) the appeal was not filed or pursued in conformity with the rules; or

(c) the appeal is moot.

(3) *Motion to Affirm.* After the appellant's brief has been filed, an appellee may file a motion to affirm the order or judgment appealed from on the ground that

(a) it is manifest that the questions sought to be reviewed are so unsubstantial as to need no argument or formal submission; or

(b) the questions sought to be reviewed were not timely or properly raised.

The decision to grant a motion to affirm must be unanimous. An order denying a motion to affirm may identify the judge or judges who would have granted it but for the unanimity requirement of this subrule.

(4) *Motion for Peremptory Reversal.* The appellant may file a motion for peremptory reversal on the ground that reversible error is so manifest that an immediate reversal of the judgment or order appealed from should be granted without formal argument or submission. The decision to grant a motion for peremptory reversal must be unanimous. An order denying a motion for peremptory reversal may identify the judge or judges who would have granted it but for the unanimity requirement of this subrule.

(5) *Motion to Withdraw.* A court-appointed appellate attorney for an indigent appellant may file a motion to withdraw if the attorney determines, after a conscientious and thorough review of the trial court record, that the appeal is wholly frivolous.

(a) A motion to withdraw is made by filing:

(i) 5 copies of a motion to withdraw (one signed) which identifies any points the appellant seeks to assert and any other matters that the attorney has considered as a basis for appeal;

(ii) 5 copies of a brief conforming to MCR 7.212(C), which refers to anything in the record that might arguably support the appeal, contains relevant record references, and cites and deals with those authorities which appear to bear on the points in question;

(iii) a notice of hearing under subrule (A)(5)(b);

(iv) proof that copies of the motion, brief in support, notice of hearing, and notice that the motion may result in the conviction or trial court judgment being affirmed were served on the appellant by certified mail; and

(v) proof that a copy of the motion only and not the brief was served the appellee.

(b) The motion to withdraw and supporting papers will be submitted to the court for decision on the first Tuesday 56 days after the appellant is served. The appellant may file with the court an answer and brief in which he or she may make any comments and raise any points that he or she chooses concerning the appeal and the attorney's motion. The appellant must file proof that a copy of the answer was served on his or her attorney.

(c) If the court finds that the appeal is wholly frivolous, it may grant the motion and affirm the conviction or trial court judgment. If the court grants the motion to withdraw, the appellant's attorney shall mail to the appellant a copy of the transcript within 14 days after the order affirming is certified and file proof of that service. If the court finds any legal point arguable on its merits, it will deny the motion and the court-appointed attorney must file an appellant's brief in support of the appeal.

(6) *Motion for Immediate Consideration.* A party may file a motion for immediate consideration to expedite hearing on another motion. The motion must state facts showing why immediate consideration is required. If a copy of the motion for immediate consideration and a copy of the motion of which immediate consideration is sought are personally served under MCR 2.107(C)(1) or (2), the motions may be submitted to the court immediately on filing. If mail service is used, motions may not be submitted until the first Tuesday 7 days after the date of service, unless the party served acknowledges receipt. The trial court or tribunal record need not be requested unless it is required as to the motion of which immediate consideration is sought.

(7) *Confession of Error by Prosecutor.* In a criminal case, if the prosecutor concurs in the relief requested by the defendant, the prosecutor shall file a confession of error so indicating, which may state reasons why concurrence in the relief requested is appropriate. The confession of error shall be submitted to one judge pursuant to MCR 7.211(E). If the judge approves the confession of error, the judge shall enter an order or opinion granting the relief. If the judge rejects the confession of error, the case shall be submitted for decision through the ordinary processes of the court, and the confession of error shall be submitted to the panel assigned to decide the case.

(D) Submission of Motions. Motions in the Court of Appeals are submitted on Tuesday of each week.

There is no oral argument on motions, unless ordered by the court.

(E) Decision on Motions.

(1) Except as provided in subrule (E)(2), orders may be entered only on the concurrence of the majority of the judges to whom the motion has been assigned.

(2) The chief judge or another designated judge may, acting alone, enter an order disposing of an administrative motion. Administrative motions include, but are not limited to:

(a) a motion to consolidate;

(b) a motion to extend the time to file a transcript or brief;

(c) a motion to strike a nonconforming brief;

(d) a motion for oral argument in a case that has not yet been placed on a session calendar;

(e) a motion to adjourn the hearing date of an application, complaint, or motion;

(f) a motion to dismiss a criminal appeal on the grounds that the defendant has absconded;

(g) a motion to file an amicus curiae brief;

(h) a motion to allow an out-of-state attorney to appear and practice.

[Effective March 1, 1985; amended effective October 1, 1989; May 1, 1995; June 2, 1995; August 1, 1995; April 1, 1996; September 1, 1997; September 1, 1998.]

1985 Staff Comment

MCR 7.211 is based on GCR 1963, 817. The provisions of the former rule are rewritten, but their substance is retained. A number of new provisions are added.

The rule requires that 5 copies of the motion and related documents be filed, rather than 4 as under GCR 1963, 817.1.

Subrule (A)(5) modifies the time periods for notice of submission of motions. Compare GCR 1963, 817.2 and 817.5(4).

Subrule (B) is a new provision covering the manner of responding to a motion.

Under subrule (C)(1), if a motion to remand is granted, proceedings in the Court of Appeals are stayed pending the proceedings on remand. In general, under MCR 7.212(A)(5), the filing of a motion does not stay the time for filing briefs.

Subrule (C) also includes several new provisions covering particular motions: motions for peremptory reversal (C)(4); motions to withdraw by appointed attorneys for indigent persons (C)(5); and motions for immediate consideration of other motions (C)(6).

Staff Comment to 1989 Amendment

There are several changes [under the October 1, 1989 amendment] in MCR 7.211. In MCR 7.211(A)(5)(b) the time within which the appellee may respond to a motion for peremptory reversal is lengthened from 21 to 35 days.

There are two changes in MCR 7.211(C)(1), the rule covering motions to remand. First, the language is modified with regard to the showing that must be made by the moving party. An affidavit or offer of proof is required. Second, language is added setting the time within which the appellant's brief is due following proceedings on remand at 42 days, unless the Court of Appeals sets another time.

Staff Comment to May, 1995 Amendment

There are several amendments of MCR 7.211 [effective May 1, 1995]. Under subrule (A), the brief requirement is changed for certain motions to affirm. Subrule (C)(1) is reorganized. New subrule (C)(1)(b) eliminates the need for a motion to remand to preserve a great weight of evidence issue in nonjury cases. Under subrule (C)(1)(c), the time for filing the appellant's brief after completion of the proceedings on remand is shortened from 42 to 21 days.

Staff Comment to June, 1995 Amendment

MCR 7.211(A)(5)(d) and (e) are amended [effective June 2, 1995] in light of the March 3, 1995, amendment of MCR 7.215(H) [effective May 1, 1995; see MCR 7.215(G) effective August 1, 1995], regarding motions for rehearing.

Staff Comment to August, 1995 Amendment

The amendment of MCR 7.211(C)(1) [effective August 1, 1995] revises the rule governing motions to remand, deleting the direction that the Court of Appeals "must" grant such motions under certain circumstances, thus giving the Court greater discretion in ruling on such motions.

Staff Comment to 1996 Amendment

New MCR 7.211(C)(7) provides a procedure for handling confessions of error by prosecutors in criminal cases.

Staff Comment to 1997 Amendment

The amendments of MCR 7.211(C)(3) and (4) [effective September 1, 1997] require orders granting motions to affirm or for peremptory reversal to be unanimous.

Staff Comment to 1998 Amendment

The June 2, 1998, amendments [effective September 1, 1998] of subchapter 7.200 deal with procedure in the Court of Appeals. The following rules are amended:

MCR 7.204(C). Require a jurisdictional checklist to be filed with the claim of appeal.

MCR 7.205(B) and (C), 7.206(D), 7.211(A) and (B). Eliminate the filing of a notice of hearing, instead specifying the time for response.

MCR 7.211(A)(2). Eliminate the requirement of filing affidavits with motions.

MCR 7.211(B)(2)(a) [former (A)(5)(a)]. Add motions to remand to the list of motions for which the notice period for submission is 21 days.

MCR 7.212(B). Require a party to obtain advance permission to file a brief in excess of the page limit set by the rule.

MCR 7.215(G)(1). Require a copy of the order with a motion for rehearing of the order.

Proposed amendments of MCR 7.212(A)(6) and (F), published for comment at 77 Mich B J 117 (January 1998), which would have prohibited parties represented by counsel from filing briefs or supplemental authority communications in propria persona, were not adopted.

RULE 7.212 BRIEFS

(A) Time for Filing and Service.

(1) *Appellant's Brief.*

(a) Filing. The appellant shall file 5 typewritten, xerographic, or printed copies of a brief with the Court of Appeals within

(i) 28 days after the claim of appeal is filed, the order granting leave is certified, or the transcript is filed with the trial court, whichever is later, in a child custody case or an interlocutory criminal appeal. This time may be extended only by the Court of Appeals on motion; or

(ii) the time provided by MCR 7.208(B)(5)(a), 7.208(B)(6), or 7.211(C)(1), in a case in which one of those rules applies;

(iii) 56 days after the claim of appeal is filed, the order granting leave is certified, or the transcript is filed with the trial court or tribunal, whichever is later, in all other cases. In a criminal case in which substitute counsel is appointed for the defendant, the time runs from the date substitute counsel is appointed or the transcript is filed, whichever is later. The parties may extend the time within which the brief must be filed for 28 days by signed stipulation filed with the Court of Appeals. The Court of Appeals may extend the time on motion.

(b) Service. Within the time for filing the appellant's brief, 1 copy must be served on all other parties to the appeal and proof of that service filed with the Court of Appeals and served with the brief.

(2) *Appellee's Brief.*

(a) Filing. The appellee shall file 5 typewritten, xerographic, or printed copies of a brief with the Court of Appeals within

(i) 21 days after the appellant's brief is served on the appellee, in an interlocutory criminal appeal or a child custody case. This time may be extended only by the Court of Appeals on motion;

(ii) 35 days after the appellant's brief is served on the appellee, in all other cases. The parties may extend this time for 28 days by signed stipulation filed with the Court of Appeals. The Court of Appeals may extend the time on motion.

(b) Service. Within the time for filing the appellee's brief, 1 copy must be served on all other parties to the appeal and proof of that service must be filed with the Court of Appeals.

(3) *Earlier Filing and Service.* The time for filing and serving the appellant's or the appellee's brief may be shortened by order of the Court of Appeals on motion showing good cause.

(4) *Late Filing.* Any party failing to timely file and serve a brief required by this rule forfeits the right to oral argument.

(5) *Motions.* The filing of a motion does not stay the time for filing a brief.

(B) Length and Form of Briefs. Except as permitted by order of the Court of Appeals, and except as provided in subrule (G), briefs are limited to 50 pages double-spaced, exclusive of tables, indexes, and appendixes. Quotations and footnotes may be single-spaced. At least one-inch margins must be used, and printing shall not be smaller than 12–point type. A motion for leave to file a brief in excess of the page limitations of this subrule must be filed at least 21 days before the due date of the brief. Such motions are disfavored and will be granted only for extraordinary and compelling reasons.

(C) Appellant's Brief; Contents. The appellant's brief must contain, in the following order:

(1) A title page, stating the full title of the case and in capital letters or boldface type "ORAL ARGUMENT REQUESTED" or "ORAL ARGUMENT NOT REQUESTED". If the appeal involves a ruling that a provision of the Michigan Constitution, a Michigan statute, a rule or regulation included in the Michigan Administrative Code, or any other action of the legislative or executive branch of state government is invalid, the title page must include the following in capital letters or boldface type:

"THE APPEAL INVOLVES A RULING THAT A PROVISION OF THE CONSTITUTION, A STATUTE, RULE OR REGULATION, OR OTHER STATE GOVERNMENTAL ACTION IS INVALID";

(2) A table of contents, listing the subject headings of the brief, including the principal points of argument, in the order of presentation, with the numbers of the pages where they appear in the brief;

(3) An index of authorities, listing in alphabetical order all case authorities cited, with the complete citations including the years of decision, and all other authorities cited, with the numbers of the pages where they appear in the brief;

(4) A statement of the basis of jurisdiction of the Court of Appeals.

(a) The statement concerning appellate jurisdiction must identify the statute, court rule, or court decision believed to confer jurisdiction on the Court of Appeals and the following information:

(i) the date of entry of the judgment or order sought to be reviewed;

(ii) the filing date of any motion claimed to toll the time within which to appeal, the disposition of such a motion, and the date of entry of the order disposing of it;

(iii) in cases where appellate counsel is appointed, the date the request for appointment of appellate counsel was filed;

(iv) in cases where appellate counsel is retained or the party is proceeding in pro per, the filing date of the claim of appeal or the date of the order granting leave to appeal or leave to proceed under MCR 7.206.

(b) If the order sought to be reviewed adjudicates fewer than all the claims, or the rights and liabilities of fewer than all the parties, the statement must provide enough information to enable the court to determine whether there is jurisdiction.

(5) A statement of questions involved, stating concisely and without repetition the questions involved in the appeal. Each question must be expressed and numbered separately and be followed by the trial court's answer to it or the statement that the trial court failed to answer it and the appellant's answer to it. When possible, each answer must be given as "Yes" or "No";

(6) A statement of facts that must be a clear, concise, and chronological narrative. All material facts, both favorable and unfavorable, must be fairly stated without argument or bias. The statement must contain, with specific page references to the transcript, the pleadings, or other document or paper filed with the trial court,

(a) the nature of the action;

(b) the character of pleadings and proceedings;

(c) the substance of proof in sufficient detail to make it intelligible, indicating the facts that are in controversy and those that are not;

(d) the dates of important instruments and events;

(e) the rulings and orders of the trial court;

(f) the verdict and judgment; and

(g) any other matters necessary to an understanding of the controversy and the questions involved;

(7) The arguments, each portion of which must be prefaced by the principal point stated in capital letters or boldface type. As to each issue, the argument must include a statement of the applicable standard or standards of review and supporting authorities. Facts stated must be supported by specific page references to the transcript, the pleadings, or other document or paper filed with the trial court. Page references to the transcript, the pleadings, or other document or paper filed with the trial court must also be given to show whether the issue was preserved for appeal by appropriate objection or by other means. If determination of the issues presented requires the study of a constitution, statute, ordinance, administrative rule, court rule, rule of evidence, judgment, order, written instrument, or document, or relevant part thereof, this material must be reproduced in the brief or in an addendum to the brief. If an argument is presented concerning the sentence imposed in a criminal case, the appellant's attorney must send a copy of the

presentence report to the court at the time the brief is filed;

(8) The relief, stating in a distinct, concluding section the order or judgment requested; and

(9) A signature.

(D) Appellee's Brief; Contents.

(1) Except as otherwise provided in this subrule, the appellee's brief must conform to subrule (C).

(2) The appellee must state whether the jurisdictional summary and the standard or standards of review stated in the appellant's brief are complete and correct. If they are not, the appellee must provide a complete jurisdictional summary and a counter-statement of the standard or standards of review, and supporting authorities.

(3) Unless under the headings "Statement of Questions Involved" and "Statement of Facts" the appellee accepts the appellant's statements, the appellee shall include

(a) a counter-statement of questions involved, stating the appellee's version of the questions involved; and

(b) a counter-statement of facts, pointing out the inaccuracies and deficiencies in the appellant's statement of facts without repeating that statement and with specific page references to the transcript, the pleadings, or other document or paper filed with the trial court, to support the appellee's assertions.

(E) Briefs in Cross Appeals. The filing and service of briefs by a cross appellant and a cross appellee are governed by subrules (A)–(D).

(F) Supplemental Authority. Without leave of court, a party may file an original and four copies of a one-page communication, titled "supplemental authority," to call the court's attention to new authority released after the party filed its brief. Such a communication,

(1) may not raise new issues;

(2) may only discuss how the new authority applies to the case, and may not repeat arguments or authorities contained in the party's brief;

(3) may not cite unpublished opinions.

(G) Reply Briefs. An appellant or a cross-appellant may reply to the brief of an appellee or cross-appellee within 21 days after service of the brief of the appellee or cross-appellee. Reply briefs must be confined to rebuttal of the arguments in the appellee's or cross-appellee's brief and must be limited to 10 pages, exclusive of tables, indexes, and appendices, and must include a table of contents and an index of authorities. No additional or supplemental briefs may be filed except as provided by subrule (F) or by leave of the Court.

(H) Amicus Curiae.

(1) An amicus curiae brief may be filed only on motion granted by the Court of Appeals. The motion must be filed within 21 days after the appellee's brief is filed. If the motion is granted, the order will state the date by which the brief must be filed.

(2) The brief is limited to the issues raised by the parties. An amicus curiae may not participate in oral argument except by court order.

(I) Nonconforming Briefs. If, on its own initiative or on a party's motion, the court concludes that a brief does not substantially comply with the requirements in this rule, it may order the party who filed the brief to file a supplemental brief within a specified time correcting the deficiencies, or it may strike the nonconforming brief.

[Effective March 1, 1985; amended effective December 1, 1987; October 1, 1989; August 1, 1991; January 1, 1994; May 1, 1995; July 1, 1995; April 1, 1996; September 1, 1997; September 1, 1998; September 1, 1999; January 1, 2002; September 1, 2002.]

1985 Staff Comment

MCR 7.212 is based on GCR 1963, 813, 814, and 815. The provisions are reorganized and rewritten, but retain most of the substance of the former rules.

Subrules (A)(1) and (2) set shorter time limits for filing briefs in child custody cases and interlocutory criminal appeals than for briefs in other appeals.

Subrule (A)(5) is a new provision explicitly stating that the filing of a motion does not stay the time for filing a brief.

Subrule (B) sets a 50–page limit on the length of briefs.

Subrule (C)(3) requires parallel citations of Michigan statutes. Compare GCR 1963, 813.1.

Subrules (F) and (G) are new provisions covering supplemental and amicus curiae briefs.

Subrule (H) is a new provision regarding the striking of nonconforming briefs.

Staff Comment to 1987 Amendment

The [December 1, 1987] amendment of MCR 7.212(C)(6) has the same purpose as Rules 21.1(f) and 34.1(f) of the Rules of the United States Supreme Court, and Rule 28(f) of the Federal Rules of Appellate Procedure.

Staff Comment to 1989 Amendment

There are a number of relatively minor changes in MCR 7.212 [under the October 1, 1989 amendment]. There are two changes in MCR 7.212(A)(1)(a) with regard to the time for filing the appellant's brief. First, new subrule (a)(ii) refers to MCR 7.208(B) and 7.211(C)(1), which include time limits for filing an appellant's brief in certain circumstances. Second, new language is added in subrule (a)(iii) to make clear that where substitute counsel is appointed in a criminal case, the time for filing the brief runs from the date substitute counsel is appointed, or from the time the transcript is filed if the substitution of counsel was made before the transcript was completed.

There are two minor changes in the language of MCR 7.212(B) regarding lengths of briefs. Appendices are added to the list of items that are excluded in determining the length. Second, single spacing of footnotes is expressly permitted.

MCR 7.212(H) is amended to provide that in the case of a nonconforming brief, the Court of Appeals is given the option of ordering the party to file a supplemental brief curing the deficiencies as an alternative to striking the brief.

Staff Comment to 1991 Amendment

In order to assist the Court of Appeals and the Supreme Court in deciding appeals in which sentencing issues are raised, the 1991 amendment of MCR 7.212(C)(6) requires a party who raises a sentencing issue to submit a copy of the presentence report. Because the copy is sent to the court for its review (not "filed" with the court), it is not included in the appellate court's public file.

Staff Comment to 1994 Amendment

The 1993 addition of MCR 7.212(G) and the accompanying change in MCR 7.212(B) [both effective January 1, 1994] were to provide direction regarding the filing of reply briefs in the Court of Appeals. Former subrules (G) and (H) were redesignated (H) and (I) when the 1993 amendment became effective [on January 1, 1994].

Staff Comment to May, 1995 Amendment

The amendment of MCR 7.212(C) [effective May 1, 1995] requires the appellant's brief to include a jurisdictional statement and to state the standard of review applicable to each issue raised. Subrule (D) requires the appellee to respond as to those matters.

Staff Comment to July, 1995 Comment

The amendment of MCR 7.212(B) [effective July 1, 1995] adds requirements regarding margins and type size for briefs in the Court of Appeals.

Staff Comment to 1996 Amendment

The amendment of MCR 7.212(C)(7) requires page references to the record showing preservation of issues.

The amendment of MCR 7.212(F) revises the rule regarding supplemental briefs. Without leave of the Court, a party may file a one-page document citing the new authority and indicating how it applies to the case. Other supplemental briefs may only be filed with leave of the Court on motion.

Staff Comment to 1997 Amendment

The amendment of MCR 7.212(C)(4) [effective September 1, 1997] requires that the jurisdictional statement in a brief filed in the Court of Appeals include information about the date of the request for appointment of counsel, if applicable.

Under the amendment of MCR 7.212(H) [effective September 1, 1997], a motion for leave to file an amicus curiae brief may be filed up to 21 days after the appellee's brief. Amicus briefs are expressly limited to the issues raised by the parties.

Staff Comment to 1998 Amendment

The June 2, 1998, amendments [effective September 1, 1998] of subchapter 7.200 deal with procedure in the Court of Appeals. The following rules are amended:

MCR 7.204(C). Require a jurisdictional checklist to be filed with the claim of appeal.

MCR 7.205(B) and (C), 7.206(D), 7.211(A) and (B). Eliminate the filing of a notice of hearing, instead specifying the time for response.

MCR 7.211(A)(2). Eliminate the requirement of filing affidavits with motions.

MCR 7.211(B)(2)(a) [former (A)(5)(a)]. Add motions to remand to the list of motions for which the notice period for submission is 21 days.

MCR 7.212(B). Require a party to obtain advance permission to file a brief in excess of the page limit set by the rule.

MCR 7.215(G)(1). Require a copy of the order with a motion for rehearing of the order.

Proposed amendments of MCR 7.212(A)(6) and (F), published for comment at 77 Mich B J 117 (January 1998), which would have prohibited parties represented by counsel from filing briefs or supplemental authority communications in propria persona, were not adopted.

Staff Comment to 1999 Amendment

This group of amendments [effective September 1, 1999] deal with various matters regarding appellate procedure. The following rules are affected:

MCR 7.201(B), 7.217(A) and (C)—Permit the Chief Judge, or another designated judge, acting alone, to enter certain orders when a party does not proceed in accordance with the rules.

MCR 7.202(6)—Delete the definition of "signed" from the rule.

New MCR 7.203(F)—Permit the chief judge, or another designated judge, acting alone, to dismiss an appeal or original proceeding for lack of jurisdiction, and create a procedure for the appellant or plaintiff to seek reconsideration of that decision.

MCR 7.212(C) and (D)—Clarify the requirement of specific page references to the record in appellate briefs.

MCR 7.215(H)—Modify several provisions in the rule governing resolution of conflicts in Court of Appeals decisions.

Staff Comment to 2002 Amendment

The November 26, 2001 amendments of MCR 4.401(D), 7.210(H), 7.212(C), 7.213(A), and 7.302(C), effective January 1, 2002, recognized numbering changes in other rules and the elimination of the "parallel citation" requirement from the Michigan Uniform System of Citation (Supreme Court AO 2001-5).

The staff comment is published only for the benefit of the bench and bar and is not an authoritative construction by the court.

Staff Comment to September 2002 Amendment

The May 17, 2002, amendments of MCR 7.204, 7.212, 7.213, 7.215, and 7.302, which are effective September 1, 2002, relate to appeals in which a Michigan constitutional provision, statute, regulation, or other governmental action has been held to be invalid.

The amendment of MCR 7.212(C)(1) requires identification of such cases on the title page of the brief on appeal.

The staff comment is published only for the benefit of the bench and bar and is not an authoritative construction by the Court.

RULE 7.213   CALENDAR CASES

(A) Pre–Argument Conference in Calendar Cases.

(1) At any time before submission of a case, the Court of Appeals may direct the attorneys for the

parties and client representatives with settlement authority to appear in person or by telephone for a pre-argument conference. The conference will be conducted by the court, or by a judge, retired judge or attorney designated by the court, known as a mediator. The conference shall consider the possibility of settlement, the simplification of the issues, and any other matters which the mediator determines may aid in the handling of or the disposition of the appeal. The mediator shall make an order that recites the action taken at the conference and the agreements made by the parties as to any of the matters considered, and that limits the issues to those not disposed of by the admissions or agreements of counsel. Such order, when entered, controls the subsequent proceedings, unless modified to prevent manifest injustice.

(2) All civil cases will be examined to determine if a pre-argument conference would be of assistance to the court or the parties. An attorney or a party may request a pre-argument conference in any case. Such a request shall be confidential. The pre-argument conference shall be conducted by

(a) the court, or by a judge, retired judge or attorney designated by the court;

(b) if the parties unanimously agree, a special mediator designated by the court or selected by unanimous agreement of the parties. The special mediator shall be an attorney, licensed in Michigan, who possesses either mediation-type experience or expertise in the subject matter of the case. The special mediator may charge a reasonable fee, which shall be divided and borne equally by the parties unless agreed otherwise and paid by the parties directly to the mediator. If a party does not agree upon the fee requested by the mediator, upon motion of the party, the Court of Appeals shall set a reasonable fee.

When a case has been selected for participation in a pre-argument conference, participation in the conference is mandatory; however, the Court of Appeals may except the case from participation on motion for good cause shown if it finds that a pre-argument conference in that case would be inappropriate.

(3) Any judge who participates in a pre-argument conference or becomes involved in settlement discussions under this rule may not thereafter consider any aspect of the merits of the case, except that participation in a pre-argument conference shall not preclude the judge from considering the case pursuant to MCR 7.215(I).

(4) Statements and comments made during the pre-argument conference are confidential, except to the extent disclosed by the pre-argument conference order, and shall not be disclosed by the mediator or by the participants in briefs or in argument.

(5) To facilitate the pre-argument conference, unless one has already been filed, an appellant must file the docketing statement required by MCR 7.204(H).

(6) Upon failure by a party or attorney to comply with a provision of this rule or the pre-argument conference order, the Court of Appeals may assess reasonable expenses caused by the failure, including attorney's fees, may assess all or a portion of appellate costs, or may dismiss the appeal.

(B) Notice of Calendar Cases. After the briefs of both parties have been filed, or after the expiration of the time for filing the appellee's brief, the clerk shall notify the parties that the case will be submitted as a "calendar case" at the next available session of the court.

(C) Priority on Calendar. The priority of cases on the session calendar is in accordance with the initial filing dates of the cases, except that precedence shall be given to:

(1) interlocutory criminal appeals;

(2) child custody cases;

(3) interlocutory appeals from the grant of a preliminary injunction;

(4) appeals of decisions holding that a provision of the Michigan Constitution, a Michigan statute, a rule or regulation included in the Michigan Administrative Code, or any other action of the legislative or executive branch of state government is invalid; and

(5) cases that the court orders expedited.

(D) Arrangement of Calendar. Twenty-one days before the first day of the session, the clerk shall mail to all parties in each calendar case notice of the designated panel, location, day, and order in which the cases will be called.

(E) Adjournment. A change may not be made in the session calendar, except by order of the court on its own initiative or in response to timely motions filed by the parties. A calendar case will not be withdrawn after being placed on the session calendar, except on a showing of extreme emergency.

[Effective March 1, 1985; amended effective May 1, 1995; January 1, 1998; January 1, 2002; September 1, 2002.]

1985 Staff Comment

MCR 7.213 is taken from GCR 1963, 816. Two parts of the former rule are moved to other rules: Most of 816.2 is placed in MCR 7.206, and 816.5 is 7.216(C).

Subrule (B) has additional language expressly requiring that interlocutory criminal appeals and child custody cases be given priority in scheduling.

Staff Comment to 1995 Amendment

New MCR 7.213(A) allows the Court of Appeals to order pre-argument conferences in appropriate cases.

Staff Comment to 1997 Amendment

The January 1, 1998 amendment of MCR 7.213 modifies the procedure for pre-argument conferences in the Court of Appeals. Ordinarily, the conference will be conducted by a judge or attorney selected by the Court of Appeals. However, the parties may agree to an alternative procedure using a special moderator.

Staff Comments to January 2002 Amendments

The amendments of MCR 7.213(A) and (C), effective January 1, 2002, were requested by the Court of Appeals. The term "mediator" was substituted for the term "moderator" in subrule (A), to be consistent with other recent rule changes governing case facilitation and mediation. In addition, subrule (A) was amended to allow the court to require the attendance of client representatives with settlement authority at pre-argument settlement conferences. (File No. 01–13.) The amendment of subrule (C) required that cases be placed on the session calendar in the order in which they are filed. (File No. 01–08.)

The staff comment is published only for the benefit of the bench and bar and is not an authoritative construction by the Court.

The November 26, 2001 amendments of MCR 4.401(D), 7.210(H), 7.212(C), 7.213(A), and 7.302(C), effective January 1, 2002, recognized numbering changes in other rules and the elimination of the "parallel citation" requirement from the Michigan Uniform System of Citation (Supreme Court AO 2001-5).

The staff comment is published only for the benefit of the bench and bar and is not an authoritative construction by the court.

Staff Comments to September 2002 Amendments

The March 12, 2002 amendments of Rules 3.310, 7.208, and 7.213, effective September 1, 2002, require trial courts to expeditiously decide actions in which preliminary injunctions have been granted, and allow them to proceed even if the Court of Appeals has granted interlocutory leave to appeal. Similarly, if the Court of Appeals grants leave to review entry of a preliminary injunction on an interlocutory basis, that Court is required to give priority to resolution of the appeal. See *Michigan Coalition of State Employee Unions* v *Michigan Civil Service Comm*, 465 Mich 212, 214, n 1 (2001).

The staff comment is published only for the benefit of the bench and bar and is not an authoritative construction by the Court.

The May 17, 2002, amendments of MCR 7.204, 7.212, 7.213, 7.215, and 7.302, which are effective September 1, 2002, relate to appeals in which a Michigan constitutional provision, statute, regulation, or other governmental action has been held to be invalid.

Language is added to MCR 7.213(C) directing that such cases be given precedence in placement on the Court of Appeals session calendar. The subrule as amended includes language previously added by an amendment dated March 12, 2002, also to be effective September 1, 2002, regarding orders granting preliminary injunctions.

The staff comment is published only for the benefit of the bench and bar and is not an authoritative construction by the Court.

RULE 7.214 ARGUMENT OF CALENDAR CASES

(A) Request for Argument. Oral argument of a calendar case is not permitted, except on order of the court, unless a party has stated on the title page of his or her brief in capital letters or boldface type "ORAL ARGUMENT REQUESTED". The failure of a party to properly request oral argument or to timely file and serve a brief waives the right to oral argument. If neither party is entitled to oral argument, the clerk will list the case as submitted on briefs.

(B) Length of Argument. In a calendar case the time allowed for argument is 30 minutes for each side. When only one side is represented, only 15 minutes is allowed to that side. The time for argument may be extended by the court on motion filed at least 21 days before the session begins, or by the presiding judge during argument.

(C) Call for Argument. The court, on each day of the session, will call the cases for argument in the order they appear on the session calendar as arranged.

(D) Submission on Briefs. A case may be submitted on briefs by stipulation at any time.

(E) Decision Without Oral Argument. * Cases may be assigned to panels of judges for appropriate review and disposition without oral argument as provided in this subrule.

(1) If, as a result of review under this rule, the panel unanimously concludes that

  (a) the dispositive issue or issues have been recently authoritatively decided;

  (b) the briefs and record adequately present the facts and legal arguments, and the court's deliberation would not be significantly aided by oral argument; or

  (c) the appeal is without merit;

the panel may enter without oral argument an appropriate order or opinion dismissing the appeal, affirming, reversing, or vacating the judgment or order appealed from, or remanding the case for additional proceedings.

(2) Any party's brief may include, at the conclusion of the brief, a statement setting forth the reasons why oral argument should be heard.

[Effective March 1, 1985; amended August 1, 1991.]

* The Michigan Supreme Court Order of July 11, 1991 which adopted MCR 7.214(E) provided that subrule (E) was "to be effective August 1, 1991 and until September 30, 1992." The Supreme Court further ordered on September 29, 1992 that "the effective date of this Court's July 11, 1991 amendment to MCR 7.214 is extended until September 30, 1993." On September 15, 1993, the Court ordered that the effective date be "extended until December 31, 1993." On December 21, 1993, the Court ordered that the effective date "is extended until further order of this Court."

1985 Staff Comment

MCR 7.214 is based on GCR 1963, 819 and 815.3. It retains the substance of the former rules, except that the rehearing provisions of GCR 1963, 819.3 are moved to MCR 7.215(H).

RULE 7.215 OPINIONS, ORDERS, JUDGMENTS, AND FINAL PROCESS FROM COURT OF APPEALS

(A) Opinions of Court. An opinion must be written and bear the writer's name or the label "per curiam" or "memorandum" opinion. An opinion of the court that bears the writer's name shall be published by the Supreme Court reporter of decisions. A memorandum opinion shall not be published. A per curiam opinion shall not be published unless one of the judges deciding the case directs the reporter to do so at the time it is filed with the clerk. A copy of an opinion to be published must be delivered to the reporter no later than when it is filed with the clerk. The reporter is responsible for having those opinions published as are opinions of the Supreme Court, but in separate volumes containing opinions of the Court of Appeals only, in a form and under a contract approved by the Supreme Court.

(B) Standards for Publication. A court opinion must be published if it:

(1) establishes a new rule of law;

(2) construes a provision of a constitution, statute, ordinance, or court rule;

(3) alters or modifies an existing rule of law or extends it to a new factual context;

(4) reaffirms a principle of law not applied in a recently reported decision;

(5) involves a legal issue of continuing public interest;

(6) criticizes existing law;

(7) creates or resolves an apparent conflict of authority, whether or not the earlier opinion was reported; or

(8) decides an appeal from a lower court order ruling that a provision of the Michigan Constitution, a Michigan statute, a rule or regulation included in the Michigan Administrative Code, or any other action of the legislative or executive branch of state government is invalid.

(C) Precedent of Opinions.

(1) An unpublished opinion is not precedentially binding under the rule of stare decisis. A party who cites an unpublished opinion must provide a copy of the opinion to the court and to opposing parties with the brief or other paper in which the citation appears.

(2) A published opinion of the Court of Appeals has precedential effect under the rule of stare decisis.

The filing of an application for leave to appeal to the Supreme Court or a Supreme Court order granting leave to appeal does not diminish the precedential effect of a published opinion of the Court of Appeals.

(D) Requesting Publication.

(1) Any party may request publication of an authored or per curiam opinion not designated for publication by

(a) filing with the clerk 4 copies of a letter stating why the opinion should be published, and

(b) mailing a copy to each party to the appeal not joining in the request, and to the clerk of the Supreme Court.

Such a request must be filed within 21 days after release of the unpublished opinion or, if a timely motion for rehearing is filed, within 21 days after the denial of the motion.

(2) Any party served with a copy of the request may file a response within 14 days in the same manner as provided in subrule (D)(1).

(3) Promptly after the expiration of the time provided in subrule (D)(2), the clerk shall submit the request, and any response that has been received, to the panel that filed the opinion. Within 21 days after submission of the request, the panel shall decide whether to direct that the opinion be published. The opinion shall be published only if the panel unanimously so directs. Failure of the panel to act within 21 days shall be treated as a denial of the request.

(4) The Court of Appeals shall not direct publication if the Supreme Court has denied an application for leave to appeal under MCR 7.302.

(E) Judgment.

(1) When the Court of Appeals disposes of an original action or an appeal, whether taken as of right, by leave granted, or by order in lieu of leave being granted, its opinion or order is its judgment. An order denying leave to appeal is not deemed to dispose of an appeal.

(2) The clerk shall send a certified copy of the opinion or order, with the date of filing stamped on it, to each party and, in an appeal, to the court or tribunal from which the appeal was received. In criminal cases, the clerk shall provide an additional copy of any opinion or order disposing of an appeal or of any order denying leave to appeal to the defendant's lawyer, which the lawyer must promptly send to the defendant. An opinion or order is notice of the entry of judgment of the Court of Appeals.

(F) Execution and Enforcement.

(1) *Routine Issuance.* Unless otherwise ordered by the Court of Appeals or the Supreme Court or as otherwise provided by these rules,

(a) the Court of Appeals judgment is effective after the expiration of the time for filing a timely application for leave to appeal to the Supreme Court, or, if such an application is filed, after the disposition of the case by the Supreme Court;

(b) execution on the Court of Appeals judgment is to be obtained or enforcement proceedings had in the trial court or tribunal after the record has been returned (by the clerk under MCR 7.210[I] or by the Supreme Court clerk under MCR 7.311[B]) with a certified copy of the court's judgment or, if a record was not transmitted to the Court of Appeals, after the time specified for return of the record had it been transmitted.

(2) *Exceptional Issuance.* The court may order that a judgment described in subrule (E) has immediate effect. The order does not prevent the filing of a motion for rehearing, but the filing of the motion does not stay execution or enforcement.

(G) Entry, Issuance, Execution on, and Enforcement of All Other Orders. An order other than one described in subrule (E) is entered on the date of filing. The clerk must promptly send a certified copy to each party and to the trial court or tribunal. Unless otherwise stated, an order is effective on the date it is entered.

(H) Rehearings.

(1) A motion for rehearing may be filed within 21 days after the date of the order or the date stamped on an opinion. The motion shall include all facts, arguments, and citations to authorities in a single document and shall not exceed 10 double-spaced pages. A copy of the order or opinion of which rehearing is sought must be included with the motion. Motions for rehearing are subject to the restrictions contained in MCR 2.119(F)(3).

(2) A party may answer a motion for rehearing within 14 days after the motion is served on the party. An answer to a motion for rehearing shall be a single document and shall not exceed 7 double-spaced pages.

(3) The clerk will not accept for filing a motion for rehearing of an order denying a motion for rehearing.

(I) Resolution of Conflicts in Court of Appeals Decisions.

(1) *Precedential Effect of Published Decisions.* A panel of the Court of Appeals must follow the rule of law established by a prior published decision of the Court of Appeals issued on or after November 1, 1990, that has not been reversed or modified by the Supreme Court, or by a special panel of the Court of Appeals as provided in this rule.

(2) *Conflicting Opinion.* A panel that follows a prior published decision only because it is required to do so by subrule (1) must so indicate in the text of its opinion, citing this rule and explaining its disagreement with the prior decision. The panel's opinion must be published in the official reports of opinions of the Court of Appeals.

(3) *Convening of Special Panel.*

(a) Poll of Judges. Except as provided in subrule (3)(b), within 28 days after release of the opinion indicating disagreement with a prior decision as provided in subrule (2), the chief judge must poll the judges of the Court of Appeals to determine whether the particular question is both outcome determinative and warrants convening a special panel to rehear the case for the purpose of resolving the conflict that would have been created but for the provisions of subrule (1). Special panels may be convened to consider outcome-determinative questions only.

(b) Effect of Pending Supreme Court Appeal. No poll shall be conducted and a special panel shall not be convened if, at the time the judges are required to be polled, the Supreme Court has granted leave to appeal in the controlling case.

(c) Order. Immediately following the poll, an order reflecting the result must be entered. The chief clerk of the Court of Appeals must provide a copy of the order to the Clerk of the Supreme Court. The order must be published in the official reports of opinions of the Court of Appeals.

(4) *Composition of Panel.* A special panel convened pursuant to this rule consists of 7 judges of the Court of Appeals selected by lot, except that judges who participated in either the controlling decision or the opinion in the case at bar may not be selected.

(5) *Consideration of Case by Panel.* An order directing the convening of a special panel must vacate only that portion of the prior opinion in the case at bar addressing the particular question that would have been decided differently but for the provisions of subrule (1). The special panel shall limit its review to resolving the conflict that would have been created but for the provisions of subrule (1) and applying its decision to the case at bar. The parties are permitted to file supplemental briefs, and are entitled to oral argument before the special panel unless the panel unanimously agrees to dispense with oral argument. The special panel shall return to the original panel for further consideration any remaining, unresolved issues, as the case may require.

(6) *Decision.* The decision of the special panel must be by published opinion or order and is binding on all panels of the Court of Appeals unless reversed or modified by the Supreme Court.

(7) *Rehearing; Appeal.* There is no appeal from the decision of the Court of Appeals as to whether to convene a special panel. As to the decision in the case at bar, the time limits for moving for rehearing or for filing an application for leave to appeal to the Supreme Court run from the date of the order declining to convene a special panel or, if a special panel is convened, from the date of the decision of the special panel, except that, if the case is returned to the original panel for further consideration in accordance

with subrule (5), the time limits shall run from the date of the original panel's decision, after return from the special panel. If a motion for rehearing is filed, it shall be submitted to the special panel, which, if appropriate, may refer some or all of the issues presented to the original panel.

[Effective March 1, 1985; amended effective April 1, 1987; October 7, 1987; October 1, 1989; November 1, 1991; May 1, 1995; August 1, 1995; September 1, 1997; September 1, 1998; September 1, 1999; April 1, 2001; Sept. 1, 2002.]

1985 Staff Comment

MCR 7.215 is based on GCR 1963, 819.4 and 821.

Subrules (B), (C), and (D) are new, covering the standards for publication of opinions, the precedential force of unpublished opinions, and the procedure by which a party can request publication.

Subrule (E) makes the Court of Appeals opinion the judgment of the court, unlike GCR 1963, 821.2.

Subrule (F) explicitly covers the matter of the enforcement of the decisions of the Court of Appeals, a matter that was left to inference under GCR 1963, 821.3. Enforcement is to be had in the trial court after the record has been returned from the Court of Appeals. See MCR 7.210(I).

Subrule (G) is a new provision covering the issuance and effective date of orders.

The rehearing provisions of subrule (H) are taken from GCR 1963, 819.4. Request for rehearing is by motion, to which MCR 7.211 would apply. The new rule explicitly provides for motions for rehearing as to orders as well as of decisions by opinion.

Staff Comment to 1987 Amendment

The [October 7, 1987] addition of MCR 7.215(C)(2) is a change from the prior rule as stated in *People* v *Phillips*, 416 Mich 63, 74–75; 330 NW2d 366 (1982).

Staff Comment to 1989 Amendment

The [October 1, 1989] amendment of MCR 7.215(C)(1) requires a party who cites an unpublished Court of Appeals decision to serve copies of the decision on the court and the opposing parties.

Changes are also made in subrules (E)–(G) with the object of treating orders which dispose of an appeal as the equivalent of an opinion for the purpose of determining when they can be enforced. Such an opinion or order is to be enforced in the trial court after the return of the record by the appellate courts (or, if a record was not transmitted, when it would have been returned had it been transmitted). Other orders are effective immediately, unless the Court of Appeals orders otherwise. An order denying leave to appeal is not considered to dispose of an appeal.

There are also several other minor changes. The Court of Appeals clerk is to send a criminal defense lawyer an extra copy of the opinion or order, including an order denying leave to appeal, which the attorney is to send to the defendant. Under former Administrative Order No. 1983–7, copies were required only of orders and opinions that disposed of an appeal.

Staff Comment to 1991 Amendment

The August 28, 1991 amendment of MCR 7.215(F) [effective November 1, 1991] clarifies the matter of the effective date of Court of Appeals judgments.

Staff Comment to May 1995 Amendment

The amendment of MCR 7.215(H) clarifies the procedure regarding motions for rehearing.

Staff Comment to August 1995 Amendment

The amendment of MCR 7.215 eliminates the procedure under which persons may request publication of Court of Appeals decisions that were originally designated as not for publication. Also, subrule (A) is modified to require that a decision to publish a per curiam or memorandum opinion must be made by a majority of the panel rather than by a single judge.

Staff Comment to 1997 Amendment

The provisions of Administrative Order 1994–4, dealing with Court of Appeals conflict resolution panels, are incorporated into the court rules as new MCR 7.215(H). Also, such panels are authorized to dispense with oral argument (by unanimous vote), and their decisions must be published in Michigan Appeals Reports.

Staff Comment 1998 Amendment

The June 2, 1998, amendments [effective September 1, 1998] of subchapter 7.200 deal with procedure in the Court of Appeals. The following rules are amended:

MCR 7.204(C). Require a jurisdictional checklist to be filed with the claim of appeal.

MCR 7.205(B) and (C), 7.206(D), 7.211(A) and (B). Eliminate the filing of a notice of hearing, instead specifying the time for response.

MCR 7.211(A)(2). Eliminate the requirement of filing affidavits with motions.

MCR 7.211(B)(2)(a) [former (A)(5)(a)]. Add motions to remand to the list of motions for which the notice period for submission is 21 days.

MCR 7.212(B). Require a party to obtain advance permission to file a brief in excess of the page limit set by the rule.

MCR 7.215(G)(1). Require a copy of the order with a motion for rehearing of the order.

Proposed amendments of MCR 7.212(A)(6) and (F), published for comment at 77 Mich B J 117 (January 1998), which would have prohibited parties represented by counsel from filing briefs or supplemental authority communications in propria persona, were not adopted.

Staff Comment to 1999 Amendment

This group of amendments [effective September 1, 1999] deal with various matters regarding appellate procedure. The following rules are affected:

MCR 7.201(B), 7.217(A) and (C)—Permit the Chief Judge, or another designated judge, acting alone, to enter certain orders when a party does not proceed in accordance with the rules.

MCR 7.202(6)—Delete the definition of "signed" from the rule.

New MCR 7.203(F)—Permit the chief judge, or another designated judge, acting alone, to dismiss an appeal or original proceeding for lack of jurisdiction, and create a procedure for the appellant or plaintiff to seek reconsideration of that decision.

MCR 7.212(C) and (D)—Clarify the requirement of specific page references to the record in appellate briefs.

MCR 7.215(H)—Modify several provisions in the rule governing resolution of conflicts in Court of Appeals decisions.

Staff Comment to 2000 Amendment

The December 13, 2000, amendments of MCR 7.202 and 7.215, effective April 1, 2001, make several changes regarding procedure in the Court of Appeals.

The amendment of MCR 7.202(7)(b)(iv) makes certain orders entered by the trial court on remand from an appellate court appealable by right.

The amendment to MCR 7.215(A) permits a single judge of the Court of Appeals panel to designate an opinion for publication.

New MCR 7.215(D) re-establishes a procedure under which a party may request publication of a Court of Appeals opinion that was not initially designated for publication. The former provision was deleted in 1995.

Staff Comment to 2002 Amendment

The May 17, 2002, amendments of MCR 7.204, 7.212, 7.213, 7.215, and 7.302, which are effective September 1, 2002, relate to appeals in which a Michigan constitutional provision, statute, regulation, or other governmental action has been held to be invalid.

New MCR 7.215(B)(8) would add decisions in such cases to the list of those in which the Court of Appeals is required to publish its decisions.

The staff comment is published only for the benefit of the bench and bar and is not an authoritative construction by the Court.

RULE 7.216   MISCELLANEOUS RELIEF

(A) Relief Obtainable. The Court of Appeals may, at any time, in addition to its general powers, in its discretion, and on the terms it deems just:

(1) exercise any or all of the powers of amendment of the trial court or tribunal;

(2) allow substitution, addition, or deletion of parties or allow parties to be rearranged as appellants or appellees, on reasonable notice;

(3) permit amendment or additions to the grounds for appeal;

(4) permit amendments, corrections, or additions to the transcript or record;

(5) remand the case to allow additional evidence to be taken;

(6) draw inferences of fact;

(7) enter any judgment or order or grant further or different relief as the case may require;

(8) if a judgment notwithstanding the verdict is set aside on appeal, grant a new trial or other relief as necessary;

(9) direct the parties as to how to proceed in any case pending before it;

(10) dismiss an appeal or an original proceeding for lack of jurisdiction or failure of the appellant or the plaintiff to pursue the case in conformity with the rules.

(B) Allowing Act After Expiration of Time. When any nonjurisdictional act is required to be done within a designated time, the Court of Appeals may permit it to be done after expiration of the period on motion showing that there was good cause for delay or that it was not due to the culpable negligence of the party or attorney.

(C) Vexatious Proceedings.

(1) The Court of Appeals may, on its own initiative or the motion of any party, assess actual and punitive damages or take other disciplinary action when it determines that an appeal or any of the proceedings in an appeal was vexatious because

(a) the appeal was taken for purposes of hindrance or delay or without any reasonable basis for belief that there was a meritorious issue to be determined on appeal; or

(b) a pleading, motion, argument, brief, document, or record filed in the case or any testimony presented in the case was grossly lacking in the requirements of propriety, violated court rules, or grossly disregarded the requirements of a fair presentation of the issues to the court.

(2) Damages may not exceed actual damages and expenses incurred by the opposing party because of the vexatious appeal or proceeding, including reasonable attorney fees, and punitive damages in an added amount not exceeding the actual damages. The court may remand the case to the trial court or tribunal for a determination of actual damages.

[Effective March 1, 1985.]

1985 Staff Comment

MCR 7.216 is based on GCR 1963, 816.5 and 820.

Subrule (A)(10) expressly authorizes the Court of Appeals to dismiss a case for lack of jurisdiction or for failure of the appellant or plaintiff to pursue the case in conformity with the rules.

Subrule (C) modifies the limitations on damages that may be imposed for vexatious proceedings. The punitive aspect of damages is measured by the adverse party's expenses, rather than the amount of the judgment in the trial court. Compare GCR 1963, 816.5.

The [March 1, 1985] amendment of MCR 7.216(C)(1) modifies the language regarding imposition of sanctions for vexatious appellate proceedings. First, references to dismissal of the appeal are deleted. That subject is covered by MCR 7.216(A)(7) and (10). Second, the limitation that a motion for costs could be brought only before a case is placed on a session calendar is deleted.

RULE 7.217   INVOLUNTARY DISMISSAL OF CASES

(A) Dismissal. If the appellant, or the plaintiff in an original action under MCR 7.206, fails to order a transcript, file a brief, or comply with court rules, the clerk will notify the parties that the appeal may be dismissed for want of prosecution unless the deficiency is remedied within 21 days after the date of the clerk's notice of deficiency. If the deficiency is not remedied within that time, the chief judge or another designated judge may dismiss the appeal for want of prosecution.

(B) Notice. A copy of an order dismissing an appeal for want of prosecution will be sent to the parties and the court or tribunal from which the appeal originated.

(C) Other Action. In all instances of failure to prosecute an appeal to hearing as required, the chief judge or another designated judge may take such other action as is deemed appropriate.

(D) Reinstatement. Within 56 days after the date of the clerk's notice of dismissal pursuant to this rule, the appellant or plaintiff may seek relief from dismissal by showing mistake, inadvertence, or excusable neglect.

[Effective March 1, 1985; amended effective February 1, 1994; September 1, 1999.]

Staff Comment to 1994 Amendment

MCR 7.217 [as amended effective February 1, 1994] is a new provision that simplifies the current procedure for dismissing no-progress cases.

Staff Comment to 1999 Amendment

This group of amendments [effective September 1, 1999] deal with various matters regarding appellate procedure. The following rules are affected:

MCR 7.201(B), 7.217(A) and (C)—Permit the Chief Judge, or another designated judge, acting alone, to enter certain orders when a party does not proceed in accordance with the rules.

MCR 7.202(6)—Delete the definition of "signed" from the rule.

New MCR 7.203(F)—Permit the chief judge, or another designated judge, acting alone, to dismiss an appeal or original proceeding for lack of jurisdiction, and create a procedure for the appellant or plaintiff to seek reconsideration of that decision.

MCR 7.212(C) and (D)—Clarify the requirement of specific page references to the record in appellate briefs.

MCR 7.215(H)—Modify several provisions in the rule governing resolution of conflicts in Court of Appeals decisions.

RULE 7.218   VOLUNTARY DISMISSAL

(A) Dismissal by Appellant. In all cases where the appellant or plaintiff in an original action under MCR 7.206 files an unopposed motion to withdraw the appeal, the clerk will enter an order of dismissal.

(B) Stipulation to Dismiss. The parties to a case in the Court of Appeals may file with the clerk a signed stipulation agreeing to dismissal of an appeal or an action brought under MCR 7.206. On payment of all fees, the clerk will enter an order dismissing the appeal or the action under MCR 7.206, except that

class actions or cases submitted on a session calendar may not be dismissed except by order of the Court of Appeals.

[Effective March 1, 1985; amended effective May 1, 1995.]

1985 Staff Comment

MCR 7.218 is based on GCR 1963, 809.

The rule includes the parts of GCR 1963, 809 that dealt with stipulations to dismiss. The clerk will not automatically dismiss a case that has been submitted on a session calendar; an order of the court is required.

The parts of GCR 1963, 809 that dealt with stipulations regarding the record are placed in MCR 7.210(A)(4).

Staff Comment to 1995 Amendment

MCR 7.218 allows dismissal of an appeal if the appellant's motion to withdraw the appeal is unopposed.

RULE 7.219   TAXATION OF COSTS; FEES

(A) Right to Costs. Except as the Court of Appeals otherwise directs, the prevailing party in a civil case is entitled to costs.

(B) Time for Filing. Within 28 days after the dispositive order, opinion, or order denying rehearing is mailed, the prevailing party may file a certified or verified bill of costs with the clerk and serve a copy on all other parties. Each item claimed in the bill must be specified. Failure to file a bill of costs within the time prescribed waives the right to costs.

(C) Objections. Any other party may file objections to the bill of costs with the clerk within 7 days after a copy of the bill is served. The objecting party must serve a copy of the objections on the prevailing party and file proof of that service.

(D) Taxation. The clerk will promptly verify the bill and tax those costs allowable.

(E) Review. The action by the clerk will be reviewed by the Court of Appeals on motion of either party filed within 7 days from the date of taxation, but on review only those affidavits or objections which were previously filed with the clerk may be considered by the court.

(F) Costs Taxable. A prevailing party may tax only the reasonable costs incurred in the Court of Appeals, including:

(1) printing of briefs, or if briefs were typewritten, a charge of $1 per original page;

(2) any appeal or stay bond;

(3) the transcript and necessary copies of it;

(4) documents required for the record on appeal;

(5) fees paid to the clerk or to the trial court clerk incident to the appeal;

(6) taxable costs allowed by law in appeals to the Supreme Court (MCL 600.2441; MSA 27A.2441); and

(7) other expenses taxable under applicable court rules.

(G) Fees Paid to Clerk. The clerk shall collect the following fees, which may be taxed as costs:

(1) the fee required by law for a claim of appeal, application for leave to appeal, application for delayed appeal, original complaint, or motion;

(2) 50¢ per page for a certified copy of a paper from a public record;

(3) $5 for certified docket entries;

(4) $1 per document for certification of a copy presented to the clerk; and

(5) 50¢ per page for a copy of an opinion; however, one copy must be given without charge to each party in a case.

A person who is unable to pay a filing fee may ask the court to waive the fee by filing a motion and an affidavit disclosing the reason for the inability.

(H) Rule Applicable. Except as provided in this rule, MCR 2.625 applies generally to taxation of costs in the Court of Appeals.

(I) Violation of Rules. The Court of Appeals may impose costs on a party or an attorney when in its discretion they should be assessed for violation of these rules.

[Effective March 1, 1985.]

1985 Staff Comment

MCR 7.219 is based on GCR 1963, 822.

Subrules (F) and (G) carry forward the provisions of GCR 1963, 822.2 and 822.3 regarding the fees and expenses that may be collected and taxed. The fee for a copy of a Court of Appeals opinion is changed to 50¢ per page, to conform with MCL 600.321(4); MSA 27A.321(4).

New subrules (A)–(E) provide the procedure for taxation of costs, formerly covered by reference to the rule governing taxation of costs in trial courts. See GCR 1963, 822.1.

Subrule (I) adds explicit authorization for the Court of Appeals to impose costs on a party or attorney for violation of the rules.

SUBCHAPTER 7.300

RULE 7.301 JURISDICTION AND TERM

(A) Jurisdiction. The Supreme Court may:

(1) review a Judicial Tenure Commission order recommending discipline, removal, retirement, or suspension (see MCR 9.223–9.226);

(2) review by appeal a case pending in the Court of Appeals or after decision by the Court of Appeals (see MCR 7.302);

(3) review by appeal a final order of the Attorney Discipline Board (see MCR 9.122);

(4) give an advisory opinion (see Const 1963, art 3, § 8);

(5) respond to a certified question (see MCR 7.305);

(6) exercise superintending control over a lower court or tribunal (see, e.g., MCR 7.304);

(7) exercise other jurisdiction as provided by the constitution or by law.

(B) Term. The Court will hold an annual term beginning on August 1 and ending on July 31. At every term, the Court will announce a date after which it will not call cases for argument except pursuant to order on a showing of special cause. Except as provided in MCR 7.312(E), the end of a term has no effect on pending cases.

[Effective March 1, 1985; amended effective October 1, 1989; January 14, 1994; September 20, 1995.]

1985 Staff Comment

MCR 7.301 is substantially the same as GCR 1963, 851.

SUPREME COURT

Staff Comment to 1989 Amendment

[Under the October 1, 1989 amendment,] MCR 7.301(B) sets an annual term of the Supreme Court beginning October 1 and ending September 30.* In cases that have not been decided by the end of the term, the parties are entitled to file supplemental briefs and request reargument. See MCR 7.312(E).

* Under the 1995 amendment, the term begins on August 1 and ends on July 31.

RULE 7.302 APPLICATION FOR LEAVE TO APPEAL

(A) What to File. To apply for leave to appeal, a party must file:

(1) 8 copies of an application for leave to appeal (one must be signed) prepared in conformity with MCR 7.212(B) and consisting of the following:

(a) a statement identifying the judgment or order appealed from and indicating the relief sought;

(b) the questions presented for review related in concise terms to the facts of the case;

(c) a table of contents and index of authorities conforming to MCR 7.212(C)(2) and (3);

(d) a concise statement of the material proceedings and facts conforming to MCR 7.212(C)(6);

(e) a concise argument, conforming to MCR 7.212(C)(7), in support of the appellant's position on each of the stated questions;

(f) any opinion, findings, or judgment of the trial court relevant to the question as to which leave to appeal is sought;

(g) the opinion or order of the Court of Appeals, unless review of a pending case is being sought;

(2) A notice for hearing stating that the application will be submitted to the Court on a date which is on a Tuesday at least 21 days after the filing of the application;

(3) Proof that a copy of the application was served on all other parties, and that a notice of the filing of the application was served on the clerks of the Court of Appeals and the trial court; and

(4) The fee provided by MCR 7.319(B)(7)(a).

(B) Grounds. The application must show that

(1) the issue involves a substantial question as to the validity of a legislative act;

(2) the issue has significant public interest and the case is one by or against the state or one of its agencies or subdivisions or by or against an officer of the state or one of its agencies or subdivisions in the officer's official capacity;

(3) the issue involves legal principles of major significance to the state's jurisprudence;

(4) in an appeal before decision by the Court of Appeals,

(a) delay in final adjudication is likely to cause substantial harm, or

(b) the appeal is from a ruling that a provision of the Michigan Constitution, a Michigan statute, a rule or regulation included in the Michigan Administrative Code, or any other action of the legislative or executive branch of state government is invalid;

(5) in an appeal from a decision of the Court of Appeals, the decision is clearly erroneous and will cause material injustice or the decision conflicts with a Supreme Court decision or another decision of the Court of Appeals; or

(6) in an appeal from the Attorney Discipline Board, the decision is erroneous and will cause material injustice.

(C) When to File.

(1) *Before Court of Appeals Decision.* In an appeal before the Court of Appeals decision, the application must be filed within 28 days

(a) after a claim of appeal is filed in the Court of Appeals;

(b) after an application for leave to appeal is filed in the Court of Appeals; or

(c) after entry of an order by the Court of Appeals granting an application for leave to appeal.

(2) *Other Appeals.* Except as provided in subrule (C)(4), in other appeals the application must be filed within 21 days

(a) after the Court of Appeals clerk mails notice of an order entered by the Court of Appeals;

(b) after the filing of the opinion appealed from; or

(c) after the Court of Appeals clerk mails notice of an order denying a timely filed motion for rehearing.

(3) *Later Application.* A delayed application may be filed, if it is accompanied by an affidavit explaining the delay. However, a delayed application may not be filed more than 56 days after the Court of Appeals decision.

(4) *Decisions Remanding for Further Proceedings.* If the decision of the Court of Appeals remands the case to a lower court for further proceedings, an application for leave may be filed within 21 days after

(a) the Court of Appeals decision ordering the remand, or

(b) the Court of Appeals decision disposing of the case following the remand procedure, in which case an application may be made on all issues raised in the Court of Appeals, including those related to the remand question.

(5) *Effect of Appeal on Decision Remanding Case.* If a party appeals a decision which remands for further proceedings as provided in subrule (C)(4)(a), the following provisions apply:

(a) If the Court of Appeals decision is a judgment under MCR 7.215 (E)(1), a timely appeal stays proceedings on remand unless the Court of Appeals or the Supreme Court orders otherwise.

(b) If the Court of Appeals decision is an order other than a judgment under MCR 7.215 (E)(1), the proceedings on remand are not stayed by an application for leave to appeal unless so ordered by the Court of Appeals or the Supreme Court.

(6) *Orders Denying Motions to Remand.* If the Court of Appeals has denied a motion to remand, the appellant may raise issues relating to that denial in an application for leave to appeal from the decision on the merits.

(D) Opposing Brief; Cross Appeal.

(1) Any party may file 8 copies of an opposing brief before the day the application is noticed for hearing. He or she must file proof that a copy of the brief was served on all other parties.

(2) An application for leave to appeal as cross appellant may be filed with the clerk by the date the appellant's application for leave is noticed for hearing or within 21 days after the appellant's application is filed, whichever is later. The application must comply with subrule (A).

(E) Emergencies. Any party may move for immediate consideration of a pending application by showing what injury would occur if usual procedures were followed. The motion or an accompanying affidavit must explain the manner of service of the motion on the other parties.

(F) Decision.

(1) *Possible Court Actions.* The Court may grant or deny the application, enter a final decision, or issue a peremptory order. There is no oral argument. The clerk shall issue the order entered and mail copies to the parties and to the Court of Appeals clerk.

(2) *Appeal Before Court of Appeals Decision.* If leave to appeal is granted, the appeal is thereafter pending in the Supreme Court only, and subchapter 7.300 applies.

(3) *Appeal After Court of Appeals Decision.* If leave to appeal is denied, the Court of Appeals decision becomes the final adjudication and may be enforced in accordance with its terms. If leave to appeal is granted, jurisdiction over the case is vested in the Supreme Court, and subchapter 7.300 applies.

(4) *Issues on Appeal.*

(a) Unless otherwise ordered by the Court, appeals shall be limited to the issues raised in the application for leave to appeal.

(b) On motion of any party, for good cause, the Court may grant a request to add additional issues not raised in the application for leave to appeal or in the order granting leave to appeal. Permission to brief and argue such additional issues does not extend the time for filing of briefs and appendixes.

(G) Stay of Proceedings. MCR 7.209 applies to appeals to the Supreme Court. When a stay bond has been filed on appeal to the Court of Appeals under MCR 7.209 or a stay has been entered, it operates to stay proceedings pending disposition of the appeal in the Supreme Court unless otherwise ordered by the Supreme Court or Court of Appeals.

[Effective March 1, 1985; amended effective October 1, 1989; September 1, 1992; June 2, 1995; January 1, 1998; September 1, 1999; January 1, 2002; September 1, 2002; January 1, 2003.]

1985 Staff Comment

MCR 7.302 is based on GCR 1963, 852 and 853. The provisions regarding applications for leave to appeal are reorganized but retain most of the substance of the former rules. The rule requires the filing of 8 copies of papers, rather than 9 as under GCR 1963, 852.2.

As in the corresponding provision in the Court of Appeals subchapter (MCR 7.205[F]), subrule (C)(3) modifies the language regarding the affidavit filed with a late appeal. It must explain the delay, but need not show the lack of "culpable negligence". Compare GCR 1963, 853.2(3).

The rules in this subchapter do not include the provision found in GCR 1963, 864.6 halving the time limits for interlocutory criminal appeals and child custody cases.

The checklist of steps on appeal found in GCR 1963, 868 is omitted.

Staff Comment to 1989 Amendment

The provisions of MCR 7.302(A) on the form of an application for leave to appeal to the Supreme Court are modified [under the October 1, 1989 amendment]. A single document

is to be filed, in contrast to the former provision, under which an application, a concise statement of the material proceedings and facts, and a supporting brief were required. The contents of the new form of application, however, generally correspond to the former provisions.

New MCR 7.302(C)(4)–(6) clarifies the parties' options when a decision of the Court of Appeals remands the case to the trial court for further proceedings. Basically, a party may immediately appeal to the Supreme Court or may await the conclusion of the proceedings in the trial court and in the Court of Appeals following the remand.

Subrule (5) specifies the effect on the remand order of an immediate application to the Supreme Court—if the order is a judgment (an opinion or an order disposing of an appeal) a timely application stays the order. Otherwise there is no stay unless the Court of Appeals or Supreme Court orders.

Subrule (6) deals with denials of motions to remand. A party who unsuccessfully moves to remand may raise issues regarding that decision in an application filed after decision on the merits.

Staff Comment to 1991 and 1992 Amendments

A 1991 amendment to MCR 7.212(C)(6) requires a person who files a sentence appeal in the Court of Appeals to submit a copy of the presentence report. The [September 1] 1992 amendment of MCR 7.302(A)(1)(e) adds a similar requirement for persons applying to the Supreme Court for leave to appeal.

Staff Comment to 1995 Amendment

Cross references in MCR 7.302(A)(1)(d) and (e) are changed in light of the renumbering of several subrules in MCR 7.212(C) in an order entered March 3, 1995.

Staff Comment to 1998 Amendment

In addition, MCR 7.302(C)(5) is amended [effective January 1, 1998] to correct cross-references to MCR 7.215.

Staff Comment to 1999 Amendment

The June 2, 1999 amendment of MCR 7.302(A)(3), effective September 1, 1999, eliminated the requirement of filing with the Court of Appeals and the trial court a copy of an application for leave to appeal that is filed with the Supreme Court. The amended rule requires that an appellant file with the Court of Appeals and the trial court only a notice that an application for leave to appeal has been filed with the Supreme Court.

Staff Comments to 2002 Amendments

The November 26, 2001 amendments of MCR 4.401(D), 7.210(H), 7.212(C), 7.213(A), and 7.302(C), effective January 1, 2002, recognized numbering changes in other rules and the elimination of the "parallel citation" requirement from the Michigan Uniform System of Citation (Supreme Court AO 2001-5).

The staff comment is published only for the benefit of the bench and bar and is not an authoritative construction by the court.

The May 17, 2002, amendments of MCR 7.204, 7.212, 7.213, 7.215, and 7.302, which are effective September 1, 2002, relate to appeals in which a Michigan constitutional provision, statute, regulation, or other governmental action has been held to be invalid.

MCR 7.302(B)(4) is amended to add as a ground for an application for leave to appeal to the Supreme Court before decision by the Court of Appeals that the appeal is from an order holding that such a provision or action is invalid.

The staff comment is published only for the benefit of the bench and bar and is not an authoritative construction by the Court.

Staff Comment to 2003 Amendment

The October 8, 2002 amendments of MCR 7.302, 7.304, 7.306, and 7.309, effective January 1, 2003, standardize the type size that is used in briefs and other papers filed with the Supreme Court. The amendments also adopt the 50–page limit set forth in MCR 7.212(B), eliminating the distinction between printed and other briefs.

The staff comment is published only for the benefit of the bench and bar and is not an authoritative construction by the Court.

RULE 7.304   ORIGINAL PROCEEDINGS

(A) When Available. A complaint may be filed in the Supreme Court to implement the Court's superintending control power when an application for leave to appeal cannot be filed. A complaint for mandamus may be filed to implement the Court's superintending control power over the Board of Law Examiners, the Attorney Discipline Board, or the Attorney Grievance Commission.

(B) What to File. To initiate an original proceeding, a plaintiff must file with the clerk:

(1) 8 copies of a complaint;

(2) 8 copies of a brief conforming as nearly as possible to MCR 7.212(B) and (C);

(3) a notice of hearing, which must state that the complaint will be submitted to the Court on a date which is a Tuesday at least 21 days after the complaint is filed;

(4) proof that a copy of the complaint and brief was served on the defendant; and

(5) the fee provided by MCR 7.319(B)(7)(b).

Copies of documents, record evidence, or supporting affidavits may be attached as exhibits to the complaint. The complaint must be entitled:

"[*Plaintiff*] v [*Court of Appeals, Board of Law Examiners, Attorney Discipline Board, or Attorney Grievance Commission*],"

and the clerk is directed to re-entitle any papers otherwise entitled.

(C) Answer.

(1) The defendant must file 8 copies of an answer and a brief conforming with MCR 7.212(B) and (D) before the date the complaint is noticed for hearing. The defendant must serve 1 copy on the plaintiff and file proof of that service with the clerk.

(2) The grievance administrator's answer to a complaint for mandamus against the Attorney Grievance Commission must show the investigatory steps taken and other pertinent information.

(D) Actions Against Attorney Grievance Commission; Confidentiality. The clerk shall keep the file in an action against the Attorney Grievance Commission or the grievance administrator confidential and not open to the public if it appears that the complaint relates to matters that are confidential under MCR 9.126. In the answer to a complaint, the grievance administrator shall certify to the clerk whether the matters involved in the action are deemed confidential under MCR 9.126. The protection provided by MCR 9.126 continues, unless the Court otherwise orders.

(E) Decision. There is no oral argument on the complaint. The Court may set the case for argument as on leave granted, grant or deny the relief requested, or enter another order it finds appropriate, including an order to show cause why the relief sought in the complaint should not be granted.

[Effective March 1, 1985; amended effective October 1, 1991; January 1, 2003.]

1985 Staff Comment

MCR 7.304 is based on GCR 1963, 862.5. The provisions are rewritten, but retain the substance of rule 862.5.

The former rule included the requirement that the defendant file an answer only in actions brought against the Attorney Discipline Board or Attorney Grievance Commission. See GCR 1963, 862.5(B). Subrule (C)(1) extends that requirement to all cases.

Staff Comment to 1991 Amendment

The September 6, 1991, amendment of MCR 7.304, effective October 1, 1991, deals with the confidentiality of files in cases brought against the attorney grievance commission or the grievance administrator.

Staff Comment to 2003 Amendment

The October 8, 2002 amendments of MCR 7.302, 7.304, 7.306, and 7.309, effective January 1, 2003, standardize the type size that is used in briefs and other papers filed with the Supreme Court. The amendments also adopt the 50–page limit set forth in MCR 7.212(B), eliminating the distinction between printed and other briefs.

The staff comment is published only for the benefit of the bench and bar and is not an authoritative construction by the Court.

RULE 7.305   CERTIFIED QUESTIONS

(A) From Michigan Courts.

(1) Whenever a court or tribunal from which an appeal may be taken to the Court of Appeals or to the Supreme Court has pending before it an action or proceeding involving a controlling question of public law, and the question is of such public moment as to require early determination according to executive message of the Governor addressed to the Supreme Court, the Supreme Court may authorize the court or tribunal to certify the question to the Supreme Court with a statement of the facts sufficient to make clear the application of the question. Further proceedings relative to the case are stayed to the extent ordered

by the court or tribunal, pending receipt of an answer from the Supreme Court.

(2) If any question is not properly stated, or if sufficient facts are not given, the Supreme Court may require a further and better statement of the question or of the facts.

(3) The answer to a certified question is given by the Supreme Court in the ordinary form of an opinion, to be published with other opinions of the Supreme Court.

(4) After the answer of the Supreme Court has been sent, the court or tribunal will proceed with or dispose of the case in accordance with the Supreme Court's answer.

(B) From Other Courts.

(1) When a federal court, state appellate court, or tribal court considers a question that Michigan law may resolve and that is not controlled by Michigan Supreme Court precedent, the court may on its own initiative or that of an interested party certify the question to the Michigan Supreme Court.

(2) A certificate may be prepared by stipulation or at the certifying court's direction, and must contain

   (a) the case title;

   (b) a factual statement; and

   (c) the question to be answered.

The presiding judge must sign it, and the clerk must certify it under seal.

(3) With the certificate, the parties shall submit

   (a) briefs conforming with MCR 7.306 and 7.309;

   (b) a joint appendix conforming with MCR 7.307, 7.308, and 7.309; and

   (c) a request for oral argument, if oral argument is desired.

(4) If the Supreme Court responds to the question certified, the clerk shall send a copy to the certifying court under seal.

(5) The Supreme Court shall divide costs equally among the parties, subject to redistribution by the certifying court.

[Effective March 1, 1985; amended effective October 1, 1989; June 16, 2000.]

1985 Staff Comment

MCR 7.305 is substantially the same as GCR 1963, 797.

Staff Comment to 1989 Amendment

The [October 1, 1989] amendment of MCR 7.305 adjusts the language to reflect the previous elimination of the requirement that briefs be printed. See 429 Mich cxxv (1987).

Staff Comment to 2000 Amendment

The June 16, 2000 amendment of MCR 7.305(B)(1) was proposed by the Representative Assembly of the State Bar of Michigan, upon the recommendation of the Standing Committee on American Indian Law. The committee is charged with improving the relationship between Michigan state courts and tribal courts.

RULE 7.306 BRIEFS IN CALENDAR CASES

(A) Form of Briefs. Briefs in calendar cases must be prepared in the form provided in MCR 7.212(B), (C), and (D) and produced as provided in MCR 7.309. For the purposes of this rule, references in MCR 7.212(C) and (D) to the "record" should be read as referring to the appendix.

(B) Length of Brief; Summary of Argument. In a brief in which the argument of any one issue exceeds 20 pages, a summary of argument must be included. The summary must be a succinct, accurate, and clear condensation of the argument actually made in the body of the brief and may not be a mere repetition of the headings under which the argument is arranged. Unless the Court allows a longer brief, a brief prepared in the manner authorized under MCR 7.309 may not exceed 50 pages, excluding the table of contents, index of authorities, and appendix, but including the summary of argument.

(C) Amicus Curiae Briefs. An amicus curiae brief may be filed only on motion granted by the Court and must conform to subrules (A) and (B) and MCR 7.309. The time for filing the brief corresponds with the time for filing the brief of the party whose position the amicus curiae supports. An amicus curiae may not participate in oral argument except by Court order.

[Effective March 1, 1985; amended effective October 1, 1987; October 1, 1989; January 1, 2003.]

1985 Staff Comment

MCR 7.306 includes the provisions of GCR 1963, 854 and 857.5.

Subrule (C) is a new provision covering the subject of amicus curiae briefs.

Staff Comment to 1987 Amendment

The [October 1, 1987] amendments of MCR 7.306, 7.307, 7.308 and 7.309 reflect, inter alia, the decision of the Court to permit the filing of typewritten briefs in calendar cases and to reduce the time for filing of briefs for the appellant in calendar cases from 91 to 56 days after leave to appeal is granted and for the appellee from 56 to 35 days after the appellant's brief and appendix are served on the appellee. MCR 7.309 as amended also mandates specific colors for the cover of briefs and appendixes filed in calendar cases.

The [October 1, 1987] amendment of MCR 7.306 adjusts the language to reflect the previous elimination of the requirement that briefs be printed. See 429 Mich cxxv (1987).

Staff Comment to 2003 Amendment

The October 8, 2002 amendments of MCR 7.302, 7.304, 7.306, and 7.309, effective January 1, 2003, standardize the type size that is used in briefs and other papers filed with the Supreme Court. The amendments also adopt the 50–page limit set forth in MCR 7.212(B), eliminating the distinction between printed and other briefs.

The staff comment is published only for the benefit of the bench and bar and is not an authoritative construction by the Court.

RULE 7.307   APPELLANT'S APPENDIX

(A) Contents of Appendix. An appendix, entitled "Appellant's Appendix", must be separately bound. Each page number must be followed by the letter "a" (e.g., 1a). The appendix must contain

(1) a table of contents;

(2) the relevant docket entries both in the lower court and in the Court of Appeals arranged chronologically in a single column;

(3) the trial court judgment, order, or decision in question and the Court of Appeals opinion or order;

(4) any relevant finding or opinion of the trial court;

(5) any relevant portions of the pleadings or other parts of the record; and

(6) any relevant portions of the transcript, including the complete jury instructions if an issue is raised regarding a jury instruction.

The items listed in subrules (A)(3)–(6) shall be arranged in chronological order.

(B) Joint Appendix.

(1) The parties may stipulate to prepare a joint appendix, so designated, containing the matters that both want the justices to read to decide fairly the questions involved. A joint appendix shall meet the requirements of this rule and shall be separately bound and served with the appellant's brief.

(2) The stipulation to use a joint appendix may provide that either party may prepare, as a supplemental appendix, any additional portion of the record not covered by the joint appendix.

[Effective March 1, 1985; amended effective October 1, 1987; October 1, 1989.]

1985 Staff Comment

MCR 7.307 is based on GCR 1963, 855.

The order of the trial court that is the subject of the appeal must be included in the appendix, but other orders of the trial court need be included only if relevant. Compare subrule (A)(3) with GCR 1963, 855(2).

Staff Comment to 1987 Amendment

The [October 1, 1987] amendments of MCR 7.306, 7.307, 7.308 and 7.309 reflect, inter alia, the decision of the Court to permit the filing of typewritten briefs in calendar cases and to reduce the time for filing of briefs for the appellant in calendar cases from 91 to 56 days after leave to appeal is granted and for the appellee from 56 to 35 days after the appellant's brief and appendix are served on the appellee. MCR 7.309 as amended also mandates specific colors for the cover of briefs and appendixes filed in calendar cases.

Staff Comment to 1989 Amendment

The [October 1, 1989] amendment of MCR 7.307 adjusts the language to reflect the previous elimination of the requirement that briefs be printed. See 429 Mich cxxv (1987).

RULE 7.308   APPELLEE'S APPENDIX

An appendix, entitled "Appellee's Appendix", may be filed, but must be separately bound. It may contain the part of the record the appellee wants the justices to read that has not been included in the appellant's appendix. The appellee's appendix must comply with the provisions of MCR 7.307. Each page number must be followed by the letter "b" (e.g., 1b). Material in the appellant's appendix may not be repeated in the appellee's appendix, except to clarify the subject matter included.

[Effective March 1, 1985; amended effective October 1, 1987; October 1, 1989.]

1985 Staff Comment

MCR 7.308 is based on GCR 1963, 856(1). GCR 856(2), which dealt with an appendix to a supplemental brief, is omitted.

Staff Comment to 1987 Amendment

The [October 1, 1987] amendments of MCR 7.306, 7.307, 7.308 and 7.309 reflect, inter alia, the decision of the Court to permit the filing of typewritten briefs in calendar cases and to reduce the time for filing of briefs for the appellant in calendar cases from 91 to 56 days after leave to appeal is granted and for the appellee from 56 to 35 days after the appellant's brief and appendix are served on the appellee. MCR 7.309 as amended also mandates specific colors for the cover of briefs and appendixes filed in calendar cases.

Staff Comment to 1989 Amendment

The [October 1, 1989] amendment of MCR 7.308 adjusts the language to reflect the previous elimination of the requirement that briefs be printed. See 429 Mich cxxv (1987).

RULE 7.309   PREPARATION, FILING, AND SERVING BRIEFS AND APPENDIXES

(A) Form.

(1) Briefs and appendixes shall be produced on good white unglazed paper by any printing, duplicating, or copying process that provides a clear image. Original typewritten pages may be used, but not carbon copies. Briefs and appendixes must be prepared in conformity with MCR 7.212(B), except that briefs must be printed on only one side of the page and appendixes must be printed on both sides of the page.

The necessary expense of preparation of briefs and appendixes to be taxed as costs pursuant to MCR 7.319 shall not exceed $2 per original page.

(2) The pages of the appendix must be numbered separately from the brief. In each appendix, brief running heads must be printed at the top of each page

indicating the character of the matter contained on the page including, for testimony, the name of the witness, and, for documents, the nature of them. The clerk must refuse to receive a brief or appendix which has not been prepared in substantial conformity with this rule. The submission to the clerk of a nonconforming brief or appendix does not satisfy the time limitations for filing briefs and appendixes.

(3) A brief and appendix must have a suitable cover of heavy paper. The cover page must follow this form:

In the Supreme Court

Appeal from the [court or tribunal appealed from] [judge or presiding officer]

_____

Plaintiff–[Appellant or Appellee],
            v   Docket No. _____

_____

Defendant–[Appellee or Appellant].

Brief on Appeal—[Appellant or Appellee]

_____

        Attorney for [Plaintiff or
        Defendant]—[Appellant or
        Appellee]

        [Business Address]
_____
_____

Appendixes shall be similarly endorsed, but shall be designated as appendixes instead of briefs. The cover of the brief of the appellant must be blue; that of the appellee, red; that of an intervenor or amicus curiae, green; that of any reply brief, gray; that of an appendix, yellow.

(B) Filing and Service; Dismissal.

(1) *Appellant's Brief and Appendix.* The appellant shall

(a) file 24 copies of a brief and appendix with the clerk within 56 days after leave to appeal is granted;

(b) serve 2 copies on each attorney who has appeared in the case for a separate party or group of parties and on each party who has appeared in person;

(c) serve 1 copy on the Attorney General in a criminal case or in a case in which the state is a party or interested; and

(d) file proof of service with the clerk.

(2) *Appellee's Brief and Appendix.* The appellee shall

(a) file 24 copies of a brief and appendix with the clerk within 35 days after the appellant's brief and appendix is served on the appellee;

(b) serve 2 copies on each attorney who has appeared in the case for a separate party or group

of parties and on each party who has appeared in person;

(c) serve 1 copy on the Attorney General in a criminal case or in a case in which the state is a party or interested; and

(d) file proof of service with the clerk.

(3) *Failure to File.* If the appellant fails to file the brief and appendix within the time required, the Court may dismiss the case and award costs to the appellee, or affirm the judgment or order appealed from. A party filing a brief late forfeits the right to oral argument. The Court may extend the time on a party's motion.

(C) Earlier Filing and Serving. The time provided for filing and serving of the appellant's or the appellee's brief and appendix may be shortened on order of the Court on motion of either party or on the Court's own initiative.

[Effective March 1, 1985; amended effective October 1, 1987; October 1, 1989; January 1, 2003.]

1985 Staff Comment

MCR 7.309 is based on GCR 1963, 857.1–857.4. The provisions are rewritten, but retain the substance of the former rule.

Staff Comment to 1987 Amendment

The [October 1, 1987] amendments of MCR 7.306, 7.307, 7.308 and 7.309 reflect, inter alia, the decision of the Court to permit the filing of typewritten briefs in calendar cases and to reduce the time for filing of briefs for the appellant in calendar cases from 91 to 56 days after leave to appeal is granted and for the appellee from 56 to 35 days after the appellant's brief and appendix are served on the appellee. MCR 7.309 as amended also mandates specific colors for the cover of briefs and appendixes filed in calendar cases.

Staff Comment to 1989 Amendment

The [October 1, 1989] amendment of MCR 7.309(B) reduces from six to one the number of copies of briefs that must be served on the Attorney General in certain cases.

Staff Comment to 2003 Amendment

The October 8, 2002 amendments of MCR 7.302, 7.304, 7.306, and 7.309, effective January 1, 2003, standardize the type size that is used in briefs and other papers filed with the Supreme Court. The amendments also adopt the 50–page limit set forth in MCR 7.212(B), eliminating the distinction between printed and other briefs.

The staff comment is published only for the benefit of the bench and bar and is not an authoritative construction by the Court.

RULE 7.310 STIPULATIONS

The parties may stipulate in writing regarding any matter constituting the basis for an application for leave to appeal, or regarding any matter relevant to a part of the record on appeal. The parties may file with the clerk a stipulation agreeing to the dismissal of an application for leave to appeal or an appeal. The clerk shall present the stipulation to the Court, which shall enter the dismissal unless it concludes that the appeal should be decided notwithstanding the stipulation.

[Effective March 1, 1985.]

1985 Staff Comment

MCR 7.310 is based on GCR 1963, 858.

Language is added to make clear that the Court, rather than the clerk, acts on the stipulation, and that the Court may refuse to enter a dismissal pursuant to stipulation.

RULE 7.311   FILING RECORD ON APPEAL

(A) Transmission of Record. An appeal is heard on the original papers, which constitute the record on appeal. When requested by the Supreme Court clerk, the Court of Appeals clerk or the lower court clerk shall send to the Supreme Court clerk all papers on file in the Court of Appeals or the lower court, certified by the clerk. For an appeal originating from an administrative board, office, or tribunal, the record on appeal is the certified record filed with the Court of Appeals clerk and the papers filed with the Court of Appeals clerk.

(B) Return of Record. After final adjudication or other disposition of an appeal, the clerk shall return the original record to the Court of Appeals clerk, to the clerk of the lower court or tribunal in which the record was made, or to the clerk of the court to which the case has been remanded for further proceedings, and the clerk of the lower court to which the original record has been sent shall promptly notify the attorneys of the receipt of the record. The Supreme Court clerk shall forward a certified copy of the order or judgment entered by the Supreme Court to the Court of Appeals clerk and to the clerk of the trial court or tribunal from which the appeal was taken.

[Effective March 1, 1985.]

1985 Staff Comment

MCR 7.311 includes the provisions of GCR 1963, 860(1) and (3). The rule omits the language found in GCR 1963, 860(2), which referred to sending part of the record for use in connection with a motion.

RULE 7.312   SUPREME COURT CALENDAR

(A) Definition. A case in which leave to appeal has been granted, or a case initiated in the Supreme Court which the Court determines will be heard and argued, is termed a "calendar case".

(B) Notice of Hearing; Request for Oral Argument.

(1) After the briefs of both parties have been filed or the time for filing the appellee's brief has expired, the clerk shall notify the parties that the case will be heard at a session of the Supreme Court not less than 35 days after the date of the notice. The Court may shorten the 35-day period.

(2) Except on order of the Court, a party is not entitled to oral argument unless that party advises the clerk, in writing, of the desire to argue orally at least 21 days before the first day of the session. If neither party is entitled to oral argument, the clerk will list the case as submitted on briefs. The Court may direct that a case be submitted on briefs without oral argument.

(C) Arrangement of Calendar. Twenty-one days before the first day of the session, the clerk will place cases on the session calendar and arrange the order in which they are to be heard. The cases will be called and heard in that order except as provided in subrule (D).

(D) Adjournments; Rearrangement of Calendar. By stipulation filed with the clerk at least 21 days before the first day of the session, a case may be specially placed on the session calendar, grouped to suit the convenience of the attorneys, or placed at the end of the call. After the rearrangement of cases by the clerk, further changes may not be made by the attorneys. A motion to adjourn to another session may be made only for good cause and on notice to the opposing attorney at least 48 hours before the time set for hearing, unless the opposing attorney consents to it in writing.

(E) Reargument of Undecided Cases. When a calendar case, other than one argued pursuant to special order under MCR 7.301(B), remains undecided at the end of the term in which it was argued, either party may file a supplemental brief. In addition, if either party requests within 14 days after the beginning of the new term, the clerk shall schedule the case for reargument.

[Effective March 1, 1985; amended effective October 1, 1989.]

1985 Staff Comment

MCR 7.312 is based on GCR 1963, 861.1–861.4 and 864.1. The provisions are rewritten, but retain the substance of the former rules.

Staff Comment to 1989 Amendment

New MCR 7.312(E) [effective October 1, 1989] relates to MCR 7.301(B), which sets an annual term of the Supreme Court beginning October 1 and ending September 30. In cases that have not been decided by the end of the term, the parties are entitled to file supplemental briefs and request reargument.

RULE 7.313   MOTIONS IN SUPREME COURT

(A) What to File. To have a motion heard, a party must file with the clerk:

(1) a motion stating briefly but distinctly the grounds on which it is based and the relief required;

(2) an affidavit supporting any allegations of fact in the motion;

(3) a notice that the motion will be heard on a Tuesday at least 7 days after the motion is filed;

(4) the fee provided by MCR 7.319(B)(7)(c); and

(5) proof that the motion and supporting papers were served on the opposing party.

Eight copies of the motion must be filed, except only 2 copies need be filed of a motion to extend time, to place a case on or withdraw a case from the session calendar, or for oral argument. The attorney must sign the motion. By filing a motion for immediate consideration, a party may obtain an earlier hearing on the motion.

(B) Motion Day. Tuesday of each week is motion day. There is no oral argument on motions, unless ordered by the Court.

(C) Answer. An answer may be filed at any time before an order is entered on the motion.

(D) Motion for Rehearing.

(1) To move for rehearing, a party must file within 21 days after the opinion was filed (the date of an opinion is stamped on the upper right corner of the first page):

(a) 24 copies of a motion prepared as provided in MCR 7.309, if the opinion decided a case placed on a session calendar; or

(b) 14 typewritten copies of a motion, if the opinion decided a noncalendar case; and

(c) proof that a copy was served on the parties.

The motion for rehearing must include reasons why the Court should modify its opinion.

(2) Unless otherwise ordered by the Court, timely filing of a motion postpones issuance of the Court's judgment order until the motion is denied by the Court or, if granted, until at least 21 days after the filing of the Court's opinion on rehearing.

(3) Any party may answer a motion within 14 days after it is served by filing

(a) 24 or 14 copies of the answer, depending on whether the motion was filed under subrule (D)(1)(a) or (b); and

(b) proof that a copy was served on the other parties.

(4) Unless ordered by the Court, there is no oral argument.

(E) Motion for Reconsideration. To move for reconsideration of a Court order, a party must file the items required by subrule (A) within 21 days after the date of certification of the order. The clerk shall refuse to accept for filing any motion for reconsideration of an order denying a motion for reconsideration.

The filing of a motion for reconsideration does not stay the effect of the order addressed in the motion.

[Effective March 1, 1985; amended effective October 1, 1989.]

1985 Staff Comment

MCR 7.313 is based on GCR 1963, 862.1–862.4 and 862.6 and 864.4. The provisions are rewritten, but retain the substance of the former rules.

Eight, rather than nine, copies of most motions and related papers are required. Compare GCR 1963, 862.1.

Staff Comment to 1989 Amendment

The [October 1, 1989] amendment of MCR 7.313 adjusts the language to reflect the previous elimination of the requirement that briefs be printed. See 429 Mich cxxv (1987).

RULE 7.314 APPEALS IN WHICH NO PROGRESS HAS BEEN MADE

(A) Designation. If a brief has not been filed under MCR 7.309(B)(1) within 182 days after the entry of the order granting leave to appeal or directing that the action be heard as a calendar case, the case shall be designated as one in which no progress has been made. In calculating the 182–day period, adjournments granted by the Court are excluded.

(B) Notice; Dismissal. When a case is so designated, the clerk shall mail to each party notice that unless cause is shown to the contrary, the case will be dismissed. The clerk shall file proof of that notice. The clerk shall place as the first item for each session calendar all cases in which notice of no progress has been mailed at least 21 days before the first day of that session. On the first day of each session, the Court shall dismiss each case appearing on the calendar as one in which no progress has been made, unless cause is shown to the contrary.

[Effective March 1, 1985.]

1985 Staff Comment

MCR 7.314 is substantially the same as GCR 1963, 863.

RULE 7.315 CALL AND ARGUMENT OF CASES IN SUPREME COURT

(A) Call; Notice of Argument; Withdrawal From Call. The Court, on the first day of each session, will call the cases for argument in the order they stand on the calendar as arranged, and proceed from day to day during the session in the same order. A case may not be withdrawn after being placed on the call, except on a showing of extreme emergency. A case may be submitted on briefs by stipulation at any time.

(B) Argument. In a calendar case, the time allowed for argument is 30 minutes for each side. When only one side is represented, only 15 minutes is allowed. The time for argument may be extended by the Court on motion filed at least 14 days before the session begins or by the Chief Justice during the argument. Oral argument should emphasize and clarify the written argument appearing in the brief filed. The Court looks with disfavor on an argument that is read from a prepared text.

[Effective March 1, 1985.]

1985 Staff Comment

MCR 7.315 is based on GCR 1963, 864.1–864.3. The part of GCR 1963, 864.1 that dealt with requesting oral argument is placed in MCR 7.312(B)(2).

RULE 7.316 MISCELLANEOUS RELIEF OBTAINABLE IN SUPREME COURT

(A) Relief Obtainable. The Supreme Court may, at any time, in addition to its general powers:

(1) exercise any or all of the powers of amendment of the court or tribunal below;

(2) on reasonable notice as it may require, allow substitution of parties by reason of marriage, death, bankruptcy, assignment, or any other cause; allow new parties to be added or parties to be dropped; or allow parties to be rearranged as appellants or appellees;

(3) permit the reasons or grounds of appeal to be amended or new grounds to be added;

(4) permit the transcript or record to be amended by correcting errors or adding matters which should have been included;

(5) adjourn the case until further evidence is taken and brought before it, as the Court may deem necessary in order to do justice;

(6) draw inferences of fact;

(7) enter any judgment or order that ought to have been entered, and enter other and further orders and grant relief as the case may require; or

(8) if a judgment notwithstanding the verdict is set aside on appeal, grant a new trial or other relief as it deems just.

(B) Allowing Act After Expiration of Time. When, under the practice relating to appeals or stay of proceedings, a nonjurisdictional act is required to be done within a designated time, the Supreme Court may at any time, on motion and notice, permit it to be done after the expiration of the period on a showing made to the Court that there was good cause for the delay or that it was not due to the culpable negligence of the appellant.

(C) Decision by Supreme Court. A motion may not be decided or an order entered by the Court unless all required documents have been filed with the Court and the requisite fees have been paid. Except for affirmance of action by a lower court or tribunal by even division of the justices, a decision of the

Supreme Court must be made by concurrence of a majority of the justices voting.

(D) Vexatious Proceedings.

(1) The Court may, on its own initiative or the motion of any party filed before a case is placed on a session calendar, dismiss an appeal, assess actual and punitive damages, or take other disciplinary action when it determines that an appeal or any of the proceedings in an appeal was vexatious because

(a) the appeal was taken for purposes of hindrance or delay or without any reasonable basis for belief that there was a meritorious issue to be determined on appeal; or

(b) a pleading, motion, argument, brief, document, or record filed in the case or any testimony presented in the case was grossly lacking in the requirements of propriety, violated court rules, or grossly disregarded the requirements of a fair presentation of the issues to the Court.

(2) Damages may not exceed actual damages and expenses incurred by the opposing party because of the vexatious appeal or proceeding, including reasonable attorney fees, and punitive damages in an added amount not exceeding the actual damages. The Court may remand the case to the trial court or tribunal for a determination of actual damages.

[Effective March 1, 1985.]

1985 Staff Comment

MCR 7.316 includes the provisions of GCR 1963, 861.5 and 865.

In subrule (D) the punitive component of damages for vexatious proceedings is measured by the expenses incurred by the opposing party, rather than by the amount of the lower court judgment.

RULE 7.317 OPINIONS, ORDERS, AND JUDGMENTS OF SUPREME COURT

(A) Opinions of Court. An opinion must be written and bear the writer's name or the label "per curiam". Each justice deciding a case must sign an opinion.

(B) Filing and Publication. The Court shall file a signed opinion with the clerk, who shall stamp the date of filing on it. The Supreme Court reporter of decisions is responsible for having the opinions printed, in a form and under a contract approved by the Court.

(C) Orders or Judgments Pursuant to Opinions.

(1) *Entry.* The clerk shall enter an order or judgment pursuant to an opinion as of the date the opinion is filed with the clerk.

(2) *Routine Issuance.*

(a) If a motion for rehearing is not timely filed under MCR 7.313(D)(1), the clerk shall send a certified copy of the order or judgment to the Court of Appeals with its file, and to the court or tribunal which tried the case with its record, not less than 21 days nor more than 28 days after entry of the order or judgment.

(b) If a motion for rehearing is timely filed, the clerk shall fulfill the responsibilities under subrule (C)(2)(a) promptly after the Court denies the motion or, if the motion is granted, enter a new order or judgment after the Court's opinion on rehearing.

(3) *Exceptional Issuance.* The Court may direct the clerk to dispense with the time requirement of subrule (C)(2)(a) and issue the order or judgment when its opinion is filed. An order or judgment issued under this subrule does not preclude the filing of a motion for rehearing, but the filing of a motion does not stay execution or enforcement.

(4) *Execution or Enforcement.* Unless otherwise ordered by the Court, an order or judgment is effective when it is issued under subrule (C)(2)(a) or (b) or (C)(3), and enforcement is to be obtained in the trial court.

(D) Entry, Issuance, Execution, and Enforcement of Other Orders and Judgments of Court. An order or judgment, other than those by opinion under subrule (C), is entered on the date of filing. Unless otherwise stated, an order or judgment is effective the date it is entered. The clerk must promptly send a certified copy to each party, to the Court of Appeals, and to the lower court or tribunal.

[Effective March 1, 1985.]

1985 Staff Comment

MCR 7.317 is substantially the same as GCR 1963, 866.

RULE 7.318   TAXATION OF COSTS

(A) Rules Applicable. The procedure for taxation of costs in the Supreme Court is as provided by MCR 7.219.

(B) Expenses Taxable. Unless the Court otherwise orders, a prevailing party may tax only the reasonable costs incurred in the Supreme Court, including the necessary expense of printing the briefs and appendixes required by these rules.

[Effective March 1, 1985.]

1985 Staff Comment

MCR 7.318 is substantially the same as GCR 1963, 867.

RULE 7.319   SUPREME COURT CLERK

(A) Appointment; General Provisions. The Supreme Court will appoint a clerk who shall keep the clerk's office in Lansing under the direction of the Court. Where the term "clerk" appears in this subchapter without modification, it means the Supreme Court clerk. The clerk may not practice law other than as clerk while serving as clerk.

(B) Duties. The clerk shall do the following:

(1) Furnish bond before taking office. The bond must be in favor of the people of the state and in the penal sum of $10,000, approved by the Chief Justice and filed with the Secretary of State, and conditioned on the faithful performance of the clerk's official duties. The fee for the bond is a state expense.

(2) Collect the fees provided for by statute or court rule.

(3) Deposit monthly with the State Treasurer the fees collected, securing and filing a receipt for them.

(4) Provide for the recording of Supreme Court proceedings as the Court directs.

(5) Care for and maintain custody of all records, seals, books, and papers pertaining to the clerk's office and filed or deposited there.

(6) After an appeal has been decided by the Court, return the original record as provided in MCR 7.311(B).

(7) Collect the following fees, which may be taxed as costs when costs are allowed by the Court:

(a) $ 250 for an application for leave to appeal;

(b) $ 250 for an original proceeding;

(c) $150 for a motion for immediate consideration or a motion to expedite appeal, except that a prosecuting attorney is exempt from paying a fee under this subdivision in an appeal arising out of a criminal proceeding, if the defendant is represented by a court-appointed lawyer;

(d) $75 for all other motions;

(e) 50¢ per page for a certified copy of a paper, from a public record;

(f) $5 for certified docket entries;

(g) $1 for certification of a copy presented to the clerk;

(h) 50¢ per page for a copy of an opinion; however, one copy must be given without charge to the attorney for each party in the case.

A person who is unable to pay a filing fee may ask the Court to waive the fee by filing a motion and an affidavit disclosing the reason for that inability.

[Effective March 1, 1985; amended effective January 1, 1990; June 1, 1998; October 3, 2000.]

1985 Staff Comment

MCR 7.319 is substantially the same as GCR 1963, 902.

The fee for a copy of an opinion is changed to 50¢ per page.

Staff Comment to 1998 Amendment

The March 24, 1998 [effective June 1, 1998], amendment of MCR 7.319(B)(7) changes the amount of the filing fees in the Supreme Court to be consistent with those applicable to the

Court of Appeals under MCL 600.321; MSA 27A.321, as amended by 1997 PA 182.

Staff Comment to 2000 Amendment

The October 3, 2000, amendment of MCR 7.319(B)(7) exempts a prosecuting attorney from paying a fee when filing a motion for immediate consideration or a motion to expedite in an appeal arising out of a criminal proceeding, if the defendant is represented by a court-appointed lawyer.

RULE 7.320 DEPUTY SUPREME COURT CLERKS

The Supreme Court may appoint deputy Supreme Court clerks. A deputy clerk shall carry out the duties assigned by the clerk and perform the duties of the clerk if the clerk is absent or unable to act.

[Effective March 1, 1985.]

1985 Staff Comment

MCR 7.320 is substantially the same as GCR 1963, 903.

RULE 7.321 REPORTER OF DECISIONS

The Supreme Court will appoint a reporter. The reporter shall:

(1) prepare the decisions, including dissenting opinions, of the Supreme Court for publication in volumes of not less than 700 nor more than 750 pages;

(2) write a brief statement of the facts of each case and headnotes containing the points made;

(3) publish each opinion in advance sheets as soon as practicable but not later than 2 months after it is issued; and

(4) publish bound volumes within 9 months after the last opinion included in it is issued.

The reasons for denying leave to appeal, required by Const 1963, art 6, § 6 and filed in the clerk's office, are not to be published, and are not to be regarded as precedent.

[Effective March 1, 1985.]

1985 Staff Comment

MCR 7.321 is substantially the same as GCR 1963, 904.

RULE 7.322 SUPREME COURT CRIER

The Supreme Court crier shall

(1) have charge of the Supreme Court room and the rooms assigned to the Supreme Court justices;

(2) have the power to serve an order, process, or writ issued by the Supreme Court; collect the fee for that service allowed by law to sheriffs; and deposit monthly with the State Treasurer all the fees collected, securing a receipt for them.

[Effective March 1, 1985.]

1985 Staff Comment

MCR 7.322 is substantially the same as GCR 1963, 905.

RULE 7.323 SELECTION OF CHIEF JUSTICE

At the first meeting of the Supreme Court in each odd-numbered year, the justices shall select by majority vote one among them to be Chief Justice.

[Effective March 1, 1985.]

1985 Staff Comment

MCR 7.323 is substantially the same as GCR 1963, 900.

CHAPTER 8.   ADMINISTRATIVE RULES OF COURT

Effective March 1, 1985

[For Table of Rules, see page 1 et seq.]

SUBCHAPTER 8.100   GENERAL ADMINISTRATIVE ORDERS

RULE 8.101   APPLICABILITY OF ADMINISTRATIVE RULES

The administrative rules of subchapter 8.100 apply to all courts established by the constitution and laws of Michigan, unless a rule otherwise provides.

[Effective March 1, 1985.]

1985 Staff Comment

MCR 8.101 is substantially the same as GCR 1963, 934.

RULE 8.103   STATE COURT ADMINISTRATOR

The state court administrator, under the Supreme Court's supervision and direction, shall:

(1) supervise and examine the administrative methods and systems employed in the offices of the courts, including the offices of the clerks and other officers, and make recommendations to the Supreme Court for the improvement of the administration of the courts;

(2) examine the status of court calendars, determine the need for assistance to a court, and report to the Supreme Court;

(3) on receipt of the monthly reports as provided in MCR 8.110(C)(5), investigate each case in an effort to determine the reason for delays, recommend actions to eliminate delays, and recommend further actions to expedite process to insure speedy trials of criminal cases;

(4) recommend to the Supreme Court the assignment of judges where courts are in need of assistance and carry out the direction of the Supreme Court as to the assignment of judges;

(5) collect and compile statistical and other data, make reports of the business transacted by the courts, and transmit the reports to the Supreme Court so that the statistics and other data may be used in taking proper action in the administration of justice;

(6) prepare and submit budget estimates of state appropriations necessary for the maintenance and operation of the judicial system;

(7) obtain reports from courts, and the judges, clerks, and other officers of the courts, in accordance with rules adopted by the Supreme Court on cases and other judicial business conducted or pending in the courts, and report on them to the Supreme Court;

(8) recommend to the Supreme Court policies for the improvement of the judicial system;

(9) approve and publish forms as required by these rules, and such other recommended forms as the administrator deems advisable;

(10) certify the adequacy of recording devices to be used for making records of different types of proceedings in trial courts pursuant to these rules and applicable statutes and publish a list of certified recording devices and the proceedings for which they are certified for use; and

(11) attend to other matters assigned by the Supreme Court.

[Effective March 1, 1985; amended effective October 1, 1989; June 1, 1991; April 1, 1998.]

1985 Staff Comment

MCR 8.103 is comparable to GCR 1963, 901.1.

New item (8) in the list of duties is based on DCR 4005.11 and PCR 901.2. Throughout the rules, the forms previously included in the General Court Rules have been deleted. The state court administrator is directed to approve forms.

Staff Comment to 1989 Amendment

MCR 8.103 has been amended [effective October 1, 1989] by the addition of a new item (3) incorporating a provision previously located in the former speedy trial rule, MCR 6.109(D). Former items (3)–(9) have been redesignated (4)–(10), but are otherwise unchanged.

Staff Comment to 1991 Amendment

The amendments to MCR 8.103 and 8.109 effective June 1, 1991, authorize the state court administrator to approve equipment for video or audio recording of trial court proceedings and require courts to use only approved equipment if such recordings are used to make the official record of proceedings.

Staff Comment to 1998 Amendment

The March 24, 1998, amendments [effective April 1, 1998] of 2.109, 2.111, 2.112, 2.119, 8.103, 8.106, 8.110, 8.111, 9.114, and 9.203, make technical changes necessary in light of statutory amendments and correct cross-references.

The amendments of MCR 2.109 and 2.112 relate to amendments of MCR 600.2912d, 600.2912e; MSA 27A.2912(d), 27A.2912(e), by 1993 PA 78.

The amendments of MCR 2.111 and 2.119 are based on statutes amended by 1996 PA 388. The change in MCR 2.111(B)(2) applies to actions filed on or after January 1, 1998, the effective date of the statute increasing the jurisdictional limit of the district court.

The amendment of MCR 8.106 corrects a statutory reference in light of 1993 PA 189.

The remaining amendments make changes in cross-references necessitated by earlier amendments. Some published versions of the rules already include several of these corrections.

RULE 8.104   JUDICIAL MEETINGS

(A) Meetings to Be Called by State Court Administrator. The state court administrator, under the Supreme Court's supervision and direction, may call

(1) an annual statewide meeting of the circuit, recorder's, and Court of Appeals judges;

(2) an annual statewide meeting of the probate judges;

(3) an annual statewide meeting of the district judges; and

(4) additional statewide or regional meetings of judges as may be desirable.

(B) Presiding Officer. The Chief Justice of the Supreme Court or another person designated by the Chief Justice shall preside at judicial meetings called by the state court administrator.

(C) Secretary. The state court administrator or deputy administrator acts as secretary at judicial meetings called by the state court administrator.

(D) Purposes. At the meetings, the judges are to

(1) study the organization, rules, methods of procedure, and practice of the judicial system in general;

(2) study the problems of administration confronting the courts and judicial system in general; and

(3) make recommendations for

(a) modifying or ameliorating existing conditions,

(b) harmonizing and improving laws, and

(c) amending the rules and statutes relating to practice and procedure.

[Effective March 1, 1985.]

1985 Staff Comment

MCR 8.104 is based on GCR 1963, 901.2.

In subrule (A)(1) a provision is added for the statewide annual meeting of the district judges.

Subrules (B) and (C) designate the presiding officer and secretary of the judicial meetings.

RULE 8.105   GENERAL DUTIES OF CLERKS

(A) Office Hours. The office of the clerk of every court of record must be open, and the clerk or deputy clerk must be in attendance, during business hours on all days except Saturdays, Sundays, and legal holidays, and at other times that the court is in session.

(B) Court Records and Reporting Duties. The clerk of every circuit court shall maintain court records and make reports as prescribed by MCR 8.119.

(C) Notice of Judgments, Orders, and Opinions. Notice of a judgment, final order, written opinion or findings filed or entered in a civil action in a court of record must be given forthwith in writing by the court clerk to the attorneys of record in the case, in the manner provided in MCR 2.107.

(D) Filing of Assurance of Discontinuance Under MCL 445.870; MSA 19.416(120). The clerk of every judicial circuit shall, without charge, receive and file an assurance of discontinuance accepted by the Attorney General under MCL 445.870; MSA 19.416(120).

[Effective March 1, 1985; amended effective October 1, 1988; July 1, 1989; January 1, 1992; November 30, 1999.]

1985 Staff Comment

MCR 8.105 corresponds to GCR 1963, 907.

The provisions of GCR 1963, 907.3 and 907.4 are placed in MCR 8.106 with the other provisions covering money paid into court.

The language of subrule (A) modifies GCR 1963, 907(1) by eliminating the requirement that the clerk be present during business hours on Saturday, except when the court is in session.

The [March 1, 1985] amendment of MCR 8.105(D) adds additional language, based on GCR 502.2, requiring the clerk to retain the original of certain judgments and orders.

Subrule (E) omits the reference found in GCR 1963, 907(7) to MCL 445.801 et seq., because that statute has been repealed.

GCR 1963, 907(6) is omitted. It required the clerk to give notice to federal district courts when the circuit court had disbarred, suspended, or reinstated an attorney.

Staff Comment to 1989 Amendment

The May 3, 1989 amendments to MCR 4.101(B) and (F), 4.102(B) and 8.105(G) [effective July 1, 1989], suggested by the Task Force on Reporting Traffic–Related Offenses, are intended to implement recent statutory changes.

Staff Comment to 1991 Amendment

The 1991 amendment added a subrule to govern the sealing of records. It was based on rules in effect in other jurisdictions, notably New York and Texas. The subrule recognizes the presumption that court records are to be open to the general public, and that the sealing of court records is a matter of public concern. The intent of the rule is to insure consistency and confidence in the way in which such matters are handled.

Staff Comment to 1999 Amendment

The amendments of MCR 2.113, 5.113, 5.901, 7.210, 8.105, 8.110, 8.116, 8.203, 8.205, and 8.302 [effective November 30, 1999] and the addition of MCR 2.518 and 8.119 [effective November 30, 1999] are to accommodate statewide records standards applicable to all courts and all clerks of the courts as developed and recommended by the Michigan Trial Court Case File Management Standards Committee.

RULE 8.106   MONEY PAID INTO COURT

(A) When Court Order Required. Except as otherwise provided by law or when the money is in the form of cash bonds, the clerk may not perform services in handling money under MCL 600.2529(1)(f); MSA 27A.2529(1)(f) without a signed order of the court.

(B) Disposition of Interest Earned. If the clerk deposits money in an interest-bearing account, the clerk retains as a fee one-tenth of the interest earned, but not more than $100 each year or part of the year. The fee must be deposited in the county general fund, as required by law. The balance of the interest earned and the principal must be disbursed to the persons entitled to the balance.

(C) Accounts; Records. The accounts of the clerk with the banks in which the money is directed to be deposited must be kept in a single trust fund, with the designation of the rights in the fund appearing on the court's records.

(D) Orders to Pay Out Funds. Orders on the banks for the payment of money out of court are made payable to the order of the person entitled to the money or of that person's duly authorized attorney, and must specify in what action or on what account the money is to be paid out, and the time when the judgment or order authorizing the payment was made.

(E) NSF Checks. A court may assess costs for reasonable expenses incurred for checks returned to the court due to nonsufficient funds.

[Effective March 1, 1985; amended effective October 18, 1990; April 1, 1998.]

1985 Staff Comment

MCR 8.106 includes the provisions of GCR 1963, 533 and 907(3) and (4).

Staff Comment to 1990 Amendment

The [October 18,] 1990 amendment added MCR 8.106(E), which permits a court to assess costs when checks are returned because of nonsufficient funds.

Staff Comment to 1998 Amendment

The March 24, 1998, amendments [effective April 1, 1998] of 2.109, 2.111, 2.112, 2.119, 8.103, 8.106, 8.110, 8.111, 9.114, and 9.203, make technical changes necessary in light of statutory amendments and correct cross-references.

The amendments of MCR 2.109 and 2.112 relate to amendments of MCR 600.2912d, 600.2912e; MSA 27A.2912(d), 27A.2912(e), by 1993 PA 78.

The amendments of MCR 2.111 and 2.119 are based on statutes amended by 1996 PA 388. The change in MCR 2.111(B)(2) applies to actions filed on or after January 1, 1998, the effective date of the statute increasing the jurisdictional limit of the district court.

The amendment of MCR 8.106 corrects a statutory reference in light of 1993 PA 189.

The remaining amendments make changes in cross-references necessitated by earlier amendments. Some published versions of the rules already include several of these corrections.

RULE 8.107   STATEMENT BY TRIAL JUDGE AS TO MATTERS UNDECIDED

Every trial judge shall, on the first business day of January, May, and September of each year, file with the state court administrator a certified statement in the form prescribed by the state court administrator, containing full information on any matter submitted to the judge for decision more than 4 months earlier which remains undecided. The judge shall also set forth in the statement the reason a matter remains undecided. For the purpose of this rule the time of submission is the time the last argument or presentation in the matter was made or the expiration of the time allowed for filing the last brief, as the case may be. If the judge has no cases to report, the word "none" on a signed report is required.

[Effective March 1, 1985.]

1985 Staff Comment

MCR 8.107 is based on GCR 1963, 910. The form of the report is deleted from the rule and will be prescribed by the state court administrator.

RULE 8.108   COURT REPORTERS AND RECORDERS

(A) Scope of Rule. This rule prescribes the duties of court reporters and recorders, the procedure for certifying them, the effect of noncertification, objections to certification, and display requirements.

(B) Attendance at Court; Taking Testimony.*

(1) The court reporter or recorder shall attend the court sessions under the direction of the court and take a verbatim record of the following:

(a) the voir dire of prospective jurors;

(b) the testimony;

(c) the charge to the jury;

(d) in a jury trial, the opening statements and final arguments;

(e) the reasons given by the court for granting or refusing any motion made by a party during the course of a trial; and

(f) opinions and orders dictated by the court and other matters as may be prescribed by the court.

This subrule does not apply to actions tried in the small claims division of the district court or in the municipal courts. In the probate court proceedings, the reporter or recorder shall take a verbatim record of proceedings as required by law and chapter 5 of these rules.

(2) The court reporter or recorder who begins to record a case shall take the record of the entire case unless he or she shows good cause for failure to do so or is otherwise excused by the court.

(C) Records Kept. The court reporter or recorder who takes the testimony on the trial or the hearing of any case shall prefix the record of the testimony of each witness with the full name of the witness and the date and time the testimony was taken. At the conclusion of the trial of the case the reporter or recorder shall secure all of the records and properly entitle them on the outside, and shall safely keep them in his or her office.

(D) Transfer of Records; Inspection. If the court reporter or recorder dies, resigns, is removed from office, or leaves the state, his or her records in each case must be transferred to the clerk of the court in which the case was tried. The clerk shall safely keep the records subject to the direction of the court. The records are a part of the record of each case and are subject to inspection in the same manner as other records. On order of the court, a transcript may be made from the records and filed as a part of the record in the case.

(E) Furnishing Transcript. The court reporter or recorder shall furnish without delay, in legible English, a transcript of the records taken by him or her (or any part thereof) to any party on request. The reporter or recorder is entitled to receive the compensation prescribed in the statute on fees from the person who makes the request.

(F) Filing Transcript.

(1) On order of the trial court, the court reporter or recorder shall make and file in the clerk's office a transcript of his or her records, in legible English, of any civil or criminal case (or any part thereof) without expense to either party; the transcript is a part of the records in the case.

(2) Except when otherwise provided by contract, the court reporter or recorder shall receive from the appropriate governmental unit the compensation specified in the statute on fees for a transcript ordered by a court.

(G) Certification.

(1) *Certification Requirement.*

(a) Except as provided in this subrule, only reporters or recorders certified pursuant to this subrule may record or prepare transcripts of proceedings held in Michigan courts or of depositions taken in Michigan pursuant to these rules. This rule applies to the preparation of transcripts of videotaped courtroom proceedings or videotaped or audiotaped depositions, but not to the recording of such proceedings or depositions by means of videotaping. A recorder holding a CEO certification under subrule (G)(7)(b) may record proceedings but may not prepare transcripts.

(b) Proceedings held pursuant to MCR 6.102 or 6.104 need not be recorded by persons certified under this rule; however, transcripts of such proceedings must be prepared by court reporters or recorders certified pursuant to this rule.

(c) An indigent party who is represented by a nonprofit legal aid program providing free civil legal services to the indigent may use persons who are not certified pursuant to this rule to transcribe and file depositions taken by videotaping or audiotaping. Such depositions shall be otherwise prepared and certified in accordance with this rule.

(d) Any person who acts in the capacity of a court reporter or recorder shall not maintain an action in the courts of this state for the collection of compensation for the performance of an act for which certification is required by this rule without alleging and proving that the person was certified under this rule at the time of the performance of the act. "Person" refers to both individuals and the entity or entities for which a court reporter or recorder performs services.

(e) Any other court rule notwithstanding, an objection to the status of a court reporter's or recorder's certification or lack thereof must be placed on the record at the outset of the court proceeding or deposition or that objection is waived. If the objection is waived, the use of transcripts of the court proceeding or deposition for any purpose provided in these rules shall be allowed.

(f) Prior to the beginning of any deposition taken under these rules, the court reporter or recorder must display to all counsel initially present, and to each other person attending the deposition who is not represented by counsel, proof that the reporter or recorder has been certified as required by this rule. Proof of such certification, by certification number, shall also be displayed on the title page and certificate page of each court and deposition transcript and on the stationery and business cards, if any, of each court reporter or recorder required to be certified by this rule.

(2) *Court Reporting and Recording Board of Review.*

(a) The Supreme Court shall appoint a Court Reporting and Recording Board of Review, composed of

(i) a Court of Appeals judge, to be the chairperson;

(ii) a circuit or recorder's judge;

(iii) a probate judge;

(iv) a district judge;

(v) a court reporter who is an employee of a Michigan court;

(vi) a court recorder who is an employee of a Michigan court;

(vii) a court reporter who is not an employee of a Michigan court;

(viii) a court recorder who is not an employee of a Michigan court; and,

(ix) an attorney.

(b) Appointments to the board shall be for terms of 4 years. A board member may be reappointed to a new term. Initial appointments may be of different lengths so that no more than 3 terms expire in the same year. The Supreme Court may remove a member at any time.

(c) If a position on the board becomes vacant because of death, resignation, or removal, or because a member is no longer employed in the capacity in which he or she was appointed, the board shall notify the Supreme Court Clerk and the Court shall appoint a successor to serve the remainder of the term.

(d) The state court administrator shall assign a staff person to serve as board secretary.

(3) *Certification by Testing.*

(a) At least twice each year the board shall administer an examination testing knowledge and speed, and, as to a recorder, familiarity with basic logging techniques and minor repair and maintenance procedures. The board shall determine the passing score.

(b) In order to be eligible for registration for an examination, an applicant must

(i) be at least 18 years of age,

(ii) be a high school graduate, and

(iii) not have been under sentence for a felony for a period of two years.

In addition, an applicant for the certified shorthand reporter examination must have satisfactorily completed an approved, accredited, or recognized course of study in court reporting.

(c) The registration fee is $60.

(4) *Reciprocal Certification.* A reporter or recorder certified in another state may apply to the board for certification based on the certification already obtained.

(5) *Temporary Certification.* A new reporter or recorder may receive one temporary certification to enable him or her to work until the results of the next test are released. If the person does not take the test, the temporary certification may not be extended unless good cause is shown. If the person takes the test and fails, the board may extend the temporary certification.

(6) *Renewal, Review, and Revocation of Certification.*

(a) Certifications under this rule must be renewed annually. The fee for renewal is $30. Renewal applications must be filed by August 1. A renewal application filed after that date must be accompanied by an additional late fee of $30. The board may require certified reporters and recorders to submit, as a condition of renewal, such information as the board reasonably deems necessary to determine that the reporter or recorder has used his or her reporting or recording skills during the preceding year.

(b) The board must review the certification of a reporter or recorder who has not used his or her skills in the preceding year, and shall determine whether the certification of such a reporter or recorder may be renewed without the necessity of a certification test.

(c) The board may review the certification of a reporter or recorder and may impose sanctions, including revoking the certification, for good cause after a hearing before the board.

(7) *Designations.* The board shall assign an identification number to each person certified. A court reporter or recorder must place the identification number assigned on his or her communications with the courts, including certificates, motions, affidavits, and transcripts. The board will use the following certification designations:

(a) certified electronic recorder (CER);

(b) certified electronic operator (CEO);

(c) certified shorthand reporter (CSR);

(d) certified stenomask reporter (CSMR).

The designations are to be used only by reporters or recorders certified by the board. A reporter or recorder may be given more than one designation by passing different tests.

[Effective March 1, 1985; amended effective April 1, 1987; April 1, 1990; June 1, 1991; January 28, 1997; amended effective as to depositions taken on or after January 1, 1998.]

* Publisher's Note: See Administrative Order 1990–7, Videotape Record of Court Proceedings, infra, which authorizes an exception to this rule.

1985 Staff Comment

MCR 8.108 is comparable to GCR 1963, 915.

In subrule (B) language is added excepting actions tried in the small claims division of the district court and in the municipal courts, and providing that probate court proceedings must be recorded as provided by law and the rules in chapter 5. See MCL 600.859; MSA 27A.859.

Subrule (D) modifies GCR 1963, 915.4 by providing that the transfer of a court reporter's records in certain circumstances is to the court clerk, rather than the county clerk.

The temporary provisions for "grandfather" certification of reporters and recorders with more than one year of experience on June 1, 1979, are omitted. See GCR 1963, 915.7(c).

In subrule (G)(7) language from Administrative Order 1977–3 is incorporated, requiring court reporters and recorders to use the identification number assigned by the Court Reporting and Recording Board of Review.

Staff Comment to 1987 Amendment

The January 27, 1987, amendments to MCR 8.108(G) are effective April 1, 1987. The principal changes are as follows:

1. Specifying that only certified reporters and recorders may record and file transcripts of proceedings in Michigan courts. Subrule (G)(1).

2. Expanding the membership of the Board of Review from 5 to 9 persons. Subrule (G)(2)(a).

3. Providing a fixed term for board members and establishing procedures for filling vacancies. Subrule (G)(2)(b) and (c).

4. Modifying the provisions regarding testing by permitting administration of more than 2 tests per year; setting minimum educational and other qualifications for persons seeking to register for a test; and raising the registration fee from $25 to $50. Subrule (G)(3).

5. Establishing a $20 fee for the annual renewal of a certification, and permitting the board to require submission of certain information as a condition of renewal. Subrule (G)(6)(a).

6. Authorizing the board to impose sanctions other than revocation of certification. Subrule (G)(6)(c).

7. Adding a new type of certification—certified electronic operator. Subrule (G)(7)(b). Persons with that certification may record proceedings but may not prepare or file transcripts. Subrule (G)(1).

Staff Comment to 1990 Amendment

The March 1, 1990, amendment of MCR 8.108, effective April 1, 1990, makes two changes. First, new subrule (F)(1)(b) is added, creating an exception to the requirement that only certified reporters or recorders may record proceedings in Michigan courts. The certification requirement will not apply to proceedings in district court under MCR 6.102 and 6.104. It is anticipated that many such proceedings will be conducted at locations other than the normal court facilities and during non-business hours. Requiring the presence of a certified reporter or recorder at all such proceedings might be difficult in some jurisdictions. However, any transcripts of such proceedings must be prepared by a certified reporter or recorder.

Second, the fee for renewal of the certification is raised from $20 to $25.

Another proposal published for comment in 1989, which would extend the certification requirement to persons who record and file depositions, remains under consideration. See 68 Michigan Bar Journal, 567 (June 1989).

Staff Comment to 1991 Amendment

MCR 8.108(G) is amended to change the fees for court reporter and recorder certification and renewal to $60 and $30, respectively, effective June 1, 1991.

Staff Comment to 1997 Amendment

The January 28, 1997, amendment of MCR 8.108(G)(3) eliminates the requirement of Michigan residency for eligibility to take the court reporter/recorder certification tests. This change is related to the amendment of MCR 8.108(G)(1), effective January 1, 1998, to provide that only certified reporters and recorders may record and prepare transcripts of depositions taken in Michigan pursuant to the Michigan Court Rules. The amendment also establishes a penalty for late filing of certification renewal applications.

Staff Comment to 1998 Amendment

The January 28, 1997, amendment of MCR 8.108(G)(1) [effective as to depositions taken on or after January 1, 1998] provides that only reporters and recorders certified by the Court Reporting and Recording Board of Review may record and prepare transcripts of depositions taken in Michigan pursuant to the Michigan Court Rules. The requirement does not apply to the videotaping of depositions, however.

RULE 8.109　MECHANICAL RECORDING OF COURT PROCEEDINGS

(A) Official Record. If a trial court uses audio or video recording devices for making the record of court proceedings, it shall use only recording devices approved by the state court administrator pursuant to MCR 8.103(10). Except where such a requirement was previously imposed by statute, this provision shall apply only to recording devices purchased after the effective date of this subrule.

(B) Other Recordings. On motion of an attorney or of a party appearing on his or her own behalf, a court may permit audio recording of a part or all of a proceeding and may permit photographic recording of visual exhibits. The court may regulate the manner of audio or photographic recording so that it does not disrupt the proceeding. An audio or photographic recording made under this rule may be used solely to assist in the prosecution or defense during the proceeding recorded; it may not be used publicly.

[Effective March 1, 1985; amended effective June 1, 1991.]

1985 Staff Comment

MCR 8.109 is substantially the same as GCR 1963, 917.

Staff Comment to 1991 Amendment

The amendments to MCR 8.103 and 8.109 effective June 1, 1991, authorize the state court administrator to approve equipment for video or audio recording of trial court proceedings and require courts to use only approved equipment if such recordings are used to make the official record of proceedings.

RULE 8.110　CHIEF JUDGE RULE

(A) Applicability. This rule applies to all trial courts: i.e., the judicial circuits of the circuit court, the districts of the district court, the probate court in each county or a probate district established by law, and the municipal courts.

(B) Chief Judge, Chief Judge Pro Tempore, and Presiding Judges of Divisions.

(1) The Supreme Court shall select a judge of each trial court to serve as chief judge. No later than October 1 of each odd-numbered year, each trial court with two or more judges may submit the names of no fewer than two judges whom the judges of that court recommend for selection as chief judge.

(2) Unless a chief judge pro tempore or presiding judge is named by the Supreme Court, the chief judge shall select a chief judge pro tempore and a presiding judge of any division of the trial court. The chief judge pro tempore and any presiding judges shall fulfill such functions as the chief judge assigns.

(3) The chief judge, chief judge pro tempore, and any presiding judges shall serve a two-year term beginning on January 1 of each even-numbered year, provided that the chief judge serves at the pleasure of the Supreme Court and the chief judge pro tempore and any presiding judges serve at the pleasure of the chief judge.

(4) Where exceptional circumstances exist, the Supreme Court may appoint a judge of another court to serve as chief judge of a trial court.

(C) Duties and Powers of Chief Judge.

(1) A chief judge shall act in conformity with the Michigan Court Rules, administrative orders of the Supreme Court, and local court rules, and should freely solicit the advice and suggestions of the other judges of his or her bench and geographic jurisdiction. If a local court management council has adopted the by-laws described in AO 1997–6 the chief judge shall exercise the authority and responsibilities under this rule in conformity with the provisions of AO 1997–6.

(2) As the presiding officer of the court, a chief judge shall:

(a) call and preside over meetings of the court;

(b) appoint committees of the court;

(c) initiate policies concerning the court's internal operations and its position on external matters affecting the court;

(d) meet regularly with all chief judges whose courts are wholly or partially within the same county;

(e) represent the court in its relations with the Supreme Court, other courts, other agencies of government, the bar, the general public, and the news media, and in ceremonial functions; and

(f) counsel and assist other judges in the performance of their responsibilities.

(3) As director of the administration of the court, a chief judge shall have administrative superintending

power and control over the judges of the court and all court personnel with authority and responsibility to:

(a) supervise caseload management and monitor disposition of the judicial work of the court;

(b) direct the apportionment and assignment of the business of the court, subject to the provisions of MCR 8.111;

(c) determine the hours of the court and the judges; coordinate and determine the number of judges and court personnel required to be present at any one time to perform necessary judicial and administrative work of the court, and require their presence to perform that work;

(d) supervise the performance of all court personnel, with authority to hire, discipline, or discharge such personnel, with the exception of a judge's secretary and law clerk, if any;

(e) coordinate judicial and personnel vacations and absences, subject to the provisions of subrule (D);

(f) supervise court finances, including financial planning, the preparation and presentation of budgets, and financial reporting;

(g) request assignments of visiting judges and direct the assignment of matters to the visiting judges;

(h) effect compliance by the court with all applicable court rules and provisions of the law; and

(i) perform any act or duty or enter any order necessarily incidental to carrying out the purposes of this rule.

(4) If a judge does not timely dispose of his or her assigned judicial work or fails or refuses to comply with an order or directive from the chief judge made under this rule, the chief judge shall report the facts to the state court administrator who will, under the Supreme Court's direction, initiate whatever corrective action is necessary.

(5) The chief judge of the court in which criminal proceedings are pending shall have filed with the state court administrator a monthly report setting forth the reasons for delay in the proceedings:

(a) in felony cases in which there has been a delay of 28 days between the hearing on the preliminary examination or the date of the waiver of the preliminary examination and the arraignment on the information or indictment;

(b) in felony cases in which there has been a delay of 6 months between the date of the arraignment on the information or indictment and the beginning of trial;

(c) in misdemeanor cases in which there has been a delay of 6 months between the date of the arraignment on the warrant and complaint and the beginning of the trial;

(d) in felony cases in which a defendant is incarcerated longer than 6 months and in misdemeanor cases in which a defendant is incarcerated longer than 28 days.

(6) A chief judge may delegate administrative duties to a trial court administrator or others.

(7) Where a court rule or statute does not already require it, the chief judge may, by administrative order, direct the clerk of the court to provide litigants and attorneys with copies of forms approved by the state court administrator. In addition, except when a court rule or statute specifies that the court or clerk of the court must provide certain forms without charge, the administrative order may allow the clerk to provide the forms at the cost of reproduction to the clerk.

(D) Court Hours; Court Holidays; Judicial Absences.

(1) *Court Hours.* The chief judge shall enter an administrative order under MCR 8.112(B) establishing the court's hours.

(2) *Court Holidays; Local Modification.*

(a) The following holidays are to be observed by all state courts, except those courts which have adopted modifying administrative orders pursuant to MCR 8.112(B):

New Year's Day, January 1;

Martin Luther King, Jr., Day, the third Monday in January in conjunction with the federal holiday;

Presidents' Day, the third Monday in February;

Memorial Day, the last Monday in May;

Independence Day, July 4;

Labor Day, the first Monday in September;

Veterans' Day, November 11;

Thanksgiving Day, the fourth Thursday in November;

Friday after Thanksgiving;

Christmas Eve, December 24;

Christmas Day, December 25; and

New Year's Eve, December 31.

(b) When New Year's Day, Independence Day, Veterans' Day, or Christmas Day falls on Saturday, the preceding Friday shall be a holiday. When New Year's Day, Independence Day, Veterans' Day, or Christmas Day falls on Sunday, the following Monday shall be a holiday. When Christmas Eve or New Year's Eve falls on Friday, the preceding Thursday shall be a holiday. When Christmas Eve or New Year's Eve falls on Saturday or Sunday, the preceding Friday shall be a holiday.

(c) Courts are encouraged to promulgate a modifying administrative order if appropriate to accommodate or achieve uniformity with the holiday practices of local governmental units regarding local public employees.

(d) With the prior approval of the chief judge, a judge may continue a trial in progress or dispose of judicial matters on any of the listed holidays if he or she finds it to be necessary.

(e) Any action taken by a court on February 12, Lincoln's birthday, or on the second Monday in October, Columbus Day, shall be valid.

(3) *Judicial Vacation Standard.* A judge is expected to take an annual vacation leave of 20 days with the approval of the chief judge to ensure docket coordination and coverage. A judge may take an additional 10 days of annual vacation leave with the approval of the chief judge. A maximum of 30 days of annual vacation unused due to workload constraints may be carried from one calendar year into the first quarter of the next calendar year and used during that quarter, if approved by the chief judge. Vacation days do not include:

(a) attendance at Michigan judicial conferences;

(b) attendance, with the chief judge's approval, at educational meetings or seminars;

(c) attendance, with the chief judge's approval, at meetings of judicial committees or committees substantially related to judicial administration of justice;

(d) absence due to illness; or

(e) administrative leave, with the chief judge's approval.

(4) *Judicial Education Leave Standard.* A judge is expected to take judicial education leave of 2 weeks every 3 years to participate in continuing legal education and training at Michigan judicial training programs and nationally recognized judicial education programs, including graduate and refresher courses. Judicial education leave does not include judicial conferences for which attendance is required. The use of judicial education leave approved by the chief judge does not affect a judge's annual leave.

(5) *Judicial Professional Leave Standard.* Judges are encouraged, as part of their regular judicial responsibilities, to participate in professional meetings and conferences that advance the administration of justice or the public's understanding of the judicial system; to serve on commissions and committees of state and national organizations that contribute to the improvement of the law or that advance the interests of the judicial system; and to serve on Supreme Court-appointed or in-house assignments or committees. The use of judicial professional leave approved by the chief judge does not affect a judge's annual leave or education leave.

(6) *Approval of Judicial Absences.* A judge may not be absent from the court without the chief judge's prior approval, except for personal illness. In making the decision on a request to approve a vacation or other absence, the chief judge shall consider, among other factors, the pending caseload of the judge involved. The chief judge shall withhold approval of vacation, judicial education, or judicial professional leave that conforms to these standards only if withholding approval is necessary to ensure the orderly conduct of judicial business. The chief judge shall maintain records of absences to be available at the request of the Supreme Court.

[Effective March 1, 1985; amended effective October 1, 1988; October 1, 1989; January 8, 1993; September 13, 1995; August 18, 1997; April 1, 1998; March 1, 1999; November 30, 1999.]

1985 Staff Comment

MCR 8.110 is based on GCR 1963, 925.

Subrule (F)(2) specifies court holidays, subject to the option of local courts to modify them by local administrative order. The list was formerly found in Administrative Order 1981–1.

The [March 1, 1985] amendment of MCR 8.110(F)(2)(a) changes the designation of Martin Luther King, Jr., Day to conform to the date set by federal statute.

In subrules (G)(1)(a) and (H)(2), the temporary provisions regarding the terms of office of the executive chief judge and the joint executive committee of the third circuit and recorder's courts have been deleted.

Staff Comment to 1988 Amendment

The 1988 amendment allows local flexibility in meeting the needs of pro per litigants and others for approved forms.

Staff Comment to 1989 Amendment

MCR 8.110 has been amended [effective October 1, 1989] by the addition of a new subrule (E)(5) incorporating a provision previously located in the former speedy trial rule, MCR 6.109(C). Former subrules (E)(5) and (6) have been redesignated (E)(6) and (7), but are otherwise unchanged.

Staff Comment to 1993 Amendment

The January 8, 1993, amendment to MCR 8.110(F) makes Christmas Eve and New Year's Eve holidays regardless of the day of the week on which they fall, and specifies when the holidays are to be observed when those days fall on Friday, Saturday, or Sunday.

Staff Comment to 1995 Amendment

In 1995, MCR 7.201(A) was amended to provide that the Supreme Court would appoint the Chief Judge of the Court of Appeals. In 1995, the Supreme Court also consolidated MCR 8.110(B), (C), and (D) into a new MCR 8.110(B), which likewise provided that the chief judges of the trial courts would be appointed by the Supreme Court. MCR 8.110(G) and (H) were repealed. MCR 8.110 was also amended to require chief judges to meet regularly with other chief judges whose courts are wholly or partially in the same county. As indicated in its 1995 order, the Supreme Court took these steps "to facilitate the Court's exercise of its constitutional responsibility to administer and superintend the courts of this state" and to "enhance the Supreme

Court's ability to implement sound policies statewide, and assure a greater degree of responsiveness to the leadership that the constitution requires this Court to exercise."

Staff Comment to 1998 Amendment

The March 24, 1998, amendments [effective April 1, 1998] of 2.109, 2.111, 2.112, 2.119, 8.103, 8.106, 8.110, 8.111, 9.114, and 9.203, make technical changes necessary in light of statutory amendments and correct cross-references.

The amendments of MCR 2.109 and 2.112 relate to amendments of MCR 600.2912d, 600.2912e; MSA 27A.2912(d), 27A.2912(e), by 1993 PA 78.

The amendments of MCR 2.111 and 2.119 are based on statutes amended by 1996 PA 388. The change in MCR 2.111(B)(2) applies to actions filed on or after January 1, 1998, the effective date of the statute increasing the jurisdictional limit of the district court.

The amendment of MCR 8.106 corrects a statutory reference in light of 1993 PA 189.

The remaining amendments make changes in cross-references necessitated by earlier amendments. Some published versions of the rules already include several of these corrections.

Staff Comment to March 1999 Amendment

The 1999 amendment to MCR 8.110(A) [effective March 1, 1999] eliminates the reference to the Recorder's Court, which was merged with the Third Circuit Court in Wayne County by 1996 Public Act 374, effective October 1, 1997.

In addition, MCR 8.110(D) was amended, effective March 1, 1999, by renumbering MCR 8.110(D)(4) as MCR 8.110(D)(6), amending MCR 8.110(D)(3), and adding new subrules MCR 8.110(D)(4) & (5) to provide standards for judicial leave and for the responsibilities of chief judges for approval of judicial leave.

Staff Comment to November 1999 Amendment

The amendments of MCR 2.113, 5.113, 5.901, 7.210, 8.105, 8.110, 8.116, 8.203, 8.205, and 8.302 [effective November 30, 1999] and the addition of MCR 2.518 and 8.119 [effective November 30, 1999] are to accommodate statewide records standards applicable to all courts and all clerks of the courts as developed and recommended by the Michigan Trial Court Case File Management Standards Committee.

RULE 8.111   ASSIGNMENT OF CASES

(A) **Application.** The rule applies to all courts defined in subrule 8.110(A).

(B) **Assignment.** All cases must be assigned by lot, unless a different system has been adopted by local court administrative order under the provisions of subrule 8.112. Assignment will occur at the time the case is filed or before a contested hearing or uncontested dispositional hearing in the case, as the chief judge directs. Civil actions must be assigned within appropriate categories determined by the chief judge. The chief judge may receive fewer assignments in order to perform the duties of chief judge.

(C) **Reassignment.** If a judge is disqualified or for other good cause cannot undertake an assigned case, the chief judge may reassign it to another judge by a written order stating the reason. To the extent feasible, the alternate judge should be selected by lot. The chief judge shall file the order with the trial court clerk and have the clerk notify the attorneys of record. The chief judge may also designate a judge to act temporarily until a case is reassigned or during a temporary absence of a judge to whom a case has been assigned.

(D) Actions Arising Out of Same Transaction or Occurrence. Subject to subrule 8.110(C),

(1) if one of two or more actions arising out of the same transaction or occurrence has been assigned to a judge, the other action or actions must be assigned to that judge;

(2) if an action arises out of the same transaction or occurrence as a civil action previously dismissed or transferred, the action must be assigned to the judge to whom the earlier action was assigned;

(3) the attorney for the party bringing the other action under subrule (1) or the new action under subrule (2) shall notify the clerk of the fact in writing in the manner prescribed in MCR 2.113(C)(2). An attorney who knowingly fails to do so is subject to disciplinary action;

(4) the chief judge may reassign cases, other than those encompassed by subrule 8.111(D)(1), in order to correct docket control problems resulting from the requirements of this rule.

[Effective March 1, 1985; amended effective July 1, 1989; April 1, 1998.]

1985 Staff Comment

MCR 8.111 is substantially the same as GCR 1963, 926.

Subrule (D)(2) adds an additional circumstance in which an action must be assigned to the judge to whom a previous action involving the same subject matter had been assigned—when the previous action has been transferred to another court.

Staff Comment to 1989 Amendment

The [July 1, 1989] amendment to MCR 8.111 authorizes the chief judge to reassign cases where necessary to correct any workload imbalance resulting from the rule's requirements.

Staff Comment to 1998 Amendment

The March 24, 1998, amendments [effective April 1, 1998] of 2.109, 2.111, 2.112, 2.119, 8.103, 8.106, 8.110, 8.111, 9.114, and 9.203, make technical changes necessary in light of statutory amendments and correct cross-references.

The amendments of MCR 2.109 and 2.112 relate to amendments of MCR 600.2912d, 600.2912e; MSA 27A.2912(d), 27A.2912(e), by 1993 PA 78.

The amendments of MCR 2.111 and 2.119 are based on statutes amended by 1996 PA 388. The change in MCR 2.111(B)(2) applies to actions filed on or after January 1, 1998, the effective date of the statute increasing the jurisdictional limit of the district court.

The amendment of MCR 8.106 corrects a statutory reference in light of 1993 PA 189.

The remaining amendments make changes in cross-references necessitated by earlier amendments. Some published versions of the rules already include several of these corrections.

RULE 8.112 LOCAL COURT RULES; ADMINISTRATIVE ORDERS

(A) Local Court Rules.

(1) A trial court may adopt rules regulating practice in that court if the rules are not in conflict with these rules and regulate matters not covered by these rules.

(2) If a practice of a trial court is not specifically authorized by these rules, and

(a) reasonably depends on attorneys or litigants being informed of the practice for its effectiveness, or

(b) requires an attorney or litigant to do some act in relation to practice before that court,

the practice, before enforcement, must be adopted by the court as a local court rule and approved by the Supreme Court.

(3) Unless a trial court finds that immediate action is required, it must give reasonable notice and an opportunity to comment on a proposed local court rule to the members of the bar in the affected judicial circuit, district, or county. The court shall send the rule and comments received to the Supreme Court clerk.

(4) If possible, the numbering of a local court rule supplementing an area covered by these rules must correspond with the numbering of these rules and bear the prefix LCR. For example, a local rule supplementing MCR 2.301 should be numbered LCR 2.301.

(B) Administrative Orders.

(1) A trial court may issue an administrative order governing only internal court management.

(2) Administrative orders must be sequentially numbered during the calendar year of their issuance. E.g., Recorder's Court Administrative Order Nos. 1984–1, 1984–2.

(3) Before its effective date, an administrative order must be sent to the state court administrator. If the state court administrator directs, a trial court shall stay the effective date of an administrative order or shall revoke it. A trial court may submit such an order to the Supreme Court as a local court rule.

[Effective March 1, 1985.]

1985 Staff Comment

MCR 8.112 is substantially the same as GCR 1963, 927.

RULE 8.113 REQUESTS FOR INVESTIGATION OF COURTS

(A) Submission of Request. A request for investigation of a court may be submitted to the state court administrator.

(B) Action by State Court Administrator. The state court administrator may

(1) attempt to informally resolve the dispute,

(2) inform the complainant that an investigation pursuant to this rule is not appropriate under the circumstances,

(3) direct the complainant to the Judicial Tenure Commission or the Attorney Grievance Commission,

(4) request an investigation by the Judicial Tenure Commission or the Attorney Grievance Commission,

(5) refer a matter to the Supreme Court for possible exercise of the Supreme Court's power of superintending control over the judiciary, or

(6) take any other appropriate action.

(C) Cooperation With Inquiry. Judges, court employees, and members of the bar shall cooperate with the state court administrator on request for assistance in inquiries pursuant to this rule.

(D) Review Prohibited; Action Without Prejudice to Other Proceedings. There is no appeal from or review of any action taken by the state court administrator under this rule, but nothing in this rule limits the right of any person to request an investigation by the Judicial Tenure Commission or the Attorney Grievance Commission or to file an action for superintending control in an appropriate court.

[Effective March 1, 1985.]

1985 Staff Comment

MCR 8.113 substantially revises the provisions of GCR 1963, 930, regarding superintendence of the judiciary.

The new rule provides for informal inquiries by the state court administrator. The formal procedures in GCR 1963, 930 were superseded to a large degree by the creation of the Judicial Tenure Commission and the related provisions under GCR 1963, 932. See subchapter 9.200.

RULE 8.115 COURTROOM DECORUM

(A) Display of Flags. The flags of the United States and of the State of Michigan must be displayed in a conspicuous place adjacent to the bench at all times when court is in session.

(B) Judicial Robe. When acting in his or her official capacity in the courtroom, a judge shall wear a black robe.

[Effective March 1, 1985.]

1985 Staff Comment

MCR 8.115 is substantially the same as GCR 1963, 916.

RULE 8.116 SESSIONS OF COURT

(A) Opening Court; Recesses. A definite time must be set for all court sessions, and the judge shall promptly open a session. Recesses shall be taken regularly, but should be short, and court must resume on time.

(B) Participants to Be Punctual. Persons having business with a court must be in court and ready to begin at the opening of the session, and must otherwise be punctual for all court business.

(C) Staggered Scheduling. A judge shall stagger the docket schedule so that an attorney or party may be heard within a time reasonably close to the scheduled time, and, except for good cause, the docket shall be called in order.

(D) Access to Court Proceedings. When a court has ordered, or has pending before it a request to order, a limitation on the access of the public to court proceedings or records of those proceedings that are otherwise public, any person may file a motion to set aside the order or an objection to entry of the proposed order. MCR 2.119 governs the proceedings on such a motion or objection. If the court denies a motion to set aside the order or enters the order after objection is filed, the moving or objecting person may file an application for leave to appeal in the same manner as a party to the action. See MCR 8.119(F)(6).

[Effective March 1, 1985; amended effective April 1, 1987; November 30, 1999.]

1985 Staff Comment

MCR 8.116 is a new rule based on former Genesee circuit local court rule 18, covering the conduct of sessions of court.

Staff Comment to 1987 Amendment

The [April 1, 1987] amendment provides for a procedure to challenge either a request to limit access of the public to court proceedings or records of the proceedings that are otherwise public, or an order which has entered accomplishing such a purpose.

Staff Comment to 1999 Amendment

The amendments of MCR 2.113, 5.113, 5.901, 7.210, 8.105, 8.110, 8.116, 8.203, 8.205, and 8.302 [effective November 30, 1999] and the addition of MCR 2.518 and 8.119 [effective November 30, 1999] are to accommodate statewide records standards applicable to all courts and all clerks of the courts as developed and recommended by the Michigan Trial Court Case File Management Standards Committee.

RULE 8.117 CASE CLASSIFICATION CODES

Use of Case–Type Code. As required by MCR 2.113(C)(1)(c), the plaintiff must assign one case-type code from a list provided by the State Court Administrator according to the principal subject matter of the action (not the nature of the proceedings), and include this code in the caption of the complaint. The case code must be included in the caption of all papers thereafter filed in the case.

[Effective March 1, 1985; amended effective March 1, 1987; June 1, 1987; July 1, 1988; March 30, 1989; May 1, 1991; January 1, 1992; September 1, 1992; February, 1, 1993; September 12, 1994; September 1, 1995; June 1, 1997; September 1, 1997; May 20, 1999; May 23, 2000.]

1985 Staff Comment

MCR 8.117 incorporates the case information control system most recently adopted in Administrative Order 1983–5. The rule covering the captioning of pleadings, MCR 2.113(C)(1)(d), requires the use of the case-type codes.

The [March 1, 1985] amendment of MCR 8.117 modifies the list of case-type codes, adding codes applicable to district and probate court.

Staff Comment to 1989 Amendment

[The March 30, 1989, amendment added (25) and (26) to subrule (D).] These two case-type codes were added to this list in response to 1988 PA 490 and 1988 PA 403.

Staff Comment to 1991 Amendment

The [May 1,] 1991 amendments of MCR 8.117(B)(3) and (C)(1) were made at the suggestion of the Negligence Law Section Council of the State Bar. The amendments of (B)(4) and (D) were made at the suggestion of the State Court Administrative Office.

Staff Comment to 1992 Amendment

The November 13, 1991 amendments to MCR 8.117(C) [effective January 1, 1992] were made at the suggestion of the Michigan District Judges Association and the State Court Administrative Office in response to 1991 PA 93, 1991 PA 95, 1991 PA 98 and 1991 PA 99.

Staff Comment to 1994 Amendment

The August 26, 1994 amendment changes several case classification code subrules in light of 1994 PA 12.

Staff Comment to June, 1997 Amendment

May 20, 1997, these amendments [effective June 1, 1997] are made to provide for the implementation of the Uniform Interstate Family Support Act, which is effective June 1, 1997. This Act was adopted so that Michigan would be in compliance with the federal Personal Responsibility and Work Opportunity Act of 1996.

Staff Comment to September, 1997 Amendment

The amendments of MCR 3.201, 3.207, and 8.117 and addition of subchapter 3.700 [effective September 1, 1997], are designed to implement the statutes providing for the issuance of personal protection orders. See MCL 600.2950; MSA 27A.2950, MCL 600.2950a; MSA 27A.29501(1).

Staff Comment to 2000 Amendment

These amendments [effective May 23, 2000] are made to allow for flexibility in making changes to case classification codes. Case classification codes are used principally for administrative purposes by trial courts and the State Court Administrator for collecting management information regarding case and for identifying the administrative processing of cases.

The notice requirements of MCR 1.201 were dispensed with in order that several changes in case classification codes required with the implementation of the Estates and Protect-

ed Individuals Code, MCL 700.1101 et seq.; MSA 27.11101 et seq. could be implemented immediately by the State Court Administrator. The Estates and Protected Individuals Code became effective April 1, 2000. This matter will be included on the Court's future public hearing agenda for the purpose of receiving comments.

The State Court Administrator will incorporate case classification codes in the Case File Management Standards maintained by that office. The State Court Administrator will publish a revised case classification code schedule immediately, and will periodically publish case classification codes for the benefit of the public and the bar.

Publisher's Note—Case Type Codes (rev. 9/2002)

The following Case Type Codes are taken from the Case File Management Standards of the State Court Administrative Office.

(A) Circuit Court Case Type Code List. The following case type code list must be used in circuit court as provided in Component 1. The bracketed letters are the case type codes.

(1) *Appeals*

(a) Agencies [AA]. All matters from administrative agencies other than the Michigan Employment Security Commission and the Michigan Secretary of State.

(b) Employment Security Commission [AE]. All matters regarding Michigan Employment Security Commission actions.

(c) Parole Board Decisions [AP]. Appeals in parole board decisions.

(d) Criminal Appeals [AR]. All criminal appeals from a lower court when filed in a higher court.

(e) Civil Appeals [AV]. All civil appeals from a lower court when filed in a higher court.

(2) *Administrative Review, Superintending Control, Extraordinary Writs*

(a) Habeas Corpus [AH]. All writs of habeas corpus except habeas corpus to obtain custody of a child.

(b) Licensing and Vehicles [AL]. All matters regarding Secretary of State actions.

(c) Superintending Control [AS]. All matters involving superintending control or supervisory control powers of the court.

(d) Writs [AW]. All actions for mandamus and quo warranto and other writs.

(e) Other Extraordinary Law Remedies [AZ]. All other extraordinary law remedies.

(3) *Criminal*

(a) Extradition/Detainer [AX]. All extradition and detainer matters initiated by Michigan to other states.

(b) Capital Felonies [FC]. Capital felony cases, in which life sentence is possible and a larger number of peremptory jury challenges is provided.

(c) Noncapital Felonies [FH].

(d) Juvenile Felonies [FJ]. Juvenile offenses committed by juveniles and waived to the criminal division of the circuit court under MCR 5.950. Includes life offenses committed by juveniles in which the prosecuting attorney has authorized the filing of a criminal complaint and warrant under MCR 6.907 instead of proceeding in the family division of the circuit court.

(4) *Civil Damage Suits*

(a) Property Damage, Auto Negligence [ND]. All complaints of property damage but not personal injury involving the use of a motor vehicle.

(b) No–Fault Automobile Insurance [NF]. All claims for first-party personal protection benefits and first-party property protection benefits under the no-fault automobile insurance act.

(c) Medical Malpractice [NH]. All claims involving health care provider malpractice.

(d) Personal Injury, Auto Negligence [NI]. All complaints of personal injury, or personal injury and property damage, involving the use of a motor vehicle.

(e) Other Professional Malpractice [NM]. All claims involving professional malpractice other than health care provider malpractice.

(f) Other Personal Injury [NO]. All other claims involving liability for personal injury not otherwise coded.

(g) Products Liability [NP]. All claims involving products liability.

(h) Dramshop Act [NS]. All claims involving liability under the dramshop act.

(i) Other Damage Suits [NZ]. All claims involving liability for personal injury.

(5) *Other Civil Matters*

(a) Business Claims [CB]. All claims involving partnership termination and other business accountings.

(b) Condemnation [CC]. All condemnation proceedings.

(c) Employment Discrimination [CD]. All complaints of employment discrimination.

(d) Environment [CE]. All environmental matters such as zoning, pollution, etc.

(e) Forfeiture Claims [CF]. All claims of interest in property seized under the Controlled Substance Act which may be subject to forfeiture.

(f) Housing and Real Estate [CH]. All housing, real estate, foreclosure, land contracts, and other property proceedings (except landlord-tenant and land contract summary proceedings).

(g) Contracts [CK]. All proceedings involving contractual obligations not otherwise coded.

(h) Labor Relations [CL]. All labor-management matters except employment discrimination.

(i) Antitrust, Franchising, and Trade Regulation [CP]. All complaints regarding unlawful trade practices including but not limited to pricing and advertising of consumer items, regulation of watercraft, restraint of trade and monopolies, Consumer Protection Act, Farm and Utility Equipment Franchise Act, franchise investment law, motor vehicle dealer agreements, and the Motor Fuel Distribution Act.

(j) Corporate Receivership [CR]. All corporate receivership proceedings.

(k) General Civil [CZ]. All other civil actions not otherwise coded.

(*l*) Proceedings to Restore, Establish, or Correct Records [PC]. All proceedings to restore, establish or correct records which are assigned a new case number (not brought under an existing case).

(m) Claim and Delivery [PD]. All complaints to recover personal property which are assigned a new case number (not brought under an existing case).

(n) Receivers in Supplemental Proceedings [PR]. All proceedings appointing a receiver which are assigned a new case number (not brought under an existing case).

(o) Supplemental Proceedings [PS]. All supplemental proceedings which are assigned a new case number (not brought under an existing case).

(p) Miscellaneous Proceedings [PZ]. All other matters assigned a new case number (not brought under an existing case), including the following matters: grand jury and multi-county grand jury.

(6) *Family Division—Domestic Relations*

(a) Custody [DC]. All habeas corpus to obtain custody of a child; order to show cause for custody of a child; other custody, or custody and support proceedings when no divorce action has been filed; or actions under the Uniform Child Custody Jurisdiction Enforcement Act.

(b) Interstate Filing [DF]. All support matters submitted for filing only under the Uniform Reciprocal Enforcement of Support Act and the Interstate Income Withholding Act.

(c) Outgoing Support Enforcement Proceedings [DI]. All support enforcement proceedings outgoing to another state under the Uniform Reciprocal Enforcement of Support Act.

(d) Divorce, Minor Children [DM]. All complaints for divorce, separate maintenance, or annulment when minor children are involved.

(e) Divorce, No Children [DO]. All complaints for divorce, separate maintenance, or annulment when no minor children are involved.

(f) Paternity [DP]. All questions of paternity; paternity and custody; or paternity, custody, and support.

(g) Registration of Foreign Orders [DR]. All registrations of foreign support orders received from another state under the Uniform Reciprocal Enforcement of Support Act.

(h) Other Support [DS]. All support matters under the Family Support Act.

(i) URESA Enforcement [DU]. All support enforcement proceedings incoming from another state under the Uniform Reciprocal Enforcement of Support Act.

(j) Interstate Income Withholding [DW]. All support orders incoming from another state under the Interstate Income Withholding Act.

(k) Other Domestic Relations Matters [DZ]. All other prejudgment matters involving domestic relations proceedings not otherwise coded.

(*l*) Transfer Custody [TC]. All intrastate transfers of postjudgment custody or custody and support proceedings where no divorce action has been filed.

(m) Transfer URESA, Initiation [TI]. All intrastate transfers of postjudgment support enforcement proceedings outgoing to another state under the Uniform Reciprocal Enforcement of Support Act.

(n) Transfer Divorce, Minor Children [TM]. All intrastate transfers of postjudgment divorce; divorce and custody; or divorce, custody, and support complaints when minor children are involved.

(o) Transfer Divorce, No Children [TO]. All intrastate transfers of postjudgment divorce complaints when no minor children are involved.

(p) Transfer Paternity [TP]. All intrastate transfers of postjudgment paternity; paternity and custody; or paternity, custody, and support complaints.

(q) Transfer Other Support [TS]. All intrastate transfers of postjudgment support matters under the Family Support Act.

(r) Transfer URESA Enforcement [TU]. All intrastate transfers of postjudgment support enforcement proceedings incoming from another state under the Uniform Reciprocal Enforcement of Support Act.

(s) Transfer Other Family Matters [TZ]. All intrastate transfers of other postjudgment matters involving domestic relations proceedings not otherwise coded.

(t) UIFSA Modification; Filing [UC]. All outgoing requests for registration of an order for the specific purpose of modification under the Uniform Interstate Family Support Act.

(u) Assist with Discovery [UD]. All proceedings under the Uniform Interstate Family Support Act to assist with discovery or to compel a response to a discovery order issued by another state's tribunal.

(v) UIFSA Establishment [UE]. All support and paternity establishment proceedings incoming from another state under the Uniform Interstate Family Support Act.

(w) UIFSA Enforcement; Filing [UF]. All outgoing requests for registration of another state's order for the specific purpose of enforcement under the Uniform Interstate Family Support Act.

(x) UIFSA Initiation [UI]. All support and paternity establishment proceedings outgoing to another state under the Uniform Interstate Family Support Act.

(y) Registration of Orders for Modification [UM]. All incoming registrations of another state's orders for the specific purpose of modification under the Uniform Interstate Family Support Act.

(z) Registration of Orders for Enforcement [UN]. All incoming registrations of another state's orders for the specific purpose of enforcement under the Uniform Interstate Family Support Act.

(aa) UIFSA Income Withholding; Filing [UO]. All outgoing requests for registration of another state's order for the specific purpose of income withholding under the Uniform Interstate Family Support Act.

(bb) Transfer UIFSA [UT]. All intrastate transfers of postjudgment support enforcement proceedings incoming from another state under the Uniform Interstate Family Support Act.

(cc) Registration of Income Withholding Orders [UW]. All incoming registrations of another state's orders for the specific purpose of income withholding under the Uniform Interstate Family Support Act.

(7) *Family Division—Proceedings under Juvenile Code*

(a) Designated Juvenile Offenses [DJ]. All juvenile offenses designated by the prosecutor or court to be heard in the family division of circuit court in the same manner as an adult criminal case is heard in the criminal division of the circuit court.

(b) Delinquency Proceedings [DL]. All delinquency proceedings initiated by petition under the juvenile code or initiated by Uniform Law Citation for various minor offenses not in the Motor Vehicle Code.

(c) Child Protective Proceedings [NA]. All child protective proceedings initiated by petition under the juvenile code.

(d) Personal Protection Actions Brought Under the Juvenile Code [PJ]. All petitions seeking a personal protection order against a respondent under the age of 18. Includes proceedings conducted for violation of personal protection orders issued under the juvenile code when heard by a county other than the county that issued the personal protection order.

(e) Traffic and Local Ordinance [TL]. All traffic and local ordinance issued on a Uniform Law Citation under the Motor Vehicle Code or local corresponding ordinance.

(8) *Family Division—Proceedings under Adoption Code*

(a) Adult Adoptions [AB]. All adult adoptions.

(b) Agency International Adoptions [AC]. All foreign children adoptions.

(c) Direct Placement Adoptions [AD]. All direct placement adoptions including temporary placements prior to filing of petition for direct placement.

(d) Relative Adoptions [AF]. All adoptions by relatives including relative guardians, but not including step-parent adoptions.

(e) Safe Delivery of Newborn Adoptions [AG]—All adoptions resulting from safe delivery of newborn proceedings.

(f) Permanent Ward Adoptions (state ward or court ward) [AM]. All state or court ward adoptions resulting from child protective proceedings.

(g) Non Relative Adoptions [AN]. All adoptions by guardians who are not relatives.

(h) Agency Other Adoptions [AO]. All other private or public agency adoptions not otherwise designated.

(i) Step–Parent Adoptions [AY]. All adoptions by stepparents.

(j) Release to Adopt; No Case [RB]. All releases to adopt; no case pending.

(k) Release to Adopt [RL]. All releases to adopt; result of a child protective case.

(9) *Family Division—Miscellaneous Proceedings*

(a) Emancipation of Minor [EM]. All emancipation proceedings initiated under the status of minors and emancipation act.

(b) Infectious Disease [ID]. All proceedings under the public health code for treatment of infectious disease or testing for infectious disease.

(c) Safe Delivery of Newborn Child [NB]. All proceedings involving a newborn child surrendered under the Safe Delivery of Newborns act (MCL 712.1 et seq.).

(d) Name Change [NC]. All name change proceedings.

(e) Personal Protection Against Stalking [PH]. All personal protection proceedings under MCL 600.2950a; MSA 27A.2950a when there is no domestic relationship between the parties and the respondent is not under the age of 18.

(f) Personal Protection in Domestic Relationships [PP]. All personal protection proceedings under MCL 600.2950; MSA 27A.2950 and/or MCL 600.2950a; MSA 27A.2950a when there is a domestic relationship between the parties and the respondent is not under the age of 18.

(g) Waiver of Parental Consent to Obtain Abortion [PW]. All waiver of parental consent proceedings under the parental rights restoration act.

(h) Violation Proceedings on Out-of-County Personal Protection Order—Revised Judicature Act [VP]. All proceedings conducted for violation of personal protection orders issued under MCL 600.2950 or MCL 600.2950a when heard by a county other than the county that issued the personal protection order. This case is filed as "In the Matter of".

(10) *Family Division—Ancillary Proceedings.* Use case type codes listed in (C) for matters filed in the probate court which may alternatively be filed in the family division of circuit court as an ancillary proceeding.

(11) *Court of Claims.*

(a) Highway Defect [MD]. All claims involving highway defects.

(b) Medical Malpractice [MH]. All claims involving health care provider malpractice.

(c) Contracts [MK]. All other proceedings involving contractual obligations not otherwise coded.

(d) Constitutional Claims [MM]. All claims for money damages brought under the Michigan Constitution.

(e) Prisoner Litigation [MP]. All claims for money damages against the State of Michigan filed by state prisoners.

(f) Tax Related Suits [MT]. All claims involving liability for state taxes.

(g) Other Damage Suits [MZ]. All other claims for money damages.

(B) District Court Case Type Code List. The following case type code list must be used in district court as provided in Component 1. The bracketed letters are the case type codes.

(1) *Criminal*

(a) Extradition/Detainer [EX]. All extradition and detainer matters initiated by Michigan to other states.

(b) Felony Criminal [FY]. All felony non-traffic cases. Includes life offenses committed by juveniles in which the prosecuting attorney has authorized the filing of a criminal complaint and warrant under MCR 6.907 instead of proceeding in the family division of the circuit court, and specified offenses committed by juveniles and waived to the criminal division of the circuit court under MCR 5.950.

(c) Ordinance Misdemeanor Criminal [OM]. All non-traffic misdemeanor offenses issued under ordinance.

(d) Statute Misdemeanor Criminal [SM]. All non-traffic misdemeanor offenses issued under statute.

(2) *Traffic*

(a) Felony Drunk Driving [FD]. All felony drunk driving cases.

(b) Felony Traffic [FT]. All felony traffic cases except drunk driving.

(c) Ordinance Misdemeanor Drunk Driving [OD]. All drunk driving misdemeanor offenses issued under ordinance.

(d) Ordinance Civil Infraction Traffic [OI]. All traffic civil infraction offenses issued under ordinance.

(e) Ordinance Misdemeanor Traffic [OT]. All traffic misdemeanor offenses issued under ordinance except drunk driving.

(f) Statute Misdemeanor Drunk Driving [SD]. All drunk driving misdemeanor offenses issued under statute.

(g) Statute Civil Infraction Traffic [SI]. All traffic civil infraction offenses issued under statute.

(h) Statute Misdemeanor Traffic [ST]. All traffic misdemeanor offenses issued under statute except drunk driving.

(3) *Non–Traffic Civil Infraction and Parking*

(a) Ordinance Parking [OK]. All parking offenses issued under ordinance.

(b) Ordinance Civil Infraction Non–Traffic [ON]. All non-traffic civil infraction offenses issued under ordinance.

(c) Statute Parking [SK]. All parking offenses issued under statute.

(d) Statute Civil Infraction Non–Traffic [SN]. All non-traffic civil infraction offenses issued under statute.

(4) *Civil Damage Suits.*

(a) General Civil [GC]. All civil cases for money damages except small claims, landlord-tenant, and land contract.

(b) Miscellaneous Civil [GZ]. All non-monetary claims including coroner's inquests, peace bonds, claim and delivery without money judgment, drug forfeitures, other summary proceedings not relating to landlord-tenant and land contract, and proceedings under the public health code for testing for infectious disease.

(c) Small Claims [SC]. All civil claims for the recovery of money which does not exceed the jurisdictional limit in MCL 600.8401; MSA 27A.8401.

(5) *Housing and Real Estate Suits.*

(a) Landlord–Tenant Summary Proceedings [LT].

(b) Land Contract Summary Proceedings [SP].

(C) Probate Court Case Type Code List. The following case type code list must be used in probate court as provided in Component. The bracketed letters are the case type codes.

(1) *Estates, Trusts, Wills*

(a) Decedent Estates, Supervised Administration [DA]. All matters involving decedent estates in which administration is supervised.

(b) Decedent Estates, Unsupervised Administration and Non–Administered Estates [DE]. All matters involving decedent estates in which either administration is unsupervised, or the estate is not administered.

(c) Determination of Heirs (separate proceeding) [DH]. All matters to determine heirs as a separate proceeding.

(d) Small Estates [PE]. All assignments of estates where gross estate assets do not exceed $15,000 (as adjusted for inflation).

(e) Trust Registration [TR]. All requests to register trusts.

(f) Trust, Testamentary [TT]. All trusts which take effect on the death of the settlor.

(g) Trust Inter Vivos [TV]. All trusts which are operative during the lifetime of the settlor.

(2) *Guardianships and Conservatorships*

These case types may also be filed in the family division of circuit court as an ancillary proceeding.

(a) Adult Conservatorship [CA]. All matters involving conservatorship of adults.

(b) Minor Conservatorship [CY]. All matters involving conservatorship of minors.

(c) Developmental Disability Guardianship [DD]. All matters involving guardianship of individuals with developmental disability, both adults and minors.

(d) Adult Guardianship [GA]. All matters involving full guardianship of incapacitated individuals.

(e) Limited Guardianship of Adult [GL]. All matters involving limited guardianship of incapacitated individuals.

(f) Minor Guardianship [GM]. All matters involving full guardianship of minors.

(g) Limited Guardianship of Minor [LG]. All matters involving limited guardianship of minors.

(h) Protective Orders [PO]. All protective orders requested under the estates and protected individuals code except when filed in conjunction with a petition for conservatorship.

(3) *Mental Illness Proceedings and Judicial Admission*

These case types may also be filed in the family division of circuit court as an ancillary proceeding.

(a) Judicial Admission [JA]. All matters involving judicial admission of individuals with developmental disability.

(b) Mental Illness Proceedings [MI]. All mental illness proceedings brought under the mental health code.

(4) *Civil and Miscellaneous Proceedings*

(a) Delayed Registration of Foreign Birth [BR].

(b) Civil [CZ]. All civil matters commenced under MCR 5.101(C).

(c) Miscellaneous Matters [ML]. All other matters filed with the probate court for judicial or administrative action including but not limited to: appeals; death by accident or disaster; filing of letters by foreign personal representative; kidney transplants; lost instruments; opening of safe deposit box; review of adoption subsidy; review of drain commission; review of mental health financial liability; secret marriage licenses; substance abuse treatment of minor; support of poor persons; and uniform gifts to minors act.

RULE 8.119 COURT RECORDS AND REPORTS; DUTIES OF CLERKS

(A) Applicability. This rule applies to all actions in every trial court except that subrule (D)(1) does not apply to civil infractions.

(B) Records Standards. The clerk of the court shall comply with the records standards in this rule and as prescribed by the Michigan Supreme Court.

(C) Filing of Papers. The clerk of the court shall endorse on the first page of every document the date on which it is filed. Papers filed with the clerk of the court must comply with Michigan Court Rules and Michigan Supreme Court records standards. The clerk of the court may reject papers which do not conform to MCR 2.113(C)(1) and MCR 5.113(A)(1).

(D) Records Kept by the Clerk. The clerk of the court of every trial court shall keep records in the form and style the court prescribes and in accordance with Michigan Supreme Court records standards and local court plans. A court may adopt a computerized, microfilm, or word-processing system for maintaining records that substantially complies with this subrule.

(1) *Indexes and Case Files.* The clerk shall keep and maintain records of each case consisting of a numerical index, an alphabetical index, a register of actions, and a case file in such form and style as may be prescribed by the Supreme Court. Each case shall be assigned a case number on receipt of a complaint, petition, or other initiating document. The case number shall comply with MCR 2.113(C)(1)(c) or MCR 5.113(A)(1)(b)(ii) as applicable. In addition to the case number, a separate petition number shall be assigned to each petition filed under the Juvenile Code as required under MCR 5.113(A)(1)(b)(ii). The case number (and petition number if applicable) shall be recorded on the register of actions, file folder, numerical index, and alphabetical index. The records shall include the following characteristics:

(a) Numerical Index. The clerk shall maintain a numerical index as a list of consecutive case numbers on which the date of filing and the names of the parties are recorded. The index may be maintained either as a central index for all cases filed in the court or as separate lists for particular types of cases or particular divisions of the court.

(b) Alphabetical Index. The clerk shall maintain a central alphabetical index or separate alphabetical indexes for particular types of cases or particular divisions of the court on which the date of filing, names of all parties, and the case number are recorded.

(c) Register of Actions. The clerk shall keep a case history of each case, known as a register of actions. The register of actions shall contain both pre-and post-judgment information. When a case is commenced, a register of actions form shall be created. The case identification information in the alphabetical index shall be entered on the register of actions. In addition, the following shall be noted chronologically on the register of actions as it pertains to the case: the offense (if one); the judge assigned to the case; fees paid; date and title of each filed document; process issued and returned; date of service; date of each event and type and result of action; date of scheduled trials, hearings, and all other appearances or reviews; orders; judgments; verdicts; the judge at adjudication and disposition; date of adjudication and disposition; manner of adjudication and disposition. Each notation shall be brief, but shall show the nature of each paper filed, each order or judgment of the court, and the returns showing execution. Each notation shall be dated with not only the date of filing,but with the date of entry and shall indicate the person recording the action.

(d) Case File. The clerk of the court shall maintain a file folder for each action, bearing the case number assigned to it, in which the clerk shall keep all pleadings, process, written opinions and findings, orders, and judgments filed in the action. Additionally, the clerk shall keep in the file all other documents prescribed by court rule, statute, or as ordered by the court. If other records of a case file are maintained separately from the file folder, the clerk shall keep them as prescribed by case file management standards.

(2) *Calendars.* The clerk may maintain calendars of actions. A calendar is a schedule of cases ready for court action that identifies times and places of activity.

(3) *Abolished Records.*

(a) Journals. Except for recording marriages, journals shall not be maintained.

(b) Dockets. A register of actions replaces a docket. Wherever these rules or applicable statutes require entries on a docket, those entries shall be entered on the register of actions.

(4) *Other Records.* The clerk shall keep in such form as may be prescribed by the court, other papers, documents, materials, and things filed with or handled by the court including but not limited to wills for safekeeping, exhibits and other discovery materials, requests for search warrants, marriage records, and administrative activities.

(E) Access to Records. The clerk may not permit any record or paper on file in the clerk's office to be taken from it without the order of the court.

(1) Unless access to a file, a document, or information contained in a file or document is restricted by statute, court rule, or an order entered pursuant to subrule (F), any person may inspect pleadings and other papers in the clerk's office and may obtain copies as provided in subrule (E)(2) and (E)(3).

(2) If a person wishes to obtain copies of papers in a file, the clerk shall provide copies upon receipt of the reasonable cost of reproduction. If the clerk prefers, the requesting person may be permitted to make copies at personal expense under the direct supervision of the clerk. Except for copies of transcripts or as otherwise directed by statute or court rule, a standard fee may be established for providing copies of papers in a file.

(3) A court is not required to create a new record, except to the extent required by furnishing copies of a file, paper, or record. A court may create a new record or compilation of records pertaining to case files or case-related information on request, provided that the record created or compiled does not disclose information that would otherwise be confidential or restricted by statute, court rule, or an order entered pursuant to subrule (F).

(4) Every court, shall adopt an administrative order pursuant to MCR 8.112(B) to

(a) make reasonable regulations necessary to protect its public records and prevent excessive and unreasonable interference with the discharge of its functions;

(b) specify the reasonable cost of reproduction of records provided under subrule (E)(2); and

(c) specify the process for determining costs under subrule (E)(3).

(F) Sealed Records.

(1) Except as otherwise provided by statute or court rule, a court may not enter an order that seals courts records, in whole or in part, in any action or proceeding, unless

(a) a party has filed a written motion that identifies the specific interest to be protected,

(b) the court has made a finding of good cause, in writing or on the record, which specifies the grounds for the order, and

(c) there is no less restrictive means to adequately and effectively protect the specific interest asserted.

(2) In determining whether good cause has been shown, the court must consider,

(a) the interests of the parties, including, where there is an allegation of domestic violence, the safety of the alleged or potential victim of the domestic violence, and

(b) the interest of the public.

(3) The court must provide any interested person the opportunity to be heard concerning the sealing of the records.

(4) For purposes of this rule, "court records" includes all documents and records of any nature that are filed with the clerk in connection with the action. Nothing in this rule is intended to limit the court's authority to issue protective orders pursuant to MCR 2.302(C).

(5) A court may not seal a court order or opinion, including an order or opinion that disposes of a motion to seal the record.

(6) Any person may file a motion to set aside an order that disposes of a motion to seal the record, or an objection to entry of a proposed order. MCR 2.119 governs the proceedings on such a motion or objection. If the court denies a motion to set aside the order or enters the order after objection is filed, the moving or objecting person may file an application for leave to appeal in the same manner as a party to the action. See MCR 8.116(D).

(7) Whenever the court grants a motion to seal a court record, in whole or in part, the court must forward a copy of the order to the Clerk of the Supreme Court and to the State Court Administrative Office.

(G) Reporting Duties.

(1) The clerk of every court shall submit reports and records as required by statute and court rule.

(2) The clerk of every court shall submit reports or provide records as required by the State Court Administrative Office, without costs.

[Adopted effective November 30, 1999; amended effective September 11, 2002.]

1999 Staff Comment

The amendments of MCR 2.113, 5.113, 5.901, 7.210, 8.105, 8.110, 8.116, 8.203, 8.205, and 8.302 [effective November 30, 1999] and the addition of MCR 2.518 and 8.119 [effective November 30, 1999] are to accommodate statewide records standards applicable to all courts and all clerks of the courts as developed and recommended by the Michigan Trial Court Case File Management Standards Committee.

Staff Comment to 2002 Amendment

The September 11, 2002, amendments of MCR 3.206, 3.214, 3.705, 3.706, 3.708, 5.982, and 8.119, which were given immediate effect, are related to the group of domestic violence statutes enacted in December 2001 that took effect April 1, 2002.

The changes in MCR 3.206 and 3.214 are related to 2001 PA 195, which adopted the Uniform Child–Custody Jurisdiction and Enforcement Act, MCL 722.1101 *et seq.* There is also some nonsubstantive reorganization of MCR 3.214.

The amendment of MCR 3.705 implements the statutory provisions regarding the statement of reasons for granting or denying personal protection orders. See 2001 PA 196.

The amendment of MCR 3.706 incorporates the statutory provisions regarding enforceability of Michigan personal protection orders in other jurisdictions. See 2001 PA 200 and 201.

MCR 3.708 and 5.982 are amended to include foreign protection orders, which are made enforceable in Michigan by 2001 PA 197.

MCR 8.119(F) is amended to conform to 2001 PA 205, which directs that when a motion to seal court records involves allegations of domestic violence, the court is to consider the safety of the potential victim in ruling on the motion.

The staff comment is published only for the benefit of the bench and bar and is not an authoritative construction by the Court.

RULE 8.120 LAW STUDENTS AND RECENT GRADUATES; PARTICIPATION IN LEGAL AID CLINICS, DEFENDER OFFICES, AND LEGAL TRAINING PROGRAMS

(A) Legal Aid Clinics; Defender Offices. Effective legal service for each person in Michigan, regardless of that person's ability to pay, is important to the directly affected person, to our court system, and to the whole citizenry. Law students and recent law graduates, under supervision by a member of the state bar, may staff public and nonprofit defender offices, and legal aid clinics that are organized under a city or county bar association or an accredited law school or for the primary purpose of providing free legal services to indigent persons .

(B) Legal Training Programs. Law students and recent law graduates may participate in legal training programs organized in the offices of county prosecuting attorneys, county corporation counsel, city attorneys, and the Attorney General.

(C) Eligible Students. A student in a law school approved by the American Bar Association who has received a passing grade in law school courses and has completed the first year is eligible to participate in a clinic or program listed in subrules (A) and (B) if the student meets the academic and moral standards established by the dean of that school. For the purpose of this rule, a "recent law graduate" is a person who has graduated from law school within the last year.

(D) Scope; Procedure.

(1) A member of the legal aid clinic, in representing an indigent person, is authorized to advise the person and to negotiate and appear on the person's behalf in all Michigan courts except the Court of Appeals and the Supreme Court.

(2) Representation must be conducted under the supervision of a state bar member. Supervision by a state bar member includes the duty to examine and sign all pleadings filed. It does not require the state bar member to be present

(a) while a law student or graduate is advising an indigent person or negotiating on the person's behalf, or

(b) during a courtroom appearance of a law student or graduate, except in a criminal or juvenile case exposing the client to a penalty of more than 6 months.

(3) A law student or graduate may not appear in a case in a Michigan court without the approval of the judge of that court. If the judge grants approval, the judge may suspend the proceedings at any stage if he

or she determines that the representation by the law student or graduate

(a) is professionally inadequate, and

(b) substantial justice requires suspension.

(4) A law student or graduate serving in a prosecutor's, county corporation counsel's, city attorney's, or Attorney General's program may be authorized to perform comparable functions and duties assigned by the prosecuting attorney, county attorney, city attorney, or Attorney General, except that

(a) the law student or graduate is subject to the conditions and restrictions of this rule; and

(b) the law student or graduate may not be appointed as an assistant prosecutor, assistant corporation counsel, assistant city attorney, or assistant Attorney General.

[Effective March 1, 1985; amended effective May 17, 1993; September 1, 2000.]

1985 Staff Comment

MCR 8.120 is based on GCR 1963, 921.

Subrule (A) allows recent law graduates to work not only in training programs organized by prosecuting attorneys or city attorneys, but also in legal aid clinics. Compare GCR 1963, 921.1. Subrule (B) defines a "recent law graduate" as a person who has graduated from law school within the last year.

Staff Comment to 1993 Amendment

The only change in the rule [under the May 17, 1993 amendment] is to include references to "county corporation counsel" in appropriate places in the rule.

Staff Comment to 2000 Amendment

The June 21, 2000 amendment of MCR 8.120, effective September 1, 2000, restructured the rule to specifically mention public and nonprofit defender organizations, and to recognize that not all clinics that provide free legal services to indigent persons are funded under the Legal Services Corporation Act, 42 USC 2996, *et seq.* The amendment also added legal training programs sponsored by the Attorney General to the list of programs in which eligible law school students and recent law school graduates may participate.

RULE 8.121 CONTINGENT FEES IN CLAIMS OR ACTIONS FOR PERSONAL INJURY AND WRONGFUL DEATH

(A) Allowable Contingent Fee Agreements. In any claim or action for personal injury or wrongful death based upon the alleged conduct of another, in which an attorney enters into an agreement, expressed or implied, whereby the attorney's compensation is dependent or contingent in whole or in part upon successful prosecution or settlement or upon the amount of recovery, the receipt, retention, or sharing by such attorney, pursuant to agreement or otherwise, of compensation which is equal to or less than the fee stated in subrule (B) is deemed to be fair and reasonable. The receipt, retention, or sharing of compensation which is in excess of such a fee shall be deemed to

be the charging of a "clearly excessive fee" in violation of MRPC 1.5(a).

(B) Maximum Fee. The maximum allowable fee for the claims and actions referred to in subrule (A) is one-third of the amount recovered.

(C) Computation.

(1) The amount referred to in subrule (B) shall be computed on the net sum recovered after deducting from the amount recovered all disbursements properly chargeable to the enforcement of the claim or prosecution of the action. In computing the fee, the costs as taxed and any interest included in or upon the amount of a judgment shall be deemed part of the amount recovered.

(2) In the case of a settlement payable in installments, the amount referred to in subrule (B) shall be computed using the present value of the future payments.

(a) If an annuity contract will be used to fund the future payments, "present value" is the actual cost of purchasing the annuity contract. The attorney for the defendant must disclose to the court and the parties the amount paid for the annuity contract, after any rebates or other discounts.

(b) If the defendant will make the future payments directly, "present value" is the amount that an entity of the same financial standing as the defendant would pay for an annuity contract. The court may appoint an independent expert to certify the "present value" as defined in this paragraph. The court may base its findings on the expert's testimony or affidavit.

(D) Agreements for Lower Fees. An attorney may enter into contingent fee arrangements calling for less compensation than that allowed by subrule (B).

(E) Advice to Client. An attorney must advise a client, before entering into a contingent fee arrangement, that attorneys may be employed under other fee arrangements in which the attorney is compensated for the reasonable value of the services performed, such as on an hourly or per diem basis. The method of compensation used by an individual attorney remains the attorney's option, and this rule does not require an attorney to accept compensation in a manner other than that chosen by the attorney.

(F) Agreements to Be in Writing. Contingent fee arrangements made by an attorney with a client must be in writing and a copy provided to the client.

(G) Applicability. This rule does not apply to agreements reduced to writing before May 3, 1975. The one-third provision of subrule (B) applies to contingent fee agreements entered into after July 9, 1981.

Earlier agreements are subject to the rule in effect at the time the agreement was made.

[Effective March 1, 1985; amended effective April 1, 1998; January 1, 2003.]

1985 Staff Comment

MCR 8.121 is based on GCR 1963, 928.

Subrule (C) adds a provision regarding computation of the maximum fee when the settlement is payable in installments. The computation is to be made using the present value of the future payments.

Staff Comment to 1998 Amendment

The amendment of subrule A adopted February 5, 1998, and effective April 1, 1998, replaced an obsolete cross reference with an updated cross reference to MRPC 1.5(a).

Staff Comment to 2002 Amendment

The October 8, 2002 amendment of MCR 8.121(C), effective January 1, 2003, defines the term "present value" as it is used to calculate a contingent attorney fee when the recovery includes a "structured settlement," a settlement that calls for future installment payments. The amendment was based on a proposal submitted by a special committee of the Civil Division of the Wayne Circuit Court.

The staff comment is published only for the benefit of the bench and bar and is not an authoritative construction by the Court.

RULE 8.122   CLAIMS BY CLIENTS AGAINST ATTORNEYS

Attorneys are officers of Michigan's one court of justice and are subject to the summary jurisdiction of the court. The circuit court of the county in which an attorney resides or maintains an office has jurisdiction, on verified written complaint of a client, and after reasonable notice and hearing, to enter an order for the payment of money or for the performance of an act by the attorney which law and justice may require. All courts have like jurisdiction over similar complaints regarding matters arising from actions or proceedings in those courts.

[Effective March 1, 1985.]

1985 Staff Comment

MCR 8.122 is substantially the same as GCR 1963, 908.

RULE 8.123.   COUNSEL APPOINTMENTS; PROCEDURE AND RECORDS

Effective Jan. 1, 2004

(A) Applicability. This rule applies to all trial courts, which means all circuit courts, district courts, probate courts, and municipal courts.

(B) Plan for Appointment. Each trial court must adopt a local administrative order that describes the court's procedures for selecting, appointing, and compensating counsel who represent indigent parties in that court.

(C) Approval by State Court Administrator. The trial court must submit the local administrative order to the State Court Administrator for review pursuant to MCR 8.112(B)(3). The State Court Administrator shall approve a plan if its provisions will protect the integrity of the judiciary.

(D) Required Records. At the end of each calendar year, a trial court must compile an annual written or electronic report of:

(1) the number of appointments given to each attorney by that court;

(2) the number of appointments given to each attorney by each judge of that court;

(3) the total public funds paid to each attorney for appointments by that court; and

(4) the total public funds paid to each attorney for appointments by each judge of that court.

Trial courts that contract for services to be provided by an affiliated group of attorneys may treat the group as a single entity when compiling the required records of appointments and compensation.

The records required by this subrule must be retained for the period specified by the State Court Administrative Office's General Schedule 16.

(E) Public Access to Records. The records must be available at the trial court for inspection by the public, without charge. The court may adopt reasonable access rules, and may charge a reasonable fee for providing copies of the records.

(F) Reports to State Court Administrator. When requested by the State Court Administrator, a trial court must:

(1) provide a copy of its most recent annual report; and

(2) provide data on an individual attorney or judge for a period specified by the request.

[Adopted effective January 1, 2004.]

Publisher's Note

This rule is effective Jan. 1, 2004.

Staff Comment to 2002 Adoption

MCR 8.123 was adopted on December 13, 2002, effective January 1, 2004. Subrule (B) requires trial courts to standardize their procedures for selecting and compensating appointed counsel. Subrule (D) requires the courts to maintain records of appointments and compensation. Subrule (E) requires that the records be public records.

The staff comment is published only for the benefit of the bench and bar and is not an authoritative construction by the Court.

RULE 8.125 ELECTRONIC FILING OF CITATION

(A) Applicability. This rule applies to all civil infraction and misdemeanor actions initiated by a Michigan Uniform Law Citation or a Michigan Uniform Municipal Civil Infraction Citation.

(B) Citation; Complaint; Filing. A citation may be filed with the court either on paper or electronically. The filing of a citation constitutes the filing of a complaint. An electronic citation must contain all the information that would be required if the citation were filed on paper. A citation that contains the full name of the police officer or authorized local official who issued it will be deemed to have been signed pursuant to MCL 257.727c(3), 600.8705(3), or 600.8805(3); MSA 9.2427(3)(3), 27A.8705(3), or 27A.8805(3).

(C) Contested Actions. If an electronic citation is contested, the court may decline to hear the matter until the citation is signed and filed on paper. A citation that is not signed and filed on paper, when required by the court, will be dismissed with prejudice.

[Adopted effective September 2, 1997.]

1997 Staff Comment

The September 1997 amendments of MCR 4.101, 4.401, and 6.615, and the addition of MCR 8.125, [effective September 2, 1997] were adopted at the request of the Michigan District Judges Association because of recent statutory changes that created new categories of civil infractions, and the availability of electronic filing. In addition, the amendment of MCR 4.401(G) was made to clarify the procedure for challenging a civil infraction judgment.

SUBCHAPTER 8.200   ADMINISTRATIVE RULES APPLICABLE IN DISTRICT COURT

RULE 8.201 ALLOCATION OF COSTS IN THIRD–CLASS DISTRICTS

(A) Duties of Clerks of Each Third-Class Control Unit Having a Clerk.

(1) On the last day of March, June, September, and December of each year, the clerk of each third-class control unit having a clerk (see MCL 600.8281; MSA 27A.8281) shall determine the total number of civil and criminal cases filed during the preceding three months in the district and each political subdivision of the district under subrule (B). These figures are the total number of cases entered and commenced in that district and each political subdivision.

(2) The clerk shall determine the total cost of maintaining, financing, and operating the district court within the district.

(3) The clerk shall determine the proper share of the costs to be borne by each political subdivision by use of the following formula: (the number of cases entered and commenced in each political subdivision divided by the total number of cases entered and commenced in the district) multiplied by the total cost of maintaining, financing, and operating the district court.

(4) The clerk shall determine the proper share of the salary of the court reporter or recorder under MCL 600.8621(1); MSA 27A.8621(1) by use of the following formula: (the number of cases entered and commenced in each political subdivision divided by the total number of cases entered and commenced in the district) multiplied by the total salary of the court reporter or recorder.

(5) The clerk shall certify the figures determined under subrules (A)(3) and (4) to the treasurer of each political subdivision in the district. Payment by each political subdivision of any unpaid portion of its certified share of the cost and salaries is then due.

(B) Determination of Cases Entered and Commenced.

(1) *In the District.* The total number of cases entered and commenced in the district is the total number of civil and criminal cases filed in the district for the time period in question, excepting those cases not attributable to a specific political subdivision under subrules (B)(2)(b) and (B)(3)(b).

(2) *In Each Political Subdivision Having a District Court Clerk.* The total number of cases entered and commenced in each political subdivision having a district court clerk is the total number of civil and criminal cases filed in the political subdivision for the time period in question, excepting those cases involving a filing plaintiff and one or more defendants whose residences are outside the political subdivision where filed.

(a) Cases in which a filing plaintiff and one or more defendants reside in the same political subdivision are deemed to have been entered and commenced in that political subdivision, even though filed elsewhere for purposes of MCL 600.8104; MSA 27A.8104.

(b) Cases in which the filing plaintiff and one or more defendants reside outside the political subdivision where the case was filed, but none of the defendants resides in the same political subdivision as the plaintiff, are to be disregarded for purposes of this rule and MCL 600.8104; MSA 27A.8104.

(3) *In Each Political Subdivision Having No District Court Clerk.*

(a) The total number of cases entered and commenced for the time period in question in each political subdivision having no district court clerk is the total number of civil and criminal cases in which the filing plaintiff and one or more defendants reside in the political subdivision, no matter where the case is filed.

(b) If more than one political subdivision qualifies under subrule (B)(3)(a), all are credited with one case for purposes of this rule and MCL 600.8104; MSA 27A.8104.

[Effective March 1, 1985.]

1985 Staff Comment

MCR 8.201 is substantially the same as DCR 4003.

RULE 8.202 PAYMENT OF ASSIGNED ATTORNEYS AND TRANSCRIPT COSTS

(A) Misdemeanor Cases. The political subdivision or subdivisions responsible for maintaining, financing, and operating the appointing court are responsible for paying assigned attorneys, regardless of whether the defendant is charged with violating a state law or an ordinance, and regardless of whether a fine or costs are actually assessed. If a county board of commissioners has taken or takes formal action to relieve cities or townships of part or all of the cost of paying assigned attorneys, that formal action shall control the payment of assigned attorneys in that county.

(B) Appeals. If an indigent defendant appealing to circuit court from a district or municipal court conviction is entitled to an assigned attorney or a transcript, the cost shall be paid by the same political subdivision or divisions that were responsible for or would have been responsible for paying an assigned attorney under subrule (A).

[Effective March 1, 1985.]

1985 Staff Comment

MCR 8.202 incorporates the provisions of Administrative Orders 1975–6 and 1975–7 regarding payment of assigned counsel costs in district court.

RULE 8.203 RECORDS AND ENTRIES KEPT BY CLERK

The clerk of every district court shall maintain court records and make reports as prescribed by MCR 8.119.

[Effective March 1, 1985; amended effective November 30, 1999.]

1985 Staff Comment

MCR 8.203 is substantially the same as DCR 4002.

Staff Comment to 1999 Amendment

The amendments of MCR 2.113, 5.113, 5.901, 7.210, 8.105, 8.110, 8.116, 8.203, 8.205, and 8.302 [effective November 30, 1999] and the addition of MCR 2.518 and 8.119 [effective November 30, 1999] are to accommodate statewide records standards applicable to all courts and all clerks of the courts as developed and recommended by the Michigan Trial Court Case File Management Standards Committee.

RULE 8.204 BONDS FOR CLERKS, DEPUTIES, MAGISTRATES, AND OFFICIAL PROCESS SERVERS

All clerks, deputy clerks, magistrates, and official process servers of the district court must file with the chief judge a bond approved by the chief judge in a penal sum determined by the state court administrator, conditioned that the officer will

(1) perform the duties as clerk, deputy clerk, magistrate, or process server of that court; and

(2) account for and pay over all money which may be received by the officer to the person or persons lawfully entitled.

The bonds must be in favor of the court and the state.

[Effective March 1, 1985.]

1985 Staff Comment

MCR 8.204 is based on DCR 4005.1.

The amount of the required bonds will be set by the state court administrator, rather than by the rule.

RULE 8.205 MAGISTRATES

The court shall provide the name, address, and telephone number of each magistrate to the clerk of the district court for the district in which the magistrate serves.

[Effective March 1, 1985; amended effective November 30, 1999.]

1985 Staff Comment

MCR 8.205 is based on DCR 3001.5.

The form of the magistrate's report is deleted and will be prescribed by the state court administrator.

Subrule (B) is a new provision emphasizing that the district court provide the name, address, and telephone number of each magistrate to the clerk of the district court.

Staff Comment to 1999 Amendment

The amendments of MCR 2.113, 5.113, 5.901, 7.210, 8.105, 8.110, 8.116, 8.203, 8.205, and 8.302 [effective November 30, 1999] and the addition of MCR 2.518 and 8.119 [effective November 30, 1999] are to accommodate statewide records standards applicable to all courts and all clerks of the courts as developed and recommended by the Michigan Trial Court Case File Management Standards Committee.

SUBCHAPTER 8.300 ADMINISTRATIVE RULES APPLICABLE IN PROBATE COURT

RULE 8.301 POWERS OF REGISTER OF PROBATE, DEPUTY REGISTERS, AND CLERKS

(A) Judicial Responsibility. The judges of probate are responsible for the direction and supervision of the registers of probate, deputy registers of probate, probate clerks, and other personnel employed by the court to assist in the work of the court.

(B) Entry of Order Specifying Authority.

(1) To the extent authorized by the chief judge of a probate court by a general order, the probate register, the deputy probate register, the clerks of the probate court, and other court employees designated in the order, have the authority, until the further order of the court, to do all acts required of the probate judge except judicial acts in a contested matter and acts forbidden by law to be performed by the probate register.

(2) The order of the chief judge may refer to the power

(a) to set the time and place for hearings in all matters; take acknowledgments; administer oaths; sign notices for adoption investigations; sign notices to fiduciaries, attorneys, and sureties; sign citations and subpoenas; conduct conferences with fiduciaries required to ensure prompt administration of estates; and take testimony as provided by law or court rule; and

(b) to sign or by device indicate the name of a judge to all orders and letters of authority of the court, with the same force and effect as though the judge had signed them. In all such cases, the register or the designated deputy must place his or her initials under the name of the judge.

(C) Statutory Authority. In addition to the powers which may be granted by order of the chief judge, the probate registers and deputy registers have the authority granted by statute and may take acknowledgments to the same extent as a notary public.
[Effective March 1, 1985; amended effective February 1, 1995.]

1985 Staff Comment
MCR 8.301 is substantially the same as PCR 907.

Staff Comment to 1995 Amendment
Former MCR 5.602(B) is incorporated into subrule (B)(2)(b).

RULE 8.302 DOCUMENTS AND FILES
Original orders and letters of authority, after being recorded, must be placed in the files of the court. For security purposes, testamentary documents of deceased persons, bonds, orders, and such other documents as the court directs must be copied by microfilming or other means promptly after filing or issuance and preserved in the records of the court separately from the files.

In addition, the clerk of every probate court shall maintain court records and make reports as prescribed by MCR 8.119.
[Effective March 1, 1985; amended effective November 30, 1999.]

1985 Staff Comment
MCR 8.302 includes the portions of PCR 917.1 that cover the recording, copying, and filing of papers.

Staff Comment to 1999 Amendment
The amendments of MCR 2.113, 5.113, 5.901, 7.210, 8.105, 8.110, 8.116, 8.203, 8.205, and 8.302 [effective November 30, 1999] and the addition of MCR 2.518 and 8.119 [effective November 30, 1999] are to accommodate statewide records standards applicable to all courts and all clerks of the courts as developed and recommended by the Michigan Trial Court Case File Management Standards Committee.

RULE 8.303 [RENUMBERED RULE 5.313]
[Renumbered effective January 1, 2002.]

CHAPTER 9. PROFESSIONAL DISCIPLINARY PROCEEDINGS

Effective March 1, 1985

[For Table of Rules, see page 1 et seq.]

SUBCHAPTER 9.100 ATTORNEY GRIEVANCE COMMISSION; ATTORNEY DISCIPLINE BOARD

RULE 9.101 DEFINITIONS

As used in subchapter 9.100:

(1) "board" means the Attorney Discipline Board;

(2) "commission" means the Attorney Grievance Commission;

(3) "administrator" means the grievance administrator;

(4) "investigator" means a person designated by the administrator to assist him or her in the investigation of alleged misconduct or requested reinstatement;

(5) "attorney" means a person regularly licensed or specially admitted to practice law in Michigan;

(6) "respondent" means an attorney named in a request for investigation or complaint;

(7) "request for investigation" means the first step in bringing alleged misconduct to the administrator's attention;

(8) "complaint" means the formal charge prepared by the administrator and filed with the board;

(9) "review" means examination by the board of a hearing panel's final order on petition by an aggrieved party;

(10) "appeal" means judicial re-examination by the Supreme Court of the board's final order on petition by an aggrieved party;

(11) "grievance" means alleged misconduct;

(12) "investigation" means fact-finding on alleged misconduct under the administrator's direction;

(13) "disbarment" means revocation of the license to practice law.

[Effective March 1, 1985; amended effective June 1, 1987.]

1985 Staff Comment

MCR 9.101 is substantially the same as GCR 1963, 950.

RULE 9.102 CONSTRUCTION; SEVERABILITY

(A) Construction. Subchapter 9.100 is to be liberally construed for the protection of the public, the courts, and the legal profession and applies to all pending matters of misconduct and reinstatement and to all future proceedings, even though the alleged misconduct occurred before the effective date of subchapter 9.100. Procedures must be as expeditious as possible.

(B) Severability. If a court finds a portion of subchapter 9.100 or its application to a person or circumstances invalid, the invalidity does not affect the remaining portions or other applications. To this end the rules are severable.

[Effective March 1, 1985.]

1985 Staff Comment

MCR 9.102 includes the provisions of GCR 1963, 951.1 and 951.3.

GCR 1963, 951.2, concerning the application of masculine or singular words to the feminine or plural, is omitted. The singular/plural point is covered by MCR 1.107.

RULE 9.103 STANDARDS OF CONDUCT FOR ATTORNEYS

(A) General Principles. The license to practice law in Michigan is, among other things, a continuing proclamation by the Supreme Court that the holder is fit to be entrusted with professional and judicial matters and to aid in the administration of justice as an attorney and counselor and as an officer of the court. It is the duty of every attorney to conduct himself or herself at all times in conformity with standards imposed on members of the bar as a condition of the privilege to practice law. These standards include, but are not limited to, the rules of professional responsibility and the rules of judicial conduct that are adopted by the Supreme Court.

(B) Duty to Assist Public to Request Investigation. An attorney shall assist a member of the public to communicate to the administrator, in appropriate form, a request for investigation of a member of the bar.

(C) Duty to Assist Administrator. An attorney shall assist the administrator in the investigation, prosecution, and disposition of a request for investigation or complaint filed with or by the administrator.

[Effective March 1, 1985.]

1985 Staff Comment

MCR 9.103 is substantially the same as GCR 1963, 952.

RULE 9.104 GROUNDS FOR DISCIPLINE IN GENERAL; ADJUDICATION ELSEWHERE

(A) The following acts or omissions by an attorney, individually or in concert with another person, are misconduct and grounds for discipline, whether or not occurring in the course of an attorney-client relationship:

(1) conduct prejudicial to the proper administration of justice;

(2) conduct that exposes the legal profession or the courts to obloquy, contempt, censure, or reproach;

(3) conduct that is contrary to justice, ethics, honesty, or good morals;

(4) conduct that violates the standards or rules of professional responsibility adopted by the Supreme Court;

(5) conduct that violates a criminal law of a state or of the United States;

(6) knowing misrepresentation of any facts or circumstances surrounding a request for investigation or complaint;

(7) failure to answer a request for investigation or complaint in conformity with MCR 9.113 and 9.115(D);

(8) contempt of the board or a hearing panel; or

(9) violation of an order of discipline.

(B) Proof of an adjudication of misconduct in a disciplinary proceeding by another state or a United States court is conclusive proof of misconduct in a disciplinary proceeding in Michigan. The only issues to be addressed in the Michigan proceeding are whether the respondent was afforded due process of law in the course of the original proceedings and whether imposition of identical discipline in Michigan would be clearly inappropriate.

[Effective March 1, 1985; amended effective June 1, 1987; July 30, 2001.]

1985 Staff Comment

MCR 9.104 is substantially the same as GCR 1963, 953.

Staff Comment to 1987 Amendment

The [June 1, 1987] amendment to MCR 9.104(6) extends the subrule to cover requests for investigation in the same manner as formal complaints.

The [June 1, 1987] amendments to the final paragraph give foreign adjudications of misconduct full faith and credit by recognizing them as conclusive proof of misconduct. The additional language is taken from the American Bar Association Standards for Lawyer Discipline and Disability Proceedings, Standard No. 10.2.

Staff Comment to 2001 Amendment

The July 30, 2001 amendment of MRPC 8.1 expressly precluded bar applicants from engaging in the unauthorized practice of law, and stated an applicant's continuing obligation to update the affidavit of personal history. The structure of MCR 9.104 was changed for greater clarity.

RULE 9.105 PURPOSE AND FUNDING OF DISCIPLINARY PROCEEDINGS

Discipline for misconduct is not intended as punishment for wrongdoing, but for the protection of the public, the courts, and the legal profession. The fact that certain misconduct has remained unchallenged when done by others or when done at other times or has not been earlier made the subject of disciplinary proceedings is not an excuse. The legal profession, through the State Bar of Michigan, is responsible for the reasonable and necessary expenses of the board, the commission, and the administrator, as determined by the Supreme Court. Commissioners of the State Bar of Michigan may not represent respondents in proceedings before the board, including preliminary discussions with commission employees prior to the filing of a request for investigation.

[Effective March 1, 1985; amended effective July 27, 1990; October 1, 1993; November 21, 1995.]

1985 Staff Comment

MCR 9.105 is substantially the same as GCR 1963, 954.

Staff Comment to 1990 Amendment

The [July 27,] 1990 amendment prevents potential conflicts of interest by disqualifying from practice before the disciplinary agencies those attorneys (and their associates) who make decisions about the level of State Bar funding for the AGC and ADB.

Staff Comment to 1993 Amendment

The July 30, 1993, amendments of MCR 9.105, 9.108, and 9.110 [effective October 1, 1993] provide that the Supreme Court, rather than the State Bar Board of Commissioners will approve the budgets of the Attorney Grievance Commission and the Attorney Discipline Board. This change had been recommended by the State Bar Representative Assembly.

Staff Comment to 1995 Amendment

The 1995 amendment eliminated language that precluded lawyers associated in the practice of law with members of the State Bar Board of Commissioners from representing respondents in attorney disciplinary proceedings. The commissioners themselves still are prohibited from such representation, however.

RULE 9.106 TYPES OF DISCIPLINE; MINIMUM DISCIPLINE; ADMONISHMENT

Misconduct is grounds for:

(1) revocation of the license to practice law in Michigan;

(2) suspension of the license to practice law in Michigan for a specified term, not less than 30 days, with such additional conditions relevant to the established misconduct as a hearing panel, the board, or the Supreme Court may impose, and, if the term exceeds 179 days, until the further order of a hearing panel, the board, or the Supreme Court;

(3) reprimand with such conditions relevant to the established misconduct as a hearing panel, the board, or the Supreme Court may impose;

(4) probation ordered by a hearing panel, the board, or the Supreme Court under MCR 9.121(C);

(5) requiring restitution, in an amount set by a hearing panel, the board, or the Supreme Court, as a condition of an order of discipline; or

(6) with the respondent's consent, admonishment by the commission without filing a complaint. An admonition does not constitute discipline and shall be confidential under MCR 9.126 except as provided by MCR 9.115(J)(3). The administrator shall notify the respondent of the provisions of this rule and the respondent may, within 21 days of service of the admonition, notify the commission in writing that respondent objects to the admonition. Upon timely receipt of the written objection, the commission shall vacate the admonition and either dismiss the request for investigation or authorize the filing of a complaint.

[Effective March 1, 1985; amended effective June 1, 1987.]

1985 Staff Comment

MCR 9.106 is substantially the same as GCR 1963, 955.

Staff Comment to 1987 Amendment

The [June 1, 1987] expansion of MCR 9.106(2) and (3) will allow the adjudicative bodies greater discretion to impose temporary restrictions or requirements such as continuing legal education, reformation of law office operations, personal counseling, and other conditions relevant to the established misconduct and the causes thereof. These conditions would be in addition to the restrictions already mandated in the case of a suspension.

[Effective June 1, 1987] Amended MCR 9.106(2) provides that all suspensions must be for a period of at least 30 days.

[Effective June 1, 1987] Amended MCR 9.106(6) conforms the rule to the present practice under which the commission, rather than the administrator, exercises the power to admonish. It also details the admonishment procedure.

RULE 9.107 RULES EXCLUSIVE ON DISCIPLINE

(A) Proceedings for Discipline. Subchapter 9.100 governs the procedure to discipline attorneys. A proceeding under subchapter 9.100 is subject to the superintending control of the Supreme Court. An investigation or proceeding may not be held invalid because of a nonprejudicial irregularity or an error not resulting in a miscarriage of justice.

(B) Local Bar Associations. A local bar association may not conduct a separate proceeding to discipline an attorney, but must assist and cooperate with the administrator in reporting and investigating alleged misconduct of an attorney.

[Effective March 1, 1985.]

1985 Staff Comment

MCR 9.107 is substantially the same as GCR 1963, 956.

RULE 9.108 ATTORNEY GRIEVANCE COMMISSION

(A) Authority of Commission. The Attorney Grievance Commission is the prosecution arm of the Supreme Court for discharge of its constitutional responsibility to supervise and discipline Michigan attorneys.

(B) Composition. The commission consists of 3 laypersons and 6 attorneys appointed by the Supreme Court. The members serve 3–year terms. A member may not serve more than 2 full terms.

(C) Chairperson and Vice–Chairperson. The Supreme Court shall designate from among the members of the commission a chairperson and a vice-chairperson who shall serve 1–year terms in those offices. The commencement and termination dates for the 1–year terms shall coincide appropriately with the 3–year membership terms of those officers and the other commission members. The Supreme Court may reappoint these officers for additional terms and may remove these officers prior to the expiration of a term. An officer appointed to fill a mid-term vacancy shall serve the remainder of that term and may be reappointed to serve a full term.

(D) Internal Rules.

(1) The commission must elect annually from among its membership a secretary to keep the minutes of the commission's meetings and issue the required notices.

(2) Five members constitute a quorum. The commission acts by majority vote of the members present.

(3) The commission must meet monthly at a time and place the chairperson designates. Notice of a regular monthly meeting is not required.

(4) A special meeting may be called by the chairperson or by petition of 3 commission members on 7

days' written notice. The notice may be waived in writing or by attending the meeting.

(E) Powers and Duties. The commission has the power and duty to:

(1) recommend attorneys to the Supreme Court for appointment as administrator and deputy administrator;

(2) supervise the investigation of attorney misconduct, including requests for investigation of and complaints against attorneys;

(3) supervise the administrator and his or her staff;

(4) seek an injunction from the Supreme Court against an attorney's misconduct when prompt action is required, even if a disciplinary proceeding concerning that conduct is not pending before the board;

(5) annually write a budget for the commission and the administrator's office (including compensation) and submit it to the Supreme Court for approval;

(6) submit to the Supreme Court proposed changes in these rules;

(7) report to the Supreme Court at least quarterly regarding its activities, and to submit a joint annual report with the Attorney Discipline Board that summarizes the activities of both agencies during the past year; and

(8) perform other duties provided in these rules.

[Effective March 1, 1985; amended effective July 27, 1990; September 14, 1990; amended September 25, 1990; amended effective February 1, 1991; October 1, 1993; July 1, 1995; January 1, 2003.]

1985 Staff Comment

MCR 9.108 is substantially the same as GCR 1963, 957.

Staff Comment to July, 1990 Amendment

The [July 27,] 1990 amendments effected the following changes: (1) The Supreme Court will select the commission members who serve as chairperson and vice-chairperson; previously, the commission elected those officers. (2) Although appointed for one-year terms, the chairperson and vice-chairperson will serve at the pleasure of the Supreme Court and may be removed from office prior to the expiration of a term. (3) The Supreme Court will select the grievance administrator and the deputy administrator, but the commission will retain an advisory role in the selection process.

Staff Comment to September, 1990 Amendment

The [September 14, 1990] court rule change provides that all members of the Attorney Grievance Commission are to be appointed by the Michigan Supreme Court. The membership is increased from seven to nine members. Of the nine members, three are to be laypersons and six are to be attorneys. Five members will constitute a quorum.

Staff Comment to 1991 Amendment

The 1991 amendment added subrule (E)(7), requiring an annual report to the Supreme Court.

Staff Comment to 1993 Amendment

The July 30, 1993, amendments of MCR 9.105, 9.108, and 9.110 [effective October 1, 1993] provide that the Supreme Court, rather than the State Bar Board of Commissioners will approve the budgets of the Attorney Grievance Commission and the Attorney Discipline Board. This change had been recommended by the State Bar Representative Assembly.

Staff Comment to 1995 Amendment

The 1995 amendment of paragraph (E) requires the Attorney Grievance Commission to submit quarterly reports to the Supreme Court. The commission previously was required to submit annual reports.

Staff Comment to 2003 Amendment

The October 8, 2002 amendments of MCR 9.108(E)(7) and 9.110(E)(8), effective January 1, 2003, require at least quarterly reports from the Attorney Discipline Board and the Attorney Grievance Commission and a joint annual report that summarizes activities of both agencies.

The staff comment is published only for the benefit of the bench and bar and is not an authoritative construction by the Court.

RULE 9.109 GRIEVANCE ADMINISTRATOR

(A) Appointment. The administrator and the deputy administrator must be attorneys. The commission shall recommend one or more candidates for appointment as administrator and deputy administrator. The Supreme Court shall appoint the administrator and the deputy administrator, may terminate their appointments at any time with or without cause, and shall determine their salaries and the other terms and conditions of their employment.

(B) Powers and Duties. The administrator has the power and duty to:

(1) employ or retain attorneys, investigators, and staff with the approval of the commission;

(2) supervise the attorneys, investigators, and staff;

(3) assist the public in preparing requests for investigation;

(4) maintain the commission records created as a result of these rules;

(5) investigate alleged misconduct of attorneys, including serving a request for investigation in his or her own name if necessary;

(6) prosecute complaints the commission authorizes;

(7) prosecute or defend reviews and appeals as the commission authorizes; and

(8) perform other duties provided in these rules or assigned by the commission.

(C) Legal Counsel for the Administrator.

(1) The administrator may appoint and retain volunteer legal counsel needed to prosecute proceedings under these rules.

(2) Legal counsel may

(a) prepare and file complaints and notices of hearings;

(b) present evidence relating to complaints or petitions for reinstatement;

(c) prepare and file arguments and briefs;

(d) inform the administrator about the progress of cases assigned; and

(e) perform other duties assigned by the administrator.

[Effective March 1, 1985; amended effective July 27, 1990.]

1985 Staff Comment

MCR 9.109 is substantially the same as GCR 1963, 958.

Staff Comment to 1990 Amendment

The [July 27,] 1990 amendment shifted the responsibility for hiring the administrator and the deputy administrator from the Attorney Grievance Commission to the Supreme Court. The AGC retains an advisory role in the process.

RULE 9.110　ATTORNEY DISCIPLINE BOARD

(A) Authority of Board. The Attorney Discipline Board is the adjudicative arm of the Supreme Court for discharge of its exclusive constitutional responsibility to supervise and discipline Michigan attorneys.

(B) Composition. The board consists of 6 attorneys and 3 laypersons appointed by the Supreme Court. The members serve 3–year terms. A member may not serve more than 2 full terms.

(C) Chairperson and Vice–Chairperson. The Supreme Court shall designate from among the members of the board a chairperson and a vice-chairperson who shall serve 1–year terms in those offices. The commencement and termination dates of the 1–year terms shall coincide appropriately with the 3–year board terms of those officers and the other board members. The Supreme Court may reappoint these officers for additional terms and may remove an officer prior to the expiration of a term. An officer appointed to fill a midterm vacancy shall serve the remainder of that term and may be reappointed to serve a full term.

(D) Internal Rules.

(1) The board must elect annually from among its membership a secretary to supervise the keeping of the minutes of the board's meetings and the issuance of the required notices.

(2) Five members constitute a quorum. The board acts by a majority vote of the members present.

(3) The board shall meet monthly as often as necessary to maintain a current docket, but no less than every 2 months, at a time and place the chairperson designates.

(4) A special meeting may be called by the chairperson or by petition of 3 board members on 7 days' written notice. The notice may be waived in writing or by attending the meeting.

(E) Power and Duties. The board has the power and duty to:

(1) appoint an attorney to serve as its general counsel and executive director;

(2) appoint hearing panels and masters;

(3) assign a complaint to a hearing panel or to a master;

(4) on request of the respondent, the administrator, or the complainant, review a final order of discipline or dismissal by a hearing panel;

(5) discipline and reinstate attorneys under these rules;

(6) file with the Supreme Court clerk its orders of suspension, disbarment, and reinstatement;

(7) annually write a budget for the board and submit it to the Supreme Court for approval;

(8) report to the Supreme Court at least quarterly regarding its activities, and to submit a joint annual report with the Attorney Grievance Commission that summarizes the activities of both agencies during the past year; and

(9) submit to the Supreme Court proposed changes in these rules.

[Effective March 1, 1985; amended effective February 1, 1991; June 3, 1991; October 1, 1993; March 1, 1994; January 1, 2003.]

1985 Staff Comment

MCR 9.110 is substantially the same as GCR 1963, 959.

Staff Comment to February, 1991 Amendment

The [February 1,] 1991 amendment added subrule (D)(8), requiring an annual report to the Supreme Court.

Staff Comment to June, 1991 Amendment

Pursuant to the amendment of June 3, 1991, the Supreme Court will appoint all members of the Attorney Discipline Board as vacancies occur.

Staff Comment to 1993 Amendment

The July 30, 1993, amendments of MCR 9.105, 9.108, and 9.110 [effective October 1, 1993] provide that the Supreme Court, rather than the State Bar Board of Commissioners will approve the budgets of the Attorney Grievance Commission and the Attorney Discipline Board. This change had been recommended by the State Bar Representative Assembly.

The amendment [to subrule (B) effective October 1, 1993] increases the composition of the Attorney Discipline Board. Per the amendment the Board now consists of 6 attorneys and 3 laypersons.

Staff Comment to 1994 Amendment

The March 1, 1994 amendments provided for Supreme Court appointment of the board's officers (new subrule [C] and related changes elsewhere); revised the responsibilities of the board's secretary (subrule [E][1]); and clarified the procedures for assigning cases and taking appeals from hearing panel decisions (subrules [E][3] and [4]).

Staff Comment to 2003 Amendment

The October 8, 2002 amendments of MCR 9.108(E)(7) and 9.110(E)(8), effective January 1, 2003, require at least quarterly reports from the Attorney Discipline Board and the Attorney Grievance Commission and a joint annual report that summarizes activities of both agencies.

The staff comment is published only for the benefit of the bench and bar and is not an authoritative construction by the Court.

RULE 9.111   HEARING PANELS

(A) Composition; Quorum. The board must annually appoint 3 attorneys to each hearing panel and must fill a vacancy as it occurs. Following appointment, the board may designate the panel's chairperson, vice-chairperson and secretary. Thereafter, a hearing panel may elect a chairperson, vice-chairperson and secretary. A hearing panel must convene at the time and place designated by its chairperson or by the board. Two members constitute a quorum. A hearing panel acts by a majority vote. If a panel is unable to reach a majority decision, the matter shall be referred to the board for reassignment to a new panel.

(B) Powers and Duties. A hearing panel shall do the following:

(1) Hold a public hearing on a complaint or reinstatement petition assigned to it within 56 days after the date the complaint is filed with the board or the date that notice of the reinstatement petition is published. A hearing must be concluded within 91 days after it is begun, unless the board grants an extension for good cause.

(2) Receive evidence and make written findings of fact.

(3) Discipline and reinstate attorneys or dismiss a complaint by order, under these rules.

(4) Report its actions to the board within 28 days after the conclusion of a hearing.

(5) Perform other duties provided in these rules.

[Effective March 1, 1985; amended effective March 1, 1994.]

1985 Staff Comment

MCR 9.111 is substantially the same as GCR 1963, 960.

Staff Comment to 1994 Amendment

The March 1, 1994 amendments to subrule (A) modified the procedures for choosing hearing panel officers and specified the procedure to be followed if a hearing panel is unable to reach a majority decision.

RULE 9.112   REQUESTS FOR INVESTIGATION

(A) Availability to Public. The administrator shall furnish a form for a request for investigation to a person who alleges misconduct against an attorney. Forms must be available to the public through each state bar office and county clerk's office. Use of the form is not required for filing a request for investigation.

(B) Form of Request. A request for investigation of alleged misconduct must

(1) be in writing;

(2) describe the alleged misconduct, including the approximate time and place of it;

(3) be signed by the complainant; and

(4) be filed with the administrator.

(C) Handling by Administrator.

(1) *Request for Investigation of Attorney.* After making a preliminary investigation, the administrator shall either

    (a) notify the complainant and the respondent that the allegations of the request for investigation are inadequate, incomplete, or insufficient to warrant the further attention of the commission; or

    (b) serve a copy of the request for investigation on the respondent by ordinary mail at the respondent's address on file with the State Bar as required by Rule 2 of the Supreme Court Rules Concerning the State Bar of Michigan. Service is effective at the time of mailing, and nondelivery does not affect the validity of service. If a respondent has not filed an answer, no formal complaint shall be filed with the board unless the administrator has served the request for investigation by registered or certified mail return receipt requested.

(2) *Request for Investigation of Judge.* The administrator shall forward to the Judicial Tenure Commission a request for investigation of a judge, even if the request arises from the judge's conduct before he or she became a judge or from conduct unconnected with his or her judicial office. MCR 9.116 thereafter governs.

(3) *Request for Investigation of Member or Employee of Commission or Board.* Except as modified by MCR 9.131, MCR 9.104–9.130 apply to a request for investigation of an attorney who is a member of or is employed by the board or the commission.

(D) Subpoenas.

(1) After the request for investigation has been served on the respondent, the commission may issue subpoenas to require the appearance of a witness or the production of documents or other tangible things concerning matters then under investigation. Documents or other tangible things so produced may be

subjected to nondestructive testing. Subpoenas shall be returnable before the administrator or a person designated by the administrator.

(2) A person who without just cause, after being commanded by a subpoena, fails or refuses to appear or give evidence, to be sworn or affirmed, or to answer a proper question after being ordered to do so is in contempt. The administrator may initiate a contempt proceeding under MCR 3.606 in the circuit court for the county where the act or refusal to act occurred.

(3) A subpoena issued pursuant to this subrule and certified by the commission chairperson shall be sufficient authorization for taking a deposition or seeking the production of evidence outside the State of Michigan. If the deponent or the person possessing the subpoenaed evidence will not comply voluntarily, the proponent of the subpoena may utilize MCR 2.305(D) or any similar provision in a statute or court rule of Michigan or of the state, territory, or country where the deponent or possessor resides or is present.

[Effective March 1, 1985; amended effective June 1, 1987; February 1, 1991; January 29, 1992; March 1, 1994.]

1985 Staff Comment

MCR 9.112 is substantially the same as GCR 1963, 961.

Staff Comment to 1987 Amendment

The [June 1, 1987] change in MCR 9.112(A) codifies an Attorney Discipline Board decision.

Staff Comment to 1991 Amendment

The [February 1,] 1991 amendment added to subrule (C)(1)(a) the requirement that the respondent attorney be given notice of the request for investigation even if the request is rejected at the preliminary investigation stage.

Staff Comment to 1992 Amendment

The amendment effective January 29, 1992 added subrule (D) dealing with subpoenas. Many of the provisions formerly appeared in MCR 9.114. The amendment also specified when investigative subpoenas may be issued and authorized the nondestructive testing of subpoenaed items.

Staff Comment to 1994 Amendment

The March 1, 1994 amendment added subrule (D)(3), which states that a subpoena issued by the AGC authorizes the holder to seek the assistance of courts in other states to compel attendance at a deposition or the production of tangible evidence.

RULE 9.113   ANSWER BY RESPONDENT

(A) **Answer.** Within 21 days after being served with a request for investigation under MCR 9.112(C)(1)(b), the respondent shall file with the administrator a signed, written answer in duplicate fully and fairly disclosing all the facts and circumstances pertaining to the alleged misconduct. The administrator may allow further time to answer. Misrepresentation in the answer is grounds for discipline. The administrator shall provide a copy of the answer and any supporting documents to the person who filed the

request for investigation unless the administrator determines that there is cause for not disclosing some or all of the documents.

(B) **Refusal or Failure to Answer.**

(1) A respondent may refuse to answer a request for investigation on expressed constitutional or professional grounds.

(2) The failure of a respondent to answer within the time permitted is misconduct. See MCR 9.104(7).

(3) If a respondent refuses to answer under subrule (B)(1), the refusal may be submitted to a hearing panel for adjudication.

(C) **Attorney-Client Privilege.** A person who files a request for investigation of an attorney waives any attorney-client privilege that he or she may have as to matters relating to the request for the purposes of the commission's investigation.

[Effective March 1, 1985; amended effective June 1, 1987; February 1, 1991.]

1985 Staff Comment

MCR 9.113 corresponds to GCR 1963, 962.

Subrule (C) is a new provision regarding waiver of the attorney-client privilege.

Staff Comment to 1987 Amendment

The [June 1, 1987] addition to MCR 9.113(A) clarifies the requirement that answers to requests for investigation must be in writing.

[Effective June 1, 1987] MCR 9.114(A)(2) has been moved and renumbered MCR 9.113(B)(3) because it more properly belongs in this rule. The submission to a hearing panel is permissive rather than mandatory since, in most cases, the administrator will not contest the propriety of respondent's exercise of a privilege, and submission to a hearing panel in such circumstances would be unnecessary.

Staff Comment to 1991 Amendment

The [February 1,] 1991 amendment to subrule (A) added the requirement that the complainant be given copies of the respondent's answer and any supporting documents.

RULE 9.114   ACTION BY ADMINISTRATOR OR COMMISSION AFTER ANSWER

(A) **Action After Investigation.** After an answer is filed or the time for filing an answer has expired, the administrator may assign the matter for further investigation, including, if necessary, an informal hearing. When the investigation is complete, the administrator shall either

(1) dismiss the request for investigation and notify the complainant and the respondent of the reasons for the dismissal, or

(2) refer the matter to the commission for its review. The commission may direct that a complaint be filed, that the request be dismissed, or that the re-

spondent be admonished with the respondent's consent.

(B) Contractual Probation. For purposes of this subrule, "contractual probation" means the placement of a consenting respondent on probation by the commission, without the filing of formal charges. Contractual probation does not constitute discipline, and shall be confidential under MCR 9.126 except as provided by MCR 9.115(J)(3).

(1) If the commission finds that the alleged misconduct, if proven, would not result in a substantial suspension or revocation of a respondent's license to practice law, the commission may defer disposition of the matter and place the respondent on contractual probation for a period not to exceed two years, provided the following criteria are met:

(a) the misconduct is significantly related to a substance abuse problem of the respondent,

(b) the terms and conditions of the contractual probation, which shall include an appropriate period of treatment, are agreed upon by the grievance administrator and the respondent prior to submission to the commission for consideration, and

(c) the commission determines that contractual probation is appropriate and in the best interests of the public, the courts, the legal profession, and the respondent.

(2) The respondent is responsible for any costs associated with the contractual probation and related treatment.

(3) Upon written notice to the respondent and an opportunity to file written objections, the commission may terminate the contractual probation and file a formal complaint or take other appropriate action based on the misconduct, if

(a) the respondent fails to satisfactorily complete the terms and conditions of the contractual probation, or

(b) the commission concludes that the respondent has committed other misconduct that warrants the filing of a formal complaint.

(4) The placing of a respondent on contractual probation shall constitute a final disposition that entitles the complainant to notice in accordance with MCR 9.114(D), and to file a mandamus action in accordance with MCR 9.122(A)(2).

(C) Assistance of Law Enforcement Agencies. The administrator may request a law enforcement office to assist in an investigation by furnishing all available information about the respondent. Law enforcement officers are requested to comply promptly with each request.

(D) Report by Administrator. The administrator shall inform the complainant and, if the respondent answered, the respondent, of the final disposition of

every request for investigation dismissed by the commission without a hearing before a hearing panel.

(E) Retention of Records. All files and records relating to allegations of misconduct by an attorney must be retained by the commission for the lifetime of the attorney, except as follows:

(1) The administrator may destroy the files or records relating to a request for investigation dismissed by the commission after 3 years have elapsed from the date of dismissal.

(2) If no request for investigation was pending when the files or records were created or acquired, and no related request for investigation was filed subsequently, the administrator may destroy the files or records after 3 years have elapsed from the date when they were created or acquired by the commission.

[Effective March 1, 1985; amended effective June 1, 1987; September 27, 1990; January 29, 1992; September 1, 1995; December 1, 1995; April 1, 1998.]

1985 Staff Comment

MCR 9.114 is substantially the same as GCR 1963, 963.

Staff Comment to 1987 Amendment

The [June 1, 1987] change in MCR 9.114(A) transfers the power to admonish from the grievance administrator to the grievance commission, in conformity with present practice and amended MCR 9.106(6). The last sentence of MCR 9.114(A) has been moved to MCR 9.113(B)(3). New subrule MCR 9.114(C)(2) provides for enforcement of the subpoena in the same manner as provided for hearing panel subpoenas in MCR 9.115(I)(2).

Staff Comment to 1990 Amendment

The [July 27,] 1990 amendment to subrule (E) modified the rules regarding the retention of commission records.

Staff Comment to 1992 Amendment

The amendment effective January 29, 1992 moved former subrule (C) [with changes] to MCR 9.112.

Staff Comment to September, 1995 Amendment

The 1995 amendment of MCR 9.114 permits the commission to defer disposition of a discipline matter and place a consenting respondent on contractual probation for up to two years, provided the alleged misconduct is significantly related to substance abuse and, if proven, would not result in a substantial suspension or revocation of the respondent's license to practice law.

Staff Comment to December, 1995 Amendment

The 1995 amendment of MCR 9.114(A) authorizes the Grievance Administrator to dismiss a request for investigation after an answer is filed, without referring the matter to the Attorney Grievance Commission.

Staff Comment to 1998 Amendment

The March 24, 1998, amendments [effective April 1, 1998] of 2.109, 2.111, 2.112, 2.119, 8.103, 8.106, 8.110, 8.111, 9.114, and 9.203, make technical changes necessary in light of statutory amendments and correct cross-references.

The amendments of MCR 2.109 and 2.112 relate to amendments of MCR 600.2912d, 600.2912e; MSA 27A.2912(d), 27A.2912(e), by 1993 PA 78.

The amendments of MCR 2.111 and 2.119 are based on statutes amended by 1996 PA 388. The change in MCR 2.111(B)(2) applies to actions filed on or after January 1, 1998, the effective date of the statute increasing the jurisdictional limit of the district court.

The amendment of MCR 8.106 corrects a statutory reference in light of 1993 PA 189.

The remaining amendments make changes in cross-references necessitated by earlier amendments. Some published versions of the rules already include several of these corrections.

RULE 9.115 HEARING PANEL PROCEDURE

(A) Rules Applicable. Except as otherwise provided in these rules, the rules governing practice and procedure in a nonjury civil action apply to a proceeding before a hearing panel. Pleadings must conform as nearly as practicable to the requirements of subchapter 2.100. The original of the formal complaint and all other pleadings must be filed with the board. The formal complaint must be served on the respondent. All other pleadings must be served on the opposing party and each member of the hearing panel. Proof of service of the formal complaint may be filed at any time prior to the date of the hearing. Proof of service of all other pleadings must be filed with the original pleadings.

(B) Complaint. Except as provided by MCR 9.120, a complaint setting forth the facts of the alleged misconduct begins proceedings before a hearing panel. The administrator shall prepare the complaint, file it with the board, and serve it on the respondent and, if the respondent is a member of or is associated with a law firm, on the firm. The unwillingness of a complainant to prosecute, or a settlement between the complainant and the respondent, does not itself affect the right of the administrator to proceed.

(C) Service. Service of the complaint and all subsequent pleadings and orders must be made by personal service or by registered or certified mail addressed to the person at the person's last known address. An attorney's last known address is the address on file with the state bar as required by Rule 2 of the Supreme Court Rules Concerning the State Bar of Michigan. A respondent's attorney of record must also be served, but service may be made under MCR 2.107. Service is effective at the time of mailing, and nondelivery does not affect the validity of the service.

(D) Answer.

(1) Within 21 days after the complaint is served, the respondent shall file and serve a signed answer as provided in subrule (A).

(2) A default, with the same effect as a default in a civil action, may enter against a respondent who fails within the time permitted to file an answer admitting, denying, or explaining the complaint, or asserting the grounds for failing to do so.

(E) Representation by Attorney. The respondent may be represented by an attorney, who must enter an appearance.

(F) Prehearing Procedure.

(1) *Extensions.* If good cause is shown, the hearing panel chairperson may grant one extension of time per party for filing pleadings and may grant one adjournment per party. Additional requests may be granted by the board chairperson if good cause is shown. Pending criminal or civil litigation of substantial similarity to the allegations of the complaint is not necessarily grounds for an adjournment.

(2) *Motion to Disqualify.*

(a) Within 14 days after an answer has been filed or the time for filing the answer has expired, each member of the hearing panel shall disclose in a writing filed with the board any information that the member believes could be grounds for disqualification under the guidelines of MCR 2.003(B). The duty to disclose shall be a continuing one. The board shall serve a copy of the disclosure on each party.

(b) Within 14 days after the board serves a copy of a written disclosure, the respondent or the administrator may move to disqualify a member of the hearing panel. The board chairperson shall decide the motion under the guidelines of MCR 2.003.

(c) The board must assign a substitute for a disqualified member of a hearing panel. If all are disqualified, the board must reassign the complaint to another panel.

(3) *Amendment of Pleadings.* The administrator and the respondent each may amend a pleading once as a matter of course within 14 days after being served with a responsive pleading by the opposing party, or within 15 days after serving the pleading if it does not require a responsive pleading. Otherwise, a party may amend a pleading only by leave granted by the hearing panel chairperson or with the written consent of the adverse party.

(4) *Discovery.* Pretrial or discovery proceedings are not permitted, except as follows:

(a) Within 21 days of the service of a formal complaint, a party may demand in writing that documentary evidence that is to be introduced at the hearing by the opposing party be made available for inspection or copying. Within 14 days after service of a written demand, the documents shall be made available, provided that the administrator need not comply prior to the filing of the respondent's answer; in such case, the administrator shall comply with the written demand within 14 days of the filing of the respondent's answer. The respondent shall comply with the written demand within 14 days, except that the respondent need not comply until the time for filing an answer to the formal complaint has expired. Any other documentary evidence to be introduced at the hearing by either party shall be supplied to the other party no later than 14 days prior to the hearing. Any documentary evidence not so supplied shall be excluded from the hearing except for good cause shown.

(b) Within 21 days of the service of a formal complaint, a party may demand in writing that the opposing party supply written notification of the name and address of any person to be called as a witness. Within 14 days after the service of a written demand, the notification shall be supplied. However, the administrator need not comply prior to the filing of the respondent's answer to the formal complaint; in such cases, the administrator shall comply with the written demand within 14 days of the filing of the respondent's answer to the formal complaint. The respondent shall comply with the written demand within 14 days, except that the respondent need not comply until the time for filing an answer to the formal complaint has expired. Except for good cause shown, a party who is required to give said notification must give supplemental notice to the adverse party within 7 days after any additional witness has been identified, and must give the supplemental notice immediately if the additional witness is identified less than 14 days before a scheduled hearing.

Upon receipt of a demand made pursuant to this rule, a party must also provide to the other party any statements given by witnesses to be called at the hearing. Witness statements include stenographic, recorded, or written statements of witnesses provided to the administrator, the respondent, or the respondent's representative. The term "written statement" does not include notes or memoranda prepared by a party or a party's representative of conversations with witnesses, or other privileged information.

(c) A deposition may be taken of a witness who lives outside the state or is physically unable to attend the hearing. For good cause shown, the hearing panel may allow the parties to depose other witnesses.

(d) The hearing panel may order a prehearing conference held before a panel member to obtain admissions or otherwise narrow the issues presented by the pleadings.

If a party fails to comply with subrule (F)(4)(a) or (b), the hearing panel or the board may, on motion and showing of material prejudice as a result of the failure, impose one or more of the sanctions set forth in MCR 2.313(B)(2)(a)–(c).

(5) *Discipline by Consent.* A respondent may offer to plead nolo contendere or to admit all essential facts contained in the complaint or any of its allegations in exchange for a stated form of discipline and on the condition that the plea or admission and discipline agreed on is accepted by the commission and the hearing panel. The respondent's offer shall first be submitted to the commission. If the offer is accepted by the commission, the administrator and the respondent shall prepare a stipulation for a consent order of discipline and file the stipulation with the hearing panel. At the time of the filing, the administrator shall serve a copy of the proposed stipulation upon the complainant. If the hearing panel approves the stipulation, it shall enter a final order of discipline. If not approved, the offer is deemed withdrawn and statements or stipulations made in connection with the offer are inadmissible in disciplinary proceedings against the respondent and not binding on the respondent or the administrator. If the stipulation is not approved, the matter must then be referred for hearing to a hearing panel other than the one that passed on the proposed discipline.

(G) Hearing Time and Place; Notice. The board or the chairperson of the hearing panel shall set the time and place for a hearing. Notice of a hearing must be served by the board or the chairperson of the hearing panel on the administrator, the respondent, the complainant, and any attorney of record at least 21 days before the initial hearing. Unless the board or the chairperson of the hearing panel otherwise directs, the hearing must be in the county in which the respondent has or last had an office or residence. If the hearing panel fails to convene or complete its hearing within a reasonable time, the board may reassign the complaint to another panel or to a master. A party may file a motion for a change of venue. The motion must be filed with the board and shall be decided by the board chairperson, in part, on the basis of the guidelines in MCR 2.221.

(H) Respondent's Appearance. The respondent shall personally appear at the hearing and is subject to cross-examination as an opposite party under MCL 600.2161; MSA 27A.2161. If the respondent, or the respondent's attorney on his or her behalf, claims physical or mental incapacity as a reason for the respondent's failure to appear before a hearing panel or the board, the panel or the board on its own initiative may suspend the respondent from the practice of law until further order of the panel or board. The order of suspension must be filed and served as other orders of discipline.

(I) Hearing; Contempt.

(1) A hearing panel may issue subpoenas (including subpoenas for production of documents and other tangible things), cause testimony to be taken under oath, and rule on the admissibility of evidence under the Michigan Rules of Evidence. The oath or affirmation may be administered by a panel member. A

subpoena must be issued in the name and under the seal of the board. It must be signed by a panel or board member, by the administrator, or by the respondent or the respondent's attorney. A subpoenaed witness must be paid the same fee and mileage as a witness subpoenaed to testify in the circuit court. Parties must notify their own witnesses of the date, time, and place of the hearing.

(2) A person who without just cause fails or refuses to appear and give evidence as commanded by a subpoena, to be sworn or affirmed, or to answer a proper question after he or she has been ordered to do so, is in contempt. The administrator may initiate a contempt proceeding under MCR 3.606 in the circuit court for the county where the act or refusal to act occurred.

(J) Decision.

(1) The hearing panel must file a report on its decisions regarding the misconduct charges and, if applicable, the resulting discipline. The report must include a certified transcript, a summary of the evidence, pleadings, exhibits and briefs, and findings of fact. The discipline section of the report must also include a summary of all previous misconduct for which the respondent was disciplined or admonished.

(2) Upon a finding of misconduct, the hearing panel shall conduct a separate hearing to determine the appropriate discipline. The hearing on discipline shall be conducted as soon after the finding of misconduct as is practicable and may be held immediately following the panel's ruling that misconduct has been established.

(3) If the hearing panel finds that the charge of misconduct is established by a preponderance of the evidence, it must enter an order of discipline. The order shall take effect 21 days after it is served on the respondent unless the panel finds good cause for the order to take effect on a different date, in which event the panel's decision must explain the reasons for ordering a different effective date. In determining the discipline to be imposed, any and all relevant evidence of aggravation or mitigation shall be admissible, including previous admonitions and orders of discipline, and the previous placement of the respondent on contractual probation.

(4) If the hearing panel finds that the charge of misconduct is not established by a preponderance of the evidence, it must enter an order dismissing the complaint.

(5) The report and order must be signed by the panel chairperson and filed with the board and the administrator. A copy must be served on the parties as required by these rules.

(K) Stay of Discipline. If a discipline order is a suspension of 179 days or less, a stay of the discipline order will automatically issue on the timely filing by the respondent of a petition for review and a petition

for a stay of the discipline. If the discipline ordered is more severe than a suspension of 179 days, the respondent may petition the board for a stay pending review of the discipline order. Once granted, a stay remains effective until the further order of the board.

(L) Enforcement. The administrator shall take the necessary steps to enforce a discipline order after it is effective.

(M) Resignation by Respondent; Admission of Charges. An attorney's request that his or her name be stricken from the official register of attorneys may not be accepted while a request for investigation or a complaint is pending, except pursuant to an order of revocation.

[Effective March 1, 1985; amended effective June 1, 1987; March 1, 1994; September 1, 1995; April 1, 1998, to apply to formal complaints filed on or after that date.]

1985 Staff Comment

MCR 9.115 is substantially the same as GCR 1963, 964.

Staff Comment to 1987 Amendment

[Effective June 1, 1987] MCR 9.115(A) specifies service and filing requirements, and adds a requirement that hearing panel members be served with copies of the pleadings.

MCR 9.115(B) is amended [effective June 1, 1987] to acknowledge the different procedure employed in MCR 9.120 (attorney convicted of a crime). Additionally, deletion of the phrase "14 days later" incorporates an intervening amendment to former GCR 1963, 964.2, the predecessor of this rule.

MCR 9.115(F)(4)(a) and (b) are amended [effective June 1, 1987] to provide for reciprocal discovery.

MCR 9.115(G) is amended [effective June 1, 1987] to provide for service of notices of hearing on the grievance administrator and the attorneys of record. It also authorizes the board to refer a complaint to a master if the hearing panel fails to act within a reasonable time.

MCR 9.115(J) is amended [effective June 1, 1987] to provide for a bifurcated hearing procedure. The first phase determines misconduct if any; the second phase determines the discipline. Subrule (J)(3) provides that prior discipline orders or admonishments, if any, should be considered by a hearing panel in the assessment of discipline.

MCR 9.115(K) is amended [effective June 1, 1987] to conform with MCR 9.122(C). Both rules will now provide for an automatic stay pending appeal when the discipline order imposes a suspension of less than 180 days. This rule governs appeals to the board. MCR 9.122(C) governs appeals to the Supreme Court.

MCR 9.115(M) is amended [effective June 1, 1987] to eliminate past uncertainty regarding the effect of a resignation while charges were still pending.

Staff Comment to 1994 Amendment

The March 1, 1994 amendments: (1) authorized the chairperson of the hearing panel to act on behalf of the panel, and the chairperson of the board to act on behalf of the board, in ruling on requests for extensions (subrule [F][1]); (2) required hearing panelists to make advance written disclosures of possible grounds for their disqualification (subrule [F][2]); (3) allowed pleadings to be amended once as a matter of right and subsequently by leave granted or if the opposing party consents (subrule [F][3]); (4) expanded the authority for taking depositions (subrule [F][4]); (5) required that an offer of consent discipline be approved by the commission before being submitted to a hearing panel (subrule [F][5]); (6) allowed a party to move for a change of venue (subrule [G]); (7) allowed a hearing panel to submit a single report covering its findings on both misconduct and discipline (subrule [J][1]); (8) allowed the hearing panel to begin the hearing on discipline immediately after announcing its findings regarding misconduct (subrule [J][2]); (9) allowed the hearing panel to specify that its discipline order shall take effect either earlier or later than the otherwise presumed 21 days after the order is entered (subrule [J][3]); (10) required the respondent to petition for a stay pending review even in situations where the stay will be granted automatically if it is requested (subrule [K]).

Staff Comment to 1995 Amendment

The 1995 amendment of MCR 9.115(J) permits a hearing panel, when determining discipline, to consider a respondent's previous placement on contractual probation under the 1995 amendment of MCR 9.114.

Staff Comment to 1997 Amendment

The 1997 amendment of the rule, which took effect April 1, 1998, added a second paragraph to MCR 9.115(F)(4)(b). The change, which was recommended by the State Bar of Michigan, permits reciprocal discovery of witness statements in lawyer discipline proceedings.

RULE 9.116 HEARING PROCEDURE; JUDGES OTHER THAN MAGISTRATES AND REFEREES

(A) Application of This Rule. This rule governs an action by the commission against a judge, except that it does not apply to an action against a magistrate or referee for misconduct separately arising from the practice of law, whether before or during the period when the person serves as a magistrate or referee.

(B) Time. The commission may not take action against a judge unless and until the Judicial Tenure Commission recommends a sanction. Then, notwithstanding the pendency of certification to and review by the Supreme Court of the Judicial Tenure Commission's action, the commission may, without an investigation, direct the administrator to file a complaint with the board.

(C) Complaint; Time and Place of Hearing; Answer. The administrator shall file a complaint setting forth the facts of the alleged misconduct within 14 days after the Judicial Tenure Commission files its order with the Supreme Court. The chairperson of the hearing panel assigned by the board shall designate a place and a time for the hearing no later than 21 days after the complaint is filed. The complaint and notice of the hearing must be served within 7 days after the complaint is filed. Within 14 days after the complaint and notice of the hearing are served, the respondent judge shall file an answer.

(D) Rules Applicable; Judicial Tenure Commission Record. To the extent it is consistent with this rule, MCR 9.115 governs hearing procedure against a respondent judge. The record of the Judicial Tenure Commission proceeding is admissible at the hearing. The administrator or the respondent may introduce additional evidence.

(E) Decision. Within 28 days after the hearing is concluded, the panel must file with the Supreme Court clerk and the board a report and order conforming with MCR 9.115(J) and serve them on the administrator and the respondent.

(1) If the Judicial Tenure Commission has recommended suspension, the panel may not disbar the respondent and may not suspend the respondent from practicing law for a period beginning earlier than or extending beyond the suspension period recommended by the Judicial Tenure Commission.

(2) If the Judicial Tenure Commission has not recommended either suspension or removal from office, and the respondent continues to hold a judicial office, then the panel may not disbar or suspend the respondent.

(3) If the Judicial Tenure Commission has recommended removal from office, or if the respondent no longer holds a judicial office, then the panel may impose any type of discipline authorized by these rules.

(F) Appeal. The respondent-judge may file a petition for review under MCR 9.118.

[Effective March 1, 1985; amended effective June 1, 1987; January 1, 1995.]

1985 Staff Comment

MCR 9.116 is substantially the same as GCR 1963, 965.

Staff Comment to 1987 Amendment

[Effective June 1, 1987] MCR 9.116(D) is amended, and MCR 9.116(E) is added to clarify the present practice.

Staff Comment to 1995 Amendment

Subrule (A) took effect in 1995. It permits the Attorney Grievance Commission to proceed against a lawyer who is a magistrate or referee and who is charged with misconduct unrelated to the duties of a magistrate or referee, without waiting for the Judicial Tenure Commission to make a recommendation. In such a case, subrule (A) also has the effect of removing the ceiling on discipline stated in subrule (E).

RULE 9.117 HEARING PROCEDURE BEFORE MASTER

If the board assigns a complaint to a master, the master shall hold a public hearing on the complaint and receive evidence. To the extent that MCR 9.115 may be applied, it governs procedure before a master. After the hearing, the master shall prepare a report containing

(1) a brief statement of the proceedings,

(2) findings of fact, and

(3) conclusions of law.

The master shall file the report with a hearing panel designated by the board and serve a copy on the administrator and the respondent. Within 14 days after the report is filed, the administrator or the respondent may file objections to the report and a supporting brief. The panel must determine if the record supports the findings of fact and conclusions of law and impose discipline, if warranted. Further proceedings are governed by MCR 9.118.

[Effective March 1, 1985.]

1985 Staff Comment

MCR 9.117 is substantially the same as GCR 1963, 966.

RULE 9.118 REVIEW OF ORDER OF HEARING PANEL

(A) Review of Order; Time.

(1) The administrator, the complainant, or the respondent may petition the board in writing to review the order of a hearing panel filed under MCR 9.115, 9.116, 9.121 or 9.124. A petition for review must set forth the reasons and the grounds on which review is sought and must be filed with the board within 21 days after the order is served. The petitioner must serve copies of the petition and the accompanying documents on the other party and the complainant and file a proof of service with the board.

(2) A cross-petition for review may be filed within 21 days after the petition for review is served on the cross-petitioner. The cross-petition must be served on the other party and the complainant, and a proof of service must be filed with the board.

(3) A delayed petition for review may be considered by the board chairperson under the guidelines of MCR 7.205(F). If a petition for review is filed more than 12 months after the order of the hearing panel is entered, the petition may not be granted.

(B) Order to Show Cause.

If a petition for review is timely filed or a delayed petition for review is accepted for filing, the board shall issue an order to show cause, at a date and time specified, why the order of the hearing panel should not be affirmed. The order shall establish a briefing schedule for all parties and may require that an answer to the petition or cross-petition be filed. An opposing party may file an answer even if the order does not require one. The board must serve the order to show cause on the administrator, respondent, and complainant at least 21 days before the hearing. Failure to comply with the order to show cause, including, but not limited to, a requirement for briefs, may be grounds for dismissal of a petition for review. Dismissal of a petition for review shall not affect the validity of a cross-petition for review.

(C) Hearing.

(1) A hearing on the order to show cause must be heard by a subboard of at least 3 board members assigned by the chairperson. The board must make a final decision on consideration of the whole record, including a transcript of the presentation made to the subboard and the subboard's recommendation. The respondent shall appear personally at the review hearing unless excused by the board. Failure to appear may result in denial of any relief sought by the respondent, or any other action allowable under MCR 9.118(D).

(2) If the board believes that additional testimony should be taken, it may refer the case to a hearing panel or a master. The panel or the master shall then take the additional testimony and make a supplemental report, including a transcript of the additional testimony, pleadings, exhibits, and briefs with the board. Notice of the filing of the supplemental report and a copy of the report must be served as an original report and order of a hearing panel.

(D) Decision.

After the hearing on the order to show cause, the board may affirm, amend, reverse, or nullify the order of the hearing panel in whole or in part or order other discipline. A discipline order is not effective until 21 days after it is served on the respondent unless the board finds good cause for the order to take effect earlier.

(E) Motion for Reconsideration; Stay.

A motion for reconsideration may be filed at any time before the board's order takes effect. An answer to a motion for reconsideration may be filed. The board may grant a stay pending its decision on a motion for reconsideration. If the board grants a stay, the stay remains effective for 21 days after the board enters its order granting or denying reconsideration. In the absence of an order by the board, the filing of a motion for reconsideration does not stay an order of discipline.

(F) Filing Orders.

The board must file a copy of its discipline order with the Supreme Court clerk and the clerk of the county where the respondent resides and where his or her office is located. The order must be served on all parties. If the respondent requests it in writing, a dismissal order must be similarly filed and served.

[Effective March 1, 1985; amended effective June 1, 1987; March 1, 1994; January 1, 2001.]

1985 Staff Comment

MCR 9.118 is substantially the same as GCR 1963, 967.

Staff Comment to 1987 Amendment

MCR 9.118(A)(3) is added [effective June 1, 1987] to codify existing practice regarding delayed petitions. New subrule (A)(2) provides for cross-petitions.

MCR 9.118(B) is amended [effective June 1, 1987] to provide for dismissal of petitions for review that are not timely prosecuted.

MCR 9.118(C) is amended [effective June 1, 1987] to require a respondent to appear at a review hearing. This is a codification of language now routinely included in board orders to show cause.

MCR 9.118(D) is amended [effective June 1, 1987] to codify present practice allowing motions for reconsideration and provide that the board may stay an order of discipline while it considers a motion for reconsideration. See also MCR 9.122(A)(1).

Staff Comment to 1994 Amendment

The March 1, 1994 amendments: (1) listed in subrule (A)(1) the orders that are appealable to the board; (2) in subrule (A)(1), added a requirement that a copy of the petition for review be served on the person who filed the request for investigation; (3) added to subrule (A)(2) a requirement that the cross-petition for review be served on the other interested parties; (4) in subrule (A)(3), authorized the board's chairperson, rather than the full board, to make the decision on whether to accept a delayed petition for review; (5) added to subrule (B) provisions for a briefing schedule; (6) moved the reconsideration and stay provisions from subrule (D) to a new subrule (E) and added language clarifying that merely filing a motion for reconsideration does not automatically stay the board's order.

Staff Comment to 2000 Amendment

The October 3, 2000 amendment of MCR 9.118(A)(3), effective January 1, 2001, made the 12–month period specified in MCR 7.205(F)(3) applicable to delayed petitions for review of hearing panel orders. Cf. *Grievance Admin v Underwood*, 462 Mich 188 (2000).

RULE 9.119 CONDUCT OF DISBARRED, SUSPENDED, OR INACTIVE ATTORNEYS

(A) Notification to Clients. An attorney whose license is revoked or suspended, or who is transferred to inactive status pursuant to MCR 9.121, or who is suspended for nondisciplinary reasons pursuant to Rule 4 of the Supreme Court Rules Concerning the State Bar of Michigan, shall, within 7 days of the effective date of the order of discipline, the transfer to inactive status or the nondisciplinary suspension, notify all of his or her active clients, in writing, by registered or certified mail, return receipt requested, of the following:

(1) the nature and duration of the discipline imposed, the transfer to inactive status, or the nondisciplinary suspension;

(2) the effective date of such discipline, transfer to inactive status, or nondisciplinary suspension;

(3) the attorney's inability to act as an attorney after the effective date of such discipline, transfer to inactive status, or nondisciplinary suspension;

(4) the location and identity of the custodian of the clients' files and records, which will be made available to them or to substitute counsel;

(5) that the clients may wish to seek legal advice and counsel elsewhere; provided that, if the disbarred, suspended or inactive attorney was a member of a law firm, the firm may continue to represent each client with the client's express written consent;

(6) the address to which all correspondence to the attorney may be addressed.

(B) Conduct in Litigated Matters. In addition to the requirements of subsection (A) of this rule, the affected attorney must, by the effective date of the order of revocation, suspension, or transfer to inactive status, in every matter in which the attorney is representing a client in litigation, file with the tribunal and all parties a notice of the attorney's disqualification from the practice of law.

(C) Filing of Proof of Compliance. Within 14 days after the effective date of the order of revocation, suspension, or transfer to inactive status pursuant to MCR 9.121, the disbarred, suspended, or inactive attorney shall file with the administrator and the board an affidavit showing full compliance with this rule. The affidavit must include as an appendix copies of the disclosure notices and mailing receipts required under subrules (A) and (B) of this rule. A disbarred, suspended, or inactive attorney shall keep and maintain records of the various steps taken under this rule so that, in any subsequent proceeding instituted by or against him or her, proof of compliance with this rule and with the disbarment or suspension order will be available.

(D) Conduct After Entry of Order Prior to Effective Date. A disbarred or suspended attorney, after entry of the order of revocation or suspension and prior to its effective date, shall not accept any new retainer or engagement as attorney for another in any new case or legal matter of any nature, unless specifically authorized by the board chairperson upon a showing of good cause and a finding that it is not contrary to the interests of the public and profession. However, during the period between the entry of the order and its effective date, the suspended or disbarred attorney may complete, on behalf of any existing client, all matters that were pending on the entry date.

(E) Conduct After Effective Date of Order. An attorney who is disbarred or suspended, or who is transferred to inactive status pursuant to MCR 9.121 is, during the period of disbarment, suspension, or inactivity forbidden from:

(1) practicing law in any form;

(2) appearing as an attorney before any court, judge, justice, board, commission, or other public authority; and

(3) holding himself or herself out as an attorney by any means.

(F) Compensation of Disbarred, Suspended, or Inactive Attorney. An attorney whose license is revoked or suspended, or who is transferred to inactive status pursuant to MCR 9.121 may not share in any legal fees for legal services performed by another attorney during the period of disqualification from the practice of law. A disbarred, suspended, or inactive attorney may be compensated on a quantum meruit basis for legal services rendered and expenses paid by him or her prior to the effective date of the revocation, suspension, or transfer to inactive status.

(G) Inventory. If the attorney whose license is revoked or suspended, or who is transferred to inactive status pursuant to MCR 9.121 was a member of a firm, the firm may continue to represent each client with the client's express written consent. If an attorney is transferred to inactive status or is disbarred or suspended and fails to give notice under the rule, or disappears or dies, and there is no partner, executor or other responsible person capable of conducting the attorney's affairs, the administrator may ask the chief judge in the judicial circuit in which the attorney maintained his or her practice to appoint a person to inventory the attorney's files and to take any action necessary to protect the interests of the attorney and the attorney's clients. The person appointed may not disclose any information contained in any inventoried file without the client's written consent. The person appointed is analogous to a receiver operating under the direction of the circuit court.

[Effective March 1, 1985; amended effective June 1, 1987.]

Staff Comment to 1987 Amendment

The new MCR 9.119 [effective June 1, 1987] is a complete revision of the present [former] rule.

RULE 9.120 CONVICTION OF CRIMINAL OFFENSE

(A) Notification of the Grievance Administrator and the Attorney Discipline Board. When a lawyer is convicted of a crime, the lawyer, the prosecutor or other authority who prosecuted the lawyer, and the defense attorney who represented the lawyer must notify the grievance administrator and the board of the conviction. This notice must be given in writing within 14 days after the conviction.

(B) Suspension.

(1) On conviction of a felony, an attorney is automatically suspended until the effective date of an order filed by a hearing panel under MCR 9.115(J). A conviction occurs upon the return of a verdict of guilty or upon the acceptance of a plea of guilty or nolo contendere. The board may, on the attorney's motion, set aside the automatic suspension when it appears consistent with the maintenance of the integrity and honor of the profession, the protection of the public, and the interests of justice. The board must set aside the automatic suspension if the felony conviction is vacated, reversed, or otherwise set aside for any reason by the trial court or an appellate court.

(2) In a disciplinary proceeding instituted against an attorney based on the attorney's conviction of a criminal offense, a certified copy of the judgment of conviction is conclusive proof of the commission of the criminal offense.

(3) The administrator may file with the board a judgment of conviction showing that an attorney has violated a criminal law of a state or of the United States. The board shall then order the attorney to show cause why a final order of discipline should not be entered, and the board shall refer the proceeding to a hearing panel for hearing. At the hearing, questions as to the validity of the conviction, alleged trial errors, and the availability of appellate remedies shall not be considered. After the hearing, the panel shall issue an order under MCR 9.115(J).

(C) Pardon; Conviction Reversed. On a pardon the board may, and on a reversal the board must, by order filed and served under MCR 9.118(E), vacate the suspension. The attorney's name must be returned to the roster of Michigan attorneys and counselors at law, but the administrator may nevertheless proceed against the respondent for misconduct which had led to the criminal charge.

[Effective March 1, 1985; amended effective June 1, 1987; January 1, 1992; March 1, 1992.]

1985 Staff Comment

MCR 9.120 is substantially the same as GCR 1963, 969.

Staff Comment to 1987 Amendment

The [June 1, 1987] amendment deletes the often overlooked requirement that the convicted attorney report the conviction to the grievance administrator. See former subrule (A)(1).

The [June 1, 1987] amendment to subrule (A)(3) limits the issues to be considered by the hearing panel. The panel is not to relitigate issues that have been or will be litigated in the criminal trial court or the appellate courts.

Staff Comment to 1991 Amendment

The 1991 amendment restored, in subrule (A), the requirement that criminal convictions be reported to the grievance authorities. See now-repealed GCR 1963, 969.1(a) and the originally enacted language of MCR 9.120(A)(1). The 1991 amendment redesignated former subrules (A) and (B) as subrules (B) and (C), respectively.

Staff Comment to 1992 Amendment

The [March 1,] 1992 amendment directed that the notice of conviction, which was required to be sent to the Grievance Administrator, must also be sent to the Attorney Discipline Board.

RULE 9.121 ATTORNEY DECLARED TO BE INCOMPETENT OR ALLEGED TO BE INCAPACITATED OR ASSERTING IMPAIRED ABILITY

(A) Adjudication by Court. If an attorney has been judicially declared incompetent or involuntarily committed on the grounds of incompetency or disability, the board, on proper proof of the fact, must enter an order effective immediately transferring the attorney to inactive status for an indefinite period and until further order of the board.

(B) Allegations of Incompetency or Incapacity.

(1) If it is alleged in a complaint by the administrator that an attorney is incapacitated to continue the practice of law because of mental or physical infirmity or disability or because of addiction to drugs or intoxicants, a hearing panel shall take action necessary to determine whether the attorney is incapacitated, including an examination of the attorney by qualified medical experts the board designates.

(2) The hearing panel shall provide notice to the attorney of the proceedings and appoint an attorney to represent him or her if he or she is without representation.

(3) If, after a hearing, the hearing panel concludes that the attorney is incapacitated from continuing to practice law, it shall enter an order transferring him or her to inactive status for an indefinite period and until further order of the board.

(4) Pending disciplinary proceedings against the attorney must be held in abeyance.

(5) Proceedings conducted under this subrule are subject to review by the board as provided in MCR 9.118.

(C) Assertion of Impaired Ability; Probation.

(1) If, in response to a formal complaint filed under subrule 9.115(B), the respondent asserts in mitigation and thereafter demonstrates by a preponderance of the evidence that

(a) during the period when the conduct which is the subject of the complaint occurred, his or her ability to practice law competently was materially impaired by physical or mental disability or by drug or alcohol addiction,

(b) the impairment was the cause of or substantially contributed to that conduct,

(c) the cause of the impairment is susceptible to treatment, and

(d) he or she in good faith intends to undergo treatment, and submits a detailed plan for such treatment,

the hearing panel, the board, or the Supreme Court may enter an order placing the respondent on probation for a specific period not to exceed 2 years if it specifically finds that an order of probation is not contrary to the public interest.

(2) If the respondent alleges impairment by physical or mental disability or by drug or alcohol addiction pursuant to subrule (C)(1), the hearing panel may order the respondent to submit to a physical or mental examination by a physician selected by the hearing panel or the board, which physician shall report to the hearing panel or board. The parties may obtain a psychiatric or medical evaluation at their own expense

by examiners of their own choosing. No physician-patient privilege shall apply under this rule. The respondent's attorney may be present at an examination. A respondent who fails or refuses to comply with an examination order, or refuses to undergo an examination requested by the administrator, shall not be eligible for probation.

(3) The probation order may

(a) specify the treatment the respondent is to undergo,

(b) require the respondent to practice law only under the direct supervision of other attorneys, or

(c) include any other terms the evidence shows are likely to eliminate the impairment without subjecting the respondent's clients or the public to a substantial risk of harm because the respondent is permitted to continue to practice law during the probation period.

(4) The probation order expires on the date specified in it unless the administrator petitions for, and the hearing panel, board, or court grants, an extension. An extension may not exceed 2 years. A probation order may be dissolved if the respondent demonstrates that the impairment giving rise to the probation order has been removed and that the probation order has been fully complied with, but only one motion to accelerate dissolution of a probation order may be filed during the probation period.

(5) On proof that a respondent has violated a probation order, he or she may be suspended or disbarred.

(D) Publication of Change in Status. The board must publish in the Michigan Bar Journal a notice of transfer to inactive status. A copy of the notice and the order must be filed and served under MCR 9.118.

(E) Reinstatement. An attorney transferred to inactive status under this rule may not resume active status until reinstated by the board's order and, if inactive 3 years or more, recertified by the Board of Law Examiners. The attorney may petition for reinstatement to active status once a year or at shorter intervals as the board may direct. A petition for reinstatement must be granted by the board on a showing by clear and convincing evidence that the attorney's disability has been removed and that he or she is fit to resume the practice of law. The board may take the action necessary to determine whether the attorney's disability has been removed, including an examination of the attorney by qualified medical experts that the board designates. The board may direct that the expense of the examination be paid by the attorney. If an attorney was transferred to inactive status under subrule 9.121(A) and subsequently has been judicially declared to be competent, the board may dispense with further evidence that the disability has been removed and may order reinstatement to active status on terms it finds proper and advisable, including recertification.

(F) Waiver of Privilege. By filing a petition for reinstatement to active status under this rule, the attorney waives the doctor-patient privilege with respect to treatment during the period of his or her disability. The attorney shall disclose the name of every psychiatrist, psychologist, physician, and hospital or other institution by whom or in which the attorney has been examined or treated since the transfer to inactive status. The attorney shall furnish to the board written consent for each to divulge whatever information and records are requested by the board's medical experts.

[Effective March 1, 1985; amended effective June 1, 1987; March 1, 1994.]

1985 Staff Comment

MCR 9.121 is substantially the same as GCR 1963, 970.

Staff Comment to 1987 Amendment

[Effective June 1, 1987] Subrule (C)(2) provides for examination of the respondent by an independent expert selected by the hearing panel or the board.

Staff Comment 1994 Amendment

The March 1, 1994 amendment to subrule (C)(2) made the examination by an independent expert appointed by the hearing panel discretionary, rather than mandatory. The amendment also added the language that denies eligibility for probation if the respondent refuses to undergo an examination by a physician selected by the grievance administrator.

RULE 9.122 REVIEW BY SUPREME COURT

(A) Kinds Available; Time for Filing.

(1) A party aggrieved, including the person who made a request for investigation, by a final order of discipline or dismissal entered by the board on review under MCR 9.118, may apply for leave to appeal to the Supreme Court under MCR 7.302 within 21 days after the order is entered. If a motion for reconsideration is filed before the board's order takes effect, the application for leave to appeal to the Supreme Court may be filed within 21 days after the board enters its order granting or denying reconsideration.

(2) If a request for investigation has been dismissed under MCR 9.112(C)(1) or 9.114(A), a party aggrieved by the dismissal may file a complaint for mandamus in the Supreme Court under MCR 7.304.

(B) Rules Applicable. Except as modified by this rule, subchapter 7.300 governs an appeal.

(C) Stay of Order. If the discipline order is a suspension of 179 days or less, a stay of the order will automatically issue on the timely filing of an appeal by the respondent. The stay remains effective until conclusion of the appeal or further order of the Supreme Court. The respondent may petition the Supreme Court for a stay pending appeal of other orders of the board.

(D) Record on Appeal. The original papers constitute the record on appeal. The board shall certify the original record and file it with the Supreme Court promptly after the briefs of the parties have been filed. The record must include a list of docket entries, a transcript of testimony taken, and all pleadings, exhibits, briefs, findings of fact, and orders in the proceeding. If the record contains material protected, the protection continues unless otherwise ordered by the Supreme Court.

(E) Disposition. The Supreme Court may make any order it deems appropriate, including dismissing the appeal. The parties may stipulate to dismiss the appeal with prejudice.

[Effective March 1, 1985; amended effective June 1, 1987.]

1985 Staff Comment

MCR 9.122 is substantially the same as GCR 1963, 971.

Staff Comment to 1987 Amendment

[Effective June 1, 1987] Amended MCR 9.122(A)(1) eliminates uncertainty by stating that the filing of a motion for reconsideration extends the deadline for filing an application for leave to appeal to the Supreme Court. See also MCR 9.118(D).

RULE 9.123 ELIGIBILITY FOR REINSTATEMENT

(A) Suspension, 179 Days or Less. An attorney whose license has been suspended for 179 days or less is automatically reinstated by filing with the Supreme Court clerk, the board, and the administrator an affidavit showing that the attorney has fully complied with the terms and conditions of the suspension order. A false statement contained in the affidavit is ground for disbarment.

(B) Revocation or Suspension More Than 179 Days. An attorney whose license to practice law has been revoked or suspended for more than 179 days is not eligible for reinstatement until the attorney has petitioned for reinstatement under MCR 9.124 and has established by clear and convincing evidence that:

(1) he or she desires in good faith to be restored to the privilege of practicing law in Michigan;

(2) the term of the suspension ordered has elapsed or 5 years have elapsed since revocation of the license;

(3) he or she has not practiced or attempted to practice law contrary to the requirement of his or her suspension or revocation;

(4) he or she has complied fully with the order of discipline;

(5) his or her conduct since the order of discipline has been exemplary and above reproach;

(6) he or she has a proper understanding of and attitude toward the standards that are imposed on members of the bar and will conduct himself or herself in conformity with those standards;

(7) taking into account all of the attorney's past conduct, including the nature of the misconduct which led to the revocation or suspension, he or she nevertheless can safely be recommended to the public, the courts, and the legal profession as a person fit to be consulted by others and to represent them and otherwise act in matters of trust and confidence, and in general to aid in the administration of justice as a member of the bar and as an officer of the court;

(8) he or she is in compliance with the requirements of subrule (C), if applicable; and

(9) he or she has reimbursed the client security fund of the State Bar of Michigan or has agreed to an arrangement satisfactory to the fund to reimburse the fund for any money paid from the fund as a result of his or her conduct. Failure to fully reimburse as agreed is ground for revocation of a reinstatement.

(C) Reinstatement After Three Years. An attorney who, as a result of disciplinary proceedings, resigns, is disbarred, or is suspended for any period of time, and who does not practice law for 3 years or more, whether as the result of the period of discipline or voluntarily, must be recertified by the Board of Law Examiners before the attorney may be reinstated to the practice of law.

(D) Petition for Reinstatement; Filing Limitations.

(1) Except as provided in subrule (D)(3), an attorney whose license to practice law has been suspended may not file a petition for reinstatement earlier than 56 days before the term of suspension ordered has fully elapsed.

(2) An attorney whose license to practice law has been revoked may not file a petition for reinstatement until 5 years have elapsed since revocation of the license.

(3) An attorney whose license to practice law has been suspended because of conviction of a felony for which a term of incarceration was imposed may not file a petition for reinstatement until six months after completion of the sentence, including any period of parole.

(4) An attorney whose license to practice law has been revoked or suspended and who has been denied reinstatement may not file a new petition for reinstatement until at least 180 days from the effective date of the most recent hearing panel order granting or denying reinstatement.

[Effective March 1, 1985; amended effective March 1, 1994; September 15, 1994; July 1, 1996; February 1, 2000.]

1985 Staff Comment

MCR 9.123 is substantially the same as GCR 1963, 972.

Staff Comment to March, 1994 Amendment

The March 1, 1994 amendments: (1) increased the automatic reinstatement eligibility threshold in subrules (A) and (B) from 119 to 179 days; and (2) added new subrule (D),

which specifies the earliest dates at which attorneys may petition for reinstatement.

The amendments to subrules (A) and (B) apply only to discipline orders issued after the amendment's effective date.

Staff Comment to 1996 Amendment

The July 1, 1996, amendment of subrule (B)(7) allows the Attorney Discipline Board to consider all an attorney's past conduct when deciding whether to grant reinstatement.

Staff Comment to 1999 Amendment

The December 1, 1999 amendment of Rule 9.123(D), effective February 1, 2000, precludes a lawyer whose license to practice law has been suspended because of a felony conviction from petitioning for reinstatement until six months after completion of any sentence of incarceration, including any term of parole. The word "parole" indicates that the lawyer was in the custody of the Michigan Department of Corrections. The rule also applies, however, to persons who were incarcerated in other jurisdictions under similar circumstances, regardless of the terminology employed.

RULE 9.124 PROCEDURE FOR REINSTATEMENT

(A) Filing of Petition. An attorney petitioning for reinstatement shall file the original petition for reinstatement with the Supreme Court clerk and a copy with the board and the commission. If the petition and the affidavit required by subrule (B)(1) are facially sufficient, and the petitioner has paid the publication fee required by subrule (B)(2), the board shall assign the petition to a hearing panel. Otherwise, the board may dismiss the petition without prejudice.

(B) Petitioner's Responsibilities.

(1) The petitioner must file, contemporaneously with and as a part of the petition for reinstatement, a personal history affidavit containing the following information:

(a) every residence address since the date of disqualification from the practice of law;

(b) employment history since the time of disqualification, including the nature of employment, the name and address of every employer, the duration of such employment, and the name of the petitioner's immediate supervisor at each place of employment;

(c) a copy of a current driver's license;

(d) any continuing legal education in which the petitioner participated during the period of disqualification from the practice of law;

(e) bank account statements, from the date of disqualification until the filing of the petition for reinstatement, for each and every bank account in which petitioner is named in any capacity;

(f) any and all professional or occupational licenses obtained or maintained during the period of disqualification and whether any were suspended or revoked;

(g) any and all names used by petitioner since the time of disqualification;

(h) petitioner's place and date of birth;

(i) petitioner's social security number;

(j) whether, since the time of disqualification, petitioner was a party or a witness in any civil case, and the title, docket number, and court in which such case occurred;

(k) whether there are any outstanding judgments against the petitioner;

(*l*) whether petitioner was a defendant or a witness in any criminal case, and the title, docket number, and court in which such case occurred.

(2) The petitioner must, contemporaneously with the filing of the petition for reinstatement and personal history affidavit, remit to the administrator the fee for publication of a reinstatement notice in the Michigan Bar Journal.

(3) A petitioner who files the petition before the term of suspension ordered has fully elapsed must file an updated petition and personal history affidavit within 14 days after the term of suspension ordered has fully elapsed. All petitioners must file updated petitions and personal history affidavits with the hearing panel when the reinstatement hearing convenes. The supplemental filings must indicate any pertinent information that has changed since the previous filing.

(4) The petitioner must cooperate fully in the investigation by the administrator into the petitioner's eligibility for reinstatement by promptly providing any information requested. If requested, the petitioner must participate in a recorded interview and answer fully and fairly under oath all questions about eligibility for reinstatement.

(C) **Administrator's Responsibilities.** Within 14 days after the commission receives its copy of the petition for reinstatement, the administrator shall submit to the Michigan Bar Journal for publication a notice briefly describing the nature and date of the discipline, the misconduct for which the petitioner was disciplined, and the matters required to be proved for reinstatement. The administrator shall investigate the petitioner's eligibility for reinstatement before a hearing on it, report the findings in writing to the board and the hearing panel within 56 days of the date the board assigns the petition to the hearing panel, and serve a copy on the petitioner. For good cause, the hearing panel may allow the administrator to file the report at a later date, but in no event later than 7 days before the hearing. The report must summarize the facts of all previous misconduct and the available evidence bearing on the petitioner's eligibility for reinstatement. The report is not a pleading and does not serve to restrict the administrator in the presentation of evidence at the hearing. Any evidence omitted from the report or received by the administrator subsequent to the filing of the report must be disclosed promptly to the hearing panel and the petitioner.

(D) **Hearing on Petition.** A reinstatement hearing may not be held earlier than 28 days after the administrator files the investigative report with the hearing panel unless the hearing panel has extended the deadline for filing the report. The proceeding on a petition for reinstatement must conform as nearly as practicable to a hearing on a complaint. The petitioner shall appear personally before the hearing panel for cross-examination by the administrator and the hearing panel and answer fully and fairly under oath all questions regarding eligibility for reinstatement. The administrator and the petitioner may call witnesses or introduce evidence bearing upon the petitioner's eligibility for reinstatement. The hearing panel must enter an order granting or denying reinstatement and make a written report signed by the chairperson, including a transcript of the testimony taken, pleadings, exhibits and briefs, and its findings of fact. A reinstatement order may grant reinstatement subject to conditions that are relevant to the established misconduct or otherwise necessary to insure the integrity of the profession, to protect the public, and to serve the interests of justice. The report and order must be filed and served under MCR 9.118(F).

(E) **Review.** Review is available under the rules governing review of other hearing panel orders.

[Effective March 1, 1985; amended effective March 1, 1994.]

1985 Staff Comment

MCR 9.124 is substantially the same as GCR 1963, 973.

Staff Comment to 1994 Amendment

The March 1, 1994 amendments: (1) clarified the subrule (A) procedures for filing a reinstatement petition; (2) added new subrule (B); (3) in subrule (C), clarified the grievance administrator's responsibilities in reinstatement proceedings and shortened the time that the administrator has to prepare the investigative report; and (4) in subrule (D), authorized conditional reinstatements and codified the existing practice under which the administrator is allowed to call witnesses and present evidence bearing on the petitioner's eligibility for reinstatement.

RULE 9.125　IMMUNITY

A person is absolutely immune from suit for statements and communications transmitted solely to the administrator, the commission, or the commission staff, or given in an investigation or proceeding on alleged misconduct or reinstatement. The administrator, legal counsel, investigators, members of hearing panels, the commission, the board, and their staffs are absolutely immune from suit for conduct arising out of the performance of their duties.

[Effective March 1, 1985; amended effective June 1, 1987.]

1985 Staff Comment

MCR 9.125 is substantially the same as GCR 1963, 974.

Staff Comment to 1987 Amendment

The [June 1, 1987] amendments to MCR 9.125 provide for absolute immunity for complainants, disciplinary officials and staff acting within the scope of their duties. The rule is patterned after the Standards for Lawyer Discipline and Disability Proceedings promulgated by the American Bar Association.

RULE 9.126 OPEN HEARINGS; CONFIDENTIAL FILES AND RECORDS

(A) Investigations. Except as provided in these rules, investigations by the administrator or the staff may not be made public. At the respondent's option, final disposition of a request for investigation not resulting in formal charges may be made public. In addition, any interested person may inspect the request for investigation and the respondent's answer thereto if a formal complaint has been filed.

(B) Hearings. Hearings before a hearing panel and the board must be open to the public, but not their deliberations.

(C) Papers. Formal pleadings, reports, findings, recommendations, discipline, reprimands, transcripts, and orders resulting from hearings must be open to the public. This subrule does not apply to a request for a disclosure authorization submitted to the board or the Supreme Court pursuant to subrules (D)(7) or (E)(5).

(D) Other Records. Other files and records of the board, the commission, the administrator, legal counsel, hearing panels and their members, and the staff of each may not be examined by or disclosed to anyone except

(1) the commission,

(2) the administrator,

(3) the respondent as provided under MCR 9.115(F)(4),

(4) members of hearing panels or the board,

(5) authorized employees,

(6) the Supreme Court, or

(7) other persons who are expressly authorized by the board or the Supreme Court.

If a disclosure is made to the Supreme Court, the board, or a hearing panel, the information must also be disclosed to the respondent.

(E) Other Information. Notwithstanding any prohibition against disclosure set forth in this rule or elsewhere, the commission shall disclose the substance of information concerning attorney or judicial misconduct to the Judicial Tenure Commission, upon request.

The commission also may make such disclosure to the Judicial Tenure Commission, absent a request, and to:

(1) the State Bar of Michigan Client Security Fund,

(2) the State Bar of Michigan Committee on Judicial Qualifications,

(3) any court-authorized attorney disciplinary or admissions agency, or

(4) other persons who are expressly authorized by the board or the Supreme Court.

(F) Summary of Disclosures. The board shall include in its annual report to the Supreme Court an accounting of all requests for disclosure that have been filed with the board pursuant to subrules (D)(7) and (E)(5). The accounting shall include the board's disposition of each request.

[Effective March 1, 1985; amended effective June 1, 1987; February 1, 1991; March 18, 1992; December 1, 1998.]

1985 Staff Comment

MCR 9.126 is substantially the same as GCR 1963, 975.

Staff Comment to 1991 Amendment

The [February 1,] 1991 amendment added subrule (E)(5), providing that the Attorney Discipline Board or the Supreme Court may authorize the Attorney Grievance Commission to release "information" about misconduct to persons other than those listed in subrules (E)(1)–(4). Subrule (D) already contained a similar provision regarding "files and records". The 1991 amendment also added subrule (F) and the second sentence of subrule (C).

Staff Comment to 1992 Amendment

The March 18, 1992 amendment to subrule (A) added the provision for public access to the request for investigation and the answer to it in situations where a formal complaint has been filed. The amendment applies to cases in which requests for investigation (which later result in the filing of formal complaints) are filed after the effective date of the rule amendment.

Staff Comment to 1998 Amendment

The December 1, 1998 amendment of MCR 9.126 and 9.222 made mandatory the disclosure of information, upon request, between the Attorney Grievance Commission and the Judicial Tenure Commission. The amendment of State Bar Rule 15, § 1 authorized the State Bar's Committee on Character and Fitness to disclose to the Attorney Grievance Commission information concerning the bar application of a disciplined lawyer who is requesting reinstatement to the practice of law. Under the amendment, the lawyer must be notified of the request, and the hearing panel must determine the relevancy of the information before permitting it to be used in a public document or proceeding.

RULE 9.127 ENFORCEMENT

(A) Interim Suspension. The Supreme Court, the board, or a hearing panel may order the interim suspension of a respondent who fails to comply with its lawful order. The suspension shall remain in effect until the respondent complies with the order or no longer has the power to comply. If the respondent is ultimately disciplined, the respondent shall not receive credit against the disciplinary suspension or disbarment for any time of suspension under this rule. All orders of hearing panels under this rule shall be reviewable immediately under MCR 9.118. All orders of the board under this rule shall be appealable immediately under MCR 9.122. The reviewing authority may issue a stay pending review or appeal.

(B) Contempt. The administrator may enforce a discipline order or an order granting or denying reinstatement by proceeding against a respondent for contempt of court. The proceeding must conform to MCR 3.606. The petition must be filed by the administrator in the circuit court in the county in which the alleged contempt took place, or in which the respondent resides, or has or had an office. Enforcement proceedings under this rule do not bar the imposition of additional discipline upon the basis of the same noncompliance with the discipline order.

[Effective March 1, 1985; amended effective June 1, 1987.]

1985 Staff Comment

MCR 9.127 is substantially the same as GCR 1963, 976.

Staff Comment to 1987 Amendment

New subrule (A) [effective June 1, 1987] provides a vehicle for prompt enforcement of preliminary orders, e.g., orders requiring a psychiatric examination.

Amended subrule (B) [effective June 1, 1987] codifies the current rule that the administrator is not compelled to make an election of remedies in enforcing an order of discipline.

RULE 9.128   COSTS

(A) Generally. The hearing panel and the board, in an order of discipline or an order granting or denying reinstatement, must include a provision directing the payment of costs within a specified period of time. Under exceptional circumstances, the board may grant a motion to reduce administrative costs assessed under this rule, but may not reduce the assessment for actual expenses. Reimbursement must be a condition in a reinstatement order.

(B) Amount and Nature of Costs Assessed. The costs assessed under these rules shall include both basic administrative costs and disciplinary expenses actually incurred by the board, the commission, a master, or a panel for the expenses of that investigation, hearing, review and appeal, if any.

(1) Basic Administrative Costs:

(a) for discipline by consent pursuant to MCR 9.115(F)(5), $750;

(b) for all other orders imposing discipline, $1,500;

(c) with the filing of a petition for reinstatement under MCR 9.124(A), where the discipline imposed was a suspension of less than 3 years, $750;

(d) with the filing of a petition for reinstatement under MCR 9.124(A), where the discipline imposed

was a suspension of 3 years or more or disbarment, $1,500.

(2) Actual Expenses. Within 14 days of the conclusion of a proceeding before a panel or a written request from the board, whichever is later, the grievance administrator shall file with the board an itemized statement of the commission's expenses allocable to the hearing, including expenses incurred during the grievance administrator's investigation. Copies shall be served upon the respondent and the panel. An itemized statement of the expenses of the board, the commission, and the panel, including the expenses of a master, shall be a part of the report in all matters of discipline and reinstatement.

(C) Certification of Nonpayment. If the respondent fails to pay the costs within the time prescribed, the board shall serve a certified notice of the nonpayment upon the respondent. Copies must be served on the administrator and the State Bar of Michigan. Commencing on the date a certified report of nonpayment is filed, interest on the unpaid fees and costs shall accrue thereafter at the rates applicable to civil judgments.

(D) Automatic Suspension for Nonpayment. The respondent will be suspended automatically, effective 7 days from the mailing of the certified notice of nonpayment, and until the respondent pays the costs assessed or the board approves a suitable plan for payment. The board shall file a notice of suspension with the clerk of the Supreme Court and the State Bar of Michigan. A copy must be served on the respondent and the administrator. A respondent who is suspended for nonpayment of costs under this rule is required to comply with the requirements imposed by MCR 9.119 on suspended attorneys.

(E) Reinstatement. A respondent who has been automatically suspended under this rule and later pays the costs or obtains approval of a payment plan, and is otherwise eligible, may seek automatic reinstatement pursuant to MCR 9.123(A) even if the suspension under this rule exceeded 179 days. However, a respondent who is suspended under this rule and, as a result, does not practice law in Michigan for 3 years or more, must be recertified by the Board of Law Examiners before the respondent may be reinstated.

[Effective March 1, 1985; amended effective June 1, 1987; March 1, 1994; November 16, 1994; July 29, 2002.]

1985 Staff Comment

MCR 9.128 is substantially the same as GCR 1963, 977.

Staff Comment to 1987 Amendment

The [June 1, 1987] amendment provides for automatic suspension in cases where a respondent fails to pay costs. This is designed to avoid the current cumbersome procedures requiring an entirely new proceeding. It is similar to the practices in other jurisdictions.

The March 1, 1994 amendments: (1) divided MCR 9.128 into two subrules; (2) clarified the rules regarding a disciplined or reinstated attorney's obligation to reimburse the State Bar for the expenses of the disciplinary proceedings; (3) provided for the accrual of interest on delinquent reimbursement obligations; and (4) added the requirement that an attorney who is suspended under this rule for more than three years must be recertified by the Board of Law Examiners.

Staff Comment to November, 1994 Amendment

The [November 16,] 1994 amendment of MCR 9.128(A) added the sentence "An attorney who is suspended for nonpayment of costs under this rule is required to comply with the requirements imposed by MCR 9.119 on suspended attorneys." The amendment reflected the Supreme Court's holding in *Grievance Administrator* v. *Floyd*, 447 Mich 422; 523 NW2d 227 (1994).

Staff Comment to 2002 Amendment

The July 29, 2002 amendment of MCR 9.128 was suggested by the Attorney Grievance Commission and the Attorney Discipline Board. It allocates a greater share of the cost of operating the discipline system to those who are disciplined. Among other changes, the new provisions permit an assessment for basic administrative costs as well as actual expenses, and expressly include investigative costs in actual expenses.

The staff comment is published only for the benefit of the bench and bar and is not an authoritative construction by the Court.

RULE 9.129   EXPENSES; REIMBURSEMENT

The state bar must reimburse each investigator, legal counsel, hearing panel member, board member, and commission member for the actual and necessary expenses the board, commission, or administrator certifies as incurred as a result of these rules.

[Effective March 1, 1985.]

1985 Staff Comment

MCR 9.129 is substantially the same as GCR 1963, 978.

RULE 9.130   MCR 8.122 CASES; ARBITRATION; DISCIPLINE; FILING COMPLAINT BY ADMINISTRATOR

(A) **Proceedings.** A proceeding on alleged misconduct to which MCR 8.122 is applicable is the same as for a request for investigation. No investigation may be made on a claim by an attorney against a client.

(B) **Arbitration.** On written agreement between an attorney and his or her client, the administrator or an attorney the administrator assigns may arbitrate a dispute and enter an award in accordance with the arbitration laws. Except as otherwise provided by this subrule, the arbitration is governed by MCR 3.602. The award and a motion for entry of an order or judgment must be filed in the court having jurisdiction

under MCR 8.122. If the award recommends discipline of the attorney, it must also be treated as a request for investigation.

(C) **Complaint.** If the administrator finds that the filing of a complaint in the appropriate court under MCR 8.122 will be a hardship to the client and that the client may have a meritorious claim, the administrator shall file the complaint on behalf of the client and prosecute it to completion without cost to the client.

[Effective March 1, 1985; amended effective September 1, 2000.]

1985 Staff Comment

MCR 9.130 is substantially the same as GCR 1963, 979.

Staff Comment to 2000 Amendment

The June 21, 2000 amendment of subrule 9.130(B), effective September 1, 2000, clarified that arbitration of attorney-discipline matters is governed by MCR 3.602, except as otherwise provided by subrule 9.130(B).

RULE 9.131   INVESTIGATION OF MEMBER OR EMPLOYEE OF BOARD OR COMMISSION; INVESTIGATION OF ATTORNEY REPRESENTING RESPONDENT OR WITNESS; REPRESENTATION BY MEMBER OR EMPLOYEE OF BOARD OR COMMISSION

(A) **Investigation of Commission Member or Employee.** If the request is for investigation of an attorney who is a member or employee of the commission, the following provisions apply:

(1) The administrator shall serve a copy of the request for investigation on the respondent by ordinary mail. Within 21 days after service, the respondent shall file with the administrator an answer to the request for investigation conforming to MCR 9.113. The administrator shall send a copy of the answer to the person who filed the request for investigation.

(2) After the answer is filed or the time for answer has expired, the administrator shall send copies of the request for investigation and the answer to the Supreme Court clerk.

(3) The Supreme Court shall review the request for investigation and the answer and shall either dismiss the request for investigation or appoint volunteer legal counsel to investigate the matter.

(4) If, after conducting the investigation, appointed counsel determines that the request for investigation does not warrant the filing of a formal complaint, he or she shall file a report setting out the reasons for that conclusion with the administrator, who shall send a copy of the report to the Supreme Court clerk, the respondent, and the person who filed the request for investigation. Review of a decision not to file a formal complaint is limited to a proceeding under MCR

9.122(A)(2). If appointed counsel determines not to file a complaint, the administrator shall close and maintain the file. MCR 9.126(A) governs the release of information regarding the investigation.

(5) If, after conducting the investigation, appointed counsel determines that the request for investigation warrants the filing of a formal complaint, he or she shall prepare and file a complaint with the board under MCR 9.115(B).

(6) Further proceedings are as in other cases except that the complaint will be prosecuted by appointed counsel rather than by the administrator.

If the request is for investigation of the administrator, the term "administrator" in this rule means a member of the commission or some other employee of the commission designated by the chairperson.

(B) Investigation of Board Member or Employee. Before the filing of a formal complaint, the procedures regarding a request for investigation of a member or employee of the board are the same as in other cases. Thereafter, the following provisions apply:

(1) The administrator shall file the formal complaint with the board and send a copy to the Supreme Court clerk.

(2) The Chief Justice shall appoint a hearing panel and may appoint a master to conduct the hearing. The hearing procedure is as provided in MCR 9.115 or 9.117, as is appropriate, except that no matters shall be submitted to the board. Procedural matters ordinarily within the authority of the board shall be decided by the hearing panel, except that a motion to disqualify a member of the panel shall be decided by the Chief Justice.

(3) The order of the hearing panel is effective 21 days after it is filed and served as required by MCR 9.115(J), and shall be treated as a final order of the board. The administrator shall send a copy of the order to the Supreme Court clerk.

(4) MCR 9.118 does not apply. Review of the hearing panel decision is by the Supreme Court as provided by MCR 9.122.

(C) Investigation of Attorney Representing a Respondent or Witness in Proceedings Before Board or Commission. If the request is for an investigation of an attorney for alleged misconduct committed during the course of that attorney's representation of a respondent or a witness in proceedings before the board or the commission, the procedures in subrule (A) shall be followed. A request for investigation that alleges misconduct of this type may be filed only by the chairperson of the commission, and only if the commission passes a resolution authorizing the filing by the chairperson.

(D) Representation By Commission or Board Member or Employee. A member or employee of the Attorney Grievance Commission or the Attorney Discipline Board and its hearing panels may not represent a respondent in proceedings before the commission, the board, or the Judicial Tenure Commission, including preliminary discussions with employees of the respective commission or board prior to the filing of a request for investigation.

[Effective March 1, 1985; amended effective October 1, 1991; July 1, 1996.]

1985 Staff Comment

MCR 9.131 is substantially the same as GCR 1963, 980.

Staff Comment to 1991 Amendment

The amendment of October 1, 1991 added subrule (C), creating a special procedure for cases in which it is alleged that an attorney acted improperly while representing a respondent or a witness in proceedings before the board or the commission.

Staff Comment to 1996 Amendment

The amendment of MCR 9.131, effective July 1, 1996, precluded members and employees of the Attorney Grievance Commission and the Attorney Discipline Board and its hearing panels from representing a respondent in proceedings before either of those bodies or the Judicial Tenure Commission.

SUBCHAPTER 9.200 JUDICIAL TENURE COMMISSION

RULE 9.201 DEFINITIONS

As used in this chapter, unless the context or subject matter otherwise requires

(1) "commission" means the Judicial Tenure Commission;

(2) "judge" means judge of an appellate or trial court or a magistrate or referee of a court appointed or elected under the laws of this state;

(3) "respondent" is a judge against whom a complaint has been filed;

(4) "chairperson" is the commission chairperson and includes the acting chairperson;

(5) "master" means one or more judges, active or retired, appointed by the Supreme Court on the commission's request to hold hearings on a complaint against a judge filed by the commission;

(6) "examiner" means one or more attorneys appointed by the commission to gather and present evidence and to act as counsel for the commission in proceedings in the Supreme Court, before a master, or before the commission;

(7) "complaint" is a written document filed by the commission's order for disciplinary action under this chapter against a judge, which alleges specific charges of misconduct in office, or mental or physical disability, which warrant commission action under Const. 1963, art. 6, § 30;

(8) "grievance" is an allegation of judicial misconduct or physical or mental disability within the commission's jurisdiction which the commission may undertake to investigate under MCR 9.207.

[Effective March 1, 1985.]

1985 Staff Comment

MCR 9.201 is substantially the same as GCR 1963, 932.3.

RULE 9.202 JUDICIAL TENURE COMMISSION; ORGANIZATION

(A) Appointment of Commissioners. As provided by Const. 1963, art. 6, § 30, the Judicial Tenure Commission consists of 9 persons. The commissioners selected by the judges are to be chosen by mail vote conducted by the state court administrator. The commissioners selected by the state bar members must be chosen by mail vote conducted by the State Bar of Michigan. Both mail elections must be conducted in accordance with nomination and election procedures approved by the Supreme Court. Immediately after a commissioner's election or appointment, the Governor, the state court administrator, and the State Bar of Michigan shall give notice of the election or appointment to the Chief Justice.

(B) Term of Office. A commissioner holds office for a term of 3 years. To achieve staggered terms, three terms expire annually. In consecutive years, the following terms expire:

(1) an appointment of the Governor, the judge of a court of limited jurisdiction, and an attorney elected by the state bar;

(2) an appointment of the Governor, the probate judge, and an attorney elected by the state bar;

(3) the Court of Appeals judge, the circuit judge, and the judge elected by the state bar.

(C) Vacancy.

(1) A vacancy in the office of a commissioner occurs:

(a) when a commissioner resigns or is incapable of serving as a member of the commission;

(b) when a judge who is a member of the commission no longer holds the office which he or she held when selected;

(c) when an attorney selected by state bar members is no longer admitted to practice in the courts of this state; and

(d) when an appointee of the Governor becomes an attorney or accepts a judicial position.

(2) Vacancies must be filled by selection of a successor in the same manner required for the selection of his or her predecessor. The commissioner selected holds office for the unexpired term of his or her predecessor. Vacancies must be filled within 3 months after the vacancy occurs.

(3) A member may retire by submitting his or her resignation to the commission, which must certify the vacancy to the selecting authority.

(D) Expenses of Commission and Staff.

(1) The commission's budget must be submitted to the Supreme Court for approval.

(2) The commission's expenses must be included in and paid from the appropriation for the Supreme Court.

(3) A commissioner may not receive compensation for his or her services but must be paid his or her reasonable and necessary expenses.

(4) The commission may employ an executive director and other employees to perform the duties it directs, subject to the availability of funds under its budget. Commission employees are exempt from the operation of Const. 1963, art. 11, § 5, as are employees of courts of record.

(E) Quorum and Chairperson.

(1) The commission elects from its members a chairperson and a vice-chairperson, each to serve 2 years. The vice-chairperson acts as chairperson when the chairperson is absent. If both are absent, the members present may select one among them to act as temporary chairperson.

(2) A quorum for the transaction of business by the commission is 5.

(3) The vote of a majority of the members constitutes the adoption or rejection of a motion or resolution before the commission. The chairperson is entitled to cast a vote as a commissioner.

(F) Meetings of Commission. Meetings must be held at the call of the chairperson, the executive director, or the written request of 3 commission members.

[Effective March 1, 1985.]

1985 Staff Comment

MCR 9.202 corresponds to GCR 1963, 932.1.

Subrule (B) rewords GCR 1963, 932.1(2), but achieves the same effect as rules 932.1(2) and 932.28 (which set the starting date for the terms of the first members of the commission).

Subrule (E)(3) is based on rule 2 of the Administrative Rules of the Judicial Tenure Commission.

RULE 9.203 JUDICIAL TENURE COMMISSION; POWERS; REVIEW

(A) Authority of Commission. The commission has all the powers provided for under Const. 1963, art. 6, § 30, and further powers provided by Supreme Court rule. Proceedings before the commission or a master are governed by these rules. The commission may adopt and publish administrative rules for its internal operation and the administration of its proceedings that do not conflict with this subchapter and submit them to the Supreme Court for approval.

(B) Review as an Appellate Court. The commission may not function as an appellate court to review the decisions of the court or to exercise superintending or administrative control of the courts, except as that review is incident to a complaint of judicial misconduct. An erroneous decision by a judge made in good faith and with due diligence is not judicial misconduct.

(C) Control of Commission Action. Proceedings under these rules are subject to the direct and exclusive superintending control of the Supreme Court. No other court has jurisdiction to restrict, control, or review the orders of the master or the tenure commission.

(D) Errors and Irregularities. An investigation or proceedings under this chapter may not be held invalid by reason of a nonprejudicial irregularity or for an error not resulting in a miscarriage of justice.

(E) Jurisdiction Over Visiting Judges. Notwithstanding MCR 9.116(B), the Attorney Grievance Commission may take action immediately against a visiting judge who currently holds no other judicial office if the allegations of misconduct pertain to professional or personal activities unrelated to the respondent's activities as a judge.

[Effective March 1, 1985; amended effective August 30, 1990; April 1, 1998.]

1985 Staff Comment

MCR 9.203 corresponds to GCR 1963, 932.2.

Subrule (B) is based on rule 1 of the Administrative Rules of the Judicial Tenure Commission.

Staff Comment to 1990 Amendment

New subrule (E) [effective August 30, 1990] resolves a potential jurisdictional conflict between the Judicial Tenure Commission and the Attorney Grievance Commission. See and compare MCR 9.116(A). The new subrule makes it clear that the AGC is free to investigate allegations of nonjudicial misconduct by a visiting judge. The AGC would continue to defer to the JTC pursuant to MCR 9.116(A) if the allegations involve judicial misconduct. But see *In the Matter of Probert*, 411 Mich 210 (1981).

Staff Comment to 1998 Amendment

The March 24, 1998, amendments [effective April 1, 1998] of 2.109, 2.111, 2.112, 2.119, 8.103, 8.106, 8.110, 8.111, 9.114,

and 9.203, make technical changes necessary in light of statutory amendments and correct cross-references.

The amendments of MCR 2.109 and 2.112 relate to amendments of MCR 600.2912d, 600.2912e; MSA 27A.2912(d), 27A.2912(e), by 1993 PA 78.

The amendments of MCR 2.111 and 2.119 are based on statutes amended by 1996 PA 388. The change in MCR 2.111(B)(2) applies to actions filed on or after January 1, 1998, the effective date of the statute increasing the jurisdictional limit of the district court.

The amendment of MCR 8.106 corrects a statutory reference in light of 1993 PA 189.

The remaining amendments make changes in cross-references necessitated by earlier amendments. Some published versions of the rules already include several of these corrections.

RULE 9.204 DISQUALIFICATION OF COMMISSION MEMBER OR EMPLOYEE

(A) Disqualification From Participation. A judge who is a member of the commission or of the Supreme Court is disqualified from participating in that capacity in proceedings involving his or her own discipline, suspension, retirement, or removal.

(B) Disqualification From Representation. A member or employee of the Judicial Tenure Commission may not represent

(1) a respondent in proceedings before the commission, including preliminary discussions with employees of the commission prior to the filing of a request for investigation; or

(2) a judge or former judge in proceedings before the Attorney Grievance Commission, or the Attorney Discipline Board and its hearing panels, as to any matter that was pending before the Judicial Tenure Commission during the member's or employee's tenure with the Judicial Tenure Commission.

[Effective March 1, 1985; amended effective July 1, 1996.]

1985 Staff Comment

MCR 9.204 is substantially the same as GCR 1963, 932.5.

Staff Comment to 1996 Amendment

The amendment of MCR 9.204, effective July 1, 1996, precluded members and employees of the Judicial Tenure Commission from representing (1) a respondent in proceedings before the Judicial Tenure Commission, and (2) a judge or former judge in proceedings before the Attorney Grievance Commission, or the Attorney Discipline Board and its hearing panels, as to matters pending before the Judicial Tenure Commission during the member's or employee's tenure with the Judicial Tenure Commission.

RULE 9.205 STANDARDS OF JUDICIAL CONDUCT

(A) Responsibility of Judge. A judge is personally responsible for his or her own behavior and for the proper conduct and administration of the court in which he or she presides.

(B) Grounds for Discipline. A judge is subject to censure, suspension, retirement, or removal for misconduct in office as defined by subrule (C) or because of disability as defined in subrule (D).

(C) Misconduct. A judge is guilty of misconduct in office if:

(1) the judge is convicted in the United States of conduct which is punishable as a felony under the laws of Michigan or federal law;

(2) the judge persistently fails to perform judicial duties;

(3) the judge is habitually intemperate within the meaning of Const 1963, art 6, § 30;

(4) the judge's conduct is clearly prejudicial to the administration of justice;

(5) the judge is persistently incompetent or neglectful in the performance of judicial duties;

(6) the judge persistently fails to treat persons fairly, with courtesy and respect; or

(7) the judge treats a person unfairly, discourteously, or disrespectfully because of the person's race, gender, or other protected personal characteristic.

(D) Disability. A judge is subject to suspension, retirement, or removal from office for physical or mental disability which significantly interferes with the capacity to perform his or her judicial duties.

(E) Code of Judicial Conduct; Rules of Professional Responsibility. Conduct in violation of the Code of Judicial Conduct or rules of professional responsibility, whether the conduct complained of occurred before or after the respondent became a judge or was or was not connected with his or her judicial office, may constitute misconduct in office, conduct that is clearly prejudicial to the administration of justice, or another ground for discipline listed in Const 1963, art 6, § 30. The question in every case is whether the conduct complained of constitutes misconduct in office, conduct that is clearly prejudicial to the administration of justice, or another ground of discipline listed in Const 1963, art 6, § 30, not whether a particular canon or disciplinary rule has been violated. All the circumstances are to be considered in deciding whether action by the commission is warranted.

[Effective March 1, 1985; amended effective May 5, 1987; October 1, 1993.]

1985 Staff Comment

MCR 9.205 corresponds to GCR 1963, 932.4.

New subrule (B) expressly states that misconduct in office or incapacity is grounds for discipline.

Staff Comment to 1987 Amendment

The 1987 amendment to MCR 9.205 is designed to permit greater flexibility in responding to the problems caused by a judge's disability.

Staff Comment to 1993 Amendment

The explanation of the 1993 amendment is found in the opening paragraphs of the Court's July 16, 1993 order, reported at 443 Mich xxiii (1993).

RULE 9.206   SERVICE AND NOTICE

(A) Service. When provision is made under these rules for serving notice of a complaint or other document on a judge or respondent, the notice must be made by service in person or by registered or certified mail to his or her judicial business office or last known residence. If an attorney has appeared for a respondent, notice may be served on the attorney in lieu of service on the respondent.

(B) Notice. Service of notice on the commission must be made by delivering or mailing by registered or certified mail to the commission's executive director at the commission's office.

[Effective March 1, 1985.]

1985 Staff Comment

MCR 9.206 is substantially the same as GCR 1963, 932.6.

RULE 9.207   PRELIMINARY INVESTIGATION

(A) Requests for Investigation. Unless the commission chooses to act on its own initiative or at the request of the Chief Justice or the state court administrator, a request for action by the commission must be made in writing and verified on oath of the complainant.

(B) Preliminary Investigation.

(1) On receiving a verified statement, found on examination and inquiry to be neither unfounded nor frivolous, alleging facts indicating that a judge is guilty of misconduct in office or suffers from physical or mental disability;

(2) on receiving a request for investigation from the Attorney Grievance Commission; or

(3) on request of the Chief Justice or the state court administrator,

the commission must conduct a preliminary investigation to determine whether a complaint is to be filed and a hearing held. The commission may, on its own initiative and without receiving a statement, make inquiry and a preliminary investigation with respect to whether a judge is guilty of misconduct in office or is physically or mentally disabled.

(C) Notice to Judge. Before filing a complaint or recommending an order of private censure, the commission must give written notice to the judge of the nature of the charges being made and afford the judge an opportunity to present in writing, within 28 days, any matters the judge chooses for consideration by the commission.

(D) Resolution of Investigation. If the preliminary examination does not disclose sufficient cause to warrant filing a complaint, the commission may:

(1) dismiss the investigation;

(2) admonish the respondent; or

(3) recommend to the Supreme Court private censure, with a statement of reasons in support of its recommendation.

The commission must promptly notify the judge of its decision to use one of these alternatives.

(E) Admonition; Order of Private Censure. An admonition or order of private censure is confidential. If the judge requests a hearing on the recommendation of private censure, the Supreme Court shall remand the case to the commission for a hearing.

(F) Notice of Disposition of Grievance. On final disposition of a grievance, the commission shall give written notice of the disposition to the complainant and may advise the judge charged with misconduct or disability.

(G) Physical or Mental Examination. In the course of an investigation of judicial misconduct or of mental or physical disability of a judge, the commission may request the judge to submit to a physical or mental examination. Failure of the judge to submit to the examination is judicial misconduct. MCR 2.311(B) is applicable to the examination.

[Effective March 1, 1985.]

1985 Staff Comment

MCR 9.207 corresponds to GCR 1963, 932.7.

Subrule (A) is taken from rule 3 of the Administrative Rules of the Judicial Tenure Commission.

Subrule (F) is taken from rule 4 of the Administrative Rules of the Judicial Tenure Commission.

RULE 9.208 COMPLAINT

(A) Filing; Service. If, after the preliminary investigation has been completed, the commission concludes that a complaint will be filed, the case must be entered in a docket to be kept for that purpose. The complaint must be filed in the commission's office, to become a public record, and a copy must promptly be served on the respondent.

(B) Form of Complaint. A complaint must be entitled:

"Complaint Against _____, Judge. No. _____."

A complaint must be in form similar to a complaint filed in a civil action in the circuit court.

[Effective March 1, 1985.]

1985 Staff Comment

MCR 9.208 corresponds to GCR 1963, 932.8. The provisions are reorganized without changing the substance of the rule.

RULE 9.209 ANSWER

(A) Filing. Within 14 days after service of the complaint, the respondent must file with the commission the original and 9 copies of an answer verified by the respondent. The answer must be in form similar to an answer in a civil action in the circuit court, and must contain a full and fair disclosure of all facts and circumstances pertaining to the respondent's alleged misconduct or physical or mental disability. Wilful concealment, misrepresentation, or failure to file an answer and disclosure are additional grounds for disciplinary action under the complaint.

(B) No Other Pleadings Allowed. The complaint and answer are the only pleadings.

[Effective March 1, 1985.]

1985 Staff Comment

MCR 9.209 is substantially the same as GCR 1963, 932.9.

RULE 9.210 SETTING FOR HEARING AND APPOINTMENT OF MASTER

(A) Notice of Hearing. On the filing of a complaint, the commission must set a time and place of hearing before it and give notice of the hearing to the respondent at least 21 days before the date set, or direct that the hearing be held before a master to be appointed by the Supreme Court.

(B) Appointment of Master. If the commission directs that the hearing be held before a master to be appointed by the Supreme Court, the commission must file an ex parte written request to the Supreme Court to appoint a master for that purpose, accompanied by a copy of the complaint. The Supreme Court must, within 14 days after receipt of the request, appoint a master to conduct the hearing. The master shall set a time and place for the hearing and give notice of the hearing to the respondent and to the examiner at least 21 days before the date set. The master shall rule on all motions and other procedural matters incident to the complaint, answer, and hearing, subject to review by the commission after the filing of the master's report.

(C) Appointment of Examiners. The executive director shall act as the examiner in every case in which a formal complaint is filed, except that the commission may appoint additional associate examiners in individual cases.

[Effective March 1, 1985.]

1985 Staff Comment

MCR 9.210 corresponds to GCR 1963, 932.10.

Subrule (C) is taken from rule 5 of the Administrative Rules of the Judicial Tenure Commission.

RULE 9.211 HEARING

(A) Procedure. At the time and place set for hearing, the commission or the master shall proceed with a public hearing, which must conform as nearly as possible to the rules of procedure and evidence governing the trial of civil actions in the circuit court. The hearing must be held whether or not the respondent has filed an answer or appears at the hearing. The examiner shall present the evidence in support of the charges set forth in the complaint. A respondent is entitled to be represented by an attorney. Any employee, officer or agent of the judge's court, law enforcement officer, public officer or employee, or attorney who testifies as a witness in the hearing, whether called by the examiner or by the judge, is subject to cross-examination by either party as an opposite party under MCL 600.2161; MSA 27A.2161.

(B) Failure to Appear. The respondent's failure to answer or to appear at the hearing may not, standing alone, be taken as evidence of the truth of the facts alleged to constitute grounds for commission action. The respondent's failure to answer, to testify in his or her own behalf, or to submit to a medical examination requested by the commission or the master may be considered as an evidentiary fact, unless it appears that the failure was due to circumstances unrelated to the facts in issue at the hearing.

(C) Record. The proceedings at the hearing must be recorded by a voice recorder or by a stenographer designated by the commission or master.

(D) Rulings. When the hearing is before the commission, at least 5 members must be present while the hearing is in active progress. Procedural and other interlocutory rulings must be made by the chairperson, and are taken as consented to by the other members of the commission unless a member calls for a vote, and then ruling must be made by a majority vote of those present.

[Effective March 1, 1985.]

1985 Staff Comment

MCR 9.211 is substantially the same as GCR 1963, 932.11.

RULE 9.212 ISSUANCE, SERVICE, AND RETURN OF SUBPOENAS

At the request of the commission, the master, the examiner, the respondent, or the respondent's attorney, subpoenas for the attendance of witnesses and the production of documents before the commission or master may be issued out of the circuit court in the county in which the hearing is to be held, in like manner and with like effect as in civil proceedings. Before the filing of a complaint, the entitlement of the

case may not disclose the name of the judge under investigation.

[Effective March 1, 1985.]

1985 Staff Comment

MCR 9.212 is substantially the same as GCR 1963, 932.12.

RULE 9.213 EVIDENCE

(A) Taking of Evidence During Preliminary Inquiry. Before filing a complaint, the commission may take evidence before it or before an individual member of the commission or its staff for purposes of its preliminary inquiry.

(B) Cooperation With Investigation. A judge, clerk, court employee, member of the bar, or other officer of the court must comply with a reasonable request made by the commission for aid in its investigation of a judge.

(C) Discovery. Pretrial or discovery proceedings are not permitted, except as follows:

(1) Within 14 days after the answer to the complaint is filed, the commission shall, on the respondent's written demand, make available for inspection or copying by the respondent documentary evidence in the commission's possession that is to be introduced as evidence at the hearing;

(2) Within the same time, the commission shall give the respondent written notification of the name and address of any person to be called as a witness. The commission shall give supplemental notice to the respondent within 5 days after any additional witness has been identified and at least 10 days before a scheduled hearing;

(3) A deposition may be taken of a witness living outside the state or physically unable to attend the hearing;

(4) The master may order a prehearing conference held before the master to obtain admissions or otherwise narrow the issues presented by the pleadings.

If the commission fails to comply with subrules (C)(1) or (2), the master may, on motion and showing of material prejudice as a result of the failure, impose one or more of the sanctions set forth in MCR 2.313(B)(2)(a)–(c).

[Effective March 1, 1985.]

1985 Staff Comment

MCR 9.213 is substantially the same as GCR 1963, 932.13.

RULE 9.214 AMENDMENTS TO COMPLAINT OR ANSWER

The master, before the conclusion of the hearing, or the commission, before its determination, may allow or require amendments to the complaint or answer. The complaint may be amended to conform to the proofs or to set forth additional facts, whether occurring before or after the commencement of the hearing. If an amendment is made, the respondent must be given reasonable time to answer the amendment and to prepare and present his or her defense against the matters charged in the amendment.

[Effective March 1, 1985.]

1985 Staff Comment

MCR 9.214 is substantially the same as GCR 1963, 932.14.

RULE 9.215   REPORT OF MASTER

Within 28 days after the conclusion of the hearing before a master, the master shall prepare and transmit to the commission in duplicate a report which must contain a brief statement of the proceedings and findings of fact and conclusions of law with respect to the issues presented by the complaint and answer. The report must be accompanied by two copies of the transcript of the proceedings before the master. On receiving the report and transcript, the commission must promptly send a copy of each to the respondent.

[Effective March 1, 1985.]

1985 Staff Comment

MCR 9.215 is substantially the same as GCR 1963, 932.15.

RULE 9.216   OBJECTIONS TO REPORT OF MASTER

Within 14 days after a copy of the master's report and transcript is mailed to the respondent, the examiner or the respondent may file with the commission an original and 9 copies of a statement of objections to the report of the master, along with a supporting brief. A copy of a statement and brief must be served on the opposite party.

[Effective March 1, 1985.]

1985 Staff Comment

MCR 9.216 is substantially the same as GCR 1963, 932.16.

RULE 9.217   APPEARANCE BEFORE COMMISSION

When the master files the report, the commission must set a date for hearing objections to the report. The respondent and the examiner must file written briefs at least 7 days before the hearing date. Both may present oral argument at the hearing.

[Effective March 1, 1985.]

1985 Staff Comment

MCR 9.217 is substantially the same as GCR 1963, 932.17.

RULE 9.218   EXTENSION OF TIME

The commission or its chairperson may extend for periods not to exceed 28 days the time for filing an answer, for the commencement of a hearing before the commission, for the filing of the master's report, and for filing a statement of objections to the report of a master. A master may similarly extend the time for the commencement of a hearing before him or her.

[Effective March 1, 1985.]

1985 Staff Comment

MCR 9.218 is substantially the same as GCR 1963, 932.18.

RULE 9.219   HEARING ADDITIONAL EVIDENCE

The commission may order a hearing, before itself or the master, for the taking of additional evidence at any time while the complaint is pending before it. The order must set the time and place of hearing and indicate the matters about which evidence is to be taken. A copy of the order must be sent to the respondent at least 14 days before the hearing.

[Effective March 1, 1985.]

1985 Staff Comment

MCR 9.219 is substantially the same as GCR 1963, 932.19.

RULE 9.220   INTERIM SUSPENSION

(A) Petition. The commission may petition the Supreme Court for an order suspending a judge from acting as a judge until final adjudication of a complaint.

(B) Contents; Affidavit or Transcript. The petition must allege facts supported by sworn affidavit or court transcript indicating that the judge is guilty of misconduct in office as defined in MCR 9.205(C) or (E) or suffers from physical or mental disability as defined in MCR 9.205(D) and that immediate suspension is necessary for the proper administration of justice.

(C) Service; Answer. A copy of the petition and supporting documents must be served on the respondent who may file an answer to the petition within 14 days after service of the petition. The commission must be served with a copy of the answer.

[Effective March 1, 1985.]

1985 Staff Comment

MCR 9.220 is substantially the same as GCR 1963, 932.20.

RULE 9.221   COMMISSION DECISION

(A) Majority Decision. The affirmative vote of 5 commission members who have considered the report of the master and objections and who were present at an oral hearing provided for in MCR 9.217, or, if the hearing was before the commission without a master, the affirmative vote of 5 commission members who were present when the evidence was taken, is required for a recommendation of discipline, removal, retirement, or suspension of a judge. Absent 5 votes, the commission must enter an order of dismissal of the complaint. A commissioner may file a written dissent.

(B) Record of Decision. The commission must make written findings of fact and conclusions of law along with its recommendations for action with respect to the issues of fact and law in the proceedings, but may adopt the findings of the master, in whole or in part, by reference.

(C) Discipline With Respondent's Consent. With the respondent's consent, the Supreme Court may enter an order of discipline, suspension, retirement, or removal at any stage of proceedings under these rules.

[Effective March 1, 1985.]

1985 Staff Comment

MCR 9.221 is substantially the same as GCR 1963, 932.21.

RULE 9.222 CONFIDENTIALITY AND PRIVILEGE OF PROCEEDINGS

(A) Before Complaint. Before a complaint is filed, a member of the commission or its staff may not disclose the existence or contents of the investigation, testimony taken, or papers filed in it, but the commission may at any time make public statements as to matters pending before it, only on its determination by a majority vote that it is in the public interest to do so, limited to the fact that:

(1) there is an investigation pending, or

(2) the investigation is complete and that there is insufficient evidence for the commission to file a complaint.

(B) After Filing of Complaint. After the complaint is filed, the proceedings are available for public inspection and must be conducted in open public hearings.

(C) Consent of Judge. On the written consent of the judge against whom a grievance has been filed or who is being investigated, the commission may disclose matters relating to it, notwithstanding the prohibition against disclosure set forth in this rule.

(D) Disclosure to State Court Administrator.

(1) The commission may refer to the state court administrator grievances and other communications received by the commission concerning the conduct of a judge, which in the opinion of the commission, are properly within the scope of the duties of the court administrator, and may provide the court administrator with files, records, investigations, and reports of the commission relating to the matter. Such referral to the court administrator does not preclude action by the commission where the judge's conduct is of such a nature as to constitute grounds for action by the commission, or which cannot be adequately resolved or corrected by action of the court administrator.

(2) The commission may disclose to the state court administrator, on his or her request, the substance of

files and records of the commission concerning a former judge who has been or may be assigned judicial duties by the state court administrator; a copy of the information disclosed must be furnished to the judge.

(E) Disclosure to Attorney Grievance Commission. Notwithstanding the prohibition against disclosure in this rule, the commission shall disclose information concerning misconduct to the Attorney Grievance Commission, upon request. Absent a request, the commission may make such disclosure to the Attorney Grievance Commission.

[Effective March 1, 1985; amended effective December 1, 1998.]

1985 Staff Comment

MCR 9.222 is substantially the same as GCR 1963, 932.22.

Staff Comment to 1998 Amendment

The December 1, 1998 amendment of MCR 9.126 and 9.222 made mandatory the disclosure of information, upon request, between the Attorney Grievance Commission and the Judicial Tenure Commission. The amendment of State Bar Rule 15, § 1 authorized the State Bar's Committee on Character and Fitness to disclose to the Attorney Grievance Commission information concerning the bar application of a disciplined lawyer who is requesting reinstatement to the practice of law. Under the amendment, the lawyer must be notified of the request, and the hearing panel must determine the relevancy of the information before permitting it to be used in a public document or proceeding.

RULE 9.223 CERTIFICATION TO SUPREME COURT

(A) Filing and Service of Documents by Commission. Within 21 days after entering an order recommending the discipline, removal, retirement, or suspension of a respondent, the commission must

(1) file in the Supreme Court:

(a) the original record arranged in chronological order and indexed and certified;

(b) 24 copies of the order;

(c) 24 copies of an appendix; and

(d) a proof of service on the respondent;

(2) serve the respondent with:

(a) notice of the filing under MCR 9.223(A)(1);

(b) 2 copies of the order and appendix;

(c) 2 copies of the index to the original record; and

(d) a copy of a portion of the original record not submitted by or previously furnished to the respondent.

(B) Contents of Appendix. The appendix must include, in chronological order,

(1) an index;

(2) all pleadings, including those filed with a master;

(3) all orders, including those issued by a master;

(4) all reports, findings of fact, and conclusions of law made by the commission or a master; and

(5) other material necessary to fairly judge the issues.

The appendix need not be printed.

[Effective March 1, 1985.]

1985 Staff Comment

MCR 9.223 is substantially the same as GCR 1963, 932.23.

RULE 9.224   REVIEW BY SUPREME COURT

(A) Petition by Respondent. Within 28 days after being served, a respondent may file in the Supreme Court 24 copies of

(1) a petition to reject or modify the commission's recommendation; the petition must:

(a) be based on the record,

(b) specify the grounds relied on,

(c) be verified, and

(d) include a brief in support; and

(2) an appendix presenting portions of the record not included in the commission's appendix which the respondent believes necessary to fairly judge the issues. The appendix need not be printed.

The respondent must serve the commission with 3 copies of the petition and 2 copies of the appendix and file proof of that service.

(B) Brief of Commission. Within 21 days after respondent's petition is served, the commission must file

(1) 24 copies of a brief supporting its finding, and

(2) proof that the respondent was served with 2 copies of the brief.

(C) Review in Absence of Petition by Respondent. If the respondent does not file a petition, the Supreme Court shall review the commission's recommendation on the record filed. The Supreme Court may order that briefs be filed or arguments be presented.

(D) Form of Briefs. A brief filed under this subrule is to be similar to a brief in an appeal to the Supreme Court, except that a brief may be typewritten.

(E) Additional Evidence. The Supreme Court may, if cause is shown, order that further evidence be taken and added to the original record.

(F) Submission. The clerk will place the case on a session calendar under MCR 7.312.   Oral argument may be requested.

[Effective March 1, 1985.]

1985 Staff Comment

MCR 9.224 is substantially the same as GCR 1963, 932.24.

RULE 9.225   DECISION BY SUPREME COURT

The Supreme Court shall review the record of the proceedings and shall file a written opinion and judgment, which may direct censure, removal, retirement, suspension, or other disciplinary action, or reject or modify the recommendations of the commission.

[Effective March 1, 1985.]

1985 Staff Comment

MCR 9.225 is substantially the same as GCR 1963, 932.25.

RULE 9.226   MOTION FOR REHEARING

The respondent may file a motion for rehearing within 14 days after the filing of the decision.   However, if the Supreme Court directs in the decision that a motion for rehearing may not be filed, the decision is final on filing.

[Effective March 1, 1985.]

1985 Staff Comment

MCR 9.226 is substantially the same as GCR 1963, 932.26.

RULE 9.227   IMMUNITY

A person is absolutely immune from suit for statements and communications transmitted solely to the Judicial Tenure Commission or the Commission staff, or given in an investigation or proceeding on alleged misconduct, and no civil action predicated upon the statements or communications may be instituted against a complainant, a witness, or their counsel. Members of the Judicial Tenure Commission and their counsel and staff are absolutely immune from suit for all conduct in the course of their official duties.

[Adopted effective September 1, 1995.]

1995 Staff Comment

The July 7, 1995, amendments of MCR 2.003, and Rules 3A, 3D, 6C, and 7B of the Michigan Code of Judicial Conduct, and new MCR 9.227 and Rule 7D of the Michigan Code of Judicial Conduct, are based on the proposed revision of the Michigan Code of Judicial Conduct submitted by the State Bar Representative Assembly.   See 442 Mich 1216 (1993).   They are effective September 1, 1995.

MICHIGAN RULES OF EVIDENCE

Effective March 1, 1978

Research Note

Use Westlaw ® to find cases citing or applying specific rules. Westlaw may also be used to search for specific terms in court rules or to update court rules. See the MI–RULES and MI–ORDERS Scope Screens for detailed descriptive information and search tips.

Amendments to these rules are published, as received, in the N.W.2d and Michigan Reporter advance sheets, and Michigan Legislative Service.

Table of Rules

INDEX

ADOPTING ORDER

On order of the Court, the notice requirements of GCR 1963, 933 having been complied with, and changes made after considering the comments received, the following new MRE 101–1102 were adopted January 5, 1978, to be effective March 1, 1978.

In adopting these rules, the Court should not be understood as foreclosing consideration of a challenge to the wisdom, validity or meaning of a rule when a question is brought to the Court judicially or by a proposal for a change in a rule. See, e.g., *Meek v Centre County Banking Co,* 268 US 426; 45 S Ct 560; 69 L Ed 1028 (1925), and *Mississippi Publishing Corp v Murphree,* 326 US 438; 66 S Ct 242; 90 L Ed 185 (1946). While these rules are binding on Michigan courts, the Court does not intend to preclude evidentiary objection in the trial court based on a challenge to the wisdom, validity or meaning of a rule and development of a separate record so as to properly present the challenge for review by this Court.

[Effective March 1, 1978.]

RULE 101. SCOPE

These rules govern proceedings in the courts of this state to the extent and with the exceptions stated in Rule 1101. A statutory rule of evidence not in conflict with these rules or other rules adopted by the Supreme Court is effective until superseded by rule or decision of the Supreme Court.

[Effective March 1, 1978.]

1978 Note

The first sentence of Michigan Rule of Evidence (MRE) 101 is identical with Rule 101 as recommended by the National Conference of Commissioners on Uniform State Laws in its Uniform Rules of Evidence (1974) and is similar to Rule 101 of the Federal Rules of Evidence. The second sentence of MRE 101 has no equivalent in the Federal Rules of Evidence or the Uniform Rules of Evidence; it is similar to GCR 1963, 16.

RULE 102. PURPOSE

These rules are intended to secure fairness in administration, elimination of unjustifiable expense and delay, and promotion of growth and development of the law of evidence to the end that the truth may be ascertained and proceedings justly determined.

[Effective March 1, 1978.]

1978 Note

MRE 102 is identical with Rule 102 of the Federal Rules of Evidence, except that the words "are intended" are substituted for the words "shall be construed".

RULE 103. RULINGS ON EVIDENCE

(a) **Effect of erroneous ruling.** Error may not be predicated upon a ruling which admits or excludes evidence unless a substantial right of the party is affected, and

(1) *Objection.* In case the ruling is one admitting evidence, a timely objection or motion to strike appears of record, stating the specific ground of objection, if the specific ground was not apparent from the context; or

(2) *Offer of proof.* In case the ruling is one excluding evidence, the substance of the evidence was made known to the court by offer or was apparent from the context within which questions were asked.

Once the court makes a definitive ruling on the record admitting or excluding evidence, either at or before trial, a party need not renew an objection or offer of proof to preserve a claim of error for appeal.

(b) **Record of Offer and Ruling.** The court may add any other or further statement which shows the character of the evidence, the form in which it was offered, the objection made, and the ruling thereon. It may direct the making of an offer in question and answer form.

(c) **Hearing of Jury.** In jury cases, proceedings shall be conducted, to the extent practicable, so as to prevent inadmissible evidence from being suggested to the jury by any means, such as making statements or offers of proof or asking questions in the hearing of the jury.

(d) **Plain Error.** Nothing in this rule precludes taking notice of plain errors affecting substantial rights although they were not brought to the attention of the court.

[Effective March 1, 1978; amended effective January 1, 2002.]

1978 Note

MRE 103 is identical with Rule 103 of the Federal Rules of Evidence.

2001 Staff Comment

The October 23, 2001 amendment of MRE 103(a), effective January 1, 2002, is identical to the amendment of FRE 103(a) that took effect on December 1, 2000. The added language says that a party need not make repetitive objections or offers of proof after the court has made a "definitive ruling".

The staff comment is published only for the benefit of the bench and bar and is not an authoritative construction by the Court.

RULE 104. PRELIMINARY QUESTIONS

(a) **Questions of Admissibility Generally.** Preliminary questions concerning the qualification of a person to be a witness, the existence of a privilege, or the admissibility of evidence shall be determined by the court, subject to the provisions of subdivision (b). In making its determination it is not bound by the Rules of Evidence except those with respect to privileges.

(b) **Relevancy Conditioned on Fact.** When the relevancy of evidence depends upon the fulfillment of a condition of fact, the court shall admit it upon, or subject to, the introduction of evidence sufficient to support a finding of the fulfillment of the condition.

(c) Hearing of Jury. Hearings on the admissibility of confessions shall in all cases be conducted out of the hearing of the jury. Hearings on other preliminary matters shall be so conducted when the interests of justice require, or when an accused is a witness, and so requests.

(d) Testimony by Accused. The accused does not, by testifying upon a preliminary matter, become subject to cross-examination as to other issues in the case.

(e) Weight and Credibility. This rule does not limit the right of a party to introduce before the jury evidence relevant to weight or credibility.

[Effective March 1, 1978; amended June 1, 1995.]

1978 Note

MRE 104 is identical with Rule 104 of the Federal Rules of Evidence.

RULE 105. LIMITED ADMISSIBILITY

When evidence which is admissible as to one party or for one purpose but not admissible as to another party or for another purpose is admitted, the court, upon request, shall restrict the evidence to its proper scope and instruct the jury accordingly.

[Effective March 1, 1978.]

1978 Note

MRE 105 is identical with Rule 105 of the Federal Rules of Evidence.

RULE 106. REMAINDER OF OR RELATED WRITINGS OR RECORDED STATEMENTS

When a writing or recorded statement or part thereof is introduced by a party, an adverse party may require the introduction at that time of any other part or any other writing or recorded statement which ought in fairness to be considered contemporaneously with it.

[Effective March 1, 1978; amended effective June 1, 1995.]

1978 Note

MRE 106 is identical with Rule 106 of the Federal Rules of Evidence.

RULE 201. JUDICIAL NOTICE OF ADJUDICATIVE FACTS

(a) Scope of Rule. This rule governs only judicial notice of adjudicative facts, and does not preclude judicial notice of legislative facts.

(b) Kinds of Facts. A judicially noticed fact must be one not subject to reasonable dispute in that it is either (1) generally known within the territorial jurisdiction of the trial court or (2) capable of accurate and ready determination by resort to sources whose accuracy cannot reasonably be questioned.

(c) When Discretionary. A court may take judicial notice, whether requested or not, and may require a party to supply necessary information.

(d) Opportunity to Be Heard. A party is entitled upon timely request to an opportunity to be heard as to the propriety of taking judicial notice and the tenor of the matter noticed. In the absence of prior notification, the request may be made after judicial notice has been taken.

(e) Time of Taking Notice. Judicial notice may be taken at any stage of the proceeding.

(f) Instructing Jury. In a civil action or proceeding, the court shall instruct the jury to accept as conclusive any fact judicially noticed. In a criminal case, the court shall instruct the jury that it may, but is not required to, accept as conclusive any fact judicially noticed.

[Effective March 1, 1978.]

1978 Note

MRE 201 is identical with Rule 201 of the Federal Rules of Evidence except that the phrase "and does not preclude judicial notice of legislative facts" is added to MRE 201(a); the phrase "and may require a party to supply necessary information" is added to MRE 201(c); and Rule 201(d) of the Federal Rules of Evidence is omitted and the subsequent subdivisions of the rule relettered accordingly. Federal Rule 201(d), which is omitted, reads as follows: "(d) When mandatory. A court shall take judicial notice if requested by a party and supplied with the necessary information."

RULE 202. JUDICIAL NOTICE OF LAW

(a) When Discretionary. A court may take judicial notice without request by a party of (1) the common law, constitutions, and public statutes in force in every state, territory, and jurisdiction of the United States; (2) private acts and resolutions of the Congress of the United States and of the Legislature of Michigan, and ordinances and regulations of governmental subdivisions or agencies of Michigan; and (3) the laws of foreign countries.

(b) When Conditionally Mandatory. A court shall take judicial notice of each matter specified in paragraph (a) of this rule if a party requests it and (1) furnishes the court sufficient information to enable it properly to comply with the request and (2) has given each adverse party such notice as the court may require to enable the adverse party to prepare to meet the request.

[Effective March 1, 1978.]

1978 Note

MRE 202 has no equivalent in the Federal Rules of Evidence. It is derived in part from Rule 9 as recommended by the National Conference of Commissioners on Uniform State Laws in its Uniform Rules of Evidence (1953).

RULE 301. PRESUMPTIONS IN CIVIL ACTIONS AND PROCEEDINGS

In all civil actions and proceedings not otherwise provided for by statute or by these rules, a presumption imposes on the party against whom it is directed the burden of going forward with evidence to rebut or meet the presumption, but does not shift to such party the burden of proof in the sense of the risk of nonpersuasion, which remains throughout the trial upon the party on whom it was originally cast.

[Effective March 1, 1978.]

1978 Note

MRE 301 is identical with Rule 301 of the Federal Rules of Evidence except that MRE 301 employs the phrase "by statute" in place of the Federal Rules phrase "by Act of Congress".

RULE 302. PRESUMPTIONS IN CRIMINAL CASES

(a) Scope. In criminal cases, presumptions against an accused, recognized at common law or created by statute, including statutory provisions that certain facts are prima facie evidence of other facts or of guilt, are governed by this rule.

(b) Instructing the Jury. Whenever the existence of a presumed fact against an accused is submitted to the jury, the court shall instruct the jury that it may, but need not, infer the existence of the presumed fact from the basic facts and that the prosecution still bears the burden of proof beyond a reasonable doubt of all the elements of the offense.

[Effective March 1, 1978.]

1978 Note

MRE 302(a) is similar to Rule 303(a) as recommended by the National Conference of Commissioners on Uniform State Laws in its Uniform Rules of Evidence (1974). MRE 302(b) is a modified version of Rule 303(c) of the Uniform Rules of Evidence.

RULE 401. DEFINITION OF "RELEVANT EVIDENCE"

"Relevant evidence" means evidence having any tendency to make the existence of any fact that is of consequence to the determination of the action more probable or less probable than it would be without the evidence.

[Effective March 1, 1978.]

1978 Note

MRE 401 is identical with Rule 401 of the Federal Rules of Evidence.

RULE 402. RELEVANT EVIDENCE GENERALLY ADMISSIBLE; IRRELEVANT EVIDENCE INADMISSIBLE

All relevant evidence is admissible, except as otherwise provided by the Constitution of the United States, the Constitution of the State of Michigan, these rules, or other rules adopted by the Supreme Court. Evidence which is not relevant is not admissible.

[Effective March 1, 1978.]

1978 Note

MRE 402 is patterned after Rule 402 of the Federal Rules of Evidence, with modifications necessary to accommodate application to the Michigan courts.

RULE 403. EXCLUSION OF RELEVANT EVIDENCE ON GROUNDS OF PREJUDICE, CONFUSION, OR WASTE OF TIME

Although relevant, evidence may be excluded if its probative value is substantially outweighed by the danger of unfair prejudice, confusion of the issues, or misleading the jury, or by considerations of undue delay, waste of time, or needless presentation of cumulative evidence.

[Effective March 1, 1978.]

1978 Note

MRE 403 is identical with Rule 403 of the Federal Rules of Evidence.

RULE 404. CHARACTER EVIDENCE NOT ADMISSIBLE TO PROVE CONDUCT; EXCEPTIONS; OTHER CRIMES

(a) Character evidence generally. Evidence of a person's character or a trait of character is not admissible for the purpose of proving action in conformity therewith on a particular occasion, except:

(1) *Character of accused.* Evidence of a pertinent trait of character offered by an accused, or by the prosecution to rebut the same; or if evidence of a trait of character of the alleged victim of the crime is offered by the accused and admitted under subdivision (a)(2), evidence of a trait of character for aggression of the accused offered by the prosecution;

(2) *Character of alleged victim of homicide.* When self-defense is an issue in a charge of homicide, evidence of a trait of character for aggression of the alleged victim of the crime offered by an accused, or evidence offered by the prosecution to rebut the same, or evidence of a character trait of peacefulness of the alleged victim offered by the prosecution in a charge of homicide to rebut evidence that the alleged victim was the first aggressor;

(3) *Character of alleged victim of sexual conduct crime.* In a prosecution for criminal sexual conduct, evidence of the alleged victim's past sexual conduct with the defendant and evidence of specific instances of sexual activity showing the source or origin of semen, pregnancy, or disease;

(4) *Character of witness.* Evidence of the character of a witness, as provided in Rules 607, 608, and 609.

(b) Other crimes, wrongs, or acts.

(1) Evidence of other crimes, wrongs, or acts is not admissible to prove the character of a person in order to show action in conformity therewith. It may, however, be admissible for other purposes, such as proof of motive, opportunity, intent, preparation, scheme, plan, or system in doing an act, knowledge, identity, or absence of mistake or accident when the same is material, whether such other crimes, wrongs, or acts are contemporaneous with, or prior or subsequent to the conduct at issue in the case.

(2) The prosecution in a criminal case shall provide reasonable notice in advance of trial, or during trial if the court excuses pretrial notice on good cause shown, of the general nature of any such evidence it intends to introduce at trial and the rationale, whether or not mentioned in subparagraph (b)(1), for admitting the evidence. If necessary to a determination of the admissibility of the evidence under this rule, the defendant shall be required to state the theory or theories of defense, limited only by the defendant's privilege against self-incrimination.

[Effective March 1, 1978; amended effective March 1, 1991; June 24, 1994; January 1, 1995; June 1, 1995; September 1, 2001.]

1978 Note

MRE 404(a) is identical with Rule 404(a) of the Federal Rules of Evidence except for the addition of MRE 404(a)(3), and language changes incident thereto, regarding evidence of the character of the victim in a case charging criminal sexual conduct. MRE 404(b) is identical with Rule 404(b) of the Federal Rules of Evidence except that the word "plan" is replaced by the phrase "scheme, plan, or system in doing an act", and there is added the phrase "when the same is material, whether such other crime, wrongs, or acts are contemporaneous with, or prior or subsequent to the crime charged".

Note to 1991 Amendment

The amendment deleted "the crime charged" and substituted "the conduct at issue in the case" in subrule (b). The rule applies in civil cases even though it is used more often in criminal cases.

Note to 1994 Amendment

The June 24, 1994 amendment codifies *People* v *Vander-Vliet*, 444 Mich 52, 89 (1993).

Note to 1995 Amendment

The January 1, 1995 amendment added the requirement that the prosecution specify its rationale for admitting the evidence.

Note to 2001 Amendment

The September 1, 2001 amendment of subrule (a)(1) allows the prosecution to introduce evidence of the defendant's aggressive character if the defendant has introduced similar evidence about the alleged victim to support a self-defense theory. This change is similar to an amendment to FRE 404(a)(1) that became effective on December 1, 2000.

The September 1, 2001 amendment of subrule (a)(2) limits the accused's use of evidence of the alleged victim's character to a character trait for aggression in a homicide case in which self-defense is an issue. These limitations mark differences between the Michigan and Federal versions of subrule (a)(2).

The September 1, 2001 amendments of subrules (a)(2) and (3) substituted "alleged victim" for "victim". The change conforms MRE 404(a) to FRE 404(a) as amended effective December 1, 2000.

Cavanagh and Kelly, JJ., dissent in part and state as follows:

"We would amend MRE 404(a)(2) as recommended by the Advisory Committee majority, making the rule applicable to all cases in which self-defense is an issue, not just to homicide cases."

RULE 405. METHODS OF PROVING CHARACTER

(a) Reputation or Opinion. In all cases in which evidence of character or a trait of character of a person is admissible, proof may be made by testimony as to reputation or by testimony in the form of an opinion. On cross-examination, inquiry is allowable into reports of relevant specific instances of conduct.

(b) Specific Instances of Conduct. In cases in which character or a trait of character of a person is an essential element of a charge, claim, or defense, proof may also be made of specific instances of that person's conduct.

[Effective March 1, 1978; amended effective March 1, 1991; June 1, 1995.]

1978 Note

MRE 405 is identical with Rule 405 of the Federal Rules of Evidence except that the phrase "or by testimony in the form of an opinion" is omitted from the first sentence of MRE 405(a), with a corresponding change in the caption; and the second sentence of MRE 405(a) is changed to limit inquiry on cross-examination to "reports of" relevant specific instances of conduct.

Note to 1991 Amendment

The 1991 amendment conformed MRE 405 to its federal counterpart by adding "or by testimony in the form of an opinion" to the first sentence in subrule (a). See also the 1991 amendment to MRE 608.

RULE 406. HABIT; ROUTINE PRACTICE

Evidence of the habit of a person or of the routine practice of an organization, whether corroborated or not and regardless of the presence of eyewitnesses, is relevant to prove that the conduct of the person or organization on a particular occasion was in conformity with the habit or routine practice.

[Effective March 1, 1978.]

1978 Note

MRE 406 is identical with Rule 406 of the Federal Rules of Evidence.

RULE 407. SUBSEQUENT REMEDIAL MEASURES

When, after an event, measures are taken which, if taken previously would have made the event less likely to occur, evidence of the subsequent measures is not admissible to prove negligence or culpable conduct in connection with the event. This rule does not require the exclusion of evidence of subsequent measures when offered for another purpose, such as proving ownership, control, or feasibility of precautionary measures, if controverted, or impeachment.

[Effective March 1, 1978.]

1978 Note

MRE 407 is identical with Rule 407 of the Federal Rules of Evidence.

RULE 408. COMPROMISE AND OFFERS TO COMPROMISE

Evidence of (1) furnishing or offering or promising to furnish, or (2) accepting or offering or promising to accept, a valuable consideration in compromising or attempting to compromise a claim which was disputed as to either validity or amount, is not admissible to prove liability for or invalidity of the claim or its amount. Evidence of conduct or statements made in compromise negotiations is likewise not admissible. This rule does not require the exclusion of any evidence otherwise discoverable merely because it is presented in the course of compromise negotiations. This rule also does not require exclusion when the evidence is offered for another purpose, such as proving bias or prejudice of a witness, negativing a contention of undue delay, or proving an effort to obstruct a criminal investigation or prosecution.

[Effective March 1, 1978.]

1978 Note

MRE 408 is identical with Rule 408 of the Federal Rules of Evidence.

RULE 409. PAYMENT OF MEDICAL AND SIMILAR EXPENSES

Evidence of furnishing or offering or promising to pay medical, hospital, or similar expenses occasioned by an injury is not admissible to prove liability for the injury.

[Effective March 1, 1978.]

1978 Note

MRE 409 is identical with Rule 409 of the Federal Rules of Evidence.

RULE 410. INADMISSIBILITY OF PLEAS, PLEA DISCUSSIONS, AND RELATED STATEMENTS

Except as otherwise provided in this rule, evidence of the following is not, in any civil or criminal proceeding, admissible against the defendant who made the plea or was a participant in the plea discussions:

(1) A plea of guilty which was later withdrawn;

(2) A plea of nolo contendere, except that, to the extent that evidence of a guilty plea would be admissible, evidence of a plea of nolo contendere to a criminal charge may be admitted in a civil proceeding to support a defense against a claim asserted by the person who entered the plea;

(3) Any statement made in the course of any proceedings under MCR 6.302 or comparable state or federal procedure regarding either of the foregoing pleas; or

(4) Any statement made in the course of plea discussions with an attorney for the prosecuting authority which do not result in a plea of guilty or which result in a plea of guilty later withdrawn.

However, such a statement is admissible (i) in any proceeding wherein another statement made in the course of the same plea or plea discussions has been introduced and the statement ought in fairness be considered contemporaneously with it, or (ii) in a criminal proceeding for perjury or false statement if the statement was made by the defendant under oath, on the record and in the presence of counsel.

[Effective March 1, 1978; amended effective October 1, 1991.]

1978 Note

MRE 410 is identical with Rule 410 of the Federal Rules of Evidence and Rule 11(e)(6) of the Federal Rules of Criminal Procedure except that the concluding phrase "if the statement was made by the defendant under oath, on the record, and in the presence of counsel" is omitted from MRE 410.

Note to 1991 Amendment

For the most part, the October 1, 1991 amendments conformed MRE 410 to the current version of its federal counterpart. The conforming changes included the placement of the commas around the phrase "in any civil or criminal proceeding". That clarified the rule's original intent as explained in *Lichon v American Universal Ins Co*, 435 Mich 408 (1990). However, the exception in subrule (2), which exception has no federal counterpart, altered one of the holdings in *Lichon* by allowing evidence of a nolo contendere plea in certain circumstances. See also MRE 803(22), which was amended concurrently.

RULE 411. LIABILITY INSURANCE

Evidence that a person was or was not insured against liability is not admissible upon the issue whether the person acted negligently or otherwise wrongfully. This rule does not require the exclusion of evidence of insurance against liability when offered for another purpose, such as proof of agency, ownership, or control, if controverted, or bias or prejudice of a witness.

[Effective March 1, 1978; amended effective June 1, 1995.]

1978 Note

MRE 411 is identical with Rule 411 of the Federal Rules of Evidence except that the words "if controverted" in the second sentence are added.

RULE 501. PRIVILEGE; GENERAL RULE

Privilege is governed by the common law, except as modified by statute or court rule.

[Effective March 1, 1978.]

1978 Note

MRE 501 is derived in part from GCR 1963, 601.

RULE 601. WITNESSES; GENERAL RULE OF COMPETENCY

Unless the court finds after questioning a person that the person does not have sufficient physical or mental capacity or sense of obligation to testify truthfully and understandably, every person is competent to be a witness except as otherwise provided in these rules.

[Effective March 1, 1978; amended effective June 1, 1995.]

1978 Note

MRE 601 is identical with Rule 601 as recommended by the National Conference of Commissioners on Uniform State Laws in its Uniform Rules of Evidence (1974) and with the United States Supreme Court version of Rule 601 of the Federal Rules of Evidence, except for the addition of the introductory clause, "[u]nless the court finds after questioning a person that he does not have sufficient physical or mental capacity or sense of obligation to testify truthfully and understandably".

RULE 602. LACK OF PERSONAL KNOWLEDGE

A witness may not testify to a matter unless evidence is introduced sufficient to support a finding that the witness has personal knowledge of the matter. Evidence to prove personal knowledge may, but need not, consist of the witness' own testimony. This rule is subject to the provisions of Rule 703, relating to opinion testimony by expert witnesses.

[Effective March 1, 1978; amended effective June 1, 1995.]

1978 Note

MRE 602 is identical with Rule 602 of the Federal Rules of Evidence.

RULE 603. OATH OR AFFIRMATION

Before testifying, every witness shall be required to declare that the witness will testify truthfully, by oath or affirmation administered in a form calculated to awaken the witness' conscience and impress the witness' mind with the duty to do so.

[Effective March 1, 1978; amended effective June 1, 1995.]

1978 Note

MRE 603 is identical with Rule 603 of the Federal Rules of Evidence.

RULE 604. INTERPRETERS

An interpreter is subject to the provisions of these rules relating to qualification as an expert and the administration of an oath or affirmation to make a true translation.

[Effective March 1, 1978; amended effective June 1, 1995.]

1978 Note

MRE 604 is identical with Rule 604 of the Federal Rules of Evidence.

RULE 605. COMPETENCY OF JUDGE AS WITNESS

The judge presiding at the trial may not testify in that trial as a witness. No objection need be made in order to preserve the point.

[Effective March 1, 1978.]

1978 Note

MRE 605 is identical with Rule 605 of the Federal Rules of Evidence.

RULE 606. COMPETENCY OF JUROR AS WITNESS

A member of the jury may not testify as a witness before that jury in the trial of the case in which the juror is sitting. No objection need be made in order to preserve the point.

[Effective March 1, 1978; amended effective June 1, 1995.]

1978 Note

MRE 606 is similar to Rule 606(a) of the Federal Rules of Evidence. MRE 606 differs from Federal Rule 606(a) in providing that as to the error committed by permitting a juror to testify as a witness, "[n]o objection need be made in order to preserve the point".

RULE 607. WHO MAY IMPEACH

The credibility of a witness may be attacked by any party, including the party calling the witness.

[Effective March 1, 1978; amended effective March 1, 1991; June 1, 1995.]

1978 Note

[Former] MRE 607 differ[ed] from Rule 607 of the Federal Rules of Evidence, which reads: "The credibility of a witness may be attacked by any party, including the party calling him."

Note to 1991 Amendment

The 1991 amendment conformed MRE 607 to its federal counterpart by eliminating the restrictions on a party impeaching its own witness.

RULE 608. EVIDENCE OF CHARACTER AND CONDUCT OF WITNESS

(a) Opinion and Reputation Evidence of Character. The credibility of a witness may be attacked or supported by evidence in the form of opinion or reputation, but subject to these limitations: (1) the evidence may refer only to character for truthfulness or untruthfulness, and (2) evidence of truthful character is admissible only after the character of the witness for truthfulness has been attacked by opinion or reputation evidence or otherwise.

(b) Specific Instances of Conduct. Specific instances of the conduct of a witness, for the purpose of attacking or supporting the witness' credibility, other than conviction of crime as provided in Rule 609, may not be proved by extrinsic evidence. They may, however, in the discretion of the court, if probative of truthfulness or untruthfulness, be inquired into on cross-examination of the witness (1) concerning the witness' character for truthfulness or untruthfulness, or (2) concerning the character for truthfulness or untruthfulness of another witness as to which character the witness being cross-examined has testified.

The giving of testimony, whether by an accused or by any other witness, does not operate as a waiver of the accused's or the witness' privilege against self-incrimination when examined with respect to matters which relate only to credibility.

[Effective March 1, 1978; amended effective March 1, 1991; June 1, 1995.]

1978 Note

MRE 608 is identical with Rule 608 of the Federal Rules of Evidence except that the first clause of Federal Rule 608(a) provides that the credibility of a witness may be attacked or supported by "evidence *in the form of opinion or* reputation"; and the last clause of Federal Rule 608(a) reads, "attacked by *opinion or* reputation evidence or otherwise". (Emphasis supplied.) In addition, the caption is modified to reflect the elimination of opinion as a means of proving character.

Note to 1991 Amendment

The 1991 amendment conformed MRE 608(a) to its federal counterpart by adding language that permits opinion testimony. See also the 1991 amendment to MRE 405.

RULE 609. IMPEACHMENT BY EVIDENCE OF CONVICTION OF CRIME

(a) General Rule. For the purpose of attacking the credibility of a witness, evidence that the witness has been convicted of a crime shall not be admitted unless the evidence has been elicited from the witness or established by public record during cross examination, and

(1) the crime contained an element of dishonesty or false statement, or

(2) the crime contained an element of theft, and

(A) the crime was punishable by imprisonment in excess of one year or death under the law under which the witness was convicted, and

(B) the court determines that the evidence has significant probative value on the issue of credibility and, if the witness is the defendant in a criminal trial, the court further determines that the probative value of the evidence outweighs its prejudicial effect.

(b) Determining Probative Value and Prejudicial Effect. For purposes of the probative value determination required by subrule (a)(2)(B), the court shall consider only the age of the conviction and the degree to which a conviction of the crime is indicative of veracity. If a determination of prejudicial effect is required, the court shall consider only the conviction's similarity to the charged offense and the possible effects on the decisional process if admitting the evidence causes the defendant to elect not to testify. The court must articulate, on the record, the analysis of each factor.

(c) Time Limit. Evidence of a conviction under this rule is not admissible if a period of more than ten years has elapsed since the date of the conviction or of the release of the witness from the confinement imposed for that conviction, whichever is the later date.

(d) Effect of Pardon, Annulment, or Certificate of Rehabilitation. Evidence of a conviction is not admissible under this rule if (1) the conviction has been the subject of a pardon, annulment, certificate of rehabilitation, or other equivalent procedure based on a finding of the rehabilitation of the person convicted, and that person has not been convicted of a subsequent crime which was punishable by death or imprisonment in excess of one year, or (2) the conviction has been the subject of a pardon, annulment, or other equivalent procedure based on a finding of innocence.

(e) Juvenile Adjudications. Evidence of juvenile adjudications is generally not admissible under this rule, except in subsequent cases against the same child in the juvenile division of a probate court. The court may, however, in a criminal case or a juvenile proceeding against the child allow evidence of a juvenile adjudication of a witness other than the accused if conviction of the offense would be admissible to attack the credibility of an adult and the court is satisfied that admission is necessary for a fair determination of the case or proceeding.

(f) Pendency of Appeal. The pendency of an appeal therefrom does not render evidence of a conviction inadmissible. Evidence of the pendency of an appeal is admissible.

[Effective March 1, 1978; amended effective May 14, 1980; March 1, 1988.]

1978 Note

MRE 609(a) is a modified version of Rule 609(a) of the Federal Rules of Evidence, differing from the Federal Rule by inserting the word "theft" before the phrase "dishonesty or false statement", and by requiring a determination by the court that "the probative value of admitting this evidence on the issue of credibility outweighs its prejudicial effect" as a condition of admissibility as to *all* convictions used for impeachment. MRE 609(b) is identical with Rule 609(b) of the Federal Rules of Evidence except for omission from the first sentence of the phrase "unless the court determines, in the interests of justice, that the probative value of the conviction supported by specific facts and circumstances substantially outweighs its prejudicial effect" and the omission of the entire second sentence. Subdivisions (c), (d) and (e) are identical with the equivalent provisions of Rule 609 of the Federal Rules of Evidence. A "pardon" within the meaning of MRE 609(c) would not include, for example, a pardon granted solely to avoid deportation.

Note to 1988 Amendment

MRE 609(a) and (b) were amended by *People* v *Allen*, 429 Mich 558 (1988), effective March 1, 1988. The *Allen* amendments use a bright-line test to automatically determine the admissibility of most prior convictions. Theft convictions, which are neither automatically admitted nor automatically excluded by the bright-lines, are tested by additional criteria.

Subdivision (c) is similar to, and subdivisions (d), (e) and (f) are virtually identical with the equivalent provisions of Rule 609 of the Federal Rules of Evidence. A "pardon" within the meaning of MRE 609(d) would not include for example, a pardon granted solely to avoid deportation.

RULE 610. RELIGIOUS BELIEFS OR OPINIONS

Evidence of the beliefs or opinions of a witness on matters of religion is not admissible for the purpose of showing that by reason of their nature the witness' credibility is impaired or enhanced.

[Effective March 1, 1978; amended effective June 1, 1995.]

1978 Note

MRE 610 is identical with Rule 610 of the Federal Rules of Evidence.

RULE 611. MODE AND ORDER OF INTERROGATION AND PRESENTATION

(a) Control by Court. The court shall exercise reasonable control over the mode and order of interrogating witnesses and presenting evidence so as to (1) make the interrogation and presentation effective for the ascertainment of the truth, (2) avoid needless consumption of time, and (3) protect witnesses from harassment or undue embarrassment.

(b) Scope of Cross-Examination. A witness may be cross-examined on any matter relevant to any issue in the case, including credibility. The judge may limit cross-examination with respect to matters not testified to on direct examination.

(c) Leading Questions.

(1) Leading questions should not be used on the direct examination of a witness except as may be necessary to develop the witness' testimony.

(2) Ordinarily leading questions should be permitted on cross-examination.

(3) When a party calls a hostile witness, an adverse party or a witness identified with an adverse party, interrogation may be by leading questions. It is not necessary to declare the intent to ask leading questions before the questioning begins or before the questioning moves beyond preliminary inquiries.

[Effective March 1, 1978; amended effective October 1, 1991.]

1978 Note

MRE 611(a) and (c) are identical with Rule 611(a) and (c) of the Federal Rules of Evidence. MRE 611(b) is inconsistent with Federal Rule 611(b), which provides: "Cross-examination should be limited to the subject matter of the direct examination and matters affecting the credibility of the witness. The court may, in the exercise of discretion, permit inquiry into additional matters as if on direct examination."

After a witness has been examined under the procedure of the last sentence of MRE 611(c), the opposing party should be permitted to ask leading questions only as to those matters covered on the direct examination of the witness; leading questions should not be permitted as to new matters.

Note to 1991 Amendment

The October 1, 1991 amendment added subrule (c)(3). That subrule permits attorneys who call adverse witnesses to begin asking leading questions at any point even if they have not declared in advance their intent to do so. Cf. *Mally* v *Excelsior Wrapper Co*, 181 Mich 568 (1914), and *Ferguson* v *Gonyaw*, 64 Mich App 685, 688–692 (1975), *lv den* 396 Mich 817 (1976). However, this right still is subject to the trial judge's authority to "exercise reasonable control over the mode and order of interrogating. . . ." Subrule (a).

RULE 612. WRITING OR OBJECT USED TO REFRESH MEMORY

(a) While Testifying. If, while testifying, a witness uses a writing or object to refresh memory, an adverse party is entitled to have the writing or object produced at the trial, hearing, or deposition in which the witness is testifying.

(b) Before Testifying. If, before testifying, a witness uses a writing or object to refresh memory for the purpose of testifying and the court in its discretion determines that the interests of justice so require, an adverse party is entitled to have the writing or object produced, if practicable, at the trial, hearing, or deposition in which the witness is testifying.

(c) Terms and Conditions of Production and Use. A party entitled to have a writing or object produced under this rule is entitled to inspect it, to cross-examine the witness thereon, and to introduce in evidence, for their bearing on credibility only unless otherwise admissible under these rules for another purpose, those portions which relate to the testimony of the witness. If production of the writing or object at the trial, hearing, or deposition is impracticable, the court may order it made available for inspection. If it is claimed that the writing or object contains matters not related to the subject matter of the testimony the court shall examine the writing or object in camera, excise any portions not so related, and order delivery of the remainder to the party entitled thereto. Any portion withheld over objections shall be preserved and made available to the appellate court in the event of an appeal. If a writing or object is not produced, made available for inspection, or delivered pursuant to order under this rule, the court shall make any order justice requires, except that in criminal cases when the prosecution elects not to comply, the order shall be one striking the testimony or, if the court in its discretion determines that the interests of justice so require, declaring a mistrial.

[Effective March 1, 1978; amended effective March 1, 1991; June 1, 1995.]

1978 Note

MRE 612 is identical with Rule 612 as recommended by the National Conference of Commissioners on Uniform State Laws in its Uniform Rules of Evidence (1974). MRE 612 is similar in some respects to Rule 612 of the Federal Rules of Evidence.

Note to 1991 Amendment

The 1991 amendment added "for their bearing on credibility only unless otherwise admissible under these rules for another purpose" in subrule (c).

RULE 613. PRIOR STATEMENTS OF WITNESSES

(a) Examining Witness Concerning Prior Statement. In examining a witness concerning a prior statement made by the witness, whether written or not, the statement need not be shown nor its contents disclosed to the witness at that time, but on request it shall be shown or disclosed to opposing counsel and the witness.

(b) Extrinsic Evidence of Prior Inconsistent Statement of Witness. Extrinsic evidence of a prior inconsistent statement by a witness is not admissible unless the witness is afforded an opportunity to explain or deny the same and the opposite party is afforded an opportunity to interrogate the witness thereon, or the interests of justice otherwise require. This provision does not apply to admissions of a party-opponent as defined in Rule 801(d)(2).

[Effective March 1, 1978; amended effective March 1, 1991; June 1, 1995.]

1978 Note

MRE 613(a) is inconsistent with Rule 613(a) of the Federal Rules of Evidence, which provides: "In examining a witness concerning a prior statement made by him, whether written or not, the statement need not be shown nor its contents disclosed to him at that time, but on request the same shall be shown or disclosed to opposing counsel." MRE 613(b) is identical with Federal Rule 613(b).

Note to 1991 Amendment

The 1991 amendment modified the provision in subrule (a), which required that a witness always be shown a copy of the witness's former statement before being questioned about the statement. The amendment requires only that the statement be disclosed "on request". The rule remains more restrictive than its federal counterpart.

RULE 614. CALLING AND INTERROGATION OF WITNESSES BY COURT

(a) Calling by Court. The court may, on its own motion or at the suggestion of a party, call witnesses, and all parties are entitled to cross-examine witnesses thus called.

(b) Interrogation by Court. The court may interrogate witnesses, whether called by itself or by a party.

(c) Objections. Objections to the calling of witnesses by the court or to interrogation by it may be made at the time or at the next available opportunity when the jury is not present.

[Effective March 1, 1978.]

1978 Note

MRE 614 is identical with Rule 614 of the Federal Rules of Evidence.

RULE 615. EXCLUSION OF WITNESSES

At the request of a party the court may order witnesses excluded so that they cannot hear the testimony of other witnesses, and it may make the order of its own motion. This rule does not authorize exclusion of (1) a party who is a natural person, or (2) an officer or employee of a party which is not a natural person designated as its representative by its attorney, or (3) a person whose presence is shown by a party to be essential to the presentation of the party's cause.

[Effective March 1, 1978; amended effective June 1, 1995.]

1978 Note

MRE 615 is identical with Rule 615 of the Federal Rules of Evidence, except that the word "may" is substituted for the word "shall" in the first clause of the first sentence.

RULE 701. OPINION TESTIMONY BY LAY WITNESSES

If the witness is not testifying as an expert, the witness' testimony in the form of opinions or inferences is limited to those opinions or inferences which are (a) rationally based on the perception of the witness and (b) helpful to a clear understanding of the witness' testimony or the determination of a fact in issue.

[Effective March 1, 1978; amended effective June 1, 1995.]

1978 Note

MRE 701 is identical with Rule 701 of the Federal Rules of Evidence.

RULE 702. TESTIMONY BY EXPERTS

If the court determines that recognized scientific, technical, or other specialized knowledge will assist the trier of fact to understand the evidence or to determine a fact in issue, a witness qualified as an expert by knowledge, skill, experience, training, or education, may testify thereto in the form of an opinion or otherwise.

[Effective March 1, 1978.]

1978 Note

MRE 702 is identical with Rule 702 of the Federal Rules of Evidence except for the addition after the word "If" of the phrase "the court determines that recognized".

RULE 703. BASES OF OPINION TESTIMONY BY EXPERTS

The facts or data in the particular case upon which an expert bases an opinion or inference may be those perceived by or made known to the expert at or before the hearing. The court may require that underlying facts or data essential to an opinion or inference be in evidence.

[Effective March 1, 1978; amended effective June 1, 1995.]

1978 Note

MRE 703 is inconsistent with Rule 703 of the Federal Rules of Evidence, which provides: "The facts or data in the particular case upon which an expert bases an opinion or inference may be those perceived by or made known to him at or before the hearing. If of a type reasonably relied upon by experts in the particular field in forming opinions or inferences upon the subject, the facts or data need not be admissible in evidence."

RULE 704. OPINION ON ULTIMATE ISSUE

Testimony in the form of an opinion or inference otherwise admissible is not objectionable because it embraces an ultimate issue to be decided by the trier of fact.

[Effective March 1, 1978.]

1978 Note

MRE 704 is identical with Rule 704 of the Federal Rules of Evidence.

RULE 705. DISCLOSURE OF FACTS OR DATA UNDERLYING EXPERT OPINION

The expert may testify in terms of opinion or inference and give reasons therefor without prior disclosure of the underlying facts or data, unless the court requires otherwise. The expert may in any event be required to disclose the underlying facts or data on cross-examination.

[Effective March 1, 1978; amended effective June 1, 1995.]

1978 Note

MRE 705 is identical with Rule 705 of the Federal Rules of Evidence.

RULE 706. COURT–APPOINTED EXPERTS

(a) Appointment. The court may on its own motion or on the motion of any party enter an order to show cause why expert witnesses should not be appointed, and may request the parties to submit nominations. The court may appoint any expert witnesses agreed upon by the parties, and may appoint expert witnesses of its own selection. An expert witness shall not be appointed by the court unless the witness consents to act. A witness so appointed shall be informed of the witness' duties by the court in writing, a copy of which shall be filed with the clerk, or at a conference in which the parties shall have opportunity to participate. A witness so appointed shall advise the parties of the witness' findings, if any; the witness' deposition may be taken by any party; and the witness may be called to testify by the court or any party. The witness shall be subject to cross-examination by each party, including a party calling the witness.

(b) Compensation. Expert witnesses so appointed are entitled to reasonable compensation in whatever sum the court may allow. The compensation thus fixed is payable from funds which may be provided by law in criminal cases and civil actions and proceedings involving just compensation under the Fifth Amendment. In other civil actions and proceedings the compensation shall be paid by the parties in such proportion and at such time as the court directs, and thereafter charged in like manner as other costs.

(c) Disclosure of Appointment. In the exercise of its discretion, the court may authorize disclosure to the jury of the fact that the court appointed the expert witness.

(d) Parties' Experts of Own Selection. Nothing in this rule limits the parties in calling expert witnesses of their own selection.

[Effective March 1, 1978; amended effective June 1, 1995.]

1978 Note

MRE 706 is identical with Rule 706 of the Federal Rules of Evidence.

RULE 707. USE OF LEARNED TREATISES FOR IMPEACHMENT

To the extent called to the attention of an expert witness upon cross-examination, statements contained in published treatises, periodicals, or pamphlets on a subject of history, medicine, or other science or art, established as a reliable authority by the testimony or admission of the witness or by other expert testimony or by judicial notice, are admissible for impeachment purposes only. If admitted, the statements may be read into evidence but may not be received as exhibits.

[Effective March 1, 1978; amended effective March 1, 1991.]

1978 Note

MRE 707 is taken from Rule 803(18) of the Federal Rules of Evidence but with the addition of the phrase "are admissible for impeachment purposes only".

Note to 1991 Amendment

The 1991 amendment deleted "or relied upon by him in direct examination" from the first sentence. It also added the entire final sentence. Compare and contrast Federal Rule of Evidence 803(18) from which MRE 707 is derived.

RULE 801. HEARSAY; DEFINITIONS

The following definitions apply under this article:

(a) Statement. A "statement" is (1) an oral or written assertion or (2) nonverbal conduct of a person, if it is intended by the person as an assertion.

(b) Declarant. A "declarant" is a person who makes a statement.

(c) Hearsay. "Hearsay" is a statement, other than one made by the declarant while testifying at the trial or hearing, offered in evidence to prove the truth of the matter asserted.

(d) Statements Which Are Not Hearsay. A statement is not hearsay if—

(1) *Prior Statement of Witness.* The declarant testifies at the trial or hearing and is subject to cross-examination concerning the statement, and the state-

ment is (A) inconsistent with the declarant's testimony, and was given under oath subject to the penalty of perjury at a trial, hearing, or other proceeding, or in a deposition, or (B) consistent with the declarant's testimony and is offered to rebut an express or implied charge against the declarant of recent fabrication or improper influence or motive, or (C) one of identification of a person made after perceiving the person; or

(2) *Admission by Party-Opponent.* The statement is offered against a party and is (A) the party's own statement, in either an individual or a representative capacity, except statements made in connection with a guilty plea to a misdemeanor motor vehicle violation or an admission of responsibility for a civil infraction under laws pertaining to motor vehicles, or (B) a statement of which the party has manifested an adoption or belief in its truth, or (C) a statement by a person authorized by the party to make a statement concerning the subject, or (D) a statement by the party's agent or servant concerning a matter within the scope of the agency or employment, made during the existence of the relationship, or (E) a statement by a coconspirator of a party during the course and in furtherance of the conspiracy on independent proof of the conspiracy.

[Effective March 1, 1978; amended effective March 1, 1991; June 1, 1995.]

1978 Note

MRE 801(a), (b) and (c) are identical with Rule 801(a), (b) and (c) of the Federal Rules of Evidence. MRE 801(d) is identical with Federal Rule 801(d) except for:

(1) The omission of (1)(A) and (B), which read: "(A) inconsistent with his testimony, or (B) consistent with his testimony and is offered to rebut an express or implied charge against him of recent fabrication or improper influence or motive";

(2) The addition in (2)(A) of the phrase: "except statements made in connection with a guilty plea to a misdemeanor motor vehicle violation";

(3) The addition in (2)(B) of the phrase: "subject to the rule announced in *People v Bobo*, 390 Mich. 355 [212 N.W.2d 190] (1973)"; and

(4) The addition in (2)(E) of the phrase: "on independent proof of the conspiracy".

Note to 1991 Amendment

The 1991 amendments added subrules (d)(1)(A) and (B), and deleted from subrule (d)(2)(B) the citation to *People v Bobo*, 390 Mich 355 (1973). These changes conformed the rule to its federal counterpart.

In subrule (d)(2)(A), the 1991 amendments added the language that recognizes the decriminalization of most traffic offenses.

RULE 802. HEARSAY RULE

Hearsay is not admissible except as provided by these rules.

[Effective March 1, 1978.]

1978 Note
MRE 802 is similar to Rule 802 of the Federal Rules of
Evidence and Rule 802 as recommended by the National
Conference of Commissioners on Uniform State Laws in its
Uniform Rules of Evidence (1974).

RULE 803. HEARSAY EXCEPTIONS; AVAILABILITY OF DECLARANT IMMATERIAL

The following are not excluded by the hearsay rule,
even though the declarant is available as a witness:

(1) Present Sense Impression. A statement describing or explaining an event or condition made
while the declarant was perceiving the event or condition, or immediately thereafter.

(2) Excited Utterance. A statement relating to a
startling event or condition made while the declarant
was under the stress of excitement caused by the
event or condition.

**(3) Then Existing Mental, Emotional, or Physi-
cal Condition.** A statement of the declarant's then
existing state of mind, emotion, sensation, or physical
condition (such as intent, plan, motive, design, mental
feeling, pain, and bodily health), but not including a
statement of memory or belief to prove the fact
remembered or believed unless it relates to the execution, revocation, identification, or terms of declarant's
will.

**(4) Statements Made for Purposes of Medical
Treatment or Medical Diagnosis in Connection
With Treatment.** Statements made for purposes of
medical treatment or medical diagnosis in connection
with treatment and describing medical history, or past
or present symptoms, pain, or sensations, or the inception or general character of the cause or external
source thereof insofar as reasonably necessary to such
diagnosis and treatment.

(5) Recorded Recollection. A memorandum or
record concerning a matter about which a witness
once had knowledge but now has insufficient recollection to enable the witness to testify fully and accurately, shown to have been made or adopted by the
witness when the matter was fresh in the witness'
memory and to reflect that knowledge correctly. If
admitted, the memorandum or record may be read
into evidence but may not itself be received as an
exhibit unless offered by an adverse party.

(6) Records of Regularly Conducted Activity. A
memorandum, report, record, or data compilation, in
any form, of acts, transactions, occurrences, events,
conditions, opinions, or diagnoses, made at or near the
time by, or from information transmitted by, a person
with knowledge, if kept in the course of a regularly
conducted business activity, and if it was the regular
practice of that business activity to make the memorandum, report, record, or data compilation, all as
shown by the testimony of the custodian or other

qualified witness, or by certification that complies with
a rule promulgated by the supreme court or a statute
permitting certification, unless the source of information or the method or circumstances of preparation
indicate lack of trustworthiness. The term "business"
as used in this paragraph includes business, institution, association, profession, occupation, and calling of
every kind, whether or not conducted for profit.

**(7) Absence of Entry in Records Kept in Accor-
dance With the Provisions of Paragraph (6).** Evidence that a matter is not included in the memoranda, reports, records, or data compilations, in any
form, kept in accordance with the provisions of paragraph (6), to prove the nonoccurrence or nonexistence
of the matter, if the matter was of a kind of which a
memorandum, report, record, or data compilation was
regularly made and preserved, unless the sources of
information or other circumstances indicate lack of
trustworthiness.

(8) Public Records and Reports. Records, reports, statements, or data compilations, in any form, of
public offices or agencies, setting forth (A) the activities of the office or agency, or (B) matters observed
pursuant to duty imposed by law as to which matters
there was a duty to report, excluding, however, in
criminal cases matters observed by police officers and
other law enforcement personnel, and subject to the
limitations of MCL 257.624; MSA 9.2324.

(9) Records of Vital Statistics. Records or data
compilations, in any form, of births, fetal deaths,
deaths, or marriages, if the report thereof was made
to a public office pursuant to requirements of law.

(10) Absence of Public Record or Entry. To
prove the absence of a record, report, statement, or
data compilation, in any form, or the nonoccurrence or
nonexistence of a matter of which a record, report,
statement, or data compilation, in any form, was regularly made and preserved by a public office or agency,
evidence in the form of a certification in accordance
with Rule 902, or testimony, that diligent search failed
to disclose the record, report, statement, or data
compilation, or entry.

(11) Records of Religious Organizations. Statements of births, marriages, divorces, deaths, legitimacy, ancestry, relationship by blood or marriage, or
other similar facts of personal or family history, contained in a regularly kept record of a religious organization.

**(12) Marriage, Baptismal, and Similar Certifi-
cates.** Statements of fact contained in a certificate
that the maker performed a marriage or other cere-
mony or administered a sacrament, made by a member of the clergy, public official, or other person
authorized by the rules or practices of a religious
organization or by law to perform the act certified,
and purporting to have been issued at the time of the
act or within a reasonable time thereafter.

(13) Family Records. Statements of fact concerning personal or family history contained in family Bibles, genealogies, charts, engravings on rings, inscriptions on family portraits, engravings on urns, crypts, or tombstones, or the like.

(14) Records of Documents Affecting an Interest in Property. The record of a document purporting to establish or affect an interest in property, as proof of the content of the original recorded document and its execution and delivery by each person by whom it purports to have been executed, if the record is a record of a public office and an applicable statute authorizes the recording of documents of that kind in that office.

(15) Statements in Documents Affecting an Interest in Property. A statement contained in a document purporting to establish or affect an interest in property if the matter stated was relevant to the purpose of the document, unless dealings with the property since the document was made have been inconsistent with the truth of the statement or the purport of the document.

(16) Statements in Ancient Documents. Statements in a document in existence twenty years or more the authenticity of which is established.

(17) Market Reports, Commercial Publications. Market quotations, tabulations, lists, directories, or other published compilations, generally used and relied upon by the public or by persons in particular occupations.

(18) Deposition Testimony of an Expert. Testimony given as a witness in a deposition taken in compliance with law in the course of the same proceeding if the court finds that the deponent is an expert witness and if the deponent is not a party to the proceeding.

(19) Reputation Concerning Personal or Family History. Reputation among members of a person's family by blood, adoption, or marriage, or among a person's associates, or in the community, concerning a person's birth, adoption, marriage, divorce, death, legitimacy, relationship by blood, adoption, or marriage, ancestry, or other similar fact of personal or family history.

(20) Reputation Concerning Boundaries or General History. Reputation in a community, arising before the controversy, as to boundaries of or customs affecting lands in the community, and reputation as to events of general history important to the community or state or nation in which located.

(21) Reputation as to Character. Reputation of a person's character among associates or in the community.

(22) Judgment of Previous Conviction. Evidence of a final judgment, entered after a trial or upon a plea of guilty (or upon a plea of nolo contendere if evidence of the plea is not excluded by MRE 410), adjudging a person guilty of a crime punishable by death or imprisonment in excess of one year, to prove any fact essential to sustain the judgment, but not including, when offered by the state in a criminal prosecution for purposes other than impeachment, judgments against persons other than the accused. The pendency of an appeal may be shown but does not affect admissibility.

(23) Judgment as to Personal, Family, or General History, or Boundaries. Judgments as proof of matters of personal, family or general history, or boundaries, essential to the judgment, if the same would be provable by evidence of reputation.

(24) Other Exceptions. A statement not specifically covered by any of the foregoing exceptions but having equivalent circumstantial guarantees of trustworthiness, if the court determines that (A) the statement is offered as evidence of a material fact, (B) the statement is more probative on the point for which it is offered than any other evidence that the proponent can procure through reasonable efforts, and (C) the general purposes of these rules and the interests of justice will best be served by admission of the statement into evidence. However, a statement may not be admitted under this exception unless the proponent of the statement makes known to the adverse party, sufficiently in advance of the trial or hearing to provide the adverse party with a fair opportunity to prepare to meet it, the proponent's intention to offer the statement and the particulars of it, including the name and address of the declarant.

[Effective March 1, 1978; amended effective March 1, 1991; October 1, 1991; June 1, 1995; April 1, 1996; September 1, 2001.]

1978 Note

MRE 803 is identical with Rule 803 of the Federal Rules of Evidence except:

(1) MRE 803(4) is less broad than Federal Rule 803(4), which reads as follows: "*Statements for purposes of medical diagnosis or treatment.* Statements made for purposes of medical diagnosis or treatment and describing medical history, or past or present symptoms, pain, or sensation, or the inception or general character of the cause or external source thereof insofar as reasonably pertinent to diagnosis or treatment."

(2) MRE 803(6) is identical with Federal Rule 803(6) except that the phrase "acts, events, conditions, opinions, or diagnosis" is replaced by the phrase "acts, transactions, occurrences, or events".

(3) MRE 803(8) is identical with Federal Rule 803(8) except for the addition to clause (B) of the phrase "and subject to the limitations of MCL 257.624; MSA 9.2324", and the deletion of the following language: "or (C) in civil actions and proceedings and against the Government in criminal cases, factual findings resulting from an investigation made pursuant to authority granted by law, unless the sources of information or other circumstances indicate lack of trustworthiness."

(4) MRE 803(18) has no parallel in the Federal Rules. It is consistent with GCR 1963, 302.4(3)[1].

(5) MRE 803(22) is identical with Federal Rule 803(22) except that the word "state" is substituted for "Government".

(6) The Michigan Rules of Evidence contain no catch-all hearsay exception such as found in Federal Rule 803(24).

Note to March, 1991 Amendment

The [March 1,] 1991 amendment conformed subrule (6) to its federal counterpart by adding the words "conditions, opinions, or diagnoses".

Note to October, 1991 Amendment

The October 1, 1991 amendment to MRE 803(22) altered one of the holdings in *Lichon v American Universal Insurance Co,* 435 Mich 408 (1990), by allowing, in narrowly defined circumstances, evidence of a conviction obtained on a plea of nolo contendere. See also MRE 410(2), which was added concurrently.

Note to 1996 Amendment

The 1996 adoption of MRE 803(24) and MRE 804(b)(6) incorporated into the Michigan Rules of Evidence the residual or "catch-all" exceptions to the hearsay rule that are part of the Federal Rules of Evidence.

Note to 2001 Amendment

The September 1, 2001 amendment of MRE 803(6) allows properly authenticated records to be introduced into evidence without requiring the records' custodian to appear and testify to their authenticity. See also MRE 902(11), which was added at the same time.

RULE 803A. HEARSAY EXCEPTION; CHILD'S STATEMENT ABOUT SEXUAL ACT

A statement describing an incident that included a sexual act performed with or on the declarant by the defendant or an accomplice is admissible to the extent that it corroborates testimony given by the declarant during the same proceeding, provided:

(1) the declarant was under the age of ten when the statement was made;

(2) the statement is shown to have been spontaneous and without indication of manufacture;

(3) either the declarant made the statement immediately after the incident or any delay is excusable as having been caused by fear or other equally effective circumstance; and

(4) the statement is introduced through the testimony of someone other than the declarant.

If the declarant made more than one corroborative statement about the incident, only the first is admissible under this rule.

A statement may not be admitted under this rule unless the proponent of the statement makes known to the adverse party the intent to offer the statement, and the particulars of the statement, sufficiently in advance of the trial or hearing to provide the adverse party with a fair opportunity to prepare to meet the statement.

This rule applies in criminal and delinquency proceedings only.

[Adopted effective March 1, 1991.]

1991 Note

New MRE 803A reinstates the Michigan common law hearsay exception known as the tender years rule. See *People v Baker,* 251 Mich 322 (1930). Cf. *People v Kreiner,* 415 Mich 372 (1982).

RULE 804. HEARSAY EXCEPTIONS; DECLARANT UNAVAILABLE

(a) **Definition of Unavailability.** "Unavailability as a witness" includes situations in which the declarant—

(1) is exempted by ruling of the court on the ground of privilege from testifying concerning the subject matter of the declarant's statement; or

(2) persists in refusing to testify concerning the subject matter of the declarant's statement despite an order of the court to do so; or

(3) has a lack of memory of the subject matter of the declarant's statement; or

(4) is unable to be present or to testify at the hearing because of death or then existing physical or mental illness or infirmity; or

(5) is absent from the hearing and the proponent of a statement has been unable to procure the declarant's attendance (or in the case of a hearsay exception under subdivision (b)(2), (3), or (4), the declarant's attendance or testimony) by process or other reasonable means, and in a criminal case, due diligence is shown.

A declarant is not unavailable as a witness if exemption, refusal, claim of lack of memory, inability, or absence is due to the procurement or wrongdoing of the proponent of a statement for the purpose of preventing the witness from attending or testifying.

(b) **Hearsay Exceptions.** The following are not excluded by the hearsay rule if the declarant is unavailable as a witness:

(1) *Former Testimony.* Testimony given as a witness at another hearing of the same or a different proceeding, if the party against whom the testimony is now offered, or, in a civil action or proceeding, a predecessor in interest, had an opportunity and similar motive to develop the testimony by direct, cross, or redirect examination.

(2) *Statement Under Belief of Impending Death.* In a prosecution for homicide or in a civil action or proceeding, a statement made by a declarant while believing that the declarant's death was imminent, concerning the cause or circumstances of what the declarant believed to be impending death.

(3) *Statement Against Interest.* A statement which was at the time of its making so far contrary to the

declarant's pecuniary or proprietary interest, or so far tended to subject the declarant to civil or criminal liability, or to render invalid a claim by the declarant against another, that a reasonable person in the declarant's position would not have made the statement unless believing it to be true. A statement tending to expose the declarant to criminal liability and offered to exculpate the accused is not admissible unless corroborating circumstances clearly indicate the trustworthiness of the statement.

(4) *Statement of Personal or Family History.*

(A) A statement concerning the declarant's own birth, adoption, marriage, divorce, legitimacy, relationship by blood, adoption, or marriage, ancestry, or other similar fact of personal or family history, even though declarant had no means of acquiring personal knowledge of the matter stated; or

(B) a statement concerning the foregoing matters, and death also, of another person, if the declarant was related to the other by blood, adoption, or marriage or was so intimately associated with the other's family as to be likely to have accurate information concerning the matter declared.

(5) *Deposition Testimony.* Testimony given as a witness in a deposition taken in compliance with law in the course of the same or another proceeding, if the party against whom the testimony is now offered, or, in a civil action or proceeding, a predecessor in interest, had an opportunity and similar motive to develop the testimony by direct, cross, or redirect examination.

For purposes of this subsection only, "unavailability of a witness" also includes situations in which:

(A) The witness is at a greater distance than 100 miles from the place of trial or hearing, or is out of the United States, unless it appears that the absence of the witness was procured by the party offering the deposition; or

(B) On motion and notice, such exceptional circumstances exist as to make it desirable, in the interests of justice, and with due regard to the importance of presenting the testimony of witnesses orally in open court, to allow the deposition to be used.

(6) *Statement by declarant made unavailable by opponent.* A statement offered against a party that has engaged in or encouraged wrongdoing that was intended to, and did, procure the unavailability of the declarant as a witness.

(7) *Other Exceptions.* A statement not specifically covered by any of the foregoing exceptions but having equivalent circumstantial guarantees of trustworthiness, if the court determines that (A) the statement is offered as evidence of a material fact, (B) the statement is more probative on the point for which it is offered than any other evidence that the proponent can procure through reasonable efforts, and (C) the

general purposes of these rules and the interests of justice will best be served by admission of the statement into evidence. However, a statement may not be admitted under this exception unless the proponent of the statement makes known to the adverse party, sufficiently in advance of the trial or hearing to provide the adverse party with a fair opportunity to prepare to meet it, the proponent's intention to offer the statement and the particulars of it, including the name and address of the declarant.

[Effective March 1, 1978; amended effective December 1, 1989; June 1, 1995; April 1, 1996; September 1, 2001.]

1978 Note

MRE 804 is identical with Rule 804 of the Federal Rules of Evidence except:

(1) MRE 804(a)(3) is identical with Federal Rule 804(a)(3) except that the word "has" is substituted for the phrase "testifies to".

(2) MRE 804(a)(5) is identical with Federal Rule 804(a)(5) except for the addition of the phrase: "and in a criminal case, due diligence is shown".

(3) MRE 804(b)(3) is identical with Federal Rule 804(b)(3) except that the phrase "reasonable person" is substituted for the phrase "reasonable man".

(4) The Michigan Rules of Evidence contain no catch-all hearsay exception such as found in Federal Rule 804(b)(5).

Note to 1989 Amendment

The new subrule (b)(5) defines several hearsay exceptions for deposition testimony. The new subrule combines a part of former subrule (b)(1) with parts of former MCR 2.308(A), which has been amended concurrently.

Note to 1996 Amendment

The 1996 adoption of MRE 803(24) and MRE 804(b)(6) incorporated into the Michigan Rules of Evidence the residual or "catch-all" exceptions to the hearsay rule that are part of the Federal Rules of Evidence.

Note to 2001 Amendment

MRE 804(b)(6) was added effective September 1, 2001. It is almost identical to FRE 804(b)(6), which was added to the federal rules effective 12/01/97. The new subrule creates a hearsay exception for prior statements by a witness who has become unavailable due to wrongful acts committed or encouraged by the party against whom the statement is to be introduced.

RULE 805.   HEARSAY WITHIN HEARSAY

Hearsay included within hearsay is not excluded under the hearsay rule if each part of the combined statements conforms with an exception to the hearsay rule provided in these rules.

[Effective March 1, 1978.]

1978 Note

MRE 805 is identical with Rule 805 of the Federal Rules of Evidence.

RULE 806. ATTACKING AND SUPPORTING CREDIBILITY OF DECLARANT

When a hearsay statement, or a statement defined in Rule 801(d)(2)(C), (D), or (E), has been admitted in evidence, the credibility of the declarant may be attacked, and if attacked may be supported, by any evidence which would be admissible for those purposes if declarant had testified as a witness. Evidence of a statement or conduct by the declarant at any time, inconsistent with the declarant's hearsay statement, is not subject to any requirement that the declarant may have been afforded an opportunity to deny or explain. If the party against whom a hearsay statement has been admitted calls the declarant as a witness, the party is entitled to examine the declarant on the statement as if under cross-examination.

[Effective March 1, 1978; amended effective June 1, 1995.]

1978 Note

MRE 806 is identical with Rule 806 of the Federal Rules of Evidence.

RULE 901. REQUIREMENT OF AUTHENTICATION OR IDENTIFICATION

(a) General Provision. The requirement of authentication or identification as a condition precedent to admissibility is satisfied by evidence sufficient to support a finding that the matter in question is what its proponent claims.

(b) Illustrations. By way of illustration only, and not by way of limitation, the following are examples of authentication or identification conforming with the requirements of this rule:

(1) *Testimony of Witness With Knowledge.* Testimony that a matter is what it is claimed to be.

(2) *Nonexpert Opinion on Handwriting.* Nonexpert opinion as to the genuineness of handwriting, based upon familiarity not acquired for purposes of the litigation.

(3) *Comparison by Trier or Expert Witness.* Comparison by the trier of fact or by expert witnesses with specimens which have been authenticated.

(4) *Distinctive Characteristics and the Like.* Appearance, contents, substance, internal patterns, or other distinctive characteristics, taken in conjunction with circumstances.

(5) *Voice Identification.* Identification of a voice, whether heard firsthand or through mechanical or electronic transmission or recording, by opinion based upon hearing the voice at any time under circumstances connecting it with the alleged speaker.

(6) *Telephone Conversations.* Telephone conversations, by evidence that a call was made to the number assigned at the time by the telephone company to a particular person or business, if (A) in the case of a person, circumstances, including self-identification, show the person answering to be the one called, or (B) in the case of a business, the call was made to a place of business and the conversation related to business reasonably transacted over the telephone.

(7) *Public Records or Reports.* Evidence that a writing authorized by law to be recorded or filed and in fact recorded or filed in a public office, or a purported public record, report, statement, or data compilation, in any form, is from the public office where items of this nature are kept.

(8) *Ancient Documents or Data Compilation.* Evidence that a document or data compilation, in any form, (A) is in such condition as to create no suspicion concerning its authenticity, (B) was in a place where it, if authentic, would likely be, and (C) has been in existence 20 years or more at the time it is offered.

(9) *Process or System.* Evidence describing a process or system used to produce a result and showing that the process or system produces an accurate result.

(10) *Methods Provided by Statute or Rule.* Any method of authentication or identification provided by the Supreme Court of Michigan or by a Michigan statute.

[Effective March 1, 1978.]

1978 Note

MRE 901(a) and (b)(1) through (9) are identical with Rule 901(a) and (b)(1) through (9) of the Federal Rules of Evidence. MRE 901(b)(10) is a modified version of Rule 901(b)(10) of the Federal Rules of Evidence. Nothing contained in MRE 901(b)(5) authorizes the admission of voiceprint evidence.

RULE 902. SELF–AUTHENTICATION

Extrinsic evidence of authenticity as a condition precedent to admissibility is not required with respect to the following:

(1) Domestic Public Documents Under Seal. A document bearing a seal purporting to be that of the United States, or of any state, district, commonwealth, territory, or insular possession thereof, or the Panama Canal Zone, or the Trust Territory of the Pacific Islands, or of a political subdivision, department, officer, or agency thereof, and a signature purporting to be an attestation or execution.

(2) Domestic Public Documents Not Under Seal. A document purporting to bear the signature in the official capacity of an officer or employee of any entity included in paragraph (1) hereof, having no seal, if a public officer having a seal and having official duties in the district or political subdivision of the officer or employee certifies under seal that the signer has the official capacity and that the signature is genuine.

(3) Foreign Public Documents. A document purporting to be executed or attested in an official capacity by a person authorized by the laws of a foreign country to make the execution or attestation, and accompanied by a final certification as to the genuineness of the signature and official position (A) of the executing or attesting person, or (B) of any foreign official whose certificate of genuineness of signature and official position relates to the execution or attestation or is in a chain of certificates of genuineness of signature and official position relating to the execution or attestation. A final certification may be made by a secretary of embassy or legation, consul general, consul, vice consul, or consular agent of the United States, or a diplomatic or consular official of the foreign country assigned or accredited to the United States. If reasonable opportunity has been given to all parties to investigate the authenticity and accuracy of official documents, the court may, for good cause shown, order that they be treated as presumptively authentic without final certification or permit them to be evidenced by an attested summary with or without final certification.

(4) Certified Copies of Public Records. A copy of an official record or report or entry therein, or of a document authorized by law to be recorded or filed and actually recorded or filed in a public office, including data compilations in any form, certified as correct by the custodian or other person authorized to make the certification, by certificate complying with paragraph (1), (2), or (3) or complying with any law of the United States or of this state.

(5) Official Publications. Books, pamphlets, or other publications purporting to be issued by public authority.

(6) Newspapers and Periodicals. Printed materials purporting to be newspapers or periodicals.

(7) Trade Inscriptions and the Like. Inscriptions, signs, tags, or labels purporting to have been affixed in the course of business and indicating ownership, control, or origin.

(8) Acknowledged Documents. Documents accompanied by a certificate of acknowledgment executed in the manner provided by law by a notary public or other officer authorized by law to take acknowledgments.

(9) Commercial Paper and Related Documents. Commercial paper, signatures thereon, and documents relating thereto to the extent provided by general commercial law.

(10) Presumptions Created by Law. Any signature, document, or other matter declared by any law of the United States or of this state to be presumptively or prima facie genuine or authentic.

(11) Certified records of regularly conducted activity. The original or a duplicate of a record, whether domestic or foreign, of regularly conducted business activity that would be admissible under rule 803(6), if accompanied by a written declaration under oath by its custodian or other qualified person certifying that-

(A) The record was made at or near the time of the occurrence of the matters set forth by, or from information transmitted by, a person with knowledge of those matters;

(B) The record was kept in the course of the regularly conducted business activity; and

(C) It was the regular practice of the business activity to make the record.

A party intending to offer a record into evidence under this paragraph must provide written notice of that intention to all adverse parties, and must make the record and declaration available for inspection sufficiently in advance of their offer into evidence to provide an adverse party with a fair opportunity to challenge them.

[Effective March 1, 1978; amended effective June 1, 1995; September 1, 2001.]

1978 Note

MRE 902 is identical with Rule 902 of the Federal Rules of Evidence, except that MRE 902(4) and (10) are identical with Rules 902(4) and (10), respectively, as recommended by the National Conference of Commissioners on Uniform State Laws in its Uniform Rules of Evidence (1974).

Note to 2001 Amendment

MRE 902(11) was added effective September 1, 2001. Together with a concurrently adopted amendment of MRE 803(6), it allows a written certification of business records to substitute for a court appearance and testimony by the records' custodian. The advance notice provision provides the opposing party a fair opportunity to challenge the certification.

RULE 903. SUBSCRIBING WITNESS'S TESTIMONY UNNECESSARY

The testimony of a subscribing witness is not necessary to authenticate a writing unless required by the laws of the jurisdiction whose laws govern the validity of the writing.

[Effective March 1, 1978.]

1978 Note

MRE 903 is identical with Rule 903 of the Federal Rules of Evidence.

RULE 1001. CONTENTS OF WRITINGS, RECORDINGS, AND PHOTOGRAPHS; DEFINITIONS

For purposes of this article the following definitions are applicable:

(1) Writings and Recordings. "Writings" and "recordings" consist of letters, words, or numbers, or their equivalent, set down by handwriting, typewriting, printing, photostating, photographing, magnetic impulse, mechanical or electronic recording, or other form of data compilation.

(2) **Photographs.** "Photographs" include still photographs, X-ray films, video tapes, and motion pictures.

(3) **Original.** An "original" of a writing or recording is the writing or recording itself or any counterpart intended to have the same effect by a person executing or issuing it. An "original" of a photograph includes the negative or any print therefrom. If data are stored in a computer or similar device, any printout or other output readable by sight, shown to reflect the data accurately, is an "original".

(4) **Duplicate.** A "duplicate" is a counterpart produced by the same impression as the original, or from the same matrix, or by means of photography, including enlargements and miniatures, or by mechanical or electronic re-recording, or by chemical reproduction, or by other equivalent techniques, which accurately reproduces the original.

[Effective March 1, 1978.]

1978 Note

MRE 1001 is identical with Rule 1001 of the Federal Rules of Evidence except for the insertion of a comma after the word "techniques" in MRE 1001(4).

RULE 1002. REQUIREMENT OF ORIGINAL

To prove the content of a writing, recording, or photograph, the original writing, recording, or photograph is required, except as otherwise provided in these rules or by statute.

[Effective March 1, 1978.]

1978 Note

MRE 1002 is identical with Rule 1002 as recommended by the National Conference of Commissioners on Uniform State Laws in its Uniform Rules of Evidence (1974). MRE 1002 is similar to Rule 1002 of the Federal Rules of Evidence.

RULE 1003. ADMISSIBILITY OF DUPLICATES

A duplicate is admissible to the same extent as an original unless (1) a genuine question is raised as to the authenticity of the original or (2) in the circumstances it would be unfair to admit the duplicate in lieu of the original.

[Effective March 1, 1978.]

1978 Note

MRE 1003 is identical with Rule 1003 of the Federal Rules of Evidence.

RULE 1004. ADMISSIBILITY OF OTHER EVIDENCE OF CONTENTS

The original is not required, and other evidence of the contents of a writing, recording, or photograph is admissible if—

(1) **Originals Lost or Destroyed.** All originals are lost or have been destroyed, unless the proponent lost or destroyed them in bad faith; or

(2) **Original Not Obtainable.** No original can be obtained by any available judicial process or procedure; or

(3) **Original in Possession of Opponent.** At a time when an original was under the control of the party against whom offered, that party was put on notice, by the pleadings or otherwise, that the contents would be a subject of proof at the hearing, and that party does not produce the original at the hearing; or

(4) **Collateral Matters.** The writing, recording, or photograph is not closely related to a controlling issue.

[Effective March 1, 1978; amended effective June 1, 1995.]

1978 Note

MRE 1004 is identical with Rule 1004 of the Federal Rules of Evidence.

RULE 1005. PUBLIC RECORDS

The contents of an official record, or of a document authorized to be recorded or filed and actually recorded or filed, including data compilations in any form, if otherwise admissible, may be proved by copy, certified as correct in accordance with Rule 902 or testified to be correct by a witness who has compared it with the original. If a copy which complies with the foregoing cannot be obtained by the exercise of reasonable diligence, then other evidence of the contents may be given.

[Effective March 1, 1978.]

1978 Note

MRE 1005 is identical with Rule 1005 of the Federal Rules of Evidence.

RULE 1006. SUMMARIES

The contents of voluminous writings, recordings, or photographs which cannot conveniently be examined in court may be presented in the form of a chart, summary, or calculation. The originals, or duplicates, shall be made available for examination or copying, or both, by other parties at reasonable time and place. The court may order that they be produced in court.

[Effective March 1, 1978.]

1978 Note

MRE 1006 is identical with Rule 1006 of the Federal Rules of Evidence.

RULE 1007. TESTIMONY OR WRITTEN ADMISSION OF A PARTY

Contents of writings, recordings, or photographs may be proved by the testimony or deposition of the party against whom offered or by that party's written admission, without accounting for the nonproduction of the original.

[Effective March 1, 1978; amended effective June 1, 1995.]

1978 Note

MRE 1007 is identical with Rule 1007 of the Federal Rules of Evidence.

RULE 1008. FUNCTIONS OF COURT AND JURY

When the admissibility of other evidence of contents of writings, recordings, or photographs under these rules depends upon the fulfillment of a condition of fact, the question whether the condition has been fulfilled is ordinarily for the court to determine in accordance with the provisions of Rule 104. However, when an issue is raised (a) whether the asserted writing ever existed, or (b) whether another writing, recording, or photograph produced at the trial is the original, or (c) whether other evidence of contents correctly reflects the contents, the issue is for the trier of fact to determine as in the case of other issues of fact.

[Effective March 1, 1978.]

1978 Note

MRE 1008 is identical with Rule 1008 of the Federal Rules of Evidence.

RULE 1101. APPLICABILITY

(a) **Rules Applicable.** Except as otherwise provided in subdivision (b), these rules apply to all actions and proceedings in the courts of this state.

(b) **Rules Inapplicable.** The rules other than those with respect to privileges do not apply in the following situations and proceedings:

(1) *Preliminary Questions of Fact.* The determination of questions of fact preliminary to admissibility of evidence when the issue is to be determined by the court under Rule 104(a).

(2) *Grand Jury.* Proceedings before grand juries.

(3) *Miscellaneous Proceedings.* Proceedings for extradition or rendition; sentencing, or granting or revoking probation; issuance of warrants for arrest, criminal summonses, and search warrants; and proceedings with respect to release on bail or otherwise.

(4) *Contempt Proceedings.* Contempt proceedings in which the court may act summarily.

(5) *Small Claims.* Small claims division of the district court.

(6) *In Camera Custody Hearings.* In camera proceedings in child custody matters to determine a child's custodial preference.

(7) *Juvenile Court Proceedings.* Proceedings in the juvenile division of the probate court wherever MCR Subchapter 5.900 states that the Michigan Rules of Evidence do not apply.

(8) *Preliminary examinations.* At preliminary examinations in criminal cases, hearsay is admissible to prove, with regard to property, the ownership, authority to use, value, possession and entry.

[Effective March 1, 1978; amended effective March 1, 1991; May 14, 2001.]

1978 Note

MRE 1101 is identical with Rule 1101 as recommended by the National Conference of Commissioners on Uniform State Laws in its Uniform Rules of Evidence (1974) except that in MRE 1101(b)(3) the words "[preliminary examination] detention hearing in criminal cases" are deleted, and MRE 1101(b)(5) is added, there being no equivalent in the Uniform Rule.

Note to 1991 Amendment

In subrule (b)(5), the 1991 amendments deleted an obsolete reference to a court that no longer exists. The amendments also added the present subrules (b)(6) and (7).

Note to 2001 Amendment

MRE 1101(8) was added effective May 14, 2001. In property crime cases, it allows the use of hearsay to prove certain elements of property crimes at the preliminary examination.

RULE 1102. TITLE

These rules are named the Michigan Rules of Evidence and may be cited as MRE.

The notes following the individual rules were drafted by the chair and the reporter of the committee which drafted the proposed rules of evidence for the benefit of the bench and bar and are not authoritative constructions by the Court.

[Effective March 1, 1978; amended effective June 1, 1995.]

INDEX TO MICHIGAN RULES OF EVIDENCE

RINGS
Engravings, statements concerning, hearsay exception, **Rule 803**

ROUTINE PRACTICE
Organizations, relevant evidence, **Rule 406**

RULINGS ON EVIDENCE
Generally, **Rule 103**

SCOPE OF RULES
Generally, **Rule 101**

Judicial notice, adjudicative facts, **Rule 201**

SEALS
Domestic public documents under or not under, extrinsic evidence of authenticity as condition precedent to admissibility not required, **Rule 902**

SEARCHES AND SEIZURES
Warrants, issuance, proceedings for, inapplicability, **Rule 1101**

SELF–INCRIMINATION
Character evidence, statement of theory of defense requirement, limitation on, **Rule 404**

Not waived by accused or other witness when examined respecting matters relating only to credibility, **Rule 608**

SENSATION
Hearsay exceptions, statement respecting, **Rule 803**

SENTENCE AND PUNISHMENT
Death Penalty, generally, this index

Impeaching credibility of witness, conviction of crime punishable by imprisonment exceeding one year, court determination, probative value, **Rule 609**

Judgment of previous conviction, crime punishable by imprisonment exceeding one year, evidence of, hearsay exception, **Rule 803**

Proceedings, inapplicability, **Rule 1101**

SEXUAL ACTS
Child's statements concerning, hearsay exception, **Rule 803A**

SHORT TITLE
Generally, **Rule 1102**

SIGNATURES
Foreign public documents, certification, genuineness and official position of executing or attesting person, etc., **Rule 902**

Self-authentication,
Commercial paper and related documents, **Rule 902**
Domestic public documents under or not under seal, **Rule 902**

SIGNS
Purporting to be affixed in course of business and indicating ownership, control or origin, self-authentication, **Rule 902**

SPECIMENS
Comparison by trier or expert witness, authentication and identification, conformity with requirements, **Rule 901**

STATE AGENCIES
Documents of under or not under seal, self-authentication, **Rule 902**

STATE OFFICERS AND EMPLOYEES
See Public Officers and Employees, generally, this index

STATEMENTS
Extrinsic evidence of prior inconsistent statement of witness, admissibility, **Rule 613**

False statements. Perjury, generally, this index

Guilty, offer to plead or withdrawn plea of, statements made in connection with, admissibility, **Rule 410**

Hearsay, this index

Made in compromise of claim negotiations, admissibility, **Rule 408**

Nolo contendere, plea of or offer to plead, statements made in connection with, admissibility, **Rule 410**

Perjury, generally, this index

Prior statements of witnesses, examination concerning, **Rule 613**

Recorded, remainder or part of, introduction, **Rule 106**

STATES
Documents of under or not under seal, self-authentication, **Rule 902**

Reputation concerning boundaries or general history important to state in which located, hearsay exception, **Rule 803**

STATUTES
Authentication or identification, methods provided by, **Rule 901**

Evidence statutes, **Rule 101**

SUBSTANCE
Authentication and identification, conformity with requirements, **Rule 901**

SUMMARIES
Voluminous writings, recordings or photographs, contents of, **Rule 1006**

SUMMONS
Criminal, proceedings for, inapplicability, **Rule 1101**

SUPPORTING CREDIBILITY OF WITNESSES
See Credibility of Witnesses, this index

SUPREME COURT
Rules of court,
Authentication and identification, methods provided by, **Rule 901**
Relevant evidence admissible except as otherwise prescribed by, **Rule 402**

SYSTEM
Used to produce result, etc., authentication and identification, conformity with requirements, **Rule 901**

TABULATIONS
Use and reliance on by public or persons in particular occupations, hearsay exception, **Rule 803**

TAGS
Purporting to be affixed in course of business and indicating ownership, control or origin, self-authentication, **Rule 902**

TELEGRAPHS AND TELEPHONES
Authentication and identification, telephone conversations, conformity with requirements, **Rule 901**

TENDER YEARS RULE
Generally, **Rule 803A**

TERRITORIES
Documents of under or not under seal, self-authentication, **Rule 902**

ADMINISTRATIVE ORDERS OF THE MICHIGAN SUPREME COURT

Research Note

Use Westlaw ® *to find cases citing or applying specific administrative orders.* Westlaw *may also be used to search for specific terms in administrative orders or to update administrative orders. See the MI–RULES and MI–ORDERS Scope Screens for detailed descriptive information and search tips.*

Administrative Orders of the Michigan Supreme Court are published, as received, in the N.W.2d *and* Michigan Reporter *advance sheets,* and Michigan Legislative Service.

*Table of Orders**

* Publisher's Note: At the request of the Supreme Court Clerk, references to rescinded orders and orders not of current interest have been deleted.

** Suggested title added by Publisher.

ADMINISTRATIVE ORDER 1968–2
JUDICIAL TENURE COMMISSION

Directed to State Bar of Michigan:

The State Bar shall publish in its journal a notice to all members that they may nominate judges and practicing attorneys who are not judges from among whom the membership will elect one judge and two attorneys as members of the judicial tenure commission. Nominating petitions, available at the State Bar office, will require the signature of 50 attorneys in good standing, and must be filed with the State Bar by a determined deadline (i.e., 30 days after publication).

In the event two nominations for each position are not received by the petition method, the board of commissioners shall thereupon nominate up to that number.

Within 10 days after the nomination of candidates therefor, the State Bar shall cause to be mailed to each member a ballot containing the names of the nominees divided into two categories,

(1) all judges nominated,

(2) all nonjudges nominated,

and space for write-in candidates.

The ballots shall be returned to the office of the State Bar of Michigan on or before (a date certain). Five tellers selected by the board of commissioners shall meet at the office of the State Bar on (a date certain), to tally the ballots. The judge receiving the highest number of votes, and the two nonjudges receiving the highest number of votes shall be declared elected.

[See GCR 1963, 932, Judicial Tenure Commission.]

[Entered November 19, 1968.]

ADMINISTRATIVE ORDER 1969–4
SEXUAL PSYCHOPATHS

It appearing upon repeal of P.A.1939, No. 165, that jurisdiction to hear petitions to test the recovery of persons committed as criminal sexual psychopaths under the provisions of said act remains unresolved, that proceedings in various courts wherein relief has been sought have been dismissed with the result that a situation has continued for several months wherein the proper forum for reviewing the propriety of continued custody of persons committed under the provisions of said law remains in question, that protection of the basic rights of such persons and the uninterrupted administration of justice requires designation of a proper forum for hearing said matters until such time as the legislature shall provide clarification, now therefore, pursuant to the provisions of Constitution 1963, art. 6, § 13, and P.A.1961, No. 236, § 601, the revised judicature act. [M.C.L.A. § 600.601].

It is ordered, that until such time as there is further legislative clarification of jurisdiction of proceedings for testing recovery of persons committed under the provisions of said P.A.1939, No. 165, as amended, jurisdiction shall continue and proceedings shall be conducted in accordance with the provisions of section 7 of said act, C.L.1948, § 780.507, as amended by P.A.1952, No. 58 (Stat.Ann.1954 Rev. § 28.967[7]) [M.C.L.A. §§ 780.501–780.509].

This order shall constitute a rule of the Supreme Court within Constitution 1963, art. 6, § 13, and shall be effective as of August 1, 1968, the date of effect of the repeal of P.A.1939, No. 165, as amended.

[Entered October 20, 1969.]

ADMINISTRATIVE ORDER 1972–1
JUDICIAL ASSIGNMENTS—
PROBATE COURTS

It is ordered that the assignment of a judge to serve as a judge of the probate court of a county in which he was not elected or appointed as a probate judge shall be made only by order of this Court or through the Court Administrator, and no judge shall so serve unless assigned in conformity herewith. This shall not apply to a judge of the circuit court for such county as provided for by M.C.L.A. 701.11.

It is further ordered that this order be given immediate effect.

[Entered January 10, 1972.]

ADMINISTRATIVE ORDER 1972–2
DEFENDERS—RECORDER'S COURT *

It appearing to the Court that the Defender's Office of the Legal Aid and Defender Association of Detroit is a nonprofit organization providing counsel to indigent defendants in the Wayne Circuit Court and the Recorder's Court of the City of Detroit, and that such method of providing counsel to indigent defendants should be encouraged for the efficient administration of criminal justice; and

It further appearing that assignments from Recorder's Court have been irregular, sometimes involving too many such assignments and sometimes too few;

Now, therefore, IT IS ORDERED that, from the date of this order until the further order of this Court, the Presiding Judge of Recorder's Court of the City of Detroit shall assign as counsel, on a weekly basis, the Defender's Office of the Legal Aid and Defender Association of Detroit in twenty-five per cent of all cases wherein counsel are appointed for indigent defendants.

Brennan, J., dissented.

[Entered May 11, 1972.]

* Publisher's Note: See Administrative Order 1997–5, entered July 25, 1997, as to the extension of the provisions of Administrative Order 1972–2 to criminal matters coming before the Third Circuit Court after the merger of the Third Circuit Court and Recorder's Court on October 1, 1997.

ADMINISTRATIVE ORDER 1972–4
MISDEMEANORS AND PETTY
OFFENSES—RIGHT TO COUNSEL

Pursuant to the general superintending control provisions of Const.1963, art. 6, § 4, and to comply with Argersinger v. Hamlin, 407 U.S. 25; 92 S.Ct. 2006; 32 L.Ed.2d 530 (6–12–72), holding inter alia "that absent a knowing and intelligent waiver, no person may be imprisoned for any offense, whether classified as petty, misdemeanor, or felony, unless he was represented by counsel at his trial."

In the absence of appropriate implemental legislation, IT IS ORDERED, from date of this order until the further order of this Court, that in any case cognizable by the District Courts, Municipal Courts, Recorder's Court and Traffic and Ordinance Division of the Recorder's Court, where the court, upon conviction either after trial with or without a jury or upon a plea of guilty, is authorized by law and expressly retains the discretionary power to impose a sentence for any period of imprisonment or incarceration, the judge or judges of said courts shall advise an accused who appears without counsel that he is entitled to the assistance of counsel and that if he is financially unable to provide counsel of his own choice the court will, upon defendant's request, appoint counsel for him at public expense and said judges shall, unless appointment of counsel is affirmatively waived on the record by defendant, appoint counsel in all said cases where defendant is determined to be indigent.

The determination of indigency shall be guided by, but not limited to, the following factors:

a. present employment, earning capacity and living expenses;

b. outstanding debts and liabilities, secured and unsecured;

c. whether defendant has qualified for and is receiving any form of public assistance;

d. availability and convertibility, without undue financial hardship to himself or to his family, of any personal or real property owned; and

e. any other circumstances which would impair the ability to pay an attorney's fee as would ordinarily be required to retain competent counsel.

IT IS FURTHER ORDERED that said judges may, pursuant to GCR 1963, 921, appoint a law student qualified under said rule, provided that said judges shall first advise defendant of the status of the appointed law student. If said defendant affirmatively indicates his desire to have a licensed member of the State Bar represent him, said judges shall appoint a licensed member of the State Bar. If the defendant consents to be represented by a law student, such consent shall be in writing and signed by the defendant, as well as on the record in the case.

IT IS FURTHER ORDERED that assigned counsel, by order of the appointing court, shall be reasonably compensated. The costs of compensating assigned counsel shall be allocated between the district control unit, municipality or county in the same proportion that fines and court costs are distributed, as provided by law.

The District Courts, Municipal Courts, Recorder's Court and Traffic and Ordinance Division of Recorder's Court may establish local procedures to screen and segregate, prior to trial on the merits, all misdemeanor cases to which this Administrative Order is applicable.

[Entered July 27, 1972.]

ADMINISTRATIVE ORDER 1973–1
COMMON PLEAS COURT—LANDLORD–
TENANT DIVISION—LEGAL AID

Directed to the Common Pleas Court of Detroit:

It appearing to the Court that there is sufficient necessity to furnish legal aid, on a case-to-case basis, to litigants in summary proceeding actions commenced in the Landlord-Tenant Division of Common Pleas Court and that existing standards of indigency preclude eligibility of said litigants for legal assistance, now therefore it is Ordered, effective from date of this order until further order of the Court, that all parties in summary proceeding actions who cannot afford an attorney in the proceedings shall be eligible for legal assistance from the legal aid clinics in the nature and manner administered under GCR 1963, 921; Provided however, that no plaintiff shall qualify for said services if he has a monetary interest in more than one income unit of real property.

[See Common Pleas Court Rule 46.]

[Entered January 12, 1973.]

ADMINISTRATIVE ORDER 1977–1
STANDARD CRIMINAL
JURY INSTRUCTIONS

Proposed GCR and DCR 516.8, which would direct the use of the Standard Criminal Jury Instructions under certain conditions, were published in the State Bar Journal in April, 1976, for comment by the bench and bar. Comments have been received from proponents and opponents of the concept of pattern instructions. The intelligent concerns expressed by both sides have caused the Court to conclude that it would be provident to observe and evaluate actual trial use of the instructions over a substantial period before making the decision regarding implementation of use of the instructions by court rule.

Accordingly all members of the bench and bar are urged to use the instructions. Such use, particularly in the manner proposed in the rules published in the April 1976 Bar Journal, would provide a basis for communicating to the Court advantages or disadvantages encountered in their use. Comments based on such use are invited immediately, and on a continuing basis. It is the intention of the Court to readdress the question of implementation of the Standard Criminal Jury Instructions by court rule after approximately one year's experience has been obtained.

[Entered January 6, 1977.]

ADMINISTRATIVE ORDER 1978–4
LAWYER ADVERTISING

A lawyer may on behalf of himself, his partner or associate, or any other lawyer affiliated with him or his firm, use or participate in the use of any form of public communication that is not false, fraudulent, misleading, or deceptive. Except for DR 2–103 and

DR 2–104, disciplinary rules in conflict with this order are suspended for a period of one year.

[Entered March 15, 1978; extended until September 15, 1979 by Administrative Order 1979–3 and continued in effect until further order of the Court by Administrative Order 1979–7.]

ADMINISTRATIVE ORDER 1978–5
STANDARD CRIMINAL
JURY INSTRUCTIONS

To assist the Supreme Court in evaluating the Standard Criminal Jury Instructions, every trial judge is requested during the four-month period beginning August 1, 1978, at the conclusion of every criminal case tried to a jury, to dictate to the court reporter a statement (outside the presence of the jury, counsel and the parties) of the offense or offenses covered by the instructions; the extent to which he used the Standard Criminal Jury Instructions; if he did not use them, why he did not; and any additional comments he may care to make to assist the Supreme Court in evaluating those instructions and in considering whether they should be made obligatory in the sense that the Standard Civil Jury Instructions are generally required to be given. The statement is not considered part of the record on appeal. The court reporter shall forward the statement to Donald Ubell, Chief Commissioner of the Supreme Court, within two weeks after the judge instructs the jury.

[Entered June 2, 1978.]

ADMINISTRATIVE ORDER 1979–4
FINGERPRINTING OF APPLICANTS
FOR ADMISSION TO BAR

On order of the Court, pursuant to the power of superintending control, Const.1963, art. VI, § 4, and MCL 600.904; MSA 27A.904, empowering the Court to provide for the organization, government and membership of the State Bar of Michigan, and to adopt rules and regulations concerning the conduct and activities of the State Bar of Michigan and the investigation and examination of applicants for admission to the bar, the Board of Law Examiners is ORDERED forthwith to require that any applicant for admission to the State Bar of Michigan by examination be fingerprinted to enable the State Bar Committee on Character and Fitness to determine whether the applicant has a record of criminal convictions in jurisdictions other than Michigan. The Board of Law Examiners and the State Bar Committee on Character and Fitness are authorized to exchange fingerprint data with the Federal Bureau of Investigation, Identification Division.

[Entered March 8, 1979.]

ADMINISTRATIVE ORDER 1981–5
REPORTING OF PENDING APPEALS
FROM PROBATE COURT ORDERS
TERMINATING PARENTAL RIGHTS

To the judges of the circuit court:

On October 29, 1981, the Court adopted new juvenile court rule 15, which provides that effective January 1, 1982, probate court orders terminating parental rights under the juvenile code are appealable to the court of appeals rather than to the circuit court. To facilitate disposition of the appeals of orders pending in the circuit court on December 31, 1981, each circuit judge is directed to:

(1) insofar as possible, expedite the consideration of pending appeals from orders terminating parental rights under the juvenile code; and

(2) on July 1, 1982, and every 6 months thereafter, file a report with the chief justice listing each such appeal that remains pending, including a statement of the reasons the appeal has not been concluded.

[Entered November 4, 1981.]

ADMINISTRATIVE ORDER 1981–6
PRIORITY TREATMENT OF APPEALS
FROM ORDERS TERMINATING
PARENTAL RIGHTS

Directed to the clerk of the court of appeals and the clerk of this Court:

On order of the Court, it appearing that there is a need to expedite consideration of appeals terminating parental rights under the juvenile code, the clerk of the court of appeals and of this Court are directed to give priority to such appeals in scheduling them for submission to their respective courts.

[Entered November 4, 1981.]

ADMINISTRATIVE ORDER 1981–7
REGULATIONS GOVERNING A SYSTEM
FOR APPOINTMENT OF APPELLATE
COUNSEL FOR INDIGENTS IN CRIMINAL
CASES AND MINIMUM STANDARDS FOR
INDIGENT CRIMINAL APPELLATE
DEFENSE SERVICES

Pursuant to 1978, P.A. 620, MCL 780.711–780.719; M.S.A. 28.1114(101)–28.1114(109), the Appellate Defender Commission submitted to this Court regulations governing a system for appointment of appellate counsel for indigents in criminal cases and minimum standards for indigent criminal appellate defense services. The Court has considered the submissions and after due consideration we approve them. However, the operation of the system and enforcement of the standards pursuant to the system requires that the legislature appropriate funds necessary to implement the system. When funds sufficient to operate the system are appropriated, this Court will promulgate an administrative order implementing the system and requiring adherence to it.

The approved regulations governing the system for appointment of appellate counsel for indigents in criminal cases, together with the commentary of the Appellate Defender Commission are as follows:

Introduction by the Commission

In order to meet its charge under MCL 780.711 et seq.; M.S.A. 28.1114(101) et seq. to design an appointment system and develop minimum performance standards, the State Appellate Defender Commission, seeking the broadest possible input, established an advisory committee, which met during 1979 and developed a set of initial proposals. After review by the commission, the proposals were circulated among the bar, presented at public hearings, further refined on the basis of the advice received, and passed on to the Supreme Court for its review, revision, and approval. The commission comments, which follow the sections of the regulations and standards, are designed to briefly present some of the thinking behind the regulations and standards as distilled from these sources.

Section 1. Establishment of the Office of the Appellate Assigned Counsel Administrator.

(1) The Appellate Defender Commission shall establish an Appellate Assigned Counsel Administrator's Office which shall be coordinated with but separate from the State Appellate Defender Office. The duty of this office shall be to compile and maintain a statewide roster of attorneys eligible and willing to accept criminal appellate defense assignments and to engage in activities designed to enhance the capacity of the private bar to render effective assistance of appellate counsel to indigent defendants.

(2) An appellate assigned counsel administrator shall be appointed by and serve at the pleasure of the Appellate Defender Commission.

(3) The appellate assigned counsel administrator shall:

(a) be an attorney licensed to practice law in this state,

(b) take and subscribe the oath required by the constitution before taking office,

(c) perform duties as hereinafter provided, and

(d) not engage in the practice of law or act as an attorney or counselor in a court of this state except in the exercise of his duties under these rules.

(4) The appellate assigned counsel administrator and supporting personnel shall be considered to be court employees and not to be classified civil service employees.

(5) The salaries of the appellate assigned counsel administrator and supporting personnel shall be established by the Appellate Defender Commission.

(6) The appellate assigned counsel administrator and supporting personnel shall be reimbursed for their reasonable actual and necessary expenses by the state treasurer upon the warrant of the state treasurer.

(7) Salaries and expenses attributable to the office of the appellate assigned counsel administrator shall be paid out of funds available for those purposes in accordance with the accounting laws of this state. The auditor general, under authority of Michigan Const.1963, art. 4, § 53, shall perform audits utilizing the same policies and criteria that are used to audit executive branch agencies.

(8) Within appropriations provided by law, the Appellate Defender Commission shall provide the office of the appellate assigned counsel administrator with suitable space and equipment at such locations as the commission considers necessary.

Commission Comment

MCL 780.711 et seq.; MSA 28.1114(101) et seq. mandates development of a mixed system of appellate defense representation containing both public defender and private assigned counsel components. The assigned counsel component is to be structured around a statewide roster of private attorneys, which the Appellate Defender Commission is to compile and maintain. The commission as an unpaid policy-making body must delegate the performance of ongoing tasks. Since establishing and administering the newly authorized roster is a large, permanent job, the first issue addressed is the organizational entity to which responsibility for the roster should be delegated.

Two administrative models for mixed systems are widely recognized and approved. The defender-administered model makes supervision of the assigned counsel panel a function of the defender office and is currently used in some states which have statewide trial defender offices. The independently administered model makes each component of the system autonomous while encouraging coordination of training and support services. See ABA Standards for Criminal Justice (2d ed. 1980), 5–1.2 (ABA Standards); National Study Commission on Defense Services, Guidelines for Legal Defense Systems in the United States (National Legal Aid and Defender Association, 1976), pp. 124–135 (hereafter NLADA); Report of the Defense Services Committee, 57 Mich.St. B.J. 242 (March 1978), recommendation 9d, p. 260; Goldberg & Lichtman, Guide to Establishing a Defender System (May 1978), pp. 71–79.

The independently administered model was perceived to be most compatible with the statute and the desires of private attorneys. It promotes the independence of assigned attorneys from the defender office and provides them with an administration which can focus exclusively on their special needs. It nonetheless permits the efficient sharing of such resources as training materials, information retrieval systems and supportive services through the coordinating efforts of the Appellate Defender Commission to which both components are ultimately responsible.

Section 2. Duties of the Appellate Assigned Counsel Administrator.

The appellate assigned counsel administrator, with such supporting staff as the commission deems appropriate, shall:

(1) After reasonable notice has been given to the members of the State Bar of Michigan, compile a roster of attorneys eligible under § 4 of these regulations and willing to accept appointments to serve as appellate counsel for indigent criminal defendants.

(a) The roster shall be updated semiannually and circulated among all probate, circuit, and appellate courts of the state. It shall also be provided, on request, to any interested party.

(b) The roster shall appear in two parts. Part one shall contain an alphabetized listing by name of all attorneys in the state who are eligible and willing to accept criminal appellate assignments. Part two shall be subdivided according to the circuits in which the attorneys' primary practices are maintained and shall contain the following information regarding each attorney: name, firm's name, business address, business telephone, and level of assignments for which the attorney is eligible.

(2) Place in the issue of the Michigan Bar Journal to be published after the results of the bar examinations have been released an announcement specifying the procedure and eligibility criteria for placement on the assigned counsel roster.

(3) Distribute by November 1 of every second year to all attorneys on the roster a standard renewal application containing appropriate questions regarding education and experience obtained during the preceding two years and notice that the completed application must be forwarded to the administrator's office within 30 days.

(a) The eligibility level of every attorney on the list shall be reviewed every second year based on the information contained in the renewal application.

(b) Where a renewal application has not been filed or reveals deficiencies in complying with any requirement for continuing eligibility, the administrator shall notify the affected attorney in writing of such deficiencies. The names of all attorneys who fail to correct deficiencies in their continuing eligibility within 60 days after the issuance of notice shall be removed from the roster, except that the administrator shall have the discretion to extend the deadline for correcting deficiencies by an additional 60 days where good cause is shown. Such extensions shall be requested and granted only in writing and shall include a summary of the pertinent facts.

(4) Notify all recipients of the roster of any change in the eligibility of any attorney within 20 days after the date on which a change occurs. Publication of a semiannual roster which reflects such changes within the time specified shall constitute adequate notice for purposes of this provision.

(5) Receive and take appropriate action as hereafter set forth regarding all correspondence forwarded by judges, defendants, or other interested parties about any attorney on the roster.

(6) Maintain a file for each case in which private counsel is appointed which shall contain:

(i) the order of appointment,

(ii) the cover page and table of contents of all briefs and memorandums filed by defense counsel,

(iii) counsel's voucher for fees, and

(iv) a case summary which shall be completed by counsel on forms provided by the administrator and which shall contain such information about filing dates, oral arguments, case disposition, and other pertinent matters as the administrator requires for statistical purposes.

(7) Forward to the Legal Resources Project copies of all briefs filed by assigned counsel for possible placement in a centralized brief bank.

(8) Select an attorney to be appointed for an appeal when requested to do so by an appellate court or by a local designating authority pursuant to § 3(4).

(9) Compile data regarding the fees paid to assigned counsel and take steps to promote the payment of reasonable fees which are commensurate with the provision of effective assistance of appellate counsel.

(10) Provide, on request of an assigned attorney or an appointing authority, information regarding the range of fees paid within the state to assigned counsel or to expert witnesses and investigators who have been retained by counsel with the prior approval of the trial court. On the request of both the attorney and the appointing authority, the administrator may arbitrate disputes about such fees in particular cases according to prevailing local standards.

(11) Take steps to promote the development and delivery of support services to appointed counsel.

(12) Present to the commission within 90 days after the end of the fiscal year an annual report on the operation of the assigned counsel system which shall include an accounting of all funds received and disbursed, an evaluation of the cost-effectiveness of the system, and recommendations for improvement.

(13) Perform other duties in connection with the administration of the assigned counsel system as the commission shall direct.

Commission Comment

The appellate assigned counsel administrator's duties described in § 2 go beyond the performance of ministerial tasks. Other functions include directing focus on efficient systems for delivery of services, adequate support services and other matters of concern to appellate practitioners. The eligibility requirements for the roster are intended to be a vehicle for upgrading as well as organizing the services of private assigned counsel. It is also important, however, that private attorneys who are willing to maintain their eligibility for the roster benefit from an organizational structure dedicated to rationalizing and improving the conditions under which they receive, perform, and are compensated for criminal appellate assignments. The view that the director of the assigned counsel system must be a competent criminal defense attorney as well as a sensitive administrator is widely shared. ABA Standards, 5–2.1; NLADA, pp. 236–239; Guide to Establishing a Defender System, pp. 84–85.

Subsections 2(1)–(4) specify the mechanics of compiling and circulating a roster which is both current and convenient. The semiannual notice and updating provisions are designed especially for new lawyers. Those who pass each bar examination will see the notice in the bar journal in time to seek placement on a semiannual roster. Eligible attorneys may join, withdraw, or be removed from the list at any time.

Subsection 2(5) recognizes that once an institutional entity with overall responsibility for assigned counsel exists, it will become the recipient of comments requiring a response. This subsection also reflects a commitment to passive rather than active review of attorneys' performance. Therefore, while the administrator is nowhere charged with overseeing the content of assigned counsel's work on a regular basis, he or she is directed to act when substantive problems come to light. Appropriate action may range from writing a letter of inquiry or clarification to removing an attorney from the roster in accordance with the due process safeguards specified in § 4. See ABA Standards, 5–2.2 and accompanying commentary.

Subsection 2(6) requires the administrator to collect such information as is needed to promote the goals of the assigned counsel system without unduly duplicating the tasks performed by other entities. The items listed in subsections (6)(i)–(iv) are adequate to inform the administrator that a case has been assigned, work is ongoing, and a case has been closed. Tracking of all pleadings in each case for timeliness is not necessary since such oversight is already provided by the courts. Should additional information be needed regarding a particular case, it can be obtained from the appropriate court file. The costly and time-consuming handling of excess paperwork is thus eliminated. On the other hand, the completion of uniform summaries after cases have been closed is a convenient way for the administrator to gather data on the operation of the system as a whole. Such data has not been collected and analyzed to date.

Subsection (7) makes the administrator's office the conduit for assigned counsel's contributions to the Legal Resources Project's brief bank. The brief bank currently serves assigned counsel but primarily contains pleadings prepared by the State Appellate Defender's staff attorneys. By performing this pass-through role, the administrator's office will have a ready means of collecting the items mentioned in subsection (6)(ii).

Subsection (8) functions are fully discussed in the commentary to § 3.

Subsections (9) and (10) reflect the commission's grave concern about the adequacy of current assigned counsel fees. Quality representation is inevitably tied to reasonable compensation. Low fees make it economically unattractive for competent attorneys to seek assignments and expend all the time and effort a case may require, and economically tempting to accept an excessive number of assignments in order to maintain a desirable income. Flat fees per case discourage attorneys from undertaking certain responsibilities, such as client visits or oral arguments, since they will be paid the same amount regardless of the work done.

While the commission recognized that specific suggestions regarding fees were outside the scope of its mandate, it also recognized that setting minimum performance standards without addressing the issue of compensation is unrealistic. Similar views have been expressed by others. See ABA Standards, 5–2.4; Report of the Defense Services Committee, recommendation 5, p. 249; NLADA, pp. 271–275. In addition, over half of the Court of Appeals judges responding to a questionnaire felt that increased fees would significantly enhance the quality of indigent defense representation. Some judges suggested rates believed to be substantially above those now being paid. Therefore, the commission included among the administrator's enumerated duties the active representation of the interests of assigned counsel and their clients in securing reasonable compensation for assigned counsel.

In subsection (10) the term "arbitrate" was substituted for the originally proposed term "mediate" at the State Bar's request.

Subsection (11) addresses counsel's need for support services in such areas as legal research, factual investigation, expert consultations and witnesses, and prison inmate problems. Some of these needs are already being filled by the Legal Resources Project and the State Appellate Defender Office. It is anticipated that close cooperation between the assigned counsel and defender components will lead to the development of additional shared services as well as continuing legal education programs. See ABA Standards, 5–1.4.

Section 3. Selection of Assigned Counsel.

(1) The judges of each circuit or group of voluntarily combined circuits shall appoint a local designating authority who shall be responsible for the selection of assigned appellate counsel from a rotating list and shall perform such other tasks in connection with the operation of the list as may be necessary at the trial court level. The designating authority may not be a judge, prosecutor or member of the prosecutor's staff, public defender or member of the public defender's staff, or any attorney in private practice who currently accepts trial or appellate criminal assignments within the jurisdiction. Circuits which have contracted with an attorney or group of attorneys to provide representation on appeal for indigent defendants must comply with these regulations within one year after implementation by the Supreme Court.

(2) Each local designating authority shall compile a list of attorneys eligible and willing to accept criminal appellate assignments as indicated on the statewide roster. In order to receive appellate assignments from a trial court, an attorney's name must appear on that circuit's local list. The local lists shall be compiled in the following manner:

(a) The name of each attorney appearing on the statewide roster who has identified the circuit in question as his or her circuit of primary practice shall automatically be placed on the local list.

(b) The name of each attorney appearing on the statewide roster who submits a written request to the local designating authority shall also be placed on the local list.

(c) The name "State Appellate Defender Office" shall be placed in every fourth position on each local list.

(3) On receiving notice from a trial judge that an indigent defendant has requested appellate counsel, the local designating authority shall select the attorney to be assigned by rotating the local list in the following manner:

(a) The opportunity for appointment shall be offered to the attorney whose name appears at the top of the list unless that attorney must be passed over for cause.

(b) When the attorney accepts the appointment or declines it for reasons other than those hereafter specified as "for cause," the attorney's name shall be rotated to the bottom of the list.

(c) When an attorney's name is passed over for cause, his or her name shall remain at the top of the list.

(d) An attorney's name must be passed over for cause in any of the following circumstances:

(i) The crime of which the defendant has been convicted carries a possible life sentence or a statutory maximum sentence exceeding 15 years and the attorney is qualified only at Level I as described in § 4(3) of these regulations.

(ii) The attorney represented the defendant at trial or plea and no exception for continued representation as specified in § 3(8) is to be made.

(iii) Representation of the defendant would create a conflict of interest for the attorney. Conflicts of interest shall be deemed to exist between codefendants whether they were jointly or separately tried. Codefendants may, however, be represented by the same attorney if they express a preference for such representation under § 3(7) of these regulations, provided that there is no apparent conflict of interest.

(iv) The attorney did not represent the defendant at trial or plea and an exception for continued representation by trial counsel as specified in § 3(8) is to be made.

(v) The defendant's request for an attorney on the list who is neither trial counsel nor next in order for appointment is to be honored pursuant to § 3(7).

(vi) The appeal to be assigned is from a habitual offender conviction and the designating authority, pursuant to § 3(9), desires to select the attorney assigned to appeal the underlying conviction.

(e) When an attorney is passed over for cause under subsections 3(d)(i), (ii), or (iii), the local designating authority shall continue systematic rotation of the list until reaching the name of an attorney willing and able to accept the appointment.

(f) When an attorney is passed over for cause under subsections 3(d)(iv), (v), or (vi) and an attorney whose name appears other than at the top of the list is selected, on accepting the appointment the latter attorney's name shall be rotated to the bottom of the list.

(g) The local designating authority shall maintain records which reflect all instances where attorneys have been passed over and the reasons therefor.

(4) Where a complete rotation of the local list fails to produce the name of an attorney willing and able to accept appointment in a particular case, the local designating authority shall refer the case to the appellate assigned counsel administrator for assignment.

(5) After selecting an attorney to be assigned in a particular case, the local designating authority shall obtain an order of appointment from the appropriate trial judge and shall forward copies of this order to the attorney named therein, the defendant, and the appellate assigned counsel administrator.

(6) All assignments other than those made to the State Appellate Defender Office shall be considered personal to the individual attorney named in the order of appointment and shall not be attributed to a partnership or firm.

(7) When advising defendants of their right to assigned counsel on appeal pursuant to GCR 1963, 785.11, trial judges shall explain that the defendant may indicate on the written request for the appointment of counsel a preference for a particular attorney. Trial judges shall further explain that the defendant's preference is not controlling and that the eligibility and willingness of the desired attorney to accept appellate assignments are controlling. When the defendant expresses a preference for counsel whose name appears on the local list, the local designating authority shall attempt to honor it.

(8) When the defendant specifically requests the appointment of his or her trial attorney for purposes of appeal and the trial attorney is otherwise eligible and willing to accept the assignment, the defendant shall be advised by the trial judge of the potential consequences of continuous representation. If the defendant thereafter maintains a preference for appellate representation by trial counsel, the advice given and the defendant's waiver of the opportunity to receive new counsel on appeal shall be by waiver on the record or by written waiver placed in the court file.

(9) Where a designating authority treats a habitual offender convicted as a separate assignment, such an assignment may be given to the attorney handling the appeal of the underlying conviction.

Commission Comment

The procedures for utilizing the statewide roster which are outlined in this section reflect a number of significant policy decisions. Foremost is the legislature's rejection of the ad hoc system of appointing counsel. This method, which involves the random selection by trial judges of attorneys who happen to be available, has been universally criticized for offering no control over the quality of representation, no basis for organizing and training a private defense bar, and no barriers to reliance on patronage or discrimination as selection criteria. See, for instance, ABA Standards, 5–2.1. MCL 780.711–780.719 meets these criticisms by requiring the selection of counsel from a roster of attorneys screened for eligibility and willingness to serve.

One incident of the ad hoc system which has been particularly troublesome in the appellate context is the practice of having the trial judge in the case select the defendant's representative on appeal. Since claims on appeal frequently allege legal error or abuse of discretion on the part of the trial judge, assigned counsel are put in the delicate position of having to criticize their "employer." Trial judges face the temptation of choosing attorneys willing to be uncritical. Defendants naturally question whether their interests are being vigorously protected. For detailed critiques see ABA Standards, 5–1.3; NLADA, p. 142; Report of the Defense Services Committee, recommendation 9a, p. 260.

MCL 780.712(6); MSA 28.1114(102)(6) states: "The appointment of criminal appellate defense services for indigents shall be made by the trial court from the roster provided by the commission or shall be referred to the office of the state appellate defender." The commission concluded that a significant difference exists between "appointment by the trial court" and "selection by the trial judge." It therefore suggested a system whereby selection of appellate attorneys from the roster would be made by nonjudicial personnel according to standardized procedures. Once designated, the attorney would still be appointed by the trial court, as opposed, for instance, to an appellate court. This method conforms to the legislative framework while avoiding potential conflicts for lawyers and judges alike. It has the added advantage of efficiency. Delegation of the selection process to a single designating authority in each circuit or in voluntarily combined circuits will relieve judges of what should be a largely ministerial task and will provide a centralized means of using the roster in multi-judge circuits.

Separate use by each circuit of the entire roster obviously would be cumbersome. Moreover, lawyers and judges would presumably be dissatisfied with a system that regularly matched attorneys and courts which are hundreds of miles apart. On the other hand, subdividing the roster into arbitrary geographical sections would preclude an attorney from seeking assignments in any circuit he or she chose. These competing concerns are both met by having shorter local lists drawn from the statewide roster in a manner which leaves to the attorney the choice of which and how many lists include his or her name. The commission assumed that normal laws of supply and demand would assure an adequate distribution of eligible counsel among the circuits. See ABA Standards, 5–2.2; NLADA, pp. 239–240.

Simplicity and evenhandedness in the allocation of cases to private counsel is assured by automatically rotating the local list with limited exceptions for cause. The commission's rotation scheme parallels those suggested in numerous published reports. ABA Standards, 5–2.3; NLADA, p. 241; Guide to Establishing a Defender System, pp. 82–83. Rotation has the inherent side effect of limiting the number of assignments available to any one attorney, and the commission chose not to adopt any additional measures for controlling caseload size. Any numerical limitation on the number of appellate assignments would be difficult to enforce and

would be inevitably arbitrary since it could not account for the remainder of a private attorney's practice.

Exceptions to strict rotation were limited to those enumerated in order to avoid reintroducing the kind of discretionary decision-making rotation is meant to eliminate. Two of these exceptions bear special mention. In general, trial counsel should not represent defendants on appeal since, like the trial judges, their performance is subject to review. While continuous representation by trial counsel may be preferred by some defendants and be desirable in some cases, it is presumptively disfavored unless the defendant makes an intelligent waiver of the right to a new attorney. Defendants considering such a waiver should therefore be advised that an appellate attorney's role includes identifying errors to which trial counsel may have failed to object and errors made by trial counsel in the first instance. If such errors exist, trial counsel may find it difficult to perceive them or to assert them most effectively on appeal. This view comports with those expressed in Report of the Defense Services Committee, recommendation 9b, p. 260, and NLADA, p. 352.

Another exception is meant to allow consideration of a defendant's preference for particular appellate counsel. While the desired attorney would have to be otherwise willing and eligible to accept the assignment, there is no reason not to accommodate the defendant's choice when possible. But for their indigency the defendants involved would have complete freedom in selecting their own attorney. Minimizing to the extent possible disparities among defendants which result from differences in financial status is a concern which has also been addressed by other groups. See Report of the Defense Services Committee, recommendation 2, alternative F, p. 245, and NLADA, pp. 477, 481–484.

Section 4. Attorney Eligibility for Assignments.

(1) Attorneys who wish to be considered for appointment as appellate counsel for indigent defendants shall file an application with the assigned counsel administrator. Based on the information contained in the application, eligible attorneys will be identified in the statewide roster as qualified for assignments at either Level I or Level II.

(2) All applicants who are members in good standing of the State Bar of Michigan and who:

(a) have been counsel of record in at least six or more appeals of felony convictions in Michigan or federal courts during the three years immediately preceding the date of application, or

(b) in exceptional circumstances, have acquired comparable experience as determined in the discretion of the Appellate Defender Commission,

shall be designated as Level II and may accept appointments to represent indigent defendants convicted of any felony and juveniles appealing their waiver decisions regarding any felony.

(3) All applicants who are members in good standing of the State Bar of Michigan who have not been designated Level II attorneys shall be designated as Level I. A Level I attorney may not be appointed to represent a defendant on appeal if the crime of which the defendant was convicted carries a possible life sentence or a statutory maximum sentence exceeding

15 years or, similarly, on appeal of juvenile waiver decisions where the maximum possible sentence for the felony charged is a life sentence or a statutory maximum exceeding 15 years.

(4) A Level I attorney shall be designated as Level II if the attorney has been counsel of record in at least two appeals of felony convictions within an 18-month period.

(5) Attorneys who are employed full time by the State Appellate Defender Office at or above the status of assistant defender need not individually prove their qualifications as Level II attorneys in order to perform the duties of their employment and may not individually appear on the statewide roster as eligible for accepting assignments during the course of their employment at the State Appellate Defender Office.

(6) In addition to demonstrating eligibility for a particular level of practice, attorneys who wish to maintain their names on the roster shall, by the filing of an application, agree to comply with the following regulations:

(a) Each attorney shall meet and shall strive to exceed the Minimum Standards for Indigent Criminal Appellate Defense Services approved by the Supreme Court and adopted by the Appellate Defender Commission.

(b) Each Level II attorney shall demonstrate continued participation in the field of criminal appellate practice by appearing as counsel of record in two felony appeals during the two years immediately preceding each eligibility renewal statement.

(c) Each attorney, in each case to which he or she is assigned as appellate counsel, shall timely forward to the assigned counsel administrator copies of the following:

(i) all briefs and memorandums filed in the defendant's behalf,

(ii) his or her voucher for fees,

(iii) a completed case summary as described in § 2(6).

(d) Each attorney shall file an eligibility renewal statement as required by § 2(3) of these regulations within 30 days after receipt of the appropriate forms from the appellate assigned counsel administrator.

(e) Each attorney shall respond promptly to notice from the appellate assigned counsel administrator that defects in the attorney's eligibility exist or that complaints about the attorney's performance have been received. Deficiencies in eligibility must be corrected within 60 days subject to the grant in writing of one 60-day extension by the administrator for good cause shown.

(f) Each attorney shall complete an educational program in criminal appellate advocacy to be pre-pared by the administrator and approved by the Supreme Court.

(7) Pursuant to 3(2)(a) and (b) each attorney on the statewide roster will automatically be placed on the local list of the circuit he or she had designated for primary practice and may, in addition, request placement on the local lists of his or her choice.

(8) The name of an attorney may be removed from the roster by the administrator for failure to comply with the preceding regulations. The administrator must give the affected attorney 60 days' notice that removal from the roster is contemplated. The attorney shall have a de novo appeal of right from administrator's decision to the Appellate Defender Commission. If the right to appeal is exercised within the 60-day notice period, removal from the roster shall be stayed pending decision by the commission. The administrator's recommendations to the commission and the commission's findings shall be in writing.

(9) Any attorney whose name is removed from the roster for a reason other than a finding of inadequate representation of a client shall complete his or her work on any cases pending at the time of removal and shall be entitled to voucher for fees in those cases in the usual manner. Where removal is predicated on a finding of inadequate representation of a client as defined in the Minimum Standards for Indigent Criminal Appellate Defense Services, the appellate assigned counsel administrator shall move the trial court for substitution of counsel, with notice to the defendant, in any pending case assigned to the attorney affected. If substitution of counsel is granted, the trial court shall determine the amount of compensation due the attorney being replaced. No attorney may accept criminal appellate defense assignments after such time as removal of his or her name from the roster has become final.

(10) Any attorney whose name has been involuntarily removed from the roster may apply for reinstatement at any time after a period of six months from the removal date has elapsed and shall be reinstated whenever renewed eligibility has been demonstrated to the satisfaction of the administrator. Refusals to reinstate by the administrator are appealable de novo to the commission. The reasons for the administrator's refusal and the commission's findings shall be in writing.

(11) Any attorney formerly eligible for assignments at Level II who has allowed his or her eligibility to lapse solely for failure to meet the continuing participation requirement of § 4(5)(b) may, on application, be reinstated at Level II if the administrator finds on review of the circumstances that reinstatement at Level I is not required to protect the quality of representation received by defendants.

Commission Comment

Establishing criteria for eligibility for the roster posed difficult and controversial questions. Criteria which were arbitrary, subjective or discriminatory in effect had to be avoided. Those which had no clear relationship to ability or which could prove misleading or unduly burdensome had to be identified. As a result, such indicators as years of membership in the bar, references, written examinations and a complicated point system were all considered and rejected. Criminal appellate experience was selected as the sole criterion which is both relevant and readily measurable.

The eligibility requirements accomplish the single but important purpose of preventing the least experienced attorneys from representing the defendants facing the most serious consequences. They serve only to prohibit attorneys with little or no criminal appellate experience from representing defendants convicted of crimes which carry an actual or potential maximum prison sentence in excess of 15 years. Attorneys who have handled a total of six felony appeals during the three years immediately preceding their initial application are automatically "grandfathered in" at Level II, i.e., they are eligible for assignment in any case. All other applicants are eligible for assignments only at Level I, i.e., to cases with actual or potential maximum sentences of 15 years or less. But the move to Level II may be made rapidly. A lawyer need only be counsel in two "Level I" appeals within an 18-month period to attain the designation "Level II."

Drawing the line dividing Levels I and II at 15 years is arbitrary and troublesome. It is not suggested that defendants with relatively lower maximum sentences are somehow less deserving of effective representation or that their appeals necessarily raise less complex legal issues. The 15 year breakpoint was selected for purely practical reasons. The most common offenses tend to divide between those which carry maximum sentences of 15 years or less, and those which have "floating" maximums (life or any term of years). While the desire to safeguard defendants is the paramount object of the entire regulatory scheme, if a sufficient number of cases is not defined as Level I, attorneys may be denied the opportunity to gain the experience required for Level II. If movement from Level I to Level II were thus systematically discouraged, the number of Level II attorneys available for appointment could become inadequate and defendants, as well as lawyers, would suffer. The 15-year demarcation is meant to insure a large enough pool of Level I appeals while still limiting the assignment of cases involving the most serious offenses and longest sentences to the more experienced appellate counsel.

Subsection (5) exempts staff attorneys employed by the State Appellate Defender Office from having to prove their qualifications as Level II attorneys for two reasons. First, they are by definition not private assigned counsel subject to the operation of the roster. They are prohibited by MCL 780.711–780.719 from accepting outside employment and therefore cannot appear on the roster as individuals. The courts' appointments in the cases they handle are made to the State Appellate Defender Office as an entity, not to them personally. Second, the State Appellate Defender Office has internal hiring and promotional procedures which provide far greater quality control than the assigned counsel system is designed to afford. Pursuant to the statute, assistant defenders must, of course, conform to the minimum standards of performance.

Having achieved eligibility for the roster, an attorney must meet certain minimal requirements in order to remain eligible. Level II attorneys are required to handle at least two felony appeals (assigned or retained) during the two years immediately preceding each eligibility renewal statement.

All participating attorneys are expected to complete a course in criminal appellate advocacy. They are also expected to perform those tasks necessary to maintain the assigned counsel system as a whole, e.g., completing case summaries and renewal applications and contributing to the brief bank. Finally, they must continue to represent their clients in conformity with the minimum standards.

Failure to maintain eligibility obviously has significant consequences to the affected attorneys. Due process safeguards are built into the administrative design through the mechanisms of written notices and findings of fact and de novo appeals to the Appellate Defender Commission. It must be remembered, however, that the potential consequences are limited to the attorney's eligibility for criminal appellate assignments. Civil work, criminal trial work, and even retained criminal appeals are not implicated. The ability of the state into set conditions on eligibility for appellate assignments stems from both the state's right to select and pay for attorneys in appointed cases and its responsibility to insure the effectiveness of counsel it selects to represent indigent defendants. The eligibility criteria and continuing participation requirements selected by the commission are in accord with the recommendations of its predecessor groups. See ABA Standards, 5–2.2. NLADA, pp. 239–241; Report of the Defense Services Committee, recommendation 10, pp. 260–261.

The approved minimum standards for indigent criminal appellate defense services, together with the commentary of the Appellate Defender Commission, are as follows:

1. Counsel shall, to the best of his or her ability, act as the defendant's counselor and advocate, undeflected by conflicting interests and subject to the applicable law and rules of professional conduct.

Commission Comment

The standard was adapted from the ABA Standards for Criminal Justice (2d ed., 1980) 4–1.1(b) and 4–1.1(c) (ABA Standards). It is meant to remind counsel of their ethical and professional responsibilities as the defendant's representative in an adversary system. The United States Supreme Court has emphasized that appellate defense counsel's task is to be an advocate, not amicus curiae. *Anders* v *California*, 386 U.S. 738, 744; 87 S.Ct. 1396; 18 L.Ed.2d 493 (1967). Speaking for a majority of the Michigan Supreme Court, Justice Williams has stated: "We hold as a fundamental precept that a lawyer's duty to his client in a criminal case is judged by the same standard regardless of the fact that his client may be indigent. The application of our Code of Professional Responsibility and Canons is not dependent upon the size of the retainer which an attorney receives." *Holt* v *State Bar Grievance Board*, 388 Mich. 50, 60; 199 N.W.2d 195, 200 (1972).

2. Counsel shall not represent more than one of multiple codefendants on appeal regardless of whether the codefendants were jointly or separately tried, unless the codefendants express a preference for joint representation and there is no apparent conflict of interest.

Commission Comment

This standard parallels GCR 1963, 785.4(4), which is intended to avoid conflicts of interest arising from the joint representation of codefendants at trial. Appellate counsel, like trial counsel, must scrupulously avoid being placed in a position where promoting the interests of one client requires minimizing or violating the interests of another client. See *State Appellate Defender* v *Saginaw Circuit Judge*, 91 Mich. App. 606; 283 N.W.2d 810 (1979). Just as at trial, arguments about the relative culpability of codefendants may be relevant to claims about the sufficiency of the evidence or the propriety of a sentence. If conflicts of interest are not investigated adequately in advance, defendants may have to face the difficulty of receiving substitute counsel weeks or months after a claim of appeal has been filed. The disrupted attorney-client relationship then must be replaced and substantial time may be added to the appellate process.

3. Except in extraordinary circumstances, counsel shall interview the defendant in person on at least one occasion during the initial stages of representation.

Commission Comment

Client interviews serve numerous purposes. They may reveal significant facts not on the record or even the fact that parts of the record are missing. They may confirm or eliminate claims of error. Interviews serve to alert counsel to circumstances which make dismissing the appeal the defendant's wisest choice. They afford the defendant the opportunity to meet the person upon whose performance his or her future depends. Personal interviews are crucial to establishing the trust and rapport which are the essence of a successful attorney-client relationship. Meeting one's client for a discussion of the case seems on its face to be a fundamental aspect of professional conduct. The commission felt strongly that attorneys must be prepared to visit their clients wherever they may be incarcerated. Compensation for travel expenses must be considered a basic cost of providing assigned appellate counsel. Court of Appeals judges who responded to a questionnaire also felt that client interviews are important to effective representation on appeal.

4. Counsel shall fully apprise the defendant of the reasonably foreseeable consequences of pursuing an appeal in the particular case under consideration.

Commission Comment

The decision whether or not to appeal belongs to the defendant, but it is a decision that can only be made intelligently with the advice of counsel. In certain circumstances, success on appeal may expose a defendant to the risk of a longer sentence or conviction on higher or additional charges. An attorney who obtains reversal of a client's conviction but fails to foresee that the client will be worse off as a result does not "conscientiously protect his client's interest." *Beasley* v *United States*, 491 F.2d 687, 696 (C.A. 6, 1974). To help the defendant make a realistic choice about appealing, counsel must explain the nature of the appellate process, the average time involved, the kind of remedies which may result, and the potential disadvantages such remedies may present. In accord see: ABA Standard 4–8.2; *Stewart* v *Wainwright*, 309 F.Supp. 1023 (M.D.Fla.1969); *Smotherman* v *Beto*, 276 F.Supp. 579, 585 (N.D.Tex.1967).

5. In any appeal of right, counsel shall comply with the applicable court rules regarding the timely and proper filing of claims of appeal and shall take any other steps which may be necessary to protect the defendant's right to review.

Commission Comment

Once a defendant chooses to exercise his state constitutional right to appeal, counsel's first duty must be to take the procedural steps necessary to protect the continued existence of that right. Despite their general reluctance to find counsel ineffective, appellate courts have not hesitated to do so when a lawyer's negligence has caused a defendant to lose even the opportunity for an appellate review provided by law. See Const 1963, art 1, § 20; GCR 1963, 803; ABA Standards, 4–8.2(b) and 4–8.4(a); *Boyd* v *Cowan*, 494 F.2d 338 (C.A. 6, 1974); *Chapman* v *United States*, 469 F.2d 634 (C.A. 5, 1972).

6. Counsel shall promptly request and review all transcripts and lower court records.

Commission Comment

While the necessity to review the record in order to perfect an appeal is self-evident, this standard reminds counsel of two additional points. First, promptness in obtaining and reviewing the record is necessary if all issues are to be researched and all facts clarified in time to prepare a thorough brief. Second, the record includes more than the bare transcript of the trial or guilty plea. Such items as docket entries, charging documents, search warrants, competency and sanity evaluations, judicial orders and presentence reports may reveal or support claims of error. Familiarity with the total record is therefore crucial to effective appellate representation. See GCR 1963, 812, and *Entsminger* v *Iowa*, 386 U.S. 748; 87 S.Ct. 1402; 18 L.Ed.2d 501 (1967).

7. Counsel shall investigate potentially meritorious claims of error not reflected in the trial court record when he or she is informed or has reason to believe that facts in support of such claims exist.

Commission Comment

Some attorneys feel that appellate representation is bound by the four corners of the record and that there is no place for factual investigation on appeal. Such a view is belied by GCR 1963, 817.6, which establishes the procedure for developing a record for appeal when the existing record is inadequate to support a claim of error. Information provided by the defendant or trial counsel or unanswered questions raised by the existing record may lead conscientious appellate counsel to the identification of potentially reversible error. This standard does not place on counsel the duty to actively search for every off-record claim that might conceivably be developed. It does, however, require counsel to be alert to the possibility of off-record claims, to verify facts which would be significant if proven, and to investigate circumstances which a criminal lawyer would recognize as potentially prejudicial to his or her client. Ignoring nonrecord claims on appeal when a procedure exists for asserting them is the equivalent of failing to "investigate all apparently substantial defenses" at trial. *Beasley* v *United States*, supra. See also ABA Standards, 4–4.1.

8. Counsel shall move for and conduct such evidentiary hearings as may be required to create or supplement a record for review of any claim of error not adequately supported by existing records which he or she believes to be meritorious.

Commission Comment

This standard is a necessary corollary to the preceding one. If investigation reveals facts off the record which would support a claim on appeal, it then becomes appellate counsel's duty to develop a testimonial record for review as GCR 1963, 817.6 provides. See *People* v *Ginther*, 390 Mich. 436, 443–444; 212 N.W.2d 922, 925–926 (1973).

9. Counsel should assert claims of error which are supported by facts of record, which will benefit the defendant if successful, which possess arguable legal merit, and which should be recognizable by a practitioner familiar with criminal law and procedure who engages in diligent legal research.

Commission Comment

The fundamental purpose served by providing counsel on appeal is to interpose between client and court the judgment of a professional familiar with the criminal law, who has assessed the facts and brought to the court's attention any errors which might entitle the defendant to relief. Competent exercise of this professional judgment is the crucial duty owed by appellate counsel to the defendant. The standard does not require that every innovative issue conceivable be raised in every case. It is addressed to the level of competence which can reasonably be expected of a conscientious criminal appellate practitioner who is not a full-time specialist. It does, however, stress the assertion of all arguably meritorious claims rather than the preselection by counsel of the one or two issues which in counsel's own opinion will in fact be successful. The "reasonableness" test of *Beasley* v *United States*, supra, was expressly adopted by the Michigan Supreme Court in *People* v *Garcia*, 398 Mich. 250, 266; 247 N.W.2d 547, 553–554 (1976). Although *Beasley* specifically addresses the conduct of trial counsel, its references to the assertion of "all apparently substantial defenses" and to "strategy and tactics which lawyers of ordinary training and skill would not consider competent" are useful and have been applied to appellate counsel. See *Rook* v *Cupp*, 18 Or.App. 608; 526 P.2d 605 (1974).

Before enunciation of the *Beasley* standard, the Michigan Supreme Court remanded for consideration by the State Bar Grievance Board a defendant's complaint against his assigned appellate counsel. The lawyer had failed to assert as error a claim identical to one then pending consideration by the Supreme Court, even though the defendant himself had pointed out the problem. Emphasizing the need for "proper legal research," the Court found "substantial evidence that suggests [the defendant] may have been inadequately represented." *Holt* v *State Bar Grievance Board*, supra, 62. The California Supreme Court requires appellate counsel to raise "all issues that are arguable." *People* v *Feggans*, 67 Cal.2d 444, 447; 62 Cal.Rptr. 419, 421; 432 P.2d 21, 23 (1967). The United States Supreme Court has said that indigent defendants must be afforded counsel to argue on appeal "any of the legal points arguable on their merits." *Anders* v *California*, supra.

10. Counsel should not hesitate to assert claims which may be complex, unique, or controversial in nature, such as issues of first impression, challenges to the effectiveness of other defense counsel, or arguments for change in the existing law.

Commission Comment

This standard complements the preceding one. While recognition of unique or complex issues cannot be required, assertion of such issues when recognized is encouraged. The attorney who, through expertise or inspiration, identifies a claim which may be conceptually difficult or controversial is obligated to pursue it in the defendant's behalf. This standard also specifically cautions appellate lawyers against avoiding legitimate ineffective assistance of counsel claims out of undue deference to their peers. In accord, see ABA Standards, 4–8.6(a) and 4–8.6(b).

11. When a defendant insists that a particular claim be raised on appeal against the advice of counsel, counsel shall inform the defendant that he or she has the right to present that claim to the appellate court in propria persona. Should the defendant choose to proceed in such manner, counsel shall provide procedural advice and such clerical assistance as may be required to conform the defendant's pleadings for acceptability to the court.

Commission Comment

This standard is the product of three strongly felt concerns. One is that the case belongs to the defendant and clients should not be foreclosed from the opportunity to act upon disagreements with their professional representatives. Nonindigent defendants who wish to have particular claims asserted are able to select retained counsel based upon the lawyer's willingness to comply with their wishes. Indigent defendants should at least be provided the aid minimally necessary to present such claims by themselves. The second concern is that in every dispute between defendants and lawyers about the merits of a claim, the defendant is not necessarily wrong. *Holt* v. *State Bar Grievance Board*, supra, is a case on point. This standard is intended to protect not only the defendant's dignity, but his or her right to prevent meritorious claims from being buried by an attorney's mistake. On the other hand, the attorney's role is to exercise professional judgment, and appellate counsel cannot be required to pursue claims which he or she had in good faith rejected as lacking any arguable merit. Counsel is only expected to provide such assistance as an indigent client, particularly one who is incarcerated, may reasonably need to place such claims before the court. The commission anticipates that compliance with other standards, particularly those that serve to promote trust and rapport between attorney and client, will result in this standard being implemented infrequently.

12. Assigned counsel shall not take any steps towards dismissing an appeal for lack of arguably meritorious issues without first obtaining the defendant's informed written consent.

Commission Comment

This standard addresses the situation where, based on the advice of counsel that no arguable grounds for relief exist, the defendant agrees to dismiss his or her appeal. Unlike cases in which an *Anders* brief is filed or a brief raising some but not all potential claims is submitted, a stipulation dismissing an appeal results in no judicial review on the merits. Nor does it result in substitution of counsel. The defendant's right to appeal is simply abandoned.

The decision to dismiss, like the decision to proceed, is ultimately the client's. Thus, counsel is prohibited from taking any unilateral action to dismiss. Counsel is obligated to be certain that the defendant understands what dismissal means and why it is being recommended. All relevant legal and factual considerations should be explored. The defendant's questions about any aspect of the proceedings which led to conviction should be answered. The practice of obtaining written consent protects the lawyer as well as the client. See ABA Standards, 4–8.2(a) and 4–8.3.

13. Counsel should seek to utilize publicly funded support services designed to enhance their capacity to present the law and facts to the extent that such services are available and may significantly improve the representation they can provide.

Commission Comment

This standard encourages counsel to avail themselves of publicly funded defense support services, e.g., the Legal Resources Project, investigative services, expert witness files. To the extent that services are provided at state expense in order to equalize the opportunities of indigent and nonindigent defendants, clients should not be denied the benefits of these services by the ignorance or negligence of attorneys who have also been provided at public expense.

14. Counsel shall be accurate in referring to the record and the authorities relied on in both written and oral presentations to the court.

Commission Comment

Accuracy is, of course, required by both court rule and professional ethics. Counsel's personal reputation for accuracy may also affect the credence given by the court to defendants' cases. Court of Appeals judges responding to a questionnaire ranked accurate representation of the facts as the most crucial aspect of appellate representation and accurate representation of the law as only marginally less crucial. See also GCR 1963, 813, and ABA Standards, 4–8.4(b).

15. Counsel shall comply with all applicable court rules regarding the timely filing of pleadings and with such other timing requirements as may be specified by the court in a particular case.

Commission Comment

It is apparent that minimum performance must include compliance with court rules and orders specifying filing dates for pleadings, hearing dates, etc. Failure to comply can have consequences to the defendant ranging from loss of oral argument to dismissal of the appeal for lack of progress. See GCR 1963, 815–819.

16. Counsel should request and appear for oral argument. In preparation for oral argument counsel shall review the briefs of both parties, file supplemental pleadings as warranted, and update his or her legal research.

Commission Comment

While opinions vary about the extent to which oral arguments affect the outcome of most appeals, defendants are entitled to have their attorneys pursue every available avenue of persuasion. Argument provides the opportunity for counsel to present recent cases, counter the prosecution's position, and answer the court's questions. Utilizing this opportunity obviously depends upon preparation. At the other extreme, counsel's failure to appear not only precludes these potential benefits but diminishes the apparent seriousness of claims which the defendant's own lawyer does not think worthy of argument.

17. Counsel shall keep the defendant apprised of the progress of the case and shall promptly forward to the defendant copies of pleadings filed in his or her behalf and orders and opinions issued by the court in his or her case.

Commission Comment

Assigned criminal appellate defense counsel represent poor clients who are usually in prison. It is an inherently unequal relationship, with the clients having little control over, and limited access to, their lawyers. It is easy for well-intentioned but busy attorneys to lose sight of the significance of a particular appeal to an individual defendant. Correspondence may be put off, phone calls unanswered, delays left unexplained. This standard reminds counsel that their clients are wholly dependent upon them for information and requires them to minimize their client's inevitable anxieties by providing such information as it becomes available. It also ensures that defendants will have the opportunity to assess the work being performed on their behalf and to express satisfaction or dissatisfaction at appropriate times on an informed basis. In accord see ABA Standards, 4–3.8, and NLADA, p. 353.

18. Upon disposition of the case by the court, counsel shall promptly and accurately inform the defendant of the courses of action which may be pursued as a result of that disposition, and the scope of any further representation counsel will provide.

Commission Comment

This standard requires appellate attorneys to complete the tasks of the counselor as well as those of the advocate. It prohibits abrupt abandonment of the attorney-client relationship upon judicial disposition of the case without due regard to the defendant's need for information and guidance. It does not require counsel to provide legal representation beyond the scope of the original order of appointment. It does assume that the original order includes a responsibility to explain the consequences of the representation already provided. When appropriate, the means and advisability of pursuing such avenues as applications to the Supreme Court or habeas corpus petitions in federal court should be discussed. Clients who have had their convictions reversed and are awaiting retrial should be represented by appellate counsel until it is clear that no further appeals will occur and trial counsel has been obtained. The goal of the standard is to prevent defendants from losing potential sources of relief because they have been left ignorant of available procedures. See ABA Standards 4–8.5.

19. At whatever point in the postconviction proceedings counsel's representation terminates, counsel shall cooperate with the defendant and any successor counsel in the transmission of records and information.

Commission Comment

This standard merely reminds counsel that even after the attorney-client relationship has been terminated certain ethical obligations remain. To the extent that counsel possesses transcripts, documents or information which the defendant needs to pursue other avenues of relief, counsel has the duty to transmit them promptly and fully at the defendant's request.

20. Counsel shall not seek or accept fees from the defendant or from any other source on the defendant's behalf other than those authorized by the appointing authority.

Commission Comment

Throughout their discussions commission members expressed deep concern about the low rates at which assigned counsel are compensated. Individuals interested in a defendant's welfare occasionally approach appointed attorneys offering supplemental fees as an incentive to hard work. Recognizing the inevitable temptation such offers present, the commission believed that the obvious ethical point made by this standard was worthy of separate attention.

To provide adequate notice of the Court's approval of the minimum standards for indigent criminal defense services, the minimum standards will apply to all counsel appointed to represent indigents on appeal after February 1, 1982.

WE REPEAT HERE THAT THE IMPLEMENTATION OF THE REGULATIONS GOVERNING THE SYSTEM FOR APPOINTMENT OF APPELLATE COUNSEL FOR INDIGENTS IN CRIMINAL CASES REQUIRES LEGISLATIVE APPROPRIATION OF FUNDS SUFFICIENT TO OPERATE THE SYSTEM. IN SUCH EVENT, ANOTHER ADMINISTRATIVE ORDER WILL BE PROMULGATED IMPLEMENTING THE SYSTEM AND REQUIRING ADHERENCE TO IT.

We further note that the comments of the commission are not a construction by the Court. The comments represent the views of the commission.

Coleman, C.J., Fitzgerald and Ryan, JJ., state:

We would defer implementation of the standards until the system has been funded because the enforcement of the standards depends on the operation of the system.

[Entered December 4, 1981; affirmed February 8, 1985 by Administrative Order 1985–3, in which the Court also stated "On the question of the regulations governing a system for appointment of appellate counsel for indigents in criminal cases, the Court is persuaded that 1978 PA 620 confides the development of such a system to the Appellate Defender Commission and not to this Court."]

ADMINISTRATIVE ORDER 1983–2
MICHIGAN COURTHOUSE GUIDELINES

The Court has received and reviewed the recommendation of the Courthouse Study Advisory Committee which urges the adoption of the Guidelines contained in Volume I of *The Michigan Courthouse Study*, pp. 53–171. The Court finds that the Guidelines reflect sound principles of court facility planning and design, application of which can greatly improve the functioning of Michigan's courts.

Accordingly, all courts and communities planning for and carrying out either construction, remodeling, or renovation of court facilities are urged to use the Guidelines.

[Entered March 2, 1983.]

ADMINISTRATIVE ORDER 1983–3
SENTENCING GUIDELINES

To assist the Supreme Court in evaluating the sentencing guidelines that have been generated by the Sentencing Guidelines Advisory Committee, every judge of the circuit court and of the Recorder's Court for the City of Detroit is invited, but not required, to use the guidelines for a period of one year, beginning May 1, 1983. These judges are urged to complete the sentencing forms to be provided by the staff of the committee and, in each case in which a minimum sentence outside the recommended minimum range is imposed, to explain on the form what aspects of the case at bar or of the guidelines have persuaded the judge to impose a sentence outside the recommended minimum range. The committee shall periodically analyze the data contained in these forms and shall provide an evaluation of such data to the Court. At the conclusion of the year, the committee shall make a final report to the Court of its findings and conclusions.

[Entered March 28, 1983.]

ADMINISTRATIVE ORDER 1983–7
ADDITIONAL COPY OF ORDER
OR OPINION IN CRIMINAL CASE *

On order of the Court, effective immediately, the Clerk of the Court of Appeals is directed to provide an additional copy of any order or opinion disposing of an appeal in a criminal case to the defendant's lawyer if the defendant was represented by counsel. Counsel shall thereupon forward the additional copy to the defendant.

[Entered October 7, 1983.]

* Suggested title added by Publisher.

ADMINISTRATIVE ORDER 1985–5
[AS AMENDED BY ADMINISTRATIVE
ORDER 1988–3] JUVENILE COURT
STANDARDS AND ADMINISTRATIVE
GUIDELINES FOR THE
CARE OF CHILDREN

Pursuant to Administrative Order 1985–5, this Court adopted the Juvenile Court Standards and Administrative Guidelines for the Care of Children, the Standards to take effect on May 1, 1985 and to expire on May 1, 1988. We now order that the Juvenile Court Standards and Administrative Guidelines continue in effect, as modified infra, until the further order of this Court:

Juvenile Court Standards and Administrative
Guidelines for the Care of Children

I. Court Administrators, Supervisory Personnel, County Juvenile Officers, Probation Officers, Caseworkers, and personnel of Court Operated Child Care Facilities shall meet the following minimum standards in order to qualify for employment. *Desired standards are those preferred qualifications that extend beyond minimal standards but are not required to perform the job function.*

These Standards shall apply only to new staff hired by the Juvenile Court on or after the effective date of these Standards. A Court employee who is currently in a position that was approved under regulations that preceded the implementation of these Standards shall be deemed qualified for that position. A court appointed person hired subsequent to the effective date of these Standards shall meet the minimum qualification of these Standards for that position.

A. *Court Administrator/Director.* The person in the Juvenile Court who is directly responsible to the Chief or Presiding Probate Judge and who is delegated administrative responsibilities for the operation of the court.

A Court Administrator, at the time of appointment, shall possess the following qualifications:

1. Education and Experience.

a. Desired Standards.

1. Master's Degree in social sciences, business or public administration, education, criminal justice or law degree with a minimum of four years of supervisory experience with Juvenile Court staff.

b. Minimum Standards.

1. Master's Degree in social sciences, business or public administration, education, criminal justice or law degree with a minimum of one year of experience working with Juvenile Court staff or related human service field.

2. A Bachelor's Degree in those same areas and two years of supervisory experience working with Juvenile Court staff or related human services field. (Courts with only one level of supervision may use two years of casework experience in lieu of supervisory experience.)

c. Knowledge, Skills and Abilities.

1. Knowledge of the juvenile justice system and overall children's services programs.

2. Knowledge of supervisory responsibilities and techniques.

3. Knowledge of the principles of administrative management.

4. Knowledge of programs and services provided by governmental agencies and the private sector.

5. Knowledge of the principles and methods concerned with personal and social problem solving.

6. Knowledge of the factors concerned in delinquency, neglect and abuse of children.

7. Knowledge of labor relations and personnel practices.

8. Ability to develop budgetary matters.

9. Ability to organize, direct and monitor service delivery work units and coordinate activities with other sections or agencies.

10. Ability to supervise professional and support staff, evaluate staff performance and assist in staff training.

11. Ability to develop policy and procedural materials and funding proposals.

12. Ability to analyze program data and recommend policy and procedural changes and program objectives.

13. Ability to interpret and effectively communicate administrative and professional policies and procedures to staff, governmental agencies, community organizations, advisory committees and the public.

14. Ability to speak and write effectively.

B. *Supervisory Personnel.* Those directly responsible for ongoing supervision of professional and support staff providing direct services to children, youth and their families.

A Supervisor, at the time of appointment, shall possess the following qualifications:

1. Education and Experience.

a. Desired Standards.

1. Master's Degree in social work or human service field with one year of professional experience in Juvenile Court work.

b. Minimum Standards.

1. A Bachelor's Degree in social sciences or human service field with two years of professional experience with a Juvenile Court staff or in a child welfare agency.

c. Knowledge, Skills and Abilities.

1. Knowledge of supervisory responsibilities and techniques.

2. Knowledge of principles, practices and techniques of child welfare work.

3. Knowledge of family dynamics and the effects of social conditions on family functioning.

4. Knowledge of factors concerned in delinquency, abuse and neglect of children.

5. Knowledge of principles and methods concerned with personal and social problem solving.

6. Knowledge of the juvenile justice system and overall children's services programs including related laws.

7. Knowledge of labor relations and personnel practices.

8. Knowledge of organizations, functions and treatment programs for children.

9. Ability to supervise professional and support staff, evaluate staff performance and assist in staff training.

10. Ability to speak and write effectively.

11. Ability to develop child welfare programs with community organizations.

12. Ability to apply social casework methods to child welfare services.

13. Ability to interpret and effectively communicate administrative and professional policies and procedures to staff, governmental agencies, community organizations, advisory committees and the public.

C. *Direct Services: Probation Officers/Casework Staff.* The professional staff who work directly with children and their families and other relevant individuals and who are primarily responsible for the development, implementation and review of plans for children, youth and their families.

Each county shall provide for a minimum of one delinquency probation officer/casework staff person (but exclusive of clinical staff and detention home personnel) for every 6,000 (or major fraction thereof) children under 19 years of age in the county.

A Probation Officer/Caseworker, at the time of appointment, shall possess the following qualifications:

1. Education and Experience.

a. Desired Standards.

1. Bachelor's Degree in social work, criminal justice, or behavioral sciences with two years of casework experience in Juvenile Court or a related child welfare agency and must complete the Michigan Judicial Institute Certification Training for Juvenile Court staff within two years after date of employment.

b. Minimum Standards.

1. Bachelor's Degree in social sciences or a related human services field and must complete the Michigan Judicial Institute Certification Training for Juvenile Court staff within two years after date of employment.

c. Knowledge, Skills and Abilities.

1. Knowledge of the principles and methods concerned with personal and social problem solving.

2. Knowledge of factors concerned in delinquency, neglect and abuse of children.

3. Knowledge of family dynamics and the effects of social conditions on family functioning.

4. Knowledge of the juvenile justice system and children's services programs.

5. Knowledge of the principles, procedures and techniques of child welfare work.

6. Ability to apply social casework methods to child welfare services.

7. Ability to develop child welfare programs with community organizations.

8. Ability to relate effectively to the public and individuals on their caseload.

9. Ability to speak and write effectively.

D. *Administrator of County Child Care Facility.* The person responsible to the Chief or Presiding Probate Judge or to the Juvenile Court Administrator and to whom is delegated overall administrative responsibility for the day-to-day operation of county child care facilities operated by the court.

The Administrator, at the time of appointment, shall possess the following qualifications:

1. Education and Experience.

a. Desired Standards.

1. Master's Degree in social work, sociology, psychology, guidance and counseling, education,

business administration, criminal justice, or public administration and two years of supervisory experience in a juvenile court, public or private child care facility.

b. Minimum Standards.

1. Same as above with a minimum of one year of supervisory experience in a Juvenile Court, public or private child care facility.

2. Bachelor's Degree in social science or human service field and two years of experience in a Juvenile Court, public or private child care facility.

c. Knowledge, Skills and Abilities.

1. Knowledge of supervisory responsibilities and techniques.

2. Knowledge of principles and methods concerned with personal and social problem solving.

3. Knowledge of factors concerned in delinquency, neglect and abuse of children.

4. Knowledge of family dynamics and effects of social conditions on family functioning.

5. Knowledge of the juvenile justice system and children's services programs.

6. Knowledge of child welfare organizations, functions and treatment programs relevant to residential care of children.

7. Knowledge of group treatment modalities.

8. Knowledge of labor relations, personnel policies and practices.

9. Ability to organize, direct and monitor service delivery work units and coordinate activities with other sections or agencies.

10. Ability to direct, monitor and coordinate several functions of a residential program.

11. Ability to supervise professional and support staff, evaluate staff performance, and assist in staff training.

12. Ability to analyze program data and recommend policy and procedural changes and program objectives.

13. Ability to analyze personal and social data and apply rehabilitative principles within the facility.

14. Ability to interpret and effectively communicate administrative and professional policies and procedures to staff, governmental agencies, community organizations, advisory committees, and the public.

15. Ability to speak and write effectively.

E. *Child Care Staff Supervisor*. The Child Care Supervisor is directly responsible for supervision of child care workers in the facility.

The Child Care Supervisor, at the time of appointment, shall possess the following qualifications:

1. Education and Experience.

a. Desired Standards.

1. Bachelor's Degree in social work, psychology, sociology, criminal justice or related human services field with two years of experience with a Juvenile Court or a public or private child care agency.

b. Minimum Standards.

1. Two years of college in a human services field and two years of work experience in a child care institution.

c. Knowledge, Skills and Abilities.

1. Knowledge of supervisory responsibilities and techniques.

2. Knowledge of the principles and methods concerned with personal and social problem solving.

3. Knowledge of factors concerned in delinquency, abuse and neglect of children.

4. Knowledge of family dynamics and the effects of social conditions on family functioning.

5. Knowledge of the juvenile justice system and children's services.

6. Knowledge of group treatment modalities.

7. Ability to supervise staff, evaluate staff performance and assist in staff training activities.

8. Ability to analyze personal and social data and apply rehabilitation principles in a practice setting.

9. Ability to interpret administrative and professional policies and procedures to staff.

10. Ability to apply social casework methods to child welfare activity.

11. Ability to speak and write effectively.

12. Basic knowledge of first aid and CPR training.

13. Knowledge of labor relations and personnel practices.

F. *Child Care Worker*. The person who provides direct care of children in the facility.

A Child Care Worker, at the time of appointment, shall possess the following qualifications:

1. Education and Experience.

a. Desired Standards.

1. Bachelor's Degree in social sciences or human services related field.

b. Minimum Standards.

1. A high school diploma or its equivalent.

c. Knowledge, Skills and Abilities.

1. Knowledge of appropriate conduct and manners.

2. Knowledge of potential facility management problems including behavior problems, food services.

3. Knowledge of potential behavior problems of children and youth.

4. Ability to provide role model for residents.

5. Ability to gain the respect, confidence and cooperation of children and youth.

6. Ability to teach children personal hygiene, proper conduct and household work.

7. Ability to understand and relate to problem children in a positive manner.

8. Ability to comprehend and follow oral and written directions.

9. Basic knowledge of first aid and CPR training within six months after date of employment.

II. Contents of Juvenile Court Case Records.

A. *Purpose.* A complete case record serves a range of purposes including, but not limited to, the following:

1. Provides an information base for planning and the delivery of services to a youth and family.

2. Provides documentation from which the worker can make appropriate recommendations for placement and services.

3. Provides an information base to assist in transfer of cases between workers and agencies.

B. *Case Record Contents for Youth Under Court Jurisdiction Placed in Their Own Home.* A separate case record shall be maintained for each youth or family under court supervision. Records shall be maintained in a uniform and organized manner and shall be protected against destruction (except as provided by court rule) and damage and shall be stored in a manner that safeguards confidentiality.

1. Records shall be typed or legibly handwritten and shall include as a minimum the following:

a. A report of the original complaint and/or petition and an appropriate social study.

b. Copies of orders of the court regarding the child and family.

c. Individual case plans with time frames where appropriate.

d. Youth Record Fact Sheet containing the following information: child's full name; date and place of birth; sex; religion of parents and child; parents' full names including mother's maiden name; address, dates and place of marriage or divorce; if deceased, date, place and cause of death; names, addresses and birth dates of other children in the family; names and addresses of near relatives; appropriate medical records.

e. Dates of casework visits or contact with child and family. Summary reports of child's

progress under care, *completed at least semi-annually.*

f. School reports, including grades, progress reports, and social and psychological reports if available and appropriate.

g. Reports of psychological tests or psychiatric examinations and follow-up treatment, if available.

h. Family financial report where appropriate.

i. Discharge summary and order for discharge.

j. Correspondence.

C. *Case Record Contents for Youth Under Court Jurisdiction in Out-of-Home Placement.* Case records for youth in *out-of-home placements* shall include the *same items as indicated for youth placed in their own home* with the following additions:

1. Individual *Case Plans* shall, where appropriate, include:

a. Description of type and appropriateness of the placement.

b. Action steps and goals expected to be accomplished by the agency.

c. Action steps and goals expected to be accomplished by the parents.

d. Action steps and goals expected to be accomplished by the child.

e. Action steps and goals expected to be accomplished by the court worker.

f. Plan for assuring proper care (supervision; review).

g. Plan for regular and frequent visitation between child and parents unless such visits, even if supervised, would not be in the best interest of the child.

h. Time frames for accomplishing elements of the case plan.

2. Record of youth's placements. Name of place, beginning and ending dates of residence.

3. Documentation of emergency medical care authorization.

4. Health Record, which includes:

a. Medical history

b. Documentation of current and prior immunizations

c. Dental information

5. Medicaid approval.

6. Governmental benefits and parental support information.

7. Foster care termination summary or residential agency summary.

[Entered April 30, 1985; amended April 29, 1988.]

ADMINISTRATIVE ORDER 1987–1
PROVIDING ACCESS TO JUROR
PERSONAL HISTORY QUESTIONNAIRES

This Court has amended MCR 2.510(C)(2), effective April 1, 1987, to direct the State Court Administrator to develop model procedures for providing attorneys and parties access to juror personal history questionnaires. Individual courts are directed to select and implement one of these procedures within two months after the State Court Administrator notifies the courts of the issuance of the model procedures.

ADMINISTRATIVE ORDER 1987–2
MICHIGAN UNIFORM SYSTEM OF CITATION

[*Publisher's Note: Order 1987–2 promulgated the Michigan Uniform System of Citation ,post.*]

ADMINISTRATIVE ORDER 1987–9
ADMINISTRATIVE ORDERS RE
SELECTION OF MEDIATORS

Subject to the approval of this Court, the State Court Administrator is to develop model procedures for establishing mediator pools and selecting mediation panels. Individual courts which desire to employ mediation are directed to select one of the model procedures within two months after the State Court Administrator notifies the courts of the issuance of the model procedures. After selecting a procedure, the individual courts shall submit an administrative order implementing it to the State Court Administrator pursuant to MCR 8.112(B). The administrative order shall be submitted to the State Court Administrator before its effective date. In the interim, any administrative orders establishing mediation pools and providing for the selection of mediation panels which have been approved by this Court shall remain in effect unless rescinded by the court which promulgated them or ordered stayed or revoked by the State Court Administrator.

[Entered December 7, 1987.]

ADMINISTRATIVE ORDER 1988–2
SUMMARY JURY TRIAL

On October 22, 1987, we ordered that a proposed court rule establishing a summary jury trial procedure be published for comment. See 66 Mich B J 1148 (November 1987). After having considered the comments received, we adopt the following summary jury trial procedure to be effective from July 1, 1988, until December 31, 1989.*

1. **Selection of Cases.** On stipulation of the parties with the approval of the court, a case that is ready for trial may be selected for a summary jury trial pursuant to this order.

2. **Pretrial Procedures.**

(A) Unless the court orders otherwise, at least 3 days before the date set for hearing, counsel shall submit proposed voir dire questions, proposed jury instructions, and briefs on any novel issues of law presented by the action. In computing the 3–day period, Saturdays, Sundays, and holidays on which the court is closed shall be excluded.

(B) Before the hearing, counsel shall confer with regard to exhibits, including documents and reports, and reach such agreement as is possible as to the use of the exhibits.

3. **Conduct of Summary Jury Trial.**

(A) The court shall adjust the time for commencement of the summary jury trial, the length of presentations by counsel, and the length of deliberations by the jury, so that the proceeding can be completed in no more than one day.

(B) *Presence of Parties.* Unless the court orders otherwise, the parties or representatives of the parties must be present at the summary jury trial.

(C) *Jury Selection.* The trial shall be conducted before a six-member jury selected from the regular jury panel. The court shall conduct a brief voir dire of the panel, and each party may exercise two challenges. No alternate jurors will be impaneled.

(D) *Presentation of Evidence.* All evidence shall be presented by the attorneys for the parties. The attorneys may summarize, quote from, and comment on pleadings, depositions, or other discovery requests and responses, exhibits, and statements of potential witnesses. No potential testimony of a witness may be referred to unless the reference is based on:

(i) the product of discovery procedures,

(ii) a written sworn statement of the witness, or

(iii) an affidavit of counsel stating:

(a) that although an affidavit of the witness is not available and cannot be obtained by the exercise of reasonable diligence, the witness would be called at trial and counsel has been told the substance of the testimony by the witness, and

(b) the substance of the witness' statement.

(E) *Length of Presentations.* Unless the court orders otherwise, presentations shall be limited to one hour for each party. In the case of multiple parties represented by separate counsel, the court shall make a reasonable adjustment of the time allowed.

(F) *Objections.* Opposing counsel may object during the course of a presentation if the presentation violates subsection 3(D) or goes beyond the limits of propriety in statements as to evidence or other comments.

(G) *Instructions to Jury.* Following the presentations by counsel, the court shall give an abbreviated set of instructions to the jury on the applicable law.

(H) *Verdict.* The jury will be encouraged to return a verdict that represents the consensus of the jurors. If after a reasonable time a consensus verdict is not possible, the jury shall be directed to return a special verdict consisting of an anonymous statement of each juror's findings on liability and damages. Following the verdict, the court may invite, but may not require, the jurors to informally discuss the case with the attorneys and the parties.

(I) *Recording of Proceedings.* Unless the court orders otherwise, the proceedings will not be recorded. However, a party may arrange for recording at its own expense.

4. Effect of Verdict. Unless the parties stipulate otherwise, the verdict is advisory only. The parties may stipulate that a consensus verdict will be deemed a final determination on the merits and that judgment may be entered on the verdict by the court, or may stipulate to any other use of the verdict that will aid in the resolution of the case.

5. Scheduling for Trial After Summary Jury Trial. If the case is not resolved within a reasonable time after the summary jury trial, the court shall schedule the case for trial as soon as practicable.

6. Statements Inadmissible in Later Proceedings. Statements in briefs or summaries submitted in connection with the summary jury trial and statements by counsel at the trial are not admissible in any evidentiary proceeding.

[Entered April 19, 1988.]

* Administrative Order 1989–5, entered December 28, 1989, ordered that "the provisions of Administrative Order 1988–2, regarding a summary jury trial procedure, are continued in effect until December 31, 1990." Administrative Order 1990–10, entered December 27, 1990, ordered the provisions "continued in effect until June 30, 1991." Administrative Order 1991–6, entered June 28, 1991, ordered the provisions "continued in effect until December 31, 1991." Administrative Order 1991–12, entered December 30, 1991, ordered the provisions "continued in effect until December 31, 1992." Administrative Order 1992–7, entered December 8, 1992, ordered the provisions "continued in effect until December 31, 1994." Administrative Order 1994–11, entered December 21, 1994, ordered the provisions "continued in effect until June 30, 1995." Administrative Order 1995–3, entered June 30, 1995, ordered the provisions "continued in effect until June 30, 1997."

Staff Comment

Administrative Order 1988–2 adopts a summary jury trial procedure based on a proposal recommended by the State Bar Representative Assembly. The procedure under Administrative Order 1988–2 is available only by stipulation of the parties in cases that are ready for trial. Following a simplified jury selection process each side is given one hour to summarize its position, utilizing the pleadings, discovery materials, exhibits, and statements of witnesses. The jury is given an abbreviated set of instructions on the applicable law and deliberates. Unless the parties have agreed otherwise, the verdict of the jury is entirely advisory. The trial court is to adjust the length of presentations and deliberations so that the proceeding can be completed within one day.

The procedure is similar to those used in a number of other jurisdictions, including the United States District Court for the Western District of Michigan. For a detailed description of the procedure as used in the Western District, see Brenneman & Wesoloski, *Blueprint for a Summary Jury Trial,* 65 Mich B J 888 (September 1986).

The procedure adopted by Administrative Order 1988–2 is in effect from July 1, 1988, through December 31, 1989.*

* Administrative Order 1989–5, entered December 28, 1989, ordered that "the provisions of Administrative Order 1988–2, regarding a summary jury trial procedure, are continued in effect until December 31, 1990." Administrative Order 1990–10, entered December 27, 1990, ordered the provisions "continued in effect until June 30, 1991." Administrative Order 1991–6, entered June 28, 1991, ordered the provisions "continued in effect until December 31, 1991." Administrative Order 1991–12, entered December 30, 1991, ordered the provisions "continued in effect until December 31, 1992." Administrative Order 1992–7, entered December 8, 1992, ordered the provisions "continued in effect until December 31. 1994." Administrative Order 1994–11, entered December 21, 1994, ordered the provisions "continued in effect until June 30, 1995." Administrative Order 1995–3, entered June 30, 1995, ordered the provisions "continued in effect until June 30, 1997."

ADMINISTRATIVE ORDER 1988–3
JUVENILE COURT STANDARDS AND
ADMINISTRATIVE GUIDELINES
FOR THE CARE OF CHILDREN

[*Publisher's Note: See Administrative Order 1985–5.*]

ADMINISTRATIVE ORDER 1988–4
SENTENCING GUIDELINES*

Administrative Order 1985–2, 420 Mich lxii, and Administrative Order 1984–1, 418 Mich lxxx, are rescinded as of October 1, 1988. The Sentencing Guidelines Advisory Committee is authorized to issue the second edition of the sentencing guidelines,** to be effective October 1, 1988. Until further order of the Court, every judge of the circuit court and of the Recorder's Court of the City of Detroit must thereafter use the second edition of the sentencing guidelines when imposing a sentence for an offense that is included in the guidelines.

In accordance with the directions found in the second edition of the sentencing guidelines, every judge of the circuit court and of the Recorder's Court of the City of Detroit must, not later than the date of sentencing, complete a sentencing information report on a form to be prescribed by and returned to the state court administrator. Whenever a judge of the circuit court or of the Recorder's Court of the City of Detroit determines that a minimum sentence outside the recommended minimum range should be imposed, the judge may do so. When such a sentence is imposed, the judge must explain on the sentencing information report and on the record the aspects of the case that have persuaded the judge to impose a sentence outside the recommended minimum range.

The Sentencing Guidelines Advisory Committee shall continue to analyze the data and the departure reasons provided by the judges of the circuit court and of the Recorder's Court of the City of Detroit and shall, at least annually, report to the Court the committee's evaluation of the status, effect, strengths, and weaknesses of the guidelines.

[Entered June 7, 1988.]

* See Administrative Order 1998-4, which rescinds the sentencing guidelines, effective January 1, 1999, for all cases in which the offense is committed on or after January 1, 1999; however, the sentencing guidelines shall remain in effect for applicable offenses committed before January 1, 1999.

** See the current edition of *Michigan Sentencing Guidelines*, available under separate cover from West.

ADMINISTRATIVE ORDER 1989-1
FILM OR ELECTRONIC MEDIA COVERAGE OF COURT PROCEEDINGS

On order of the Court, the report of the Cameras in the Courtroom Committee having been received and considered, the following exception to the Michigan Code of Judicial Conduct, Canon 3A(7) is adopted to permit film or electronic media coverage in all Michigan Courts effective March 1, 1989:

The following guidelines shall apply to film or electronic media coverage of proceedings in Michigan courts:

1. Definitions.

(a) "Film or electronic media coverage" means any recording or broadcasting of court proceedings by the media using television, radio, photographic, or recording equipment.

(b) "Media" or "media agency" means any person or organization engaging in news gathering or reporting and includes any newspaper, radio or television station or network, news service, magazine, trade paper, professional journal, or other news reporting or news gathering agency.

(c) "Judge" means the judge presiding over a proceeding in the trial court, the presiding judge of a panel in the Court of Appeals, or the Chief Justice of the Supreme Court.

2. Limitations.

(a) Film or electronic media coverage shall be allowed upon request in all court proceedings. Requests by representatives of media agencies for such coverage must be made in writing to the clerk of the particular court not less than three business days before the proceeding is scheduled to begin. A judge has the discretion to honor a request that does not comply with the requirements of this subsection. The court shall provide that the parties be notified of a request for film or electronic media coverage.

(b) A judge may terminate, suspend, limit, or exclude film or electronic media coverage at any time upon a finding, made and articulated on the record in the exercise of discretion, that the fair administration of justice requires such action, or that rules established under this order or additional rules imposed by the judge have been violated. The judge has sole discretion to exclude coverage of certain witnesses, including but not limited to the victims of sex crimes and their families, police informants, undercover agents, and relocated witnesses.

(c) Film or electronic media coverage of the jurors or the jury selection process shall not be permitted.

(d) A trial judge's decision to terminate, suspend, limit, or exclude film or electronic media coverage is not appealable, by right or by leave.

3. Judicial Authority.
Nothing in these guidelines shall be construed as altering the authority of the Chief Justice, the Chief Judge of the Court of Appeals, trial court chief judges, or trial judges to control proceedings in their courtrooms, and to ensure decorum and prevent distractions and to ensure the fair administration of justice in the pending cause.

4. Equipment and Personnel.
Unless the judge orders otherwise, the following rules apply:

(a) Not more than two videotape or television cameras, operated by not more than one person each, shall be permitted in any courtroom.

(b) Not more than two still photographers, utilizing not more than two still cameras each with not more than two lenses for each camera, and related necessary equipment, shall be permitted in any courtroom.

(c) Not more than one audio system for radio and/or television recording purposes shall be permitted in any courtroom. If such an audio system is permanently in place in the courtroom, pickup shall be made from that system; if it is not, microphones and wires shall be placed as unobtrusively as possible.

(d) Media agency representatives shall make their own pooling arrangements without calling upon the court to mediate any dispute relating to those arrangements. In the absence of media agency agreement on procedures, personnel, and equipment, the judge shall not permit the use of film or electronic media coverage.

5. Sound and Light Criteria.

(a) Only television, photographic, and audio equipment which does not produce distracting sound or light shall be utilized to cover judicial proceedings. Courtroom lighting shall be supplemented only if the judge grants permission.

(b) Only still camera equipment which does not produce distracting sound or light shall be employed to cover judicial proceedings. No artificial lighting device of any kind shall be employed with a still camera.

(c) Media agency personnel must demonstrate in advance, to the satisfaction of the judge, that the equipment proposed for utilization will not detract from the proceedings.

6. Location of Equipment and Personnel.

(a) Television camera equipment and attendant personnel shall be positioned in such locations in the courtroom as shall be designated by the judge. Audio and video tape recording and amplification equipment which is not a component of a camera or microphone shall be located in a designated area remote from the courtroom.

(b) Still camera photographers shall be positioned in such locations in the courtroom as shall be designated by the judge. Still camera photographers shall assume fixed positions within the designated areas and shall not move about in any way that would detract from the proceedings.

(c) Photographic or audio equipment may be placed in, moved about in, or removed from, the courtroom only during a recess. Camera film and lenses may be changed in the courtroom only during a recess.

(d) Representatives of the media agencies are invited to submit suggested equipment positions to the judge for consideration.

7. Conferences. There shall be no audio pickup, broadcast or video closeup of conferences between an attorney and client, between co-counsel, between counsel and the judge held at the bench at trial, or between judges in an appellate proceeding.

8. Conduct of Media Agency Personnel. Persons assigned by media agencies to operate within the courtroom shall dress and deport themselves in ways that will not detract from the proceedings.

9. Nonexclusivity. These guidelines shall not preclude coverage of any judicial proceeding by news reporters or other persons who are employing more traditional means, such as taking notes or drawing pictures.

[Entered January 13, 1989.]

ADMINISTRATIVE ORDER 1989–3 IN RE THE APPOINTMENT OF APPELLATE ASSIGNED COUNSEL

On order of the Court, 1978 PA 620 authorized the Appellate Defender Commission to develop a system of indigent appellate defense services to include services provided by the Office of the State Appellate Defender and locally appointed private counsel. This legislation also authorized the Commission to compile and keep current a statewide roster of attorneys eligible for and willing to accept appointment by an appropriate court to serve as criminal appellate defense counsel for indigents. The Legislature provided that the appointment of criminal appellate defense attorneys for indigents was to be made by the trial court from the roster provided by the Commission or should be referred to the Office of the State Appellate Defender. Since that time the Appellate Defender Commission has adopted the Michigan Appellate As-

signed Counsel System Regulations. We have examined those regulations, as adopted by the Appellate Defender Commission effective November 15, 1985 and as amended January 28, 1988, and, pursuant to our power of general superintending control over all courts under Const 1963, art 6, § 4, we ORDER the judges of each circuit and of the Recorder's Court of the City of Detroit to comply with § 3 of those regulations. The text of § 3 follows:

"**(1)** The judges of each circuit and of Recorder's Court shall appoint a local designating authority who may be responsible for the selection of assigned appellate counsel from the local list provided by the appellate assigned counsel administrator pursuant to § 2(2) of these regulations and who shall perform such other tasks in connection with the operation of the list as may be necessary at the trial court level.

"(a) The designating authority may not be a judge, prosecutor or member of the prosecutor's staff, public defender or member of the public defender's staff, or any attorney in private practice who currently accepts trial or appellate criminal assignments within the jurisdiction.

"(b) Circuits which have contracted with an attorney or group of attorneys to provide representation on appeal for indigent defendants shall comply with these regulations within one year after the statewide roster becomes operational.

"**(2)** Appellate assignments shall be made by each trial court only from its local list or to the State Appellate Defender Office except pursuant to § 3(7) of these regulations or an order of an appellate court.

"(a) Each trial bench shall review its local list and, within 56 days of an attorney's appearance on that list, shall notify the appellate assigned counsel administrator if it has actual knowledge that the attorney has, within the last three years, substantially violated the Minimum Standards for Indigent Criminal Appellate Defense Services or the Code of Professional Conduct. Each bench shall thereafter notify the administrator of such violations by attorneys on its list within 56 days of learning that a violation has occurred.

"(b) Upon receiving notice from a trial court that an attorney has substantially violated the Minimum Standards or the Code of Professional Conduct, the administrator shall promptly review the allegations and take appropriate action. Any determination that an attorney should be removed from the roster shall be made in compliance with § 4(8) of these regulations.

"**(3)** Appellate counsel shall be assigned within 14 days after a defendant submits a timely request.

"**(4)** In each circuit and Recorder's Court, the chief judge shall determine whether appellate assigned counsel are to be selected by the chief judge or by the local designating authority.

"(a) If the chief judge chooses to retain the discretion to select counsel, he or she shall personally exercise that discretion in all cases as described in § 3(5).

"(b) If the chief judge chooses to delegate the selection of counsel, the local designating authority shall, in all cases, rotate the local list as described in § 3(6).

"(5) The chief judge may exercise discretion in selecting counsel, subject to the following conditions:

"(a) Pursuant to § 2(2)(d), every third, fourth, or fifth assignment, or such other number of assignments as the Appellate Defender Commission may determine, shall be made to the State Appellate Defender Office. That office may also be assigned out of sequence pursuant to § 3(13) or 3(15).

"(b) All other assignments must be made to attorneys whose names appear on the trial court's local list.

"(i) The attorney must be eligible for assignment to the particular case, pursuant to § 4(2).

"(ii) Where a Level I attorney has received an even-numbered amount of assignments and any other Level I attorney has less than half that number, an assignment shall be offered to each of the latter attorneys before any additional assignments are offered to the former.

"(iii) Where a Level II or Level III attorney has received an even-numbered amount of assignments and any other Level II or Level III attorney has less than half that number, an assignment shall be offered to each of the eligible latter attorneys before any additional assignments are offered to the former.

"(iv) If an order of appointment is issued and the attorney selected refuses the appointment for any reason not constituting a pass for cause as defined in § 3(6)(c), the assignment shall be counted in the attorney's total.

"(6) When directed to select counsel by the chief judge, the local designating authority shall select the attorney to be assigned in the following manner:

"(a) The local designating authority shall first determine whether assignment is to be made to the State Appellate Defender Office, to a particular attorney on the local list pursuant to § 3(6)(f), 3(12), or 3(13), or by rotation of the local list.

"(i) Pursuant to § 2(2)(d), every third, fourth, or fifth assignment, or such other number of assignments as the Appellate Defender Commission may determine, shall be made to the State Appellate Defender Office. That office may also be assigned out of sequence pursuant to § 3(13) or 3(15).

"(ii) An attorney whose name appears on the local list may be selected out of sequence pursuant to § 3(6)(f), 3(12), or 3(13). That attorney's name shall then be rotated to the bottom of the list.

"(iii) All other assignments shall be made by rotating the local list.

"(b) Local lists shall be rotated in the following manner:

"(i) The local designating authority shall identify the first attorney on the list who does not have to be passed for cause and shall obtain an order appointing that attorney from the appropriate trial judge.

"(ii) The name of the attorney appointed shall be rotated to the bottom of the local list.

"(iii) The names of any attorneys passed by the local designating authority for cause shall remain in place at the top of the list and shall be considered for the next available appointment.

"(c) An attorney's name must be passed for cause in any of the following circumstances:

"(i) The attorney is not qualified at the eligibility level appropriate to the offense as described in § 4(2). A Level II or III attorney may be assigned a Level I case only if no Level I attorney is available.

"(ii) The attorney represented the defendant at trial or plea and no exception for continued representation as specified in § 3(12) is to be made.

"(iii) Representation of the defendant would create a conflict of interest for the attorney. Conflicts of interest shall be deemed to exist between codefendants whether they were jointly or separately tried. Codefendants may, however, be represented by the same attorney if they express a preference for such representation under § 3(6)(f) of these regulations, provided that there is no apparent conflict of interest.

"(d) An attorney's name may be passed for cause if the defendant has been sentenced only to probation or incarceration in the county jail, and the attorney's office is located more than 100 miles from the trial court.

"(e) If the attorney selected thereafter declines appointment for reasons which constitute a pass for cause, the attorney's name shall be reinstated at the top of the list. If the attorney selected declines the appointment for any other reason, his or her name shall remain at the point in the rotation order where it was placed when the order of appointment was issued.

"(f) When the defendant expresses a preference for counsel whose name appears on the local list, and who is eligible and willing to accept the appointment, the local designating authority shall honor it.

"(7) Where a complete review of the local list fails to produce the name of an attorney eligible and willing to accept appointment in a particular case, the local designating authority shall refer the case to the appellate assigned counsel administrator for selection of counsel to be assigned from the statewide roster.

"(8) When an attorney has declined to accept three consecutive assignments for which the attorney was eligible under these regulations, the local designating authority may request the appellate assigned counsel administrator to remove the attorney's name from the jurisdiction's local list.

"**(9)** The trial court shall maintain, on forms provided by the Appellate Assigned Counsel System, records which accurately reflect the basis on which all assignments have been made, whether by the chief judge or the local designating authority, and shall provide duplicates of those records to the Appellate Assigned Counsel System at regular intervals specified by the administrator.

"**(10)** The local designating authority shall provide copies of each order appointing appellate counsel and written evidence of each defendant's request for counsel, including any waiver executed pursuant to § 3(12).

"**(11)** All assignments other than those made to the State Appellate Defender Office shall be considered personal to the individual attorney named in the order of appointment and shall not be attributed to a partnership or firm.

"**(12)** When the defendant specifically requests the appointment of his or her trial attorney for purposes of appeal and the trial attorney is otherwise eligible and willing to accept the assignment, the defendant shall be advised by the trial judge of the potential consequences of continuous representation. If the defendant thereafter maintains a preference for appellate representation by trial counsel, the advice given and the defendant's waiver of the opportunity to receive new counsel on appeal shall appear on a form signed by the defendant. Appropriate forms shall be supplied to the trial courts by the Appellate Assigned Counsel System.

"**(13)** Where counsel represents the defendant on a currently pending appeal of another conviction, or represented the defendant on appeal of a prior conviction for the same offense, the designating authority may select that attorney out of sequence to conduct a subsequent appeal on the defendant's behalf if that attorney is otherwise eligible and willing to accept the additional appointment.

"**(14)** Where the trial judge determines that a Level I or II case is sufficiently more complex than the average case of its type to warrant appointment of an attorney classified at a higher level than required by § 4(2), the judge shall provide to the chief judge or the local designating authority a written statement of the level believed to be appropriate and the reasons for that determination. The local designating authority shall, and the chief judge in his or her discretion may, select counsel accordingly.

"**(15)** When, in exceptional circumstances, the complexity of the case or the economic hardship the appeal would cause the county makes the selection of private assigned counsel impractical, the State Appellate Defender Office may, after confirmation of that office's ability to accept the assignment, be selected for appointment out of sequence. When such an out-of-sequence assignment is made, it shall be treated as a substitute for the next in-sequence assignment the State Appellate Defender Office would have otherwise received."

Boyle, J., dissents and states as follows:

I abstain from today's action. I do so because I have reservations regarding the wisdom of the decision. More importantly, I have grave doubts regarding this use of the authority of superintending control, Const 1963, art 6, § 4.

The apparent goal of the system is to improve the quality of appellate representation of indigent defendants. To accomplish this, the Court orders compliance with a regulation which has as a central feature elimination of the role of the one person in any given trial whose sole responsibility it is to uphold the constitution and the laws of this state: the trial judge. In lieu of the appointing authority of the trial judge, the regulations substitute a right in the defendant to counsel of choice, a preference that "shall be" honored if the attorney selected is willing and eligible, § 3(7). I cannot endorse regulations that suggest we trust the trial court judiciary of this state less than we trust a convicted defendant.

We direct the trial courts to comply with this regulation, although not adopted by this Court. We do so without a studied comparison of the quality of representation currently provided and that which would be provided under such a system. Thus, we act without independent validation of the premise that perceived inadequacies are attributable to the selection of counsel by trial judges, or that the system will produce a level of performance that justifies severing the tie of political accountability between the local funding unit and locally elected judicial officers. Nor has there been any independent examination of those states that have such a system to determine the fiscal implications for local governments which will bear the cost of the system.

I am even more deeply troubled, however, by our assertion of authority in this matter. We act in a hypothetical context, without a record, hearing, or the benefit of opposing viewpoints. In doing so, we impinge upon such significant justiciable issues as, among others, the Separation of Powers Clause of our constitution, art 3, § 2, the section of our constitution that provides that "as provided by law, when the trial court so orders," appellate counsel shall be provided, art 1, § 20, a legislative directive that appointment of counsel for the indigent "shall be made by the trial court," MCL 780.712(6); MSA 28.1114(102)(6), the propriety of the delegation of judicial functions to nonjudicial personnel, as well as the lawfulness of compelling compliance with a regulation the Court has not adopted.

To the extent that today's order interdicts litigation, our action frustrates the primary purpose of this institution: the resolution of lawsuits. To the extent that today's order expresses our prejudgment on these or any other legal questions, we call into question our impartiality in resolving such issues.

The assertion of unreviewable authority stands in opposition to the most fundamental principles of a democratic government and is justified in the last analysis only by the consent of the governed. "That all lawful power derives from the people and must be held in check to preserve their freedom is the oldest and most central tenet of American constitutionalism," Tribe, American Constitutional Law (2d ed), § 1–2, p 2. Precisely because the authority of superintending control is unreviewable, the indispensable ingredient for its proper exercise is a highly refined respect for our own limits, lest we threaten public confidence and institutional integrity.

The *MAACs* regulations may be a good idea whose time has come. They ultimately may improve the quality of appellate representation for indigents. However, not even the authority of superintending control empowers us to act outside the restraints imposed by our traditional adjudicative role simply to accomplish what Cardozo called our "own ideal of beauty or of goodness."

Therefore, I abstain from today's order.

[Entered March 15, 1989.]

ADMINISTRATIVE ORDER 1989–4
USE OF FACSIMILE COMMUNICATION EQUIPMENT IN MENTAL HEALTH PROCEEDINGS

On order of the Court, the probate courts for the Counties of Calhoun, Kalamazoo and Oceana are authorized until further order of this Court, to conduct an experimental program which will utilize facsimile communication equipment to transmit petitions, physicians' certificates and other supporting documents from the Kalamazoo Regional Psychiatric Hospital for filing in the aforementioned courts. In all cases, the court will consider the documents filed when they are received by the facsimile equipment, and the court will initiate all notices so that the hearings are held within the time frames required by the Mental Health Code and Rules.

The facsimile documents shall be file-stamped when received and treated like an original, until the original documents are received by mail. If the original is not received within five days, the facsimile documents shall be copied on ordinary paper.

When the original documents are received by mail, the court shall file-stamp the originals with the date they were received and place them in the court file. A statement shall also be placed in the file, itemizing the documents received by facsimile, and indicating the date received. After comparing the facsimile documents with the original documents, the facsimile documents and any copies thereof shall be discarded.

The State Court Administrative Office shall provide assistance in the implementation of the pilot project and shall conduct an evaluation of the experimental program after the individual courts submit a report on the pilot project within 15 days after June 30, 1990. The pilot courts shall cooperate with the State Court Administrative Office.

This order shall be effective upon entry.

[Entered November 22, 1989.]

ADMINISTRATIVE ORDER 1990–2
INTEREST ON LAWYER TRUST ACCOUNTS

On order of the Court, Administrative Order No. 1987–3 is VACATED and this order replaces it. The provisions of this order are adopted February 21, 1990, to be effective immediately.

1. Lawyer Trust Account Program. The Board of Trustees of the Michigan State Bar Foundation has been designated and has agreed to organize and administer the Lawyer Trust Account Program.

2. Powers and Duties.

(A) The Board shall have general supervisory authority over the administration of the Lawyer Trust Account Program.

(B) The Board shall receive funds from lawyers' interest-bearing trust accounts established in accordance with MRPC 1.15 of the Code [Rules] of Professional Conduct and shall make appropriate temporary investments of such funds pending disbursement of them.

(C) The Board shall, by grants and appropriations it deems appropriate, disburse funds as follows:

[*Publisher's Note: See, now, Administrative Order 1997–9.*]

(D) The Board shall maintain proper books and records of all Program receipts and disbursements and shall have them audited annually by a certified public accountant. The Board shall annually within 90 days after the close of its fiscal year cause to be presented an audited financial statement of its Program receipts and expenditures for the year. The statement shall be filed with the clerk of this Court and shall be published in the next available issue of the Michigan Bar Journal.

(E) The Board shall monitor the operation of the Lawyer Trust Account Program, propose to this Court changes in this order or in MRPC 1.15, and may, subject to approval by this Court, adopt and publish such instructions or guidelines not inconsistent with this order which it deems necessary to administer the Lawyer Trust Account Program.

3. Executive Director.

(A) The Board may appoint an executive director of the Lawyer Trust Account Program to serve on a full- or part-time basis at the pleasure of the Board. The executive director shall be paid such compensation as is fixed by the Board.

(B) The executive director shall be responsible and accountable to the Board for the proper administration of this Program.

(C) The executive director may employ persons or contract for services as the Board may approve.

4. Compensation and Expenses of the Board.

(A) The President and other members of the Board shall administer the Lawyer Trust Account Program without compensation, but shall be paid their reasonable and necessary expenses incurred in the performance of their duties.

(B) All expenses of the operation of the Lawyer Trust Account Program shall be paid from funds which the Board receives from the Program.

(C) The Board may borrow from the State Bar of Michigan or a commercial lender monies needed to finance the operation of the Lawyer Trust Account Program from the time it is constituted until the Program becomes operational. Any sum so borrowed shall be repaid, together with interest at prevailing market rates, as promptly as the initial receipts from the Program permit.

5. Disposition of Funds Upon Dissolution. If the Program or its administration by the Michigan State Bar Foundation is discontinued, any Program funds then on hand shall be transferred in accordance with the order of this Court terminating the Program or its administration by the Michigan State Bar Foundation.

[Entered February 21, 1990.]

ADMINISTRATIVE ORDER 1990–3
IN RE RECOMMENDATIONS OF THE
TASK FORCE ON GENDER ISSUES IN
THE COURTS AND THE TASK FORCE ON
RACIAL/ETHNIC ISSUES IN THE COURTS

In September, 1987, the Michigan Supreme Court appointed two nineteen-member task forces to examine the court system and to recommend changes to assure equal treatment for men and women, free from race or gender bias. The task forces were the Task Force on Racial/Ethnic Issues in the Courts and the Task Force on Gender Issues in the Courts.

The task forces submitted their final reports to this Court in December, 1989. They made a total of 167 recommendations for eliminating bias in the court-

room and among court personnel, in professional organizations, and in legal education. Many of these proposals can be implemented fairly quickly. Others will require long-range planning. All merit serious consideration.

This Court is in the process of reviewing all of the recommendations in order to determine the appropriate steps to be taken. We are persuaded upon preliminary examination that several of the proposals ought to be acted upon immediately. Therefore, we direct:

That judges, employees of the judicial system, attorneys and other court officers commit themselves to the elimination of racial, ethnic and gender discrimination in the Michigan judicial system;

That the State Bar of Michigan review the process for this Court's appointment of members of the Board of Commissioners of the State Bar and recommend to this Court whether the process should be changed in order to assure full participation by women and minority lawyers;

That the State Bar of Michigan make recommendations to this Court with regard to the proposals by the task forces that the Rules of Professional Conduct and the Code of Judicial Conduct be amended to specifically prohibit sexual harassment and invidious discrimination;

That members of the State Bar of Michigan support the Michigan Minority Demonstration Project and the American Bar Association Minority Demonstration Project; and

That the Michigan Judicial Institute continue its efforts to eliminate gender and racial/ethnic bias in the court environment through the education of judges, court administrators and others.

This Court is committed to assuring the fair and equal application of the rule of law for all persons in the Michigan court system. To that end, we support the principles that underlie the 167 recommendations that have been made. We are indebted to the thirty-eight men and women who gave of their time and talents to serve on the two task forces, and commend them for their dedication.

[Entered June 12, 1990.]

ADMINISTRATIVE ORDER 1990–4
PILOT PROJECT FOR DISTRICT COURT
JUDGES ACCEPTING GUILTY PLEAS
IN FELONY CASES

On order of the Court, effective July 1, 1990, for a period of one year or until further order of the Court,* the judges of the 61st District Court are assigned as circuit judges in the 17th Circuit for an experimental pilot project for the purpose of taking guilty pleas in criminal cases cognizable in the circuit court.

If the defendant, the defense attorney, and the prosecutor consent on the record, these pleas may be taken after bind over following the conclusion or waiver of the preliminary examination. Following the plea, cases will be transferred to the 17th Circuit Court for sentencing.

The State Court Administrative Office shall conduct an assessment of the experimental project and report to the Court. The 61st District Court and the 17th Circuit Court shall cooperate with the State Court Administrative Office.

[Entered June 27, 1990.]

* Publisher's Note: See Administrative Order 1991–5, entered June 25, 1991.

ADMINISTRATIVE ORDER 1990–7
VIDEOTAPE RECORD OF
COURT PROCEEDINGS

On order of the Court, the State Court Administrator is authorized to approve, until further order of this Court, trial courts to use videotape record systems for the purpose of making the verbatim court record of proceedings in individual courtrooms. Courts desiring approval to use the videotape record system in a courtroom must apply to the State Court Administrator and must submit a local administrative order to implement the videotape record procedures. Upon approval by the State Court Administrator of the application and the local administrative order, the court may use the videotape record system in the courtroom until further order of this Court or of the State Court Administrator.

The State Court Administrator is authorized to certify which videotape record equipment may be utilized by trial courts for the purposes of making the verbatim court record.

The applications by the trial courts and approval by the State Court Administrator shall be based upon criteria established by this Court.

The previous authorizations by this Court and by the State Court Administrator pursuant to Administrative Order 1989–2 to the twelve pilot courtrooms for utilization of the videotape record systems is continued until further order of this Court or the State Court Administrator.

This order authorizes exceptions to the Michigan Code of Judicial Conduct, Canon 3(A)(7), which currently prohibits such recording, and to MCR 8.108, which requires that certified court reporters and recorders furnishing transcripts of proceedings be in attendance at those proceedings.

The following guidelines shall apply to the courts authorized to use videotape record systems for the purpose of making the court record:

1. At least two videotape recordings, recorded simultaneously, shall constitute part of the original record in the case. One videotape shall be retained by the clerk of the court to be forwarded, or for portions to be copied and forwarded, if an appeal is taken and if requested by the Court of Appeals, to the Court of Appeals pursuant to MCR 7.210. The other videotape shall be stored off the court premises in a location to be designated by the chief judge.

2. The judge shall:

(a) Be charged with the responsibility of ensuring, through routine checks of the videotape system by a suitably trained person, that the videotape system is operating in keeping with specifications.

(b) Keep a proper index of proceedings that have been videotaped, including a list of witnesses and exhibits.

3. If an appeal is taken in an action which has been videotaped under this order, a transcript of the proceedings must be prepared in the same manner as in the case of proceedings recorded in other ways. However, a court reporter or recorder need not certify attendance at the proceedings being transcribed from the videotaped record, but need only certify that the transcript represents the complete, true and correct rendition of the videotape of the proceeding as recorded.

4. Transcripts of videotape recordings of 25 pages or less must contain, on each page, a reference to the number of the videotape and the month, day, year, hour, and minute at which the reference begins as recorded on the videotape. For example: (Tape No. 1, 10–1–87, 13:12). Transcripts of 26 or more pages must contain this reference on the first page, on every 25 pages thereafter, and on the last page.

5. Film or electronic media coverage in these courts, if utilized, shall be governed by the guidelines set out in Administrative Order 1989–1.

6. The State Court Administrative Office shall provide assistance in implementation of the use of videotape record system in each approved courtroom and shall continue to conduct an evaluation of the program. The courts using videotape record systems shall cooperate with the State Court Administrative Office.

7. This order shall be effective upon entry. Administrative Order 1989–2 is rescinded.

[Entered October 15, 1990.]

ADMINISTRATIVE ORDER 1990–8
USE OF FACSIMILE COMMUNICATION
EQUIPMENT IN MENTAL HEALTH
PROCEEDINGS

Until further order of the court, the probate courts in the Kalamazoo Regional Psychiatric Hospital catchment area are authorized to utilize facsimile communication equipment to transmit petitions, physician's certificates and other supporting documents from the Kalamazoo Regional Psychiatric Hospital for filing in the courts.

Participation by the probate courts listed below shall be subject to the discretion of the Chief Judge of the probate court and with the approval of the State Court Administrator.

The probate courts in the Kalamazoo Regional Psychiatric Hospital catchment area are located in the following counties: Allegan, Barry, Benzie, Berrien, Calhoun, Cass, Gratiot, Ionia, Kalamazoo, Kent, Lake, Manistee, Mason, Mecosta, Montcalm, Muskegon, Newaygo, Oceana, Osceola, Ottawa, St. Joseph, and Van Buren.

In all cases, the court will consider the documents filed when they are received by the facsimile equipment, and the court will initiate all notices so that the hearings are held within the time frames required by the Mental Health Code and Rules.

The facsimile documents shall be file-stamped when received and treated like an original, until the original documents are received by mail. If the original is not received within five days, the facsimile documents shall be copied on ordinary paper.

When the original documents are received by mail, the court shall file-stamp the originals with the date they were received and place them in the court file. A statement shall also be placed in the file, itemizing the documents received by facsimile and indicating the date received. After comparing the facsimile documents with the original documents, the facsimile documents and any copies thereof shall be discarded.

The State Court Administrative Office shall assist in the implementation of the use of facsimile equipment in mental health proceedings for those courts electing to participate.

The State Court Administrative Office shall review the pilot projects after the participating courts submit a report within 15 days after November 1, 1991.

[Entered October 22, 1990.]

ADMINISTRATIVE ORDER 1990-9
VOICE AND FACSIMILE COMMUNICATION EQUIPMENT FOR THE TRANSMISSION AND FILING OF COURT DOCUMENTS

On order of the Court, the State Court Administrative Office may authorize pilot courts to use on an experimental basis, voice and facsimile communication equipment for the transmission and filing of court documents.

The State Court Administrator shall select a sufficient number of courts of diverse case volume, so as to be able to evaluate the feasibility of facsimile transmission and filing of documents, the feasibility of the

proposed rules, and whether or not other issues and questions require further clarification by rule or statute or whether further study and experiments are needed.

The State Court Administrative Office shall provide assistance in the implementation of the pilot project, and shall conduct an assessment of the experimental program and report to the Court. The pilot courts shall cooperate with the State Court Administrative Office.

The following experimental court rules shall govern the pilot courts:

EXPERIMENTAL RULE: Use of Communication Equipment

(A) Definition. "Voice communication equipment" means a conference telephone or other electronic device that permits all those appearing or participating to hear and speak to each other.

(B) Use. A court may, on its own initiative or on the written request of a party, direct that voice communication equipment be used for a motion hearing, pretrial conference, or status conference. The court must give notice to the parties before directing on its own initiative that voice communication equipment be used. A party's written request must be made at least 7 days before the day on which the communication equipment is sought to be used, and a copy must be served on the other parties. The court may, with the consent of all parties, direct that the testimony of a witness be taken through voice communication equipment. A verbatim record of the proceedings must still be made.

(C) Burden of Expense. The cost for the use of the voice communication equipment is to be shared equally, unless the court otherwise directs.

(D) Facsimile Communication Equipment. Courts, by local court rules established pursuant to MCR 8.112(A), may permit the filing of 8½″ × 11″ pleading, motions, affidavits, opinions, orders, or other documents by the use of facsimile (FAX) communication equipment. Except as provided in MCR 2.002, a clerk shall not permit the filing of any document for which a filing fee is required unless the full amount of the filing fee has been paid or deposited in advance with the clerk. Documents intended to be filed in any court shall be on paper not subject to more rapid deterioration than ordinary typewritten material on ordinary paper.

(E) The local court rule established pursuant to MCR 8.112(A) shall establish for facsimile filing of documents with the court by the public:

(1) a reasonable fee, in addition to statutory filing fees, to be charged by the clerk, which may take into account the cost of equipment, paper, supplies and telephone line charges;

(2) a maximum number of pages which may be sent at one time for any document or documents;

(3) the hours during which documents may be received;

(4) other reasonable requirements to promote the efficient filing of facsimile documents; and

(5) the method of giving notice to attorneys and litigants of any facsimile filing requirements.

(F) Oath. A judge or magistrate may administer an oath to a witness or affiant by voice communication equipment.

(G) Signature. For purposes of MCR 2.114, a signature includes a signature transmitted by facsimile communication equipment.

(H) Warrants. Facsimile communication equipment and voice communication equipment may be used as provided for in 1990 PA 41, 43, 44 and 45.

[Entered October 22, 1990.]

ADMINISTRATIVE ORDER 1991–1
USE OF FACSIMILE COMMUNICATION EQUIPMENT IN MENTAL HEALTH PROCEEDINGS

Until further order of the court, all Michigan probate courts are authorized to utilize facsimile communication equipment to transmit petitions, physician's certificates and other supporting documents from the state regional psychiatric hospitals for filing in the courts.

Participation by Michigan probate courts shall be subject to the discretion of the Chief Judge of the probate court and with the approval of the State Court Administrator.

In all cases, the probate court will consider the documents filed when they are received by the facsimile equipment, and the probate court will initiate all notices so that the hearings are held within the time frames required by the Mental Health Code and Court Rules.

The facsimile documents shall be file-stamped when received and treated like originals, until the original documents are received by mail. If the originals are not received within five days, the facsimile documents shall be copied on ordinary paper.

When the original documents are received by mail, the probate court shall file-stamp the originals with the date they are received and place them in the court file. A statement shall also be placed in the file itemizing the documents received by facsimile and indicating the date received. After comparing the facsimile documents with the original documents, the facsimile documents and any copies thereof shall be discarded.

The State Court Administrative Office shall assist in the implementation of the use of facsimile equipment in mental health proceedings for those courts electing to participate.

The State Court Administrative Office shall review the pilot project after the participating courts submit a report within 15 days after January 1, 1992.

[Entered April 10, 1991.]

ADMINISTRATIVE ORDER 1991–4
CASEFLOW MANAGEMENT

The Court, having considered the reports of the Caseflow Management Coordinating Committee and the Caseflow Management Rules Committee, has determined that the management of the flow of cases is properly the responsibility of the judiciary. The judiciary has a responsibility to balance the rights and interests of individual litigants; the limited resources of the judicial branch and other participants in the adjudication process; and the interests of the citizens of this state in having an effective, fair and efficient system of justice.

The Court has further determined that establishing goals for case processing can serve as an important component of a program to ensure the efficient administration of the state's trial court caseload. However, meeting guidelines for case processing, such as those proposed by the Caseflow Management Coordinating Committee is contingent upon an appropriate level of managerial and financial resources at both the local and state level, and reassessment of such goals in light of changes in the environment in which courts operate and changes in rules and statutes.

Accordingly, ON ORDER OF THE COURT, effective immediately until further order of the Court,

A. The State Court Administrator is directed, within available resources, to:

1. Assist trial courts in the implementation of caseflow management plans, including provisions for local bench-bar justice system advisory committees;

2. Establish goals for case processing adapted as necessary to reflect changes in statutes, rules and the litigation environment;

3. Assist trial courts in the implementation of the caseflow management goals established under paragraph A.2., above;

4. Develop case-age tracking and caseflow monitoring systems to serve as performance measurement devices for the benefit of individual trial courts and the Supreme Court; and

5. Make an assessment of the effect of caseflow management plans, time guidelines for case processing and the development of tracking and monitoring systems and provide the Court with a report within two years.

B. All trial courts of this state are directed to:

1. Develop and implement caseflow management plans, which include case processing goals as established under Section A.2. above, and provide for local bench-bar justice system advisory committees, in cooperation with the State Court Administrative Office;

2. Report to the State Court Administrative Office caseflow management statistics and other caseflow management data required by that office; and

3. Cooperate with the State Court Administrative Office in the assessment of the caseflow management goals and plans implemented pursuant to this Administrative Order.

The time guidelines for case processing appended to this order, adapted from those recommended by the Caseflow Management Coordinating Committee, shall be the model used by the State Court Administrative Office and the trial courts in developing caseflow management plans and goals pursuant to this order. Time guidelines adopted as part of a caseflow management plan shall not be the basis for procedural or substantive rulings in individual cases.

TIME GUIDELINES FOR CASE PROCESSING

A. Probate Court Guidelines.

1. *Delinquency and Neglect Proceedings.*

a. In–Custody. Where a minor is being detained or is held in court custody, 90% of all petitions or complaints should have adjudication and disposition completed within 84 days from the authorization of the petition, and 100% within 98 days.

b. Non-custody. Where a minor is not being detained or held in court custody, 75% of all petitions or complaints should have adjudication and disposition completed within 119 days from authorization of the petition, 90% within 6 months and 100% within 7 months.

2. *Probate Proceedings.* 75% of all contested probate matters should be resolved within 6 months from the time the issue is joined, 90% within 9 months and 100% within 12 months except for individual cases in which the court determines exceptional circumstances exist and for which a continuing review should occur.

B. District Court Guidelines.

1. *Civil Proceedings.*

a. General Civil. 90% of all civil cases should be settled, tried or otherwise concluded within 6 months from the date of case filing, 98% within 9 months and 100% within 12 months except for individual cases in which the court determines exceptional circumstances exist and/or for which a continuing review should occur.

b. Summary Civil. Proceedings using summary hearing procedures, as in small claims, landlord/tenant and claim and delivery actions should be settled, tried or otherwise concluded within 35 days from the date of service. In those cases where a jury is demanded, actions should be concluded within 63 days from the date of service.

2. *Criminal and Traffic Proceedings.*

a. Misdemeanor. 90% of all misdemeanors, civil infractions, and other non-felony cases should be adjudicated or otherwise concluded within 63 days from the date of the first appearance, 98% within 91 days and 100% within 126 days.

b. Felonies. 100% of preliminary examinations to be concluded within 12 days of arraignment unless good cause is shown.

NOTE: When a case is removed from circuit to district court, the district court Time Guidelines should apply and the time should commence when the case is received by the district court.

C. Circuit and Recorder's Court Guidelines.

1. *Civil Proceedings.* 75% of all civil cases should be settled, tried or otherwise concluded within 12 months from the date of case filing, 95% within 18 months and 100% within 24 months except for individual cases in which the court determines exceptional circumstances exist and for which a continuing review should occur.

2. *Domestic Relations Proceedings.*

a. Divorce Without Children. 90% of all divorce cases without children should be settled, tried or otherwise concluded within 91 days from the date of case filing, 98% within 9 months and 100% within 12 months.

b. Divorce With Children. 90% of all divorce cases with children should be settled, tried or otherwise concluded within 8 months of the date of case filing, 98% within 10 months and 100% within 12 months.

c. Paternity. 90% of all paternity cases should be settled, tried or otherwise concluded within 3 months of the date of service of process, 98% within 6 months and 100% within 12 months.

d. Initiating Uniform Reciprocal Enforcement of Support Act (URESA). 100% of all URESA orders should be forwarded to the court of the responding state having reciprocal legislation within 24 hours of the filing of the Certificate of Support.

e. Child Support/Responding Uniform Reciprocal Enforcement of Support Act (URESA). 90% of all child support/responding URESA cases should be adjudicated or otherwise concluded within 91 days from the date of case filing or receipt of order from initiating state, 98% within 6 months and 100% within 12 months.

f. Child Custody Issues. 100% of all child custody issues should be adjudicated or otherwise concluded within 91 days from notice of request for custody hearing.

3. *Criminal Proceedings.* 90% of all felony cases should be adjudicated or otherwise concluded within 91 days from the date of entry of order binding the defendant over to circuit court, 98% within 154 days and 100% within 10 months. Incarcerated persons should be afforded priority for trial.

4. *Appeals to Circuit Court.*

a. Appeals From Courts of Limited Jurisdiction. 100% of all appeals to the circuit court from courts of limited jurisdiction should be settled or otherwise concluded within 154 days from the filing of the Claim of Appeals.

b. Appeals From Administrative Agencies. 100% of all appeals to the circuit court from administrative agencies should be settled or otherwise concluded within 154 days from the filing of the Claim of Appeals.

c. Extraordinary Writs. 98% of all extraordinary writ requests should be adjudicated within 35 days from the date of filing, and 100% within 91 days.

5. *Matters Submitted to the Judge.* Matters under submission to a judge or judicial officer should be promptly determined. Short deadlines should be set for presentation of briefs and affidavits and for production of transcripts. Decisions, when possible, should be made from the bench or within a few days of submission; except in extraordinarily complicated cases, a decision should be rendered no later than 35 days after submission.

NOTE: In the Time Guidelines for criminal cases, the phrase "adjudicated or otherwise concluded" refers to the date of conviction or acquittal for the purpose of measuring the age of the cases. These Guidelines contemplate that an incarcerated defendant will be sentenced within 2 weeks and a non-incarcerated defendant will be sentenced within 4 weeks of a finding of guilt.

[Entered June 11, 1991.]

ADMINISTRATIVE ORDER 1991–5
PILOT PROJECTS FOR DISTRICT
COURT JUDGES ACCEPTING GUILTY
PLEAS IN FELONY CASES

On order of the Court, effective July 1, 1991 and until July 1, 1992, or until further order of the Court,* the State Court Administrator is authorized to approve the assignment of judges of the district court as judges in the court with trial jurisdiction over felony cases for experimental projects for the purpose of taking guilty pleas in criminal cases cognizable in the court with trial jurisdiction over felony cases.

If the defendant, the defense attorney, and the prosecutor consent on the record, these pleas may be taken after bind over following the conclusion or waiver of the preliminary examination. Following the pleas, the cases will be transferred to the court with trial jurisdiction over felony cases.

The previous authorization by this Court and the State Court Administrator pursuant to Administrative Order 1990–4 for a pilot project for the judges of the 61st District Court to be assigned as Circuit Judges in the 17th Circuit Court (Kent County) to take guilty pleas in criminal cases cognizable in the circuit court is continued until further order of this Court or the State Court Administrator.

Each court requesting an authorization is directed to expeditiously submit a Local Administrative Order to the State Court Administrator pursuant to MCR 8.112(B) to implement the pilot program.

The State Court Administrative Office shall conduct an assessment of the experimental programs and report to the Court.

[Entered June 25, 1991.]

* Publisher's Note: See Administrative Order 1992–5, entered June 30, 1992.

ADMINISTRATIVE ORDER 1991–7
ELECTION PROCEDURES FOR
JUDICIAL MEMBERS OF THE
JUDICIAL TENURE COMMISSION

Administrative Order 1980–3 is hereby RESCINDED, and the following procedure is established for the election of judicial members of the Judicial Tenure Commission.

Each year in which the term of a commissioner selected by the judges of the courts of this state expires, the state court administrator shall send a notice to all judges eligible to vote for the commissioner position to be filled that they may nominate judges to fill the position. The notice, with a nominating petition, shall be mailed before July 17, with the instruction that, to be valid, nominating petitions must be filed at the office of the administrator in Lansing before September 1.

For a judge to be nominated petitions must be signed by at least ten judges eligible to vote for the nominee, except that a judge of the Court of Appeals may be nominated by petitions signed by five judges of that court. The administrator shall determine the validity of each nomination.

Before September 20, the administrator shall mail a ballot to every judge eligible to vote. A ballot will not be counted unless marked and returned in a sealed envelope addressed to the office of the administrator in Lansing with a postmark of not later than October 20.

In the event there is only one nominee, a ballot will not be mailed, and the nominee will be declared elected. The state court administrator will certify the declared election to the Chief Justice of the Supreme Court, Supreme Court Clerk and Executive Director of the Judicial Tenure Commission before December 15.

The administrator or designee, and three tellers appointed by the administrator, shall canvass the ballots and certify the count to the Supreme Court Clerk before November 1. The nominee receiving the highest number of votes will be declared elected. If there is a tie vote, the administrator shall mail a second ballot, consisting of those nominees receiving the highest count, by November 1. The second ballot must be marked and returned in a sealed envelope addressed to the office of the administrator in Lansing with a postmark of not later than November 30. The four tellers shall canvass these second ballots and, if a tie vote still results, they shall determine the successful nominee by lot. They shall certify the count or the result of the selection by lot to the Supreme Court Clerk before December 15.

If a vacancy occurs or is impending, the Judicial Tenure Commission shall notify the administrator promptly. The procedure set forth above shall be followed, except that time limits may be shortened to insure that the election occurs within 90 days, and the dates set forth above shall not be applicable.

[Entered July 29, 1991.]

ADMINISTRATIVE ORDER 1991–8
STATE JUDICIAL COUNCIL

Administrative Order 1982–2 is hereby RESCINDED, and the following procedure is established for the election of members of the State Judicial Council.

A. The State Court Administrator shall send a notice to all judges regarding the statutorily required composition of the State Judicial Council and informing them that:

1. Two of the four nominees by the circuit/recorder's bench must be judges of the recorder's court or of the circuit court in judicial circuits in which the employees who serve in the court or circuit are employees of the State Judicial Council.

2. Two of the four nominees by the district court judges must be judges of the district court in judicial districts in which the employees who serve in the district are employees of the State Judicial Council.

3. No more than one of the appointees nominated by the circuit/recorder's judges, no more than one of the appointees nominated by the district judges, and no more than one of the appointees nominated by the probate judges may be a judge elected or appointed within a county having a population of more than 2,000,000.

4. Judges may seek election to the list of nominees (four for each court type) from which the Chief Justice will appoint the judicial members (two for each court type) of the State Judicial Council.

B. The notice, with a nominating petition, shall be mailed before June 4, with the instruction that, to be valid, nominating petitions must be received at the office of the State Court Administrator in Lansing before June 29 and must meet the following criteria:

1. Petitions for any nominee must be signed by at least five judges eligible to vote for the nominee;

2. Each petition filed must indicate:

a. whether the judge seeking nomination serves on the circuit or recorder's court, the district court, or the probate court, and

b. whether the judge seeking nomination is a judge or a court in which the employees are State Judicial Council employees.

The State Court Administrator shall determine the validity of each nomination.

C. Before July 20, the State Court Administrator shall mail a ballot to every judge eligible to vote. Each ballot mailed to judges of the circuit, recorder's, or district court shall have two classifications: State-Financed and General. Each ballot mailed to judges of the probate court shall have no classifications. Each judge may vote for no more than two names on the ballot.

A ballot will not be counted unless marked and returned in a sealed envelope addressed to the office of the State Court Administrator in Lansing and received in that office no later than August 17.

D. In the event there is only one nominee, a ballot will not be mailed, and the Chief Justice shall appoint the nominee to the respective four-year term.

E. The State Court Administrator and three tellers appointed by the State Court Administrator shall canvass the ballots and certify the count to the Supreme Court Clerk before August 31. The two judges in each classification (State-Financed and General) for circuit/recorder's receiving the highest and second-highest number of votes will be placed on the list of nominees to be submitted to the Chief Justice. The two judges in each classification (State-Financed and General) for district receiving the highest and second-highest number of votes will be placed on the list of nominees to be submitted to the Chief Justice. The two probate judges receiving the highest and second-highest number of votes will be placed on the list of nominees to be submitted to the Chief Justice. If there is a tie vote, the tellers shall determine the successful candidate by lot.

F. Before September 30, the Chief Justice shall appoint one judge from each list of nominees to the State Judicial Council for a term of four years.

G. The procedure set forth above shall be followed each year in which the term of a judicial member of the State Judicial Council expires. The notice shall be sent by the State Court Administrator to all judges eligible to vote for the position, shall indicate that they may nominate a judge to fill the position, and shall indicate whether the position to be filled is in the classification of "State–Financed" or "General."

H. If a vacancy occurs, the Chief Justice may appoint from the previous list of nominees or may order that the procedure set forth above shall be followed. If this procedure is followed, the time limits may be shortened to insure that the election of nominees occurs within 60 days, and the dates set forth above shall not be applicable.

[Entered July 29, 1991.]

ADMINISTRATIVE ORDER 1991–9
[AS AMENDED BY ADMINISTRATIVE ORDER 1992–6] TEMPORARY JUDGES ON COURT OF APPEALS PANELS *

For the purpose of addressing the serious problem of the volume of cases presently awaiting disposition in the Court of Appeals, IT IS HEREBY ORDERED that the provision of MCR 7.201(D) which requires that only one temporary judge may sit on a three-judge panel is suspended. This suspension is for the limited purpose of permitting the assignment of panels of former judges of the Court of Appeals and former justices of the Supreme Court. In all other respects the aforementioned provision of MCR 7.201(D) shall remain in effect. The suspension of MCR 7.201(D) for the limited purpose which is provided for in this order shall be effective until September 30, 1993.**

[Entered August 14, 1991; amended September 29, 1992.]

* Suggested title added by Publisher.

** Administrative Order 1993–6, entered September 29, 1993, ordered that "the terms and conditions of Administrative Order 1992–6 are continued in effect until September 30, 1994 or until the further order of this Court." Administrative Order 1994–7, entered September 16, 1994, ordered the terms and conditions "continued in effect until January 15, 1995." Administrative Order 1995–1, entered January 31, 1995, ordered the terms and conditions "continued in effect until October 1, 1995." Administrative Order 1995–4, entered August 18, 1995, ordered the terms and conditions "continued in effect until December 31, 1995." Administrative Order 1995–6, entered November 3, 1995, ordered the terms and conditions "extended until March 31, 1996." Administrative Order 1996–3, entered March 22, 1996, ordered the terms and conditions "extended until September 30, 1996." Administrative Order 1996–10, entered August 22, 1996, ordered the terms and conditions "extended until March 31, 1997."

ADMINISTRATIVE ORDER 1992–2
COURT OF APPEALS
DOCKETING STATEMENT

On order of the Court, the Court of Appeals is authorized to require appellants in that Court to file a docketing statement in appeals of right. The Court of Appeals will supply the docketing statement form after the appeal has been filed. This requirement will govern appeals of right filed after April 1, 1992.

[Entered January 22, 1992.]

ADMINISTRATIVE ORDER 1992–3
USE OF FACSIMILE EQUIPMENT IN
MENTAL HEALTH PROCEEDINGS

Until further order of the Court, all Michigan probate courts are authorized to utilize facsimile communication equipment to transmit petitions, physician's certificates and other supporting documents from the state regional psychiatric hospitals or private hospitals for filing in the courts.

Participation by Michigan probate courts shall be subject to the discretion of the Chief Judge of the probate court and with the approval of the State Court Administrator.

In all cases, the probate court will consider the documents filed when they are received by the facsimile equipment, and the probate court will initiate all notices so that the hearings are held within the time frames required by the Mental Health Code and Court Rules.

The facsimile documents shall be file-stamped when received and treated like an original, until the original documents are received by mail. If the original is not received within five days, the facsimile documents shall be copied on ordinary paper.

When the original documents are received by mail, the probate court shall file-stamp the originals with the date they are received and place them in the court file. A statement shall also be placed in the file, itemizing the documents received by facsimile and indicating the date received. After comparing the facsimile documents with the original documents, the facsimile documents and any copies thereof shall be discarded.

The State Court Administrative Office shall assist in the implementation of the use of facsimile equipment in mental health proceedings for those courts electing to participate.

[Entered April 3, 1992.]

ADMINISTRATIVE ORDER 1992–5
DISTRICT COURT JUDGES ACCEPTING
PLEAS IN FELONY CASES

On order of the Court, the State Court Administrator is authorized to approve, until further order of this Court, the assignment of judges of the district court as judges in the court with trial jurisdiction over felony cases for the purpose of taking not guilty and guilty pleas in criminal cases cognizable in the court with trial court jurisdiction over felony cases. Courts desiring approval to accept felony pleas must submit a local administrative order signed by the chief judges of the circuit and district courts. Upon approval by the State Court Administrator of the local administrative order and assignment of judges, the court may accept not guilty and guilty pleas in cases cognizable in the circuit court until further order of this Court or of the State Court Administrator.

If the defendant, the defense attorney, and the prosecutor consent on the record, these pleas may be taken after bind over following the conclusion or waiver of the preliminary examination. Following the pleas, the cases will be transferred to the court with trial court jurisdiction over felony cases.

The previous authorization by this Court and the State Court Administrator pursuant to Administrative Order 1991–5 to the eleven pilot courts to take guilty pleas in criminal cases cognizable in the circuit court is continued until further order of this Court or the State Court Administrator.

[Entered June 30, 1992.]

ADMINISTRATIVE ORDER 1992–6
TEMPORARY JUDGES ON COURT
OF APPEALS PANELS*

[*Publisher's Note: See Administrative Order 1991–9.*]

* Suggested title added by Publisher.

ADMINISTRATIVE ORDER 1993–2
SILICONE GEL IMPLANT PRODUCT
LIABILITY LITIGATION

On order of the Court, it appearing that a large number of actions have been filed alleging personal injuries due to silicone gel implant devices, and that coordination of pretrial proceedings in those cases will promote the economical and expeditious resolution of that litigation, pursuant to Const 1963, art 6, § 4, we direct all state courts to follow the procedures set forth in this administrative order.

1. This order applies to all pending and future personal injury silicone gel implant product liability actions pending or to be filed in Michigan courts other than the Third Judicial Circuit. For the purposes of this order, "silicone gel implant product liability actions" include all cases in which it is alleged that a party has suffered personal injury or economic loss caused by any silicone gel implant, regardless of the theory of recovery. Until the transfer of the action under paragraph 2 of this order, the parties to such an action shall include the words "Implant Case" on the top right-hand corner of the first page of any papers subsequently filed in this action.

2. Each court in which a silicone gel implant product liability action is pending shall enter an order changing venue of the action to the Third Judicial Circuit within 14 days of the date of this order. Upon

the filing of a new silicone gel implant product liability action, the court shall enter an order changing venue to the Third Judicial Circuit within 14 days after the action is filed. The court shall send a copy of the order to the State Court Administrator. A party who objects to the transfer of an action under this paragraph may raise the objection by filing a motion in the Third Judicial Circuit. Such a motion must be filed within 14 days after the transfer of the action. Nothing in this order shall be construed as a finding that venue is proper in Wayne County.

3. Proceedings in each action transferred under this order shall be conducted in accordance with the Initial Case Management Order entered in Third Circuit Civil Action Number 93–302061 MP on February 8, 1993, and such further orders as may be entered by the Third Judicial Circuit. The Third Judicial Circuit shall cooperate with the State Court Administrator in monitoring the proceedings in the actions. Orders entered by the court in which the action was originally filed that are inconsistent with orders entered by the Third Judicial Circuit are superseded.

4. After the close of discovery, the Third Judicial Circuit shall conduct a settlement conference or conferences. If settlement is not reached as to all claims, the Third Judicial Circuit shall enter an order changing venue to the court in which the action was originally filed, or if appropriate to some other court, for further proceedings. A copy of the order shall be sent to the State Court Administrator.

5. Depositions taken in *In Re: Silicone Gel Breast Implants Products Liability Litigation* (MDL–926), Master File No. CV 92–P–10000–S (N.D.Ala) [hereinafter MDL], may be used in any actions governed by Third Judicial Circuit case management orders as provided in this paragraph notwithstanding that they were not taken in these actions. Such depositions may be used against a party in a Michigan state court action who is not also a party in an MDL proceeding only if the party proposing to use the MDL deposition gives written notice of that intention. The notice shall specifically designate the portions of the MDL deposition to be used and the noticing party must provide a transcript of the testimony being offered and a copy of the videotape of the deposition, if any, to the party against whom the deposition is proposed to be offered. That party may file a motion for further examination of the MDL witness, specifying the subjects as to which further examination is sought. If the motion is granted, the further deposition of the MDL witness may cover only those subjects designated in the order. The judge of the Third Judicial Circuit shall specify the times within which notices and motions under this paragraph may be filed.

6. If discovery proceedings have been conducted in an action prior to a transfer under this order, those discovery materials remain part of the record in the action in which they were produced, and may be used in further proceedings where otherwise appropriate

notwithstanding the transfer under this rule. The materials are not part of the record in other cases governed by Third Judicial Circuit case management orders.

7. MCR 2.222, MCR 2.223, and MCR 2.224 do not apply to changes of venue pursuant to this order.

[Entered March 31, 1993.]

ADMINISTRATIVE ORDER 1993–3
PILOT PROJECT TO IMPLEMENT THE RECOMMENDATIONS OF THE COMMISSION ON COURTS IN THE 21ST CENTURY

On order of the Court, effective immediately, the following jurisdictions are authorized to participate in experimental pilot projects to implement concepts of the Commission on the Courts in the 21st Century issued in its final report, entitled *Michigan's Courts in the 21st Century.*

BERRIEN COUNTY
Second Circuit Court
Fifth District Court
Berrien County Probate Court

CALHOUN COUNTY
Thirty–Seventh Circuit Court
Tenth District Court
Calhoun County Probate Court

MUSKEGON COUNTY
Fourteenth Circuit Court
Sixtieth District Court
Muskegon County Probate Court

WASHTENAW COUNTY
Twenty–Second Circuit Court
Fourteen–A District Court
Fourteen–B District Court
Fifteenth District Court
Washtenaw County Probate Court

The chief judges of each of the courts will cooperate with the State Court Administrative Office to establish the specific procedural requirements for the project, as needed, pursuant to MCR 8.112. This Order will remain in effect until further order of the Court.

[Entered March 31, 1993.]

ADMINISTRATIVE ORDER 1993–5
STATE BAR OF MICHIGAN ACTIVITIES

IT IS ORDERED that Administrative Order 1992–4 is RESCINDED effective October 1, 1993; however, as to its 1993–1994 fiscal year budget, the State Bar of Michigan need not publish a calculation of the pro rata share of a member's dues that are eligible for diversion and deduction as required by Administrative Order 1992–4.

IT IS FURTHER ORDERED that:

I. Ideological Activities Generally. The State Bar of Michigan shall not, except as provided in this order, use the dues of its members to fund activities of an ideological nature that are not reasonably related to:

(a) the regulation and discipline of attorneys;

(b) matters relating to the improvement of the functioning of the courts, judicial efficacy and efficiency;

(c) increasing the availability of legal services to society;

(d) regulation of attorney trust accounts; and

(e) the education, ethics, competence, integrity and regulation of the legal profession.

On or about August 15 of each year, the State Bar of Michigan shall publish in the Michigan Bar Journal a notice advising members of these limitations on the use of dues and the State Bar budget for the next fiscal year.

II. Activities Intended to Influence Legislation.

(A) The State Bar of Michigan may use the mandatory dues of all members to review and analyze pending legislation.

(B) The State Bar of Michigan may use the mandatory dues of all members to provide content-neutral technical assistance to legislators, provided that:

(1) a legislator requests the assistance;

(2) the president of the State Bar of Michigan approves the request in a letter to the legislator stating that providing technical assistance does not imply either support for or opposition to the legislation; and

(3) the president of the State Bar of Michigan annually prepares and publishes in the Michigan Bar Journal a report summarizing all technical assistance provided during the preceding year.

(C) No other activities intended to influence legislation may be funded with members' mandatory dues, unless the legislation in question is limited to matters within the scope of ideological activities requirements in Section I.

(D) Neither the State Bar of Michigan nor any person acting as its representative shall take any action to support or oppose legislation unless the position has been approved by a two-thirds vote of the Board of Commissioners or Representative Assembly taken after all members were advised, by notice published in the Michigan Bar Journal at least 2 weeks prior to the Board or Assembly meeting, that the proposed legislation would be discussed at the meeting. The published notice shall include a brief summary of the legislation and a statement that members may express their opinion at the meeting, or by written or telephonic communication to the State Bar of Michigan. When time constraints prevent timely publication of a notice in the Michigan Bar Journal, the notice may be provided by any alternative method that will deliver individual written notices to all members at least 7 days before the meeting.

(E) The results of all Board and Assembly votes on proposals to support or oppose legislation shall be published in the next Michigan Bar Journal. When either body adopts a position by a less-than-unanimous vote, a roll call vote shall be taken, and each commissioner's or assembly-person's vote shall be included in the published notice.

(F) Those sections of the State Bar of Michigan that are funded by the voluntary dues of their members are not subject to this order, and may engage in ideological activities on their own behalf.

III. Challenges Regarding State Bar Activities.

(A) A member who claims that the State Bar of Michigan is funding ideological activity in violation of this order may file a challenge by giving written notice to the executive director.

(a) A challenge involving legislative advocacy must be postmarked on or before the last day of the month following the month in which notice of adoption of that legislative position is published in the Michigan Bar Journal pursuant to section II(E).

(b) A challenge involving ideological activity appearing in the annual budget of the State Bar of Michigan must be postmarked on or before October 20 following the publication of the budget funding the challenged activity.

(c) A challenge involving any other ideological activity must be postmarked on or before the last day of the month following the month in which disclosure of that ideological activity is published in the Michigan Bar Journal.

Failure to challenge within the time allotted shall constitute a waiver.

(B) After a written challenge has been received, the executive director shall promptly determine the pro rata amount of the member's dues used to fund the challenged activity and shall place that amount in an escrow account pending determination of the merits of the challenge.

(C) Upon the expiration of the deadline for receipt of written challenges to the same activity, the Board of Commissioners shall decide whether to give a pro rata refund to the challengers or to refer the challenge to arbitration.

(D) A challenge that is not resolved between the parties shall be submitted to an arbitrator appointed by the American Arbitration Association, who shall determine whether the funding of the activity complies with the limitations of this order. If not, the arbitrator shall determine the pro rata share of dues, plus statutory judgment interest from the date of payment of those dues to the State Bar of Michigan, that is to be refunded. The State Bar of Michigan has the burden of proving by a preponderance of the evidence that the activity is permitted by this order. The necessary costs of the arbitration shall be paid by the State Bar of Michigan.

(E) A challenger or the State Bar of Michigan may seek review by this Court of the arbitrator's decisions as to whether the challenged activity violates the limitations on State Bar ideological activities set forth in this order, and any pro rata share of dues to be refunded.

IV. Other State Bar Activities. The State Bar of Michigan shall:

(A) annually publish in the Michigan Bar Journal a notice informing members that, upon request, their names will be removed from the mailing list that is used for commercial mailings;

(B) annually publish in the Michigan Bar Journal a notice informing members of the Young Lawyers Section that, upon request, their membership in that section will be terminated;

(C) limit its funding of the Michigan Lawyers Auxiliary to $5000 per year with adjustments for inflation after 1981, the funding to continue for as long as Michigan Lawyers Auxiliary continues its Law Day activities, specifically including the Law Day essay contest.

[Entered July 30, 1993.]

Staff Comment

Administrative Order 1993–5 limits State Bar use of members' mandatory dues for ideological purposes and legislative advocacy. This change had been recommended by the State Bar Representative Assembly.

Publisher's Note: The Michigan Supreme Court Order of June 30, 2000, provides:

This administrative matter presents the straightforward and narrow question whether the State Bar of Michigan may use its membership mailing to solicit for a political action committee (PAC). After considerable public comment and response from the State Bar of Michigan, this Court concludes that the use of the annual membership dues form of the State Bar (or any other mailing by the State Bar) to solicit or collect financial contributions for any political action committee is inconsistent with the State Bar's public role.

The State Bar is an organization established under state law to which all attorneys who wish to practice law in Michigan must belong. The State Bar is a "public body corporate."[1] The question whether the State Bar is a "public entity" for all purposes is not before this Court and need not be decided today. The fact that one must be a member of the State Bar to participate as a lawyer in the public activity of the court system is sufficient to establish the public character of the bar for purposes of resolving this matter administratively. The Court resolves this administrative matter under the provisions of MCL 600.904; MSA 27A.904 which grant this Court exclusive authority to "adopt rules and regulations concerning the conduct and activities of the state bar of Michigan." In resolving this matter administratively, the Court rejects the invitation of the Michigan Chamber of Commerce to interpret the Michigan Campaign Finance Act or the terms of LAWPAC's conciliation agreement with Secretary of State, or to pronounce upon the First Amendment implications of bar assistance to LAWPAC.

Today's order is based on the following determinations:

1) Given the mandatory nature of attorney membership in the bar, the solicitation on membership dues forms for funds for LAWPAC or any other PAC selected by the bar for inclusion on the forms involves the bar in appearing to

endorse or promote partisan candidates and political positions that may be opposed by individual members of the Bar.

2) No attorney should be required to join an organization that engages, through the conferring of direct or indirect benefit or assistance, in the promotion of partisan or political activities. Lawyers who disfavor the positions of a political committee or who disfavor the political candidates supported by a committee should not, as a condition of engaging in their profession, be required to join an organization providing benefits to such a political committee.

3) The inclusion of a solicitation of funds for a PAC on the annual dues notice of the State Bar confers a benefit upon the PAC.[2]

For the reasons stated above, IT IS ORDERED that the State Bar of Michigan shall not include a solicitation for funds for any PAC on any mailing to its membership.

This order does not prevent individual attorneys from exercising their rights to contribute to any PAC, including LAWPAC.

IT IS FURTHER ORDERED that this order shall be effective immediately.

IT IS FURTHER ORDERED that Administrative Order No. 1993–5 shall remain in effect.

Cavanagh, J., dissents and states as follows:

In February 1999, the Michigan Chamber of Commerce, through counsel, requested this Court to prohibit the State Bar of Michigan from soliciting LAWPAC contributions on its 1999–2000 dues notice and to require the State Bar to sever completely its connection with LAWPAC. It was asserted by the chamber that the bar's connection with LAWPAC violated provisions of the Michigan Campaign Finance Act, 1976 PA 388, MCL 169.201 et seq.; MSA 4.1703(1) et seq., and impinged upon the First Amendment rights of attorneys.

Earlier in February, the State Bar, LAWPAC, and the Secretary of State entered into "conciliation agreements" to resolve a complaint in which the president of the Michigan Chamber of Commerce alleged that the State Bar's involvement with LAWPAC violated the Michigan Campaign Finance Act (MCFA). Those conciliation agreements require LAWPAC to reimburse the State Bar for supplies and services provided in the past. In addition, the State Bar has agreed to bill LAWPAC "at commercially reasonable rates" for any supplies or services provided in the future.

But the conciliation agreements did not address specifically the manner in which the State Bar solicits LAWPAC contributions on its dues notices. The language utilized certainly, however, contemplated the continuation of the current practice. The conciliation agreements also did not specify the "commercially reasonable [value]" of being the only non-bar entity to have that privilege.

LAWPAC was formed in 1973 under the State Bar's sponsorship. It functions as a political action committee that solicits contributions from attorneys and uses the money to conduct lobbying activities and to make contributions to candidates.

In 1978, LAWPAC became a "separate segregated fund" of the State Bar. That is a term of art used in § 55 of the MCFA.[3] At the time, the statute allowed a "corporation or a joint stock company" to establish and administer a separate segregated fund. The State Bar is neither of those things. The State Bar's enabling legislation describes it as a "public body corporate."[4] The fact that the State Bar was not

expressly authorized to have a separate segregated fund was one of the points made by the Michigan Chamber of Commerce in the complaint that it filed with the Secretary of State last year. That point had gone unraised for twenty years. Shortly after the chamber filed its complaint, the State Bar filed an amended campaign finance report that recharacterized LAWPAC as an "independent committee," a term defined in MCFA, § 8.[5]

From 1978–79 continuing through the current fiscal year, the State Bar has solicited contributions to LAWPAC via a "reverse checkoff" on the annual dues invoices. The form adds a suggested $35 LAWPAC contribution to the base State Bar dues. Below that is a space that allows a member to subtract the $35 and pay only the base dues. But, unless the member acts affirmatively to make that subtraction, the invoice requires payment of a gross total that includes a LAWPAC contribution. Personal and clerical inertia make that reverse checkoff procedure advantageous to LAWPAC. The request for this administrative action asserts that ninety-six percent of the money that LAWPAC received from 1996 through 1998 came in with State Bar dues payments.[6]

The State Bar processes the dues payments and separates the LAWPAC component. Special processing sometimes is required. For example, some attorneys pay their dues with corporate checks, but corporations may not contribute to LAWPAC, so reprocessing of those payments by the State Bar is necessary.

As explained previously, the State Bar never has been a type of entity that is expressly authorized by MCFA, § 55 to sponsor a "separate segregated fund." As passed originally, the MCFA did not say exactly what a "public body corporate" such as the State Bar could or could not do. A new § 57 was added to the MCFA by 1995 PA 264. That new section, which was then amended by 1996 PA 590, now reads as follows:

(1) A public body or an individual acting for a public body shall not use or authorize the use of funds, personnel, office space, property, stationery, postage, vehicles, equipment, supplies, or other public resources to make a contribution or expenditure or provide volunteer personal services....

(2) A person who knowingly violates this section is guilty of a misdemeanor.... [MCL 169.257; MSA 4.1703(57).]

These points, and others, were raised by E. James Barrett, President of the Michigan Chamber of Commerce, in a MCFA complaint that was filed with the Secretary of State on May 7, 1998. The State Bar's position is that, while it might be described as a "quasi-public" body, it certainly is not a "state agency," the intended object of the amendment. In any event, that filing led to the State Bar and LAWPAC signing the February 12, 1999, conciliation agreements. While refraining from making explicit findings about past MCFA violations, the conciliation agreements required corrective and preventive measures.

At the time of this request from the chamber, I recall my puzzlement about why, suddenly, this twenty-year-old practice was suddenly now deemed to deserve a fatal blow. One would have thought that such new-found urgency would have arisen closer to the annual dues notification date in July of earlier years, or in 1998, the immediately preceding year. Be that as it may, in an apparent attempt to accomplish, through our administrative procedures, what the chamber had failed to effect through its Secretary of State Conciliation Agreement, it requested this Court to terminate the bar's connection with LAWPAC, asserting, as previously stated, that such connection entailed statutory and constitutional violations. A majority of this Court, in May of last year, considered just such a swift administrative demise of LAWPAC appearing on the bar's dues notice, but action was deferred in recognition of our rules that, absent an emergency, require publication and a public hearing. Then, following a public hearing in May 1999, the Chief Justice, in July 1999, notified the bar that the Court was giving serious consideration to the chamber's request because, "in light of MCL 169.257; MSA 4.1703(57), we are troubled by the solicitation method." By that correspondence, the bar was further notified that the matter would reappear on a September 1999 public hearing agenda and that no changes would be required in the 1999–2000 dues notice. The Court also indicated it would be most interested in hearing the bar's response to the chamber's request. Additional public hearings have been held, and, pursuant to our direction, the State Bar had the matter considered by its Dues Statement Review Committee, which made recommendations for formulation of bar policies and procedures for the annual dues statement. These recommendations were subsequently approved by the State Bar Board of Commissioners and have been presented to this Court for consideration.

The Court's perfunctory order today, following public hearings and receipt of the bar's recommendations in response to our request, simply closes the circle commenced by the chamber's initial request.

I dissent from the Court's action in response to this request. Although the conciliation agreements supposedly resolved the complaint filed by the chamber's president, the reality seems to be that the dispute continues. The request to this Court effectively asked the Court to issue a declaratory interpretation of the MCFA and the conciliation agreements and to infer constitutional violations from LAWPAC's relationship with the bar. No lower court has ruled on those questions. Neither the Secretary of State nor the Attorney General has asserted that the State Bar's anticipated future conduct would violate either the MCFA or the conciliation agreements, nor has any lower court considered and ruled upon any asserted constitutional violations. I would deny the chamber's request and suggest it seek an adjudication of its statutory or constitutional claims or an administrative ruling or amendatory legislation. While the Court's order today deems the bar's conduct inconsistent with its public role, I would suggest that what is really inconsistent and inappropriate is this Court's resolution of what, in essence, is an adjudicative matter, while purporting to wear its administrative hat, its protestations to the contrary notwithstanding.

Kelly, J., dissents and states as follows:

I disagree with the majority's decision to order the State Bar of Michigan to discontinue permitting LAWPAC to solicit donations on the State Bar's annual membership dues notice.[7] The majority's action circumvents an established legislative procedure for addressing the issue raised here. Also, it fails to recognize the true nature of the transaction between LAWPAC and the State Bar.

Our public hearings on this matter have provided us insight into the underlying facts. In early 1999, the State Bar, LAWPAC and the Michigan Secretary of State entered into conciliation agreements to resolve a complaint by the Michigan Chamber of Commerce. It alleged that the State Bar's involvement with LAWPAC violated the Michigan Campaign Finance Act (MCFA).[8] The conciliation agreements required LAWPAC to reimburse the State Bar for

supplies and services provided in the past. In addition, the State Bar agreed to bill LAWPAC "at commercially reasonable rates" for any supplies or services provided in the future.

The conciliation agreements did not, however, address specifically the manner in which LAWPAC solicits contributions on the State Bar's dues notices. Nor did they specify the commercially reasonable value of being the only non-bar entity to have that privilege.

Three Michigan attorneys have asserted that the conciliation agreements actually prohibit the State Bar from allowing LAWPAC to solicit donations on its dues notices.[9] They assert that, despite the conciliation agreements, the State Bar will continue to allow LAWPAC to solicit donations in its traditional manner. Thus, they have requested this Court to amend Administrative Order No. 1993–5 to prohibit the practice.[10]

We have the authority "to adopt rules and regulations concerning the conduct and activities of the state bar of Michigan.... " **MCL 600.904; MSA 27A.904; see also Const 1963, art 6, § 5.** However, the Legislature has provided a specific method for parties to seek relief from a violation of the MCFA. In the act, it provides that, when a party to a conciliation agreement violates that agreement,

the secretary of state may refer the matter to the attorney general for the enforcement of any criminal penalty provided by this act or commence a hearing.... [MCL 169.215(5); MSA 4.1703(15)(5).]

If the Secretary of State decides to commence a hearing and determines

that a violation of this act has occurred, the secretary of state may issue an order requiring the person to pay a civil fine equal to the amount of the improper contribution or expenditure plus not more than $1,000.00 for each violation. [MCL 169.215(6); MSA 4.1703(15)(6).]

If, instead, the Secretary of State refers the matter to the Attorney General, the latter is authorized to pursue a criminal prosecution for the alleged violation of § 57.

A person who knowingly violates this section is guilty of a misdemeanor punishable ... if the person is not an individual, by 1 of the following, whichever is greater: (a) A fine of not more than $20,000.00. (b) A fine equal to the amount of the improper contribution or expenditure. [MCL 169.157(2); MSA 4.1703(57)(2).]

In essence, the complainants here allege that the State Bar is violating the conciliation agreements and the MCFA by allowing LAWPAC to solicit donations on bar dues notices. The MCFA specifies the proper manner for obtaining relief. In fact, its provisions state that they furnish the exclusive manner to address a violation of the act. MCL 169.215(9); MSA 4.1703(15)(9).[11] In the absence of a violation, "a conciliation agreement is a complete bar to any further action with respect to matters covered in the conciliation agreement." MCL 169.215(5); MSA 4.1703(15)(5).

Despite that fact, the complaining parties have prompted the majority to grant them relief without adjudicating whether the State Bar is in violation of its agreements and the MCFA. The action taken by the majority today clearly circumvents the legislative framework provided for resolving the issue.

There has yet to be a determination by the Secretary of State or a lower court that a violation of the MCFA has occurred or is occurring. Hence, the issue whether the State

Bar can properly solicit funds for LAWPAC is not properly before us. I dissent from the majority's action and would direct the complaining parties to address their complaint to the Secretary of State for disposition through the provisions of the MCFA.

The majority fails to address how this issue came before the Court and instead focuses on policy reasons for justifying its action. A close examination of the reasons cited indicates that, in actuality, the majority is basing its decision on the State Bar's purported violation of the MCFA.

The majority asserts that the State Bar confers a benefit upon LAWPAC by allowing the PAC to solicit donations on the State Bar's annual dues notice. Considering the public character of the State Bar and the mandatory nature of attorney membership, the majority concludes that the State Bar should not be involved in endorsing or assisting any PAC.

The property of the State Bar is public property. *State Bar of Michigan v City of Lansing*, 361 Mich 185, 197–198; 105 NW2d 131 (1960). If the State Bar is assisting LAWPAC by contributing space on its annual dues statement to LAWPAC or reducing the postage costs LAWPAC would otherwise incur, such assistance would violate § 57. The allegation of such "assistance" is exactly the subject of the conciliation agreements between LAWPAC, the State Bar, and the Secretary of State. Thus, it can be seen that the policy reasons cited by the majority for its decision are really nothing more than "smoke and mirrors." They hide the basic issue whether the State Bar's continuing practice of allowing LAWPAC to solicit contributions on its annual dues notice violates the conciliation agreements and the MCFA.

The majority merely "presumes" that LAWPAC receives a benefit from the arrangement and that providing a benefit to LAWPAC equates to providing assistance to LAWPAC. It ignores the fee that LAWPAC pays to the State Bar to include its solicitation on the annual membership dues statements.[12]

Admittedly, LAWPAC has had exclusive access to the State Bar's annual membership dues notices, but counsel for the State Bar has advised us that no other PAC has requested to be included. Regardless, the State Bar has recently approved guidelines by which any PAC can be included on the annual dues notices for the purpose of soliciting donations.[13] The State Bar will charge the PAC a minimum annual fee of $10,000 for that opportunity. Thus, the "assistance" offered by the State Bar is in the form of a value-for-value transaction.

The issue whether a value-for-value transaction of this sort violates § 57 of the MCFA and confers a benefit on LAWPAC has never been decided in the proper forum. The majority's reliance on conclusory statements and observations clouds the issue. Because the Court has not undertaken proper consideration of the issue, I disagree with the order issued today.

In addition, how does a value-for-value transaction open to any PAC constitute an endorsement or promotion by the bar of a particular ideological or political perspective? Whatever contributions LAWPAC, or any other PAC, receives by way of a dues notice or solicitation of bar members are voluntary. The State Bar does not give LAWPAC any portion of the mandatory member's dues. Therefore, those whom the law requires to join the State Bar are not made members of an organization that supports interests adverse or objectionable to their own.

The appropriate action for this Court is to direct the complaining parties to lodge their concerns with the Secretary of State in accordance with the requirements of the MCFA.

1. "The State Bar of Michigan is the association of the members of the bar of this state, organized and existing as a public body corporate pursuant to powers of the Supreme Court over the bar of the state." State Bar Rule 1

2. The Court has studied a thoughtful proposal from the bar intended to "cure" this problem by allowing the bar to sell dues mailing solicitation services to organizations that meet the bar's predetermined criteria. However, even if a commercially reasonable rate for the cost of the benefit conferred could be determined and imposed, given the finite number of solicitations possible on any given dues notice and the need for the bar to "vet" applications for inclusion, we are persuaded that such provisions do not alter the essential fact that a benefit is conferred.

3. MCL 169.255; MSA 4.1703(55).

4. MCL 600.901; MSA 27A.901.

5. MCL 169.208(3); MSA 4.1703(8) (3).

6. Speaking as an individual attorney, I would note that I have never been enamored of the LAWPAC solicitation on my State Bar dues notice. The solicitation—more particularly the "reverse checkoff" method—always has been bothersome to me, even though I can subtract the suggested contribution before paying my bar dues.

7. LAWPAC is a political action committee formed for the purpose of identifying and contributing to the campaigns of public officials who share an interest in the legal profession.

8. MCL 169.201 *et seq*; MSA 4.1703(1) *et seq*. The complaint alleged that the State Bar contributed supplies and services to LAWPAC in violation of MCL 169.257; MSA 4.1703(57). Subsection 57(1) states:

A public body ... shall not use or authorize the use of funds, personnel, office space, property, stationery, postage, vehicles, equipment, supplies, or other public resources to make a contribution or expenditure....

The Secretary of State, pursuant to the authority in MCL 169.215(5); MSA 4.1703(15)(5), investigated the complaint and negotiated conciliation agreements with LAWPAC and the State Bar to resolve the chamber's objections.

9. The attorneys proceed on the theory that the State Bar has conferred a benefit to LAWPAC in the nature of a contribution in violation of § 57.

10. Administrative Order No. 1993–5, 443 Mich xci, sets forth permissible and impermissible activities of the State Bar.

11. MCL 169.215(9); MSA 4.1703(15)(9) reads:

There is no private right of action, either in law or in equity, pursuant to this act. The remedies provided in this act are the exclusive means by which this act may be enforced and by which any harm resulting from a violation of this act may be redressed.

12. Counsel for the State Bar submitted an affidavit from the Assistant Executive Director for Financial Affairs of the State Bar showing that, for fiscal year 1998, LAWPAC paid the State Bar $8,732 to include its solicitation on the dues notice.

13. The majority appears to conclude that, because space is limited on the annual dues statement, the State Bar will choose among applicants selecting only some for inclusion. Thus, it remains in a position to confer a benefit.

The majority's conclusion is based on conjecture that a high number of PACs will take advantage of the opportunity. It assumes that there will not be room on the notice to accommodate all those desiring to be included. I believe that it is premature to make such a conclusion. We should not automatically assume that, in the event that there is insufficient space, the State Bar will exercise its discretion in a prejudicial or referential manner.

Furthermore, every PAC that applies to be included on the annual dues notice is subject to the condition contained in the State Bar's guidelines. Neither LAWPAC, nor any other PAC, is guaranteed placement on the dues notice in the event that space is limited.

ADMINISTRATIVE ORDER 1994-2 FACSIMILE AND COMMUNICATION EQUIPMENT FOR THE FILING AND TRANSMISSION OF COURT DOCUMENTS

Until further order of the Court, the State Court Administrative Office may authorize courts to use facsimile communication equipment for the transmission and filing of court documents.

The State Court Administrative Office shall provide assistance in the implementation of the use of facsimile equipment for the filing and transmission of court documents for those courts electing to participate. Participating courts shall cooperate with the State Court Administrative Office and provide information regarding the use of facsimile equipment for the filing and transmission of court documents.

The previous authorizations by this Court and by the State Court Administrator pursuant to Administrative Order 1990-9, are continued until further order of this Court or the State Court Administrator.

The following experimental court rules shall govern the participating courts:

(A) Facsimile Communication Equipment. Courts, by local court rules established pursuant to MCR 8.112(A), may permit the filing of 8½″ × 11″ pleadings, motions, affidavits, opinions, orders, or other documents by the use of facsimile (FAX) communication equipment. Except as provided by MCR 2.002, a clerk shall not permit the filing of any document for which a filing fee is required unless the full amount of the filing fee is paid or deposited in advance with the clerk. Documents intended to be filed in any court shall be on paper not subject to more rapid deterioration than ordinary typewritten material on ordinary paper.

(B) The local court rule established pursuant to MCR 8.112(A) shall establish for facsimile filing of documents with the court by the public:

(1) a reasonable fee, in addition to statutory filing fees, to be charged by the clerk, which may take into account the cost of equipment, paper, supplies and telephone line charges;

(2) a maximum number of pages which may be sent at one time for any document or documents;

(3) the hours during which documents may be received;

(4) other reasonable requirements to promote the efficient filing of facsimile documents;

(5) the method of giving notice to attorneys and litigants of any facsimile filing requirements.

(C) Signature. For purposes of MCR 2.114, a signature includes a signature transmitted by facsimile communication equipment.

(D) Warrants. Facsimile communication equipment and voice communication equipment may be used as provided for in 1990 PA 41, 43, 44 and 45.

[Entered February 3, 1994.]

ADMINISTRATIVE ORDER 1994-4 RESOLUTION OF CONFLICTS IN COURT OF APPEALS DECISIONS [REPEALED]

[Repealed effective September 1, 1997.]

Staff Comment to 1997 Repeal

The provisions of Administrative Order 1994-4, dealing with Court of Appeals conflict resolution panels, are incorporated into the court rules as new MCR 7.215(H). Also, such panels are authorized to dispense with oral argument (by unanimous vote), and their decisions must be published in Michigan Appeals Reports.

ADMINISTRATIVE ORDER 1994-6 REDUCTIONS IN TRIAL COURT BUDGETS BY FUNDING UNITS

On order of the Court, it appearing that a number of court funding units have reduced their original appropriations for the courts for the current fiscal year, this Administrative Order, applicable to all trial courts as defined in MCR 8.110(A), is adopted to be effective September 16, 1994.

1. If a court is notified by its funding unit of a reduction of the original appropriation for the court for the current fiscal year, the court shall immediately file a copy of that notice with the State Court Administrative Office.

2. Within 10 days after filing the notice, the chief judge must provide the following to the State Court Administrative Office Regional Administrator:

a. A copy of the court's original budget.

b. A copy of a revised budget in light of the reduced appropriation.

c. A statement of the amount of the reduction in court revenue by source, and a statement of anticipated revenues for the remainder of this fiscal year by source.

d. A budget reduction plan to reduce court operations in light of anticipated reductions in revenue, and an impact statement describing,

i. Any anticipated reduction in the trial court work force that would be required.

ii. Any anticipated reduction in court hours that would be required.

iii. Any anticipated reductions in revenues that are anticipated, by source and by recipient.

iv. The impact on other entities that would occur, including at a minimum potential service reductions, work flow backlogs, and revenue shortfalls.

Other entities to be reviewed should include, at a minimum, the youth home (if any), the local jail, the prosecuting attorney (county and municipal), local law enforcement agencies, community mental health agencies, and county clerk's office.

v. The schedule to be used for implementing reductions and for distributing notices to employees, other agencies, etc., and the date funds are estimated to be depleted under the revised budget plan.

e. An emergency services plan which outlines what services are essential and must be provided by the court. The emergency services plan should consider services which at a minimum will preserve rights guaranteed by the Michigan and U.S. Constitutions, and those guaranteed by statute.

If a copy of such a notice of reduction of appropriation has already been sent to the State Court Administrative Office, the additional information required by this section must be provided within 10 days of the effective date of this order. The State Court Administrative Office may grant an extension of time in its sole discretion.

3. After reviewing the revised budget and impact statement a designee of the State Court Administrator shall meet with the chief judge to discuss implementation of the plan and any anticipated need for assistance from other courts to assure provision of emergency services. Thereafter, the implementation of the plan shall begin immediately.

4. The State Court Administrative Office shall monitor the implementation of the plan. The chief judge shall notify the SCAO when budgeted funds are anticipated to be depleted and the date the emergency services plan filed pursuant to this Order will be implemented.

5. The State Court Administrator shall re-assign sitting judges as necessary to ensure as nearly as possible the maximum use of judicial resources in light of reduced operations, and to assist in the provision of emergency services to affected trial courts.

6. The procedures set forth in Administrative Order 1985–6 are not affected by this order and must be followed before the court may institute litigation against the funding unit.

[Entered September 9, 1994.]

ADMINISTRATIVE ORDER 1994–8
ALLOCATION OF FUNDS FROM
LAWYER TRUST ACCOUNT PROGRAM

On order of the Court, effective October 4, 1994, until further order of the Court, Administrative Order 1990–2 is MODIFIED so as to provide that the funds to be distributed by the Board of Trustees of the Michigan State Bar Foundation shall be disbursed as follows:

[Publisher's Note: See, now, Administrative Order 1997–9.]

Administrative Order 1991–10 is rescinded.

[Entered October 4, 1994; amended October 12 and 13, 1994.]

ADMINISTRATIVE ORDER 1994–9
SUSPENSION OF INTEREST ON
DELINQUENT COSTS IMPOSED IN
ATTORNEY DISCIPLINE PROCEEDINGS

The Attorney Discipline Board has proposed that a 60–day period be provided during which interest would not be assessed on costs paid by suspended or disbarred attorneys who are in default on their obligations to pay costs in connection with discipline proceedings. On order of the Court, we AUTHORIZE the Attorney Discipline Board to notify persons delinquent in payment of costs that interest will not be assessed if the costs are paid within 60 days of the date of the notice.

[Entered November 16, 1994.]

ADMINISTRATIVE ORDER 1994–10
DISCOVERY IN CRIMINAL CASES*

On May 4, 1994, the Governor signed House Bill 4227, concerning discovery by the prosecution of certain information known to the defendant in a criminal case. 1994 PA 113, MCL 767.94a; MSA 28.1023(194a). On November 16, 1994, this Court promulgated MCR 6.201, which is a comprehensive treatment of the subject of discovery in criminal cases.

On order of the Court, effective January 1, 1995, discovery in criminal cases heard in the courts of this state is governed by MCR 6.201 and not by MCL 767.94a; MSA 28.1023(194a). Const 1963, art 6, § 5; MCR 1.104.

[Entered November 16, 1994.]

*Suggested title added by Publisher.

ADMINISTRATIVE ORDER 1995–2
PROBATE COURT FEE SCHEDULE

On order of the Court, the following fee schedule is adopted June 1, 1995 for use in probate court, to be effective July 1, 1995.

Probate Court Fees

How to Use This Schedule. This schedule is divided into four sections:

(1) Proceedings by Subject Matter,

(2) Generally Applicable Procedures,

(3) Fees for Copies, and

(4) Waiving Fees.

Be familiar with the contents of the generally applicable procedures and waiving fees sections, as these may apply in any type of proceeding. In general, there is a $70.00 fee for filing papers (documents) which open a file and a $15.00 fee for filing additional papers. The fees for starting certain proceedings are increased on an annual time table set out at the end of this schedule. These fees are marked with an asterisk. Some parties do not have to pay filing fees. See Waiving Fees section.

Proceedings by Subject Matter

Decedent Estates:

Small Estate—generally $20,000 or less, MCL 700.101; MSA 27.5101	$70.00 *
Small Estate—$15,000 or less, MCL 700.102; MSA 27.5102 (plus inventory fee)	$25.00
Petition to Determine Heirs (in pending case, even if in petition to commence proceedings)	$15.00
Petition for Commencement of Proceedings	$70.00 *
—If the petition requests appointment of a temporary personal representative in addition to a personal representative or independent personal representative	$15.00
—Each other request at any time	$15.00
Petition to Reopen a Closed File	$70.00 *
Claims (statement and proof)	$15.00
Disallowance of Claim	No Fee
Civil Action (summons and complaint)	$70.00 *
Motions in Civil Actions, per document	$15.00
Inventory	
—No fee for filing	No Fee
—An inventory fee, set by MCL 600.871; MSA 27A.871 is due with the final account or within one year of commencement, whichever occurs first	See RJA 871
Account (any type: annual, amended, final, interim, supplemental, including account with zero receipts and disbursements)	$15.00
Account with Assets less than $15.00	No Fee

Petition for Allowance of Account (if separate)	$15.00
Each Additional Petition, Motion, Objection or other Paper, no matter how titled, which requests relief or requires a hearing or ruling of the court, for instance:	$15.00

—Petition for Partial Distribution of Assets
—Report of Sale of Real Estate, Petition for Confirmation
—Petition for Authority to Settle Wrongful Death Claim
—Petition for Supervision
—Report, Petition and Order for Continuing Pendency
—Petition for Removal of Personal Representative and Appointment of Successor
—Petition for Reinstatement of Personal Representative after Suspension

Proceedings Involving Testamentary or Inter Vivos Trusts:

Initiating a Proceeding Involving a Testamentary Trust (unless the trust proceeding is processed as part of a decedent estate)	$70.00 *
Initiating a Proceeding Involving a Testamentary Trust (if processed as part of a decedent estate)	$15.00
Petition to Commence a Proceeding Relating to an Inter Vivos Trust	$70.00 *
Registration of Trust	$25.00
Each Additional Petition, Motion, Objection or other Paper, no matter how titled, which requests relief or requires a hearing or ruling of the court, for instance:	$15.00

—Petition to Remove a Trustee and Appoint a Successor
—Petition to Review the Fees of a Trustee
—Petition to Require, Hear, and Settle Interim or Final Accounts
—Petition to Ascertain Beneficiaries
—Petition for Construction
—Petition for Instructions

Conservatorship/Guardianship of Estate:

Petition for Conservator/Protective Order (There are two fees if a conservator [$70.00 *] and guardian [$50.00] are requested for the same person) $70.00 *

Petition to Add Conservator or Protective Order (filed after Proceeding Opened) $15.00

Petition for Preliminary Protective Order (special conservatorship—petition for conservator/protective order must be pending) $15.00

Account (any type: annual, amended, final, interim, supplemental, including account with zero receipts and disbursements) $15.00

Account with Assets less than $15.00   No Fee

Petition for Allowance of Account (if separate from account) $15.00

Claims (statement and proof) $15.00

Disallowance of Claim   No Fee

Civil Action (summons and complaint) $70.00 *

Motions in Civil Actions (per document) $15.00

Motion to Release Restricted Funds of a Minor   No Fee

Any Petition if the subject of the proceeding (the Ward) is the Petitioner   No Fee

Each Additional Petition, Motion, Objection or other Paper, no matter how titled, which requests relief or requires a hearing or ruling of the court, for instance: $15.00

—Petition for Successor or Special Conservator
—Petition for Removal of Conservator
—Proof of Sale of Real Estate, Petition to Confirm

Guardianships (Legally Incapacitated Persons and Minors): [1]

Petition for Full or Limited Guardianship (There are two fees if a conservator and guardian are requested for the same person) $50.00

Petition for Temporary Guardianship (whether filed with or after initial pe- $15.00

tition, petition for full appointment must be pending)

Annual Report on Condition of Ward   No Fee

Any Petition where the Ward is the Petitioner   No Fee

Petitions by Court Appointed Attorney in Response to Guardianship Review   No Fee

Each Additional Petition, Motion, Objection or other Paper, no matter how titled, which requests relief or requires a hearing or ruling of the court, for instance: $15.00

—Petition for Authority
—Petition for Authority to Adopt (minor guardianship)
—Petition for Modification or Termination

Adoption Proceedings:

Commencement of Proceeding for Adoption—first paper of any title (petition, two day report, etc.) in a new proceeding for a child and specified prospective parents $70.00 *

Petition for Adoption (in a proceeding which has already been commenced for the child and specified prospective parents) $15.00

Motion to Establish Delayed Registration of Foreign Birth (if new proceeding) $70.00 *

Request for Release of Non–Identifying Information, if no court ruling required   No Fee (except for copy)

Request (Petition) for Release of Non–Identifying Information, if court ruling required $15.00

Petition to Appoint Confidential Intermediary (A Confidential Intermediary may be charged a regular copy fee for copies of documents) $15.00

Petition for Release of Confidential Information from Confidential Intermediary and Court $15.00

Petition for Approval of Confidential Intermediary Fee $15.00

Petition to Return Child	$15.00
Petition to Determine Custody	$15.00
Motion for Immediate Confirmation	No Fee
Petition for Hearing to Identify Father	$15.00
Supplemental Petition to Terminate Rights of Non–Custodial Parent	$15.00
Release of Information concerning Adoption, see MCL 710.68(18); MSA 27.3178(555.68)(18)	Cost up to $60.00
Declaration of Inability to Locate or Identify Father	No Fee
Petition of Adult to Rescind Adoption by Stepparent	$15.00
Petition to Determine if Consent is being Arbitrarily or Capriciously Withheld	$15.00
Each Subsequent Petition, Motion, Objection, or other Paper, no matter how titled, which requests relief or requires a hearing or ruling of the court	$15.00

Other Specific Proceedings: [2]

Entry of Order Changing Name (does not include a certified copy, $10.00)	$10.00
Petition for Emancipation	$70.00 *
Petition to Open Safe Deposit Box	$10.00
Wills Filed for Safekeeping	$25.00
Civil Action, Summons and Complaint	$70.00 *
Civil Action, Motion	$15.00
Performing a Marriage	$10.00
Secret Marriage License	$3.00
Issuance of a Commission to Take Testimony	$7.00
Petition to Change Name (adult or minor)	$70.00 *
Proceedings on Waiving Parental Consent (any filing)	No Fee
Proceedings on Infectious Disease (any filing)	No Fee

Proceedings on Substance Abuse (any filing)	No Fee
Petition for Settlement of Personal Injury Claim	$15.00
Petition to Establish Death of Victim of Accident or Disaster	$70.00 *
Petition to Determine Heirs (in separate proceeding)	$70.00 *
Acknowledgment of Paternity	No Fee
Petition for Leave to File Acknowledgment of Paternity	$70.00 *

Generally Applicable Procedures

Demand for Jury Trial (except Juvenile Division and mental health proceedings for which there is no fee)	$30.00
Motion to Change Venue	$15.00
Objection (for example to inventory, account, will, appointments)	$15.00
Answer, Brief, Response (distinguish from objections)	No Fee
Motion to Show Cause	$15.00
Motion to Recuse	$15.00
Amended Petition (any kind)	$15.00
Writ of Garnishment or Execution	$15.00
Petition for Temporary Restraining Order (main petition must be filed with or before this petition)	$15.00
Petition to Withdraw a Petition, if hearing required (no fee if no hearing)	$15.00
Motion for Rehearing (distinguish from a petition to reopen)	$15.00
Petition for Fees by Fiduciary (if separate from account)	$15.00
If More Than One Account is Filed at the Same Time	$15.00 per account
Petition for Attorney Fees (if separate from account)	$15.00

Petition for Instruction (after the case has been opened) $15.00

Petition to Surcharge Fiduciary $15.00

Petition for Removal of Fiduciary and Appointment of Successor $15.00

Petition and Order for Reinstatement of Fiduciary after Suspension $15.00

Petition for Appointment for Guardian ad Litem $15.00

Single Account Filed by Temporary Personal Representative/Personal Representative for Same Accounting Period $15.00

Petition to Allow Account (if separate from account) $15.00

Appeals from Probate Court to Circuit Court or Court of Appeals $25.00

Petition to Withdraw as Attorney (if hearing required) $15.00

Petition to Allow Fees of Guardian ad Litem $15.00

Petition and Order for Authority $15.00

Annual Report on Condition of Ward   No Fee

Copy Fees (Certified or Exemplified Copies)

Letter of Authority to Fiduciary or Fiduciary's Attorney (first copy only)   No Fee

Each Subsequent Letter of Authority, first page $10.00
—Each additional page $1.00

Order Changing Name $10.00

Order of Adoption $10.00

Order for Small Estate Assignment $11.00

Acknowledgment of Paternity $10.00

Order for Use of Funds, adult ward $10.00
—if for minor   No Fee

Certified copies of Papers in Connection with Commitment Proceedings   No Fee

Certified copies of Papers in Proceedings for Determining Inheritance Tax   No Fee

Taking, Certifying, Sealing, and Forwarding Depositions $5.00 plus $0.10 per folio

Each copy of deposition furnished $0.03 per folio

Certified Copies of any Other Paper
—First Page $10.00
—Each Additional Page $1.00

Waiving Fees

No fees are charged in the following situations:

—There is no fee for proceedings for admission and commitment of persons under the mental health code, except for matters affecting an estate from other than public sources. See note 1.

—After filing of the initial petition, there are no $15.00 fees where the ward is the petitioner or moving party (guardianship and conservatorship).

—There are no fees where the petitioner or moving party is indigent or has an inability to pay. Procedures for determining indigency are appropriate for local administrative rule. See also MC 20.

—Where the petitioner is the Attorney General, Department of Treasury, Department of Social Services, State Public Administrator, Administrator of Veterans Affairs, or a county governmental agency.

—Where the value of a small estate, not exceeding $5,000.00 is less than $500.00, the Court might consider waiving the $11.00 order fee.

—There may be other instances where the Court might exercise discretion to waive fees.

Commencement Fee Schedule:

Present	through	9/30/95	$ 70.00
10/1/95	through	9/30/96	$ 80.00
10/1/96	through	9/30/97	$ 90.00
10/1/97 and after			$100.00

1. MCL 600.880(3); MSA 27A.880(3), as amended by 1993 PA 189 states, in part, "[A] fee shall not be charged for commencing a proceeding in probate court pursuant to any provision of the mental health code." The statute is silent as to fees for matters other than commencement of proceedings. Until the statute is clarified, no fee should be charged after commencement except for matters affecting

an estate which is derived from other than public sources, for example an inheritance or personal injury recovery.

2. There may be many different petitions, motions, objections or similar papers filed in any of the listed proceedings. There will be a fee of $15.00 per paper (document) filed.

[Entered June 7, 1995; corrected June 14, 1995 and June 20, 1995.]

ADMINISTRATIVE ORDER 1996–1
AUTHORIZATION OF DEMONSTRATION PROJECTS TO STUDY COURT CONSOLIDATION

In its report entitled "Justice in Michigan: A Program for Reforming the Judicial Branch of Government; a Report to the People of Michigan from the Justices of the Michigan Supreme Court," the Supreme Court stated its intention to authorize demonstration projects to study and evaluate the merger of the circuit, probate and district courts into a fully consolidated trial court.

The following courts shall begin a two-year demonstration project, effective January 1, 1996:

> Barry County
> 5th Circuit Court
> 56–1 District Court
> Barry County Probate Court

During the two-year term of the demonstration project, these courts shall be referred to as the Barry County Trial Court.

The Hon. James H. Fisher is appointed as the Chief Judge of the Barry County Trial Court. He shall have all of the authorities and responsibilities of a chief judge under MCR 8.110 as to all of the participating courts.

The judges, magistrates and referees within the Barry County Trial Court are assigned to serve the whole court. Subject to the direction of the chief judge, each judge may exercise the jurisdiction of a judge of the circuit, probate, and district court. Subject to the direction of the chief judge, each magistrate or referee may perform the functions of a domestic relations referee, a district court magistrate or a juvenile court referee, with the authority to conduct proceedings as allowed by law and court rule.

The Barry County Trial Court may form divisions. These divisions may correspond to the existing workload of the circuit, probate, and district courts, or may reflect another partition of the workload of the court; provided that the Barry County Trial Court will incorporate into one general division issues affecting the family.

During this demonstration project, the Barry County Trial Court may enter into cooperative agreements with state and local non-judicial branch agencies to test the feasibility of the court to carry out essential court functions, such as record-keeping, felony proba-

tion services, information systems management, personnel management and financial management.

The chief judge of the trial court shall cooperate with the State Court Administrative Office by abiding by the terms of the project agreement, which include reporting and evaluation requirements.

Specific administrative and procedural requirements for each project, as needed, will be implemented through local administrative order or local court rule pursuant to MCR 8.112.

The State Court Administrative Office shall submit a status report to the Supreme Court at the end of each year of the demonstration project.*

[Entered March 20, 1996; extended until further order of the Court by Administrative Order 1997–12.]

* Administrative Order 1997–12, entered December 19, 1997, ordered that the "State Court Administrator shall provide a report on the status of each of the projects by November, 1998, and annually thereafter."

ADMINISTRATIVE ORDER 1996–2
AUTHORIZATION OF DEMONSTRATION PROJECTS TO STUDY COURT CONSOLIDATION

In its report entitled "Justice in Michigan: A Program for Reforming the Judicial Branch of Government; a Report to the People of Michigan from the Justices of the Michigan Supreme Court," the Supreme Court stated its intention to authorize demonstration projects to study and evaluate the merger of the circuit, probate and district courts into a fully consolidated trial court.

The following courts shall begin a two-year demonstration project, effective January 1, 1996:

> WASHTENAW COUNTY

> 22nd Circuit Court
> 14A District Court
> 14B District Court
> 15th District Court
> Washtenaw County Probate Court

During the two-year term of the demonstration project, these courts shall be referred to as the Washtenaw County Trial Court.

The Hon. Kurtis T. Wilder is appointed as the Chief Judge of the Washtenaw County Trial Court. He shall have all of the authorities and responsibilities of a chief judge under MCR 8.110 as to all of the participating courts.

The judges, magistrates and referees within the Washtenaw County Trial Court are assigned to serve the whole court. Subject to the direction of the chief judge, each judge may exercise the jurisdiction of a judge of the circuit, probate, and district court. Subject to the direction of the chief judge, each magistrate or referee may perform the functions of a domestic relations referee, a district court magistrate or a juvenile court referee, with the authority to conduct proceedings as allowed by law and court rule.

The Washtenaw County Trial Court may form divisions. These divisions may correspond to the existing workload of the circuit, probate, and district courts, or may reflect another partition of the workload of the court; provided that the Washtenaw County Trial Court will incorporate into one general division issues affecting the family.

During this demonstration project, the Washtenaw County Trial Court may enter into cooperative agreements with state and local non-judicial branch agencies to test the feasibility of the court to carry out essential court functions, such as record-keeping, felony probation services, information systems management, personnel management and financial management.

The chief judge of the trial court shall cooperate with the State Court Administrative Office by abiding by the terms of the project agreement, which include reporting and evaluation requirements.

Specific administrative and procedural requirements for each project, as needed, will be implemented through local administrative order or local court rule pursuant to MCR 8.112.

The State Court Administrative Office shall submit a status report to the Supreme Court at the end of each year of the demonstration project.*

[Entered March 20, 1996; extended until further order of the Court by Administrative Order 1997–12.]

* Administrative Order 1997–12, entered December 19, 1997, ordered that the "State Court Administrator shall provide a report on the status of each of the projects by November, 1998, and annually thereafter."

ADMINISTRATIVE ORDER 1996–4
RESOLUTION OF CONFLICTS IN COURT OF APPEALS DECISIONS

On order of the Court, the terms and conditions of Administrative Order 1994–4 * are continued in effect until the further order of this Court.

[Entered April 23, 1996.]

* Administrative Order 1994–4, was repealed effective September 1, 1997. The provisions of Administrative Order 1994–4 were incorporated into MCR 7.215(H). The Staff Comment to the 1997 Repeal of Administrative Order 1994–4, states:

"The provisions of Administrative Order 1994–4, dealing with Court of Appeals conflict resolution panels, are incorporated into the court rules as new MCR 7.215(H). Also, such panels are authorized to dispense with oral argument (by unanimous vote), and their decisions must be published in Michigan Appeals Reports."

ADMINISTRATIVE ORDER 1996–5
AUTHORIZATION OF DEMONSTRATION PROJECTS TO STUDY COURT CONSOLIDATION

In its report entitled "Justice in Michigan: A Program for Reforming the Judicial Branch of Government; a Report to the People of Michigan from the Justices of the Michigan Supreme Court," the Supreme Court stated its intention to authorize demonstration projects to study and evaluate the merger of the circuit, probate and district courts into a fully consolidated trial court.

The following courts shall begin a two-year demonstration project, effective January 1, 1996:

> BERRIEN COUNTY
> 2nd Circuit Court
> 5th District Court
> Berrien County Probate Court

During the two-year term of the demonstration project, these courts shall be referred to as the Berrien County Trial Court.

The Hon. Ronald J. Taylor is appointed as the Chief Judge of the Berrien County Trial Court. He shall have all of the authorities and responsibilities of a chief judge under MCR 8.110 as to all of the participating courts.

The judges, magistrates and referees within the Berrien County Trial Court are assigned to serve the whole court. Subject to the direction of the chief judge, each judge may exercise the jurisdiction of a judge of the circuit, probate, and district court. Subject to the direction of the chief judge, each magistrate or referee may perform the functions of a domestic relations referee, a district court magistrate or a juvenile court referee, with the authority to conduct proceedings as allowed by law and court rule.

The Berrien County Trial Court may form divisions. These divisions may correspond to the existing workload of the circuit, probate, and district courts, or may reflect another partition of the workload of the court; provided that the Berrien County Trial Court will incorporate into one general division issues affecting the family.

During this demonstration project, the Berrien County Trial Court may enter into cooperative agreements with state and local nonjudicial branch agencies to test the feasibility of the court to carry out essential court functions, such as record-keeping, felony probation services, information systems management, personnel management and financial management.

The chief judge of the trial court shall cooperate with the State Court Administrative Office by abiding by the terms of the project agreement, which include reporting and evaluation requirements.

Specific administrative and procedural requirements for each project, as needed, will be implemented through local administrative order or local court rule pursuant to MCR 8.112.

The State Court Administrative Office shall submit a status report to the Supreme Court at the end of each year of the demonstration project.*

[Entered April 25, 1996; extended until further order of the Court by Administrative Order 1997–12.]

* Administrative Order 1997–12, entered December 19, 1997, ordered that the "State Court Administrator shall provide a report on the status of each of the projects by November, 1998, and annually thereafter."

ADMINISTRATIVE ORDER 1996–6
AUTHORIZATION OF DEMONSTRATION PROJECTS TO STUDY COURT CONSOLIDATION

In its report entitled "Justice in Michigan: A Program for Reforming the Judicial Branch of Government; a Report to the People of Michigan from the Justices of the Michigan Supreme Court," the Supreme Court stated its intention to authorize demonstration projects to study and evaluate the merger of the circuit, probate and district courts into a fully consolidated trial court.

The following courts shall begin a two-year demonstration project, effective January 1, 1996:

ISABELLA COUNTY
21st Circuit Court
76th District Court
Isabella County Probate Court

During the two-year term of the demonstration project, these courts shall be referred to as the Isabella County Trial Court.

The Hon. Paul H. Chamberlain is appointed as the Chief Judge of the Isabella County Trial Court. He shall have all of the authorities and responsibilities of a chief judge under MCR 8.110 as to all of the participating courts.

The judges, magistrates and referees within the Isabella County Trial Court are assigned to serve the whole court. Subject to the direction of the chief judge, each judge may exercise the jurisdiction of a judge of the circuit, probate, and district court. Subject to the direction of the chief judge, each magistrate or referee may perform the functions of a domestic relations referee, a district court magistrate or a juvenile court referee, with the authority to conduct proceedings as allowed by law and court rule.

The Isabella County Trial Court may form divisions. These divisions may correspond to the existing workload of the circuit, probate, and district courts, or may reflect another partition of the workload of the court; provided that the Isabella County Trial Court will incorporate into one general division issues affecting the family.

During this demonstration project, the Isabella County Trial Court may enter into cooperative agreements with state and local nonjudicial branch agencies

to test the feasibility of the court to carry out essential court functions, such as record-keeping, felony probation services, information systems management, personnel management and financial management.

The chief judge of the trial court shall cooperate with the State Court Administrative Office by abiding by the terms of the project agreement, which include reporting and evaluation requirements.

Specific administrative and procedural requirements for each project, as needed, will be implemented through local administrative order or local court rule pursuant to MCR 8.112.

The State Court Administrative Office shall submit a status report to the Supreme Court at the end of each year of the demonstration project.*

[Entered May 2, 1996; extended until further order of the Court by Administrative Order 1997–12.]

* Administrative Order 1997–12, entered December 19, 1997, ordered that the "State Court Administrator shall provide a report on the status of each of the projects by November, 1998, and annually thereafter."

ADMINISTRATIVE ORDER 1996–7
AUTHORIZATION OF DEMONSTRATION PROJECTS TO STUDY COURT CONSOLIDATION

In its report entitled "Justice in Michigan: A Program for Reforming the Judicial Branch of Government; a Report to the People of Michigan from the Justices of the Michigan Supreme Court," the Supreme Court stated its intention to authorize demonstration projects to study and evaluate the merger of the circuit, probate and district courts into a fully consolidated trial court.

The following courts shall begin a two-year demonstration project, effective January 1, 1996:

LAKE COUNTY
51st Circuit Court
78th District Court
Lake County Probate Court

During the two-year term of the demonstration project, these courts shall be referred to as the Lake County Trial Court.

The Hon. Mark S. Wickens is appointed as the Chief Judge of the Lake County Trial Court. He shall have all of the authorities and responsibilities of a chief judge under MCR 8.110 as to all of the participating courts.

The judges, magistrates and referees within the Lake County Trial Court are assigned to serve the whole court. Subject to the direction of the chief judge, each judge may exercise the jurisdiction of a judge of the circuit, probate, and district court. Subject to the direction of the chief judge, each magistrate or referee may perform the functions of a domestic relations referee, a district court magistrate or a juvenile court referee, with the authority to conduct proceedings as allowed by law and court rule.

The Lake County Trial Court may form divisions. These divisions may correspond to the existing workload of the circuit, probate, and district courts, or may reflect another partition of the workload of the court; provided that the Lake County Trial Court will incorporate into one general division issues affecting the family.

During this demonstration project, the Lake County Trial Court may enter into cooperative agreements with state and local nonjudicial branch agencies to test the feasibility of the court to carry out essential court functions, such as record-keeping, felony probation services, information systems management, personnel management and financial management.

The chief judge of the trial court shall cooperate with the State Court Administrative Office by abiding by the terms of the project agreement, which include reporting and evaluation requirements.

Specific administrative and procedural requirements for each project, as needed, will be implemented through local administrative order or local court rule pursuant to MCR 8.112.

The State Court Administrative Office shall submit a status report to the Supreme Court at the end of each year of the demonstration project.*

[Entered May 6, 1996; extended until further order of the Court by Administrative Order 1997–12.]

* Administrative Order 1997–12, entered December 19, 1997, ordered that the "State Court Administrator shall provide a report on the status of each of the projects by November, 1998, and annually thereafter."

ADMINISTRATIVE ORDER 1996–9
AUTHORIZATION OF DEMONSTRATION PROJECTS TO STUDY COURT CONSOLIDATION

In its report entitled "Justice in Michigan: A Program for Reforming the Judicial Branch of Government; a Report to the People of Michigan from the Justices of the Michigan Supreme Court," the Supreme Court stated its intention to authorize demonstration projects to study and evaluate the merger of the circuit, probate and district courts into a fully consolidated trial court.

The following courts shall begin a two-year demonstration project, effective January 1, 1996:

CRAWFORD, KALKASKA AND OTSEGO COUNTIES
46th Circuit Court
83rd District Court (Crawford County)
87th District Court (Kalkaska and Otsego Counties)
Crawford County Probate Court

Kalkaska County Probate Court
Otsego County Probate Court

During the two-year term of the demonstration project, these courts shall be referred to as the 46th Circuit Trial Court.

The Hon. Alton T. Davis is appointed as the Chief Judge of the 46th Circuit Trial Court. He shall have all of the authorities and responsibilities of a chief judge under MCR 8.110 as to all of the participating courts.

The judges, magistrates and referees within the 46th Circuit Trial Court are assigned to serve the whole court. Subject to the direction of the chief judge and the limits on the authority of a nonlawyer probate judge, each judge may exercise the jurisdiction of a judge of the circuit, probate, and district court. Subject to the direction of the chief judge, each magistrate or referee may perform the functions of a domestic relations referee, a district court magistrate or a juvenile court referee, with the authority to conduct proceedings as allowed by law and court rule.

The 46th Circuit Trial Court may form divisions. These divisions may correspond to the existing workload of the circuit, probate, and district courts, or may reflect another partition of the workload of the court; provided that the 46th Circuit Trial Court will incorporate into one general division issues affecting the family.

During this demonstration project, the 46th Circuit Trial Court may enter into cooperative agreements with state and local nonjudicial branch agencies to test the feasibility of the court to carry out essential court functions, such as record-keeping, felony probation services, information systems management, personnel management and financial management.

The chief judge of the trial court shall cooperate with the State Court Administrative Office by abiding by the terms of the project agreement, which include reporting and evaluation requirements.

Specific administrative and procedural requirements for each project, as needed, will be implemented through local administrative order or local court rule pursuant to MCR 8.112.

The State Court Administrative Office shall submit a status report to the Supreme Court at the end of each year of the demonstration project.*

[Entered May 31, 1996; extended until further order of the Court by Administrative Order 1997–12.]

* Administrative Order 1997–12, entered December 19, 1997, ordered that the "State Court Administrator shall provide a report on the status of each of the projects by November, 1998, and annually thereafter."

ADMINISTRATIVE ORDER 1996–11
HIRING OF RELATIVES BY COURTS

In order to ensure that the Michigan judiciary is able to attract and retain the highest quality work force, and make most effective use of its personnel, IT IS ORDERED that the following anti-nepotism policy is effective December 1, 1996, for all courts of this state.

1. **Purpose.** This anti-nepotism policy is adopted to avoid conflicts of interest, the possibility or appearance of favoritism, morale problems, and the potential for emotional interference with job performance.

2. **Application.** This policy applies to all full-time and part-time non-union employees, temporary employees, contractual employment, including independent contractors, student interns, and personal service contracts. This policy also applies to all applicants for employment regardless of whether the position applied for is union or non-union.

3. **Definitions.**

a) As used in this policy, the term "Relative" is defined to include spouse, child, parent, brother, sister, grandparent, grandchild, first cousin, uncle, aunt, niece, nephew, brother-in-law, sister-in-law, daughter-in-law, son-in-law, mother-in-law, and father-in-law, whether natural, adopted, step or foster.

b) As used in this policy, "State Court System" is defined to include all courts and agencies enumerated in Const 1963, art 6, § 1 and the Revised Judicature Act of 1961, MCL 600.101 et seq.; MSA 27A.101 et seq.

c) As used in this policy, the term "Court Administrator" is defined to include the highest level administrator, clerk or director of the court or agency who functions under the general direction of the chief justice or chief judge, such as, state court administrator, agency director, circuit court administrator, friend of the court, probate court administrator, juvenile court administrator, probate register and district court administrator/clerk.

4. **Prohibitions.**

a) Relatives of justices, judges or court administrators shall not be employed within the same court or judicial entity. This prohibition does not bar the assignment of judges and retired judges by the Supreme Court to serve in any other court in this state for a limited period or specific assignment, provided those assigned shall not participate in any employment related matters or decisions in the court to which they are assigned.

b) Relatives of employees not employed as justices, judges or court administrators shall not be employed, whether by hire, appointment, transfer or promotion, in any court within the state court system (i) where one person has any degree of supervisory authority over the other, whether direct or indirect; (ii) where the employment would create favoritism or a conflict of interest or the appearance of favoritism or a conflict of interest; or (iii) for reasons of confidentiality.

c) Should two employees become relatives by reason of marriage or other legal relationship after employment, if possible, one employee shall be required to transfer to another court within the state court system if the transfer would eliminate the violation. If a transfer is not possible or if the violation cannot be eliminated, one employee shall be required to resign. The decision as to which employee shall transfer or resign may be made by the employees. If the employees fail to decide between themselves within thirty days of becoming relatives, the employee with the least seniority shall be required to transfer or resign. However, if one of the two employees holds an elective office, is a judge or is covered by a union contract, the other employee shall be required to transfer or resign.

5. **Required Submissions.** If any person, whether employed by hire, appointment, or election, contemplates the creation of a contractual relationship that may implicate this policy, whether directly or indirectly, the proposed contract shall be submitted to the State Court Administrative Office for review to ensure compliance with this policy.

6. **Required Disclosure.** All current employees, including persons who are elected or appointed, shall disclose in writing to the State Court Administrative Office the existence of any familial relationship as described in this policy within thirty (30) days of the issuance of this policy or creation of the relationship, whichever is sooner.

7. **Affected Employees.** This policy shall not apply to any person who is an employee of the state court system on December 1, 1996, except that from December 1, 1996, forward, no person shall be transferred or promoted or enter into a nepotic relationship in violation of this policy.

[Entered November 8, 1996.]

ADMINISTRATIVE ORDER 1997–1
IMPLEMENTATION OF THE FAMILY DIVISION OF THE CIRCUIT COURT

Public Act 388 of 1996 provides for the implementation of a family division of the circuit court. Chief circuit and probate judges are to develop a plan for the implementation and operation of the family division, and to identify the manner in which services will be coordinated to provide effective and efficient services to families by the family division of the circuit court.

In order to ensure effective administration of the family division of the circuit court, IT IS ORDERED that chief circuit and probate judges shall file plans for implementation and operation of the family division of the circuit court with the State Court Administrative Office by July 1, 1997. In developing the plans, chief circuit and probate judges shall seek the input of all judges of the circuit and probate court, staff of the circuit and probate courts, and other entities providing service to families within that jurisdiction, or who will be affected by the operation of the family division.

Upon the filing of the plan, the State Court Administrative Office shall accept the plan for filing, or may return the plan to the chief circuit and probate judge for amendment in accordance with Public Act 388 of 1996 and requirements and guidelines provided by the State Court Administrative Office for family division implementation plans.[1]

The State Court Administrative Office, upon approval by the Supreme Court, may provide an extension of time for filing of implementation plans for good cause upon a written request of the chief circuit and probate judge required to file a plan, and a showing that there is substantial progress on the development of the implementation plan.

Any amendment to a family division implementation and operation plan must be filed with the State Court Administrative Office and accepted by that office for filing prior to the implementation of amended provisions of the plan.

The State Court Administrative Office, upon acceptance of the filing of a family division implementation and operation plan, shall provide for assignment of judges of the probate court to the family division of the circuit court, and if appropriate, to other divisions of the circuit court in accordance with the implementation and operation plan.

In any circuit court where the chief circuit and probate judges are unable to agree upon a family division implementation and operation plan by July 1, 1997, or a later date approved by the State Court Administrative Office, the State Court Administrative Office will develop a plan for implementation and operation of the family division of the circuit court in that circuit.

The State Court Administrator shall provide periodic reports to the Supreme Court regarding the status of development of family division implementation and operation plans. Those reports shall include identification of barriers to development of or implementation of plans and recommendations for remedial action.

1. The State Court Administrative Office must approve the plan prior to accepting it for filing and provide written notification of such approval. The plan must be approved and accepted for filing prior to implementation. This process is similar to the process for approval of local administrative orders under MCR 8.112(B).

[Entered February 25, 1997.]

ADMINISTRATIVE ORDER 1997–2
SUSPENSION OF LICENSE TO PRACTICE LAW—PURSUANT TO 1996 PA 236, 1996 PA 238 and 1996 PA 239

On order of the Court, in light of 1996 PA 236, 1996 PA 238 and 1996 PA 239, we authorize circuit courts to issue suspensions of licenses to practice law subject to the conditions specified in the above-mentioned legislative enactments. The order shall be effective upon entry by the circuit court. The Office of the Friend of the Court shall send a copy of the suspension order or rescission of a prior suspension order to the Clerk of the Supreme Court, the State Court Administrative Office, the State Bar of Michigan, the Attorney Grievance Commission, and the Attorney Discipline Board.

[Entered April 1, 1997.]

ADMINISTRATIVE ORDER 1997–4
APPOINTMENT OF EXECUTIVE CHIEF JUDGE FOR THIRD CIRCUIT COURT AND RECORDER'S COURT; ESTABLISHMENT OF EXECUTIVE COMMITTEE

On order of the Court, it appearing that the administration of justice would be served by the appointment of an Executive Chief Judge to oversee the administration of the Third Circuit Court and Recorder's Court in order to facilitate the orderly transition to a single court; it is ORDERED that the Honorable Michael F. Sapala is appointed as Executive Chief Judge of the Third Circuit and Recorder's Courts, effectively immediately.

The Executive Chief Judge of the Third Circuit Court and Recorder's Court has all of the responsibility and authority of chief judge pursuant to Michigan Court Rule 8.110 and as otherwise indicated in the Michigan Court Rules.

The Chief Judge of the Recorder's Court and Chief Judge of the Third Circuit Court shall continue to have responsibility for docket management, facilities and security, day to day management of personnel, budget and purchasing activity; and other responsibilities delegated by the Executive Chief Judge.

It is further ORDERED, that effective 10–01–97, the Hon. Michael F. Sapala shall be the Chief Judge of the Third Circuit Court.

It is further ORDERED, effective immediately, that an Executive Committee of the Third Circuit Court and Recorder's Court is established to provide assistance to the Executive Chief Judge in developing administrative policy. The Chief Justice shall appoint members of the Executive Committee from the benches of the Third Circuit Court and Recorder's Court. Effective 10–01–97, and until further order of this Court, the Executive Committee shall serve the Third Circuit Court, and shall provide assistance to the Chief Judge of the Third Circuit Court.

[Entered June 4, 1997.]

1997 Staff Comment

This order has been entered by the Court in anticipation of the merger of the Third Circuit Court and Recorder's Court as mandated by 1996 PA 374, which will take place effective 10–01–97. The appointment of an Executive Chief Judge is designed to facilitate planning for the merger and to assure a consistent approach to policy issues affecting both courts which will have an impact on the administration of the Third Circuit Court after 10–01–97.

ADMINISTRATIVE ORDER 1997–5
DEFENDERS—THIRD CIRCUIT COURT

The Court has determined that the efficient administration of justice requires the extension of the provisions of Administrative Order 1972–2 to criminal matters coming before the Third Circuit Court after the merger of the Third Circuit Court and Recorder's Court on October 1, 1997. IT IS THEREFORE ORDERED that effective October 1, 1997 and until further order of the Court, that the Chief Judge of the Third Circuit Court shall provide for the assignment as counsel, on a weekly basis, of the Legal Aid and Defender Association in twenty five percent of all cases wherein counsel are appointed for indigent defendants.

[Entered July 25, 1997.]

ADMINISTRATIVE ORDER 1997–8
ESTABLISHMENT OF COURT
DATA STANDARDS

In order to ensure effective administration of trial court information systems and facilitate the efficient exchange of trial court case information, IT IS ORDERED that the State Court Administrator establish court data standards. Chief judges shall take necessary action to ensure their courts' information systems comply with data standards established by the State Court Administrator.

The State Court Administrator shall provide reasonable time frames for compliance with court data standards. Not less than two years will be provided for compliance with data standards initially established pursuant to this order.

[Entered November 12, 1997.]

ADMINISTRATIVE ORDER 1997–9
ALLOCATION OF FUNDS FROM
LAWYER TRUST ACCOUNT PROGRAM

On order of the Court, effective November 14, 1997, until further order of the Court, Administrative Order 1994–8, which modified Administrative Order 1990–2, is modified so as to provide that the funds to be distributed by the Board of Trustees of the Michigan State Bar Foundation shall be disbursed as follows:

1. Seventy percent of the net proceeds of the Lawyer Trust Account Program to support the delivery of civil legal services to the poor;

2. Fifteen percent of the net proceeds of the Lawyer Trust Account Program to support programs to promote improvements in the administration of justice;

3. Ten percent of the proceeds of the Lawyer Trust Account Program to support implementation, within the judiciary, of the recommendations of the Task Force on Gender Issues in the Courts and the Task Force on Racial/Ethnic Issues in the Courts; and

4. Five percent of the net proceeds of the Lawyer Trust Account Program to support the activities of the Michigan Supreme Court Historical Society.

[Entered November 14, 1997.]

ADMINISTRATIVE ORDER 1997–10
ACCESS TO JUDICIAL BRANCH
ADMINISTRATIVE INFORMATION

On order of the Court, the following order is effective February 1, 1998. The Court invites public comment on ways in which the objectives of the policy expressed in this order—an informed public and an accountable judicial branch—might be achieved most effectively and efficiently, consistent with the exercise of the constitutional responsibilities of the judicial branch. Comments should be sent to the Supreme Court Clerk by January 31, 1998.

(A) Scope, Coverage, and Definitions.

(1) This order does not apply to the adjudicative function of the judicial branch. It neither broadens nor restricts the availability of information relating to a court's adjudicative records.

(2) Solely as used in this order:

(a) "Adjudicative record" means any writing of any nature, and information in any form, that is filed with a court in connection with a matter to be adjudicated, and any writing prepared in the performance of an adjudicative function of the judicial branch.

(b) "Administrative function" means the nonfinancial, managerial work that a court does, outside the context of any particular case.

(c) "Administrative record" means a writing, other than a financial record or an employee record, prepared in the performance of an administrative function of the judicial branch.

(d) "Employee record" means information concerning an employee of the Supreme Court, State Court Administrative Office, Michigan Judicial Institute, and Board of Law Examiners.

(e) "Financial record" means the proposed budget, enacted budget, judicial salary information, and annual revenues and expenditures of a court.

(f) "Judge" means a justice of the Supreme Court or a judge of the Court of Appeals, circuit court, probate court, district court, or municipal court.

(g) "Person" means any individual or entity, except an individual incarcerated in a local, state, or federal correctional facility of any kind.

(h) "Supreme Court administrative agency" means the State Court Administrative Office, the Office of the Clerk, the Office of the Chief Justice, the Supreme Court Finance Department, and the Public Information Office.

(B) Access to Information Regarding Supreme Court Administrative, Financial, and Employee Records.

(1) Upon a written request that describes an administrative record, an employee record, or a financial record sufficiently to enable the Supreme Court administrative agency to find the record, a person has a right to examine, copy, or receive copies of the record, except as provided in this order.

(2) Requests for an administrative or employee record of a Supreme Court administrative agency must be directed to the administrative agency or to the Public Information Office. Requests for a financial record must be directed to the Supreme Court Finance Department. An administrative record, employee record, or financial record must be available for examination during regular business hours.

(3) A Supreme Court administrative agency may make reasonable rules to protect its records and to prevent unreasonable interference with its functions.

(4) This order does not require the creation of a new administrative record, employee record, or financial record.

(5) A reasonable fee may be charged for providing a copy of an administrative record, employee record, or financial record. The fee must be limited to the actual marginal cost of providing the copy, including materials and the time required to find the record and delete any exempt material. A person requesting voluminous records may be required to submit a deposit representing no more than half the estimated fee.

(6) A copyrighted administrative record is a public record that may not be re-published without proper authorization.

(7) The following are exempt from disclosure:

(a) Personal information if public disclosure would be an unwarranted invasion of an individual's privacy. Such information includes, but is not limited to:

(i) The home address, home telephone number, social security account number, financial institution record, electronic transfer fund number, deferred compensation, savings bonds, W–2 and W–4 forms, and any court-enforced judgment of a judge or employee.

(ii) The benefit selection of a judge or employee.

(iii) Detail in a telephone bill, including the telephone number and name of the person or entity called.

(iv) Telephone logs and messages.

(v) Unemployment compensation records and worker's disability compensation records.

(b) Information that would endanger the safety or well-being of an individual.

(c) Information that, if disclosed, would undermine the discharge of a constitutional or statutory responsibility.

(d) Records or information exempted from disclosure by a statutory or common law privilege.

(e) An administrative record or financial record that is to a substantial degree advisory in nature and preliminary to a final administrative decision, rather than to a substantial degree factual in nature.

(f) Investigative records compiled by the State Court Administrative Office pursuant to MCR 8.113.

(g) An administrative record or financial record relating to recommendations for appointments to court positions, court-sponsored committees, or evaluation of persons for appointment to court positions or court-sponsored committees.

(h) Trade secrets, bids, or other commercial information if public disclosure would give or deny a commercial benefit to an individual or commercial entity.

(i) Examination materials that would affect the integrity of a testing process.

(j) Material exempt from disclosure under MCL 15.243; MSA 4.1801(13).

(k) The identity of judges assigned to or participating in the preparation of a written decision or opinion.

(*l*) Correspondence between individuals and judges. Such correspondence may be made accessible to the public by the sender or the recipient, unless the subject matter of the correspondence is otherwise protected from disclosure.

(m) Reports filed pursuant to MCR 8.110(5), and information compiled by the Supreme Court exclusively for purposes of evaluating judicial and court performance, pursuant to MCL 600.238; MSA 27A.238. Such information shall be made accessible to the public as directed by separate administrative order.

(n) An administrative record, employee record, or financial record in draft form.

(*o*) The work product of an attorney or law clerk employed by or representing the judicial branch in the regular course of business or representation of the judicial branch.

(p) Correspondence with the Judicial Tenure Commission regarding any judge or judicial officer, or materials received from the Judicial Tenure Commission regarding any judge or judicial officer.

(q) Correspondence with the Attorney Grievance Commission or Attorney Discipline Board regarding any attorney, judge, or judicial officer, or materials received from the Attorney Grievance Commission or Attorney Discipline Board regarding any attorney, judge, or judicial officer.

(8) A request for a record may be denied if the custodian of the record determines that:

(a) compliance with the request would create an undue financial burden on court operations because of the amount of equipment, materials, staff time, or other resources required to satisfy the request.

(b) compliance with the request would substantially interfere with the constitutionally or statutorily mandated functions of the court.

(c) the request is made for the purpose of harassing or substantially interfering with the routine operations of the court.

(d) the request is submitted within one month following the date of the denial of a substantially identical request by the same requester, denied under substantially identical rules and circumstances.

(9) A person's request to examine, copy, or receive copies of an administrative record, employee record, or financial record must be granted, granted in part and denied in part, or denied, as promptly as practicable. A request must include sufficient information to reasonably identify what is being sought. The person requesting the information shall not be required to have detailed information about the court's filing system or procedures to submit a request. A Supreme Court administrative agency may require that a request be made in writing if the request is complex or involves a large number of records. Upon request, a partial or complete denial must be accompanied by a written explanation. A partial or complete denial is not subject to an appeal.

(10) Employee records are not open to public access, except for the following information:

(a) The full name of the employee.

(b) The date of employment.

(c) The current and previous job titles and descriptions within the judicial branch, and effective dates of employment for previous employment within the judicial branch.

(d) The name, location, and telephone number of the court or agency of the employee.

(e) The name of the employee's current supervisor.

(f) Any information authorized by the employee to be released to the public or to a named individual, unless otherwise prohibited by law.

(g) The current salary of the employee. A request for salary information pursuant to this order must be in writing. The individual who provides the information must immediately notify the employee that a request for salary information has been made, and that the information has been provided.

(11) The design and operation of all future automated record management systems must incorporate processing features and procedures that maximize the availability of administrative records or financial records maintained electronically. Automated systems development policies must require the identification and segregation of confidential data elements from database sections that are accessible to the public. Whenever feasible, any major enhancements or upgrades to existing systems are to include modifications that segregate confidential information from publicly accessed databases.

[Entered December 9, 1997.]

ADMINISTRATIVE ORDER 1997–11
ACCESS TO JUDICIAL BRANCH ADMINISTRATIVE DECISIONMAKING

On order of the Court, the following order is effective February 1, 1998. The Court invites public comment on ways in which the objectives of the policy expressed in this order—an informed public and an accountable judicial branch—might be achieved most effectively and efficiently, consistent with the exercise of the constitutional responsibilities of the judicial branch. Comments should be sent to the Supreme Court Clerk by January 31, 1998.

(A) Scope, Coverage, and Definitions. This order neither broadens nor restricts the extent to which court proceedings are conducted in public.

(B) Supreme Court Administrative Public Hearings.

(1) At least three times annually the Supreme Court will conduct an administrative public hearing on rules or administrative orders significantly affecting the delivery of justice proposed for adoption or amendment. An agenda of an administrative public hearing will be published not less than 28 days before the hearing in the manner most likely to come to the attention of interested persons. Public notice of any amendments to the agenda after publication will be made in the most effective manner practicable under the circumstances. Persons who notify the clerk of the Supreme Court in writing not less than 7 days before the hearing of their desire to address the Court at the hearing will be afforded the opportunity to do so.

(2) Unless immediate action is required, the adoption or amendment of rules or administrative orders that will significantly affect the administration of justice will be preceded by an administrative public hearing under subsection (1). If no public hearing has been held before a rule is adopted or amended, the matter will be placed on the agenda of the next public hearing, at which time the Supreme Court will hear public comment regarding whether the rule should be retained or amended.

(3) The adoption or amendment of a court rule or administrative order by the Supreme Court shall be by a recorded vote, and shall be available upon request from the Supreme Court Clerk.

(C) State Court Administrative Office; Administrative Public Hearings.

(1) Task forces, commissions, and working groups created at the direction of the Supreme Court and convened to advise the State Court Administrative Office and the Michigan Supreme Court on matters significantly affecting the delivery of justice must provide an opportunity for public attendance at one or more meetings.

(2) Notice of a meeting that is open to the public pursuant to this order must be provided in a manner reasonably likely to come to the attention of interested persons.

(3) A meeting held pursuant to this section must be held at a reasonably convenient time and in a handicap accessible setting.

(4) Persons interested in making a public comment at a meeting held pursuant to this section must be afforded the opportunity for public comment to the extent practicable. If the business of the meeting precludes the opportunity for public comment by any person wishing to comment, the person must be allowed to speak at a subsequent meeting or, if no future meeting will be held, be given the opportunity to have a written public comment recorded in the minutes and distributed to members of the task force, commission, or working group.

[Entered December 9, 1997.]

ADMINISTRATIVE ORDER 1997–12
AUTHORIZATION OF DEMONSTRATION PROJECTS TO STUDY COURT CONSOLIDATION

The Court having decided that the Court Consolidation Demonstration Projects authorized by Supreme Court Administrative Orders 1996–1, 1996–2, 1996–5, 1996–6, 1996–7, 1996–9 have provided valuable information regarding the effective consolidation of courts and the process of consolidation of courts, and that there would be benefit from extending the projects, orders that the provisions of the following Supreme

Court Administrative Orders are extended until further order of the Court:

  1996–1 Barry County Trial Court
  1996–2 Washtenaw County Trial Court
  1996–5 Berrien County Trial Court
  1996–6 Isabella County Trial Court
  1996–7 Lake County Trial Court
  1996–9 46th Circuit Trial Court

The State Court Administrator shall provide a report on the status of each of the projects by November, 1998, and annually thereafter.

It is further ordered that the chief judges of the trial courts created through those administrative orders will be as designated by the Supreme Court in its order dated October 30, 1997.

[Entered December 19, 1997.]

ADMINISTRATIVE ORDER 1998–1
REASSIGNMENT OF CIRCUIT COURT ACTIONS TO DISTRICT JUDGES

In 1996 PA 374 the Legislature repealed former MCL 600.641; MSA 27A.641, which authorized the removal of actions from circuit court to district court on the ground that the amount of damages sustained may be less than the jurisdictional limitation as to the amount in controversy applicable to the district court. In accordance with that legislation, we repealed former MCR 4.003, the court rule implementing that procedure. It appearing that some courts have been improperly using transfers of actions under MCR 2.227 as a substitute for the former removal procedure, and that some procedure for utilizing district judges to try actions filed in circuit court would promote the efficient administration of justice, we adopt this administrative order, effective immediately, to apply to actions filed after January 1, 1997.

A circuit court may not transfer an action to district court under MCR 2.227 based on the amount in controversy unless: (1) The parties stipulate to the transfer and to an appropriate amendment of the complaint, see MCR 2.111(B)(2); or (2) From the allegations of the complaint, it appears to a legal certainty that the amount in controversy is not greater than the applicable jurisdictional limit of the district court. Circuit courts are directed to send to the State Court Administrator copies of all orders transferring actions to district court under MCR 2.227 based on the amount in controversy.

Circuit courts and the district courts within their geographic jurisdictions are strongly urged to enter into agreements, to be implemented by joint local administrative orders, to provide that certain actions pending in circuit court will be reassigned to district judges for further proceedings. An action designated for such reassignment shall remain pending as a circuit court action, and the circuit court shall request the State Court Administrator assign the district judge to the circuit court for the purpose of conducting proceedings. Such administrative orders may specify the categories of cases that are appropriate or inappropriate for such reassignment, and shall include a procedure for resolution of disputes between circuit and district courts as to whether a case was properly reassigned to a district judge.

Because this order was entered without having been considered at a public hearing under Administrative Order 1997–11, the question whether to retain or amend the order will be placed on the agenda for the next administrative public hearing, currently scheduled for September 24, 1998.

[Entered June 16, 1998, to apply to actions filed after January 1, 1997.]

ADMINISTRATIVE ORDER 1998–2
SENTENCING GUIDELINES
[VACATED]*

* Publisher's Note: See Administrative Order 1998–4, entered December 15, 1998, relating to the Michigan Sentencing Guidelines.

ADMINISTRATIVE ORDER 1998–3
FAMILY DIVISION OF THE
CIRCUIT COURT;
SUPPORT PAYMENTS

The family division of the circuit court is responsible for the receipt and disbursement of child and spousal support payments. Those transactions require substantial public resources in order to ensure that the funds are properly receipted and disbursed on a timely basis for the benefit of those who receive the funds. Michigan circuit courts have an exemplary record for the rapid and efficient receipt and disbursement of support payments. The implementation of electronic funds transfer processes for receipt and disbursement of funds provides the opportunity for more timely processing support payments, and the opportunity for reducing the cost of such transactions. Furthermore, it is apparent that the implementation of electronic funds transfers for support payments will facilitate the implementation of central distribution processes required by the federal Personal Responsibility and Work Opportunity Act of 1996.

Therefore, it is ordered that circuit courts, in receiving and disbursing support payments, shall use electronic funds transfer to the fullest extent possible.

In implementing electronic funds transfers, circuit courts will follow guidelines established by the State Court Administrator for that purpose.

[Entered November 24, 1998.]

ADMINISTRATIVE ORDER 1998–4
SENTENCING GUIDELINES

On order of the Court, Administrative Order 1998–2, 459 Mich xvi (1998), is vacated.

The sentencing guidelines promulgated by the Supreme Court in Administrative Order 1988–4, 430 Mich ci (1988) are rescinded, effective January 1, 1999, for all cases in which the offense is committed on or after January 1, 1999. The sentencing guidelines promulgated in Administrative Order 1988–4, as governed by the appellate case law concerning those guidelines, remain in effect for applicable offenses committed before January 1, 1999.*

[Entered December 15, 1998.]

* See the current edition of *Michigan Sentencing Guidelines*, available from West.

ADMINISTRATIVE ORDER 1998–5
CHIEF JUDGE RESPONSIBILITIES;
LOCAL INTERGOVERNMENTAL
RELATIONS

On order of the Court, the following order is effective immediately. This order replaces Administrative Order No. 1997–6, which is rescinded.

I. APPLICABILITY

This Administrative Order applies to all trial courts as defined in MCR 8.110(A).

II. COURT BUDGETING

A court must submit its proposed and appropriated annual budget and subsequent modifications to the State Court Administrator at the time of submission to or receipt from the local funding unit or units. The budget submitted must be in conformity with a uniform chart of accounts. If the local funding unit requests that a proposed budget be submitted in line-item detail, the chief judge must comply with the request. If a budget has been appropriated in line-item detail, without prior approval of the funding unit, a court may not transfer between line-item accounts to: (a) create new personnel positions or to supplement existing wage scales or benefits, except to implement across the board increases that were granted to employees of the funding unit after the adoption of the court's budget at the same rate, or (b) reclassify an employee to a higher level of an existing category. A chief judge may not enter into a multiple-year commitment concerning any personnel economic issue unless: (1) the funding unit agrees, or (2) the agreement does not exceed the percentage increase or the duration of a multiple-year contract that the funding unit has negotiated for its employees. Courts must notify the funding unit or a local court management council of transfers between lines within 10 business days of the transfer. The requirements shall not be construed to restrict implementation of collective bargaining agreements.

III. FUNDING DISPUTES; MEDIATION AND LEGAL ACTION

If, after the local funding unit has made its appropriations, a court concludes that the funds provided for its operations by its local funding unit are insufficient to enable the court to properly perform its duties and that legal action is necessary, the procedures set forth in this order must be followed.

1. Legal action may be commenced 30 days after the court has notified the State Court Administrator that a dispute exists regarding court funding that the court and the local funding unit have been unable to resolve, unless mediation of the dispute is in progress, in which case legal action may not be commenced within 60 days of the commencement of the mediation. The notice must be accompanied by a written communication indicating that the chief judge of the court has approved the commencement of legal proceedings. With the notice, the court must supply the State Court Administrator with all facts relevant to the funding dispute. The State Court Administrator may extend this period for an additional 30 days.

2. During the waiting period provided in paragraph 1, the State Court Administrator must attempt to aid the court and the involved local funding unit to resolve the dispute.

3. If, after the procedure provided in paragraph 2 has been followed, the court concludes that a civil action to compel funding is necessary, the State Court Administrator must assign a disinterested judge to preside over the action.

4. Chief judges or representatives of funding units may request the assistance of the State Court Administrative Office to mediate situations involving potential disputes at any time, before differences escalate to the level of a formal funding dispute.

IV. LOCAL COURT MANAGEMENT COUNCIL OPTION

Where a local court management council has been created by a funding unit, the chief judge of a trial court for which the council operates as a local court management council, or the chief judge's designee, may serve as a member of the council. Unless the local court management council adopts the bylaws described below, without the agreement of the chief judge, the council serves solely in an advisory role with respect to decisions concerning trial court management otherwise reserved exclusively to the chief judge of the trial court pursuant to court order and administrative order of the Supreme Court.

A chief judge, or the chief judge's designee, must serve as a member of a council whose nonjudicial members agree to the adoption of the following bylaws:

1) Council membership includes the chief judge of each court for which the council operates as a local court management council.

2) Funding unit membership does not exceed judicial membership by more than one vote. Funding unit membership is determined by the local funding unit; judicial membership is determined by the chief judge or chief judges. Judicial membership may not be an even number.

3) Any action of the council requires an affirmative vote by a majority of the funding unit representatives on the council and a majority vote of the judicial representatives on the council.

4) Once a council has been formed, dissolution of the council requires the majority vote of the funding unit representatives and the judicial representatives of the council.

5) Meetings of the council must comply with the Open Meetings Act.[1] Records of the council are subject to the Freedom of Information Act.[2]

If such bylaws have been adopted, a chief judge shall implement any personnel policies agreed upon by the council concerning compensation, fringe benefits, and pensions of court employees, and shall not take any action inconsistent with policies of the local court management council concerning those matters. Management policies concerning the following are to be established by the chief judge, but must be consistent with the written employment policies of the local funding unit except to the extent that conformity with those policies would impair the operation of the court: holidays, leave, work schedules, discipline, grievance process, probation, classification, personnel records, and employee compensation for closure of court business due to weather conditions.

As a member of a local court management council that has adopted the bylaws described above, a chief judge or the chief judge's designee must not act in a manner that frustrates or impedes the collective bargaining process. If an impasse occurs in a local court management council concerning issues affecting the collective bargaining process, the chief judge or judges of the council must immediately notify the State Court Administrator, who will initiate action to aid the local court management council in resolving the impasse. It is expected that before and during the collective bargaining process, the local court management council will agree on bargaining strategy and a proposed dollar value for personnel costs. Should a local court management council fail to agree on strategy or be unable to develop an offer for presentation to employees for response, the chief judge must notify the State Court Administrator. The State Court Administrator must work to break the impasse and cause to be developed for presentation to employees a series of proposals on which negotiations must be held.

V. PARTICIPATION BY FUNDING UNIT IN NEGOTIATING PROCESS

If a court does not have a local court management council, the chief judge, in establishing personnel policies concerning compensation, fringe benefits, pensions, holidays, or leave, must consult regularly with the local funding unit and must permit a representative of the local funding unit to attend and participate in negotiating sessions with court employees, if desired by the local funding unit. The chief judge shall inform the funding unit at least 72 hours in advance of any negotiating session. The chief judge may permit the funding unit to act on the chief judge's behalf as negotiating agent.

VI. CONSISTENCY WITH FUNDING UNIT PERSONNEL POLICIES

To the extent possible, consistent with the effective operation of the court, the chief judge must adopt personnel policies consistent with the written employment policies of the local funding unit. Effective operation of the court to best serve the public in multi-county circuits and districts, and in third class district courts with multiple funding units may require a single, uniform personnel policy that does not wholly conform with specific personnel policies of any of the court's funding units.

1. *Unscheduled Court Closing Due to Weather Emergency.* If a chief judge opts to close a court and dismiss court employees because of a weather emergency, the dismissed court employees must use accumulated leave time or take unpaid leave if the funding unit has employees in the same facility who are not dismissed by the funding unit. If a collective bargaining agreement with court staff does not allow the use of accumulated leave time or unpaid leave in the event of court closure due to weather conditions, the chief judge shall not close the court unless the funding unit also dismisses its employees working at the same facility as the court. Within 90 days of the issuance of this order, a chief judge shall develop and submit to the State Court Administrative Office a local administrative order detailing the process for unscheduled court closing in the event of bad weather. In preparing the order, the chief judge shall consult with the court's funding unit. The policy must be consistent with any collective bargaining agreements in effect for employees working in the court.

2. *Court Staff Hours.* The standard working hours of court staff, including when they begin and end work, shall be consistent with the standard working hours of the funding unit. Any deviation from the standard working hours of the funding unit must be reflected in a local administrative order, as required by the chief judge rule, and be submitted for review and comment to the funding unit before it is submitted to the SCAO for approval.

VII. TRAINING PROGRAMS

The Supreme Court will direct the development and implementation of ongoing training seminars of judges and funding unit representatives on judicial/legislative relations, court budgeting, expenditures, collective bargaining, and employee management issues.

VIII. COLLECTIVE BARGAINING

For purposes of collective bargaining pursuant to 1947 PA 336, a chief judge or a designee of the chief judge shall bargain and sign contracts with employees of the court. Notwithstanding the primary role of the chief judge concerning court personnel pursuant to MCR 8.110, to the extent that such action is consistent with the effective and efficient operation of the court, a chief judge of a trial court may designate a representative of a local funding unit or a local court management council to act on the court's behalf for purposes of collective bargaining pursuant to 1947 PA 336 only, and, as a member of a local court management council, may vote in the affirmative to designate a local court management council to act on the court's behalf for purposes of collective bargaining only.

IX. EFFECT ON EXISTING AGREEMENTS

This order shall not be construed to impair existing collective bargaining agreements. Nothing in this order shall be construed to amend or abrogate agreements between chief judges and local funding units in effect on the date of this order. Any existing collective bargaining agreements that expire within 90 days may be extended for up to 12 months.

If the implementation of 1996 PA 374 pursuant to this order requires a transfer of court employees or a change of employers, all employees of the former court employer shall be transferred to, and appointed as employees of, the appropriate employer, subject to all rights and benefits they held with the former court employer. The employer shall assume and be bound by any existing collective bargaining agreement held by the former court employer and, except where the existing collective bargaining agreement may otherwise permit, shall retain the employees covered by that collective bargaining agreement. A transfer of court employees shall not adversely affect any existing rights and obligations contained in the existing collective bargaining agreement. An employee who is transferred shall not, by reason of the transfer, be placed in any worse position with respect to worker's compensation, pension, seniority, wages, sick leave, vacation, health and welfare insurance, or any other terms and conditions of employment that the employee enjoyed as an employee of the former court employer. The rights and benefits thus protected may be altered by a future collective bargaining agreement.

X. REQUESTS FOR ASSISTANCE

The chief judge or a representative of the funding unit may request the assistance of the State Court

tion

Administrative Office to facilitate effective communication between the court and the funding unit.

[Entered December 28, 1998.]

1. MCL 15.261 *et seq.*; MSA 4.1800(11) *et seq.*
2. MCL 15.231 *et seq.*; MSA 4.1801(1) *et seq.*

ADMINISTRATIVE ORDER 1999–1 ASSIGNMENT OF MEDICAL SUPPORT ENFORCEMENT MATTERS TO THE THIRD CIRCUIT FOR DISCOVERY PURPOSES

Administrative Order No. 1997–3 is rescinded. On order of the Court, it appears that the administration of justice would be served in matters pending in circuit courts relating to support of minor children; any sitting judge of the Third Circuit Court assigned to the family division of the Third Circuit Court may act in proceedings involving the financial and medical support of minor children in jurisdictions other than the Third Circuit Court according to the following procedures:

1. This order applies to all pending and future actions involving the enforcement of financial or medical support of minor children filed in jurisdictions other than the Third Circuit Court.

2. In actions where the circuit court, office of the friend of the court, requires the discovery of information relating to the availability of health or medical care insurance coverage to the parents of children subject to orders of support pending in that court, the chief circuit judge may refer those actions by writing or through electronic means to the Third Circuit Court Friend of the Court Office for assistance in the discovery of such information.

3. Upon acceptance of the referral under section 2 by the Chief Judge of the Third Circuit or his or her designee, a judge of the Family Division of the Third Circuit Court designated by the Chief Judge of the Third Circuit Court may issue appropriate orders in that action for the purpose of discovery of information related to the availability of medical or health care insurance to the parents of minor children who are the subjects of that action. The judge(s) so assigned may by subpoena or other lawful means require the production of information for that purpose through single orders which apply to all cases referred from all jurisdictions making referrals under section 2.

4. The State Court Administrative Office shall be responsible to oversee the administration of this order and shall report to the Supreme Court as needed regarding administration of this order.

[Entered January 21, 1999.]

1998 Staff Comment

This order is issued to facilitate the Medical Support Enforcement System Project, which is a cooperative effort of the Family Independence Agency and the judiciary. The intent of the program is to ensure that courts are able to effectively establish and enforce child support orders that include provision of health care coverage for minor children pursuant to MCL 552.452(5), 722.27(5), 722.3(6), and 722.717(6); MSA 25.222(2)(5), 25.312(7)(5). 25.244(3)(6), and 25.497(6). The Supreme Court issued Administrative Order No. 1997–3 on a short term basis, and through this order provides for discovery of medical information through the Third Circuit Court until further order of the Court.

ADMINISTRATIVE ORDER 1999–2 AUTHORIZATION OF ADDITIONAL DEMONSTRATION PROJECT TO STUDY COURT CONSOLIDATION

The Court, having determined that the Court Consolidation Demonstration Projects authorized by Supreme Court Administrative Orders Nos. 1996–1, 1996–2, 1996–5, 1996–6, 1996–7 and 1996–9, and extended until further order of the Court pursuant to Supreme Court Administrative Order No. 1997–12, have provided valuable information regarding the effective consolidation of courts and the process of consolidation of courts and the potential for better, more cost-effective service to the public, and that there would be benefit from extending the projects to additional locations in Michigan, orders that the following courts shall begin a court consolidation demonstration project, effective February 1, 1999, and until further order of the Court:

Iron County

41st Circuit Court

95–B District Court

Iron County Probate Court

During the term of the demonstration project, these courts shall be referred to as the Iron County Trial Court.

The Hon. C. Joseph Schwedler is appointed as the Administrative Chief Judge of the Iron County Trial Court. He shall have all of the authorities and responsibilities of a chief judge under MCR 8.110 as to all of the participating courts in the demonstration project. The trial court shall form a judicial council consisting of at least all chief judges of the Iron County courts listed above.

The judges, magistrates, and referees within the Iron County Trial Court are assigned to serve the whole court. Subject to the direction of the chief judge, each judge may exercise the jurisdiction of a judge of the circuit, probate, and district courts. Subject to the direction of the administrative chief judge, each magistrate or referee may perform the functions of a domestic relations referee, a district court magistrate or a juvenile court referee, with the authority to conduct proceedings as allowed by law and rule.

The Iron County Trial Court may form divisions. These divisions may correspond to the existing workload of the circuit, probate, and district courts, or may reflect another partition of the workload of the court, provided that the Iron County Trial Court will incorporate into one general division issues affecting the family pursuant to 1996 PA 388 and Supreme Court Administrative Order No. 1997–1.

During this demonstration project, the Iron County Trial Court may enter into cooperative agreements with state and local nonjudicial branch agencies to test the feasibility of the court to carry out essential court functions, such as record-keeping, felony probation services, information systems management, personnel management, and financial management.

The administrative chief judge of the trial court shall cooperate with the State Court Administrative Office by abiding by the terms of the project agreement, which include reporting and evaluation requirements.

Specific and procedural requirements for each project, as needed, will be implemented through local court order or local court rule pursuant to MCR 8.112.

The State Court Administrative Office shall submit a status report to the Supreme Court at the end of each year of the demonstration project.

[Entered January 21, 1999.]

ADMINISTRATIVE ORDER 1999–3
DISCOVERY IN MISDEMEANOR CASES

On order of the Court, in the case of *People* v *Sheldon*, 234 Mich App 68; 592 NW2d 121 (1999) (COA Docket No. 204254), the Court of Appeals ruled that MCR 6.201, which provides for discovery in criminal felony cases, also applies to criminal misdemeanor cases. That ruling was premised on an erroneous interpretation of our Administrative Order No. 1994–10. By virtue of this Administrative Order, we wish to inform the bench and bar that MCR 6.201 applies only to criminal felony cases. Administrative Order No. 1994–10 does not enlarge the scope of applicability of MCR 6.201. See MCR 6.001(A) and (B).

[Entered April 30, 1999]

ADMINISTRATIVE ORDER 1999–4
ESTABLISHMENT OF MICHIGAN TRIAL COURT CASE FILE MANAGEMENT STANDARDS

In order to improve the administration of justice; to improve the service to the public, other agencies, and the judiciary; to improve the performance and efficiency of Michigan trial court operations; and to enhance the trial courts' ability to preserve an accurate record of the trial courts' proceedings, decisions, orders, and judgments pursuant to statute and court rule, IT IS ORDERED that the State Court Administrator establish Michigan Trial Court Case File Management

Standards and that trial courts conform to those standards. The State Court Administrative Office shall enforce the standards and assist courts in adopting practices to conform to those standards.

[Entered November 30, 1999.]

ADMINISTRATIVE ORDER 2000–1
ESTABLISHMENT OF COUNCIL OF CHIEF JUDGES

On order of the Court, the following order is effective immediately.

It appearing that the administration of justice would be served by the establishment of a Council of Chief Judges to advise the Chief Justice and the Court on administrative matters; it is ORDERED that the Council of Chief Judges is established.

The Council is advisory in nature and is charged with the following duties:

1. To advise and make recommendations on administrative matters as requested by the Chief Justice.

2. To provide information for the improvement of the administration of justice.

The Council shall consist of sixteen (16) members. Council members shall be chief judges appointed by the Michigan Supreme Court. Fifteen (15) members shall be chief judges of circuit, probate, and district courts; one (1) member shall be the chief judge of the Court of Appeals.

The term of appointment shall be consistent with the term of the Chief Justice. Appointments to the Council shall be made by the Chief Justice. Reappointment is at the discretion of the Chief Justice.

The Council shall meet as convened by the Chief Justice.

[Entered January 27, 2000.]

ADMINISTRATIVE ORDER 2000–3
VIDEO PROCEEDINGS
(CIRCUIT AND DISTRICT COURTS)

On order of the Court, Administrative Orders 1990–1, 1991–2, 1992–1, and 1993–1 are rescinded.

The State Court Administrator is authorized, until further order of this Court, to approve the use of two-way interactive video technology in the criminal divisions of the circuit and district courts to conduct the following proceedings between a courtroom and a prison, jail, or other place of detention: initial arraignments on the warrant, arraignments on the information, pretrials, pleas, sentencing for misdemeanor offenses, show cause hearings, waivers and adjournments of extradition, referrals for forensic determination of competency, and waivers and adjournments of preliminary examinations.

Each court seeking to use interactive video technology must submit a local administrative order for approval by the State Court Administrator pursuant to MCR 8.112(B), describing how the program will be implemented and the administrative procedures for each type of hearing for which interactive video technology will be used. Upon a court's filing of a local administrative order, the State Court Administrative Office shall either approve the order or return the order to the chief circuit or district judge for amendment in accordance with requirements and guidelines provided by the State Court Administrative Office.

Courts that previously were authorized to use interactive video technology pursuant to Administrative Orders 1990-1, 1991-2, 1992-1, or 1993-1 may continue to do so until further order of this Court or the State Court Administrator.

The State Court Administrative Office shall assist courts in implementing the technology, and shall report periodically to this Court regarding its assessment of the program. Those courts using the technology shall provide statistics and otherwise cooperate with the State Court Administrative Office in monitoring the use of two-way video proceedings.

[Entered July 18, 2000.]

2000 Staff Comment

Administrative Order 2000-3 [entered July 18, 2000] added waivers and adjournments of preliminary examinations and extradition hearings, and hearings on referrals for forensic determination of competency, to those proceedings for which interactive video technology may be used in the circuit and district courts.

ADMINISTRATIVE ORDER 2000-5
IN RE MICROSOFT ANTITRUST LITIGATION

On order of the Court, it appearing that a number of actions have been filed alleging violation of the Michigan Antitrust Reform Act (hereafter "MARA") by Microsoft Corporation, and that coordination of pretrial and trial proceedings in those cases will promote the economical and expeditious resolution of that litigation, pursuant to Const 1963, art 6, sec 4, we direct all state courts to follow the procedures set forth in this administrative order.

1. This order applies to all pending and future Microsoft MARA actions pending or to be filed in Michigan courts other than the Third Judicial Circuit, including any Microsoft MARA cases remanded by a federal court to a Michigan court other than the Third Judicial Circuit. For purposes of this order, "Microsoft MARA actions" include all cases in which it is alleged that a party has suffered harm due to violations of MARA by Microsoft Corporation.

2. Any orders in place in Michigan courts staying proceedings in a Microsoft MARA action as a result of

Administrative Order 2000-2 may now be rescinded. Administrative Order 2000-2 is RESCINDED.

3. Each court in which a Microsoft MARA action is pending shall enter an order changing venue of the action to the Third Judicial Circuit within 14 days of the date of this order. Upon the filing of a new Microsoft MARA action, the court shall enter an order changing venue to the Third Judicial Circuit within 14 days after the action is filed. The court shall send a copy of the order to the State Court Administrator. A party who objects to the transfer of an action under this paragraph may raise the objection by filing a motion in the Third Judicial Circuit. Such a motion must be filed within 14 days after the transfer of the action. Nothing in this order shall be construed as a finding that venue is proper in Wayne County.

4. Until the transfer of an action under paragraph 3, the parties to the action shall include the words "Microsoft MARA case" on the top right-hand corner of the first page of any papers subsequently filed in this action.

5. The Third Judicial Circuit shall cooperate with the State Court Administrator in monitoring the proceedings in the actions.

6. MCR 2.222 and MCR 2.223 do not apply to changes of venue pursuant to this order.

[Entered August 8, 2000.]

ADMINISTRATIVE ORDER 2001-1
RELATING TO SECURITY POLICIES FOR COURT FACILITIES

It appearing that the orderly administration of justice would be best served by prompt action, the following order is given immediate effect. The Court invites public comment regarding the merits of the order. Comments may be submitted in writing or electronically to the Supreme Court Clerk by *June 1, 2001.* P.O. Box 30052, Lansing, MI 48909, or MSC_clerk@jud.state.mi.us. When submitting a comment, please refer to File No. **01-15.**

This matter will be considered by the Court at a public hearing to be held June 14, 2001, in Kalamazoo. Persons interested in addressing this issue at the hearing should notify the Clerk by *June 12, 2001.* Further information about the hearing will be posted on the Court's website, www.supremecourt.state.mi.us. When requesting time to speak at the hearing, please refer to File No. **01-15.**

The issue of courthouse safety is important not only to the judicial employees of this state, but also to all those who are summoned to Michigan courtrooms or who visit for professional or personal reasons. Accordingly, the Supreme Court today issues the following declaration regarding the presence of weapons in court facilities.

It is ordered that weapons are not permitted in any courtroom, office, or other space used for official court business or by judicial employees unless the chief judge or other person designated by the chief judge has given prior approval consistent with the court's written policy.

Each court is directed to submit a written policy conforming with this order to the State Court Administrator for approval, as soon as is practicable. In developing a policy, courts are encouraged to collaborate with other entities in shared facilities and, where appropriate, to work with local funding units. Such a policy may be part of a general security program or it may be a separate plan.

[Entered March 27, 2001.]

ADMINISTRATIVE ORDER 2001–2
UNIFORM EFFECTIVE DATES
FOR COURT RULE AMENDMENTS

On the basis of a request from the Appellate Practice Section of the State Bar of Michigan, the Supreme Court published for comment a proposed amendment of Rule 1.201 of the Michigan Court Rules. File No. 00–11. 463 Mich 1219 (No. 4, 2000). The matter also was on the agenda of the public hearing held March 29, 2001, in Lansing. The proposal provided that an amendment of the court rules would not take effect until at least two months after its adoption, and that the effective date would be either April 1 or October 1, absent the need for immediate action.

The Court understands the concerns expressed by those who submitted written comments and those who addressed this proposal at the public hearing. After careful consideration, however, the Court is persuaded that the best approach to more uniformity in the rulemaking process is not a court rule amendment, but rather an administrative order that provides for three effective dates during the year.

Accordingly, on ORDER of the Court, unless there is a need for immediate action, amendments of the Michigan Court Rules will take effect on January 1, May 1, or September 1.

[Entered April 5, 2001.]

ADMINISTRATIVE ORDER 2001–3
SECURITY POLICY FOR THE MICHIGAN
SUPREME COURT

Effective immediately, in accordance with Article 6, sections 1, 4, and 5 of the Michigan Constitution, and Administrative Order 2001–1, the following policy is adopted for the Supreme Court.

IT IS ORDERED THAT

1. No weapons are allowed in the courtroom of the Supreme Court or in other facilities used for official business of the Court. This prohibition does not apply to security personnel of the Court in the performance of their official duties, or to law enforcement officers in the performance of their official duties, if the officer is in uniform (or otherwise properly identified) and is not a party to a matter then before the Court. The Chief Justice may authorize additional exceptions under appropriate circumstances.

2. All persons and objects are subject to screening by Court security personnel, for the purpose of keeping weapons from entering Court facilities.

3. Notice shall be posted that "No weapons are permitted in this Court facility."

4. Persons in violation of this order may be held in contempt of Court.

[Entered May 25, 2001.]

ADMINISTRATIVE ORDER 2001–4
VIDEO PROCEEDINGS
(FAMILY DIVISION OF CIRCUIT
COURT AND PROBATE COURT)

On order of the Court, the State Court Administrator is authorized, until July 1, 2003, or until further order of this Court, to approve the experimental use of two-way interactive video technology to conduct proceedings between a courtroom and a hospital, mental health facility, jail, detention facility, or other placement facility, in the following circumstances:

(1) Hearings concerning initial involuntary treatment and continuing treatment in mental health cases in the probate court in the counties of Calhoun, Chippewa, Genesee, Gogebic, Livingston, Ottawa, Saginaw, Washtenaw, and Wayne.

(2) Preliminary hearings and review hearings in child protective proceedings in the family division of the circuit court in the counties of Calhoun, Chippewa, Genesee, Gogebic, Kalamazoo, Kent, Livingston, Ottawa, Saginaw, Washtenaw, and Wayne.

(3) Preliminary hearings held in juvenile delinquency proceedings to satisfy the requirements of MCR 5.935(A)(1), and post-dispositional progress reviews and dispositional review hearings, where the court does not order a more physically restrictive level of placement or more restrictive treatment of the juvenile, in the family division of the circuit court in the counties of Calhoun, Chippewa, Genesee, Gogebic, Kalamazoo, Kent, Livingston, Ottawa, Saginaw, Washtenaw, and Wayne.

Each court seeking to participate must submit a local administrative order for approval by the State Court Administrator pursuant to MCR 8.112(B), describing how the program will be implemented, and the administrative procedures for each type of hearing for which interactive video technology will be used. Upon a court's filing of a local administrative order, the State Court Administrative Office shall either approve the order or return the order to the chief circuit or probate judge for amendment in accordance with requirements and guidelines provided by the State Court Administrative Office.

The State Court Administrative Office shall assist courts in implementing the technology, and shall report to this Court regarding its assessment of the program. Those courts using the technology shall provide statistics and otherwise cooperate with the State Court Administrative Office in monitoring the use of two-way video proceedings.

Administrative Order 2000–4 is rescinded.

[Entered June 1, 2001.]

2001 Staff Comment

Administrative Order 2000–4 authorized the experimental use of two-way interactive video technology for specified involuntary commitment and child protective proceedings in the probate court and the family division of the circuit court in certain counties. Administrative Order 2001–4 reauthorizes this use, but expands the number of counties in the pilot project and includes authorization to use interactive video technology in select juvenile delinquency proceedings.

ADMINISTRATIVE ORDER 2001–5 AMENDMENT OF MICHIGAN UNIFORM SYSTEM OF CITATION (ADMINISTRATIVE ORDER 1987–2)

On order of the Court, the Michigan Uniform System of Citation (Administrative Order 1987–2) is amended, effective immediately, to provide as follows:

[Publishers Note: See Michigan Uniform System of Citation, post.]

[Entered June 26, 2001.]

ADMINISTRATIVE ORDER 2001–6 COMMITTEE ON MODEL CIVIL JURY INSTRUCTIONS

Forty years ago, in response to a resolution of the Michigan Judicial Conference, the Supreme Court appointed a committee to prepare jury instructions for use in civil cases. In 1970, the Court amended former Rule 516 of the General Court Rules to authorize the use of these instructions by trial courts. Later that year, the Court approved general instructions and instructions governing personal injury actions. In 1975, at the request of the committee that had developed the instructions, the Court appointed a new Committee on Standard Jury Instructions to oversee the task of maintaining the accuracy of existing model instructions and developing new instructions. Five years later, the Court amended the court rules to give the committee express standing authority to propose and modify standard instructions.

The Court has reconstituted the Committee on Standard Jury Instructions from time to time to pro-

vide for new members and to make permanent the status of the committee's reporter. But the committee has until now operated without a defined structure and without a fixed number of members.

The Court is appreciative of the faithful and distinguished service that has been rendered over the years by members of the current and predecessor committees. Many of the present members have given long and selfless service, and their contributions have greatly enhanced the administration of justice. As part of an effort to regularize all the working groups that the Court has established, and to ensure continuity, we are persuaded that it now would be beneficial to develop a formal structure and membership for this committee. In addition, we are renaming the committee to clarify that the instructions apply to civil cases and that they are model instructions.

Therefore, on order of the Court, a new Committee on Model Civil Jury Instructions is established. The committee shall 2 consist of 21 persons to be appointed by the Supreme Court. The Supreme Court will designate one member to serve as the chairperson of the committee. Generally members will be appointed for three-year terms and may be reappointed for two additional terms. However, to facilitate the transition and the staggering of terms, some initial appointments will be for abbreviated terms and those appointees who are members of the current Committee on Standard Jury Instructions will not be eligible for reappointment.

Effective January 1, 2002, the following persons are appointed to the new Committee on Model Civil Jury Instructions:

For terms ending December 31, 2002

Honorable Susan D. Borman

Peter L. Dunlap

R. Emmet Hannick

Honorable Harold Hood

Honorable Robert M. Ransom

George T. Sinas

Sheldon J. Stark

For terms ending December 31, 2003

David C. Coey

Honorable Pat M. Donofrio

Honorable Bruce A. Newman

Honorable Wendy L. Potts

Michael B. Rizik, Jr.

Valerie P. Simmons

Susan H. Zitterman

For terms ending December 31, 2004

Thomas Blaske

Honorable William J. Giovan

Mark R. Granzotto

Maurice G. Jenkins

Steven W. Martineau

Honorable Susan Bieke Neilson

Mary Massaron Ross

Judge Hood is designated as chairperson for the duration of his term, after which Judge Giovan shall assume that position. Sharon M. Brown is appointed reporter for the committee.

It shall be the duty of the committee to ensure that the Model Civil Jury Instructions accurately state applicable law, and that the instructions are concise, understandable, conversational, unslanted, and not argumentative. In this regard, the committee 3 shall have the authority to amend or repeal existing instructions and, when necessary, to adopt new instructions. Before doing so, the committee shall provide a text of the proposal to the secretary of the State Bar and the state court administrator, who shall give the notice specified in Rule 1.201 of the Michigan Court Rules. The notice shall state the time and method for commenting on the proposal. Following the comment period and any public hearing that the committee may hold on the matter, the committee shall provide notice of its decision in the same manner in which it provided notice of proposed instructions.

By separate order, the Court is amending Rule 2.516 of the Michigan Court Rules to reflect the name of the new committee.

[Entered December 18, 2001.]

ADMINISTRATIVE ORDER 2002–1
CHILD SUPPORT LEADERSHIP COUNCIL

On order of the Court, the following order is effective immediately.

Recognizing the integral role played by the judicial branch in the operation of programs affecting Michigan's families, this Court joined the Governor in 1997 in establishing the Child Support Coordinating Council to set statewide goals for the efficient and prompt delivery of adequate child support to the children of Michigan. Administrative Order 1997–7. In continuing cooperation with the Executive Branch, we now reconstitute that committee as the Child Support Leadership Council to resume a coordinated effort to provide Michigan families with optimal child support and related services.

It is therefore ordered, concurrent with the Executive Order issued today by Governor John Engler, that the Child Support Leadership Council is established. The Council is advisory in nature and is charged with the following responsibilities:

1. Establish statewide goals and objectives for the child support program.

2. Review and recommend policy for the child support program.

3. Share information with appropriate groups regarding program issues.

4. Analyze and recommend state positions on pending and proposed changes in court rules and federal and state legislation.

The Council shall consist of nine members. Four shall be appointed by the Governor, four shall be appointed by the Supreme Court, and one shall be appointed by the Prosecuting Attorneys Association of Michigan.

The term of appointment is two years, except that two of the Governor's first appointments and three of the Court's first appointments shall serve terms of one year. Reappointment is at the discretion of the respective appointing authority.

Two members shall be appointed each January to serve as co-chairs of the Council, except that the first appointments shall occur coincident with this order. The Governor shall appoint one co-chair and the Court shall appoint the other co-chair.

The Council shall meet quarterly or more frequently as it deems necessary. The co-chairs shall organize the time and location of each meeting, develop an agenda, and facilitate the conduct.

Each year the Council shall submit to the Governor and the Court its recommendations for annual goals and strategies. Within sixty days, the Governor and the Court may approve or amend the recommendations.

By January 31 of each year, the Council shall submit an annual report to the Governor and the Court for the previous year.

By-laws for the operation of the Council shall be developed and approved by the members.

Policy changes warranted by federal or state law shall be presented to the Council by the Office of Child Support (federal or state law) or the State Court Administrative Office (state law or court rule), or shall be submitted to one of the co-chairs by other sources. The Council shall develop a format for presenting and discussing issues, which shall include an opportunity for raising issues during a regular meeting or placing them on the agenda through one of the co-chairs before the meeting.

In developing recommendations, members may seek comment as appropriate, including comment from various child support advocacy organizations, through a process determined by the members.

If the Council cannot reach agreement on an issue requiring its recommendation, the alternative positions shall be documented in writing for decision by the Governor and the Court.

Administrative Order 1997–7 is rescinded, effective immediately.

[Entered April 11, 2002.]

ADMINISTRATIVE ORDER 2002–2
FACSIMILE TRANSMISSION OF DOCUMENTS IN THE COURT OF APPEALS

On order of the Court, the Court of Appeals is authorized, beginning September 1, 2002, and until further order of the Supreme Court, to accept the facsimile transmission of documents in the following circumstances:

(1) The Court of Appeals shall accept the filing of the following documents by facsimile (fax) transmission:

(a) answers to motions filed under MCR 7.211(B)(2)(e);

(b) answers to pleadings that were accompanied by a motion for immediate consideration under MCR 7.211(C)(6).

(2) The Court of Appeals may expand or restrict the other types of filings accepted by fax upon notice published in its Internal Operating Procedures.

(3) Allowable fax filings will be received by the Court of Appeals at any time. However, fax filings received on weekends, designated Court of Appeals holidays, or after 4:00 p.m. Eastern Time will be considered filed on the next business day. The time of receipt will be the time the cover sheet is received by the Court of Appeals, except if less than the entire document is received through no fault of the Court of Appeals or its facsimile equipment. If less than the entire document is received through no fault of the Court of Appeals or its facsimile equipment, there is no filing.

(4) A cover sheet provided by the Court of Appeals must accompany every transmission. The following information must be included on the cover sheet:

(a) case name and Court of Appeals docket number (or applicable case names and docket numbers of cases consolidated by the Court of Appeals to which the faxed filing applies);

(b) county of case origin;

(c) title of document being filed;

(d) name, attorney P-number (if applicable), telephone number, and fax number of the attorney or party sending the fax;

(e) if fees have not already been paid, the credit card number, expiration date, and authorized signature of the cardholder;

(f) number of pages in the transmission, including the cover sheet.

(5) All fax filings must be on 8½″ × 11″ paper, in at least 12–point type. Every page must be numbered consecutively, and the background and print must contrast sufficiently to be easily readable.

(6) The fax filing shall be considered the document filed in the Court of Appeals. The attorney or party filing the document shall retain the original document, to be produced only at the request of the Court of Appeals. No further copies should be mailed to the Court of Appeals unless requested.

(7) Attachments to a filing must be labeled in the format of "Attachment X" on the lower right-hand corner of either a separate page or the first page of the attachment.

(8) All other requirements of the court rules apply to fax filings, including the signature, page limitations, filing fees, and service on other parties.

(9) A service fee shall be charged for the receipt of each fax transmission in the amount published in the Internal Operating Procedures. Fax filings in multiple Court of Appeals docket numbers must be transmitted separately under separate cover sheets unless the cases have already been consolidated by the Court of Appeals.

(10) Service fees and filing fees must be paid, or permission to charge the fees to an authorized credit card must be allowed by the filing party on the cover sheet, at the same time the fax filing is sent. A credit card transaction must be approved by the issuing financial institution before the document will be accepted as filed by the Court of Appeals.

[Entered April 23, 2002.]

Staff Comment

MCR 7.211(B)(2)(e) provides that answers to certain motions must be filed 7 days after the motions are served on the other parties. A filing made in person may be served by mail. When service is accomplished through mailing, it is complete "at the time of mailing." MCR 2.107(C)(3). In Michigan, where the mail process can consume two or three days of the seven-day response time, attorneys or parties who are located at a distance from a district office of the Clerk of the Court are disadvantaged in their ability to timely answer such motions.

This administrative order, adopted April 23, 2002, effective September 1, 2002, remedies this geographical disparity by permitting all parties or attorneys to make certain filings by fax. This administrative order will apply statewide, ensuring that all rights and responsibilities under it will affect each case and each filing in the same manner. Consistent with practice in the Court of Appeals under the court rules, it is *not* anticipated that service of the faxed filings on the other parties must be by facsimile. Service may be accomplished by any means that is otherwise acceptable under the court rules.

The staff comment is published only for the benefit of the bench and bar and is not an authoritative construction by the Court.

ADMINISTRATIVE ORDER 2002–3 FAMILY VIOLENCE INDICATOR (FAMILY DIVISION OF CIRCUIT COURT AND PROBATE COURT)

On order of the Court, the need for immediate action having been found, the Court adopts the following requirements for friends of the court, to be effective upon implementation of an automated child support enforcement system within the Family Independence Agency, MCL 400.231 *et seq.*, and the availability of necessary programming. The provisions of this order will be considered further by the Court at a public hearing. Notice of future public hearings will be provided by the Court and posted at the Court's website, http://www.courts.michigan.gov/supremecourt.

The friends of the court shall adhere to the following rules in managing their files and records:

(1) When the Family Violence Indicator is set in the statewide automated child support enforcement system for an individual in an action, that individual's address shall be considered confidential under MCR 3.218(A)(3)(f).

(2) Friend of the court offices shall cause a Family Violence Indicator to be set in the statewide automated child support enforcement system on all the files and records in an action involving an individual when:

(a) a personal protection order has been entered protecting that individual,

(b) the friend of the court becomes aware of an order of any Michigan court that provides for confidentiality of the individual's address, or denies access to the individual's address,

(c) an individual files a sworn statement with the office setting forth specific incidents or threats of domestic violence or child abuse, or

(d) the friend of the court becomes aware that a determination has been made in another state that a disclosure risk comparable to any of the above risk indicators exists for the individual.

(3) When the Family Violence Indicator has been set for an individual in any action, the Family Violence Indicator shall be set in all other actions within the statewide automated child support enforcement system concerning that same individual.

(4) When the Family Violence Indicator has been set for a custodial parent in any action, the Family Violence Indicator shall also be set for all minors for which the individual is a custodial parent. When the Family Violence Indicator has been set for any minor in an action, the Family Violence Indicator shall also be set for the minor's custodian.

(5) The friend of the court office shall cause the Family Violence Indicator to be removed:

(a) by order of the circuit court,

(b) at the request of the protected party, when the protected party files a sworn statement with the office that the threats of violence or child abuse no longer exist, unless a protective order or other order of any Michigan court is in effect providing for confidentiality of an individual's address, or

(c) at the request of a state that had previously determined that a disclosure risk comparable to the risks in paragraph two existed for the individual.

(6) When the Family Violence Indicator has been removed for an individual in any action, the Family Violence Indicator that was set automatically for other persons and cases associated with that individual shall also be removed.

[Entered May 2, 2002.]

2002 Staff Comment

Administrative Order 2002–3 implements 42 USC 654(26), which precludes friends of the court from disclosing information concerning the location of a party or a child when there is evidence of domestic violence or child abuse against the party or the child, and the disclosure could be harmful to the party or the child. 45 CFR 307.11(f)(1)(x) creates a "Family Violence Indicator" to track such circumstances. The Administrative Order does not provide protection beyond requiring measures to implement restrictions on addresses and is not designed to be a substitute for statutory and injunctive measures to provide protection to victims of domestic abuse. The staff comment is published only for the benefit of the bench and bar and is not an authoritative construction by the Court.

A copy of this order will be given to the secretary of the State Bar and to the State Court Administrator. Comments on this order may be sent to the Supreme Court clerk in writing or electronically by *August 1, 2002.* Clerk, P.O. Box 30052, Lansing, MI 48909, or MSC_clerk@jud.state.mi.us. When filing a comment, please refer to File No. 2002–07.

ADMINISTRATIVE ORDER 2002–4 CASES INVOLVING CHILDREN ABSENT FROM COURT-ORDERED PLACEMENT WITHOUT LEGAL PERMISSION

In Michigan, the family division of the circuit court is entrusted with protecting the welfare of children who are under its jurisdiction. This includes thousands of victims of abuse or neglect who are placed by court order in a variety of environments, such as foster care, to ensure their safety.

Recently, there have been reports of several hundred children in Michigan who are absent from court-ordered placements without permission from the court. In some situations, the child has run away. Other times, especially in the case of younger children, there has been an abduction, often by a family member. Regardless of the reason, there can be no justification for the unauthorized disappearance from court-ordered placement of even one child.

The Legislature has given the Family Independence Agency the responsibility of supervising children who are under court jurisdiction because of abuse or neglect. Any effort to locate children who are absent from court-ordered placements thus must include both the agency and the courts. Accordingly, on order of the Court, each circuit court must develop a plan for reviewing cases involving children who are absent from court-ordered placements without permission from the court. Such plans must include the establishment of a special docket or other expedited process for review of such cases, either through the dispositional review hearings that are required by statute and court rule in all child-protective proceedings, or through formal status conferences or emergency status reviews. In addition, the plans should:

A. identify the judge who has responsibility for ensuring compliance with the plan;

B. address the coordination of the efforts of the Family Independence Agency and the court to locate absent children;

C. describe the process for reviewing such cases;

D. address any special problems that the court has identified;

E. describe the court's procedures for obtaining information regarding the whereabouts of absent children and for promptly scheduling hearings to determine their legal status; and

F. describe the court's procedures for giving priority to cases involving children ages 15 and younger, particularly if the child may have been abducted.

Each circuit court must submit a local administrative order to the State Court Administrative Office by February 1, 2003, describing its plan for reviewing cases involving children who are absent from court-ordered placements without permission from the court.

[Entered November 19, 2002.]

ADMINISTRATIVE ORDER 2002–5 DIFFERENTIATED CASE SCHEDULING AT THE COURT OF APPEALS

The Court of Appeals is engaged in a delay-reduction initiative, with the goal of disposing of 95 percent of its cases within 18 months of filing beginning in October 2003. To assist in reaching that goal, the Supreme Court orders that the Court of Appeals may give precedence on the session calendar under Rule 7.213(C) of the Michigan Court Rules to any appeals that the Court of Appeals determines are appropriate for differentiated case management. Specifically, the Court of Appeals may schedule such cases on the session calendar as soon as the time for filing the briefs has elapsed, the record has been received, and the matter has been prepared for submission in accordance with internal procedure.

This order is effective immediately and will remain in effect until December 31, 2003, at which time the Court will decide whether to amend Rule 7.213(C) on a permanent basis, consistent with this administrative order. In the meantime, the Court will further consider this interim order at a public hearing. The schedule of future public hearings will be posted on the Court's website, www.courts.mi.gov/supremecourt. Please refer to Administrative File No. 2002–44 in any correspondence or inquiry.

[Entered December 23, 2002.]

Publisher's Note

This order remains in effect until Dec. 31, 2003, by its terms.

LOCAL COURT RULES

Research Note

Use Westlaw ® *to find cases citing or applying specific rules.* Westlaw *may also be used to search for specific terms in court rules or to update court rules. See the* MI–RULES *and* MI–ORDERS *Scope Screens for detailed descriptive information and search tips.*

Amendments to these rules are published, as received, in the N.W.2d *and* Michigan Reporter *advance sheets,* and Michigan Legislative Service.

Summary of Contents

Thirty-Sixth Judicial District [City of Detroit]
Forty-Eighth Judicial District [Parts of Oakland County]
54–A Judicial District [City of Lansing]
54–B Judicial District [City of East Lansing]
Fifty-Sixth Judicial District, First Division [Barry County]
Sixty-First Judicial District [City of Grand Rapids]
62–A Judicial District [City of Wyoming]
Sixty-Fifth Judicial District, First Division [Gratiot County]
Sixty-Eighth Judicial District [City of Flint]
Seventy-Fourth Judicial District [Bay County]
Eighty-First Judicial District [Iosco and Arenac Counties]
Eighty-Second Judicial District [Alcona, Oscoda and Ogemaw Counties]
Eighty-Ninth Judicial District [Cheboygan and Presque Isle Counties]
95–B Judicial District [Dickinson and Iron Counties]

Probate Courts

Allegan Probate Court
Barry Probate Court
Charlevoix and Emmet Probate Court [Rescinded]
Eaton Probate Court
Genesee Probate Court
Ingham Probate Court
Kalamazoo Probate Court
Marquette Probate Court [Rescinded]
Menominee Probate Court
Oakland Probate Court
Oscoda Probate Court
St. Joseph Probate Court

LOCAL RULES OF THE THIRD JUDICIAL CIRCUIT

[WAYNE COUNTY]

Effective March 1, 1985

Table of Rules

* Suggested title added by Publisher.

RULE 2.100 AT ISSUE PRAECIPES— FORMS AND PROCEDURE

(A) At Issue Praecipes—Forms. The following forms shall be used for "At Issue Praecipes":

(1) *Yellow Form*—Domestic relations default judgments.

(2) *Blue form*—Contested domestic relations actions.

(3) *White form*—All other civil actions.

(B) At Issue Praecipes—Filing. An "At Issue Praecipe" shall be filed with Docket Management and a copy served on the attorneys of record or parties in propria persona, with the answer to the complaint.

(C) Added Parties or Appearance After Praecipe is Filed (Notice to Docket Management). If any party is added to an action or an attorney appears in an action after the "At Issue Praecipe" is filed, the party or attorney shall immediately notify Docket Management.

(D) Domestic Relations Actions. In uncontested domestic relations actions the action shall be considered "at issue" when the default has been taken, and an "At Issue Praecipe" shall be filed with the affidavit of default.

[Amended effective May 15, 2001.]

Staff Comment to 2001 Amendment

The May 15, 2001 amendments of Local Court Rules 2.100 and 8.108 of the Third Judicial Circuit were made at the request of that court, effective immediately.

RULE 2.107 SERVICE AND FILING OF PLEADINGS AND OTHER PAPERS *

(A) Service of Pleadings. At the time of service of the summons and complaint, the plaintiff shall serve upon the opposing parties the pre-printed caption labels provided pursuant to LCR 2.113(C).

[Adopted to be effective from April 1, 1987, until March 31, 1988; order entered March 25, 1988 providing rule shall remain in effect until further order of Supreme Court.]

* Suggested title added by Publisher.

RULE 2.113 FORM OF PLEADINGS AND OTHER PAPERS *

(C) Pleadings—Requirement of Preprinted Labels. All pleadings hereinafter filed shall bear on the face thereof preprinted caption labels to be furnished by the Office of the County Clerk.

[Adopted to be effective from April 1, 1987, until March 31, 1988; order entered March 25, 1988 providing rule shall remain in effect until further order of Supreme Court.]

* Suggested title added by Publisher.

RULE 2.119 MOTION PRACTICE

(A) Motion Praecipe Forms. A white form is to be used for a general motion praecipe and a yellow form for a domestic relations motion praecipe.

(B) Additional Motion Requirements.

(1) *Certification by Attorney.* The following certificate signed by the attorney of record or the party in propria persona must be placed on the face sheet of each motion filed in the county clerk's office:

I hereby certify that I have complied with all provisions of LCR 2.119(B) on motion practice.

Attorney of Record

(2) *Ascertaining Opposition; Contents.* The moving party must ascertain whether a contemplated motion will be opposed. The motion must affirmatively state that the concurrence of counsel in the relief sought has been requested on a specified date, and that concurrence has been denied or has not been acquiesced in, and hence, that it is necessary to present the motion.

(C) Motions and Orders to Show Cause in Domestic Relations Cases; Objections to Friend of the Court Recommendations; Referee Hearings.

(1) *Motions and Orders to Show Cause in Domestic Relations Cases.*

(a) A verified motion for custody, support, or alimony, including a motion for modification of a custody, support, or alimony order or judgment, is a "general" motion. All other motions are "miscellaneous" motions.

(b) A written motion or order to show cause will not be heard unless the proper praecipe is filed and a copy of the motion and the notice of hearing is served in accordance with MCR 2.107 and MCR 2.119.

(c) The party filing a general motion shall file a praecipe and a copy of the verified motion with the Friend of the Court for an investigation and recommendation. The hearing date for all general motions shall be set by the Friend of the Court unless otherwise ordered by the court. Except as to an order to show cause filed by an attorney, the Friend of the Court shall provide written notice of the hearing in accordance with MCR 2.119(C).

(d) A miscellaneous motion, or an order to show cause, and the praecipe must be filed at the same time, and in compliance with MCR 2.119(C)(1), unless the time has been shortened by the court. The original motion or order to show cause must be filed with the county clerk, who shall indicate on the praecipe that the motion fee has been paid.

(e) When an order to show cause for contempt is presented for the signature of the judge, it must be accompanied by a verified motion and praecipe setting forth the date, time, and place of the hearing.

(f) The praecipe, with a copy of the motion or order to show cause attached, must be delivered to the Friend of the Court.

(g) If the moving attorney or party in propria persona does not appear at the hearing on a miscellaneous motion, the praecipe will be dismissed and a new praecipe will be required. An order to show cause filed by an attorney will be dismissed in its entirety if the attorney does not appear for the hearing.

(2) *Objections to Friend of the Court Recommendations.* Objections to the recommendations of the Friend of the Court shall be filed in writing and shall be served on the Friend of the Court and the opposing attorney or party in propria persona at least 1 day before the scheduled hearing date.

(3) *Notice of Dispute Form.* In all cases in which there is a dispute as to child custody, visitation, child support, or alimony, a party who requests a temporary or final order or modified order shall file with the Friend of the Court a Notice of Dispute Form, which shall include the information required by MCR 3.204 and the nature of the dispute. (Forms to be supplied by the Friend of the Court's office.)

(4) *Referee Hearings.*

(a) Pursuant to MCL 552.507; MSA 25.176(7), hearings in domestic relations motions and actions, including actions and motions under the Support and Visitation Enforcement Act and Paternity Act, shall be heard by a Friend of the Court referee, unless waived by the judge to whom the case is assigned.

(b) The recommendation of the Friend of the Court referee shall be subject to a de novo hearing by a designated circuit judge at the request of either party or on the court's own motion.

(5) *Rehearing on Motions.* Motions for rehearing of matters which were originally reviewed by a circuit judge shall be heard by the same judge who heard the matter in the first instance.

(D) Motions and Orders to Show Cause in Civil Cases Other Than Domestic Relations Cases. The original motion must be filed with the county clerk, who shall indicate payment of the motion fee on the praecipe. The praecipe, with a copy of the motion or order to show cause and the brief, if any, attached, must be delivered to the judge who is to hear the motion or order to show cause. Any party filing any pleading, brief, or other document relating to a pending motion or order to show cause shall indicate the hearing date and time for oral argument of the motion or order to show cause in the upper right corner of the front page of each document, file the original with the county clerk, and deliver a copy to the judge who is to hear the motion or order to show cause.

[Amended effective April 1, 1992; continued effective April 30, 1993 until further order of the Supreme Court.]

Staff Comment to 1992 Amendment

The 1992 amendment of Local Rule 2.119(D) added the final sentence of subrule (D).

RULE 2.301   TIME LIMITS, WITNESS LIST [REPEALED]

[Repealed effective May 15, 2001.]

RULE 2.401   SETTLEMENT CONFERENCE [REPEALED]

[Repealed effective May 15, 2001.]

RULE 2.503   ADJOURNMENTS [REPEALED]

[Repealed effective May 15, 2001.]

RULE 3.204   CERTIFICATE ON BEHALF OF PLAINTIFF REGARDING EX PARTE INTERIM SUPPORT ORDER

A completed "Certificate on Behalf of Plaintiff Regarding Ex Parte Interim Support Order" must be filed in all actions for divorce, separate maintenance or annulment of marriage, where the complaint alleges that minor children were born to the parties or during the marriage. The original must be filed with the county clerk. Copies must be served on the

Friend of the Court and the defendant. A proof of service must be provided to the Friend of the Court.

[Adopted and amended effective October 1, 1987; continued effective April 30, 1993 until further order of the Supreme Court.]

RULE 3.206   EX PARTE INTERIM ORDERS FOR SUPPORT, CUSTODY OF CHILDREN AND ATTORNEY FEES; NOTICE OF DISPUTE

(A) Before an ex parte interim order for the support of minor children or for attorney fees in a domestic relations action is presented to the judge, the party seeking the order must complete a "Certificate on Behalf of Plaintiff Regarding Ex Parte Interim Support Order," and a "Certificate of Conformity." The originals must be filed with the county clerk, and copies provided to the Friend of the Court. The party also must submit a Verified Statement as required by MCR 3.204(B).

(B) After the ex parte interim order for support is entered, the party who obtained the order must serve on the opposite party completed copies of the "Certificate on Behalf of Plaintiff Regarding Ex Parte Interim Support Order," the "Certificate of Conformity," the complaint (or counterclaim or petition), the custody affidavit required by MCL 600.659; MSA 27A.659, and the ex parte interim order for support. A proof of service of these documents must be filed with the county clerk and the Friend of the Court.

(C) In all cases in which there is a dispute as to child custody, visitation, child support, or alimony, a party who requests the temporary or final order shall file with the Friend of the Court a written Notice of Dispute which shall include the information required by MCR 3.204 and the nature of the dispute. (Forms to be supplied by the Friend of the Court's Office.)

[Amended effective October 1, 1987; continued effective April 30, 1993 until further order of the Supreme Court.]

RULE 3.209   JUDGMENTS AND ORDERS

(B) Certificate of Conformity. Domestic relations orders and judgments, when presented for the court's signature, shall be certified as to content on an appropriate Certificate of Conformity. The forms shall be provided by the Friend of the Court's office.

[Continued effective April 30, 1993 until further order of the Supreme Court.]

RULE 6.100   RULES APPLICABLE IN THE THIRD JUDICIAL CIRCUIT

(A) Criminal Division, Assignment of Judges, Case Processing. The Criminal Division of the Third Judicial Circuit shall consist of a presiding judge and such other judges as may be assigned by the chief judge. The number and term of said judges shall be determined by the chief judge.

(B) Appearance in Lower Court Constitutes Appearance in Circuit Court. Appearance by an attorney in a municipal or district court in any criminal action where the defendant is bound over to the Third Judicial Circuit shall constitute an appearance in the Third Judicial Circuit in said criminal action. An attorney may by motion for cause shown be permitted to withdraw from further representation of said defendant.

(C) Method of Assignment, Reassignment; Adjournments. Cases shall be assigned by lot to a trial judge. If the trial judge is unavailable on the date set for trial, the case shall be reassigned to an available judge within the Criminal Division or, if no such judge is available, then to a judge available in the Civil Division.

No trial of a criminal case shall be adjourned except by the presiding judge for good cause shown upon motion of the party seeking the adjournment or by the presiding judge for good cause.

(D) Implementation of Court-Administered Final Plea Conference in Criminal Felony Matters. A final plea conference shall be held prior to trial of all criminal felony cases bound over to the Third Judicial Circuit. The final plea conference shall be scheduled by the court after the conclusion of the arraignment on the information and no later than 3 weeks prior to the scheduled trial date. The final plea conference shall be administered by the presiding judge of the criminal division. The defendants, defense attorneys, and the Wayne County Prosecuting Attorney's office shall be notified in writing of the court-scheduled final conference and shall appear at the time and location specified in the notice. The failure of the defendant to appear for the final conference may result in the issuance of a warrant for his or her arrest and the revocation of bond. All requests for adjournment of the final conference are to be taken in open court before the presiding judge of the Criminal Division.

THIRD CIRCUIT AND RECORDER'S COURT JOINT LOCAL COURT RULE 6.102. PROCEEDINGS ON THE CONSOLIDATED CRIMINAL DOCKET [VACATED]

[Vacated effective October 10, 1995.]

RULE 6.410   SELECTION OF JURIES FOR TRIALS OF FORMER RECORDER'S COURT CASES

(A) Application. This rule only applies to defendants who are

(1) charged with committing a felony in the City of Detroit, and

(2) arraigned on the warrant or complaint before October 1, 1997.

(B) Selection of Jurors. For trials of defendants described in subrule (A), the court will draw potential jurors from all of Wayne County, unless the defendant elects in writing, on or before the final pretrial conference, to be tried by a jury composed of persons drawn only from the City of Detroit.

[Adopted effective October 1, 1997.]

1997 Staff Comment

Local Rule 6.410 was adopted at the request of the Wayne Circuit Court.

RULE 8.108   TRANSCRIPT FOR APPEAL

A request or order for a transcript of proceedings in the Third Judicial Circuit for use on appeal must be made to Court Reporting Services or a designee of that office by completing and filing the required form with Court Reporting Services.

All transcripts will be filed with and can be obtained through Court Reporting Services by the ordering party, upon completion.

[Amended effective May 15, 2001.]

Staff Comment to 2001 Amendment

The May 15, 2001 amendments of Local Court Rules 2.100 and 8.108 of the Third Judicial Circuit were made at the request of that court, effective immediately.

LOCAL RULES OF THE FOURTH JUDICIAL CIRCUIT

[JACKSON COUNTY]

Effective March 1, 1985

Table of Rules

RULE 2.402 FACSIMILE TRANSMISSION OF DOCUMENTS

(1) This court will permit the filing of pleadings and court documents by the use of facsimile (FAX) equipment. All filings shall be on 8½ by 11 inch paper.

(2) Documents which require a filing fee will not be accepted unless the filing fee and service fee are paid in full. Payment may be made to the county clerk's office by use of Visa or MasterCard charges.

(3) In addition to the statutory filing fee, a fax service fee of $3 for the first page and $1 for each additional page shall be assessed to be paid per credit card.

(4) Documents will be received by the clerk's office between the hours of 8:00 A.M. and 4:00 P.M. FAX-ES received after 4:00 P.M. will be considered filed on the following business day.

(5) A cover sheet provided by the county clerk's office must accompany every transmission. The following information must be included on this sheet: case name, case number (not applicable for new filings), document title, name and telephone number of sender, Visa or MasterCard number, expiration of card, signature of authorized agent for card.

(6) Signature. For purposes of MCR 2.114, a signature includes a signature transmitted by facsimile equipment.

[Adopted effective September 21, 1994.]

RULE 2.403 MEDIATION

(A) **Obtaining Briefs or Summary.** The mediation clerk shall, immediately after the deadline for filing a document, brief, or summary, make those received available to the assigned mediators. The assigned mediators shall thereafter obtain the same as soon as possible from the administrative office of the court.

(B) **Disposition and Adjournment.**

(1) Adjournment of mediation hearings is to be avoided whenever possible. Adjournments are to be approved by the judge assigned to the case or, in the absence of the assigned judge, the chief judge or, in the absence of the chief judge, the chief judge pro tempore.

Whenever possible, the attorney in principal charge of the case shall delegate responsibility for attendance at the hearing to another attorney when necessary so as to avoid adjournment.

(2) When a case is set for mediation as provided in MCR 2.403, and is thereafter settled or otherwise disposed of before the mediation, it shall be the responsibility of both counsel immediately to notify the mediation clerk of the disposition, and to provide the mediation clerk with a signed, true copy of the judge's order of disposition as soon as possible.

(3) When a true copy of a final order of disposition is submitted to the mediation clerk before the documents, briefs, or summaries have been turned over to the assigned mediators, the fees paid for that hearing shall be returned to the parties paying such fees; except for those fees subject to penalty under the terms of this rule.

LOCAL RULES OF THE SIXTH
JUDICIAL CIRCUIT

[OAKLAND COUNTY]

Effective March 1, 1985

Table of Rules

RULE 2.119 MOTION PRACTICE

(A) Miscellaneous Calendar. Motions and petitions shall be heard on Wednesday mornings unless otherwise ordered by the court. An attorney desiring to have a hearing on any pro confesso, default, motion or miscellaneous matter shall file a praecipe with the assignment clerk on or before the Wednesday preceding the Wednesday of the desired hearing. Each Thursday the assignment clerk shall, under the direction of the chief judge, prepare a list of all matters to be heard the following Wednesday. The list shall show the name of the judge before whom the matter will be heard. A copy of the list shall be published in a newspaper as defined in MCR 2.106(F) before the Wednesday on which the matters will be heard.

(B) Motion Praecipe; Motion Certification by Attorney.

(1) A motion praecipe must be filed at least 7 days before the hearing.

(2) Motion certification by attorney.

(a) The following certificate signed by the attorney of record or by the party in propria persona shall be attached to or incorporated in the praecipe filed with the assignment clerk:

I HEREBY CERTIFY that I have made personal contact with _____ on _____, 19__, requesting concurrence in the relief sought with this motion and that concurrence has been denied or that I have made reasonable and diligent attempts to contact counsel requesting concurrence in the relief sought with this motion.

(C) Appearance at the Hearing. If counsel for the moving party on a motion praeciped for hearing does not check in with the court clerk by 9:30 a.m., the court may dismiss the motion praecipe on its own motion or upon request of counsel for the opposing party.

If counsel for the opposing party in a motion praeciped for hearing does not check in with the clerk by 9:30 a.m., upon request of the moving party the clerk shall call the motion for hearing. If appropriate, the court shall grant the requested relief.

RULE 2.202 SUBSTITUTION OF PARTIES; SUBSTITUTION OF COUNSEL

(A) Substitution of Parties. Any attorney granted leave to add or delete a party to or from a pending case shall promptly notify the assignment office.

(B) Substitution of Counsel. Any attorney granted leave to substitute into a pending case shall promptly notify the assignment office.

RULE 2.315 VIDEO TAPE DEPOSITIONS

(A) Filing of Petition. A producer of a videotaped deposition or a party may file a petition in a closed case, identifying the tape produced for use in the case, stating facts showing the case is closed, and requesting return of the video tape.

(B) Filing of Affidavit and Stipulation. Along with the petition, the following shall be filed:

(1) An affidavit by the petitioner affirming there is a written transcript in the court file for each requested video-taped deposition, and stating that the petitioner is the owner of the requested video tape or that the owner has waived any rights to the requested video tape;

(2) A stipulation from each party litigant or all counsel of record agreeing there is no objection to releasing the requested video tape and stating there is no appeal pending or contemplated.

(C) Discretion of Court. Upon review of the petition and supporting documents, the court may enter an order permitting release of the requested video tape, may refuse to return the video tape, or may order release of the video tape upon any conditions it deems appropriate.

RULE 3.205 PRIOR AND SUBSEQUENT ORDERS AND JUDGMENTS AFFECTING MINORS

(A) Venue. This rule applies whenever the prior and subsequent courts are Oakland County courts.

(B) Notice to Prior Court, Friend of the Court, Juvenile/Probate Register or Prosecuting Attorney.

(1) As used in this rule, "appropriate official" means the friend of the court, juvenile/probate register, or Prosecuting Attorney, depending on the nature of the prior or subsequent action and the court involved.

(2) If a minor is known to be subject to the prior continuing jurisdiction of an Oakland County court, the plaintiff or other initiating party must file written notice of proceedings in the subsequent court with

(a) the clerk or register of the prior court, and

(b) the appropriate official of the prior court.

(3) The notice must be filed at least 21 days before the date set for hearing. If the fact of continuing jurisdiction is not then known, notice must be given immediately when it becomes known.

(4) The notice requirement of this subrule is not jurisdictional and does not preclude the subsequent court from entering interim orders before the expiration of the 21–day period, if required by the best interests of the minor.

(C) Prior Orders.

(1) Each provision of a prior order remains in effect until the provision is superseded, changed, or terminated by a subsequent order.

(2) A subsequent court must give due consideration to prior continuing orders of other courts, and may

not enter orders contrary to or inconsistent with such orders, except as provided by law.

(D) Duties of Officials of Prior and Subsequent Courts.

(1) Upon receipt of the notice required by subrule (B), the appropriate official of the prior court

(a) must provide the assigned judge of the subsequent court with the docket sheet;

(b) may appear in person at proceedings in the subsequent court, as the welfare of the minor and the interests of justice require.

(2) The appropriate official of the prior court shall furnish documents upon request of the subsequent court.

(3) Upon request of the prior court, the appropriate official of the subsequent court

(a) must notify the appropriate official of the prior court of all proceedings in the subsequent court, and

(b) must send copies of all orders entered in the subsequent court to the attention of the clerk or register and the appropriate official of the prior court.

(4) If a circuit court awards custody of a minor pursuant to MCL 722.26b; MSA 25.312(6b), the clerk of the circuit court must send a copy of the judgment or order of disposition to the probate court that has prior or continuing jurisdiction of the minor as a result of the guardianship proceedings, regardless of whether there is a request.

(5) Upon receipt of an order from the subsequent court, the appropriate official of the prior court must take the steps necessary to implement the order in the prior court.

[Adopted effective November 1, 1995.]

1995 Staff Comment

Local Court Rule 3.205 of the Sixth Judicial Circuit and the Oakland County Probate Court was adopted at the joint request of those courts.

RULE 3.207 POWERS AND DUTIES OF FRIEND OF THE COURT [RESCINDED]

[Rescinded effective May 1, 1993.]

RULE 3.208 POWERS AND DUTIES OF FRIEND OF THE COURT

(B) Friend of the Court Pre–arraignment Review.

(1) All bench warrants issued for failure to appear pursuant to an order to show cause in friend of the court matters must contain a provision for bail and be returnable to a friend of the court referee.

(2) A person arrested pursuant to such a bench warrant will be brought before a referee for review at the Oakland County Jail. The referee is empowered to:

    (a) enter into a consent agreement for payment of support;

    (b) lower the bond if appropriate; and

    (c) continue the bond until the next court date for friend of the court matters.

(3) Either party may request an immediate arraignment before the court.

[Adopted effective April 30, 1993 until further order of the Supreme Court.]

RULE 6.101 TERMINATION OF CIRCUIT COURT APPOINTMENT OF ATTORNEYS AND SUBMISSION OF FEE VOUCHERS

(A) Termination of Circuit Court Appointment of Attorneys. The appointment of counsel in indigent cases shall terminate at the time of dismissal or sentencing, whether the dismissal or sentencing has occurred at circuit or district court.

(B) Date Certain for Attorney Fee Vouchers. Appointed attorneys shall submit their vouchers to the court administrator no later than one month after dismissal of the case or sentencing of their client.

(C) For purposes of this rule, sentencing shall include granting of YTA status and delayed sentence.

RULE 6.107 GRAND JURIES

Petitions for a grand jury shall be presented to the chief judge and submitted by him or her to the bench for decision. No such petition shall be granted except by affirmative majority action of the bench. If a one-man grand jury is called, the judges of the circuit, by majority action, shall designate the judge who shall act as the grand juror.

LOCAL RULES OF THE SEVENTH JUDICIAL CIRCUIT

[GENESEE COUNTY]

Effective March 1, 1999

Table of Rules

RULE 2.119 MOTION PRACTICE

(A) Motion Certification by Attorney. The following certificate signed by the attorney of record or by the party *in propria persona* shall be attached to or incorporated in the motion and notice of hearing filed with the clerk:

I hereby certify that I have made personal contact with _____ [name] on _____, [date] requesting concurrence in the relief sought with this motion and that concurrence has been denied, or that I have made reasonable and diligent attempts to contact counsel requesting concurrence in the relief sought with this motion.

(B) Proposed Orders. A proposed order must be attached to and served with the motion.

(C) Application. This rule applies to all motions filed in the circuit court and to motions filed in civil actions in the probate court.

[Adopted effective March 1, 1999.]

1998 Staff Comment

Local Court Rule 2.119 of the Seventh Judicial Circuit and the Genesee Probate Court was adopted February 2, 1999, effective March 1, 1999, at the request of those courts.

LOCAL RULES OF THE NINTH JUDICIAL CIRCUIT

[KALAMAZOO COUNTY]

Effective March 1, 1985

Table of Rules

RULE 2.119 MOTION PRACTICE

(A) Motion day is Monday. The following court matters are scheduled and ordinarily heard on motion day:

(1) Criminal: sentences, pleas, arraignments, 15-minute motions, driver's license restorations, and driver's license reviews.

(2) Civil: pro confesso and consent judgments, 15-minute motions, paternity arraignments, non-support matters, URESA matters, and Friend of the Court matters.

If a court holiday is on a Monday, motion day is held the following day, Tuesday.

(B) Courtrooms A and C hear civil matters in the morning and criminal matters, including civil matters involving the prosecutor's office, in the afternoon.

(C) Courtrooms B, D, and E hear criminal matters, including civil matters involving the prosecutor's office, in the morning and civil matters in the afternoon.

(D) All motion day hearings are to be requested by a telephone call to the court administrator's office. *DO NOT* praecipe the above cited hearings.

(E) Petitions and motions MUST be filed in the circuit court clerk's office, with the applicable filing fee BEFORE a court date is assigned.

(F) The attorney requesting a hearing on motion day is responsible for noticing ALL appropriate parties of the scheduled date.

(G) Motion day hearings are scheduled for 15 minutes per case.

(H) Motion day hearings may be cancelled or adjourned only by the requesting attorney or the court. The requesting attorney is responsible for notifying ALL appropriate parties of the cancellation or adjournment. A stipulation and order is not required for adjournment of a motion day hearing.

(I) A motion day hearing may be cancelled or adjourned by the court. The court is responsible for notifying the attorney that requested the hearing. That attorney is responsible for notifying all other appropriate parties.

[Approved February 27, 1985.]

RULE 2.401 PRETRIAL PROCEDURES— CIVIL [RESCINDED]

[Rescinded effective May 2, 1995.]

RULE 2.403 MEDIATION [RESCINDED]

[Rescinded effective May 2, 1995.]

RULE 2.501 COURT CALENDAR: CIVIL AND DOMESTIC HEARINGS

(A) Civil matters and domestic relations matters requiring hearings of more than 15 minutes are normally scheduled on Friday. All such hearings are requested by praecipe.

(B) Full-day hearings begin at 9:30 a.m. and half-day hearings are scheduled at 9:30 a.m. or 1:30 p.m. All other matters are heard as indicated in the Notice of Hearing.

RULE 3.200 DOMESTIC CASES: JUDG-MENTS; SUPPORT AND CUSTODY ORDERS [RESCINDED]

[Rescinded effective May 1, 1993.]

RULE 6.000 COURT CALENDAR: EVIDENTIARY HEARINGS— CRIMINAL CASES

(A) Each judge will normally hold evidentiary hearings every 5 or 6 weeks.

(B) A request for an evidentiary hearing shall be initiated by motion and praecipe filed with the court clerk and court administrator's office. The praecipe shall specify the type of hearing requested and length of court time estimated for the hearing.

(C) The court administrator's office will notice attorneys of record for the scheduled hearing date and time.

RULE 6.001 CRIMINAL PROCEDURES— PRETRIALS

(A) A criminal pretrial conference will be held in every case which is not disposed of at the circuit court arraignment.

(B) The defendant and his or her attorney, as well as the prosecuting attorney or a representative, shall attend the pretrial conference. The defendant shall not participate in the conference, but shall be immediately available for consultation. Incarcerated defendants need not be present, unless required by the judge.

(C) All attorneys shall be prepared to conduct a meaningful pretrial conference. Unexcused failure to appear at the pretrial conference or to be prepared to accomplish the purposes stated herein, or to cooperate in the conduct of the pretrial conference, shall subject an attorney to such action or sanctions as the judge shall deem appropriate. The unexcused or unwarranted absence of the defendant shall be grounds for forfeiture of bond and issuance of a bench warrant.

(D) Copies of the Pretrial Conference Summary and Order Scheduling Events and Controlling Proceedings shall be provided by the court to all parties at the conclusion of the conference.

(E) The purpose of the pretrial conference shall be:

(1) To determine whether the parties intend to proceed to trial or to enter a plea to the original charge, a lesser charge, or an added charge.

(2) To determine whether any pretrial motions or matters not yet heard are to be filed or heard. Motions not having been timely filed and noticed for hearing will not be cause for delay or adjournment of trial. Failure to comply with this requirement may result in a waiver of claims and defenses or imposition of sanctions, except in the discretion of the court upon good cause shown.

(3) To stipulate which witnesses will be called at trial and which witnesses will be waived, if any; and to determine the availability of witnesses for trial.

(4) To determine if trial is to be jury or nonjury and the estimated trial time necessary.

(5) To determine that the case is ready for trial and disclose any scheduling problems.

(6) To discuss freely the theories of the case, requested jury instructions, legal issues, and the need for briefs and memoranda of law.

[Amended effective April 27, 1995.]

LOCAL RULES OF THE SIXTEENTH JUDICIAL CIRCUIT

[MACOMB COUNTY]

Effective March 1, 1985

Table of Rules

RULE 2.119 MOTION PRACTICE

(A) Motion Day. Monday of each week shall be motion day, except when on a legal holiday, in which case it will be the day following. Uncontested matters will be given preference over contested matters at the morning session.

(B) Filing. Counsel shall notice motions for hearing by filing a praecipe with the County Clerk at least 7 days prior to the scheduled hearing date. The praecipe shall contain the following information:

1. Names of the parties and the number of the case.

2. Nature of the motion.

3. Names of the attorneys.

4. Scheduled hearing date.

5. Name of the judge to whom the case is assigned.

If an order to show cause has been issued and a hearing scheduled for a Monday, 7 days or more from the date of issuance, a praecipe shall be filed to notify the clerk of that fact.

The original motion must be filed with the County Clerk, who shall indicate payment of the motion fee on the praecipe. If not consented to by the opposing party, a copy of the motion and brief, if any, must be filed with the judge who is to hear the motion. The same procedure shall apply for any responses made to the motion by the opposing party.

All motions shall be scheduled for 9:00 a.m. unless otherwise scheduled by or with the approval of the court, and opposing counsel has been so notified.

(C) Opening of Court. Motions will be called by the court clerk in the order as attorneys appear. All counsel entering the courtroom should notify the court clerk of their readiness for hearing.

(D) Dismissal for Non-appearance. Motions not responded to when called by the court clerk may be dismissed without prejudice one hour after being called. The court clerk will grant consent adjournments if notified by telephone or written stipulation.

(E) Assignment. By 8:45 a.m. each motion day, the assignment clerk and respective court clerks will have posted on the main floor bulletin board of the court building and on each court bulletin board the list of matters scheduled for that day and before which judge the case is assigned.

(F) Hearing on Other Than Motion Day. All motions should be specifically noticed before the judge assigned to the case. Short matters may be heard on days other than motion days promptly at 9:00 a.m., but only when confirmed and scheduled in advance by the judge and when properly noticed for hearing.

(G) Duty to Examine File. Counsel are charged with the responsibility of examining the court file to see that all papers necessary to the hearing are in the file, including proof of service or notice of hearing.

(H) Motion Certification. The attorney of record or the party in propria persona shall certify on the notice of hearing that the attorney or party either has made personal contact with the other party or the party's attorney and requested concurrence in the relief sought, but concurrence has been denied, or that the attorney or party has made reasonable and diligent attempts to contact the other party or the party's attorney, but was unable to do so. The certification must specify the date or dates that contact was made or attempted.

[Amended effective February 6, 1986; November 1, 1991; December 1, 1999.]

Subrule (H) was addded to Local Court Rule 2.119, effective December 1, 1999, at the request of the Sixteenth Circuit Court (Macomb County).

RULE 2.402   FACSIMILE TRANSMISSION OF DOCUMENTS

(1) Pursuant to Michigan Supreme Court Administrative Order 1994–2, the Macomb County Circuit Court authorizes the Macomb County Bar Association to operate a service for filing documents transmitted by facsimile communication equipment with the Court.

(2) The Clerk of the Court, Friend of the Court, the Mediation Clerk and other Court employees may accept for filing pleadings, motions, briefs, affidavits, orders and other documents from the Macomb County Bar Association which were received by facsimile transmission pursuant to this local court rule.

(3) All facsimile filings shall be on 8½″ × 11″ standard, plain paper, and any required filing fee must be paid at the time the document is filed.

(4) For documents presented for filing pursuant to this local court rule, a "signature," as defined in MCR 2.114, includes a signature transmitted by facsimile communication equipment.

(5) Attorneys or parties representing themselves shall keep a copy of the original document to be produced at the Court's request.

(6) The Macomb County Bar Association shall establish policies and procedures for the operation of the fax filing service and may limit the type of pleadings, motions, briefs, and other documents it will accept for filing. The Macomb County Bar Association's policies and procedures, and any changes thereto, shall be submitted to and approved by the Chief Judge of the Court prior to adoption.

(7) The Macomb County Bar Association may charge a reasonable fee for providing a facsimile filing service.

[Adopted effective July 6, 1995.]

RULE 2.501   TRIAL CALENDAR [RESCINDED]

[Rescinded effective June 22, 1993.]

RULE 2.602   ORDERS AND JUDGMENTS

(A) Presentation for Signature. Judgments and orders to which all parties have consented in writing as to form or form and substance shall be presented for the signature or attention of the judge through the court clerk, the court officer, or the judge's secretary. Such documents shall be presented before court convenes, during recess, at the close of court in the forenoon or afternoon, or left at the judge's chambers for presentation to the judge. If the document is presented for signature while the judge is on the bench and it would be a hardship upon the attorney to return later to pick up the signed document, it may be given to the court clerk who will present it to the judge as soon as possible.

(B) Distracting Conduct. Papers should not be presented to the clerk in the court during trial arguments to the court or jury.

RULE 3.200   DOMESTIC RELATIONS [RESCINDED]

[Rescinded effective May 1, 1993.]

LOCAL RULES OF THE NINETEENTH JUDICIAL CIRCUIT

[BENZIE AND MANISTEE COUNTIES]

Effective March 3, 1995

Table of Rules

RULE 2.402 FACSIMILE TRANSMISSION OF DOCUMENTS

Pursuant to Michigan Supreme Court Administrative Order 1994–2, the 19th Judicial Circuit will permit the use of facsimile equipment for the filing of court documents. The following regulations have been established to govern the use of facsimile equipment for the filing of documents with the 19th Judicial Circuit:

1. This Court will permit the filing of pleadings and court documents *which do not require a filing fee* by the use of facsimile (FAX) communications equipment. Any document for which a filing fee is required will not be accepted through the use of facsimile equipment unless the fee is tendered prior to or simultaneously with receipt of the facsimile. All filings shall be on 8½″ × 11″ standard paper.

2. The original document shall be sent to the Court within three business days. The Court Clerk shall retain the entire facsimile filing.

3. A fax service fee of $1.00 per page (including cover sheet) will be charged by the Court for receiving a facsimile transmission. Payment for the fax service fee shall be sent with the original document.

4. Documents will be received by the Court between the hours of 8:30 a.m. and 4:45 p.m. Documents received after 4:45 p.m. will be considered filed on the next following business day.

5. The maximum number of pages which may be sent to the Court at one time is limited to twenty pages.

6. A cover sheet must accompany every transmission which includes the following information: case name, case number, document title, name and telephone number of sender.

7. For purposes of MCR 2.114, a signature includes a signature transmitted by facsimile communication equipment.

[Adopted effective March 3, 1995.]

RULE 6.445 PROBATION VIOLATIONS; AUTHORITY OF PROBATION AGENT TO APPREHEND, DETAIN AND CONFINE

(A) Authorization to Apprehend. Probation officers assigned to the Manistee/Benzie Circuit Court are, pursuant to MCL 771.4; MSA 28.1134, authorized without further order of the court to apprehend, detain, and confine any probationer of the Manistee/Benzie Circuit Court accused of violating a term of probation.

(B) Prompt Arraignment. A probationer apprehended, detained or confined under this rule must be brought promptly before the court for arraignment.

(C) Written Charges and Hearing. A probationer apprehended, detained, or confined under this rule is entitled to a written copy of the charge, setting forth the alleged violation of probation, and is entitled to a hearing conducted in accordance with law and the court rules.

[Adopted effective June 24, 1997.]

LOCAL RULES OF THE TWENTY-FIRST JUDICIAL CIRCUIT

[ISABELLA COUNTY]

Effective March 24, 2000

Table of Rules

Rule
2.402   Facsimile Transmission of Documents.

RULE 2.402 FACSIMILE TRANSMISSION OF DOCUMENTS

(1) "Facsimile Communication Equipment' means a plain paper electronic device that permits the filing of 8-1/2 x 11-inch pleadings, motions, affidavits, opinions, orders and other documents to be filed in the Isabella County Trial Court by use of facsimile (FAX) communication equipment. Fax/documents are considered originals.

(2) Documents which require a filing fee will not be accepted unless fees are paid in full.

(3) The maximum number of pages which may be sent at one time for any pleading will be limited to 15 pages per document.

(4) Documents may be transmitted via fax 24 hours a day. Pleadings received before 4:15 P.M. will be filed the same day. Pleadings received after 4:15 P.M. will be filed the next business day. Confirmation of receipt beyond the fax confirmation sheet can be determined by telephoning the Clerk's office..

(5) A cover sheet must accompany every transmission which includes the following information: case name, case number, document title, name and telephone number of the sender.

(6) True copies of documents submitted via FAX will not be provided.

(7) For purposes of MCR 2.114, a signature includes a signature transmitted by facsimile communication equipment.

[Adopted effective March 24, 2000.]

LOCAL RULES OF THE TWENTY– THIRD JUDICIAL CIRCUIT

[IOSCO AND OSCODA COUNTIES]

Effective July 6, 1995

Table of Rules

RULE 2.119 MOTION PRACTICE

(A) An attorney of record may secure a date for hearing from the trial judge's secretary for matters such as uncontested divorce cases, brief motion arguments, and hearings.

(B) Motion Days.

(1) Circuit court motions shall be heard in Iosco County on the first and third Mondays of each month, and on the morning of the fourth Monday. Circuit court motions shall be heard in Oscoda County on the second Monday of each month.

(2) Motions shall be scheduled in the family division of the circuit court as ordered by the court.

(3) If a motion day falls on a legal holiday, the motion day shall be the following Wednesday.

(C) A copy of a motion or response (including brief) filed under this rule must be provided by counsel to the office of the judge hearing the motion. The judge's copy must be clearly marked JUDGE'S COPY on the cover sheet; the notation may be handwritten.

(D) Any matter requiring testimony or hearing of more than 15 minutes shall be scheduled by the assignment clerk other than on motion day.

(E) Motion Certification by Attorney.

(1) The following certificate signed by the attorney of record or by the party in propria persona shall be attached to or incorporated in the motion and notice of hearing filed with the clerk:

I hereby certify that I have made personal contact with _____ on _____
        [name]   [date]
requesting concurrence in the relief sought with this motion and that concurrence has been denied, or that I have made the following reasonable and diligent attempts to contact counsel requesting concurrence in the relief sought with this motion: _____

(2) A proposed order must be attached to and served with the motion.

[Adopted effective October 1, 2000.]

2000 Staff Comment

Local Court Rule 2.119 was approved by the Supreme Court on August 16, 2000, to be effective October 1, 2000, at the request of the 23rd Circuit Court.

RULE 2.402 FACSIMILE TRANSMISSION OF DOCUMENTS

1. This Court will permit the filing of pleadings and court documents by the use of facsimile (FAX) communications equipment. All filings shall be on 8½″ × 11″ standard paper.

2. Documents which require a filing fee will not be accepted unless the filing fee and service fee are paid in full. Payment may be made to the county clerk's office by use of Visa or MasterCard charges.

3. In addition to the statutory filing fee, a FAX service fee of $3 for the first page and $1 for each additional page shall be assessed to be paid per credit card.

4. Documents will be received by the Court between the hours of 8:00 a.m. and 4:00 p.m. Documents received after 4:00 p.m. will be considered filed on the next following business day.

5. The maximum number of pages which may be sent to the Court at one time is limited to twenty (20) pages except for pleadings.

6. A cover sheet must accompany every transmission. The following information must be included on this sheet: case name, case number (not applicable for new filings), document title, name and telephone number of sender, Visa or MasterCard number, expiration date of card, signature of authorized agent for card.

7. *Signature.* For purposes of MCR 2.114, a signature includes a signature transmitted by facsimile communication equipment.

[Adopted effective July 6, 1995.]

RULE 3.208(B) TAKING OF CASH BONDS AND MODIFICATION OF CASH BONDS IN FRIEND OF THE COURT BENCH WARRANT CASES

(A) In addition to the sheriff or his deputy, court officers authorized by the chief judge may accept the payment of money in fulfillment of a cash bond from a person arrested pursuant to a bench warrant issued under MCL 552.631; MSA 25.164(31) or MCR 3.208(B)(4) and (6); immediately upon arrest or at any point thereafter prior to court appearance, subject to the conditions set forth at MCL 552.632; MSA 25.164(32).

(B) If the respondent is not brought before the court within 24 hours of arrest and is unable, thereafter, to post the required cash bond, or if the respondent cannot be lodged at the county jai because of a declared jail overcrowding emergency and a circuit judge is not readily available to arraign the respondent, the friend of the court or deputy friend of the court may conduct a prearraignment bond review and authorize a lower cash bond, pending the respondent's arraignment on the bench warrant before the court.

(C) In determining whether to lower a cash bond, the friend of the court or deputy friend of the court must take into account factors such as the respondent's available resources and the likelihood that he or she will appear before the court as further directed by the friend of the court or deputy friend of the court. The friend of the court or deputy friend of the court may authorize release upon personal recognizance pending arraignment before the court.

[Adopted effective April 26, 2000.]

2000 Staff Comment

Local Court Rules 3.208, 6.113, and 6.445 were approved by the Supreme Court, effective April 26, 2000, at the request of the 23rd Circuit Court.

RULE 6.113 PRETRIAL CONFERENCES

(A) Pretrial conferences in Criminal Cases.

(1) On the date scheduled for arraignment, a pretrial conference shall be held unless the defendant enters a plea of guilty or *nolo contendere* when arraigned.

(a) The pretrial conference may be adjourned or continued by order of the court.

(b) The defendant shall be present at the pretrial conference unless excused by order of the court.

(2) *Scope of Conference.* At the pretrial conference, the court shall:

(a) Determine the need for pretrial motions, establish a cutoff date for the filing of said motions, and schedule said motions for hearing;

(b) Determine whether there are additional witnesses sought to be endorsed by the prosecution or defendant;

(c) Determine whether the defendant is raising any defense that requires notice (alibi, insanity, or incompetency) and require the filing of such notice as required by law and ordered by the court;

(d) Estimate the time required for trial;

(e) Determine whether plea negotiations are completed;

(f) Determine whether the defense will waive any endorsed witnesses;

(g) Determine whether there will be any unusual legal issues or requested special jury instructions;

(h) Consider all other matters that may aid in the disposition of the action; and

(i) Fix a date for trial.

[Adopted effective April 26, 2000.]

2000 Staff Comment

Local Court Rules 3.208, 6.113, and 6.445 were approved by the Supreme Court, effective April 26, 2000, at the request of the 23rd Circuit Court.

RULE 6.445 PROBATION VIOLATIONS; AUTHORITY OF PROBATION AGENT TO APPREHEND, DETAIN AND CONFINE

(A) Authorization to Apprehend. Probation officers assigned to the 23rd Circuit Court (Iosco and Oscoda Counties) are, pursuant to MCL 771.4; MSA 28.1134, authorized without further order of the court to apprehend, detain, and confine any probationer of the 23rd Circuit Court accused of violating a term of probation.

(B) Prompt Arraignment. A probationer apprehended, detained or confined under this rule must be brought promptly before the court for arraignment.

(C) Written Charges and Hearing. A probationer apprehended, detained, or confined under this rule is entitled to a written copy of the charge, setting forth the alleged violation of probation, and is entitled to a hearing conducted in accordance with law and the court rules.

[Adopted effective April 26, 2000.]

2000 Staff Comment

Local Court Rules 3.208, 6.113, and 6.445 were approved by the Supreme Court, effective April 26, 2000, at the request of the 23rd Circuit Court.

LOCAL RULES OF THE TWENTY–FOURTH JUDICIAL CIRCUIT

[SANILAC COUNTY]

Effective March 1, 1985

Table of Rules

RULE 2.401   PRETRIAL CONFERENCES; TRIAL DATE ASSIGNMENTS

The assignment clerk shall, based upon the term calendar, determine which cases are ready for pretrial conference and notify counsel of record as to the date, time, and place thereof; however, all pretrial conferences shall, as far as practicable, be held a reasonable time prior to trial. Failure of counsel to appear at pretrial conferences without notice may result in such action as is provided by the Michigan Court Rules. The pretrial conference may be waived in writing by both counsel through stipulation, except where a pretrial conference is expressly ordered by the court. All counsel for the respective parties shall attend the pretrial hearing, unless excused by the court, and they may, at their discretion, and the discretion of the court, be accompanied by their respective clients. As far as possible, trial dates will be assigned to counsel at the pretrial conference, and no further notice of trial shall be given. Post pretrial discovery shall be allowed; however, failure to complete discovery prior to trial shall not be a basis for adjournment of the trial date set at the pretrial hearing, except for good cause shown.

RULE 2.602   SIGNING OF PROPOSED JUDGMENTS AND ORDERS

All proposed judgments or orders shall be delivered to the assignment clerk or the county clerk, who shall attach them to the appropriate court file. However, if an attorney is desirous of obtaining a signed order or judgment without delay, the appropriate file may be checked out of the county clerk's office with the proposed order or judgment attached and presented to the judge for signature.

RULE 3.207   JUDGMENTS AND ORDERS IN DOMESTIC RELATIONS CASES [RESCINDED]

[Rescinded effective May 1, 1993.]

LOCAL RULES OF THE TWENTY-FIFTH JUDICIAL CIRCUIT

[MARQUETTE COUNTY]

Table of Rules

RULE 8.123   CONCURRENT JURISDICTION CASES [RESCINDED]

[Rescinded effective March 22, 2000.]

Staff Comment to 2000 Rescission

Joint Local Court Rule 8.123 was rescinded March 22, 2000, in light of the establishment of the family division of circuit court.

LOCAL RULES OF THE TWENTY–EIGHTH JUDICIAL CIRCUIT

[MISSAUKEE AND WEXFORD COUNTIES]

Effective March 1, 1985

Table of Rules

RULE 2.401 PRETRIAL CONFERENCES

(A) Pretrial Conferences in Criminal Cases.

(1) On the date scheduled for arraignment pursuant to Local Administrative Order 1985–2, a pretrial conference shall be held unless the defendant enters a plea of guilty or nolo contendere when arraigned.

(a) The pretrial conference may be adjourned or continued by order of the court.

(b) The defendant shall be present at the pretrial conference unless excused by order of the court.

(2) *Scope of Conference.* At the pretrial conference, the court shall:

(a) Determine the need for pretrial motions, establish a cutoff date for the filing of said motions, and schedule said motions for hearing;

(b) Determine whether or not there are additional witnesses sought to be endorsed by the prosecution or defendant;

(c) Determine whether the defendant is raising any defense which requires notice (alibi, insanity, or incompetency) and require the filing of such notice as required by law;

(d) Estimate the time required for trial;

(e) Determine whether plea negotiations are completed;

(f) Determine whether the defense will waive any endorsed witness;

(g) Determine whether there will be any unusual legal issues or requested special jury instructions;

(h) Consider all other matters that may aid in the disposition of the action; and

(i) Fix a date certain for trial.

RULE 3.206 ATTORNEYS FEES; EXPENSES; INTERIM AND TEMPORARY ORDERS FOR ALIMONY OR CHILD SUPPORT [RESCINDED]

[Rescinded effective May 1, 1993.]

RULE 3.207 POWERS AND DUTIES OF FRIEND OF THE COURT [RESCINDED]

[Rescinded effective May 1, 1993.]

RULE 3.209 JUDGMENTS AND ORDERS [RESCINDED]

[Rescinded effective May 1, 1993.]

LOCAL RULES OF THE THIRTIETH JUDICIAL CIRCUIT *

[INGHAM COUNTY]

Effective March 1, 1985

Table of Rules

* Publisher's Note: The Court of Claims is a division of the 30th Judicial Circuit Court. The Court of Claims Act, set forth following the Local Rules of the St. Joseph Probate Court, infra, governs practice and procedure in the Court of Claims.

RULE 2.119   MOTION PRACTICE

(A) An attorney of record may secure a date for hearing from the trial judge's secretary for matters such as uncontested divorce cases, brief motion arguments, and hearings.

(B) Motion day shall be Wednesday. If a legal holiday coincides in some manner, the assignment clerk shall set a new motion day and provide appropriate notice.

(C) Any hearing time secured by telephone shall be cancelled if a written notice of hearing is not filed within seven days with a copy to the assignment clerk or judge's secretary, as appropriate.

(D) Any matter requiring testimony or hearings of more than 15 minutes shall be scheduled by the assignment clerk other than on motion day.

[Adopted effective May 31, 1985; amended effective September 4, 1985.]

RULE 2.404   DOMESTIC RELATIONS MEDIATION [RESCINDED]

[Rescinded effective May 1, 1993.]

RULE 2.510   IMPANELING THE JURY

Jurors: Term of Service.

(1) All persons summoned to appear as circuit court petit jurors shall serve a term of one calendar week, or for the duration of the trial, if selected to serve on a trial jury.

(2) During the term of the jury service jurors shall report for actual jury service only when so directed by the court.

[Adopted effective March 1, 1985.]

RULE 3.209   JUDGMENTS AND ORDERS [RESCINDED]

[Rescinded effective May 1, 1993.]

RULE 6.107   GRAND JURY

(A) **Grand Juries; Presentation of Petition; Granting of Petition.**

(1) Petitions for a grand jury shall be presented to the chief judge, and submitted to the bench for decision.

(2) No such petition shall be granted except by affirmative majority action of the entire bench.

(B) **Grand Juries; One-Person Grand Jury.** If a one-person grand jury is called, the judge who shall act as the grand juror shall be selected by blind draw.

(C) **Grand Juries; Citizens' Grand Jury; Selection.** If a citizens' grand jury is called, the chief judge shall direct the jury board to draw the names of a specified number of persons to appear for selection to serve as grand jurors. A judge shall be selected by blind draw and shall preside over the selection of a sufficient number of the persons to serve as grand jurors and subsequent grand jury proceedings.

[Adopted effective March 1, 1985.]

LOCAL RULES OF THE THIRTY–THIRD
JUDICIAL CIRCUIT

[CHARLEVOIX COUNTY]

Table of Rules

RULE 8.123 CONCURRENT JURISDICTION CASES [RESCINDED]

[Rescinded effective March 22, 2000.]

Staff Comment to 2000 Rescission

Joint Local Court Rule 8.123 was rescinded March 22, 2000, in light of the establishment of the family division of circuit court.

LOCAL RULES OF THE THIRTY–SEVENTH JUDICIAL CIRCUIT

[CALHOUN COUNTY]

Effective March 1, 1985

Table of Rules

RULE 2.119　MOTION PRACTICE

(A) Examination of File. Counsel must ensure that all papers necessary to a hearing are in the court file and properly executed, including proof of service and notice of hearing, whether contested or not.

(B) No motion will be heard wherein the motion fee is due and unpaid at the time of the scheduled hearing unless such fee has been waived or suspended in accordance with the Michigan Court Rules.

RULE 2.401　PRETRIAL CONFERENCES [RESCINDED]

[Rescinded effective September 20, 1993.]

RULE 2.402　FASCIMILE TRANMISSION OF DOCUMENTS

(1) The clerk is authorized to accept the filing of pleadings and court documents by the use of facsimile (fax) communication equipment. All filings shall be on 8½ by 11–inch standard paper.

(2) Documents which require a filing fee will not be accepted unless the filing fee and service fee are paid in full in advance. In addition to the statutory filing fee, a fax service fee of $3 for the first page and $1 for each additional page shall be assessed.

(3) Documents will be received by the clerk between the hours of 8:00 a.m. and 4:00 p.m. Monday through Friday, except designated court holidays. Documents received after 4:00 P.M. will be considered filed on the next following court business day.

(4) The clerk will establish a designated telephone number exclusively used for fax filings. Further, the clerk will notify attorneys and litigants of any fax filing requirements.

(5) The maximum number of pages which may be sent to the court at one time is limited to twenty (20) pages except for pleadings.

(6) A cover sheet must accompany every transmission. The following information must be included on the sheet: case name, case number (not applicable for new filings), document title, and the name and telephone number of the sender. In the event the clerk accepts payments by credit card, the cover sheet shall also include the Visa or MasterCard number, expiration date of card, and signature of the authorized agent for the card.

(7) **Signature.** For purposes of MCR 2.114, a signature includes a signature transmitted by facsimile communication equipment.

[Adopted effective February 6, 1998.]

RULE 2.403　MEDIATION

(A) Mediators. Property division in divorce proceedings shall be heard by one mediator unless a greater number is ordered by the court or is requested by the parties at the time the case is ordered to mediation.

(B) Scheduling of Hearings. The mediation clerk may establish a monthly standard mediation day or days, as needed, for hearings. Cases will generally be assigned to such date in the month ordered by the court; provided, if the court has not designated a specific month for mediation, then the month assigned by the mediation clerk will be that which will allow sufficient time for post-mediation procedures prior to trial, unless the parties stipulate otherwise.

(C) Mediation Fees.

(1) If a matter is settled or adjourned but notification is not given by the parties to the mediation clerk until after the eighth day prior to the scheduled hearing, no refund of fees will be made and the mediators shall be paid their fees. Any subsequently rescheduled hearing shall require the parties to pay an additional $75 per party fee.

(2) Parties qualified for waiver or suspension of fees by reason of indigency are not required to pay a mediation fee or late filing fee unless or until they recover upon a money judgment or settlement in the suit.

(3) If a party fails to pay any fees required within the time limits prescribed, the mediators may refuse to accept or consider the written and oral presentations of that party in mediating the case. The mediation clerk shall send a past due notice for any unpaid fees. If any fees remain unpaid after 20 days from the mailing of the past due notice, then the mediation clerk shall petition the court for an order to show cause directed to the delinquent party or counsel if the parties are represented by counsel. Additionally, if the party fails to pay fees or the late filing penalty, the panel's evaluation may include a provision that the party not be entitled to recovery of costs if the matter proceeds to trial. This provision shall not apply to any party for whom fees have been waived or suspended by reason of indigency.

(D) Submission of Documents.
All communications among the parties and the mediators concerning the issues in mediation shall be made in the presence of all parties, or, if in writing, by immediately forwarding copies of such communication to other parties to the proceeding. This provision does not apply to communications between mediators in evaluating the case.

(E) Conduct of Hearings.

(1) At the hearing, the plaintiff's statement shall be made first and the defendant's thereafter, if any. Rebuttal may be made if a counterclaim is asserted, or, if authorized by the panel.

(2) Mediation hearings shall be subject to the same decorum and conduct rules as court proceedings. Any violations thereof shall be reported by the mediators to the mediation clerk for appropriate enforcement action. Any such action shall be brought before the chief judge.

(3) Attendance at mediation hearings will be limited to the mediators, the parties and their attorneys, and the mediation clerk unless attendance by others is specifically authorized by the mediation panel or by court order.

RULE 3.208(B) TAKING OF CASH BONDS AND MODIFICATION OF CASH BONDS IN FRIEND OF THE COURT BENCH WARRANT CASES

(1) In addition to the sheriff or his deputy, court officers authorized by the chief judge may accept the payment of money in fulfillment of a cash bond from a person arrested pursuant to a bench warrant issued under MCL 552.631; MSA 25.164(31) or MCR 3.207(D)(5)*, immediately upon arrest or at any point thereafter prior to court appearance, subject to the conditions set forth at MCL 552.632; MSA 25.164(32).

(2) If the respondent is not brought before the court within 24 hours of arrest and is unable, thereafter, to post the required cash bond, or if the respondent cannot be lodged at the county jail because of a declared jail overcrowding emergency and a circuit judge is not readily available to arraign the respondent, a friend of the court referee may conduct a pre-arraignment bond review and authorize a lower cash bond pending the respondent's arraignment on the bench warrant before the court.

(3) In determining whether to lower a cash bond, the referee must take into account factors such as the respondent's available resources and the likelihood that he or she will appear before the court as further directed by the referee. The referee is without authority to authorize release upon personal recognizance pending arraignment before the court.

[Adopted as Rule 3.207(D) effective April 12, 1993 until further order of the Supreme Court; redesignated as Rule 3.208(B) effective May 1, 1993.]

* Publisher's Note: See MCR 3.208(B)(6).

RULE 3.209 JUDGMENTS AND ORDERS [RESCINDED]

[Rescinded effective May 1, 1993.]

RULE 6.445 PROBATION VIOLATIONS; AUTHORITY OF PROBATION AGENT TO APPREHEND, DETAIN AND CONFINE

(A) Authorization to Apprehend. Probation officers assigned to the Calhoun Circuit Court are, pursuant to MCL 771.4; MSA 28.1134, authorized without further order of the court to apprehend, detain, and confine any probationer of the Calhoun Circuit Court accused of violating a term of probation. The director and the assistant director of the Calhoun Community Alternatives Program Residential Probation Center may apprehend, detain, and confine a probationer of this court who is assigned to that program and who is accused of violationg a term of probation.

(B) Prompt Arraignment. A probationer apprehended, detained or confined under this rule must be brought promptly before the court for arraignment.

(C) Written Charges and Hearing. A probationer apprehended, detained, or confined under this rule is entitled to a written copy of the charge, setting forth the alleged violation of probation, and is entitled to a hearing conducted in accordance with law and the court rules.

[Adopted effective September 20, 1993.]

LOCAL RULES OF THE THIRTY–EIGHTH JUDICIAL CIRCUIT

[MONROE COUNTY]

Effective June 1, 1989

Table of Rules

RULE 2.119   MOTION PRACTICE

(C) Time for Service of Motion Praecipe. Except in an emergency, a motion praecipe must be filed at least 7 days before the scheduled hearing date.

[Adopted effective June 1, 1989.]

LOCAL RULES OF THE THIRTY–NINTH JUDICIAL CIRCUIT

[LENAWEE COUNTY]

Effective March 1, 1985

Table of Rules

RULE 3.207 POWERS AND DUTIES OF FRIEND OF THE COURT [RESCINDED]

[Rescinded effective May 1, 1993.]

RULE 8.110 CHIEF JUDGE RULE

(A) Terms and Sessions. There shall be four terms of court each year beginning the first Monday of January, April, July, and October, unless falling on a legal holiday, in which case the next weekday of the month shall be the first day of the term. Each term of the court shall be deemed to continue from the first day of the term until the first day of the succeeding term.

(B) Arraignments. When the district court binds any respondent over to the circuit court for trial, said respondent shall be ordered to appear before the Thirty-Ninth Circuit Court on the Tuesday or Friday morning next following four days after the district court orders said respondent bound over. The appearance shall be at 8:15 a.m. on said Tuesday or Friday.

(C) Nonsupport Orders. Nonsupport orders to show cause will be noticed at 8:30 a.m., Monday.

(D) Motions. Motions, petitions, defaults, pro confesso, ex parte, and miscellaneous matters, and other short causes not requiring more than 20 minutes, shall be heard on Monday of each week beginning at 9:00 a.m., unless a legal holiday, in which case they shall be heard the following day at 9:00 a.m.

(E) Monday Matters. Monday matters will be heard by the court. If others attorneys are waiting, a matter being heard will be recessed after 20 minutes until all other matters are heard.

LOCAL RULES OF THE FORTIETH JUDICIAL CIRCUIT

[LAPEER COUNTY]

Effective March 1, 1985

Table of Rules

RULE 1.101 SCOPE OF RULES

(A) These rules govern the practice of the Fortieth Judicial Circuit in civil and criminal cases.

(B) These rules are supplemental to the Michigan Court Rules of 1985, which shall be controlling in the event of any conflict in the rules.

(C) These rules shall supersede all earlier local court rules of this circuit and shall rescind all related administrative orders of this circuit.

RULE 1.102 NUMBER OF RULES

(A) These rules are numbered in conformity with the Michigan Court Rules of 1985 as closely as is feasible.

(B) These rules may be cited as "LCR," i.e., this rule may be referred to as LCR 1.102(B).

RULE 2.119 MOTION DAY PRACTICE

(A) Motion days shall be held on the first four Mondays of each month. If a Monday is a legal holiday, then the following day shall be motion day, unless otherwise designated.

(B) The chief judge shall determine on which motion days criminal matters will be heard.

(C) All motion day matters shall be noticed for hearing on a regularly scheduled motion day of the judge to whom the action is assigned.

(D) Matters may be scheduled for hearing on motion days by filing a motion praecipe no later than noon of the previous Thursday.

(E) Unless otherwise provided by notice published in the term calendar, criminal matters (including appeals), paternity, arraignments, family support mat-

ters, and driver's license petitions shall be noticed for hearing on assigned motion days at 1:30 p.m.; all other matters shall be heard at 9:00 a.m.

(F) At each session of motion day, attorneys shall notify the court clerk when their matters are ready for hearing and those matters shall be called in the order in which notice is received.

RULE 2.401 CIVIL PRETRIAL CONFERENCE PROCEDURES

(A) Preparing for Pretrial Conference. Attorneys or parties in propria persona shall be prepared to participate in a pretrial conference pursuant to MCR 2.401 and these rules.

(B) Submitting Pretrial Statements. Each party shall submit to the court and to the opposing counsel, at the beginning of every scheduled pretrial conference, a pretrial statement that sets forth:

(1) a brief statement of the party's claims and defenses;

(2) a statement of factual issues;

(3) a statement of legal issues;

(4) citations of law in support of the party's positions including, in negligence actions, all statutes the other party is claimed to have violated;

(5) a statement of required amendments to pleadings and the reasons of the delayed request to amend pleadings;

(6) a statement of required discovery;

(7) an estimate of the time required for trials; and

(8) any other information that will enable the court and parties to conduct a meaningful pretrial conference.

(C) Using Forms in Lieu of Statement. Blank forms for pretrial statements for different types of actions shall be available in the clerk's office and may be completed and submitted in lieu of the pretrial statement described in subrule (B).

RULE 2.602 PRESENTING ORDERS AND JUDGMENTS FOR SIGNATURE OF JUDGE

Proposed judgments and orders shall be deposited with the clerk, who will check them against the clerk's minutes before they are presented to the judge for signature; this procedure need not be followed with respect to the following judgments and orders:

(1) those approved by opposing counsel,

(2) those presented for signature at the same session of court, and

(3) interim support orders.

RULE 3.201 DOMESTIC RELATIONS MATTERS [RESCINDED]

[Rescinded effective May 1, 1993.]

RULE 6.100 CRIMINAL PROCEDURE

(A) Criminal Pretrial Conferences.

(1) Pretrial conferences shall be held in all criminal cases to be tried in circuit court. The purposes of a pretrial conference shall be:

(a) to determine whether the parties intend to proceed to trial or to enter a plea to the original charge, a lesser charge, or an added charge;

(b) to determine whether pretrial motions have been completed;

(c) to stipulate which witnesses will be called at trial and which witnesses will be waived, if any;

(d) to determine the number of trial days required;

(e) to determine when the case will be ready for trial and disclose any scheduling problems.

(2) The defendant and his or her attorney, as well as the prosecuting attorney or a representative, shall attend the pretrial conference. The defendant shall not participate in the conference, but shall be immediately available for consultation. Incarcerated defendants need not be present, unless required by the judge.

(3) Copies of the pretrial conference summary shall be available from the clerk on request.

(B) Arraignments and Motions.

(1) Arraignments shall be noticed for a regularly scheduled motion day of the judge to whom the case is assigned. The district court judge who binds the case over to circuit court for arraignment will ordinarily assign a date for arraignment. If no date is assigned, the case will automatically be noticed by the clerk for the next regularly scheduled criminal motion day of the assigned judge.

(2) A defendant represented by a lawyer may enter a plea of not guilty or stand mute without arraignment in accordance with the provisions of MCR 6.101(D)(2). In such a case, the defendant shall state, in addition, what pretrial motions will be filed, how much time will be required to hear them, and the earliest date the defendant will be ready to proceed with them. A copy of the statement shall be served on the prosecuting attorney no later than the date set for arraignment.

(3) At the arraignment or on receipt of the statement required in subsection (2), the court shall set a date for hearing pretrial motions. Except in the discretion of the trial court for good cause and not as the result of failure to exercise due diligence on the part of counsel or the parties and in those matters concerning jurisdiction, no pretrial motions shall be accepted by the court for hearing after the pretrial conference is completed.

LOCAL RULES OF THE FORTY-FIRST JUDICIAL CIRCUIT

[DICKINSON, IRON AND MENOMINEE COUNTIES]

Effective September 21, 1994

Table of Rules

RULE 2.402 FACSIMILE TRANSMISSION OF DOCUMENTS

(1) This court will permit the filing of pleadings and court documents by the use of facsimile (FAX) communications equipment. All filings shall be on 8½ by 11 inch standard paper.

(2) Documents which will require a filing fee will not be accepted unless the filing fee is paid in full.

(3) In addition to the statutory filing fee, a FAX service fee of $1 per page will be charged by the court for receiving facsimile transmission. Documents will not be accepted from anyone who is 30 days or more delinquent in payment of a FAX service fee.

(4) Documents will be received by the court between the hours of 8:00 A.M. and 4:15 P.M. C.S.T. (Dickinson Co.), and between the hours of 8:00 A.M. and 3:45 P.M. C.S.T. (Iron and Menominee Cos.). Documents received after 4:15 P.M. C.S.T. (Dickinson Co.), and after 3:45 P.M. C.S.T. (Iron and Menominee Cos.), will be considered filed on the next following business day.

(5) The maximum number of pages which may be sent to the court at one time is limited to 20 pages.

(6) A cover sheet must accompany every transmission which includes the following information: case name, case number, document title, name and telephone number of sender.

(7) **Signature.** For purposes of MCR 2.114, a signature includes a signature transmitted by facsimile communication equipment.

[Adopted effective September 21, 1994.]

LOCAL RULES OF THE FORTY-SECOND JUDICIAL CIRCUIT

[MIDLAND COUNTY]

Effective July 6, 1995

Table of Rules

RULE 2.402 FACSIMILE TRANSMISSION OF DOCUMENTS

1. Filings by FAX. This court will permit the filing of pleadings and court documents by the use of facsimile (FAX) equipment. All filings shall be on 8½" by 11" inch paper.

2. Filing Fee. Documents which require a filing fee will not be accepted unless the filing fee and service fee are paid in full. Payment may be made to the Clerk of the Circuit Court's office by use of Visa or MasterCard charges.

3. Service Fee. In addition to the statutory filing fee, a FAX service fee of $3 for the first page and $1 for each additional page shall be assessed to be paid by credit card.

4. Hours of Acceptance. Documents will be received by the clerk's office between the hours of 8:00 a.m. and 4:00 p.m. FAXES received after 4:00 p.m. will be considered filed on the following business day.

5. Cover Sheet. A cover sheet provided by the Clerk of the Circuit Court's office must accompany every transmission. The following information must be included on this sheet: case name, case number (not applicable for new filings), document title, name and telephone number of sender, Visa or MasterCard number, expiration of card, and signature of authorized agent for card.

6. Signature. For purposes of MCR 2.114, a signature includes a signature transmitted by facsimile equipment.

[Adopted effective July 6, 1995.]

LOCAL RULES OF THE FORTY–FIFTH JUDICIAL CIRCUIT

[ST. JOSEPH COUNTY]

Effective May 31, 1985

Table of Rules

RULE 2.403 MEDIATION

(A) All mediation procedures shall be in accordance with MCR 2.403.

(B) After a mediation order is entered, the parties must serve upon the mediation clerk a copy of any motion, stipulation, order, or pleading concerning scheduling.

(C) The parties may object to the form of mediation or to the composition of a mediation panel by following the procedures and time periods specified in MCR 2.403(C).

(G) Mediation shall be conducted in the courthouse on the last Friday of each month or, by stipulation, at any other time and place convenient to the mediators.

(H) If a matter is settled or otherwise concluded, and a notice of disposition is given to the mediation clerk at least 14 days prior to the hearing date, any fees paid pursuant to MCR 2.403(H) shall be returned. Failure to notify the mediation clerk within the specified time shall preclude the return of fees.

[Adopted effective January 21, 1987.]

RULE 2.502 DISMISSAL FOR LACK OF PROGRESS

(A) Notice of Proposed Dismissal. If an attorney or party is directed to appear in court pursuant to MCR 2.502(A) in order to prevent an action from being dismissed for lack of progress, such appearance may be made either by letter or in person.

LOCAL RULES OF THE FORTY–SIXTH JUDICIAL CIRCUIT

[KALKASKA, CRAWFORD AND OTSEGO COUNTIES]

Effective July 1, 1988

Table of Rules

RULE 2.403   MEDIATION

(A) All mediation procedures shall be in accordance with MCR 2.403.

(B) After a mediation order is entered, the parties must serve upon the mediation clerk a copy of any motion, stipulation, order, or pleading concerning scheduling.

(C) Adjournment of mediation hearings is to be avoided whenever possible. Adjournments are to be approved by the judge assigned to the case or, in the absence of the assigned judge, the chief judge. Whenever possible, the attorney in principal charge of the case shall delegate responsibility for attendance to another attorney so as to avoid adjournment.

(D) If a matter is adjourned, settled or otherwise disposed of before mediation, it shall be the responsibility of both counsel to immediately notify the mediation clerk of the disposition. If a notice of disposition or adjournment is given to the mediation clerk at least 7 days prior to the hearing date, any fees paid pursuant to MCR 2.403(H) shall be returned. Failure to notify the mediation clerk within the specified time shall preclude the return of fees; any subsequent rescheduled hearing shall require the parties to pay an additional $75 fee per party.

LOCAL RULES OF THE FORTY–EIGHTH JUDICIAL CIRCUIT

[ALLEGAN COUNTY]

Effective July 6, 1995

Table of Rules

RULE 2.402 FACSIMILE TRANSMISSION OF DOCUMENTS

1. This Court will permit the filing of pleadings and court documents by the use of facsimile (FAX) equipment. All filings shall be on 8½″ by 11″ paper.

2. Documents which require a filing fee will not be accepted unless the filing fee and service fees are paid in full. Payment must be made to the County Clerk's Office by use of Visa or MasterCard charges.

3. In addition to the statutory filing fee, a fax service fee of $3.00 for the 1st page and $1.00 for each additional page shall be assessed to be paid by credit card.

4. Documents will be received by the Clerk's office between the hours of 9:00 A.M. and 4:00 P.M. Faxes received after 4:00 P.M. will be considered filed on the following business day.

5. Documents requiring duplicate copies (e.g., for the Friend of the Court), must include the appropriate number of copies or authorization must be given on the transmittal form for a $2.00 per page copy fee to be paid by Visa or MasterCard.

6. The maximum number of pages which may be sent at one time for any document or documents is 25.

7. A cover sheet provided by the County Clerk's office must accompany every transmission. The following information must be included on this sheet: case name, case number (not applicable for new filings, document title, name and telephone number of sender, Visa or MasterCard number, expiration of card, signature of authorized agent for card.

8. Signature. For purposes of MCR 2.114, a signature includes a signature transmitted by facsimile equipment.

[Adopted effective July 6, 1995.]

RULE 3.206 PLEADING

All new cases filed in the family division of the 48th Circuit Court must be accompanied by a completed case file information form, in addition to any other document or information required by statute or court rule. Forms may be obtained from the Office of the County Clerk.

[Adopted effective January 1, 1999.]

1998 Staff Comment

Local Court Rule 3.206 was adopted October 7, 1998, at the request of the circuit court, to be effective January 1, 1999.

LOCAL RULES OF THE FIFTIETH JUDICIAL CIRCUIT

[CHIPPEWA AND MACKINAC COUNTIES]

Effective March 3, 1995

Table of Rules

RULE 2.402   FACSIMILE TRANSMISSION OF DOCUMENTS

1. Filing of pleadings and court documents by use of facsimile (FAX) communications equipment shall be permitted by this Court. All filings shall be on 8½″ × 11″ ordinary copy paper.

2. No document will be accepted by facsimile equipment where a filing fee is required.

3. A fee for receiving of pleadings by facsimile transmission shall be $5.00 for the first page and $1.00 for each additional page. A statement shall be forwarded to sender and must be paid by return mail. Failure to pay said fee shall result in the refusal to accept future fax transmissions.

4. A fee for returning of pleadings by facsimile transmission shall be $1.00 for each page.

5. The number of pages which will be accepted by facsimile transmission shall be limited to twenty (20). Each page shall be appropriately numbered.

6. Documents will be received by the County Clerk's Office between the hours of 8:30 a.m. and 4:45 p.m. Documents received after 4:45 p.m. will not be processed or time stamped until the following day.

7. A cover page must accompany every facsimile transmission and include the following information: case name, case number, document title, name and telephone number of sender.

8. For purposes of MCR 2.114, a signature includes a signature transmitted by facsimile communication equipment.

9. Warrants. Facsimile communication equipment and voice communication equipment may be used as provided for in 1990 PA 41, 43, 44 and 45.

[Adopted effective March 3, 1995.]

LOCAL RULES OF THE FIFTY–SIXTH JUDICIAL CIRCUIT

[EATON COUNTY]

Effective September 21, 1994

Table of Rules

RULE 2.402   FACSIMILE FILING AND TRANSMISSION OF COURT DOCUMENTS

(1) This court will permit the filing of pleadings and court documents by the use of facsimile (FAX) communications equipment. All filings shall be on 8½ by 11 inch standard paper.

(2) Any document for which a filing fee is required will *not* be accepted through the use of facsimile equipment.

(3) No fee will be charged by the court for receiving a facsimile transmission.

(4) Documents will be received by the court between the hours of 8:00 A.M. and 4:45 P.M. Documents received after 4:45 P.M. will be considered filed on the next following business day.

(5) The maximum number of pages which may be sent to the court at one time is limited to twenty pages.

(6) A cover sheet must accompany every transmission which includes the following information: the name of the person/department for whom the fax is intended, case name, case number, name and telephone number of sender.

(7) **Signature.** For purposes of MCR 2.114, a signature includes a signature transmitted by facsimile communication equipment.

[Adopted effective September 21, 1994.]

LOCAL RULES OF THE FIFTY–SEVENTH JUDICIAL CIRCUIT

[EMMET COUNTY]

Table of Rules

Rule
8.123   Concurrent Jurisdiction Cases [Rescinded].

RULE 8.123 CONCURRENT JURISDICTION CASES [RESCINDED]

[Rescinded effective March 22, 2000.]

Staff Comment to 2000 Rescission

Joint Local Court Rule 8.123 was rescinded March 22, 2000, in light of the establishment of the family division of circuit court.

LOCAL RULES OF THE RECORDER'S COURT

[CITY OF DETROIT]

Effective March 1, 1985

Table of Rules

RULE 2.302 DISCOVERY OF DOCUMENTS AND EXHIBITS

(A) On a motion in open court at the arraignment on the information or by a subsequent proper motion, the trial court may order that the prosecution make copies of the following available to defense counsel:

(1) All statements known to the police and prosecutor by all endorsed witnesses;

(2) All statements by the defendant which have been recorded or written;

(3) The investigator's report and all preliminary complaint reports (PCR's) concerning the case;

(4) The defendant's arrest and conviction record;

(5) All scientific and laboratory reports;

(6) All corporeal and photographic lineup sheets.

(B) The trial court may also order that the prosecution permit defense counsel to view the following:

(1) All photographs, diagrams, or other visual evidence pertaining to the case that are in police custody;

(2) All physical or tangible evidence pertaining to the case that are in police custody.

(C) Additionally, the court may order that the prosecution permit defense counsel to view or receive copies of any and all other documents pertaining to the case that are in the possession or control of the police or prosecution. This shall be in effect whenever such documents or items may be material to the defense, regardless of whether they are intended to evidence at trial.

RULE 2.401 PRETRIAL CONFERENCES

(A) The pretrial stage begins after the arraignment on the information. The purpose of the pretrial conference is to review the legal issues, to advise the court of any motions, and to fix time limitations on such motions and filings. Guilty plea possibilities are to be discussed as well as other matters the court may determine to be necessary to expedite the orderly progression of the case. The pretrial stage consists of three phases:

(1) The calendar conference for setting the calendar of events;

(2) Motion and evidentiary hearings; and

(3) Final conference for terminating plea negotiations, certifying readiness for trial, and setting a firm trial date.

(B) Attendance is required. The presence of the defendant, defense counsel, and the prosecutor is required at each conference.

RULE 2.503 CONTINUANCES AND ADJOURNMENTS

Adjournments, postponements, or continuances of any trial or other proceeding shall occur only on a written order of the chief judge or a designee.

RULE 2.506 WITNESSES AND SUBPOENAS

(A) Filing of Witness Lists. The court clerk may assume responsibility for the service of subpoenas on witnesses for either party provided that either party, the prosecution, or defense, files in the clerk's office, no later than 28 days prior to the scheduled trial date, a complete list of the respective witnesses for whom subpoenas are sought, together with their addresses.

(B) Subpoenas, Preparation, and Service. When witness lists are filed in accordance with subrule (A), the court clerk shall direct the timely and proper preparation of subpoenas for each of the witnesses listed and shall be responsible for seeing that the proper officers of the Detroit Police Department receive the subpoenas timely with directions that they be promptly served and that a return of service for each subpoena is filed with the court before the trial date or the date of such other proceeding for which the attendance of the witness is required.

(C) Whenever the procedure for service of subpoenas which is outlined in this rule is not followed, and due diligence is not shown with respect to the service of subpoenas on any witness, no adjournment, postponement, or continuance will be granted because of the failure of the witness to appear.

RULE 2.511   JURORS; JURY SERVICE

(A) Supervision of Jurors. The chief judge shall supervise persons summoned for jury duty in Recorder's Court and shall exercise the other responsibilities required by law or court rules pertaining to jury service. The trial judge, however, shall supervise jurors summoned before him or her for voir dire and the entire jury selection process, and shall supervise those jurors selected to sit on a case until they are discharged by the trial judge.

(B) Term of Juror Services. Persons summoned for jury duty shall serve one day, or the duration of any trial for which they are jurors.

(C) Communication Between Jurors, Attorneys, and Court Personnel. Deputy clerks, prosecuting or defense attorneys, police officers, or other officials or employees on duty in the Recorder's Court building who must perform any duty, directly or indirectly, with or for any jurors or panel of jurors, shall not converse with them at any time or place during their period of service. Only necessary social civility or the transaction of necessary court business are excepted from this rule.

RULE 6.101   PRETRIAL PROCEEDINGS; ARRAIGNMENT ON THE INFORMATION

(A) Immediately after a defendant is bound over for trial, the defendant, the defense counsel, and the prosecuting attorney shall be notified of the date and time of arraignment on the information.

(B) When a defendant is confined in jail, he or she shall be arraigned on the information before the chief judge or a designee on the seventh calendar day after the magistrate signs the return; when a defendant is free on bail or recognizance, he or she shall be arraigned on the fourteenth calendar day after the magistrate signs the return. Court holidays shall not be counted in computing time.

(C) At the arraignment on the information, the chief judge, or a designee, may accept a plea of guilty and may consider an application for youthful trainee or diversionary status.

THIRD CIRCUIT AND RECORDER'S COURT JOINT LOCAL COURT RULE 6.102. PROCEEDINGS ON THE CONSOLIDATED CRIMINAL DOCKET [VACATED]

[Vacated effective October 10, 1995.]

LOCAL RULES OF THE 2A JUDICIAL DISTRICT

[LENAWEE COUNTY]

Effective November 2, 1999

Table of Rules

RULE 4.201 SUMMARY PROCEEDINGS TO RECOVER POSSESSION OF PREMISES

(C) Summons.

(1) The summons must comply with MCR 2.102, and shall command the defendant to appear in accord with MCL 600.5735(4); MSA 27A.5735(4), as follows:

(a) within 10 days after service of the summons upon the defendant, in proceedings under MCL 600.5726; MSA 27A.5726;

(b) within 5 days after service of to summons upon the defendant in all other proceedings.

[Adopted effective November 2, 1999.]

1999 Staff Comment

Local Rule 4.201(C) of the 2A District Court was adopted November 2, 1999, at the request of that court, to be effective immediately.

LOCAL RULES OF THE
3–b JUDICIAL DISTRICT

[ST. JOSEPH COUNTY]

Effective July 16, 1997

Table of Rules

Rule
2.402   Facsimile Transmission of Documents.

RULE 2.402   FACSIMILE TRANSMISSION OF DOCUMENTS

(1) The court permits the filing of documents by use of facsimile (FAX) equipment. Each document shall be on 8½ by 11–inch paper. A document for which a filing fee is required will not be filed until the fee is received by the clerk.

(2) Filing fees, service fees and FAX service fees shall be paid to the court within three (3) business days of the transmission. The original documents should be kept by the sender, unless otherwise ordered.

(3) The service fee for receipt of documents is $1.00 per page (including the cover page). The service fee for the sending of documents by the court is $2.00 per page.

(4) No document in excess of 10 pages will be accepted.

(5) Stipulations for adjournment filed by FAX will not be considered unless (a) they comply with MCR 2.503, and (b) they are received at least two (2) business days before the scheduled court appearance.

(6) Documents must be accompanied by a notice of transmittal, stating the name of the contact person, phone number, FAX number, the number of pages being sent, and the case number. The case number is not required if a new file will be assigned by the clerk.

(7) Documents will be received between 9:00 A.M. and 4:30 P.M. on business days.

(8) Appropriate notice of this rule has been provided by the court through posting in court facilities and mailing to all attorneys who regularly practice in St. Joseph County.

(9) For purposes of MCR 2.114, a signature includes a signature transmitted by FAX and the documents received will become a part of the court file.

(10) Facsimile communication equipment and voice communication equipment may be used as provided for in 1990 PA 41, 43, 44 and 45.

[Adopted effective July 16, 1997.]

LOCAL RULES OF THE TWELFTH JUDICIAL DISTRICT

[JACKSON COUNTY]

Effective July 6, 1995

Table of Rules

RULE 2.402   FACSIMILE TRANSMISSION OF DOCUMENTS

The following regulations have been established to govern the use of facsimile (fax) equipment for the filing of documents with the Twelfth District Court:

1. The Court will permit the filing of pleadings and court documents by the use of facsimile (FAX) communications equipment. All filings shall be on 8½″ × 11″ standard paper.

2. Any document for which a filing fee is required will not be accepted through the use of facsimile equipment.

3. No fee will be charged by the Court for receiving a facsimile transmission.

4. Documents will be received by the Court between the hours of 8:00 a.m. and 4:45 p.m. Documents received after 4:45 p.m. will be considered filed on the next following business day.

5. The maximum number of pages which may be sent to the Court at one time is limited to ten (10) pages.

6. A cover sheet must accompany every transmission of documents. The cover sheet is to include the following information: case name, case number, document title, name and telephone number of sender.

7. **Signature.** For purposes of MCR 2.114, a signature includes a signature transmitted by facsimile communication equipment.

[Adopted effective July 6, 1995.]

RULE 4.201 SUMMARY PROCEEDINGS TO RECOVER POSSESSION OF PREMISES

(C) Summons.

(1) The summons must comply with MCR 2.102, and shall command the defendant to appear in accord with MCL 600.5735(4), as follows:

(a) within 10 days after service of the summons upon the defendant, in proceedings under MCL 600.5726,

(b) within 5 days after service of the summons upon the defendant in all other proceedings.

[Adopted effective May 1, 2002.]

2002 Staff Comment

Local Rule 4.201(C) of the 12th District Court was adopted January 15, 2002, at the request of that court, to be effective May 1, 2002.

The staff comment is published only for the benefit of the bench and bar and is not an authoritative construction by the Court.

LOCAL RULES OF THE EIGHTEENTH JUDICIAL DISTRICT

[CITY OF WESTLAND]

Effective December 2, 1992

Table of Rules

RULE 2.402 FACSIMILE TRANSMISSION OF DOCUMENTS

1. This Court will permit the filing of pleadings and court documents by the use of facsimile (FAX) communications equipment. All filings shall be on 8½″ × 11″ standard paper.

2. Any document for which a filing fee is required will not be accepted through the use of facsimile equipment.

3. No fee will be charged by the Court for receiving a facsimile transmission.

4. Documents will be received by the Court between the hours of 8:45 a.m. and 4:00 p.m. Documents received after 4:00 p.m. will be considered filed on the next following business day.

5. The maximum number of pages which may be sent to the Court at one time is limited to ten (10).

6. A cover sheet must accompany every transmission which includes the following information: case name, case number, document title, name and telephone number of sender.

7. Signature. For purposes of MCR 2.114, a signature includes a signature transmitted by facsimile communication equipment.

[Adopted effective July 6, 1995.]

RULE 4.201 SUMMARY PROCEEDINGS TO RECOVER POSSESSION OF PREMISES

(C) Summons.

(1) The summons must comply with MCR 2.102, and shall command the defendant to appear in accord with MCL 600.5735(4); MSA 27A.5735(4), as follows:

(a) within 10 days after service of the summons upon the defendant, in proceedings under MCL 600.5726; MSA 27A.5726;

(b) within 5 days after service of the summons upon the defendant in all other proceedings.

[Adopted effective December 2, 1992.]

1992 Staff Comment

Local Rule 4.201(C)(1) of the 18th District Court was adopted in 1992 at the request of that court.

LOCAL RULES OF THE 27–2 JUDICIAL DISTRICT

[CITY OF RIVERVIEW]

Effective May 6, 1997

Table of Rules

RULE 4.201 SUMMARY PROCEEDINGS TO RECOVER POSSESSION OF PREMISES

(C) Summons.

(1) The summons must comply with MCR 2.102, and shall command the defendant to appear in accord with MCL 600.5735(4); MSA 27A.5735(4), as follows:

(a) within 10 days after service of the summons upon the defendant, in proceedings under MCL 600.5726; MSA 27A.5726;

(b) within 5 days after service of the summons upon the defendant in all other proceedings.

[Adopted effective May 6, 1997.]

1997 Staff Comment

Local Rule 4.201(C)(1) of the 27–2 District Court was adopted in May 1997 at the request of that court.

LOCAL RULES OF THE THIRTY–SIXTH
JUDICIAL DISTRICT

[CITY OF DETROIT]

Effective March 1, 1985

Table of Rules

RULE 2.113   FORM OF PLEADING AND OTHER PAPERS

(E) Praecipe [Rescinded].

[Amended effective March 25, 1991.]

RULE 2.119   MOTION PRACTICE FOR MOTIONS IN GENERAL CIVIL CASES

(A) Application. The provisions of this rule apply to motions filed in general civil cases in the 36th District Court. This rule does not apply to motions filed in small claims, real estate, traffic, or criminal cases. The judge's copy of motions and responses shall be filed with the clerk at the same time as the originals.

(B) Motion Praecipe Forms. A motion praecipe form provided by the clerk of the court must be attached to the judge's copy of all motions.

(C) No Oral Argument; Decision/Review Date; Notice. There is no oral argument on motions unless a request is made and is granted by the assigned judge. The moving party shall choose a decision/review date that shall be a Tuesday and shall constitute "the time set for hearing" under MCR 2.119(C) and MCR 2.116(B)(2) for purposes of providing adequate notice to the opposing party. The moving party must provide notice of the decision/review date to the opposing party or that party's attorney. The notice must advise that there will be no oral argument unless the assigned judge grants a request.

(D) Certification of Attempt to Obtain Concurrence. The attorney for the moving party or the moving party must certify on the praecipe form that the opposing party or that party's attorney has been contacted and asked to concur in the relief sought, and

that concurrence has been denied or otherwise not obtained.

(E) Responses; Notation of Decision/Review Date. A response to a motion must be filed no later than 3 days before the decision/review date. That date must appear on the upper right corner of the first page of any pleading, brief, or other document relating to a pending motion.

[Adopted effective January 1, 2003.]

Staff Comment to 2002 Adoption

Local Rule 2.119 of the 36th District Court was adopted September 11, 2002, at the request of that court, to be effective January 1, 2003.

The staff comment is published only for the benefit of the bench and bar and is not an authoritative construction by the Court.

RULE 2.603   DEFAULT AND DEFAULT JUDGMENTS

The provisions of MCR 2.603 apply in the Thirty-Sixth Judicial District except when in conflict with the following:

(1) At any time within 14 days after the entry of a default, the plaintiff may prove his or her claim in an amount not exceeding that set forth in the statement of claim served on the defendant. The time for taking a default judgment may be extended 30 days, but only if an application for this extension is made within the 14-day period for taking a default judgment.

(2) If the plaintiff fails to seek a default judgment within the time provided by this rule, the action will be dismissed without prejudice. However, if another defendant in the action has filed a responsive pleading or motion, judgment against the defendant in default may be entered at the time of the trial or other disposition of the action as to the defendant who has responded.

RULE 3.101 GARNISHMENT AFTER JUDGMENT

(F) Service of Writ. The writ of garnishment and the disclosure form, and a copy of the writ for each principal defendant, must be served on the garnishee defendant in the manner provided for the service of a summons and complaint in MCR 2.105 within 14 days after the writ was issued.

RULE 4.201 SUMMARY PROCEEDINGS TO RECOVER POSSESSION OF PREMISES

(G) Claims and Counterclaims.

(1) *Joinder*.

(c) In the Thirty-Sixth District Court a money claim or counterclaim must be tried separately from a claim for possession unless joinder is allowed by leave of the court pursuant to MCR 4.201(G)(1)(e).

RULE 4.202 SUMMARY PROCEEDINGS; LAND CONTRACT FORFEITURE

(I) Joinder; Removal.

(2) In the Thirty-Sixth District Court a money claim or counterclaim must be tried separately from a claim for possession unless joinder is allowed by leave of the court pursuant to MCR 4.202(I)(3).

LOCAL RULES OF THE FORTY–EIGHTH JUDICIAL DISTRICT

[PARTS OF OAKLAND COUNTY]

Effective September 21, 1994

Table of Rules

RULE 2.402   FACSIMILE TRANSMISSION OF DOCUMENTS

The court will permit the filing of pleadings, motions, affidavits, opinions, and orders by the use of FAX equipment, on the conditions set forth herein.

(1) No pleading requiring a filing fee will be accepted.

(2) No document will be accepted unless it is on 8½ by 11 inch paper. MCR 1.109.

(3) No document will be accepted which is in excess of 10 pages.

(4) Stipulations for adjournment filed by fax will not be considered unless (a) they comply with MCR 2.503, and (b) they are received at least 2 business days before the scheduled court appearance.

(5) Documents must be accompanied by a notice of transmittal stating the name of a contact person, phone number, fax number, the number of pages being sent, and the case number.

(6) The faxed documents and transmittal cover sheets will become part of the court file.

[Adopted effective September 21, 1994.]

LOCAL RULES OF THE 54–A JUDICIAL DISTRICT

[CITY OF LANSING]

Effective January 3, 1996

Table of Rules

RULE 2.402. USE OF FACSIMILE COMMUNICATION EQUIPMENT

(1) Parties may file pleadings with the 54–A District Court by facsimile machines, with the exceptions of original complaints and any document for which a filing fee is required.

(2) There will be a limit of 10 pages which may be sent at one time for any document.

(3) Each transmission shall include the case name, docket number, document title, name and telephone number of the sender.

(4) The equipment may be used at any hour. Any transmission after 4:45 P.M. will be considered filed the next business day.

(5) The parties may establish proof of service on attorney or litigants by providing a copy of the journal which is prepared by the facsimile machine of the server or by preparing a proof of service.

(6) For purposes of MCR 2.114, a signature includes a signature transmitted by facsimile communication equipment.

[Adopted effective January 3, 1996; amended effective April 3, 1998.]

LOCAL RULES OF THE 54–B JUDICIAL DISTRICT

[CITY OF EAST LANSING]

Effective July 6, 1995

Table of Rules

Rule
2.402 Facsimile Transmission of Documents.

RULE 2.402 FACSIMILE TRANSMISSION OF DOCUMENTS

1. Parties may file pleadings with the 54–B District Court by facsimile machines.

2. There will be a limit of 10 pages which may be sent at one time for any document.

3. The equipment may be used at any hour. Any transmission after 4:45 p.m. will be considered filed the next day.

4. The original document with any required fee shall be mailed contemporaneously with the fax transmittal.

5. Filing with the court will be considered as being made when the document is received by the court's fax machine if no fee is required. If a filing fee is required, the filing shall not be effective until the filing fee is received.

6. In addition to any required statutory filing fee, a fax service fee of $1.00 per page will be charged by the court for receiving facsimile filings.

7. The parties may establish proof of service on attorneys or litigants by providing a copy of the journal which is prepared by the facsimile machine or by preparing a proof of service.

[Adopted effective July 6, 1995.]

LOCAL RULES OF THE FIFTY–SIXTH JUDICIAL DISTRICT, FIRST DIVISION

[BARRY COUNTY]

Effective March 3, 1995

Table of Rules

RULE 2.402 FACSIMILE TRANSMISSION OF DOCUMENTS

1. This Court will permit the filing of pleadings and court documents by the use of facsimile (FAX) Communications equipment. All filings shall be on 8½ ″ × 11″ standard paper.

2. Any document for which a filing fee is required will not be accepted through the use of facsimile equipment.

3. No fee will be charged by the Court for receiving a facsimile transmission.

4. Documents will be received by the Court between the hours of 8:00 A.M. and 4:45 P.M. Documents received after 4:45 P.M. will be considered filed on the next following business day.

5. The maximum number of pages which may be sent to the Court at one time is limited to twenty pages.

6. A cover sheet must accompany every transmission which includes the following information: case name, case number, document title, name and telephone number of sender.

7. Signature. For purposes of MCR 2.114, a signature includes a signature transmitted by facsimile communication equipment.

[Adopted effective March 3, 1995.]

LOCAL RULES OF THE SIXTY–FIRST JUDICIAL DISTRICT

[CITY OF GRAND RAPIDS]

Effective September 21, 1994

Table of Rules

RULE 2.402 USE OF FACSIMILE AND COMMUNICATION EQUIPMENT FOR THE FILING AND TRANSMISSION OF COURT DOCUMENTS

(1) This court will permit the filing of pleadings and court documents by the use of facsimile (FAX) communications equipment. All filings shall be on 8½ by 11 inch standard paper.

(2) Any document for which a filing fee is required will not be accepted through the use of facsimile equipment.

(3) No fee will be charged by the court for receiving a facsimile transmission.

(4) Documents will be received by the court between the hours of 8:00 A.M. *and* 4:45 P.M. Documents received after 4:45 P.M. will be considered filed on the next following business day.

(5) The maximum number of pages which may be sent to the court at one time is limited to twenty pages.

(6) A cover sheet must accompany every transmission which includes the following information: case name, case number, document title, name and telephone number of sender.

(7) **Signature.** For purposes of MCR 2.114, a signature includes a signature transmitted by facsimile communication equipment.

[Adopted effective September 21, 1994.]

LOCAL RULES OF THE 62–A JUDICIAL DISTRICT

[CITY OF WYOMING]

Effective March 3, 1995

Table of Rules

RULE 2.402 FACSIMILE TRANSMISSION OF DOCUMENTS

1. This court will permit the filing of pleadings and court documents by use of facsimile (fax) communication equipment. All filings shall be on 8½ × 11 inch standard paper.

2. Any document for which a filing fee is required will not be accepted through the use of facsimile equipment.

3. No fee will be charged by the court for receiving a facsimile transmission.

4. Documents will be received by the court 24 hours a day. Documents received after 5:00 p.m. will be considered filed on the following business day.

5. The maximum number of pages which may be sent to the court at one time is limited to 20 pages.

6. A cover sheet must accompany every transmission which includes the following information:

    Case name
    Case number
    Document title
    Name and telephone number of sender.

7. Signature. For purposes of MCR 2.114, a signature includes a signature transmitted by facsimile communication equipment.

8. Warrants. Facsimile communication equipment and voice communication equipment may be used as provided by 1990 PA 41, 43, 44 and 45.

[Adopted effective March 3, 1995.]

LOCAL RULES OF THE SIXTY–FIFTH JUDICIAL DISTRICT, FIRST DIVISION

[GRATIOT COUNTY]

Effective July 6, 1995

Table of Rules

RULE 2.402   FACSIMILE TRANSMISSION OF DOCUMENTS

(1) Parties may file pleadings with the 65–1 District Court by facsimile machines.

(2) There will be no fee required for the use of the equipment.

(3) Any documents requiring filing fees will not be accepted by facsimile.

(4) There will be a limit of (10) ten pages which may be sent at one time for any document and only on 8½″ × 11″ standard paper.

(5) Documents will be received by the court between the hours of 9:00 a.m. and 5:00 p.m. Documents received after 5:00 p.m. will be considered filed on the next following business day. Original documents shall be retained by the sender, but should be made available upon request of the court.

(6) A cover sheet must accompany every transmission which includes the following information: Case name, case number, document title, name and telephone number of sender.

(7) Where service is made by facsimile machine, proof of service shall be made by affidavit of the person making the service, or by certificate of an attorney. Attached to such affidavit or such certificates shall be the printed confirmation of receipt of the message generated by the transmitting machine.

(8) For purposes of MCR 2.114, a signature includes a signature transmitted by facsimile communication equipment.

[Adopted effective July 6, 1995.]

LOCAL RULES OF THE SIXTY–EIGHTH JUDICIAL DISTRICT

[CITY OF FLINT]

Effective March 1, 1985

Table of Rules

RULE 2.503 ADJOURNMENT POLICY

Requests must be made by motion or stipulation in writing or orally in open court based on good cause, except as specifically exempted below:

(1) Felony pretrial can be adjourned by the prosecutor who shall note the adjournment and new date on the Register of Actions.

(2) The clerk's office can grant adjournment of misdemeanor arraignments for a period not exceeding 1 week from the originally scheduled date. At the option of the defendant, the new date can be set for any day within the period at 8:30 a.m. or 3 p.m.

(3) Alias dates (i.e., no service by date originally scheduled) can be given by the clerk's office, however, this cannot be done on the phone. All copies of the summons must be returned to the clerk's office so the new date and time can be noted on the stipulation. The person making the change must put his or her initials on the strip, and, at the bottom, put the date the change was made and the initials again.

(4) The scheduling office may adjourn initial misdemeanor pretrials as necessary, except that it must occur prior to the final pretrial. Final misdemeanor pretrials may not be adjourned except pursuant to MCR 2.503.

(5) The scheduling office may adjourn civil pretrials no more than two times upon receipt of written stipulation and order.

(6) The scheduling office may adjourn nonjury trials no more than one time upon receipt of written stipulation and order.

(7) Jury trials may not be adjourned except pursuant to MCR 2.503.

LOCAL RULES OF THE SEVENTY–FOURTH JUDICIAL DISTRICT

[BAY COUNTY]

Effective January 8, 1998

Table of Rules

RULE 2.402. FACSIMILE TRANSMISSION OF DOCUMENTS

(1) The court will permit the filing of pleadings and court documents by the use of facsimile (FAX) communication equipment. All filings shall be on 8-½ by 11-inch standard paper.

(2) Any document for which a filing fee is required *will not* be accepted through the use of facsimile equipment.

(3) *No fee* will be charged by the court for receiving a facsimile.

(4) Documents will be received by the court between the hours of 8:30 A.M. and 4:30 P.M. Documents received after 4:30 P.M. will be considered filed on the following working day.

(5) A maximum of twenty pages per transmission will be received.

(6) A cover sheet must accompany every transmission, which includes: case name, case number, document title, name, and telephone number of the sender.

(7) *Signature*: For the purpose of MCR 2.114, a signature includes a signature transmitted by facsimile communication equipment.

(8) This Court will not respond to requests for criminal background check received via facsimile transmission.

[Adopted effective January 8, 1998.]

LOCAL RULES OF THE EIGHTY–FIRST JUDICIAL DISTRICT

[IOSCO AND ARENAC COUNTIES]

Effective March 25, 1993

Table of Rules

RULE 4.201 SUMMARY PROCEEDINGS TO RECOVER POSSESSION OF PREMISES

(C) Summons.

(1) The summons must comply with MCR 2.102, and shall command the defendant to appear in accord with MCL 600.5735(4); MSA 27A.5735(4), as follows:

(a) within 10 days after service of the summons upon the defendant, in proceedings under MCL 600.5726; MSA 27A.5726;

(b) within 5 days after service of the summons upon the defendant in all other proceedings.

[Adopted effective March 25, 1993.]

Staff Comment

Local Rule 4.201(C)(1) of the 81st District Court was adopted in 1993 at the request of that court.

LOCAL RULES OF THE EIGHTY–SECOND JUDICIAL DISTRICT

[ALCONA, OSCODA AND OGEMAW COUNTIES]

Effective February 1, 1989

Table of Rules

RULE 2.402 FACSIMILE TRANSMISSION OF DOCUMENTS

1. This Court will permit the filing of pleadings and court documents by the use of facsimile (FAX) communications equipment. All filings shall be on 8½″ × 11″ standard paper.

2. Any documents for which a filing fee is required will not be accepted through the use of facsimile equipment.

3. No fee will be charged by the Court for receiving a facsimile transmission.

4. Documents will be received by the Court between the hours of 9:00 A.M. and 4:00 P.M. Documents received after 4:00 P.M. will be considered filed on the next business day.

5. The maximum number of pages which may be sent to the Court at one time is limited to 15 pages.

6. A cover sheet must accompany every transmission which includes the following information: case name, case number, document title, name and telephone number of sender.

7. **Signature.** For purposes of MCR 2.114, a signature includes a signature transmitted by facsimile communication equipment.

[Adopted effective March 3, 1995.]

RULE 4.201 SUMMARY PROCEEDINGS TO RECOVER POSSESSION OF PREMISES

(C) Summons.

(1) The summons must comply with MCR 2.102, and shall command the defendant to appear in accord with MCL 600.5735(4); MSA 27A.5735(4), as follows:

(a) within 10 days after service of the summons upon the defendant, in proceedings under MCL 600.5726; MSA 27A.5726;

(b) within 5 days after service of the summons upon the defendant in all other proceedings.

[Adopted effective February 1, 1989.]

LOCAL RULES OF THE EIGHTY–NINTH JUDICIAL DISTRICT

[CHEBOYGAN AND PRESQUE ISLE COUNTIES]

Effective March 3, 1995

Table of Rules

RULE 2.402 FACSIMILE TRANSMISSION OF DOCUMENTS

1. This court will permit the filing of pleadings and court documents by the use of facsimile (FAX) communications equipment. All filings shall be on 8½″ × 11″ standard paper.

2. Documents which require a filing fee will not be accepted through the use of the facsimile equipment in Presque Isle County.

In Cheboygan County, documents which require a filing fee will not be accepted unless the filing fee is paid in full. Payment may be made to the Court through use of a credit card, MasterCard or Visa.

3. Documents will be received by the Cheboygan County court office between the hours of 8:30 a.m. and 4:00 p.m. Documents received after 4:00 p.m. will be considered filed on the next following business day.

Documents will be received by the Presque Isle County court office between the hours of 8:30 a.m. and 4:30 p.m. Documents received after 4:30 p.m. will be considered filed on the next following business day.

Documents for filing in Presque Isle County will not be accepted at the Cheboygan County office and documents for filing in Cheboygan County will not be accepted at the Presque Isle County office.

4. No fee will be charged by the court for receiving a facsimile transmission.

5. The maximum number of pages which may be sent to the court at one time is limited to twenty pages.

6. A cover sheet must accompany every transmission which includes the following information: case number, case name, document title, name and telephone number of sender.

7. **Signature.** For purposes of MCR 2.114, a signature includes a signature transmitted by facsimile communication equipment.

[Adopted effective March 3, 1995.]

LOCAL RULES OF THE 95–B JUDICIAL DISTRICT

[DICKINSON AND IRON COUNTIES]

Effective May 1, 1992

Table of Rules

RULE 4.201 SUMMARY PROCEEDINGS TO RECOVER POSSESSION OF PREMISES

(C) Summons.

(1) The summons must comply with MCR 2.102, and shall command the defendant to appear in accord with MCL 600.5735(4); MSA 27A.5735(4), as follows:

(a) within 10 days after service of the summons upon the defendant, in proceedings under MCL 600.5726; MSA 27A.5726;

(b) within 5 days after service of the summons upon the defendant in all other proceedings.

[Adopted effective May 1, 1992.]

1992 Staff Comment

Local Rule 4.201(C)(1) of the 95–B Judicial District Court was adopted in 1992 at the request of that court.

LOCAL RULES OF THE ALLEGAN PROBATE COURT

Effective July 6, 1995

Table of Rules

RULE 2.402   FACSIMILE TRANSMISSION OF DOCUMENTS

1. Scope. The Allegan County Probate Court will permit the filing of certain documents by the use of facsimile (FAX) communication equipment.

A. Documents permitted for filing by FAX are pleadings, motions, affidavits, opinions, orders and other documents to be filed in the Probate or Juvenile Courts.

B. All FAX documents shall be limited to those not requiring a filing fee, or required filing fee is prepaid.

C. All persons transmitting documents to the Court shall use a FAX transmittal certificate which shall state the number and type of documents being transmitted, number of pages of each document, the title of the matter, and names, addresses and telephone number of sender and any other pertinent information.

D. Filing with the Court will be considered as being made when the document is received by the Court's FAX machine. It is the responsibility of the transmitting party to serve documents on all interested parties and file with the Court an affidavit of service.

E. In the event the Probate Court should be authorized to accept filing fees by way of Visa or MasterCard charges, then such faxed materials should include the charge card number, name, expiration date and signature of person authorized to charge upon such card.

2. Method.

A. The Allegan County Probate Court shall consider all documents received by FAX prior to 4:45 p.m. on a business day as filed that day. For documents received after 4:45 p.m. or received when the Court is closed, the Court shall consider them filed on the first business day thereafter.

B. All FAX documents received shall be file-stamped by a Court employee if the documents meet filing requirements and copied by a Court employee, if necessary, for inclusion in the Court's file.

C. All documents transmitted shall be 8½″ by 11″, and a maximum length of fifteen (15) pages per transmission, excluding the transmittal certificate. Transmissions during business hours beyond 15 pages may be made with advanced permission of Court register or at any time on weekdays and outside of normal business hours.

3. Fees. A fee, in addition to any statutory fee otherwise applicable, shall be assessed at the amount of $.50 per page taking into consideration the cost of equipment, paper, supplies, and telephone line charges for receiving a FAX transmission. If a responding FAX is necessary, a charge shall be assessed in the amount of $2.00 per first page and $1.00 per additional page for sending the FAX to the transmitting party. Documents will not be filed unless the full amount of any filing fee has been paid. The FAX service fee shall be billed directly to the transmitting party, payable within 10 days.

4. Signatures. For purposes of MCR 2.114, a signature includes a signature transmitted by facsimile communication equipment.

[Adopted effective July 6, 1995.]

LOCAL RULES OF THE BARRY PROBATE COURT

Effective July 6, 1995

Table of Rules

RULE 2.402 FACSIMILE TRANSMISSION OF DOCUMENTS

1. The document or paper filed by use of FAX does not exceed the standard paper size of $8\frac{1}{2}'' \times 11''$.

2. Any document for which a filing fee is required will not be accepted through the use of FAX.

3. No fee will be charged by the Court for receiving a FAX transmission. If a responding FAX is necessary, a charge shall be assessed in the amount of $2.00 per first page and $1.00 for each additional page for sending the FAX to the requesting party. The FAX service fee shall be billed directly to the requesting party, payable within 10 days.

4. Documents will be received by the Court between the hours of 8:00 a.m. and 4:30 p.m. Documents received after 4:30 p.m. will be considered filed on the next following business day except in exigent circumstances. The time and date stamp of the FAX equipment shall be used to verify the date and time of the filing for compliance of this provision.

5. The maximum number of pages which may be sent to the Court at one time is limited to twenty-eight (28) pages including the cover sheet.

6. A cover sheet must accompany every transmission which includes the following information: case name, case number, document title, name and telephone number of sender.

7. Upon the receipt of the FAXed document or paper, the Court shall ensure that the FAXed document is on paper that is not subject to more rapid deterioration than ordinary typewritten material on ordinary paper. This may require the Court to transfer the FAXed document or paper by use of photocopy equipment to standard paper.

8. All FAX documents received shall be file-stamped by a Court employee if the documents meet the filing requirements.

9. **Signature.** For purposes of MCR 2.114 and MCR 5.114, a signature includes a signature transmitted by facsimile communication equipment, and such signature shall be recognized as an original signature.
[Adopted effective July 6, 1995.]

LOCAL RULES OF THE CHARLEVOIX AND EMMET PROBATE COURT

Table of Rules

RULE 8.123   CONCURRENT JURISDICTION CASES [RESCINDED]

[Rescinded effective March 22, 2000.]

Staff Comment to 2000 Rescission

Joint Local Court Rule 8.123 was rescinded March 22, 2000, in light of the establishment of the family division of circuit court.

LOCAL RULES OF THE EATON PROBATE COURT

Effective September 21, 1994

Table of Rules

RULE 2.402   USE OF COMMUNICATION EQUIPMENT

(A) Form of Documents Generally.

(1) Documents transmitted by facsimile equipment, which require a statutory filing fee shall not be accepted for filing by the court.

(2) All documents must be typed, excluding any required signatures, on 8½ inch by 11 inch plain white paper.

(3) The total number pages of any faxed document or single faxed transmission shall not exceed twenty (20) pages.

(4) Documents shall be received for filing by the court between the hours of 8:00 A.M. E.S.T. and 4:30 P.M. E.S.T., Monday through Friday, only. Documents received after 4:30 P.M. will be considered filed on the next following business day.

(5) A cover sheet must accompany every transmission which includes the following information: the name of the person/department for whom the fax is intended, case name, case number, name, address and telephone number of the sender.

(6) Signature—For purposes of MCR 2.114, a signature includes a signature transmitted by facsimile communication equipment.

[Adopted effective September 21, 1994.]

LOCAL RULES OF THE GENESEE PROBATE COURT

Effective March 1, 1999

Table of Rules

RULE 2.119   MOTION PRACTICE

(A) Motion Certification by Attorney. The following certificate signed by the attorney of record or by the party *in propria persona* shall be attached to or incorporated in the motion and notice of hearing filed with the clerk:

I hereby certify that I have made personal contact with _____ [name] on _____, [date] requesting concurrence in the relief sought with this motion and that concurrence has been denied, or that I have made reasonable and diligent attempts to contact counsel requesting concurrence in the relief sought with this motion.

(B) Proposed Orders. A proposed order must be attached to and served with the motion.

(C) Application. This rule applies to all motions filed in the circuit court and to motions filed in civil actions in the probate court.

[Adopted effective March 1, 1999.]

1998 Staff Comment

Local Court Rule 2.119 of the Seventh Judicial Circuit and the Genesee Probate Court was adopted February 2, 1999, effective March 1, 1999, at the request of those courts.

LOCAL RULES OF THE INGHAM PROBATE COURT

Effective March 3, 1995

Table of Rules

RULE 2.402 FACSIMILE TRANSMISSION OF DOCUMENTS

1. This Court will permit the filing of pleadings and court documents by the use of facsimile (FAX) communications equipment. All filings shall be on 8½" × 11" standard paper.

2. Any document for which a filing fee is required will not be accepted through the use of facsimile equipment.

3. No fee will be charged by the Court for receiving a facsimile transmission.

4. Documents received after 4:45 P.M. will be considered filed on the next business day.

5. No more than fifteen pages may be included in each FAX transmission.

6. A cover sheet must accompany every transmission which includes the following information: case name, case number, document title, name and telephone number of sender.

7. Signature. For purposes of MCR 2.114, a signature includes a signature transmitted by facsimile communication equipment.

8. The fax transmitter will be responsible to retain the original document to be available for Court review.

9. Court employees will only file-stamp facsimile documents if they meet filing requirements; nonconforming documents will be returned by ordinary mail.

10. Documents concerning probate matters, including, but not limited to, deceased estates, wills, trusts, guardianships and conservatorships, which are not set for hearing within two business days, should be faxed to our Mason office at (517) 676–7344. Documents concerning adoptions, mental illness, juvenile matters or probate matters scheduled for hearing in Lansing within two business days should be faxed to our Lansing office at (517) 483–6150.

[Adopted effective March 3, 1995.]

LOCAL RULES OF THE KALAMAZOO PROBATE COURT

Effective March 3, 1995

Table of Rules

RULE 2.402 FACSIMILE TRANSMISSION OF DOCUMENTS

The following regulations have been established to govern the use of facsimile equipment for the filing of documents with the Kalamazoo County Probate Court.

1. Scope.

A. Documents permitted for filing by facsimile communication equipment ("FAX") on 8½″ × 11″ paper are: pleadings, motions, affidavits, opinions, orders and other documents.

B. All FAX documents shall be limited to those not requiring a filing fee, or the required filing fee is prepaid.

C. All persons transmitting documents to the court shall use a cover sheet, which includes the case name, case number, name and telephone number of the sender, number of pages transmitted and any special instructions.

D. This local court rule shall apply to all documents filed by FAX relating to mental health proceedings.

2. Method.

A. The Kalamazoo County Probate Court shall consider all documents received by FAX prior to 4:30 p.m. on a business day as filed that day. For documents received after 4:30 p.m. or received when the court is closed, the court shall consider them filed on the first business day thereafter.

B. If the documents meet filing requirements, all FAX documents received shall be file-stamped by a court employee, and copied for inclusion in the court's file.

C. If the FAX document is not legible, the court may request the original document to be filed.

D. It is the responsibility of the transmitting party to serve documents on all interested parties and file with the court an affidavit of service.

3. Fees.

A. There will be no fee required for the use of the FAX equipment.

[Adopted effective March 3, 1995.]

LOCAL RULES OF THE MARQUETTE PROBATE COURT

Table of Rules

RULE 8.123   CONCURRENT JURISDICTION CASES [RESCINDED]

[Rescinded effective March 22, 2000.]

Staff Comment to 2000 Rescission

Joint Local Court Rule 8.123 was rescinded March 22, 2000, in light of the establishment of the family division of circuit court.

LOCAL RULES OF THE MENOMINEE PROBATE COURT

Effective March 3, 1995

Table of Rules

RULE 2.402   FACSIMILE TRANSMISSION OF DOCUMENTS

(A) Pursuant to Administrative Order 1994–2, the filing of 8½″ × 11″ pleadings, motions, affidavits, opinions, orders, or other documents is permitted, subject to this rule.

(B) Except as provided by MCR 2.002, a clerk shall not permit the filing of any document for which a filing fee is required unless the full amount of the filing fee is paid or deposited in advance with the clerk. Documents intended to be filed in any court shall be on paper not subject to more rapid deterioration than ordinary typewritten material on ordinary paper.

(C) The person filing shall:

(1) Pay a fee in the amount of $.25 per page, which fee is in addition to any filing fee imposed.

(2) Be permitted to file no more than 20 pages at one time.

(3) Arrange for the receipt by the Court of said documents during the hours of 8:00 a.m. to 4:00 p.m. central time.

[Adopted effective March 3, 1995.]

LOCAL RULES OF THE OAKLAND PROBATE COURT

Effective May 1, 1992

Table of Rules

RULE 2.402 USE OF COMMUNICATION EQUIPMENT

(A) Scope. The Oakland County Probate Court will permit the filing of documents by the use of the court's facsimile (fax) communication equipment.

(1) Documents permitted for filing by facsimile communication equipment include pleadings, petitions, motions, affidavits, opinions, orders and other documents in the probate or juvenile courts.

(2) Documents which require a filing fee will not be accepted for filing unless the filing fee is received simultaneously.

(B) Method.

(1) All facsimile transmissions must be accompanied by a fax transmittal sheet which includes the following information: name of the person or department for whom the fax is intended, type of document, case name, case number, number of pages in the transmission, and the name, address and telephone number of the sender.

(2) All facsimile documents received by the court's facsimile equipment prior to 4:30 p.m. on a business day shall be considered filed that day. Documents received after 4:30 p.m. or received when the court is closed, shall be considered filed on the first business day thereafter.

(3) All facsimile documents received shall be file-stamped by a court employee if the documents meet filing requirements.

(4) All documents transmitted shall be 8½ by 11 inches and a maximum length of fifteen (15) pages per transmission, excluding the transmittal sheet.

(5) The transmitter of the facsimile documents is responsible for retaining the original document for purposes of court review.

(C) Fees. No fee will be charged by the court for receiving a facsimile transmission.

(D) Signature. For purposes of MCR 2.114, a signature includes a signature transmitted by facsimile communication equipment.

[Adopted effective April 4, 1996.]

RULE 3.205 PRIOR AND SUBSEQUENT ORDERS AND JUDGMENTS AFFECTING MINORS

(A) Venue. This rule applies whenever the prior and subsequent courts are Oakland County courts.

(B) Notice to Prior Court, Friend of the Court, Juvenile/Probate Register or Prosecuting Attorney.

(1) As used in this rule, "appropriate official" means the Friend of the Court, juvenile/probate register or Prosecuting Attorney, depending on the nature of the prior or subsequent action and the court involved.

(2) If a minor is known to be subject to the prior continuing jurisdiction of an Oakland County court, the plaintiff or other initiating party must file written notice of proceedings in the subsequent court with

  (a) the clerk or register of the prior court, and

  (b) the appropriate official of the prior court.

(3) The notice must be filed at least 21 days before the date set for hearing. If the fact of continuing jurisdiction is not then known, notice must be given immediately when it becomes known.

(4) The notice requirement of this subrule is not jurisdictional and does not preclude the subsequent

court from entering interim orders before the expiration of the 21–day period, if required by the best interests of the minor.

(C) Prior Orders.

(1) Each provision of a prior order remains in effect until the provision is superseded, changed, or terminated by a subsequent order.

(2) A subsequent court must give due consideration to prior continuing orders of other courts, and may not enter orders contrary to or inconsistent with such orders, except as provided by law.

(D) Duties of Officials of Prior and Subsequent Courts.

(1) Upon receipt of the notice required by subrule (B), the appropriate official of the prior court

(a) must provide the assigned judge of the subsequent court with the docket sheet;

(b) may appear in person at proceedings in the subsequent court, as the welfare of the minor and the interests of justice require.

(2) The appropriate official of the prior court shall furnish documents upon request of the subsequent court.

(3) Upon request of the prior court, the appropriate official of the subsequent court

(a) must notify the appropriate official of the prior court of all proceedings in the subsequent court, and

(b) must send copies of all orders entered in the subsequent court to the attention of the clerk or register and the appropriate official of the prior court.

(4) If a circuit court awards custody of a minor pursuant to MCL 722.26b; MSA 25.312(6b), the clerk of the circuit court must send a copy of the judgment or order of disposition to the probate court that has prior or continuing jurisdiction of the minor as a result of the guardianship proceedings, regardless whether there is a request.

(5) Upon receipt of an order from the subsequent court, the appropriate official of the prior court must take the steps necessary to implement the order in the prior court.

[Adopted effective November 1, 1995.]

1995 Staff Comment

Local Court Rule 3.205 of the Sixth Judicial Circuit and the Oakland County Probate Court was adopted at the joint request of those courts.

RULE 5.503 ADJOURNMENTS IN THE ESTATES DIVISION

(A) General. This rule governs adjournments in the estates division of the Oakland Probate Court. Adjournment of hearings shall be limited to those situations where the party requesting adjournment demonstrates verifiable good cause. Where the court has issued an order to show cause, adjournments may be only granted by the judge at hearing.

(B) Adjournment Request Procedure in the Estates Division.

(1) All requests must be made in writing or by telephone.

(2) Subject to the limitations set forth in subrules (B)(3), and (D) all requests for adjournment will be acted upon by the deputy probate register with oversight by the manager of estates and mental health, or, in the manager's absence, by the division's staff attorney.

(3) Only the assigned judge has authority to approve:

(a) requests submitted within 24 hours of the scheduled hearing,

(b) requests involving contested matters, or

(c) requests made during a hearing.

(4) The form of the request for adjournment must conform with MCR 2.503(B)(2).

(5) A stipulation and a proposed order for adjournment will be accepted from any party to the stipulation.

(C) Adjournment Requests From Attorneys of Record.

(1) An attorney of record who seeks an adjournment shall contact the court by telephone or in writing. An attorney who contacts the court in writing shall submit a stipulation and a proposed order.

(2) If the request for adjournment is made by telephone, the requesting attorney shall immediately prepare a stipulation and proposed order and forward it to the court.

(3) If the request is made in writing through a stipulation and a proposed order, it will be acted upon in accordance with subrule (B)(2) or (3).

(D) Adjournment Requests From Unrepresented Parties. When a party not represented by an attorney requests an adjournment, either in writing or by telephone, the request shall be received and acted upon by the deputy probate register.

(E) Adjournment to Date Certain. If the court grants an adjournment, it shall simultaneously establish an adjourned hearing date.

(1) Court employees handling the request must coordinate the adjourned date and time with the assigned judge's court calendar.

(2) The adjourned hearing date shall be no more than 28 days after the originally scheduled date.

(3) If the adjournment occurs at a hearing, the court shall announce the adjourned date on the record.

(F) Sanctions for Noncompliance. Failure to file the required stipulation and proposed order by the hearing date may result in court-imposed sanctions, including but not limited to dismissal of the petition, costs, and/or fees. If a petition dismissed under this rule is later refiled, a new petition filing fee must be paid.

(G) Statistical Monitoring. The court staff may record and catalog all requests for adjournment as to party, reason, and result.

[Adopted effective May 1, 1992.]

1992 Staff Comment

Local Rule 5.503 of the Oakland Probate Court was adopted in 1992 at the request of that court.

LOCAL RULES OF THE OSCODA PROBATE COURT

Effective September 21, 1994

Table of Rules

RULE 2.402 FACSIMILE TRANSMISSION OF DOCUMENTS

(1) The court will permit the filing of pleadings and court documents by the use of facsimile (fax) communications equipment. All filings shall be on 8½ by 11 inch standard paper.

(2) Any document for which a filing fee is required will not be accepted through the use of facsimile equipment.

(3) No fee will be charged by the court for receiving a facsimile transmission.

(4) Documents will be received by the court between the hours of 9:00 A.M. and 4:00 P.M. Documents received after 4:00 P.M. will be considered filed on the next business day.

(5) The maximum number of pages which may be sent to the court at one time is limited to 15 pages.

(6) A cover sheet must accompany every transmission which includes the following information: case name, case number, document title, name and telephone number of sender.

(7) **Signature.** For purposes of MCR 2.114, a signature includes a signature transmitted by facsimile communications equipment.

[Adopted effective September 21, 1994.]

LOCAL RULES OF THE ST. JOSEPH PROBATE COURT

Effective September 21, 1994

Table of Rules

RULE 2.402 USE OF FACSIMILE COMMUNICATION EQUIPMENT FOR PURPOSES OF FILING COURT DOCUMENTS

(1) Scope. The St. Joseph County Probate Court will permit the filing of certain documents by the use of facsimile (fax) communication equipment.

(A) Documents permitted for filing by fax are pleadings, motions, affidavits, opinions, orders and other documents to be filed in the probate or juvenile courts.

(B) All fax documents shall be limited to those not requiring a filing fee, or required filing fee is prepaid.

(C) All persons transmitting documents to the court shall use a fax transmittal certificate which shall state the number and type of documents being transmitted, number of pages of each document, as well as the title of the matter and any other pertinent information.

(D) Filing with the court will be considered as being made when the document is received by the court's fax machine. It is the responsibility of the transmitting party to serve documents on all interested parties and file with the court an affidavit of service.

(2) Method.

(A) The St. Joseph County Probate Court shall consider all documents received by fax prior to 4:30 P.M. on a business day as filed that day. For documents received after 4:30 P.M. or received when the court is closed, the court shall consider them filed on the first business day thereafter.

(B) All fax documents received shall be file-stamped by a court employee if the documents meeting filing requirements and copied by a court employee for inclusion in the court's file.

(C) All documents transmitted shall be 8½ by 11 inches, and a maximum length of fifteen (15) pages per transmission, excluding the transmittal certificate.

(3) Fees.

(A) A fee, in addition to any statutory fee otherwise applicable, shall be assessed at the amount of 50 cents per page, taking into consideration the cost of equipment, paper, supplies and telephone line charges for receiving a fax transmission. If a responding fax is necessary, a charge shall be assessed in the amount of $2 per first page and $1 per additional page for sending the fax to the transmitting party. Documents will not be filed unless the full amount of any filing fee has been paid. The fax service fee shall be billed directly to the transmitting party, payable within 10 days.

(4) Signatures.

(A) For purposes of MCR 2.114 a signature includes a signature transmitted by facsimile communication equipment.

[Adopted effective September 21, 1994.]

THE COURT OF CLAIMS ACT

Table of Sections

Publisher's Note

Includes text updates through the 2002 Regular Session.

§ 600.6401 SHORT TITLE

This chapter shall be known and may be cited as "the court of claims act".

§ 600.6404 CREATION OF COURT; JUDGES

The court of claims is created as a function of the circuit court for the thirtieth judicial circuit. A circuit judge of the thirtieth judicial circuit and any judge assigned into the thirtieth judicial circuit by the state court administrator may exercise the jurisdiction of the court of claims as provided by law.

(2)* In case of the disability or absence from the place of holding court of a circuit judge before whom while sitting as the judge of the court of claims a case has been tried or motion heard, another circuit judge designated to sit as the judge of the court of claims to** may continue, hear, determine, and sign all matters that his or her predecessor could have continued, heard, determined, and signed.

(3) In case a circuit judge designated to sit as the judge of the court of claims dies before signing a judgment and after filing a finding of fact or rendering an opinion upon proof submitted and argument of counsel disposing of all or part of the issues in the case involved, a successor as judge of the court of claims may proceed with that action in a manner consistent with the finding or opinion and the judge is given the same powers as if the finding of fact had been made or the opinion had been rendered by the successor judge.

* So in enrolled bill; there is no subsec. (1).

** So in enrolled bill.

§ 600.6407 SESSIONS, LOCATION; COURT OFFICER

The court shall hold at least 4 sessions in each year. Sessions of the court of claims may be held in the various circuits in the state as the supreme court administrator may determine. If the hearing in a particular case is to be held at a place other than the city of Lansing, due notice shall be given to all interested persons. The sheriff of the county within which a case is heard, or 1 of his deputies, shall serve as court officer without additional compensation therefor. The department of management and budget shall furnish the court with suitable space and equipment in the city of Lansing.

§ 600.6410 CLERKS; FEES; SERVICE OF PROCESS

(1) The circuit judges of the thirtieth judicial circuit shall appoint or remove the clerk of the court of claims.

(2) For making copies of records, proceedings, and testimony and furnishing the same at the request of the claimant, or any other person, the clerk of the court of claims, or any reporter or recorder serving in the court of claims shall be entitled in addition to salary, to the same fees as are by law provided for court reporters or recorders in the circuit court. No charge shall be made against the state for services rendered for furnishing copies of records, proceedings, or testimony or other papers to the attorney general.

(3) Process issued by the court may be served by any member of the Michigan state police as well as any other officer or person authorized to serve process issued out of the circuit court.

§ 600.6413 INGHAM COUNTY REIM-BURSEMENT OF COSTS; TRANSFER OF EMPLOYEES; SENIORITY RIGHTS; RETIREMENT BENEFITS

(1) The state shall reimburse the county of Ingham for the reasonable and actual costs incurred by that county for implementing jurisdictional duties in the circuit court imposed on that county by this chapter.

(2) The county of Ingham shall submit quarterly its itemized costs as described in this section to the state court administrative office. After determination by the state court administrator of the reasonableness of the amount to be paid, payment shall be made pursuant to the accounting laws of this state. Determination of reasonableness by the state court administrator shall be conclusive.

(3) Full-time employees of the court of claims are transferred to the circuit court for the thirtieth judicial circuit. Seniority rights, annual leave, sick leave, longevity pay and retirement benefits to which employees of the court of claims are now entitled shall be preserved and the employees shall be continued in their positions in the court of claims in the thirtieth judicial circuit in a manner not inferior to their prior status. The obligation of the state for retirement benefits to employees of the court of claims for their accrued service in the court of claims shall not be transferred. The retirement system available to public employees in Ingham county shall provide retirement benefits to employees of the court of claims not inferior to those provided therefor under their prior status.

§ 600.6416 REPRESENTATION OF STATE BY ATTORNEY GENERAL OR ASSISTANTS

The attorney general, or his assistants, shall appear for and represent the interests of the state in all matters before the court.

§ 600.6419 JURISDICTION; CLAIMS LESS THAN $1,000; COUNTERCLAIMS

(1) **Power and Jurisdiction.** Except as provided in sections 6419a and 6440,* the jurisdiction of the court of claims, as conferred upon it by this chapter, shall be exclusive. The state administrative board is hereby vested with discretionary authority upon the advice of the attorney general, to hear, consider, determine, and allow any claim against the state in an amount less than $1,000.00. Any claim so allowed by the state administrative board shall be paid in the same manner as judgments are paid under section 6458** upon certification of the allowed claim by the secretary of the state administrative board to the clerk of the court of claims. The court has power and jurisdiction:

(a) To hear and determine all claims and demands, liquidated or unliquidated, ex contractu or ex delicto, against the state and any of its departments, commissions, boards, institutions, arms, or agencies.

(b) To hear and determine any claims or demands, liquidated or unliquidated, ex contractu or ex delicto, which may be pleaded by way of counterclaim on the part of the state or any department, commission, board, institution, arm, or agency of the state against any claimant who may bring an action in the court of claims. Any claim of the state or of any department, commission, board, institution, arm, or agency of the state may be pleaded by way of counterclaim in any action brought against the state, or any other department, commission, board, institution, arm, or agency of the state.

(2) **Judgment; Counterclaims; Process.** The judgment entered by the court of claims upon any such claim, either against or in favor of the state or any department, commission, board, institution, arm, or agency of the state, upon becoming final shall be res adjudicata of that claim. Upon the trial of any cause in which any demand is made by the state or any department, commission, board, institution, arm, or agency of the state against the claimant either by way of setoff, recoupment, or cross declaration, the court shall hear and determine each claim or demand, and if the court finds a balance due from the claimant to the state, the court shall render judgment in favor of the state for the balance. Writs of execution or garnishment may issue upon the judgment the same as from the circuit court of this state. The judgment entered by the court of claims upon any claim, either for or against the claimant, shall be final unless appealed from as provided in this chapter.

(3) **Jurisdiction, Workers' Compensation, Peace Officers.** The court of claims shall not have jurisdiction of any claim for compensation under the provisions of either of the following:

(a) The worker's disability compensation act of 1969, Act No. 317 of the Public Acts of 1969, being sections 418.101 to 418.941 of the Michigan Compiled Laws.

(b) Act No. 329 of the Public Acts of 1937, as amended, being sections 419.101 to 419.104.

(4) Jurisdiction, Circuit Courts, Sales Tax, Declaratory or Equitable Relief, Other Statutory Claims, Review of Unemployment Claims. This chapter shall not deprive the circuit court of this state of jurisdiction over actions brought by the taxpayer under the general sales tax act, Act No. 167 of the Public Acts of 1933, being sections 205.51 to 205.78 of the Michigan Compiled Laws, or proceedings for declaratory or equitable relief, or any other actions against state agencies based upon the statutes of this state in such case made and provided, which expressly confer jurisdiction thereof upon the circuit court, or proceedings to review findings as provided in the Michigan employment security act, Act No. 1 of the Public Acts of the Extra Session of 1936, being sections 421.1 to 421.72 of the Michigan Compiled Laws, or any other similar proceedings expressly authorized by the statutes of this state in such case made and provided.

* M.C.L.A. §§ 600.6419a and 600.6440.

** M.C.L.A. § 600.6458.

§ 600.6419a COURT OF CLAIMS; CONCURRENT JURISDICTION

In addition to the powers and jurisdiction conferred upon the court of claims by section 6419,* the court of claims has concurrent jurisdiction of any demand for equitable relief and any demand for a declaratory judgment when ancillary to a claim filed pursuant to section 6419. The jurisdiction conferred by this section is not intended to be exclusive of the jurisdiction of the circuit court over demands for declaratory and equitable relief conferred by section 605.**

* M.C.L.A. § 600.6419.

** M.C.L.A. § 600.605.

§ 600.6420 CLAIMS OF $500 OR LESS, DELEGATION OF STATE ADMINISTRATIVE BOARD'S AUTHORITY TO DETERMINE AND ALLOW CLAIMS; PAYMENT

The state administrative board may delegate the authority vested in it by section 6419(1)* for any claim of $500.00 or less for damage or loss of personal property by a claimant who is an employee of the state, to the head of the department in which the claimant was employed. Payment of the claim shall be made upon the written certificate of the department head that the loss or damage occurred in the course of the claimant's employment, without fault on the part of the claimant and that the claimant has not otherwise been reimbursed for the loss.

* M.C.L.A. § 600.6419(1).

§ 600.6421 JOINDER OF CASES; TRIAL BY JUDGE

Cases in the court of claims may be joined for trial with cases arising out of the same transaction or series of transactions which are pending in any of the various trial courts of the state. A case in the court of claims shall be tried and determined by the judge even though the trial court action with which it may be joined is tried to a jury under the supervision of the same trial judge.

§ 600.6422 PRACTICE AND PROCEDURE

Practice and procedure in the court of claims shall be in accordance with the statutes and court rules prescribing the practice in the circuit courts of this state, except as herein otherwise provided. The supreme court shall have power to make special rules for said court.

§ 600.6425 DEPOSITIONS

The statutes and rules governing the taking of depositions in suits in the circuit courts of this state shall govern in the court of claims, except that it is not sufficient that the witness resides more than 50 miles from the place of holding court to enable the deposition to be used for any purpose.

§ 600.6428 WITNESSES, POWER TO COMPEL ATTENDANCE

The court of claims is hereby given the same power to subpoena witnesses and require the production of books, papers, records, documents and any other evidence and to punish for contempt as the circuit courts of this state now have or may hereafter have. The judge and clerk of said court may administer oaths and affirmations, and take acknowledgments of instruments in writing.

§ 600.6431 NOTICE OF INTENTION TO FILE CLAIM, CONTENTS, TIME, VERIFICATION, COPIES

(1) No claim may be maintained against the state unless the claimant, within 1 year after such claim has accrued, files in the office of the clerk of the court of claims either a written claim or a written notice of intention to file a claim against the state or any of its departments, commissions, boards, institutions, arms or agencies, stating the time when and the place where such claim arose and in detail the nature of the same and of the items of damage alleged or claimed to have been sustained, which claim or notice shall be

signed and verified by the claimant before an officer authorized to administer oaths.

(2) Such claim or notice shall designate any department, commission, board, institution, arm or agency of the state involved in connection with such claim, and a copy of such claim or notice shall be furnished to the clerk at the time of the filing of the original for transmittal to the attorney general and to each of the departments, commissions, boards, institutions, arms or agencies designated.

(3) In all actions for property damage or personal injuries, claimant shall file with the clerk of the court of claims a notice of intention to file a claim or the claim itself within 6 months following the happening of the event giving rise to the cause of action.

§ 600.6434 PLEADINGS, SERVICE, COPIES

(1) Except as provided in this section, the pleadings shall conform to the rules for pleadings in the circuit courts.

(2) The complaint shall be verified. The pleadings of the state need not be verified.

(3) The complaint shall be served upon any department, commission, board, institution, arm, or agency of the state involved in the litigation, in the same manner as a complaint filed in the circuit court.

(4) With each paper, including the original complaint filed by the claimant, 1 copy of each shall be furnished to the clerk who shall immediately transmit the copy to the attorney general.

§ 600.6437 JUDGMENT ON STIPULATED FACTS

The court may order entry of judgment against the state or any of its departments, commissions, boards, institutions, arms or agencies based upon facts as stipulated by counsel after taking such proofs in support thereof as may be necessary to satisfy the court as to the accuracy of such facts and upon being satisfied that such judgment is in accordance with applicable law.

§ 600.6440 REMEDY IN FEDERAL COURT AS BAR TO JURISDICTION

No claimant may be permitted to file claim in said court against the state nor any department, commission, board, institution, arm or agency thereof who has an adequate remedy upon his claim in the federal courts, but it is not necessary in the complaint filed to allege that claimant has no such adequate remedy, but that fact may be put in issue by the answer or motion filed by the state or the department, commission, board, institution, arm or agency thereof.

§ 600.6443 TRIAL BY COURT WITHOUT JURY; NEW TRIAL

The case shall be heard by the judge without a jury. The court may grant a new trial upon the same terms and under the same conditions and for the same reasons as prevail in the case of the circuit courts of this state, in a case at law without a jury.

§ 600.6446 APPEAL TO COURT OF APPEALS; PROCEDURE

(1) Appeals shall lie from the court of claims to the court of appeals in all respects as if the court of claims was a circuit court.

(2) The procedure for the taking of appeals to the court of appeals from the court of claims shall be governed by the statutes and court rules governing the taking of appeals from a circuit court to the court of appeals in a case at law, without a jury.

(3) The clerk of the court of claims shall immediately furnish the parties to every action with a notice of entry of any final order or judgment, and the time within which an appeal as of right may be taken shall be governed by the Michigan court rules.

§ 600.6449 COSTS, SECURITY FOR COSTS ON APPEAL

(1) If the state shall put in issue the right of claimant to recover, the court may allow costs to the prevailing party from the time of the joining of the issue. The costs, however, shall include only witness fees and officers' fees for service of subpoenas actually paid, and attorney fees in the same amount as is provided for trial of cases in circuit court.

(2) Costs upon an appeal to the court of appeals shall be allowed in like amounts and for the same items as in a case appealed to the court of appeals from the circuit court.

(3) In the case of costs allowed against a claimant, judgment shall be entered thereon and writs of execution or garnishment may issue as from the circuit court.

(4) In the event of an appeal to the court of appeals by a claimant the judge may, upon motion by the attorney general, require security for costs from the claimant in connection with such an appeal.

§ 600.6452 LIMITATION OF ACTIONS; RIGHTS OF ATTORNEY GENERAL, PETITIONS FOR ADMINISTRATION OF ESTATE OR APPOINTMENT OF GUARDIAN

(1) **Filing of Claim.** Every claim against the state, cognizable by the court of claims, shall be forever barred unless the claim is filed with the clerk

of the court or suit instituted thereon in federal court as authorized in section 6440,* within 3 years after the claim first accrues.

(2) Limitation of Actions. Except as modified by this section, the provisions of RJA chapter 58,** relative to the limitation of actions, shall also be applicable to the limitation prescribed in this section.

(3) Attorney General; Petition for Administration of Estate of a Deceased Person. The attorney general shall have the same right as a creditor under the provisions of the statutes of the state of Michigan in such case made and provided, to petition for the granting of letters of administration of the estate of any deceased person.

(4) Petition for Appointment of Guardian of Minor or Person Under Disability. The attorney general shall have the same right as a superintendent of the poor under the provisions of the statutes of the state of Michigan in such case made and provided, to petition for the appointment of a guardian of the estate of a minor or any other person under disability.

* M.C.L.A. § 600.6440.

** M.C.L.A. § 600.5801 et seq.

§ 600.6455 COURT OF CLAIMS; JUDGMENT, INTEREST

(1) Interest shall not be allowed upon any claim up to the date of the rendition of judgment by the court, unless upon a contract expressly stipulating for the payment of interest. All judgments from the date of the rendition of the judgment shall carry interest at the rate of 12% per annum compounded annually, except that judgment upon a contract expressly providing for interest shall carry interest at the rate provided by the contract in which case provision to that effect shall be incorporated in the judgment entered. This subsection shall apply to any civil action based on tort filed on or after July 9, 1984 but before January 1, 1987 and any action pending before the court of claims on July 9, 1984. This subsection shall apply to any action, other than a civil action based on tort, filed on or after July 1, 1984 and any action pending before the court of claims on July 9, 1984.

(2) Except as otherwise provided in this subsection, for complaints filed on or after January 1, 1987, interest on a money judgment recovered in a civil action shall be calculated from the date of filing the complaint at a rate of interest which is equal to 1% plus the average interest rate paid at auctions of 5–year United States treasury notes during the 6 months immediately preceding July 1 and January 1, as certified by the state treasurer, and compounded annually, pursuant to this section.

(3) For complaints filed on or after October 1, 1986, interest shall not be allowed on future damages from the date of filing the complaint to the date of entry of the judgment.

(4) If a bona fide, reasonable written offer of settlement in a civil action based on tort is made by the party against whom the judgment is subsequently rendered, the court shall order that interest shall not be allowed beyond the date the written offer of settlement which is made and rejected by the plaintiff, and is filed with the court.

(5) Except as otherwise provided in subsection (3), if a bona fide, reasonable written offer of settlement in a civil action based on tort is not made by the party against whom the judgment is subsequently rendered, or is made and that offer is not filed with the court, the court shall order that interest be calculated from the date of filing the complaint to the date of satisfaction of the judgment.

(6) Except as otherwise provided in subsection (3), if a bona fide, reasonable written offer of settlement in a civil action based on tort is made by a plaintiff for whom the judgment is subsequently rendered and that offer is rejected and the offer is filed with the court, the court shall order that interest be calculated from the date of the rejection of the offer to the date of satisfaction of the judgment at a rate of interest equal to 2% plus the rate of interest computed under subsection (2).

(7) An offer made pursuant to this section which is not accepted within 21 days after the offer is made shall be considered rejected. A rejection, under this subsection or otherwise, does not preclude a later offer by either party.

(8) As used in this section:

(a) "Bona fide, reasonable written offer of settlement" means:

(i) With respect to an offer of settlement made by a defendant against whom judgment is subsequently rendered, an offer of settlement that is not less than 90% of the amount actually received by the plaintiff in the action through judgment.

(ii) With respect to an offer of settlement made by a plaintiff, an offer of settlement that is not more than 110% of the amount actually received by the plaintiff in the action through judgment.

(b) "Defendant" means a defendant, a counter-defendant, or a cross-defendant.

(c) "Party" means a plaintiff or a defendant.

(d) "Plaintiff" means a plaintiff, a counter-plaintiff, or a cross-plaintiff.

§ 600.6458 JUDGMENT AGAINST STATE, PAYMENT

(1) In rendering any judgment against the state, or any department, commission, board, institution, arm or agency, the court shall determine and specify in that judgment the department, commission, board, institution, arm or agency from whose appropriation that judgment shall be paid.

(2) Upon any judgment against the state or any department, commission, board, institution, arm or agency becoming final, or upon allowance of any claim by the state administrative board and upon certification by the secretary of the state administrative board to the clerk of the court of claims, the clerk of the court shall certify to the state treasurer the fact that that judgment was entered or that the claim was allowed and the claim shall thereupon be paid from the unencumbered appropriation of the department, commission, board, institution, arm or agency if the state treasurer determines the unencumbered appropriation is sufficient for the payment. In the event that funds are not available to pay the judgment or allowed claim, the state treasurer shall instruct the clerk of the court of claims to issue a voucher against an appropriation made by the legislature for the payment of judgment claims and allowed claims. In the event that funds are not available to pay the judgment or allowed claim, that fact, together with the name of the claimant, date of judgment, date of allowance of claim by the state administrative board and amount shall be reported to the legislature at its next session, and the judgment or allowed claim shall be paid as soon as money is available for that purpose. The clerk shall not certify any judgment to the state treasurer until the period for appeal from that judgment shall have expired, unless written stipulation between the attorney general and the claimant or his attorney, waiving any right of appeal or new trial, is filed with the clerk of the court.

(3) The clerk shall approve vouchers under the direction of the court for the payment of the several judgments rendered by the court. All warrants issued in satisfaction of those judgments shall be transmitted to the clerk for distribution; and all warrants issued in satisfaction of claims allowed by the state administrative board shall be transmitted to the secretary of the state administrative board for distribution.

§ 600.6461   CLERK'S REPORT TO LEGISLATURE, STATE TREASURER, AND BUDGET DIRECTOR

(1) At the commencement of each session of the legislature and at such other times during the session as he or she may consider proper, the clerk of the court shall report to the legislature the claims upon which the court has finally acted, with a statement of the judgment rendered in each case.

(2) The clerk shall submit a detailed statement of the amount of each claim allowed by the court to the state treasurer and the budget director.

§ 600.6464   JUDGMENT, DISCHARGE

The payment of any amount due as found by the judgment of the court of claims, including interest and costs, shall operate as a discharge of such judgment.

§ 600.6467   STATE AGENCIES TO FURNISH INFORMATION UPON REQUEST

The court shall have power to call upon any officer, department, institution, board, arm or agency of the state government for any examination, information or papers pertinent to the issues involved in any case then pending before the court. No state employee shall receive any additional fees or compensation for rendering such services or appearing as a witness before the court upon behalf of the state.

§ 600.6470   FRAUD IN CONNECTION WITH CLAIM; FORFEITURE

Any person who corruptly practices, or attempts to practice, any fraud against the state of Michigan, in the proof, statement, establishment, or allowance of any claim or of any part of a claim, against the state, shall thereby forfeit the same to the state and it shall be the duty of the court of claims in such case to find specifically that such fraud was practiced, or attempted to be practiced, and thereupon to give judgment that such claim is forfeited to the state and that the claimant be forever barred from prosecuting the same.

§ 600.6475   ACTIONS INVOLVING NEGLIGENT OPERATION OF MOTOR VEHICLES OR AIRCRAFT; DEFENSE OF GOVERNMENTAL FUNCTION

In all actions brought in the court of claims against the state to recover damages resulting from the negligent operation by an officer, agent or employee of the state of a motor vehicle or an aircraft, other than a military aircraft, of which the state is owner, the fact that the state, in the ownership or operation of such motor vehicle or aircraft, was engaged in a governmental function shall not be a defense to such action. This act shall not be construed to impose upon the state a liability other or greater than the liability imposed by law upon other owners of motor vehicles or aircraft.

MICHIGAN RULES OF PROFESSIONAL CONDUCT

Adopted Effective October 1, 1988

Research Note

Use Westlaw ® *to find cases citing or applying specific rules.* Westlaw *may also be used to search for specific terms in court rules or to update court rules. See the MI–RULES and MI–ORDERS Scope Screens for detailed descriptive information and search tips.*

Amendments to these rules are published, as received, in the N.W.2d *and* Michigan Reporter *advance sheets*, and Michigan Legislative Service.

Table of Rules

RULE 1.0 SCOPE AND APPLICABILITY OF RULES AND COMMENTARY

(a) These are the Michigan Rules of Professional Conduct. The form of citation for this rule is MRPC 1.0.

(b) Failure to comply with an obligation or prohibition imposed by a rule is a basis for invoking the disciplinary process. The rules do not, however, give rise to a cause of action for enforcement of a rule or for damages caused by failure to comply with an obligation or prohibition imposed by a rule. In a civil or criminal action, the admissibility of the Rules of Professional Conduct is governed by the Michigan Rules of Evidence and other provisions of law.

(c) The text of each rule is authoritative. The comment that accompanies each rule does not expand or limit the scope of the obligations, prohibitions, and counsel found in the text of the rule.

Comment

The rules and comments were largely drawn from the American Bar Association's Model Rules of Professional Conduct. Prior to submission of those Model Rules to the Michigan Supreme Court, the State Bar of Michigan made minor changes in the rules and the comments to conform them to Michigan law and preferred practice. The Supreme Court then adopted the rules, with such substantive changes as appeared proper to the Court. Additional changes in the comments were then made by staff to conform the comments to the rules as adopted by the Supreme Court. The Supreme Court has authorized publication of the comments as an aid to the reader, but the rules alone comprise the Supreme Court's authoritative statement of a lawyer's ethical obligations.

PREAMBLE: A LAWYER'S RESPONSIBILITIES

This preamble is part of the comment to Rule 1.0, and provides a general introduction to the Rules of Professional Conduct.

A lawyer is a representative of clients, an officer of the legal system and a public citizen having special responsibility for the quality of justice.

As a representative of clients, a lawyer performs various functions. As advisor, a lawyer provides a client with an informed understanding of the client's legal rights and obligations and explains their practical implications. As advocate, a lawyer zealously asserts the client's position under the rules of the adversary system. As negotiator, a lawyer seeks a result advantageous to the client but consistent with requirements of honest dealing with others. As intermediary between clients, a lawyer seeks to reconcile their divergent interests as an advisor and, to a limited extent, as a spokesperson for each client. A lawyer acts as evaluator by examining a client's legal affairs and reporting about them to the client or to others.

In all professional functions a lawyer should be competent, prompt and diligent. A lawyer should maintain communication with a client concerning the representation. A lawyer should keep in confidence information relating to representation of a client except so far as disclosure is required or permitted by the Rules of Professional Conduct or other law.

A lawyer's conduct should conform to the requirements of the law, both in professional service to clients and in the lawyer's business and personal affairs. A lawyer should use the law's procedures only for legitimate purposes and not to harass or intimidate others. A lawyer should demonstrate respect for the legal system and for those who serve it, including judges, other lawyers and public officials. While it is a lawyer's duty, when necessary, to challenge the rectitude of official action, it is also a lawyer's duty to uphold legal process.

As a public citizen, a lawyer should seek improvement of the law, the administration of justice and the quality of service rendered by the legal profession. As a member of a learned profession, a lawyer should cultivate knowledge of the law beyond its use for clients, employ that knowledge in reform of the law and work to strengthen legal education. A lawyer should be mindful of deficiencies in the administration of justice and of the fact that the poor, and sometimes persons who are not poor, cannot afford adequate legal assistance, and should therefore devote professional time and civic influence in their behalf. A lawyer should aid the legal profession in pursuing these objectives and should help the bar regulate itself in the public interest.

Many of a lawyer's professional responsibilities are prescribed in the Rules of Professional Conduct, as well as substantive and procedural law. However, a lawyer is also guided by personal conscience and the approbation of professional peers. A lawyer should strive to attain the highest level of skill, to improve the law and the legal profession and to exemplify the legal profession's ideals of public service.

A lawyer's responsibilities as a representative of clients, an officer of the legal system, and a public citizen are usually harmonious. Thus, when an opposing party is well represented, a lawyer can be a zealous advocate on behalf of a client and at the same time assume that justice is being done. So also, a lawyer can be sure that preserving client confidences ordinarily serves the public interest because people are more likely to seek legal advice, and thereby heed their legal obligations, when they know their communications will be private.

In the nature of law practice, however, conflicting responsibilities are encountered. Virtually all difficult ethical problems arise from conflict between a lawyer's responsibilities to clients, to the legal system, and to the lawyer's own interest in remaining an upright person while earning a satisfactory living. The Rules of Professional Conduct prescribe terms for resolving such conflicts. Within the framework of these rules many difficult issues of professional discretion can arise. Such issues must be resolved through the exercise of sensitive professional and moral judgment guided by the basic principles underlying the rules.

The legal profession is largely self-governing. Although other professions also have been granted powers of self-government, the legal profession is unique in this respect because of the close relationship between the profession and the processes of government and law enforcement. This connection is manifested in the fact that ultimate authority over the legal profession is vested largely in the courts.

To the extent that lawyers meet the obligations of their professional calling, the occasion for government regulation is obviated. Self-regulation also helps maintain the legal profession's independence from government domination. An independent legal profession is an important force in preserving government under law, for abuse of legal authority is more readily challenged by a profession whose members are not dependent on government for the right to practice.

The legal profession's relative autonomy carries with it special responsibilities of self-government. The profession has a responsibility to assure that its regulations are conceived in the public interest and not in furtherance of parochial or self-interested concerns of the bar. Every lawyer is responsible for observance of the Rules of Professional Conduct. A lawyer should also aid in securing their observance by other lawyers. Neglect of these responsibilities compromises the independence of the profession and the public interest which it serves.

Lawyers play a vital role in the preservation of society. The fulfillment of this role requires an understanding by lawyers of their relationship to our legal system. The Rules of Professional Conduct, when properly applied, serve to define that relationship.

Scope. The Rules of Professional Conduct are rules of reason. They should be interpreted with reference to the purposes of legal representation and of the law itself. Some of the rules are imperatives, cast in the terms "shall" or "shall not." These define proper conduct for purposes of professional discipline. Others, generally cast in the term "may," are permissive and define areas under the rules in which the lawyer has professional discretion. No disciplinary action should be taken when the lawyer acts or chooses not to act within the bounds of such discretion. Other rules define the nature of relationships between the lawyer and others. The rules are thus partly obligatory and disciplinary and partly constitutive and descriptive in that they define a lawyer's professional role. Many of the comments use the term "should." Comments do not add obligations to the rules, but provide guidance for practicing in compliance with the rules.

The rules presuppose a larger legal context shaping the lawyer's role. That context includes court rules and statutes relating to matters of licensure, laws defining specific obligations of lawyers, and substantive and procedural law in general. Compliance with the rules, as with all law in an open society, depends primarily upon understanding and voluntary compliance, secondarily upon reinforcement by peer and public opinion, and finally, when necessary, upon enforcement through disciplinary proceedings. The rules do not, however, exhaust the moral and ethical considerations that should inform a lawyer for no worthwhile human activity can be completely defined by legal rules. The rules simply provide a framework for the ethical practice of law.

Furthermore, for purposes of determining the lawyer's authority and responsibility, principles of substantive law external to these rules determine whether a client-lawyer relationship exists. Most of the duties flowing from the client-lawyer relationship attach only after the client has requested the lawyer to render legal services and the lawyer has agreed to do so. But there are some duties, such as that of confidentiality under Rule 1.6, that may attach when the lawyer agrees to consider whether a client-lawyer relationship shall be established. Whether a client-lawyer relationship exists for any specific purpose can depend on the circumstances and may be a question of fact.

Under various legal provisions, including constitutional, statutory and common-law, the responsibilities of government lawyers may include authority concerning legal matters that ordinarily reposes in the client in private client-lawyer relationships. For example, a lawyer for a government agency may have authority on behalf of the government to decide upon settlement or whether to appeal from an adverse judgment. Such authority in various respects is generally vested in the attorney general and the prosecuting attorney in state government, and their federal counterparts, and the same may be true of other government law officers. Also, lawyers under the supervision of these officers may be authorized to represent several government agencies in intragovernmental legal controversies in circumstances where a private lawyer could not represent multiple private clients. They also may have authority to represent the "public interest" in circumstances where a private lawyer would not be authorized to do so. These rules do not abrogate any such authority.

As indicated earlier in this comment, a failure to comply with an obligation or prohibition imposed by a rule is a basis for invoking the disciplinary process. The rules presuppose that disciplinary assessment of a lawyer's conduct will be made on the basis of the facts and circumstances as they existed at the time of the conduct in question and in recognition of the fact that a lawyer often has to act upon uncertain or incomplete evidence of the situation. Moreover, the rules presuppose that whether or not discipline should be imposed for a violation, and the severity of a sanction, depend on all the circumstances, such as the wilfulness and seriousness of the violation, extenuating factors and whether there have been previous violations.

As also indicated earlier in this comment, a violation of a rule does not give rise to a cause of action, nor does it create any presumption that a legal duty has been breached. The rules are designed to provide guidance to lawyers and to provide a structure for regulating conduct through disciplinary agencies. They are not designed to be a basis for civil liability. Furthermore, the purposes of the rules can be subverted when they are invoked by opposing parties as procedural weapons. The fact that a rule is a just basis for a lawyer's self-assessment, or for sanctioning a lawyer under the administration of a disciplinary authority, does not imply that an antagonist in a collateral proceeding or transaction has standing to seek enforcement of the rule. Accordingly, nothing in the rules should be deemed to augment any substantive legal duty of lawyers or the extradisciplinary consequences of violating such a duty.

Moreover, these rules are not intended to govern or affect judicial application of either the client-lawyer or work-product privilege. Those privileges were developed to promote compliance with law and fairness in litigation. In reliance on the client-lawyer privilege, clients are entitled to expect that communications within the scope of the privilege will be protected against compelled disclosure. The client-lawyer privilege is that of the client and not of the lawyer. The fact that in exceptional situations the lawyer under the rules has a limited discretion to disclose a client confidence does not vitiate the proposition that, as a general matter, the client has a reasonable expectation that information relating to the client will not be voluntarily disclosed and that disclosure of such information may be judicially compelled only in accordance with recognized exceptions to the client-lawyer and work-product privileges.

The lawyer's exercise of discretion not to disclose information under Rule 1.6 should not be subject to reexamination. Permitting such reexamination would be incompatible with the general policy of promoting compliance with law through assurances that communications will be protected against disclosure.

The comment accompanying each rule explains and illustrates the meaning and purpose of the rule. The Preamble and this note on scope provide general orientation. The comments are intended as guides to interpretation, but the text of each rule is authoritative.

Terminology. "Belief" or "believes" denotes that the person involved actually supposed the fact in question to be true. A person's belief may be inferred from circumstances.

"Consult" or "consultation" denotes communication of information reasonably sufficient to permit the client to appreciate the significance of the matter in question.

"Firm" or "law firm" denotes a lawyer or lawyers in a private firm, lawyers employed in the legal department of a corporation or other organization, and lawyers employed in a legal services organization. See comment, Rule 1.10.

"Fraud" or "fraudulent" denotes conduct having a purpose to deceive and not merely negligent misrepresentation or failure to apprise another of relevant information.

"Knowingly," "known," or "knows" denotes actual knowledge of the fact in question. A person's knowledge may be inferred from circumstances.

"Partner" denotes a member of a partnership and a shareholder in a law firm organized as a professional corporation.

"Reasonable" or "reasonably," when used in relation to conduct by a lawyer, denotes the conduct of a reasonably prudent and competent lawyer.

"Reasonable belief" or "reasonably believes," when used in reference to a lawyer, denotes that the lawyer believes the matter in question and that the circumstances are such that the belief is reasonable.

"Reasonably should know," when used in reference to a lawyer, denotes that a lawyer of reasonable prudence and competence would ascertain the matter in question.

"Substantial," when used in reference to degree or extent, denotes a material matter of clear and weighty importance.

CLIENT–LAWYER RELATIONSHIP

RULE 1.1   COMPETENCE

A lawyer shall provide competent representation to a client. A lawyer shall not:

(a) handle a legal matter which the lawyer knows or should know that the lawyer is not competent to handle, without associating with a lawyer who is competent to handle it;

(b) handle a legal matter without preparation adequate in the circumstances; or

(c) neglect a legal matter entrusted to the lawyer.

Comment

Legal Knowledge and Skill. In determining whether a lawyer is able to provide competent representation in a particular matter, relevant factors include the relative complexity and specialized nature of the matter, the lawyer's general experience, the lawyer's training and experience in the field in question, the preparation and study the lawyer is able to give the matter, and whether it is feasible to refer the matter to, or associate or consult with, a lawyer of established competence in the field in question. In many instances, the required proficiency is that of a general practitioner. Expertise in a particular field of law may be required in some circumstances.

A lawyer need not necessarily have special training or prior experience to handle legal problems of a type with which the lawyer is unfamiliar. A newly admitted lawyer can be as competent as a practitioner with long experience. Some important legal skills, such as the analysis of precedent, the evaluation of evidence and legal drafting, are required in all legal problems. Perhaps the most fundamental legal skill consists of determining what kind of legal problems a situation may involve, a skill that necessarily transcends any particular specialized knowledge. A lawyer can provide adequate representation in a wholly novel field through necessary study. Competent representation can also be provided through the association of a lawyer of established competence in the field in question.

In an emergency, a lawyer may give advice or assistance in a matter in which the lawyer does not have the skill ordinarily required where referral to or consultation or association with another lawyer would be impractical. Even in an emergency, however, assistance should be limited to that reasonably necessary in the circumstances, for ill-considered action under emergency conditions can jeopardize the client's interest.

A lawyer may offer representation where the requisite level of competence can be achieved by reasonable preparation. This applies as well to a lawyer who is appointed as counsel for an unrepresented person. See also Rule 6.2.

Thoroughness and Preparation. Competent handling of a particular matter includes inquiry into and analysis of the factual and legal elements of the problem, and use of methods and procedures meeting the standards of competent practitioners. It also includes adequate preparation. The required attention and preparation are determined in part by what is at stake; major litigation and complex transactions ordinarily require more elaborate treatment than matters of lesser consequence.

Maintaining Competence. To maintain the requisite knowledge and skill, a lawyer should engage in continuing study and education. If a system of peer review has been established, the lawyer should consider making use of it in appropriate circumstances.

RULE 1.2   SCOPE OF REPRESENTATION

(a) A lawyer shall seek the lawful objectives of a client through reasonably available means permitted by law and these rules. A lawyer does not violate this rule by acceding to reasonable requests of opposing counsel that do not prejudice the rights of the client, by being punctual in fulfilling all professional commitments, or by avoiding offensive tactics. A lawyer shall abide by a client's decision whether to accept an offer of settlement or mediation evaluation of a matter. In a criminal case, the lawyer shall abide by the client's decision, after consultation with the lawyer, with respect to a plea to be entered, whether to waive jury trial, and whether the client will testify. In representing a client, a lawyer may, where permissible, exercise professional judgment to waive or fail to assert a right or position of the client.

(b) A lawyer may limit the objectives of the representation if the client consents after consultation.

(c) A lawyer shall not counsel a client to engage, or assist a client, in conduct that the lawyer knows is illegal or fraudulent, but a lawyer may discuss the legal consequences of any proposed course of conduct with a client and may counsel or assist a client to make a good-faith effort to determine the validity, scope, meaning, or application of the law.

(d) When a lawyer knows that a client expects assistance not permitted by the Rules of Professional Conduct or other law, the lawyer shall consult with the client regarding the relevant limitations on the lawyer's conduct.

[Amended effective October 1, 1993.]

Comment

Scope of Representation. Both the lawyer and the client have authority and responsibility in the objectives and means of representation. The client has ultimate authority to determine the purposes to be served by legal representation, within the limits imposed by law and the lawyer's professional obligations. Within those limits, a client also has a right to consult with the lawyer about the means to be used in pursuing those objectives. At the same time, a lawyer is not required to pursue objectives or employ means simply because a client may wish that the lawyer do so. A clear distinction between objectives and means sometimes cannot be drawn, and in many cases the client-lawyer relationship partakes of a joint undertaking. In questions of means, the lawyer should assume responsibility for technical and legal tactical issues, but should defer to the client regarding such questions as the expense to be incurred and concern for third persons who might be adversely affected.

In a case in which the client appears to be suffering mental disability, the lawyer's duty to abide by the client's decisions is to be guided by reference to Rule 1.14.

Independence from Client's Views or Activities. Legal representation should not be denied to people who are unable to afford legal services or whose cause is controversial or the subject of popular disapproval. By the same token, representation of a client, including representation by appointment, does not constitute an endorsement of the client's political, economic, social, or moral views or activities.

Services Limited in Objectives or Means. The objectives or scope of services provided by a lawyer may be limited by agreement with the client or by the terms under which the lawyer's services are made available to the client.

For example, a retainer may be for a specifically defined purpose. Representation provided through a legal-aid agency may be subject to limitations on the types of cases the agency handles. When a lawyer has been retained by an insurer to represent an insured, the representation may be limited to matters related to the insurance coverage. The terms upon which representation is undertaken may exclude specific objectives or means. Such limitations may exclude objectives or means that the lawyer regards as repugnant or imprudent.

An agreement concerning the scope of representation must accord with the Rules of Professional Conduct and other law. Thus, the client may not be asked to agree to representation so limited in scope as to violate Rule 1.1, or to surrender the right to terminate the lawyer's services or the right to settle litigation that the lawyer might wish to continue.

Illegal, Fraudulent and Prohibited Transactions. A lawyer is required to give an honest opinion about the actual consequences that appear likely to result from a client's conduct. The fact that a client uses advice in a course of action that is illegal or fraudulent does not, of itself, make a lawyer a party to the course of action. However, a lawyer may not knowingly assist a client in illegal or fraudulent conduct. There is a critical distinction between presenting an analysis of legal aspects of questionable conduct and recommending the means by which an illegal act or fraud might be committed with impunity.

When the client's course of action has already begun and is continuing, the lawyer's responsibility is especially delicate. The lawyer is not permitted to reveal the client's wrongdoing, except where permitted by Rule 1.6. However, the lawyer is required to avoid furthering the purpose, for example, by suggesting how it might be concealed. A lawyer may not continue assisting a client in conduct that the lawyer originally supposes is legally proper but then discovers is illegal or fraudulent. Withdrawal from the representation, therefore, may be required.

Where the client is a fiduciary, the lawyer may be charged with special obligations in dealings with a beneficiary.

Paragraph (c) applies whether or not the defrauded party is a party to the transaction. Hence, a lawyer should not participate in a sham transaction; for example, a transaction to effectuate criminal or fraudulent escape of tax liability. Paragraph (c) does not preclude undertaking a criminal defense incident to a general retainer for legal services to a lawful enterprise. The last clause of paragraph (c) recognizes that determining the validity or interpretation of a statute or regulation may require a course of action involving disobedience of the statute or regulation or of the interpretation placed upon it by governmental authorities.

RULE 1.3 DILIGENCE

A lawyer shall act with reasonable diligence and promptness in representing a client.

Comment

A lawyer should pursue a matter on behalf of a client despite opposition, obstruction or personal inconvenience to the lawyer, and may take whatever lawful and ethical measures are required to vindicate a client's cause or endeavor. A lawyer should act with commitment and dedication to the interests of the client and with zeal in advocacy upon the client's behalf. However, a lawyer is not bound to press for every advantage that might be realized for a client. A lawyer has professional discretion in determining the means by which a matter should be pursued. See Rule 1.2. A lawyer's workload should be controlled so that each matter can be handled adequately.

Perhaps no professional shortcoming is more widely resented than procrastination. A client's interests often can be adversely affected by the passage of time or the change of conditions; in extreme instances, as when a lawyer overlooks a statute of limitations, the client's legal position may be destroyed. Even when the client's interests are not affected in substance, however, unreasonable delay can cause a client needless anxiety and undermine confidence in the lawyer's trustworthiness.

Unless the relationship is terminated as provided in Rule 1.16, a lawyer should carry through to conclusion all matters undertaken for a client. If a lawyer's employment is limited to a specific matter, the relationship terminates when the matter has been resolved. If a lawyer has served a client over a substantial period in a variety of matters, the client sometimes may assume that the lawyer will continue to serve on a continuing basis unless the lawyer gives notice of withdrawal. Doubt about whether a client-lawyer relationship still exists should be clarified by the lawyer, preferably in writing, so that the client will not mistakenly suppose the lawyer is looking after the client's affairs when the lawyer has ceased to do so. For example, if a lawyer has handled a judicial or administrative proceeding that produced a result adverse to the client but has not been specifically instructed concerning pursuit of an appeal, the lawyer should advise the client of the possibility of appeal before relinquishing responsibility for the matter.

RULE 1.4 COMMUNICATION

(a) A lawyer shall keep a client reasonably informed about the status of a matter and comply promptly with reasonable requests for information. A lawyer shall notify the client promptly of all settlement offers, mediation evaluations, and proposed plea bargains.

(b) A lawyer shall explain a matter to the extent reasonably necessary to permit the client to make informed decisions regarding the representation.

Comment

The client should have sufficient information to participate intelligently in decisions concerning the objectives of the representation and the means by which they are to be pursued to the extent the client is willing and able to do so. For example, a lawyer negotiating on behalf of a client should provide the client with facts relevant to the matter, inform the client of communications from another party, and take other reasonable steps that permit the client to make a decision regarding an offer from another party. A lawyer who receives an offer of settlement or a mediation evaluation in a civil controversy, or a proffered plea bargain in a criminal case, must promptly inform the client of its substance. See Rule 1.2(a). Even when a client delegates authority to the lawyer, the client should be kept advised of the status of the matter.

Adequacy of communication depends in part on the kind of advice or assistance involved. For example, in negotiations where there is time to explain a proposal, the lawyer should review all important provisions with the client before pro-

ceeding to an agreement. In litigation, a lawyer should explain the general strategy and prospects of success and ordinarily should consult the client on tactics that might injure or coerce others. On the other hand, a lawyer ordinarily cannot be expected to describe trial or negotiation strategy in detail. The guiding principle is that the lawyer should fulfill reasonable client expectations for information consistent with the duty to act in the client's best interests and consistent with the client's overall requirements as to the character of representation.

Ordinarily, the information to be provided is that appropriate for a client who is a comprehending and responsible adult. However, fully informing the client according to this standard may be impracticable, for example, where the client is a child or suffers from mental disability. See Rule 1.14. When the client is an organization or group, it is often impossible or inappropriate to inform every one of its members about its legal affairs; ordinarily, the lawyer should address communications to the appropriate officials of the organization. See Rule 1.13. Where many routine matters are involved, a system of limited or occasional reporting may be arranged with the client. Practical exigency may also require a lawyer to act for a client without prior consultation.

Withholding Information. In some circumstances, a lawyer may be justified in delaying transmission of information when the client would be likely to react imprudently to an immediate communication. Thus, a lawyer might withhold a psychiatric diagnosis of a client when the examining psychiatrist indicates that disclosure would harm the client. A lawyer may not withhold information to serve the lawyer's own interest or convenience. Rules or court orders governing litigation may provide that information supplied to a lawyer may not be disclosed to the client. Rule 3.4(c) directs compliance with such rules or orders.

RULE 1.5 FEES

(a) A lawyer shall not enter into an agreement for, charge, or collect an illegal or clearly excessive fee. A fee is clearly excessive when, after a review of the facts, a lawyer of ordinary prudence would be left with a definite and firm conviction that the fee is in excess of a reasonable fee. The factors to be considered in determining the reasonableness of a fee include the following:

(1) the time and labor required, the novelty and difficulty of the questions involved, and the skill requisite to perform the legal service properly;

(2) the likelihood, if apparent to the client, that the acceptance of the particular employment will preclude other employment by the lawyer;

(3) the fee customarily charged in the locality for similar legal services;

(4) the amount involved and the results obtained;

(5) the time limitations imposed by the client or by the circumstances;

(6) the nature and length of the professional relationship with the client;

(7) the experience, reputation, and ability of the lawyer or lawyers performing the services; and

(8) whether the fee is fixed or contingent.

(b) When the lawyer has not regularly represented the client, the basis or rate of the fee shall be communicated to the client, preferably in writing, before or within a reasonable time after commencing the representation.

(c) A fee may be contingent on the outcome of the matter for which the service is rendered, except in a matter in which a contingent fee is prohibited by paragraph (d) or by other law. A contingent-fee agreement shall be in writing and shall state the method by which the fee is to be determined. Upon conclusion of a contingent-fee matter, the lawyer shall provide the client with a written statement of the outcome of the matter and, if there is a recovery, show the remittance to the client and the method of its determination. See also MCR 8.121 for additional requirements applicable to some contingent-fee agreements.

(d) A lawyer shall not enter into an arrangement for, charge, or collect a contingent fee in a domestic relations matter or in a criminal matter.

(e) A division of a fee between lawyers who are not in the same firm may be made only if:

(1) the client is advised of and does not object to the participation of all the lawyers involved; and

(2) the total fee is reasonable.

[Amended effective April 1, 1998.]

Comment

Basis or Rate of Fee. When the lawyer has regularly represented a client, they ordinarily will have evolved an understanding concerning the basis or rate of the fee. In a new client-lawyer relationship, however, an understanding as to the fee should be promptly established. It is not necessary to recite all the factors that underlie the basis of the fee, but only those that are directly involved in its computation. It is sufficient, for example, to state that the basic rate is an hourly charge or a fixed amount or an estimated amount, or to identify the factors that may be taken into account in finally fixing the fee. When developments occur during the representation that render an earlier estimate substantially inaccurate, a revised estimate should be provided to the client. A written statement concerning the fee reduces the possibility of misunderstanding. Furnishing the client with a simple memorandum or a copy of the lawyer's customary fee schedule is sufficient if the basis or rate of the fee is set forth.

Terms of Payment. A lawyer may require advance payment of a fee, but is obliged to return any unearned portion. See Rule 1.16(d). A lawyer may accept property in payment for services, such as an ownership interest in an enterprise, providing this does not involve acquisition of a proprietary interest in the cause of action or subject matter of the litigation contrary to Rule 1.8(j). However, a fee paid in property instead of money may be subject to special scrutiny because it involves questions concerning both the value of the services and the lawyer's special knowledge of the value of the property.

An agreement may not be made whose terms might induce the lawyer improperly to curtail services for the client or perform them in a way contrary to the client's interest. For example, a lawyer should not enter into an agreement whereby services are to be provided only up to a stated amount when it is foreseeable that more extensive services probably will be required, unless the situation is adequately explained to the client. Otherwise, the client might have to bargain for further assistance in the midst of a proceeding or transaction. However, it is proper to define the extent of services in light of the client's ability to pay. A lawyer should not exploit a fee arrangement based primarily on hourly charges by using wasteful procedures. When there is doubt whether a contingent fee is consistent with the client's best interest, the lawyer should offer the client alternative bases for the fee and explain their implications. Applicable law may impose limitations on contingent fees, such as a ceiling on the percentage. See MCR 8.121.

Division of Fee. A division of fee is a single billing to a client covering the fee of two or more lawyers who are not in the same firm. A division of fee facilitates association of more than one lawyer in a matter in which neither alone could serve the client as well, and most often is used when the fee is contingent and the division is between a referring lawyer and a trial specialist. Paragraph (e) permits the lawyers to divide a fee on agreement between the participating lawyers if the client is advised and does not object. It does not require disclosure to the client of the share that each lawyer is to receive.

Disputes Over Fees. If a procedure has been established for resolution of fee disputes, such as an arbitration or mediation procedure established by the bar, the lawyer should conscientiously consider submitting to it. Law may prescribe a procedure for determining a lawyer's fee, for example, in representation of an executor or administrator, of a class, or of a person entitled to a reasonable fee as part of the measure of damages. The lawyer entitled to such a fee and a lawyer representing another party concerned with the fee should comply with the prescribed procedure.

Staff Comment to 1998 Amendment

The amendment of paragraph c, adopted February 5, 1998, and effective April 1, 1998, clarified that this rule's provisions apply to all contingent fee agreements, not just to those covered by MCR 8.121.

RULE 1.6 CONFIDENTIALITY OF INFORMATION

(a) "Confidence" refers to information protected by the client-lawyer privilege under applicable law, and "secret" refers to other information gained in the professional relationship that the client has requested be held inviolate or the disclosure of which would be embarrassing or would be likely to be detrimental to the client.

(b) Except when permitted under paragraph (c), a lawyer shall not knowingly:

(1) reveal a confidence or secret of a client;

(2) use a confidence or secret of a client to the disadvantage of the client; or

(3) use a confidence or secret of a client for the advantage of the lawyer or of a third person, unless the client consents after full disclosure.

(c) A lawyer may reveal:

(1) confidences or secrets with the consent of the client or clients affected, but only after full disclosure to them;

(2) confidences or secrets when permitted or required by these rules, or when required by law or by court order;

(3) confidences and secrets to the extent reasonably necessary to rectify the consequences of a client's illegal or fraudulent act in the furtherance of which the lawyer's services have been used;

(4) the intention of a client to commit a crime and the information necessary to prevent the crime; and

(5) confidences or secrets necessary to establish or collect a fee, or to defend the lawyer or the lawyer's employees or associates against an accusation of wrongful conduct.

(d) A lawyer shall exercise reasonable care to prevent employees, associates, and others whose services are utilized by the lawyer from disclosing or using confidences or secrets of a client, except that a lawyer may reveal the information allowed by paragraph (c) through an employee.

Comment

The lawyer is part of a judicial system charged with upholding the law. One of the lawyer's functions is to advise clients so that they avoid any violation of the law in the proper exercise of their rights.

The observance of the ethical obligation of a lawyer to hold inviolate confidential information of the client not only facilitates the full development of facts essential to proper representation of the client, but also encourages people to seek early legal assistance.

Almost without exception, clients come to lawyers in order to determine what their rights are and what is, in the maze of laws and regulations, deemed to be legal and correct. The common law recognizes that the client's confidences must be protected from disclosure. Upon the basis of experience, lawyers know that almost all clients follow the advice given and that the law is upheld.

A fundamental principle in the client-lawyer relationship is that the lawyer maintain confidentiality of information relating to the representation. The client is thereby encouraged to communicate fully and frankly with the lawyer even as to embarrassing or legally damaging subject matter.

The principle of confidentiality is given effect in two related bodies of law, the client-lawyer privilege (which includes the work-product doctrine) in the law of evidence and the rule of confidentiality established in professional ethics. The client-lawyer privilege applies in judicial and other proceedings in which a lawyer may be called as a witness or otherwise required to produce evidence concerning a client. The rule of client-lawyer confidentiality applies in situations other than those where evidence is sought from the lawyer through compulsion of law. The confidentiality rule applies to confidences and secrets as defined in the rule. A lawyer

may not disclose such information except as authorized or required by the Rules of Professional Conduct or other law. See also Scope, ante.

The requirement of maintaining confidentiality of information relating to representation applies to government lawyers who may disagree with the policy goals that their representation is designed to advance.

Authorized Disclosure. A lawyer is impliedly authorized to make disclosures about a client when appropriate in carrying out the representation, except to the extent that the client's instructions or special circumstances limit that authority. In litigation, for example, a lawyer may disclose information by admitting a fact that cannot properly be disputed, or, in negotiation, by making a disclosure that facilitates a satisfactory conclusion.

Lawyers in a firm may, in the course of the firm's practice, disclose to each other information relating to a client of the firm, unless the client has instructed that particular information be confined to specified lawyers, or unless the disclosure would breach a screen erected within the firm in accordance with Rules 1.10(b), 1.11(a), or 1.12(c).

Disclosure Adverse to Client. The confidentiality rule is subject to limited exceptions. In becoming privy to information about a client, a lawyer may foresee that the client intends to commit a crime. To the extent a lawyer is prohibited from making disclosure, the interests of the potential victim are sacrificed in favor of preserving the client's confidences even though the client's purpose is wrongful. To the extent a lawyer is required or permitted to disclose a client's purposes, the client may be inhibited from revealing facts which would enable the lawyer to counsel against a wrongful course of action. A rule governing disclosure of threatened harm thus involves balancing the interests of one group of potential victims against those of another. On the assumption that lawyers generally fulfill their duty to advise against the commission of deliberately wrongful acts, the public is better protected if full and open communication by the client is encouraged than if it is inhibited.

Generally speaking, information relating to the representation must be kept confidential as stated in paragraph (b). However, when the client is or will be engaged in criminal conduct or the integrity of the lawyer's own conduct is involved, the principle of confidentiality may appropriately yield, depending on the lawyer's knowledge about and relationship to the conduct in question, and the seriousness of that conduct. Several situations must be distinguished.

First, the lawyer may not counsel or assist a client in conduct that is illegal or fraudulent. See Rule 1.2(c). Similarly, a lawyer has a duty under Rule 3.3(a)(4) not to use false evidence. This duty is essentially a special instance of the duty prescribed in Rule 1.2(c) to avoid assisting a client in illegal or fraudulent conduct. The same is true of compliance with Rule 4.1 concerning truthfulness of a lawyer's own representations.

Second, the lawyer may have been innocently involved in past conduct by the client that was criminal or fraudulent. In such a situation the lawyer has not violated Rule 1.2(c), because to "counsel or assist" criminal or fraudulent conduct requires knowing that the conduct is of that character. Even if the involvement was innocent, however, the fact remains that the lawyer's professional services were made the instrument of the client's crime or fraud. The lawyer, therefore, has a legitimate interest in being able to rectify the consequences of such conduct, and has the professional right, although not a professional duty, to rectify the situation. Exercising that right may require revealing information relating to the representation. Paragraph (c)(3) gives the lawyer professional discretion to reveal such information to the extent necessary to accomplish rectification. However, the constitutional rights of defendants in criminal cases may limit the extent to which counsel for a defendant may correct a misrepresentation that is based on information provided by the client. See comment to Rule 3.3.

Third, the lawyer may learn that a client intends prospective conduct that is criminal. Inaction by the lawyer is not a violation of Rule 1.2(c), except in the limited circumstances where failure to act constitutes assisting the client. See comment to Rule 1.2(c). However, the lawyer's knowledge of the client's purpose may enable the lawyer to prevent commission of the prospective crime. If the prospective crime is likely to result in substantial injury, the lawyer may feel a moral obligation to take preventive action. When the threatened injury is grave, such as homicide or serious bodily injury, a lawyer may have an obligation under tort or criminal law to take reasonable preventive measures. Whether the lawyer's concern is based on moral or legal considerations, the interest in preventing the harm may be more compelling than the interest in preserving confidentiality of information relating to the client. As stated in paragraph (c)(4), the lawyer has professional discretion to reveal information in order to prevent a client's criminal act.

It is arguable that the lawyer should have a professional obligation to make a disclosure in order to prevent homicide or serious bodily injury which the lawyer knows is intended by the client. However, it is very difficult for a lawyer to "know" when such a heinous purpose will actually be carried out, for the client may have a change of mind. To require disclosure when the client intends such an act, at the risk of professional discipline if the assessment of the client's purpose turns out to be wrong, would be to impose a penal risk that might interfere with the lawyer's resolution of an inherently difficult moral dilemma.

The lawyer's exercise of discretion requires consideration of such factors as magnitude, proximity, and likelihood of the contemplated wrong; the nature of the lawyer's relationship with the client and with those who might be injured by the client; the lawyer's own involvement in the transaction; and factors that may extenuate the conduct in question. Where practical, the lawyer should seek to persuade the client to take suitable action. In any case, a disclosure adverse to the client's interest should be no greater than the lawyer reasonably believes necessary to the purpose. A lawyer's decision not to make a disclosure permitted by paragraph (c) does not violate this rule.

Where the client is an organization, the lawyer may be in doubt whether contemplated conduct will actually be carried out by the organization. Where necessary to guide conduct in connection with this rule, the lawyer should make an inquiry within the organization as indicated in Rule 1.13(b).

Paragraph (c)(3) does not apply where a lawyer is employed after a crime or fraud has been committed to represent the client in matters ensuing therefrom.

Withdrawal. If the lawyer's services will be used by the client in materially furthering a course of criminal or fraudulent conduct, the lawyer must withdraw, as stated in Rule 1.16(a)(1).

After withdrawal the lawyer is required to refrain from making disclosure of the client's confidences, except as otherwise provided in Rule 1.6. Neither this rule nor Rule 1.8(b) nor Rule 1.16(d) prevents the lawyer from giving notice of the fact of withdrawal, and the lawyer may also withdraw or disaffirm any opinion, document, affirmation, or the like.

Dispute Concerning Lawyer's Conduct. Where a legal claim or disciplinary charge alleges complicity of the lawyer in a client's conduct or other misconduct of the lawyer involving representation of the client, the lawyer may respond to the extent the lawyer reasonably believes necessary to establish a defense. The same is true with respect to a claim involving the conduct or representation of a former client. The lawyer's right to respond arises when an assertion of complicity or other misconduct has been made. Paragraph (c)(5) does not require the lawyer to await the commencement of an action or proceeding that charges complicity or other misconduct, so that the defense may be established by responding directly to a third party who has made such an assertion. The right to defend, of course, applies where a proceeding has been commenced. Where practicable and not prejudicial to the lawyer's ability to establish the defense, the lawyer should advise the client of the third party's assertion and request that the client respond appropriately. In any event, disclosure should be no greater than the lawyer reasonably believes is necessary to vindicate innocence, the disclosure should be made in a manner which limits access to the information to the tribunal or other persons having a need to know it, and appropriate protective orders or other arrangements should be sought by the lawyer to the fullest extent practicable.

If the lawyer is charged with wrongdoing in which the client's conduct is implicated, the rule of confidentiality should not prevent the lawyer from defending against the charge. Such a charge can arise in a civil, criminal, or professional disciplinary proceeding, and can be based on a wrong allegedly committed by the lawyer against the client, or on a wrong alleged by a third person, for example, a person claiming to have been defrauded by the lawyer and client acting together.

A lawyer entitled to a fee is permitted by paragraph (c)(5) to prove the services rendered in an action to collect it. This aspect of the rule expresses the principle that the beneficiary of a fiduciary relationship may not exploit it to the detriment of the fiduciary. As stated above, the lawyer must make every effort practicable to avoid unnecessary disclosure of information relating to a representation, to limit disclosure to those having the need to know it, and to obtain protective orders or make other arrangements minimizing the risk of disclosure.

Disclosures Otherwise Required or Authorized. The scope of the client-lawyer privilege is a question of law. If a lawyer is called as a witness to give testimony concerning a client, absent waiver by the client, paragraph (b)(1) requires the lawyer to invoke the privilege when it is applicable. The lawyer must comply with the final orders of a court or other tribunal of competent jurisdiction requiring the lawyer to give information about the client.

The Rules of Professional Conduct in various circumstances permit or require a lawyer to disclose information relating to the representation. See Rules 2.2, 2.3, 3.3 and 4.1. In addition to these provisions, a lawyer may be obligated or permitted by other provisions of law to give information about a client. Whether another provision of law supersedes Rule 1.6 is a matter of interpretation beyond the scope of these rules, but a presumption should exist against such a supersession.

Former Client. The duty of confidentiality continues after the client-lawyer relationship has terminated. See Rule 1.9.

RULE 1.7 CONFLICT OF INTEREST: GENERAL RULE

(a) A lawyer shall not represent a client if the representation of that client will be directly adverse to another client, unless:

(1) the lawyer reasonably believes the representation will not adversely affect the relationship with the other client; and

(2) each client consents after consultation.

(b) A lawyer shall not represent a client if the representation of that client may be materially limited by the lawyer's responsibilities to another client or to a third person, or by the lawyer's own interests, unless:

(1) the lawyer reasonably believes the representation will not be adversely affected; and

(2) the client consents after consultation. When representation of multiple clients in a single matter is undertaken, the consultation shall include explanation of the implications of the common representation and the advantages and risks involved.

[Amended effective June 7, 1989.]

Comment

Loyalty to a Client. Loyalty is an essential element in the lawyer's relationship to a client. An impermissible conflict of interest may exist before representation is undertaken, in which event the representation should be declined. The lawyer should adopt reasonable procedures, appropriate for the size and type of firm and practice, to determine in both litigation and nonlitigation matters the parties and issues involved and to determine whether there are actual or potential conflicts of interest.

If such a conflict arises after representation has been undertaken, the lawyer should withdraw from the representation. See Rule 1.16. Where more than one client is involved and the lawyer withdraws because a conflict arises after representation, whether the lawyer may continue to represent any of the clients is determined by Rule 1.9. See also Rule 2.2(c). As to whether a client-lawyer relationship exists or, having once been established, is continuing, see comment to Rule 1.3 and Scope, ante.

As a general proposition, loyalty to a client prohibits undertaking representation directly adverse to that client without that client's consent. Paragraph (a) expresses that general rule. Thus, a lawyer ordinarily may not act as advocate against a person the lawyer represents in some other matter, even if it is wholly unrelated. On the other hand, simultaneous representation in unrelated matters of clients whose interests are only generally adverse, such as competing economic enterprises, does not require consent of the respective clients. Paragraph (a) applies only when the representation of one client would be directly adverse to the other.

Loyalty to a client is also impaired when a lawyer cannot consider, recommend, or carry out an appropriate course of action for the client because of the lawyer's other responsibilities or interests. The conflict in effect forecloses alternatives that would otherwise be available to the client. Paragraph (b) addresses such situations. A possible conflict does not itself preclude the representation. The critical questions are the likelihood that a conflict will eventuate and, if it does, whether it will materially interfere with the lawyer's independent professional judgment in considering alternatives or foreclose courses of action that reasonably should be pursued on behalf of the client. Consideration should be given to whether the client wishes to accommodate the other interest involved.

Consultation and Consent. A client may consent to representation notwithstanding a conflict. However, as indicated in paragraph (a)(1) with respect to representation directly adverse to a client, and paragraph (b)(1) with respect to material limitations on representation of a client, when a disinterested lawyer would conclude that the client should not agree to the representation under the circumstances, the lawyer involved cannot properly ask for such agreement or provide representation on the basis of the client's consent. When more than one client is involved, the question of conflict must be resolved as to each client. Moreover, there may be circumstances where it is impossible to make the disclosure necessary to obtain consent. For example, when the lawyer represents different clients in related matters and one of the clients refuses to consent to the disclosure necessary to permit the other client to make an informed decision, the lawyer cannot properly ask the latter to consent.

Lawyer's Interests. The lawyer's own interests should not be permitted to have adverse effect on representation of a client. For example, a lawyer's need for income should not lead the lawyer to undertake matters that cannot be handled competently and at a reasonable fee. See Rules 1.1 and 1.5. If the probity of a lawyer's own conduct in a transaction is in serious question, it may be difficult or impossible for the lawyer to give a client detached advice. A lawyer may not allow related business interests to affect representation, for example, by referring clients to an enterprise in which the lawyer has an undisclosed interest.

Conflicts in Litigation. Paragraph (a) prohibits representation of opposing parties in litigation. Simultaneous representation of parties whose interests in litigation may conflict, such as coplaintiffs or codefendants, is governed by paragraph (b). An impermissible conflict may exist by reason of substantial discrepancy in the parties' testimony, incompatibility in positions in relation to an opposing party, or the fact that there are substantially different possibilities of settlement of the claims or liabilities in question. Such conflicts can arise in criminal cases as well as civil. The potential for conflict of interest in representing multiple defendants in a criminal case is so grave that ordinarily a lawyer should decline to represent more than one codefendant. On the other hand, common representation of persons having similar interests is proper if the risk of adverse effect is minimal and the requirements of paragraph (b) are met. Compare Rule 2.2 involving intermediation between clients.

Ordinarily, a lawyer may not act as advocate against a client the lawyer represents in some other matter, even if the other matter is wholly unrelated. However, there are circumstances in which a lawyer may act as advocate against a client. For example, a lawyer representing an enterprise with diverse operations may accept employment as an advocate against the enterprise in an unrelated matter if doing so will not adversely affect the lawyer's relationship with the enterprise or conduct of the suit and if both clients consent upon consultation. By the same token, government lawyers in some circumstances may represent government employees in proceedings in which a government agency is the opposing party. The propriety of concurrent representation can depend on the nature of the litigation. For example, a suit charging fraud entails conflict to a degree not involved in a suit for a declaratory judgment concerning statutory interpretation.

Interest of Person Paying for a Lawyer's Service. A lawyer may be paid from a source other than the client if the client is informed of that fact and consents and the arrangement does not compromise the lawyer's duty of loyalty to the client. See Rule 1.8(f). For example, when an insurer and its insured have conflicting interests in a matter arising from a liability insurance agreement, and the insurer is required to provide special counsel for the insured, the arrangement should assure the special counsel's professional independence. So also, when a corporation and its directors or employees are involved in a controversy in which they have conflicting interests, the corporation may provide funds for separate legal representation of the directors or employees if the clients consent after consultation and the arrangement ensures the lawyer's professional independence.

Other Conflict Situations. Conflicts of interest in contexts other than litigation sometimes may be difficult to assess. Relevant factors in determining whether there is potential for adverse effect include the duration and intimacy of the lawyer's relationship with the client or clients involved, the functions being performed by the lawyer, the likelihood that actual conflict will arise, and the likely prejudice to the client from the conflict if it does arise. The question is often one of proximity and degree.

For example, a lawyer may not represent multiple parties in a negotiation whose interests are fundamentally antagonistic to each other, but common representation is permissible where the clients are generally aligned in interest even though there is some difference of interest among them.

Conflict questions may also arise in estate planning and estate administration. A lawyer may be called upon to prepare wills for several family members, such as husband and wife, and, depending upon the circumstances, a conflict of interest may arise. In estate administration the identity of the client may be a question of law. The lawyer should make clear the relationship to the parties involved.

A lawyer for a corporation or other organization who is also a member of its board of directors should determine whether the responsibilities of the two roles may conflict. The lawyer may be called on to advise the corporation in matters involving actions of the directors. Consideration should be given to the frequency with which such situations may arise, the potential intensity of the conflict, the effect of the lawyer's resignation from the board, and the possibility of the corporation's obtaining legal advice from another lawyer in such situations. If there is material risk that the dual role will compromise the lawyer's independence of professional judgment, the lawyer should not serve as a director.

Conflict Charged by an Opposing Party. Resolving questions of conflict of interest is primarily the responsibility of the lawyer undertaking the representation. In litigation, a court may raise the question when there is reason to infer that the lawyer has neglected the responsibility. In a criminal case, inquiry by the court is generally required when a lawyer represents multiple defendants. See MCR 6.101(C)(4). Where the conflict is such as clearly to call in question the fair or efficient administration of justice, opposing counsel may properly raise the question. Such an objection should be viewed with caution, however, for it can be misused as a technique of harassment. See Scope, *ante.*

Staff Comment

The 1989 amendment inserts a phrase ("the relationship with") that was part of Rule 1.7(a)(1) of the American Bar Association's Model Rules, but which was omitted when Rule 1.7 was originally promulgated by the Michigan Supreme Court.

RULE 1.8 CONFLICT OF INTEREST: PROHIBITED TRANSACTIONS

(a) A lawyer shall not enter into a business transaction with a client or knowingly acquire an ownership, possessory, security, or other pecuniary interest adverse to a client unless:

(1) the transaction and terms on which the lawyer acquires the interest are fair and reasonable to the client and are fully disclosed and transmitted in writing to the client in a manner that can be reasonably understood by the client;

(2) the client is given a reasonable opportunity to seek the advice of independent counsel in the transaction; and

(3) the client consents in writing thereto.

(b) A lawyer shall not use information relating to representation of a client to the disadvantage of the client unless the client consents after consultation, except as permitted or required by Rule 1.6 or Rule 3.3.

(c) A lawyer shall not prepare an instrument giving the lawyer or a person related to the lawyer as parent, child, sibling, or spouse any substantial gift from a client, including a testamentary gift, except where the client is related to the donee.

(d) Prior to the conclusion of representation of a client, a lawyer shall not make or negotiate an agreement giving the lawyer literary or media rights to a portrayal or account based in substantial part on information relating to the representation.

(e) A lawyer shall not provide financial assistance to a client in connection with pending or contemplated litigation, except that

(1) a lawyer may advance court costs and expenses of litigation, the repayment of which shall ultimately be the responsibility of the client; and

(2) a lawyer representing an indigent client may pay court costs and expenses of litigation on behalf of the client.

(f) A lawyer shall not accept compensation for representing a client from one other than the client unless:

(1) the client consents after consultation;

(2) there is no interference with the lawyer's independence of professional judgment or with the client-lawyer relationship; and

(3) information relating to representation of a client is protected as required by Rule 1.6.

(g) A lawyer who represents two or more clients shall not participate in making an aggregate settlement of the claims of or against the clients, or, in a criminal case, an aggregated agreement as to guilty or nolo contendere pleas, unless each client consents after consultation, including disclosure of the existence and nature of all the claims or pleas involved and of the participation of each person in the settlement.

(h) A lawyer shall not:

(1) make an agreement prospectively limiting the lawyer's liability to a client for malpractice unless permitted by law and the client is independently represented in making the agreement; or

(2) settle a claim for such liability with an unrepresented client or former client without first advising that person in writing that independent representation is appropriate in connection therewith.

(i) A lawyer related to another lawyer as parent, child, sibling, or spouse shall not represent a client in a representation directly adverse to a person whom the lawyer knows is represented by the other lawyer except upon consent by the client after consultation regarding the relationship.

(j) A lawyer shall not acquire a proprietary interest in the cause of action or subject matter of litigation the lawyer is conducting for a client, except that the lawyer may:

(1) acquire a lien granted by law to secure the lawyer's fee or expenses; and

(2) contract with a client for a reasonable contingent fee in a civil case, as permitted by Rule 1.5 and MCR 8.121.

Comment

Transactions Between Client and Lawyer. As a general principle, all transactions between client and lawyer should be fair and reasonable to the client. In such transactions a review by independent counsel on behalf of the client is often advisable. Furthermore, a lawyer may not exploit information relating to the representation to the client's disadvantage. For example, a lawyer who has learned that the client is investing in specific real estate may not, without the client's consent, seek to acquire nearby property where doing so would adversely affect the client's plan for investment. Paragraph (a) does not, however, apply to standard commercial transactions between the lawyer and the client for products or services that the client generally markets to others, for example, banking or brokerage services, medical services, products manufactured or distributed by the client, and utilities' services. In such transactions, the lawyer has no advantage in dealing with the client, and the restrictions in paragraph (a) are unnecessary and impractical.

A lawyer may accept a gift from a client if the transaction meets general standards of fairness. For example, a simple gift such as a present given at a holiday or as a token of appreciation is permitted. If effectuation of a substantial gift requires preparing a legal instrument such as a will or conveyance, however, the client should have the detached advice that another lawyer can provide. Paragraph (c) recognizes an exception where the client is a relative of the donee or the gift is not substantial.

Literary Rights. An agreement by which a lawyer acquires literary or media rights concerning the conduct of the representation creates a conflict between the interests of the client and the personal interests of the lawyer. Measures suitable in the representation of the client may detract from the publication value of an account of the representation. Paragraph (d) does not prohibit a lawyer representing a client in a transaction concerning literary property from agreeing that the lawyer's fee shall consist of a share in ownership in the property, if the arrangement conforms to Rule 1.5 and paragraph (j).

Person Paying for Lawyer's Services. Paragraph (f) requires disclosure of the fact that the lawyer's services are being paid for by a third party. Such an arrangement must also conform to the requirements of Rule 1.6 concerning confidentiality and Rule 1.7 concerning conflict of interest. Where the client is a class, consent may be obtained on behalf of the class by court-supervised procedure.

Limiting Liability. Paragraph (h) is not intended to apply to customary qualifications and limitations in legal opinions and memoranda.

Family Relationships Between Lawyers. Paragraph (i) applies to related lawyers who are in different firms. Related lawyers in the same firm are governed by Rules 1.7, 1.9, and 1.10. The disqualification stated in paragraph (i) is personal and is not imputed to members of firms with whom the lawyers are associated.

Acquisition of Interest in Litigation. Paragraph (j) states the traditional general rule that lawyers are prohibited from acquiring a proprietary interest in litigation. This general rule, which has its basis in common-law champerty and maintenance, is subject to specific exceptions developed in decisional law and continued in these rules, such as the exception for reasonable contingent fees set forth in Rule 1.5 and the exception for certain advances of the costs of litigation set forth in paragraph (e).

Sexual Relations with Clients. After careful study, the Supreme Court declined in 1998 to adopt a proposal to amend Rule 1.8 to limit sexual relationships between lawyers and clients. The Michigan Rules of Professional Conduct adequately prohibit representation that lacks competence or diligence, or that is shadowed by a conflict of interest. With regard to sexual behavior, the Michigan Court Rules provide that a lawyer may be disciplined for "conduct that is contrary to justice, ethics, honesty, or good morals." MCR 9.104(3). Further, the Legislature has enacted criminal penalties for certain types of sexual misconduct. In this regard, it should be emphasized that a lawyer bears a fiduciary responsibility toward the client. A lawyer who has a conflict of interest, whose actions interfere with effective representation, who takes advantage of a client's vulnerability, or whose behavior is immoral risks severe sanctions under the existing Michigan Court Rules and Michigan Rules of Professional Conduct.

[Comment amended effective October 15, 1998.]

RULE 1.9   CONFLICT OF INTEREST: FORMER CLIENT

(a) A lawyer who has formerly represented a client in a matter shall not thereafter represent another person in the same or a substantially related matter in which that person's interests are materially adverse to the interests of the former client unless the former client consents after consultation.

(b) Unless the former client consents after consultation, a lawyer shall not knowingly represent a person in the same or a substantially related matter in which a firm with which the lawyer formerly was associated has previously represented a client

(1) whose interests are materially adverse to that person, and

(2) about whom the lawyer had acquired information protected by Rules 1.6 and 1.9(c) that is material to the matter.

(c) A lawyer who has formerly represented a client in a matter or whose present or former firm has formerly represented a client in a matter shall not thereafter:

(1) use information relating to the representation to the disadvantage of the former client except as Rule 1.6 or Rule 3.3 would permit or require with respect to a client, or when the information has become generally known; or

(2) reveal information relating to the representation except as Rule 1.6 or Rule 3.3 would permit or require with respect to a client.

[Amended effective August 1, 1990.]

Comment

After termination of a client-lawyer relationship, a lawyer may not represent another client except in conformity with this rule. The principles in Rule 1.7 determine whether the interests of the present and former client are adverse. Thus, a lawyer could not properly seek to rescind on behalf of a new client a contract drafted on behalf of the former client. So also a lawyer who has prosecuted an accused person could not properly represent the accused in a subsequent civil action against the government concerning the same transaction.

The scope of a "matter" for purposes of this rule may depend on the facts of a particular situation or transaction. The lawyer's involvement in a matter can also be a question of degree. When a lawyer has been directly involved in a specific transaction, subsequent representation of other clients with materially adverse interests clearly is prohibited. On the other hand, a lawyer who recurrently handled a type of problem for a former client is not precluded from later representing another client in a wholly distinct problem of that type even though the subsequent representation involves a position adverse to the prior client. Similar considerations can apply to the reassignment of military lawyers between defense and prosecution functions within the same military jurisdiction. The underlying question is whether the lawyer was so involved in the matter that the subsequent representation can be justly regarded as a changing of sides in the matter in question.

Lawyers Moving Between Firms. When lawyers have been associated in a firm but then end their association, the problem is more complicated. First, the client previously represented must be reasonably assured that the principle of loyalty to the client is not compromised. Second, the rule of disqualification should not be so broadly cast as to preclude other persons from having reasonable choice of legal counsel. Third, the rule of disqualification should not unreasonably hamper lawyers from forming new associations and taking on new clients after having left a previous association. In this connection, it should be recognized that today many lawyers practice in firms, that many, to some degree, limit their practice to one field or another, and that many move from one association to another several times in their careers. If the concept of imputed disqualification were applied with unqualified rigor, the result would be radical curtailment of the opportunity of lawyers to move from one practice setting to another and of the opportunity of clients to change counsel.

Reconciliation of these competing principles in the past has been attempted under two rubrics. One approach has been to seek rules of disqualification per se. For example, it has been held that a partner in a law firm is conclusively presumed to have access to all confidences concerning all clients of the firm. Under this analysis, if a lawyer has been a partner in one law firm and then becomes a partner in another law firm, there is a presumption that all confidences known by a partner in the first firm are known to all partners in the second firm. This presumption might properly be applied in some circumstances, especially where the client has been extensively represented, but may be unrealistic where the client was represented only for limited purposes. Furthermore, such a rigid rule exaggerates the difference between a partner and an associate in modern law firms.

The other rubric formerly used for dealing with vicarious disqualification is the appearance of impropriety proscribed in Canon 9 of the Michigan Code of Professional Responsibility. Two problems can arise under this rubric. First, the appearance of impropriety might be understood to include any new client-lawyer relationship that might make a former client feel anxious. If that meaning were adopted, disqualification would become little more than a question of subjective judgment by the former client. Second, since "impropriety" is undefined, the term "appearance of impropriety" begs the question. Thus, the problem of imputed disqualification cannot readily be resolved either by simple analogy to a lawyer practicing alone or by the very general concept of appearance of impropriety.

A rule based on a functional analysis is more appropriate for determining the question of vicarious disqualification. Two functions are involved: preserving confidentiality and avoiding positions adverse to a client.

Under Rule 1.10(b), screening may be employed to preserve the confidences of a client when a lawyer has moved from one firm to another. Rule 1.10(b) applies not just to cases in which a lawyer's present and former firms are involved on the date the lawyer moves. The paragraph also applies where the lawyer's present firm later wishes to enter a case from which the lawyer is barred because of information acquired while associated with the prior firm.

Confidentiality. Preserving confidentiality is a question of access to information. Access to information, in turn, is essentially a question of fact in particular circumstances. The determination of that question of fact can be aided by inferences, deductions, or assumptions that reasonably may be made about the way in which lawyers work together. A lawyer may have general access to files of all clients of a law firm and may regularly participate in discussions of their affairs; it should be inferred that such a lawyer in fact is privy to all information about all the firm's clients. In contrast, another lawyer may have access to the files of only a limited number of clients and participate in discussion of the affairs of no other clients; in the absence of information to the contrary, it should be inferred that such a lawyer in fact is privy to information about the clients actually served but not those of other clients.

Application of paragraph (b) depends on a situation's particular facts. In any such inquiry, the burden of proof should rest upon the lawyer whose disqualification is sought.

Rule 1.10(b), incorporating paragraph (b) of this rule, operates to disqualify the firm only when the lawyer involved has actual knowledge of information protected by Rules 1.6 and 1.9(c). Thus, if a lawyer while with one firm acquired no knowledge of information relating to a particular client of the firm, and that lawyer later joined another firm, neither the lawyer individually nor the second firm is disqualified from representing another client in the same or a related matter even though the interests of the two clients conflict. See Rule 1.10(c) for the restrictions on a firm once a lawyer has terminated association with the firm.

Independent of the question of disqualification of a firm, a lawyer changing professional association has a continuing duty to preserve confidentiality of information about a client formerly represented. See Rule 1.6.

Adverse Positions. The second aspect of loyalty to a client is the lawyer's obligation to decline subsequent representations involving positions adverse to a former client arising in substantially related matters. This obligation requires abstention from adverse representation by the individual lawyer involved, but does not properly entail abstention of other lawyers through imputed disqualification. Thus, if a lawyer left one firm for another, the new affiliation would not preclude the firms involved from continuing to represent clients with adverse interests in the same or related matters, so long as the conditions of Rule 1.10(b) and (c) have been met.

Information acquired by the lawyer in the course of representing a client may not subsequently be used or revealed by the lawyer to the disadvantage of the client. However, the fact that a lawyer has once served a client does not preclude the lawyer from using generally known information about that client when later representing another client.

Disqualification from subsequent representation is for the protection of clients and can be waived by them. A waiver is effective only if there is disclosure of the circumstances, including the lawyer's intended role in behalf of the new client.

With regard to an opposing party raising a question of conflict of interest, see comment to Rule 1.7. With regard to disqualification of a firm with which a lawyer is or was formerly associated, see Rule 1.10.

RULE 1.10 IMPUTED DISQUALIFICATION: GENERAL RULE

(a) While lawyers are associated in a firm, none of them shall knowingly represent a client when any one

of them practicing alone would be prohibited from doing so by Rules 1.7, 1.8(c), 1.9(a) or (c), or 2.2.

(b) When a lawyer becomes associated with a firm, the firm may not knowingly represent a person in the same or a substantially related matter in which that lawyer, or a firm with which the lawyer was associated, is disqualified under Rule 1.9(b), unless:

(1) the disqualified lawyer is screened from any participation in the matter and is apportioned no part of the fee therefrom; and

(2) written notice is promptly given to the appropriate tribunal to enable it to ascertain compliance with the provisions of this rule.

(c) When a lawyer has terminated an association with a firm, the firm is not prohibited from thereafter representing a person with interests materially adverse to those of a client represented by the formerly associated lawyer, and not currently represented by the firm, unless:

(1) the matter is the same or substantially related to that in which the formerly associated lawyer represented the client; and

(2) any lawyer remaining in the firm has information protected by Rules 1.6 and 1.9(c) that is material to the matter.

(d) A disqualification prescribed by this rule may be waived by the affected client under the conditions stated in Rule 1.7.

[Amended effective August 1, 1990.]

Comment

Definition of "Firm". For purposes of these rules, the term "firm" includes lawyers in a private firm and lawyers employed in the legal department of a corporation or other organization or in a legal services organization. Whether two or more lawyers constitute a firm within this definition can depend on the specific facts. For example, two practitioners who share office space and occasionally consult or assist each other ordinarily would not be regarded as constituting a firm. However, if they present themselves to the public in a way suggesting that they are a firm or conduct themselves as a firm, they should be regarded as a firm for purposes of the rules. The terms of any formal agreement between associated lawyers are relevant in determining whether they are a firm, as is the fact that they have mutual access to confidential information concerning the clients they serve. Furthermore, it is relevant in doubtful cases to consider the underlying purpose of the rule that is involved. A group of lawyers could be regarded as a firm for purposes of the rule that the same lawyer should not represent opposing parties in litigation, while it might not be so regarded for purposes of the rule that information acquired by one lawyer is attributed to another.

With respect to the law department of an organization, there is ordinarily no question that the members of the department constitute a firm within the meaning of the Rules of Professional Conduct. However, there can be uncertainty as to the identity of the client. For example, it may not be clear whether the law department of a corporation represents a subsidiary or an affiliated corporation, as well as the corporation by which the members of the department are directly employed. A similar question can arise concerning an unincorporated association and its local affiliates.

Similar questions can also arise with respect to lawyers in legal aid. Lawyers employed in the same unit of a legal service organization constitute a firm, but not necessarily those employed in separate units. As in the case of independent practitioners, whether the lawyers should be treated as being associated with each other can depend on the particular rule that is involved and on the specific facts of the situation.

Where a lawyer has joined a private firm after having represented the government, the situation is governed by Rule 1.11(a) and (b); where a lawyer represents the government after having served private clients, the situation is governed by Rule 1.11(c)(1). The individual lawyer involved is bound by the rules generally, including Rules 1.6, 1.7, and 1.9.

Principles of Imputed Disqualification. The rule of imputed disqualification stated in paragraph (a) gives effect to the principle of loyalty to the client as it applies to lawyers who practice in a law firm. Such situations can be considered from the premise that a firm of lawyers is essentially one lawyer for purposes of the rules governing loyalty to the client, or from the premise that each lawyer is vicariously bound by the obligation of loyalty owed by each lawyer with whom the lawyer is associated. Paragraph (a) operates only among the lawyers currently associated in a firm. When a lawyer moves or has recently moved from one firm to another, the situation is governed by Rules 1.9(b) and 1.10(b).

Rule 1.10(b) operates to permit a law firm, under certain circumstances, to represent a person with interests directly adverse to those of a client represented by a lawyer who formerly was associated with the firm. The rule applies regardless of when the formerly associated lawyer represented the client. However, the law firm may not represent a person with interests adverse to those of a present client of the firm, which would violate Rule 1.7. Moreover, the firm may not represent the person where the matter is the same or substantially related to that in which the formerly associated lawyer represented the client and any other lawyer currently in the firm has material information protected by Rules 1.6 and 1.9(c), unless this rule's provisions are followed.

RULE 1.11 SUCCESSIVE GOVERNMENT AND PRIVATE EMPLOYMENT

(a) Except as law may otherwise expressly permit, a lawyer shall not represent a private client in connection with a matter in which the lawyer participated personally and substantially as a public officer or employee, unless the appropriate government agency consents after consultation. No lawyer in a firm with which that lawyer is associated may knowingly undertake or continue representation in such a matter, unless:

(1) the disqualified lawyer is screened from any participation in the matter and is apportioned no part of the fee therefrom; and

(2) written notice is promptly given to the appropriate government agency to enable it to ascertain compliance with the provisions of this rule.

(b) Except as law may otherwise expressly permit, a lawyer having information that the lawyer knows is confidential government information about a person, acquired when the lawyer was a public officer or employee, may not represent a private client whose interests are adverse to that person in a matter in which the information could be used to the material disadvantage of that person. A firm with which that lawyer is associated may undertake or continue representation in the matter only if the disqualified lawyer is screened from any participation in the matter and is apportioned no part of the fee therefrom.

(c) Except as law may otherwise expressly permit, a lawyer serving as a public officer or employee shall not:

(1) participate in a matter in which the lawyer participated personally and substantially while in private practice or nongovernmental employment, unless under applicable law no one is, or by lawful delegation may be, authorized to act in the lawyer's stead in the matter; or

(2) negotiate for private employment with any person who is involved as a party or as an attorney for a party in a matter in which the lawyer is participating personally and substantially, except that a lawyer serving as a law clerk to a judge, other adjudicative officer, or arbitrator may negotiate for private employment in accordance with Rule 1.12(b).

(d) As used in this rule, the term "matter" includes:

(1) any judicial or other proceeding, application, request for a ruling or other determination, contract, claim, controversy, investigation, charge, accusation, arrest, or other particular matter involving a specific party or parties; and

(2) any other matter covered by the conflict of interest rules of the appropriate government agency.

(e) As used in this rule, the term "confidential government information" means information that has been obtained under governmental authority and that, at the time this rule is applied, the government is prohibited by law from disclosing to the public or has a legal privilege not to disclose, and that is not otherwise available to the public.

Comment

This rule prevents a lawyer from exploiting public office for the advantage of a private client. It is a counterpart of Rule 1.10(b), which applies to lawyers moving from one firm to another.

A lawyer representing a government agency, whether employed or specially retained by the government, is subject to the Rules of Professional Conduct, including the prohibition against representing adverse interests stated in Rule 1.7 and the protections afforded former clients in Rule 1.9. In addition, such a lawyer is subject to Rule 1.11 and to statutes and government regulations regarding conflict of interest. Such statutes and regulations may circumscribe the extent to which the government agency may give consent under this rule.

Where the successive clients are a public agency and a private client, the risk exists that power or discretion vested in public authority might be used for the special benefit of a private client. A lawyer should not be in a position where benefit to a private client might affect performance of the lawyer's professional functions on behalf of public authority. Also, unfair advantage could accrue to the private client by reason of access to confidential government information about the client's adversary obtainable only through the lawyer's government service. However, the rules governing lawyers presently or formerly employed by a government agency should not be so restrictive as to inhibit transfer of employment to and from the government. The government has a legitimate need to attract qualified lawyers as well as to maintain high ethical standards. The provisions for screening and waiver are necessary to prevent the disqualification rule from imposing too severe a deterrent against entering public service.

When the client is an agency of one government, that agency should be treated as a private client for purposes of this rule if the lawyer thereafter represents an agency of another government, as when a lawyer represents a city and subsequently is employed by a federal agency.

Paragraphs (a)(1) and (b) do not prohibit a lawyer from receiving a salary or partnership share established by prior independent agreement. They prohibit directly relating the attorney's compensation to the fee in the matter in which the lawyer is disqualified.

Paragraph (a)(2) does not require that a lawyer give notice to the government agency at a time when premature disclosure would injure the client; a requirement for premature disclosure might preclude engagement of the lawyer. Such notice is, however, required to be given as soon as practicable in order that the government agency will have a reasonable opportunity to ascertain that the lawyer is complying with Rule 1.11 and to take appropriate action if it believes the lawyer is not complying.

Paragraph (b) operates only when the lawyer in question has knowledge of the information, which means actual knowledge; it does not operate with respect to information that merely could be imputed to the lawyer.

Paragraphs (a) and (c) do not prohibit a lawyer from jointly representing a private party and a government agency when doing so is permitted by Rule 1.7 and is not otherwise prohibited by law.

Paragraph (c) does not disqualify other lawyers in the agency with which the lawyer in question has become associated.

RULE 1.12 FORMER JUDGE OR ARBITRATOR

(a) Except as stated in paragraph (d), a lawyer shall not represent anyone in connection with a matter in which the lawyer participated personally and substantially as a judge or other adjudicative officer, arbitrator, or law clerk to such a person, unless all parties to the proceeding consent after consultation.

(b) A lawyer shall not negotiate for employment with any person who is involved as a party, or as an attorney for a party, in a matter in which the lawyer is participating personally and substantially as a judge or other adjudicative officer or arbitrator. A lawyer

serving as a law clerk to a judge, other adjudicative officer, or arbitrator may negotiate for employment with a party or attorney involved in a matter in which the clerk is participating personally and substantially, but only after the lawyer has notified the judge, other adjudicative officer, or arbitrator.

(c) If a lawyer is disqualified by paragraph (a), no lawyer in a firm with which that lawyer is associated may knowingly undertake or continue representation in the matter, unless:

(1) the disqualified lawyer is screened from any participation in the matter and is apportioned no part of the fee therefrom; and

(2) written notice is promptly given to the appropriate tribunal to enable it to ascertain compliance with the provisions of this rule.

(d) An arbitrator selected as a partisan of a party in a multimember arbitration panel is not prohibited from subsequently representing that party.

Comment

This rule generally parallels Rule 1.11. The term "personally and substantially" signifies that a judge who was a member of a multimember court, and thereafter left judicial office to practice law, is not prohibited from representing a client in a matter pending in the court, but in which the former judge did not participate. So also the fact that a former judge exercised administrative responsibility in a court does not prevent the former judge from acting as a lawyer in a matter where the judge had previously exercised remote or incidental administrative responsibility that did not affect the merits. Compare the comment to Rule 1.11. The term "adjudicative officer" includes such officials as judges pro tempore, referees, special masters, hearing officers and other parajudicial officers, and also lawyers who serve as part-time judges.

RULE 1.13 ORGANIZATION AS CLIENT

(a) A lawyer employed or retained to represent an organization represents the organization as distinct from its directors, officers, employees, members, shareholders, or other constituents.

(b) If a lawyer for an organization knows that an officer, employee, or other person associated with the organization is engaged in action, intends to act, or refuses to act in a matter related to the representation that is a violation of a legal obligation to the organization, or a violation of law which reasonably might be imputed to the organization, and that is likely to result in substantial injury to the organization, the lawyer shall proceed as is reasonably necessary in the best interest of the organization. In determining how to proceed, the lawyer shall give due consideration to the seriousness of the violation and its consequences, the scope and nature of the lawyer's representation, the responsibility in the organization, and the apparent motivation of the person involved, the policies of the organization concerning such matters, and any other relevant considerations. Any measures taken shall be designed to minimize disruption of the organization and the risk of revealing information relating to the representation to persons outside the organization. Such measures may include among others:

(1) asking reconsideration of the matter;

(2) advising that a separate legal opinion on the matter be sought for presentation to appropriate authority in the organization; and

(3) referring the matter to higher authority in the organization, including, if warranted by the seriousness of the matter, referral to the highest authority that can act in behalf of the organization as determined by applicable law.

(c) When the organization's highest authority insists upon action, or refuses to take action, that is clearly a violation of a legal obligation to the organization or a violation of law which reasonably might be imputed to the organization, and that is likely to result in substantial injury to the organization, the lawyer may take further remedial action that the lawyer reasonably believes to be in the best interest of the organization. Such action may include revealing information otherwise protected by Rule 1.6 only if the lawyer reasonably believes that

(1) the highest authority in the organization has acted to further the personal or financial interests of members of that authority which are in conflict with the interests of the organization; and

(2) revealing the information is necessary in the best interest of the organization.

(d) In dealing with an organization's directors, officers, employees, members, shareholders, or other constituents, a lawyer shall explain the identity of the client when the lawyer believes that such explanation is necessary to avoid misunderstandings on their part.

(e) A lawyer representing an organization may also represent any of its directors, officers, employees, members, shareholders, or other constituents, subject to the provisions of Rule 1.7. If the organization's consent to the dual representation is required by Rule 1.7, the consent shall be given by an appropriate official of the organization other than the individual who is to be represented, or by the shareholders.

Comment

The Entity as the Client. In transactions with their lawyers, clients who are individuals can speak and decide for themselves, finally and authoritatively. In transactions between an organization and its lawyer, however, the organization can speak and decide only through agents, such as its officers or employees. In effect, the client-lawyer relationship is maintained through an intermediary between the client and the lawyer. This fact requires the lawyer under certain conditions to be concerned whether the intermediary legitimately represents the client.

When officers or employees of the organization make decisions for it, the decisions ordinarily must be accepted by the lawyer even if their utility or prudence is doubtful.

Decisions concerning policy and operations, including ones entailing serious risk, are not as such in the lawyer's province. However, different considerations arise when the lawyer knows that the organization may be substantially injured by action of an officer or employee that is in violation of law. In such a circumstance, it may be reasonably necessary for the lawyer to ask the officer, employee, or other agent to reconsider the matter. If that fails, or if the matter is of sufficient seriousness and importance to the organization, it may be reasonably necessary for the lawyer to take steps to have the matter reviewed by a higher authority in the organization. Clear justification should exist for seeking review over the head of the officer or employee normally responsible for it. The stated policy of the organization may define circumstances and prescribe channels for such review, and a lawyer should encourage formulation of such a policy. Even in the absence of organization policy, however, the lawyer may have an obligation to refer a matter to higher authority, depending on the seriousness of the matter and whether the officer in question has apparent motives to act at variance with the organization's interest. Review by the chief executive officer or by the board of directors may be required when the matter is of importance commensurate with their authority. At some point it may be useful or essential to obtain an independent legal opinion.

In an extreme case, it may be reasonably necessary for the lawyer to refer the matter to the organization's highest authority. Ordinarily, that is the board of directors or similar governing body. However, applicable law may prescribe that under certain conditions highest authority reposes elsewhere, for example, in the independent directors of a corporation. The ultimately difficult question is whether the lawyer should be permitted to circumvent the organization's highest authority when it persists in a course of action that is clearly violative of law or a legal obligation to the organization and that is likely to result in substantial injury to the organization.

In such a situation, if the lawyer can take remedial action without a disclosure of information that might adversely affect the organization, the lawyer as a matter of professional discretion may take such actions as the lawyer reasonably believes to be in the best interest of the organization. For example, a lawyer for a close corporation may find it reasonably necessary to disclose misconduct by the board to the shareholders. However, taking such action could entail disclosure of information relating to the representation with consequent risk of injury to the client. When such is the case, the organization is threatened by alternative injuries: the injury that may result from the governing board's action or refusal to act, and the injury that may result if the lawyer's remedial efforts entail disclosure of confidential information. The lawyer may pursue remedial efforts even at the risk of disclosure in the circumstances stated in subparagraphs (c)(1) and (c)(2).

Relation to Other Rules. The authority and responsibility provided in Rules 1.13(b) and (c) are concurrent with the authority and responsibility provided in other rules. In particular, this rule does not limit the lawyer's authority under Rule 1.6, the responsibilities to the client under Rules 1.8 and 1.16 and the responsibilities of the lawyer under Rule 3.3 or 4.1. If the lawyer's services are being used by an organization to further an illegal act or fraud by the organization, Rule 1.2(c) can be applicable. In connection with complying with Rule 1.2(c), 3.3 or 4.1, or exercising the discretion conferred by Rule 1.6(c), a lawyer for an organization may be in doubt whether the conduct will actually be carried out by the organization. To guide conduct in such circumstances, the lawyer ordinarily should make inquiry within the organization as indicated in Rule 1.13(b).

When the lawyer involved is a member of a firm, the firm's procedures may require referral of difficult questions to a superior in the firm. In that event, Rule 5.2 may be applicable.

Unincorporated associations. The duty defined in this rule applies to unincorporated associations.

Governmental Agency. The duty defined in this rule applies to governmental organizations. However, when the client is a governmental organization, a different balance may be appropriate between maintaining confidentiality and assuring that the wrongful official act is prevented or rectified because public business is involved. In addition, duties of lawyers employed by the government or lawyers in military service may be defined by statutes and regulations. Therefore, defining precisely the identity of the client and prescribing the resulting obligations of such lawyers may be more difficult in the government context. In some circumstances, it may be a specific agency, but in others it may be the government as a whole. For example, if the action or failure to act involves the head of a bureau, the department of which the bureau is a part may be the client for purposes of this rule. With these qualifications, the lawyer's substantive duty to the client and reasonable courses of action are essentially the same as when the client is a private organization.

Clarifying the Lawyer's Role. The fact that the organization is the client may be quite unclear to the organization's officials and employees. An organization official accustomed to working with the organization's lawyer may forget that the lawyer represents the organization and not the official. The result of such a misunderstanding can be embarrassing or prejudicial to the individual if, for example, the situation is such that the client-lawyer privilege will not protect the individual's communications to the lawyer. The lawyer should take reasonable care to prevent such consequences. The measures required depend on the circumstances. In routine legal matters, a lawyer for a large corporation does not have to explain to a corporate official that the corporation is the client. On the other hand, if the lawyer is conducting an inquiry involving possible illegal activity, a warning might be essential to prevent unfairness to a corporate employee. See also Rule 4.3.

Dual Representation. Paragraph (e) recognizes that a lawyer for an organization may also represent a principal officer or major shareholder. Such common representation, although often undertaken in practice, can entail serious potential conflicts of interest.

Derivative Actions. Under generally prevailing law, the shareholders or members of a corporation may bring suit to compel the directors to perform their legal obligations in the supervision of the organization. Members of unincorporated associations have essentially the same right. Such an action may be brought nominally by the organization, but usually is, in fact, a legal controversy over management of the organization.

The question can arise whether counsel for the organization may defend such an action. The proposition that the organization is the lawyer's client does not alone resolve the issue. Most derivative actions are a normal incident of an organization's affairs, to be defended by the organization's lawyer like any other suit. However, if the claim involves serious charges of wrongdoing by those in control of the organization, a conflict may arise between the lawyer's duty to the organization and the lawyer's relationship with the board. In those circumstances, Rule 1.7 governs whether independent counsel should represent the directors.

RULE 1.14   CLIENT UNDER A DISABILITY

(a) When a client's ability to make adequately considered decisions in connection with the representation is impaired, whether because of minority or mental disability or for some other reason, the lawyer shall, as far as reasonably possible, maintain a normal client-lawyer relationship with the client.

(b) A lawyer may seek the appointment of a guardian or take other protective action with respect to a client only when the lawyer reasonably believes that the client cannot adequately act in the client's own interest.

Comment

The normal client-lawyer relationship is based on the assumption that the client, when properly advised and assisted, is capable of making decisions about important matters. When the client is a minor or suffers from a mental disorder or disability, however, maintaining the ordinary client-lawyer relationship may not be possible in all respects. In particular, an incapacitated person may have no power to make legally binding decisions. Nevertheless, a client lacking legal competence often has the ability to understand, deliberate upon, and reach conclusions about matters affecting the client's own well-being. Furthermore, to an increasing extent the law recognizes intermediate degrees of competence. For example, children as young as five or six years of age, and certainly those of ten or twelve, are regarded as having opinions that are entitled to weight in legal proceedings concerning their custody. So also, it is recognized that some persons of advanced age can be quite capable of handling routine financial matters while needing special legal protection concerning major transactions.

The fact that a client suffers a disability does not diminish the lawyer's obligation to treat the client with attention and respect. If the person has no guardian or legal representative, the lawyer often must act de facto as guardian. Even if the person does have a legal representative, the lawyer should as far as possible accord the represented person the status of client, particularly in maintaining communication.

If a legal representative has already been appointed for the client, the lawyer should ordinarily look to the representative for decisions on behalf of the client. If a legal representative has not been appointed, the lawyer should see to such an appointment where it would serve the client's best interests. Thus, if a disabled client has substantial property that should be sold for the client's benefit, effective completion of the transaction ordinarily requires appointment of a legal representative. In many circumstances, however, appointment of a legal representative may be expensive or traumatic for the client. Evaluation of these considerations is a matter of professional judgment on the lawyer's part.

If the lawyer represents the guardian as distinct from the ward, and is aware that the guardian is acting adversely to the ward's interest, the lawyer may have an obligation to prevent or rectify the guardian's misconduct. See Rule 1.2(c).

If the lawyer seeks the appointment of a legal representative for the client, the filing of the request itself, together with the facts upon which it is predicated, may constitute the disclosure of confidential information which could be used against the client. If the court to whom the matter is submitted thereafter determines that a legal representative is not necessary, the harm befalling the client as the result of the disclosure may be irreparable. Consequently, consideration should be given to initially filing the petition seeking the appointment of a legal representative ex parte so that the court can decide how best to proceed to minimize the potential adverse consequences to the client by, for example, issuing a protective order limiting the disclosure of the confidential information upon which the request is predicated.

Disclosure of the Client's Condition. Rules of procedure in litigation generally provide that minors or persons suffering mental disability shall be represented by a guardian or next friend if they do not have a general guardian. However, disclosure of the client's disability can adversely affect the client's interests. For example, raising the question of disability could, in some circumstances, lead to proceedings for involuntary commitment. The lawyer's position in such cases is an unavoidably difficult one. The lawyer may seek guidance from an appropriate diagnostician.

RULE 1.15 SAFEKEEPING PROPERTY

(a) A lawyer shall hold property of clients or third persons that is in a lawyer's possession in connection with a representation separate from the lawyer's own property. All funds of the client paid to a lawyer or law firm, other than advances for costs and expenses, shall be deposited in an interest-bearing account in one or more identifiable banks, savings and loan associations, or credit unions maintained in the state in which the law office is situated, and no funds belonging to the lawyer or the law firm shall be deposited therein except as provided in this rule. Other property shall be identified as such and appropriately safeguarded. Complete records of such account funds and other property shall be kept by the lawyer and shall be preserved for a period of five years after termination of the representation.

(b) Upon receiving funds or other property in which a client or third person has an interest, a lawyer shall promptly notify the client or third person. Except as stated in this rule or otherwise permitted by law or by agreement with the client, a lawyer shall promptly deliver to the client or third person any funds or other property that the client or third person is entitled to receive and, upon request by the client or third person, shall promptly render a full accounting regarding such property.

(c) When in the course of representation a lawyer is in possession of property in which both the lawyer and another person claim interests, the property shall be kept separate by the lawyer until there is an accounting and severance of their interests. If a dispute arises concerning their respective interests, the portion in dispute shall be kept separate by the lawyer until the dispute is resolved.

(d)(1) Except as set forth in paragraph (d)(2), a lawyer who or a law firm which receives client funds shall maintain a pooled interest-bearing trust account for deposit of client funds, other than advances for costs and expenses, which at the time of receipt and deposit the lawyer or law firm reasonably anticipates will generate $50 or less in interest during the period for which it is anticipated such funds are to be held. Such an account shall comply with the following:

(A) No interest from the account shall be made available to the lawyer or law firm.

(B) The account shall include all client funds which are not expected to earn more than $50 in interest during the period it is anticipated such funds are to be held unless such funds are deposited in an interest-bearing account specified in paragraph (d)(2). The good-faith decision by the lawyer as to whether funds are expected to earn this amount is not reviewable by a disciplinary body.

(C) Funds deposited with a bank, savings and loan association, or credit union shall be subject to withdrawal upon request and without delay, and the account shall be insured by an agency of the federal government.

(D) The interest paid on the account shall not be less than the rate paid by the bank, savings and loan association, or credit union to any other non-lawyer customers on accounts of the same class within the institution.

(E) The lawyer or law firm shall direct the bank, savings and loan association, or credit union to:

(i) remit the interest, less reasonable service charges, at least quarterly to the Michigan State Bar Foundation.

(ii) transmit, with each remittance to the Michigan State Bar Foundation, a report which shall identify each lawyer or law firm and the amount of the remittance attributable to each account maintained by each lawyer or law firm; and

(iii) transmit to the depositing lawyer or law firm, in accordance with normal procedures for reporting to depositors, a report which shall indicate account balances, the rate of interest applied, interest earned, service charges, and the amount remitted to the Michigan State Bar Foundation.

(2) All client funds shall be deposited in the account specified in paragraph (d)(1) unless they are deposited in:

(A) a separate interest-bearing trust account for the particular client or client's matter on which the interest will be paid to the client; or

(B) a pooled interest-bearing trust account with subaccounting by the financial institution or by the lawyer or law firm that will provide for computation of interest earned by each client's funds and the payment thereof to the client.

[Amended effective October 1, 1990.]

Comment

A lawyer should hold property of others with the care required of a professional fiduciary. Securities should be kept in a safe deposit box, except when some other form of safekeeping is warranted by special circumstances. All property which is the property of a client or a third person should be kept separate from the lawyer's business and personal property and, if funds, should be kept in one or more trust accounts. Separate trust accounts may be warranted when administering estate funds or acting in similar fiduciary capacities.

Lawyers often receive from third persons funds from which the lawyer's fee will be paid. If there is risk that the client may divert the funds without paying the fee, the lawyer is not required to remit the portion from which the fee is to be paid. However, a lawyer may not hold funds to coerce a client into accepting the lawyer's contention. The disputed portion of the funds should be kept in trust and the lawyer should suggest means for prompt resolution of the dispute, such as arbitration. The undisputed portion of the funds shall be promptly distributed.

A third person, such as a client's creditors, may have a just claim against funds or other property in a lawyer's custody. A lawyer may have a duty under applicable law to protect such a third-party claim against wrongful interference by the client, and accordingly may refuse to surrender the property to the client. However, a lawyer should not unilaterally assume to arbitrate a dispute between the client and the third person.

The obligations of a lawyer under this rule are independent of those arising from activity other than rendering legal services. For example, a lawyer who serves as an escrow agent is governed by the applicable law relating to fiduciaries even though the lawyer does not render legal services in the transaction.

RULE 1.16 DECLINING OR TERMINATING REPRESENTATION

(a) Except as stated in paragraph (c), a lawyer shall not represent a client or, where representation has commenced, shall withdraw from the representation of a client if:

(1) the representation will result in violation of the Rules of Professional Conduct or other law;

(2) the lawyer's physical or mental condition materially impairs the lawyer's ability to represent the client; or

(3) the lawyer is discharged.

(b) Except as stated in paragraph (c), a lawyer may withdraw from representing a client if withdrawal can be accomplished without material adverse effect on the interests of the client, or if:

(1) the client persists in a course of action involving the lawyer's services that the lawyer reasonably believes is criminal or fraudulent;

(2) the client has used the lawyer's services to perpetrate a crime or fraud;

(3) the client insists upon pursuing an objective that the lawyer considers repugnant or imprudent;

(4) the client fails substantially to fulfill an obligation to the lawyer regarding the lawyer's services and has been given reasonable warning that the lawyer will withdraw unless the obligation is fulfilled;

(5) the representation will result in an unreasonable financial burden on the lawyer or has been rendered unreasonably difficult by the client; or

(6) other good cause for withdrawal exists.

(c) When ordered to do so by a tribunal, a lawyer shall continue representation notwithstanding good cause for terminating the representation.

(d) Upon termination of representation, a lawyer shall take reasonable steps to protect a client's interests, such as giving reasonable notice to the client, allowing time for employment of other counsel, surrendering papers and property to which the client is entitled, and refunding any advance payment of fee that has not been earned. The lawyer may retain papers relating to the client to the extent permitted by law.

Comment

A lawyer should not accept representation in a matter unless it can be performed competently, promptly, without improper conflict of interest and to completion.

Mandatory Withdrawal. A lawyer ordinarily must decline or withdraw from representation if the client demands that the lawyer engage in conduct that is illegal or violates the Rules of Professional Conduct or other law. The lawyer is not obliged to decline or withdraw simply because the client suggests such a course of conduct; a client may make such a suggestion in the hope that a lawyer will not be constrained by a professional obligation.

When a lawyer has been appointed to represent a client, withdrawal ordinarily requires approval of the appointing authority. See also Rule 6.2. Difficulty may be encountered if withdrawal is based on the client's demand that the lawyer engage in unprofessional conduct. The court may wish an explanation for the withdrawal, while the lawyer may be bound to keep confidential the facts that would constitute such an explanation. The lawyer's statement that professional considerations require termination of the representation ordinarily should be accepted as sufficient.

Discharge. A client has a right to discharge a lawyer at any time, with or without cause, subject to liability for payment for the lawyer's services. Where future dispute about the withdrawal may be anticipated, it may be advisable to prepare a written statement reciting the circumstances.

Whether a client can discharge appointed counsel may depend on applicable law. A client seeking to do so should be given a full explanation of the consequences. These consequences may include a decision by the appointing authority that appointment of successor counsel is unjustified, thus requiring the client to represent himself.

If the client is mentally incompetent, the client may lack the legal capacity to discharge the lawyer, and in any event the discharge may be seriously adverse to the client's interests. The lawyer should make special effort to help the client consider the consequences and, in an extreme case, may initiate proceedings for a conservatorship or similar protection of the client. See Rule 1.14.

Optional Withdrawal. A lawyer may withdraw from representation in some circumstances. The lawyer has the option to withdraw if it can be accomplished without material adverse effect on the client's interests. Withdrawal is also justified if the client persists in a course of action that the lawyer reasonably believes is illegal or fraudulent, for a lawyer is not required to be associated with such conduct even if the lawyer does not further it. Withdrawal is also permitted if the lawyer's services were misused in the past even if that would materially prejudice the client. The lawyer also may withdraw where the client insists on a repugnant or imprudent objective.

A lawyer may withdraw if the client refuses to abide by the terms of an agreement relating to the representation, such as an agreement concerning fees or court costs, or an agreement limiting the objectives of the representation.

Assisting the Client Upon Withdrawal. Even if the lawyer has been unfairly discharged by the client, a lawyer must take all reasonable steps to mitigate the consequences to the client. The lawyer may retain papers as security for a fee only to the extent permitted by law.

Whether a lawyer for an organization may under certain unusual circumstances have a legal obligation to the organization after withdrawing or being discharged by the organization's highest authority is beyond the scope of these rules.

RULE 1.17 SALE OF A LAW PRACTICE

(a) A lawyer or a law firm may sell or purchase a private law practice, including good will, pursuant to this rule.

(b) The fees charged clients shall not be increased by reason of the sale, and a purchaser shall not pass on the cost of good will to a client. The purchaser may, however, refuse to undertake the representation unless the client consents to pay fees regularly charged by the purchaser for rendering substantially similar services to other clients prior to the initiation of the purchase negotiations.

(c) Actual written notice of a pending sale shall be given at least 91 days prior to the date of the sale to each of the seller's clients, and the notice shall include:

(1) notice of the fact of the proposed sale;

(2) the identity of the purchaser;

(3) the terms of any proposed change in the fee agreement permitted under paragraph (b);

(4) notice of the client's right to retain other counsel or to take possession of the file; and

(5) notice that the client's consent to the transfer of the client's file to the purchaser will be presumed if the client does not retain other counsel or otherwise object within 90 days of receipt of the notice.

If the purchaser has identified a conflict of interest that the client cannot waive and that prohibits the purchaser from undertaking the client's matter, the notice shall advise that the client should retain substitute counsel to assume the representation and arrange to have the substitute counsel contact the seller.

(d) If a client cannot be given actual notice as required in paragraph (c), the representation of that client may be transferred to the purchaser only upon entry of an order so authorizing by a judge of the judicial circuit in which the seller maintains the practice. The seller or the purchaser may disclose to the judge in camera information relating to the representation only to the extent necessary to obtain an order authorizing the transfer of a file.

(e) The sale of the good will of a law practice may be conditioned upon the seller ceasing to engage in the private practice of law for a reasonable period of time within the geographical area in which the practice had been conducted.

[Adopted effective October 1, 1991.]

Comment

This rule permits a selling lawyer or law firm to obtain compensation for the reasonable value of a private law practice in the same manner as withdrawing partners of law firms. See Rules 5.4 and 5.6. This rule does not apply to the transfer of responsibility for legal representation from one lawyer or firm to another when such transfers are unrelated to the sale of a practice; for transfer of individual files in other circumstances, see Rules 1.5(e) and 1.16. Admission to or retirement from a law partnership or professional association, retirement plans and similar arrangements, and a sale of tangible assets of a law practice, do not constitute a sale or purchase governed by this rule.

A lawyer participating in the sale of a law practice is subject to the ethical standards that apply when involving another lawyer in the representation of a client. These include, for example, the seller's obligation to act competently in identifying a purchaser qualified to assume the representation of the client and the purchaser's obligation to undertake the representation competently, Rule 1.1, the obligation to avoid disqualifying conflicts and to secure client consent after consultation for those conflicts that can be waived, Rule 1.7, and the obligation to protect information relating to the representation, Rules 1.6 and 1.9.

If approval of the substitution of the purchasing attorney for the selling attorney is required by the rules of any tribunal in which a matter is pending, such approval must be obtained before the matter can be included in the sale, Rule 1.16. See also MCR 2.117(C).

All the elements of client autonomy, including the client's absolute right to discharge a lawyer and transfer the representation to another, survive the sale of the practice.

Selling Entire Practice. When a lawyer is closing a private practice, the lawyer may negotiate with a purchaser for the reasonable value of the practice that has been developed by the seller. A seller may agree to transfer matters in one legal field to one purchaser, while transferring matters in another legal field to a separate purchaser. However, a lawyer may not sell individual files piecemeal. A seller closing a practice to accept employment with another firm may take certain matters to the new employer while selling the remainder of the practice.

Although the rule contemplates the sale of substantially all of the law practice, a seller retiring from private practice generally may continue to represent a small number of clients while transferring the balance of the practice.

The seller remains responsible for handling all client matters until the files are transferred under this rule.

Termination of Practice by the Seller. The rule allows the parties to agree that the seller cease practice in the geographical area for a reasonable time as a condition of the sale. In certain situations, a blanket prohibition on the seller's practice would not be appropriate or warranted, such as a judicial appointee who might subsequently be defeated for reelection, or a seller elected full-time prosecutor. The parties should be allowed to negotiate, for instance, whether any geographical or duration restrictions apply to the seller's employment as a lawyer on the staff of a public agency or of a legal services entity that provides legal services to the poor, or as inside counsel to a business.

Conflicts. The practice may be sold to one or more lawyers or firms, provided that the seller assures that all clients are afforded competent representation. Since the number of client matters and their nature directly bear on the valuation of good will and therefore directly relate to selling the law practice, conflicts that cannot be waived by the client and that prevent the prospective purchaser from undertaking the client's matter should be determined promptly. If the purchaser identifies a conflict that the client cannot waive, information should be provided to the client to assist in locating substitute counsel. If the conflict can be waived by the client, the purchaser should explain the implications and determine whether the client consents to the purchaser undertaking the representation. Initial screening with regard to conflicts, for the purpose of determining the good will of the practice, need be no more intrusive than conflict screening of a walk-in prospective client at the purchaser's firm.

Client Confidences, Consent, and Notice. Negotiations between the seller and prospective purchaser prior to disclosure of information relating to a specific representation of an identifiable client can be conducted in a manner that does not violate the confidentiality provisions of Rule 1.6, just as preliminary discussions are permissible concerning the possible association of another lawyer or mergers between firms, with respect to which client consent is not required. Providing the purchaser access to client-specific information relating to the representation and to the file, however, requires client consent. The rule provides that before such information can be disclosed by the seller to the purchaser the client must be given actual written notice of the fact of the contemplated sale, including the identity of the purchaser, and must be told that the decision to consent or make other arrange-

ments must be made within 90 days. If nothing is heard from the client within that time, consent to the transfer of the client's file to the identified purchaser is presumed.

A lawyer or law firm ceasing to practice cannot be required to remain in practice because some clients cannot be given actual notice of the proposed purchase. Since these clients are not available to consent to the purchase or direct any other disposition of their files, the rule requires an order from a judge of the judicial circuit in which the seller maintains the practice, authorizing their transfer or other disposition. The court can be expected to determine whether reasonable efforts to locate the client have been exhausted, and whether the absent client's legitimate interests will be served by authorizing the transfer of the file so that the purchaser may continue the representation. Preservation of client confidences requires that the petition for a court order be considered in camera.

The client should be told the identity of the purchaser before being asked to consent to disclosure of confidences and secrets or to consent to transfer of the file.

MCR 9.119(G) provides a mechanism for handling client matters when a lawyer dies and there is no one else at the firm to take responsibility for the file.

Fee Arrangements Between Client and Purchaser. Paragraph (b) is intended to prohibit a purchaser from charging the former clients of the seller a higher fee than the purchaser is charging the purchaser's existing clients. The sale may not be financed by increases in fees charged to clients of the practice that is purchased. Existing agreements between the seller and the client as to fees and the scope of the work must be honored by the purchaser, unless the client consents after consultation.

Adjustments for differences in the fee schedules of the seller and the purchaser should be made between the seller and purchaser in valuing good will, and not between the client and the purchaser. The purchaser may, however, advise the client that the purchaser will not undertake the representation unless the client consents to pay the higher fees the purchaser usually charges. To prevent client financing of the sale, the higher fee the purchaser may charge must not exceed the fees charged by the purchaser for substantially similar service rendered prior to the initiation of the purchase negotiations.

Deceased Lawyer. Even though a nonlawyer seller representing the estate of a deceased lawyer is not subject to the Michigan Rules of Professional Conduct, a lawyer who participates in a sale of a law practice must conform to this rule. Therefore, the purchasing lawyer can be expected to see that its requirements are met.

COUNSELOR

RULE 2.1 ADVISOR

In representing a client, a lawyer shall exercise independent professional judgment and shall render candid advice. In rendering advice, a lawyer may refer not only to law but to other considerations such as moral, economic, social, and political factors that may be relevant to the client's situation.

Comment

Scope of Advice. A client is entitled to straightforward advice expressing the lawyer's honest assessment. Legal advice often involves unpleasant facts and alternatives that a client may be disinclined to confront. In presenting advice, a lawyer endeavors to sustain the client's morale and may put advice in as acceptable a form as honesty permits. However, a lawyer should not be deterred from giving candid advice by the prospect that the advice will be unpalatable to the client.

Advice couched in narrowly legal terms may be of little value to a client, especially where practical considerations, such as cost or effects on other people, are predominant. Purely technical legal advice, therefore, can sometimes be inadequate. It is proper for a lawyer to refer to relevant moral and ethical considerations in giving advice. Although a lawyer is not a moral advisor as such, moral and ethical considerations impinge upon most legal questions and may decisively influence how the law will be applied.

A client may expressly or impliedly ask the lawyer for purely technical advice. When such a request is made by a client experienced in legal matters, the lawyer may accept it at face value. When such a request is made by a client inexperienced in legal matters, however, the lawyer's responsibility as advisor may include indicating that more is involved than strictly legal considerations.

Matters that go beyond strictly legal questions may also be in the domain of another profession. Family matters can involve problems within the professional competence of psychiatry, clinical psychology, or social work; business matters can involve problems within the competence of the accounting profession or of financial specialists. Where consultation with a professional in another field is itself something a competent lawyer would recommend, the lawyer should make such a recommendation. At the same time, a lawyer's advice at its best often consists of recommending a course of action in the face of conflicting recommendations of experts.

Offering Advice. In general, a lawyer is not expected to give advice until asked by the client. However, when a lawyer knows that a client proposes a course of action that is likely to result in substantial adverse legal consequences to the client, the duty to the client under Rule 1.4 may require that the lawyer act if the client's course of action is related to the representation. A lawyer ordinarily has no duty to initiate investigation of a client's affairs or to give advice that the client has indicated is unwanted, but a lawyer may initiate advice to a client when doing so appears to be in the client's interest.

RULE 2.2 INTERMEDIARY

(a) A lawyer may act as intermediary between clients if:

(1) the lawyer consults with each client concerning the implications of the common representation, including the advantages and risks involved and the effect on the client-lawyer privileges, and obtains each client's consent to the common representation;

(2) the lawyer reasonably believes that the matter can be resolved on terms compatible with the clients' best interests, that each client will be able to make adequately informed decisions in the matter, and that there is little risk of material prejudice to the interests of any of the clients if the contemplated resolution is unsuccessful; and

(3) the lawyer reasonably believes that the common representation can be undertaken impartially and without improper effect on other responsibilities the lawyer has to any of the clients.

(b) While acting as intermediary, the lawyer shall consult with each client concerning the decisions to be made and the considerations relevant in making them, so that each client can make adequately informed decisions.

(c) A lawyer shall withdraw as intermediary if any of the clients so requests, or if any of the conditions stated in paragraph (a) is no longer satisfied. Upon withdrawal, the lawyer shall not continue to represent any of the clients in the matter that was the subject of the intermediation.

Comment

A lawyer acts as intermediary under this rule when the lawyer represents two or more parties with potentially conflicting interests. A key factor in defining the relationship is whether the parties share responsibility for the lawyer's fee, but the common representation may be inferred from other circumstances. Because confusion can arise as to the lawyer's role where each party is not separately represented, it is important that the lawyer make clear the relationship.

The rule does not apply to a lawyer acting as arbitrator or mediator between or among parties who are not clients of the lawyer, even where the lawyer has been appointed with the concurrence of the parties. In performing such a role the lawyer may be subject to applicable codes of ethics, such as the Code of Ethics for Arbitration in Commercial Disputes prepared by a joint committee of the American Bar Association and the American Arbitration Association.

A lawyer acts as intermediary in seeking to establish or adjust a relationship between clients on an amicable and mutually advantageous basis, for example, in helping to organize a business in which two or more clients are entrepreneurs, working out the financial reorganization of an enterprise in which two or more clients have an interest, arranging a property distribution in settlement of an estate, or mediating a dispute between clients. The lawyer seeks to resolve potentially conflicting interests by developing the parties' mutual interests. The alternative can be that each party may have to obtain separate representation, with the possibility in some situations of incurring additional cost, complication, or even litigation. Given these and other relevant factors, all the clients may prefer that the lawyer act as intermediary.

In considering whether to act as intermediary between clients, a lawyer should be mindful that if the intermediation fails the result can be additional cost, embarrassment, and recrimination. In some situations the risk of failure is so great that intermediation is plainly impossible. For example, a lawyer cannot undertake common representation of clients between whom contentious litigation is imminent or who contemplate contentious negotiations. More generally, if the relationship between the parties has already assumed definite antagonism, the possibility that the clients' interests can be adjusted by intermediation ordinarily is not very good.

The appropriateness of intermediation can depend on its form. Forms of intermediation include informal arbitration (where each client's case is presented by the respective client and the lawyer decides the outcome), mediation, and common representation where the clients' interests are substantially, though not entirely, compatible. One form may be appropriate in circumstances where another would not. Other relevant factors are whether the lawyer subsequently will represent both parties on a continuing basis and whether the situation involves creating a relationship between the parties or terminating one.

Confidentiality and Privilege. A particularly important factor in determining the appropriateness of intermediation is the effect on client-lawyer confidentiality and the client-lawyer privilege. In a common representation, the lawyer is still required both to keep each client adequately informed and to maintain confidentiality of information relating to the representation. See Rules 1.4 and 1.6. Complying with both requirements while acting as intermediary requires a delicate balance. If the balance cannot be maintained, the common representation is improper. With regard to the client-lawyer privilege, the prevailing rule is that as between commonly represented clients the privilege does not attach. Hence, it must be assumed that if litigation eventuates between the clients, the privilege will not protect any such communications, and the clients should be so advised.

Since the lawyer is required to be impartial between commonly represented clients, intermediation is improper when that impartiality cannot be maintained. For example, a lawyer who has represented one of the clients for a long period and in a variety of matters might have difficulty being impartial between that client and one to whom the lawyer has only recently been introduced.

Consultation. In acting as intermediary between clients, the lawyer is required to consult with the clients on the implications of doing so, and proceed only upon consent based on such a consultation. The consultation should make clear that the lawyer's role is not that of partisanship normally expected in other circumstances.

Paragraph (b) is an application of the principle expressed in Rule 1.4. Where the lawyer is intermediary, the clients ordinarily must assume greater responsibility for decisions than when each client is independently represented.

Withdrawal. Common representation does not diminish the rights of each client in the client-lawyer relationship. Each has the right to loyal and diligent representation, the right to discharge the lawyer as stated in Rule 1.16, and the protection of Rule 1.9 concerning obligations to a former client.

RULE 2.3 EVALUATION FOR USE BY THIRD PERSONS

(a) A lawyer may, for the use of someone other than the client, undertake an evaluation of a matter affecting a client if:

(1) the lawyer reasonably believes that making the evaluation is compatible with other aspects of the lawyer's relationship with the client; and

(2) the client consents after consultation.

(b) Except as disclosure is required in connection with a report of an evaluation, information relating to the evaluation is protected by Rule 1.6.

Comment

Definition. An evaluation may be performed at the client's direction, but for the primary purpose of establishing information for the benefit of third parties; for example, an opinion concerning the title of property rendered at the behest of a vendor for the information of a prospective purchaser, or at the behest of a borrower for the information of a prospective lender. In some situations, the evaluation may be required by a government agency, for example, an opinion concerning the legality of the securities registered for sale under the securities laws. In other instances, the evaluation may be required by a third person, such as a purchaser of a business.

Lawyers for the government may be called upon to give a formal opinion on the legality of contemplated government agency action. In making such an evaluation, the government lawyer acts at the behest of the government as the client, but for the purpose of establishing the limits of the agency's authorized activity. Such an opinion is to be distinguished from confidential legal advice given agency officials. The critical question is whether the opinion is to be made public.

A legal evaluation should be distinguished from an investigation of a person with whom the lawyer does not have a client-lawyer relationship. For example, a lawyer retained by a purchaser to analyze a vendor's title to property does not have a client-lawyer relationship with the vendor. So also, an investigation into a person's affairs by a government lawyer, or by special counsel employed by the government, is not an evaluation as that term is used in this rule. The question is whether the lawyer is retained by the person whose affairs are being examined. When the lawyer is retained by that person, the general rules concerning loyalty to client and preservation of confidences apply, which is not the case if the lawyer is retained by someone else. For this reason, it is essential to identify the person by whom the lawyer is retained. This should be made clear not only to the person under examination, but also to others to whom the results are to be made available.

Duty to Third Person. When the evaluation is intended for the information or use of a third person, a legal duty to that person may or may not arise. That legal question is beyond the scope of this rule. However, since such an evaluation involves a departure from the normal client-lawyer relationship, careful analysis of the situation is required. The lawyer must be satisfied as a matter of professional judgment that making the evaluation is compatible with other functions undertaken in behalf of the client. For example, if the lawyer is acting as advocate in defending the client against charges of fraud, it would normally be incompatible with that responsibility for the lawyer to perform an evaluation for others concerning the same or a related transaction. Assuming no such impediment is apparent, however, the lawyer should advise the client of the implications of the evaluation, particularly the lawyer's responsibilities to third persons and the duty to disseminate the findings.

Access to and Disclosure of Information. The quality of an evaluation depends on the freedom and extent of the investigation upon which it is based. Ordinarily a lawyer should have whatever latitude of investigation seems necessary as a matter of professional judgment. Under some circumstances, however, the terms of the evaluation may be limited. For example, certain issues or sources may be categorically excluded, or the scope of search may be limited by time constraints or the noncooperation of persons having relevant information. Any such limitations which are material to the evaluation should be described in the report. If after a lawyer has commenced an evaluation the client refuses to comply with the terms upon which it was understood the evaluation was to have been made, the lawyer's obligations are determined by law, having reference to the terms of the client's agreement and the surrounding circumstances.

Financial Auditors' Requests for Information. When a question concerning the legal situation of a client arises at the instance of the client's financial auditor and the question is referred to the lawyer, the lawyer's response may be made in accordance with procedures recognized in the legal profession. Such a procedure is set forth in the American Bar Association Statement of Policy Regarding Lawyers' Responses to Auditors' Requests for Information, adopted in 1975.

ADVOCATE

RULE 3.1 MERITORIOUS CLAIMS AND CONTENTIONS

A lawyer shall not bring or defend a proceeding, or assert or controvert an issue therein, unless there is a basis for doing so that is not frivolous. A lawyer may offer a good-faith argument for an extension, modification, or reversal of existing law. A lawyer for the defendant in a criminal proceeding, or the respondent in a proceeding that could result in incarceration, may so defend the proceeding as to require that every element of the case be established.

Comment

The advocate has a duty to use legal procedure for the fullest benefit of the client's cause, but also has a duty not to abuse legal procedure. The law, both procedural and substantive, establishes the limits within which an advocate may proceed. However, the law is not always clear and never is static. Accordingly, in determining the proper scope of advocacy, account must be taken of the law's ambiguities and potential for change.

The filing of an action or defense or similar action taken for a client is not frivolous merely because the facts have not first been fully substantiated or because the lawyer expects to develop vital evidence only by discovery. Such action is not frivolous even though the lawyer believes that the client's position ultimately will not prevail. The action is frivolous, however, if the client desires to have the action taken primarily for the purpose of harassing or maliciously injuring a person. Likewise, the action is frivolous if the lawyer is unable either to make a good-faith argument on the merits of the action taken or to support the action taken by a good-faith argument for an extension, modification, or reversal of existing law.

RULE 3.2 EXPEDITING LITIGATION

A lawyer shall make reasonable efforts to expedite litigation consistent with the interests of the client.

Comment

Although a judge bears the responsibility of assuring the progress of a court's docket, dilatory practices by a lawyer can bring the administration of justice into disrepute. Delay should not be indulged merely for the convenience of the advocates, or for the purpose of frustrating an opposing party's attempt to obtain rightful redress or repose. It is not a justification that similar conduct is often tolerated by the bench and bar. Even though it causes delay, a course of action is proper if a competent lawyer acting in good faith would regard the course of action as having some substantial purpose other than delay. Realizing financial or other benefit from otherwise improper delay in litigation is not a legitimate interest of the client.

RULE 3.3 CANDOR TOWARD THE TRIBUNAL

(a) A lawyer shall not knowingly:

(1) make a false statement of material fact or law to a tribunal;

(2) fail to disclose a material fact to a tribunal when disclosure is necessary to avoid assisting a criminal or fraudulent act by the client;

(3) fail to disclose to a tribunal controlling legal authority in the jurisdiction known to the lawyer to be directly adverse to the position of the client and not disclosed by opposing counsel; or

(4) offer evidence that the lawyer knows to be false.

If a lawyer has offered material evidence and comes to know of its falsity, the lawyer shall take reasonable remedial measures.

(b) The duties stated in paragraph (a) continue to the conclusion of the proceeding, and apply even if compliance requires disclosure of information otherwise protected by Rule 1.6.

(c) A lawyer may refuse to offer evidence that the lawyer reasonably believes is false.

(d) In an ex parte proceeding, a lawyer shall inform the tribunal of all material facts that are known to the lawyer and that will enable the tribunal to make an informed decision, whether or not the facts are adverse.

Comment

The advocate's task is to present the client's case with persuasive force. Performance of that duty while maintaining confidences of the client is qualified by the advocate's duty of candor to the tribunal. However, an advocate does not vouch for the evidence submitted in a cause; the tribunal is responsible for assessing its probative value.

Representations by a Lawyer. An advocate is responsible for pleadings and other documents prepared for litigation, but is usually not required to have personal knowledge of matters asserted therein, because litigation documents ordinarily present assertions by the client or by someone on the client's behalf and not assertions by the lawyer. Compare Rule 3.1. However, an assertion purporting to be on the lawyer's own knowledge, as in an affidavit by the lawyer or in a statement in open court, may properly be made only when the lawyer knows the assertion is true or believes it to be true on the basis of a reasonably diligent inquiry. There are circumstances where failure to make a disclosure is the equivalent of an affirmative misrepresentation. The obligation prescribed in Rule 1.2(c) not to counsel a client to commit or assist the client in committing a fraud applies in litigation. Regarding compliance with Rule 1.2(c), see the comment to that rule. See also the comment to Rule 8.4(b).

Misleading Legal Argument. Legal argument based on a knowingly false representation of law constitutes dishonesty toward the tribunal. A lawyer is not required to make a disinterested exposition of the law, but must recognize the existence of pertinent legal authorities. Furthermore, as stated in paragraph (a)(3), an advocate has a duty to disclose directly controlling adverse authority in the jurisdiction which has not been disclosed by the opposing party. The underlying concept is that legal argument is a discussion seeking to determine the legal premises properly applicable to the case.

False Evidence. When evidence that a lawyer knows to be false is provided by a person who is not the client, the lawyer must refuse to offer it regardless of the client's wishes.

When false evidence is offered by the client, however, a conflict may arise between the lawyer's duty to keep the client's revelations confidential and the duty of candor to the court. Upon ascertaining that material evidence is false, the lawyer should seek to persuade the client that the evidence should not be offered or, if it has been offered, that its false character should immediately be disclosed. If the persuasion is ineffective, the lawyer must taken reasonable remedial measures.

Except in the defense of a criminal accused, the rule generally recognized is that, if necessary to rectify the situation, an advocate must disclose the existence of the client's deception to the court or to the other party. Such a disclosure can result in grave consequences to the client, including not only a sense of betrayal but also loss of the case and perhaps a prosecution for perjury. But the alternative is that the lawyer cooperate in deceiving the court, thereby subverting the truth-finding process which the adversary system is designed to implement. See Rule 1.2(c). Furthermore, unless it is clearly understood that the lawyer will act upon the duty to disclose the existence of false evidence, the client can simply reject the lawyer's advice to reveal the false evidence and insist that the lawyer keep silent. Thus the client could in effect coerce the lawyer into being a party to fraud on the court.

Perjury by a Criminal Defendant. Whether an advocate for a criminally accused has the same duty of disclosure has been intensely debated. While it is agreed that the lawyer should seek to persuade the client to refrain from perjurious testimony, there has been dispute concerning the lawyer's duty when that persuasion fails. If the confrontation with the client occurs before trial, the lawyer ordinarily can withdraw. Withdrawal before trial may not be possible, however, because trial is imminent, or because the confrontation with the client does not take place until the trial itself, or because no other counsel is available.

The most difficult situation, therefore, arises in a criminal case where the accused insists on testifying when the lawyer knows that the testimony is perjurious. The lawyer's effort to rectify the situation can increase the likelihood of the client's being convicted as well as opening the possibility of a prosecution for perjury. On the other hand, if the lawyer does not exercise control over the proof, the lawyer participates, although in a merely passive way, in deception of the court.

Three resolutions of this dilemma have been proposed. One is to permit the accused to testify by a narrative without

guidance through the lawyer's questioning. This compromises both contending principles; it exempts the lawyer from the duty to disclose false evidence, but subjects the client to an implicit disclosure of information imparted to counsel. Another suggested resolution of relatively recent origin, is that the advocate be entirely excused from the duty to reveal perjury if the perjury is that of the client. This is a coherent solution, but makes the advocate a knowing instrument of perjury.

The other resolution of the dilemma is that the lawyer must reveal the client's perjury if necessary to rectify the situation. A criminal accused has a right to the assistance of an advocate, a right to testify, and a right of confidential communication with counsel. However, an accused should not have a right to assistance of counsel in committing perjury. Furthermore, an advocate has an obligation, not only in professional ethics but under the law as well, to avoid implication in the commission of perjury or other falsification of evidence. See Rule 1.2(c).

Remedial Measures. If perjured testimony or false evidence has been offered, the advocate's proper course ordinarily is to remonstrate with the client confidentially. If that fails, the advocate should seek to withdraw if that will remedy the situation. If withdrawal will not remedy the situation or is impossible, the advocate should make disclosure to the court. It is for the court then to determine what should be done—making a statement about the matter to the trier of fact, ordering a mistrial, or perhaps nothing. If the false testimony was that of the client, the client may controvert the lawyer's version of their communication when the lawyer discloses the situation to the court. If there is an issue whether the client has committed perjury, the lawyer cannot represent the client in resolution of the issue, and a mistrial may be unavoidable. An unscrupulous client might in this way attempt to produce a series of mistrials and thus escape prosecution. However, the second such encounter could be construed as a deliberate abuse of the right to counsel and as such a waiver of the right to further representation.

Constitutional Requirements. The general rule—that an advocate must disclose the existence of perjury with respect to a material fact, even that of a client—applies to defense counsel in criminal cases, as well as in other instances. However, the definition of the lawyer's ethical duty in such a situation may be qualified by constitutional provisions for due process and the right to counsel in criminal cases. The obligation of the advocate under these rules is subordinate to such a constitutional requirement.

Duration of Obligation. A practical time limit on the obligation to rectify the presentation of false evidence must be established. The conclusion of the proceeding is a reasonably definite point for the termination of the obligation.

Refusing to Offer Proof Believed to Be False. Generally speaking, a lawyer has authority to refuse to offer testimony or other proof that the lawyer believes is untrustworthy. Offering such proof may reflect adversely on the lawyer's ability to discriminate in the quality of evidence and thus impair the lawyer's effectiveness as an advocate. In criminal cases, however, a lawyer may be denied this authority by constitutional requirements governing the right to counsel.

Ex Parte Proceedings. Ordinarily, an advocate has the limited responsibility of presenting one side of the matters that a tribunal should consider in reaching a decision; the conflicting position is expected to be presented by the opposing party. However, in an ex parte proceeding, such as an application for a temporary restraining order, there is no balance of presentation by opposing advocates. The object of an ex parte proceeding is nevertheless to yield a substantially just result. The judge has an affirmative responsibility to accord the absent party just consideration. The lawyer for the represented party has the correlative duty to make disclosures of material facts that are known to the lawyer and that the lawyer reasonably believes are necessary to an informed decision.

RULE 3.4 FAIRNESS TO OPPOSING PARTY AND COUNSEL

A lawyer shall not:

(a) unlawfully obstruct another party's access to evidence; unlawfully alter, destroy, or conceal a document or other material having potential evidentiary value; or counsel or assist another person to do any such act;

(b) falsify evidence, counsel or assist a witness to testify falsely, or offer an inducement to a witness that is prohibited by law;

(c) knowingly disobey an obligation under the rules of a tribunal except for an open refusal based on an assertion that no valid obligation exists;

(d) in pretrial procedure, make a frivolous discovery request or fail to make reasonably diligent efforts to comply with a legally proper discovery request by an opposing party;

(e) during trial, allude to any matter that the lawyer does not reasonably believe is relevant or that will not be supported by admissible evidence, assert personal knowledge of facts in issue except when testifying as a witness, or state a personal opinion as to the justness of a cause, the credibility of a witness, the culpability of a civil litigant, or the guilt or innocence of an accused; or

(f) request a person other than a client to refrain from voluntarily giving relevant information to another party, unless:

(1) the person is a relative or an employee or other agent of a client; and

(2) the lawyer reasonably believes that the person's interests will not be adversely affected by refraining from giving such information.

Comment

The procedure of the adversary system contemplates that the evidence in a case is to be marshalled competitively by the contending parties. Fair competition in the adversary system is secured by prohibitions against destruction or concealment of evidence, improper influence of witnesses, obstructive tactics in discovery procedure, and the like.

Documents and other items of evidence are often essential to establish a claim or defense. Subject to evidentiary privileges, the right of an opposing party, including the government, to obtain evidence through discovery or subpoena is an important procedural right. The exercise of that right can be frustrated if relevant material is altered, con-

cealed or destroyed. Other law makes it an offense to destroy material for purpose of impairing its availability in a pending proceeding or one whose commencement can be foreseen. Falsifying evidence is also generally a criminal offense. Paragraph (a) applies to evidentiary material generally, including computerized information.

With regard to paragraph (b), it is not improper to pay a witness' expenses or to compensate an expert witness on terms permitted by law. It is, however, improper to pay an occurrence witness any fee for testifying beyond that authorized by law, and it is improper to pay an expert witness a contingent fee.

Paragraph (f) permits a lawyer to advise employees of a client to refrain from giving information to another party, because the employees may identify their interests with those of the client. See also Rules 4.2 and 4.3.

RULE 3.5 IMPARTIALITY AND DECORUM OF THE TRIBUNAL

A lawyer shall not:

(a) seek to influence a judge, juror, prospective juror, or other official by means prohibited by law;

(b) communicate ex parte with such a person concerning a pending matter, except as permitted by law; or

(c) engage in undignified or discourteous conduct toward the tribunal.

Comment

Many forms of improper influence upon a tribunal are proscribed by criminal law. Others are specified in the Michigan Code of Judicial Conduct, with which an advocate should be familiar. A lawyer is required to avoid contributing to a violation of such provisions.

The advocate's function is to present evidence and argument so that the cause may be decided according to law. Refraining from undignified or discourteous conduct is a corollary of the advocate's right to speak on behalf of litigants. A lawyer may stand firm against abuse by a judge, but should avoid reciprocation; the judge's default is no justification for similar dereliction by an advocate. An advocate can present the cause, protect the record for subsequent review, and preserve professional integrity by patient firmness no less effectively than by belligerence or theatrics.

RULE 3.6 TRIAL PUBLICITY

A lawyer shall not make an extrajudicial statement that a reasonable person would expect to be disseminated by means of public communication if the lawyer knows or reasonably should know that it will have a substantial likelihood of materially prejudicing an adjudicative proceeding.

Comment

It is difficult to strike a balance between protecting the right to a fair trial and safeguarding the right of free expression. Preserving the right to a fair trial necessarily entails some curtailment of the information that may be disseminated about a party prior to trial, particularly where trial by jury is involved. If there were no such limits, the result would be the practical nullification of the protective effect of the rules of forensic decorum and the exclusionary rules of evidence. On the other hand, there are vital social interests served by the free dissemination of information about events having legal consequences and about legal proceedings themselves. The public has a right to know about threats to its safety and measures aimed at assuring its security. It also has a legitimate interest in the conduct of judicial proceedings, particularly in matters of general public concern. Furthermore, the subject matter of legal proceedings is often of direct significance in debate and deliberation over questions of public policy.

No body of rules can simultaneously satisfy all interests of fair trial and all those of free expression. Moreover, the confidentiality provisions of Rule 1.6 may prevent the disclosure of information which might otherwise be included in an extrajudicial statement. In addition, special rules of confidentiality may validly govern proceedings in juvenile, domestic relations, and mental disability proceedings, and perhaps other types of litigation. Rule 3.4(c) requires compliance with such rules.

For guidance in this difficult area, one may consider the following language adapted from the American Bar Association's Model Rule 3.6:

(a) A statement referred to in Rule 3.6 ordinarily is likely to have such a prejudicial effect when it refers to a civil matter triable to a jury, a criminal matter, or any other proceeding that could result in incarceration, and the statement relates to:

(1) the character, credibility, reputation or criminal record of a party, of a suspect in a criminal investigation or of a witness, or the identity of a witness, or the expected testimony of a party or witness;

(2) in a criminal case or proceeding that could result in incarceration, the possibility of a plea of guilty to the offense or the existence or contents of any confession, admission, or statement given by a defendant or suspect, or that person's refusal or failure to make a statement;

(3) the performance or results of any examination or test, or the refusal or failure of a person to submit to an examination or test, or the identity or nature of physical evidence expected to be presented;

(4) any opinion as to the guilt or innocence of a defendant or suspect in a criminal case or proceeding that could result in incarceration;

(5) information that the lawyer knows or reasonably should know is likely to be inadmissible as evidence in a trial and that would, if disclosed, create a substantial risk of prejudicing an impartial trial; or

(6) the fact that a defendant has been charged with a crime, unless there is included therein a statement explaining that the charge is merely an accusation and that the defendant is presumed innocent until and unless proven guilty.

(b) Notwithstanding Rule 3.6 and paragraphs (a)(1–5) of this portion of the comment, a lawyer involved in the investigation or litigation of a matter may state without elaboration:

(1) the general nature of the claim or defense;

(2) the information contained in a public record;

(3) that an investigation of the matter is in progress, including the general scope of the investigation, the offense or claim or defense involved and, except when prohibited by law, the identity of the persons involved;

(4) the scheduling or result of any step in litigation;

(5) a request for assistance in obtaining evidence and information necessary thereto;

(6) a warning of danger concerning the behavior of a person involved, when there is reason to believe that there exists the likelihood of substantial harm to an individual or to the public interest; and

(7) in a criminal case:

(A) the identity, residence, occupation and family status of the accused;

(B) if the accused has not been apprehended, information necessary to aid in apprehension of that person;

(C) the fact, time and place of arrest; and

(D) the identity of investigating and arresting officers or agencies and the length of the investigation.

RULE 3.7 LAWYER AS WITNESS

(a) A lawyer shall not act as advocate at a trial in which the lawyer is likely to be a necessary witness except where:

(1) the testimony relates to an uncontested issue;

(2) the testimony relates to the nature and value of legal services rendered in the case; or

(3) disqualification of the lawyer would work substantial hardship on the client.

(b) A lawyer may act as advocate in a trial in which another lawyer in the lawyer's firm is likely to be called as a witness unless precluded from doing so by Rule 1.7 or Rule 1.9.

Comment

Combining the roles of advocate and witness can prejudice the opposing party and can involve a conflict of interest between the lawyer and client.

The opposing party may properly object where the combination of rules may prejudice that party's rights in the litigation. A witness is required to testify on the basis of personal knowledge, while an advocate is expected to explain and comment on evidence given by others. It may not be clear whether a statement by an advocate-witness should be taken as proof or as an analysis of the proof.

Paragraph (a)(1) recognizes that if the testimony will be uncontested, the ambiguities in the dual role are purely theoretical. Paragraph (a)(2) recognizes that where the testimony concerns the extent and value of legal services rendered in the action in which the testimony is offered, permitting the lawyers to testify avoids the need for a second trial with new counsel to resolve that issue. Moreover, in such a situation the judge has firsthand knowledge of the matter in issue; hence, there is less dependence on the adversary process to test the credibility of the testimony.

Apart from these two exceptions, paragraph (a)(3) recognizes that a balancing is required between the interests of the client and those of the opposing party. Whether the opposing party is likely to suffer prejudice depends on the nature of the case, the importance and probable tenor of the lawyer's testimony, and the probability that the lawyer's testimony will conflict with that of other witnesses. Even if there is risk of such prejudice, in determining whether the lawyer should be disqualified due regard must be given to the effect of disqualification on the lawyer's client. It is relevant that one or both parties could reasonably foresee that the lawyer would probably be a witness. The principle of imputed disqualification stated in Rule 1.10 has no application to this aspect of the problem.

Whether the combination of roles involves an improper conflict of interest with respect to the client is determined by Rule 1.7 or 1.9. For example, if there is likely to be substantial conflict between the testimony of the client and that of the lawyer or a member of the lawyer's firm, the representation is improper. The problem can arise whether the lawyer is called as a witness on behalf of the client or is called by the opposing party. Determining whether or not such a conflict exists is primarily the responsibility of the lawyer involved. See comment to Rule 1.7. If a lawyer who is a member of a firm may not act as both advocate and witness by reason of conflict of interest, Rule 1.10 disqualifies the firm also.

RULE 3.8 SPECIAL RESPONSIBILITIES OF A PROSECUTOR

The prosecutor in a criminal case shall:

(a) refrain from prosecuting a charge that the prosecutor knows is not supported by probable cause;

(b) make reasonable efforts to assure that the accused has been advised of the right to, and the procedure for obtaining, counsel and has been given reasonable opportunity to obtain counsel;

(c) not seek to obtain from an unrepresented accused a waiver of important pretrial rights, such as the right to a preliminary hearing;

(d) make timely disclosure to the defense of all evidence or information known to the prosecutor that tends to negate the guilt of the accused or mitigates the degree of the offense, and, in connection with sentencing, disclose to the defense and to the tribunal all unprivileged mitigating information known to the prosecutor, except when the prosecutor is relieved of this responsibility by a protective order of the tribunal; and

(e) exercise reasonable care to prevent investigators, law enforcement personnel, employees, or other persons assisting or associated with the prosecutor in a criminal case from making an extrajudicial statement that the prosecutor would be prohibited from making under Rule 3.6.

Comment

A prosecutor has the responsibility of a minister of justice and not simply that of an advocate. This responsibility carries with it specific obligations to see that the defendant is accorded procedural justice and that guilt is decided upon the basis of sufficient evidence. Precisely how far the prosecutor

is required to go in this direction is a matter of debate. Cf. Rule 3.3(d), governing ex parte proceedings, among which grand jury proceedings are included. Applicable law may require other measures by the prosecutor, and knowing disregard of those obligations or a systematic abuse of prosecutorial discretion could constitute a violation of Rule 8.4.

Paragraph (c) does not apply to an accused appearing pro se with the approval of the tribunal. Nor does it forbid the lawful questioning of a suspect who has knowingly waived the rights to counsel and silence.

The exception in paragraph (d) recognizes that a prosecutor may seek an appropriate protective order from the tribunal if disclosure of information to the defense could result in substantial harm to an individual or to the public interest.

In paragraphs (b) and (e), this rule imposes on a prosecutor an obligation to make reasonable efforts and to take reasonable care to assure that a defendant's rights are protected. Of course, not all of the individuals who might encroach upon those rights are under the control of the prosecutor. The prosecutor cannot be held responsible for the actions of persons over whom the prosecutor does not exercise authority. The prosecutor's obligation is discharged if the prosecutor has taken reasonable and appropriate steps to assure that the defendant's rights are protected.

RULE 3.9 ADVOCATE IN NONADJUDICATIVE PROCEEDINGS

A lawyer representing a client before a legislative or administrative tribunal in a nonadjudicative proceeding shall disclose that the appearance is in a representative capacity and shall conform to the provisions of Rules 3.3(a) through (c), 3.4(a) through (c), and 3.5.

Comment

In representation before bodies such as legislatures, municipal councils, and executive and administrative agencies acting in a rule-making or policy-making capacity, lawyers present facts, formulate issues, and advance argument in the matters under consideration. The decision-making body, like a court, should be able to rely on the integrity of the submissions made to it. A lawyer appearing before such a body should deal with the tribunal honestly and in conformity with applicable rules of procedure.

Lawyers have no exclusive right to appear before nonadjudicative bodies, as they do before a court. The requirements of this rule therefore may subject lawyers to regulations inapplicable to advocates who are not lawyers. However, legislatures and administrative agencies have a right to expect lawyers to deal with them as they deal with courts.

This rule does not apply to representation of a client in a negotiation or other bilateral transaction with a governmental agency; representation in such a transaction is governed by Rules 4.1 through 4.4.

TRANSACTIONS WITH PERSONS OTHER THAN CLIENTS

RULE 4.1 TRUTHFULNESS IN STATEMENTS TO OTHERS

In the course of representing a client, a lawyer shall not knowingly make a false statement of material fact or law to a third person.

Comment

Misrepresentation. A lawyer is required to be truthful when dealing with others on a client's behalf, but generally has no affirmative duty to inform an opposing party of relevant facts. A misrepresentation can occur if the lawyer incorporates or affirms a statement of another person that the lawyer knows is false.

Statements of Fact. This rule refers to statements of fact. Whether a particular statement should be regarded as one of fact can depend on the circumstances. Under generally accepted conventions in negotiation, certain types of statements ordinarily are not taken as statements of material fact. Estimates of price or value placed on the subject of a transaction and a party's intentions as to an acceptable settlement of a claim are in this category, and so is the existence of an undisclosed principal except where nondisclosure of the principal would constitute fraud.

Fraud by Client. Making a false statement may include the failure to make a statement in circumstances in which silence is equivalent to making such a statement. Thus, where the lawyer has made a statement that the lawyer believed to be true when made but later discovers that the statement was not true, in some circumstances failure to correct the statement may be equivalent to making a statement that is false. When the falsity of the original statement by the lawyer resulted from reliance upon what was told to the lawyer by the client and if the original statement if left uncorrected may further a criminal or fraudulent act by the client, the provisions of Rule 1.6(c)(3) give the lawyer discretion to make the disclosure necessary to rectify the consequences.

RULE 4.2 COMMUNICATION WITH A PERSON REPRESENTED BY COUNSEL

In representing a client, a lawyer shall not communicate about the subject of the representation with a party whom the lawyer knows to be represented in the matter by another lawyer, unless the lawyer has the consent of the other lawyer or is authorized by law to do so.

Comment

This rule does not prohibit communication with a party, or an employee or agent of a party, concerning matters outside the representation. For example, the existence of a controversy between a government agency and a private party, or between two organizations, does not prohibit a lawyer for either from communicating with nonlawyer representatives of the other regarding a separate matter. Also, parties to a matter may communicate directly with each other and a

lawyer having independent justification for communicating with the other party is permitted to do so. Communications authorized by law include, for example, the right of a party to a controversy with a government agency to speak with government officials about the matter.

In the case of an organization, this rule prohibits communications by a lawyer for one party concerning the matter in representation with persons having a managerial responsibility on behalf of the organization, and with any other person whose act or omission in connection with that matter may be imputed to the organization for purposes of civil or criminal liability or whose statement may constitute an admission on the part of the organization. If an agent or employee of the organization is represented in the matter by separate counsel, the consent by that counsel to a communication will be sufficient for purposes of this rule. Compare Rule 3.4(f).

This rule also covers any person, whether or not a party to a formal proceeding, who is represented by counsel concerning the matter in question.

RULE 4.3 DEALING WITH AN UNREPRESENTED PERSON

In dealing on behalf of a client with a person who is not represented by counsel, a lawyer shall not state or imply that the lawyer is disinterested. When the lawyer knows or reasonably should know that the unrepresented person misunderstands the lawyer's role in the matter, the lawyer shall make reasonable efforts to correct the misunderstanding.

Comment

An unrepresented person, particularly one not experienced in dealing with legal matters, might assume that a lawyer is disinterested in loyalties or is a disinterested authority on the law even when the lawyer represents a client. During the course of a lawyer's representation of a client, the lawyer should not give advice to an unrepresented person other than the advice to obtain counsel.

RULE 4.4 RESPECT FOR RIGHTS OF THIRD PERSONS

In representing a client, a lawyer shall not use means that have no substantial purpose other than to embarrass, delay, or burden a third person, or use methods of obtaining evidence that violate the legal rights of such a person.

Comment

Responsibility to a client requires a lawyer to subordinate the interests of others to those of the client, but that responsibility does not imply that a lawyer may disregard the rights of third persons. It is impractical to catalogue all such rights, but they include legal restrictions on methods of obtaining evidence from third persons.

LAW FIRMS AND ASSOCIATIONS

RULE 5.1 RESPONSIBILITIES OF A PARTNER OR SUPERVISORY LAWYER

(a) A partner in a law firm shall make reasonable efforts to ensure that the firm has in effect measures giving reasonable assurance that all lawyers in the firm conform to the Rules of Professional Conduct.

(b) A lawyer having direct supervisory authority over another lawyer shall make reasonable efforts to ensure that the other lawyer conforms to the Rules of Professional Conduct.

(c) A lawyer shall be responsible for another lawyer's violation of the rules of professional conduct if:

(1) the lawyer orders or, with knowledge of the relevant facts and the specific conduct, ratifies the conduct involved; or

(2) the lawyer is a partner in the law firm in which the other lawyer practices or has direct supervisory authority over the other lawyer, and knows of the conduct at a time when its consequences can be avoided or mitigated but fails to take reasonable remedial action.

Comment

Paragraphs (a) and (b) refer to lawyers who have supervisory authority over the professional work of a firm or a legal department of a government agency. This includes members of a partnership and the shareholders in a law firm organized as a professional corporation. This also includes lawyers having supervisory authority in the law department of an enterprise or government agency and lawyers who have intermediate managerial responsibilities in a firm.

The measures required to fulfill the responsibility prescribed in paragraphs (a) and (b) can depend on the firm's structure and the nature of its practice. In a small firm, informal supervision and occasional admonition ordinarily might be sufficient. In a large firm, or in practice situations in which intensely difficult ethical problems frequently arise, more elaborate procedures may be necessary. Some firms, for example, have a procedure whereby junior lawyers can make confidential referral of ethical problems directly to a designated senior partner or special committee. See Rule 5.2. Firms, whether large or small, may also rely on continuing legal education in professional ethics. In any event, the ethical atmosphere of a firm can influence the conduct of all its members and a lawyer having authority over the work of another may not assume that the subordinate lawyer will inevitably conform to the rules.

Paragraph (c)(1) expresses a general principle concerning responsibility for acts of another. See also Rule 8.4(a).

Paragraph (c)(2) defines the duty of a lawyer having direct supervisory authority over performance of specific legal work by another lawyer. Whether a lawyer has such supervisory authority in particular circumstances is a question of fact. Partners of a private firm have at least indirect responsibility for all work being done by the firm, while a partner in charge of a particular matter ordinarily has direct authority over other firm lawyers engaged in the matter. Appropriate remedial action by a partner would depend on the immediacy of the partner's involvement and the seriousness of the misconduct. The supervisor is required to intervene to prevent avoidable consequences of misconduct if the supervisor knows that the misconduct occurred. Thus, if a supervising lawyer knows that a subordinate misrepresented a matter to an opposing party in negotiation, the supervisor as well as the subordinate has a duty to correct the resulting misapprehension.

Professional misconduct by a lawyer under supervision could reveal a violation of paragraph (b) on the part of the supervisory lawyer even though it does not entail a violation of paragraph (c) because there was no direction, ratification, or knowledge of the violation.

Apart from this rule and Rule 8.4(a), a lawyer does not have disciplinary liability for the conduct of a partner, associate, or subordinate. Whether a lawyer may be liable civilly or criminally for another lawyer's conduct is a question of law beyond the scope of these rules.

RULE 5.2 RESPONSIBILITIES OF A SUBORDINATE LAWYER

(a) A lawyer is bound by the rules of professional conduct notwithstanding that the lawyer acted at the direction of another person.

(b) A subordinate lawyer does not violate the rules of professional conduct if that lawyer acts in accordance with a supervisory lawyer's reasonable resolution of an arguable question of professional duty.

Comment

Although a lawyer is not relieved of responsibility for a violation by the fact that the lawyer acted at the direction of a supervisor, that fact may be relevant in determining whether a lawyer had the knowledge required to render conduct a violation of the rules. For example, if a subordinate filed a frivolous pleading at the direction of a supervisor, the subordinate would not be guilty of a professional violation unless the subordinate knew of the document's frivolous character.

When lawyers in a supervisor-subordinate relationship encounter a matter involving professional judgment as to ethical duty, the supervisor may assume responsibility for making the judgment. Otherwise a consistent course of action or position could not be taken. If the question can reasonably be answered only one way, the duty of both lawyers is clear and they are equally responsible for fulfilling it. However, if the question is reasonably arguable, someone has to decide upon the course of action. That authority ordinarily reposes in the supervisor, and a subordinate may be guided accordingly. For example, if a question arises whether the interests of two clients conflict under Rule 1.7, the supervisor's reasonable resolution of the question should protect the subordinate professionally if the resolution is subsequently challenged.

RULE 5.3 RESPONSIBILITIES REGARDING NONLAWYER ASSISTANTS

With respect to a nonlawyer employed by, retained by, or associated with a lawyer:

(a) a partner in a law firm shall make reasonable efforts to ensure that the firm has in effect measures giving reasonable assurance that the person's conduct is compatible with the professional obligations of the lawyer;

(b) a lawyer having direct supervisory authority over the nonlawyer shall make reasonable efforts to ensure that the person's conduct is compatible with the professional obligations of the lawyer; and

(c) a lawyer shall be responsible for conduct of such a person that would be a violation of the rules of professional conduct if engaged in by a lawyer if:

(1) the lawyer orders or, with knowledge of the relevant facts and the specific conduct, ratifies the conduct involved; or

(2) the lawyer is a partner in the law firm in which the person is employed or has direct supervisory authority over the person and knows of the conduct at a time when its consequences can be avoided or mitigated but fails to take reasonable remedial action.

Comment

Lawyers generally employ assistants in their practice, including secretaries, investigators, law student interns, and paraprofessionals. Such assistants, whether employees or independent contractors, act for the lawyer in rendition of the lawyer's professional services. A lawyer should give such assistants appropriate instruction and supervision concerning the ethical aspects of their employment, particularly regarding the obligation not to disclose information relating to representation of the client, and should be responsible for their work product. The measures employed in supervising nonlawyers should take account of the fact that they do not have legal training and are not subject to professional discipline.

As does Rule 3.8, this rule may in certain situations impose on a prosecutor an obligation to make reasonable efforts to assure that a defendant's rights are protected. Of course, not all of the individuals who might encroach upon those rights are under the control of the prosecutor, but where this rule applies, the prosecutor must take reasonable and appropriate steps to assure that the defendant's rights are protected.

RULE 5.4 PROFESSIONAL INDEPENDENCE OF A LAWYER

(a) A lawyer or law firm shall not share legal fees with a nonlawyer, except that:

(1) an agreement by a lawyer with the lawyer's firm, partner, or associate may provide for the payment of money, over a reasonable period of time after the lawyer's death, to the lawyer's estate, or to one or more specified persons;

(2) a lawyer who purchases the practice of a deceased, disabled, or disappeared lawyer may pay to the estate or other representative of that lawyer the agreed-upon purchase price pursuant to the provisions of Rule 1.17; and

(3) a lawyer or law firm may include nonlawyer employees in a compensation or retirement plan, even though the plan is based in whole or in part on a profit-sharing arrangement.

(b) A lawyer shall not form a partnership with a nonlawyer if any of the activities of the partnership consist of the practice of law.

(c) A lawyer shall not permit a person who recommends, employs, or pays the lawyer to render legal services for another to direct or regulate the lawyer's professional judgment in rendering such legal services.

(d) A lawyer shall not practice with or in the form of a professional corporation or association authorized to practice law for a profit, if:

(1) a nonlawyer owns any interest therein, except that a fiduciary representative of the estate of a lawyer may hold the stock or interest of the lawyer for a reasonable time during administration;

(2) a nonlawyer is a corporate director or officer thereof; or

(3) a nonlawyer has the right to direct or control the professional judgment of a lawyer.

[Amended effective October 1, 1991.]

Comment

The provisions of this rule express traditional limitations on sharing fees. These limitations are to protect the lawyer's professional independence of judgment. Where someone other than the client pays the lawyer's fee or salary, or recommends employment of the lawyer, that arrangement does not modify the lawyer's obligation to the client. As stated in paragraph (c), such arrangements should not interfere with the lawyer's professional judgment.

A lawyer does not violate this rule by affiliating with or being employed by an organization such as a union-sponsored prepaid legal services plan, provided the structure of the organization permits the lawyer independently to exercise professional judgment on behalf of a client.

RULE 5.5 UNAUTHORIZED PRACTICE OF LAW

A lawyer shall not:

(a) practice law in a jurisdiction where doing so violates the regulation of the legal profession in that jurisdiction; or

(b) assist a person who is not a member of the bar in the performance of activity that constitutes the unauthorized practice of law.

Comment

Limiting the practice of law to members of the bar protects the public against rendition of legal services by unqualified persons. Paragraph (b) does not prohibit a lawyer from employing the services of paraprofessionals and delegating functions to them, so long as the lawyer supervises the delegated work and retains responsibility for their work. See Rule 5.3. Likewise, it does not prohibit lawyers from providing professional advice and instruction to nonlawyers whose employment requires knowledge of law, for example, claims adjusters, employees of financial or commercial institutions, social workers, accountants and persons employed in government agencies. In addition, a lawyer may counsel nonlawyers who wish to proceed pro se.

RULE 5.6 RESTRICTIONS ON RIGHT TO PRACTICE

A lawyer shall not participate in offering or making:

(a) a partnership or employment agreement that restricts the right of a lawyer to practice after termination of the relationship, except an agreement concerning benefits upon retirement or as permitted in Rule 1.17; or

(b) an agreement in which a restriction on the lawyer's right to practice is part of the settlement of a controversy between private parties.

[Amended effective October 1, 1991.]

Comment

An agreement restricting the right of a lawyer to practice after leaving a firm not only limits the lawyer's professional autonomy but also limits the freedom of clients to choose a lawyer. Paragraph (a) prohibits such agreements except for restrictions incident to provisions concerning retirement benefits for service with the firm or restrictions included in the terms of a sale pursuant to Rule 1.17.

Paragraph (b) prohibits a lawyer from agreeing not to represent other persons in connection with settling a claim on behalf of a client.

[Comment amended effective October 1, 1991.]

PUBLIC SERVICE

RULE 6.1 PRO BONO PUBLICO SERVICE

A lawyer should render public interest legal service. A lawyer may discharge this responsibility by providing professional services at no fee or a reduced fee to persons of limited means, or to public service or charitable groups or organizations. A lawyer may also discharge this responsibility by service in activities for improving the law, the legal system, or the legal profession, and by financial support for organizations that provide legal services to persons of limited means.

Comment

The ABA House of Delegates has formally acknowledged "the basic responsibility of each lawyer engaged in the practice of law to provide public interest legal services" without fee, or at a substantially reduced fee, in one or more of the following areas: poverty law, civil rights law, public rights law, charitable organization representation and the administration of justice. This rule expresses that policy, but is not intended to be enforced through disciplinary process.

The rights and responsibilities of individuals and organizations in the United States are increasingly defined in legal terms. As a consequence, legal assistance in coping with the web of statutes, rules and regulations is imperative for persons of modest and limited means, as well as for the relatively well-to-do.

The basic responsibility for providing legal services for those unable to pay ultimately rests upon the individual lawyer, and personal involvement in the problems of the disadvantaged can be one of the most rewarding experiences in the life of a lawyer. Every lawyer, regardless of professional prominence or professional workload, should find time to participate in or otherwise support the provision of legal services to the disadvantaged. The provision of free legal services to those unable to pay reasonable fees continues to be an obligation of each lawyer as well as the profession generally, but the efforts of individual lawyers are often not enough to meet the need. Thus, it has been necessary for the profession and government to institute additional programs to provide legal services. Accordingly, legal aid offices, lawyer referral services and other related programs have been developed, and others will be developed by the profession and government. Every lawyer should support all proper efforts to meet this need for legal services.

RULE 6.2 ACCEPTING APPOINTMENTS

A lawyer shall not seek to avoid appointment by a tribunal to represent a person except for good cause, such as:

(a) representing the client is likely to result in violation of the Rules of Professional Conduct or other law;

(b) representing the client is likely to result in an unreasonable financial burden on the lawyer; or

(c) the client or the cause is so repugnant to the lawyer as to be likely to impair the client-lawyer relationship or the lawyer's ability to represent the client.

Comment

A lawyer ordinarily is not obliged to accept a client whose character or cause the lawyer regards as repugnant. The lawyer's freedom to select clients is, however, qualified. All lawyers have a responsibility to assist in providing pro bono publico service. See Rule 6.1. An individual lawyer fulfills this responsibility by accepting a fair share of unpopular matters or indigent or unpopular clients. A lawyer may also be subject to appointment by a court to serve unpopular clients or persons unable to afford legal services.

Appointed Counsel. For good cause, a lawyer may seek to decline an appointment to represent a person who cannot afford to retain counsel or whose cause is unpopular. Good cause exists if the lawyer could not handle the matter competently (see Rule 1.1) or if undertaking the representation would result in an improper conflict of interest. Good cause also exists if the client or the cause is so repugnant to the lawyer as to be likely to impair the client-lawyer relationship or the lawyer's ability to represent the client. A lawyer may also seek to decline an appointment if acceptance would be unreasonably burdensome, for example, when it would impose a financial sacrifice so great as to be unjust.

An appointed lawyer has the same obligations to the client as retained counsel, including the obligations of loyalty and confidentiality, and is subject to the same limitations on the client-lawyer relationship, such as the obligation to refrain from assisting the client in violation of the rules.

RULE 6.3 LEGAL SERVICES ORGANIZATIONS AND LAWYER REFERRAL SERVICES

(a) A lawyer may serve as a director, officer, or member of a legal services organization, apart from the law firm in which the lawyer practices, notwithstanding that the organization serves persons having interests adverse to a client of the lawyer. The lawyer shall not knowingly participate in a decision or action of the organization:

(1) if participating in the decision or action would be incompatible with the lawyer's obligations to a client under Rule 1.7; or

(2) where the decision or action could have a material adverse effect on the representation of a client of the organization whose interests are adverse to a client of the lawyer.

(b) A lawyer may participate in and pay the usual charges of a not-for-profit lawyer referral service that recommends legal services to the public if that service:

(1) maintains registration as a qualified service with the State Bar, under such rules as may be adopted by the State Bar, consistent with these rules;

(2) is operated in the public interest for the purpose of referring prospective clients to lawyers; pro bono and public service legal programs; and government, consumer or other agencies that can best provide the assistance needed by clients, in light of their financial circumstances, spoken language, any disability, geographical convenience, and the nature and complexity of their problems;

(3) is open to all lawyers licensed and eligible to practice in this state who maintain an office within the geographical area served, and who:

(i) meet reasonable and objective requirements of experience, as established by the service;

(ii) pay reasonable registration and membership fees not to exceed an amount established by the State Bar to encourage widespread lawyer participation; and

(iii) maintain a policy of errors and omissions insurance, or provide proof of financial responsibility, in an amount at least equal to the minimum established by the State Bar;

(4) ensures that the combined fees and expenses charge a prospective client by a qualified service and a lawyer to whom the client is referred not

exceed the total charges the client would have incurred had no referral service been involved; and

(5) makes no fee-generating referral to any lawyer who has an ownership interest in, or who operates or is employed by, the qualified service, or who is associated with a law firm that has an ownership interest in, or operates or is employed by, a qualified service.

(c) The requirements of subrule (b) do no apply to

(1) a plan of prepaid legal services insurance authorized to operate in the state, or a group or prepaid legal plan, whether operated by a union, trust, mutual benefit or aid association, corporation or other entity or person, which provides unlimited or a specified amount of telephone advice or personal communications at no charge to the members or beneficiaries, other than a periodic membership or beneficiary fee, and furnishes to or pays for legal services for its members or beneficiaries;

(2) individual lawyer-to-lawyer referrals;

(3) lawyers jointly advertising their services in a manner that discloses that such advertising is solely to solicit clients for themselves; or

(4) any pro bono legal assistance program that does not accept fees from lawyers or clients for referrals.

(d) The State Bar or any aggrieved person may seek an injunction in the circuit court to enjoin violations of subrule (b). In the event the injunction is granted, the petitioner shall be entitled to reasonable costs and attorney fees.

(e) A lawyer may participate in and pay the usual charges of a plan or organization defined in subrule (c)(1), if that plan or organization:

(1) has filed with the State Bar of Michigan a written plan disclosing the name under which it operates; the name, address, and telephone number of its chief operating officer; and the plan terms, conditions of eligibility, schedule of benefits, subscription charges and agreements with counsel;

(2) updates its filings within 30 days of any material change;

(3) in January of each year following its inception files a statement representing that it continues to do business under the terms and conditions reflected in its filings as amended to date.

These filing requirements shall not apply to not-for-profit legal aid associations.

[Amended effective January 1, 1990; March 1, 1990; April 1, 1998.]

Comment

Lawyers should be encouraged to support and participate in legal service organizations. A lawyer who is an officer or a member of such an organization does not thereby have a client-lawyer relationship with persons served by the organization. However, there is potential conflict between the interests of such persons and the interests of the lawyer's clients. If the possibility of such conflict disqualified a lawyer from serving on the board of a legal services organization, the profession's involvement in such organizations would be severely curtailed.

It may be necessary in appropriate cases to reassure a client of the organization that the representation will not be affected by conflicting loyalties of a member of the board. Established, written policies in this respect can enhance the credibility of such assurances.

The restriction on lawyer participation with legal services and lawyer referral service organizations to those that file their plans with the State Bar of Michigan is intended to facilitate the establishment of a single, central repository of all such organizations in Michigan and of the terms and conditions under which they operate. The existence of that repository would make it possible for the State Bar of Michigan annually to prepare and make publicly available a directory of legal services and lawyer referral service organizations in Michigan. Absent such a central repository, reliable information concerning the status of all such organizations might not be available.

Staff Comment to 1990 Amendment

The 1990 amendment to MRPC 6.3(b) was made at the request of the State Bar of Michigan.

Staff Comment to 1998 Amendment

The April 1998 amendment of MRPC 6.3 was recommended by the State Bar of Michigan. The amended rule provides that a lawyer referral service may not make fee-generating referrals to lawyers who have an ownership or employment interest in the service. The rule also distinguishes services established and operated in the public interest from for-profit ventures and those of private law firms; establishes minimum uniform standards for making referrals and operating the referral business in the public interest; and helps clarify the public understanding of the types of services advertised and offered by different delivery systems.

RULE 6.4   LAW REFORM ACTIVITIES AFFECTING CLIENT INTERESTS

A lawyer may serve as a director, officer, or member of an organization involved in reform of the law or administration of the law notwithstanding that the reform may affect the interests of a client of the lawyer. When the lawyer knows that the interests of a client may be materially benefitted by a decision in which the lawyer participates, the lawyer shall disclose that fact but need not identify the client.

Comment

Lawyers involved in organizations seeking law reform generally do not have a client-lawyer relationship with the organization. Otherwise, it might follow that a lawyer could not be involved in a bar association law reform program that might indirectly affect a client. See also the comment to Rule 1.2. For example, a lawyer specializing in antitrust litigation might be regarded as disqualified from participating in drafting revisions of rules governing that subject. In determining the nature and scope of participation in such activities, a lawyer should be mindful of obligations to clients under other rules, particularly Rule 1.7. A lawyer is professionally obligated to protect the integrity of the program by making an appropriate disclosure within the organization when the lawyer knows a private client might be materially benefitted.

RULE 6.5   PROFESSIONAL CONDUCT

(a) A lawyer shall treat with courtesy and respect all persons involved in the legal process. A lawyer shall take particular care to avoid treating such a person discourteously or disrespectfully because of the person's race, gender, or other protected personal characteristic. To the extent possible, a lawyer shall require subordinate lawyers and nonlawyer assistants to provide such courteous and respectful treatment.

(b) A lawyer serving as an adjudicative officer shall, without regard to a person's race, gender, or other protected personal characteristic, treat every person fairly, with courtesy and respect. To the extent possible, the lawyer shall require staff and others who are subject to the adjudicative officer's direction and control to provide such fair, courteous, and respectful treatment to persons who have contact with the adjudicative tribunal.

[Adopted effective October 1, 1993.]

Comment

Duties of the Lawyer. A lawyer is an officer of the court who has sworn to uphold the federal and state constitutions, to proceed only by means that are truthful and honorable, and to avoid offensive personality. It follows that such a professional must treat clients and third persons with courtesy and respect. For many citizens, contact with a lawyer is the first or only contact with the legal system. Respect for law and for legal institutions is diminished whenever a lawyer neglects the obligation to treat persons properly. It is increased when the obligation is met.

A lawyer must pursue a client's interests with diligence. This often requires the lawyer to frame questions and statements in bold and direct terms. The obligation to treat persons with courtesy and respect is not inconsistent with the lawyer's right, where appropriate, to speak and write bluntly. Obviously, it is not possible to formulate a rule that will clearly divide what is properly challenging from what is impermissibly rude. A lawyer's professional judgment must be employed here with care and discretion.

A lawyer must take particular care to avoid words or actions that appear to be improperly based upon a person's race, gender, or other protected personal characteristic. Legal institutions, and those who serve them, should take leadership roles in assuring equal treatment for all.

A judge must act "[a]t all times" in a manner that promotes public confidence in the impartiality of the judiciary. Canon 2(B) of the Code of Judicial Conduct. See also Canon 5. By contrast, a lawyer's private conduct is largely beyond the scope of these rules. See Rule 8.4. However, a lawyer's private conduct should not cast doubt on the lawyer's commitment to equal justice under law.

A supervisory lawyer should make every reasonable effort to ensure that subordinate lawyers and nonlawyer assistants, as well as other agents, avoid discourteous or disrespectful behavior toward persons involved in the legal process. Further, a supervisory lawyer should make reasonable efforts to ensure that the firm has in effect policies and procedures that do not discriminate against members or employees of the firm on the basis of race, gender, or other protected personal characteristic. See Rules 5.1 and 5.3.

Duties of Adjudicative Officers. The duties of an adjudicative officer are included in these rules, since many legisla-tively created adjudicative positions, such as administrative hearing officer, are not covered by the Code of Judicial Conduct. For parallel provisions for judges, see the Code of Judicial Conduct.

INFORMATION ABOUT LEGAL SERVICES

RULE 7.1 COMMUNICATIONS CONCERNING A LAWYER'S SERVICES

A lawyer may, on the lawyer's own behalf, on behalf of a partner or associate, or on behalf of any other lawyer affiliated with the lawyer or the lawyer's law firm, use or participate in the use of any form of public communication that is not false, fraudulent, misleading, or deceptive. A communication shall not:

(a) contain a material misrepresentation of fact or law, or omit a fact necessary to make the statement considered as a whole not materially misleading;

(b) be likely to create an unjustified expectation about results the lawyer can achieve, or state or imply that the lawyer can achieve results by means that violate the Rules of Professional Conduct or other law; or

(c) compare the lawyer's services with other law-yers' services, unless the comparison can be factually substantiated.

Comment

This rule governs all communications about a lawyer's services, including advertising permitted by Rule 7.2. Whatever means are used to make known a lawyer's services, statements about them should be truthful. The prohibition in paragraph (b) of statements that may create "an unjusti-fied expectation" would ordinarily preclude advertisements about results obtained on behalf of a client, such as the amount of a damage award or the lawyer's record in obtain-ing favorable verdicts, and would ordinarily preclude adver-tisements containing client endorsements. Such information may create the unjustified expectation that similar results can be obtained for others without reference to the specific factual and legal circumstances.

RULE 7.2 ADVERTISING

(a) Subject to the provisions of these rules, a law-yer may advertise.

(b) A copy or recording of an advertisement or communication shall be kept for two years after its last dissemination along with a record of when and where it was used.

(c) A lawyer shall not give anything of value to a person for recommending the lawyer's services, except that a lawyer may:

(i) pay the reasonable cost of advertising or commu-nication permitted by this rule;

(ii) participate in, and pay the usual charges of, a not-for-profit lawyer referral service or other legal service organization that satisfies the requirements of Rule 6.3(b); and

(iii) pay for a law practice in accordance with Rule 1.17.

[Amended effective January 1, 1990; October 1, 1991.]

Comment

To assist the public in obtaining legal services, lawyers should be allowed to make known their services not only through reputation but also through organized information campaigns in the form of advertising. Advertising involves an active quest for clients, contrary to the tradition that a lawyer should not seek clientele. However, the public's need to know about legal services can be fulfilled in part through advertising. This need is particularly acute in the case of persons of moderate means who have not made extensive use of legal services. The interest in expanding public informa-tion about legal services ought to prevail over considerations of tradition. Nevertheless, advertising by lawyers entails the risk of practices that are misleading or overreaching.

Neither this rule nor Rule 7.3 prohibits communications authorized by law, such as notice to members of a class in a class action.

Record of Advertising. Paragraph (b) requires that a record of the content and use of advertising be kept in order to facilitate enforcement of these rules.

Paying Others to Recommend a Lawyer. A lawyer is allowed to pay for advertising permitted by these rules and for the purchase of a law practice in accordance with the provisions of Rule 1.17, but otherwise is not permitted to pay another person for channeling professional work. But see Rule 1.5(e). This restriction does not prevent an organiza-tion or person other than the lawyer from advertising or recommending the lawyer's services. Thus, a legal aid agen-cy or prepaid legal services plan may pay to advertise legal services provided under its auspices. Likewise, a lawyer may participate in not-for-profit lawyer referral programs and pay the usual fees charged by such programs. Para-graph (c) does not prohibit paying regular compensation to an assistant, such as a secretary, to prepare communications permitted by these rules.

[Comment amended effective October 1, 1991.]

RULE 7.3 DIRECT CONTACT WITH PROSPECTIVE CLIENTS

(a) A lawyer shall not solicit professional employ-ment from a prospective client with whom the lawyer has no family or prior professional relationship when a significant motive for the lawyer's doing so is the lawyer's pecuniary gain. The term "solicit" includes contact in person, by telephone or telegraph, by letter or other writing, or by other communication directed to a specific recipient, but does not include letters addressed or advertising circulars distributed generally to persons not known to need legal services of the kind provided by the lawyer in a particular matter, but who are so situated that they might in general find such services useful, nor does the term "solicit" include "sending truthful and nondeceptive letters to potential clients known to face particular legal problems" as elucidated in *Shapero v Kentucky Bar Ass'n*, 486 US 466; 108 SCt 1916; 100 LEd2d 475 (1988).

(b) A lawyer shall not solicit professional employment from a prospective client by written or recorded communication or by in-person or telephone contact even when not otherwise prohibited by paragraph (a), if:

(1) the prospective client has made known to the lawyer a desire not to be solicited by the lawyer; or

(2) the solicitation involves coercion, duress or harassment.

[Amended effective January 1, 1990.]

Comment

There is a potential for abuse inherent in direct contact by a lawyer with a prospective client known to need legal services. These forms of contact between a lawyer and a prospective client subject the layperson to the private importuning of the trained advocate in a direct interpersonal encounter. The prospective client, who may already feel overwhelmed by the circumstances giving rise to the need for legal services, may find it difficult to evaluate fully all available alternatives with reasoned judgment and appropriate self-interest in the face of the lawyer's presence and insistence upon being retained immediately. The situation is fraught with the possibility of undue influence, intimidation, and overreaching.

However, the U.S. Supreme Court has modified the traditional ban on written solicitation. *Shapero v Kentucky Bar Ass'n*, 486 US 466; 108 SCt 1916; 100 LEd2d 475 (1988). Paragraph (a) of this rule is therefore modified to the extent required by the *Shapero* decision.

The potential for abuse inherent in direct solicitation of prospective clients justifies its partial prohibition, particularly since lawyer advertising and the communication permitted under these rules are alternative means of communicating necessary information to those who may be in need of legal services.

Advertising and permissible communication make it possible for a prospective client to be informed about the need for legal services, and about the qualifications of available lawyers and law firms, without subjecting the prospective client to impermissible persuasion that may overwhelm the client's judgment.

The use of general advertising and communications permitted under *Shapero* to transmit information from lawyer to prospective client, rather than impermissible direct contact, will help to assure that the information flows cleanly as well as freely. Advertising is out in public view, thus subject to scrutiny by those who know the lawyer. The contents of advertisements and communications permitted under Rule 7.2 are permanently recorded so that they cannot be disputed and may be shared with others who know the lawyer.

This potential for informal review is itself likely to help guard against statements and claims that might constitute false or misleading communications, in violation of Rule 7.1. The contents of some impermissible direct conversations between a lawyer and a prospective client can be disputed and are not subject to third-party scrutiny. Consequently they are much more likely to approach (and occasionally cross) the dividing line between accurate representations and those that are false and misleading.

There is far less likelihood that a lawyer would engage in abusive practices against an individual with whom the lawyer has a prior family or professional relationship or where the lawyer is motivated by considerations other than the lawyer's pecuniary gain. Consequently, the general prohibition in Rule 7.3(a) is not applicable in those situations.

This rule is not intended to prohibit a lawyer from contacting representatives of organizations or groups that may be interested in establishing a group or prepaid legal plan for its members, insureds, beneficiaries, or other third parties for the purpose of informing such entities of the availability of, and detail concerning, the plan or arrangement that the lawyer or the lawyer's firm is willing to offer. This form of communication is not directed to a specific prospective client known to need legal services related to a particular matter. Rather, it is usually addressed to an individual acting in a fiduciary capacity seeking a supplier of legal services for others who may, if they choose, become prospective clients of the lawyer. Under these circumstances, the activity which the lawyer undertakes in communicating with such representatives and the type of information transmitted to the individual are functionally similar to and serve the same purpose as advertising permitted under these rules.

The 1989 amendment to MRPC 6.3 [effective January 1, 1990] and the corresponding amendment to 7.2(c) [effective January 1, 1990] were made in response to a proposal by the State Bar of Michigan. As indicated in the revised commentary for MRPC 6.3, the changes are intended to facilitate the establishment of a single, central repository of information concerning programs of the sort described in the rule, and of the terms and conditions under which they operate. With such a repository, it will be possible for the State Bar of Michigan annually to prepare and make publicly available a directory of such organizations in Michigan.

The 1989 amendment to MRPC 7.3 [effective January 1, 1990], a corresponding change in MRPC 7.2, and the accompanying changes in the commentary are in response to the U.S. Supreme Court's decision in *Shapero v Kentucky Bar Ass'n*, 486 US 466; 108 SCt 1916; 100 LEd2d 475 (1988).

RULE 7.4 COMMUNICATION OF FIELDS OF PRACTICE

A lawyer may communicate the fact that the lawyer does or does not practice in particular fields of law.

Comment

This rule permits a lawyer to indicate areas of practice in communications about the lawyer's services, for example, in a telephone directory or other advertising. If a lawyer practices only in certain fields, or will not accept matters except in such fields, the lawyer is permitted to indicate that fact.

RULE 7.5 FIRM NAMES AND LETTERHEADS

(a) A lawyer shall not use a firm name, letterhead or other professional designation that violates Rule 7.1. A trade name may be used by a lawyer in private practice if it does not imply a connection with a government agency or with a public or charitable legal services organization and it is not otherwise in violation of Rule 7.1.

(b) A law firm with offices in more than one jurisdiction may use the same name in each jurisdiction, but identification of the lawyers in an office of the firm shall indicate the jurisdictional limitations on those not licensed to practice in the jurisdiction where the office is located.

(c) The name of a lawyer holding a public office shall not be used in the name of a law firm, or in communications on its behalf, during any substantial period in which the lawyer is not actively and regularly practicing with the firm.

(d) Lawyers may state or imply that they practice in a partnership or other organization only when that is the fact.

Comment

A firm may be designated by the names of all or some of its members, by the names of deceased members where there has been a continuing succession in the firm's identity or by a trade name such as the "ABC Legal Clinic." Although the United States Supreme Court has held that legislation may prohibit the use of trade names in professional practice, use of such names in law practice is acceptable so long as it is not misleading. If a private firm uses a trade name that includes a geographical name such as "Springfield Legal Clinic," an express disclaimer that it is a public legal aid agency may be required to avoid a misleading implication. It may be observed that any firm name including the name of a deceased partner is, strictly speaking, a trade name. The use of such names to designate law firms has proven a useful means of identification. However, it is misleading to use the name of a lawyer not associated with the firm or with a predecessor of the firm.

With regard to paragraph (d), lawyers sharing office facilities, but who are not in fact partners, may not denominate themselves as, for example, "Smith and Jones," for that title suggests partnership in the practice of law.

MAINTAINING THE INTEGRITY OF THE PROFESSION

RULE 8.1 BAR ADMISSION AND DISCIPLINARY MATTERS

(a) An applicant for admission to the bar, or a lawyer in connection with a bar admission application or in connection with a disciplinary matter, shall not

(1) knowingly make a false statement of material fact, or

(2) fail to disclose a fact necessary to correct a misapprehension known by the person to have arisen in the matter, or knowingly fail to respond to a lawful demand for information from an admissions or disciplinary authority, except that this rule does not require disclosure of information protected by Rule 1.6.

(b) An applicant for admission to the bar

(1) shall not engage in the unauthorized practice of law (this does not apply to activities permitted under MCR 8.120), and

(2) has a continuing obligation, until the date of admission, to inform the standing committee on character and fitness, in writing, if any answers in the applicant's affidavit of personal history change or cease to be true.

[Amended effective July 30, 2001.]

Comment

The duty imposed by this rule extends to persons seeking admission to the bar as well as to lawyers. Hence, if a person makes a material false statement in connection with an application for admission, it may be the basis for subsequent disciplinary action if the person is admitted, and in any event may be relevant in a subsequent admission application.

The duty imposed by this rule applies to a lawyer's own admission or discipline as well as that of others. Thus, it is a separate professional offense for a lawyer to knowingly make a misrepresentation or omission in connection with a disciplinary investigation of the lawyer's own conduct. This rule also requires affirmative clarification of any misunderstanding on the part of the admissions or disciplinary authority of which the person involved becomes aware.

This rule is subject to the provisions of the Fifth Amendment of the United States Constitution and to article 1, section 17 of the Michigan Constitution. A person relying on such a provision in response to a question, however, should do so openly and not use the right of nondisclosure as a justification for failure to comply with this rule.

A lawyer representing an applicant for admission to the bar, or representing a lawyer who is the subject of a disciplinary inquiry or proceeding, is governed by the rules applicable to the client-lawyer relationship.

Staff Comment to 2001 Amendment

The July 30, 2001 amendment of MRPC 8.1 expressly precluded bar applicants from engaging in the unauthorized practice of law, and stated an applicant's continuing obligation to update the affidavit of personal history. The structure of MCR 9.104 was changed for greater clarity.

RULE 8.2 JUDICIAL AND LEGAL OFFICIALS

(a) A lawyer shall not make a statement that the lawyer knows to be false or with reckless disregard as to its truth or falsity concerning the qualifications or integrity of a judge, adjudicative officer, or public legal officer, or of a candidate for election or appointment to judicial or legal office.

(b) A lawyer who is a candidate for judicial office shall comply with the applicable provisions of the Code of Judicial Conduct.

Comment

Assessments by lawyers are relied on in evaluating the professional or personal fitness of persons being considered for election or appointment to judicial office and to public legal offices, such as attorney general, prosecuting attorney and public defender. Expressing honest and candid opinions on such matters contributes to improving the administration of justice. Conversely, false statements by a lawyer can unfairly undermine public confidence in the administration of justice.

When a lawyer seeks judicial office, the lawyer should be bound by applicable limitations on political activity.

To maintain the fair and independent administration of justice, lawyers are encouraged to continue traditional efforts to defend judges and courts unjustly criticized.

RULE 8.3 REPORTING PROFESSIONAL MISCONDUCT

(a) A lawyer having knowledge that another lawyer has committed a significant violation of the Rules of Professional Conduct that raises a substantial question as to that lawyer's honesty, trustworthiness, or fitness as a lawyer shall inform the Attorney Grievance Commission.

(b) A lawyer having knowledge that a judge has committed a significant violation of the Code of Judicial Conduct that raises a substantial question as to the judge's honesty, trustworthiness or fitness for office shall inform the Judicial Tenure Commission.

(c) This rule does not require disclosure of:

(1) information otherwise protected by Rule 1.6; or

(2) information gained by a lawyer while serving as an employee or volunteer of the substance abuse counseling program of the State Bar of Michigan, to the extent the information would be protected under Rule 1.6 from disclosure if it were a communication between lawyer and client.

[Amended effective January 6, 1993.]

Comment

Self-regulation of the legal profession requires that members of the profession initiate disciplinary investigation when they know of a violation of the Rules of Professional Conduct. Lawyers have a similar obligation with respect to judicial misconduct. An apparently isolated violation may indicate a pattern of misconduct that only a disciplinary investigation can uncover. Reporting a violation is especially important where the victim is unlikely to discover the offense.

A report about misconduct is not required where it would involve violation of Rule 1.6. However, a lawyer should encourage a client to consent to disclosure where prosecution would not substantially prejudice the client's interests. Because confidentiality is essential to encourage lawyers and judges to seek treatment, information received in the course of providing counseling services in the State Bar's lawyers and judges assistance program is exempt from the reporting requirement to the extent it would be protected under Rule 1.6 if it were a communication between lawyer and client.

If a lawyer were obliged to report every violation of the rules, the failure to report any violation would itself be a professional offense. Such a requirement existed in many jurisdictions but proved to be unenforceable. This rule limits the reporting obligation to those offenses that a self-regulating profession must vigorously endeavor to prevent. A measure of judgment is, therefore, required in complying with the provisions of this rule. The term "substantial" refers to the seriousness of the possible offense and not the quantum of evidence of which the lawyer is aware.

The duty to report professional misconduct does not apply to a lawyer retained to represent a lawyer whose professional conduct is in question. Such a situation is governed by the rules applicable to the client-lawyer relationship.

[Comment amended effective January 6, 1993.]

RULE 8.4 MISCONDUCT

It is professional misconduct for a lawyer to:

(a) violate or attempt to violate the Rules of Professional Conduct, knowingly assist or induce another to do so, or do so through the acts of another;

(b) engage in conduct involving dishonesty, fraud, deceit, misrepresentation, or violation of the criminal law, where such conduct reflects adversely on the lawyer's honesty, trustworthiness, or fitness as a lawyer;

(c) engage in conduct that is prejudicial to the administration of justice;

(d) state or imply an ability to influence improperly a government agency or official; or

(e) knowingly assist a judge or judicial officer in conduct that is a violation of the Code of Judicial Conduct or other law.

Comment

Many kinds of illegal conduct reflect adversely on fitness to practice law, such as offenses involving fraud and the offense of wilful failure to file an income tax return. However, some kinds of offenses carry no such implication. Traditionally, the distinction was drawn in terms of offenses involving "moral turpitude." That concept can be construed to include offenses concerning some matters of personal morality, such as adultery and comparable offenses, that have no specific connection to fitness for the practice of law. Although a lawyer is personally answerable to the entire criminal law, a lawyer should be professionally answerable only for offenses that indicate lack of those characteristics relevant to law practice. Offenses involving violence, dishonesty, breach of trust, or serious interference with the administration of justice are in that category. A pattern of repeated offenses, even ones of minor significance when considered separately, can indicate indifference to legal obligation.

A lawyer may refuse to comply with an obligation imposed by law upon a good-faith belief that no valid obligation exists. The provisions of Rule 1.2(c) concerning a good-faith challenge to the validity, scope, meaning, or application of the law apply to challenges of legal regulation of the practice of law. See also Rule 3.4(c).

Lawyers holding public office assume legal responsibilities going beyond those of other citizens. A lawyer's abuse of public office can suggest an inability to fulfill the professional role of attorney. The same is true of abuse of positions of private trust such as trustee, executor, administrator, guardian, agent, and such as officer, director, or manager of a corporation or other organization.

RULE 8.5   JURISDICTION

A lawyer licensed to practice in this jurisdiction is subject to the disciplinary authority of this jurisdiction, regardless of whether the lawyer is engaged in practice elsewhere. A lawyer who is licensed to practice in another jurisdiction and who is admitted to practice in this jurisdiction is subject to the disciplinary authority of this jurisdiction.

[Amended effective October 6, 1995.]

Comment

In modern practice lawyers frequently act outside the territorial limits of the jurisdiction in which they are licensed to practice, either in another state or outside the United States. In doing so, they remain subject to the governing authority of the jurisdiction in which they are licensed to practice. If their activity in another jurisdiction is substantial and continuous, it may constitute practice of law in that jurisdiction. See Rule 5.5. A lawyer admitted to practice in Michigan pro hac vice is subject to the disciplinary authority of this state for actions and inactions occurring during the course of the representation of a client in Michigan.

If the rules of professional conduct in the two jurisdictions differ, principles of conflict of laws may apply. Similar problems can arise when a lawyer is licensed to practice in more than one jurisdiction.

Where the lawyer is licensed to practice law in two jurisdictions which impose conflicting obligations, applicable rules of choice of law may govern the situation. A related problem arises with respect to practice before a federal tribunal, where the general authority of the states to regulate the practice of law must be reconciled with such authority as federal tribunals may have to regulate practice before them.

Staff Comment to 1995 Amendment

The 1995 amendment of Rule 8.5 was based on a proposal from the State Bar of Michigan. The word "licensed" was substituted for the word "admitted" in the first sentence and the beginning part of the second sentence; the words "regardless of whether the lawyer is" were substituted for the word "although" in the first sentence; and the words "admitted to practice" were substituted for the word "practicing" in the second part of the second sentence.

RULES CONCERNING THE STATE
BAR OF MICHIGAN

Effective January 12, 1972

Research Note

Use Westlaw® to find cases citing or applying specific rules. Westlaw may also be used to search for specific terms in court rules or to update court rules. See the MI–RULES and MI–ORDERS Scope Screens for detailed descriptive information and search tips.

Amendments to these rules are published, as received, in the N.W.2d and Michigan Reporter advance sheets, and Michigan Legislative Service.

Table of Rules

RULE 1. STATE BAR OF MICHIGAN

The State Bar of Michigan is the association of the members of the bar of this State, organized and existing as a public body corporate pursuant to powers of the Supreme Court over the bar of the State. The State Bar of Michigan shall, under these rules, aid in promoting improvements in the administration of justice and advancements in jurisprudence, in improving relations between the legal profession and the public, and in promoting the interests of the legal profession in this State.

Publisher's Note: The Michigan Supreme Court Order of June 30, 2000, provides:

This administrative matter presents the straightforward and narrow question whether the State Bar of Michigan may use its membership mailing to solicit for a political action committee (PAC). After considerable public comment and response from the State Bar of Michigan, this Court concludes that the use of the annual membership dues form of the State Bar (or any other mailing by the State Bar) to solicit or collect financial contributions for any political action committee is inconsistent with the State Bar's public role.

The State Bar is an organization established under state law to which all attorneys who wish to practice law in Michigan must belong. The State Bar is a "public body corporate."[1] The question whether the State Bar is a "public entity" for all purposes is not before this Court and need not be decided today. The fact that one must be a member of the State Bar to participate as a lawyer in the public activity of the court system is sufficient to establish the public character of the bar for purposes of resolving this matter administratively. The Court resolves this administrative matter under the provisions of MCL 600.904; MSA 27A.904 which grant this Court exclusive authority to "adopt rules and regulations concerning the conduct and activities of the state bar of Michigan." In resolving this matter administratively, the Court rejects the invitation of the Michigan Chamber of Commerce to interpret the Michigan Campaign Finance Act or the terms of LAWPAC's conciliation agreement with Secretary of State, or to pronounce upon the First Amendment implications of bar assistance to LAWPAC.

Today's order is based on the following determinations:

1) Given the mandatory nature of attorney membership in the bar, the solicitation on membership dues forms for funds for LAWPAC or any other PAC selected by the bar for inclusion on the forms involves the bar in appearing to endorse or promote partisan candidates and political positions that may be opposed by individual members of the Bar.

2) No attorney should be required to join an organization that engages, through the conferring of direct or indirect benefit or assistance, in the promotion of partisan or political activities. Lawyers who disfavor the positions of a political committee or who disfavor the political candidates supported by a committee should not, as a condition of engaging in their profession, be required to join an organization providing benefits to such a political committee.

3) The inclusion of a solicitation of funds for a PAC on the annual dues notice of the State Bar confers a benefit upon the PAC.[2]

For the reasons stated above, IT IS ORDERED that the State Bar of Michigan shall not include a solicitation for funds for any PAC on any mailing to its membership.

This order does not prevent individual attorneys from exercising their rights to contribute to any PAC, including LAWPAC.

IT IS FURTHER ORDERED that this order shall be effective immediately.

IT IS FURTHER ORDERED that Administrative Order No. 1993–5 shall remain in effect.

Cavanagh, J., dissents and states as follows:

In February 1999, the Michigan Chamber of Commerce, through counsel, requested this Court to prohibit the State Bar of Michigan from soliciting LAWPAC contributions on its 1999–2000 dues notice and to require the State Bar to sever completely its connection with LAWPAC. It was asserted by the chamber that the bar's connection with LAWPAC violated provisions of the Michigan Campaign Finance Act, 1976 PA 388, MCL 169.201 *et seq.*; MSA 4.1703(1) *et seq.*, and impinged upon the First Amendment rights of attorneys.

Earlier in February, the State Bar, LAWPAC, and the Secretary of State entered into "conciliation agreements" to resolve a complaint in which the president of the Michigan Chamber of Commerce alleged that the State Bar's involvement with LAWPAC violated the Michigan Campaign Finance Act (MCFA). Those conciliation agreements require LAWPAC to reimburse the State Bar for supplies and services provided in the past. In addition, the State Bar has agreed to bill LAWPAC "at commercially reasonable rates" for any supplies or services provided in the future.

But the conciliation agreements did not address specifically the manner in which the State Bar solicits LAWPAC contributions on its dues notices. The language utilized certainly, however, contemplated the continuation of the current practice. The conciliation agreements also did not specify the "commercially reasonable [value]" of being the only non-bar entity to have that privilege.

LAWPAC was formed in 1973 under the State Bar's sponsorship. It functions as a political action committee that solicits contributions from attorneys and uses the money to conduct lobbying activities and to make contributions to candidates.

In 1978, LAWPAC became a "separate segregated fund" of the State Bar. That is a term of art used in § 55 of the MCFA.[3] At the time, the statute allowed a "corporation or a joint stock company" to establish and administer a separate segregated fund. The State Bar is neither of those things. The State Bar's enabling legislation describes it as a "public body corporate."[4] The fact that the State Bar was not expressly authorized to have a separate segregated fund was one of the points made by the Michigan Chamber of Commerce in the complaint that it filed with the Secretary of State last year. That point had gone unraised for twenty years. Shortly after the chamber filed its complaint, the State Bar filed an amended campaign finance report that recharacterized LAWPAC as an "independent committee," a term defined in MCFA, § 8.[5]

From 1978–79 continuing through the current fiscal year, the State Bar has solicited contributions to LAWPAC via a "reverse checkoff" on the annual dues invoices. The form adds a suggested $35 LAWPAC contribution to the base

State Bar dues. Below that is a space that allows a member to subtract the $35 and pay only the base dues. But, unless the member acts affirmatively to make that subtraction, the invoice requires payment of a gross total that includes a LAWPAC contribution. Personal and clerical inertia make that reverse checkoff procedure advantageous to LAWPAC. The request for this administrative action asserts that ninety-six percent of the money that LAWPAC received from 1996 through 1998 came in with State Bar dues payments.[6]

The State Bar processes the dues payments and separates the LAWPAC component. Special processing sometimes is required. For example, some attorneys pay their dues with corporate checks, but corporations may not contribute to LAWPAC, so reprocessing of those payments by the State Bar is necessary.

As explained previously, the State Bar never has been a type of entity that is expressly authorized by MCFA, § 55 to sponsor a "separate segregated fund." As passed originally, the MCFA did not say exactly what a "public body corporate" such as the State Bar could or could not do. A new § 57 was added to the MCFA by 1995 PA 264. That new section, which was then amended by 1996 PA 590, now reads as follows:

(1) A public body or an individual acting for a public body shall not use or authorize the use of funds, personnel, office space, property, stationery, postage, vehicles, equipment, supplies, or other public resources to make a contribution or expenditure or provide volunteer personal services....

(2) A person who knowingly violates this section is guilty of a misdemeanor.... [MCL 169.257; MSA 4.1703(57).]

These points, and others, were raised by E. James Barrett, President of the Michigan Chamber of Commerce, in a MCFA complaint that was filed with the Secretary of State on May 7, 1998. The State Bar's position is that, while it might be described as a "quasi-public" body, it certainly is not a "state agency," the intended object of the amendment. In any event, that filing led to the State Bar and LAWPAC signing the February 12, 1999, conciliation agreements. While refraining from making explicit findings about past MCFA violations, the conciliation agreements required corrective and preventive measures.

At the time of this request from the chamber, I recall my puzzlement about why, suddenly, this twenty-year-old practice was suddenly now deemed to deserve a fatal blow. One would have thought that such new-found urgency would have arisen closer to the annual dues notification date in July of earlier years, or in 1998, the immediately preceding year. Be that as it may, in an apparent attempt to accomplish, through our administrative procedures, what the chamber had failed to effect through its Secretary of State Conciliation Agreement, it requested this Court to terminate the bar's connection with LAWPAC, asserting, as previously stated, that such connection entailed statutory and constitutional violations. A majority of this Court, in May of last year, considered just such a swift administrative demise of LAWPAC appearing on the bar's dues notice, but action was deferred in recognition of our rules that, absent an emergency, require publication and a public hearing. Then, following a public hearing in May 1999, the Chief Justice, in July 1999, notified the bar that the Court was giving serious consideration to the chamber's request because, "in light of MCL 169.257; MSA 4.1703(57), we are troubled by the solicitation method." By that correspondence, the bar was further notified that the matter

would reappear on a September 1999 public hearing agenda and that no changes would be required in the 1999–2000 dues notice. The Court also indicated it would be most interested in hearing the bar's response to the chamber's request. Additional public hearings have been held, and, pursuant to our direction, the State Bar had the matter considered by its Dues Statement Review Committee, which made recommendations for formulation of bar policies and procedures for the annual dues statement. These recommendations were subsequently approved by the State Bar Board of Commissioners and have been presented to this Court for consideration.

The Court's perfunctory order today, following public hearings and receipt of the bar's recommendations in response to our request, simply closes the circle commenced by the chamber's initial request.

I dissent from the Court's action in response to this request. Although the conciliation agreements supposedly resolved the complaint filed by the chamber's president, the reality seems to be that the dispute continues. The request to this Court effectively asked the Court to issue a declaratory interpretation of the MCFA and the conciliation agreements and to infer constitutional violations from LAWPAC's relationship with the bar. No lower court has ruled on those questions. Neither the Secretary of State nor the Attorney General has asserted that the State Bar's anticipated future conduct would violate either the MCFA or the conciliation agreements, nor has any lower court considered and ruled upon any asserted constitutional violations. I would deny the chamber's request and suggest it seek an adjudication of its statutory or constitutional claims or an administrative ruling or amendatory legislation. While the Court's order today deems the bar's conduct inconsistent with its public role, I would suggest that what is really inconsistent and inappropriate is this Court's resolution of what, in essence, is an adjudicative matter, while purporting to wear its administrative hat, its protestations to the contrary notwithstanding.

Kelly, J., dissents and states as follows:

I disagree with the majority's decision to order the State Bar of Michigan to discontinue permitting LAWPAC to solicit donations on the State Bar's annual membership dues notice.[7] The majority's action circumvents an established legislative procedure for addressing the issue raised here. Also, it fails to recognize the true nature of the transaction between LAWPAC and the State Bar.

Our public hearings on this matter have provided us insight into the underlying facts. In early 1999, the State Bar, LAWPAC and the Michigan Secretary of State entered into conciliation agreements to resolve a complaint by the Michigan Chamber of Commerce. It alleged that the State Bar's involvement with LAWPAC violated the Michigan Campaign Finance Act (MCFA).[8] The conciliation agreements required LAWPAC to reimburse the State Bar for supplies and services provided in the past. In addition, the State Bar agreed to bill LAWPAC "at commercially reasonable rates" for any supplies or services provided in the future.

The conciliation agreements did not, however, address specifically the manner in which LAWPAC solicits contributions on the State Bar's dues notices. Nor did they specify the commercially reasonable value of being the only non-bar entity to have that privilege.

Three Michigan attorneys have asserted that the conciliation agreements actually prohibit the State Bar from allowing LAWPAC to solicit donations on its dues notices.[9] They assert that, despite the conciliation agreements, the State Bar will continue to allow LAWPAC to solicit donations in its traditional manner. Thus, they have requested this Court to amend Administrative Order No. 1993–5 to prohibit the practice.[10]

We have the authority "to adopt rules and regulations concerning the conduct and activities of the state bar of Michigan.... " **MCL 600.904; MSA 27A.904; see also Const 1963, art 6, § 5.** However, the Legislature has provided a specific method for parties to seek relief from a violation of the MCFA. In the act, it provides that, when a party to a conciliation agreement violates that agreement,

the secretary of state may refer the matter to the attorney general for the enforcement of any criminal penalty provided by this act or commence a hearing.... [MCL 169.215(5); MSA 4.1703(15)(5).]

If the Secretary of State decides to commence a hearing and determines

that a violation of this act has occurred, the secretary of state may issue an order requiring the person to pay a civil fine equal to the amount of the improper contribution or expenditure plus not more than $1,000.00 for each violation. [MCL 169.215(6); MSA 4.1703(15)(6).]

If, instead, the Secretary of State refers the matter to the Attorney General, the latter is authorized to pursue a criminal prosecution for the alleged violation of § 57.

A person who knowingly violates this section is guilty of a misdemeanor punishable ... if the person is not an individual, by 1 of the following, whichever is greater: (a) A fine of not more than $20,000.00. (b) A fine equal to the amount of the improper contribution or expenditure. [MCL 169.157(2); MSA 4.1703(57)(2).]

In essence, the complainants here allege that the State Bar is violating the conciliation agreements and the MCFA by allowing LAWPAC to solicit donations on bar dues notices. The MCFA specifies the proper manner for obtaining relief. In fact, its provisions state that they furnish the exclusive manner to address a violation of the act. MCL 169.215(9); MSA 4.1703(15)(9).[11] In the absence of a violation, "a conciliation agreement is a complete bar to any further action with respect to matters covered in the conciliation agreement." MCL 169.215(5); MSA 4.1703(15)(5).

Despite that fact, the complaining parties have prompted the majority to grant them relief without adjudicating whether the State Bar is in violation of its agreements and the MCFA. The action taken by the majority today clearly circumvents the legislative framework provided for resolving the issue.

There has yet to be a determination by the Secretary of State or a lower court that a violation of the MCFA has occurred or is occurring. Hence, the issue whether the State Bar can properly solicit funds for LAWPAC is not properly before us. I dissent from the majority's action and would direct the complaining parties to address their complaint to the Secretary of State for disposition through the provisions of the MCFA.

The majority fails to address how this issue came before the Court and instead focuses on policy reasons for justifying its action. A close examination of the reasons cited indicates that, in actuality, the majority is basing its decision on the State Bar's purported violation of the MCFA.

The majority asserts that the State Bar confers a benefit upon LAWPAC by allowing the PAC to solicit donations on the State Bar's annual dues notice. Considering the public character of the State Bar and the mandatory nature of attorney membership, the majority concludes that the State Bar should not be involved in endorsing or assisting any PAC.

The property of the State Bar is public property. *State Bar of Michigan v City of Lansing,* 361 Mich 185, 197–198; 105 NW2d 131 (1960). If the State Bar is assisting LAWPAC by contributing space on its annual dues statement to LAWPAC or reducing the postage costs LAWPAC would otherwise incur, such assistance would violate § 57. The allegation of such "assistance" is exactly the subject of the conciliation agreements between LAWPAC, the State Bar, and the Secretary of State. Thus, it can be seen that the policy reasons cited by the majority for its decision are really nothing more than "smoke and mirrors." They hide the basic issue whether the State Bar's continuing practice of allowing LAWPAC to solicit contributions on its annual dues notice violates the conciliation agreements and the MCFA.

The majority merely "presumes" that LAWPAC receives a benefit from the arrangement and that providing a benefit to LAWPAC equates to providing assistance to LAWPAC. It ignores the fee that LAWPAC pays to the State Bar to include its solicitation on the annual membership dues statements.[12]

Admittedly, LAWPAC has had exclusive access to the State Bar's annual membership dues notices, but counsel for the State Bar has advised us that no other PAC has requested to be included. Regardless, the State Bar has recently approved guidelines by which any PAC can be included on the annual dues notices for the purpose of soliciting donations.[13] The State Bar will charge the PAC a minimum annual fee of $10,000 for that opportunity. Thus, the "assistance" offered by the State Bar is in the form of a value-for-value transaction.

The issue whether a value-for-value transaction of this sort violates § 57 of the MCFA and confers a benefit on LAWPAC has never been decided in the proper forum. The majority's reliance on conclusory statements and observations clouds the issue. Because the Court has not undertaken proper consideration of the issue, I disagree with the order issued today.

In addition, how does a value-for-value transaction open to any PAC constitute an endorsement or promotion by the bar of a particular ideological or political perspective? Whatever contributions LAWPAC, or any other PAC, receives by way of a dues notice or solicitation of bar members are voluntary. The State Bar does not give LAWPAC any portion of the mandatory member's dues. Therefore, those whom the law requires to join the State Bar are not made members of an organization that supports interests adverse or objectionable to their own.

The appropriate action for this Court is to direct the complaining parties to lodge their concerns with the Secretary of State in accordance with the requirements of the MCFA.

1. "The State Bar of Michigan is the association of the members of the bar of this state, organized and existing as a public body corporate pursuant to powers of the Supreme Court over the bar of the state." State Bar Rule 1

2. The Court has studied a thoughtful proposal from the bar intended to "cure" this problem by allowing the bar to sell dues mailing solicitation services to organizations that meet the bar's predetermined criteria. However, even if a commercially reasonable rate for the cost of the benefit conferred could be determined and

imposed, given the finite number of solicitations possible on any given dues notice and the need for the bar to "vet" applications for inclusion, we are persuaded that such provisions do not alter the essential fact that a benefit is conferred.

3.   MCL 169.255; MSA 4.1703(55).

4.   MCL 600.901; MSA 27A.901.

5.   MCL 169.208(3); MSA 4.1703(8) (3).

6.   Speaking as an individual attorney, I would note that I have never been enamored of the LAWPAC solicitation on my State Bar dues notice. The solicitation—more particularly the "reverse checkoff" method—always has been bothersome to me, even though I can subtract the suggested contribution before paying my bar dues.

7.   LAWPAC is a political action committee formed for the purpose of identifying and contributing to the campaigns of public officials who share an interest in the legal profession.

8.   MCL 169.201 *et seq*; MSA 4.1703(1) *et seq*. The complaint alleged that the State Bar contributed supplies and services to LAWPAC in violation of MCL 169.257; MSA 4.1703(57). Subsection 57(1) states:

A public body ... shall not use or authorize the use of funds, personnel, office space, property, stationery, postage, vehicles, equipment, supplies, or other public resources to make a contribution or expenditure....

The Secretary of State, pursuant to the authority in MCL 169.215(5); MSA 4.1703(15)(5), investigated the complaint and negotiated conciliation agreements with LAWPAC and the State Bar to resolve the chamber's objections.

9.   The attorneys proceed on the theory that the State Bar has conferred a benefit to LAWPAC in the nature of a contribution in violation of § 57.

10.   Administrative Order No. 1993–5, 443 Mich xci, sets forth permissible and impermissible activities of the State Bar.

11.   MCL 169.215(9); MSA 4.1703(15)(9) reads:

There is no private right of action, either in law or in equity, pursuant to this act. The remedies provided in this act are the exclusive means by which this act may be enforced and by which any harm resulting from a violation of this act may be redressed.

12.   Counsel for the State Bar submitted an affidavit from the Assistant Executive Director for Financial Affairs of the State Bar showing that, for fiscal year 1998, LAWPAC paid the State Bar $8,732 to include its solicitation on the dues notice.

13.   The majority appears to conclude that, because space is limited on the annual dues statement, the State Bar will choose among applicants selecting only some for inclusion. Thus, it remains in a position to confer a benefit.

The majority's conclusion is based on conjecture that a high number of PACs will take advantage of the opportunity. It assumes that there will not be room on the notice to accommodate all those desiring to be included. I believe that it is premature to make such a conclusion. We should not automatically assume that, in the event that there is insufficient space, the State Bar will exercise its discretion in a prejudicial or referential manner.

Furthermore, every PAC that applies to be included on the annual dues notice is subject to the condition contained in the State Bar's guidelines. Neither LAWPAC, nor any other PAC, is guaranteed placement on the dues notice in the event that space is limited.

RULE 2. MEMBERSHIP

Those persons who are licensed to practice law in this state shall constitute the membership of the State Bar of Michigan, subject to the provisions of these rules. Law students may become law student section members of the State Bar. None other than a member's correct name shall be entered upon the official register of attorneys of this state. Each member, upon admission to the State Bar and in the annual dues statement, must provide the State Bar with the member's correct name and address, and such addi-

tional information as may be required. If the address provided is a mailing address only, the member also must provide a street or building address for the member's business or residence. No member shall practice law in this state until such information has been provided. Members shall notify the State Bar promptly in writing of any change of name or address. The State Bar shall be entitled to due notice of, and to intervene and be heard in, any proceeding by a member to alter or change the member's name. The name and address on file with the State Bar at the time shall control in any matter arising under these rules involving the sufficiency of notice to a member or the propriety of the name used by the member in the practice of law or in a judicial election or in an election for any other public office. Every active member shall annually provide a certification as to whether the member or the member's law firm has a policy to maintain interest-bearing trust accounts for deposit of client and third-party funds. The certification shall be placed on the face of the annual dues notice and shall require the member's signature.

[Amended December 11, 1975; amended effective August 1, 1991; August 19, 1993; September 26, 2001.]

Staff Comment to 2001 Amendment

The September 26, 2001 amendment of Rule 2 was made at the request of the State Bar of Michigan. The amendment eliminated the requirement that members of the Bar provide their home addresses to the Bar. Under the amendment, a business address will be sufficient unless it is a mailing address only. Although Rule 2 had included a "residence address" requirement since its inception, the Bar had not requested such information for many years. The other changes were made for clarity and style.

The staff comment is published only for the benefit of the bench and bar and is not an authoritative construction by the Court.

RULE 3. MEMBERSHIP CLASSES

(a) **Active.** A person engaged in the practice of law in Michigan must be an active member of the State Bar. In addition to its traditional meaning, the term "person engaged in the practice of law" in this rule includes a person licensed to practice law in Michigan or another jurisdiction and employed in Michigan in the administration of justice or in a position which requires that the person be a law school graduate, but does not include (1) a judicial law clerk who is a member or is seeking to become a member of the bar of another jurisdiction and who does not intend to practice in Michigan after the clerkship ends, or (2) an instructor in law. Only an active member may vote in a State Bar election or hold a State Bar office. A person not an active member who engages in the practice of law is subject to discipline or prosecution for unauthorized practice.

(b) **Inactive.** An active member may request an inactive classification. The member may later be classified as an active member by

(1) applying to the State Bar secretary;

(2) paying the annual dues;

(3) demonstrating that no disciplinary action has been taken or is currently pending in another jurisdiction; and

(4) if the member was inactive for 3 years or more, obtaining a certificate from the Board of Law Examiners that the member currently possesses sufficient ability and learning in the law to enable the member to properly practice as an attorney and counselor in Michigan.

If the inactive member has been or is currently subject to disciplinary action in another jurisdiction, the application must be referred to the Attorney Discipline Board and action on the application delayed until the board makes a decision.

(c) Law Student. A student in good standing at a law school approved by the Board of Law Examiners or the American Bar Association may be a member of the law student section.

(d) Affiliate. A legal assistant as defined in the State Bar bylaws may become an affiliate member of the State Bar of Michigan and shall thereupon be a member of the legal assistants section. A legal administrator as defined in the State Bar bylaws may become an affiliate member of the State Bar of Michigan and shall thereupon be a member of the legal administrators section.

[Amended May 12, 1972; December 11, 1975; October 1, 1978; May 4, 1979; amended effective April 1, 1990; August 1, 1991.]

RULE 4. MEMBERSHIP DUES

(a) An active member's dues for each fiscal year (October 1 through September 30), are payable at the State Bar's principal office by October 1 of each year. The dues consist of two components: $160 for State Bar expenses other than the attorney discipline system and an amount to be set annually by the Supreme Court to fund the Attorney Grievance Commission and Attorney Discipline Board, to be separately stated in the dues notice. However, for a member admitted between April 1 and September 30, the fiscal year of admission, dues are one-half of the full-year amount.

(b) Dues notices must be sent to all active members before September 20. A 10 percent late charge is added to a dues payment postmarked after November 30. The State Bar must send a written notice of delinquency (by registered or certified mail to the last recorded business address) to a member who fails to pay dues by November 30. If the dues and the late charge are not paid within 30 days after the notice is sent, the individual is suspended from active membership in the State Bar. If an individual is not subject to a disciplinary order and the suspension is for less than 3 years, the member is automatically reinstated on the payment of dues and late charges owing from the date of the suspension to the date of the reinstatement. If the suspension is for 3 years or more, the individual must also apply for recertification under Rule 8 for the Board of Law Examiners.

(c) An active member does not have to pay dues after becoming 70.

(d) Annual dues for affiliate members and law student section members are established annually by the Board of Commissioners in an amount not to exceed one-third of the portion of dues for active members which fund State Bar activities other than the attorney discipline system and are payable at the State Bar's principal office by October 1 of each year.

(e) All dues are paid into the State Bar treasury and maintained in segregated accounts to pay State Bar expenses authorized by the Board of Commissioners and the expenses of the attorney discipline system within the budget approved by the Supreme Court, respectively.

[Amended March 15, 1973; December 11, 1975; December 28, 1976; October 1, 1978; amended effective October 1, 1989; April 1, 1990; August 1, 1991; October 1, 1993.]

Staff Comment

The July 30, 1993, amendment of State Bar Rule 4 bifurcates State Bar dues into two components, one for State Bar activities other than the attorney discipline system and the other to fund the Attorney Grievance Commission and the Attorney Discipline Board. This change had been recommended by the State Bar Representative Assembly. In addition, the amendment sets the nondiscipline component at $160.

RULE 5. BOARD OF COMMISSIONERS

Sec. 1. Powers, Functions, and Duties.

(a) The Board of Commissioners shall

(1) implement policy adopted by the assembly;

(2) establish policy for the State Bar between assembly meetings not inconsistent with prior action of the assembly;

(3) manage the State Bar, adopt a budget for it, and supervise receipt and disbursements of State Bar funds;

(4) prescribe the function and duties of committees;

(5) provide for the organization of sections (including a law student section) of the State Bar, membership in which is voluntary, and determine the amount and regulate the collection and disbursement of section dues;

(6) receive and review committee and section reports and recommendations proposing action by the board and take interim or final action that the board finds feasible, in the public interest, and germane to the functions and purposes of the State Bar; and

(7) arrange for the publication of a journal to be issued at least 4 times a year and sent to the active members without charge.

(b) The Board of Commissioners may

(1) adopt bylaws;

(2) appoint standing and special committees, including

    (A) character and fitness,

    (B) civil procedure,

    (C) court administration,

    (D) criminal jurisprudence,

    (E) fiscal,

    (F) grievance,

    (G) judicial qualifications,

    (H) legal education,

    (I) legislation,

    (J) professional and judicial ethics,

    (K) scope and correlation, and

    (L) unauthorized practice of law;

(3) at the request of the governor, the legislature, or the supreme court, or on its own initiative, conduct an investigation of any matter relating to the state's courts or tribunals, to the practice and procedure in them, or to the administration of justice, and report to the officer or body making the request;

(4) acquire and hold real and personal estate by lease, purchase, gift, devise, or bequest, and sell, convey, mortgage, pledge, or release property;

(5) borrow money and pledge for repayment in annual installments, in anticipation of future revenues from annual membership dues, and issue notes, but the total indebtedness outstanding may not at any time exceed 40 percent and the principal installment due in one year may not exceed 8 percent of the revenues from required annual membership dues for the 5 preceding fiscal years;

(6) accept and hold real and personal estate in trust for any use or purpose germane to the general functions and purposes of the State Bar;

(7) bring an action or proceeding at law or in equity in a state or federal court or tribunal and intervene and be heard on an issue involving the membership or affairs of the State Bar in an action or proceeding pending in a state or federal court or tribunal.

(c) The board may assign these powers, functions, and duties to another State Bar agency but the board may reverse or modify the exercise of a power, function, or duty by a delegated agency.

Sec. 2. Membership; Terms. The board consists of:

(1) 20 elected members, each serving a 3-year term commencing upon the adjournment of the meeting of the outgoing Board of Commissioners held at the annual meeting following the member's election.

(2) 5 members appointed by the Supreme Court, each serving a 3-year term commencing upon the adjournment of the meeting of the outgoing Board of Commissioners held at the annual meeting following the member's appointment. In the event that a commissioner appointed by the Supreme Court is not appointed before the adjournment of the annual meeting at which time he or she would ordinarily take office, that member shall begin to serve immediately upon appointment. Except where appointment is made under Section 5, such appointed commissioner shall be considered to have been in office at the beginning of the term for which the appointment is made.

(3) The chairperson-elect, the chairperson and the immediate past chairperson of the State Bar young lawyers section, each serving for the years during which they hold those positions.

(4) The chairperson, vice-chairperson, and clerk of the assembly, each serving for the years during which they hold those positions.

Sec. 3. Election Districts; Apportionment. The board shall establish commissioner election districts consisting of contiguous judicial circuits and containing, as nearly as practicable, an equal lawyer population. The largest geographic area may have the highest deviation from population equality.

The board shall review and revise election districts every 6 years. If, as the result of a revision in election districts, no elected commissioner maintains his or her principal office in a district or a district has fewer elected commissioners than it is entitled to, the board may designate an elected commissioner or commissioner at large for the district until the next annual election when the vacancy will be filled.

To provide for an orderly transition and to preserve the requirement that approximately one-third of the elected board members are elected each year, the board may extend the term of an elected commissioner for a period not exceeding one year and the authorized membership of the board will be enlarged for the period affected.

An elected commissioner whose district is merged with another district as the result of a revision of commissioner election districts may nevertheless serve the full term for which the commissioner was elected and the authorized membership of the board will be temporarily enlarged for that purpose.

Sec. 4. Nomination and Election of Commissioners. A commissioner is elected by the active members having their principal offices in the election district. To be nominated, a member must have his or her principal office in the election district and file a petition signed by at least 5 persons entitled to vote for the nominee with the secretary at the principal office of the State Bar between April 1 and April 30. Voting eligibility is determined annually on May 1. Before June 2, the secretary shall mail a ballot to everyone entitled to vote. A ballot will not be counted unless marked and returned to the secretary at the principal office of the State Bar in a sealed envelope bearing a postmark date not later than June 15. A board of 3 tellers appointed by the president shall canvass the ballots, and the secretary shall certify the count to the supreme court clerk. A member of or a candidate for the board may not be a teller. The candidate receiving the highest number of votes will be declared elected. In the case of a tie vote, the tellers shall determine the successful candidate by lot. In an election in which terms of differing length are to be filled, the successful candidate with the lowest vote shall serve the shortest term to be filled.

Sec. 5. Vacancy. The board shall fill a vacancy among the elected commissioners and the Supreme Court shall fill a vacancy among the appointed commissioners, to serve the remainder of an unexpired term. If an elected commissioner moves his or her principal office out of his or her election district, the board shall declare that a vacancy exists. If an elected or appointed commissioner does not attend two consecutive meetings of the board without being excused by the president because of a personal or professional emergency, the president shall declare that a vacancy exists.

Sec. 6. Meetings. The board shall meet during the annual meeting of the State Bar and before the convening of the assembly and shall hold not less than 4 meetings each year. The interval between board meetings may not be greater than 3 months. A special meeting may be held at the president's call and must be held at the secretary's call at the request of three or more board members. At a meeting, a majority of the board constitutes a quorum.

Sec. 7. Voting. Each member of the board may cast only one vote. Voting by proxy is not permitted.

[Amended October 24, 1972; March 15, 1973; April 22, 1975; May 28, 1975; December 11, 1975; November 25, 1977; June 29, 1979; amended effective February 11, 1986; January 10, 1989; August 1, 1991; May 16, 1995; May 10, 1996.]

Staff Comment to 1996 Amendment

The May 10, 1996, amendment rescinds the prohibition on service by judges on the State Bar Board of Commissioners or in the Representative Assembly. However, judges may not be elected or appointed officers of either body.

RULE 6. REPRESENTATIVE ASSEMBLY

Sec. 1. Powers, Functions and Duties. The Representative Assembly is the final policy-making body of the State Bar. No petition may be made for an increase in State Bar dues except as authorized by the Representative Assembly.

Sec. 2. Membership. The assembly consists of:

(1) 142 elected representatives.

(2) 8 commissioner representatives who are the members of the executive committee of the Board of Commissioners. No other member of the board may serve in the assembly.

Notwithstanding the provisions of this section, all representatives previously appointed by the Supreme Court shall serve until the end of their terms. The provisions of Section 6 with regard to the declaration of a vacancy shall also apply, where applicable, to the remaining appointed representatives. Vacancies in appointed positions shall not be filled. In order to achieve the increase in the number of elected representatives from 130 to 142, the assembly shall allocate additional seats each year as necessary to replace former appointed representatives whose terms expire or whose seats have become vacant.

Sec. 3. Election Districts; Apportionment. The assembly shall apportion the representatives every 6 years. The judicial circuits are the election districts. Each judicial circuit is entitled to one representative. The remaining seats are to be apportioned among the circuits on the basis of lawyer population, determined on February 1 of the reapportionment year. If as a result of the reapportionment any circuit becomes entitled to fewer representatives than are currently elected therefrom, the assembly representatives from that circuit may nevertheless serve the full terms for which they were elected and the authorized membership of the assembly will be temporarily enlarged for that purpose.

Sec. 4. Nomination and Election of Representatives. A representative is elected by the active members having their principal offices in a judicial circuit. To be nominated, a member must have his or her principal office in the judicial circuit and file a petition signed by at least 5 persons entitled to vote for the nominee with the secretary at the principal office of the State Bar between April 1 and April 30. Voting eligibility is determined annually on May 1. Before June 2, the secretary shall mail a ballot to everyone entitled to vote. When an assembly member seeks reelection, the election notification must disclose his or her incumbency and the number of meetings of the assembly that the incumbent has attended in the following form: "has attended _____ of _____ meetings during the period of [*his or her*] incumbency." A ballot may not be counted unless marked and returned to the secretary at the principal office of the State Bar in a sealed envelope bearing a postmark date not later than June 15. A board of tellers appointed by the president shall canvass the ballots and the secretary shall certify the count to the supreme court clerk. A member of or candidate for the assembly may not be a teller. The candidate receiving the highest number of votes will be declared elected. In the case of a tie vote, the tellers shall determine the successful candidate by lot. An election will occur in each judicial circuit every 3 years, except that in a judicial circuit entitled to 3 or more representatives, one-third will be elected each year. If a short-term representative is to be elected at the same election as a full-term one, the member with the higher vote total is elected to the longer term.

Sec. 5. Terms. An elected representative shall serve a three-year term beginning with the adjournment of the annual meeting following the representative's election and until his or her successor is elected. A representative may not continue to serve after completing two successive three-year terms unless service is extended under the provisions of Rule 7, Section 2.

Sec. 6. Vacancy. If an elected representative ceases to be a member of the State Bar of Michigan, dies during his or her term of office, moves his or her principal office out of the judicial circuit he or she represents, or submits a written resignation acceptable to the chairperson, the chairperson shall declare that a vacancy exists. If an elected representative does not attend two consecutive meetings of the assembly without being excused by the chairperson because of a personal or professional emergency, or does not attend three consecutive meetings of the assembly for any reason or reasons, the chairperson shall declare that a vacancy exists.

When a vacancy exists, the remaining representatives from the affected judicial circuit or, if there are none, the State Bar-recognized local bar associations in the affected judicial circuit, shall nominate a successor prior to the next meeting of the assembly. The assembly may appoint such nominee or, in the event of failure to receive such nomination, any lawyer from the affected judicial circuit, to fill the vacancy, effective immediately upon such appointment and continuing until the position is filled by the election process.

In the event that at the time a vacancy arises under this rule more than eighteen months remain in the term of an elected representative, there will be an election for the unexpired term at the next annual election of representatives. If there are less than eighteen months remaining in the term of an elected representative when a vacancy arises, no interim election will be held. The interim appointment ends when the secretary certifies the election count, and the person elected shall take his or her seat immediately.

Sec. 7. Meetings. The assembly shall meet:

(1) during the annual meeting of the State Bar;

(2) annually in March or April; and

(3) at any other time and place it determines.

A special meeting may be called by the Board of Commissioners, or by the chairperson and clerk, who shall determine the time and place of such meeting. A special meeting must be called by the chairperson on the written request of a quorum of the Representative Assembly. Fifty members constitute a quorum. The chairperson of the assembly presides at all of its meetings. The assembly may adopt rules and procedures for the transaction of its business not inconsistent with these rules or the bylaws of the State Bar. A section chairperson is entitled to floor privileges without a vote when the assembly considers a matter falling within the section's jurisdiction.

Sec. 8. Voting. Each member of the assembly may cast only one vote. Voting by proxy is not permitted.

[Amended September 10, 1974; April 22, 1975; April 29, 1976; June 29, 1979; amended effective February 2, 1981; February 11, 1986; January 10, 1989; May 16, 1995; May 10, 1996.]

Staff Comment to 1996 Amendment

The May 10, 1996, amendment rescinds the prohibition on service by judges on the State Bar Board of Commissioners or in the Representative Assembly. However, judges may not be elected or appointed officers of either body.

RULE 7. OFFICERS

Sec. 1. President, President-elect, Vice-president, Secretary, and Treasurer. The officers of the Board of Commissioners of the State Bar of Michigan are the president, the president-elect, the vice-president, the secretary, and the treasurer. The officers serve for the year beginning with the adjournment of the annual meeting following their election and ending with the adjournment of the next annual meeting. A person may serve as president only once.

After the election of board members but before the annual meeting each year, the Board of Commissioners shall elect from among its members, by majority vote of those present and voting, if a quorum is present:

(1) a vice-president who, after serving a one-year term, automatically succeeds to the office of president-elect for a one-year term, and then to the office of president, for a one-year term;

(2) a secretary; and

(3) a treasurer.

If a vice-president is not able to assume the duties of president-elect, the Board of Commissioners also shall elect from among its members, by majority vote of those present and voting, if a quorum is present, a president-elect who becomes president on the adjournment of the next succeeding annual meeting.

A commissioner whose term expires at the next annual meeting is not eligible for election as an officer unless the commissioner has been reelected or reappointed for another term as a commissioner. If the remaining term of a commissioner elected vice-president or president-elect will expire before the commissioner completes a term as president, the term shall be extended to allow the commissioner to complete the term as president. If the term of an elected commissioner is so extended, the authorized membership of the board is increased by one for that period; a vacancy in the district the vice-president or president-elect represents exists when the term as a commissioner would normally expire, and an election to choose a successor is to be held in the usual manner.

No person holding judicial office may be elected or appointed an officer of the Board of Commissioners. A judge presently serving as an officer may complete that term but may not thereafter, while holding judicial office, be elected or appointed an officer. A person serving as an officer who, after the effective date of this amendment, is elected or appointed to a judicial office, must resign as an officer of the board on or before the date that person assumes judicial office.

Sec. 2. Chairperson, Vice-Chairperson, and Clerk of the Assembly. A clerk of the Representative Assembly chosen from the elected or appointed membership of the assembly must be elected by the assembly at each annual meeting by majority vote of those present and voting, if there is a quorum present. The clerk serves a one-year term beginning with the adjournment of the annual meeting at which he or she is elected and ending with the adjournment of the next annual meeting at which he or she becomes vice-chairperson for a one-year term concluding with the next annual meeting, at which time he or she becomes chairperson for a one-year term concluding with the next annual meeting. If a representative is elected clerk of the assembly with only one or two years of his or her term remaining, the term of the representative is extended for an additional year or years to permit him or her to serve consecutive terms as vice-chairperson, and chairperson. If the term of an elected representative is so extended, the authorized membership of the assembly is increased by one for the appropriate period; a vacancy in the judicial circuit the chairperson-elect or chairperson represents exists when his or her term would normally expire and an election conducted to choose a successor having the vote to which the representative for that judicial circuit is entitled is to be held in the usual manner. Assembly officers may not concurrently hold another State Bar office and may not be reelected as assembly officers.

No person holding judicial office may be elected or appointed an officer of the Representative Assembly. A judge presently serving as an officer may complete that term but may not thereafter, while holding judicial office, be elected or appointed an officer. A person serving as an officer who, after the effective date of this amendment, is elected or appointed to a judicial office, must resign as an officer of the assembly on or before the date that person assumes judicial office.

Sec. 3. Duties. The president shall preside at all State Bar meetings and at all meetings of the Board

of Commissioners and perform other duties that are usually incident to that office.

The president-elect shall perform the duties assigned by the president. If the president is unable to perform his or her duties or is absent from a meeting of the board or the State Bar, the president-elect shall perform the duties of the president while the disability or absence continues.

The vice-president shall perform the duties assigned by the president and if the president and president-elect are unable to perform their duties or are absent from a meeting of the board or the State Bar, the vice-president shall perform the duties of the president while the disability or absence continues.

The secretary shall act as secretary of the Board of Commissioners, prepare an annual report, and perform the duties usually incident to that office.

The treasurer shall prepare an annual report and perform the duties usually incident to that office. The treasurer will furnish bond that the Board of Commissioners directs.

The Board of Commissioners may assign other duties to the president, president-elect, vice-president, secretary, and treasurer.

The chairperson of the Representative Assembly shall preside at all of its meetings and perform the other duties usually incident to that office, together with additional duties the assembly may assign. The vice-chairperson shall perform duties assigned by the chairperson or as the assembly may assign. The clerk of the assembly shall act as secretary of the assembly and perform the other duties the assembly assigns. If the chairperson is unable to perform his or her duties or is absent from a meeting of the assembly, the vice-chairperson shall perform the chairperson's duties while the disability or absence continues.

Sec. 4. Vacancies. If any office other than that of president or chairperson or vice-chairperson or clerk of the Representative Assembly becomes vacant, the Board of Commissioners shall fill the office for the unexpired term. If the office of president becomes vacant, the president-elect becomes president for the unexpired term, and may continue as president at the adjournment of the next annual meeting. If the office of president becomes vacant when the office of president-elect is also vacant, the Board of Commissioners shall fill both vacancies for the unexpired term. If the office of chairperson of the Representative Assembly becomes vacant, the vice-chairperson becomes chairperson for the unexpired term, and may continue as chairperson at the adjournment of the next annual meeting. If the office of chairperson becomes vacant when the office of vice-chairperson or clerk is also vacant, the assembly shall fill all vacancies for the unexpired term at its next meeting; the secretary shall convene and preside at the meeting until successors are elected.

[Amended May 24, 1978; June 29, 1979; amended effective August 1, 1991; May 10, 1996; July 1, 2001.]

Staff Comment to 1996 Amendment

The May 10, 1996, amendment rescinds the prohibition on service by judges on the State Bar Board of Commissioners or in the Representative Assembly. However, judges may not be elected or appointed officers of either body.

Staff Comment to 2001 Amendment

The April 3, 2001 amendment of § 1, effective July 1, 2001, provides that persons elected vice president of the Board of Commissioners succeed to the office of president-elect and then to the office of president.

RULE 8.   EXECUTIVE DIRECTOR

The Board of Commissioners may appoint an Executive Director, and such assistants, who shall serve on a full-time or part-time basis during such period and for such compensation as the Board of Commissioners may determine, but shall at all times be subject to removal by the board with or without cause. The Executive Director shall perform such duties as the Board of Commissioners may from time to time prescribe. The Executive Director shall have the privilege of the floor at all meetings of the Board of Commissioners, Representative Assembly, sections, section councils, committees, or subcommittees, without vote.

[Amended effective August 1, 1991.]

Staff Comment

The 1991 amendments effected several changes. They added a vice-chairperson for the Representative Assembly, and gave this new officer a seat on the Board of Commissioners. They also altered the membership of the Board of Commissioners by assigning a seat to the chairperson-elect of the Young Lawyers Section, in addition to the immediate past chairperson and the chairperson of the section. They increased the number of Supreme Court appointees on the Board of Commissioners from three to five. Finally, the 1991 amendments rendered these rules in gender-neutral language.

RULE 9.   DISBURSEMENTS

The Board of Commissioners shall make the necessary appropriations for disbursements from the funds of the treasury to pay the necessary expenses of the State Bar of Michigan, its officers, and committees. It shall be the duty of the board to cause proper books of account to be kept and to have them audited annually by a certified public accountant. On or before December 31 each year the board shall cause to be presented an audited financial statement of the receipts and expenditures of the State Bar of Michigan for the fiscal year ending the preceding September 30. Such a statement shall also be filed with the Clerk of the Supreme Court and shall be published in the January issue of the official publication of the State Bar of Michigan.

No officer, member of the Board of Commissioners, member of the Representative Assembly, or member of a committee or section of the State Bar of Michigan shall receive compensation for services rendered in connection with the performance of his or her duties. They may, however, be reimbursed for the necessary expenses incurred in connection with the performance of their duties.

[Amended effective February 11, 1986.]

RULE 10.   ANNUAL MEETING

The State Bar shall hold an annual meeting, which shall include a meeting of the Board of Commissioners and the Representative Assembly and, if requested, the annual congress, as well as meetings of sections and committees that the Board of Commissioners may set. The Board of Commissioners shall designate the time (no later than November 1) and place of the annual meeting.

[Amended June 29, 1979.]

RULE 11.   COMMITTEES

Sec. 1.   Appointment. Committees of the State Bar of Michigan may be established for the promotion of the objects of the State Bar of Michigan, and shall consist of limited numbers of members appointed by the President with their number, jurisdiction, method of selection and tenure determined in accordance with the bylaws and the resolution establishing the committee. In the event of the resignation, death or disqualification of any member of a committee, the President shall appoint a successor to serve for the unexpired term.

Sec. 2.   Classes. The classes of committees of the State Bar of Michigan shall be:

(a) Standing committees, for the investigation and study of matters relating to the accomplishment of the general purposes, business and objects of the State Bar of Michigan of a continuous and recurring character, within the limitation of the powers conferred.

(b) Special committees, created by resolution of the Board of Commissioners defining the powers and duties of such committees, to investigate and study matters relating to the specific purposes, business and objects of the State Bar of Michigan of an immediate or non-recurring character. The life of any special committee shall expire at the end of the next annual meeting following its creation unless continued by action of the Board.

Sec. 3.   Powers. The Committee on Arbitration of Disputes Among Lawyers, which has the authority to arbitrate disputes voluntarily submitted by lawyers, has the power to issue subpoenas (including subpoenas duces tecum), to take testimony under oath, and to rule on the admissibility of evidence according to the rules of evidence applicable to civil cases.

[Amended May 4, 1977; August 12, 1977.]

RULE 12. SECTIONS

Sec. 1. Establishment and Discontinuance. New sections may be established and existing sections may be combined or discontinued or their names changed by the Board of Commissioners in a manner provided by the bylaws.

Sec. 2. Bylaws. Each section shall have bylaws not inconsistent with these Rules or the bylaws of the State Bar of Michigan. Section bylaws or amendments thereof shall become effective when approved by the Board of Commissioners.

Sec. 3. Existing Sections. Sections in existence at the time of the adoption of these Rules shall continue unless changed by action of the Board of Commissioners.

RULE 13. INITIATIVE

Three percent or more of the active members of the State Bar may by written petition require consideration by the Representative Assembly of any question of public policy germane to the function and purposes of the State Bar; the assembly may take action on it that it finds proper. The petition must be filed with the clerk at least 90 days before any meeting of the Representative Assembly at which the subject matter is to be considered.

[Amended June 29, 1979.]

RULE 14. CONGRESS

Sec. 1. Membership and Meeting. Twenty-five or more active members of the State Bar may file a written petition with the secretary at the principal office of the State Bar no later than 90 days before the annual meeting of the State Bar, to require the convening of a congress of the active members of the State Bar in conjunction with the annual meeting to consider the subject matter raised in the petition. One hundred active members constitute a quorum. The president is the presiding officer of the congress and the secretary is the secretary of the congress.

Sec. 2. Agenda. The congress shall consider all matters proposed for inclusion on its agenda in the petition requesting its convening. The congress may take action on the matters arising on its agenda that it deems warranted. The action is advisory only and must be communicated to the Board of Commissioners and to the Representative Assembly, but the congress may by a two-thirds vote place an issue on the agenda of the board or assembly. If an issue so initiated is first considered by the board, the board shall notify

the assembly of its action, and the assembly shall concur with, modify, or reverse the board's action.

[Amended April 22, 1975; June 29, 1979.]

RULE 15. ADMISSION TO THE BAR

Section 1. Character and Fitness Committees.

(1) A standing committee on character and fitness consisting of 18 active members of the bar shall be appointed annually by the president of the State Bar of Michigan, who shall designate its chairperson. District character and fitness committees consisting of active members of the bar in each commissioner election district shall be appointed, and their chairpersons designated, by the State Bar commissioners within the respective districts, subject to approval by the State Bar Board of Commissioners.

(2) The standing committee and the district committees under its supervision shall investigate and make recommendations with respect to the character and fitness of every applicant for admission to the bar by bar examination and, upon request of the Board of Law Examiners, the character and fitness of any other applicant for admission.

(3) The State Bar of Michigan shall assign staff to assist the standing and district committees in the discharge of their duties.

(4) The standing committee and each district committee shall meet at the times and places designated by their respective chairpersons. Five members of the standing committee or 3 members of a district committee shall constitute a quorum. The action of a majority of those present constitutes the action of a committee.

(5) State Bar recommendations concerning the character and fitness of an applicant for admission to the bar shall be transmitted to the Board of Law Examiners in accordance with the following procedure:

(a) An applicant shall be recommended favorably by State Bar staff without referral to committee when investigation of all past conduct discloses no significant adverse factual information.

(b) In all other instances, applicants shall be referred to the appropriate district committee for personal interview unless the chairperson or other member of the standing committee designated by the chairperson determines that any adverse information reflected in the file would under no circumstance justify a committee determination that the applicant does not possess the character and fitness requisite for admission, in which event the application shall be transmitted to the Board of Law Examiners with a favorable recommendation.

(c) District committees shall, under the supervision and direction of the standing committee, investigate the character and fitness (other than scholastic) of every applicant referred to them. They shall do so by informal interview and any additional investigation which to them seems appropriate. District committees shall make a written report and recommendation to the standing committee concerning each applicant referred to them.

(d) Upon receiving a district committee report and recommendation, the standing committee shall endorse the recommendation, take the recommendation under advisement pending the receipt of additional information that it deems necessary, remand the recommendation to the district committee with instructions for further proceedings, or reject the recommendation and conduct a hearing de novo.

(e) If the standing committee endorses a report and recommendation of a district committee that an applicant has the requisite character and fitness for admission to the bar, it shall transmit that recommendation to the Board of Law Examiners.

(f) If the standing committee endorses a report and recommendation of a district committee that an applicant does not have the requisite character and fitness for admission to the bar, it shall furnish the applicant with a copy of the report and recommendation and advise the applicant of the right to a formal hearing before the standing committee provided request therefor is made in writing within 20 days. If the applicant requests a formal hearing within the time permitted, a hearing shall be scheduled before the standing committee. If the applicant does not request a formal hearing before the standing committee within the time permitted, the standing committee shall thereupon transmit the report and recommendation of the district committee to the Board of Law Examiners.

(g) At the conclusion of any hearing conducted by the standing committee it shall transmit its report and recommendation to the Board of Law Examiners.

(6) Each applicant is entitled to be represented by counsel at the applicant's own expense at any stage of character and fitness processing.

(7) Information obtained in the course of processing an application for admission to the bar may not be used for any other purpose or otherwise disclosed without the consent of the applicant or by order of the Supreme Court.

(8) Notwithstanding any prohibition against disclosure in this rule or elsewhere, the committee on character and fitness shall disclose information concerning a bar application to the Attorney Grievance Commission during the course of the commission's investigation of a disciplined lawyer's request for reinstatement to the practice of law. Upon receiving a request for character and fitness information and proof that a disciplined lawyer is seeking reinstatement to the practice of law, the committee shall notify the lawyer that the commission has requested the lawyer's confidential file. The committee then shall disclose to the commission all information relating to the lawyer's bar application. The commission and the grievance administrator shall protect such information, as provided in MCR 9.126(D). The administrator shall submit to a hearing panel, under seal, any information obtained under this rule that the administrator intends to use in a reinstatement proceeding. The hearing panel shall determine whether the information is relevant to the proceeding, and only upon such a determination may the administrator use the information in a public pleading or proceeding.

(9) Any information pertaining to an application for admission to the bar submitted to a district committee, the standing committee, the Board of Law Examiners or the Supreme Court must also be disclosed to the applicant.

(10) A person is absolutely immune from suit for statements and communications transmitted solely to the State Bar staff, the district committee, the standing committee or the Board of Law Examiners, or given in the course of an investigation or proceeding concerning the character and fitness of an applicant for admission to the bar. The State Bar staff, the members of the district and standing committees and the members and staff of the Board of Law Examiners are absolutely immune from suit for conduct arising out of the performance of their duties.

(11) The standing committee has the power to issue subpoenas (including subpoenas duces tecum), to take testimony under oath, and to rule on the admissibility of evidence guided, but not strictly bound, by the rules of evidence applicable to civil cases. An applicant is entitled to use the committee's subpoena power to obtain relevant evidence by request submitted to the chairperson of the standing committee.

(12) Formal hearings conducted by the standing committee shall be suitably recorded for the later production of transcripts, if necessary.

(13) An applicant is entitled to a copy of the entire record of proceedings before the standing committee at the applicant's expense.

(14) An applicant is entitled to at least 10 days notice of scheduled district committee interviews and standing committee hearings. The notice shall contain the following information:

(a) The time and place of the interview or hearing;

(b) A statement of the conduct which is to be the subject of the interview or hearing;

(c) The applicant's right to be represented by counsel; and

(d) A description of the procedures to be followed at the interview or hearing, together with copies of any applicable rules.

(15) An applicant has the burden of proving by clear and convincing evidence that he or she has the current good moral character and general fitness to warrant admission to the bar.

(16) Upon request made no later than 5 days prior to a scheduled interview or hearing, the applicant and State Bar staff may demand of the other that they be furnished with the identity of any witnesses to be produced at the interview or hearing as well as an opportunity for inspecting or copying any documentary evidence to be offered or introduced.

(17) If an application is withdrawn following an adverse recommendation by a district committee or the standing committee, or, if following such an adverse recommendation the applicant fails to appear for further proceedings, the standing committee shall notify the applicant that the application for admission to the bar may not be renewed until the expiration of three years or such lesser period as the committee specifies.

(18) An applicant who has been denied character and fitness certification for admission to the bar by the Board of Law Examiners may not reapply for character and fitness certification for a period of five years following the denial or such lesser period specified in the decision denying certification.

(19) The standing committee may adopt rules of procedure governing the processing and investigation of applications for admission to the bar and proceedings before district committees and the standing committee not inconsistent with these rules.

(20) An applicant is entitled to review by the Board of Law Examiners of any report and recommendation filed with the Board concluding that the applicant does not have the character and fitness requisite for admission.

(21) Every applicant for admission by examination and any other applicant whose application is submitted to the standing committee on character and fitness for evaluation and recommendation shall pay to the State Bar of Michigan a fee of $225 for the character and fitness investigation authorized by this rule. An additional fee of $100 shall be required for character and fitness evaluations related to applications for the February examination that are postmarked after November 1, and applications for the July examination that are postmarked after March 1.

Sec. 2. Foreign Attorney; Temporary Permission. Any person who is duly licensed to practice law in another state or territory, or in the District of Columbia, of the United States of America, or in any foreign country, may be permitted to engage in the trial of a specific case in a court or before an administrative tribunal in this State when associated with and on motion of an active member of the State Bar of Michigan who appears of record in the case. Such

temporary permission may be revoked by the court summarily at any time for misconduct.

Sec. 3. Procedure for Admission; Oath of Office.

(1) Each applicant to whom a certificate of qualification has been issued by the Board of Law Examiners is required to appear personally and present such certificate to the Supreme Court or one of the circuit courts of this State. Upon motion made in open court by an active member of the State Bar of Michigan, the court may enter an order admitting such applicant to the bar of this State. The clerk of such court is required to forthwith administer to such applicant in open court the following oath of office:

I do solemnly swear (or affirm):

I will support the Constitution of the United States and the Constitution of the State of Michigan;

I will maintain the respect due to courts of justice and judicial officers;

I will not counsel or maintain any suit or proceeding which shall appear to me to be unjust, nor any defense except such as I believe to be honestly debatable under the law of the land;

I will employ for the purpose of maintaining the causes confided to me such means only as are consistent with truth and honor, and will never seek to mislead the judge or jury by any artifice or false statement of fact or law;

I will maintain the confidence and preserve inviolate the secrets of my client, and will accept no compensation in connection with my client's business except with my client's knowledge and approval;

I will abstain from all offensive personality, and advance no fact prejudicial to the honor or reputation of a party or witness, unless required by the justice of the cause with which I am charged;

I will never reject, from any consideration personal to myself, the cause of the defenseless or oppressed, or delay any cause for lucre or malice;

I will in all other respects conduct myself personally and professionally in conformity with the high standards of conduct imposed on members of the bar as conditions for the privilege to practice law in this State.

(2) The applicant is required to subscribe to such oath of office by signing a copy and to register membership in the State Bar of Michigan in the manner prescribed in Rule 2 of these rules and to pay the required dues before practicing law in this State. The clerk shall record such admission, in the journal of such court, and shall preserve such oath of office in the records of the court. A roll of all persons admitted to the bar shall be kept in the office of the clerk of the Supreme Court.

(3) Admission to the bar of this State is an authorization to practice as an attorney and counselor in every court in this State.

[Renumbered June 29, 1979; amended effective October 4, 1985; February 10, 1987; September 25, 1987; July 30, 1992; November 1, 1996; December 1, 1998; July 18, 2001; September 12, 2001; November 1, 2002.]

Staff Comment to 1996 Amendment

The November 1, 1996 amendment of Rule 15, section 1, paragraph (20), was requested by the State Bar of Michigan. The amendment will permit the State Bar to charge an additional fee for character and fitness evaluations related to late applications.

Staff Comment to 1998 Amendment

The December 1, 1998 amendment of MCR 9.126 and 9.222 made mandatory the disclosure of information, upon request, between the Attorney Grievance Commission and the Judicial Tenure Commission. The amendment of State Bar Rule 15, § 1 authorized the State Bar's Committee on Character and Fitness to disclose to the Attorney Grievance Commission information concerning the bar application of a disciplined lawyer who is requesting reinstatement to the practice of law. Under the amendment, the lawyer must be notified of the request, and the hearing panel must determine the relevancy of the information before permitting it to be used in a public document or proceeding.

Staff Comment to 2001 Amendment

The July 18, 2001, amendment of Rule 15, § 1, ¶ 21 was proposed by the State Bar of Michigan to more accurately reflect the actual cost of character and fitness investigations. It was approved by the Supreme Court as to new applications for the February 2002 bar examination and any other applications submitted to the character and fitness committee of the State Bar during that time period. The request to make the fee increase permanent remained under consideration by the Court. [The amendment was made permanent by order of the Court effective September 12, 2001.]

Staff Comment to 2002 Amendment

The November 1, 2002, amendment of Rule 15 of the Rules Concerning the State Bar of Michigan increased the number of members on the Standing Committee on Character and Fitness from 12 to 18.

The staff comment is published only for the benefit of the bench and bar and is not an authoritative construction by the Court.

RULE 16. UNAUTHORIZED PRACTICE OF THE LAW

The State Bar of Michigan is hereby authorized and empowered to investigate matters pertaining to the unauthorized practice of law and, with the authority of its Board of Commissioners, to file and prosecute actions and proceedings with regard to such matters.

[Renumbered June 29, 1979.]

RULE 17. MANDATORY LEGAL EDUCATION PROGRAM FOR NEW ADMITTEES TO THE MICHIGAN BAR [RESCINDED]

[Rescinded effective April 1, 1994.]

RULES FOR THE BOARD OF LAW EXAMINERS

Revised August 26, 1976

Research Note

Use Westlaw ® *to find cases citing or applying specific rules. Westlaw may also be used to search for specific terms in court rules or to update court rules. See the MI–RULES and MI–ORDERS Scope Screens for detailed descriptive information and search tips.*

Amendments to these rules are published, as received, in the N.W.2d and Michigan Reporter advance sheets, and Michigan Legislative Service.

Table of Rules

RULE 1. GENERAL REQUIREMENTS

An applicant for admission to the practice of law must

(A) be 18 years old or older;

(B) possess good moral character; and

(C) have completed, before entering law school, at least 60 semester hours or 90 quarter hours toward an undergraduate degree from an accredited school or while attending an accredited junior or community college.

RULE 2. ADMISSION BY EXAMINATION

(A) An application must be filed by November 1 for the February examination, or March 1 for the July examination. Late applications will be accepted until December 15 for the February examination, or May 15 for the July examination. An application must be accompanied by payment of the fee. All materials filed are confidential.

(B) Before taking the examination, an applicant must obtain a JD, LLB, or LLM degree from a reputable and qualified law school that

(1) is incorporated in the United States, its territories, or the District of Columbia; and

(2) requires for graduation 3 school years of study for full-time students, and 4 school years of study for part-time or night students. A school year must be at least 30 weeks.

A law school approved by the American Bar Association is reputable and qualified. Other schools may ask the Board to approve the school as reputable and qualified. If the applicant has obtained an LLM degree from an approved law school, the applicant's JD or LLB need not be from an approved law school.

(C) The State Bar character and fitness committee will investigate each applicant. The applicant must disclose any criminal conviction which carries a possible penalty of incarceration in jail or prison that has not been reversed or vacated and comply with the committee's requirements and requests. The committee will report the results of its investigation to the Board. If the committee report shows that an applicant lacks the necessary character and fitness, the Board will review the application, record, and report. If the Board accepts the report, the applicant is entitled to a hearing before the Board and may use the Board's subpoena power. The Board may permit an applicant to take the examination before the character and fitness committee reports. The Board will release the applicant's grade if character and fitness committee approval is obtained.

(D) Every applicant for admission must achieve a passing score, as determined by the Board, on the Multistate Professional Responsibility Examination.

(E) The Board may permit an applicant entering the armed forces before the examination immediately following graduation to take an earlier examination. The applicant must have completed, before the examination, 2½ years full-time or 3½ years part-time study. The Board will release the applicant's grade when the school certifies the applicant's graduation.

(F) The applicant is responsible for meeting all requirements before the examination. The Board may act on information about an applicant's character whenever the information is received.

[Amended July 11, 1979; January 15, 1981; amended effective January 1, 1990; June 1, 1995; February 1, 1996.]

Staff Comment to 1990 Amendment

The [January 1, 1990] amendment conforms the Rules for the Board of Law Examiners concerning admission to the practice of law by examination to the requirements of MCL 600.940, MSA 27A.940, which requires, inter alia, that every applicant for the bar examination be a graduate of a reputable and qualified law school. The amendment rescinds the summer school exception which allowed students attending summer law school to sit for the bar exam if the student would be graduated at the end of the summer term.

Staff Comment to 1996 Amendment

This rule change in section 2(D), effective February 1, 1996, replaces present Rule 2(D) in its entirety as of that date and requires all applicants for admission to the State Bar of Michigan to receive a passing score on the Multistate Professional Responsibility Examination.

RULE 3. EXAMINATION SUBJECTS AND GRADING

(A) The examination consists of two sections:

(1) The Multistate Bar Examination prepared by the National Conference of Bar Examiners and administered on dates and under regulations set by the Conference.

(2) An essay examination prepared by or under the supervision of the Board or by law professors selected by the Board, on these subjects:

(a) Real and Personal Property

(b) Wills and Trusts

(c) Contracts

(d) Constitutional Law

(e) Criminal Law and Procedure

(f) Corporations, Partnerships, and Agency

(g) Evidence

(h) Creditor's Rights, including mortgages, garnishments and attachments

(i) Practice and Procedure, trial and appellate, state and federal

(j) Equity

(k) Torts (including no-fault)

(*l*) The sales, negotiable instruments, and secured transactions articles of the Uniform Commercial Code

(m) Michigan Rules of Professional Conduct

(n) Domestic Relations

(o) Conflicts of Laws

(p) Worker's Compensation.

(B) The National Conference of Bar Examiners will grade the Multistate section. The Board or its agents will grade the essay section, with the Board having final responsibility. The Board will determine a method for combining the grades and select a passing score.

[Amended effective August 10, 1995; April 21, 1998; January 1, 2000.]

Staff Comment to April, 1998 Amendment

The rule change gives Board Members the authority to author their own questions and model answers for the essay portion of the bar exam.

Staff Comment to October, 1998 Amendment

The October 1998 amendment of Rule 3(A)(2) of the Rules for the Board of Law Examiners, effective January 1, 2000, adds to the list of subjects for essay questions. The category of "no fault" is added to the subject of "Torts." See (k). In addition, the categories of "Domestic Relations", "Conflicts of Laws" and "Worker's Compensation" have been added.

RULE 4. POST–EXAMINATION PROCEDURES

(A) The Assistant Secretary will release examination results at the Board's direction. Blue books will be kept for 3 months after results are released.

(B) Within 30 days after the day the results are released, the applicant may ask the Board to reconsider the applicant's essay grades. The applicant shall file with the Assistant Secretary two (2) copies of

(1) the request;

(2) the answer given in the applicant's blue books; and

(3) an explanation why the applicant deserves a higher grade.

(C) An applicant for re-examination may obtain an application from the Assistant Secretary. The application must be filed at least sixty (60) days before the examination. If the applicant's clearance is more than three (3) years old, the applicant must be approved by the State Bar Committee on Character and Fitness.

[Amended effective June 1, 1995; July 7, 1995; corrected July 17, 1995; amended effective August 10, 1995.]

RULE 5. ADMISSION WITHOUT EXAMINATION

(A) An applicant for admission without examination must

(1) qualify under Rules 1 and 2(B);

(2) be licensed to practice law in the United States, its territories, or the District of Columbia;

(3) be a member in good standing of the Bar where admitted;

(4) intend in good faith to maintain an office in this state for the practice of law;

(5) intend to practice law in Michigan, or to be a full-time instructor in a reputable and qualified Michigan law school; and

(6) have, after being licensed and for 3 of the 5 years preceding the application,

    (a) actively practiced law as a principal business or occupation in a jurisdiction where admitted (the practice of law under a special certificate pursuant to Rule 5[D] or as a special legal consultant pursuant to Rule 5[E] does not qualify as the practice of law required by this rule);

    (b) been employed as a full-time instructor in a reputable and qualified law school in the United States, its districts, or its territories; or

    (c) been on active duty (other than for training or reserve duty) in the United States armed forces as a judge advocate, legal specialist, or legal officer. The judge advocate general (or a comparable officer) or delegate must certify the assignment and the inclusive dates.

The Supreme Court may, for good cause, increase the 5–year period. Active duty in the United States armed forces not satisfying Rule 5(A)(6)(c) may be excluded when computing the 5–year period.

(B) An applicant must submit the National Conference of Bar Examiners' Request for Preparation of a Character Report along with other material required by the Board and payment of the fees.

(C) An applicant not satisfying Rule 5(A) will be notified and given an opportunity to appear before the Board. The applicant may use the Board's subpoena power.

(D) An attorney

(1) ineligible for admission without examination because of the inability to satisfy Rule 5(A)(6); and

(2) practicing law in an institutional setting, e.g., counsel to a corporation or instructor in a law school,

may apply to the Board for a special certificate of qualification to practice law. The applicant must satisfy Rule 5(A)(1)–(4), and comply with Rule 5(B). The Board may then issue the special certificate, which will entitle the attorney to continue current employment if the attorney becomes an active member of the State Bar. If the attorney leaves the current employment, the special certificate automatically expires; if the attorney's new employment is also institutional, the attorney may reapply for another special certificate.

(E) Special Legal Consultants.

(a) To qualify for admission without examination to practice as a special legal consultant one must:

(1) be admitted to practice in a foreign country and have actually practiced, and be in good standing, as an attorney or counselor at law or the equivalent in such foreign country for at least three of the five years immediately preceding the application; and

(2) possess the good moral character and general fitness requisite for a member of the bar of this state; and

(3) fulfill the requirements of MCL 600.934 and 600.937; and

(4) be a resident of this or another state of the United States, its territories or the District of Columbia and maintain an office in this state for the practice of law; and

(5) be over 18 years of age.

(b) In considering whether to license an applicant to practice pursuant to Rule 5(E), the Board may in its discretion take into account whether a member of the bar of this state would have a reasonable and practical opportunity to establish an office for the giving of legal advice to clients in the applicant's country of admission (as referred to in Rule 5[E][a][1]), if there is pending with the Board a request to take this factor into account from a member of the bar of this state actively seeking to establish such an office in that country which raises a serious question as to the adequacy of the opportunity for such a member to establish such an office.

(c) An applicant for a license as a special legal consultant shall submit to the Board:

(1) a certificate from the authority in such foreign country having final jurisdiction over professional discipline, certifying as to the applicant's admission to practice and the date thereof and as to the good standing of such attorney or counselor at law or the equivalent, together with a duly authenticated English translation of such certificate if it is not in English; and

(2) a letter of recommendation from one of the judges of the highest law court or intermediate appellate court of such foreign country, together with a duly authenticated English translation of such letter if it is not in English; and

(3) the National Conference of Bar Examiners questionnaire and affidavit along with the payment

of the requisite fee and such other evidence of the applicant's educational and professional qualifications, good moral character and general fitness, and compliance with the requirements of Rule 5(E)(a)(1)–(5) as the Board may require; and

(4) shall execute and file with the Assistant Secretary of the State Board of Law Examiners, in such form and manner as the Board may prescribe,

(i) a duly acknowledged instrument in writing setting forth the special legal consultant's address in the state of Michigan and designating the Assistant Secretary of the State Board of Law Examiners an agent upon whom process may be served, with like effect as if served personally upon the special legal consultant, in any action or proceeding thereafter brought against the special legal consultant and arising out of or based upon any legal services rendered or offered to be rendered by the special legal consultant within or to residents of the state of Michigan whenever after due diligence service cannot be made upon the special legal consultant at such address or at such new address in the state of Michigan as the special legal consultant shall have filed in the office of the Assistant Secretary of the State Board of Law Examiners by means of a duly acknowledged supplemental instrument in writing; and

(ii) the special legal consultant's commitment to notify the Assistant Secretary of the State Board of Law Examiners of any resignation or revocation of the special legal consultant's admission to practice in the foreign country of admission, or of any censure, suspension or expulsion in respect of such admission.

Service of process on the Assistant Secretary of the State Board of Law Examiners shall be made by personally delivering to and leaving with the Assistant Secretary, or with a deputy or assistant authorized by the Assistant Secretary to receive such service, at the Assistant Secretary's office, duplicate copies of such process together with a fee of $10.00. Service of process shall be complete when the Assistant Secretary has been so served. The Assistant Secretary shall promptly send one of such copies to the special legal consultant to whom the process is directed, by certified mail, return receipt requested, addressed to such special legal consultant at the address specified by the special legal consultant as aforesaid.

(d) A person licensed to practice as a special legal consultant must maintain active membership in the State Bar of Michigan and must discharge the responsibilities of State Bar membership and is authorized to render professional legal advice:

(1) on the law of the foreign country where the legal consultant is admitted to practice;

(2) may use the title "special legal consultant" either singly or in connection with the authorized title or firm name in the foreign country of the legal consultant's admission to practice, provided that in each case the name of such foreign country be identified.

[Amended October 1, 1978; amended effective March 26, 1982; August 23, 1983; November 27, 1985; September 9, 1988; June 1, 1995; August 10, 1995; September 1, 1996.]

Staff Comment to 1988 Amendment

The amendment conforms the Rules for the Board of Law Examiners concerning admission to the practice of law without examination to the requirements of MCL 600.946; MSA 27A.946, which requires, inter alia, that for admission to the practice of law without examination, an applicant must intend in good faith either to maintain an office in the state for the practice of law and to practice actively in this state, or to engage in the teaching of law as a full-time instructor in a reputable and qualified law school duly incorporated under the laws of this state. The residency requirement formerly a part of Rule 5(A)(4) of the Rules for the Board of Law Examiners is rescinded so that the Rules conform with MCL 600.946; MSA 27A.946, and the United States Supreme Court decision of *Supreme Court of Virginia* v *Friedman*, 487 US 59; 108 SCt 2260; 101 LEd2d 56 (1988).

Staff Comment to 1996 Amendment

The July 16, 1996 amendment of subrule 5(A)(5), proposed by the State Bar of Michigan, eliminated the requirement that applicants for admission without examination intend to practice law in Michigan "as a principal occupation."

RULE 6. FEES

The fees are: an application for examination, $175 and an additional fee for the late filing of an application or transfer of an application for examination, $100; an application for re-examination, $100; an application for recertification, $100; an application for admission without examination, $400 plus the requisite fee for the National Conference of Bar Examiners' report. Checks must be payable to the State of Michigan.

[Amended effective July 5, 1989.]

Staff Comment to 1989 Amendment

The [July 5, 1989] amendments reflect increases in filing fees required by 1989 PA 100, signed by the Governor, June 21, 1989 and given immediate effect.

RULE 7. EXCEPTIONS

An applicant may ask the Board to waive any requirement except the payment of fees. The applicant must demonstrate why the request should be granted.

[Amended effective June 1, 1995.]

RULE 8. RECERTIFICATION

An applicant for recertification shall file an application and other material required by the Board. After a hearing the Board shall either recertify the applicant or require that the applicant pass the examination described in Rule 3. An applicant may use the Board's subpoena power for the hearing. An applicant who is an inactive State Bar member and who has been employed in another jurisdiction in one of the ways listed in Rule 5(A)(6) is entitled to recertification by the Board.

[Added October 1, 1978; amended effective June 1, 1995.]

MICHIGAN CODE OF JUDICIAL CONDUCT

Adopted October 1, 1974

Research Note

Use Westlaw ® *to find cases citing or applying specific rules. Westlaw may also be used to search for specific terms in court rules or to update court rules. See the MI–RULES and MI–ORDERS Scope Screens for detailed descriptive information and search tips.*

Amendments to these rules are published, as received, in the N.W.2d and Michigan Reporter advance sheets, and Michigan Legislative Service.

Table of Canons

Canon

1. A Judge Should Uphold the Integrity and Independence of the Judiciary.
2. A Judge Should Avoid Impropriety and the Appearance of Impropriety in All Activities.
3. A Judge Should Perform the Duties of Office Impartially and Diligently.
4. A Judge May Engage in Activities to Improve the Law, the Legal System, and the Administration of Justice.

Canon

5. A Judge Should Regulate Extra-Judicial Activities to Minimize the Risk of Conflict With Judicial Duties.
6. A Judge Should Regularly File Reports of Compensation Received for Quasi-Judicial and Extra-Judicial Activities and of Monetary Contributions.
7. A Judge or a Candidate for Judicial Office Should Refrain From Political Activity Inappropriate to Judicial Office.
8. Collective Activity By Judges.

CANON 1
A Judge Should Uphold the Integrity and Independence of the Judiciary

An independent and honorable judiciary is indispensable to justice in our society. A judge should participate in establishing, maintaining, and enforcing, and should personally observe, high standards of conduct so that the integrity and independence of the judiciary may be preserved. A judge should always be aware that the judicial system is for the benefit of the litigant and the public, not the judiciary. The provisions of this code should be construed and applied to further those objectives.

[Amended effective October 1, 1993.]

CANON 2
A Judge Should Avoid Impropriety and the Appearance of Impropriety in All Activities

A. Public confidence in the judiciary is eroded by irresponsible or improper conduct by judges. A judge must avoid all impropriety and appearance of impropriety. A judge must expect to be the subject of constant public scrutiny. A judge must therefore accept restrictions on conduct that might be viewed as burdensome by the ordinary citizen and should do so freely and willingly.

B. A judge should respect and observe the law. At all times, the conduct and manner of a judge should promote public confidence in the integrity and impartiality of the judiciary. Without regard to a person's race, gender, or other protected personal characteristic, a judge should treat every person fairly, with courtesy and respect.

C. A judge should not allow family, social, or other relationships to influence judicial conduct or judgment. A judge should not use the prestige of office to advance personal business interests or those of others. A judge should not appear as a witness in a court proceeding unless subpoenaed.

D. A judge may respond to requests for personal references.

E. A judge should not allow activity as a member of an organization to cast doubt on the judge's ability to perform the function of the office in a manner consistent with the Michigan Code of Judicial Conduct, the laws of this state, and the Michigan and United States Constitutions. A judge should be particularly cautious with regard to membership activities that discriminate, or appear to discriminate, on the basis of race, gender, or other protected personal characteristic. Nothing in this paragraph should be interpreted to diminish a judge's right to the free exercise of religion.

[Amended effective October 1, 1993.]

CANON 3
A Judge Should Perform the Duties of Office Impartially and Diligently

The judicial duties of a judge take precedence over all other activities. Judicial duties include all the duties of office prescribed by law. In the performance of these duties, the following standards apply:

A. Adjudicative Responsibilities.

(1) A judge should be faithful to the law and maintain professional competence in it. A judge should be unswayed by partisan interests, public clamor, or fear of criticism.

(2) A judge may require lawyers, court personnel, and litigants to be appropriately attired for court and should enforce reasonable rules of conduct in the courtroom.

(3) A judge should be patient, dignified, and courteous to litigants, jurors, witnesses, lawyers, and others with whom the judge deals in an official capacity, and should require similar conduct of lawyers, and of staff, court officials, and others subject to the judge's direction and control.

(4) A judge shall not initiate, permit, or consider ex parte communications, or consider other communications made to the judge outside the presence of the parties concerning a pending or impending proceeding, except as follows:

(a) A judge may allow ex parte communications for scheduling, administrative purposes, or emergencies that do not deal with substantive matters or issues on the merits, provided:

(i) the judge reasonably believes that no party or counsel for a party will gain a procedural or

tactical advantage as a result of the ex parte communication, and

(ii) the judge makes provision promptly to notify all other parties and counsel for parties of the substance of the ex parte communication and allows an opportunity to respond.

(b) A judge may obtain the advice of a disinterested expert on the law applicable to a proceeding before the judge if the judge gives notice to the parties of the person consulted and the substance of the advice, and affords the parties reasonable opportunity to respond.

(c) A judge may consult with court personnel whose function is to aid the judge in carrying out the judge's adjudicative responsibilities or with other judges.

(d) A judge may, with the consent of the parties, confer separately with the parties and their lawyers in an effort to mediate or settle matters pending before the judge.

(e) A judge may initiate or consider any ex parte communications when expressly authorized by law to do so.

(5) A judge should dispose promptly of the business of the court.

(6) A judge should abstain from public comment about a pending or impending proceeding in any court, and should require a similar abstention on the part of court personnel subject to the judge's direction and control. This subsection does not prohibit a judge from making public statements in the course of official duties or from explaining for public information the procedures of the court or the judge's holdings or actions.

(7) A judge should prohibit broadcasting, televising, recording, or taking of photographs in or of the courtroom during sessions of court or recesses between sessions except as authorized by the Supreme Court.*

(8) A judge may properly intervene in a trial of a case to promote expedition, and prevent unnecessary waste of time, or to clear up some obscurity, but the judge should bear in mind that undue interference, impatience, or participation in the examination of witnesses, or a severe attitude on the judge's part toward witnesses, especially those who are excited or terrified by the unusual circumstances of a trial, may tend to prevent the proper presentation of the cause, or the ascertainment of truth in respect thereto.

Conversation between the judge and counsel in court is often necessary, but the judge should be studious to avoid controversies that are apt to obscure the merits of the dispute between litigants and lead to its unjust disposition. In addressing counsel, litigants, or witnesses, the judge should avoid a controversial manner or tone.

A judge should avoid interruptions of counsel in their arguments except to clarify their positions, and should not be tempted to the unnecessary display of learning or a premature judgment.

(9) A judge should adopt the usual and accepted methods of doing justice, avoid the imposition of humiliating acts or discipline, not authorized by law in sentencing and endeavor to conform to a reasonable standard of punishment and not seek popularity or publicity either by exceptional severity or undue leniency.

(10) Without regard to a person's race, gender, or other protected personal characteristic, a judge should treat every person fairly, with courtesy and respect. To the extent possible, a judge should require staff, court officials, and others who are subject to the judge's direction and control to provide such fair, courteous, and respectful treatment to persons who have contact with the court.

B. Administrative Responsibilities.

(1) A judge should diligently discharge administrative responsibilities, maintain professional competence in judicial administration, and facilitate the performance of the administrative responsibilities of other judges and court officials.

(2) A judge should direct staff and court officials subject to the judge's control to observe high standards of fidelity, diligence, and courtesy to litigants, jurors, witnesses, lawyers, and others with whom they deal in their official capacity.

(3) A judge should take or initiate appropriate disciplinary measures against a judge or lawyer for unprofessional conduct of which the judge may become aware. However, a judge is not obliged to take or initiate disciplinary measures on the basis of information gained while serving with the substance abuse counseling program of the State Bar of Michigan, to the extent the information would be protected under MRPC 1.6 from disclosure if it were a communication between lawyer and client.

(4) A judge should not cause unnecessary expense by making unnecessary appointments. All appointments shall be based upon merit.

(5) A judge should not approve compensation beyond the fair value of services rendered.

C. Disqualification. A judge should raise the issue of disqualification whenever the judge has cause to believe that grounds for disqualification may exist under MCR 2.003(B).

D. Remittal of Disqualification. A disqualification of a judge may be remitted as provided by MCR 2.003(D).

[Amended effective October 1, 1993; January 18, 1994; September 1, 1995.]

*Publisher's Note: See Administrative Order 1990–7, Videotape Record of Court Proceedings, supra, which authorizes an exception to this paragraph.

Staff Comment to 1994 Amendment

The 1994 amendment of Canon 3.B(3) was proposed by the State Bar of Michigan. It was designed to parallel the language of MRPC 8.3(c)(2), and to help assure confidentiality for those seeking assistance in the Bar's substance-abuse counseling program.

Staff Comment to 1995 Amendment

The July 7, 1995, amendments of MCR 2.003, and Rules 3A, 3D, 6C, and 7B of the Michigan Code of Judicial Conduct, and new MCR 9.227 and Rule 7D of the Michigan Code of Judicial Conduct, are based on the proposed revision of the Michigan Code of Judicial Conduct submitted by the State Bar Representative Assembly. See 442 Mich 1216 (1993). They are effective September 1, 1995.

CANON 4
A Judge May Engage in Activities to Improve the Law, the Legal System, and the Administration of Justice

As a judicial officer and person specially learned in the law, a judge is in a unique position to contribute to the improvement of the law, the legal system, and the administration of justice, including revision of substantive and procedural law and improvement of criminal and juvenile justice. To the extent that time permits, the judge is encouraged to do so, either independently or through a bar association, judicial conference, or other organization dedicated to the improvement of the law.

A judge, subject to the proper performance of judicial duties, may engage in the following quasi-judicial activities:

A. A judge may speak, write, lecture, teach, and participate in other activities concerning the law, the legal system, and the administration of justice.

B. A judge may appear at a public hearing before an executive or legislative body or official on matters concerning the law, the legal system, and the administration of justice, and may otherwise consult with such executive or legislative body or official on such matters.

C. A judge may serve as a member, officer, or director of an organization or governmental agency devoted to the improvement of the law, the legal system, or the administration of justice. A judge may assist such an organization in raising funds and may participate in their management and investment, but should not individually solicit funds. A judge may make recommendations to public and private fund-granting agencies on projects and programs concerning the law, the legal system, and the administration of justice.

[Amended effective October 1, 1993.]

CANON 5
A Judge Should Regulate Extra-Judicial Activities to Minimize the Risk of Conflict With Judicial Duties

A. Avocational Activities. A judge may write, lecture, teach, speak, and consult on nonlegal subjects, appear before public nonlegal bodies, and engage in the arts, sports, and other social and recreational activities, if such avocational activities do not detract from the dignity of the office or interfere with the performance of judicial duties.

B. Civic and Charitable Activities. A judge may participate in civic and charitable activities that do not reflect adversely upon the judge's impartiality or interfere with the performance of judicial duties. A judge may serve as an officer, director, trustee, or nonlegal advisor of a bona fide educational, religious, charitable, fraternal, or civic organization, subject to the following limitations:

(1) A judge should not serve if it is likely that the organization will be engaged in proceedings that would ordinarily come before the judge or will be regularly engaged in adversary proceedings in any court.

(2) A judge should not individually solicit funds for any educational, religious, charitable, fraternal, or civic organization, or use or permit the use of the prestige of the office for that purpose, but may be listed as an officer, director, or trustee of such an organization. A judge may, however, join a general appeal on behalf of an educational, religious, charitable, or fraternal organization, or speak on behalf of such organization.

C. Financial Activities.

(1) A judge should refrain from financial and business dealings that tend to reflect adversely on the judge's impartiality or judicial office, interfere with the proper performance of judicial duties, exploit the judicial position, or involve the judge in frequent transactions with lawyers or persons likely to come before the court on which the judge serves.

(2) Subject to the requirements of C(1), a judge may hold and manage investments, including real estate, and engage in other remunerative activity, but should not serve as director, officer, manager, advisor, or employee of any business. Provided, however, with respect to a judge holding office and serving as an officer, director, manager, advisor, or employee of any business not prohibited heretofore by law or judicial canon, the effective date of the prohibition contained herein shall be the date of expiration of the judge's current judicial term of office.

(3) A judge should manage investments and other financial interests to minimize the number of cases in which the judge is disqualified. As soon as it can be done without serious financial detriment, the judge should dispose of investments and other financial interests that require frequent disqualification.

(4) Neither a judge nor a family member residing in the judge's household should accept a gift, bequest, favor, or loan from anyone except as follows:

(a) A judge may accept a gift or gifts not to exceed a total value of $100, incident to a public testimonial; books supplied by publishers on a complimentary basis for official use; or an invitation to the judge and spouse to attend a bar-related function or activity devoted to the improvement of the law, the legal system, or the administration of justice.

(b) A judge or a family member residing in the judge's household may accept ordinary social hospitality; a gift, bequest, favor, or loan from a relative; a wedding or engagement gift; a loan from a lending institution in its regular course of business on the same terms generally available to persons who are not judges; or a scholarship or fellowship awarded on the same terms applied to other applicants.

(c) A judge or a family member residing in the judge's household may accept any other gift, bequest, favor, or loan only if the donor is not a party or other person whose interests have come or are likely to come before the judge, and, if its value exceeds $100, the judge reports it in the same manner as compensation is reported in Canon 6C.

(5) For the purposes of this section, "family member residing in the judge's household" means any relative of a judge by blood or marriage, or a person treated by a judge as a family member, who resides in the judge's household.

(6) A judge is not required by this code to disclose income, debts, or investments, except as provided in this canon and Canons 3 and 6.

(7) Information acquired by a judge in a judicial capacity should not be used or disclosed by the judge in financial dealings or for any other purpose not related to judicial duties.

D. Fiduciary Activities. A judge should not serve as an executor, administrator, testamentary trustee, or guardian, except for the estate, testamentary trust, or person of a member of the judge's immediate family, and then only if such service will not interfere with the proper performance of judicial duties. As a family fiduciary, a judge is subject to the following restrictions:

(1) A judge should not serve if it is likely that as such fiduciary the judge will be engaged in proceedings that would ordinarily come before the judge or if the estate, trust, or ward becomes involved in adversary proceedings in the court on which the judge serves or one under its appellate jurisdiction.

(2) While acting as such fiduciary, a judge is subject to the same restrictions on financial activities that apply in the judge's personal capacity.

E. Arbitration. A judge should not act as an arbitrator or mediator, except in the performance of judicial duties.

F. Practice of Law. A judge should not practice law for compensation except as otherwise provided by law.

G. Extra–Judicial Appointments. A judge should not accept appointment to a governmental committee, commission, or other position that is concerned with issues of fact or policy on matters other than the improvement of the law, the legal system, or the administration of justice. A judge, however, may represent the country, state, or locality on ceremonial occasions or in connection with historical, educational, and cultural activities.

[Amended effective October 1, 1993.]

CANON 6
A Judge Should Regularly File Reports of Compensation Received for Quasi-Judicial and Extra-Judicial Activities and of Monetary Contributions

A judge may receive compensation and reimbursement of expenses for the quasi-judicial and extra-judicial activities permitted by this code, if the source of such payments does not give the appearance of influencing the judge in judicial duties or otherwise give the appearance of impropriety, subject to the following restrictions:

A. Compensation. Compensation should not exceed a reasonable amount nor should it exceed what a person who is not a judge would receive for the same activity.

B. Expense Reimbursement. Expense reimbursement should be limited to the actual cost of travel, food, and lodging reasonably incurred by the judge and, where appropriate to the occasion, by the judge's spouse. Any payment in excess of such an amount is compensation.

C. Public Reports. A judge shall report the date, place, and nature of any activity for which the judge received compensation, and the name of the payor and the amount of compensation so received. The judge's report shall be made at least annually and shall be filed as a public document in the office of the State Court Administrator or other office designated by law.

[Amended effective April 21, 1980; October 1, 1993; September 1, 1995.]

Staff Comment to 1995 Amendment

The July 7, 1995, amendments of MCR 2.003, and Rules 3A, 3D, 6C, and 7B of the Michigan Code of Judicial Conduct, and new MCR 9.227 and Rule 7D of the Michigan Code of Judicial Conduct, are based on the proposed revision of the Michigan Code of Judicial Conduct submitted by the State Bar Representative Assembly. See 442 Mich 1216 (1993). They are effective September 1, 1995.

CANON 7
A Judge or a Candidate for Judicial Office Should Refrain From Political Activity Inappropriate to Judicial Office

A. Political Conduct in General.

(1) A judge or a candidate for judicial office should not:

    (a) hold any office in a political party;

    (b) make speeches on behalf of a political party or non-judicial candidate or publicly endorse a candidate for non-judicial office.

(2) A judge or candidate for judicial office may:

    (a) attend political gatherings;

    (b) speak to such gatherings on the judge's own behalf or on behalf of other judicial candidates;

    (c) contribute to a political party.

(3) A judge should resign the judicial office before becoming a candidate either in a party primary or in a general election for nonjudicial office.

B. Campaign Conduct.

(1) A candidate, including an incumbent judge, for a judicial office:

    (a) should maintain the dignity appropriate to judicial office, and should encourage family members to adhere to the same standards of political conduct that apply to the judge;

    (b) should prohibit public employees subject to the judge's direction or control from doing for the judge what the judge is prohibited from doing under this canon;

    (c) should not make pledges or promises of conduct in office other than the faithful and impartial performance of the duties of the office;

    (d) should not knowingly, or with reckless disregard, use or participate in the use of any form of public communication that is false.

(2) These provisions govern a candidate, including an incumbent judge, for a judicial office:

    (a) A judge should not personally solicit or accept campaign funds, or solicit publicly stated support by improper use of the judicial office in violation of B(1)(c). A judge may send a thank-you note to a contributor.

    (b) A judge may establish committees of responsible persons to secure and manage the expenditure of funds for the campaign and to obtain public statements of support for the candidacy.

(c) Such committees are prohibited from soliciting campaign contributions from lawyers in excess of $100 per lawyer, but may solicit public support from lawyers. It is not a violation of this provision for a committee, in undertaking solicitations that are not directed exclusively to lawyers but may in fact go to lawyers who are members of a group or found on a mailing list, to solicit more than $100 per person, provided that the following disclaimer appears on the letter or on a response card, in print that is at least the same size as the remainder of the print in the letter or the response card:

"Canon 7 of the Michigan Code of Judicial Conduct prohibits a judicial campaign committee from soliciting more than $100 per lawyer. If you are a lawyer, please regard this as informative and not a solicitation for more than $100."

(d) A candidate's committee may solicit funds for the campaign no earlier than February 15 of the year of the election, and may not solicit or accept funds after the date of the general election.

(e) A candidate should not use or permit the use of campaign contributions for the private benefit of the candidate or the candidate's family.

(f) If a candidate is not opposed for such judicial office, the candidate or the candidate's committee shall return to the contributors funds raised in excess of the actual costs incurred or contribute such funds to the client security fund of the State Bar of Michigan, not later than January 1 following the election. Likewise, any candidate or committee having funds remaining after payment of all campaign expenses shall either return such funds to the contributors thereof or donate the funds to the client security fund of the State Bar of Michigan, not later than January 1 following the election.

(3) No judge should personally sell or permit any court or public employee working for or assigned to any court to sell fund-raising tickets or accept contributions of any kind on the judge's behalf or on behalf of any other judicial candidate.

C. Fund Raising Other Than for Campaign Purposes Prohibited. Except as provided in 7B(2)(b), (c),

(1) No judge shall accept a testimonial occasion on the judge's behalf where the tickets are priced to cover more than the reasonable costs thereof, which may include only a nominal gift,

(2) No judge or other person, party, committee, organization, firm, group or entity may accept any contribution of money or of a tangible thing of value, directly or indirectly, to or for a judge's benefit for any purpose whatever, including, but not limited to, contribution for a campaign deficit, expenses associat-

ed with judicial office, testimonial, honorarium (other than for services, subject to Canon 6) or otherwise.

D. Applicability.

(1) A successful candidate, whether or not an incumbent, and an unsuccessful candidate who is a judge, are subject to judicial discipline for campaign misconduct. An unsuccessful candidate who is a lawyer is subject to lawyer discipline for judicial campaign misconduct.

(2) A successful elected candidate who was not an incumbent has until midnight December 31 following the election to wind up the candidate's law practice, and has until June 30 following the election to resign from organizations and activities, and divest interests that do not qualify under Canon 4 or 5.

(3) Upon notice of appointment to judicial office, a candidate shall wind up the candidate's law practice prior to taking office, and has six months from the date of taking office to resign from organizations and activities and divest interests that do not qualify under Canon 4 or 5.

[Amended effective October 1, 1993; September 1, 1995; January 1, 2000; March 30, 2000.]

Staff Comment to 1995 Amendment

The July 7, 1995, amendments of MCR 2.003, and Rules 3A, 3D, 6C, and 7B of the Michigan Code of Judicial Conduct, and new MCR 9.227 and Rule 7D of the Michigan Code of Judicial Conduct, are based on the proposed revision of the Michigan Code of Judicial Conduct submitted by the State Bar Representative Assembly. See 442 Mich 1216 (1993). They are effective September 1, 1995.

Staff Comment to 1999 Amendment

With regard to the December 28, 1999 amendment of Canon 7B(2)(a), effective January 1, 2000, both the Michigan Judges Association and the State Bar of Michigan Standing Committee on Professional and Judicial Ethics supported this clarification concerning thank-you notes. Further, several witnesses at the Supreme Court's public hearings questioned how a simple expression of common courtesy could be unethical. As attorney John Felton stated during the hearing on November 4, 1999, in Gaylord:

"One other comment, if I might, with respect to thank you notes. Having donated to campaigns, and I know I have talked to other lawyers that donate to campaigns, I just can't conceive of how the good manners our mother taught us would lead to bad ethics. So I think it's perfectly appropriate, and I don't think as a lawyer I would draw any inference from a judge thanking a lawyer for a contribution."

The Court considered concerns expressed by some members of the State Bar Representative Assembly that a thank-you note might circumvent the intent of the code to prohibit a candidate's personal involvement in fund-raising, but was persuaded that the requirement of the Michigan Campaign Finance Act, 1976 PA 388, that judicial candidates verify the truth of campaign finance statements that list contributors, MCL 169.237; MSA 4.1703(37), effectively negates that concern. The reference in the proposed rule that would have allowed "other acknowledgments" was not adopted.

With regard to Canon 7B(2)(c), the $100 limitation concerning solicitation of lawyers had been the rule since 1974. If adjusted for inflation, the amount would have been in excess of $300. Nevertheless, the Court declined to raise the amount judicial candidate committees may solicit from lawyers from $100 to $300 for the year 2000 judicial elections. The Court explained, however, that its duty to keep its rules in compliance with the United States Supreme Court's understanding of First Amendment law concerning free speech and rights of association might require it to revisit this question after the United States Supreme Court decides *Shrink Missouri Government PAC v Nixon*, 161 F3d 519 (CA 8, 1998) cert granted 119 S Ct 901; 142 L Ed 2d 901 (1999), because that case involves a constitutional challenge to limits on contributions that have not been raised for many years to account for the effects of inflation.

The Court adopted language in Canon 7B(2)(c) allowing for a disclaimer in solicitation letters in excess of $100 that may inadvertently be sent to lawyers because it is virtually impossible for a candidate to assure that a solicitation sent to any group believed to consist primarily of nonlawyers will not include at least one lawyer.

With regard to Canon 7B(2)(d)-(f), the Court established a fixed date that made clear to the public and to candidate committees, when fund-raising may begin, eliminating the need to count backwards 180 days from the date of the primary election or the varying dates of the parties' nominating conventions in order to arrive at the applicable date. As the Court had no desire to increase the length of time for fund-raising, it chose February 15 as the starting date, a change that has the effect of decreasing the amount of time available for fund-raising, given the historic practice of using the primary election date as the applicable date from which to count back.

The Court rejected the proposal to allow solicitation or acceptance of funds up to 45 days after the general election because of comments suggesting that such a rule could lead to abuses and the appearance of impropriety.

Parts of Canon 7B(2)(d)-(f) also were restructured.

The December 28, 1999 amendment of Canon 7C, effective January 1, 2000, eliminated obsolete language pertaining to campaign year 1974.

Staff Comment to 2000 Amendment

The March 30, 2000 amendment of Canon 7 is explained in *In re Chmura*, 461 Mich [517]; [608] NW2d [31] (2000).

CANON 8
Collective Activity By Judges

The canons of this Code concerning the conduct of individual judges and judicial candidates also apply to judges' associations or any other organization consisting exclusively of judges.

[Adopted Effective January 1, 2000.]

1999 Staff Comment

The addition of Canon 8 on December 28, 1999, effective January 1, 2000, clarified that judges remain accountable for their actions under the Code of Judicial Conduct when acting collectively in concert with other judges.

RULES CONCERNING THE JUDICIAL CONFERENCE OF MICHIGAN

Effective November 1, 1955

Research Note

Use Westlaw ® *to find cases citing or applying specific rules.* Westlaw *may also be used to search for specific terms in court rules or to update court rules. See the* MI–RULES *and* MI–ORDERS *Scope Screens for detailed descriptive information and search tips.*

Amendments to these rules are published, as received, in the N.W.2d *and* Michigan Reporter *advance sheets, and Michigan Legislative Service.*

---

1. There is hereby constituted the judicial conference of Michigan, hereinafter called the conference, of which the justices of the Supreme Court and the judges of the circuit courts, recorder's court of the city of Detroit, and superior court of Grand Rapids shall be members. The chief justice, with the approval of the Supreme Court, may invite lawyers and laymen to attend sessions of the conference or to participate in its programs.

2. The directors of the conference shall consist of the chief justice, as chairman, the court administrator, as secretary, the president of the Michigan Judges' Association, the president of the State Bar, the president of the State Bar Foundation, the attorney general of Michigan, the chairman of the senate judiciary committee, the chairman of the house judiciary committee, 3 other members of the conference designated, with the approval of the Supreme Court, by the chief justice, and such others as the chief justice, with the approval of the Supreme Court, may from time to time determine.

3. The directors shall meet at the call of the chief justice. They shall assign subjects to the conference study committees for study, report and recommendations. The directors shall receive and consider the reports of such committees and refer them, together with their own recommendations thereon, to the Supreme Court. The directors may, either on the basis of such committee reports or otherwise, make recommendations to the Supreme Court for amendments, changes or additions to the Michigan Court Rules, and, with the approval of the Supreme Court, make recommendations to the judges who are members of this conference with respect to local practice, and to the governor, the legislature and the people for statutory or constitutional amendments, enactments or changes. The directors shall also, subject to the direction, approval and control of the Supreme Court, inaugurate and maintain, in behalf of the conference and its members, a program of relations with the Michigan State Bar, the State Bar Foundation, the Federal courts, the governor, the legislature and the public.

4. The study committees of the conference shall consist of the following and such others as the chief justice, with the approval of the Supreme Court, shall from time to time determine, namely, study committees on:

(a) Civil procedure.

(b) Criminal jurisprudence.

(c) Substantive law.

(d) Local court organization and administration.

(e) Professional and judicial ethics.

(f) Domestic relations.

(g) Miscellaneous and special questions.

Each study committee shall be composed of a chairman and members designated, with the approval of the Supreme Court, by the chief justice, including the following: A justice of the Supreme Court, at least 2 trial judges who are members of the conference, at least 2 members of the bar, and at least 2 laymen, and shall meet at the call of its chairman.

5. The study committees shall study subjects assigned to them by the chief justice or the directors and make reports and recommendations thereon to the directors, for consideration by the latter and reference to the Supreme Court. Such recommendations

may include proposed amendments, changes and additions to the statutory and constitutional law and Court Rules of Michigan.

6. Each member of the conference shall from time to time, as he encounters problems in the administration of justice and operation of the courts, forward a statement thereof to the court administrator for consideration by the directors and assignment to the appropriate study committee.

7. At the annual meeting of the conference, the directors shall make a report of their work and that of the several study committees during the preceding year.

8. The Supreme Court shall from time to time make such other and further provisions with respect to the conference as it shall deem necessary and proper.

9. The foregoing rules are promulgated pursuant to the general superintending control of the Court over all inferior courts, its powers over the bar of the State and the members thereof, and P.A. 1954, No. 195. They shall take effect on November 1, 1955, and remain in effect until altered or abrogated.

MICHIGAN UNIFORM SYSTEM
OF CITATION

Effective February 10, 1987 (Administrative Order 1987–2). As amended, eff. June 26, 2001 (Administrative Order 2001–5).

Research Note

Use Westlaw ® *to find cases citing or applying specific rules.* Westlaw *may also be used to search for specific terms in court rules or to update court rules. See the MI–RULES and MI–ORDERS Scope Screens for detailed descriptive information and search tips.*

Amendments to these rules are published, as received, in the N.W.2d *and* Michigan Reporter *advance sheets,* and Michigan Legislative Service.

Table of Contents

---

* Suggested title added by Publisher.

INTRODUCTION*

On order of the Court [Administrative Order 1987-2, effective February 10, 1987], Administrative Orders Nos. 1971–3 and 1973–5, which adopted and amended the Michigan Uniform System of Citations, are rescinded. Effective February 10, 1987, all reported decisions of the Supreme Court and the Court of Appeals shall adhere to and follow the revised Michigan Uniform System of Citation as follows:

MICHIGAN UNIFORM SYSTEM
OF CITATION

The Michigan Uniform System of Citation provides a comprehensive scheme for citation of authority in documents filed with or issued by Michigan courts. This revision reflects the style currently used in the opinions of the Supreme Court as published in *Michigan Reports*. It is based on the former Uniform System of Citations, Administrative Order No. 1971–3, 385 Mich xxvi–xxxv, and Administrative Order No. 1973-5, 390 Mich xxxi, and the Proposed Rules of Citation, 402A, Mich 455–468.

For matters not covered, refer to *A Uniform System of Citation*, 13th ed., for guidance, but conform citations to Michigan citation style.

* Suggested title added by Publisher.

I. CITATION OF AUTHORITY

A. CITATION OF CASES

1. Initial Citation.

a. The first time a case is cited, either in the text or a footnote, cite it in full, including parallel citations. See part (A)(5)(m)(2).

b. Cite the name of a case from the first page of the case in the *official* report as fully as necessary to enable the reader to recognize it. Do not show *et al.*, *et ux.*, or like references to other parties in a case name, but do show *ex rel* or *on the Relation of* and the relator's name.

c. Where the name of the case as it appears in the official report is too long or involved, it should be shortened. Names of cases should show only the first plaintiff's surname or corporate name and the first defendant's surname or corporate name.

Examples:

The title in the official report of 262 US 447 is Commonwealth of Massachusetts v Mellon, Secretary of the Treasury, et al., and should be cited as Massachusetts v Mellon, 262 US 447; 43 S Ct 597; 67 L Ed 1078 (1923).

International Union of Electrical, Radio and Machine Workers, AFL–CIO Frigidaire Local 801 v NLRB, 113 US App DC 342; 307 F2d 679 (1962), may be shortened to Electrical Workers Union v NLRB, etc.

d. If a case is initially cited only in a footnote, recite it *in full* if it is referred to subsequently in the text. However, once cited *in full* in the text, a case need not be cited in full in a subsequent footnote.

2. Subsequent Citation. Subsequent reference in the text or in a footnote to a case previously cited in full *in the text* may be in any of the following shortened forms:

E.g., Mayberry v Pryor, 422 Mich 579; 374 NW2d 683 (1985), once cited in full in the text, may be referred to as Mayberry, supra; Mayberry; Mayberry v Pryor. (N.B., "*id.*" may be used as a subsequent reference *only* if no other authority intervenes between the previous citation of the same source and "*id.*")

3. Where a case is cited in full *in a footnote*, a subsequent short-form citation may be used *in a footnote* to refer the reader to the footnote in which the full citation occurs.

Example:

Mayberry, n 4 supra.

4. Point or "Jump" Citation.

a. To refer to a particular page in the official report of a case:

(1) include the "jump" page in the initial citation:

Mayberry v Pryor, 422 Mich 579, 587; 374 NW2d 683 (1985);

(2) append the "jump" page to any short form citation:

Mayberry, supra, p 587; Mayberry, supra at 587; Mayberry, 587; id., p 587; id. at 587; 422 Mich 587.

b. If the official report of a case is not available, refer to the "jump" page in an unofficial report:

(1) Initial Citation. Galster v Woods (On Rehearing), 173 Cal App 3d 529, _____; 219 Cal Rptr 500, 509 (1985);

(2) Subsequent Citation. Galster, supra, 219 Cal Rptr 509; or id., 219 Cal Rptr 509; or 219 Cal Rptr 509; etc. (N.B.: it is mandatory in this situation that the identity of the *unofficial* reporter be shown because references to pages not otherwise identified are presumed to be to the *official* reporter.)

(3) The citation form used within a document should be uniform, i.e., do not mix id., p 270, with id. at 270, or Ensign, supra, p 270, with Ensign, supra at 270.

5. a. *Case Names.* Names of cases are to be italicized in both the text of an opinion and in a footnote. Italicizing is indicated on typed copy by underscoring.

b. Where two separate cases with the same citable title are referred to in a document, add the first names of the parties in order to distinguish the cases.

c. *Officials as Parties.*

(1) Michigan Cases. If a person was sued in an official capacity, use the title of the official capacity, not the name of the person.

Examples:

Jones v Secretary of State, not Jones v Austin; Giannotta v Governor, not Giannotta v Milliken

(2) United States Supreme Court Cases and Cases From Other States. Use the commonly accepted practice within the jurisdiction referred to as to the surname or title of the party. In United States Supreme Court and some sister state court cases, the title of a party is not ordinarily used.

Example:

Massachusetts v Mellon, not Massachusetts v Secretary of Treasury

d. *State or City as a Party.* Use only the name of the state or city.

Example:

The title which appears at 383 Mich 579 is Consumers Power Company v State of Michigan; cite it as Consumers Power Co v Michigan.

However, if the name of the city may also commonly be used as a surname, such as City of Warren, cite as Jones v City of Warren; but, Jones v Detroit.

e. *County, Township or School District as a Party.* Place the name of the county, township or school district first and then Co, Twp, or School Dist.

Examples:

Oakland Co v Smith; Bush v Waterford Twp; Jones v Waverly School Dist

f. Where names of railroads occur in citations, abbreviate all geographical words other than the first word of the railroad name unless the words complete the name of a state, city, or other entity begun by the first word. Do *not* follow these with a period. Use "R Co" instead of "RR" or "Ry" in a railroad name.

Examples:

New York, NH & HR Co v Smith

Grand Rapids & IR Co v Michigan Railroad Comm

Fletcher Paper Co v Detroit & MR Co

La Croix v Grand Trunk WR Co

g. *Second Name of Case.* Do not give a second name for a case if the first one fully identifies it.

Examples (second name required):

Harvey v Lewis (Appeal of List) and Harvey v Lewis (In re Disqualification of Judge)

h. *Rehearing or Remand.* If the opinion cited was decided on rehearing or remand, the specification (*On Rehearing*) or (*On Remand*) is part of the title if the earlier opinion was published and *must* be included in the citation.

Example:

People v Walker, 371 Mich 599; 124 NW2d 761 (1963); People v Walker (On Rehearing), 374 Mich 331; 132 NW2d 87 (1965).

i. *Supplemental Opinion.*

Example:

In re Ernst, 373 Mich 337, Supplemental Opinion, 349, 354; 129 NW2d 430 (1964).

j. *Punctuation in Case Citations.*

(1) The group of data showing volume, report, page, and year is in nonrestrictive apposition with the case name and must be preceded by a comma and followed by a comma, semicolon, period, or other punctuation (except where parenthetical matter postpones it).

Example:

". . . resolved in Village of Kingsford v Cudlip, 258 Mich 144; 241 NW2d 893 (1932), where the Court . . ."

(2) Parallel citations are separated from official citations and from other parallel citations by semicolons to avoid confusion with the commas which frequently separate page numbers in one citation. These semicolons should not be viewed as punctuation; they are merely separators.

Example:

People ex rel Gummow v Larson, 35 Ill 2d 280, 282; 220 NE2d 165 (1966)

However, where a string of citations is conjoined by "and," use commas to separate the citations.

Example:

See Nicholls v Charlevoix Circuit Judge, 155 Mich 455; 120 NW 343 (1909), Kemp v Stradley, 134 Mich 676; 97 NW 41 (1903), and Backus v Detroit, 49 Mich 110; 13 NW 380 (1882).

k. *Abbreviations.*

(1) Abbreviate frequently occurring parts of names in case citations as follows. Do not use a period with these abbreviations. For example:

Name	Abbreviation
Association	Ass'n
Brothers	Bros
Commission	Comm
Commissioner	Comm'r
Company	Co
Corporation	Corp
County	Co
Department	Dep't
District	Dist
Incorporated	Inc
Insurance	Ins
Manufacturing	Mfg
Number	No
Township	Twp

The list is *not* exclusive, and other words may be added where abbreviation will not cause confusion.

(2) Use the ampersand "&," in place of the word "and" wherever that word is spelled out in the name of a case.

(3) The proper abbreviation of "versus" in a citation is "v," not "vs."

(4) The proper abbreviation for "footnote" is "n"; the plural, "footnotes" is "ns."

l. *Jurisdiction.*

(1) Jurisdiction is usually shown by the abbreviation of the title of the official reporter. (Mich: Michigan Supreme Court; Mich App: Michigan Court of Appeals.) When a title is not so shown, as where official reports are no longer published, the jurisdiction must be indicated in the parentheses at the end of the citation along with the date of the decision. For the highest court of a state, only the name of the state should be shown. Use the abbreviations of state names listed in Appendix A. For lower appellate courts, abbreviate the name of the court in addition to the state name.

Examples:

People v Blythe, 417 Mich 430; 339 NW2d 399 (1983);

State v Gallion, 572 P2d 683 (Utah, 1977);

Miller v Stumbo, 661 SW2d 1 (Ky App, 1983).

(2) Federal courts of appeal are shown in parentheses with the date of decision as CA plus the circuit number. E.g.: CA 6, not 6 Cir or 6th Cir or CCA 6. The Court of Appeals for the District of Columbia Circuit is *not* shown in parentheses because there is an official reporter: US App DC, and a citation to the official reporter indicates the jurisdiction.

Examples:

Kirkland v Preston, 128 US App DC 148; 385 F2d 670 (1967)

Ierardi v Gunter, 528 F2d 929, 930–931 (CA 1, 1976)

(3) Federal districts, but not divisions, are shown in parentheses, if there is one. (ED Mich, not ND ED Mich.) If a state comprises one district, use D plus the state abbreviation, not the state abbreviation alone.

Example:

United States ex rel Mayberry v Yeager, 321 F Supp 199, 211 (D NJ, 1971)

(4) Early US reports, through 90 US, must be cited by consecutive volume number in the US series, with the corresponding reporter's name (abbreviated) and volume number in parentheses.

Example:

Sexton v Wheaton, 21 US (8 Wheat) 229; 5 L Ed 603 (1823)

(5) Jurisdiction Not Shown in Official Report. Where jurisdiction is not shown in the official report, show it in parentheses with the year of decision unless indicated by the parallel citation.

Examples:

Beekman v Frost, 18 Johns 543 (NY, 1820); People ex rel Meredith v Meredith, 272 App Div 79; 69 NYS 2d 462 (1947). (Here the parallel citation to the New York Supplement shows the jurisdiction.)

m. *Parallel.*

(1) Parallel citations for United States Supreme Court reports are to be given in the order S Ct, L Ed.

(2) A parallel citation to the National Reporter System Regional Reports must be given if there is one. For New York or California cases, the New York Supplement or California Reporter citation also *must* be given if there is *no* regional reporter citation (e.g., Cal App), and *may* be given in addition to the regional reporter citation.

(3) Parallel citations to other reports, e.g., ALR, *may* be given if the case is reported in full.

n. *Year of Decision.* Insert the year in which the case was decided, not the year of publication or the term of the court, after the final reporter citation.

o. *Citations Not Yet Available.*

(1) When an official or parallel citation is not yet available, provide blanks in which the information later can be inserted.

Example:

__ Mich __; __ NW2d __ (1978)

Do not use this form where the citation will *never* be available because the reports have been discontinued. See Appendix B.

(2) USLW or other advance reports or abstract citations should be given only if *both* the official *and* the regional or other permanent unofficial report citations are not yet available.

Examples:

Comm'r of Internal Revenue v Kowalski, __ US __; __ S Ct __; __ L Ed 2d __; 46 USLW 4015 (November 29, 1977).

Pechter v Lyons, __ F Supp __; 46 USLW 2251 (SD NY, November 8, 1977).

p. *Periods and Spacing of Report Names and Capitalization.*

(1) Use no periods in abbreviations of report names, even if there are two or more words, and do not insert a space where single letters abbreviate the words.

Examples:

NE; NW; NY; RI; US; ALR

(2) Insert a space between parts of abbreviations where more than one letter is used to abbreviate the individual words and capitalize the first letter of each word.

Examples:

Mich App; F Supp; US App DC; S Ct; L Ed

(3) Insert a space between the report name and series designation (2d, etc.) if the last individual word abbreviation in the report name has more than one letter; otherwise do not.

Examples:

(No space) F2d; NYS2d; ALR3d; A2d; NE2d; SW2d

(Space) Wis 2d; So 2d; Misc 2d; L Ed 2d

(Exception—space) LRA NS

q. *Subsequent History or Explanation.* Citation of *denial* of discretionary action such as rehearing, leave to appeal, certiorari, reconsideration, or the like, is not required. If it is necessary to give the subsequent history of a case or an explanation, use the following abbreviations without periods, *not* followed by a comma:

affirmed	aff'd
affirming	aff'g
appeal dismissed	app dis
certiorari denied	cert den
leave to appeal denied	lv den
leave to appeal granted	lv gtd

modified	no abbreviation
rehearing denied	reh den
rehearing granted	reh gtd
reversed	rev'd
reversed on other grounds	rev'd on other grounds
reversing	rev'g
vacated	no abbreviation

Citation of the official report of subsequent action alone is sufficient.

r. *Unreported Cases.* Cite unpublished Michigan cases as follows and foreign cases by analogy:

A v B, unpublished opinion per curiam of the Court of Appeals, decided [month, day, year] (Docket No. _____).

Unpublished opinion of the Attorney General (No. _____, [month, day, year]).

B. CITATION OF CONSTITUTIONS, STATUTES, REGULATIONS, COURT RULES AND JURY INSTRUCTIONS

1. Constitutions.

a. *Michigan.* Give year of the constitution (not the year of an amendment), article, and section number in *Arabic* numerals.

Example:

Const 1963, art 6, § 1; Const 1963, sched § 1

If the section has been amended since adoption of the constitution, the reference is presumed to be to the section current at the time of the writing unless otherwise indicated.

b. *United States.* Give article or amendment number in *Roman* numerals, section number in *Arabic* numerals: US Const, art III, § 1. For amendment: US Const, Am XIV (*not* Art XIV).

c. *Other States.* Cite by analogy to the Michigan and United States Constitutions.

2. Statutes.

a. *Michigan Statutes.*

(1) Public and Local Acts. Cite the year, "PA" or "LA," and the act number.

Examples:

1974 PA 296; 1974 LA 1, *not* Act 296, 1974.

If enacted at an extra session, the extra session designation follows the year in parentheses.

Examples:

1912 (1st Ex Sess) PA 10, part 2, § 9; 1967 (Ex Sess) PA 3

(2) Amended Act. Cite as: 1961 PA 236, as amended (or, as added) by 1974 PA 52, MCL 600.103.

(3) Compiled Laws. The official compilations of 1948, 1970, and 1979 of Michigan Compiled Laws, the Michigan Compiled Laws Annotated, and the

Michigan Compiled Laws Service have the same numbering system. Citation should be to the *official* compilation, e.g., MCL 750.316.

Inclusion of the public act number is optional. If used, the form is: 1978 PA 368, MCL 333.20175. Subsequent references in the same document may be shortened as follows:

§ 20175   or act 368, § 20175.

b. *Federal Statutes.* Cite title and section numbers of the United States Code without punctuation or section symbol: 11 USC 29, 17 USC 8, 18 USC 922. The official United States Code (USC), the United States Code Annotated (USCA), and the United States Code Service (USCS) all use the same numbering system. Cite the *official* version (USC). Citation of the Statutes at Large is unnecessary, except where there is no corresponding citation of USC or where the particular title of USC has not been enacted into positive law and the wording of USC is materially different from that in the Statutes at Large.

c. *Other Statutes.* Cite in the way usually followed in the jurisdiction of the statute, preferably in the official reports. The jurisdiction must appear clearly in or with the citation.

Examples:

Ariz Rev Stat 13–4032, *not* ARS 13–4032

N H Rev Stat Ann 651:57, *not* NHRSA 651:57

3. Court Rules.

a. *Michigan Court Rules of 1985.* Cite as MCR and the rule number. (MCR 2.625.)

b. *Michigan Rules of Evidence.* Cite as MRE and the rule number. (MRE 801.)

c. *Former Court Rules.*

(1) General Court Rules of 1963. Cite as GCR 1963, comma, and the rule number. (GCR 1963, 105.4.)

(2) Court Rules of 1945. Cite as Court Rule No 8, § 7 (1945).

(3) Earlier Court Rules. Cite analogously to the Court Rules of 1945.

(4) Former District Court Rules. Cite as DCR and the rule number.

(5) Former Probate Court Rules. Cite as PCR and the rule number.

(6) Former Juvenile Court Rules. Cite as JCR 1969, comma, and the rule number.

d. *Local Court Rules.* Cite as: [jurisdiction] Local Rule and the rule number.

Example:

Ingham Circuit Court Local Rule 2.119.

e. *Proposed Court Rules.* Cite as Proposed MCR and the rule number.

f. *Code of Professional Responsibility and Canons.*

(1) Canons. Cite as: Code of Professional Responsibility and Canons, Canon 1.

(2) Disciplinary Rules. Cite as: Code of Professional Responsibility and Canons, DR 1–101.

g. *Code of Judicial Conduct.* Cite as: Code of Judicial Conduct, Canon 1.

h. *Rules Concerning the State Bar of Michigan.* Cite as State Bar Rule (number), and, if applicable, a comma, section symbol, and section number. (State Bar Rule 6, § 3.)

i. *Federal Rules.*

(1) Federal Rules of Civil Procedure. Cite as FR Civ P and the rule number. (FR Civ P 52[a].)

(2) Federal Rules of Criminal Procedure. Cite as FR Crim P and the rule number. (FR Crim P 11.)

(3) Federal Rules of Evidence. Cite as FRE and the rule number. (FRE 12.)

j. *Court Rules of Other Jurisdictions.* Cite in the same manner as cited by the official reporter of the court.

4. Jury Instructions.

a. *Standard Jury Instructions—Civil.* Cite as SJI2d and an instruction number.

Examples:

SJI2d 1.03;

SJI2d 2.01;

SJI2d 25.32(c).

b. *Criminal Jury Instructions.* Cite as CJI and the three-part instruction number with colons separating the parts.

Example:

CJI 3:1:02.

5. Administrative Rules.

a. Cite the 1979 Administrative Code as follows: 1979 AC, R 408.41863.

b. If the rule has been amended or superseded, cite the appropriate Annual Administrative Code Supplement where available:

1983 AACS, R 408.41863,

or to a more recent revision in the *Michigan Register*:

1985 MR 7, R 408.30495c.

(N.B.: Revisions contained in the *Michigan Register* are cumulated annually in AACS. Thus, regulations published in 1985 MR, vols. 1–12, are later reprinted in 1985 AACS.)

Subsequent references can be shortened to:

Rule 408.41863.

[Amended effective June 26, 2001.]

C. MISCELLANEOUS CITATIONS

1. Attorney General Opinions. Cite as:

1 OAG, 1956, No 3,010, p 407 (August 26, 1957).

OAG, 1947–1948, No 146, p 217 (March 7, 1947).

2. Municipal Charters and Ordinances.

a. *Charters.* Cite the name of the municipality, the charter, and sufficient data to identify the particular section of interest uniquely, but not redundantly. For example, if all the sections of chapter 6 of a charter are numbered as 6.1, 6.2, etc., and sections in no other chapter are so numbered, 6.2 is sufficient and ch 6 should not be added to the citation.

Example:

Detroit Charter, tit VI, ch VII, § 11.

b. *Ordinances.*

(1) Codified Ordinances. Cite the name of the municipality, the ordinance code, and sufficient data to identify the particular section of interest uniquely, but not redundantly.

Example:

Detroit Ordinances, § 38–5–7.

(2) Uncodified Ordinances. Cite the name of the municipality and the ordinance number and section; the date is unnecessary for ordinances currently in force, but should be added in parentheses when necessary to distinguish from other versions.

Example:

Saginaw Ordinance D–511, § 203.

3. Administrative decisions. Cite cases as follows:

A v B, 1978 MERC Lab Op 328

(Employment Relations Commission)

A v B, 95 LRRM 1274 (1977)

(Labor Relations Reference Manual)

A v B, 1 MTTR 95 (Docket No. 3799, May 15, 1975)

(Tax Tribunal Reports)

A v B, 1979 WCABO 2617

(Workers' Compensation Appeal Board)

Cite other reports by analogy.

4. Constitutional Convention. 2 Official Record, Constitutional Convention 1961, p 2038.

5. Legislative Materials.

a. *Bills.*

HB 4015

SB 481

b. *Legislative Journals.*

(1) Bound Volumes. Cite the year of the session and the page number:

1965 Journal of the House 77–78

1983 Journal of the Senate 2280

(2) Advance Sheets. Cite, in addition, the pamphlet number and the date of issue:

1986 Journal of the House 76 (No. 6, January 22, 1986).

1986 Journal of the Senate 449 (No. 26, March 6, 1986).

c. *Legislative Analyses.* House Legislative Analysis, HB 6037, September 29, 1980.

6. Legal Treatises and Texts.

Examples:

3 Callaghan's Michigan Pleading & Practice (2d ed), § 16.23, p 564.

12 Michigan Law & Practice, Fraud, § 10, pp 409, 410.

2 Am Jur 2d, Administrative Law, § 698, p 597.

26 CJS, Declaratory Judgment, § 108, p 214.

1 Gillespie, Michigan Criminal Law & Procedure (2d ed), § 312, p 374.

1 McCormick, Evidence (2d ed), § 202, p 484.

6 Wigmore, Evidence (Chadbourn rev), § 1747, p 195.

Prosser, Torts (4th ed), § 103, p 673.

12 McQuillin, Municipal Corporations (3d ed, 1976 Cum Supp), § 32.133, p 141.

2 Honigman & Hawkins, Michigan Court Rules Annotated (2d ed), p 334.

1 Cooley, Constitutional Limitations (2d ed), p 10.

Lewis, Trusts (13th ed), p 91.

3 Restatement Torts, 2d, § 520, p 41.

2 Restatement Torts, 2d, Appendix (1966), § 344, p 237.

Restatement Contracts, 2d (Tentative Draft No 8, 1973), § 267, pp 77–78.

Anno: Fraud or undue influence in conveyance from child to parent, 11 ALR 735, 746.

78 ALR2d 218, § 2, pp 220, 221.

7. Nonlegal Books.
Cite author, editor, or issuing institution, title in italics, and, in parentheses, the place of publication, colon, publisher, edition number, and year of publication; followed by, if appropriate, sufficient data to identify the matter of interest, such as chapter and page number.

Examples:

Inbau & Reid, Lie Detection and Criminal Interrogation (Baltimore: Williams & Wilkins Co, 3d ed, 1953), pp 110–111.

Greenfield & Sternbach, eds, Handbook of Psychophysiology (New York: Holt, Rinehart & Winston, Inc, 1972), ch 19, p 749.

Yung-Ping Chen & The Technical Committee on Income, Income: Background & Issues (Washington, DC: White House Conference on Aging, 1971).

United States Bureau of the Census, Census of Population: 1970, Detailed Characteristics; Final Report PC(1)—D24 Michigan (Washington, DC: United States Government Printing Office, 1972).

Bernstein, The Careful Writer (New York: Atheneum, 1973).

Follett, Modern American Usage (New York: Hill & Wang, 1966).

Evans, A Dictionary of Contemporary American Usage (New York: Random House, 1957).

Dictionaries:

Webster's Third New International Dictionary, Unabridged Edition (1966).

The Random House Dictionary of the English Language: Unabridged Edition.

Funk & Wagnalls New Standard Dictionary of the English Language (1963).

The American Heritage Dictionary of the English Language (1973).

8. Law Review Material.

a. Any citation of law review material must include the volume number, abbreviated name of the law review or journal, page number or numbers, and, in parentheses, the year.

b. Articles, whether denominated article, commentary, or note, having a named author, whether student or not, and a title, should be cited by surname of author (unless more is needed for certainty) and *italicized* title. If it is called commentary or note, that should precede the title.

c. A commentary or note having a title but no author's name should be cited as Commentary (or Note), comma, and *italicized* title.

d. Matter in the nature of a regular department of the periodical having a number of contributors or anonymous contributors should be cited by the usual title, e.g., Current Law Notes, Recent Legislation, Recent Developments, not italicized.

Examples:

Comment, Prosecutorial discretion in the duplicative statutes setting, 42 U Colo L R 455 (1971).

Kutak & Gottschalk, In search of a rational sentence: A return to the concept of appellate review, 53 Neb L R 463 (1974).

Conyers, The politics of revenue sharing, 52 J Urban L 61 (1974).

Moley, The use of the information in criminal cases, 17 ABAJ 292 (1931).

II. QUOTATION OF AUTHORITY

A. OFFICIAL SOURCES*

Where available, official sources should be quoted. E.g., the official source of opinions of the Michigan Supreme Court is *Michigan Reports* (Mich), not the *North Western Reporter* or *Michigan Reporter* (NW2d); the official source of the opinions of the United States Supreme Court is *United States Reports* (US), not the *Supreme Court Reporter* (S Ct), the *United States Supreme Court Reports, Lawyers Edition* (L Ed, L Ed 2d), or *United States Law Week* (USLW). The official source of Michigan statutes is the Public or Local Acts (PA, LA) or the Michigan Compiled Laws of 1979 (MCL), not Michigan Compiled Laws Annotated (MCLA) or Michigan Statutes Annotated (MSA).

* Suggested title added by Publisher.

B. ERRORS*

Authority should be quoted *exactly*. If it appears that the text of an authority contains an error, "[sic]" should be inserted in the text immediately following the error.

* Suggested title added by Publisher.

C. PUBLISHED OPINIONS*

Published opinions of Michigan, federal, or foreign courts should be quoted *exactly* with respect to the text; *however*, citation form and punctuation style should be *altered* and bracketed to conform to *current* publication style where parallel citations are required or where the original citation form is confusing.

Examples:

In 378 Mich 195, the following citation appears:

Brown v City of Highland Park (1948), 320 Mich 108.

If the paragraph containing the citation is quoted, only the parallel citation need be added:

Brown v Highland Park, (1948) 320 Mich 108 [30 NW2d 798].

In 199 Mich 316, "Jones v Berkey, 181 Mich 472 (148 NW 375)," should be quoted:

"Jones v Berkey, 181 Mich 472 (148 NW 375) [1914]." (NB.: periods after "Mich" and "NW" are deleted.)

In 225 Mich 568, "See Act No. 163, Pub.Acts 1921 (Comp.Laws Supp. 1922, § 1989 [1–20])," should be quoted:

"See [1921 PA 163]."

In 417 Mich 119, the following sentence appears:

There is no question that the "until the first election" language in that situation becomes inoperative.

It should be quoted:

"There is no question that the 'until the first election' language in that situation becomes inoperative."

* Suggested title added by Publisher.

D. STATUTES*

1. The boldface catchlines found at the beginning and sometimes elsewhere in statutes in the Public and Local Acts, MCL, MCLA, and MSA were inserted by an editor, not enacted by the Legislature. They are *not* part of the statute and should not be included when quoting a statute. Similarly, catchlines found in a statute following the section number, as in many sections of the Michigan Penal Code, are not part of the statute.

2. Generally speaking any section number appearing at the beginning of a statute should also be omitted from the quotation unless needed for clarity, e.g., if the sections of the act are not evident and will be used later for reference.

3. The statutory history which follows each section also is *not* part of the legislative enactment and should *not* be included in quoted material.

Examples:

~~691.1412 Claims under act; defenses available.~~ (delete)

[~~Sec. 12.~~] (delete) Claims under this act are subject to all of the defenses available to claims sounding in tort brought against private persons.

[~~HISTORY: New 1964, p. 224, Act 170, Eff. Jul. 1, 1965.~~] (delete)

* Suggested title added by Publisher.

E. QUOTING A FOOTNOTE

If the material quoted contains a footnote which will be included in the quotation, use the same footnote numbering as the original and add the footnote at the end of the block of quoted material. Separate the footnote from the main quotation by a line from margin to margin above and below the quoted footnote. For clarity, cite the material in the text of the opinion *before* beginning the block quotation.

Example:

A discussion of presumptions and their effect upon the burden of producing evidence appears in In re Wood Estate, 374 Mich 278, 289; 132 NW2d 35; 54 ALR3d 1 (1965):

"The immediate legal effect of a presumption is procedural—it shifts the burden of going forward with the evidence relating to the presumed fact.[5] Once there is a presumption that fact C is true, the opposing party must produce evidence tending to disprove either facts A and B or presumed fact C; if he fails to do so, he risks jury instruction that they must presume fact C to have been established.

"[5] Baker v Delano, 191 Mich 204, 208 [157 NW 427 (1916)], citing 1 Elliott on Evidence, § 91: ' "The office or effect of a true presumption is to cast upon the party against whom it works the duty of going forward with evidence." ' "

The thrust of the Wood case was to change the law in this state concerning the effect that a presumption has after rebuttal evidence has been introduced.

F. PLACEMENT OF CITATION

A citation indicating the source of a block quotation preferably should be supplied in the text preceding the quotation.

Example:

The Equal Protection Clause, US Const, Am XIV, § 5, provides:

"The Congress shall have power to enforce, by appropriate legislation, the provisions of this article."

A citation may follow the quotation in the block, immediately after the quoted material, without additional separation, and followed by a closing period.

The no-fault insurance act provides, in part:

"An agreement for assignment of a right to benefits payable in the future is void." MCL 500.3143; MSA 24.13143.

G. BRACKETS

1. Use brackets [ ]:

(a) to enclose explanatory remarks, extraneous data, editorial interpolations, or additional citations within quoted passages:

There is no doubt that the April 23, 1973 finding was that defendant was guilty of civil contempt. Judge O'Hair specifically told the defendant that she would be jailed until she purged herself. She therefore was able to "carry the 'keys of [the] prison in [her] own pocket' [and] the action is essentially civil." People v Goodman, 17 Mich App 175, 177; 169 NW2d 120 (1969).

If one substitutes "warehouse owner, lessee or operator" for "consignee," then the exclusion would read "no portion of any premises owned or leased or operated by a [warehouse owner, lessee or operator] shall be deemed to be a public warehouse." The expansive meaning sought by the city does not work unless there can be a consignor without a consignee.

The proscription of "unreasonable searches and seizures" and the warrant requirement

"must be read in light of 'the history that gave rise to the words'—a history of 'abuses so deeply felt by the Colonies as to be one of the potent causes of the Revolution.' [United States v Rabinowitz], 339 US [56], 69 [70 S Ct 430; 94 L Ed 653 (1950)]. The amendment was in large part a reaction to the general warrants and warrantless searches that had so alienated the colonists and had helped speed the movement for independence."

(b) to indicate a change in capitalization to conform to the sense of the context in quoted source material:

"[W]e cannot agree that the Fourth Amendment interests at stake in these [administrative] inspection cases are merely 'peripheral.' It is surely anomalous to say that the individual and his private property are fully protected by the Fourth Amendment only when the individual is suspected of criminal behavior."

(c) to indicate a misspelled or misused word in the text accompanied by the word "sic":

"Any person who shall commit the offense of larceny, by steeling [sic], shall be guilty of a felony ."

(d) to function as parentheses within parentheses:

The statute (MCL 418.551[2]; MSA 17.237[551][2]) provides . . .

APPENDICES

APPENDIX A. STATE ABBREVIATIONS

Ala	Ky	ND
Alas	La	Ohio
Ariz	Me	Okla
Ark	Md	Or
Cal	Mass	Pa
Colo	Mich	RI
Conn	Minn	SC
Del	Miss	SD
DC	Mo	Tenn
Fla	Mont	Tex
Ga	Neb	Utah
Hawaii	Nev	Vt
Idaho	NH	Va
Ill	NJ	Wash
Ind	NM	W Va
Iowa	NY	Wis
Kan	NC	Wy

APPENDIX B. COURTS NO LONGER PUBLISHING OFFICIAL REPORTS

State	Last Volume	Last Year
Alabama	295	1976
Alabama Appeals	57	1976

State	Last Volume	Last Year
Alaska	17	1958
Arizona Appeals	27	1976
Colorado	200	1980
Colorado Appeals	44	1980
Delaware	59	1966
Delaware Chancery	43	1966
Florida	160	1948
Indiana	275	1981
Indiana Appeals	182	1981
Iowa	261	1968
Kentucky	314	1951
Louisiana	263	1972
Louisiana Appeals	19	1932
Maine	161	1965
Minnesota	312	1977
Mississippi	254	1966
Missouri	365	1956
Missouri Appeals	241	1955
North Dakota	79	1953
Oklahoma	208	1953
Oklahoma Criminal Appeals	97	1953
South Dakota	90	1976
Tennessee	225	1971
Tennessee Appeals	63	1971
Tennessee Civil Appeals	8	1918
Texas	163	1962
Texas Criminal Appeals	172	1963
Utah	30 Utah 2d	1974
Wyoming	80	1959

†